W9-AGM-060

THE WRITER'S HANDBOOK

The Writer's Handbook

Edited by

SYLVIA K. BURACK

Editor, The Writer

Publishers   THE WRITER, INC.   Boston

CONTENTS

BACKGROUND FOR WRITERS

HOW TO WRITE—TECHNIQUES
GENERAL FICTION

SPECIALIZED FICTION

NONFICTION: ARTICLES AND BOOKS

POETRY

PLAYWRITING

JUVENILE AND YOUNG ADULT

EDITING AND MARKETING

WHERE TO SELL

Background
for Writers

>> 1

THE JOURNEY INWARD

BY KATHERINE PATERSON

DO YOU KEEP A JOURNAL?" NO, I ANSWER A BIT RED-FACED, BECAUSE I know that *real* writers keep voluminous journals so fascinating that the world can hardly wait until they die to read the published versions. But it's not quite true. I do make journal-like entries in used schoolgirl spiral notebooks, on odd scraps of paper, in fairly anonymous computer files. These notations are all so embarrassing that I am hoping for at least a week's notice to hunt them down and destroy all the bits and pieces before my demise.

I write these entries, you see, only when I can't write what I want to write. If they were collected and published, the reader could logically conclude that I was not only totally inept as a writer but that I lacked integration of personality at best, and at worst, was dangerously depressed.

If I had kept a proper journal, these neurotic passages would be seen in context, but such is not the case. If my writing is going well, why would I waste time talking about it? I'd be doing it. So if these notes survive me, they will give whatever segment of posterity might happen upon them a very skewed view of my mental state.

The reason I am nattering on about this is that I have come to realize that I am not alone. As soon as my books (after years of struggle) began to be published, I started to get questions from people that I had trouble answering in any helpful way: "Do you use a pen and pad or do you write on a typewriter?" (Nowadays, "computer" is always included in this question, but I'm talking about twenty years ago.)

"Whatever works," I'd say. Which was true. Sometimes I wrote first drafts by hand, sometimes on the typewriter; often I'd switch back and forth in an attempt to keep the flow going. The questioner would thank me politely, but, looking back, I know now that I had failed her.

3

"Do you have a regular schedule everyday or do you just write when you feel inspired?" the person would ask earnestly. I am ashamed to say, I would often laugh at this. "If I wrote only when I was inspired," I'd say, "I'd write about three days a year. Books don't get written in three days a year."

Occasionally, the question (and now, I know, all these were the same question) would be framed more baldly. "How do you begin?" "Well," I would say, "you sit down in front of the typewriter, roll in a sheet of paper and . . ."

If I ever gave any of you one of those answers, or if any other writer has ever given you similar tripe, I would like to apologize publicly. I was asked, in whatever disguise, a truly important question, and I finessed the answer into a one-liner.

How *do* you begin? It is not an idle or trick question. It is a cry from the heart.

I know. That's what all those aborted journal notes are about. They are the cry when I simply cannot begin. When no inspiration ever comes, when neither pen, nor pencil, nor typewriter, nor state-of-the-art computer can unloose what's raging about inside me.

So what happens? Well, something must. I've begun and ended over and over again through the years. There are several novels out there with my name on the cover. Somehow I figured out how to begin. Once the book is finished, the memory of the effort dims—until you're trying to begin the next one.

Well, I'm there now. I have to begin again. What have I done those other times? How have I gotten from that feeling of stony hopelessness? How do I break through that barrier as hard as sunbaked earth to the springs of creativity?

Sometimes, I know, I have a conversation with myself on paper:

What's the matter?
What do you mean "what's the matter?" You know perfectly well. I want to write, but I can't think of a thing to say.
Not a single thing?
Not a single thing worth saying.
You're scared what you might say won't be up to snuff? Scared people might laugh at you? Scared you might despise yourself?
Well, it is scary. How do I know there's still anything in here?

4

You don't. You just have to let it flow. If you start judging, you'll cut off the flow—you've already cut off the flow from all appearances—before it starts.

Grump.

Ah yes, we never learn, do we? Whatever happened to that wonderful idea of getting up so early in the morning that the critic in you was still asleep?

How do I know it will work this time?

You won't know if you don't try. But then, trying is risky, and you do seem a bit timid to me.

You don't know what it's like pouring out your guts to the world.

I don't?

Well, you don't care as much as I do.

Of course I do. I just happen to know that it is so important to my psychic health to do this that I'm willing to take the risk. You, my friend, seem to want all the creative juices inside you to curdle and poison the whole system.

You're nothing but a two-bit psychologist.

Well, I've been right before.

But how do I begin?

I don't know. Why don't we just get up at five tomorrow, come to the machine and type like fury for an hour and see what happens? Could be fun. Critic won't be up, and we won't ever have to show anybody what we've done.

Now you understand why I have to burn this stuff before I die. My posthumous reputation as a sane person of more than moderate intelligence hangs in the balance. But living writers, in order to keep writing, have to forget about posthumous reputations. We have to become, quite literally, like little children. We have to remember our early griefs and embarrassments. Talk aloud to ourselves. Make up imaginary companions. We have to play.

Have you ever watched children fooling with play dough or finger-paint? They mess around to see what will emerge, and they fiddle with what comes out. Occasionally, you will see a sad child, one that has decided beforehand what he wants to do. He stamps his foot because the picture on the page or the green blob on the table falls short of the vision in his head. But he is, thankfully, a rarity, already too concerned with adult approval.

The unspoiled child allows herself to be surprised with what comes out of herself. She takes joy in the material, patting it and rolling it and shaping it. She is not too quick to name it. And, unless some grownup interferes, she is not a judge but a lover of whatever comes from her heart through her hands. This child knows that what she has created is marvelous simply because she has made it. No one else could make this wonderful thing because it has come out of her.

What treasures we have inside ourselves—not just joy and delight but also pain and darkness. Only I can share the treasures of the human spirit that are within me. No one else has *these* thoughts, *these* feelings, *these* relationships, *these* experiences, *these* truths.

How do I begin? You could start, as I often do, by talking to yourself. The dialogue may help you understand what is holding you back. Are you afraid that deep down inside you are really shallow? That when you take that dark voyage deep within yourself, you will find there is no treasure to share? Trust me. There is. Don't let your fear stop you. Begin early in the morning before that critical adult within wakes up. Like a child, pour out what is inside you, not listening to anything but the stream of life within you. Read Dorothea Brande's classic *On Becoming a Writer,* in which she suggests that you put off for several days reading what you have written in the wee hours. Then when you do read it you may discern a repeated theme pointing you to what you want to begin writing about.

Begin, Anne Lamott suggests in her wonderful book *Bird by Bird,* in the form of a letter. Tell your child or a trusted friend stories from your past. Exploring childhood is almost always an effective wedge into what's inside you. And didn't you mean to share those stories with your children someday anyhow?

While I was in the midst of revising this article, my husband happened to bring home Julia Cameron's book, *The Artist's Way.* Cameron suggests three pages of longhand every morning as soon as you get up. I decided to give the "morning pages" a try and heartily recommend the practice, though these pages, too, will need to be destroyed before I die.

When I was trying to begin the book which finally became *Flip-Flop Girl* (and you should see the anguished notes along the way!), I just began writing down the name of every child I could remember from the fourth grade at Calvin H. Wiley School. Sometimes I appended a note that explained why that child's name was still in my head. Early-morning exercises explored ways the story might go, and I rejected most of them, but out of those fourth-grade names and painful betrayals a story began to grow. Judging from the notes, it was over a year in developing and many more months in the actual writing. But I did begin, and I did finish. There's a bit of courage for the next journey inward.

Now it's your turn. Bon voyage.

>> 2

BETWEEN THE REAL AND THE BELIEVABLE

BY CHARLES MCCARRY

SOME TWENTY YEARS AGO I PUBLISHED A NOVEL IN WHICH ONE OF the characters, a pathologically jealous young woman, was so obsessed with her husband, an American spy who kept his operational life secret from her, that she embarked on a series of joyless adulteries in order to accumulate secrets of her own, and so become his romantic equal.

Soon after this work appeared, I found myself at a dinner party in Northampton, Mass., seated next to an agitated feminist, who, like my unhappy character, was young and beautiful and a recent bride. Throughout dinner, she told me how much she hated the girl in the book, whose behavior she had found to be utterly unrealistic and an insult to women—"male chauvinist propaganda," she called it.

I was not surprised by the onslaught. For a writer in America, going out to dinner is like living as an American in Europe: Total strangers think they can say anything they like to you. Still, I had trouble grasping the point. Why did a 1950s fictional character have to conform to an ideological model that had not yet been invented at the period in which the novel took place?

I asked my critic to tell me in plain English why she disliked and distrusted my character so. After a moment of angry silence the woman threw half a glass of California burgundy on my best gray suit and replied, "Because I used to be just like her!"

On the way home, my wife wisely told me I should take this happening as a compliment. But there was more to it than that, as is perhaps demonstrated by the fact that I have never even considered using the wine episode as a scene in a novel. Truth in life and truth in art are not the same, and for the reader—that passive collaborator who must complete the author's work by developing it in his mind as if it were

8

a strip of exposed film—suspension of belief is quite different from believing what one is expected to believe.

Unlike speech, which slips into the consciousness obsequiously through the ear, the written word clambers into the mind through the window of the eye. It is more likely to be welcome if it wears the mask and costume of a harmless guest at a masked ball than if it carries the blackjack and clinking tool kit of a real burglar. People do not like to be surprised, but fiction that abjures the element of surprise is mere bedtime story.

Over the years I have moved back and forth between novels and nonfiction, including collaborations on the memoirs of well-known public figures—"like a polygamist moving from bedchamber to bedchamber," as a friend, monogamous in literary matters, put it. Others have suggested that what I learn from writing about the real world must be of direct use to me in writing novels.

Not really. For one thing, writing is famously a cure: By the mystical process of transforming the invisible contents of the mind into black ink on a white page, you get rid of the damn stuff forever. For another, though reality checks are part of the process, no true novel can be made from anything but the imagination and its silent partner, experience, which is not at all the same thing as research.

Knowledge of the world of affairs does confer certain secondary benefits on the novelist: He learns for a fact that the great are only the small made large. But there is very little he can carry back and forth between the two forms, though they are much alike from a technical standpoint—he uses the technique of fiction (action proceeds from character, dialogue reveals inner meaning, surprise is the soul of narrative) to write about real people in real life, and the fundamental problem is the same in both forms: The greater the verisimilitude, the greater the will to resist it.

For a decade at the height of the Cold War, I worked abroad under cover as an intelligence agent. After I resigned, intending to spend the rest of my life writing fiction and knowing what tricks the mind can play when the gates are thrown wide open, as they are by the act of writing, between the imagination and that part of the brain in which information is stored, I took the precaution of writing a closely remembered narrative of my clandestine experiences. After correcting the manuscript, I burned it.

9

What I kept for my own use was the atmosphere of secret life: How it worked on the five senses and what it did to the heart and mind. All the rest went up in flames, setting me free henceforth to make it all up. In all important matters, such as the creation of characters and the invention of plots, with rare and minor exceptions, that is what I have done. And, as might be expected, when I have been weak enough to use something that really happened as an episode in a novel, it is that piece of scrap, buried in a landfill of the imaginary, readers invariably refuse to believe.

>> 3

"I" Is Not Me

By Margaret Maron

RECENTLY, AN IRATE READER TOOK ME TO TASK FOR MY NOVEL, *Shooting at Loons*. Offended when my first-person narrator remarked that someone was "not much taller than me," the reader acidly inquired if grammar were no longer important.

"It is clear that you don't know any better than to let your character—a judge with a law degree, for heaven's sake!—use bad grammar," he fumed, "but why didn't your editor catch it? Don't editors edit anymore?"

Fortunately for me, my editor is more astute than that particular reader. She knows the stylistic difference between an author's formal voice and a character's narrative voice and would never try to smooth away my "I" character's verbal idiosyncrasies. Nevertheless, that letter did make me stop and reconsider how, as writers, we often do use a first-person voice as a shorthand method to convey character and personality without actually having to spell them out.

The omniscient author's voice pays strict attention to the laws of grammar and punctuation; the narrative voice pays strict attention to the character of the "I" who is telling the story.

As someone who reads Fowler's *Modern English Usage* for sheer pleasure, I do know the difference between subjective and objective pronouns; and yes, I do try to use them correctly when writing third-person or formally. (Actually, Fowler prefers "Not much taller than me" over "Not much taller than I," which "strikes the reader as pedantic.") But that is neither here nor there. The truth is that when I write first-person fiction, I deliberately mimic language that will let my readers know this person's social class, present emotional status, and whether he is likeable or mean-minded, brave or timorous, a whining pessimist or a cheerful optimist.

11

This is especially useful in the short story form, where every word counts.

In my short story, "Deadhead Coming Down," no third-person description of an easily bored trucker can match the immediacy of his own voice saying,

> There's not one damn thing exotic about driving a eighteen-wheeler. Next to standing on a assembly line and screwing Bolt A into Hole C like my no-'count brother-in-law, driving a truck's got to be the dullest way under God's red sun to make a living. 'Specially if it's just up and down the eastern seaboard like me.

The trucker speaks in short blunt words and his coarse denial of his brother-in-law's worth foreshadows his truly callous actions in the story.

Conversely, when I wrote "On Windy Ridge," I hoped that the slower, dreamlike pacing and choice of elegiac language would help convey the image of a middle-aged mountain woman who possesses both intelligence and a slightly psychic sensitivity:

> Waiting is more tiresome than doing, and I was weary. Bone weary . . . but my eyes lifted to the distant hills, beyond trees that burned red and gold, to where the ridges misted into smoky blue. The hills were real and everlasting and I had borrowed of their strength before.

In *Shooting at Loons,* the novel that so exercised my overly pedantic reader, my narrator is Deborah Knott, a district court judge in her mid-thirties. Even though she knows better, Deborah is a breezily colloquial Southerner who makes grammatical slips because she is the daughter and sister of semiliterate dirt farmers who will use dialect, split infinitives, double negatives, sentence fragments, dangling participles, and a host of other colorful grammatical errors till the day they die. True, she has a law degree; true, she is a judge. Neither has turned her into a grammarian. (I was once sent to the principal's office because I would not agree when the English teacher insisted that *it's* was the possessive of *it*. She, too, possessed an advanced degree.)

With one foot in North Carolina's agrarian past and the other firmly planted in its high-tech present, Deborah is never going to "get above her raising." Not if I have anything to say about it.

After all, I have a classic precedent for claiming the right to a narrative voice that is not necessarily my own.

12

In a preface to one of his books many years ago, a certain writer used his formal voice to explain the technical side of creation: "In this book a number of dialects are used . . . . The shadings have not been done in a haphazard fashion, or by guesswork, but painstakingly, and with the trustworthy guidance and support of personal familiarity with these several forms of speech." Then switching into his first-person narrative voice, that same author wrote, "You don't know about me without you have read a book by the name of *The Adventures of Tom Sawyer,* but that ain't no matter."

Had Mark Twain written the whole book as omniscient and highly literate author, *The Adventures of Huckleberry Finn* would be a forgotten piece of 19th-century esoterica. Instead he gave us Huck's distinctly ungrammatical *"I"* voice and the book remains a living, breathing masterpiece a hundred years later.

$\gg\gg$ 4

WRITER—OR FRAUD?

BY DIANE LEFER

IN MY MANY YEARS OF TEACHING IN A CREATIVE WRITING PROGRAM, I've watched students go on to publish stories, articles, essays, and books, but most of them—including some of the most talented and committed—sooner or later ask the same anguished question: Am I really a writer? Or am I a fraud?

I used to respond with pep talks and reassurance but I now suspect that if boosts to self-confidence come from outside instead of inside, a writer learns to demonstrate bravado without ever feeling secure. The feelings of fraudulence linger and no matter how much success and accomplishment the person eventually achieves, any conviction of being the genuine article remains elusive. So I've tried to debunk a few of the "tests" that are commonly applied as a measure of Real Writerhood.

A Real Writer writes every day and can't be stopped.

To me, this is one of our most dangerous misconceptions: the idea that unless you sit in the chair in front of the blank paper for so many hours a day you're not for real. If you're a real writer, you write even though you're in emotional turmoil. Nothing can stop you. And if you don't—YOU'RE NOT A REAL WRITER. Ridiculous! This false notion of discipline and commitment leads to mediocre writing and also to writers who behave irresponsibly.

Like so many false notions, however, there is a kernel of truth in it. I do think if you're a writer, you feel compelled to write. It's what you do. Not every day. Some days you don't have anything to say. And some days, other human matters can and do and *should* take priority. Sometimes you *do* write because you *want* to, you *have* to, and nothing else makes any difference, even if it happens to be Christmas morning. If you don't know how *not* to do it, you're a writer.

I've published close to fifty short stories, including one collection, plus a number of non-literary books, dozens of articles and essays, and hundreds of reviews. I've also written several unpublished novels. Do I write every day? No. I tried to. Years ago, unable to pay the rent with my free-lance work and part-time jobs, I took a full-time job that took over my life, and I wondered if I would ever have time to write again. I set the alarm for 4:00 every morning and got up and wrote before taking the subway to work. Almost two years later, with a series of magazine assignments awaiting me, I was able to quit the job. For the first time, I had a breathing space, sat down, and looked back over the hundreds of pages I'd written in those early mornings. Worthless. Not even anything worth revising. For me, getting enough sleep and writing occasionally on the weekends would have made for a happier, healthier life—and for better fiction.

A writer's raw material is life. You're working as a writer when you're reading. When you're spending time with family or friends or strangers. When you're thinking. Staring out the window or day-dreaming. When you're hiking or sitting by the sea—even if you manage to come up with only two lines. When I'm stuck, I read a lot—often nonfiction so I don't get lost in someone else's fictional voice. I read poetry aloud. I listen to music; problems I'm having with stories often untangle and become resolved while I'm listening to blues or jazz. A *lot* of the work—and it's genuine work—takes place away from the page. In fact, I believe procrastination and avoidance are often the mind's way of stopping us from putting poorly formed ideas on paper. When you think you know what you want to say but can't say it, that's often a sign that the material is more complex than you'd realized. It may take more time, more exploration—subconscious percolation—and thought.

For me, writers block isn't the Valley of the Shadow: It's permission to spend time with people I've neglected, or to go to the movies, watch TV, talk on the phone, or catch up on sleep. The well's gone dry on me often enough that I recognize that one way to fill it is to relax and participate in life instead of agonizing because I think I have nothing to say. I reassure myself that I've done it before and I'll do it again.

None of this means I like getting stuck. It's uncomfortable. When I'm not writing, there's an absence of rightness in my life, but I don't see any reason to make it worse by beating up on myself.

When you feel the pressure to produce, remember: There is no quantitative measure of being a *Real Writer.*

A Real Writer is published.

First of all, there are two sides of "being a writer." In the personal, inward sense, you *know* you're a writer. Being a writer is how you make sense of the world; when you're writing and it's going well, your sense of identity is absolutely clear. But we're constantly asked to present a social identity as well. *Who are you? What are you?* People label what they do for a living. We may live to write and sometimes feel we have to write to live, but that often has little to do with earning money.

In the social world, when people ask what you are or what you do, if you say, "A writer," you often get that sneering, "Yeah? What have you published?" Now you may feel you're on thin ice. Maybe you've been working on a novel for years, and it's still far from completion, or you've been sending your work around to publishers and gathering mostly rejection slips. Even extensive publication may not protect you. A friend of mine has published close to 100 books: family sagas, men's adventure novels, nonfiction on a wide range of subjects. Aside from a brief stint as a cab driver in the 1950s, he's earned his living as a writer for more than 40 years. But when someone asked his occupation and my friend said he was a writer, the man responded, "Was your last book reviewed in *The New York Times*?" When my friend said no, the man replied, "Oh, then you're not a writer." No wonder we're often nervous about our social identity. We want to be able to call ourselves writers in public, but just like the revelation of any other deeply personal information, it carries a risk.

A Real Writer takes rejection in stride.

On the one hand, we're told we aren't "real" if we don't publish. On the other, we're criticized for wanting publication so much.

Has this ever happened to you? Your best, most recent story is rejected—again—and you turn to someone you love and admit you're frustrated and depressed. And this ordinarily supportive, loving person tells you, "You're supposed to love the work itself. Why do you need so much external validation?" As though if you were a Real Writer, rejection slips wouldn't hurt.

Of course they hurt! You wrote that story because it meant something to you. That's your heart on the page, along with hopes for the future. Of course you want other people to read it and be moved by it. If you didn't write that story desiring to connect with others, there would have been no point in submitting it.

What's wrong with wanting validation? It isn't a sign of crassness to want success. I'm not talking about unrealistic dreams of fame and fortune. Most of us wish we had more time to devote to writing, but without publication, external validation, and reward, that goal remains elusive.

At times we probably all feel, *Who cares what I have to say? What makes me think I have anything to add to all the words in the universe? Why don't I give this up and do something useful with my life?* Most days, I manage to believe that art, literature, writing (the products) really matter. Other times, I say, *Maybe I'm being self-indulgent,* but that's not the worst thing in the world. Basically, I come back to the idea that even if what I'm writing at the moment lacks great merit, I believe that just the fact that I sit quietly and think about life and transform experience into words is helpful not just to me but maybe to others. It's impossible to write without demonstrating your belief in inner and imaginative values.

We all go through periods of writers block and darkness. We pass through them, and *that* is where self-confidence comes from. Only the confidence that comes of experience can quiet those inner voices.

➤➤ 5

TALKING ABOUT WRITING

BY URSULA K. LE GUIN

PEOPLE COME UP TO YOU IF YOU'RE A WRITER, AND THEY SAY, I WANT to be a writer. How do I become a writer?

I have a two-stage answer to that. The first-stage answer is this: You learn to type (or to word-process). The only alternative is to have an inherited income and hire a full-time stenographer. If this seems unlikely, don't worry. Keyboards are easy to learn.

Well, the person who asked, How do I become a writer, is a bit cross now, and mumbles, but that isn't what I meant. (And I say, I know it wasn't.) I want to write short stories, what are the rules for writing short stories? I want to write a novel, what are the rules for writing novels?

Now I say Ah! and get really enthusiastic. You can find all the rules of writing in the book called *Elements of Style,* by Strunk and White, and a good dictionary—I recommend the *Shorter Oxford*; Webster's is too wishy-washy. There are only a very few rules of writing not covered in those two volumes, and I can summarize them thus: Your story may begin in longhand on the backs of old shopping lists, but when it goes to an editor, it should be typed, double-spaced, on one side of the paper only, with generous margins—especially the left-hand one—and not too many really grotty corrections per page.

Your name and its name and the page number should be on the top of every single page; and when you mail it to the editor it should have enclosed with it a stamped, self-addressed envelope. And those are the Basic Rules of Writing.

I'm not being funny. Those are the basic requirements for a readable, therefore publishable, manuscript. And, beyond grammar and spelling, they are the only rules of writing I know.

All right, that is stage one of my answer. If the person listens to all

18

that without hitting me, and still says All right all right, but how *do* you become a writer, then I can deliver stage two. How do you become a writer? Answer: You write.

It's amazing how much resentment and evasion this answer can arouse. Even among writers, believe me.

The most frequent evasive tactic is for the would-be writer to say, But before I have anything to say, I must get *experience.*

Well, yes; if you want to be a journalist. But I don't know anything about journalism, I'm talking about fiction. And of course fiction is made out of experience, your whole life from infancy on, everything you've thought and done and seen and read and dreamed. But experience isn't something you go and *get*—it's a gift, and the only prerequisite for receiving it is that you be open to it. A closed soul can have the most immense adventures, go through a civil war or a trip to the moon, and have nothing to show for all that "experience"; whereas the open soul can do wonders with nothing. I invite you to meditate on a pair of sisters. Emily and Charlotte. Their life experience was an isolated vicarage in a small, dreary English village, a couple of bad years at a girls' school, another year or two in Brussels, and a lot of housework. Out of that seething mass of raw, vital, brutal, gutsy Experience they made two of the greatest novels ever written: *Jane Eyre* and *Wuthering Heights.*

Now of course they were writing from experience; writing about what they knew, which is what people always tell you to do; but what was their experience? What was it they knew? Very little about "life." They knew their own souls, they knew their own minds and hearts; and it was not a knowledge lightly or easily gained. From the time they were seven or eight years old, they wrote, and thought, and learned the landscape of their own being, and how to describe it. They wrote with the imagination, which is the tool of the farmer, the plow you plow your own soul with. They wrote from inside, from as deep inside as they could get by using all their strength and courage and intelligence. And that is where books come from. The novelist writes from inside.

I'm rather sensitive on this point, because I often write science fiction, or fantasy, or about imaginary countries—stuff that, by definition, involves times, places, events that I could not possibly experience in my own life. So when I was young and would submit one of these things about space voyages to Orion or dragons or something, I was told, at extremely regular intervals, "You should try to write about things you know." And I would say, But I do; I know about Orion, and dragons, and imaginary countries. Who do you think knows about my own imaginary countries, if I don't?

But they didn't listen, because they don't understand. They think an artist is like a roll of photographic film: You expose it and develop it and there is a reproduction of Reality in two dimensions. But that's all wrong, and if any artist tells you "I am a camera," or "I am a mirror," distrust them instantly; they're fooling you. Artists are people who are not at all interested in the facts—only in the truth. You get the facts from outside. The truth you get from inside.

O.K., how do you go about getting at that truth? You want to tell the truth. You want to be a writer. So what do you do?

You write.

Why do people ask that question? Does anybody ever come up to a musician and say, Tell me, tell me—how should I become a tuba player? No! it's too obvious. If you want to be a tuba player you get a tuba, and some tuba music. And you ask the neighbors to move away or put cotton in their ears. And probably you get a tuba teacher, because there are quite a lot of objective rules and techniques both to written music and to tuba performance. And then you sit down and you play the tuba, every day, every week, every month, year after year, until you are good at playing the tuba; until you can—if you desire—play the truth on the tuba.

It is exactly the same with writing. You sit down, and you do it, and you do it, and you do it, until you have learned how to do it.

Of course, there are differences. Writing makes no noise, except groans, and it can be done anywhere, and it is done alone.

It is the experience or premonition of that loneliness, perhaps, that drives a lot of young writers into this search for rules.

Writing cannot be shared, nor can it be taught as a technique, except on the most superficial level. All a writer's real learning is done alone, thinking, reading other people's books, or writing—practicing. A really good writing class or workshop can give us some shadow of what musicians have all the time—the excitement of a group working together, so that each member outdoes himself—but what comes out of that is not a collaboration, like a symphony performance, but a lot of totally separate, isolated works, expressions of individual souls. And therefore there are no rules, except those each individual makes up.

I know. There are lots of rules. You find them in the books about The Craft of Fiction and The Art of the Short Story and so on. I know some of them. One of them says: Never begin a story with dialogue! People won't read it; here is somebody talking and readers don't know who, and so they don't care, so—Never begin a story with dialogue.

Well, there is a story I know, it begins like this:

"*Eh bien, mon prince!* so Genoa and Lucca are now no more than private estates of the Bonaparte family!"

It's not only a dialogue opening, the first four words are in *French,* and it's not even a French novel. What a horrible way to begin a book! The title of the book is *War and Peace.*

There's another Rule I know: Introduce all the main characters early in the book. That sounds perfectly sensible, mostly I suppose it is sensible, but it's not a rule, or if it is somebody forgot to tell it to Charles Dickens. He didn't get Sam Weller into the *Pickwick Papers* for ten chapters—that's five months, since the book was coming out as a serial in installments.

Now you can say, all right, so Tolstoy can break the rules, so Dickens can break the rules, but they're geniuses; rules are made for geniuses to break, but for ordinary, talented, not-yet-professional writers to follow, as guidelines.

And I would accept this, but very grudgingly. Put it this way: If you feel you need rules and want rules, and you find a rule that appeals to you, or that works for you, then follow it. Use it. But if it doesn't appeal to you or work for you, then ignore it; in fact, if you want to and are able to, kick it in the teeth, break it, fold staple mutilate and destroy it.

See, the thing is, as a writer you are free. You are about the freest person that ever was. Your freedom is what you have bought with your solitude, your loneliness. You are in the country where *you* make up the rules, the laws. It is a country nobody has ever explored before. It is up to you to make the maps, to build the cities. Nobody else in the world can do it, or ever could do it, or ever will be able to do it again.

Absolute freedom is absolute responsibility. The writer's job, as I see it, is to tell the truth. The writer's truth—nobody else's. It is not an easy job. You know how hard it is to say to somebody, just some-

21

body you know, how you *really* feel, what you *really* think—with complete honesty? You have to trust them, and you have to *know yourself,* before you can say anything anywhere near the truth. And it's hard. It takes a lot out of you.

You multiply that by thousands; you replace the listener, the live flesh-and-blood friend you trust, with a faceless unknown audience of people who may possibly not even exist; and you try to write the truth to them, you try to draw them a map of your inmost mind and feelings, hiding nothing and trying to keep all the distances straight and the altitudes right and the emotions honest. . . . And you never succeed. The map is never complete, or even accurate. You read it over and it may be beautiful, but you realize that you have fudged here, and smeared there, and left this out, and put in some stuff that isn't really there at all, and so on—and there is nothing to do then but say O.K.; that's done; now I come back and start a new map, and try to do it better, more truthfully. And all of this, every time, you do alone—absolutely alone. The only questions that really matter are the ones you ask yourself.

⇉ 6

Cultivating the Library Habit

By John Jakes

LIBRARIES ARE MAGICAL PLACES. THERE'S NOTHING QUITE LIKE strolling the hushed aisles, letting your eye rove along dimly lit shelves. Each spine, each title, seems to beckon with a promise of incredible wonders, surprises and adventures.

Libraries not only take us into new and exciting realms, but also help us grow. They answer questions, solve problems, enable us to better ourselves. If I did not have the library habit—which is passed on by families—I certainly couldn't research and write the first chapter of a historical novel.

Whatever the need—from simple escape reading to learning gourmet cookery, or evaluating mutual funds, or confronting dire illness—as my son, Mike, said in his 20s, when he set out to master the handling of small boats: "There's always a book."

I've never forgotten those words. A majority of Americans know how true they are. According to the American Library Association, 66 percent of us use one of the nation's 15,000-plus public libraries annually. And the usage numbers go up each year.

But finding the books we need or want, when we want them, is getting harder. Our libraries are in trouble. And we'd better take notice and remedy the situation before one of our nation's most precious assets becomes a skinny, starving shell of its old self.

With today's tax dollars stretched to the limit, states and towns facing a budget crisis find the library a tempting target. But when they do, bad things happen. Services are curtailed, hours shrink. Worst of all, libraries are closing all over the country. Even in the Great Depression, I don't know of *one* library going out of business.

It's a terrible situation—and here's the paradox: Americans as a whole don't want it to happen! Individually, we want our libraries to succeed. We want *more* for them, not less.

So what's wrong? I'm afraid we must round up the usual suspects—politicians and their Frill Mentality. This is a mindset that perceives public libraries as less important than unfilled potholes.

The Frill Mentality is sometimes bolstered by the assertion that libraries are dinosaurs, doomed to extinction by the computer age. I doubt it. I suspect it will be many years before every home has a computer and the money and expertise to use it.

And will we then give up the children's story hours? Book discussion groups? The librarian who helps us find exactly what we're searching for?

But the Frill Mentality is widespread and insidious. It attacks the very life blood of our nation—information, knowledge. Because a library isn't just some pleasant, dusty building under the trees that's nice to have but not really essential. I believe passionately that the library is one of the cornerstones of a healthy community. It gives us the opportunity to encounter great ideas, great minds, great art.

And spare me the argument that reading is declining because of TV. It may be true in some quarters, but I've seen TV adaptations of my novels drive hordes of new readers straight *to* the libraries, hunting for Jakes books. Some of those readers send me letters saying mine is the first novel they've ever read.

What, then, can you or I do as individuals do to protect and promote our public libraries?

• First, get the facts and figures. Is your library adequately funded? If not, what's a reasonable higher goal to work toward? If you have a good local or county library board, its members can be helpful here.

• Second, watch for elected or appointed officials who exhibit symptoms of the Frill Mentality. If one of them starts blathering about "unnecessary" library hours and "expendable" services, jump on that person with calls or letters. If he or she is unreasonable, elect someone else next time.

• Third, for muscle in your own locality, it helps to have an organized Friends group. If there's one where you are, join it. If there isn't, start one. Friends of Libraries U.S.A. (1700 Walnut St., Suite 715, Philadelphia, PA 19103) will be glad to help.

Finally, as a strategic objective, work to have the library operating tax removed from the general tax fund, and always put it to a public vote separately.

"There's always a book," our son said. That's a promise we absolutely have to keep.

>> 7

Myths About Writing

By Diane C. Arkins

I'm a firm believer in the "author as a sponge" school of writing. I've racked up 20 years as a published author, and correspondingly 20 years' worth of *reading* about writing. I've studied, pondered, memorized, and applied all the varied and sundry hints, tips, caveats, and suggestions the pros have to offer. Yet the more I test and try the truisms, the more I've discovered that "expert" advice isn't always the bottom line to writing satisfaction and success.

It isn't that the experts don't know their stuff. It's just important for the average writer to know that sometimes the rules are meant to be broken, and that even if you march to the beat of a different drummer, the road can still lead to publishing success. Here's the lowdown on Writers' Mythology.

Address your submission to someone on the masthead. If you've been dealing with a particular editor who's interested in your work, this approach makes a lot of sense. But using a masthead from any magazine's current issue can be just as hazardous as risking the disdain of an editor by using the "to whom it may concern" or "Articles Editor" approach.

A potentially salable Christmas piece of mine once met with a sadly delayed fate when I followed the prescribed "masthead etiquette." In June, I'd mailed the story to a specific editor, by name, from the current masthead. Unbeknown to me, the magazine was undergoing a major change in its editorial staff, and anything directed to the outgoing crew was being unceremoniously referred to B.O.B. (Bottom of the Basket), while the new staffers settled in. In December, I received a letter from a new editor, saying, "It's a shame that your piece didn't arrive in time for our Christmas issue, as we had a similar theme." Ouch. I could groan only to myself that, of course, it had "arrived in time."

Manuscripts directed to specific editors can also lose precious weeks of editorial attention awaiting a specific editor's (a) return from vacation, (b) free time to peruse the "slush" pile, (c) completion of other projects at hand, or (d) all of the above. A generic salutation may not always win you points in an editor's book, but it won't necessarily work against you. Let the addresser beware.

Don't submit anything "different." The experts judiciously advise prospective writers to study six months' worth of a target magazine's most recent issues as examples of what the magazine is looking for. While every writer should have a working familiarity with potential markets, submitting carbon copies of what's already being published can actually eliminate or reduce a wide spectrum of creative opportunities: *What if* the magazine is planning an editorial change, or is simply on the lookout for a "one-shot" that's slightly different from their usual fare? *What if* there's been a recent change in staff and the new editor falls in love with your unique article or query? *What if* your originality and creativity shine through in an article, and the editor offers you an assignment based on the submission that in itself wasn't quite right? *What if* your piece is absolutely perfect for a new spin-off magazine being planned that you hadn't heard of?

As long as you're level-headed enough not to submit a story on day-care centers to *National Fisherman,* don't be afraid to be different—to take a chance—to be fresh and exciting! Your ideas and prose may well be the pot of gold at the end of a very grateful editor's rainbow.

Don't write for payment-upon-publication markets. The world would undoubtedly be a much better place if all periodicals issued checks the moment a manuscript was accepted. Some experts argue that payment upon publication will cease to exist if you refuse to write for these periodicals. In reality, all that happens is that you will eliminate some prospective markets that will eventually pay and publish your manuscript.

Certainly, don't make these markets your first choice. But realistically, your story is always better off waiting for possible payment upon publication than hibernating in your desk drawer. Some authors will be selling to these markets . . . why shouldn't that someone be you?

You can't query humor. As a humorist, I'm convinced that the only

27

experts who espouse this theory are *non*-humor writers. Positive-thinking, sales-oriented writers can query on any topic or in any style in which they can produce an article. Some writing fields may simply require a more creative or unconventional approach. For example, my humor essay about living with a self-professed handyman began with a series of questions on how to identify a real do-it-yourselfer. I began my query with those same questions and continued to entice the editor by promising that:

> Life with a handyman could drive you crazy, but fortunately help is available in the form of my short humor essay.

and

> If you've ever done dishes in the bathtub while your Better Half desperately "plumbs" away at the kitchen sink, you may be interested in returning the enclosed SASE for a copy of my story.

Lifting enticing lines and phrases from your article can help to sell virtually *any* type of article.

Always start at the "bottom." Many experts try to steer novice writers to self-imposed "internships" at low-paying, less prestigious markets. When you write and revise a piece to make it the very best you can, don't shortchange yourself by setting self-defeating limitations on your editorial horizons. Always believe in yourself and aim as high as your talents and dreams can take you.

The first three articles I ever wrote for publication sold the first time out—to *Woman's Day, Seventeen,* and *Co-Ed.* This three-time "beginner's luck" became the cornerstone of a very enjoyable part-time/after-hours writing career. It doesn't cost any more to mail your manuscript to the highest echelons in the publishing marketplace than to send it to your hometown paper. Don't sell yourself short. The confidence you show in yourself will shine through in your writing. Aim for the stars. The "top" is a great place to begin!

>> 8

FOURTEEN REASONS FOR REJECTIONS

BY GENE FEHLER

FOR EVERY WRITER WHO HAS A POEM, ARTICLE, PLAY, STORY, ESSAY, filler, or book accepted by a publisher and has seen that work finally appear in print, dozens of "wannabes" just hope. Some of these wannabes have not yet submitted a manuscript for publication; others send out work only to have it returned, unwanted and unloved.

The world of publishing is a cold and hard one for the aspiring writer, and rejections come easy. It helps if you happen to be more talented than ninety-nine percent of all the writers with whom you're competing. But ninety-nine percent of all writers are not more talented. You have to compensate by at least being competent, by working harder at your craft than most other writers do, and by trying to analyze why your work hasn't been accepted as widely as you think it deserves to be.

Here are fourteen key factors that keep aspiring writers from having their work published:

1) **You really don't want to write; you just want to be published.** You are a dreamer; you visualize your byline in a major magazine, your name on the cover of a novel. You dream of topping the bestseller list. While dreams are the lifeblood of a writer, dreams minus work equals rejection. "I'm a novelist," you tell people, not adding that your novel is still unwritten. You've told yourself, "All I have to do is take a couple hours to sit down and write it." But when you actually do sit down and start to write, you discover that the process requires effort. You discover you don't really want to write, you want to have written something—anything—that will get your name in print, that will identify you forevermore as an exalted Author. Only rarely do you discipline yourself to complete even a first draft. When that

29

first draft is rejected, you blame those obtuse editors for not recognizing your genius.

2) **You haven't read widely the kind of material you are trying to write.** If you want to write young adult novels, you must spend the necessary hours in the library and in bookstores finding and reading the best young adult books. Writing mysteries? Read them by the dozens, the hundreds. Tens of thousands of self-proclaimed poets have written far more poems than they have read. Almost all of those "poets" remain unpublished. It's virtually impossible to write quality poetry without having immersed yourself in the poetry of the masters and in the best contemporary poetry. You can't develop a sense of poetic language, of sounds, of form, of imagery, of tone, of structure, without *seeing* and *hearing* how those elements are handled by great poets. If you want to write poems with subtleties and layers of meaning and striking images, you need to read the best of that kind of poetry. If you want to write homey or inspirational poetry, light verse or accessible poetry or street poetry, you must read widely the best of those types. Otherwise, you simply can't know the diverse techniques that go into building those literary works.

The same holds true for every field of writing: picture books, westerns, horror, romance, science fiction, mainstream novels, plays, to name only a few. Libraries and bookstores are filled with thousands of great teachers. Be receptive to all they have to offer—unless, of course, you were born with an intuitive understanding of your genre's techniques, with a style so fresh, mature, and distinctive, that no other writer has anything to teach you.

3) **You haven't mastered writing techniques.** Having read widely the kinds of novels or poems or articles you're trying to write, you may be able to recognize the techniques that make a piece of writing good. But you can give yourself even more of an edge by learning as much as possible about specific writing techniques. In addition to magazines for writers and books on how to write various kinds of works, creative writing classes or groups can help you learn how to handle a flashback, develop characters, sharpen your language, build plot, create atmosphere, sustain suspense.

4) **You've been too easily discouraged.** The fact that your work is not on the level of Stephen King's or Robert Penn Warren's or

Chekhov's shouldn't cause you to stop trying. Only a small number of writers will ever reach those levels of accomplishment. But after you write a few hundred thousand words, you may discover that your style can hold its own against many published writers.

Some writers are discouraged and give up after one or two rejections. Just because your first submission comes back rejected is no reason to call it quits. There are countless examples of manuscripts that are accepted only after thirty or forty rejections. Remember that most magazines, especially the top markets, publish less than one percent of the material submitted to them. Hundreds of best sellers would never have been published if the authors had stopped after only half a dozen rejections.

5) **You haven't studied the market.** All editors have horror stories about manuscripts they have received that were totally inappropriate for their target audience. Don't waste your time or the publishers' by sending an erotic novel to a religious book publisher, a picture book to a publisher of romance novels, a short story to a publisher of historical novels. If you are submitting poetry, study *The International Directory of Little Magazines and Small Presses,* and the poetry market listings in this book and in writers' magazines. Send for sample copies of magazines you think you might like to write for to determine whether your style and subject are appropriate for that publication. (There is usually a small fee for sample copies.) Browse at newsstands and bookstores and libraries. Many writers use a scattergun approach, submitting their manuscripts to markets at random, hoping to get lucky and hit the right editor with the right manuscript. You can *make* your own luck by studying the markets *before* submitting your work.

6) **You failed to follow up leads.** Have you ever received an encouraging word from an editor and then failed to follow up on it, or to respond to an editor's invitation to "send more," or ignored an editor's encouragement? If an editor bothers to write "try again," or "close, but not quite," submit new, appropriate material to that editor as soon as possible. Some writers get angry at being rejected: "Why should I send that editor anything else? I sent my best work and it was rejected!" If an editor invites you to submit, the odds have shifted in your favor. If you respond, your new manuscript may be rejected, the editor may ask to see more, or your work will be accepted. Even if

you get another rejection, the editor who has invested time in considering your work may make suggestions for revision or suggest other markets.

7) **You can't take criticism.** You think angrily, "My story works for me," or "My article says what I want it to say." Or, "They're missing my point; they didn't read my poem carefully enough." Many writers refuse to accept advice, either through stubbornness, false pride, or arrogance. Some writers want their work published their way or not at all. They don't recognize the fact that the suggestions editors make for revisions will often make the difference between acceptance and rejection.

In critique groups, opinions flow freely. Some suggestions have merit; others don't. But the writer who is willing to listen with an open mind and not get defensive when a story or poem doesn't work has the benefit of a supportive group, in effect, a personal editorial staff.

8) **Your writing is commonplace or lacks imaginative spark.** Sometimes a piece of writing looks good at first reading; it's grammatically sound and competently written. But a closer reading shows that it does not fulfill the expectations initially promised, which would make it disappointing to readers. The topic alone does not make a story. What makes it stand out is your ability to handle the subject or theme in a fresh, unique, distinctive way. It's been said that some writers can write about the end of the world and make it seem trite and boring, while others can write about a napkin or a blade of grass and make it seem exciting. You must always strive to make "the unknown familiar, the familiar unique."

9) **Your query letters don't "sell" your idea.** Many potentially salable manuscripts are summarily rejected because of a poor query letter. Here's an example:

This is my first try at writing a novel. It's just as scary as any Stephen King has written, so I know you'll want to publish it.

Or:

I don't know if you publish poetry or not, but here are three poems that I just wrote last night. Please let me know right away what you think about them.

A strong query is one way to improve your chances of getting your work published. Learn what you should and should not put into a query. Here's a quick summary: a) Find out from market listings if you should first send a query or whether a publisher wants to see the complete manuscript with a cover letter. b) Don't be cocky or arrogant about your work. c) Include a list of relevant credits. d) Make your query brief and to the point. e) Give your qualifications and experience for writing the work you are submitting. f) Let your query letter show editors that you are a writer they would like to work with.

10) **You don't revise before submitting your manuscript.**
"Revision is boring. I'll let the editor polish my manuscript." Who do you suppose has the better odds, the writer who submits the first draft of a manuscript or the writer who has written five or ten or even twenty drafts, setting the manuscript aside for a time between each draft to gain a fresh perspective, then polishing and tightening it with each revision?

After a few rejections, take a new look at your work more objectively. Perhaps you will discover new approaches, more precise wording to improve the piece. You can make any piece of writing better.

11) **You are too concerned with writing for a specific market.**
Some writers simply do not fully explore the wide range of possible markets. An acceptance from *The New Yorker* or *The Atlantic* would be nice, but your success as a writer does not depend on it. Don't fall into the trap of many beginning writers who get rejected again and again by the same magazine, or handful of magazines, without exploring other markets. You may have the right ammunition but the wrong target, or too small a target area. You've failed to explore the hundreds of other magazines that are realistically more appropriate for your work.

12) **You haven't learned the editorial requirements of a specific market.**
Is there a special field that you feel competent to write about? If so, make the most of it. Find out which markets want articles or books about that specialty, because you are probably more qualified to write about it than most writers. Writing extensively about it will open up other opportunities for you and give you more exposure and the confidence to explore new areas.

13) **You make excuses for not writing.** "I could have published a novel, but I just didn't have time to write it." No matter how busy you are, if you really want to write, you can find a period of time each day—however short—to get started on a piece of writing. And gradually, writing will take priority over other activities that had consumed your time. Excuses are easy; writing is hard. You have to decide that writing is worth the time and effort it takes to do it well.

14) **You may not have the talent or skill to succeed at the level you'd envisioned.** A good deal of published writing may not be outstanding, but what the authors did have was perseverance. They kept at it until an editor or publisher felt their manuscripts were worthy of publication. That's the key to getting published: Keep writing. Keep improving. Keep studying the markets. Keep your manuscripts in circulation. As you continue to work at your craft, analyze your limitations and your strengths. Recognize that there are markets you cannot realistically hope to break into; focus on those you're capable of writing for successfully, and try to develop whatever skills can make you succeed in those markets.

If you are an unpublished writer or a published writer hoping that your work will find greater acceptance by publishers, take a close look at the reasons you may have fallen short of your publication goals. Once you've faced and overcome the reasons for rejection, you'll increase your chances of having an editor say, "You're just the writer we've been looking for!"

➢➢ 9

IMAGINING WHAT YOU DON'T KNOW

BY PAULA FOX

I HAVE BEEN UNABLE TO PUT OUT OF MY MIND, THOUGH I HAVE TRIED, a sentence I glimpsed in the last paragraph of an interview with a novelist that appeared in a national magazine a few years ago. The novelist, when asked about her plans, replied, "Now that I have succeeded as a writer, I'm looking for new forms of stimulation."

Such fatuousness is not exceptional, perhaps not even surprising during these days when one of the more intrusive catchwords has become *lifestyle*, with its implication that how one lives is entirely by choice, by will, and when the director of a national self-help organization announces from his platform that "We must applaud everything equally and give up the useless habit of evaluation."

Life is not a style, any more than death is a style, although if we give up the "useless habit of evaluation," we may not be able to tell the difference. And as for succeeding as a writer, a claim that in the days of my own youth no writer would have been caught dead making, and wouldn't, I venture to say, have secretly thought, here is what Cesare Pavese says about such self-congratulation in his diary, *This Business of Living:*

Complacency is a deficiency whose penalty is a special perennial adolescence of the spirit. It is doubt which alone can make us probe and glimpse the depth of consciousness.

I have written and published six adult novels and twenty books for young people. Save for an occasional sentence, a paragraph here and there, I haven't been content with my work. "Eased" is closer to describing the sense of deliverance I feel when the last galley is corrected, when I am, for a time, free of the enveloping tension of work.

During those quiet days, a kind of truce prevails in me. I am relatively untroubled, either by doubt or certainty, volatile states in any

35

case. In fact, for a little while, I rest almost in a torpor, its surface only faintly ruffled by mild, vague thoughts. I can hardly recall, in this state, the days of the years when work was like digging a trench in hard ground. I forget the times of confusion, of tedium, of a failure of nerve, of pulling myself together once more to go to my workroom, wishing the telephone would ring, resenting it when it does, wishing for any distraction, yet dreading all distraction. I forget, too, the moments when writing seems nearly effortless (there are few of those!), and a voice seems to speak through me. And I forget the deep pleasure of an absorption so complete that time itself weighs nothing.

Before the book is actually published, any judgment of mine on the possible failure or success of the book I have written bears on how effectively reviewers will encourage or discourage readers from buying it and reading it; the significance of that kind of success or failure is that it will—or will not—result in buying me time so I can begin once again.

The calm is soon over. A few reviews trickle in. A painful prospect opens up. My book will not be understood by anyone. It will not be read by anyone. Or if it is read and written about somewhere, it will be by that same happy and successful novelist whose words I quoted at the start of this article. And she will say about my book: It has not succeeded! Let the writer seek a new form of stimulation!

Hard and unremitting labor is what writing is. It is in that labor that I feel the weight and force of my own life. That is its great and nettlesome reward.

It is not easy to convince people who take writing courses just how much labor is required of a writer.

After all, their mouths are full of words. They need only transfer those words to paper. Writing can't be really difficult, like learning to play the oboe, for example, or studying astrophysics.

Pavese, in his diary, also writes:

They say that to create while actually writing is to reach out beyond whatever plan we have made, searching, listening to the deep truth within. But often the profoundest truth we have is the plan we have created by slow, ruthless, weary effort and surrender.

Most students of writing need little convincing about the deep truth they have within them, but they are not always partial to "slow, ruthless, weary effort." Few of us are. Yet there comes a time when you know that ruthless effort is what you must exert. There is no other way. And on that way you will discover such limitations in yourself as to make you gasp. But you work on. If you have done that for a long time, something will happen. You will succeed in becoming dogged. You will become resolute about one thing: to go to your desk day after day and try. You will give up the hope that you can come to a conclusion about yourself as a writer. You will give up conclusions.

The English critic, John Middleton Murry, wrote:

A writer does not really come to conclusions about life, he discovers a quality in it. His emotions, reinforcing one another, gradually form in him a habit of emotion; certain kinds of objects and incidents impress him with a peculiar weight and significance. This emotional bias or predilection is what I have ventured to call the writer's mode of experience; it is by virtue of this mysterious accumulation of past emotions that the writer, in his maturity, is able to accomplish the miracle of giving to the particular the weight and force of the universal.

People who see themselves as having succeeded so thoroughly at writing there is nothing left for them except to search out fresh fields of endeavor are not, in my view, in the right profession. Conclusions about life are just what such authors like best. They wish to believe there are answers to everything, and everything is defined by them as that for which they have answers.

I think that the character, the temperament, of their products, exhibit a kind of perverted social-workerism. And their fiction trivializes even as it sentimentalizes our lives no less than did the older, didactic literature of the past, toward which these new didactic writers often express such lofty contempt.

These are not tellers of tales, imaginers. They are answerers, like those voices on the telephone, which, for a fee, can provide a caller with a prayer, a joke, sexual stimulation, weather reports, or a list of antidotes in case one has swallowed poison.

In *The Tragic Sense of Life,* Miguel de Unamuno tells of Solon weeping over the death of his son. When asked why he is weeping, since it will avail him nothing, "That," replied Solon, "is why I was weeping."

Complacency is a deadweight on the spirit. It smothers imagination. But one rarely hears talk about imagination, especially in the classroom. This is partly due, I think, to an insidious kind of censorship. Censors have always been around, wanting to ban books because they contain some sexual or social or political content that frightens or repels them.

But the new censors tell us that, as writers, our only valid subject is ourselves, or those identical to ourselves, as though we were clumps of clones distributed about the earth. Men are to write only about men, women about women, black people about black people, and so on.

What a foretaste of the intolerable boredom that lies ahead! What is to be done with Tolstoy's reflective hunting dog, with Gogol's Nose, with Turgenev's singers of the Brezhin meadow, with Sancho Panza's imaginary kingdom, with all the men and women and children and ghosts and gods and animals that have been imagined and made living for us in all the stories that witness and record our pleasures and our sufferings, the mystery of our lives?

Narrowing, ever narrowing, the new censors, their tiny banners inscribed with ominous declarations: *I can't identify with that! I can't relate to this!* seem to want to ban humanity itself, in all its disarray and difference!

"Maybe we're here," the poet, Rainer Maria Rilke, said, "only to say: house, bridge, well, gate, jug, olive-tree, window—at most, pillar, tower—but to say them, remember, oh! to say them in a way that the things themselves never dreamed of so intensely."

As I write Rilke's words, I think of the great silence into which we hold up our small bundle of words; it is like the blue light of our small planet glimmering in the darkness that is all around.

$\succ\succ$ 10

WHAT IS SUCCESS?

BY JOANNA HIGGINS

UNTIL RECENTLY, I'VE FELT LITTLE NEED TO THINK ABOUT SUCCESS in any systematic way, or to question conventional definitions. It was something to dream about, but in my case it was also something that seems to happen only to others. Since the publication of my first book, though, after twelve years of writing, I *have* been thinking about it, especially when friends say, "You must be *so* excited!"

I agree, of course, not wanting to deflate their enthusiasm. But I don't add that it's not as exciting as the book's acceptance, months ago. And nowhere near the stratospheric excitement I felt while *writing* the stories.

Here's the thing. If I'm not writing, if I haven't written that day when I wanted to, needed to, and could have, had I managed my time better, then in my own eyes I'm not much of a success at that moment. Nor do I feel "victorious" or "prosperous" or "famous," all synonyms of the word. Just a little disconcerted, in the presence of that awesome gap between illusion and reality.

All this has led me to come up with my own definition for success, a personal, existential one: success as *process* as well as result. Journey as well as arrival. For without the journey, there can be no arrival. No success story.

Here, then, are the tenets of my definition:
• Success, above all, is writing—daily, if possible. A little bit or a lot. Writing: making words appear where there were none before—on page or computer monitor. Writing when I feel like it—and when I don't, when I'm high on some idea or in a slump or anywhere in between, when I've been "accepted" or "rejected." Writing. Journal entries, essays, lines of poetry, character sketches, plot ideas, fragments of description, bits of dialogue, three pages, one page; even letters,

39

but really get into them, take time, craft them and enjoy the crafting; don't skimp.

• Success is having a system to help you work through your frustration over rejections. I give myself a day or two, sometimes, to mope, then go out and buy a new ream of paper and say to myself, "Well you have to keep going now until you use this batch up, *then* you can quit, if you want to." The date for this decision, like the millennium, is always pushed ahead, and in the meantime, I get more words down.

• Success is schooling myself to acknowledge and praise previous accomplishments, including—and most important—the writing done that day, not devaluing these victories in light of what I hope to achieve but haven't—yet. So, once in a while I take time to look over a list of my published work and say to myself, "Now, *there.* See?" This exercise also helps the rejection blues. Which leads to the next tenet:

• Success is thinking positively. This really works. The unconscious needs to hear good things. Say, "I can *do* this. It's going to take lots of time and effort and patience, but I can do it, and it'll be terrific. So let's get moving!" And off we go. But if I allow myself to whine—"Oh, I don't think I can do this novel, this poem, this story, I'm not good enough, I'm no writer, look at all these rejections! I'm too old (or too young), too inexperienced, too tired, too fragmented, I have no time, no talent, no one believes in my work, how am I supposed to *write!*"— guess what? Words wither. Pages stay blank or hopelessly botched. What follows is more internal whining—about writer's block. A vicious circle. The real pity is that so much valuable time and energy are spent in the creation of—nothing. Fight these "negs" with positive imagery. Last thing every night, first thing every morning, say a kind of writer's prayer: *I can do this, I will do it.* Repeat ten times. Then see yourself doing it, and sit down and write. That is success.

But exerting one's will and inculcating discipline shouldn't obscure the fact that a sense of *play* is at the heart of all creativity. *Play,* and the freedom—and joy—that true creativity embodies. I once took a beginner's class in acrylic painting and was struck by how much fun it was, learning to mix colors and create the illusion of shapes and perspective on canvas. Another woman in the class, far more accomplished than the rest of us, seemed awfully anxious and tense. Why?

I asked her, when she was obviously so good. She said she'd really enjoyed painting when she first began, but as she started entering competitions, winning prizes, getting commissions, the less she enjoyed painting, and the more stressful it all became.

I immediately thought of parallels to writing. Entering contests, getting rejected, sending a manuscript out again and again over the years, having one's work continually judged in competition with others'—especially in a glutted market—how truly hard it is to retain that sense of play, to be joyful in the doing. *To have fun.* There's bound to be some emotional erosion over time. Success provides the nutrients necessary to rejuvenate the soil: Design a *writer's* sabbatical. Take a course in a field other than writing. Or read works that speak deeply to the writer's soul. My favorites include Dorothea Brande's *Becoming a Writer* and John Gardner's *On Becoming a Novelist.*

• Success is also finding time to read for pure pleasure, so we don't ever forget what we're about, as writers: To give pleasure—through the stories, poems, or creative essays we write. It's important to read the best writers in order to develop an instinct for "the best" and to cultivate it in our own work.

• Above all, success is forgetting about success and just doing the work at hand: finishing a first draft, setting it aside before rewriting, then digging deeper, maybe after weeks of doubt, misgivings, premature judgments, and all the other "negs" we need to fight. It is sending out that story again and again, while continuing to work on other things. *No matter what.*

Prizes, accolades are fine—wonderful, in fact—as testimonials to where we've been. Where I *am,* though, at the moment is what counts. Right now I'm at my desk writing, and it feels just great. Congratulations are definitely in order.

>> 11

Books on Top

By E. Annie Proulx

EVERY OTHER WEEK SOMEONE SAYS THAT BOOKS ARE DEAD OR DYING, that just around the corner is the black hour when they will be curiosities like stereopticon slides or milk stools—probably the same thing they said when radio was invented, when television flickered its way into our living rooms.

To some the phrase means sluggish book sales in the recent and lingering recession; to others it means that the old gray novel ain't what it used to be. Not a few associate the obliteration of distinguished literary houses and imprints in the age of the corporate takeover as synonymous with the inevitable disappearance of books. The hearse followers mournfully announce that no one reads these days, can't read, won't read. It doesn't strike them as peculiar that there is a fierce scramble among corporate interests to buy the publishing houses that put out these dying books.

It's possible that the premature obituaries merely cover our confusion about the clouded direction of change in the culture. As the big publishers try for bestsellers at the expense of serious books, it is increasingly the small publishers and university presses that are finding and publishing the books of interesting new writers.

Books once rather scornfully considered grist for the small publisher's mill are catching the reading public's interest. Among the new books published last year were important works of fiction from Arab-Americans, African-Americans, Chinese-Americans, Mexican-Americans, Caribbean-Americans, Native Americans, and others. The so-called gay and lesbian novel is beginning to escape the genre closet and stand on bookstore shelves alongside traditional works.

Book groups, an old idea, are everywhere. Books are moving into motel and hotel rooms, where a year ago one could find only a single title in a black binding. Now thousands of copies of Joel Conarroe's *Six American Poets* engage travelers in lonely rooms across the continent. There are guidebooks to used bookshops, and a few imaginative independent booksellers thrive in the shadow of ever-increasing numbers of superstores.

Those who say the book is moribund often cite the computer as the asp on the mat. But the electronic highway is for bulletin boards on esoteric subjects, reference works, lists and news—timely utilitarian information, efficiently pulled through the wires. Nobody is going to sit down and read a novel on a twitchy little screen. Ever.

In a curious way, the computer emphasizes the unique virtues of the book:

The book is small, lightweight and durable, and can be stuffed in a coat pocket, read in the waiting room, on the plane. What are planes but flying reading rooms?

Books give esthetic and tactile pleasure, from the dust jacket art to the binding, paper, typography and text design, from the moment of purchase until the last page is turned.

Books speak even when they stand unopened on the shelf. If you would know a man or woman, look at their books, not their software.

>> 12

THE ONE AND THE MANY

BY MICHAEL DIRDA

AMONG THE TENDEREST SCENES IN LITERATURE ARE THOSE IN WHICH a benevolent, often elderly scholar shuffles off to a snug little study to reread for the nth time some favorite book. There he or she, with a sigh of anticipatory pleasure, takes down from the shelf a much-loved copy of *Pride and Prejudice* or *The Decline and Fall of the Roman Empire* or Boswell's *Life of Johnson*. In years past such people might be referred to as the man—or more rarely, the woman—"of one book," and were frequently the occasion for dire warning: Make any single volume a personal scripture and some kind of gleaming fanaticism was sure to result. The model here, of course, was the hellfire preacher who could quote his Bible by chapter and verse as he thunderously delivered sinful unbelievers into the hands of a God even angrier than he was. But there are other examples too: the young Maoist with his *Little Red Book,* the pale Joycean with his marked-up copy of *Finnegans Wake.*

Being one who has read thousands of books—a statement that sounds more than a little grotesque even to me—I have always secretly wished to be a one-title guy. E. B. White, for instance, toted *Walden* around in his pocket for years; he could quote Thoreau, aptly, humorously on just about any subject. Samuel Johnson famously recommended that would-be writers devote their days and nights solely to Addison's essays. Even Alexander the Great, who admittedly didn't have quite as much reading material to choose from as we do, never left for Central Asia without his bejeweled copy of Homer's *Iliad.*

There have been occasions when I've daydreamed about reducing my overflowing library to just one small bookcase of essential volumes, maybe even a single shelf. Surely this would make one feel light and clean, like a bather in a Whitman poem. In a sense, of course, the books that reside permanently on my bedside night table represent just such a selection—the Bible, the Concise Oxford English Dictionary, the five-volume Auden and Pearson *Poets of the English Language,* Montaigne's essays, *The Oxford Book of Aphorisms,* Jules Renard's journal, F. W. Bateson's *Guide to English Literature,* Brewer's *Dictionary of Phrase and Fable,* Lempriere's Classical Dictionary and a dozen or so others (I have a crowded night table). But these are all, for the most part, browsing books, classic references more suitable for insomniac diversion than for passionate devotion.

Unfortunately, like most readers, I lack the single-mindedness to restrict myself to one favorite title. To begin with, I'm not precisely what you would call a rereader, except of poetry. I try to go through novels and nonfiction slowly, with great attention to detail, flipping back and forth to check points, aiming to "see" the book as a whole. Since I mark favorite passages, I can and sometimes do pick up a book to refresh my memory of its contents. Still, I don't suppose there are more than a score of titles I have ever reread from cover to cover.

Not that I don't want to reread more. But in truth I'm a flighty creature, always darting from one bright blossom to the next; I contemplate my groaning bookshelves and see only fresh fields and pastures new. With so many treats still before me, how can I turn away and go back to works I have already read, no matter how deeply enjoyed?

Of course, it is utterly ludicrous of me to say that I already know, say, Thomas Mann's *The Magic Mountain.* I haven't looked at the novel since devouring it one long-ago summer when I was 15. I recall the X-ray taken of the heroine's tubercular chest. I can dredge up the names of some of the main characters—Hans Castorp, Peeperkorn, Settembrini, Naphta. And I am certain that the novel concludes with Hans Castorp leaving the sanitarium to fight in World War I. Unfortunately, these few altogether paltry sentences sum up virtually everything I know about *The Magic Mountain.* How can I say that I've read it?

Here is when I begin to grow depressed and start daydreaming about knowing at least one book inside out. Think of any novel you've ever read, and what do you really possess? Perhaps a few vague memories of its plot, characters and tone; more likely than not, you remember, in the most general way, only how much or how little you liked the book. In truth, next to nothing. Just so, detective-story fans regularly grumble about being halfway through some Agatha Christie whodunit before realizing that they've already pored over its clues and suspects before.

Alas, one carries away so little from even the greatest works of art. Of the longer classics I have read more than once and, in some instances, actually taught to students—*Hamlet, The Divine Comedy, Walden, Huckleberry Finn, Crime and Punishment,* a few others—I am shocked at how little I retain, especially for one often credited with a good memory: only a handful of quotations, a spotty sense of plot. Obviously, were I to open these books again my understanding of them would prove—I hope—deeper than this: Familiarity with the action allows one, at the very least, to focus on the artistry. But stay away for a few years and even the most analyzed text utterly vanishes from the conscious mind.

The memory of a tone, the rhythm of an author's sentences, the sorrow we felt on a novel's last page—perhaps that is all that we can expect to keep from books. As we turn their pages, they amuse/shock/inspire/console/instruct us; but after we return them to our shelves or the public library, they linger in our souls only like the distant images of childhood.

So is it with the novels and nonfiction we read long ago and now only vaguely recall. But fortunately we can still reopen *Lolita* or *Invisible Man* and plunge once more into the lived experience itself. Perhaps poems and stories, like paintings and music, truly exist only when we are actively engaged with them. Afterwards they lose their substance, grow wispy and vague, or find themselves diminished to little more than a few cold facts. The actual art, all that makes a great work funny, sorrowful and real, fades away like a dream at morning.

So when I think back over the books I have loved, I seldom feel any unalloyed pleasure. This copy of *The Good Soldier* made me weep, and now I merely remember its opening sentence and Ford Madox Ford's twisty narrative technique. I can only hope that deep within me, in my soul or subconscious, more of the novel lingers on. Only by rereading it could I reexperience its quite overwhelming artistic and emotive power. But maybe I ought to spend the time on some other classic—*The Good Soldier Schweik,* perhaps. On second—or is that third—thought, I definitely should look into Carol Shields's award-winning *The Stone Diaries.* Only a fool would miss out on the literature of his own time.

Amid such an internal *tohubohu,* is it any wonder that I think fondly of the man of one book, the hedgehog who—in the phrase made famous by Isaiah Berlin—knows one big thing and doesn't need to know any other? In very low moments I sometimes think that a passion for omnivorous reading has seduced me into a lifetime of one-night stands, while the less promiscuous have managed to find a single true and more fulfilling love. But it's too late for me and my kind to change now, no matter how much we may yearn for those carpet slippers and one or two well-worn volumes. How, after all, can I resist that flashy new thriller or sloe-eyed biography, let alone the new novel that promises hitherto unimagined pleasures? Sirens all. Of the reading of many books there is no end.

>> 13

MIXED SIGNALS

By Nancy Springer

THE YOUNG MAN ENTHRONES HIMSELF ATOP A CLASSROOM DESK, FACing me, swinging his combat-booted feet. He is holding a copy of one of my novels; I have just signed it for him. "So how do you do this, anyway?" he asks, keeping his voice deep and casual. "How do you get a book published?"

He is a student in the writing class I teach at a post-secondary school attended mostly by youngsters who are not academically inclined. He wears a lot of leather, always dresses entirely in black, has a bizarre haircut, some tattoos, a ring in one nostril. He wrote his how-to paper on "How to Throw a Hand Grenade" and his "If I Had Three Days to Live" paper on suicide-bombing his former employer. He is muscular and struts when he walks; other male students get out of his way. He is rowdy in class. Yet whenever I ask him to please shut up, he smiles with genuine sweetness and does so—for a few minutes. He is always in attendance, always on time, he writes unusually well, and a lot of what he says—out of turn and between Elvis impersonations—is off-the-wall funny and brilliant. He upstages me constantly. I like him, yet feel deeply unsure about him—mixed signals put me off balance, keep me thinking about him. A friendly, intelligent youth who dresses like death incarnate and is fascinated by weapons? What is he really like? I can't tell.

Now, though, I recognize the glimmer nearly hidden deep in his wise-guy eyes. Or maybe I merely think I recognize it. Maybe I'm just hoping.

How do you get a book published? I have a dozen glib responses at the ready to provide me with quick escape in social situations, but for this young man I think a moment, trying to give him a good, true answer. He waits. "It's a twofold process," I say, "and most people concentrate too much on one aspect or the other."

48

He is listening attentively, his mouth firmly shut.

"First you have to write something good," I say, "which means you really have to learn how to write. That part usually takes years. And then, once you have something worthwhile, you need to market it. Go to conferences, meet people, learn your way around publishing. I see people who write great stuff and stick it in a drawer, and I see a lot more people who write crap and think that if they could just find an agent they could get it published. It doesn't work that way. You have to write good stuff first."

My student nods seriously. I remember he called me at home one evening about an assignment—"Hi, this is Jason." For a moment I couldn't place him; I needed a surname, so in a light tone I asked, "And which Jason might that be?" "The good Jason," he said. This response, as bizarre as his haircut, gives me a shadowy feeling—presumably I have always experienced "the good Jason"? What is the other Jason like? I'm not sure I want to know.

Now, back in my classroom, he says shyly, "I'm writing this book. It's about this kind of hero-type guy, they killed his girlfriend, he's gonna get revenge. He was Army Intelligence, and now he's a bounty hunter. He knows weapons and explosives, he knows how to track people, he can do everything. But I don't want him to be just, you know, a stereotype."

I knew it, I knew it, I knew he was writing a novel! That glimmer deep in his eyes was pure writerly yearning. But I do not inflict any effusions upon him. I try to be as casual and low-key as he is trying to be. "The last book I did with a hero-type guy in it," I say, "I made him short, fat and bald."

"Yeah!" He sits straight up, his face alight with childlike enthusiasm above his metal-studded black-leather jacket collar. "That's what I mean, I need to do something unexpected. Surprise people. I mean, like real life, like me. The way I dress, people don't expect me to be nice."

I nearly laugh out loud, mostly at myself. It is so simple now that he has given me the key. "Jason," I say, "I have hopes for you." He might just do it. He might really be a writer.

"Why?" he asks anxiously, as if my opinion can make it happen.

"You're a twofold person," I say. And maybe that's what a writer has to be. A layered person. The private, hidden person who writes. And the public person who sells what the other has written.

He's a rebel as well. A rebel against appearances and conventional expectations. One who defies What People Think. One who ascribes to secrets and complexities. One who tries to surprise. And maybe a writer needs to be those things, too.

He smiles; we talk awhile longer. I silently and gratefully note that he does not ask me to read his novel manuscript. He has the right instincts: He will do this on his own. I tell him to let me know when he is ready, and I will help him plug into the publishing network. He thanks me, hops off the desk and swaggers out, turning at the door. "Thankyouvermuch." He bows over an imaginary microphone, going into his Elvis routine. In addition to all the rest of it, he's a clown.

A clown obsessed with weapons and combat.

After he is gone, my warm and happy sense of sureness about him deserts me, and doubts shadow me again. Who or what is he? He is built in layers like an onion, and I hope he is not bitter at the core.

Or if he is, I hope writing can help him.

I hope he really is a writer. He is a layered person, and writing is a layered process, draft upon draft upon text upon subtext upon symbol upon subconscious self-expression; it is fitting that writing might be his calling. I hope so. I hope he is writer, because someday I want to read his book. I hope he is a writer, because I want to know what's at the core of this particular onion. I hope he is a writer, because I hope writing will save him from the other Jason.

>> 14

CHOOSING A WRITERS CONFERENCE

BY SHIRL THOMAS

FROM MY OBSERVATIONS AS A CONFEREE, AS WELL AS A SPEAKER AND workshop leader at writers conferences, I have found that those who attend often feel shortchanged, for a variety of reasons: They may find speakers uninterested, hard to approach, or disappointing; are unclear about a conference's procedures and available services; or feel that they don't get the most out of workshop sessions, particularly when writers at varying levels of competence are in the same group.

There are countless writers conferences—local, regional, and national; they can be as short as one day or as long as one week. The conference locale, cost, and theme or focus can vary greatly; subject matter may be geared to beginners or cover advanced writing or marketing techniques. So, how do you decide if a particular conference is worth the time and money? One important factor to consider is your motivation. Are you writing for love of the written word, or striving for a professional career? Prospective goals can make a difference in your determination.

If you write primarily for self-expression, speakers who deal extensively with the literary marketplace or small presses would be of interest. These "little" magazines often publish only experimental works and poetry, and usually offer modest compensation—sometimes, "payment in copies only." However, they are receptive to beginning writers who can gain valuable experience from contributing to these markets and have a better chance of getting published.

If you have professional goals, attending workshops on business and marketing would be beneficial, along with hearing speakers from the more prestigious magazines and publishing houses, as well as literary agents who could be helpful in placing your work later on.

In any case, some research is necessary before making an informed decision about attending one conference over another. Here are some guidelines:

1. Does it fit your needs?

You should have a direct interest in the market categories represented. Most conferences will offer a range of several different fields, while others are organized around a specific theme or topic, such as "Writing for Children" or "Articles in the Making." Find out in advance what market categories will be covered. Do they match your writing interests?

For example, if workshops and seminars emphasize "whodunits" and you're concentrating more on "how-tos," you may want to choose a different conference. (There is much to be said, however, for mixing fiction techniques with nonfiction styles.)

2. What type of help will be offered?

There are four popular conference formats: lectures; workshops; writer discussion groups; and speaker roundtables, or a combination of two or three. Choose the one most appropriate to your taste and needs, taking into account whether a conference is geared to your level of writing. Ask yourself these questions: Will discussions include beginning fundamentals or be restricted to more advanced techniques and the business side of writing? Will detailed instruction be offered? Will there be an opportunity to have your manuscript critiqued at the conference? By whom? Other conferees, or workshop leaders—editors, publishers or agents? May manuscripts be sent in advance and appointments set up so that you can be sure of being able to discuss your work with a professional? Should you bring a writing sample— or a portfolio?

Determine the level of your participation well in advance, and be prepared to take advantage of these opportunities.

NOTE: Make sure any material you do bring with you is professionally typed and ready for the market. No first drafts!

3. Who are the speakers?

Research the qualifications of speakers and the genres and specific areas they will cover, and decide whether they warrant your time and effort. Will appointments for private consultation be available? If not, ask whether speakers will have question-and-answer sessions or will mind being approached by participants at the conference. And when the time comes, remember: Don't be too timid or too pushy.

4. How much will it cost?

In addition to the registration fee, will the costs for food, lodging, and travel fit your budget? Conferences at luxury hotels may be prohibitive, so you may want to consider going to a conference held on a college campus. (Don't expect to recoup expenses with the money you'll make from your writing!)

5. What are the proposed schedules?

Will there be a conflict in the schedules for the lectures or workshops in which you have a special interest? If so, will you be able to buy tapes of the overlapping seminars? Do you object to early-morning or late-evening sessions?

NOTE: If you are restricted by time or finances, you may want to check to see if you can be a part-time participant.

Attending the right conference at the right time can open doors of opportunity for a writer, provide an often needed change of scenery, a fresh point of view, and insight into how others are pursuing the craft. Although some writers may find the prospect of being around professional authors intimidating, keep in mind that successful published writers were once beginners, too, and are usually sensitive to newcomers' trepidations. Though some speakers' egos may interfere with the goal of addressing writers' concerns, most are dedicated to assisting writers and are prepared to help—otherwise, they would not agree to participate.

If you leave a conference feeling only that it provided entertainment or perhaps a diversion, then there may have been little merit in having attended. But if the time spent at a writers conference helps you improve, or has given you a push in the right direction, then it was a worthwhile endeavor—whether you write for the love of the craft or with the goal of becoming a professional. In any case, it's a personal choice. Decide what you want to derive from the experience, and then go for it.

➤➤ 15

Gertrude Stein's Secret

By Helen Marie Casey

"And that is all there is to good writing," Gertrude Stein wrote, "putting down on the paper words which dance and weep and make love and fight and kiss and perform miracles."

Who can argue with a description that creates its own miracle of synopsis, that uses action verbs to show as well as tell, that mirrors the magic of words at work?

Without explicitly mentioning stories or poems, Stein's collection of highly charged, extraordinarily visual action words takes us to the realm of imaginative writing, to poems, plays, and novels we love.

We know what she is talking about because we know where words in the hands of an artist can take us. We've been there. We've been in that magic kingdom where "Let's pretend" ends by taking us deep into meanings we didn't know we could find.

Stein's words focus us on the raw power of language, of even the simplest words: *dance; weep; make; love; fight; kiss; perform; miracles*. At the same time, they humble and they energize us. These words are choreographed. They are alive. They are in motion. They sing. They are compelling.

Is it the content of what she has to tell us that arrests us, or is it the phrasing itself? Does the magic, in fact, lie in the way she has placed her words on the page?

We look again and are struck by the cadence she has achieved by the balanced use of that small word *and*: "And that is all there is to good writing, putting down on the paper words which dance *and* weep *and* make love *and* fight *and* kiss *and* perform miracles." There's a lilt in the movement of the sentence that rises with each succeeding action word. This is no accidental arrangement of thoughts. The statement has the economy of a tightly crafted short story at the same time that it has the grace of a lyric poem.

What do we learn from so brief—and eloquent—an observation about good writing? We're reminded all over again that words work. They do not achieve their effect by serendipity. They cannot be selected at random. All words are not equal. After they are selected, words must be properly shaped and chiseled if they are going to leap when they must.

Words cannot be partnered willy-nilly. Strong, simple verbs do not want to be overpowered. They must be trusted to carry their full weight.

Words that the tongue savors require time for the savoring. Duration. They want pauses around them, pauses created by other words that slow us down and pauses created by careful line breaks and intelligent punctuation.

The hard work of writing is not the initial setting down of words but the listening to them to hear what they are telling us about themselves, about how they want to work, how they want to go about saying what they want—and know how—to say. Words in fresh combination, words in patterned repetitions, words doing work they've never done before: All have their own requirements.

In a sense, each word or image becomes a hinge. That word-hinge has dictates of its own about precisely what may follow. The heft of each word must be taken before it can be entrusted with carrying on its work on the page.

What Gertrude Stein knew about language she tried to tell us. She wrote and spoke about language. She experimented with language, spending a lifetime letting words play through her fingers to the page. She listened to words with the intensity of an artist who, while moving away from conventional approaches, is listening all the while for new direction. Her ear became her great ally in writing. It taught her to follow the rhythm of language; it taught her the importance of repetition, particularly nuanced repetition; and it taught her to create and value the dense linguistic texture created by words—often seemingly devoid of meaning—reverberating off each other.

Gertrude Stein was thoroughly unconventional in her writing. She broke syntactical rules. She thumbed her nose at traditional approaches to narrative. She created new patterns in every genre she touched. She left us an immense body of work, and she shared her secret: *If the communication is perfect, the words have life, and that is all there is to good writing, putting down on the paper words which dance and weep and make love and fight and kiss and perform miracles.*

➤➤ 16

Writer's Block—and What to Do About It

By Jeffrey Skinner and Stephen Phillip Policoff

Now here's a subject and a cry near and dear to every writer's heart: I can't think of a single thing to say!

You wake bright and early. You note the weather and the stirring of the few birds earlier than yourself carrying on their bird business in the yard. You brew the coffee, eat your bran muffin, settle in to that magical corner of your room. In the past, this spot has reliably carried you to the height of the American Parnassus. You touch extra-fine-point felt-tip pen to paper. Two hours pass and, upon lifting pen from paper you discover . . . a dot! It's round! The same color as the ink in your pen! Never mind that every pencil within reach may now be sharpened to acuity, and your desk beautifully organized and dusted for the first time in six months, and a second pot of coffee consumed, and all neighborhood bird life and car movements scrupulously observed and mentally noted. You have not written a word.

This is an old story. Every writer has a tale of woe to tell about going blank, dry, empty, blocked. Even when I first began writing and would turn out poems at an alarming rate, day after day, I eventually got wind of this thing called writer's block and, of course, immediately came down with an acutely painful case of it. "I'm afraid," I said archly to a friend, "that each poet has a finite stock of images given to him in a lifetime, and that I may be approaching the end of my store."

The problem is that we have amnesia. Sometimes we forget that we have written before, that we are essentially the same person, and that we will touch that true place of poetry within us and write again. We mistake a momentary pause for a permanent condition. I don't know why writers are so susceptible to this fear; perhaps because, by temperament, we have such a strong interest and investment in the very notion of permanence.

In any case, it is common among writers to experience periods of block, or dryness, or times when the muse does not return our calls—however we choose to characterize those stretches when nothing comes, and we simply do not write. And the fact that virtually every one among us, in this loose tribe called writers, at one time or another, or repeatedly, shares this problem, should and can be the beginning of our calm as we face writer's block individually. We are not alone; others have worked through blocks to write more and better than ever before, and so can we. So the first thing to do when facing the scary void of writer's block is to relax, to rest easy in the knowledge that you *will* write again.

The fact is that there are probably times in any writer's life when it is a good idea not to be writing. "To every thing," Ecclesiastes said, "there is a season." The marathoner must rest at the end of a race, and poet who has written hard under the white heat of inspired composition has also expended great energy and needs time to regroup and recover mentally, physically, and spiritually. This is natural, and it may well be that an inability to write the next poem, at the time you want to write it, is a deep expression of the body/mind/spirit's need for solitude, silence, new reading, or simply just loafing around. Loafing is good: "I loaf and invite my soul, I lean and loaf at my ease observing a spear of summer grass," said Walt Whitman. All of us, in this time and this country, are more driven than is good for our souls. Walt had the right idea. There is a time for writing, and there is a time for contemplation, for just being.

After we have taken a few deep breaths, gained some healthy perspective on the problem, and had our proper fill of loafing, there are some concrete steps we can take to "prime the pump"—to slip back into the writing head. I'll list a few that have worked for me and for other poets I've known. As with all my suggestions, not every one will work for you, but if you keep trying I'm pretty sure that something will, by and by, shake loose inside, letting the words through again.

Vary writing locations

Generally, it's a good idea to establish a writing routine, if at all possible: writing in the same place, at the same time, for the same period, every day. This is the ideal, but any schedule approaching this regularity can work.

Writing under these circumstances becomes a sort of conditioned response; somehow the body/mind/psyche learns through repetition that there is a time and place to write and slips faster and deeper into the writing mode with familiarity and practice. The unconscious (whatever that may mean) gets into the act.

An hour a day on a regular basis is better than ten hours all at once at unpredictable intervals. We understand only too well how hard this is to put into practice in our harried world, but we also have experienced (at those blissful times when we were able to write on a regular, daily basis) the benefits of such perseverance.

This is one of those general principles that was made to be broken. And if you are blocked, vary your writing routine. Maybe just the thing you need to stir up fresh stuff is to write in the park instead of at your desk; to write first thing in the morning, if you are a usually a night writer; to use a pen instead of a typewriter or a typewriter instead of a pen. Writers tend to be ritualistic, at least about writing process and paraphernalia, and sometimes turning our usual ritual on its head can result in a poem (or a story or a play) we never dreamed could come from us—one that can "stand on its hands." Experiment!

Give up the fixed ideas you've had about your own writing ("I can write only when it's absolutely quiet") and try the opposite. You can change the rules of the game. Why not? It's your game.

Vary your reading

Writers tend to be readers ("A writer is a reader who is moved to emulation," said Saul Bellow), so we probably don't have to tell you how important it is to the enrichment of your own work to read the work of others. But it is. Read the work of those who are doing, this moment, what you want to do—living, publishing poets and fiction writers. Read lots of it. You're not going to like all of what you read, but that's natural; nobody likes all of anything. But we hope you find enough to fall in love with: those chosen writers that seem to speak to you personally, whom you read with absolute wonder that they know so much about your inner life, who change you in ways sometimes more profound than the three-dimensional, living-color people you speak to and dance with and love and can't stand, every day. The passion of our reading feeds the passion of our writing, in some way both mysterious and absolutely real.

So if we find ourselves in a slump, we can easily change one of the things that most directly and deeply affects our writing: our reading. As in location, sometimes it's very fruitful to make a radical change— to pick up the kind of book we never thought we'd be interested in, something ordinarily far from our tastes. If we have a passion for Kurt Vonnegut, we might try the more mainstream (but also highly readable and accomplished) novels of Anne Tyler. If our tastes in poetry ordinarily run to the high-speed surrealism of, for example, James Tate, we might try the firmly grounded, statuesque poems of Louise Gluck. If you don't know enough about the scene to find such new resources, ask your friends for recommendations.

But this suggestion about varying your reading does not only apply to "fine literary writing." Most writers are voracious readers of anything printed. There is nothing wrong with "escapist" literature! Or instruction manuals, biographies, fairy tales, geology textbooks, rock star interviews, science journals, *People* magazine, or, anything in words—it can all be grist for the writer's mill. Pick up the *National Enquirer* at the supermarket checkout. Maybe the two-headed baby story will spark your next story or poem. We don't suggest that you make this kind of thing your only pleasure reading; it's essential that you read the best published examples of contemporary fiction and poetry and lots of it. But ideas come from the oddest places, and for a writer to divide all printed matter into the two categories of *literature* and *trash,* boasting of the former and sneering at the latter, is simply self-imposed limitation. It's more liberating to think of ourselves as scientists of the sentence, the line, the word; on some level every specimen is worth examining. Read with an alert sensitivity to language, and everything you read will give you something—perhaps the beginnings of your next poem or story.

Jump-starts

Freewrite in your journal to help you rev up your creative engine and jump-start your failed battery. Write down everything that comes into your head. Describe the smirk on a colleague's face; scold your friend on the page; write the stupidest, foulest things you can think of. Any writing helps the act of writing seem less daunting.

Write a letter, not a real letter but one that you have no intention of mailing. Write a letter to someone you admire but could never bring yourself to talk to. Write a letter to the friend you wish you had. Write a letter to someone in which you say everything you've ever wanted to say—then throw it away. Or, better still, read it over; maybe you'll find a poem lurking in there; maybe there's a character you've invented without even knowing it.

Exercise. Creative people often use physical exercise as a way of forcing their minds to work in a different way. Sitting and brooding over the blank page in front of you is probably the worst thing you can do. Jog around your neighborhood; take your dog for the longest walk he's ever been on; go for a swim; ride your bike to that secret place where you can scream, and no one will hear you—or care, anyway. But while you're doing these things, be sure you keep your eyes open, and observe everything around you. Be a sponge; soak up the atmosphere, even if it's the same atmosphere you see every day.

People-watch—intensively. If you can, go somewhere, sit down, and watch the world go by. Go to the mall, the local diner, the donut shop, the bus station, the train station, a busy downtown street—somewhere, anywhere, as long as there are lots of people going by. Bring your journal, and just sit and watch. Sooner or later someone will do something or say something or walk by wearing a weird hat, and maybe you'll get an idea. Maybe you won't, but you will have removed yourself from the place where ideas are not flowing, and put yourself in a position to make them flow. There is probably no better way to invite ideas than simply to allow yourself to observe and think and laugh.

Sit in the dark and listen to music. The idea is to jolt your mind out of its usual mode of thinking, and try to get into a sort of trance state. That's what freewriting does, to an extent, and what physical exercise does. Some music nudges us into that state. You must experiment with the sort of music that will work for you. It probably won't be the kind of music you listen to for fun, to dance to, or when you're bored. Instead, try some instrumental music—classical or jazz—or what is often called "New Age" music, music that washes over you, like waves of the ocean. You may hate it, but the point is that this sort of music (and weirder music, like that of Philip Glass and Laurie Anderson) often acts in an almost hypnotic way and may coax your imagination out of hiding.

61

Go to a museum. Looking at pictures, especially unusual ones, or pictures you are unfamiliar with, can be a valuable goad to the creative process. If there's no museum accessible, go to the library or to a bookstore and look at art or photography books. Try to find an image or two that intrigues you or gives you the creeps, then without trying to figure out why you like or hate it, write down everything you can remember about it: what it made you think of, what you think the artist was up to, what you saw in that picture.

There are lots of other gambits that writers have dreamed up to coax them out of writer's block. Ernest Hemingway always stopped for the day in mid-sentence so that when he returned the next day, he would have a way of beginning again without thinking about what he was doing.

Remember, too, that all writers write badly most of the time. All writers—young ones, old ones, famous ones, desperate ones. Feeling compelled to write brilliantly, or even passably well, all the time is a sure-fire way to thwart your ability to write at all.

Ultimately, the most important lesson to be learned from writer's block is this: You just have to write. You can put it off, you can worry about it, you can tear up each page because you hate it so much, you can swear you'll never write again, but still you know that you will. Writing is the best cure for not writing. Writing nonsense, writing stuff you know stinks to high heaven, writing because you want to, have to write—that's all that counts.

➤➤ 17

DIGGING UP THE FACTS

BY RICHARD S. SMITH

THE STORY HAD BEEN PROGRESSING SMOOTHLY, ALMOST EFFORT-
lessly, until I got to the part where my protagonist, Matthew McClure,
was forced to open the lid of a coffin. This stopped me dead, if you'll
pardon the expression.

I did not have the foggiest idea how a coffin lid works.

Does anybody? Maybe undertakers and grave robbers, I thought,
but I have never had the misfortune to exchange pleasantries with
either of them.

What I wanted to say in the story was something like this: "Matt
reached under the coffin, unfastened the latch, and raised the lid
quickly so that . . ."

But is it a latch? Maybe coffins have more of a catch. Or a hasp,
bolt, fastener, clinch, clip or clasp. And it might be located on the top,
rather than on the bottom.

It's not that I'm too lazy to do a little research now and then, but
this was ridiculous. Would any of my readers really care? Yes, they
would. A casket manufacturer, for instance. I could already see the
sales manager's irate letter:

Dear Mr. Smith:
After reading your story, "Six Feet Under," I realize how true it is that
writers should write about what they know. You obviously wouldn't know a
casket if it fell on you. The lid will open only if you release the fradestan
buckle which is located, not under the coffin, but just to the left of the catary
elbow coupler near the head handle. So now you know. And when your time
is nigh, and you feel death's soft breath on your cheeks, remember our name.
Our coffins are known as the Cadillacs of the industry. Incidentally, why wait?
If you order now, we can offer you a ten percent discount.

Heaven help me I should get such a letter.

But to get back to my story, the situation was as follows: Matthew, a

North Carolina mountain man, is attending the funeral of his eccentric brother, Arvel. Just as the coffin is being lowered into the ground, Matt remembers a pledge he made to Arvel on his deathbed. He promised to bury with him two of his most prized possessions: his harmonica, on which he could play only one tune, "Home on the Range," and his box of dead bugs.

Are you still with me?

Anyway, Matthew forgets all about it until it's almost too late. The two items are still not in the casket as it begins to disappear into the hold, so he has to have it brought back up to the surface. To make matters even worse, Arvel's body has not been embalmed (to save the family, which is very po', money) and by now the flesh is ripe enough to fall off the bones. So what Matt has to do is get the lid up as fast as possible and slide the bugs and harmonica in before something foul slides out.

I called the library and asked if they had any books on the construction of caskets. They wanted to know if I was serious. I said, "Hell, yes, I'm *dead* serious. This knowledge is absolutely essential to the authenticity of a story I'm writing."

They suggested I call a funeral home.

O.K. There were fifteen of them listed in the phone book, confirming my suspicions that death, while not very advantageous to the deceased, must be highly profitable for those who care for the remains.

My first call was to the Swan Song Mortuary, where I got a busy signal. The phone was also busy at the Eternal Rest Funeral Parlor, the Last Sleep Embalmment Center, and a joint called Terminally Yours. Business must be booming, I thought. Had a horrible plague struck the area? I finally got an answer at a place called The Debt Which Cancels All Others.

"I'm a free-lance writer," I said. "In the story I'm writing one of the characters has to open a coffin. How does the lid work?"

There was a long pause, followed by a chuckle, and then, "Is that you, Marty?"

"Marty?" I said.

"Come on," said the voice. "I know it's you. Ha-ha. That's really a good one. How does the lid work."

I hung up and dialed the Swan Song again. This time I got an answer and briefly explained my problem.

"Is the coffin a single or double-lidder?" the man asked.

"What's the difference?"

"Well, with a single-lidder, the whole lid comes up. On the double model, only the top half raises, the half where the deceased's head is located. The lower half of the body remains covered with the bottom half of the lid."

Isn't research wonderful? I had already learned something new and useful, but it didn't alter the fact that I had no particular coffin preferences.

"Make it a double," I said absently.

"It's really very simple," the man said. "by the way, my name's Fogg, as in London."

"Mine's Smith," I said. "As in under the spreading chestnut tree."

"I could probably explain it over the phone," said Fogg, "but I think it would behoove you to come in and let me demonstrate."

Sure. Why not? I needed a break, anyway. I said goodbye to the wife and told her I was going into town to look at some coffins. She immediately turned deathly pale, if you'll pardon the expression.

"My God!" she cried, clawing at her hair curlers. "I didn't even know you were ill!'

It took the better part of an hour to pacify her.

Fogg was a tiny gnome of a man who looked a little like Yoda in *Star Wars*. Long, pointy ears, scraggly hair, and a wrinkled face. After introductions, he led me through a dark chamber, with a single candle burning, to a well-lighted room in which there was a coffin surrounded by racks of flowers. The top half of the double lid was open, and I noticed there was a gray-haired old man in it, taking the long sleep. Was Fogg going to demonstrate the lid functions on a coffin that was occupied? Yes, he was. He started to lower the lid over this poor old guy's face, and I began to feel the way I did when the horse kicked me in the stomach.

"Couldn't you demonstrate on an empty one?" I asked.

"I'm afraid we don't have any empty ones at the moment," he said. "The minute they come in, we fill them."

"Oh," I said.

He was pointing to some kind of doohickey on the side of the lid, but I was staring at the old guy. I couldn't take my eyes off him. He was the first dead person I had ever seen. Yes, I thought, research is truly wonderful. Now I know what a corpse looks like. Actually, he didn't look too bad. A splash of rouge on his cheeks for color, gray hair carefully combed, nice suit, shirt and tie. He probably looked better here in the other world than he had in the real one.

"If you press this and turn it counter-clockwise," Fogg was saying— but I had turned my head at the sound of voices behind me. Six other people, three men and three women, had entered the room, and I suddenly found myself in the middle of a group of bereaved friends or relatives. Slowly, they all began to file past the open coffin, the women wailing, knuckling their eyes, sniffling, blowing their noses and muttering, "poor Emil," the men merely looking down silently at the body. Fogg had retreated to the rear of the bier.

This was enough for me. Maybe some other time; right now I need some fresh air. A casket, after all, is not a computer. It's only a box. Since I'm in charge of the story I can do anything I want to. I'll have Matthew build a homemade one out of pine, to my specifications, of course. Six feet long, two feet wide, and two feet deep. The latch will be one of those simple little hooks they put on screen doors. Nothing complicated. Arvel will never know the difference, and think of the money Matthew can save.

And that's exactly what I plan on doing, one of these days. Maybe tomorrow. Next week would be even better. I'd get at it right away, but after all that running around, doing important and valuable casket research, I'm dead tired.

If you'll pardon the expression.

>> 18

A PLATTER OF ADMONITIONS

BY EDITH PEARLMAN

BECAUSE I WRITE AND PUBLISH SHORT FICTION, I AM OFTEN APproached at parties by young writers, or new writers, or accomplished writers in a temporary funk. They want to discuss the ways of making stories.

So I natter about craft. I refer my colleagues to Poe's "Essay on the Art of Composition" as precept, and I urge them to read anything by Sylvia Townsend Warner as example. These suggestions don't seem to satisfy. I grab another potato skin. "Send me something you've written," I rashly invite. "Oh, maybe I will," they say, all at once shy.

But they do send me something. The something is usually a story whose protagonist strongly resembles the author. This protagonist, often the narrator, is in a situation of emotional turmoil. There is a lot of comment and not much incident. The resolution is not prefigured, just affixed. Adjectives flourish, crowding out metaphors.

Still, I never regret asking for the stories. There is always something to delight in—a bit of dialogue expertly controlled; a believable action which also flares with symbolic meaning; or simply—simply!—a new pairing of verb with noun.

"Would appreciate feedback," says a note stuck to the first page, apparently an afterthought.

Dear and Promising Young Writer, here is your feedback, prospectively—four chunks of advice, served on a skewer, sauced with my admiration and good wishes.

1) First—stop rifling your journal! Perhaps the stories you are destined to write will originate in your own experience, though as time goes on, you may, like Henry James, seek material in other people's lives; and you may even, like Jorge Luis Borges, make everything up. But wherever your stories originate, they must result in a revelation.

Your own recent biography should be left to ferment, gather accretions, even decompose—in short, to grow rich; only then will it yield its particular candescent truth.

2) Next—beware the first person! Twain and Nabokov and Dickens did write masterpieces with first-person narrators. But Huck and Humbert Humbert and Pip are rounded, flexible, fictional characters with biographies quite different from their authors'. They have their own idiosyncratic vocabularies and sensibilities. They are artistic creations, not stand-ins for their begetting geniuses.

The rest of us not-yet geniuses, when tempted by the available "I," settle down to write unmediated autobiography. We fall into uncritical habits: Something that really happened seems worth telling; something we really felt must of course be interesting. Invention fails and language flattens.

The first person is a beguiling friend who begs you to play, not work. Just say no.

3) Now—cut your stories by a third! That's too much, your widening eyes object. No—it's too little! Cut them by half.

Writing is nine-tenths revision. To revise is, nine times out of ten, to shorten. Some shortening is simple deletion—crumpling that introductory page and beginning *in medias res,* for instance, or slashing the ironic final paragraph. But most shortening is compression, sentence by sentence, draft after draft. You are the ruthless captain of your pitching tale; every word must work to keep you afloat. Allow nouns to cling to one adjective at most. Let metaphoric verbs do the rowing; toss flabby ones overboard.

4) Finally—read; and read further back than your own contemporaries. Our predecessors knew a lot about our trade. Get chummy with the generation before yours, and observe the all-seeing eye of John Cheever. Track down the generation before that, and emulate the simplicity of Sherwood Anderson. Acquaint yourself with Chekhov's elliptical dialogue and Saki's inventiveness and Balzac's thorough psychology. Go back further . . . back, back, back. Don't stop until you trip over Aesop, who's dying to teach you economy.

If you find yourself respecting these warnings so rigidly that you lose your appetite for writing, turn to my own favorite, Colette. She obeyed all the rules when she began to write, and by the end of her long and glorious career she had broken every one.

How To Write—
Techniques

≫ GENERAL FICTION

19

CREATING VILLAINS YOU HATE TO LIKE

BY EILEEN GOUDGE

LADY MACBETH HAS A SPOT. SHYLOCK FEELS PERSECUTED. MRS. Danvers is obsessed. Hannibal Lecter is fastidious. Even Frankenstein is more misunderstood than monstrous. But these fictional villains all have one thing in common: They're memorable. Why? What *is* it about these characters that makes them stand out in a crowd of men in black hats? What makes their crimes so compelling?

It's simple, really. What makes a villain—or any character—unforgettable is dimension. Most writers know that for a hero or heroine to be interesting, he or she must be more than a one-note Pollyanna. A touch of angst, a shameful past, a dark side—all of these devices serve to contour and shade what might otherwise be the literary equivalent of cream cheese. But often, the same skilled writer will make the mistake of painting the villain of the piece all in black, a sociopath with no redeeming features and all the staying power of a tabloid headline.

Yes, such misfits *do* exist in real life . . . but unless we know what makes them tick, what makes them human, what to some extent explains their actions, they're not terribly interesting. Witness Truman Capote's chilling nonfiction tour de force, *In Cold Blood*. Had Capote not portrayed his subjects as men to be pitied as much as abhorred, would the book hold quite the same fascination for us? Instead, we find ourselves squirming as the date of their execution approaches, unable to beat a safe retreat into our own righteousness. These young killers clearly have no place in civilized society—but they are human. Through them, we begin to see ourselves in a different light, a kind of there-but-for-the-grace-of-God view that tends to be thought-provoking, and even disturbing as it cuts a little too close to home.

Fictional predators, when richly drawn, can come alive in the same way. By behaving in less than predictable ways, and by virtue of past actions that might cast them in a gentler light, they become not only less evil, but more interesting. Let's face it, pure evil is boring. You can pretty much predict what the man in the black hat is going to do, because he has no conscience to get in his way. It's even kind of comforting, because you don't have to worry too much about anticipating his actions; all you have to do is root for the hero to escape his clutches. All well and good for Spiderman and the Green Hornet, but don't we look for more in novels than the stuff of comics? And doesn't a worthy protagonist deserve more than a good chase? Give me a villain with a higher purpose, a soupçon of remorse, a dash of leading man in him, and I'll guarantee you a duel you won't want to miss.

Ken Follett's *Eye of the Needle* is a good example of how a multi-faceted villain can help build pulse-pounding suspense. In Chapter One, Faber, the Nazi spy known as *Die Nadel,* is discovered with a short-wave radio by his landlady, whom he then feels he has no choice but to kill. Upon stabbing her to death, he throws up. At once, our interest is piqued. Who is this cold-blooded killer with so weak a stomach for blood-letting? Might there be more to him than meets the eye? Indeed there is. More than a threat to Western civilization, someone whose actions could drastically alter the outcome of World War II, Faber is a man with a soft spot for a particular woman—a man capable even of gallantry. In the cat-and-mouse chase that ensues, Faber's conflicted nature leads us down a path far more circuitous than any traveled by a stock spy in a standard thriller. Nearing the climax, we almost root for him, while hating ourselves for doing so. Faber, of course, falls victim to his own Achilles heel, while forever securing a place for himself among the Great Villains of Modern Fiction.

In my own novels, I strive to make my antagonists complex, and yet easily fathomable. Often, they come dangerously close to being *likable.* I wouldn't go so far as to say that David Sloane, in my novel *Garden of Lies,* is anyone you'd want your daughter to bring home, and especially not the kind of person you'd want as your gynecologist. But by my weaving in strands of memory from David's childhood and adolescence, readers can sympathize with, if not forgive, the actions of a man who has not escaped the long shadow of his abusive alcoholic father, or his own shame about his roots. In the courtroom climax, when David is publicly humiliated by the woman he set out to destroy, he evokes pity even while no one would deny there is poetic justice in his comeuppance.

The same applies to Rudy in *Such Devoted Sisters.* For all his Machiavellian grotesqueness, he is in many ways a more engaging villain than his handsome, self-serving half-brother, Val, because Rudy is motivated, even *twisted,* you might say, by his obsessive love for his niece Laurel. At the dark heart of his evil machinations lies the tender ache of knowing he can never possess the kind of beauty and purity embodied in a young woman like Laurel. Trapped within his own ugliness, he is nearly driven mad by his yearning.

While writing the scenes in which Rudy plots to gain custody of Laurel's illegitimate baby, I found myself remembering how I'd felt reading "Rumpelstiltskin" for the first time, when I was eight or nine. How could I have pitied the princess when her baby was taken from her and at the same time, have felt a little sorry for Rumpelstiltskin at being thwarted in the end? Such is the dichotomy that defines the very best fiction, and makes it as timeless as a Grimms' fairy tale. For in art, as in life, the real story is often told between the lines and in the subtle shadings between black and white. In reflecting on the eternal puzzle of what makes good people do bad things and vice versa, we learn to know ourselves better.

How, you might ask, can you achieve this uneasy balance in your own antagonists? The answer is: not easily. It's a juggling act, and too heavy a hand in either direction can end up looking like something that came out of the oven too soon—in other words, a soggy mess. In rendering David Sloane (*Garden of Lies*), I realized that he needed a motive in addition to his tortured past for turning so nasty in the end. He needed to feel justified—and not entirely without reason—for his vicious attack on Rachel. And so I gave him a motivation that would make almost any man, nice or nasty, squirm. Early in the novel, after Rachel has told him she's pregnant with his baby, and he's insisted that she have an abortion, she informs him that the only way she'll even consider such a thing is if *he* performs it. This isn't as farfetched as you'd think. David is a doctor, after all, and ob/gyn is his specialty. Pushed into a corner, he reluctantly acquiesces—and becomes impotent in the years that follow. Imagine his rage at Rachel then! In a way, who could blame him for lashing out?

Oddly enough, in writing *Blessing in Disguise,* the shadings of gray

I had given Cordelia in my earlier drafts eventually transformed her from an antagonist into a protagonist. She was never really bad to begin with, but through her willfulness, as well as her stubborn avoidance of the truth, she had managed to alienate one grown daughter and make a spineless lump out of the other. What differentiates Cordelia from Rudy and from David Sloane is that Cordelia, at some point, sees that her old methods aren't working and finds the courage to strike out into the new and frightening territory of self-discovery. She and her daughter Grace manage a reconciliation of sorts, but as in real life, it's both less than it might have been and more than either of them had dared hope for. Cordelia even finds true love in the form of her poetic gardener.

But without Cordelia, a reader could say that *Blessing in Disguise* has no real villain. Which brings me to my next point: Not every novel *needs* a villain. When mining for conflict, I often find the richest dramatic ore lies in situations, particularly family situations, rather than in one particular person, or a cat-and-mouse chase. Broken promises, shameful deeds, dark secrets—these are the ingredients that can make a plot simmer, as well as light a path to the villain that lurks in the heart of all of us. In Peter Benchley's novel *Jaws,* you could say the shark is the bad guy—but is it? The shark has no personality and no motive for killing other than to fill its stomach. The real evil in *Jaws,* as I see it, is the town's inertia and the pig-headed avariciousness of petty bureaucrats. The hero, in bucking the system, finds himself up against an antagonist more formidable—and, in a way, unbeatable—than any snack-happy shark. After all, it's a lot easier simply to stay out of the water than to remove oneself from life situations rife with conflict!

But let's say you've already written your novel. Maybe you've sent it out to a few publishers who rejected it. You've been told it has a terrific plot, but the characters are somewhat flat. You're prepared to rewrite it, but you don't know where to begin. So let's start with your villain, since the chances are good that this is where artificial resuscitation is most needed. You've done your job in most respects. Your villain's modus operandi is well established: He's clever; he's ruthless; he's a perfect foil to your hero. But is he a little too perfect? You might want to season him a bit by introducing a new strand—a past injustice, a tortured memory, a dysfunctional family—but feel that it would alter the plot in an adverse way or require you to start all over from scratch. If at all possible, you absolutely *should* do what is necessary to make this the best character and the best book it can be. But maybe the same goal can be achieved in another, less tricky way. This is where odd quirks and unlikely characteristics can be used in fleshing out cardboard villains.

Take Hannibal Lecter, in *The Silence of the Lambs.* Who would imagine a cannibal could be a dilettante? A deranged sociopath who also happens to be brilliant and, yes, even gentlemanly. This study in contrasts is part of what makes him so fascinating, far more so, in fact, than the main villain, whose most interesting feature is his penchant for human hides.

Hard Fall, by Ridley Pearson, is another example of how life can be breathed into a villain. I was privileged to read that novel in an early draft, in which the antagonist, Kort, came dangerously close to appearing like a character from Central Casting. On the advice of his agent, Pearson added an extra dimension, giving Kort not angst or some moral quandary, but a toothache! Imagine plotting to blow up an airplane full of passengers while in the throes of a throbbing toothache. Desperate to get to a dentist, Kort becomes human to us in a very immediate way, someone we can relate to whether we want to or not.

In *Such Devoted Sisters,* I gave Rudy a similar weakness: He's allergic to chocolate. What makes it ironic is that Annie, the object of his ire, is the owner of a successful chocolate shop. I used this device in *Blessing in Disguise,* as well. Teen-aged Hannah (more a wannabe than a real villainess) has an allergy to nuts—which she uses to her advantage in the opening chapter, when her father's girlfriend, Grace, accidentally serves her a piece of chocolate-nut torte.

And who could forget Don Corleone, the patriarch of *The Godfather,* tending his garden and playing so sweetly with his grandson? This, from the mafioso responsible for chopping off a horse's head and having it placed in a man's bed. Contradictory? Yes, but such is the stuff of real life. People are seldom what they appear to be on the surface, and in some cases, they can surprise even themselves. Part of what made *Schindler's List,* the novel and the movie, so compelling was the duality of Schindler's nature. He was a far-from-perfect man, a philanderer and opportunist, who found himself cast in the unlikely role of savior—a role that bewildered Oskar Schindler himself as much as it did anyone who knew him. Fate had brought his sterling qualities to the fore and made him a hero. It follows then that the same war (as the story suggests) made monsters out of ordinary men who might otherwise have led uneventful lives. Allow this uneasy stretch to apply to your fictional villains and you could come up with something that will have readers turning the pages even as they scratch their heads.

Recently, at Stratford-on-Avon, I had the matchless experience of seeing *Macbeth* performed by the Royal Shakespeare Company. I had never seen the play on any stage, and was overwhelmed by something that somehow had escaped my notice in reading it: Lady Macbeth, one of the most ruthless villainesses of all time, isn't *all* bad. She's a snake—but she has a conscience. O.K., so it isn't *much* of a conscience. In fact, it's about the size of—well, a *spot*. In her famous closing speech, as she scrubs at her palm in a vain attempt to remove the imaginary spot, she becomes, for a singular, nearly poignant moment, vulnerable, an object of pity rather than contempt.

What would Lady Macbeth have been without her spot? Not nearly as enduring, I can assure you. In its marvelous complexity, hers is a role that any actress would kill for, but which few can carry off. Not because they aren't talented or skilled, but because it isn't easy to project, or even to imagine, the spot of warmth that lies at the core of even the coldest heart.

As writers, we must bring empathy into our craft along with our imaginations. For in the very best fiction, every larger-than-life hero has a small devil on his shoulder, and every villain wears, if not a tarnished halo, then at least a hat more gray than black.

>> 20

IT REALLY HAPPENED

BY CHET VITTITOW

AT A RECENT WRITERS CONFERENCE, EIGHT OF US WERE GATHERED in a small room, reading manuscripts aloud and analyzing them. I was about to comment on a story that had just been read when the writer said, "The man was my grandfather . . ." and I knew what was coming next. She went on, "It really happened."

Writers seem to consider those three words—*it really happened*—as a kind of incantation, as if by uttering them a bad story could be elevated to Pulitzer Prize status. In this case, however, the writer did not take our well-intentioned criticism lying down. Instead, she fired back a question worth more than all the comments that had been made so far in the session.

"Tell me," she demanded. "Why is it that everyone tells you to write from your experiences, then criticizes you when you do?"

She had a point. Moreover, it is a basic question, a fundamental question. Reiterating fundamentals is as important to developing writing skill as mastering any new technique.

Write from experience. Write what you know. Do such self-evident statements demand explanation? If they lead to *it really happened* criticism—then, yes, they do.

To write *from* experience is not the same as writing *about* your experiences. At the most basic level, we have all experienced a different variety of words. I know words that you do not; you know words that I do not know. I grew up in the marginally southern state of Kentucky, and I speak fluent Hillbilly. I am not familiar enough with Cockney English to try to pull it off on the page.

I have stood in front of a jury and cross-examined witnesses. I have never given birth. I can play several musical instruments, but I cannot draw a recognizable picture of a dog. I believe that I can act, but I am mistaken.

These are the experiences I use to enrich my characters. If my heroine plays the violin, you can bet the strings will appear in the correct position. If she gets herself pregnant, she will have a "difficult labor." I will not try to give a blow-by-blow account.

"Oh?" you ask. "So I can't write science fiction unless I've been on a spacecraft? And just how many people, on the average, do you have to kill to write a mystery story?"

Well, of course you can write science fiction. If you need to describe a shuttle launch, there are plenty of firsthand accounts. Use them. See if the descriptions match anything you *have* experienced. Just be careful not to force it.

Actually, I did stumble across a corpse once, though I was not responsible for the demise of the person. When my character found a body, his reaction was the same as my own:

> Priding himself on his composure, Ozro began making his way back to the Castle to phone the police. He was halfway there before he realized that he was running as fast as he could.

I used only that, a reaction. All the other circumstances were different. I did not try to plug my own story into Ozro's life. No one who has read it has criticized me for it. I have never had to say, "It really happened."

But what is so wrong with, "It really happened"? What is wrong with using the events in my life to craft a story?

Maybe nothing. Maybe there are episodes in your life that need only be mildly "fictionalized." Maybe your entire life is so glittering a series of vignettes as to warrant an autobiography. Maybe. For those writers who simply wish to insert the more interesting chapters of their lives into a story, I have found four stumbling blocks, one or more of which will occur when "it really happens":

The first is *improbable coincidence*. Life is full of improbable coincidences. An old friend and mentor told the tale of being mustered out of Korea the day before Christmas Eve. Upon arriving in Seoul, he met an old high school buddy, who put him on the next flight to the Philippines. There, he met *another* old buddy who got him to Hawaii, where he met *another* old buddy who got him to San Francisco. . . .

You get the point. He "old buddied" his way back to Georgia in time for Christmas Eve. Who is going to believe it? Moreover, such a coincidence, if merely related, is simply curious. An author's job is to further the plot, not just relate amusing anecdotes. In advancing that plot, the writer must make it show that it's *essential* that the character arrive home by Christmas Eve. Once the plot is shown to turn on the event, the coincidence becomes not just fortuitous, but completely un-believable.

To be sure, there are writers who do use improbable coincidence, and use it to great effect. Clive Cussler piles coincidences one on top of the other, until they all become part of a grand, adventurous roller-coaster ride. The reader doesn't think of them as coincidences, and just enjoys the trip. But as the writer you must be deft, confident, and—most of all—aware of what you are doing. Do not throw in a coincidence just because it made an impression on you at the time.

Did I say, "made an impression"? It must have been a segue into what I call *the honeymoon effect.*

My wife and I honeymooned in New Orleans. What a city! What people! Oh, what a great time we had! Well, what do you expect? We were on our honeymoon! Every memory is affected by the event itself. But what was a profound emotional experience for me may not come across as such for the reader.

Should I abandon these experiences, throw them in a sort of literary lock-box, never to be used? No. I like to think of them as photographs, rather than as a videotape. We have all seen those interminable videos Uncle Fewmet took on the trip to Disney World, complete with a shot (and narrative) of the place where Aunt Dewlap got that corndog, and a riveting explanation of what happened to it on Space Mountain. The point is, such films are boring. They ramble; they evoke memories only for the participants, not the viewer. A still photo seeks to capture the moment in one frame. You should try to make words do the same. A single image will serve better than a four-page description. The reader does not need to know every detail of a trip—only that it was fun.

In a worst-case scenario, the writer's emotional memory of an event may simply not mesh with even the most objective recitation of events.

When my first wife left me—listen up, this *really happened*—she did so out of the blue. I came home, no wife. The next day she left a sort of "Dear John" message *on my answering machine.* I was devas-tated.

A year later, I was watching *Buffy the Vampire Slayer* with the woman I would later marry. At one point, Buffy blurts out incredulously: "You mean you broke up with my *answering machine?!*" We howled. Time had passed. What had been subjectively agonizing was objectively funny.

I do not worry about answering machine breakups these days. That would not be my wife's style. It would be an *incongruous action.*

Sometimes a writer has a wonderful experience that warrants telling, but does not have a character suitable to carry the story effectively. Do not force it. Your personal experience may be as pointless to the plot as it is incongruous to the character. A pointless vignette in the middle of an otherwise logical story does nothing but show a lack of narrative skill. No matter how funny—or sad, or moving, or frightening—an event may be, make sure it is something the character would do, and make sure it advances the plot.

Which brings me to the final pitfall. I call it the *reality defense.* You could also call it *hiding behind your life.*

In this case, the event described will usually be painful. It will also be improbably coincidental, "honeymooned," or incongruous. When challenged, the writer tosses out those three magic words: *It really happened.* By questioning the validity of the writing, is the validity of the writer's life being questioned? Think of the reality defense as a sort of literary guilt trip. Fortunately, there is a two-word response to the reality defense: *So what?* This may sound cruel, but it's not. It is literally "tough love."

Perhaps your writers group wants to bare its collective soul. Sobs will be sobbed. Tears will fall. I think such emotional feeding frenzies are fine! Exorcising the painful parts of your life is wonderful. It is therapeutic, but it will not produce good writing. Do not be afraid to give tough criticism, and do not be upset when it is offered. Do not hide behind your hurt; use the experience to make the reader see that your *character* is hurt.

Remember, when you push your manuscript from the proverbial nest, it must fly on its own. You will not be there to nurture or protect it. You will not be there to defend it. You can't call every potential reader and say, "It really happened."

>> 21

Plotting Your Novel

By M. K. Lorens

I've always suspected that the old dictum "Write what you know" would be far better expressed as "Know what you write."

Maybe you're one of those disgustingly organized writers who works out plots in advance and carefully inscribes each scene on a file card or stores it away in the memory bank of your PC. Or maybe, like me, you are that almost-extinct critter, the Blank Page Writer, and you simply throw your unsuspecting characters into ice-cold water and yell, "Swim, damn you!," as you hammer out your novel on the old manual Remington you bought in 1964.

However you do it, you still have to fulfill the basic responsibility of any storyteller. You have to start your story, move it forward, and keep it moving to the end.

Profluence.

That's the fancy word for it. "Character isolated by a deed / To engross the present and dominate memory" is what the poet William Butler Yeats called it. What I have always thought it meant is that the kind of story you write depends upon the people who inhabit your imagination, the intensity of their fictional life. Character isolated by a deed.

But the practical fact is that unless you know what sort of plot your characters are suited for, you're likely to come out with a chaotic mass of incidents instead of a forward-thrusting plot. Suppose, for instance, that Mary Shelley had written Victor Frankenstein and his Creature into a neat little social comedy like *Pride and Prejudice,* or that Jane Eyre somehow turned up not in Mr. Rochester's country house but in that inn on the road to London where Tom Jones had so much fun.

Mary Shelley, of course, began with the plot already dictated, more or less. She wrote *Frankenstein* on a sort of dare from her husband

Percy's intellectual pals to come up with a better Gothic novel than they did. But what if you have no preconceptions about the kind of plot you want to write? Where do you start, and how can you be sure you're doing it right?

The answers are simple. You start with imagination. (Not self-expression, please. Leave that for your diary.) And there's only one way to tell if you're doing it right. Do it, and see if it works.

Right, then. Let's try a little experiment. Suppose we begin with a simple statement that could belong in any sort of modern novel, with almost any cast of characters.

"The bus pulled away without them."

Chapter One, Page One. Point of Attack.

As the beginning of our plot, the line assumes that some things have happened before the bus pulled away and that some other things will happen now that it's gone, and we're standing there in the dust.

What these things are depends entirely upon who "they" may be. We now have to decide who our main characters will be, and I choose to make one of "them" a woman. She needs a name straightaway. Andrea? Elizabeth? If I want to write a romance, maybe. Those names are elegant and a bit remote, and they have nothing to do with the woman whose somewhat bony, rumpled figure I have already caught a glimpse of, standing in the dust, inhaling exhaust fumes of that departing bus.

No, no! No Andreas or Elizabeths. Let's call her Jimmy.

That choice of name gets our plot up and running. Because this woman, my Jimmy—whose name is almost certainly not *really* Jimmy—is carrying a lot of baggage already, and I don't mean suitcases. It's a small-town name—as a matter of fact I happen to have had a female cousin named Jimmy—and you don't bump into a lot of women called Jimmy on Park Avenue.

Besides, I've decided that her real name is Germaine, and being Jimmy was better than what the boys called her in school. She's heavily freckled, with reddish-brown hair, and everybody called her Germaine Measles.

There she is, my Jimmy, standing on the dusty shoulder of a back road at the edge of a small midwestern town. Blue Creek, Kansas. Why? Why not? I once lived in western Kansas, and almost nothing there was blue, including the sky when the oil refineries were running.

Jimmy's wearing a Toronto Blue Jays baseball cap—high treason in Kansas City Royals country—and her luggage consists of a bulging backpack and two plastic shopping bags. Has she been to Toronto, or is Canada a cool, blue dream to which she hoped that bus would take her?

But the word isn't "her." It's "them." She's traveling with a little boy, scrawny, bratty, but real. Named? Weasel Karloff. You guessed it. Real name Boris.

Now, then. Jimmy and Weasel have missed the bus. We have opened the plot—not the story, because that's what we've just been fishing out of my nefarious subconscious—in the middle of things. *In medias res.* In the middle of events that will be built upon and will grow into a climax.

We have begun our plot at the point at which something has to happen. Our characters have to go on or turn back, fight or sink into the dust and be defeated. They have to make a choice, and so do I, as the writer. Write what you know. Know what you write.

What kind of novel is this likely to become?

That depends on what Jimmy and Weasel do next. If they go back to the place next to the mortuary where Jimmy keeps house for her eighty-seven-year-old mother, and Jimmy marries Pete Redwing, the half-Sioux Vietnam vet who runs the filling station, and they adopt Weasel and live happily ever after . . . then we've got a romance, though not the kind in which Andrea or Elizabeth would feel at home.

But suppose Pete has flashbacks and patrols his gas pumps with an M-1 and shoots the social worker who's headed for Jimmy's house to take custody of Weasel?

Tragedy? Mystery? Melodrama?

Or suppose Jimmy and Weasel, having missed the bus, hitch a ride with a crazy half-Sioux named Pete Redwing, and light out with him for Canada, experiencing on their journey all the virtues and brutalities of modern America at the end of the twentieth century?

This is a picaresque, an episodic novel about a rascal off to seek his fortune, in the manner of Huckleberry Finn.

Or suppose that instead of Jimmy, we focus on Weasel, watch him grow up under Jimmy's care, go to school, become a politician, run for the Senate, and at last run for President, to be defeated and return at last to Blue Creek, Kansas, as the bus he came home on leaves him standing—what else?—in the dust. This time we've got what's sometimes called a growth-and-education novel, like *David Copperfield.*

The point of the exercise is that the combination of characters and setting dictates the profluence of plot. They begin as separate elements, but they quickly merge to establish a line of scenes or episodes of mounting intensity. One cardinal law of plotting—which most of us break at some time or other—is that the line of story must never be confused, muddied up or twisted to fit some external factor, like the need to preach a sermon or put in another sex scene or chop up a few more body parts. Everything must move the plot forward to its inevitable climax. In *The Fugitive,* Lieutenant Gerard *must* catch Richard Kimball. Henry the Fifth *must* fight the Battle of Agincourt. Subplots, flashbacks, everything you use must in some way contribute to the inevitability of that climactic scene.

> Character isolated by a deed
> To engross the present and dominate memory.

Most of the time, when I sit down to write a novel, I know only two things about the plot—where it starts and what that great crucial scene will have to be. Sometimes I even dream it. But that is because by that time, I know the characters far better than I know myself.

Far too well to leave them standing in the dust of Blue Creek, Kansas, while the last bus to their future pulls away.

➤➤ 22

LET DIALOGUE DRIVE YOUR STORY

BY SONIA LEVITIN

"LET ME TELL YOU A STORY," SHE BEGAN, "ABOUT ONE OF THE MOST fascinating, bizarre, and evil people I have ever met." Such a beginning is bound to charm a listener or a reader into paying attention, asking for more. Dialogue is a powerful tool for the writer. Used well, it will define your characters, move your plot, and amplify your theme—and it is fun to read.

Something about a line set between quotation marks adds life and realism to a scene. A few lines of narrative can do wonders in moving the time and place of your story and doing it quickly. But dialogue infuses fiction with emotion and action, and sustains the tension better than narrative can.

Characters joined in action naturally speak to one another. When they speak, readers learn not only what is going on, but how each person reacts to the events and, further, how he or she either disguises or admits true feelings.

What makes good dialogue?

In a word, I believe it is intensity. A few well-chosen, carefully honed words of dialogue work better than several paragraphs of explanation. For example, in my historical novel *Escape from Egypt,* I chose dialogue to open the story, having decided that it was the most efficient and immediate way to show not only time and place, but also the very strained circumstances of my hero Jesse's life:

"You! What are you carrying in that basket?"
"Only a few vegetables from our garden, my lord. Would my lord like some for his table?"
"What poor harvests you Israelites produce, and after we give you everything you need! It's disgusting."

87

Immediately we see the fear and servility of the slave pitted against the arrogance and authority of the master. From the dialogue, we can well imagine the resentment of our hero, and indeed, the following narrative emphasizes what the dialogue has begun. It affirms that Jesse is an Israelite slave in ancient Egypt, mistreated and miserable, but still vital.

Thus, dialogue can lead adroitly into several paragraphs of description, making the narrative seem less boring, less pedantic. Our goal as fiction writers is to avoid pedantry, to create the illusion of an effortlessly flowing tale unfolding before the reader's very eyes. To do so, we must offer information smoothly, so the reader gains knowledge almost without realizing he has acquired facts he needs to know.

It is much better to describe a character's looks, disposition, and station through dialogue than merely to chronicle this information. So, to show Jesse's age, status, and physical features, I used brief dialogue with a woman who, like him, is run down by a gang of Egyptian teenagers with their horses:

"Let me dress that cut for you," the woman said. "It's a shame to scar that fine face of yours."

And, she goes on:

"Jesse, son of Nathan and Devorah! Why, you've grown a hand's breadth since I last saw you!"

Thus, the reader knows the names of Jesse's parents, that he is probably in his mid-teens, having experienced a growth spurt, and that he is handsome. When the woman asks Jesse, "Where have you been keeping yourself?" Jesse replies,

"I've been working in the home of In-Hop Tep."
"Ah, In-Hop Tep," says the woman, much impressed, "you're coming up in the world. No wonder you don't have time to work in our small garden."
"I do my share, Ima. At night I weed and make furrows. . . ."

From this small bit of dialogue, readers learn that Jesse is privileged to work in an illustrious household, and that he is a person who takes responsibility seriously. He becomes immediately heroic through these traits, first by being specially privileged and then by being humble.

A good deal of the tension in a story has to do with the actions and reactions not only of the main characters, but also of minor characters and what I call the "Greek chorus."

Sometimes the impact of events that occur in a story needs to be put into focus for the reader. That's where the Greek chorus comes in. Basically, this "chorus" is a bit of generalized dialogue or "mob reaction":

"Kill him . . ."
"Don't let him go . . ."
"He is evil . . . evil!"

Likewise, in a scene of joy, we can expect the chorus to augment and elucidate the prevailing emotion:

"Happy father! Happy mother! Joyous reunion!"

I used a similar technique—bits of dialogue uttered by various unnamed people—in my book *Adam's War,* after the tragic outcome of a mock battle:

"It's a miracle one of the children wasn't shot."
"They say that rifle was pointed toward the swings."
"A good thing Adam jumped on that boy."
"People shouldn't keep guns. You see what happens."

Adam is not a direct participant in this scene. The effect of this talk is powerful; it shows how the tragedy has affected everyone in the community, not only Adam and his friends. The "chorus" can also serve as a bridge between scenes, finally narrowing in on a specific character, who continues the action.

Dialogue in a story is very different from real dialogue—but the trick is to make it *appear* realistic. Real dialogue is repetitive, boring, and often inconclusive. The famous dialogue in the movie *Marty* comes to mind as an example of dialogue that is static, but is for that very reason funny and affecting.

"What do you want to do tonight?"
"I don't know, what do you want to do?"
"I don't know—what do you want to do?"

Obviously, one cannot go on this way too long. In a story, one or two repetitions of a word or a phrase are enough to indicate a pattern. Suppose you have a character who is not truthful. To highlight this trait you have decided, like Shakespeare, to use protestations to prove the opposite. When this liar speaks, he is apt to preface his remarks with, "Well, to be totally honest. . . ." Two or three repetitions are enough to alert your reader to this character's machinations. Likewise, any other speech perversion or mannerism should be used judiciously, sparingly, just enough to make the point. This also goes for dialect, incorrect grammar, or foreign words. To suggest a mere flavor of the exotic, it must not dominate, or it becomes intrusive, overwhelming the plot.

One way to make dialogue appear realistic is to offer digressions— just a few. Remember, characters do not always answer questions directly.

"What are you asking for that old Samovar?"
"My grandmother brought it over from Russia, you know."
"It's lovely—I've seen them in antique stores."
"So have I. Many are very valuable indeed."
"What are you asking for it?"
"Well, suppose you make me an offer."
"I don't know—I'm not really into antiques."

A certain amount of verbal fencing goes on, especially in a negotiation. The inquirer attempts one tactic and, failing to get what he wants (the price), he tries another. Negotiation applies not only to money matters; every time one character wants something from another, negotiation takes place. Thus, to help your dialogue come alive, think of it as a contest. In his book, *The Art of Dramatic Writing,* Lajos Egri explains that good dialogue shows truth revealed *under pressure.* Don't make it too easy for your character to get answers or solutions. By presenting evasion, misunderstanding, exaggeration, and even downright lies, you keep the pressure on. Then, when true facts and feelings are finally revealed, the character and the reader experience a literary high—catharsis.

Novelists can learn a great deal from reading plays. A good playwright must move the plot and express all the emotions through dialogue, with only minor action to accompany the words. In a successful dramatic scene, the pitch of the dialogue rises gradually, each line intensifying the stakes, the conflict, until a climax is reached. Then, in an outburst of emotion, resolution is achieved, the truth is finally told, the scene ends. That is the best and most satisfying use of dialogue, to bring a highly charged scene to fruition by doling out the revelations little by little, then letting the "point" explode.

A couple of "don'ts" about dialogue are in order. First, don't repeat in dialogue what has already been explained in narrative. It is much more effective to let your reader in on the surprise *as your character reveals it to another person* than to broadcast the character's intention in advance.

For instance, one might say in narrative: Veronica decided to tell Stan that she did not want to see him again.

Stan came to the door. "We're through, Stan," said Veronica.

This is a complete flop, because there is no tension, no surprise.

Consider, however, Veronica getting dressed, fixing her hair, listening to her favorite CD, making herself a drink, pacing, pondering, remembering their times together while she waits for Stan. The doorbell rings. She answers.

"Hi, gorgeous."
"Hi, Stan."
"What's wrong? Aren't you glad to see me?"
"Sure, I'm glad to see you."
"You don't look it. Come here. Give us a kiss."
"Stan—don't."
"What's the matter, baby? Aren't you feeling well?"
"I can't—I don't want to see you anymore, Stan. Please don't say anything. I mean it this time. We're through."

Another "don't": Don't have too many dangling speeches. People do interrupt, they do speak at cross-purposes, but a sequence of dialogue must be easy to follow, and too many unfinished phrases cause confusion and become annoying to readers.

As you practice writing dialogue, keep in mind that every person's speech is unique. Just as we know our friends by their voices on the telephone, we also know them by the content of their talk, by their speech rhythms, and the peculiar ways in which they use words.

An old-fashioned character, for example, uses old-fashioned words, a homespun style, a slow cadence of speech. "He's slow as molasses." Or, "I packed me a grip and left."

A hip teenager speaks quickly, incorporating slang and references to pop culture. "Hey, I'm not into dancing—let's go grab a Starbucks."

A Swiss college professor sounds different from a Portuguese gardener. A child's speech differs from an adult's. Some speech differences reflect status and education, others interests and lifestyle. A horse-trainer will speak in terms of horses and the out-of-doors; the seamstress describes things in terms of close, careful concentration; the sailor's speech reflects his visual and emotional connection with the sea. We need to know a great deal about the characters speaking, and be able to put ourselves visually, emotionally and psychologically in their place before we can accurately portray their speech.

In my novel, *The No-Return Trail,* when a young husband who is an unschooled Kentucky woodsman compliments his wife by saying, "Your hair shines just like a blackbird's wing," he speaks in terms of what he knows and loves, reflecting his experience and his status. Were he a professor or a cabinet maker, surely his comment would be different.

It is interesting and creative to produce dialogue that provides a clue to your characters' personalities. It deepens your story to know how characters speak, and why. The boss who laughs too much is unknowingly revealing his own insecurities. A doctor who speaks mostly in monosyllables has trouble articulating his feelings. A boy who always argues is probably in desperate need of attention. The mother who constantly scolds may be masking her deep anxiety and concern.

Consider carefully who your characters are, what they know, and what they reveal—both consciously and unconsciously—by the way they speak. Make their revelations come about in a lively give-and-take, under pressure, remembering that dialogue drives your story.

➤➤ 23

On Location: You Are There!

By Winifred Madison

Obviously, a story has to happen somewhere. Readers want to feel that they are right where the action takes place or they will suffer disappointment, or even a sense of displacement, if the location is undefined. One of the joys of reading is that it takes you somewhere else or, by comparison, makes the place where you live more understandable.

More important, characters and plots are so deeply influenced by where the story takes place that they cannot be divorced from it, even though the themes are universal. Can you imagine *Wuthering Heights* taking place anywhere but on the lonely moors of England, or *Tom Sawyer* and *Huckleberry Finn* far from the Mississippi River? While Shakespeare's *Romeo and Juliet* is clearly set in Italy—more exactly, in Verona—*West Side Story,* based on the same theme, could take place only in New York City.

Choosing the setting is a tremendous pleasure for the writer who has a love for place. Certain cities, such as Venice, Paris, New York, New Orleans, or Los Angeles, act as magnets for writers. However, the temptation to choose a background about which a writer may dream romantically—perhaps the French Riviera or the American Southwest or a village in the English countryside—is chancy if you do not know the area well. You run the danger of sounding like a travel brochure, which will be immediately clear to those who do know the place. Even with maps and research, it's all too easy to make the kind of mistake that will lose your reader's confidence. For example, if you choose to write about San Francisco although you have seen it only in the movies, you might slip up by confusing the Bay Bridge with the Golden Gate Bridge, and will immediately lose your credibility. Creating a place realistically is as tricky as committing the perfect crime.

93

Write about places you know. "But the place where I live is so *dull!*" you may complain, or, in the words of Gertrude Stein, "There is no there there." Be assured there is, but you may have become so accustomed to it, that you cannot "see" it any more. You may rediscover your home by leaving it for a day, a week, or even a year, and viewing it from a distance.

The prairies were considered dull until Laura Ingalls Wilder's *The Little House on the Prairie.* Monterey was once a sleepy California coastal village until John Steinbeck brought it to life in *Cannery Row.*

A location need not be dramatic or bizarre or unusual; what matters is how you view it and what understanding you bring to it. A fast-food restaurant, a supermarket, or an ordinary suburban home may have as much emotional drama in it as the secluded estate of a billionaire or a grand hotel in Venice, depending on what you do with it. Experience any place, even one you know well, as though you were seeing it for the first time. Let the air brush against your cheek, and listen to the sounds—whether it's the distant crowing of a rooster or the impatient horn-blowing of a traffic jam—and soon it will come alive.

To make the most of a setting, *be there.* Use all your senses. Your first gut reaction is important. Does the place make you feel elated or gloomy, strange, bored or excited? What does it do to your plot and characters?

1. *See it as a painter would.* Is the tone of the place light, dark, or grayish? What are the colors that come to mind? Is the landscape predominantly mild, with the easy rises and falls of a rural setting, with fields and woodlands? Or is the skyline harshly geometric with the architectural complexities of a modern city?

2. *Consider the climate.* A fiercely hot atmosphere will produce characters who speak, move and act differently from those in a temperate climate, just as the colors of Arizona or New Mexico with their hot pinks, terra cottas, and turquoise skies will vary markedly from the cool greens and cloudy blues of the Northwest.

3. *Make the weather work for you,* bringing out the emotional quality your story needs. It's possible to orchestrate it. A continual rain may be soothing and gentle, or the same rain may become increasingly depressing. A sunny day may be sparkling and light, yet too much sun can be harsh and punishing.

4. *Odors play a part in the scene.* A street in a large city with

garbage piled up will not smell like a field of newly mown hay. The tempting whiff of baking bread from a bakery, the familiar smell of chlorine from a swimming pool, the medicinal smell in a hospital, the scent of perfume on a woman passing by . . . the list is endless, and each olfactory detail will help bring your setting to life.

5. *Atmosphere is filled with sound,* even the sound of silence. Heavy traffic with the screech of brakes, the incessant repetition of horns and the terror induced by sirens may be only part of the background, but they will say a great deal about the mood of your story. Use different kinds of noise, like a soundtrack underscoring the spirit of the scene: a loud rock band, the noise of children at play, a student practicing a violin or a saxophone, the lapping of water against a boat, the intermittent roar of a plane flying overhead, the sudden silence in a lonely room.

6. *Become a sky watcher,* and see how this will increase your repertory of atmosphere; skies are theaters in which all moods may pass at one time or another. Bright sunlit skies with a few puffs of cloud may suggest a playful mood, just as a glowering sky with blackening clouds will foreshadow danger or violence. Skies may be one of a hundred shades of blue, each with a different emotional message. But blue is not the only color. Sometimes all traces of color disappear from the sky, leaving it seemingly blank. Let a flock of black crows fly across this colorless sky, or have a single plane leave a diminishing white trail.

Beware of the predictable. It is easy to think of a funeral on a cold dreary day, but on a bright day, when the earth becomes alive and joyful with spring, death may be even more poignant. Describe a garden wedding caught in a sudden storm that drenches everyone. Have a gale of wind come up at an outdoor concert, throwing the music off the stands into the audience.

Location. Focus on environment—buildings, houses, and rooms, as well as a geographical area. A character's immediate surroundings are of prime importance. Houses, whether grand or humble, carry intense emotional weight. Among those "fictional" houses that play unforgettable roles are Tara, in *Gone with the Wind* (Margaret Mitchell) and Manderley in *Rebecca* (Daphne Du Maurier).

Lofty structures like bridges, towers, churches, lighthouses, and nuclear reactors are important symbolically as they rise into the sky and dominate the landscape, either elevating, as the spires of Oxford, or threatening, as the nuclear reactors in P. D. James's novel, *Devices and Desires*. Conversely, settings hidden from daylight—caves, cellars, tunnels and basements—suggest the dark underground of mind and spirit.

Falling in love with a place is an experience so common to many writers that stories seem to rise out of it. During the year I spent in Vancouver, I frequently rode the ferry through the Gulf Islands, and this led to my writing a novel that takes place there—*The Genessee Queen*. Here is a paragraph from it:

> At the moment it is a blue day, everything blue, so blue that Monica feels herself drenched in blueness. She leans on the rail of *The Genessee Queen* as it leaves the mainland and wonders that she has never tired of the trip, though she has made it many times. She knows exactly how on this day the cool northern light will bathe the islands that rise in the distance a chilled gunmetal blue. She has also seen on other days the water gleaming in the sun. A ferry sailing in the distance and the gulls screeching mournfully as they circle above, remain insistently white. But it can change. In the north, the sun lurks in a furrow of moody clouds and possibly all the blueness will drain away in a matter of minutes, becoming colorless, as if the whole view were an overexposed film.

Names. Collect names of places; they can be magical in setting a mood to your story. If you wish to avoid naming a particular place because you do not really know it, you can make up a name, but most readers will want to know the general location of your story, whether it's the Arctic circle, Los Angeles, or an island in the Mediterranean.

Being a name freak or a map junkie will help writers in pursuit of exactly the right name. Among my favorites are Illyria (in Greece) or Elyria (in Ohio and Kansas) and the Isle of Skye, which actually are as poetic as they sound. Such names as the Firth of Forth, Lands End (in England or San Francisco), or Giggleswick in England have a style about them and suggest different emotional moods. Among the many names in Northern California are Cool, Rough and Ready, Shirttail Canyon, and Fiddletown. I also admit a fondness for the name of Boring, Oregon. Unless you know these places, it would be unwise to set your story there, but knowing such names may help you choose exactly the right one for the location of your story or novel.

A last word. Be careful. You may fall so in love with your setting that you will want to go on and on about it. Don't. You may lose a reader who is not ready to wade through page after page of description. Your reader wants to get on with the plot. Catch the mood of the setting; ask yourself if it is right for your story; find the telling details; and do whatever you can to make the reader believe he is actually there, and that's all you need to do.

>> 24

ENDINGS

BY BARNABY CONRAD

WE'VE ALL READ ARTICLES ON BEGINNINGS THAT ADVISE US TO start our stories fast, grab the reader's attention, begin with something happening, hook the reader, and so forth.

Not so easy is the elusive subject of how and when to end a story. Just about the only firm rule one can make is this imprecise admonition:

The endings of stories should satisfy the reader, being consistent with the actions and characterizations that we have been shown during the telling of the story.

Consider the disparate endings of some classic stories and you will find they have one thing in common: Their ends justify what has gone on before, and usually they stem from the character and actions of the protagonists.

For example, one of the most famous stories ever written is O. Henry's "Gift of the Magi." It is Christmastime, and a young unselfish couple is very much in love, but also very poor. Each of them wants to surprise the other with a wonderful gift, but how, with no money? On Christmas Day they discover that he, in order to buy an ornate comb for her beautiful hair, has sold his cherished pocket watch, while she, to buy a gold chain for his watch, has had her hair cut off and sold it. It is a touching, bittersweet ending which, while sad, is totally right.

There are many conclusions to famous stories and novels that do not "end happily" but which are, nevertheless, satisfying.

Certain stories, even when the protagonist dies a violent death, have "happy" endings because they are appropriate and therefore acceptable to the reader. In Jack London's astonishing story, "Lost Face," for example, the hero tricks the cruel Indian chief into beheading him, claiming to have a magic potion that will render his neck invulnerable to the chief's axe. The "trick" allows the protagonist to avoid the horribly prolonged torture death the rest of his men have endured:

> Alone, of all their prisoners, he had escaped the torture. That had been the stake for which he played. A great roar of laughter went up. Makamuk bowed his head in shame. The fur-thief had fooled him. He had lost face before all his people. . . . He knew that thenceforth he would be no longer known as Makamuk. He would be Lost Face; the record of his shame would be with him until he died; and whenever the tribes gathered . . . the story would pass back and forth across the camp-fire of how the fur-thief died peaceably, at a single stroke, by the hand of Lost Face.

Because the hero succeeds in outwitting the Indian, he emerges victorious, albeit posthumously, so the ending is entirely satisfactory and not really sad.

Hemingway's novel, *For Whom the Bell Tolls,* begins this way:

> He lay flat on the brown, pine-needled floor of the forest, his chin on his folded arms, and high overhead the wind blew in the tops of the pine trees.

Four hundred seventy pages later, the book ends with Robert Jordan again lying on pine needles, his hip broken, his submachine gun at the ready, awaiting certain death:

> Lieutenant Berrendo, watching the trail, came riding up, his thin face serious and grave. His submachine gun lay across his saddle in the crook of his left arm. Robert Jordan lay behind the tree, holding onto himself very carefully and delicately to keep his hands steady. He was waiting until the officer reached the sunlit place where the first trees of the pine forest joined the green slope of the meadow. He could feel his heart beating against the pine needle floor of the forest.

The end. Once again, it is a sad ending but a correct one. Jordan was willing to give his young life for a cause he believed in.

The next two examples point up the key issue about endings: When and how should the final scene of a story or a novel end? This, of course, depends on the needs of the story line itself. In *For Whom the Bell Tolls,* Hemingway felt that the reader did not need to see the actual death of Robert Jordan and its aftermath; it was neither artistic nor necessary to show it, so he didn't. In *A Farewell to Arms,* on the other hand, after the protagonist's beloved Catherine dies in childbirth, in long and detailed scenes, Hemingway even adds a touching conclusion. It is said that he rewrote it some thirty-three times in order to get it right and he did so with the proper restraint. The devastated narrator goes to the hospital room where the dead woman lies and says to the nurses:

"You get out," I said. "The other one too."
But after I had got them out and shut the door and turned off the light it wasn't any good. It was like saying good-by to a statue. After a while I went out and left the hospital and walked back to the hotel in the rain.

So, when to end a final scene? What to leave to the reader's imagination? What *feels* right varies from story to story. Some can be ended obliquely, especially when the moral or tangible issues are broad. Other stories—plot-driven stories with specific payoff devices—demand a more "on-the-nose" expository conclusion. A story by Raymond Carver would seem heavy-handed if it didn't end on an oblique note; a Frederick Forsyth short story demands specificity in the payoff.

For example, in a story that ends in a suicide, it is not obligatory that the readers see the act itself. In my novel, *Dangerfield,* I planted the fact several times that although the great writer had been sober for many years, if he were to drink again doctors said he would die. At the end of the book, his son finds the locked liquor cabinet smashed open and several bottles gone. That is all the reader needed to know about what was tantamount to a suicide, and I felt it was a more artistic way to end the book because it invited the reader to use his imagination rather than following the man to his last boozy gasp.

On the other hand, Ambrose Bierce in his classic short story, "Occurrence at Owl Creek Bridge," feels obliged to give us every last graphic minute of the young soldier Peyton Farquhar's execution.

In the opening paragraph Farquhar is about to be hanged from the bridge. He thinks of escaping; it then appears that he does break loose and makes his way down the river to his home and to his beloved wife:

At the bottom of the steps she stands waiting, with a smile of ineffable joy, an attitude of matchless grace and dignity. Ah, how beautiful she is! He springs forward with extended arms. As he is about to clasp her he feels a stunning blow upon the back of the neck; a blinding white light blazes all about him with a sound like the shock of a cannon—then all is darkness and silence!
Peyton Farquhar was dead; his body, with a broken neck, swung gently from side to side beneath the timbers of the Owl Creek Bridge.

The reader then realizes that the escape was all in his mind, that there was no escape from death for many of the young men in the Civil War, and that war is hell.

Another famous story is Shirley Jackson's 1948 shocker, "The Lottery." A nice "normal" New England town has an annual lottery, after which the owner of the losing ticket is ritually stoned to death; the last chilling sentence is: "'It isn't fair, it isn't right,' Mrs. Hutchinson screamed, and then they were upon her."

The message to writers here is clear: When your story in intended to frighten or shock readers, make sure you have a scene in which a character is vulnerable to some imminent danger.

Some oft-anthologized stories depend totally on their surprise endings—tales like Faulkner's "A Rose for Emily," at the end of which the heroine's lover is found to be a longtime skeleton with whom she sleeps in the nuptial bed; Roald Dahl's "A Lamb to Slaughter," in which the matronly murderer gets rid of the murder weapon, a frozen lamb shank, by serving it to the detectives for dinner; W. W. Jacobs' classic, "The Monkey's Paw," in which the third wish that the old couple makes to restore their son to them results in his almost returning in his decayed dead state; and most of O. Henry's stories.

I confess to a weakness for this kind of a story. I still love a tale with a beginning, middle, and snapper at the end, but over the years stories with the so-called O. Henry endings have fallen in disfavor. There are, however, still magazines around, like *Alfred Hitchcock Mystery Magazine* and *Ellery Queen's Mystery Magazine,* that specialize in this genre.

Few novels have an ending sentence as famous as its opening one. An exception is Charles Dickens's *A Tale of Two Cities,* which begins "It was the best of times, it was the worst of times. . . ."

And the book ends at the guillotine with the lyrical sentence: "It is a far, far better thing that I do, than I have ever done; it is a far, far better rest that I go to, than I have ever known."

Some writers, like Mark Twain, like to tie up all loose ends neatly at the end of their stories. In *The Adventures of Huckleberry Finn,* which starts out with Huck chatting amiably with the reader, Twain wraps up matters in a similar way:

Tom's most well now, and got his bullet around his neck on a watch-guard for a watch, and is always seeing what time it is, and so there ain't nothing more to write about, and I am rotten glad of it, because if I'd 'a' knowed what a trouble it was to make a book I wouldn't 'a' tackled it, and ain't a-going to no more. But I reckon I got to light out for the Territory ahead of the rest, because Aunt Sally she's going to adopt me and sivilize me, and I can't stand it. I been there before.

At least one famous old story leaves the ending entirely up to the reader. Frank Stockton's "The Lady or the Tiger?" tells of a jealous princess who must choose whether a beautiful young bride for her lover will come out of a tunnel in the arena or a vicious tiger that will claw him to bits. The story has prompted many a heated debate over why her choice would be for one or the other.

And what are we to make of the trend for the last several decades toward "slice of life" stories in which, rather than ending a story, the authors simply abandon the characters in midstream with little resolved? Readers are often left to make up their own endings.

Change is an important element in a successful story's ending; things and people and the situation we saw at the beginning are now different. A good example is in Flannery O'Connor's story "A Good Man is Hard to Find," in which readers see a querulous, selfish old woman die a surprisingly brave death at the hands of some criminals. "She would have been a good woman," The Misfit said, "if it had been somebody there to shoot her every minute of her life."

Sometimes a writer, after tying up the strands of the plot, will add a sort of coda or general summing up of the story. Chekhov once said, "My instinct tells me that at the end of a story or a novel I must artfully concentrate for the reader an impression of the entire work. . . ."

Fitzgerald does this in *The Great Gatsby*. After the enigmatic protagonist is dead and buried and the plot has run its course, the narrator ruminates on the tragedy at length, ending with:

Gatsby believed in the green light, the orgiastic future that year by year recedes before us. It eluded us then, but that's no matter—tomorrow we will run faster, stretch out our arms farther. . . . And one fine morning—

So we beat on, boats against the current, borne back ceaselessly into the past.

Many stories indicate and almost *require* that at the end the protagonist be shot, like Gatsby, or guillotined, like Sydney Carton, or commit suicide like Emma Bovary, or that virtually everyone die by cold steel as in *Hamlet*; any other ending in those cases would not be satisfactory to the reader, bearing in mind what has gone on before.

But things don't always have to end badly in fiction. There are many happy endings in great literature. Alice returns safe and sound from Wonderland, "and she would remember the happy summer days." We know Scarlett O'Hara is going to survive somehow, with or without Rhett Butler; Don Quixote gets back to La Mancha in one piece; Ulysses makes it home and slays his wife's suitors; Tom Jones ends up with the girl and the money; and Elizabeth nabs Darcy in *Pride and Prejudice*.

Most good stories end the way they *must* end; the agendas of the protagonists or antagonists dictate the outcome, and in this way the endings satisfy the reader. Many beginning writers, instead of having the characters decide the outcome, bring in Mother Nature (or the Marines) to help them wind up things tidily: a well-timed earthquake, or a flood, storm, or forest fire. The gods stepping in, *deus ex machina,* rarely satisfies, except, perhaps, on the wide, wide silver screen.

Also, using a coincidence to resolve matters rarely satisfies; you may launch a story with a coincidence ("Honey, you're not going to believe this, but two seats ahead of us in this plane to Paris sits my first wife!"), but not conclude it.

Satisfy—that, ultimately, is the operative word. Whether the hero or heroine lives or, like Romeo and Juliet, dies, whether the villain does or does not achieve his objectives, whether happy or sad, the end of the story must satisfy.

And always keep in mind Longfellow's words:

"Great is the art of the beginning, but greater the art of ending."

>> 25

CREATING A CHARACTER THE READER HAS NEVER MET

BY SHELBY HEARON

LAST SPRING, I GOT A LETTER FROM A TALENTED FORMER STUDENT, a fine writer who said she was stuck working on her novel. She didn't know where to go with it. What did I suggest? I knew she had sold her first story to *Mademoiselle,* and had an agent, so I didn't take her predicament lightly. Her impasse is one all writers share. And I sent her back a postcard that summed up the basic rule for writing fiction:

Dear Elizabeth,
Forget everything else and create a character the reader has never met before.
          Love,
          Shelby

I think we all know this is the secret heart of fiction. When we recall those books we most loved growing up, or discovered last year and passed around to our friends, we loved them because they introduced us to someone we had never met before and couldn't get out of our minds.

I saw in the bookstore that my writer friend Max Apple had a non-fiction book about his grandfather, who, at 93, had gone off to college with him. The book is called *Roommates.* And I thought, for Max, his granddaddy (who later, at 103, moved into the house with him and helped him out when his first wife was very ill) is the unforgettable character. But for a fiction writer, the young man who went off to college with his 93-year-old granddaddy in tow would be the person readers couldn't forget. What became of him? How did it work out? What did he do on dates, when he was studying, after he (they) graduated? I wouldn't use the real-life events: Max Apple remarries, this time a vital rabbi, and writes a bestseller about his grandfather. If it were fiction, I'd start with the idea of someone doing something we'd never encountered before, would never have imagined, and can't forget once we've read it.

I was thinking along the lines that we have to make sure the character we are creating is not just one of a class of people (boy coming of age, unhappy wife, victim and killer, star-crossed lovers, old man has a change of heart), but someone who, although in that class, is at the same time distinct from it. A misfit or a standout, a winner among losers, a loser among winners, a participant among observers, an observer among participants. A lemon in a bowl of cherries. That is the attraction of books in which someone with limited mental capacities is born to a family of Ph.Ds, or someone who breaks the tape for the 100-meter dash has parents who are home eating chips and watching the game on TV.

So I made that my first rule for writers: Write about someone who is not like everyone else in the group. I recalled the stories I'd judged or taught in the past year, trying to figure out what had made a select few out of hundreds stick in my mind. The plots themselves did not sound that different. There was a boy meeting a man in a mall; a minority student from the Texas Valley accepted to Yale; a Cuban woman tearing her legs fleeing her country; a security guard duped into crime; a probation officer deciding to help one more kid before throwing in the towel; an unmarried woman in the sixties deciding to keep her baby; a divorcée who recited in her mind like a litany all the men she'd ever been with when she met someone new. But what made these memorable, made them recalled not as stories similar to other stories I'd read, was that the people in the stories were unforgettable.

The writer of each had chosen some specific detail that still stood out in my mind. And had taken this one characteristic or habit or way of behaving and exaggerated it. Emphasized it. Enlarged it. Made that particular quirk or dream the starting place and built on that. So that the one alive, interesting, revealing part of the character became the kickoff, the yeast, from which the whole person could grow into someone I, the reader, had never encountered before. And about whom I wanted to know much more.

But this turned out to be only half the story. I realized it wasn't enough to create bizarre people with odd handicaps in weird predicaments having peculiar epiphanies. And I realized that "memorable" doesn't just mean strange; that freaky situations don't necessarily create depth of character.

In a recent *New York Times Book Review,* I read about a book by the real woman who became known as Jane Roe in *Roe* v. *Wade,* and I was intrigued at once. Here was not the person I'd expected to encounter, but rather someone in jeans, who worked in a bar, and wore a bandanna around her left leg in what was supposed to be a signal that she didn't have a girlfriend. What a wonderful fictional character that would make, I thought. Someone so unlikely, becoming a symbol for all of us. Then when I read the review of a novel about a teenager who loses his hearing after swimming in a forbidden pool, I realized that here was the missing key to how we create someone the reader has never met before. It is not enough to make your character unusual; your character must also teach us something new.

I went back to the Max Apple book and thought, if I were writing a fictional account of a boy going off to college, rooming with his grand-dad, I would need to be saying to the reader: We are all roommates on this planet, as reluctant and mismatched as we sometimes are. We are all going through the school of life together. And I understood that what had caught my interest about the woman who became Jane Roe was not only that she was unlikely candidate, but that her life made the point that those we least expect to can become symbols of something larger and finer and more important than our individual lives. I read again the review of the illicit swimmer and realized that what had made me want to buy the book was the suggestion that the tale was going to say that we are all deaf to our parents, that our children are all deaf to us. That in each case the character would be someone we had never met before because the character would be telling us a truth we had not thought about before.

I remembered those *Reader's Digest* features on "My Most Unforgettable Character" that I'd read as a girl: where the person, usually a parent or a teacher, but perhaps a bum or a stranger on a train, teaches us a lesson. That the person remains unforgettable not only because of special quirks, language, attitudes, but also for the way they make the writer, and us, the readers, see something we had not seen before about our lives.

I thought back to my gifted student, Elizabeth, and her own life. A lovely WASP woman who fell in love with a Jewish man, already a father, married him, had two more babies. And I asked myself: What would I do with that in a fictional way to make a fictional Elizabeth you had never met before? Certainly I would detail special things about her likes and dislikes, oddities about her upbringing, some funny, perhaps sad, thing she always did when she met someone she liked, something she kept hidden in a drawer, maybe, that no one ever saw, a talisman—all those details we use to build character. But then, to make her someone you had never met before, I would also have to let her tell you something true that you had never thought about that way before. Perhaps that all of us marry strangers, that all of us couple with people whose lives we don't share and can never wholly know, that every marriage is mixed, a mixed-bag, a mixed-metaphor, a mixture of intimacy and distance.

That got me thinking about my own recent novel, *Life Estates,* and the two women in it and readers' responses to them. And I saw that in my own case there was more to creating someone readers had never met before than just unusual loves and hates, attitudes and possessions, being different from others in the group. The novel is the story of two women who have been friends for forty years, since boarding school, and takes place the spring and summer before one of them dies. Harriet, the one who lives in east Texas, at fifty-five is very vain about her Betty Grable legs. She has an emerald green bedroom and wears emerald green satin mules and robe. She has a deer rifle in the corner by her bed and carries a .38 caliber handgun in her beaded evening bag. When she has to start chemotherapy, she arranges to get an eye-tuck at the same time. She has a crush on a man fifteen years younger.

Readers either loved her ("how spunky," "how brave") or hated her ("what a narcissistic twit," "what a self-centered snob"). But it was Sarah that they remembered, the woman in western South Carolina with the braid down her back, the wallpaper shop, the black lab named Gentle Ben, the peach orchards, the seventy-year-old lover, the daughter pregnant with her fifth son. They remembered her not because of these details, but because she refused to accept the money provided for her by her banker husband's will. The idea of men supporting their wives from the grave seemed to Sarah a denial of death, and sexist besides. And it was this declaration, this decision, and what it said about her view of life and loss and men and women that caused readers to remember her. It wasn't only because she possessed a juxtaposition of contradictions they hadn't encountered before, as was the case with Harriet, but because her actions caused them to think about something in a way they hadn't thought about before.

And so I dropped another postcard to my former student, now working away on her novel about a younger sister, and said:

Dear Elizabeth,
Don't forget that the character we have never met before must also teach us something we have never learned before.
Love,
Shelby

>> 26

HOLD THAT EDGE OF EXCITEMENT

BY PHYLLIS A. WHITNEY

THERE ARE A GOOD MANY EXCITING MOMENTS IN A WRITER'S LIFE.
These happenings are all the more gratifying because of the rejections
and discouragement that have gone before. I will never forget my first
encouragement from an editor, or the first acceptance and appearance
of my words in print. Of course I felt ecstatic when I held my first
book in my hands.

However, I'm sure that the true "high" for any writer of fiction lies
elsewhere. Fortunately, it is something that can come again and again,
and we learn to treasure and encourage it. I mean that magical moment
when the first glimmer of an idea for a story stirs in our minds. There
can be a sense of marvelous "shimmer" around the flashing of those
early indications of a story (or novel) to come. We always feel that
this will be the best thing we've ever written.

While this miracle can occur for me in an instant—perhaps when
I'm not even searching—it is something I may carry about with me
for days or weeks, while the shining nucleus in my mind gathers more
of its special sparkle, developing as if by magic. Perhaps creativity in
any field is one of life's most satisfying experiences. That it doesn't
last must be accepted and dealt with, so that it can be transferred to
something that exists in the real world.

At first, the experience can be so invigorating that I need to hold
back and not run around telling everyone what a remarkable book I
am going to write. After seventy-three books, I can still be eager and
even naive, though I know by this time that too much talking is a sure
way to dampen the glow—and possibly even kill my own interest in
what is happening.

Getting the idea down on paper in some form is much safer than
bragging about it. Even a few words can capture it sufficiently so it

109

won't get away for good. I do know, by now, that this glimmer is only that, and it won't be ready to become a full story or novel for quite a while. So, impatient though I may be, I have learned to wait.

When I was twelve years old, I discovered that I enjoyed making up stories. I could tell exciting stories to neighborhood children, making them up as I went along and delivering them with a dramatic flair that made up for their shortcomings. But I wanted something more permanent that could be read over again—by others, and by me.

My young brain teemed with stories, and I began to set them down on paper. I started out gloriously with story after story, but only now and then did I finish one. Whatever I wrote was never as wonderful as the dream. I was in too much of a hurry, and when I found I had created only the beginning of a story and must then find out where I was going, I lost interest. The magic disappeared and I gave up repeatedly.

There are two kinds of writers. I envy the writer who *can* run with the initial idea and develop it into a story or novel. (I have a private theory that these writers may need even more revision than I want or expect to do.) But my mind doesn't work that way; I can't find my story by writing it immediately, so I will deal here with my sort of writer. *We* need to find out where we're going before we attempt to write. I have developed a few methods that I use to hold onto that early shimmer and help it to grow. Or to be reborn. Somehow, in the course of three hundred pages or more, I must keep the initial excitement going so my interest will stay high until I finish the project.

How long that first edge of excitement will last differs with each book. I spend time with my notebook, developing my characters, collecting odds and ends of plot, discovering my direction, simply jotting down whatever comes to me—until the moment I *must* write. This always arrives before my planning is complete, and I know better than to deny the urge. At least I may get the opening for my story down. So I reward myself by writing several pages. My actors come onstage and begin to live. This is good for future planning, and I don't mind when the desire to write dies and I must go back to work on my characters and plotting.

When I read over what I've written, exhilaration runs high again, and I want to share this remarkable piece of writing with a reader. I never seem to learn, but perhaps it doesn't matter, since one part of my brain is being realistic and doesn't expect too much too soon. Of course, what I want is warm applause, approval—the same response to the "shimmer" that *I* have been feeling, even though I know that I am the worst possible judge of my own work when I am too close to the creative phase to see its faults.

Usually, my chosen reader, knowing the game, provides encouragement, with a hint of gentle suggestion that brings me down to earth. Sooner or later, I take another look at the first chapter and see if I can do a better version with a little more thought. For the beginner, there may be a danger in asking for criticism too soon. Our excitement over that first shining vision can be damaged all too easily. It's a lot safer to get the work done before we call on that necessary reader/critic.

Though I no longer expect that high point of excitement to last, I know it will return to engage and delight me—and keep me going. The writing of several hundred pages cannot be achieved on a single wave of exhilaration. Still, I can manage to lose myself in individual scenes that I feel are good. Along the way, wonderful new ideas attach themselves, and I take unexpected turns that lift me to the heights again. Fiction writers are allowed to be emotional people. If we write coldly and automatically, it will show.

It isn't wise to wait for these spurts of inspiration to come from out of the blue. I ask myself deliberate questions: What unexpected action can a character take at this point? What surprise event can I supply that will be logical and lift the story? I dream, see pictures in my mind, invent—and encourage lightning to strike repeatedly.

Let's consider three types of excitement that are involved in fiction writing. First and most important is the author's feeling about the story he or she is going to write. That's what I've been talking about. The second is the excitement the characters themselves feel as they play their roles in the story. If you examine what will excite each character and move him or her to action, you'll raise the excitement level.

The third type concerns the reader. If your interest and the interest of the characters remain high, the reader will live your story and take satisfaction from the experience. As writers, our purpose is to make the reader feel emotion along with the characters. But how does a writer retain that high interest level, often so difficult to achieve, when it's necessary to work on the same novel for months, or even years?

Boredom for what we're writing and loss of perspective remain a real threat.

To avoid this and keep a certain freshness about the work, I make it a rule not to go back very far over what I've written. When I start work each day, I read only the last finished pages before moving ahead. This gives me a needed impetus to continue. Though I am dying to know what I've done and whether it's any good, I never allow myself to look back for more than a few pages—not for a while, anyway.

Eventually the time comes when I begin to feel sure that what I've written is a mess. I lose interest and courage. Since I expect this to happen, I now go back and read all those earlier pages that I'd stayed away from—read them up to the point where my writing stalled. They always seem much better than I expected, and I'm caught up again in the excitement of the story and can move ahead. I find that I even know my characters better after that rereading. This can be repeated a number of times in the course of writing a novel.

Often I receive letters from young writers—or even older ones who are still beginners—who are experiencing "writer's block." "Writer's block" is not a label I believe in. These pauses and stoppages are never incurable. We learn to set aside the "real" world with its worries and sorrows that can pull us away from our fictional scenes. The healing that results from our writing can be remarkable. We learn to turn the blows life gives us into stories, thus helping not only ourselves, but perhaps our readers as well. Nothing that happens to a writer ever needs to be wasted. We adapt and change and *use,* whether a happening is good or bad. For me the only writer's block occurs when excitement over my creation dies and my interest is suddenly gone. That could be fatal if I accepted the condition!

The problem came home to me repeatedly in the writing of my Charleston, South Carolina, novel, *Woman Without A Past.* I found myself breaking one of my own major rules: *to give my main character a strong, life-or-death drive*—a struggle she must engage in and deal with in order to save herself. In the course of writing this novel, I often failed to achieve this and my excitement for the story died along the way.

In the early stages of the novel, my heroine took action only when she was forced to by the characters around her. *They* all had plenty of drive and purpose, much of it tremendously important to them. My heroine's one goal was to solve the mystery of her birth. But that wasn't strong enough in itself and she drifted along without much drive behind her actions. I worried about her, but couldn't seem to correct the flaw. When I asked myself what she was striving for, fighting for, I came up with nothing strong enough. I ploughed through dull (to me) transition scenes, hoping I could fix them later. (Transition scenes are always hard for me to make interesting, so that was nothing new.)

During this struggle (on my part, if not on my heroine's) I called in every device I knew to keep myself interested in a character who wasn't fighting for her life, or for much of anything else. I examined my other characters—interesting enough—to discover how they would challenge my heroine and force her to act. This worked pretty well. My own interest quickened, and my excitement level rose—at times.

When the action sagged, I worked on emotion. It is all too easy in the middle deserts of a novel to lose contact with the main character's feeling. Each writer must find a way to recover lost emotion. Some play music that moves or stirs them; others take long walks that seem to free the creative mind. Or you may have a trusted friend—not necessarily another writer—with whom to discuss the problem. There are times when talking helps.

My own method is to read. Certain fiction speaks to me. I read, not to imitate or to get ideas, but to find a mood. My attention will wander from the page as something touches some emotion in me. Then I can write, because I have transferred that feeling to my main character. I rewrite the wooden love scene, and this time it works. Once you evoke your memories, they are endlessly useful and can be adapted to the needs of the scene you are working on. My heroine, I find, has a good deal to worry about.

I have also discovered that a good way to cure my loss of interest is to feed something new into my mind. Long ago, when I was teaching writing at New York University, I adopted a slogan: *Interest follows action.* When students would look at me blankly, with not a story idea stirring, I'd tell them to go out and *do* something new. Study something they knew nothing about—have fresh experiences. These need not be earthshaking, but just something to open the possibility of exploring a new field. They were always surprised that their own interest came to life when they took this sort of action, and very quickly they found themselves filled with fresh story ideas. First, you *do* something, and then you get interested. It never fails. While writing *The Singing Stones,* I went up in a hot air balloon. I had no idea how I could get that into a story—but it churned away at the back of my mind and gave me a lovely climax scene.

So when I was baffled by my problems with *Woman Without A Past,* I investigated a new subject, for me: what is known in the psychic field as "channeling," when a voice (from another dimension?) speaks through a living person. Or through a story character! My interest came to life, and I was able to develop several scenes that tied in with the plot. I even investigated cats for this novel, reading several books about them so I could understand and write about the cat in my story. Research about practically anything that will fit in can give you more material than you can handle. You, your characters, and your readers will profit from what you learn.

Nevertheless, when I finished the book, I had no great confidence in what I'd written. I knew there were some good dramatic scenes, and my Charleston setting offered wonderful material. Yet, my heroine's drifting continued to worry me, and I waited anxiously for editorial response. To my surprise, my agent and my daughter thought the story strong, exciting, satisfying. No one seemed to notice that my main character was more done-to than doing. By all the rules I know, it wasn't supposed to work—but it did. Why?

It took me some time to find the answer, and it's a useful one. I discovered the explanation in a book by Dwight Swain: *Creating Characters.* One of the goals he lists for a character is "relief from. . . ." Now I knew why my heroine had succeeded in spite of the author! I had written about a sympathetic young woman who is much put-upon (that's important) and who deserves to win out in the end. The goal of *relief-from-adversity* is legitimate and can be very satisfying to the reader.

A great deal of anxiety can be involved, in spite of having the main character take only minor action on her own. Often she is afraid, and this helped with my own interest as I became aware of her desperate, threatened state. She certainly needed relief from a number of unpleasant actions by other characters.

Anxiety can be a good tool to think about and use. However, I don't recommend that this rather negative goal be the sole direction of your main character. In my next novel, I shall make sure that my main character has a strong drive against tough opposition, though I'll certainly use the element of "relief-from" as well.

All such methods and devices are part of a writer's tool kit. We use them to keep our characters in a state of excitement that will convey itself to the reader and will grow from our own effort to hold that first shimmer of an idea alive—that edge of magical excitement that is the best reward of all to the fiction writer.

>> 27

TELLING DETAILS

BY MARCIE HERSHMAN

WRITERS, BY NATURE, LOVE DETAILS. THERE'S SOME PART OF US that's gotten trained to notice and hold on to them, even in the midst of our own personal tumult. *This detail,* we might say to ourselves upon entering a room, *this fact of X's eyelids lowering, and her slow, seemingly casual half-turn away as I walk through the doorway, unannounced, means she's ashamed by what she did last month to me. This slight flutter of her pale eyelids—yes; the half-turn of her torso, begun with a twitch of the narrow shoulders—yes.* In times when we later need a boost, we might call up the particulars of X's apparent embarrassment to give ourselves the energy to explore some other feeling we have, as yet inexplicable. Or perhaps we summon these details in order to begin moving in a new direction, to push ourselves more confidently along a path that will lead us to the next necessary interaction.

In professional terms, we also hold on to and use details in our work. Sometimes we hold on to one or another of the darn things for years. The process might start when we're working on an early draft of a story or chapter—and we "discover" the detail in the attempt to show the sudden lurch in our main character's gait, say, at the moment he spies his ex-wife coming toward him as they cross the same busy street. In our second pass at the story, however, we realize that as brilliantly put as the descriptive detail about Mr. XX's physical stride originally seemed, it's no longer right for his emotional stride—now that we've finished the story and have come to understand XX in all his complexity. So, we edit. The detail that struck us in the first run-through is itself struck: Out it goes.

Only trouble is, it doesn't leave, not all the way. It might be excised from the page, but it's taken up a whispering residency in our mind.

If, out of weakness or love, we try to reinsert it into the same story, it will make only a semi-honest fit. Why? Because it's a bit of rhetoric now, just bunched-up words, empty as the jacket some stranger threw onto our doorstep on a day grown too warm for its use or comfort. Again, the editing pencil comes out.

Denied a place to lodge, this detail might float back into view at odd moments. "A sudden hitch in an effortlessly long, loose-legged gait" might be exactly what we need to have in another tale—the one we haven't written yet. It might serve as the grain of sand that irritates our literary imagination long enough so that thin layers of gleaming substance adhere to it. The sand that makes the pearl; the pearl that makes the story.

Well and truly used, a detail is indissoluble.

But.

But of course I've been going on here about a certain kind of detail. The *telling* detail. One of that company of absolutely select particulars that possesses not only enough self-assurance to reward both writer and reader with a further insight into a character, but also enough physical reality to push that person a bit farther along in the outside world. In other words, the telling detail is versatile; it can speak to both theme and plot. It reveals a sly, inward-gazing intentionality (character and theme) in addition to a more public purpose (action and plot).

The telling detail is the essential detail. It wastes nothing. It is crucial, rather than self-important. Instead of just filling up space on the page, it takes what might seem *plausible* and hammers it down as *inevitable*.

I'd like to illustrate this with the first sentence from a short story by the writer, Lynne Sharon Schwartz. "Mrs. Saunders Writes to the World" (1978) was among the first stories Schwartz published. Even at this early stage in her career, Schwartz exercised great selectivity in her details.

You need to know the plot that follows to understand how *telling* the details are. "Mrs. Saunders Writes to the World" concerns a widow who longs to hear someone call her by her first name; but those who would have been intimate enough to do so have died or moved away, and the young people in her apartment complex don't think to ask. Mrs. Saunders is from a generation "too polite" to make any such direct request. What happens after that? She takes to spray painting her name on the sly. Her name, as graffiti, appears all over the building; but, of course everyone assumes it's the work of a youngster, until. . . .

But back to the lead sentence:

Mrs. Saunders placed her white plastic bag of garbage in one of the cans behind the row of garden apartments and looked about for a familiar face, but finding nothing except two unknown toddlers in the playground a short distance off, she shrugged, gazed briefly into the wan early spring sun, and climbed the stairs back to her own door.

Now that you, too, have the writer's advantage of knowing the sweep of the plot, you can see how each seemingly casual action speaks to the work as a whole. Since Mrs. Saunders will feel discarded in life, Schwartz shows it first by having her disposing of inessentials—trash. Since she will remain outside of reciprocal friendships, here she sees "toddlers"—those who are not only unequal to her but are also "unknown"—that is, unnamed. And "having a name" will prove to be Franny Saunders' central struggle. The sentence ends with a climb "back to her own door." In fact, she shuts both a real and a metaphorical "door" seventeen pages later.

All this—*told* in the first sentence. It's a sentence that most likely got reworked once the story was completed. After all, an author can make a character do anything in the world. Mrs. Saunders could have been introduced singing in the shower; she could have been watching TV. But Schwartz searched for the best details. Without giving the story away, she subtly gave it shape, with each and every word.

There are those who argue you can't write solely with *telling* details. More often you need—they assert—common detail.

Well, sometimes you do need the merely factual common detail. But sometimes comes, in my experience as a writer of literary fiction, rarely.

Here's a way to explore this argument. You may have noticed how writers-in-training often begin a story with a character's eyes opening from sleep to focus on the numbers on the alarm clock. The next sentence says that it's eight-fifteen, one-twenty-six, or five o'clock, precisely. A common use of common details.

Can a writer forgo using these blandly efficient numbers about time of day, and instead use *telling* details to speak more to the internal and external action of the story, right off the bat? Also, is it possible to avoid the usual next part of the problem—where the writer takes up the better part of the same page to get her character, XXX, over to a bathroom mirror, in order to give the reader an accurate description of XXX's face?

Since we know that most people leave bed in the morning and trudge over to the bathroom, the choice this writer has made just to use common details (clock numerals, bathroom mirror) yields for the reader the picture of a generic person, rather than a unique, specific individual—a character already caught, let's say, in the middle of some unique situation. The unique situation? Well, that's surely the start of the story-to-come. So, even from the first moment, the *telling* detail—the non-generic or non-common detail—will hold more potential.

Let me offer now some of my own ways of addressing the above technical challenges. The next two paragraphs are taken from the beginning of my novel, *Safe in America,* and focus the reader on a main character, Evan Eichenbaum:

First, his left arm stiffened, though he hadn't been sleeping on it, at least not that he knew; he'd awakened on his back. Slowly, he raised the bare arm above his head. No pain, just the cool air bathing it. Second, he began kneading the area that didn't hurt, his neck and shoulder. As he worked these muscles over hard, the few hairs on the back of his hand caught the low light in the room. The day had only just started; the creamy slats of the venetian blinds were edged pink. Evan was then sixty-seven years old, and of course he knew what to do with his own body's aches and pains. Third, lowering his arm, he slipped his hand just under the sheet, where the best heat was trapped.

Vera was sleeping on her stomach. When he ran his fingers along her spine, the silky nightgown rippled. By habit she turned toward him, eyes still closed, and sighed. She didn't yet know that during the night mostly everything had unraveled. The tiny crossed swords of her black bobby pins had slipped from the curls she'd hoped to keep coiled; a piece of the tissue paper wadded to support the waves of her hairdo now beat loosely against the pulse in her neck. Her disarray and abandon were full of trust. He watched her, breathing. He cuddled into her and could smell part of the secret between them: the warm skin on her neck, the beautiful Vera-is-here perfume. How long did he stay like that? Fourth, his chest tightened with a fierce warmth. It was true, nothing hurt him.

These two paragraphs are paced not by a clock, but by a man's movements, as he tries to determine what has awakened him. From the start, we understand something is not quite right with Evan because he slowly raises one bare arm into the cool air, as if seeking some kind of relief; we see him kneading the muscles, quietly, gingerly. These are details that tell something about him (how methodical he is, how cautious) and they're details that foretell, too: There's a heart attack to come.

Yet even when the focus isn't on Evan, but on his sleeping wife, Vera, the details in her description underscore our uneasiness. Take the detail of the "tiny crossed swords" and supporting tissue paper, all coming undone in Vera's hairdo—the point being made that despite the care being taken, "during the night mostly everything had unraveled." Telling details, and foretelling, too. They give us insight into the characters' personalities, and make Vera and Evan particular individuals; they also move the action along in the current situation, and hint of the situation to come.

Finally, let's go back and address the first problem, that of the alarm clock. Which sentence of the following is more telling in terms of establishing that Evan has awakened in early morning? "The numerals of the clock read: 5:23"; or: "The creamy slats of the venetian blinds were edged pink." My decision when rewriting was to cut the former and keep only the latter. Why? Because with the blinds' slats limned with dawn, the reader enters the sleeping couple's room, and gets not only a sense of its decor, but an awareness, too, of the world outside as it fills with the quivering color signaling the start of a process that is large, quiet, natural, unstoppable.

My hope is that these two paragraphs yield more than what I can take up the space here to explain. But that's what using details— carefully chosen, essential, versatile, telling details—can do: give us a vivid sense of the larger picture.

The truth is: In terms of our writing, we must not only be drawn to details, we must sweat them.

>> 28

REWRITING—WITH A FOCUS

BY REX BURNS

IF THERE IS A SINGLE CAVEAT THAT WILL HELP A WRITER STRENGTHEN the structure of a detective story or any piece of fiction, it would be, Know What You Want to Say. That is, if you know precisely the conclusion of your work before you start, you will discover the way to get there, and usually discover it with the least effort. But if, like me, you are not so lucky, if you're not quite sure what you're groping toward in a story, if the process of creating is a process of discovery for you, then there's no easy way, but only the hard one: Rewrite. And rewrite. And . . .

To say rewrite may be good advice, but it's a pretty vague directive. I rewrite for various purposes: In addition to going through a manuscript to correct basic spelling, language, and punctuation errors, I find other problems that may require me to do more rewrites. For example, one pass through a manuscript might be to look at diction, to be certain that the words I used achieved not only clarity, but euphony and effectiveness. Are there too many -ing endings too close together ("Seeing and hearing the running dog, Fred . . ." *vs.* "Fred jumped up")? Another kind of rewrite might look closely at sentences to see if the length suits the action. Did I vary my sentence patterns effectively? Did I use unnecessarily convoluted sentences? What excess words can I cut?

Less cosmetic but more fundamental is the rewrite that focuses on such elements of narrative structure as plot, multiple story lines, and in mysteries, puzzle.

The conventional distinction between story and plot—"story" is what happens, "plot" is why it happens—is a convenient and generally accurate one. Plot does answer the whys of an action: Why does Fred visit his father? Why does his father feel as he does toward Fred?

When we start to understand the whys of actions, we say, "Aha—the plot thickens!"

But plot has at least two main aspects, and examining them separately can often contribute to your perception of the manuscript and, thus, to how well the rewrite works. Let's call these the *psychological* and the *mechanical* aspects. Henry James argued that plot and character were synonymous, and there's truth in that: Psychological motivation, derived from character, often explains a lot of the whys of an event. Fred, a selfish young man, is greedy for his inheritance and, to sate that greed, he tries to convince his rich father that he is a dutiful son. That's the *psychological* reason behind Fred's decision to visit the old man.

The *mechanical* aspect of plot is the result of forces external to a character. For example, for years, Fred has ignored his father, except to ask for money, but now the old man has a terminal illness. This external circumstance prompts Fred to visit his father before it's too late. Moreover, the combination of Fred's past behavior and the discovery of his father's illness, both external to the father's character, generate in the father resentment and suspicion of his son's sudden solicitude.

Recognizing this distinction between the psychological and the mechanical aspects of plot by careful rewriting can help you focus the story more sharply. Depending upon the length of the story, Fred's greed, for example, can be explored for development and consistency. What made him so selfish? Was it a trait inherited from an over-acquisitive grandmother? Was it the result of his being the smallest at the dinner table? Was he imitating a similar fault in his father? Or has he a sense of alienation from other people? In other words, by singling out the psychological aspect of plot for rewriting, you can more readily trace the protagonist's character through the story and assess it for probability and consistency. On the other hand, by focusing on the mechanical aspect, you can rewrite in anticipation of an event: Is it likely that Fred could avoid his father for years and yet ask him for money? Is it possible that the old man has terminal cancer? Could Fred easily arrange a visit home?

Broken down into a series of questions like this about the sequence of events and their psychological or mechanical causes, the job of rewriting becomes not just one of determining the believability of an action, but also of seeing the proper proportion of narrative space required to describe that action. So the writer can see more clearly which events are the most vital and consequently most likely to demand "scenic" treatment. Conversely, actions identified as less vital can be treated by mere reference or inference. For example, Fred may have a memory of fighting for that last slice of bread on the dinner table, but perhaps the event with the greater psychological impact, and therefore necessitating greater detail, was seeing his father, as master of the house, help himself first to the best. Or, the father's cancer could be mentioned briefly in a letter or telephone call, while Fred's decision to go back home might call for somewhat more expanded treatment.

The relationship between Fred and his father might be sufficient for a short story or a one-act play, but a novel would require more strands. Fred's mother or sister or brother may come on stage. There may be longtime servants present or a family lawyer to draw up a new will. In other words, given that Fred's is the central story, other story lines might also exist. Often when I'm partway through writing a novel, I've discovered that my protagonist or chief villain needs an accomplice, or that the suspense element calls for a red herring, or the pacing of the action requires the tension provided by adding another suspect. Thus, even before a book is completed, I usually face a rewrite to look closely at multiple story lines.

Again, an analysis of the psychological and mechanical aspects of plot often applies to the secondary story lines as well. Fred's mother, for instance, may have suffered silently in the conflict between her son and her husband. What events have caused her to be silent? Does she eventually speak out? Why? But in addition to examining these issues, you must also ask how (and whether) the secondary line clarifies or adds tension to or resolves issues in the main narrative. If Fred's mother does finally speak out, what effect does that have on the main narrative? Or do the actions of an old and privileged servant contribute to the father-son conflict? If so, how? What about Fred's sister Mary? What has she been doing all these years, and how does she feel about her brother's sudden reappearance? Note further that in making revisions in these other story lines, the extent of their effect on the central narrative will determine their importance and consequent space appropriate in the overall structure.

Sometimes, a subsidiary story line will gain in importance either in

123

the first draft or in the rewrite. If it's in the first draft, my practice is to let it grow, because at that point I don't usually know where the story's going. But in the rewrite stage, painful though it may be, my method is usually to share and pare. Does the subsidiary story line compete with the main story and blur the focus, thus requiring you to cut? Where and how can it be expanded to add enrichment—thematic or psychological—to the principal narrative? Obviously, there's no clear-cut answer to these questions, but the relationship between the subsidiary story line and the central narrative helps clarify the development and presentation needed. Is it important that Fred's sister has an illegitimate child? It is if her father sees that child as a better son than Fred has been, or if Fred believes that's the case; it is if the child is old enough and willing to act in some way that affects the main story. If, however, that child serves no purpose in the central narrative, then it may be best to delete it or not even put Fred's sister, poor thing, through the trauma of an unwanted pregnancy.

A third element that the writer of mystery and detection fiction must emphasize is puzzle, which is often confused with plot. *Who*dunit is often related to *why* it was done, and thus the confusions. But whereas the writer must deal with both plot and puzzle, readers are often interested primarily in puzzle, while plot is only on the fringe of their attention. You must keep this difference in emphasis in mind as you write. Who was it that knocked on the door two hours after Fred returned home, and why? What was it that Fred's sister didn't want overheard when she was on the phone? Why was the lawyer standing outside the door when Fred and his father had their first meeting in years? And where did the old and trusted servant disappear to on the night Fred's father was murdered?

Such puzzling elements may or may not be integral to the structure of the story. If that is the case, however, chances are that they have already figured as mechanical aspects of the plot. But if they are solely elements of the puzzle, they can be considered or possibly added in a rewrite as useful red herrings, or used to heighten tension, or even be used as genuine clues in either the primary or the secondary story line. Again, in dealing with puzzle elements, the principle of effective rewriting is the same: analysis of the element, focus of attention on that element, and assessment of its relationship to the narrative's climactic ending.

>> 29

WHAT WE WRITE ABOUT WHEN WE WRITE ABOUT LOVE

By Nancy Willard

THE FIRST BOOK I EVER WANTED TO STEAL WAS A SLIM BLUE PAPER-back called *Tales of French Love and Passion.* It showed a woman in a low-cut gown and elbow-length gloves eyeing a man with a goatee and moustache: the devil, I supposed, or one of his minions. Because the devil wore a striped polo shirt and a beret, I assumed he was on vacation—a cruise, perhaps. The woman was giving him a sly smile; she had one arm raised, as if she were waving at someone just out of the picture.

I was twelve, going on sixteen. Every summer my mother and sister and I moved from Ann Arbor, Michigan, to a ramshackle cottage sixty miles away, in the sleepy settlement of Stoney Lake. My father, who was teaching summer school, drove to Stoney Lake every Friday after his last class, and on Sunday he drove the family car back to Ann Arbor.

All week long the old men of Stoney Lake went fishing and the young men went to work in town or at the gravel pit across the lake, and the mothers and grandmothers sat on their front porches and watched the dust rise and fall in the dirt road, and gossiped in Italian, and so the air hung heavy with their secrets. Only our house felt as dull as a convent.

Thank God for my mother's younger sister, Nell, whose chose to spend the first month of her summer vacation with us and whose *Tales of French Love and Passion* showed me what I was missing. She kept the book on the nightstand, next to her Madame DuBarry Beauty Box, and her favorite story, "Room Eleven," was no secret; when I picked up that slim blue volume, it obligingly opened to p. 33:

She picked all her lovers from the army and kept them three years, the time of their sojourn in the garrison. In short, she not only had love, she had sense. . . . She gave the preference to men of calm allurement, like herself, but they must be handsome. She also wished them to have had no previous entanglements, any passion having the power to leave traces, or that had made any trouble. Because the man whose loves are mentioned is never a very discreet man.

After having decided upon the one she would love for the three years of his regulation sojourn, it only remained to throw down the gauntlet.

—From *Stories of Love and Passion: A Collection of Complete Short Stories Chosen from the Works of Guy de Maupassant*

Not for her second-graders at Northville Elementary did Nell pluck her eyebrows, oil her eyelashes, and rouge her cheeks. She was young, pretty, and thrice divorced. When she scanned the *Oxford Weekly,* she was appalled to find that God hosted all the regular social events announced in its pages; even square dancing was held in the basement of the Methodist church. The only gatherings that escaped His watchful eye were auctions.

The auctions always took place on somebody's front lawn. On one hot Sunday in July, we stood in the crowd that milled around the front yard opposite the high school, listening to the to the auctioneer's patter and laughing at his jokes.

Nell bid on whatever looked like a bargain. Who knows why we suddenly want what we don't need? When an upright piano was pushed into view and the auctioneer shouted, "What am I bid for this piano?" my mother bid ten dollars.

"Ten dollars!" sneered the auctioneer. "Madam, I'd buy it myself for ten dollars if I had a place to put it. Look at the work on this thing."

"Do it play?" called a voice from the back of the crowd.

"Play? Play?" The auctioneer touched middle C. "Can anyone here give us a demonstration?"

Nell was on the platform in an instant. She pulled up a kitchen chair, and she played "You Are My Sunshine" and "Four Leaf Clover," then eased into the rippling improvisation she used to quiet her second-graders.

"Twenty!" shouted the voice in the back.

"Twenty-five!" shouted my mother.

"Twenty-five going once, twenty-five going twice—"

The auctioneer paused. The silence was deafening.

"All done at twenty-five!"

"My God," whispered Mother, "where will we put a piano?"

While the auctioneer's assistant was smoothing Mother's five-dollar bills and tucking them into the cashbox, Nell was talking to one of the movers, a man whose sweat-soaked shirt stuck to his back in ragged patches. He was the only mover with black hair, and it fell around his eyes in tight curls. Nell signaled to my mother.

"His name is Lou Lubbock," she said. "For two dollars, he'll move the piano on his pick-up truck."

By the time Mother had counted her change, Lou had rolled the piano up a ramp into the back of the red pick-up and was sitting in the cab beside a man whose face we couldn't see.

"Did you tell him where we live?" asked my mother.

"I told him to follow us," said Nell.

"You did?" exclaimed Mother. "Who's that old gentleman with him?"

"His father."

The piano, which had looked almost diminutive among wardrobes and breakfronts at the auction, appeared monstrous when Lou tried to bring it through the front door of the cottage. Mother cast anxious glances at Lou Lubbock's father. He did not look as though he'd ever moved anything heavier than a telephone book.

"Won't go through the front door," he remarked, as the two men set the piano on the grass.

"I guess we'll have to take it back to the auction," said Mother. She sounded relieved.

"What doesn't go through the door goes through the window," said Lou. "Trust me."

With the practiced hand of a burglar, he pried out the top half of the big window in the living room and pushed his father through. Then he lifted the front end of the piano, letting it straddle the sill.

There was a sudden thud, and all at once the piano was standing in the living room as if had always been there. As Lou Lubbock took his leave, somewhere between our front door and his truck, he invited Nell to go roller skating.

That summer Nell kept company with the piano mover and I read *Tales of French Love and Passion* and mooned around the visible borders of their passion like a twelve-year-old voyeur. But when school started in September and our teacher asked us to write about what we did on our vacation, did I write about Aunt Nell and the piano mover? No. I wrote about the lake, the fish, and the turtles. What I learned about love that summer sank out of sight but not out of mind. Like so many visitors from the invisible world, those memories come unannounced and never when I call them.

Writers believe they choose the stories they want to write, but this is an illusion. Our stories choose us, and they are as patient and sure as the heroine in that tale I found on my aunt's nightstand. Not until ninth grade did I meet it again when I happened to check out of the school library a modest gray hardcover called *The Complete Stories of Guy de Maupassant*. As I reread it with astonishment and awe, the longing that had infused the summer of the piano mover washed over me. I wanted to write a love story. And de Maupassant made it look so easy.

There are two ways of beginning such a story. The first lets you know right away that you're reading a love story. The second does not; indeed, it takes pains to hide its true intent. A beginning of the first kind can make you feel you're eavesdropping on a telephone with a party line. Here is the opening of John Updike's "Love Song for a Moog Synthesizer":

> She was good in bed. She went to church. Her I.Q. was 145. She repeated herself. Nothing fit; it frightened him. Yet Tod wanted to hang on, to hang on to the bits and pieces, which perhaps were not truly pieces but islands, which a little lowering sea level would reveal to be rises on a sunken continent, peaks of a subaqueous range, secretly one, a world.
> —From *Problems and Other Stories,* by John Updike (Alfred A. Knopf)

What Updike gives us is a close-up: the raw surface of the lover's confusion as he picks over the bits and pieces of a relationship, puzzling over them, gathering them into the lap of a long sentence, trying to understand love through the sum of its parts.

Now turn the telescope of the lover's vision around. The moment you step back and put a little distance between you and the characters, you have space to examine their motives, as Alice Walker does here in the opening sentence of her story, "The Lover": "Her husband had wanted a child and so she gave him one as a gift, because she liked her husband and admired him greatly."

No writer can surpass Isaac Babel for opening sentences that perfectly balance distance with immediacy. Take the beginning of a story called "First Love," which, by its very title, announces its subject—a dangerous practice for the novice writer:

> When I was ten years old, I fell in love with a woman called Galina. Her surname was Rubtsov. Her husband, an officer, went off to the Russo-Japanese War and returned in October, 1905. He brought a great many trunks back with him. These trunks, which weighed nearly half a ton, contained Chinese souvenirs such as screens and costly weapons. Kurma the yardman used to tell us that Rubtsov had bought all these things with money he had embezzled while serving in the engineer corps of the Manchurian Army.
> —From *The Collected Stories,* edited and translated by Walter Morison (Criterion Books)

Though Babel's impassioned opening sentence seems to give the whole story away, he follows it, not with a description of Galina, but with three purely factual statements: her name, her husband's occupation, and what he brought home from the war. The last sentence in the paragraph turns from fact to rumor and gives us a little of the husband's character through the eyes of the yardman. The husband is a crook. Babel knows that part of telling a story well is holding back and that Chekhov's advice on writing about grief also applies to writing about love:

> When you . . . wish to move your reader to pity, try to be colder. It will give a kind of backdrop to . . . grief, make it stand out more. . . . Yes, be cold. . . .
> —From *Chekhov,* by Henri Troyat (Ballantine Books)

Why am I seeking advice from Chekhov? Because Nell's story is knocking at a locked door in the back of my mind, and I can't find the key to let it out. The key is the right voice to tell it. Should the teller be a twelve-year-old child, narrating the events with an innocent eye? Or the child, grown up now, looking back? Should I tell it in the voice of my mother, looking askance? Or should I hand the story over to Aunt Nell, who is not looking at all but stepping headlong into love?

Here's one possible way into the story:

> The piano went for twenty-five dollars, plus three dollars extra if you wanted the auctioneer's assistant to move it. Nell asked him if he would move it for two as she and her sister were short of cash. Watching him push it up the ramp into his pick-up truck she thought, I could run away with that man.

The instant I've written these lines, I know I'm lying. It was not love at first sight. Every evening Lou Lubbock called for Nell in his pick-up truck, and every night I dozed but did not fall asleep until two in the morning, when his truck clattered down the dirt road to our house, and Nell let herself in through the kitchen door, and my mother tiptoed downstairs in her nightgown. Together my mother and Nell sat in front of the empty fireplace and went over the day, piece by piece. A hole in the floor under my bed gave me a clear view of the living room. If I pressed my ear to the hole, I could catch most of their conversation. It might go something like this:

Mother: So where did he take you?
Nell: We went roller skating.
Mother: Oh, you love roller skating.
Nell: Not with him. He's a terrible skater. All he wants to do is eat.
Mother: Where'd you eat?
Nell: He took me to the Harvest Table.
Mother: That's a nice restaurant.
Nell: But he chews with his mouth full. And he always has dirt under his nails. I said to him, "Lou, just because you work on cars all day doesn't mean you can't wash up afterwards."
Mother: Why do you go out with him?
Nell: Because he's there.

Oh, he was certainly there. Though he was always on her mind, she made it clear to us that she would leave him at the end of the summer. Even she would never have called what passed between them love.

Who knows better than Chekhov the power of love that begins with mild curiosity and ends with obsession? In "The Lady With The Pet Dog," a man has an affair with a woman he meets at a resort hotel, expecting to forget her when the affair ends, as he has forgotten other women. In a single paragraph, Chekhov shows us the lover's inability to forget:

A month or so would pass and the image of Anna Sergeyevna, it seemed to him, would become misty in his memory, and only from time to time he would dream of her with her touching smile as he dreamed of others. But more than a month went by, winter came into its own, and everything was still clear in his memory as though he had departed from Anna Sergeyevna only yesterday. And his memories glowed more and more vividly. In the street he followed the women with his eyes, looking for someone who resembled her.
—From *The Portable Chekhov,* edited by Avrahm Yarmolinsky (Viking)

To tell Nell's story the way it happened, I need the kind of beginning that doesn't appear to be part of a love story at all. Take, for example, the opening of Rachel Ingalls' "Faces of Madness."

Four other boys in William's class shared his name. At home he was Will. At school someone else was called Will; two were Bill, and one went under a middle name. Only William was given the full, formal version.
—From *The Literary Lover,* edited by Larry Dark (Viking Penguin)

Nothing in the opening hints at how the main character, William, will spend his life and fortune looking for the woman his parents prevented him from marrying.

After the summer ended, Nell rarely mentioned Lou Lubbock. A week before Christmas, one of the women who lived in the cottage next door called to say Lou's truck had skidded on a patch of ice and flipped over on him. "He was trapped for six hours before he died," she added. "Thank God he was alone when it happened."

That winter when Nell came to visit on weekends, I could feel the ghost of Lou Lubbock listening, invisible and helpless, as she told the story of how she'd met her first husband in the laundromat. She'd just put two quarters into the dryer.

"I went to get a Coke from the machine, and he snuck over and opened the door of the dryer and threw all his stuff in with mine. When we tried to sort it out, my bra was hooked around his undershirt. One thing sort of led to another."

Now let me interrupt myself with a story which I hope will illuminate the problem facing any writer who has ever set out to write a love story. Three years after the summer of Nell and the piano mover, my sister, who was living in a sorority house in Ann Arbor, accepted the fraternity pin of the boy she was dating, and called home, four blocks away, to announce the good news.

"I've been 'pinned'!"

I was fifteen and thought the choice of words was unfortunate; it made me think of wrestlers on a mat, of butterflies skewered under labels. But to those wiser than I, it meant she was one step away from being engaged. It also meant that on a Monday night in the middle of May the whole fraternity would assemble under her window and serenade her. Of course my mother and father and I were not invited. But she explained that if we brought binoculars and hid behind the trees or in the bushes that flourished in the front yard of the First Presbyterian Church across the street, we could get a view of the whole ceremony.

On the appointed evening, my mother and father concealed themselves behind two large oaks, and I tucked myself into a honeysuckle bush between the church and the parking lot, with its single car, and waited for the show to begin. The fragrance of honeysuckle filled me with a nameless sorrow. Because I had the worst view, my mother had entrusted me with the binoculars. The sorority house was dark save for a single upstairs window, at which my sister stood, holding a candle so that love could find her. Presently I heard the clatter of footsteps in the distance. What appeared to be a well-trained army of salesmen was marching toward my sister's light, two by two, on the opposite side of the street. They assembled under her window, and after a small silence—during which I could almost hear the squeak of a pitchpipe—they burst into song.

A love song, no doubt. I've forgotten the words. In the middle of it, the young man paying court to my sister held up something large and lobed—his heart, I thought, till it lit up and through the binoculars I saw it was a model of his fraternity pin. Was it my fear of the dark that made me turn the binoculars away from my sister to the parking lot? What did it matter that I had the worst view of the pinning ceremony? I had an extraordinary view of the couple necking in the car in the parking lot.

Writing a love story is a little like finding yourself with a pair of binoculars in your hand, caught between passion and scruples, ceremony and sex. If you err too far in either direction, you can end up on the side of pornography or romance. The difference between a love story and a romance is one of intent. When you write a romance, you carefully follow where many have trod, so that your readers can recognize the genre through its conventions. But in a love story, you try to show love as if your characters had just invented it. Follow your characters, and they will give you the story, but you can't tell ahead of time exactly where they'll lead you. Rousseau's advice for writing a love letter is also useful for writing a story: ". . . you ought to begin

132

without knowing what you mean to say, and to finish without knowing what you have written."

Love has its roots in the particular and the ordinary. Surely one of the writer's greatest challenges is to show how imagination can transform an ordinary human being into one whose absence turns day into night, heaven into hell, happiness into an abyss. Weather, light, fragrance, memory and loneliness have more to do with the alchemy of love than beauty or grace; Maurice Chevalier once remarked that "many a man has fallen in love with a girl in a light so dim he would not have chosen a suit by it." For showing that alchemy, I know of few writers who can surpass Thomas Mann in this passage from "Tonio Kroger":

> Strange how things come about! He had seen her a thousand times; then one evening he saw her again; saw her in a certain light, talking with a friend in a certain saucy way, laughing and tossing her head; saw her lift her arm and smooth her back hair with her schoolgirl hand, that was by no means particularly fine or slender, in such a way that the thin white sleeve slipped down from her elbow; heard her speak a word or two, a quite indifferent phrase, but with a certain intonation, with a warm ring in her voice; and his heart throbbed with ecstasy . . .
> —From *Death in Venice and Seven Other Stories.*
> Translated by H. T. Lowe-Porter (Vintage Books)

We are in love, and love what vanishes; isn't that why the sight of a thin white sleeve slipping down a girl's arm can break someone's heart? While lovers lie in each other's arms, the world is singing an older tune: "Golden lads and girls all must/ As chimney-sweepers, come to dust."

But though the teller vanishes, the tale does not. Several years ago when I started to work on a novel called *Sister Water,* the voices of women—in the living room at two in the morning—these voices I thought I'd forgotten did not forget me. As I wrote the chapter in which the main character receives word that her husband has been killed in a car accident, I knew what Aunt Nell would say.

"Death is so ordinary," she whispers. "Write about love."

>> 30

CREATING DYNAMIC OUTLINES FOR YOUR NOVELS

BY WILLIAM H. LOVEJOY

IF YOU'RE LIKE MOST WRITERS I'VE TALKED TO, YOU DISLIKE BOTH the thought and the act of outlining a story or writing a synopsis of it. I *know* I've got this hummer mapped out in my mind, and all I need to do is sit down and transfer it from my frail memory to the more reliable memory of the machine, one sentence after another.

The trouble is, no matter what you and I think we can accomplish as writers, there's always someone—an agent, an editor, a publisher—who wants to see that outline or synopsis at some point in the process. Sometimes, the request comes before we write the novel. Then, too, there's always that nagging little suspicion that we could drop the ball on one of the subplots, forgetting to resolve some of the minor issues before reaching the end.

Over the past several years, I've developed a system of outlining that I find flexible and easy to use; certainly it's less rigid than that *I, II, III, A, B, C, i, ii, iii* format that Miss Turpin drummed into me in sophomore English. It changes as I go long, adapting to those strange little turns that my characters take as they begin to control the keyboard and do things that I had never predicted for them. When I discover, sixty pages into the book, that I've developed an interesting little subplot that was unplanned, the outline reshapes itself to accommodate my fickle side.

For one thing, the day never begins with a blank page. The first screen that appears on the machine when I power up in the morning looks like this:

OUTLINE
Title:
Theme:
Plot:

Protagonist:
Antagonist:
Locale:
Details:
Characters:

   ONE
   Scene 1
   Scene 2
   Scene 3
   Etc. . . .

   TWO
   Scene 1
   Scene 2
   Etc. . . .

   THREE

You can start anywhere. If you wake up in the middle of the night with a super title in mind, plug it in. Work up a description or biography for your protagonist. Spend some time creating a villain, and if that doesn't work, simply delete him from the antagonist slot and paste him in as one of your characters, for possible use in another place.

In no time at all, you'll find the slots filling in, and before you know it, you'll have enough flesh and bone to develop a summary of one or two pages. That's as far as I go in the first step, since my proposals are generally based on my summary. Here's an example of how the partially completed outline of my novel *China Dome* took shape:

Title:	*China Dome*
Theme:	Chinese desire to maintain capitalism in Hong Kong after 1997 and become a global commercial power. Suspense with high-tech.
Plot:	
Protagonist:	Dan Kerry, Vice President for Far Eastern Development, 6' 1", 40s, ruggedly handsome, blonde/silver/sun-bleached hair, deep tan, gray eyes, permanent squint, rebuilt teeth, Vietnam F-4s— Silver Star, Air Medal, Air Force Academy-aeronautical engineering
Antagonist:	
Locale:	Hong Kong, Pacific Rim
Details:	American, French, German, Russian SSTs

135

Characters: James Lee, (Hu Ziyang) undercover at China Dome, bulky, thick-torsoed, long arms, obscene tattoos on arms, right eye has an ugly scar, missing left little finger
Charley Whitlock
Karen Meyer, El Al (Mossad agent)
Hyun Oh, North Korean, tall

Once most of the headings are filled in (you'll keep adding to them as you write), you can begin thinking about the chapters. Let's say you're writing a 150,000-word novel. This will average thirty chapters of twenty pages each, coming out just right to six hundred pages. This will help you maintain the pacing, though you'll probably deviate from the average at times. That's all right though, since the outline will reshape itself as you progress. *China Dome* actually ended up with twenty-six chapters.

Under each chapter number, note the number of scenes, whether you're writing from an omniscient, first-person, or single point of view. I use multiple points of view for most of my novels, with each scene shown through the eyes of a different character. That being the case, under each chapter number I list the name of each character whose point of view I expect to use in that chapter when I come to writing it. For a first-person historical romance, you may wish to list the scenes by number, by location, by time, or by any device that fits your objective.

From my summary, or from actions that I've played out in my mind, I know approximately where particular scenes should go throughout the novel. I jump back and forth in the outline, plugging them into various chapters, keeping the exposition and explanation short—using just enough to trigger the details of the scene I've envisioned. The first time I go through the outline, I lay out the primary plot, then insert the subplots. Approximate placement is sufficient. As the book grows, I often shift the scenes to other chapters. If I know through whose point of view the reader should view a particular scene, I assign it to that character. If I don't know, I just list the scene ideas at the bottom of the chapter, assigning them to a specific character later. Mystery writers frequently work backward, starting with the resolution of the crime. This type of outline works very well for mysteries.

The outline for a few chapters of *China Dome* looked like this in the early stages:

ONE

Kerry—arrives at China Dome, explosion

TWO

Kerry—rescues men from tower
Broussard—reaches scene of explosion, stopped by Yichang
Carroll—
Yichang—
Sun—learns of disaster, background to Chinese education
Hua—
Jackson—
Wehmeier—

Another of the tools that helps build suspense is the use of time to point out the approach of impending doom. And with the approach of the high-tech supersonic aircraft, each of the scenes has to be timed to take into consideration the speed of the aircraft, a couple of much slower ships, and a few helicopters. At about Chapter Fourteen, I decided to give each scene a specific time and place, and I made some carefully calculated additions to the outline. (It was important to watch for the transitions between time zones and crossing the International Date Line):

TWENTY-FOUR

October 1, 12:30 p.m., Deng Xiaoping International Superport
  Sun—welcoming dignitaries
October 1, 12:32 p.m., over the South China Sea
  Carroll—approaching the mainland, F-16 joins up
October 1, 12:34 p.m., Deng Xiaoping International Superport
  Yichang—tension in the tower
October 1, 12:52 p.m., over the South China Sea
  Hua—on patrol, notes operating powerful radar
October 1, 12:55 p.m., Southern China
  Jackson—first sight of airport
October 1, 12:57 p.m., Taya Wan, China
  Wehmeier—getting ready, radio scanner listening to aircraft
October 1, 12:59 p.m., 45 kilometers west of Deng Xiaoping International Superport
  Broussard—approaching from the west
October 1, 1:07 p.m., Deng Xiaoping International Superport
  Kerry—getting worried
October 1, 1:11 p.m., South China
  Carroll—joins with other SSTs, on approach to China Dome, loses control

Each of those time-and-place entries became the subheadings in the final manuscript to divide scenes to help readers understand that the

137

point of view was changing. The subheads also preclude the need to establish the time and place in narrative or dialogue in scenes in which the timing and location of aircraft and lethal weaponry are critical.

When I've finished the novel, I've also finished the outline, and with a little cutting and the insertion of a few verbs, I have a *final* sentence synopsis for the editors who require one. And I also have a framework to help me stay with my characters when they veer unexpectedly or raise questions that require an answer somewhere back in Chapter One or Twenty-Six. *China Dome* involves fifty-four major and minor characters (not counting the walk-ons).

If you shy away from outlining, perhaps this process will ease the task for you and prove its value. Start with the title . . . or the hero . . . or Chapter One . . . or Chapter Thirty. But start.

≫≫31

MAKE DIALOGUE WORK FOR YOUR STORY

BY ALYCE MILLER

WRITING DIALOGUE IN FICTION IS A NEVER-ENDING LESSON IN LIStening. Writers often become so preoccupied with plot and characterization that they forget how essential dialogue is to both. They must develop a keen sense not only of observation, but also of hearing how people (both real and fictional) speak.

When your characters are allowed to talk, you begin to learn who they are. Trial runs at conversations between characters can tell you things about them you didn't know. Try sketching out various exchanges of dialogue between characters as part of your daily writing exercise.

You might try placing your characters in various situations of conflict to find out how they would respond. How would your character respond if someone accused him or her of cheating on a spouse? What would your character say if asked if she or he believes in God?

Be aware of not only *what* your characters say, but *how* they say it. What words do they choose or repeat? There's a difference between a character who says, "She's a nice woman" and one who says, "She's a terrific gal." What does that difference reveal about the character?

The following dialogue ideas are just that: ideas. Read through them quickly at first, then go back and develop your own dialogue exercises from them.

• Dialogue in fiction should never be used simply to convey information. This is what I call the soap-opera approach to writing. If you tune in to a soap opera, you can generally find out from the repeated histories and explanations in the characters' dialogue exactly what's going on in the tangled web of plot. Example: "Remember when John

139

was married to Ginny, the year his sister died of breast cancer, right before Ollie was jailed for murder, and Ginny cheated on him with Sam, and John had to shoot Sam with the gun he borrowed from Max?" This is an exaggeration, of course, but not too far from many soap opera scenes. Real people, familiar with each other's backgrounds, don't engage in rehashing details. They may refer to them, but they don't use the language of exposition to do it. One might rewrite the above to show tension between two characters. For example: Jane: "I think John had something to do with Sam's death." Mabel: "You're crazy. Sam was shot. John has never gone near a gun in his life."

People often use dialogue to *conceal* information. Example: The woman who has just cheated on her husband probably isn't going to announce it. Instead she may choose to conceal what she has just done and say, "I've been thinking maybe we should have another baby." Or dialogue can be ironic, as when a character who obviously has no idea he is about to be run over by a car says, "What a beautiful fall day this is!" That line resonates with meaning that the character never intended.

• Dialogue should not just mirror the action of the characters. Example: "Jane was thirsty so she poured herself a glass of lemonade. 'God, I'm so thirsty and this lemonade is just the thing to hit the spot,' she said." In this case, you could cut the dialogue altogether, and just record the gesture—"Jane poured herself a glass of lemonade"—or keep the dialogue simple, with Jane saying, "This really hits the spot."

Sometimes dialogue works against the action. Example: "'I don't care,' she said, and burst into tears." Obviously, we can tell she *does* care, but she's not admitting it. Notice that tension has been introduced at the moment her words contradict her actions.

• In tense situations, people in real life rarely talk about what they really want to talk about, either because their conscious mind resists the truth or they aren't sure how to express their feelings. A man may criticize his sister's bad marriage because he can't stand to talk about his own troubled one. Or in speaking to her neighbor, a woman goes on and on about the bad weather because she can't bring herself to complain about the neighbor's mean dog.

• Try paraphrasing what a character says when it is not essential that the reader hear every word. Don't have a character talk on and on about her wonderful son if we already know she worships him and what she has to say about him is not crucial to the story. Simply write, "For the rest of the evening, she talked endlessly about her son."

However, if the character has been estranged from her son and is going to meet him after a long separation, you don't want to cheat your reader of the chance to see how mother and son interact when reunited. In this case, you probably wouldn't say, "Marge and her son were thrilled to see each other and talked for hours, catching each other up on the last five years." The reader would want to hear the dialogue, to watch the dynamics unfold.

• Real-life people communicate a lot through small talk and silence. They also fill in gaps in conversation with "um," "like," and "well." Of course, this is not advisable in fiction; it would grow tedious quickly. Readers will not patiently sit through pages of "how's-the-weather" dialogue. This does not mean that everything a character says should be complex and profound. You can convey the impression of small talk through paraphrase and gesture.

Stick to small talk when it overlays a larger tension. The above scene with the reuniting mother and son might be an excellent case for small talk in the opening dialogue. People under the stress of deep emotion will frequently revert to comfortable subjects. Example: Mary and Jane, who are both in love with Karl, are trapped on an elevator to the fiftieth floor. The reader knows they are mortal enemies, but they refuse to discuss Karl. In that situation their small talk could be used to heighten tension and develop the dramatic action. "Mary kept her eyes on the elevator door, as if expecting it to open at any second. Jane said, 'So, Mary, what brings you out this way?' Mary didn't answer right away. When she did, her voice was flat and indifferent. 'I like to shop here. The prices are better.'"

• Gestures may actually convey far more than a line of dialogue. Instead of saying, "'I'm furious with you, Helen,' said John," why not try, "John moved briskly to the other side of the room"?

• When you have finished a scene or a story, always read your dialogue aloud. *Hear* what is on the page. Don't simply listen for content. Pay attention to the rhythms and pacing of speech. Think about not only the meaning of what is said, but the difference in sound and rhythm, in saying "I'm hot!" or "I'm burning up!" or "This heat is killing me."

• Avoid long-winded soliloquies. They are usually full of repetition and information that is not crucial to the story; in addition, long passages of dialogue are difficult to write, and even more important, difficult to read. Convey characters' emotions, outlooks, and beliefs through shorter, crisper, tighter dialogue.

• If you have a character who speaks in dialect or with a particular accent or speech impediment, avoid odd spellings to convey it, and stay away from clichés that signal caricature. Example: "'Thtay with me, Thoothie,' he lisped. "Promith you'll thit here all night long.'" This becomes ludicrous, cumbersome, and intrusive. If a character lisps, simply tell us that. You might write, "It irritated Susie that John could not pronounce the letter 's' in her name." Allow the reader to supply the rest.

If you use dialect or slang or colloquialisms, be sure you really know how a person with a particular background or from a certain region would sound. There's nothing worse than serving up stereotypes. Not only may it offend readers, it's a cop-out on the writer's part because it doesn't ring true; the writer hasn't really *listened*. If you are writing about a character whose class or background or culture is very unfamiliar to you, you might want to reconsider using that character in your story, or else make a point of listening to how real-life people from that culture or background speak. It is easy to listen only superficially and miss subtle nuances of others' speech. Hone your ear. Really listen without imposing your own preconceptions.

• Drop unnecessary dialogue tags ("he said" and "she said"). They become repetitive and tedious. Traditionally, writers show change of speaker by moving to a new paragraph. When you do need to differentiate between speakers, particularly in longer exchanges of dialogue, an occasional "he said" is the least noticeable way of doing so. Readers don't stumble over it the way they do with showy tags like "he hissed" or "she exclaimed." Avoid the temptation to include modifying adverbs ("he said peevishly" or "she exclaimed dramatically"). Make your dialogue reveal who is speaking and what the mood is. If necessary, you can supply a gesture. Or, if you must use tags other than "said," stick to words that convey what cannot be shown in dialogue itself, as in "she whispered" or "he shouted." But use them sparingly!

Remember that writing dialogue is a skill that you can perfect through listening carefully and reading aloud passages of your own dialogue and those written by other writers you admire. Resist the influence of "television dialogue," which often tends to be overly clever or downright silly.

Keep in mind that it is your character who tells you how he or she should speak. Open your ears and listen.

➢➢ 32

REVISING YOUR FICTION MANUSCRIPT

By John Dufresne

REVISION IS NOT A MATTER OF CHOICE, YET MANY BEGINNING FICTION writers either resist, resent, or misunderstand its importance. When we read an impressive ten-page story, we may not be aware of the numerous discarded pages that preceded the finished product. If you were taught that writing is product and not process, that it's the articulation of thought and not thought itself, then revision may seem like punishment for not getting it right the first time. But writing is not supposed to be easy or extemporaneous. The writer has the duty and the opportunity to rework a story to try to find the best word, phrase, or scene, or do it over again until it is right.

If you are like Dorothy Parker, your revision begins with the first sentence of the first draft. She claimed that in writing seven words she revised five. The writing process itself is repetitive, erratic, messy. Planning, drafting, and revising seldom proceed in a linear fashion and, perhaps, should not be thought of as distinct tasks. All three go on in the first draft, as well as in the second and the tenth. But if we think of revision as a "seeing again," then we might say it starts when you have a beginning, middle, and end to your story. Now you can read it. Now you can see what you've said and sense what still needs to be said.

Revising means casting a critical eye on your work, and doing so makes the revision different from your first draft. You reorganize material; examine words, phrases, and paragraphs; consider character and plot; look at beginnings, endings, transitions, and composition. You add, delete, reshape. You examine your choices. There are a thousand steps in the process. It is in the revision stage that your imagination becomes deeply engaged with your material, when you come to know your characters and begin to perceive their motivations and values. Revision is not the end of the creative process, but a new beginning; it's a chance not simply to clean up and edit, but to open up and discover.

When you've completed a draft of your story, it's a good idea to set the manuscript aside and return to it later. Each time you read it over, you'll see something new. Read it aloud and note the places where the rhythms are smooth or hard, the prose graceful or awkward, a character's diction consistent and revealing, or jarring and unconvincing. Note the connections and tangents. Listen to your story. What is it trying to tell you? Try to visualize your characters, and before you go on to the next draft, imagine what they're doing or what they think they're doing and how they feel about it.

As the creator of a piece of fiction, you see what no one else sees. That's your job. Just as you notice every significant detail about your character's appearance—the thin scar on his left index finger, say—so you notice the confusing shift in tense, the awkward transition, the intrusive or extraneous adverb. You see what you wrote, not what you thought you wrote.

You look at your current draft and you ask yourself the right questions: Have I shown and not told? Is every scene necessary? Have I chosen the point of view that is likely to add interest and afford the reader clear access to the central conflict? Is the plot a causal sequence of events or a simple chronology? Has my central character changed? If so, how? Is the purpose of the change clear? Does each character have a distinctive voice? Have I made it difficult enough for my central character to get what she wants? Is the setting evocative? the theme fresh? Are the details vivid, precise, and revealing?

Answer the questions honestly. Make all necessary changes, and see if they necessitate additional ones. The substitution of a single word may sharpen the vision of an entire story. A character's precisely described gesture may be as effective as a page of exposition. Ask yourself more questions: What is my story about? Was that my intention? What emotional experience do I want the reader to have? Have I made that happen? Is the story as clear as it can be? If a scene drags, cut it; if dialogue rambles, tighten it. Make every word count.

All these rewrites and changes can't be done at once. Some writers may revise as they go along. Each of us has a different approach and process and needs to learn what works best. But for every writer, the first draft is an act of discovery; then the real labor begins. Be ruthless. The story should improve with each revision. Make a list of your "obsessions." Challenge your characters to take responsibility for their actions. Read each draft closely, because you must find the solution to the problems in the story itself. You begin to write better than you thought you could. You fix the problem, a new one appears, you persevere, and write on. If you never revise, you never learn to write. You see that the made-up characters you have created have become vivid and intriguing people who live interesting, but often heartbreaking, lives. You begin to resent the time spent away from them.

I write many drafts longhand, because it slows me down, gives me time to think. I change sentences, words, phrases as I write, often recopying the entire annotated draft from the first line to the point at which the corrections get so messy and confusing that I have to stop and make a fresh copy. In this way, I get to feel the rhythm of the prose, hear the tone of the narrative voice.

When I'm finally satisfied that the elements of plot are in place and I think I know what my characters want, I type this draft into the computer. I print it out, then put the copy away for a few days. When I read it again, I immediately begin to tear it apart. What I couldn't see in the heat of writing usually becomes clear now. I see that a story that I thought was good can be made even stronger. I make the changes, wait, reread, and start over.

There are some common stylistic problems that you will want to address in each stage of revision or at some point before the manuscript is finished. The following checklist may help you do that. By "challenge," I mean take out the offending word or phrase, read the piece again and only if the word or words in question are essential should you put them back in.

1. *Challenge every adverb.* Mark Twain said, "The adverb is the enemy of the verb." Often, what we need are not two words, one qualifying, thus weakening, the other, but one stronger word. Not "He walked unsteadily" but "He staggered." Adverbs modifying verbs of attribution are particularly intrusive and offensive. "'I see the problem,' she said confidently." *Show* us her confidence; don't tell us.

2. *Challenge every adjective.* Like adverbs, most adjectives are unnecessary. Often the adjectival concept is in the noun. A night *is* dark, an ache painful, a needle sharp. Color is often redundant, as in *blue* sky, *green* grass, and so on. Other adjectives are too conventional to

be either vivid or significant, like a *tender* heart or a *sly* fox. An adjective should never be simply a decoration; it must always be essential.

3. *Challenge every verb with an auxiliary.* Replace passive voice verbs with active ones that are immediate, clear, and vigorous. "I kissed her" is better than "She was kissed by me"—and shorter. Also, replace progressive forms of verbs with the simple tenses: "I brewed coffee" indicates a more definite time than "I was brewing coffee." (On the other hand, be sure to use the past perfect tense if denoting an action completed before a time in the past: "My mother had already called the plumber by the time I arrived.")

4. *Challenge the first paragraph.* Sometimes the first paragraph helps get the story going, but often it merely introduces the reader to the story we are about to tell. Action may actually begin in the second paragraph.

5. *Challenge the last paragraph.* If the last paragraph unnecessarily summarizes or explains the meaning of the story, cut it out.

6. *Challenge every line that you love.* Delete every word that is there only for effect, every phrase you think is clever, every sentence for which there is no purpose or point. Your concern must be with the characters and not with your own wit or style. Check your list of "obsessions" and correct them. Watch for your "pet" words—"just," "very," and "that" are common offenders—and delete them if they're not essential. Or perhaps your first-person narrators do too much telling and not enough showing, or you tend to shift tenses needlessly.

7. *Challenge every exclamation point.* Like adverbs, they are intrusive.

8. *Be alert for every cliché* or hackneyed word or phrase, every overused or unnecessary modifier. If you've heard it often, don't use it.

9. *Cut every nonessential dialogue tag.* In a conversation between two people you may need only a single tag:

"Doris, I'm home," Lefty said.
"In the kitchen, dear. Did you remember the milk?"
"Got it right here."

The new paragraphs clearly indicate who is speaking. When you're attributing dialogue, use "said" or "asked." Anything else focuses attention away from the dialogue.

10. *Eliminate those colloquial introductory words* in dialogue, like "yes," "no," "well," "oh," etc. What follows usually tells enough.

11. *Eliminate everything you're not sure of.* If you doubt whether a sentence, word, or behavior belongs, it doesn't.

12. *Read the draft aloud and listen* for awkward and repetitious words, inadvertent rhyme, faulty rhythm.

13. *Proofread* for clarity, consistency, grammar, punctuation, economy. And then proofread again.

Revision is not just a time to edit. It's a time to invent and surprise, to add texture and nuance. In writing fiction, you must be honest and rigorous. You cannot judge your characters or want to say something so much that you manipulate them, twist the plot, or ignore what *their* reactions and responses would be. You owe it to your characters to do justice to *their* lives. Revision continues until you feel that you have done all you can to make the story as compelling and honest as possible. Ask yourself if you care enough about these characters to put in the time, energy, and thought it takes to work a story into its best possible shape. If you quit, if you don't revise, then you don't care enough.

➤➤33

MAKING SENSE OF "SHOW, DON'T TELL"

BY LUCY JANE BLEDSOE

A FEW YEARS AGO, WHEN I WAS TRYING TO BREAK INTO THE FICTION market, I thought I'd scream if I heard one more person say, "*Show, don't tell.*" These words were repeated over and over at all the writing classes and workshops I attended. Though I understand what this expression means, it has never helped me write better stories. Whenever I heard it, I wanted to ask, "*How* exactly do I 'show'?"

The truth is, "Show, don't tell" has become a catch phrase, a cliché, an easy criticism to make of any story that "doesn't work." The words offer nothing positive and are often misapplied.

Over the years, by asking critics and from my own experience, I've come up with five ways to "show."

Write in scenes

Think of your story in *scenes* rather than in terms of *what happens*. A scene takes place in time and space. A scene is about people in a specific setting, showing how they interact with each other and that setting. In other words, a scene is dynamic and multifaceted, while plot, or what happens, is static and linear. Your whole story should move from one scene to the next.

Consider these two examples:

Telling: Doris went to the party and met a man who attracted her enormously.

Showing: At the party, Doris tried to talk to lots of people, but found herself circling back, time and again, to the man with the beard.

In the example, the reader is told that Doris is attracted to the man she met at a party, which is the plot. In the second version, we *see*

Doris's attraction, because she can't keep away from the man, and the narrator doesn't ever mention it directly.

Appeal to the five senses

You've probably heard about the old ploy for selling a house. When prospective buyers come to look at it, have a freshly baked apple pie filling the house with its irresistible aroma; a red Jaguar parked in the driveway; and soothing music playing on the stereo. No matter that the buyers wanted something smaller with a fireplace and a big yard. They will be overcome by the sensual appeal, leave reason at the door, and buy your large house with no fireplace and no yard.

The same goes for a story. To sell readers on your story, appeal to their senses. Make them *see, hear, smell, taste,* and *feel* the textures in your story. Even better, make them crave or be repulsed by the sensory details. If you do, they will stay with you till *The End.*

Willa Cather said that each of the five senses should come into play on every page you write! This may be difficult to accomplish in most stories, but trying to do it is an instructive and amusing exercise.

Appealing to the five senses as a technique for developing your plot into connected scenes is the best way to place your characters in the story rather than simply pushing them through a plot.

Consider Doris at the party again:

Telling: The party is gross. People are drinking too much. The place smells of stale beer and is too hot.

Showing: Doris *smells* spilt beer; *sees* the men passed out on the couch; *tastes* soggy chips; *hears* a bass beat, but no melody from the amps; *feels* her own perspiration soak her shirt.

Use dialogue

A good way to show what a character is like is through dialogue. Remember that a scene is interaction in a setting. Dialogue is the main way people interact. A married woman who is having an affair might be evasive when her friend asks about her husband. A man who has a big self-esteem problem might use lofty words in conversation to puff up his ego.

However, be sure to know the difference between showing character through dialogue and simply having characters "tell." For example, the narrator in a story can say to a friend, "Mom and Dad were always fighting." It *is* dialogue, and it may work fine in a particular story. But if it's the writer's intention to make the reader really feel the pain of the parents' fighting, then the reader must *see* and *hear* Mom and Dad fighting as they speak to one another in loud, angry tones.

Try writing an entire story in dialogue—not a simple conversation, but a real story in which something happens in a setting. Make each of your characters distinct by choosing the kinds of words and phrases each of them would use. You'll discover that it's possible to make a character come alive just through his or her speech.

Use action rather than description

Emotion is essential to almost any story. Kinetic energy, or bodily energy, is also important in many stories. This does not mean a story needs shoot-outs and chase scenes, but should show your characters' physical actions; mannerisms, habits, and movements reveal a lot about the character. When a man learns of his mother's death, does he throw himself on the bed sobbing, immediately rush to the phone to make arrangements for the funeral, stand stiff and still, or go out and have sex? The way a character *acts* and *reacts* draws the reader into the kinetic energy of the story and demands a response.

Which of the following two examples is more convincing?

Telling: Bob was nosy.

Showing: Bob dashed through the house, room by room, inspecting photo albums and reading the notes on the refrigerator.

Hone your story's point of view

A story is told from a particular point of view. An omniscient point of view—writing the story as if you were God—is the most difficult to use if you are prone to telling rather than showing, because it tends to make you explain and describe.

To avoid this, try writing in the first-person point of view. This limits your story to one person's perceptions (your own) and helps you develop your writer's voice. A first-person point of view helps you avoid lengthy explanations of motives; instead, the character acts out the story. A close third-person viewpoint—writing as if you were perched on the character's shoulder—is another good way to avoid too much telling. Whatever point of view you use, the key is to know your narrator and not to stray from his or her way of looking at the story or the world.

Is "telling" always bad? When is it appropriate? Some writers believe that telling never has a place in a story, but reading great writers will probably tell you otherwise.

Sometimes background on a story is best given in a paragraph that simply gives—or tells—necessary information. An example of this might be describing a main character's family background, where his parents and grandparents are from, etc. Your story may not be about the great-grandparents coming over on the *Mayflower,* but that fact may be pertinent to your story. A paragraph here and there giving the background of the story and its characters is often appropriate.

A short section of telling in a story can help slow down the pace of a story or just shift gears a bit. The effect of a vivid and highly charged scene can be enhanced by a paragraph or two of information that allows readers to absorb the action scenes. Telling can also provide contrast in a story. Just as a good photograph has bright and dark parts, a good story needs contrast so that each part stands out clearly.

Finally, a paragraph or two of telling can serve as a transition between scenes. For example, moving from a scene in which a couple has taken a long romantic hike in the woods to a scene in which they are entering a house where a large party is underway may require a bit of exposition about who's at the party, why the couple must attend, or some other detail.

The point is to be aware of when you are telling and to use it sparsely and appropriately.

All five of these suggestions can be summarized in this way: Showing is illustrating and giving examples; it respects the reader's ability to draw conclusions about the story and characters from the information presented. Your goal in writing a story is to *evoke*—not *order*—a response from the reader.

Look again at the example about nosy Bob. If you write, "Bob is nosy," the best you can hope for from the passive reader is acceptance of your assertion. If you write, "Bob dashed through the house, room by room, inspecting photo albums and reading the notes on the refrigerator," readers on their own will think, "Bob sure is nosy!," and be convinced. You will have hooked your audience.

>> 34

WHAT YOU NEED TO KNOW ABOUT FICTION WRITING

BY SIDNEY SHELDON

Q. *How can writers learn to be their own critics?*

A. While writing the first draft of a novel, it's very important to let the creator take over and to keep the critic away. Once the first draft is finished, the critic should go to work. Being a critic of your work initially as you go along is much too inhibiting.

Q. *How do you invent characters for your novels?*

A. I think doing a profile for a character prior to starting a novel is a good idea. I work a little differently. My characters come to life on their own as I dictate the story.

Q. *How can you "write about what you know," which is common advice, and at the same time use what is considered the writer's most important tool: the imagination?*

A. I believe that a writer can get wonderful material by what he experiences or witnesses around him, but I don't think his imagination would destroy what he observes—only embellish it.

Q. *Does a character's name help to determine the way the reader feels about him or her? How do you come up with just the right name for a character?*

A. I try to choose names for my characters that fit the persona. For example, if I were writing about a homeless person, I wouldn't name him Trump.

Q. *During the writing process, some characters—important as they may be to the story—refuse to come alive on the page. Has this happened to you? What can writers do to overcome this common problem?*

A. Once you know your characters, the rest gets easier. They speak in an individual way, they get involved in appropriate situations. The characters really write the story.

Q. *Is there any point during the novel-writing process at which you often feel bogged down—beginnings? middles? endings? How can you work your way out of it?*

A. One way to prevent getting bogged down is to end each day's work with the beginning of the following day's scene, so that when you sit down to write the next morning, your scene has already been started.

Q. *Are there any writing experiments you've conducted lately (in characterization, transitions, viewpoints) that you could share? Whether successful or not, how did you learn from them?*

A. Writing *The Doomsday Conspiracy* was a departure for me in several ways. Aside from *The Naked Face,* I had never used a male protagonist in any of my novels, and I had never done anything approaching science fiction before. I talked to a dozen astronauts, among other experts, and was rather startled by the experiences they recounted to me. The question in my mind is: Is *The Doomsday Conspiracy* science fiction?

Q. *Writers have so many decisions to make in constructing a story (point of view, tone, background, locale). What approach do you advise storytellers to take in confronting these decisions?*

A. Before I begin writing a novel, I do extensive research. I won't write about a city that I haven't visited or about a meal that I haven't eaten—the more details that fill in the picture, the better. By doing this, I experience fewer problems and less interruption once I begin writing.

Q. *Do you think the dominance of movies and television in our cul-*

ture has had an impact on the types of novels written today? How has your own scriptwriting experience shaped you as a novelist?

A. I think the world has a shorter attention span, largely because of TV and "news bites." On the other hand, if another Thomas Wolfe comes along with his love of language, I think publishers would be very happy to publish such a book.

The motion pictures, TV shows, and Broadway plays I've written have made a great difference in my life as a novelist. They have taught me to keep the action moving and to write dialogue that's realistic.

Q. *Self-discipline is a problem for writers in all genres, but especially for novelists, who must spend months and even years on one project. How does a writer stay focused on a project over a long period of time?*

A. I work from 9:30 in the morning until 6:00 in the afternoon every day during the week. Sometimes I'll continue the same schedule over the weekend, or use that time to edit and make additional notes for future chapters. It's really not a matter of discipline for me; I write every day because I enjoy it.

Q. *Some books get off to a great start and then lag in the middle. How can writers deal with problems in pacing their stories?*

A. I think it's very important for new writers to work with a complete outline before they start a book, so they can plan the degree of action or emotion they wish to achieve.

Q. *Discuss the importance of setting in fiction, and its influence on plot and character. How do you settle on the right setting for the story you want to tell?*

A. For me, a character or characters come to mind first, then the setting. In order for the story to be intriguing, the characters must be interesting. I let the characters dictate the plot through their personality and interaction with others. When I wrote *Nothing Lasts Forever*, I was inspired by the arena of a hospital because it is packed with drama—it deals with life and death. I thought it would be interesting

155

to write about three women doctors, their adventures and the problems they face in that setting.

Q. *Do you think it's true that some writers have only one novel in them?*

A. Some writers seem to have only one novel in them, especially if that novel is autobiographical. Carl Reiner wrote a wonderful play called *Exit Laughing*, about a playwright who wrote a smash hit and had trouble writing a second play until he moved back into the poverty-stricken life he was living when he wrote his hit play!

Q. *Could you talk about the effects of overt censorship (book banning in schools and libraries, for instance) on the average writer as he sits at his desk, day to day, trying to create a publishable manuscript?*

A. I am against censorship in any form. The reader should decide what he wants to read.

Q. *Can a writer get so close to his novel-in-progress that he can't see the big picture? What are some signs that a major overhaul is necessary?*

A. A major overhaul is necessary when you no longer believe in your book. John D. MacDonald told me that he worked without an outline, and when he came to a place where he found the novel was no longer working, he backed up to the point where it did work, then took the character on a different tangent.

Q. *Have you ever had to scrap a book manuscript after writing a substantial portion of it?*

A. No. It takes me several months to finish the first draft of a manuscript. My secretary types it, and I go back to page one and start rewriting. This version can number anywhere from 1,000 to 2,000 pages, and I'll throw away 100 to 200 pages at a time, ripping all the scenes apart, getting rid of and creating new characters. Two months later that draft will be finished and I'll start all over again. I do that for 12 to 18 months, doing up to a dozen different rewrites.

Q. *What techniques or devices can be used in dialogue to distinguish one character from another? For instance, how do you handle a long exchange between two characters so the reader won't become confused about who is speaking?*

A. Each character has his own personality. If the characters are clear in your mind, no two of them will speak alike. A mobster uses one language, a socialite another. It should be possible to write a book with no description at all, only dialogue, and the reader should be able to tell by the dialogue who is speaking.

>> 35

CIRCUMSTANTIAL EVIDENCE: SOURCE OF FICTION PLOTS

BY LEILA DAVIS

CREATING A CHARACTER BASED ON CIRCUMSTANTIAL EVIDENCE PRESents a writer with a different approach—and challenge. Law enforcement officers are often faced with that situation, a classic example being the "contents of a dead man's pockets." Identification may be missing, leaving as clues only what "John Doe" carried and wore. For example:

1) In John Doe's pockets they may find: a key chain with gold-tone golf cart medallion and seven assorted keys, nail clippers, black comb, two large rubber bands, partial book of matches from Tony's, one white shirt button, golf tee, receipt for three rolls of film, partial pack of mint Tic Tacs, two ticket stubs from a hockey game, a ⅜-inch brass nut, three nickels, six pennies, one quarter. A crumpled grocery list with these items: grapefruit, bread, coffee, chicken, light bulbs, Coors, cheese, carrots, tuna, hamburger, meat sauce, VCR tapes. No wallet was found.

The police have already taken the body to forensics; fingerprints and dental charts may eventually identify the man. Let's assume his body was found on the shores of Lake Michigan. Given the size of the Great Lakes, a boat could capsize and/or sink without ever being noticed or reported.

One writer might invent the following story: The victim, Mark, a cautious man, always stashed his wallet in the cabin so he wouldn't lose it if he fell overboard. He needed the ⅜-inch brass nut to repair the boat railing. Brass fittings are expensive, used mainly where equipment is subjected to a high degree of corrosion, such as a cabin cruiser. Mark also enjoys golf, but neither golf nor his boat gives him enough exercise to control the weight he's gained from frequent meals at

Tony's Ristorante. The shirt button, strained to the limit, popped into his lasagna, and ended up in his pocket.

He'd left the three rolls of film on July 7 to be developed, pictures taken during a holiday get-together with other boating/golfing enthusiasts. Mark bought the groceries for the weekend he had custody of his son, who tapes movies off Dad's cable TV. The pair spent one evening at an exhibition hockey game.

Quite another story could be developed by a novelist: Randy, with the same items in his pocket, is found in an alley, victim of a mugger. Randy plays golf with the same foursome every week during the golfing season. The author imagines the button came off when Randy forgot to undo the left sleeve before pulling off his shirt in his rush to make starting time. He and one of his golf buddies are also rabid hockey fans, vocal in expressing their opinions. After a game, they often stop at Tony's to hash over the highlights of the day's game.

Smoking is not allowed in Randy's office, so he sucks a Tic Tac when he can't have a cigarette. The brass nut is to repair his leaking kitchen sink, too long neglected by the apartment manager. Randy pulled the large rubber bands off the bundle of magazines and letters delivered that day.

In addition to the key to his apartment and two car keys, he has a key to his basement storage locker, another to the apartment of one of his golf partners, as well as one to his parents' home, and one to his office. But, inexplicably, his key to the executive washroom is missing. Against company policy, Randy was having duplicates made. When his boss hears that Randy was killed, he's more upset about the missing executive washroom key than about Randy's death.

And here's a third possibility for developing a story from the same "evidence": Joe has never really liked golf, but his wife, Vanessa, loves it; he's more her caddy than her partner. The key chain was a stocking stuffer at Christmas, and now he carries on it a key to the apartment of his mistress, Melanie, who shares his love of hockey, a game Vanessa considers "common" and "vulgar." Melanie also shares Joe's interest in restoring antique cars. She picked up the brass nut for him at the hardware store where she works, and where they met. She and Joe occasionally meet at Tony's Lounge, a bar with a dim interior and high-backed booths.

The film is still at the drugstore where he'd left it because Joe's handwriting is so illegible that the envelope with the developed pictures is filed under Joshua, not J. Fisher. Vanessa has been nagging him for losing the pictures of their Miami vacation, but it was the crumpled grocery list she found in Joe's pocket that signed his death warrant. On it are chicken, hamburger, meat sauce. An ardent animal rights' activist and a vegetarian, Vanessa would never have asked Joe to buy these items. Enraged by his infidelity, she hired a hit-man to shoot Joe and make it look like a robbery.

2) Women usually carry handbags, and a woman carrying a Gucci handbag with gold-plated fittings is very different from one who carries a denim patchwork bag. Alison carried a red leather shoulder bag, gold-tone trim, one outside pocket, with one inside zipper pocket. Suppose a purse-snatcher removes Alison's wallet before disposing of the handbag in a trash can?

The person who discovers it opens the purse and finds these items in the zipper pocket: a twice-folded $20 dollar bill inside an address book, two community theater season tickets, a Hilton sewing kit, three Band-Aids, four safety pins, a pair of silver hoop pierced earrings. Loose in the purse are a black ball-point pen, a short Garfield pencil with worn-down eraser, three keys on a key ring, a small memo pad, a checkbook with scenic mountain "designer" checks, a receipt for dry cleaning—one suit, two sweaters—a packet of Kleenex tissues. Also in the purse is a floral cosmetic kit containing Clinique cosmetics—pink lipstick, mauve eyeshadow, brown/black mascara—a medium beige compact, comb, mirror, emery board, and an open pack of Tums. In the outside pocket are sunglasses and a Hallmark pocket calendar noting birthdays, anniversaries, teacher conference dates and orthodontist appointments for her daughter.

A writer may conclude that Alison is an upper-middle income mother. Her cosmetics are in a separate bag, not rattling around the bottom of her purse, demonstrating organization and the importance she places on her makeup. She can afford to keep $20 stashed away for emergencies, and supports the local theater. She has her sweaters dry cleaned, not hand-washed at home. At least one child has braces, seldom covered in full by dental insurance. The fact that she's willing to pay for her daughter's orthodontia and to arrange conferences with her teacher indicates a caring mother, but the Tums show she sometimes suffers from indigestion. Her scenic checks are another little luxury. Imprinted with her name and address, they may get her handbag back.

The Band-Aids, safety pins, sewing kit, tissues, and extra earrings indicate she's prepared for emergencies. With an address book in her purse, she has instant access to necessary information when she's away from home.

An alternative view casts Alison as a second-grade teacher keeping track of parent conferences and *her* orthodontist appointments. As an adult, she's opted to have the dental work her parents couldn't afford when she was a child. Her allergies led her to choose Clinique cosmetics, and the earrings were left at her home by an absent-minded guest. Alison plans to return them when she sees the woman at the next meeting of the community theater play selection committee. On the way to school, she dropped her husband's clothes at the cleaners; Alison is allergic to wool.

The red leather handbag was a birthday present from her mother, who lectures Alison about becoming dowdy. Mom also ordered the checks, a reminder of the annual family ski vacations in Vermont. Her mother's final gift was the address book listing all their relatives, including some Alison would like to forget.

A pupil gave Alison his Garfield pencil for her birthday. The memo pad is a necessity for a woman who writes notes to herself about everything. With her sensitive eyes, Alison wears sunglasses outdoors year-round.

3) Lacking a John Doe with pockets for you to explore, or a lost handbag, try to analyze character traits of fellow diners. Imagine a thirty-something couple seated across from you at a moderately priced restaurant at six on a weekday evening. The man is wearing a conservative suit but a flashy tie. His companion's raspberry suit is accented with a large pearl and rhinestone brooch. Both wear wedding rings.

He starts with a cocktail, but she shakes her head and drinks ice water. They share an appetizer of crab-stuffed mushrooms, then go on to soup, caesar salad, hers with peppercorn dressing, his with Roquefort. When the entrees arrive, he has a thick filet mignon that covers a platter, with large baked potato and sour cream on the side. She ordered chicken Kiev on a bed of rice. Later, the waitress brings two glasses of champagne, and offers congratulations. After clinking their glasses in a toast, the woman takes a few sips, then sets it aside. His dessert is "Chocolate Sin Pie," hers fresh strawberries and yogurt. Before leaving, she places three $20 bills on the table, under the check. What could the occasion be?

They could be celebrating an anniversary, or the birth of their first child. The early hour suggests they plan to go elsewhere after dinner, or perhaps their babysitter has an early curfew on a school night. The woman may have chosen not to drink much because she's on a medication that precludes alcohol, or she's more conscious of her health. In their haste to leave home, she forgot to give her husband the cash she'd picked up at the bank that day. Budget-conscious, they keep their credit cards locked in a desk at home unless they're traveling, also forgotten on this occasion.

But the writer reveals this couple is not married to each other. They're business rivals in the firm both work for. She lost her bet that she could outdo his sales figures for the month. Fearful that her husband—a tight man with a dollar—may find out how much the dinner cost, she paid cash, inwardly seething because her co-worker chose the most expensive items on the menu. The waitress offered congratulations after the man boasted they were celebrating a major triumph at work.

Whatever your basic information, try viewing it from at least three angles. "Circumstantial evidence" too often depends on personal interpretation. That's why it's seldom accepted in a courtroom. You see the teenager next door, with his deafening boombox and reckless driving, as a menace to society. To his girlfriend, he's a second Tom Cruise. His father glows with pride when he thinks of his son as a future partner in the family tire dealership. And you're *all* right.

>> 36

DIALOGUE: THE MEANING BEYOND THE WORDS

BY TIM SANDLIN

THE FIRST NIGHT OF MY FICTIONAL FICTION CLASS, I WALK TO THE front of the room, open the roll form conveniently provided by Central Wyoming College, and begin.

"George Singleton."

"Yo."

"Irene Bukowski."

"Present."

One by one, I call their names and they respond.

"Here."

"You got me."

"Yes."

"It is I."

One girl doesn't say anything, just raises her hand a half-inch off the desk.

"Accounted for."

"Sorry, I'm late."

And with each response, I learn something about the characters. The "Yo" guy will write comic pieces that start with the hero waking up hung over. The girl who won't speak will write a poem featuring death. The "It is I" girl won't take criticism, "You got me" is sneaky, and "Sorry, I'm late" will drop out after we read his first story.

Your snap judgments based on one or two words of dialogue may not match mine, but the point is that each member of the class gave a different response. And they stayed in character.

In real life, half the class would say "Here" and the other half raise their right hand about chin high, but this is fiction, and fiction is not real life. Don't forget that. If you write so realistically you can't stand

163

the thought of that much diversification in a group, skip calling the roll and go right to the scene where each student says a few words on "Why I'm taking this creative writing class."

Won't be any repeat answers there.

In fiction with energy, no two characters put any one thought the same. There are four primary ways to build a character—description, dialogue, and action, plus thought in your viewpoint people. To pass up the smallest opportunity to differentiate and build on your fictional people is a waste. Worse, it's stagnant. Even a story about stagnation can't be stagnant.

Several years ago in a show called "Charlie's Angels," three women with teeth and hair brought bad guys to bay with perkiness and spunk. But without dialogue. As far as the lines went, the women were interchangeable. Mostly, they took turns saying, "Come on, Charlie."

In putting words on paper, no one has enough teeth or hair to get away with this sloppiness. P. G. Wodehouse believed every sentence in a book must have entertainment value. That may or may not be true with every style of book, but it sure is true of dialogue. If the reader doesn't learn something new every time he ventures between the quotation marks, the writer has botched his or her job.

So what are these gems the reader is supposed to learn between the squiggly floating marks? Oversimplified, dialogue must do four things—show character, advance plot, give information, and set the voice, tone, and scene.

Show character. There are people in the English-speaking world of a certain cultural and educational background who actually say, "It is I." Imagine that. The secret is to nail down a character as quickly as possible. If you have her say "It is I," then follow up with a tight bun on her head and dark purple nail polish, you've pretty much done the job. Give her some matching action and send her down the road.

The idea is to supply one or two details that are so distinct, the reader can fill in all the others. A character who says, "I'm going to snatch you kids baldheaded," won't wear the same clothes or drive the same car as a character who says, "I have difficulty interfacing with children."

Even non-dialogue is dialogue. The girl who wouldn't answer but held up her hand a half-inch revealed character by not speaking. From there, you can have her go with the grain by keeping her in sweaters four sizes too large and afraid to ride on an elevator unless it's empty, or you can blast against the grain—and be almost as trite—by turning her into a sex-crazed tigress when she lets down her hair.

Not speaking often says more than speaking, especially in tense climactic showdowns. It's a lot easier to write a scene where a man punches out his boss than a scene in which his anger is beyond words, and he walks away. That makes sense. By definition, "beyond words" is harder to put into words than a punch in the nose.

Here's a trick for keeping your characters in character. When I wrote a book about two 13-year-olds and their awkward struggles to overcome strange upbringings, I found my old junior high yearbook from 1963. Whenever one of my kids said something precocious, wise, or cornball, I looked at a photo of my 13-year-old classmates, and said, "Could this have come from Ronnie Craig's mouth, or Ann Humphrey's, or Annette Gilliam's?" The answer was usually "No," and the line got thrown out.

Advance action. This one should be self-explanatory. Story is how characters react to conflict, and much of the conflict between people in our modern world is caused by words. Communication—the thing that is supposed to resolve problems—actually causes more than it resolves.

We advance action by arguing, seducing, planning, slighting, gossiping, giving ultimatums—I could go find a thesaurus and stretch this into twelve column inches, but you get the idea.

Here's another place where fiction differs from real life. Most of those heart-to-hearts you have with your mother/husband/wife go in circles and dead-end. The same thoughts are constantly reported in slightly different ways, and when all this communicating is done, nothing has changed.

You don't have time for this jive in fiction. Each conversation must end with some condition different from what it was at the beginning. The relationship between the speakers has been slightly altered, or someone has grown wiser, or the speakers—at the very least, the readers—have information they didn't know before. Your viewpoint character is in more trouble or thinks he is moving closer to the solution to

165

the conflict. Or maybe all she's done is order lunch. Ordering lunch reveals more about a character than his or her resumé.

A sidetrack on dialect. Anyone who tries it is braver than I am. Mark Twain pulled it off. John Kennedy Toole pulled it off. People think Eudora Welty pulls it off, but if you read her work carefully, you'll see she does it more with sentence rhythm and word choice than by dropping g's off walkin' and talkin'.

Check this out from her "My Life at the P.O.":

I says, "Papa-Daddy, you know I wouldn't any more want you to cut off your beard than the man in the moon. It was the farthest thing from my mind. Stella-Rondo sat there and made that up while she was eating breast of chicken."

Not a misspelled word in the quote, yet after I read this story to my class, they all swore it was written in Deep Mississippi dialect.

Give information. This is the easiest one to mess up. The worst example I can think of in conveying information through dialogue happens on the soap operas.

MAMA: "I saw Mildred Kinnicknick at the grocery store yesterday."
DAUGHTER: "Is that the same Mildred Kinnicknick whose father was tried for murder, then he got off by claiming insanity because he'd eaten too many Twinkies and whose mother used to be married to Doc Watson, then she divorced him and married his brother Spud, only now she's back with Doc but carrying the baby of his older brother Bubba?"
MAMA: "Yes."

Uh-uh. Dialogue doesn't work that way. To get information across, you have to be sneaky. This is part of the Show-Don't-Tell lesson you've heard 200 times. Don't say, "I see you wear glasses." Do say, "Your glasses are always dirty." This gets across that the character does wear glasses, and it also says something about his personality that they're always dirty and it says something about the speaker's personality that she notices the dirt and is brazen enough to comment on it.

This is especially true when you use dialogue to foreshadow. In mysteries by unskilled writers, there's always a line where someone says, "I notice you have a gun in your closet," or "We're spraying the rose bushes with Fetadetamiacin today, so don't stick any petals in your mouth or you'll die." Right then, I know that 200 pages from now, the gun or the Fetadetamiacin will pop up and kill somebody.

Foreshadowing, especially in mysteries, has to be done so when readers come to the place where the gun is used, they're totally surprised, but then they think about it and say, "Gee, that makes sense."

Anticipated surprises—they're what make endings fun. And the sneakiest way to foreshadow without getting caught is in dialogue.

Set the voice, tone and scene. Choosing the tone may be the most important decision you make when starting a story. I was once assistant editor at a literary magazine, and I read something like 200 stories in a weekend. Every one of those stories was competent—not a total loser in the batch—but what made an exceptional story rise above the others were the voice and tone.

The Holy Trinity of fiction is plot, character, and voice—Father, Son, and Holy Ghost. And, like the Holy Ghost, voice is the hardest to understand. Voice is that attitude of the writer to the story. It's the attitude of the writer toward his or her readers.

Sometimes I have my students write a two-page story, then rewrite it Erma Bombeck-style, then Edgar Allan Poe-style, then Louis L'Amour. The growth of these stories is amazing. And the easiest place to establish these styles is in the dialogue. People in Valley Girl High School speak differently from people in 1880s Bitter Creek or Transylvania. People about to be murdered on the moors speak differently from people chasing down the blue light special at K Mart. Doesn't take a Guggenheim grant to figure out that one.

Not everything to do with dialogue happens between the quote marks. The reader has to know who is talking and in what tone of voice. For this we use dialogue tags.

Dialogue tags seem to come in styles, like hats. What worked in 1932 looks slightly ridiculous now. There are no absolute rules in writing dialogue tags or anything else. If it works, you got away with it. But there are certain ways to playing it that work more often than not.

The easiest tag is none. Compare—Laurie crossed her arms on her chest. "Why do you say that?" to— "Why do you say that?" Laurie asked defensively.

If you can set the tone of the speech with a bit of action, you're better off than "Blah-blah," he said, adverb. If it isn't crystal clear who is speaking, use *he said* or *she said*. Once every couple of pages, sneak in a *he asked*. Don't, under penalty of personal castigation, use *he stated, she observed, the boy piped, George groaned,* or any other word for *said*. If you want George to groan, have him do it first.

George groaned. "I can't get up this morning."
Not—"I can't get up this morning," George groaned.

Trust me on this. You can't groan and talk at the same time.

And, if at all possible, avoid adverbs in dialogue tags. In the 1950s, riding the wave of the Hemingway revolution, adverbs were words to be avoided like the plague. I look at them as tools, and no tool should be banned forever.

However, use them with care. Hand grenades don't kill—people who throw hand grenades do kill. Pretend the adverb, when used in a dialogue tag, is a hand grenade. Don't play with it.

A word about typographical tricks. Say your character is really hacked off.

"GET OUT OF MY HOUSE." "Get out of my house!"
"Get out of my house."

Every editor in America is going to hate two of those three sentences, but I can't tell you which two, because it depends on the editor. Personally, I'd rather snort barbwire than use an exclamation point, and I can't even think of a metaphor disgusting enough to compare to dialogue in ALL CAPS, so I'm stuck with italics. Some editors can't stand italics. It's a pet peeve deal. If possible, work it into the action.

George smashed a glass on the linoleum floor.
"Get out of my house."

If that isn't strong enough for you, try one of the other three. I highly recommend against any combinations. *"GET OUT OF MY HOUSE!"*

And the worst, absolutely bottom-of-the-barrel method of expressing quoted frenzy is multiple punctuation.

"Get out of my house!!?!"

This was once Batman-style, but no more. I just looked in one of my son's *Ghost Rider* comic books, and do you think Mephisto himself screams questions!? Heck, no @#%&!

Of course, as soon as I say that, someone will mail in an example of James Joyce and the double exclamation point. Which brings us back to rule number one: There are no rules.

$\leftleftarrows$ 37

A Story's Five Senses

By Thomas E. Kennedy

EACH STORY HAS ITS OWN LOGIC OR STYLE. SOME ARE AS REALISTIC as a cheap diner or a smack in the mouth, others magical as a circus. But one thing all stories have in common is that they are founded on illusion, and all illusions are based on the five senses.

As the great story writer Flannery O'Connor said, "Fiction begins where human knowledge begins—with the senses." We have only five ways of perceiving reality: We can *see* it, *hear* it, *taste* it, *smell* it, *touch* it. Or, in the case of fiction, writers can *seem* to do these things.

The novels and the eighty or so stories I've published vary considerably in approach. Some are straight realism, like "Landing Zone X-Ray," which is apparently so believable that *The New Yorker* rejected it as being more of a memoir than a story. Yet it is pure fiction. Others are surreal or magical realism, like "Murphy's Angel." That story was initially rejected by one editor as being too unreal; a year later, as he had continued to think about it, he wrote to ask if it was still available. But it had already been sold to *New Delta Review* and included in *The Pushcart Prize 1990*.

In addition to stories that aim to mirror everyday life and in which no laws of nature are transcended, I have published short fiction from the point of view of a snail ("Escargots," *The North American Review*), and of a fly ("The Ant, the Wasp, the Fly," *Asylum*), as well as stories in which God or the devil appears as a character.

Yet every one of those stories builds upon the same basic trick: to convince the reader to believe that the story is "real," that it might have happened—in the real world of the imagination. The trick is to get the reader to *smell* the story's reality, to *taste* it, to *feel* it.

For example, in "Landing Zone X-Ray," the narrator, a twenty-year-old college man harboring a military deserter, smells coffee and bacon on the breath of the FBI agent who comes to arrest the deserter at six in the morning. When the deserter resists and is hit in the face, the narrator sees lines of blood between his teeth. When he stands by as his father is shaving, he hears the scrape of the razor as the older man pulls it across his jowl. An important part of the trick, of course, is not to use just *any* sensory detail, but to let your imagination present the *right* detail for that moment of the story's reality—and remember, sometimes the imagination needs a couple of tries. The smell of bacon and coffee on the breath of the FBI man was just the detail I needed to provide the contrast from which the story evolved: A man who enforces the law wakes in the morning and is fed breakfast by his wife before he goes out to arrest two hungry young men living on their own outside the law.

At first, I had the narrator smell chewing gum (spearmint) on the policeman's breath, but that didn't quite do it. So I closed my eyes, and my imagination offered bacon and coffee. Thus, in the story of establishment and rebellion, the representatives of the law were well fed; the rebels were not, and what food scent is as sharp and memorable as that of bacon? Similarly, the scrape of the razor as the father shaves sets up a father-son/civilized adult vs. wild youth contrast. All the way back to the Bible, the cutting of hair is a symbol of emasculation or taming.

I did not, however, "invent" the detail; it came from my imagination. After examining it, I felt it was right. When, in writing a story, an author enters the world of imagination, his or her senses must be alert to the details that exemplify the story thematically as well as "physically." We need to be open to the sounds and the aromas that lure us around the corner.

Another story of mine, "Color of Darkness, Color of Night" (*Four Quarters*), begins with a successful, affluent man walking home from his commuter bus and noticing the Big Dipper sparkling in the windy night sky above his house. His wife is visiting her mother that night, and he is alone with his three-year-old daughter, who is coming down with something. She has a nosebleed, and he changes her T-shirt, goes to the bathroom for a towel and sees a spider on the T-shirt that he had dropped on the floor; the spider is on the blood spot. Then, as I was writing, I realized that these details were accumulating to infuse a very ordinary, realistic story with a sense of doom, suggesting astrol-

171

ogy and evil in everyday events, and the primitive fears that assail us when a child is ill.

During the course of the night, the child grows sicker, begins to throw up; outside the wind becomes violent and the windows rattle as they are slashed with rain. Lightning flashes and the electricity and phone go out. He worries also now about his wife and mother-in-law who have gone to the theater in Manhattan. These details are used to strip away the character's defenses, to reveal and dramatize his helplessness, the impotence we all have experienced standing over the bed of a sick child.

But these effects all come through the senses or sensory memories of the reader as well as of the writer—the flash of lightning, the rattle of window glass, the girl's eyes bright with fever in the shadows of the room, the father's anxiety in keeping her from strangling on her vomit—all ordinary details which I attempted to imbue with a kind of magic to heighten their realism. In creating surreal images, you must bring your story from the realm of abstraction into the physical world.

Sometimes a story develops directly from the sensory details that suggested it. The creative starting point often is simply some detail of the senses, and recording that detail starts an imaginative process from which a story evolves.

When I was in high school, I worked afternoons assisting a shoemaker. I liked the job, the sensual smells of the shop—the aroma of raw leather straps, smell of glue, dye, tins of polish—the grumbling stitch of the heavy sewing machine, the whack of the nailer, the scrape of the sander, and the moan of the waxing wheels. Those sensory memories were embodied in my unconscious.

I knew that one day I would write a story set in a shoemaker's shop, inspired by those particulars, although I did not then know why or how they would fit a still unknown story. Nearly thirty years passed before I got around to writing it. One day I began to sketch a scene of a high school boy working an afternoon job in a shoemaker's shop, surrounded by the smells and sounds I so clearly recalled. From those details, the scene took on a life of its own. The boy and shoemaker looked out the narrow shop window as they worked, watching people walk by. The shoemaker is on the lookout for passing females; he likes to tell the boy, who is a virgin, about his experiences with women, experiences as narrow as the view outside the shop and as crude as the

172

smells of his shop. The boy, innocent of the world, is at first attracted to the shoemaker's spicy, knowledgeable comments, and tries to apply them to his own life, but finally he comes to see how narrow his boss's view really is—how he dehumanizes in words every woman he has come in contact with.

The idea behind the title—"A View of the World" (*The Chariton Review*)—is also captured in a sensory detail: the narrow glass window that faces the street. I didn't know I wanted to write that story until I had established the sensory details that brought me—and my main character—into the cobbler's shop, a shop similar to the one I had known as a boy, though reshaped by my imagination into a stage and a scene that could tell more of life than my raw, literal memories could.

Sometimes a single detail in a story is enough to bring it to life for the reader, and keep it alive in memory. As a college student, I was once mugged. The mugger had a switchblade, and I will never forget the silken sound of the knife blade springing from its shaft, the pink scar on the mugger's lip, or the sound of his voice, ordering me in broken grammar, "Open you wallet can I see you got." I recall vividly the sight of his long fingers snaking in to pluck out the two dollar bills I had there. Later, I wrote these details down, realizing they all suggested violation, and they were perfect for the story I ultimately wrote and sold to *Four Quarters* for two *hundred* dollars. The story does not recount what happened to me, but the details that evoked the "life" of that central incident came from my own sensory experience, which I transformed into words.

So whether your main character is a human being or an angel, a snail or a fly, a god or a devil, a mugger or a shoemaker, he, she or it lives in the world of your imagination through the basic channels of human communication—the five senses. Without the appropriate use of sensory detail, your story is not likely to come to life for your readers, because it will never become "real" for them. By using such details, however, you will find that the story will come to life on the page and be a better story than you ever dreamed possible!

$\mathbf{\succ\succ 38}$

BACK IN A FLASH

BY GAIL RADLEY

FLASHBACKS OCCUR SO NATURALLY IN EVERYDAY LIFE THAT YOU MAY scarcely notice them. In fiction a flashback is a valuable device for conveying information and revealing character and motivation. Whether you are writing juvenile or adult works, short stories or novels, a few simple techniques will enable you to ease in and out of the past gracefully.

There are times when the current events of a story just don't carry the full impact without background information. These are good times to consider flashbacks. In my juvenile novel, *The Golden Days,* it is important that the reader know eleven-year-old Cory's background of disappointment and abandonment to appreciate why he is having trouble trusting his new foster parents. I conveyed this information in a quick montage of memories:

. . . he could remember [his mother] much better than he could remember his father. She had been with him longer—until he was nine. He remembered her staring out the window for what seemed like hours, while he tugged at her hand and begged her to play. He remembered burying his face in her long blond hair while she rocked him, and how her face twisted up when she screamed at him. He remembered chasing her down the stairs and running after that beat-up old Volkswagen van until he could run no more. He remembered the hollow feeling when he realized she wasn't going to stop and he couldn't catch up to her—and how he wished for tears that did not come until nightfall. She had put a loaf of bread, a jar of peanut butter, and a jar of Marshmallow Fluff on the kitchen table and walked out of his life.

Without this passage, and the passages that describe Cory's previous foster fathers, it would be difficult to sympathize with Cory when he rebuffs his foster parents' overtures.

When the information is dramatic and central to the story, you may want to expand the flashback into a scene that allows the reader to experience its impact fully. In *Cracker Jackson,* by Betsy Byars, a boy learns that his former baby sitter is being abused by her husband. Two things are critical to Jackson's response—his fear and his love for the sitter. Byars established both with a flashback:

> Jackson's earliest memory was of fear.
> Alma, his new baby sitter, had taken him down to the creek behind the apartment house to wade. He was five years old, but he had never been allowed to wade before, and stomping around in the muddy water made him happier than he had known it was possible to be.
> When he and Alma got out of the creek, they noticed there were some brown things on their ankles. Jackson was pleased, and Alma was, too.
> "What are they, Cracker? Mine don't want to come off, do yours?"

In the next two pages we learn that the "brown things" were leeches. We see Mrs. Hunter's horror when she discovers them and hear her restrained anger toward Alma. We experience Mrs. Hunter's caution and fear as contributing to Jackson's fears. But his fear does not surpass his devotion to Alma:

> "Is Alma coming back?" Jackson asked as he and his mother went up the stairs.
> The leech danger had passed. He now had on his hightop, orthopedic, Stride-Rite shoes, laced tight. He was safe.
> "Is she?" Alma was his newest, youngest, and already his favorite baby sitter.
> The only answer his mother would give was the one he hated most: "We'll see."
> His mother did let Alma come back, but Alma was never at ease with his mother after that.

Flashing in

Notice that Byars introduced the flashback by having Jackson evoke a memory, which is a commonly used and effective technique for signaling a shift into the past. Sometimes the character is actually reliving the memory at the point in the story where it occurs. But too much stopping to remember makes the reader uneasy. Byars has avoided this problem by making the transition into flashback through narration, rather than by having Jackson lapse into reminiscence.

There are many ways of introducing a flashback other than evoking memory. Katherine Paterson moves into a flashback boldly in *Jacob Have I Loved* with the phrase "This is the story that the old people told." The story concerns the past of a former resident of a tiny island

175

community who has recently returned. Since his identity and purpose in returning are mysterious to Louise, the main character, and since he figures importantly in the story, the episode deserved to be set off in such a prominent way. A shift to the past perfect tense—which you may have noticed in the preceding examples—eases the transition. Note that the past perfect need only be used for a sentence or two. Simple past tense can be used for the main part of the flashback:

> This is the story that the old people told: Captain Wallace and his son, Hiram, had let down their sails and were waiting out the storm. The lightning was so bright and near that it seemed to flash through the heavy canvas of the sail. . . . [Hiram] had rushed out from under his sail cover, taken an ax, and chopped the mast to the level of the deck. After the storm passed, they were sighted drifting mastless on the Bay and were towed home by an obliging neighbor. . . . Not long after, he left the island for good. . . .
>
> Unless, of course, the strong old man rebuilding the Wallace house was the handsome young coward who had left nearly fifty years before.

Usually, you will want to slide into a flashback less conspicuously. There is a whole range of subtle transitional words and phrases that can announce your flashing into a different time zone, such as "once," "yesterday," and "when she was in fifth grade." Watch for such phrases in your reading.

Flashing out

When returning to the time of the story, continue in the past tense for a sentence or two. Use of a common link makes transitions smoother—and flashbacks are no exception. In the preceding Paterson example, Hiram Wallace, past and present, provides the necessary link. An object, an idea, or a feeling are other possible links you can use. Put in another transitional word or phrase, such as "now" or "today," to further clarify the return to the present.

Of course, any time you ask readers to step out of the chronological time flow, you run the risk of losing or confusing them. This is especially true for young readers who live in the here and now, and for whom it is easy to become confused by a disjointed chronology. So use flashbacks judiciously. Allow your reader the opportunity to care about what is happening in the story's present. Don't break into a tense or emotional scene with a flashback: You have worked too hard to build that emotion to step away before it is completed.

The alternatives

You don't need to rely on flashbacks whenever you want to say something about the past. Consider alternatives. If the scene is important enough to dramatize, you might begin your story at that point in time. Jerry Spinelli summarizes the first ten years in the life of *Maniac Magee* in under three pages. *Jacob Have I Loved* actually begins at the end of the story, with the main character returning to the island where she grew up. The remainder of the book recalls her growing-up experiences there, and her early history is briefly summarized.

Another alternative is to work the information in through dialogue or narration. If your story is told from the main character's viewpoint, you will *have* to present background information about other characters through dialogue and narration. *The Golden Days* is told through Cory's viewpoint. But background information about his elderly friend Carlotta is important. Cory learns her story along with the reader—through dialogue:

"Tell me about when you were with the circus, Carlotta."
A little puff of sound escaped her, and Cory waited. "When I was sixteen, I saw Philo's circus. It was the first circus I had ever seen." There was a silence in which Cory settled himself cross-legged on the rollaway bed. . . . Then Carlotta spoke again, her voice low and soothing. "I thought this was the most beautiful thing in the world. The costumes flashing like colored stars, the animals so strong and wild. Only later did I understand how trapped they were, and how faded the stars. . . ."

Realism is the watchword for presenting the past through dialogue and narration. Your characters must not sound as if they have stepped out of the story to give the reader a necessary bit of information. Listen to the words. Does the dialogue sound natural? Does the narration seem too weighed down with information? Does the story seem to stop when the information begins?

Information can also be conveyed through official reports. My novel-in-progress, *Dear Gabby,* uses a newspaper article to tell some of the story. Since reading the newspaper figures naturally into the story, it does not seem contrived. A detective story might lend itself to using police reports, a school story could naturally use school records.

Although the flashback is not the only way to present past information, it is an important device. Using a flashback, you can highlight past events quickly, or invite the reader to step back and experience the past with your character. And with careful use of verb tenses and transitions, you can slip into the past and be back in a flash.

➤➤ 39

READING AS A WRITER, WRITING AS A READER

BY SHARON OARD WARNER

LAST WEEK I RECEIVED A LETTER FROM A NOVELIST FRIEND. SHE began by telling me about her hectic summer schedule. Her new novel has just been published, and she's about to leave for her first big tour of bookstores. She included a scrawled list of cities and dates, so many that I felt a little daunted, sitting comfortably on my front porch. So far, twenty newspapers are committed to reviewing her book, and of course she's worried about what the reviewers will say. Will they be generous, and if they are, will their good words translate into sales? But that's not all she had to say. She also reported that her adult daughter has come down with chicken pox in Europe and is now confined to an American hospital. Do I know how awful chicken pox is in adults? (As a matter of fact, I do.) And how do you suppose my friend ends the letter? This way: "I'm reading Jane Hamilton's *Map of the World*. It's a knockout."

Writers are first of all readers—avid, life-long readers who consume books the way other people do hamburgers or beer. As children, we crave the cool silence of libraries and summer afternoons draped over an armchair, the hours we spend suspended between the real world and the one we hold between our two sweaty hands. We covet the feel of books, their rigid covers and the pages that blow in the breeze. When our eyes scan a book we've just borrowed or bought, we writers feel buoyed with anticipation, hopeful and content.

Most often, though, we are taught to consider writing and reading as separate activities. We do one or the other, and most of us would agree that reading is the easier of the two. Sometimes, if we sit down dutifully in front of the computer or typewriter, we reward ourselves with an hour of reading. Other times, we put off writing by reading.

I've certainly indulged in this sort of guilty reading over the years, although I no longer call it procrastination. Now, I dip briefly into books before I write in order to remind myself that I am first of all a reader, that I write because I read. For me at least, the two activities have been mingled; it's difficult to say where one leaves off and the other begins.

What do I mean? Well, lately, I've been writing my first novel after many years of devoting myself to short stories. When I began this novel two years ago, short stories were what I knew how to write—familiar territory, so to speak—and I was inclined to approach the first chapter of my novel as I would have a short story: with a vague sense of theme, or a strong image, or maybe even a bit of dialogue.

I'm not suggesting that I launched into the novel itself without a plan; I had a plan and one hundred note cards to prove it. I also had legal pads full of notes on my main characters, but none of those things told me how to begin the first chapter of my book. What does a novelist want to accomplish in the first chapter of a novel? A chapter shares some common features with a short story, but when push comes to shove, the two are also different. Just how different, I wasn't sure.

In some ways, I have found short-story writing a useful apprenticeship for that longer endeavor, the novel. To begin with, short-story writers get ample experience developing characters. In fact, one of the disappointing parts about writing stories is that you just get good and comfortable with a character when the story is finished. It's a little like going to a two-week camp, where you begin by bunking with strangers and end by parting with friends. The goodbyes are wrenching, but they're also clean because you haven't spent enough time with these people to get good and sick of them.

Short-story writers also learn the A to Z of settings. We eventually realize that characters are like the rest of us: They live in particular rooms in specific cities; they despair of cigarette wrappers in the gutters or atrazine in the farm fields; they suffer through cold snaps and sweat when the weather is humid. They even have their own ideas about interior decorating. Some characters line their mantels with Coke bottles from all fifty states, while others prefer Precious Moments figurines or half-burned candles.

All this experience holds the writer in good stead when it comes to writing the first chapter of a novel. But where plotting is concerned, short-story writers draw up short. We're like day hikers who suddenly find ourselves at the foot of Mt. Everest. It's a hell of a climb, and we have no idea where to start or how long it will take to get there. This is especially true for those writers in the habit of writing "sudden fiction," although even longer stories are a little thin where plot is concerned.

Take "Cathedral," by Raymond Carver, for instance. I admire this story and wouldn't change a word of it, but in some sense, not much really happens. A blind man has dinner with a couple; they drink a lot and smoke a lot; and then the husband and the blind man draw a cathedral together. That's the gist of the story—that's what happens on the outside, anyway. But if you've read the story, you realize I've left out the important part: After spending an evening with a blind man, the narrow-minded main character of Carver's magnificent story has been given sight, or rather, insight. He has experienced what we short story writers call an epiphany. Unfortunately, epiphanies do not a novel make.

If experience is not the best teacher when it comes to writing chapter one, what's a short-story writer turned novelist to do? The answer is simple: Read a good book. To get a sense of what's crucial to include in the first chapter of your novel, try taking a look at the initial chapters of novels you admire. Reread the first chapter of three novels you have read recently, and then ask yourself this question: What did the writer do in the first chapter to get my attention and keep it? Make a very specific list. These will be your objectives in writing a first chapter.

Once you begin your first chapter, you'll find it's necessary to change gears. Reading as a writer will only take you so far. Eventually, you'll have to write as a reader, too. Otherwise, the book won't get done. Now, I'm not suggesting you become a critic. That comes later, after you've written chapter one and all those subsequent chapters. For the time being, while you're getting something down on paper, you should read as a fan. We all need fans, don't we? According to my novelist friend, we need as many fans as we can get. So be a fan of your own work. Write the sort of novel you love to read. Chances are that if you truly enjoy reading as you write, others will enjoy reading *what* you write.

While this may seem an obvious bit of advice, some of us have to learn our lessons the hard way. For instance, a few years ago, I had a

181

bit of success with selling stories to a particular women's magazine. When summer came around and I had a little more time, I decided to write a story specifically for the editor of this one women's magazine. Likely, you can guess the result. Here's part of the letter I received from the fiction editor: "I have found that whenever a writer tells me she or he wrote a story especially for us, it lacks a certain special quality that we are looking for—a quality that comes, I think, only when the writer is writing a story she or he wants or has to write for personal reasons." She was right. My reasons weren't personal at all. I was in it for the buck, not for the joy of the process. Since I seldom read women's magazine fiction, I didn't really care about what I was writing.

Fortunately, when I began my novel, I knew better than to write for an editor or the market or a favorite teacher. Instead, I wrote the kind of novel I like to read. Where a first chapter is concerned, here are a few suggestions for writing as a reader:

1. In Chapter One, introduce at least one character who is both familiar and yet somewhat puzzling. As the writer, you should know and understand this character to the degree that you've done your homework—written character inventories and profiles. But as a reader, you must feel some mysterious pull to this person, some curiosity or intrigue. In his essay "The Magic Show," Tim O'Brien writes that "the object is not to 'solve' a character—to expose some hidden secret— but instead to deepen and enlarge the riddle itself." Part of the pleasure of intimacy is the element of surprise. This should also be true of writers and their characters.

2. Don't allow your first chapter to get bogged down in exposition. Because we're beginning something big, as novelists we often feel the first chapter should indicate seriousness of purpose. And nothing is more serious than page after page of summary and description. Nothing's more deadening to write or read, either. If you must begin with exposition, dispense with it quickly, and be on your way to writing a scene. Readers yearn for scenes, for life taking place. That's where the unexpected is likely to happen, and the unexpected is what keeps readers and writers (one and the same for our purposes) turning the pages. Here's the opening sentence to Rosellen Brown's *Before and After:* "She wasn't on ER, never was during the day when she had

patients, but they called her in on it." Immediately, we are immersed in a scene. What's going to happen? What's she been called in on?

3. Get your plot underway immediately. After reading the first chapter of my novel, an editor remarked that she was happy to see something significant happening in the first twenty pages. (The character I introduce in Chapter One attends a pro-life rally, where she witnesses a car accident.) Short-story writers turned novelists often proceed slowly because they're used to the exposition/complication/crisis/climax mode of story development. In something as big as a novel, they may reason, surely the first chapter should be devoted to exposition alone. Here's where thinking as a reader comes in handy. Readers crave action, and they're most likely to stay interested in characters who are *doing* things, preferably interesting, inexplicable things.

4. As you climb slowly toward the summit—the end of your novel—return to the first chapter for inspiration and guidance. Be your own best reader. Often, part of the larger design of the book is imbedded in your initial chapter. This design can manifest itself in different ways. For instance, the first chapter of my novel ends with the accident. As I progressed through the novel, I began to see that accidents of various sorts were the novel's means for exploring the notion of fate. Not surprisingly, then, the culminating incident in the book is also an accident, one which is, in many respects, the logical outcome of the accident in Chapter One.

5. Lastly, enjoy yourself. Have fun with the first chapter and with the rest of the book, too. I can honestly say that writing my first novel has been a pleasure, and I'm convinced that my enjoyment of the process has as much to do with my love of reading as it does my love of writing. For me, writing is a way of responding to what I read; it's a way of conversing with myself and others, a way of paying homage to all those writers who have written so beautifully and so well.

≻≻ SPECIALIZED FICTION

$\ggg$ **40**

Why Oh Why?
Motivation in the Crime Novel

By Robert Barnard

MOTIVATION IN THE CRIME NOVEL HAS SUFFERED A SEA CHANGE IN recent decades, with the decline of respectability. George Eliot declared that respectability was "the only religion possible to the mass of English people," and this made things comparatively easy for the writers of English "cozies" in the between-the-wars period, when respectability still counted, especially with the professional middle classes. The point of a "cozy" is in the initial presentation of a stable, conventional environment, and the gradual revelation of the sleazy underbelly which at some stage leads to murder. The word "cozy" is a sad misnomer, because it is the reverse of cozy that suggests that the sort of people you know and mix with (and reading detective stories is essentially a middle-class taste) are as riddled with corruption and obsession as the sleazier characters that the superficially more "realistic" American mystery writers prefer.

Motive is therefore more important to the cozy mystery than it is to the American private eye mystery. The typical cozy presents a smiling English village or a stable, prosperous household, and then gradually renders the reader uncertain and uneasy, by suggesting that all is not as it seems. One familiar element is blackmail, as for example in Agatha Christie's *The Murder of Roger Ackroyd,* and its use depends on establishing a setting in which traditional standards still matter, and where a career or a position in the local hierarchy can be destroyed by the revelation of some form of dishonesty or deviance. By the end of a cozy, the reader is left considerably more skeptical of small-town morals or the gentry's right to the forelock-tugging respect they still tried to enforce in the twenties and thirties.

Things are more difficult now. On the one hand, we can deal with areas that the Golden Age detective writers barely touched: sexual deviance, for example. Even homosexuality, so common in the artistic life of the time, was barely touched on in the novels of Christie, Ngaio Marsh, and Margery Allingham. On the other hand, the decline in monogamy, the widespread acceptance of almost any form of sexual conduct, removes one of the most common motives. Closets are out of fashion, but they were devilishly useful to crime writers. Similarly, the decline in professional standards weakens one of the most common motivations in the traditional crime story: the fear of being found out in something that would ruin one's career.

Today, then, the challenge to writers is to invent new and surprising motivations for their crime novels. In this they are not free to follow or copy the absurdities of real life: People commit murder because they can't stand someone's voice, or their suede shoes, or in order to inherit a worthless china cat. If that sort of triviality of motive is used in a crime novel, the reader flings the book away in disgust. And perhaps he is right to do so, for though such murderers undoubtedly exist, they are of a mental and psychological inconsequence that would make it impossible for the writer to arouse the reader's interest in them as characters.

But it is possible to use a new or unusual motive in a way that surprises the reader yet convinces him, and many modern crime writers have done this. If I talk for the moment about motives in my own novels, it is because it seems unfair to reveal the solutions of any of my contemporaries. My experience is that often a motive that seems perfectly convincing on one side of the Atlantic can seem strained or ridiculous on the other. In one of my books, the motive depended on the obsessive love of a woman for her dog. Nobody commented on this in Britain, but many reviewers in the States found it implausible. In another of my novels, the motive for murder was the desperate need of an American academic to gain tenure as a professor. Again, nobody in the States thought this worth commenting on, but people in Britain who were unaware of the American system and the paranoia it often produces, found this much too slight a motive. Sometimes a writer simply does not realize that his motive will be all but incomprehensible on the other side of the herring pond. One of my novels concerned a murder that was committed to precipitate a by-election in the constituency of the murdered MP. Since the procedure in the States is so different on the death of a Congressman or Senator, this motive was a mystery in itself to American readers, and the book sold fewer copies than any other book of mine.

The search for unusual motives will often turn up an obsession that can be subtly but persistently suggested as the book progresses. I once started a novel that hinged on a woman's obsession that no one should find out that one of her ancestors was black (Dr. Johnson's servant and residual legatee Francis Barber). I made her South African to add point to her obsession. But as laws changed and reforms snowballed in that country, the motive seemed less and less plausible, and I felt that the book was likely to be out-of-date before it was published, so I gave it up. In any case, obsession with one's family tree is something I consider rather silly, so I found it difficult to present it sympathetically or with understanding.

Families, however, interest me very much, and if there is one area that has been opened up by modern crime novels, it is the secrets of the nuclear family. Sexual abuse that would have been thought by Golden Age writers too horrible and too outré to use becomes central to the motivation of many present-day British crime novels (and still they get called cozies!). But physical abuse that would have been thought standard disciplinary practice by a Victorian father or schoolmaster can be revealed by the present-day crime writer for what it really is (as it was in a recent Sharyn McCrumb novel).

Again, more and more novels depend these days on family relationships that are not what they seem, or lead to murder. In one novel, I dealt with an outwardly loving relationship between a dreadful mother and her two sons, who are in fact conspiring to murder her to escape her suffocating embrace. My then editor desperately wanted to reject it on the grounds that "boys don't murder their mothers!" In the months after she said that, it seemed as if one could not open a newspaper without finding an account of a son who had murdered, or tried to murder, his mother. "Obviously mercy-killing," said my editor. In fact the modern family is far from the close and loving stereotype of yesteryear, and probably it never was. At least nowadays we can say so.

So watch out for relationships that are not what they seem in the crime novels that are coming out these days: for parents who are more than parents to their children; for people who are not in fact the sex they seem; for sisters who are really lesbian lovers, and for loving mothers and sons who are not that at all. All of which suggests that the detective novel remains today, though in differing form, what it always has been: a masquerade, in which the masks are slowly and painfully stripped off.

>> 41

WRITING THE FRONTIER NOVEL

BY JOHN EDWARD AMES

NOVELS SET ON THE AMERICAN FRONTIER ARE OFTEN DISMISSED AS formula fiction, quaint "horse operas" about the long-gone past. But in fact they continue to attract and hold readers because their courageous, decent, tough-but-seldom-mean protagonists satisfy an enduring need for homegrown heroic myths—prose versions of the original epic-heroic poems that eventually evolved into modern literature.

"Frontier fiction" is a general category that includes short, action-oriented Westerns (averaging 50,000 to 60,000 words and most often set in the 19th century—what Elmer Kelton calls the familiar "utility Western") as well as series novels and many but not all of the more ambitious, less rigidly defined historical novels. While this category enjoys fewer best sellers than do most other genres, it is certainly enduring.

One reason for this longevity is the loyalty and enthusiasm of the readers drawn to frontier and historical fiction. They expect the basic elements of all good fiction, of course: believable characters, intriguing dialogue, compelling plots and vivid settings. But writers who understand these readers also understand some important conventions of the frontier genre.

1) *Obscure research is less valuable than accurate and interesting details about everyday life.* Just as students of a foreign language start by memorizing the most important, high-frequency words, frontier writers need to compile basic details about daily life in the past: details about foods and beverages, leisure activities, occupations, household objects and furnishings, medicine and doctors, monetary systems and typical prices for common items.

Your editor may or may not know that Indians mounted their horses from the right side, white men from the left. But you had better know it, because some of your readers surely will—and they will resent your ignorance of such basic details. They also expect you to know such things as the value of a double-eagle gold piece or the various steps involved in loading and firing a percussion rifle. Too many writers don't respect the genre enough to go beyond the television clichés from the days of *Bonanza* and *Gunsmoke.*

Nor should you treat "the past" as one vague, fuzzy, undifferentiated period. It's not enough, for example, to know what a hoop skirt is: Do you know exactly when the hoop skirt was all the rage last century, and in what diameters during which decades? Nineteenth-century fashions changed dramatically from decade to decade, and a woman dressed for the theater in 1820 looked very different from her counterpart of 1860.

One good reference source is Marc McCutcheon's *Everyday Life in the 1800's.* Other more general sources for good details include David Lavender's *The Great West* and Mark Twain's *Roughing It.*

2) *Convey research indirectly.* Even though period information is essential, it should never take over or interrupt the dramatic flow of your story. Beginning writers often over-research, sometimes to postpone the more difficult task of composition. Thus armed with stacks of notecards, they produce prose that matches the narrative cadence of a parts catalogue.

One good strategy to help you avoid this pitfall is to skip exposition, when possible, and let your characters inform the readers more naturally in dialogue. Writers tend to report too much when they use exposition; dialogue, in contrast, forces them to select only the most germane details, just as taciturn cowboys are famous for uttering terse sentences stripped down to their bare semantic bones.

In an early draft of my first historical novel, *Unwritten Order,* I included an expository paragraph about the hazards posed by the Comanche penchant for making arrow points out of metal instead of flint. This information was useful, but during revision I realized that a more logical way to convey this relevant information was in the words of the contract surgeon who removed such an arrow from my hero:

"See there?" Enis Hagan said, holding a palm-size iron triangle out in the fading light. "Cut from white man's sheet iron. I'd rather get hit by a flint arrowhead any day over one of these. See there how it bent and clinched when

192

it hit bone? Made it a sonofapup to extract. I had to hook it with a looped wire and pray the shaft didn't come loose."

3) *In frontier fiction, setting itself often assumes the status of a character, usually an antagonist.* This basic rule is necessitated by geography and history, not by the laws of drama. One stark and important fact defines not only the American West, but the main focus of much writing about that vast region west of the hundredth meridian: "The West can count only a very few rivers," wrote Donald Worster in *Under Western Skies,* "all well distanced from one another and many of them drying up by summer's end."

Don't dismiss that quiet sentence as too obvious or irrelevant for writers. The aridity and other harsh physical features of the American West caused far more suffering than gun slingers, the Cavalry, and wild Indians combined, and writers of frontier fiction should reflect this important fact. Indeed, man against nature is a crucial element in much good frontier fiction: The ability to cauterize a wound, find water and shade in the desert, or interpret the warning calls of birds could mean the survival edge in a harsh and unforgiving environment.

4) *Diction or word choice is especially important.* A strong sense of time and place is crucial to frontier fiction. One way writers satisfy this requirement, besides providing vivid descriptions and apt topical references, is through mastery of historically accurate diction.

I've found it useful to remain aware of three major influences on 19th-century frontier diction, each distinct though often overlapping the others: a) the fur-trapping era (circa 1800 to 1850); b) the brief but important cowboy era (circa 1865 to 1890); c) words used by or traditionally associated with Native Americans. I recommend that writers "collect" frontier words and phrases in notebooks, learning the differences among the three main influences and noticing which characters would logically speak which words.

The nomadic fur traders who explored the intermountain West also left perhaps the most colorful influence on frontier speech. Characterized by an earthy directness and a quirky taboo against saying "I" or "me," this mountain-man argot dominated frontier speech during the first half of last century. Three fascinating American novels showcase this unique language and are must reading for frontier writers: *The Big Sky,* by A. B. Guthrie, Jr.; *Lord Grizzly,* by Frederick Manfred; and

Mountain Man, by Vardis Fisher (basis for the movie *Jeremiah Johnson*). Excellent nonfiction sources include Osborne Russell's *Journal of A Trapper* and Irving Stone's *Men to Match My Mountains.*

While the speech of the fur traders has been neglected, cowboy-era lingo is more familiar to many of us. Even so, much of its original color and power have been lost and trivialized by over-reliance on pat words and phrases associated with utility Westerns. The plot of Owen Wister's classic novel *The Virginian* has aged somewhat, but his book is rich with authentic cowboy-era speech. So are the novels of Zane Grey and Frederick Faust (a.k.a. Max Brand). Excellent nonfiction sources include Andy Adams' *Log of A Cowboy* and E. C. "Teddy Blue" Abbott's *We Pointed Them North.*

Diction used by or related to Native Americans poses more problems, especially because many North American Indian languages were never recorded in writing and thus have been lost. Others are too typographically complicated to print; many "Indian" words conventional to frontier fiction are either English translations or mistaken permutations.

All this confusion suggests that would-be frontier writers are well advised to familiarize themselves with the Native American point of view as a precursor to apt word choices for expressing it. One logical place to begin is with the title voted number one on the Western Writers of America's list of the best Western nonfiction books: Dee Brown's *Bury My Heart at Wounded Knee,* a history of the West from the Native American point of view (it includes an excellent bibliography of further sources).

5) *Innovate or evaporate!* Those who don't read frontier novels believe this genre is a crusty old codger, hidebound and resistant to change. They are wrong, but their attitude is understandable. For most of this century Western movies and fiction have been dominated by what Bernard DeVoto called "the cowboy on a pedestal" mentality. The relatively brief cowboy era was certainly important. But it has been vastly overblown, distorting our perception of the larger history of the frontier.

Variety has always been there for readers who sought it out. Indeed, fans of Western movies and fiction have shown strong interest lately in the Indian point of view and in other previously "marginalized" characters and perspectives. My *Cheyenne* series was intended as a six-book project to test the market; twenty books later, reader interest shows no sign of flagging. Curiosity about Native American culture and history has never been stronger, in part because more and more writers are seriously recognizing the practical and inspirational value of such study. Editors welcome well-written alternatives to the standard plots and heroes. Judy Alter's *Libbie* offers a thoughtful new look at George Armstrong Custer from his wife's point of view, reminding readers that the West was far more complicated and diverse than the dime novels and shilling-shockers will allow. Pete Dexter's *Deadwood* provides a fascinating version of the Wild Bill Hickok story, as told from the point of view of such hitherto "peripheral" characters as Chinese laborers. Cormac McCarthy's haunting *Blood Meridian* depicts the violent conquest of Apacheria with uncompromising grace and power. It has also convinced even the most dubious critics of "shoot-'em-ups" that innovative frontier fiction can be important literature, too.

Every genre features conventions that endure and help define it for loyal readers. But only a dead fish swims with the stream. Frontier fiction that pleases readers will survive and even flourish in the 21st century if we writers show true pioneer spirit and continually breathe new life into it.

$\gg\!\!\gg 42$

WRITING GHOST STORIES

BY JOAN AIKEN

Like one that, on a lonely road
Doth walk in fear and dread
And, having once turn'd round, walks on
And turns no more his head:
Because he knows a frightful fiend
Doth close behind him tread.
—Coleridge *(The Rime of the Ancient Mariner)*

WHY DO WE READ GHOST STORIES? PARTLY OUT OF CURIOSITY. NO one—except Lazarus—ever *has* come back from the dead; most people, at one time or another, wonder if there is another life, if souls linger after death, if the effect of some violent happening can remain, like an imprint or an echo, affecting the locality where it took place. And the discoveries of modern science do nothing to diminish such speculations; the knowledge that matter is not at all what it appears to be, that space is full of gravitational waves, and time wholly different from our conception of it, makes the idea of ghosts—*revenants,* "the ones who come back," as the French call them—more credible, not less.

Ghosts themselves have changed, though. In contemporary stories, they no longer clank chains and trail white sheets; they do not inhabit ruined abbeys and crumbling castles. They are to be found in subway trains and elevators, peering out of TV screens and car windows, sending postcards through the mail, or uttering threats over the telephone. Ghosts are more sophisticated than they were in the days of our grandparents, but they are just as potent.

In the course of my writing career I have put together five or six collections of ghost/horror stories, and among my novels, three short ones had definitely supernatural themes (*The Shadow Guests, Voices*—in the United States retitled *Return to Harken House*—and *The*

196

Haunting of Lamb House); significantly, all of those have sold rather better, and continued to stay in print longer, than my non-supernatural works. And a tiny ghost tale, *The Erl-King's Daughter,* actually found its way onto a best-seller list. All of which proves, to me at least, that readers like ghosts and need them. Perhaps ghost stories are a kind of homeopathic remedy against real terrors: Take one a day to guard against anything of this kind happening to you. Most modern readers lead lives which are, to a great extent, insulated from primitive fears. But this, I believe, leads to a build-up of unacknowledged anxiety that may be liberated and drawn to the surface by the artificial alarms of ghost stories.

Henry James said that ghost stories were on a par with fairy tales, and there is a generally accepted theory that the human race needs fairy tales and myths; that children who grow up without this kind of mental nourishment are permanently impoverished. Perhaps it is such people, deprived of fantasy in their early years, who turn so eagerly to ghost stories in adult life.

Be that as it may, ghost stories do seem to be in perennial demand; any writer who gets into the ghostly habit may be sure of regular requests from editors for "a Christmas ghost story," "a summer holiday ghost story," or one related to some theme for a specialized anthology. I once even—believe it or not—received a request for a "Regency ghost story." And even more incredibly, I happened to have, in my unsold story drawer, a manuscript that, with a little editorial work, would suit the purpose: a story I had written in my twenties about a girl bedeviled by the ghost of a swashbuckling Restoration ancestor. A few changes of costume and dialogue shifted Lord Harlowe from the reign of Charles II to that of George III. And this reinforced the lesson drummed into me by my first literary agent: Never throw any work away; something that is not wanted now may be just what editors are asking for in five, ten, fifteen years.

That story (it was called "Peer Behind the Scenes") was a light-weight, not meant to be taken seriously; but if you can write a *real* ghost story, the sort that keeps the reader breathlessly attentive through half a dozen pages of mounting tension, torn between an incli-nation to shut the book and think of something else, and an inability to do so—and if you can then finish the story with a genuine freezing *frisson*—then you may be sure of a permanent market for anything

197

you are able to produce. And, of course, if you can do this, you hardly need me to be making suggestions about the technique of writing ghost stories. But one may always pick up a clue or two from the ideas of other practitioners.

It is never too late to study the advice of the masters. M. R. James, who might be called the Grand Old Man of ghost-story writing, said that *reticence* was just as necessary in a ghost story as horror and malevolence; and with this I most emphatically agree. It is always a mistake to ladle on the grue too fast and too lavishly; just a delicate touch at a time achieves a much stronger effect.

Henry James, the other old master of the supernatural, likewise advised that the writer should make use of what he called his "process of adumbration," that is, making the reader use his own imagination to envisage the horror that threatens the hero. "Only make the reader's general vision intense enough . . . and that already is a charming job . . . his own experience . . . will supply him quite sufficiently with all the particulars.

This is brilliant advice. It was brilliant when Henry James wrote it, and it has lost none of its force now.

The worst, the most frightening stories, are those in which the reader is not told precisely what happens, but is left to guess. Another thing that James said, in discussing *The Turn of the Screw,* is still sadly true: If the threat in the story is to children, it makes it much worse. This has been a period of dreadful happenings: Wars, floods, earthquakes, bombs, every kind of horror has been presented on TV news. But to me the worst, most unforgettable image was during the hunt in Liverpool for the killers of a three-year-old boy whose body had been found: His abduction by two older boys had actually been recorded on a shopping-mall TV. I cannot think of anything more dreadful than the hazy picture of those two young, thin figures receding into the crowd with the little, trustful one going off between them.

Of the stories by M. R. James that after nearly a hundred years still hold great potency, the most terrifying is "Oh Whistle and I'll Come to You." Yet, what happens? The hero picks up a whistle, and has a dream of a half-glimpsed creature chasing a terrified man through the dusk along a wintry beach. At the climax of the story, the bedclothes from the unoccupied bed in his hotel room assemble themselves into a shape and come at him. He sees a face *of crumpled linen* (James's italics). But what could a creature made out of bedclothes really do to an active, golf-playing university professor? The secret of the story is that the reader is not given time to ask such a question; he is completely caught up in the carefully assembled and graded action: first, the character of Parkins, a fussy, fidgety, old-maidish academic; then the detailed description of the English east-coast area, the hotel, the "pale ribbon of sand intersected by black wooden groynings" [breakwaters], and the monastic ruins where Parkins picks up the whistle.

The story seems to proceed at a leisurely pace, but all along the way, small hints are dropped. Parkins, having picked up the whistle, glances back and sees "a rather indistinct personage who seemed to be making great efforts to catch up with him but made little, if any, progress." He makes little of this glimpse—though the reader makes more—but it serves to remind him of the moment in *The Pilgrim's Progress* where Christian sees a foul fiend coming over the field to meet him. And from then on, tension builds steadily. When Parkins tries to blow the whistle, there is a sudden gust of wind, and an image comes into his mind of a desolate, windswept landscape, with a solitary figure. He then has the frightening dream, and the reader is conned into thinking that perhaps all the fear, all the threat, is in Parkins's own mind. But no; the bedding on the second bed is disturbed at night and a local boy, outside, is terrified by the sight of a white figure—"not a *right* person"—in the hotel bedroom window. Notice that all through the story the impressions given the reader are always as observed by one of the characters in the story. And even in the final climax, it is through Parkins's eyes that we see: "The spectator realized, with some horror and some relief, that it must be blind, for it seemed to feel about it. . . ." (The fact that the creature is blind makes it *more* frightening, not *less*.)

Does a writer have to believe in ghosts himself in order to be able to portray them?

My answer to that is no, or, at least, it depends on what you mean by ghosts. I do not believe in sheeted spectres clanking chains, and I have not seen anything of the kind. But I know several people who have experienced supernatural manifestations. (One was my stepfather, an entirely rational, level-headed, skeptical person.) I have had experience with telepathy and nonnatural happenings, and I am perfectly ready to believe that paraphysical phenomena take place all around us all the time, but we have hardly begun to be aware of, or to understand them. I have lived in various old houses in which odd things happen, some of which I used in a story called "The Legacy." "Would you shut the window, Basil?" said my aunt Helen. "The curtain keeps billowing in." But, behind the curtain, the window was already tight and locked. Also in that house, a pair of shoes were found in the cellar, inexplicably packed with foil milk-bottle caps. Nobody could have done this, and there was no reason for it. That is generally the case with supernatural, or paranormal occurrences: They are odd, trivial, meaningless. The art of the ghost story writer is to turn these inexplicable little oddities into something meaningful and threatening.

The way I build a ghost story is to start with what I call *the moment*—the climax, though it may not be the end. The classic example of this is the person waking in a fright, putting out a hand in the dark, and the hand goes into a *mouth,* hot and wet, with sharp teeth. . . . Other examples: You ring the bell of a familiar house, but when the door is opening, the interior is completely unfamiliar, and the person who opens the door is a stranger. You answer the phone, and the voice of a long-dead person says, "See you later." You confidently put your hand in your pocket for keys and encounter—what? Something hideously out of place.

E. F. Benson was a great exponent of The Moment; several of his stories, such as "Naboth's Vineyard," rise to an almost unbearably frightening climax. But I think the best of all is in another M. R. James story, "The Treasure of Abbot Thomas," in which, following clues, a treasure hunter climbs down a spiral stair into a well, and opens a door in the masonry, only have Something slither out and *put its arms round his neck.*

In my case, The Moment comes first. Then follows the slow, structural part of working back to causes and building up to the scene. To whom has this happened? Why? And, tremendously important, where? To be frightening, a story does not have to be set in some wild, desolate Edgar Allan Poe-type region. Elizabeth Bowen, who wrote some very haunting supernatural stories, used modern housing estates and prosperous stockbrokers' residences. One of her most sinister ghosts is a taxi driver.

E. F. Benson tended to build his stories on a traditional pattern: Some evil, violent episode has occurred in the past—murder, hostility, cruelty, oppression. Into the place where this happened comes a present-day character who somehow contrives to disturb old vibrations and set off a replay of what took place before. The present-day protagonists may come to a sticky end. Or there may be some kind of exorcism. This is a reliable framework; the skill lies in making the setting as real, and the characters as sympathetic as possible, so that the reader may become involved and empathize more and more, up to the moment of climax.

I find it enriching to the story if the protagonists have aims and intentions and plans of their own, so that there are two themes intertwined, as happens so often in life. The story, therefore, is not simply A goes to Place X and sees Ghost B, but A, having decided to leave his wife and children and go off with C, arrives at Place X and meets Ghost B; whereupon the writer is at once given various interesting choices: Does C also see the ghost? If not, why not? Is A seeing the ghost because he is in a vulnerable psychological state? Does this affect his relationship with C? And so on.

A couple of years ago, I was approached by the National Trust, the body that cares for ancient houses in England, and asked if I would like to write a story about one of their properties. Enchanted, I at once said, Yes, I would like to write a story about Lamb House. This ancient house stands at the top of the hill where I was born, in Rye, Sussex, England. Up to 1918, it belonged to Henry James, who wrote many novels there, including *The Turn of the Screw;* after his death, it passed into the hands of E. F. Benson, who wrote his Lucia books and many ghost stories there. Then later, it was occupied by Rumer Godden, who had several strange psychic experiences (described in her autobiography *A House with Four Rooms*). Both James and Benson had fallen in love with the house, and both said they had practically been *summoned* to live in it by what seemed a meaningful chain of events. Comparing their lives, I found many interesting parallels: They both came from large, talented families; their sisters had breakdowns; they had supernatural experiences. . . . I began planning a series of three tales, one to be wholly invented, preceding the lives of James and Benson, but linking them. I thought I would write the stories about James and Benson each in a pastiche of their own style, and the climax of each would be the type they themselves used in ghost stories: In the case of James, a kind of nebulous, sinister fade-out; in Benson's case, a more robust and dramatic confrontation with the Powers of Evil, ending in an exorcism.

At this point the National Trust got in touch with me and said they were afraid that Lamb House was not at all suitable for such a project, as there was no shop on the premises in which the book could be sold.

But by that time (several months had elapsed) I was fired with enthusiasm and wrote the book anyway and had a lot of fun inventing appropriate happenings. (Both men had written ghost stories—which I took pains to read—using Lamb House as a setting. Although mine was not a book that would ever reach a best-seller list, I was lucky enough to find publishers on both sides of the Atlantic, and even in Spain and Germany, and it did rather better than expected for such an oddity. Which shows that there is always a market for a ghost!

Like all writers, I keep a notebook—a whole series of notebooks— in which I jot down ideas for future stories. Many of these might develop into ghost stories: "Hotel wallpaper with spooky little catlike creatures." "Somebody whose memory skips a day. Why?" "Churchyard full of grave slabs that look like a chessboard." "Floor covered with fingernails." "Sign: DANGER. Keep clear of unpropped body." "Taking ghost on travels."

These are all waiting for The Moment.

Being a writer is not at all unlike being a medium. Sometimes the message comes through loud and clear. Sometimes you simply have to wait for it.

>> 43

A Novel by Any Other Name . . .

By Elizabeth George

I'VE FOUND THAT ONE OF THE BENEFITS OF ACHIEVING THE STATUS of published writer is that I've been able to meet and talk with hundreds upon hundreds of readers and unpublished writers since my first novel hit the bookstores in 1988. My role when asked to speak to neophyte writers is to give a shot-in-the-arm discourse about persevering through doubts and dead ends that go hand in hand with completing a project, as well as weathering the maddening frustrations of trying to get someone to read, to represent, to believe in, and—*mirabile dictu*—to purchase their work.

But every so often, a conversation develops that carries me in another direction, prompting me to evaluate what I do when I sit down in front of my word processor every day and, more important, why I do it.

I had such a conversation not long ago with a psychologist-cum-novelist who told me that he intended to write mystery novels only until such a time as he became good enough to write "a real novel." The fact that a mystery (or thriller or crime or suspense or psychological) novel is indeed "a real novel" possessing all the requirements of "a real novel" appeared to escape him. As far as he was concerned, writing a mystery was going to be a way to practice his craft, rather like baking cookies in the hope that one day he could work himself up to the challenge of a layer cake.

Let's ignore the questionable sense our psychologist displayed in sharing this peculiar literary plan of action with a mystery-suspense writer. Instead, let's examine what he failed to realize about the well-crafted mystery. First, it *is* a novel of character, of plot, of setting, of dialogue, of metaphor, of allusion, of landscape, of drama, of conflict, of love, of death, and most important, of imagination. And second, to deny the mystery-suspense its place among the world's "real novels" is to deny a place among "real novelists" to such writers as Thomas Hardy *(Desperate Remedies)*, William Faulkner *(Intruder in the Dust)*, Charles Dickens *(Bleak House)*, Wilkie Collins *(The Woman in White)*, Edgar Allan Poe *(Murders in the Rue Morgue)*, Dorothy L. Sayers *(Gaudy Night)*, George Eliot *(Silas Marner)*, Nathaniel Hawthorne *(The House of the Seven Gables)*, and more recent writers like Alice Hoffman *(Turtle Moon)*, Scott Turow *(Presumed Innocent)*, Kem Nunn *(Pomona Queen)*, and a host of others whose mysteries and suspenses have stood and will stand the test of time.

This is not to argue that there are no deplorable mystery-suspense novels being written. On the contrary, dozens of writers seem to turn them out on an annual basis. But the novelist who commits herself to the process, the product, and the passion of writing is, believe me, writing "a real novel" from start to finish.

The mystery-suspense novel provides the writer with a natural structure, and it is perhaps because this structure exists in the first place that the uninformed neophyte writer might evaluate the mystery-suspense as a lesser creature in the world of literature. The natural structure is generally the same: A situation of grave import (like a murder) has occurred or is threatening to occur or a dramatic question is presented to the reader; this situation or this dramatic question must be resolved in some way by the final pages of the book. But it is what the individual writer does with this natural structure that can, and often does, alter the tiresome label "piece of genre fiction" to "literary classic."

Because a given structure exists, the writer of the mystery-suspense can choose to provide her readers with little more than a skeleton of a novel and still get away with constructing a whodunit that not only entertains, but also stimulates the reader's perspicacity. In this sort of novel, the hero or heroine—be the character a spymaster, a police detective, a private investigator, an FBI agent, or an amateur sleuth caught up in unexpected circumstances that try the intellect if not the soul—marches fairly directly to the conclusion of the story, encountering the expected road blocks, clues, red herrings, and conflicts along the way. Or the writer can take that same skeleton and hang upon it the organs, muscles, and flesh of subplot, theme, character development, exploration of social issues, and the complex psychology of human relationships. It's my belief that the novels that stand the test of time, that move out of genre because of their refusal to be bound by the mundane rules of genre, follow this latter course of action.

To write a mystery-suspense that is "a real novel" is to write largely about character. In these novels, the characters and the circumstances engendered by those characters drive the story forward, and not vice versa. Characters do not exist to be set pieces in a contrived drama whose value is ultimately revealed in a single indecipherable clue or a "gotcha" ending whose sole purpose is surprise rather than provocation of thought. Mystery-suspense novels that are "real novels" end where they begin: with an examination of the human heart—in conflict, in despair, in peace, in anguish, in love, in happiness, in fear.

When a writer decides to create a novel of character within this genre of mystery-suspense, she challenges herself to move beyond the simple mechanics of plotting, to drive from her mind the temptation to adhere to a formula, and to take a risk. She decides to begin with character and to use character as the foundation for the hundreds of pages and thousands of words that will follow that character's creation.

This is what I have attempted to do with my novels, which are sometimes called literary mysteries, sometimes novels of psychological suspense, sometimes detective stories, sometimes police procedurals, sometimes British novels, but are always—at least to my way of thinking—"real novels" from start to finish. I begin with a kernel of killer, victim, and motive. I plant that kernel into the soil of imagination, and I begin to people a world in which killer and victim move.

In peopling the world of the novel, I create individuals. I begin with their names, knowing that the name I give to a character will have a large influence upon the way a reader feels about him. So when I wanted the victim in *Missing Joseph* to be seen as a gentle and thoughtful country vicar, I named him Robin Sage, just as when I wanted the schoolboy bully in *Well-Schooled in Murder* to be believable as a mutilator of self and others, I gave him the name Clive Pritchard with the hard sound of that initial *C* and the surname reminiscent of a farming tool.

Once I have named my cast of characters, I begin the process of making them real. Each is given a personality that has—as we all do— a core need in life. Perhaps the core need is to be seen as competent, perhaps it is to be in control of self and others, perhaps it is to belong,

205

to be of service, to be perceived as authentic. The character's personality arises out of his backstory, which may or may not become part of the novel but is indeed part of the groundwork that leads up to the writing of the novel. The character's backstory includes his family relationships, his growing up, any pivotal events that shaped him, his friendships or the lack thereof. Within this backstory is woven the character's interior landscape: what his agenda is with other characters, what his throughline is for the entire novel, how he reacts to stress, what he experiences as joy or pleasure. To this are added the telling details that will appear in the novel and act as a means by which the reader can view the character in a more direct light: that peculiar article of clothing worn by a teen-aged boy but once belonging to his absent father; that bullet-like line of ear studs and the silver nose ring donned by the girl who always wears black; the hairlip covered inadequately by a mustache; the perfect sitting room with no mote of dust floating in the air; the bitten fingernails; the choice of artwork; the music listened to; the car driven; the condition of the curtains hanging at the windows; the collection of tea cups lovingly displayed. The character is given a place of birth, a place in society, and a place within his individual family. He is described physically, mentally, psychologically, and emotionally. And when that is done, he stands on the brink, ready to come to life in the manuscript itself.

But my preliminary work does not end here. Because the novel will not exist in outer space, I must create an inner space for it. This is its setting. The setting may be a place as simple to construct as was the Yorkshire village of Keldale in *A Great Deliverance* where a farmer met a hideous end in an old stone barn. What was required of that little village: two pubs, an inn, a churchyard containing the grave of an abandoned newborn, a huge ruined abbey with a legend descending from the time of Cromwell. Having seen many such villages and abbeys during my time in Yorkshire, I needed only to assembly my photographs and map out my locations.

Or setting may be as challenging as the creation of Bredgar Chambers, the public school founded by Henry VII that sat in West Sussex and served as the setting of *Well-Schooled in Murder*. Here I needed all the accouterments of the English public school—the great chapel, the dining hall, the houses of residence, the quadrangle, etc.—and the only way to make them authentic was to blend myself into the world of the English public school for a period of time until I knew it well enough to create my own, from its prospectus to its architecture.

Or setting may require that I bring a real place to life, jockeying its streets and buildings a little in order that it might accommodate just one more college. This was the case in *For the Sake of Elena,* where St. Stephen's College was slid into the new space I created between Trinity College and Trinity Hall. But to make it real—and thus to integrate it into an atmosphere that felt authentic to the reader—St. Stephen's had to be a place of architectural significance, for such is the case of every college in the city of Cambridge.

With setting and characters well in hand, I begin to outline the plot. Sometimes I use a step outline only, creating a preliminary list of scenes with fragments of information to guide me in the construction of those scenes. Sometimes I use a running plot outline, in which entire sections of the novel are outlined in depth, including description, narration, and dialogue. And sometimes I have to feel my way slowly into the novel, allowing an initial scene or the glimpse of a character to dictate what will follow.

The story I ultimately tell grows out of all of this: these characters who have been created in my imagination from that initial kernel of killer, victim, and motive; this setting that I have labored over like a loving god; this plot that I am always unsure of, partly in terror of, but determined to carry onward. And when that story has reached its conclusion, if it's successful and not a tosser, it comprises plot and subplot, internal and external conflict, theme, drama, moments of reflection and evaluation, landscape, setting, metaphor, and allusion.

It is, because of how it has been written, in every way a real novel.

207

WRITING EFFECTIVE DIALOGUE

BY JEREMIAH HEALY

LET ME ASK YOU BEFORE YOU BEGIN THIS PIECE TO READ THE FOL-lowing exchange:

Beginning Draft

John Jeffers walked into the room. He saw Mary Edwards standing at the window. John exclaimed, "Mary, what are you doing here?"

Mary turned to him. "Aw, John, I am just so upset about Martha," she blurted.

John walked across the room, taking her in his arms. He whispered, "Aw, Mary, I am sorry about Martha, too, but we cannot let it ruin our lives."

Mary held him tightly. "I know, but it is all just so hard," she murmured. "And besides," she added, "I think I know where Geoff hid the knife."

If you feel the above passage represents good dialogue, then stop reading this article. On the other hand, if you don't like the John/Mary exchange, but you recognize in it, uncomfortably, some of your own tendencies as a writer, then the following may be helpful to you.

Though I write mystery novels, most of my comments will apply to many types of fiction. As a premise, let's assume that dialogue should serve three purposes: story advancement, character development, and writing style. I'm going to spend a little less time here on the first two purposes and a little more on the third.

In order to use dialogue to advance the story in a mystery novel, you have to have some idea of what information must be communicated to the reader in each chapter. In my opinion, the best example of a writer who uses dialogue to inform the reader about the story is Elmore Leonard. Pick up any of his street thrillers (*Glitz, Stick,* etc.), and notice how he tells the reader most of his plot through dialogue. Leonard's high point is the opening chapter of his Edgar Award novel, *LaBrava,* in which the entire setting of the story is explained by a two-character exchange of dialogue.

Does the passage I use at the beginning of this article advance the story? Hard to tell, since we don't know what information the writer wants to communicate to the reader or where in the story line the passage appears. At the very least, though, we know the male character is surprised to find the female character in the setting; the female character is upset about someone else; there is some pre-existing relationship between the male and female characters; and, somehow, another character and a knife are involved in a sinister way. Let's say, then, that the story has been advanced by the John/Mary exchange.

The second purpose of dialogue is character development. The reader has to see your characters as more than just ciphers or the novelistic version of operatic spear-carriers for the plot. Here, we know that the female character is upset; that the male character is empathetic ("I am sorry . . ."), yet forward-looking ("We cannot let it ruin . . ."); and that the female character is also troubled by a secret she believes she's discovered. While there is some overlap with the story advancement purpose, the writer has done a credible job with character development, too. Read any of Mary Higgins Clark's novels for other examples of the use of dialogue to develop character.

I think, then, that the major failing of my first exchange is in writing style, and I'd like to focus upon this third purpose of dialogue. Reread my opening passage. Stylistically, what's wrong with it? Answer: technically nothing. The characters in the exchange speak perfect English in perfect sentence structure, with thesaurus "cue" words like "exclaimed" and "blurted" (and "whispered" and "murmured") that tell the reader exactly what intensity of emotion the author meant the characters to reveal.

However, judged from a novelist's standpoint, the dialogue is dreadful. It's stilted and unnatural, because people in the real world having actual conversations don't speak in complete sentences and do use contractions. Also, through the dialogue *itself,* a writer ought to be able to convey the intensity of expression without thesaurus cues. The word "said" is virtually the only expression cue you should ever need, and even that often isn't necessary, since in a two-character scene the break in paragraphs "cues" the reader that the other character is now speaking, and the character action (stage directions of "she turned" or "he walked") usually can cover the rest.

Now, let's rewrite the opening passage using just the foregoing suggestions (incomplete sentences, contractions, and stage directions, but no cues other than "said"):

First Revision

Walking into the study, John Jeffers saw Mary Edwards standing at the window and stopped short. "Mary, what are you doing here?"

Mary turned to him. "Aw, John, I'm just so upset about . . . you know." She turned back to the window. "Martha."

John walked across the room, taking her in his arms. "Aw, Mary, I'm sorry, too. But we can't let it. . . . We have to go on with our lives."

Mary held him tightly. "I know. It's just so . . ." In a different tone, she said, "Besides, I think I know where Geoff hid the knife."

An improvement? I think the answer is clearly yes. Are we there yet? Clearly not. Why?

A couple of subtler, even subliminal problems. The writer has named the male character "John Jeffers." There's nothing wrong with a common first name like "John," or an alliterated surname like "Jeffers." However, the writer has used up or "burned" the possibility of another character with the first name "Jeff" by having a surname with that "root" in it. Otherwise, the reader would be subliminally confused in the dialogue by references to the "Jeff" sound in a name, and thus "Geoff" in the last phrase would have to be changed. In my private investigator novels, the protagonist's name is "John Francis Cuddy." If I were to have another character's first or last name sound like or contain "John" or "Francis," I'd subliminally confuse even longstanding fans of the ten-book series.

This reasoning also applies to the similarity of "Mary" and "Martha." I try to avoid even the same first *initials* for more than one of my characters, and I keep an alphabet of first and last names, listed vertically, when I begin any novel, to be sure I don't accidentally have several characters with a first name beginning with a specific letter. Though not technically related to dialogue, the naming of characters does affect dialogue directly.

A continuing problem with names in our first revision of the opening passage is that John, Mary, *and the author* use the names themselves too much. To get around this, the author can inject a last name in stage direction prose, while the characters in dialogue occasionally address each other by first name (or even better, nickname). Pronouns, also, if the antecedent is clear, provide the reader with both variety and necessary cues.

Finally, the author should give a pet phrase to only one character, so that for the reader the phrase becomes that character's subliminal signature. Therefore, Mary and John should not both use "Aw" as a pet phrase.

Let's do a second revision of the opening passage, cumulating these last observations (different names, different initials, nicknames, and different pet phrases) into the first revision:

Second Revision

Walking into the study, John Jenkins saw Mary Eberson standing at the window and stopped short. "What are you doing here?"

Eberson turned to him. "Oh, Jack, I'm just so upset about . . . you know." She turned back to the window. "Karen."

Jenkins walked across the room, taking her in his arms. "Hey-ey-ey, Mary, I'm upset too, but we can't—Look, we have to get on with our lives, right?"

Eberson held him tightly. "I know, it's just so . . ." In a different tone, she said, "Besides, I think I know where Geoff hid the knife."

Better? I think so, though we still have some stylistic problems, as in the two usages of "walk." However, in fixing some problems we've created others. For one thing, I don't like the way the author's use of the surnames in stage directions "feels" in this scene.

How can I be writing an article implying that you can and should revise dialogue mechanically, even suggesting some "tricks" on how to do it, when some of the best writers have told me they don't revise at all? Simple. Mechanical revisions showing how *not* to write will improve many authors' dialogue immediately, but while I can "tell" you how some of the best do it, I can't "teach" you that method. Each writer learned his or her own "tricks" intuitively by writing.

I come down midway between the mechanical model and the intuitive one. To write what I hope will be natural, effective dialogue, I first imagine a real person with the characteristics of a given character. I try to imagine that person/character having an actual conversation with another person/character in some real-world setting (people speak differently in bars from the way they do in doctors' offices). Then, instead of *creating* the dialogue as an author, I just *transcribe* it as a stenographer would. I key into my computer what I "hear" each person/character saying to the other during this scene in my head. I would, of course, already have done some planning to determine how the dialogue must advance the story and develop the characters, as suggested earlier. Then, with just a little revision, I can make the dialogue stylistically smooth, and thereafter, I can read the exchange aloud, as a quality control for "natural sound."

So the opening passage again, as a third revision:

Third Revision

Entering the study, John Jenkins saw Mary Eberson standing at the window. "Mary, what the hell are you doing here?"

She turned to him. "Jack, I've just been . . ." Back to the window. "I'm still upset about Karen."

He crossed the room, closing his arms around her gently. "Hey-ey-ey, you got the right, o.k.? But don't let it run your life."

"Or ruin it?" Mary put her left hand on his right forearm. "Good advice. It's just . . ."

"What?"

"The knife."

"The knife?"

"Yes, I think I know where Geoff hid it."

Is this third revision the best yet? I think so. The story is advanced, the characters are developed, and now even contrasted as well. (The reader may be curious about why John and Mary seem to be close when he "sounds" less well educated than she does.) When read silently, the writing is "stylish." When read aloud, the exchange sounds "natural."

Of course, I may like the third revision best because it's *my* way of doing the scene, "transcribing" what I "hear" the characters saying to each other. Accordingly, I'd advise you to use the hints in this article as vehicles for immediately improving your dialogue. Then, slowly develop your *own* way of writing effective dialogue thereafter.

>> 45

THE USES OF SUSPENSE

BY ANDREW KLAVAN

WANT TO LEARN ABOUT WRITING SUSPENSE FICTION? TRY THIS SIMple experiment at home. Invite a friend over to your house, preferably someone better-looking than you are and with more money. Let's call him Nigel. Let's say he's been trying to make time with your wife. (Women can try this experiment, too! It's easy! Just change Nigel's sex!) Seat Nigel in a chair close to yours, one of those wooden Windsors with the fanning spoked backs. Now, for approximately fifteen minutes, engage Nigel in conversation about something excruciatingly dull: the latest deficit debates, say, or Madonna's inner life.

A yawn-fest, am I wrong? O.K. Now, tie Nigel to the chair with a strong rope (this is where that spoked back comes in handy). Produce a .38 caliber revolver with only one bullet in it (prepare this earlier). Spin the revolver's wheel so you don't know where the bullet is, and then level the barrel at Nigel's head. Continue the conversation on exactly the same subject in exactly the same way as before—except, every minute on the minute, pull the trigger of the gun.

I think you'll find that those next five minutes of conversation—if there are five more minutes of conversation—are a lot more interesting and suspenseful than the first fifteen, especially to Nigel. Thus, you have just demonstrated several important aspects of the nature of suspense. And, as I hope and pray you'll be spending the rest of your life in some sort of high-security institution, you should have a lot of time to think about them, too.

But what exactly have we learned? To begin with, suspense is not about the things that are happening; it's about the things that might happen, that threaten to happen. Obviously, if you'd merely continued chatting away about the deconstructionist profundities of "Like A Virgin," there would have been no suspense at all, though you might eventually have been given tenure. But it's also true that if you had simply whipped a fully loaded gun out and blown Nigel away, it might have been surprising, it would certainly have been messy, but the suspense factor would still have stood at zero. Suspense is in the pauses between the pulls of the trigger; between the time the reader knows what might happen and the time it actually happens or doesn't.

It follows from this that the more readers know about the threat to your characters, and the earlier they know, the more suspense there is. All sorts of interesting stories can be told in which the audience, mystified, waits to be enlightened. But in suspense fiction, whatever else you hold back, your readers should be in on the threat of danger as soon as possible and as much as possible.

For example, in a novel I wrote called *Don't Say A Word,* the story revolves around a psychiatrist, his wife and child, and a beautiful but disturbed young woman who becomes his patient. For the first hundred pages or so, the psychiatrist tends to his practice, plays with his child, makes love to his wife, and treats the young woman. Then, the psychiatrist's little girl is kidnapped, and he spends the rest of the book in a desperate attempt to get her back. I like to think that those first hundred pages are interesting and mysterious and compelling and all that, but if they're suspenseful, it's because of the ten-page prologue during which the bad guys worm their way into an apartment that has a view through the psychiatrist's window. They brutally murder the old lady who lives there and set up camp, watching every move the psychiatrist makes. When the psychiatrist plays with his child, the reader knows they're watching. When he makes love to his wife, the reader knows they're watching. And because of what they did to the old lady, the reader knows that whatever the bad guys eventually do to the psychiatrist, it's going to be very bad. Right up front, I tell the reader who the bad guys are, what they're like, and whom they're after. The only mystery about them is their motive, which has nothing to do with the present danger and so can be saved for a revelation at the end. The less I can hold back, in other words, the more the reader comes with me for the ride.

Of course, any editor or agent will tell you to begin a suspense novel with a scene of danger or violence like that. But it's amazing how often they want you to cut out precisely the piece of information that switches on the suspense. In this particular case, they liked the old lady getting killed, but they didn't want me to mention that it was the psychiatrist the bad guys were watching. Editors and agents know that a little violence at the beginning sells books, but somewhere along the line someone told them that you're not supposed to give too much away. I think, to create suspense, you should give as much away as you can. So in the event you should meet with this problem, try saying something like this: "Sweetheart—baby—you're the best editor or agent I've ever met, and I love you like my own brother, and I'm going to give that a lot of thought, let me tell you." Then leave it in.

This brings us to the next lesson we learned from killing Nigel (and what an oleaginous little son-of-a-gun he was, wasn't he?). Once you have established suspense, once readers know exactly where the danger lies, you really have a lot of room to work in. Even if you and Nige are discussing the latest trade agreement and its effect on deficit spending, no one's attention is going to wander once you've pulled out that gun. Likewise, in a work of fiction, the firm pressure of suspense gives you the time you need to establish your characters, work out your plot elements, expound your ridiculous metaphysical theories, or hawk your half-baked political notions—whatever meat your story feeds on. In *Don't Say A Word,* I wanted to draw a fairly full picture of this psychiatrist's life; I wanted readers to see his fault-lines, where he might crack once the going got tough. The killing of the old woman and the men watching through the window, gave me time to do a fairly in-depth study of the man, all the while keeping the pressure on.

This use of suspense is particularly important to me because of the kinds of books I write. I don't generally deal with stories about world leaders or terrorists or guys in ties who grab the phone and shout, "Get me Quantico! Now!" I like stories like that quite a lot actually, but as a writer, I'm more interested in the inner worlds of regular people, and I generally make up stories in which the glitches and nightmares of those inner worlds are played out in reality. Now, if you introduce the President of the United States as a character, readers all know he's important, and if you bring in the best FBI agent west of the Tappan Zee, readers know he or she is likely to be where the action is. But establishing the inner worlds of clerks and housewives, small-time shrinks and would-be poets—and drawing readers into their ordinary lives—takes more time and involves a lot of mundane action.

215

Suspense—the danger that the audience can see coming—gives you that time and brings those actions to life.

But the effect of suspense on commonplace events can be brought into play in all sorts of ways, scene by scene. I love to create episodes in which something perfectly ordinary happens while the reader (one hopes) tears his hair out wishing it would stop. In my novel *The Animal Hour,* one of my heroes, Oliver, gets trapped into what is to him the horrible situation of *having tea with his grandmother*! The way it works out is this: Oliver is trying to prevent the murder of his grandmother, which he knows will take place at a certain time. He trails the villain, who knows the plan of his grandmother's house. Both she and Oliver also know that Granny has a very bad heart; any sort of fuss will likely cause the old woman to die. So, when Oliver tries to force the villain out of the room, she, in turn, offers to make everyone a lovely cup of tea. As a result, Oliver, a hulking bear of a man, is forced to sit through a dainty tea party with Granny and the villain, while the minutes tick away toward the time of the killing.

What I like about this situation is that the trivial is heightened with the threat of death, and since both the trivial and the threat of death are always with us, it provides the story with a sort of metarealism. If you do it well enough, you can make the reader feel that even the dullest tea party takes place under an inexorably ticking clock. Which, of course, it does.

Finally, the now-famous Nigel Experiment demonstrates a more subtle aspect of suspense and one that is, in my opinion, too rarely put to good use; that is, suspense is amoral. It slams the reader into the endangered character's point of view, no matter who that character is or what he's done. Let's say we tell the story of our experiment from Nigel's viewpoint. We know he's a no-good sort of guy; just look at him: Anyone who's richer and better-looking than you are probably deserves whatever he gets. But when you pull that gun out, when your finger begins to tighten on the trigger, readers can't help putting themselves in his place. Every time the hammer goes back, they'll worry about him and fear for him, whether they like him or not. You can take it to the limit—a thief, a rapist, a killer. Write the scene from his point of view, put him under threat of danger, and part of the reader's mind will automatically root for him to escape.

This gives the suspense writer a wonderful opportunity to drag readers kicking and screaming into the lives of the very people they most condemn. What's more, you can do it without romanticizing the villain, without pardoning his behavior, and without even explaining that his mother never loved him and that's why he's such a bad hat. I suppose you could say that danger—suspense—forces the reader to recognize the villain's humanity without losing sight of his own moral verities.

Nowhere have I seen this done better than in Simon Brett's novel *A Shock to the System*. I adapted this book for the movie that starred Michael Caine, and what I most wanted to recreate in the film was the way Brett used suspense to make the reader an accomplice to murder. The story involves a man who begins to realize that he can kill his way to the top of his profession. At first, he escapes through pure good luck. But with each successive killing, he becomes more and more adept at covering his tracts. Brett didn't stint in his depiction of the homicidal personality. His protagonist is bitter, vengeful, impotent, sweaty-palmed, and full of petty deceit (I stinted a little in my screenplay: Movie stars don't play impotent). All the same, whenever something threatens to go wrong with one of the killer's plans, whenever the police seem to be closing in, the audience holds its collective breath. They don't want the bad guy to get away exactly; they just don't want him to be caught right now. As a result, bit by bit, they are drawn into the killer's activities nearly as completely as he is himself. I love that. It's wicked and it's funny, but it also reminds us that even the things of darkness must ultimately be acknowledged as our own.

So, though Nigel is no longer with us, we can take comfort in the fact that he gave his sleazy little life to show some of the methods through which suspense can be well used. Indeed, I think if he were here today, what he would tell us, in his smarmy way, is that all fiction is merely a series of thrills, some deeper and more subtle than others, but thrills all the same. In suspense, the basic thrills are pretty obvious and immediate, and they naturally lend themselves to being used mechanically and on the cheap. Used skillfully, though, they give the writer the time and the narrative drive he needs to pull his readers into heightened worlds of thought and sensation that are, at the same time, not much different from everyday life. Well, that's what Nigel would've said. He was a verbose, pompous guy, what can I tell you? I never liked him.

217

➤➤ 46

The Plot's the Thing

By Reginald Hill

It is a truth universally acknowledged that everybody's got one good novel in them.

It is a delusion generally untested that everybody can write it. Which is just as well for us writers who can go about quietly cannibalizing our friends' lives and experiences for our own plots.

I want to talk here about plotting, the process by which we take the raw materials of our fiction and serve them up in a digestible mode. Get it wrong, and what you planned as soufflé may turn out as scrambled eggs.

Of course, when that happens, professional writers don't blow their brains out; they start looking for a market for scrambled eggs. But if what they've got is cold porridge, they feed it to the pigs and start again.

So let's start with what a plot is not. It isn't just narrative, not even moving narrative. Tell your friends that you got mugged in the elevator, and they'll be truly shocked and sympathetic, but that's because they're your friends, and even your nearest and dearest will show signs of irritation if you're still going on about it the following week. To turn it into the kind of anecdote that people ask you to repeat to others who haven't heard it takes a bit of art, which, as Sir Thomas Browne said, is the perfection of nature. So, if you were on your way to an important job interview when the mugging happened, and you put the experience behind you and went straight in anyway, forgetting that the mugger, attracted by the handsome gold buckle on your belt, had made you remove it . . . . Now it's a funny recyclable story, but still a long way from a plot. At best there might be the germ of a short story there, but so what? Great short stories are made by concentration, not expansion.

218

What I'm laboring to stress is that plot and story are not the same thing. A plot is both the structure in which the narrative takes place and a function of that narrative. To describe the way I see plot, I'm going to take the writer's easy way out and resort once more to metaphor.

Think of it as a house: A conventional arrangement would be a living room, a dining room, and a kitchen on the first floor, and three bedrooms and a bathroom on the second. Of course, if people are to live comfortably in the house, there must be access to each room from a common area—a hallway downstairs and a landing upstairs, plus a stairway connecting the two floors. There will probably be an attic, possibly a cellar. Some of the rooms may interconnect directly—say, the kitchen and dining room, or two of the bedrooms, one of which is a nursery. Each of the rooms will have specific functions with occasional variation, as when you have the living room serve as a bedroom when you have too many overnight guests. Some rooms, like the bathroom, may be locked without causing surprise. But a locked bedroom may, in certain circumstances, cause unease, and a locked kitchen, downright alarm. There are certain areas in which the presence of certain people is expected, but others in which their presence will require explanation. Some windows are more private than others: One window looks into the back garden, while another looks out onto the street. People living outside the house use these windows, too: sometimes to see in, sometimes to get in.

Corbusier's definition of a house as a machine for living in works only if we see people as the machine's moving parts, and so it is in my analogy. You start your story with a shell, and your characters move in. The shell they move into is going to direct and restrict their activities, but your characters are the forces that will shape the way the shell comes to life, sometimes dramatically. When I started writing decades ago, I thought it was pretty easy, especially once I'd opted for the conventionally structured crime novel. I could decide whether I wanted a country cottage or a town house, a gothic castle or a condo. Narrative was linear: People moved in at the start of a book, and the survivors arranged themselves photogenically at the end.

But pretty soon I began to realize that art is harder, not easier, than life; that having total control is no soft option; that being the Mighty Oz requires a hell of a lot of huffing and puffing from that small man behind the curtain. With control over your house—your plot—you can knock down walls as well as open doors and build extensions if you find you're short of space. Like Faustus, you'll find that your dominion can stretch as far as the mind of man.

Now I realize that all I'm doing here is telling you what it's like, not how to do it. To be honest, I feel that to give practical advice, I really should have written this article years ago, before I learned just how complicated it all was. If you yourself have reached that happy stage at which it all seems pretty simple, then don't let me discourage you. It may be that you are one of the really lucky ones who can construct a flow chart on paper or in your computer that will keep your plot straight as a ploughman's furrow. If you have this gift, treasure it, refine it; don't distract yourself with the wildflowers growing at the edge of the field.

But if once you start writing a story you never stop thinking about it no matter what you're doing, not even after you've finished it; and if your idea of making notes is to scribble things in margins, on the backs of envelopes, under your watch strap—then you need more than a flow chart to plot your story. If you're happy to spend half an hour tracking the right word through a thesaurus or dictionary and another half hour tracking all the other lovely words you chance upon; if you can read the hundred pages you've labored over for a week and accept what your sinking heart tells you and go back to the beginning and write them all again—then you, too, are tempted by the freedom in plotting I've been talking about. If you feel that in holding a mirror up to life, fiction may have to select but must never simplify; if you think a typewriter and a stack of paper are the best company in the world—then here for you alone are the few crumbs of anything resembling practical advice I can give:

- The simpler the plot, the subtler the plotting.
- Girl meets boy is not the same as boy meets girl.
- The three touchstones of plotting are pace, point of view, and continuity.

Pace doesn't mean speed; it means the *right* speed. Diagnosis and cure are simple. If you've reached where you want to be in your story too quickly, ask yourself what you've left out. If you've come to a certain point too slowly, ask yourself what kept you so long. When Charlotte Brontë wrote, "Reader, I married him," in *Jane Eyre,* it was enough. But if Herman Melville had written, "Reader, it killed him," when Captain Ahab finally confronts Moby Dick, he would have left readers dissatisfied. Always try the most direct route first. If it works, it works, and the 50 pages of explication you'd planned are superfluous. On the other hand, because I generally find I need to know far more about my characters and their context than my readers do, I spend a great deal of revision time paring away unnecessary detail.

Point of view is obviously of prime importance in plotting. If you go for the single eye (or I), then you limit your options in a way that can either be attractively simple or simply frustrating. If you want to let the reader know what's going on in the bathroom, you can't just tell it; you've got to put your I's eye to the keyhole, which is only a partial *view,* or have another character describe what's happening, which is a partial *version.* But if you go for godlike ubiquity in your viewpoint, then you give yourself a much greater problem of selection. This must be related to pace: Are you going at a gallop or taking a stroll? But it also relates to tone. The temptation of first-person narrative is to take on the tone of a smart-mouth, as with the traditional hard-boiled P.I., for example. The tone taken with the omniscient narrator can be one of patronizing preachiness. Some Victorian writers were particularly prone to having an uplifting chat with their readers. In writing my novel, *Pictures of Perfection,* I was faced with the problem of how best to introduce information about the past: flashback? straight history? character reminiscence? I opted for excerpts from a history of the local parish written by a former vicar. This device allowed me not only to give information, but also to make the kind of general observations I wanted to make without (I hope) sounding pompously *ex cathedra.* Throughout the book, in fact, I confronted the same problem. What happened in the fairly distant past was essential to an understanding of what was going on in the present, and I indulged in many experiments before I settled on the version that was finally published. All the versions were, of course, subject to the tests of pace and point of view. Some leeway and difference of opinion may be permissible here, but the last of my three touchstones—continuity—permits no compromise.

Put simply, no matter how well paced your plotting is or how clever you are with your point of view, without continuity, the overall effect is a jerky and disjointed novel. By continuity I do not mean making

221

sure your hero's shirt doesn't change color between scenes. Instead, continuity means wholeness, "hanging togetherness," integrity. I enjoy the interweaving of complex plots, I love tying and untying knots, but I'm always aware that one false move could result in a messy tangle rather than a pleasing pattern.

Plotting is not the story you want to tell, it is finding the best way of telling that story. And if, as you write, the reference books and scribbled notes to yourself and last month's mail pile up around you, then you are probably capable of enduring the uncertainties, mysteries, and doubts necessary to tell that story, without any irritable reaching after fact and reason (that quality Keats called *negative capability*). You will be able to because you are confident your unconsciousness or intuition will show you the way. If you're my kind of plotter, then the best advice I can give you is, don't let anything go till you feel it's right.

>> 47

SERIES CHARACTERS: LOVE 'EM OR LEAVE 'EM

BY ELIZABETH PETERS

CONAN DOYLE LEARNED TO LOATHE HOLMES SO INTENSELY, HE TRIED to murder him. At the opposite end of the spectrum are such writers as Dorothy Sayers, whose affection for Lord Peter Wimsey has prompted a certain amount of rude speculation. What is it about series characters? Is there a happy medium between loving and loathing them? Do the advantage of series characters outweigh the disadvantages? Should you, if you haven't done so already, consider starting a series?

In addition to the non-series Barbara Michaels novels, I write three different series, featuring Jacqueline Kirby, librarian; Vicky Bliss, art historian; and the notorious Amelia Peabody, Victorian gentlewoman Egyptologist.

None of the novels in which these three characters first appeared was intended to be the beginning of a series. The reason the series developed is simple and crass: There was a demand. I don't know why publishers suddenly decided that series characters were "in." They had always been popular, as witness Holmes, Poirot, Wimsey, et al., but it was not until ten or fifteen years ago that interest resurfaced. Now, many mystery writers have a series character, and those who do not are being pressured to create one.

The demand of the market is important. If publishers aren't buying a particular type of book, there is not much point in writing it, except for your own satisfaction. However, it is a big mistake to write only for the market, and a bigger mistake to do something you detest simply for the sake of sales.

There are certain disadvantages to a series. It does limit the author to some extent; a given plot may not be suitable for your character.

Another disadvantage is that you have to reintroduce the character in every book, and it requires some skill to tell a new reader what he needs to know without boring those who have read earlier books and without slowing the action. Publishers want series, but they also insist that each book stand on its own. This may not be literally oxymoronic, but it's darned hard to do.

However, this last problem is simply one of craftsmanship, and I find that the advantages of a series character far outweigh the disadvantages. Over the space of several books, you can develop the character far more richly and convincingly than is possible in one book, and I believe character has become increasingly important in the mystery novel. Readers are no longer satisfied with stereotypical robots—the Young Lovers, the Detective, the Sinister Lawyer, and so on. The most successful writers of the New Golden Age have succeeded in large part, not so much because of the ingenuity of their plots, but because readers like their characters and want to know more about them.

And, in my opinion, the author should feel the same way about the characters. If, as you hope, the series is a success, you are going to live with these characters for a long time. If you don't like them, they will get on your nerves, and you will either loathe them or become horribly bored by them. (Readers are less likely to become bored than you are. If they do lose interest in your characters, you will know about it; they will stop buying the books.) But there's no reason for you to take on a task you despise when, with a few relatively simple tricks, you can learn to enjoy your characters and look forward to the next visit with them. After writing seven books in the Amelia Peabody series, I am finding her and her family more fascinating every time around.

The most important thing is to begin by creating realistic characters. This may sound paradoxical when applied to Amelia, but in fact she is far less of a caricature than some readers believe. I had read an enormous number of contemporary novels, biographies, social histories, and travel books before I began writing the series, and there are many real-life parallels to Amelia's career, opinions, and behavior, as well as those of her eccentric husband, Emerson. Even Ramses, their catastrophically precocious son, is based to some extent on actual Victorian children, and, to an even greater extent, on normal boys of all eras who exhibit similar tendencies.

If the protagonists of the novel are properly conceived, they will behave consistently and comprehensibly. Of course this requirement is true of character development in general, but it is particularly important with series characters, whom the reader comes to know well. One useful result of consistently drawn characters is that you will find their personalities often determine the way the plot is going to develop. By now I am so familiar with the behavioral patterns of the Emersons that I have only to set up a situation and describe how they will inevitably react.

Just because a character is consistent, however, doesn't mean his behavior should always be predictable. In fact, seemingly irrational behavior makes a character more realistic; real people don't always behave sensibly either. Yet, if we examine the true motives that govern their behavior, we find it is not inconsistent, that we ought to have anticipated it. It is the author's task to establish this. The reaction you want from a reader is a shock of surprise, followed immediately by a shock of recognition: "Oh, yes, of course. I ought to have realized . . ." that despite her constant criticism of her son, Amelia would kill to protect him; that though Emerson complains about his wife's recklessness, he is secretly amused by and appreciative of her courage; that while Ramses sounds like a pompous little snob, he is as insecure as are most young children.

The best way of establishing character is through actions rather than words. This is particularly true if you are writing in the first person. Amelia describes herself as hard-headed and unsentimental, but it should be apparent by page ten of the first book in the series that she is a soft touch who acts on impulse, and then has to scramble desperately to find logical reasons for her actions.

But the smartest thing I did with the Amelia series wasn't done deliberately; it was pure serendipity, or luck, or as I would like to believe, "a writer's instinct."

Crocodile on the Sandbank, the first book in the series, ended like any conventional romantic mystery novel, with Amelia happily married to the hero. This should have been the end of the story; conventional literary wisdom maintains that the protagonist of a series should remain single and therefore open to further adventures, amatory and otherwise. But when I decided to resurrect Amelia, I had to resurrect Emerson as well. I mean, there he was. Worse—he and I had got

225

Amelia pregnant. Emerson may have done it on purpose, but I certainly didn't. The demands of a husband interfere considerably with a heroine's activities as a detective; the demands of a baby are almost impossible to dismiss.

If I had intended *Crocodile* to be the first in a series, I wouldn't have been as specific about dates. Not only did Amelia inform the reader of her age (curse her!), but historical events mentioned in the book tied it to a particular year. As the series continued, there was no way I could get around this, or fudge the date of Ramses' birth, or keep him and his parents from aging a year every twelve months.

I decided to regard these developments not as limitations but as challenges. Could a spouse and a baby be advantages to a heroine, instead of the reverse?

There are two ways of dealing with a detective's spouse. The first and perhaps most common method is to make the spouse a minor character (babies are particularly useful in keeping wives in the background). I chose the second alternative: husband and wife operating as equal, active partners in a genuine team. Note that word *equal.* I wanted my readers to feel that it would be inconceivable for either Amelia or Emerson to function independently of the other.

Insofar as the romantic element was concerned. . . . Well, that was another challenge. I couldn't see any reason husband and wife shouldn't be enthusiastic lovers as well as affectionate, supportive mates, but in order to maintain the "sexual tension" editors are always demanding, the marriage had to be questioned, even threatened, periodically. Rivals who crop up from time to time keep both Amelia and Emerson on their toes (so to speak). In the Amelia novel *The Snake, the Crocodile and the Dog,* I resorted to an even more drastic expedient, which resulted in a severe, potentially destructive strain on their relationship. However, the real conflict stems from the personalities of the major characters themselves. Amelia's air of smug self-confidence conceals a painful inferiority complex, particularly with regard to her personal appearance. She'll always be jealous of more beautiful women, and Emerson will never stop wondering what *really* happened when his wife was in the clutches of her devoted admirer the Master Criminal. Their marriage will never be boring and neither of them will ever take the other for granted.

The birth of Ramses presented even greater difficulties, and more provocative possibilities. In the second book of the series, I hadn't quite come to grips with the difficulties, so I did what most writers do with inconvenient babies: I left Ramses at home and allowed his parents to continue their activities without him. By the third book, *The Mummy Case,* I was ready to cope not only with Ramses, but with the tripartite relationship.

During this novel, Ramses developed into one of the most perniciously obnoxious children in all of mystery fiction—or so I have been told. I'm rather fond of the poor little devil myself, and I do not respond politely to readers who want me to drown him. However, by the fifth book I decided he was getting a little out of hand, so I copied a device by another writer, and introduced two children who were so awful they made Ramses look sympathetic by comparison. They also forced Amelia to reevaluate her feelings for her son. He becomes a full and active participant in his parents' adventures, supplying both comic relief and much-needed assistance in critical situations. His participation stems naturally and inevitably from his own character traits, which are the result not only of heredity but of upbringing; as he matures he will undoubtedly play a larger and quite different part. His relationship with his parents will change as well; a young adult can't (or shouldn't!) be treated like a child.

So the baby, who might have been a liability, is developing into an individual with considerable future potential. Ramses is about to enter adolescence, and I await this development with much interest.

The minor characters who populate a series are almost as important as the protagonists, and this, I think, is another way in which the New Golden Age mysteries differ from those of the first Golden Age. Instead of a single sidekick or bumbling foil from Scotland Yard, the Emersons have acquired a group of friends, enemies, and hangers-on who form a pool from which I can draw: Gargery, the cudgel-wielding butler; Kevin O'Connor, the brash young reporter; Abdullah, the loyal foreman; Evelyn, Amelia's sister-in-law; Nefret, the golden-haired beauty who has won Ramses' adolescent heart; and above all, Emerson's hated rival, the Master Criminal. The utility of a cast of supporting characters should be obvious. Like the major characters, they have changed and developed during the course of the books, and their occasional reappearances add to the reader's feeling that these are real people with decided personalities and distinctive foibles.

This is why I do not anticipate ever becoming bored with my series characters. Like real people, they change. Like real people, they are not always predictable. I have a rough idea of what is going to happen to them, but I could not emulate Agatha Christie and write the last book in the series now. I don't know what the Emersons are going to do until they do it—but when they do it, I am not really surprised. "Of course. I should have known. . . ."

From a purely practical viewpoint, there is one simple way to avoid being bored by your series characters: Don't confine yourself to a single series. Some writers can do this; I don't believe I could. The Barbara Michaels novels give me the opportunity to use plot ideas that don't fit any of the series characters, and the two other series I write as Elizabeth Peters allow me to employ themes and interests unsuited to Amelia and company.

To a lesser extent—probably because I have written less about them—Vicky and Jacqueline are also maturing and changing. Jacqueline has become a best-selling writer of romances, a development she regards with a distinctly jaundiced eye, and somewhere in her background there is a Mr. Kirby. Who is he and what happened to him? Some day I may find out.

As for Vicky, she's not getting any younger, and when I began *Night Train to Memphis,* I decided it was time for Vicky to sort out her feelings, not only for the dashing Sir John Smythe, but for her exasperating but engaging boss, Herr Direktor Schmidt. By the time I finished the book, I was a trifle surprised, and decidedly intrigued, to discover how Vicky, as well as John and Schmidt, have changed since they first appeared on the literary scene.

And that, dear Reader (to quote Amelia), is the real trick. Let your characters grow; allow them to mature and develop; put them into situations that will force them to exhibit hitherto unsuspected aspects of their personalities. The other day I was talking with a friend who inquired interestedly, "Is Vicky going to get pregnant in this book?" My reaction was instantaneous, spontaneous, and, I am afraid, typical of the generation in which I was raised. "Pregnant?" I squawked indignantly. "She isn't even married!"

I am fairly sure Vicky's reaction would be, if not identical, equally indignant. But one never knows. At least *I* never know, and that's why I like writing about my series characters.

If you don't like yours and can't make them into people whose company you enjoy, be brutal. No, not that brutal; I do not recommend killing off major characters, no matter how much you detest them. You can be sure some of your readers have become attached to them and will resent you for bumping them off. Just ignore them for a while. Shrug and smile politely when readers ask when you are going to return to Harry or Jennifer or whoever. Start another series, with characters who do appeal to you. You may find, after enough time has elapsed, that Harry and Jennifer aren't as repellent as you thought. If they still don't appeal to you, let them languish in the limbo of forgotten literary figures. The bottom line is simple: Enjoy your characters or leave them alone.

>>48

BUILDING CONFLICT IN THE HISTORICAL ROMANCE

BY PATRICIA WERNER

CONFLICT, SET IN A COLORFUL BACKGROUND, IS WHAT DRIVES THE historical romance. Here are some of the techniques for weaving threads of conflict into a complex tapestry that will appeal to readers.

Plotting opposites

History itself offers barriers an author can use to create obstacles between lovers. One popular technique is having the hero and heroine on opposite sides of two warring factions (such as the North and South during the Civil War or the British and the Colonists during the American Revolution).

Another possible choice could be to make the main characters members of feuding families. Or they might be from different social classes or ethnic backgrounds. By using incidents in the story to show the characters' personal goals, you can bring them into conflict with each other. Such incidents move the plot forward.

For example, a railroad baron may want to buy a widow's land to lay track through the mountains. But the widow wants to hold on to her land because it's her son's birthright, and she promised her father she would never sell it. Or perhaps the land offers her a chance to prove that she can be a successful rancher.

In this plot, the railroad baron and the widow have different ideas for proper use of the land. But if, in spite of this conflict, the baron and the widow are attracted to each other, you have the set-up for a valid historical romance plot. Your challenge as the author is to let those two characters work out their conflicts and acknowledge their love by the end of the book.

Motivation and purpose

Motivation provides the reason your characters take certain actions.

Although in life people sometimes seem to do things for no apparent reason, your characters must act *with* reason, and their actions must be consistent with their personalities. Plant these reasons, or motives, either in the thoughts of the character, or in dialogue in which the character confides hopes, dreams, and secrets to another character. This will reveal your characters' motives and show the reader how and why the hero's and heroine's purposes are truly in conflict.

For example, in my historical romance *The Falcon and the Sword,* set in the early barbarian kingdoms of what later became known as France, the heroine, Judith, has attached herself to her childhood friend, a princess who has just married the king of Neustria. (Neustria, Austrasia, and Burgundy were Frankish territories in 567 A.D.) Judith's purpose is to protect the newly married princess from an evil, jealous concubine. Thus Judith's friendship with the princess *motivates* her to keep watch over her friend.

The hero, Marcus, is an envoy from the kingdom of Austrasia and his political purpose is to serve *his* king. The two kings are warring brothers. Judith finds herself in a position to act as a spy for Marcus. It would have been easy to end the book there and have him take her back to Austrasia. But being people bound by the moral code of the Franks called for a blood feud. Hence, when the princess is murdered, Judith's moral code *motivates* her to avenge her friend's death, keeping her apart from Marcus, whose purpose is to wage a war for his king.

Your characters' motives must be believable, and to achieve this credibility, you must put yourself into your characters' thoughts and get to know them. Try to live the scene as you write it, so you will know which motives are logical for each character. Ask yourself, does this character have a reason for his or her actions? Don't write anything that seems vague to you, or it will certainly seem even vaguer to your readers.

Emotional conflicts

Let emotional conflicts provide an undercurrent for the larger historical issues. Emotions draw the reader into a story. The characters react emotionally to the need to meet the social or political challenges of the plot, and this advances the story.

Here is how I showed social conflicts arousing emotions in *Velvet Dreams*: The impoverished Duke of Sunderland goes to America to seek an American heiress to pay his bills. He doesn't intend to marry for love. Socialite Amanda Whitney wants to marry only for love, so from the start their actions are at cross-purposes. Amanda's mother threatens to kill herself if Amanda marries the ne'er-do-well American whom Amanda is secretly pledged to, thus putting her under emotional pressure.

But Amanda has misjudged her American suitor, who jilts her. Her anger at the Duke's overt desire to marry her for money and her desire to prove her mother wrong motivate her to rebel and turn to a French scholar for solace. She is in conflict with the Duke, with her mother, and with the societal values with which she was raised. All of these conflicts provide excitement, danger, and action, which hold the readers' interest.

One man, one woman

When your hero and heroine fall in love with each other, they must be free of all ties. The one woman-one man historical romance is standard for the genre, which has well-defined conventions when it comes to love—though both hero and heroine may have had previous relationships or even marriages. They must not, however, indulge in romantic dalliances with anyone else *while their relationship is developing,* especially not after they have gone to bed together. Timing here is the key to emotional entanglement.

In some circumstances, it is permissible for the heroine to become romantically and physically involved with another man before falling in love with or consummating her relationship with the hero. This adds to the original conflict and makes the reader turn the pages to find out which man will win. But this should always be very carefully done and well motivated, or it will offend readers.

In *The Falcon and the Sword,* Judith takes a barbarian lover for protection. Though she cares for him, according to the conventions of historical romance, he has to leave or die before she can form a relationship with Marcus. Her barbarian lover is killed in battle; Judith grieves; Marcus rescues her from the Saxons. Only then, after a slow, emotional build-up, does their love take root, and they finally consummate their relationship.

Setting

Setting can provide another wedge between characters. Perhaps the heroine is in a place she despises, but she has to be there to carry out her mission. Or the place represents something from her past that must be avenged or purged. Her resentment of the hero may stem from the fact that he is so much a part of that place that he could never think of leaving. Or perhaps he cannot leave because he has responsibilities there.

In a historical romance, the characters may be sent on journeys, thus separating the hero and heroine for several chapters. In a novel this long, there is room for adventures. It is a convention of this genre that when hero and heroine are apart, they should continue to think of one another.

Complications

Complicate the conflicts wherever possible. Carefully weave together the historical, romantic, and goal-oriented conflicts. Every step the heroine takes toward *her* goal should inadvertently antagonize the hero or frustrate *his* goal. This action and reaction will advance the plot, but at the same time, you must draw the hero and the heroine deeper and deeper into their relationship. In spite of all their conflicts, make them care about what will happen to the other person if their own goal is met.

Push your heroine into such a tight corner that she has few choices that would help to get her out. Use motives that make for difficult choices. And the result of each choice should throw her back into the path, or arms, of the hero.

Secrets

Give either the hero or heroine a secret: One can wear a disguise to obtain information or to hide something. Here the conflict stems from the fact that the disguised character must pretend to be another person, at the same time wishing deeply to reveal the truth.

In my novel, *Cimarron Seductress,* Roslyn Dwayne, an ex-outlaw named Cimarron Rose, decides to leave the outlaw life. She goes to live in Indian territory with distant relatives who know nothing of her past. There, she is attracted to Marshal Luke McBride. But she learns to her horror that he is looking for Cimarron Rose, a woman he believes can lead him to the Doolin gang, who accidently killed his sister in a shootout during a bank robbery at Southwest City.

Can Roslyn admit that she is Cimarron Rose? No. Because by this

233

point in the story, her uncle, who's lost his wife, has come to depend on her to take care of his sons, her cousins. If she tells the truth, she'll not only lose Luke but will also disappoint her new family. But she cannot live the lie forever. When an old crony of Doolin's shows up, saying that Doolin's been hurt, is nearby, and needs help, the old loyalty tears at her. The Doolin gang took her in when she was small—orphaned when her parents died in a train wreck. Bill Doolin taught her how to survive in a tough situation. Surely she owes him something, too.

Build the conflicts one on the other. You are not simply retelling a well-known historical event; you must entangle the central characters deeper and deeper into multiple plot conflicts. It must appear as if they cannot escape but of course they must. How does the author achieve this without jarring the reader or making one of the characters do such a sudden about-face that it appears ridiculous?

Make your characters undergo change. Plant the seed early on that the character actually wants to change, so that when it occurs, the change will be motivated. For example, Roslyn had already decided to become a law-abiding citizen *before* she met Marshal McBride. He had already decided to give up his badge and turn to ranching once the culprits were caught. So their resolution at the end seems convincing.

At the resolution of the story, self-revelation brings hero and heroine to accept their mutual love in spite of the difficult conflicts. Luke realizes that Roslyn really is no longer a woman on the wrong side of the law, that she acted as she did because of loyalty, not cowardice. He would want her to be no less loyal to him. Love conquers all? Yes, but it must do so in a believable and well-motivated way.

What about sex?

Make the passion sizzle while the conflicts grow. These two characters burn for each other, but they are in conflict with one another because of their opposing goals. Their inner conflict keeps them from acknowledging their love at first. Their passion for each other should be followed by denial, or a feeling of guilt, or anger. Sexual encounters as well as their arguments must ring true.

Most editors leave the number of love scenes and the degree of explicit sex up to the author. Historical romances are categorized by editors as sweet, spicy, or sensual. Sweet romances do not lack in sexual attraction that leads to passionate embraces; the characters may even go to bed together near the end of the novel—but the curtains are drawn.

Spicy romances take time out from plot developments and other adventures to present a few steamy scenes. Sensual romances have many explicit love scenes, but even so, they should be well integrated into the story line; each love scene—justified and well motivated—should intensify the conflict.

Length

Most historical romances run from 100,000 to 135,000 words. The novel must have a happy ending, otherwise it will be classified as a saga or mainstream historical novel. Your manuscript will be from 400 to 550 typewritten double-spaced pages, producing a book that will run from about 364 to 474 printed pages.

Do enough research to make the setting and story come alive in your mind, and to write a salable book, keep the conflict going till THE END.

>> 49

WHY HORROR?

BY GRAHAM MASTERTON

FEW PEOPLE UNDERSTAND THAT WRITERS ARE WRITING ALL THE time.

To think that a writer is writing only when he or she is actually hammering a keyboard is like believing that a police officer's job is "arresting people."

Even while they're not sitting down at the word processor, writers are writing in their heads. Inventing stories. Playing with words. Thinking up jokes and riddles and metaphors and similes. These days, I write both historical sagas and horror novels. Most people relish historical sagas, but I'm often asked, "Why do people like horror?"

I think they like horror novels because they depict ordinary people dealing with extraordinary threats. They like to imagine, what would *I* do if a dark shadow with glowing red eyes appeared in my bedroom at night? What would *I* do if I heard a sinister scratching inside the walls of my house? What would *I* do if my husband's head turned around 360 degrees?

I've found my inspiration for horror stories in legends from ancient cultures, and my research into how these demons came to be created by ordinary men and women is fascinating. Each of them represents a very real fear that people once felt, and often still do.

There are beguiling men who turn into evil demons. There are monsters that suck your breath when you're asleep. There are gremlins that steal children. There are horrible gorgons that make you go blind just to look at them, and vampires that drain all of the energy out of you. There are zombies who come back from the dead and torment you.

My favorite Scottish demons were the glaistigs, hideous hags who were supposed to be the ghosts of women haunting their former homes.

They were frequently accompanied by a child who was called "the little plug" or "the whimperer." If you didn't leave out a bowl of milk for the glaistigs, they would suck your cows dry or drain their blood. Sometimes a glaistig would carry her little whimperer into the house, and bathe it in the blood of the youngest infant in the house, and the victim would be found dead and white in the morning.

Now, this is a legend, but you can understand what genuine fears it expresses. A woman's fear of other women intruding into her home, as in the film, *Fatal Attraction*; a man's fear of losing his livelihood; parents' fear of losing their children to malevolent and inexplicable illnesses, such as crib death. What I do is take these ancient demons, which are vivid and expressive manifestations of basic and genuine fears, and write about them in an up-to-date setting, with modern characters.

The very first horror novel I wrote was called *The Manitou*. A manitou is a Native American demon, and in this novel a 300-year-old medicine man was reborn in the present day to take his revenge on the white man. I was inspired to write that by *The Buffalo Bill Annual, 1956*.

Since then I have written books based on Mexican demons, Balinese demons, French demons and Biblical demons, two dozen in all, and I'm working on another one about the Glasgow woman who makes a pact with Satan so that her house disappears every time the rent collector calls.

I started writing horror novels at school, when I was 11. I used to read them to my friends during recess. Reading your work out loud is always invaluable training. When I met one of my old school friends only recently, he said, "I'll never forget the story you wrote about the woman with no head who kept singing 'Tiptoe Through the Tulips.' It gave me nine years of sleepless nights, and I still can't have tulips in the house."

Horror books seem to sell well all over the world, with some notable exceptions, like Germany. The French love horror, and the Poles adore it. In France, *Le Figaro* called me "Le Roi du Mal," the King of Evil. I was the first Western horror novelist to be published in Romania, home of Dracula. I received a letter from a reader this week saying, "I have to write to congratulate you on a wonderful book, rich with ideas and shining with great metaphors. Also very good printing, and excellent paper, which is appreciated here because of bathroom tissue shortage."

How extreme can you be when you write horror? As extreme, I think, as your talent and your taste permit, although gruesomeness is no substitute for skillful writing. I had several complaints about a scene in my book *Picture of Evil,* in which the hero kills two young girls with a poker. People protested my graphic description of blood spattering everywhere. In fact, I never once mentioned blood. All I said was, "He clubbed them to death like two baby seals." The reader's imagination was left to do the rest.

It is catching the mood and feel of a moment that makes your writing come to life. Most of the time you can dispense with whole realms of description if you catch one vivid image; catching those images requires thought and research. When I write historical novels, I frequently rent period costumes which my wife and I try on so I can better understand how my characters would have moved and behaved when wearing them. How do you rush to meet your lover when wearing a hobble skirt? How do you sit down with a bustle?

We also prepare food and drink from old recipes, using cookbooks by Fannie Farmer, Mrs. Beeton, and Escoffier. One of the least successful period drinks we prepared was the King's Death, drunk by King Alfonso of Spain in the Men's Bar of the Paris Ritz. The King's Death is made with wild strawberries marinated in Napoleon brandy, then topped up with half a bottle of champagne—each! We served it to some dinner party guests, and they became incoherent and had to go home.

Whether you're writing history or horror, thrillers or love stories, the most important technique is to live inside the book instead of viewing it from the outside. Your word processor or typewriter is nothing more than a key that opens the door to another world. When I'm writing, I step into that world, so that it surrounds me. So many writers as they write look only forward at the page, or screen, forgetting what's all around them.

Think of the rain on the side of your face and the wind against your back. Think of what you can hear in the distance. Think of the fragrances you can smell. Most of all, *be* all your characters: Act out their lives, act out their movements and their facial expressions, and speak their dialogue out loud. Get up from your keyboard sometimes, and do what you've imagined; then sit down and write it. The Disney artist Ward Kimball used to draw Donald Duck by making faces in the mirror. You can do the same when you're writing about the way your characters act and react.

Your best research is watching real live people living out their real lives. Watch every gesture, every nuance, listen to people's conversations and accents. Try to propel your story along at the pace that *you* would like to read it. Avoid showing off in your writing; all that does is slow down your story and break the spell you have been working so hard to conjure up. How many times has your suspension of disbelief been broken by ridiculous similes, like "her bosoms swelled like two panfuls of overboiling milk."

Two similes that really caught my attention and which I later used in novels were an old Afrikaner's description of lions roaring "like coal being delivered," and the hideous description by an Australian prisoner of war of two of his fellow prisoners being beheaded: "the blood spurted out of their necks like red walking-sticks."

To my mind, the greatest achievement in writing is to create a vivid, spectacular novel without readers being aware that they are reading at all. My ideal novel would be one that readers put down, and discover that they're still in it, that it's actually come to life.

The other day I was reading *Secrets of the Great Chefs of China,* and apart from the eel recipe, where you throw live eels into boiling water and have to clamp the lid down quickly to stop them from jumping out of the pot, the most memorable advice the book gave was, "A great chef prepares his food so that it is ready for the mouths of his guests; it is both a courtesy and a measure of his professionalism." That goes for writing, too.

>> 50

IT'S NO MYSTERY

BY CAROLYN G. HART

WHAT CAN MAKE *YOUR* MYSTERY AN EDITOR'S CHOICE? THE ANSWER is no mystery—or it shouldn't be.

Superb books grab the editor in the very first paragraphs, the very first lines.

Superb books are as individual and as idiosyncratic as crusty Aunt Edith or affable Cousin Charles.

So these, in my view, are the two essential elements for a successful mystery novel:

Action.

Voice.

Action is creating the story as the reader watches.

Voice is the unmistakable reflection of the author's personality.

If your novel successfully combines action and voice, editors will vie to publish you.

I've always loved beginning novels with action, and in my Death on Demand mystery series, I use a technique I adore: the vignette.

A vignette is a small, swift cameo of a scene, featuring a character who is important to the novel in an act that relates to the theme of the novel.

Here are the opening sentences of the vignettes in the fourth book in the series, *Honeymoon with Murder:*

Vignette One: Jesse Penrick didn't miss much on his solitary nocturnal rambles. Lights at an odd hour. A visitor never before seen. An unfamiliar car.

Vignette Two: Lucinda Burrows darted through the crowd, her brown alligator heels clicking excitedly against the concrete. She'd done just as instructed, and the whole operation had gone without a hitch.

Vignette Three: The perfect crime. Who said it couldn't be done?

Vignette Four: Ingrid Jones had no idea she was being observed, she and the whole expanse of Nightingale Court.

What is accomplished? The reader is immediately plunged into the action. The reader knows things are happening, and the reader is made a part of the action.

Perhaps the single most enervating and deadly mistake a beginning writer makes is in trying to tell the reader what is happening.

Never *tell* a reader anything.

Let the reader become a part of the scene.

Look at it this way: People who read are smart or they wouldn't read. They've been going to films all their lives. When the movie opens with a chase scene, big guys with guns chasing Michael Douglas down an alley, the viewers don't know what's going on, but they are quite willing to find out *as the story unfolds.*

Let your story unfold.

For example, in *The Christie Caper,* my protagonist Annie Laurance, owner of the Death on Demand mystery bookstore, is planning a celebration of the centennial of the birth of Agatha Christie. What could be more boring than beginning a book with that information? For example, Annie might be talking on the telephone with her mother-in-law, Laurel, and she could tell Laurel, "I'm going to have a convention here on the island to celebrate the centennial, etc., etc."

That is telling the reader. Instead here is the beginning of the opening chapter:

Annie counted the magnums of champagne. Four. Five. Six. Surely that would be enough. She whirled on her heel and dashed out of the storeroom.

I don't *tell* the reader anything. The reader is there as Annie frantically readies the bookstore for an evening cocktail party for the convention attendees.

Action. Use it. Enjoy it. Live that scene, and your reader will live it, too.

There is always a way to provide information through action. When I received the editorial letter on *Deadly Valentine,* my editor suggested that readers needed to know more about the people who would be the focus at the Valentine Ball *before* the Ball began.

I created a scene before the party, when Annie and her mother-in-law, Laurel, walk down to the pier and look at the houses around Scarlet King lagoon, where Annie and Max live in their new house. If they'd walked down to the pier and Annie had simply described the houses and their occupants, it would have been what writing teachers call "tea party conversation," that is, the contrived exchange of information in a scene that doesn't move the story. Instead, there is action because of a subtle struggling between Laurel and Annie, Laurel intent upon gaining information, Annie reluctant to part with it. What makes it credible is that Annie is certain Laurel has some ulterior motive in asking for this information, and, as the reader discovers later, indeed Laurel did. This moves the story along and, at the same time, it satisfies the author's objective of introducing to the reader some of the people who will be at the Valentine Ball. Often, the author has several objectives in a scene in addition to the objectives of the characters. The characters' objectives in this scene are twofold: Annie wants to find out what her madcap mother-in-law is up to, and Laurel is quite determined to learn all about the neighbors.

Action can be mental. In *Design for Murder,* I used a vignette to give readers a clear picture of Corinne Prichard Webster's character:

. . . Her eyes narrowed, and she no longer looked at her reflection so she didn't see the transformation. At one instant, the mirrored face was soft and beguiling, almost as beautiful with its classic bones, silver-blonde hair, and Mediterranean blue eyes as on her wedding day at nineteen almost forty years before. Then, as Corinne Prichard Webster thought about her niece, Gail, throwing herself at a totally unsuitable man, the face hardened and looked all of its fifty-nine years, the eyes cold and hard, the mouth, thin, determined, and cruel.

In *A Little Class on Murder,* Annie is teaching a course at a college in Chastain on the Three Great Ladies of the Mystery: Agatha Christie, Dorothy L. Sayers, and Mary Roberts Rinehart. This is Annie's first teaching venture, and she's very self-conscious and certainly doesn't want anyone in the class whom she knows. I decided (unknown to Annie, of course) to enroll in the class Annie's ditzy mother-in-law, Laurel, her most opinionated customer, Henny, and the curmudgeon of Chastain, Miss Dora.

The day arrives for Annie's first class:

She was skimming her lecture notes when she stiffened, her senses assaulted.
Scent.
Sound.

242

Sight.

The scent came first. The unmistakable fragrance of lilac, clear and sharp and sweet.

Annie's hands tightened in a death grip on the sides of the lectern. Surely it couldn't—

It could.

Laurel swept through the doorway, beaming, of course. . . .

In short order, Miss Dora and Henny also arrive.

. . . The back of her (Annie's) neck prickled. That thump behind her!

It took every vestige of her will to turn her head to face the door to the hallway.

Thump. Thump. Thump.

Quick, purposeful, decisive thumps.

The ebony cane with its black rubber tip poked around the corner, followed by its mistress.

The tiny old lady (Miss Dora) stood motionless in the doorway. . . .

And then . . .

Oh God.

The sight framed in the doorway was almost too much for her to accept. Laurel was bad enough. Miss Dora would cast a pall on the Addams family tea party.

But this—

It wasn't as though she didn't recognize the costume: a large gray flannel skirt with a droopy hem, a full blouse with a lacy panel down the front, a shapeless rust-colored cardigan, lisle stockings, extremely sensible brown shoes, and hair bobbing in springy sausage-curl rolls.

"Henny," she moaned.

And poor Annie is facing her first class.

The reader saw it happen.

Action is yours for the asking. Pretend you're training a camera on your characters. Watch the scene unfold *with* your readers.

And with action, you will discover voice.

How you see the world, how you create scenes, will be a product of your personality, your experiences, and your willingness to dare.

Voice is perhaps the easiest element to recognize in successful fiction and, for uncertain writers, the most difficult to attain.

What is voice? It is the quality of writing that makes a passage instantly identifiable. If you handed me five unidentified pages written by Nancy Pickard, Sara Paretsky, Dorothy Cannell, and Joan Hess, I would have no difficulty at all in knowing who wrote what. Because each author's voice is so distinctive, so unmistakable.

This is perhaps the most elusive concept in writing. Maybe a few don'ts will make it clearer.

If you look at the bestseller lists, then write a book and send it to an agent or editor, saying this is just like Robert B. Parker or Mary Higgins Clark, that book won't sell.

Don't try to be another Parker or Clark. Don't imitate. Study, observe, absorb, but when you write, write it your way. You must write a book that absolutely no one in the world could have written except you. Each human being is unique. The passions and prejudices, the obsessions and revulsions that drive each person are different. Take advantage of this. Listen to your heart. Then you will have a voice.

You must write a book that matters enormously to you, not a Native American mystery because Tony Hillerman is hot, or a cat mystery because Lillian Jackson Braun is hot, or a serial killer because Thomas Harris is hot.

This isn't to say you can't set a book in New Mexico. Walter Satterthwaite and Judith Van Gieson are using that locale, but their books are succeeding because they are unmistakably their own, not Hillerman spinoffs.

If I look deeply into the books I have written, I realize that paramount to me is the exercise of power in relationships. This is my obsession, the element that fuels my books. I want everyone to be accountable for the way they treat others, so that is my focus.

And the way I write?

I love language. The sound of words matters to me. Is my fiction distinctive enough for readers to mark the words as mine? I can't answer that. That is for readers to say. But I know there are passages in what I have written that reflect the essence of my soul.

That is the price a writer pays to achieve voice. The writer must be willing to reveal what matters most of all to him.

If I were to select a passage that perhaps says the most about me, it would be from my novel, *Dead Man's Island*. This is the first novel in a new series featuring a retired newspaperwoman, Henrietta O'Dwyer Collins, as the protagonist. She's known as Henri O, a nickname given to her by her late husband, Richard, because he said she provided more surprises in a single day than O. Henry ever put in a short story.

Dead Man's Island is the story of a woman who responds to a call for help from a voice out of her past. She travels to a private island where murder and a hurricane threaten the survival of the stranded guests.

Toward the close of *Dead Man's Island,* Henri O awaits the return of the storm:

As I stood, fatigue washed over me. It would be so easy to drop down beside Valerie and close my eyes, let the warmth of the sunlight touch me with fingers of life and let my mind drift, taking memories and thoughts as they came.

But anger flickered beneath the exhaustion.

I suppose I've always been angry. That's what drives most writers, the hot steady consuming flame of anger against injustice and dishonesty and exploitation, against sham and artifice and greed, against arrogance and brutality and deceitfulness, against betrayal and indifference and cruelty.

I would not give up.

This passage is what Henri O is all about.

Should you as a reader care, this passage also tells you everything you'd ever need to know about me, the author. So when you write a book that offers your heart and mind and soul to readers, it will have voice.

Your voice.

>> 51

BEFORE YOU WRITE YOUR HISTORICAL NOVEL

BY THOMAS FLEMING

THERE IS NO SUBSTITUTE FOR RESEARCH WHEN A WRITER TACKLES A historical novel. The first and most important reason is the commitment every writer, both in fiction and nonfiction, has to the truth. Another reason, seldom grasped by beginning writers, is how much impact research can have on a novel's development.

In the course of publishing 17 novels, most of them in that category amorphously described as historical (I prefer to call them novels of the historical imagination), I have found that research can deepen an imaginary character, transform a key scene, and even alter a novel's plot.

In my novel *Loyalties,* about an American who becomes involved in the German resistance to Hitler, I have a scene in which the main American character, Jonathan Talbot, must rescue from Nazi hands the German woman, Berthe von Hoffmann, who is trying to make contact with the Americans on behalf of the resistance. The encounter takes place in the deserted palace of the Alhambra, in Granada, Spain. The American, disguised as a German businessman, must choose a moment to murder the Nazi SS Oberfuhrer, who is close to forcing Berthe to reveal the identity of the leaders of the resistance.

I knew little about the Alhambra Palace when I started the book. After considerable research, I acquired a lot more knowledge, but something remained missing in my sense of the appropriate place to commit the murder. I went back and did more research. I discovered that there was a palace within the palace, an ugly monstrosity built by one of the Spanish kings after the Moors fled. On the wall of one of the central rooms was an immense painting depicting the expulsion of the Jews from Spain in 1492. At its center was a tragic column of refugees winding over the horizon.

Here was the detail I wanted. As the SS Oberfuhrer gazes up at the painting and smugly tells Talbot he plans to persuade General Franco to let him bring it back to Berlin and hang it in the Reichchancellery, Talbot whips a silk cord around his throat and begins strangling him. That painting transformed more or less ordinary hugger-mugger into a symbolic scene of great power.

In researching my previous novel, *Over There,* I discovered on a dusty shelf in the stacks of the Yale Library about forty memoirs of women who had gone to France during World War I. No one had looked at these volumes for fifty years. In many, the pages were still uncut.

By the time I finished devouring these books, I had completely re-plotted the novel. Instead of a drama about an eccentric general and the men in his division, I created one of my best women characters, Polly Warden, a feminist who, like most of these women, goes to France to prove that a woman can face the horrors of the western front as courageously as a man.

In one of those Yale memoirs, I discovered an entire scene describing the author's arrival at a French hospital just behind the front lines in the middle of the night. Without an iota of training as a nurse, she found herself giving tetanus injections, bandaging desperately wounded men. I transplanted that scene into Polly's story, making it her defining moment in France.

Historical novel research is not something "extra"—a lot of facts that embroider or support the central imaginary story, sort of the way a frame surrounds a painting. In a good novel, the imagination blends the imaginary and the factual into the very warp and woof of the story. They become a single element—the narrative flowing through the landscape of the past.

A novelist does not look for the same sort of facts that historians need to buttress claims of authenticity or arguments. Historians are seldom interested in personal emotion. For a novelist, that is the essence of his search. For my novel, *The Spoils of War,* I spent months researching the Republican theft of the presidency in 1876. I acquired enough information about this famous scandal to write a good history book—or at least a solid article—on it. But I did not find what I wanted until I uncovered the astonishing fact that the managing editor of *The New York Times,* then the Republican Party's flagship paper, was the man who orchestrated the plot. The same paper that had won the moral admiration of the world for uncovering the machinations of Boss Tweed and his corrupt Tammany henchmen in New York!

For the first time, I was able to portray my main character, Jonathan Stapleton, who carried some of the money south to bribe electors in key southern states to switch their votes, as a man who saw himself performing a moral mission. He was preventing the Democratic Party—the party of secession and rebellion, responsible, in his (and the managing editor's) mind, for the million deaths of the Civil War—from regaining the presidency. That discovery enabled me to give that part of the book a spiritual depth that led directly to the tragic development of the next phase of the story: the breakup of Jonathan Stapleton's marriage because his southern-born wife could not accept his reason for participating in the scandal.

As a writer gets into a historical novel, he or she has to keep feeding the imagination fresh facts. I favor doing about sixty percent of the research at the start and then completing the rest as the ongoing narrative tells you what you need. Often small details can play a tremendous part in a later scene. In my research for *Time and Tide,* my novel set in the Pacific during World War II, I came across an incident in which American sailors discovered a huge Japanese torpedo washed up on Guadalcanal. It was far superior to any torpedo then in use in the U.S. Navy.

I fed this fact into my narrative. My main character, Captain Arthur McKay, commander of the imaginary ship that sails through the book—the *USS Jefferson City*—reports the discovery of the torpedo to his superiors. But the Navy bureaucracy ignores him, and in the next battle, a flotilla of Japanese destroyers wreaks havoc on the American fleet, firing these torpedoes from long range. McKay's disillusion with the Navy deepens, and the reader watches him plunge into a drinking bout that almost wrecks his career.

How do you do such research? Often, by rummaging around in diaries or oral histories of the participants in the history you are writing about. Research for a novel covers some of the same ground as research for nonfiction—you need to know the big picture—but in the novel the focus is on what fits into your smaller picture, on things that intensify the emotional dimensions of your story.

If your novel involves the politics and social life of a period, like my book, *The Spoils of War,* which is set in New York in the decades after the Civil War, newspapers of the day provide another source of background information. These are available on microfilm in many big public libraries, or may be borrowed through interlibrary loan.

I could not have written *Over There* without the 1918–19 issues of the *Paris Herald,* which contained fascinating, day-by-day coverage of Americans in Paris and at the front during World War I. Reading the reactions of people who were in Paris when the Germans were shelling the city by day and bombing it by night was like a trip in a nightmare time machine.

Biographies or memoirs of minor figures, generals of the second rank, diplomats, and politicians provide another valuable source of material for historical fiction. These are often full of the minutiae you need to bring scenes to life. You can often transplant one of these characters to your story under another name, bolstering your novel's authenticity.

Even better are interviews with some of the people involved in the events you use in your novel, if you can locate them. I spent a fascinating weekend with the late General Albert Wedemeyer (who was 91 at the time) discussing the leak of Rainbow Five, the top-secret U.S. plans for World War II. On December 4, 1941, this story created blazing headlines in papers across the country. Wedemeyer was suspected of leaking the plans and for a while was threatened with a firing squad. I attributed much of this experience to my novel's main character, Jonathan Talbot.

For *The Officers' Wives,* I interviewed at length two Army wives who had followed their husbands through Korea and Vietnam, which gave me priceless insights into a woman's reaction to the turmoil these wars created in the Army. Neither woman resembled even faintly the three women I later created as main characters in the novel. That is not the way the historical imagination works. It does not literally copy, but transforms the research facts as required by the plot into the blend of imagination and history that the writer is creating in the novel.

Sometimes, as you work on a novel, you find the research-writing process reversing itself: Instead of research helping you create a character, the character inspires you to do more research, which often adds a whole new dimension to your book.

The historical novelist's ultimate challenge is to discover a new interpretation of a major aspect of the past. Here the novelist is brushing shoulders with the historians, and he must be very very sure of the available facts. At the same time, he is more free to deal in probabilities. In *The Spoils of War*, I decided from my research that the battleship *Maine*, which blew up in Havana harbor in 1898, was almost certainly not sunk by the Spanish, as the history books long told us. Nor did its magazines explode accidentally, as recent historians have suggested, influenced by a study of the event written by Admiral Hyman Rickover. Far more probably, the ship was sunk by the Cuban revolutionaries, who despised the Americans and had no compunction about manipulating them into the war on their side.

To bolster this conclusion, I hired an expert on naval architecture, who wrote me a devastating critique of Rickover's book. My expert told me that after reading the Admiral's so-called evidence, he was convinced that the *Maine* had been sunk by a mine. With this reassurance, I made the destruction of the *Maine* by the Cuban revolutionaries part of the final scenes of *The Spoils of War*.

In *Loyalties,* I encountered an even more momentous reinterpretation. I started the book with the assumption that Franklin D. Roosevelt never made a major mistake during World War II. As I dug deeper into the unexplored world of wartime Washington, I slowly began to perceive a very different president, a fatally ill, even dying man who nursed a pathological hatred of all things German, to the point of refusing to negotiate with the decent Germans who were trying to overthrow Hitler. I spent six months confirming this interpretation from dozens of sources, eventually writing a 50-page essay with over 100 footnotes. I showed this to several historian friends before including this characterization of Roosevelt in the novel.

These experiences have taught me that a historical novelist should take nothing for granted in the so-called history of even the recent past. Every writer should approach his story with the skepticism of the reporter, looking for the truth about men and measures, about events great and small, in the maze of yesterday. At the same time, historical novelists must never forget that they are storytellers, struggling to shape a narrative into the novel's demands as art.

>> 52

SCIENCE IN SCIENCE FICTION: MAKING IT WORK

BY JOAN SLONCZEWSKI

"WHERE DO YOU GET THOSE *IDEAS?*" THAT IS THE NUMBER ONE QUES-tion I get as a writer of science fiction. The next question is, how do you make science ideas into a story? Most important, how do you extrapolate from known science to make it convincing and intriguing?

First it's important to realize that there are various kinds of science fiction today, in which science functions differently. Michael Crichton builds a thriller around technical details, even tables of data; character and "art" are less emphasized. Ursula Le Guin writes anthropological science fiction, emphasizing the social sciences and subtleties of char-acter. A recent trend is the "future historical" novel such as Maureen McHugh's *China Mountain Zhang,* in which scientific extrapolation provides details of a vivid future setting for everyday people. My own work explores the interactions between science and society, and the human beings caught between them—even when, as in *A Door into Ocean,* we are not sure at first who is "human."

As a writer, you need to decide what role (if any) science extrapola-tion can play in your work. In fact, much of what is labeled "science fiction" today could as easily be labeled fantasy; and if your own style is distinctive enough, that may be the route for you. On the other hand, to take science seriously requires special attention. I can suggest some approaches that work for me.

Where to find ideas

The freshest ideas come straight from experience in an actual scien-tific laboratory. In my own lab and those of my colleagues, I regularly experience natural phenomena stranger than the strangest of science fiction: a superconducting magnet that suspends paper clips in the

251

room next door; a dish of bacteria that generate thousands of mutations overnight; a flask of chemicals that "magically" turns color every few seconds. As a research scientist, and a teacher needing to range widely, I have an advantage. But any writer can telephone a research lab and even request a visit; most scientists love to talk about their work. INTERNET bulletin boards are another good source of expertise.

Next to the lab itself, the best source of ideas is research journals such as *Science* and *Nature.* These sources provide primary research reports of the latest discoveries, those of interest to a wide range of scientists. While the reading is a challenge even for a veteran scientist, most of the exciting finds reported here will never reach the popular science magazines. For example, I came across a report in *Science* of a bacterium that actually eats uranium. This fit right into the plot of my science fiction novel *Daughter of Elysium,* which required an organism to eat something no other creature would touch!

For readable reviews of emerging fields, use periodicals aimed at the scientifically literate readership such as *Scientific American* and Sigma Xi's *American Scientist.* Be wary of newspapers and the less sophisticated popular science magazines, whose accounts are likely to be superficial and contain errors.

Once you have a good idea, it's worth checking it out with experts, just as you might check out any other aspect of setting. Thus you can avoid obvious bloopers, as well as ideas considered total clichés by experts who would otherwise be sympathetic to your work. For example, physicists told me that an anti-gravity device would be written off as a cliché, but the use of a white hole as an energy source might be taken seriously.

In the end, you can take heart from the fact that "mistakes" may not be fatal, as far as popular success is concerned. Frank Herbert's bestseller *Dune* showed settlers on a desert planet distilling water from the air. This would work in an Earth desert only because Earth's atmosphere carries water from the oceans. Even if your science is "right" when the book is written, some aspects are bound to get outdated soon. *A Door into Ocean* depicted women who generate children by fusion of ova. Even before the proofs reached me, research had shown this to be impossible because paternal chromosomes carry essential modifications.

Credibility and consistency

What makes an idea "credible," then, is hard to define. Getting the facts exactly "right" and up-to-date is helpful; yet if none of your assumptions or extrapolations could be challenged, your work would not be science fiction.

Interestingly, the more common complaint I hear from inexperienced writers is that the "real science" they have carefully researched is declared false or unbelievable by readers or editors. What do we do when truth is stranger than fiction?

One way to make your ideas credible is to tie each invention to some easily verifiable event or fact on Earth. This can be done more or less subtly as a sort of in-text footnote. When Crichton shows his dinosaurs chomping through steel bars, "like hyenas," he offers a fact that I could verify. We can be sure that some hyena enthusiast out there will complain loudly if he gets it wrong! Similarly, when I created an alien organism with infrared vision in *The Wall around Eden,* I noted that known animals such as rattlesnakes possess infrared sensor organs. The focusing lens of the alien "eyes" was of sodium chloride, an infrared-focusing substance that living creatures commonly contain in their bodies.

Another source of credibility is consistency: Make sure that your facts and extrapolations, however reasonable on their own, make sense together in the story. If your imagined planet has twice the mass of earth, what is its gravity? The composition of its atmosphere? How close is it to its sun, and how long does it take to complete a year? Do the native animals on such a planet have thick, ponderous limbs, or delicate long ones? If voracious monsters descend upon your space visitors, what fauna do they normally prey upon?

The biological questions are frequently overlooked. In *Door into Ocean,* I created an entire ecosystem complete with microbial plants to photosynthesize, small phosphorescent grazers, both aerial and marine predators of a range of sizes, and scavengers, "legfish" that crawl up upon floating vegetation.

It may seem exhausting and frustrating to get all the parts to work together, but this extra craft is what distinguishes stories like *Dune* from more forgettable attempts. In my own work, I have come to rely upon a layered approach, in which I start at the beginning, write in a chapter or two until inconsistencies build up, then start all over from the beginning and try to get a couple of chapters farther. Inevitably the first chapter gets rewritten twenty times; but the reward is that my last one virtually writes itself.

A writer who develops a particularly complex worldview, or "universe," may choose to write several books within the same universe, exploring different aspects of its setting or theme. Just as Doris Lessing wrote a series of novels about Martha Quest in Africa, Ursula Le Guin wrote several books, including *Left Hand of Darkness,* within one imagined universe, where humanity's far-flung colonial worlds are linked by the "ansible" communication device. One must however take care to come up with enough fresh material to justify each new story in its own right.

Explaining your ideas

The biggest mistake is to lecture your readers, however intriguing an idea may be. The writer must blend science ideas seamlessly with all other aspects of experience that form the story. As always, "show, not tell" is the rule.

Try to let science ideas lead into character development, and vice versa. An example of this process occurred as I wrote *A Door into Ocean,* in which a population of women called Sharers inhabit a planet covered entirely by ocean. One day a researcher in my laboratory excitedly showed me a flask of purple protein he had just isolated from photosynthetic bacteria. When light shined upon the protein, it bleached clear, as it absorbed the light energy. This demonstration gave me the idea that my aquatic women characters would carry purple bacteria as symbionts in their skin, providing extra oxygen underwater. When their oxygen ran low, the Sharers' skin would bleach white dramatically. This ability to "bleach white" later developed a spiritual significance as well; the Sharers can enter a special kind of trance, called "whitetrance," which enables them to endure extreme physical stress while upholding their religious beliefs.

Another example from *A Door into Ocean* works in the opposite direction, of character development leading to science: The Sharers use Gandhian pacifist resistance to repel an armed invasion of their planet. I sought a metaphor from science to help describe the unexpected success of their resistance, which from the invaders' limited perspective seemed doomed to fail. The metaphor had to fit into the perspective of the Sharers, who have advanced biological technology. I hit upon the idea of "electron tunneling," a phenomenon in which electrons can penetrate a seemingly impenetrable energy barrier. Electron tunneling occurs in the hemoglobin molecule as it collects oxygen in the blood, so the Sharers would know about it.

Some explanation is always necessary; the trick is, how much. It helps to weave necessary explication into dialogue, a sentence at a time, at a point where events demand it. For example, in *Daughter of Elysium,* a visiting scientist (new to the planet) discovers that his discarded culture dishes have come alive and are trying to gobble up his two-year-old son. A student comes to the rescue and explains that the "intelligent" culture-dish material (composed of billions of microscopic robots) has malfunctioned; it is designed to enclose tissue cultures, not children.

This example, by the way, also illustrates the time-honored gimmick for explaining any new setting: the naive "visitor," who needs everything explained. It works, if you don't make the lecture too obvious and do keep the plot moving. Michael Crichton's *Jurassic Park* essentially consists of a long lecture on cloning dinosaurs, kept moving by a fast-paced, and blood-thirsty, series of events.

One approach to the problem of explanation is to include all that the story seems to need in the first draft, even though you know it's too much for the reader to take. In later drafts, cut it drastically. Omit terms known only to experts, or redefine in simple language. (*Oogenesis* is "making eggs.") A typical science course introduces more new words than a first year of language. So try to use scientific terminology as you would use words from a foreign language—sparingly, for effect.

An occasional phrase of jargon may be worth keeping if it takes on a life of its own in the story. In *Daughter of Elysium,* I did keep one phrase of fetal development about the "primordial germ cells" which undergo a lengthy migration to reach the developing gonads before the fetus is born. The phrase set up a distinctive metaphor for the life journey of my central characters. But countless similar phrases were cut or redefined before my final draft.

How science and technology can advance plot

Complex technical information is best fed to the reader a little at a time and in such a way that it feels "inevitable" where it comes up.

This task is a challenge, but if done skillfully the development of ideas can advance your plot, heightening dramatic tension, much more so than if you had revealed all the implications at the start.

Daughter of Elysium depicts research connecting fetal development and aging, a field of daunting complexity. My opening chapter shows how the fetal heart tube forms and begins to pulse; later chapters depict more subtle processes of cells and tissues, and much later, the critical molecular events that determine whether the embryo will live or die—or live without aging. In between, various subplots incidental to research take up the scientist's time, much as they would in real life. Often the subplots make an ironic contrast to his work; for instance, when he faces his dying relatives back home, who will never benefit from his research on aging.

Another role for science in your plot can be to show how various characters react to change, and are themselves changed (or not). In *A Door into Ocean,* the invaders of the ocean world respond to the Sharers' life science in diverse ways. Some simply try to destroy it, and none of the bizarre setbacks they face changes their outlook. Others become intrigued by the new science, with its implications for their own medicine and agriculture. A few even take up the symbiotic purple microbes into their own skin.

The points I've made about finding ideas and using them have served me well in my own novels, and have worked for other writers too. At the same time, it is important not to get lost in the science. Remember that what makes a science fiction novel "work" in the long run is what makes any good novel work: connection, consistency, and characters that make us care.

>> 53

No Detail Too Small

By Rosalind Laker

THERE IS A LINE IN A SONG THAT SAYS IT IS THE LITTLE THINGS THAT mean so much.

Surprisingly, perhaps, this is good to remember when writing anything set back in time, whether the fifteenth century or World War II. The writer must make the period become alive and real, often to readers who know little or nothing about it. Every century offers a panoramic backdrop to the action of a plot, but it is in the details—frequently no more than snippets gathered from research—that the whole texture of the past can be summoned up.

One of my forebears, Richard Walling, was a master of small, descriptive detail, and yet his diary, handed down in the family, was never meant for publication. Being a miller, he took a great interest in the local weather and kept a daily record of it from 1822 until 1895, interspersed with a line or two on family happenings.

During an abnormally wet July he wrote: *The hay is swimming in the meadows.* One of several entries showed the difficulties of getting about in the countryside after dark, since there were no street lamps: *I had forgot my lantern, and the night was so mourning black I lost my way.* On the day he entered the death of his wife in his diary, he revealed the formality of address between Victorian married couples, at the same time conveying the quiet depths of his grief: *This morning at eleven o'clock Mrs. Walling died without a murmur. I held her hand all night before and a long time afterwards.* His final entry, written shortly before his own death, was made during the worst winter that he could remember. He summed it all up in a single despairing sentence: *Ground hard as stone, starvation everywhere.*

Although he was unaware of evoking the age in which he lived, I see his diary as an example of how it is possible through little details to make men and women of the past (not forgetting the setting) as vivid and understandable as in the present day. Out of it all comes atmosphere, as in Tolstoy's *Anna Karenina,* when the tea is poured into *porcelain cups of moonlike transparency.* What an elegant scene that conjures up!

Frequently, a detail uncovered in research can in its own small way help guide a plot along. Often, it can give a deeper insight into the character of an historical personage that might otherwise be overlooked. In my novel *Banners of Silk,* I wrote of Empress Eugenie leaving France for exile in England in 1870. Every year afterward, Worth, the great courturier in Paris, sent her a bunch of her favorite violets. She had always worn them in her heyday. A tiny fragment of history, and yet it showed poignantly what receiving these French violets must have meant to her, bereaved and lonely, in an alien land. It also emphasized still further the thoughtfulness and kindness of Worth, who had featured strongly in my story, and showed that he was never to forget that it was she who had been responsible for his worldwide fame.

It was not long after this book was published that an elderly American lady wrote to tell me how much she had enjoyed it and enclosed a Victorian photograph of her great-aunt. It was hand-tinted and showed a young woman in a beautiful yellow taffeta ball gown. The woman in the picture was the niece of the American ambassador in Paris and had been staying with him and his wife in 1870. The gown was designed by Worth, and it was worn by the young woman at the last ball given by Napoleon III and Empress Eugenie before he lost his imperial throne.

I have shown the photograph many times while lecturing, both as an example of a Worth gown and also to illustrate how old photographs can be a valuable source of research for the period in which a novel is set. Another source that can prove invaluable is found within the pages of many illustrated books of paintings from previous centuries available in public libraries. These show in detail the lives and customs of working people, as well as the rich, and the backgrounds in these paintings provide everything from furnished interiors to methods of transport, scenery, food, and much more.

In *The Sugar Pavilion,* the subplot tells of the Prince Regent's secret morganatic marriage to Maria Fitzherbert. It was a doomed love, in that the Prince Regent, never faithful, finally abandoned her when his own wild extravagance led to such debts that he was forced to agree to a political marriage with a foreign princess. Then I discovered an interesting item during my research: On his deathbed, he had asked the Duke of Wellington to promise that the locket that he wore night and day be buried with him. After the Prince Regent's death, the Duke could not resist looking inside the locket. It contained a miniature of Maria, showing that in spite of the Prince Regent's scandalous life, she had remained the only woman he had ever truly loved. Thus I was able to show that there was yet another facet to this man's complex character.

As a postscript to my research for this book, I went to Buckingham Palace when the State Apartments were opened to the public for the first time. I was intrigued to find from the catalogue that much of the lovely furniture, the glorious porcelain, and the priceless paintings had been purchased by the Prince Regent before he became George IV. The true cost of these treasures had been his personal happiness.

It was an earlier snippet, gleaned from some French records, that resulted in my presenting Marie Antoinette in a sympathetic light when I wrote *To Dance with Kings*. I have been asked many times why I did this, and explained that having discovered that two French queens before Marie Antoinette had said contemptuously that the starving peasants should eat cake when there was no bread, I began to investigate further. What I found was that the ill-fated Marie Antoinette had never uttered those words. Many other details about her came to light, and there emerged for me a woman who had matured from being a foolish girl to a loyal wife and a devoted mother. On the night the mob advanced on Versailles, she could have fled to safety with the children, but she stayed courageously at her husband's side, even though she knew she was the main target of the mob's hatred.

Nobody was more pleased than I when in October 1993, the unfortunate queen was finally vindicated, exactly two hundred years after her dreadful death at the guillotine; France finally acknowledged that she had been much maligned in the past, and it had been political plotting against her during her lifetime that had blackened her name unfairly throughout the years. Memorial services were held for her in Paris and throughout France.

Although I always set a fictional story against an historical background, I make absolutely sure that nothing in the real sequence of events is untrue. This is the reason I have always done my own research. In this way I familiarize myself with every aspect of the period about which I'm writing.

All the research I did for *Orchids and Diamonds* brought a host of colorful, small but important details to light. My fictional characters move against a background created by the Spanish dress designer, Fortuny, who scorned the Parisian world of haute couture for many years, preferring to work unobtrusively in Venice. He kept to the prototype of a deceptively simple silk gown with minuscule pleats made by his own secret method. Even today nobody is exactly sure how this was done. During the Twenties these gowns were all the rage. Today, however old they are, they are dateless and still flatter the wearer, but are now accepted as works of art and are found only in private costume collections and in the great museums of the world.

The details I gathered enabled my heroine to work for Fortuny and see for herself the Arabian Nights effect he created with fabrics of his own design in the Venetian palace where he lived and displayed his creations. Yet I had a setback in my research when I went to visit the palace (now the Museum Fortuny). I made a special trip to Venice, and found, to my dismay, that the palace was closed during preparations for a special Fortuny exhibition, and unfortunately, it was not due to reopen until after I had to return to England.

As I never travel without a camera when visiting a site to feature in my books, I made the best of things by taking pictures of the palace's fifteenth-century façade and what I could see of an inner courtyard as the workmen came in and out. Finally, I went down a long passageway at the side of the great building to photograph the water-entrance at the far end where customers would have once arrived by gondola. Suddenly, a man called to me, his voice echoing down the walls of the passageway along which I had come.

"Are you the writer from England researching Fortuny? I'm the director of the exhibition, and I'll show you around!"

It proved to me once again that people are extraordinarily helpful to writers doing research. The Arabian Nights atmosphere still prevails in Fortuny's palace, with its exotically draped fabrics stamped in gold, silver, and bronze, all enhanced by Fortuny's works of art. But a detail I noticed, which was of significance in the finished plot, was the deep comfort of the velvet couch and cushioned chairs where Fortuny and his wife had entertained friends. Any little thing, no matter how mundane it might appear, that registers when you are viewing it or reading about it, should be noted for possible later use. It is this seeking after detail—much of which may be generally unknown—that will enable you to make your novel informative as well as entertaining to your readers.

Yet nothing must be dropped like a heavy rock into the story. Details can be used only if they form an integral part of a setting or situation, for above all else, your research should never be obvious. What you leave out is as important as what you put in. Some years ago, I read a book set in the Civil War, and it was coming to a climax when soldiers were about to burst into a house and capture the hero. But as they thundered toward the door, the author went off on a tangent about the pay they earned, and the whole impact of the scene was lost.

Research, collect, and then prune is an old but golden rule. Being ruthless with what you have gathered will yield good results. Keep only the most interesting and fascinating details to dramatize and enhance the finished work.

>> 54

THE CRAFT OF THE ESPIONAGE THRILLER

BY JOSEPH FINDER

WHEN I WAS IN MY MID-TWENTIES AND STRUGGLING TO WRITE MY first novel, *The Moscow Club,* I got to know another aspiring writer, a cynical and embittered (but very funny) man, and told him I was immersed in the research for a spy thriller I hadn't begun to write. He shook his head slowly and scowled. "That's a sign of desperation," he intoned ominously. "Research is an excuse for not writing."

This ex-friend has given up trying to write and is working at some job he despises, while I'm making a living writing novels, so I think there may be a moral here. That old dictum writers are always accosted by—"Write what you know"—is, in the espionage-thriller genre, at least, a fallacy.

Obviously, research is no substitute for good writing, good storytelling, or the ability to create flesh-and-blood characters. But even the masters of the spy novel plunge into research for the worlds they create. John le Carré (the pen name for David Cornwell) was for a short while a spy for the British secret service, but nevertheless, he assiduously researches his spy tales. In the extensive acknowledgements at the end of *The Night Manager,* he thanks numerous sources in the U.S. Drug Enforcement Agency and the U.S. Treasury, mercenary soldiers, antiques dealers, and the "arms dealers who opened their doors to me." The novel only *reads* effortlessly.

I suppose you can just make it up, but it will always show, if you do, and the spy thriller must always evoke an authentic, fully realized world. Readers want to believe that the author is an authority, an expert, an insider who's willing to let them in on a shattering secret or two.

But no one can be expert in everything. My first novel was about a

262

CIA analyst who learns of an impending coup attempt in Moscow and is drawn into the conspiracy. In the first draft, however, the hero, Charles Stone, was instead a ghostwriter for a legendary American statesman. Luckily, my agent persuaded me that no one wants to read about the exploits of a ghostwriter.

Transforming Charlie into a CIA officer took a lot of rethinking, but fortunately, I had sources: While a student at Yale, I'd been recruited by the CIA (but decided against it), and I had some friends in the intelligence community. They helped me make Charlie Stone a far more interesting, more appealing and believable character.

The best ideas, I believe, spring from real-life events, from reading newspapers and books, and from conducting interviews. Frederick Forsyth came up with the idea for his classic thriller, *The Day of the Jackal* (a fictional plot on the life of Charles de Gaulle), from his experience working as a Reuters correspondent in Paris in the early 1960s, when rumors kept circulating about assassination attempts on de Gaulle. Robert Ludlum was watching TV news in a Paris hotel when he happened to catch a report about an international terrorist named Carlos; this became the seed for one of his best novels, *The Bourne Identity*.

When I first began thinking about writing the novel that later became *The Moscow Club,* I was a graduate student at the Harvard Russian Research Center, studying the politics of the Soviet Union. I remember reading Forsyth's *The Devil's Alternative,* which concerns intrigue in the Kremlin. Why not try my hand at this? I thought. After Mikhail Gorbachev became head of the Soviet Union and began the slow-motion revolution that would eventually lead to the collapse of that empire, I began to hear bizarre rumors about attempts in Moscow to unseat Gorbachev. The rumors didn't seem so far-fetched to me. But when *The Moscow Club* came out at the beginning of 1991, I was chided for my overly active imagination. Then, in August of that year, the real thing happened: The KGB and the military banded together to try to overthrow the Gorbachev government—and suddenly, I was a prophet!

My second novel, however, was a significant departure from this political background. *Extraordinary Powers* concerns Ben Ellison, an attorney for a prestigious Boston law firm (and former clandestine operative for the CIA). He is lured into a top-secret government experiment and emerges with a limited ability to "hear" the thoughts of others. This sprang from a reference I'd come across in a study of the KGB to some highly secret programs in the U.S. and Soviet governments that attempted to locate people with telepathic ability to serve in various espionage undertakings. Whether or not one believes in ESP, the fact that such projects really do exist was irresistible to me. I sent *Extraordinary Powers* to a friend who does contract work for the CIA; he confided in me that he'd received a call from a highly placed person in a government agency who actually runs such a project and had used psychics during the Gulf War. He wanted to know whether I'd been the recipient of a leak.

With this seemingly fantastic premise at the center of my novel, it was crucially important that the world in which this plot takes place be a very real, very well-grounded one. Because I wanted the telepathy project to hew as closely to reality as possible, I spent a great deal of time talking to patent lawyers, helicopter pilots, gold experts, and even neurologists. I was relieved to get letters from a world-famous neurobiologist and from the editor of *The New England Journal of Medicine* saying that they were persuaded that such an experiment was within the realm of possibility.

In one crucial scene in *The Moscow Club,* Charlie had to smuggle a gun through airport security, but I had no idea how this might actually work, so I tracked a knowledgeable gun dealer, and after I'd convinced him I was a writer, not a criminal, he became intrigued by the scenario and agreed to help. It turned out that this fellow had a friend who used to be in the Secret Service and had actually taken a Glock pistol and got it past the metal detectors and X-ray machines in security at Washington's National Airport and onto a plane to Boston. He then showed me exactly how he'd done it, so I could write about it accurately. (I left out a few key details to foil any potential hijacker.)

Can readers tell when a scene or a detail is authentic? I believe so. I'm convinced that painstaking research can yield a texture, an atmosphere of authenticity, that average readers can feel and smell. (There will always be a few experts waiting to pounce. In *Extraordinary Powers,* I mistakenly described a Glock 19 as having a safety, and I continue to get angry letters about it.)

The longer I write, it seems, the more research I do. For my forthcoming novel, *Prince of Darkness,* whose hero is a female FBI counter-terrorism specialist, I managed to wangle official cooperation from the FBI, and I spent a lot of time talking to several FBI Special Agents. I also interviewed past and present terrorism experts for the CIA, asking them such questions as, would they really be able to catch a skilled professional terrorist—as well as some seemingly trivial ones.

Since the other main character in *Prince of Darkness* is a professional terrorist-for-hire, I thought it was important to talk to someone who's actually been a terrorist. This was not easy. In fact, it took me months to locate an ex-terrorist (through a friend of a friend) who was willing to talk. But it was worth the time and effort: My fictional terrorist is now, I think, far more credible than he'd have been if I'd simply invented him.

I've done interviews with a convicted forger for details on how to falsify a U.S. passport; with a bomb disposal expert about how to construct bombs; with an expert in satellite surveillance to help me describe authentically how the U.S. government is able to listen in on telephone conversations. I've often called upon the expertise of police homicide detectives, retired FBI agents, helicopter pilots, pathologists, even experts in embalming (or "applied arts," as they are called).

Since an important character in *Prince of Darkness* is a high-priced call girl, I spent a lot of time interviewing prostitutes, expensive call girls, and madams. As a result of this groundwork, I think this particular character is more sympathetic, more believable, than I'd have drawn her otherwise.

Because international settings are often integral parts of spy novels, I strongly believe that travel—really being there in Paris, say, or Rome, or wherever—not only can help you create plausible settings, make them look and smell and feel real, but can suggest scenes and ideas that would otherwise never occur to you. But not everyone can afford to travel (or likes to; ironically, Robert Ludlum, whose plots traverse the globe, abhors traveling). No doubt you can get by tolerably well consulting a good guidebook or two.

Gathering research material is a strange obsession, but it's by far the best part of writing thrillers. I will admit, however, that this passion can go too far. In Rome, I was pickpocketed while standing in a *gelato* shop. When I realized that my passport and all my cash and travelers checks were gone, I panicked. I searched for the perpetrator and came upon a man who looked somewhat shifty. I approached him and pleaded, in my pathetic Italian, *"Per favore, signore! Per favore!* My passport! *Per piacere!"* When the man responded by unzipping his travel bag to prove he didn't have my belongings, that he was innocent, I knew I'd found my man. I told him quietly: "Look, I'm on my honeymoon. If you give me back my passport and my money, I promise I won't turn you in."

He looked around and furtively put my passport and wallet back in my bag.

At this point any sane tourist would flee, but, I went on, "One more thing. If you'll agree to be interviewed, I won't call the police."

He looked at me as if I were out of my mind. "I'm quite serious," I said. "Let me buy you an espresso."

He sat down at a table with me as I explained that I was doing research for a novel partly set in Rome. Flattered that a writer would take an interest in his life, he began to tell me all about how he got into this line of work, about his childhood in Palermo spent snatching purses, about how he travels around Europe frequenting international gatherings of the rich and famous, how he lives in hotels and is often lonely. He explained how he spots an easy mark, how he fences passports, which travelers checks he has no interest in. He demonstrated how he picks pockets and handbags, and taught me how to make sure it never happened to me again.

Much of the information I gleaned from this pickpocket later turned up in the Italy sequence in *Extraordinary Powers.*

I'm certainly not suggesting that a committed espionage novelist must go out of his way to get his pockets picked in Rome, or consort with convicted forgers, assassins, or terrorists. But the longer I write espionage fiction, the more strongly I'm convinced that if you're going to write about unusual people and circumstances in a compelling and plausible way, there's really no substitute for firsthand experience.

$\gg$ 55

A Mystery in Three Acts

By Stephen Greenleaf

IN WRITING A MYSTERY NOVEL, I'VE FOUND THAT IT IS HELPFUL TO follow the basic structure of the play in three acts, a foundation that has been central to dramatic prose since Aristotle.

Act I introduces the crime and the mystery to be solved; the sleuth who will solve it; and the setting in which the crime occurred. Act II describes the investigation that points to a conclusion, but later proves erroneous. Act III depicts the final confrontation between the sleuth and the villain, reveals the deductions that led to the true solution, and suggests the ramifications of the secrets that have emerged along the way. If supported by the persuasive prose and imaginative incident that make for a well-crafted novel, this approach to plotting will produce a good book.

To this end, you should begin your story dramatically. Since the premise of a mystery is that the crime to be solved has already taken place and the sleuth (the point-of-view character) didn't witness it, your opening requires imaginative improvisation.

There are at least three ways to achieve a beginning that will engage the reader at once: One is to open with a prologue that describes in vivid detail the crime as it occurs, narrated either in the third-person omniscient point of view or in the voice of the victim or villain. The second is to begin with the sleuth in a devilish predicament, then flash back to show how he got into such a fix. The third is to have the person who reveals the details of the crime do so in such a way that the reader feels as if he or she were there when the crime took place.

Once the crime is set forth, you must establish several plot elements within the first few chapters, first and foremost revealing the voice of the sleuth and making his personality sufficiently unique and engaging that readers will want to spend several hours with him.

Your sleuth must be, in Raymond Chandler's phrase, a person "fit for adventure," which should be established quickly. In the opening pages, the hero should say something and do something so clever and unexpected to reveal him as unusual and in some ways unique. All aspects of the hero's personality need not be revealed at the outset, of course; some should remain an enigma until well into the heart of the novel. The job of Act I is merely to establish the existence of a complex and compelling and credible person.

The crime that propels the story—the mystery the sleuth is to solve—must be a serious one; it doesn't have to be murder, but it has to be the moral equivalent of murder—kidnapping, child abuse, sexual assault, etc. It must also be intriguing in and of itself: committed in an unusual way, in an unusual place, or involving an unusual person—or all three. Also, readers should learn enough about the victim to care that the perpetrator is brought to justice.

To be most effective, the opening scenes should include a symbol— a person, an object, a natural phenomenon—that can serve as a metaphor for what is happening in the overall setting. Having his symbol reappear at the end will give the story a sense of closure. For an example, see the way Ross Macdonald used the forest fire in *The Underground Man.*

The opening crime should generate two essential aspects of the plot. First, it should provide two clues to a solution—physical and psychological. Some clues obviously point in a specific direction; others aren't recognized as clues until later, e.g., the hound that didn't bark (as in Sherlock Holmes' *The Hound of the Baskervilles*). You should include a variety of clues in your story so that the clever reader can solve the mystery by analyzing the details that you have supplied.

The opening crime also suggests a line of investigation in which the suspects and motives will carry the sleuth to the end of Act I. Chapter 2 is the logical first step the sleuth would take to solve the crime described in Chapter 1: If a wife is dead, the first thing you must do is talk to the husband. How do you come up with other suspects? Make a chart of the people who touched the victim's life, personally and professionally. Then select those characters who would be believable and powerful suspects—a jealous lover, an envious sibling, an ambitious rival—and have the sleuth question them. Editors say they want "character-driven" rather than "plot-driven" novels, so choose a few well-rounded suspects to enliven your story.

The major suspects who appear in Act I should reappear later in the novel, after the sleuth has learned that they are not as disinterested as they seemed. A good plot is often circular, bringing the reader back to the beginning of the quest but in an atmosphere that has been redefined by the work of the detective. One of the suspects who appears in Act I must turn out to be the real villain; it's not fair to discount him, or to have the solution depend on luck or coincidence or information that the sleuth knew but the reader didn't.

After the investigation is underway, it is time to introduce the subplot. While your plot carries the story, the subplot carries the theme. This means that the subplot is where you move the tale from the particular to the universal—where the events in the novel correspond with the events in the reader's life.

Most subplots arise from two sources: a crisis in the sleuth's private life—divorce, alcoholism, unemployment; and the fact that the investigation causes the sleuth to confront issues of courage, honesty, or fidelity, creating dilemmas that call into question his sense of himself or his purpose in life. An important part of the dramatic arc of the novel is the change that takes place within the sleuth as the subplot is resolved.

The subplot also offers a way to alter the pace of the story by moving back and forth between the personal and professional obstacles the sleuth encounters. It is also a way to broaden the author's canvas by introducing scenes of romance or pathos or humor that are not part of the main investigation.

At the mid-point of Act I, something happens that indicates the crime may be more complicated than it first appeared. There is no elucidation, just hints that there are depths and densities still to be revealed—for example, a hint that the victim was not the upstanding citizen he was reputed to be. At this point the reader may see the hints more clearly than the sleuth does.

At the end of Act I there is a change in the focus and scope of the inquiry. The initial line of investigation proves unproductive: The major suspect dies or the crime turns out to be other than it first appeared—a murder instead of a disappearance, a kidnapping instead of a runaway. The story takes a new direction, plunging into the heart of Act II, in which the following things should happen:

a) A sense of urgency must be developed. If the crime is not solved soon, even worse things will happen.

b) The investigation should expand to include other characters from different walks of life. Every scene, whether an interview or a fist fight or the discovery of physical evidence, must yield a fact that points toward the solution, even though the relevance is not always obvious at the time.

c) As the subplot evolves, the sleuth's backstory is revealed: how he got to be the way he is, what's lacking in his life, what's kept him from achieving his goal previously.

d) The writer reveals that the sleuth has a personal stake in the case—because his life has been threatened, or his investigation may expose issues that disturb him, or a suspect is emotionally linked to him in some way.

e) Hidden motives proliferate as the result of the discovery of secret relationships—love affairs, business shenanigans, family feuds. The depths and densities only hinted at in Act I become clear in Act II.

f) At the mid-point of this Act, the sleuth is stymied; a solution seems impossible.

g) By the end of Act II, the force of logic and the elimination of alternatives point to a conclusion—a villain and a motive emerge from the uncertainties, and the sleuth reveals the results of his investigation. But he still hasn't got it quite right.

His mistaken conclusion can take various forms. He may have incorrectly identified the villain, but his reasoning may be right: The prime suspect actually turns out to be a victim who has been framed. Or he points to the perpetrator, but his reasoning is wrong: The case is more complex than it had appeared, which presupposes that others are involved in ways previously unknown to him. Or the sleuth has misinterpreted a clue and needs to retrace his steps to find out where he went wrong.

In contrast to the end of Act I, where the error was obvious to all, at the end of Act II the error is known only to the sleuth (and perhaps to the clever reader), who finally recognizes the scheme that provoked the crime. The crucial clue turns out to be some action or event that

270

seemed innocuous in Act I, but now takes on new meaning because of information obtained by the end of Act II.

In Act III, the sleuth reevaluates what he has learned and resumes his quest. The subplot resolves itself; the sleuth is stronger for his private ordeal and strengthened for the final drive toward the true solution. The story climaxes in a confrontation between the sleuth and the villain—a meeting of the forces of good and evil.

The climactic scene should be a memorable conflict in which the villain's own weapons are turned against him, and the sleuth triumphs against what had appeared to be all odds. The case is solved, the client is satisfied, the closing symbol tells us that the story has ended, and even the clever reader has been outwitted.

It's easier said than done, of course. Plotting is hard work, a feat of imagination, a riff of theme and variation, a game of "what if" played out in the clever corners of the mind. Some writers work it out ahead of time; others improvise along the way. You'll sleep better if you work it out, but you probably won't have as much fun.

≫ 56

CREATING SUPERHEROES IN SCIENCE FICTION AND FANTASY

BY JOSEPHA SHERMAN

WHAT DOES THE WORD "SUPERHERO" CONJURE UP FOR YOU? DO YOU picture someone who possesses some amazing, more-than-human ability, who wears an odd costume while battling an equally odd villain? That's one aspect of the superhero, but only one.

You can also create a less fantastic, more believable superhero, a character who is larger than life because of cleverness, intelligence, or strength, but still seems like a real person. When creating such a character, you must keep in mind that if readers are going to accept your superhero as credible, there must be some definite limits to his or her powers. Your superhero can't be strong enough to leap over buildings or have the talent to read people's minds—*unless* you can provide a logical explanation for those abilities.

Before you can begin to create a convincing superhero, you must decide what type of story you want to tell. Is it going to be science fiction, in which reasonably real science is necessary? Or is it going to be fantasy, in which the presumption is that magic works and more fabulous events are possible?

Let's say you've decided that you want to write a science fiction story. Now you need to figure out what type of superhero you want to create. What traits make him superior to a normal person? Maybe your superhero is an alien from a planet with a much heavier gravity than Earth. This would mean that he would be much stronger than anyone on our planet, but if he came to Earth, he would still be limited by the laws of physics, the same law that applied to the astronauts making those easy jumps on the Moon, thanks to its lesser gravity. This means that while your hero might be able to make the long jump in an athletics competition seem easy, he couldn't leap over anything

272

taller than a very low building, or fly without some mechanical device, or lift objects as heavy as trucks or airplanes.

But what would such an alien want to do on Earth? He doesn't have to become a crime fighter; that's much too ordinary. Try to think of something more original. Each question you pose to yourself will raise more questions, but if you can answer most of them, you'll have a believable character. For instance, you might ask: What if your superhero decides that he's come to Earth to become a great sports hero? Would people accept that? Or would they be fearful of his great strength? Would your superhero fight the people on Earth, or would he try to find a way to prove that he came in peace? And how would he manage to convince athletes to let him on their teams?

Maybe you've decided that your superhero isn't an alien at all. Maybe he or she is an Earthling, a genius whom people fear because of his or her intelligence. What would such superheroes be like? Could they lead a normal social life? Would they be shy or angry because no human being can match their brilliance? And how would they use their superior intelligence? Would your superhero develop vaccines that could cure all diseases? What if these miracle medicines could keep everyone young—but prevent them from having children?

What if, instead, your superhero invents an FTL spaceship drive (FTL is the accepted science fiction shorthand for "Faster Than Light") that allows people on Earth to travel to other worlds? How would that change their lives? How would they feel about the superhero?

But maybe you've decided that your superhero isn't going to be either an alien or a scientific genius. Maybe he's just unusually clever. Is he nice, too? Or is he a bit of a scoundrel, likable but not always law-abiding? What made him this way? Does he mean to hurt people with his schemes, or is he just a sort of interstellar Robin Hood? What if he steals something that turns out to be sacred to another planet's inhabitants? What if stealing that object gets him involved in an interplanetary war, or a fight for freedom from an intergalactic oppressor? How can your superhero use his one gift—his clever wits—to save himself and everyone else?

As you can see, each question leads deeper and deeper into a possible story.

Now let's take a look at the fantasy side of things. Here you have a little more room for your superhero's unique powers, but you still can't get too bizarre. Nothing will destroy readers' acceptance of your character faster than a story that's too illogical and therefore totally incredible. And nothing is more frustrating to a reader than a superhero who can develop a new magical power every time he's in danger, or who casts spells simply by snapping his fingers! If your story is to be properly entertaining, magic must be as carefully thought out as science, with definite rules and regulations.

As with science fiction, the same technique of asking yourself a series of questions works well in creating a credible fantasy superhero. In fact, if you want to create a hero who's a bit of a scoundrel or a daring thief, you can ask and answer almost the same questions as if he were a science fiction rogue, remembering that he's going to run into magical traps rather than lasers.

But suppose you want to create a superhero who isn't a rogue? Then you'll need to ask a new set of questions. What if your character possesses great magical powers? Did she inherit them, or is she unique? Does she have a family, and if so, how do they feel about her powers? For that matter, how does society feel about magic? Do they accept it, or is it the government's policy to kill all magicians? Where did your character learn her magical powers, and how does she hope to use them?

How is the magic in your fantasy story supposed to work? Remember that you can't create a believable superhero who can do anything at all too easily, or without some difficulty. Where does the power to fuel spells come from? Does casting spells dissipate the magician's strength? Does the magic require some exotic, difficult-to-find objects to make it work?

Of course, your fantasy character doesn't have to be a magician. You might want to make him a heroic warrior, maybe even a knight—though not a clone of one of King Arthur's knights; you want to create someone original. How? This can lead you to yet another set of questions.

First, does your character have great strength, or is his talent having superior skills with weapons? Was he born with that strength or skill? You can state that he was granted these gifts by some supernatural force—but then you must ask yourself why. Do his gods plan to use him for some evil or good purpose? What if he rebels?

Your character can't come by his talent magically; only in comic books does a hero gain superior powers overnight. It takes training and time. Where did he get that training? Even in a fantasy adventure, your warrior hero must have physical limits; he cannot fight all day without getting hungry and tired. He can't do anything that's physically impossible, like tearing down a castle wall with his bare hands, and unless he's been given a spell to protect him, he's bound to get hurt sooner or later.

Let's say your hero once saved a wizard who gave him a protection spell as a reward. He's a good fighter because he was born with great strength and was trained by his tribe. Now you need to ask: Why is he fighting? For whom? Is he loyal to a specific ruler or cause? Is he a paladin, a wandering warrior in search of noble deeds to do? This may look like the easiest type of character to create, but it can lead a writer into a major plot problem. While it may seem like fun to have your hero travel continuously through strange new lands, your readers will find a superhero who wanders aimlessly along, fighting battle after battle, pretty pointless after a time. Even a superhero needs some realistic goals.

And it's up to you as the writer to give him a worthwhile goal. That may be your hardest task. But if you can create a believable, larger-than-life superhero and put him or her into a believable setting and situation, you are going to do more than come up with a story that works. You are going to make your readers think that *you* are the superhero!

➤➤ 57

CREATING MEMORABLE ENDINGS

BY PETER ROBINSON

JUST AS YOU HAVE TO HOOK READERS AT THE BEGINNING OF YOUR story, you have to hook them again at the end. The final hook is different in kind from the opening one—after all, you are not trying to make someone turn the pages faster at the end—but last impressions do count a lot.

Writers trying to get published are far more concerned about making their openings, plots, characters, and narrative structures so strong that an editor will actually read their manuscripts all the way to the end. Beginnings get all the polish; endings are often just left to fizzle out. Yet if you plan to write more than one novel, a powerful ending can be an important way of building up a loyal readership. And if your beginning and middle are so good, then why should you skimp on your ending? Imagine how an audacious and unusual final page or paragraph might just sway an editor who already likes the manuscript enough to have read that far.

Many endings, particularly in the crime field, are trite and conventional. This is partly because mystery fiction often demands some variation of the "Golden Age" ending, in which the detective explains to the suspects assembled in the vicarage drawing-room how he solved the crime.

But mystery fiction—or any other kind of fiction, for that matter—doesn't have to end like that if you remember that every book can have *two* endings: The first ties up the strands of the plot, whereas the second presents some powerful image, action, or dramatic scene, leaving the reader with something to think about after finishing the book. If you are lucky, of course, both endings merge into one.

The first ending is relatively easy to handle if you keep in mind one or two basic points. After all, if you have spent so much time working out your plot, planting the clues and red herrings, you must not leave anything hanging. Keep a written record of all your clues and tick them off as you tie them up. Make sure you explain all your red herrings away. Your ending should stem logically and naturally from situations and events you have already set up in the narrative, with no new material thrown in at the last minute.

The most interesting decision with the first ending is whether you should tie up *all* the loose ends. This depends very much on how close to reality you want your story to appear. In real life, few loose ends are tied up; threads are left hanging; important events may remain unexplained, and we can rarely see a person's motives with the clarity of a novelist.

I recall something P. D. James said some years ago about the modern mystery: Justice may be done and order may be restored at the end of the story, but the cost, in human terms, is often very high. Some characters' lives have been so contaminated by their contact with the criminal investigation that they will never be the same.

Modern mysteries can and do reflect this duality. Often, the guilty go unpunished, and the innocent suffer. Many mysteries have just and logical solutions that, nonetheless, leave a legacy of misery and disruption behind. Occasionally, the villain gets away, which we know happens often enough in real life. Patricia Highsmith created an interesting villain in her "Ripley" novels—a character who literally gets away with murder. Whether this kind of first ending is for you or not depends on how morally complex your plot is. It is no mean feat to write a book in which your villain escapes, and your readers praise you for it.

In writing a series, you also have the option toward the end of introducing a twist in the lives of one or more series characters. An affair begins, perhaps, or seems about to, and the reader has to wait until the next book to find out exactly what happens. This loses its effect if you overdo it, but a few subtle hints that there are changes in store for your series characters next time around certainly won't be amiss.

The second ending has not so much to do with plot and loose ends as with leaving the reader *something to remember you by.* It may consist of your final sentence, paragraph, or a brief scene, and it involves taking risks and daring to be unconventional.

When I came to the end of writing *The Hanging Valley,* I wanted to avoid the conventional gathering of suspects and explanation of the crime, so I took care of all that obliquely in an earlier scene and ended, instead, with dramatic action. That ending has always been associated in my mind with the final piano chord of The Beatles' "A Day in the Life." It comes with a loud crash and reverberates long after.

Most readers responded positively to my ending, but one person told me she took the book back to the shop because she thought there must be some pages missing from the end. That's what happens when you take risks.

Sometimes you don't finish your story until, literally, the last sentence. To illustrate what I mean, I will give away the ending of my book *Past Reason Hated.* For those who haven't read it, this won't ruin the plot element because it deals more with theme and subtext.

Throughout *Past Reason Hated,* my series character, Inspector Banks, is at odds with a new police image being foisted on the public. It is a paternalistic image of bobbies on the beat and your friendly neighborhood copper showing you the way, telling you the time. This false, nostalgic image is symbolized for Banks by the antiquated blue light outside the police station.

At the end of the book, Banks is walking back to the police station on an icy night after solving a particularly tragic murder and explaining the ironies of the case to the bereaved lover. Earlier, he had confiscated a catapult (British term for slingshot) from a teenager who was using it to shoot pebbles at the ducks on the river:

About twenty yards beyond the station, on Market Street, he stopped and turned. That damn blue light was still shining above the door like a beacon proclaiming benign, paternal innocence and simplicity. Almost without thinking, he took the catapult from his pocket, scraped up a couple of fair-sized stones from the icy gutter, put one in the sling and took aim. The stone clattered on the pavement somewhere along North Market Street. He took a deep breath, sighed out a plume of air, then aimed again carefully, trying to recreate his childhood accuracy. This time the lamp disintegrated in a burst of powder-blue glass, and Banks took off down a side-street, the back way home, feeling guilty and oddly elated, like a naughty schoolboy.

And so the book ends. While I make no claims for this as a great ending, it does illustrate some points I want to make about the often overlooked *second* ending.

First, it is *unusual.* We don't normally expect our fictional police heroes to go around acting the way Banks does here. Secondly, though this ending is not essential to the plot, it ties in strongly with one *theme,* that of the difference between public image and reality, and it reveals the main character's reactions to this.

Thirdly, it ends the book on a note of *action,* an image rather than a dry statement. It proffers a strongly *visual* scene that is likely to stick in the reader's mind. Fourthly, it adds something to our understanding of the *character.* We have never seen Banks act this way before. He is a policeman, not a common vandal, but here we watch him destroy public property and, I hope, sympathize with his motives. Because in fiction you can be with someone even when he is alone, you see Banks here in a private moment, when he thinks nobody is watching. Usually he is the responsible, if slightly irreverent, cop, but here you get some insight into the mischievous child inside him.

Most writers, and some readers, know that characters in a novel have no life beyond what they are given on the page. If it were important for readers to know what happens to someone after the narrative, then the author would have to add an extra chapter or write a sequel.

On the other hand, anyone who loves books knows that characters can live on in the imagination and haunt a reader long after the story is over. In the same way, fictional events can often resonate well beyond the pages in which they were "lived." If you follow this line of thinking, you will see that the more memorable you make your ending, the more a scene of action reverberates like a piano chord; and the more strongly a visual image is lodged in the reader's mind, then the more chance you have of hooking readers into buying your next book, and the one after that.

➤➤ 58

WHAT HAPPENS NEXT?
WRITING FOR PLOT

BY KARIN MCQUILLAN

IT WAS A GREAT SHOCK TO ME, WHEN EXAMINING THE FIRST DRAFT of my first novel, to realize that after half a lifetime of reading books and watching movies, I still didn't understand what a plot was well enough to create my own. I'd come up with a solid framework for the story, a mystery called *Deadly Safari*: The heroine, Jazz Jasper, is a spunky American woman who has started her own safari company in Africa, and the story begins as a murder occurs on her first trip with a group of important clients. I'd filled each chapter with exciting events involving clues, wild animals, Maasai warriors, and a vivid set of characters. And yet it didn't hold together, at the end of each chapter you could close the book with a satisfied sigh, instead of reading on till two in the morning. Something was missing: a plot.

I spent the next year on a quest to discover how to write a tight, gripping plot. I analyzed successful novels; I took copious notes on how to create suspense, how to structure scenes; and I tore apart and put together my own book over and over. By the end, I had distilled a few basic principles of excellence and methods of applying them that worked for me.

A strong plot is not a mystical achievement of inborn talents, but like ninety percent of writing, one more element of craft that can be broken down into comprehensible parts, practiced, and eventually mastered. Even after three published works, I don't claim that plotting is the easiest part of writing, but it is often the most satisfying. Nothing equals that wonderful feeling when you get it right, and your story flows from that first paragraph that hooks readers until you let go of them in the final pages.

The three essential elements of creating an excellent plot are the three C's: causality, character, and complication.

Causality: Everything happens for a reason

The key to plot is causality, without which the events of your book are essentially static. What you want to create is a game of billiards, where the initial action sets off a chain of events, A leading to B and C, C ricocheting off D, and B off E, until the last ball falls into the pocket. Since each event has an effect, you create in readers' minds the question, "Given this event, what will happen next?" Will readers keep turning the pages to find out? Without causality, after a given event anything or nothing could happen, and your reader would likely not go on reading.

You can and must make each step seem logical and believable by using foreshadowing, a powerful tool that prepares the reader to accept plot development by planting information earlier in the book that makes later action believable. The foreshadowing may be an object, a fact, a character's values or personality, or an event. As Chekhov said, if you show a gun in Act One, it must go off in Act Three. Conversely, if a gun goes off in Act Three, you must have brought it on stage in Act One. No matter how unusual or heroic the events are, if your foreshadowing is skillfully done, your readers will be willing to suspend disbelief and stay within the fantasy of the story.

Near the beginning of my novel, *The Cheetah Chase,* Jazz Jasper goes to a fancy party in the capital city where she meets a visiting Saudi princess who is presented with a tiny cheetah cub. Jazz is appalled that an endangered wild animal is being used as a pet. She finds out that the princess and her husband are in Kenya on a camping safari in the northern desert. Later in the book, when Jazz is flying in a two-seater plane to a remote part of the northern desert, retracing the last days of the murder victim in an effort to find out what information he might have stumbled on that led to his murder, the reader is prepared for her to discover some place that is secret and dangerous. Her small plane has to make an emergency landing, and Jazz has to trek to her destination—a tribe of nomadic warriors and herders recently visited by the murder victim—where she discovers that the Saudi camp is nearby, and is involved in illegal hunting.

This series of events gives readers one surprise after another, but nothing they haven't been prepared for earlier in the story. I foreshadowed the plane crash with a chapter in which Jazz takes a test flight at the airport and finds that the airplane had not been fixed properly. Therefore, although readers are shocked when the fuel tank springs a leak, they believe it could happen, because the plane was badly maintained. Coming upon the Saudis would have seemed a mere coincidence if readers had not already learned in the party scene about the existence and location of the camp. Through foreshadowing, the plot elements are linked in a meaningful chain of events: The victim's murder after a visit to the desert leads Jazz to retrace his steps; poor maintenance leads to a plane crash; searching in the desert leads Jazz to find the Saudi camp, which the reader already knew was in that area. The reader will happily give in to the adventure, and be carried along.

No matter how many dramatic surprises you spring on your readers, if you have included the necessary links in the chain of causality, you will give them the feeling of an inevitable working out of fate. This inexorable rightness is one of the reasons people read novels: It gives the comforting illusion that our crazy world can make logical sense, that things happen for a reason! In the real world, fate is capricious, and random events happen all the time, but in the fictional world, coincidences will make your story seem artificial. Because something really happened that way can never justify its use in a story. The story has its own requirements in order to seem believable, and the primary one is causality.

The unity of character and action

E. M. Forster, in *Aspects of the Novel,* distinguishes between a story and a plot this way: "The king died and then the queen died" is a story. "The king died and then the queen died of grief" is a plot. What makes a plot is causality, which relates the first death to the second death. The queen dying of grief is obviously characterization as well, which brings us to a second key element of plot: the unity of character and action.

Every event in a novel must grow out of and simultaneously build character. The characters are known through their actions; the prime adage of fiction is show, don't tell. At the same time, actions are believable because of who that character is, given her history, personality, and relationships with the other characters.

Readers know that my heroine Jazz is impulsive, brave, and passionate in defense of wildlife. Furthermore, the reader has seen Jazz's barely controlled outrage when the Saudi princess is given a cheetah cub as a pet. Still, would she seem a believable character when I later have her steal the cub from the princess's tent? I needed even more preparation to convince the reader that Jazz would risk her life to save an animal. So when the princess shows off the cub to Jazz in the desert chapter, I make the cub look miserable and sick, wearing a tight diamond collar and showing signs of severe dehydration. To bring matters to an emotional head, the cub wriggles to escape the princess's grasp, and she slaps it around.

Identifying with Jazz, the average reader will be incensed and want her to do anything to get that cub away from captivity, abuse, and certain death. Given Jazz's character, she has to try and rescue that cub, and the playing out of this action not only shows new levels of bravery and resourcefulness in Jazz that the reader didn't know she had, it also brings her up against the most severe physical and moral challenges she has ever faced.

If you force a character to act "out of character" just to serve your plot, you will lose plausibility. If it is vital for a given character to take a particular action, then you must prepare the reader to accept and understand why this character would do such a thing by providing convincing motivation earlier in the book. Solving problems like this will make your characters more complex and unique.

If at any time you throw in an irrelevant event because "the character took over," you have lost control of your plot. Instead of A leading to B and C, suddenly readers are wandering down Y, wondering how they got there and what it has to do with anything. It is wonderful when your understanding of a character gives you ideas for the next logical step in the plot; it is a disaster when meandering after a character muddies and even destroys the chain of causality. Actions must be true to character, but they grow out of and lead to other actions.

Complication

Perhaps the most famous definition of plot is: Boy meets girl, boy loses girl, boy gets girl. But this definition is inadequate, because it

283

leaves out causality. It does a good job, however, of capsulizing the basic building blocks of plot: problem, complication, resolution. This little trio repeats itself over and over, from the small scale of every scene to the large scale of the entire book. It is the engine that moves the plot. Your protagonist is confronted with a problem, which arises from his or her goal meeting either internal or external opposition, or both. The most common form for the complication is conflict within and between characters, but it can also be shown in a confrontation with an outside force of circumstance or nature. In meeting the initial problem, the protagonist faces further complications that create an even worse problem, building up to a climax of complete disaster. In the climax, the protagonist meets this seemingly unsolvable problem head on, and either fails or succeeds.

The goal and the conflict will be more meaningful and have greater impact if they are personalized rather than abstract. Instead of having Jazz fight impersonal forces endangering cheetahs, I have her fight for the life of one particular cheetah cub named Comet. The villains are not a generalization about people who buy wild animals as pets, or hunters who bribe officials so they can kill endangered wildlife, but specific characters with faces and names and personal quirks. The idea that saving wildlife requires determination and self-sacrifice on everyone's part is embodied in Jazz's heroic qualities.

The structure of your plot can be drawn as a staircase leading to the climax. Each stair is made of a goal, complication, and partial resolution leading to the next goal. In my book, *Elephants' Graveyard,* the wealthy head of an organization that fights ivory poaching is murdered. One of the first people Jazz wishes to question is Joseph, the victim's confidant, but here the first complication arises: Joseph has abruptly quit his job as family butler, and disappeared. In trying to find him, Jazz is faced with a series of obstacles that are circumstantial, human, and cultural. A relative who is taking care of Joseph's apartment refuses to say where Joseph has gone despite Jazz's most persuasive efforts. When Jazz tries to question neighbors, the relative loudly announces that a juju (magic charm) will harm anyone who talks about Joseph's whereabouts. Jazz and her partner, Inspector Omondi of the Nairobi police, manage to discover that Joseph is driving a cab, and after scouring various colorful Nairobi neighborhoods, trace him to the city's most dangerous shantytown. Just as they are being led to him, Jazz and Omondi are attacked by a gang of thugs with machetes, and Joseph takes off. This is the climax of the sequence: A minor setback has led to a deadly threat, and Jazz's quarry has escaped just as she thought she'd found him.

Through her sense of humor and quick thinking, Jazz turns the thugs into allies, and in a reversal of fortune, the thugs help her nab Joseph. Joseph mistakenly thinks Jazz and Omondi have saved him from attack, and in recompense, is willing to talk to them. But he will tell them only so much, giving them a clue that will lead them into further adventures. And so the next goal—and the next series of complications—are set in motion. Notice that to overcome each difficulty, Jazz and Omondi have to take positive action, which moves the plot forward.

Often a plot falters because the writer has not put complication into a scene. After you have finished the first draft, make an outline that analyzes each chapter: State the goal; the obstacle to achieving that goal; and the partial solution that results from action the protagonists take, leading to a new goal. Read authors whose plots move well, and identify the conflict/resolution sequences that build up to the climax.

Causality, character, and complication: Keep a firm grasp on these principles and you will create tight, dynamic plots that will keep your satisfied audience reading into the wee hours of the morning.

➤➤ 59

FROM GUMSHOE TO GAMMA RAYS: HIGH-TECH ADVANCES IN CRIMINAL INVESTIGATION

BY ROBERT L. SNOW

NOT LONG AGO IN INDIANAPOLIS, WE SOLVED A FOUR-YEAR-OLD MURder that we had previously believed would go unsolved. The victim had been bound and then strangled with an electric cord ripped from a lamp. Although at first we thought we might get lucky when an evidence technician lifted a partial fingerprint from the lamp, the fingerprint, it turned out, didn't match anyone connected with the case or acquainted with the victim, so the case stalled for four years.

The incident that broke the case came about because Indianapolis, like most major cities, has recently installed an Automated Fingerprint Identification System (AFIS). This very expensive computer compares fingerprints fed into it with the millions that can be stored in its memory. In setting up the system, the technicians needed to do a number of test runs, and they decided to use the fingerprint from this murder during one of the tests. Within a half hour, the computer gave us a suspect, a young street hustler who, when confronted by detectives, confessed to the murder and named his accomplice.

This incident started me thinking about all of the technological advances that have been introduced into law enforcement during just the last five or six years, and how important they can be to writers. Although police work in the 1990s still involves bringing the bad guys to justice, how the police do this has changed, and writers of mysteries, police procedurals, or those who simply include the police in a novel or short story must know about these changes because if they don't, somewhere a reader will spot the mistakes and omissions and point them out!

With the introduction of AFIS, fingerprints have increased dramatically in importance in solving crimes, particularly in cases where there are no suspects. Before AFIS, if there were no specific suspects, there was really no practical way to search through the fingerprint file of a large city like Indianapolis, which has 4,000,000 individual fingerprints on file; any fingerprints recovered in a major case that didn't match the suspect's were kept in an open file, and only as time was available were they *manually* compared against the fingerprints taken from newly arrested people. Occasionally, we would be lucky and hit a match. Now, however, a fingerprint recovered at the scene of a crime can be inserted into the AFIS computer, and its recognition points compared at enormous speed with the millions of prints already in the computer's memory.

The actual collection of fingerprints has also gone high-tech in the last five or six years, and writers need to be aware of these changes. The traditional method for collecting fingerprints involves brushing fingerprint powder onto smooth surfaces. But on many surfaces fingerprints are not visible, and in many cases—particularly when large areas are involved—the traditional method is not only messy but often impractical.

Thanks to recent developments in light technology, however, the detection of these fingerprints is now much easier. Scientists have found that the amino acids and other compounds in fingerprint residue will fluoresce under certain lighting conditions. Because of this discovery, police officers are now able to detect previously invisible fingerprints by using such devices as a Laser Print Finder, a pulsating laser beam, and Luma-Lite, a high-intensity light source. The beam of these light sources causes the amino acids and other compounds to produce glowing fingerprints that can be seen by wearing special goggles.

Finding the fingerprint is only half of the job. It must then be recovered, and rather than going high-tech, police use a simple substance to do this: the chemical cyanoacrylate, which is the main ingredient in Super Glue. Objects with fingerprints are placed in a closed container with cyanoacrylate that is either heated or simply allowed to vaporize naturally. The chemical vapors stick to the fingerprint residue and then harden.

Several years ago in California, the police recovered a vehicle believed driven by the infamous "Nightstalker." A structure was built around the car and filled with cyanoacrylate vapor. A print recovered

287

from the car was sent to the AFIS computer in Sacramento, where a match was made, and the "Nightstalker" arrested.

In addition to fingerprints, there is another personal identifier that suspects often leave behind at the scene of a crime: samples of their DNA in the form of blood, saliva, semen, or other bodily fluids. Contained in most human cells, DNA is the blueprint for a person's body, and it is now accepted as an identifier by a number of courts. While still in its infancy, DNA testing will become extremely important to the police departments of the future. Unfortunately, however, there is currently no AFIS computer for DNA, as there is for fingerprints, and so a suspect must be available in order for a match to be made. In a number of celebrated cases, however, DNA analysis has been used to free suspects rather than convict them, since it can prove that the semen, blood, or other substance left at a crime scene was not theirs.

Many times, there are no fingerprints, DNA, or live witnesses at a crime scene, but again, science has filled the gap. The police are now able to do "criminal profiling" from the evidence left at a crime scene, from the type of crime it was, and from how the crime was committed. This profiling will often suggest the perpetrator's age, sex, race, educational level, and other attributes, even though there were no witnesses.

Several years ago in Indianapolis, a woman was kidnapped from a shopping center, raped and murdered, and then left in the trunk of her car. Even though there were no witnesses to the crime, through criminal profiling we were able to develop a clear enough picture of the perpetrator to identify a likely suspect, who was arrested and later convicted of the crime.

Since the apprehension of criminals can quite often be dangerous, as in the murder case above, safety devices for officers have also gone high-tech. For example, while body armor has been around for many years, until recently it was so bulky and hot—and so obvious—that many officers decided just to take their chances. Within the last few years, however, body armor for police has become thinner, lighter, cooler, and much less obvious, and now in many high-crime areas almost all officers wear it.

Science has also improved on the old standard nightstick or billy club. Police officers today are much more likely to be carrying a PR-24, or side-handled baton, which can be used, in martial arts fashion, much more effectively than the old nightstick. And liquid tear gas has

288

been replaced by a new chemical that is much more potent and effective, disorienting a person as well as irritating the eyes and nasal passages. One form of spray now offered even uses the chemical found in red peppers.

Along with saving lives, however, saving time has also become high-tech, and computers are now firmly established in law enforcement. They are everywhere, from Computer-Aided Dispatching to in-car terminals, from in-car navigational systems to computer mug shot terminals that can age, remove hair, grow beards, add moustaches, etc. And of course, many police departments now routinely computerize their records.

Writers also need to know that in the last five or six years video cameras have become standard law enforcement equipment. Crime scenes are now routinely videotaped, as are suspect line-ups and confessions. A number of police departments are also installing video cameras in police cars to record everything the officer sees and hears through the windshield. These are, of course, of immeasurable help in convicting anyone committing a crime that's visible through the windshield, and they have actually recorded the murder of police officers by the occupants of stopped vehicles.

The above examples are only a few of the dozens of recent innovations in law enforcement technology that writers need to be aware of if they want their work to be authentic. There are many more, including laser-sighted weapons, night-vision goggles, Tasers (electric stun guns), multi-channel walkie-talkies with scrambling capability, signalling devices that allow the police to track stolen cars, robots for high-risk entry, quick and accurate kits for field testing drugs (police officers NEVER, NEVER test drugs by tasting them!), and many more high-tech advances.

There are several ways for a writer to learn about these high-tech advances: reading police journals such as *Law and Order* (1000 Skokie Boulevard, Wilmette, IL 60091); *Police* (6300 Yarrow Drive, Carlsbad, CA 92009); or *Law Enforcement Technology* (445 Broad Hollow Road, Melville, NY 11747). If these are not available in your local or community library, try the library at a university that has a Criminal Justice program. You might also try inviting a police officer to your writers club meeting; most police departments will send an officer to groups that request them, and they are usually glad to discuss the details of their work and investigation procedures.

Still another way for writers to get a firsthand view of police work in action: Most large police departments have ride-along programs for citizens who want to see police work up close. Be prepared, however, for salty talk, filthy homes, and bloody situations, which are all part of police work. And if, as occasionally happens, you ride on a slow night when nothing is happening, don't be discouraged; this will give you eight uninterrupted hours to pick the officer's brain.

I suspect that some writers, particularly those without a firm grounding in the sciences, will be discouraged by all of this new police technology because they don't believe they'll be able to understand it. Don't be. Your viewpoint character doesn't have to have the in-depth knowledge of a scientist, but if you want your work to ring of authenticity *you* must know at least as much as the police do.

➤➤ Nonfiction: Articles and Books

➤➤ 60

CREATIVE NONFICTION: WHERE JOURNALISM AND STORYTELLING MEET

BY MARK H. MASSÉ

A DEDICATED FIFTH-GRADE TEACHER GIVES HER STRUGGLING STU-
dents hope in a depressed New England mill town (*Among Schoolchildren*, by Tracy Kidder). A power-hungry Southern sheriff clashes
with a proud African-American community leader in rural Georgia
(*Praying for Sheetrock*, by Melissa F. Greene). Innovative crisis workers in Oregon help clients battle mental illness as they heal their own
emotional pain in my book, *FRONTLINE*.

These may sound like fictional narratives, but they are factual accounts—products of extensive research and reportage, combined with
dramatic storytelling techniques. Welcome to the exciting world of
creative nonfiction. In the 1960s and 1970s, when Truman Capote (*In
Cold Blood*), Gay Talese (*Honor Thy Father*), and Tom Wolfe (*The
Right Stuff*) were melding in-depth reporting with literary writing,
their work was called New Journalism. Currently, the term "creative
nonfiction" is increasingly popular. The good news for today's writers
is that this genre offers new, expanding opportunities to craft distinctive, evocative stories using a combination of fiction and nonfiction
techniques.

To produce successful creative nonfiction, you must have a credible
and compelling story to tell. It should inform and enlighten the reader
and be based on verifiable facts. Yet, a good creative nonfiction writer
will transcend the conventions of fact-based journalism by portraying
characters with psychological depth, providing riveting details and descriptions, and presenting a true story that uses dramatic scenes to
engage the reader's interest and emotions.

293

A telling comparison

Compare the following two treatments of a scene from a 24-hour crisis hotline. First, a straight news approach:

Pat, a veteran crisis worker, sits in one of the clinic's cluttered offices and answers another call.

"I got a .45 here on my lap, and I've spent the last week convincing myself that I shouldn't pull the trigger," the man on the line says. "But I've run out of reasons. I'll give you five minutes to convince me that I shouldn't kill myself."

"That's not going to work," Pat says firmly. "You could give me five minutes or five years, and I still might not have an answer that I could give you. What I can do is help you to find you own reasons to go on living—if that's what you want to do."

The same scene in creative nonfiction style (from *FRONTLINE*):

A dozen steps away in the cluttered buckstopper office, which overlooks the wide, sagging front porch, Pat instinctively takes a deep breath and plants his bare feet firmly on the scruffy brown carpet before answering the phone.

"I got a .45 here on my lap, and I've spent the last week convincing myself that I shouldn't pull the trigger. But I've run out of reasons." The voice on the other end is deep and gruff-sounding, the craggy voice of a longtime pack-a-day man. His words are flat, emotionless. "I'll give you five minutes to convince me that I shouldn't kill myself."

The first thing that pops into Pat's mind is the one-liner that he told the crisis team at last Monday's group debriefing session: "Suicide is our way of telling God—you can't fire me, I quit!" But Pat isn't smiling. The familiar queasy feeling of fear is welling up inside him.

"That's not going to work," he tells the caller. "You could give me five minutes or five years, and I still might not have an answer that I could give you." He pauses, not knowing if he'll hear the click of a receiver. "What I can do is help you to find your own reasons to go on living—if that's what you want to do."

By including concrete details and sensory imagery to describe the scene (e.g., bare feet on a scruffy carpet; craggy voice of a longtime pack-a-day man), I tried to evoke a mood and make an impact on the reader. The use of extended dialogue and internal monologue—other techniques of creative nonfiction—heightened the tension in this life-and-death drama. Through numerous interviews, oral histories, and months of "participant observation," I learned firsthand about the demanding life of a crisis worker. Tom Wolfe calls this approach "saturation reporting," getting to know people, settings, and story background in sufficient detail to craft a literary journalistic tale.

Extensive research into the inner world of crisis intervention enabled me to write the kind of dramatic scene typically found in fiction. In the excerpt from *FRONTLINE,* I was able to "get inside the head" of the crisis worker and share his thoughts, feelings, and fears with the reader. Ultimately, this scene worked because of the same dynamic that drives successful short stories and novels: a sympathetic protagonist confronted with a complicated problem, conflict, and crisis in which the outcome is uncertain.

To write creative nonfiction successfully, focus on these fundamentals:

1) An appropriate subject
2) Research
3) A dramatic story

Choosing an appropriate subject

The first consideration in approaching a creative nonfiction project is the author's interest in and connection to a given subject. An appropriate topic is one that can be presented with sufficient scope to achieve the intimacy, insight, and drama required of a well-written work of creative nonfiction. In my study of the Eugene, Oregon, crisis intervention team, access to crisis workers' personal and professional lives over several months gave me the opportunity to compile detailed material that I would later rely on when writing my nonfiction narrative.

There is a wide range of subjects suitable for creative nonfiction treatment. Here is a list of possible categories for your consideration:

- Adventure
- Biography
- Business
- Communities
- Crime stories
- Family sagas
- Government & politics
- History
- Institutions
- Personal experience
- Popular culture
- Science & technology
- Sports
- Travel

Before embarking on a work of creative nonfiction, ask yourself: What is this story going to be about? What are the broader themes and/or ramifications of this subject? How can I marshal the facts, the emotions, and the deeper meanings of this story?

For example, in telling his story of friendships in a Massachusetts nursing home (*Old Friends*), Pulitzer Prize-winning creative nonfiction writer Tracy Kidder examined a much larger landscape: aging in America. My tale of Oregon crisis workers on the "front line of pain" isn't merely about mental illness; ultimately, it is a universal story of heroism in everyday life—how "ordinary" people (caregivers) are capable of extraordinary achievements in serving others in need. This theme is appropriate for any good story, whether fiction or nonfiction.

Research

Maybe you don't fancy yourself as brilliant a chronicler of popular culture and the American scene as Tom Wolfe. Perhaps you aren't as renowned for your powers of observation and reporting as John McPhee. Do Joan Didion's remarkable insights into the seemingly ordinary events of everyday life intimidate you? Don't despair. In deciding whether to tackle a work of creative nonfiction, go back to the basics of what makes a writer in the first place.

Are you a good people watcher? Observe the particulars of how a person dresses, walks, eats, gestures. Train your ear to hear the subtleties of a conversation—the trace of an accent, the tone of a voice, an inflection. By putting gestures and conversation together, try to detect any underlying meaning to the dialogue. Concentrate on the recurring details of the environment you are studying, such as "official or unofficial" norms, customs, and rituals.

As a careful and sensitive observer of individuals and groups, you may be able to conduct the saturation reporting that is the foundation of creative nonfiction. Excellent interviewing skills will be vital to your research. In studying people over an extended period of time, you must be adept at gaining their confidence and cooperation. This is achieved by your personal credibility and persuasiveness, combined with sensitive, creative interviewing techniques. Your ability to converse with rather than interrogate your sources will determine how successful you will be in portraying your characters accurately and with the detail required of a fully developed, complex story.

Creative nonfiction has been called the "literature of fact" for good reason: Writers in this field depend on information to generate a story.

In addition to observing and conducting interviews, you must immerse yourself in your subject by reading voraciously, using electronic information retrieval services (computerized databases) and contacting experts. When collecting facts, you must "sweat the details."

Creative nonfiction writers must not violate the rules of accuracy and honesty. In the words of Gay Talese, "All that we write should be verifiable." Before you write a single line of internal monologue for a character, make sure you have in your interview notes the actual words from the person about what he or she was thinking at a given time.

A dramatic story

The years I have spent as a fiction writer—honing my narrative skills, structuring dramatic scenes, developing complex characters, drafting realistic dialogue—gave me the confidence to write creative nonfiction. Before you attempt a work of creative nonfiction, you must know the difference between such basics as narration, description, and exposition. Once you have mastered these storytelling techniques and acquired research and reporting skills, you may have the tools to produce vivid, innovative nonfiction narratives.

A creative nonfiction story begins with sound research. Cull your notes for scenes with dramatic potential (e.g., arguments, crises, confrontations, discoveries), including names of the characters involved, a description of the complication, and the resolution—if there was one. Also, list your scenes chronologically—a valuable aid when it comes time to plot your story.

Selecting the appropriate narrative structure is just as essential for a work of creative nonfiction as it is for a novel. Review your material carefully, and remember that form should follow function. How can you best present this story in a way that informs, enlightens, and engages the reader? If there is a natural progression to the story, then a chronological structure may be appropriate. But even with a chronological structure, you may choose to begin the story *in medias res* (in the middle of the action) with a dramatic opening, before flashing back or forward to resume the story.

When chronicling the accounts of several individuals in a creative nonfiction story, you may find it helpful to use parallel narratives that converge at a climactic point in the "plot." Another tried-and-true method is the quest or journey story, in which characters pursue a dream, destination, or goal and the plot develops accordingly.

Like the fiction writer, the author of creative nonfiction must decide on the proper point of view of his or her story. The best approach is to let the strength of your material determine whether you use first- or third-person viewpoint or a combination of the two. Another key decision you must make is how much of a role (if any) you will play in the story: Remember, the presence of the writer as a character may detract from the story's dramatic action.

Although a creative nonfiction story uses a mixture of narrative techniques, it remains a fact-driven literary form, emphasizing concrete, verifiable details about characters, events, settings, and dialogue. Unlike the fiction writer, who can rely solely on his or her imagination to weave a story, the creative nonfiction writer is bound by facts, opinions, observations, and other information collected during the research phase. But, the imagination of the dramatic nonfiction author plays an important role in the creative and persuasive "telling" of a true story.

➤➤ 61

AT LEAST TWO SIDES TO EVERY STORY

BY HARRIET WEBSTER

IMAGINE THIRTY CARRIER PIGEONS WINGING THROUGH THE UNIVERSE, each one looking for a congenial place to nest. That's how I envision my queries—a flock of message-bearing birds searching for just the right homes.

I support myself as a full-time free lancer, and I've discovered that in order always to have enough work, I need to keep 25–30 queries in circulation all the time, and to produce fresh ideas continually. That's not such a problem since I embraced what I call the at-least-two-sides-to-every-story approach, which basically involves treating one subject from several angles. It's a great way to refuel and increase the number of queries you have in circulation and consequently the number of positive responses you get back. You may not be able to locate a publication that wants to run your feature story on that fantastic children's museum you visited, but perhaps an editor will take the bait when you suggest a piece describing ten great children's museums across the country.

The more well-crafted queries you submit, the more likely you are to catch an editor's interest. By looking at your article idea through the prism of your imagination, you'll soon find you can generate several proposals from what began as a single subject. Ideally, your inquiries will result in an assignment or an encouraging although less committed "go ahead." Don't turn away if, as frequently happens, you are asked to do the piece on speculation—that is, when an editor expresses interest in seeing your article but does not make a firm commitment to publish it.

I've found that an important key to getting solid assignments is putting together clips of your published work to show editors the quality of writing you can do. In the best scenario, by writing on spec you will produce a published piece as evidence of your competence, which will lead to a productive working relationship with a satisfied editor who may publish more of your articles down the road. Beginning writers who refuse to work on spec are in effect slamming the door in their own faces. The truth is that there's a speculation aspect to any piece, even if it's assigned. After seeing one of your queries, an editor may ask you to write a specific piece based on it, but that doesn't mean he has to publish it. If he does not accept it, he may pay what is called a "kill fee" (usually no more than 25% of the previously agreed upon price), assuming that the publication does in fact pay "kill fees." Many publications do not.

Now, after nearly 25 years of free-lancing, most of my work is assigned. However, I still write an occasional piece on spec, usually when I want to break into a new publication and an editor there says to go ahead with the article even though he isn't willing to make a commitment in advance to buy it. I know that, having expressed interest, he will give my piece a thorough reading, particularly if I deliver it in a reasonable length of time, while it's still fresh in his memory.

Looking at one subject from several angles and fashioning several queries around it helps me get moving when I'm stuck for ideas and enables me to query several different publications at the same time. While one editor may be willing to assign a piece on one aspect of my subject, another might express interest in a different approach, on spec. For a couple of years now, I've wanted to write an article about adult sibling relationships, particularly between sisters and brothers. I still haven't found an interested editor, but I did get a go-ahead on a related piece, one centered on a new bride's relationship with her husband's siblings. *Bride's Magazine* accepted it.

Sometimes the fresh perspective comes from a magazine editor. If you're willing to envision the subject you've proposed through someone else's eyes, you may be able to place your manuscript. I queried *Family Circle* about a piece profiling a mother-daughter housecleaning business. Though the editors weren't interested in that angle, they asked me if I would interview the mother and daughter to get their hints for the magazine's annual spring cleaning feature.

Here are some other ways to use the at least-two-sides-to-every-story approach to boost your queries and, ultimately, your sales.

1. *Individualize your queries.* Personally disorganized, I used to worry that I'd pass my bad habits on to my children. To help me figure out ways to keep that from happening, I developed a piece for *Working Mother* on how to teach your child organizational skills. In the course of doing that, I also suggested a piece to *Seventeen* showing teens how to organize their time. The magazine took it.

The point is this: Ideas are adaptable. If you want to do a piece on how to create kitchen storage space for a home magazine, why not also submit a query to a craft magazine on storage options for a basement workroom? Or, a parenting publication might be interested in a piece on how to solve storage problems in a child's room.

2. *Vary the point of view.* To write about a magnificent new playground built by volunteers, why not write one query homing in on a key figure—perhaps a teenager or a group of teens who immersed themselves in the project. Then write another suggesting a piece from the point of view of the school principal or adults in the community who spearheaded the project.

I was fortunate enough to sell a piece on peer education to *Better Homes & Gardens* (how to start a program in your child's school) and another to *Seventeen* (focusing on some teenagers involved in such a program). The first piece was heavy on advice from guidance counselors and school administrators, while the second relied on the voices of teenagers who have been involved in such a program.

3. *Approach varied markets.* Let's say your child is an avid soccer fan and you want to write about soccer. Query a sports magazine about a piece on the enormous growth of the sport nationally. Try a parenting magazine with a query on what makes a good coach; what to do when parents act like poor sports; what it feels like to be a soccer parent (spending your weekends freezing your toes at remote fields). Then pitch an article on safety considerations in soccer to a health publication and a consumer-oriented piece to a newspaper sports section in which you focus on the type of equipment needed and how to buy it at bargain prices.

4. *Experiment with opposites.* Suppose you are interested in writing a human-interest piece about a single woman who adopted a baby

301

from China. You envision a warm, heartfelt article that chronicles her feelings from the moment the agency called and asked if she was interested in the little girl, right up to the present. You send your query off to the lifestyle section of a number of newspapers and also submit it to several women's magazines. Have you covered all the possible markets? Perhaps not.

How about writing a second query that deals with the problems single women encounter when they try to adopt a child? Or perhaps you could suggest a piece about the frustrations involved in international adoptions. By proposing an article targeting the *problems* involved, as well as one describing a successful *experience,* you'll multiply your number of queries.

5. *Take your specialty apart.* The idea here is to take your main idea and turn it inside out. Interested in travel writing? Find out what kinds of travel pieces various publications run. Flip through a few issues and note the titles that intrigue you. Also check the features and departments and even the ads. You may find that in addition to destination pieces, a magazine runs personality and business profiles, and features on food, sports, shopping, museums, environmental issues, celebrations, and dozens of other subjects.

When I visited Colorado with my teen-age son, I figured I might be able to sell a travel piece about our trip. I was delighted when *The Boston Globe* assigned one on Glenwood Springs, a town we discovered by mistake and loved. And I was also able to expand my sales by writing several special-interest queries. Out of these, *FamilyFun* bought a first-person essay describing what it felt like to watch my son undertake his first serious rock-climbing experience.

I'm still circulating a query describing our experiences camping and hiking in Rocky Mountain National Park. I'm also thinking of querying a magazine that does an annual roundup of family-friendly resorts to see if they might be interested in a short piece about a splendid Victorian era hotel we visited.

6. *Big picture, little picture.* If you are an avid researcher, you may well find yourself feeling frustrated when, in the course of preparing a query for a piece, you collect tons of exciting material that doesn't fit into the article you're planning to write. Don't let the leftover material

go to waste. I once wrote a piece for *Americana Magazine* describing the technique used by guides at the Plimouth Plantation, a Massachusetts living history museum, to bring visitors into the lives of the people who lived in the village in the 17th century: Each of the guides plays the role of a specific individual who inhabited the plantation.

I was so fascinated by it that by the time I'd finished writing it, I had a great deal of material that I just couldn't fit in. In particular, I wanted to write about the reenactment of a Wampanoag Indian wedding ceremony I had attended. It turned out the reenactment is held several times a year, so I was able to work up a "weekender" piece for *Newsday,* a Long Island, NY, newspaper with a Sunday travel section that usually features a timely event or activity within a day's drive of the city.

Another possible approach is to write a query geared to a local publication and then to expand it to create a version appropriate for a regional or national magazine or newspaper. The moral of the story is that looking at both the big picture and the little picture is a great way to increase your query inventory.

By increasing the number of proposals you submit and the number and types of publications you submit them to—ranging from well-known national magazines to regional periodicals, from special-interest magazines to trade journals to newspapers—you up your chances of finding editors who will encourage you and may eventually publish your work. By looking at your ideas from many different angles, you will discover that you need never run out of material for intriguing queries.

Ideas are waiting to be discovered by article writers every day. Remember that "conversation" you had with your daughter this morning as she ran out the door to catch the school bus without taking time for breakfast . . . again? Parents all over the country can identify with that. What kinds of queries can you generate from it? A piece on teenage nutrition issues. An article focusing on how skipping breakfast affects school performance. A food piece listing ready-to-grab-and-eat-on-the-run nutritious breakfasts for kids. A first-person piece about the difficulty of letting go as your child verges on adulthood and makes her own sometimes dubious decisions. A nostalgic piece on eating breakfast with the kids when they were little. Whom will you interview? Nutritionists, teachers, teens, other parents, a pediatrician. . . .

Where will you send the queries? Health and parenting publications, magazines for young women, op-ed pages. . . . Soon you'll find yourself armed with a substantial batch of queries ready to circulate. With patience, perseverance, and a pinch of good luck, some of them will find good markets.

⪼ 62

When a Biographer's Subject Is Less than Perfect

By David Robertson

Recently, I had the pleasure of reading in a national newspaper a favorable, front-page review of my first biography. The book's subject is James F. Byrnes, a former U.S. Secretary of State, who was an unrepentant segregationist, a firm advocate of the atomic bombings in Japan, and the architect of the Republican "southern strategy" that has given us such leaders as Newt Gingrich. Stating that I had chosen a "sometimes wholly unsympathetic subject," the reviewer praised the book as a "balanced, deeply researched and sympathetic history of the man."

My first reaction to the review was like that of a boy who had learned how to aim a pellet gun, but who then shot and killed a songbird: I felt pride in my skills, but was appalled at the results. What had I done by raising in public memory the life of such an apparently unsympathetic figure? And if I, as the biographer, had been found sympathetic to such a life, what did that say about me, and the uses to which I had put my life and literary work?

Upon reflection, however, I decided to accept the praise for what it is. Even unsympathetic subjects deserve an accurate accounting of their minor virtues, as well as their major vices. If nothing else, such a biographical account can help explain to the reader how the subject failed to achieve a good, or at least decent, life by choices taken or not taken. And, frankly, for a biographer searching for a modern subject, twentieth-century history offers far more major figures whose lives will provide shock and disapproval than admiration and self-identification. Think, for example, of the number of twentieth-century leaders who were "great" in the sense that Stalin was great, rather than that Eleanor Roosevelt was a great leader.

Whether in dealing with a public or a private figure, with a sympathetic or unsympathetic subject, the writing of all biographies is, I believe, a deliberate grappling with the "other," an entity different from us, a person whose life we cannot fully comprehend or approve. The first biographer to learn this hard lesson was the biblical Jacob, who spent all night wrestling with an angel in an attempt to learn the other being's true name. (Jacob got his hip broken for his trouble.) But the resulting struggles, particularly with an unsympathetic subject, can strengthen a biographer's skills, just as I feel mine were strengthened by my struggles to determine whether Secretary Byrnes led an admirable or unadmirable life.

Currently, I am grappling with my own dark angel; I am writing a second biography of a man who, unlike Byrnes, is largely an admirable figure, but whose personality and actions are disturbing to me. The subject is Denmark Vesey (1767?–1822), a former slave who purchased his own freedom and then attempted the largest slave insurrection in the history of the United States at Charleston, South Carolina. In many ways, we are similar: Vesey, like me, was in his late forties when he attempted his uprising; we could have spoken in several foreign languages; we both spent much of our free time as manual laborers, and have no illusions about the horrors of American slavery. But as I walk the nineteenth-century streets of Charleston at night, passing Vesey's carpentry shop where he had planned his revolution, one thought is inescapable to me: I am a white southerner. Had Vesey's plot succeeded, his followers were under his strict orders to kill *every* white person at Charleston, including men, women, and small children, before burning the city and seizing ships at harbor to sail for Africa. Hence, although I am Vesey's biographer and intend to write sympathetically of his life, there is no doubt that, had we chanced to meet, Denmark Vesey would have cut David Robertson's throat.

My experience in writing and researching lives of subjects whose actions appear malevolent or whose historical image resists a biographer's self-identification has led me to adopt certain techniques. I offer these techniques to other biographers struggling with a less-than-sympathetic subject.

Write the life your subject lived. Some subjects, as disparate and attractive as Alice James or Adlai Stevenson, engage a biographer's admiration for what they could not or did not do. But frequently in writing of public or famous figures, the biographer is tempted to scold or rebuke the subject for not living the life the biographer expected. This can be great fun at the expense of the dead, of course, as Lytton Strachey demonstrated in *Eminent Victorians*. But recent biographies of John Kennedy and Lyndon Johnson have been marred, in my opinion, by the biographers' refusal to consider the historical and political limits to their subjects' actions and their personal failings. Byrnes, for example, as a Supreme Court Justice, U.S. Senator, and the "Assistant President" during World War II, did far less than he should have to protect civil liberties for blacks and the rights of organized labor. But in researching the careers of other prominent southern politicians— including Justice Hugo Black of Alabama, who served with Byrnes on the Supreme Court—I discovered that Byrnes often did more than his contemporaries expected of him, and sometimes did so to his personal disadvantage. Justice Black chose to remove himself from electoral politics and try to do what was right; Jimmy Byrnes chose to remain in politics and to do what was possible. I chose to write the life of the politician, not the jurist.

Such a decision means that the biographer must emphasize historical context as well as personality. Expect to do far more research in history and social sciences if you choose to write on an unsympathetic subject. (My bibliography and endnotes to the Byrnes biography ran to 69 small-type pages.) That research helped me comprehend—if not fully approve—the planned ferocity of Denmark Vesey's attempted revolt. I discovered that during Denmark Vesey's lifetime, South Carolina contained more African-born people in bondage than any other slave-holding state at the time. These proud men and women considered themselves to be *African,* not African-American, and in a type of "ethnic cleansing," their masters were attempting to destroy their ties to marriage, parenthood, their religion, and their nations. Vesey, who probably had traveled to Africa, preached to these first-generation slaves that he was attempting to liberate not only them, but also their right as a people to exist unmolested in their own homeland. Considered historically as an armed struggle against physical and cultural genocide, Vesey's actions appear more expedient. Do we blame the Cheyenne for taking no prisoners at Little Big Horn?

307

Don't be surprised by surprises. In writing a biography of an unre-deemably selfish or cruel individual, don't be surprised by occasional acts of generosity or sentimentality. Include them, not as unaccount-able surprises, but as further evidence for your case. Sentimentality is the weakling brother of brutality. Even human monsters will occasion-ally show pity or indulgence as if to convince themselves, if not the reader of their biographies, that they really *aren't* monsters. Hitler, an acquaintance told me, was very fond of lighthearted movies and large, friendly dogs. Stalin, with his baggy-seat trousers, his beloved pipe tobacco, and his crinkly brown eyes, could appear as Uncle Joe from the Old Country. The contiguous existence of pity and brutality within one uneasy individual is a concept as twentieth-century as Freud, who warned us that inside each sadist is a powerless child terrified of be-coming a victim, and as ancient as Tacitus, who wrote of one cruel Caesar that if we could see his soul at night, we would see a face self-lacerated in fear.

Occasionally, a subject acting against type can illuminate the larger personality the biographer wishes he had been. Byrnes, who after his retirement from the Department of State spent much of his life frustrat-ing efforts to put civil rights legislation into effect in the South, was outraged when a black friend of his was denied the use of a public restroom in South Carolina in the 1960s. Byrnes wrote angry letters, and considered all sorts of political retribution, in an effort to convince a white segregationist that Byrnes' black friend was "special," and therefore deserving of all the civil liberties and rights of any U.S. citi-zen. Yet Byrnes seemed never to have considered that, legally and morally, all individuals are special, regardless of their skin color. Byrnes' failure to make an intuitive and ethical leap toward all U.S. citizens, regardless of his good intentions in this single episode, illumi-nates both his possibilities and his limitations as a national leader.

Shake hands with your dark side. "If Hitler could have had any friends, I would certainly have been among his close friends," Albert Speer tells us in his memoirs of the Third Reich. Speer's account of how he became Hitler's chief architect and armaments minister is in many ways also the "best" biography of Hitler, but it is in no way an *apologia* for the madness and unadulterated evil of Adolf Hitler. Speer's book is, rather, a disturbing account of how a possibly decent individual came in his writing to identify with such an evil person. Speer's account is plainly self-serving. But it offers a statement *in extremis* of the final temptations and difficulties besetting the biographer of an unsympathetic subject.

Leon Edel has warned us of what he called "transference," whereby a biographer's subject becomes an idealized self-portrait of the biographer. Transference occurs most commonly when the subject is considered admirable. Conversely, when writing of an unsympathetic subject, the biographer is in danger of being unnerved by recognizing his own baser impulses in the actions of the subject. I began to be concerned with my own past untruthfulness, for example, after years of seeing in Jimmy Byrnes' life how easily a lie can advance a career. Similarly, I have never felt the lash of slavery; but what if I had? And what if I had then met Denmark Vesey, a man of biblical presence and authority, who secretly handed me a weapon and told me, as he told his other followers at Charleston, "And they shall utterly destroy all that was in the city, with the edge of the sword"?

In recognizing the parts of our personality we wish to deny, we can to a degree control them or change them. In writing about an unsympathetic subject, you must expect to learn as much about your own darker side as about your subject's. When the subject's baser motives hit too close to home, the biographer can be tempted to write an overlong justification of the subject's actions, or be cowed into an embarrassed silence. But if a biographer is honest about his or her own strengths and weaknesses, then that biographer can write about an unsympathetic subject with uncommon honesty and strength.

All of which brings us back to Jacob struggling with his angel at night. Jacob, you will recall, never learned the angel's true name. But in acknowledgement of Jacob's struggles, and the wound he received, the angel told Jacob *his* true name. Jacob became a better, and different, person for knowing it. Similarly, the struggles and personal wounds a biographer sustains in writing about an unsympathetic subject can, at the end of the subject's life, leave the biographer with a different and better identity: as a researcher, biographer, and as literary artist.

➤➤ 63

FACTS AND THE NONFICTION WRITER

BY TRACY KIDDER

WHEN I STARTED WRITING NONFICTION A COUPLE OF DECADES AGO there was an idea in the air, which for me had the force of a revelation: that all journalism was inevitably subjective. I was in my twenties then, and although my behavior was somewhat worse than it has been recently, I was quite a moralist. I decided that writers of nonfiction had a moral obligation to write in the first person—really write in the first person, making themselves characters on the page. In this way, I would disclose my biases. I would not hide the truth from the reader. I would proclaim that what I wrote was just my own impression of events. In retrospect it seems clear that this prescription for honesty often served as a license for self-absorption on the page. I was too young and self-absorbed to realize what should have been obvious: that I was less likely to write honestly about myself than about anyone else on earth.

I wrote a book about a murder case in a swashbuckling first person. After it was published and disappeared without a trace, I went back to writing articles for the *Atlantic Monthly*. For about five years, during which I didn't dare attempt another book, I worked on creating what many writer friends of mine call "voice." I didn't do this consciously. If I had, I probably wouldn't have gotten anywhere. But gradually, I think, I found a writing voice, the voice of a person who was informed, fair-minded, and always temperate—the voice, not of the person I was, but of the person I wanted to be. Then I went back to writing books, and discovered other points of view besides the first person.

Choosing a point of view is a matter of finding the best place from which to tell a story. The process shouldn't be determined by theory, but driven by immersion in the material itself. The choice of point of view, I've come to think, has nothing to do with morality. It's a choice

310

among tools. On the other hand, the wrong choice can lead to dishonesty. Point of view is primary; it affects everything else, including voice. I've made my choices by instinct sometimes and sometimes by experiment. Most of my memories of time spent writing have merged together in a blur, but I remember vividly my first attempts to find a way to write *Among Schoolchildren,* a book about an inner-city teacher. I had spent a year inside her classroom. I intended, vaguely, to fold into my account of events I'd witnessed there a great deal about the lives of particular children and about the problems of education in America. I tried every point of view that I'd used in previous books, and every page I wrote felt lifeless and remote. Finally, I hit on a restricted third-person narration.

That approach seemed to work. The world of that classroom seemed to come alive when the view of it was restricted mainly to observations of the teacher and to accounts of what the teacher saw and heard and smelled and felt. This choice narrowed my options. I ended up writing something less comprehensive than I'd planned. The book became essentially an account of a year in the emotional life of a schoolteacher.

My choice of the restricted third person also obliged me to write parts of the book as if from within the teacher's mind. I wrote many sentences that contained the phrase "she thought." I felt I could do so because the teacher had told me how she felt and what she thought about almost everything that happened in her classroom. And her descriptions of her thoughts and feelings never seemed self-serving. Believing in them myself, I thought that I could make them believable on the page.

For me, part of the pleasure of reading comes from the awareness that an author stands behind the scenes adroitly pulling the strings. But the pleasure quickly palls at painful reminders of that presence— the times when, for instance, I sense that the author strains to produce yet another clever metaphor. Then I stop believing in what I read, and usually stop reading. Belief is what a reader offers an author, what Coleridge famously called "That willing suspension of disbelief for the moment, which constitutes poetic faith." All writers have to find ways to do their work without disappointing readers into withdrawing belief.

In fiction, believability may have nothing to do with reality or even plausibility. It has everything to do with those things in nonfiction.

I think that the nonfiction writer's fundamental job is to make what

311

is true believable. But for some writers lately the job has clearly become more varied: to make believable what the writer thinks is true (if the writer wants to be scrupulous); to make believable what the writer wishes were true (if the writer isn't interested in scrupulosity); or to make believable what the writer thinks might be true (if the writer couldn't get the story and had to make it up).

I figure that if I call a piece of my own writing nonfiction it ought to be about real people, with their real names attached whenever possible, who say and do in print nothing that they didn't actually say and do. On the cover page of my new book I put a note that reads, "This is a work of nonfiction," and I listed the several names that I was obliged to change in the text. I feared that a longer note would stand between the reader and the spell that I wanted to create, inviting the reader into the world of a nursing home. But the definition of "nonfiction" has become so slippery that I wonder if I shouldn't have written more. So now I'll take this opportunity to explain that I spent a year doing research, that the name of the place I wrote about is its real name, that I didn't change the names of any major characters, and that I didn't invent dialogue or put any thoughts in characters' minds that the characters themselves didn't confess to.

I no longer care what rules other writers set for themselves. If I don't like what someone has written, I can stop reading, which is, after all, the worst punishment a writer can suffer. But the expanded definitions of "nonfiction" have created problems for those writers who define the term narrowly. Many readers now view with suspicion every narrative that claims to be nonfiction. But not all writers make up their stories or the details in them. In fact, scores of very good writers do not—writers such as John McPhee (*Coming into the Country*), Jane Kramer (*The Last Cowboy*), J. Anthony Lucas (*Common Ground*). There are also special cases, which confound categories and all attempts to lay down rules for narrative. I have in mind especially Norman Mailer's *Executioner's Song,* a hybrid of fact and fiction, labeled as such, which I loved reading.

Most writers lack Mailer's powers of invention. Some nonfiction writers do not lack his willingness to invent, but the candor to admit it. Some writers proceed by trying to discover the truth about a situation, and then invent the facts as necessary. Even in these suspicious times, a writer can get away with this. Often no one will know, and the subjects of the story may not care. They may approve. They may not notice. But the writer always knows. I believe in immersion in the events of a story. I take it on faith that the truth lies in the events somewhere, and that immersion in those real events will yield glimpses of that truth. I try to hew to a narrow definition of nonfiction partly in that faith and partly out of fear. I'm afraid that if I started making things up in a story that purported to be about real events and people, I'd stop believing it myself. And I imagine that such a loss of conviction would infect every sentence and make each one unbelievable.

I don't mean to imply that all a person has to do to write good nonfiction is to take accurate notes and reproduce them. The kind of nonfiction I like to read is at bottom storytelling, as gracefully accomplished as good fiction. I don't think any technique should be ruled out to achieve it well. For myself, I rule out only invention. But I don't think that honesty and artifice are contradictory. They work together in good writing of every sort. Artfulness and an author's justified belief in a story often combine to produce the most believable nonfiction.

>> 64

CONDUCTING THE "SENSITIVE" INTERVIEW

BY KATHLEEN WINKLER

A DAUGHTER WHO WAS STALKED AND KILLED BY A FORMER LOVER. Surgery that left impotence in its wake. An abortion kept secret for years. A past that includes painful abuse.

Occasionally in your writing career you may find yourself interviewing people about topics that are very hard to talk about. Sometimes it's because they are physically unpleasant or embarrassing. Sometimes it's because they are emotionally wrenching. In either case, you as the writer have a great challenge: to make your subjects feel comfortable enough to share sensitive, intimate experiences with you so your readers can benefit from them.

An awkward interviewer, trampling on the subject's sensibilities, will not only not get a good story, but can also do great damage to the subject, who may never again trust anyone enough to open up.

A skilled and sympathetic interviewer, on the other hand, will not only elicit a moving story from the subject, but may actually help him or her come to terms with an experience kept hidden or repressed for years.

It all depends on how you go about it.

As a medical writer for fifteen years, I've interviewed people on such intimate topics as sexual function, emotional responses to physical scars from surgery, and life-threatening illness. In the course of writing *When the Crying Stops: Abortion, the Pain and the Healing* (Northwestern Publishing House), I interviewed twenty women about their abortion experiences and subsequent reactions. Some of these women had never told their stories to anyone before the interview.

As a result of these often painful interviews, I've developed an approach to sensitive interviewing and some helpful ways to make such interviews easier for me and for the subject, and more productive.

I believe that the number one rule for interviewing on any topic, especially a sensitive one, is respect for the person sitting across from you. Always keep in mind that he or she doesn't *owe* you anything. In most cases your subject is telling his or her story out of a simple desire to help others cope with the same or a similar problem, with no expectation of any kind of reward. The subject, therefore, has the right to decide how much to share. While as the interviewer you can encourage the sharing and make it as free of stress as possible, you must not try to force the person to reveal more than he or she is willing to. The subject has the right to end the interview at any point, or to say, "I don't want to talk about that"—and you must respect that decision.

There are some things you can do to make a sensitive interview as tension-free as possible for the subject, and, at the same time, get the information you need to write an honest and moving piece.

• Since it's absolutely essential to use a tape recorder during the interview—especially if there are likely to be any legal aspects to the project—ask the subject for permission to do so, explaining that you want to be sure your quotes are accurate. But get the permission on tape before you begin.

• Preparation is important. Never try to "wing" an interview. Learn as much as you can about the person in advance. If the story is likely to have a psychological or medical slant, do your research: Familiarize yourself with the problem and the various treatments and side effects. In dealing with a social problem—child abuse, spouse battering, etc.—read current background material on all aspects of it.

• Prepare your questions carefully ahead of time. Start with the general, less threatening questions and move on to those dealing with the more difficult, personal aspects of the experience. Begin by asking about the subject's childhood and the events that led up to the traumatic experience. This will help relax your subject and get the dialogue flowing.

• When you arrive at the interview, the subject is likely to be nervous. A warm smile, a handshake, and a friendly comment—"I'm so happy to meet you; I think it's wonderful that you are willing to share your experience with others"—will go a long way toward putting the subject at ease.

• If your subject is especially nervous, confront that fact—don't ignore it—saying, "I know this may be difficult for you. That's understandable. Many people are uneasy at first, but it won't be as hard as you may think."

• Start with a disclaimer, if you think it will help. Say, frankly, "I hope you will want to share your thoughts and feelings, but I won't pressure you to say any more than you want to." If you have agreed to anonymity for the subject, emphasize at the outset that you will not, under any circumstances, break that promise.

• Use broad, general questions at first, asking such non-threatening questions as, "Tell me a little about yourself: Where are you from? What was it like growing up in your family? How did you get along with your siblings? Parents?" If this leads to an appropriate opening, you might follow the answer with, "Can you tell me a little more about that?" Obviously avoid questions that can be answered with "yes" or "no." Have a summary question ready for the end—"What's the most important effect this experience has had on you? What is the most helpful thing you would like to share with the readers?"

• Move gradually, in chronological order, through the part of the person's life that is relevant to the story. If the subject wanders and gets off track, bring the interview back to the main topic by saying something like, "We're going to get to that in a minute, but right now I'd like to hear more about—." A little humor never hurts: "Hold on a bit; we're getting way ahead of ourselves."

• When you are ready to deal with the sensitive topic, warn the person by saying, "We've come to the point where I need to ask you some more specific questions about what happened." If the subject becomes emotional, confront that directly, saying, "Go ahead and cry if you feel like it. I certainly understand. I would have cried, too, in that situation." Don't try to hide your emotional reaction; if you actually do respond with tears, that's O.K. I've never done a sensitive interview in which the subject cried and I didn't shed a few tears, too.

• Give your subject plenty of time to respond to your questions. If she or he stops at a critical point, pause, too, and then make a casual comment to start the conversation flowing again: "That must have been very hard for you. What happened next?" Keep your voice warm and sympathetic.

• Never make a judgmental comment. Obviously, remarks like, "How could you have done that!" are taboo, but so are even subtle gestures or verbal responses, no matter how repellent you may find what the subject says.

• Get on tape the subject's wishes about using real names in your feature.

• When you have finished the interview, thank the person warmly, and leave your card so she or he can reach you if she wishes to give you some additional information. Don't be reluctant to call her back for clarification or more details. Store the tapes in a fireproof safe. It is not advisable to show the subject a transcript of the tape recording or the manuscript prior to its publication.

Though telephone interviews on sensitive subjects can be done, they do present a different challenge. Sometimes the anonymity of the phone allows a nervous subject to talk more freely, but it can, in some instances, be inhibiting.

• Always tell the person that the phone interview is being tape recorded. I usually say, "I'm taping this, so you don't have to worry about talking slowly enough for me to take notes."

• As in a face-to-face interview, you must establish a personal relationship over the telephone, which presents some difficulties. Chat casually at first, in a warm, friendly tone, asking about the weather, how the person likes living in his or her hometown, how he or she spent the weekend. Get to know the subject a bit before jumping into the interview.

• Schedule your phone interview at a time when you are not likely to be interrupted. Disconnect your call-waiting! Late night often works best for me. There's something about quiet houses and low lights that encourages the flow of conversation.

Talking to people about their most intimate, personal problems and experiences can be exhausting and emotionally draining, for you as well as for your subject. Don't schedule too many such interviews back to back or you may find yourself on overload. Allow time for a break between interviews.

Some of your subjects may well be in need of professional counseling and may try to put you into the role of therapist. Remember that your job is only to ask the questions and listen—which may in itself be therapeutic for the subject. Never offer advice. It may in some instances be appropriate to ask, "Have you ever had professional help in dealing with this problem? You might find it helpful."

Sharing the darker side of pain often helps the teller and the reader to know that they are not alone, that other human beings have had similar experiences and survived.

As writers, we have a tremendous responsibility in doing sensitive interviews. We have a responsibility to our subjects not to betray their trust. And, in addition, we have a responsibility to our readers to present these stories as honestly and with as much empathy as we can. Conducting ourselves with the utmost professionalism is the only way to live up to it.

➤➤ 65

PROBING THE MIND OF THE TRUE CRIME DETECTIVE

BY KRIST BOARDMAN

NONFICTION WRITERS CAN NEVER TRULY GET INSIDE THE MIND OF A real person, not to the point where we know everything about him. Fiction writers are the only gods on the planet who can wholly create persons and imbue their personalities with all the complexities of real people.

Writers of nonfiction can do only what other keen observers might do: listen and record what the person says about himself and what he did, what other people said he said and did, and what they observe directly.

A true crime writer uses indirect and direct observation to describe his protagonist, but his main subject is the crime itself. The writer should never make the mistake of speculating what is in the dectective's mind, unless he has reliable information to support his observations.

For the true crime article, information is assembled from courthouse and newspaper research and interviews. While characterizations of the important players in each crime are important, they should be supported by the researched material. Invented, undocumented dialogue and situations should be avoided.

The true crime article is most effective when written from the perspective of the detective. There are a number of very good reasons for this. One is that policemen and detectives love to read about themselves or others in their profession; also, other people like to read about the everyday heroes on local police forces.

Editors of true crime magazines know that cops aren't perfect either in the personal or professional aspects of their lives, but their magazines are an appropriate place to show detective work at its best.

The ideal protagonist for a true crime article is a seemingly ordinary detective with extraordinary skills or just plain dogged persistence, who faces numerous obstacles in his efforts to bring a criminal to justice.

Remember also that police officers usually can't take shortcuts: They have to obey the law and follow proper procedures, or they may blow their cases. When they get frustrated, they can't just pull out high-caliber weapons and blow people's heads off, as Clint Eastwood does in the Dirty Harry movies. And they can't break into people's homes and offices with lock picks or credit cards to search for incriminating evidence and documents when new evidence is needed.

These impediments to frontier-style and private-eye justice help make a better true crime story, because the challenge of the investigation is increased. In today's real world, the investigator's techniques must remain within the confines of the law. Legal issues are very much part of the overall article, as they play an increasingly important role in the resolution of a case.

There are limits to what a beginning true crime writer can write about when describing an investigation. A fiction writer might describe a disorder in the unusual life of a homicide detective—a gambling habit, womanizing, alcoholism, problems with a relationship or with another person. This makes a more interesting story, particularly if the detective's personal problems can be woven into the main mystery. But it is not appropriate for the true crime magazine piece, unless it becomes part of the official record of the court case, which is unlikely.

If the true crime writer exposes the personal weaknesses of detectives, he may never regain the confidence and trust of officers working in that department. Furthermore, the focus of the true crime article would be straying too far from the resolution of the crime itself. Yet it is often helpful—and it makes for a more effective article—if as part of the narrative the writer does note and include a short profile of the detective. After all, readers want to know something about the main person or persons who solve the crime. That's what makes the article human and interesting.

You must try to humanize the components of your article, often despite the tendency of investigators to depersonalize everything about the investigation in their accounts of it. Anyone who has read detailed applications for search warrants and reports by detectives to their supervisors understands this. Many documents are written in stilted police bureaucratese in which the detective describes himself and his actions as the activities of "the writer," "the applicant," or "your affiant."

These detective-written narratives are usually the best sources of information about a case, barring a long interview. They should be used as guidelines to describe the progress of the investigation and as supporting documentation for your article. But you must rework the material, weaving in information from other sources to bring your article to life.

To the extent possible, official documents should also be evaluated for information the detective may purposely not have included. There is plenty that never gets into these official records for a variety of reasons—for instance, the interplay among various persons working on the case or in the investigative unit. This kind of information can be obtained only from interviews or court transcripts of trials where it was brought out under the rules of discovery or in cross-examination in the courtroom.

For example, one of my favorite true crime articles described a detective's obsession with a human leg bone retrieved by a junkyard dog from a swamp. The detective was an unheralded policeman from a small agency who tenaciously followed up the discovery with an investigation that lasted several years. His coworkers derisively nicknamed him "Bones" and made fun of his efforts to solve what appeared to be an unsolvable crime. Yet "Bones" did go on to solve the case, much to his credit, and he removed from the streets a dangerous man who had been involved in other criminal activity.

That particular case was unusual because the detective succeeded almost in spite of the efforts of others in his department. Most detectives are not usually in such an untenable position, but are accepted members of tightly knit investigative units and are careful not to attract undue attention to themselves. Nevertheless, a resourceful crime writer may find ways to characterize the detective while working within these limits.

In addition to the constraints within police departments, there are often problem cases that prosecutors and detectives feel uncomfortable discussing even after a conviction, because of possible appeals that may be cause for retrial. If an interview can be obtained, the

321

source will usually be reluctant to discuss anything that was not said or did not actually occur in the courtroom. Newspaper accounts of the trial and investigation will then have to serve as primary sources, unless the writer has the time and opportunity to attend the court trial himself.

Nevertheless, even with all these restrictions, detectives are talkative and anxious to explain a point that is not clear. You as the true crime writer should first study all the sources that are available so that you can ask only informed questions. You may then be able to elicit over the phone off-the-cuff remarks that will be very useful even if someone up the chain of command has refused a formal interview. This usually works best if you say at the outset that the comments will not be attributed to that particular source.

One true crime article I wrote involved a crime committed in a northern Virginia county. The suspect had family ties to a very small, remote county in the mountains of southwest Virginia that the investigator and his partner had never heard of. The detectives' trip to the county was eventful because there was no available lodging, nor could the locals understand how black and white detectives could work together. None of this material about the detectives' trip was included in official documents, but in an interview the investigator gave me material that added color, perspective, and insight into the life of the suspect.

The myriad problems real detectives face, such as pleading with supervisors for funds to travel, mistaken identities, foul-ups within the jail system, courtroom maneuverings, not to mention the craftiness and elusiveness of suspects, make up the interesting though often frustrating lives of real detectives. The more of this kind of detail a crime writer can provide, the better job he has done in profiling the work of America's frontline investigators.

➤➤ 66

Turn Your Travels into Sales

By Barbara Petoskey

Even if you have no interest in star ratings of hotels, there are many undiscovered opportunities for you to use your vacation or other out-of-town trips to increase your manuscript sales. Best of all you can capitalize on your experiences, whether you write nonfiction, fiction or poetry.

We're all familiar with the traditional travel piece, packed with food and lodging tips and a hearty dollop of local color. But there are many other ways to get extra mileage from your travel.

The facts

If you'd like to write just a brief piece about your journey without getting into "how to get there and where to stay," find a small niche market. Consider, for example:

- Annual events (such as the Garlic Festival/Gilroy, California)
- Historical events (battle of Tippecanoe/Indiana)
- Well-known people (Motown Records Museum/Detroit)
- Distinctive architecture (Baltimore rowhouses)
- A clustering of a particular art or business (Native American silversmiths or Amish quiltmakers, antique malls or flea markets)
- Any regional specialty, sport, or style

Even an article that relies primarily on library research may benefit from in-person experience. For me, a half-day stop in Amherst, Massachusetts, on my way from Boston to Michigan enriched two differently focused biographical essays I wrote on Emily Dickinson: One sold to a literary magazine, the other to a book lover's newsletter.

Multiple slanting options abound. A tour of, say, Ernest Hemingway's home in Key West could yield salable pieces for fans of either literature or cats. And watch for the famous person in an unexpected spot: While we naturally link Samuel Clemens and Hannibal, Missouri, his final resting place is Elmira, New York, where he also wrote some of his finest novels. (Incidentally, his grave marker is "Two Fathoms"— or "mark twain"—high; could there be an article in that?)

When hunting for markets for these travel capsules, don't overlook regional, hobby, or trade publications. A magazine that wouldn't consider a standard travel piece may snap up an article about a place with a clever tie-in for its audience. So whether you choose to focus on the Trap Shooting Hall of Fame in Vandalia, Ohio, or the Tupperware Museum in Kissimmee, Florida, your mini-account of a place off the beaten track may capture an editor's imagination.

Facts plus

Fresh perceptions evoked by new surroundings can make travel the perfect springboard for the personal experience essay. Many magazines and newspaper Sunday supplements—a good weekly market—may buy such features if you have a unique story to tell, even if you're not a big-name byline. Only·you can recount the unique experience of your drive to the Grand Canyon as a late-spring snowstorm howled out of the Rockies, or your reactions to visiting the village from which your ancestors came. I've turned twelve days in Maracaibo into three essays: Venezuelan cab drivers, celebrating Christmas in the tropics, and getting along in a foreign country whose language you don't know well. Also, consider writing an account of your unique situation: as a solo traveler after divorce; a visit to Disneyland *without* children or to Club Med *with* kids; travel using a wheelchair.

And don't overlook the absurd. The common denominator of most trips is something that goes wrong: That missed turn, lost key, or noisy hotel guest next door may provide you with anything from a humorous filler to a full-blown misadventure.

The flavor: fiction

Obviously, if you write fiction, your travels can provide you with authentic details to help you develop that vivid sense of place that pulls readers into your story. Scout sites for action: streets, landmarks, centers of activity. And, of course, such details must all be accurate. Just try writing that your heroine took the Lincoln Tunnel from Manhattan to Queens, and your credibility will plunge into the East River. (The Lincoln Tunnel goes to Jersey).

A good city map can give you the general geographic layout, so you'll want to watch for the unusual quirk, custom, or telling detail that captures the essence of the place or that can play a role in your fiction. When I set my comic-suspense short story "After Hours" in Chicago, I noted that "the lighted faces of the Tribune Tower clocks watched like eerie moons"—a point not featured in the average tour-book. While you don't have to go everywhere your characters do, if the events of your story or novel unfold in San Francisco, it can't hurt to have heard the clang of a cable car or your thumping heart as you scaled those hills.

Even if your fiction never mentions events that occurred before page one, the influence of the "backstory" on present action will help make your characters three-dimensional. Perhaps this shows up in a regional expression or taste or in a turn of phrase in your dialogue. If your Harvard-educated lawyer reveals her fondness for a breakfast of huevos rancheros, she may hint at Southwestern roots. Wherever you go, watch, listen, store it up, and jot it down. Such tidbits may later help define a character's personality.

The feeling: poetry

Travel broadens not only the mind, but stirs the soul as well. How can a poet fail to be touched by new sensations? Whether on a trip to the Great Wall or to your grandmother's house, your emotions and reactions may send you scrambling for paper.

Impressions come in all varieties. I've published descriptive poems about the New Orleans French Quarter, the rugged Oregon coast, and autumn in New England. I've also used an exotic place or experience as a metaphorical jumping-off point: the "fall" of returning from a brief get-away on an island aptly named Paradise; sensing kinship with a pair of dolphins sighted off a Gulf of Mexico beach. None of these poems would ever have come to me in my own backyard.

On site

Serendipity accounts for much of travel's pleasure. Whether you've pursued your plan or simply stumbled onto the unexpected, make notes for future writing; take photographs; pick up brochures, postcards, maps, newspapers, hotel "visitors' guides," matchbooks, or even those paper placemats found in mom-and-pop restaurants that highlight tourist attractions—anything that will help you later to recreate that local experience.

Also be sure to note:

- Food (local fruits and vegetables, spices, unusual preparation)
- Architecture (brick, frame, adobe, ranch-style, Cape Cod, high-rise)
- Fashions (conservative or trendy, formal or casual)
- Music (country, soul, reggae, jazz, bluegrass)
- Major ethnic influences (Asian, African, Scandinavian, Italian, Jewish)
- Regional words (*soda* vs. *pop*)
- Regional brands or store names
- Weather (sunny or cloudy, humid or dry)
- Vegetation, landscaping (deciduous, conifer, cactus, palm, fenced yards, no yards)

When you get back home, organize your notes and materials—by place, topic, plot, whatever works—so you don't find later that you "can't get there from here."

The next time you hit the road, for whatever reason, have a good time. Maybe soak up a little sun. And be sure to soak up some atmosphere to put into your writing.

>>67

TURNING A PERSONAL EXPERIENCE
INTO AN ARTICLE

BY KATHRYN LAY

HAVE YOU EVER READ AN ARTICLE THAT HAS TOUCHED YOU IN A special way? You think, "That happened to me" or "That's the way I feel" or even, "Maybe I could write about my experience with . . ."

Someone else's story has communicated a feeling or emotion that relates to your life, or has shown you how to solve a similar problem. Personal experience articles can be humorous, sad, informative, or thought-provoking. They remind readers how they felt in a similar situation, or they warn others how to avoid a problem. Many times, readers learn how to cope with or overcome similar events. And most often, personal experience articles offer hope.

If something special has happened in your life that you think would touch others, there are several ways in which you can turn it into a publishable article. Personal experiences can be written in as few as fifty words or run to several thousand. Here are the three most popular types:

1) *Your story.* This is an account of something you or someone close to you has experienced that will interest other people—something they can relate to or identify with.

After I went through a false pregnancy following years of infertility, I wrote the article, "No Less A Woman," which has been published four times. Many readers wrote to say it touched, encouraged, helped, or educated them.

2) *Real-life drama.* Most people have not had the experience of being mauled by a bear or surviving a plane crash, but the fact that someone else went through this adventure or trauma and survived can make compelling reading. "As told to" articles are one way to write

someone else's dramatic story. You must first, of course, get the person's permission. Also, it's important to capture the emotion and descriptions as if you were there when it happened.

3) *The how-to.* In this type of piece, you share what you've experienced emotionally and/or physically while you were pursuing a particular goal, and show others how they might achieve a similar goal.

For instance, has an experience with your children, friends, relatives, or even strangers, or your success in a new venture, given you insight and information that would be valuable to others? Use anecdotes, emotion, and firsthand experience to write your how-to personal experiences.

In "Make a Date to Plan Together," I described how my husband and I set up planning sessions that helped us reach our goals and strengthened our relationship. The article was originally published in *Sunday Digest* and has been reprinted many times.

Once you have found a personal experience you want to write about, study different magazines to find where your story would fit best; each publication has its own needs and style. For example, women's magazines have specific preferences, most often dealing with women's or parenting issues. An article on how you or someone you know overcame bulimia might find a home in *Family Circle* or *Woman's World.* And a personal experience how-to about your camping trip through the Rockies would have a good chance of acceptance at a travel, outdoors, or regional magazine, as long as you give it an unusual twist. Inspirational magazines could be the market for a personal experience piece on a battle with cancer, domestic abuse or violence, or the death of a family member.

Personal experience articles aren't necessarily about momentous events. They might deal with a more common experience, such as your relationship with your mother-in-law. Or in an informative article you may explain how your runaway dog gave you an idea for a new business. Humorous personal experience pieces are always in demand. Most people can relate to the problems of moving; in an article I wrote about my own moving experience, there was nothing deep or life-threatening, yet readers could understand and laugh along with my misadventures.

There are four basic steps that will help you write a successful personal experience piece:

1) *Hook your readers immediately.* My article "No Less A Woman" began in this way:

"You are about six weeks pregnant," the doctor informed me. After two years of waiting to hear those words, I wanted to laugh, to cry!

This tells readers at the outset what the piece will be about. If it concerns your struggle with a disease and readers are facing the same problem or know someone who is, there is a good chance they will want to read about your experience.

2) *Follow the hook with a statement that explains what the article is about.* In "Make a Date . . ." I let the reader know right away what to expect:

Four times a year my husband and I spend time alone planning creative ways to meet common goals. There are five steps to setting up such goal-planning sessions.

Once you have captured your readers' attention, or stirred their memories or longings, they will want to know whether your article will give them a story of hope, or solutions to a problem.

3) *The body of the piece must be well organized and interesting.* Get your experience down on paper first. During the rewrite see if it can or should be structured differently. Describe your experience as it happened; leave out unnecessary details, but include emotion and tension. Did you reach a point of no return? Did you give up hope at any point? Readers who may have struggled with the same problem want to laugh or cry with you; they want to see that someone else feels as they do. Imagine how you would tell your story to a special friend, not to a reporter who wants "just the facts."

4) *Wind your article up by returning to your beginning idea.* Give your readers something to think about after they've finished reading your article—an idea, a feeling, or a plan of action they can follow for a similar problem. I ended "And Baby Makes Three," a piece about our daughter's adoption, by bringing readers back to a common emotion.

When others see Michelle, they speak of how wonderful it is that she has parents who love her. But I always correct them. We are the ones who have been blessed.

At the end of "No Less A Woman," I went back to my original problem of infertility and the emotional change I'd experienced:

Does my infertility make me less of a woman? It may seem to, if I allow the world to tell me what a woman should be. I know, however, that in the eyes of my loving husband, I am no less a woman.

Everyone has had at least one personal experience, perhaps many, that would make good articles. Keep a journal. Reflect on events of the day or week. If you think something has the potential for a personal experience piece, ask yourself these questions:

- Can others relate to my experience?
- Could an article about it encourage, teach, warn, or help others, or is the audience too limited?
- Can I write it with emotion, yet step back from it so that it won't become a "self-portrait account" or a "soap-box tirade"?
- Is there a market for this? Even more than one?

These questions can later be used as guidelines when you begin to write. Once you know your target audience and what you hope to give your reader, the piece will flow more easily.

How do you submit personal experience articles? Although many magazines will accept unsolicited manuscripts, some prefer query letters first. For several reasons, this may be the better approach for the writer. If there is a limited market for your personal experience, you may not want to spend time writing the complete article. And if, after reading your query, an editor does ask to see the manuscript, you will be able to gear it toward *that* magazine's audience. An editor may ask to see your article and give you ideas of what slant or information she prefers. Your chances of selling your article will increase if you know in advance what the editor expects.

As with your article, begin your query with a "grabber" sentence, stating what your piece will be about. If it is humorous, say so in a funny way. If it is meant to be dramatic, make sure the opening sentence is intriguing. Make sure your query reflects whatever emotion you expect your article to evoke in your readers.

Your query should also stress the unique angle of your article, mention expert sources, if any, and why your personal experience may help or make a difference in the lives of the magazine's readers. Show the editor that you will give its readers accurate, authoritative information, and that what you have to say will touch them. If you have had articles published previously, send tear sheets, especially if they were personal experience pieces.

Even after you receive a go-ahead to your query, your article may not sell to that magazine . . . but don't panic. Submit it to the next magazine on your list of possible markets. Some of my personal experience articles have sold the first time out; others have sold after ten or more rejections. As with all writing, persistence and market research will increase your chances of selling.

If you enjoy reading personal experience articles, there is a good chance you'll enjoy writing them, and get satisfaction from touching readers' hearts and lives.

➤➤ 68

HOW TO WRITE A BETTER OP-ED

BY LES KOZACZEK

THE SPEED OF ELECTRONIC COMMUNICATIONS HAS FORCED PRINT ME-
dia to rely heavily on interpreting, rather than breaking, news stories.
Some of this interpretation is performed in-house, but a significant
amount is supplied by free-lance writers in the form of op-eds.

Most of the country's newspapers have op-ed (or commentary)
pages. These short, insightful essays, usually on current issues, are
always in demand. They offer an excellent turnover time from idea to
publication, a rare thing in the writer's world of months-long lead
times. Not all publications pay for op-eds, and competition is stiff, but
writing, and possibly self-syndicating your informed opinion on any of
a broad range of issues can provide you with an excellent source of
regular income.

Here are fourteen tips on how to write a salable op-ed:

1) Avoid the crescendo conclusion. This type of op-ed begins slowly
and builds up to a final, earth-shattering conclusion. While this may
be an effective technique in telling a joke, it demands too much patience from op-ed readers. Make your strongest point first—in your
lead or second paragraph. Never forget that, as important as your topic
is to you, to the majority of your readers it will be just one more
demand on a busy mind. If you don't tell your readers up front why
they should read on, they won't.

For instance, if you believe that Ukraine's new prime minister is
going to have a hard time overcoming the resistance of his obstruction-
ist parliament, then that's your lead, not an analysis of how the Ukrain-
ian government works, which will eventually lead us "Ta dum!" to
your opinion.

2) Be timely, topical and original. Giving your opinion piece a topical hook will increase your chances of seeing it in print. Most opinion pieces are about current events. (There are perennial topics, such as abortion, women in the military, etc., but it's very difficult coming up with something new to say on those issues. They're also issues that editors tend to ration, otherwise their pages could very quickly become monotonous.) Even timely pieces need an original slant, not just the standard point of view on an issue. For instance, instead of writing about why somebody won a recent election, analyze why his opponent lost.

3) Write fast when necessary. Be prepared to respond and write very quickly about current issues. When an insightful opinion piece runs the day after a major event, it's most likely that the op-ed editor has a file filled with informed, reliable writers who can produce quality work in just hours. Try to get your name in that file.

4) Be selective. Address as many issues as you wish, but just make sure each one is in a separate opinion piece. If your issue is the military's lack of sensitivity toward parents who are both in the service— it often sends them both to war, forcing them to "abandon" their children—then don't get caught up in an argument about the morality of war, or about how so many children of military parents have contracted Desert Storm Syndrome.

5) Get the length right. A piece that runs 700 to 900 words (about three double-spaced pages) is fairly standard for an op-ed, but some papers want more or fewer words to fit specific spaces on their op-ed page. *USA Today,* for instance, prefers 500-word pieces from free lancers. Few editors will have the time or be willing to lop hundreds of words off even the best op-ed.

6) Don't be picky about minor changes! While you should certainly insist on maintaining your opinion in your op-ed, so will the editor. Don't be too picky about wording or minor changes. It's your opinion that counts, not its wrapping. Newspapers have their own forms and will use them.

7) Have respect for the reader. No editor wants opinion pieces that

333

talk down to his readers, so don't condescend. If your readers don't understand what you're trying to tell them, that's your fault. And it's a fault an editor simply won't tolerate. An op-ed about a complex matter such as banking, for instance, should be written just as much for the reader with $5 in his pocket as for the reader with $500,000 in stocks and bonds. Yes, the material can be complex enough to satisfy the expert, but the language should be crystal clear.

8) Don't try for balance. Opinion pieces should be just that. Phrases like "On the other hand" or "Although it might be said that . . ." will kill your piece . . . dead. The op-ed editor is likely to have an in-tray full of articles on the same subject that contradict your views. Neither the editor nor the reader is looking for balance in an opinion piece; both want a single, forcefully argued, plausible statement.

An op-ed in *The Baltimore Evening Sun* offering advice to black college students begins, "As an African American college freshman on a predominantly white campus, you'll learn an important and startling lesson before you ever pick up a book: You'll still be judged as much by the color of your skin as by the content of your character."

Clearly, there are millions who would disagree with that statement, but that's their opinion, which they should write in their own op-eds.

9) Avoid jargon. Jargon—a language recognizable only by others who share your expertise—is unclear and frustrating to general readers, who make up the audience of a popular daily newspaper. One paragraph that didn't even make it to the editor was from a political scientist: "Clinton surely doesn't need to reconceptualize and dualize his too obviously zero-optioned platform." (Eh?) If jargon is simply unavoidable, explain it as briefly as possible and then get back to English.

10) Show that you can be passionate. If you don't seem to care about your topic, then neither will anybody else. A recent piece that ran in *The Chicago Tribune* began, "Cracked concrete walls, a water-spotted ceiling, stained linoleum, chemically indestructible ants, a deafening air-conditioner that quit in May and reinforced windows dotted with bullet holes. Though this sounds like a prison cell or a battlefield shack, it's an urban third-grade classroom and a glaring testament to the US

334

education system, particularly to the way it treats poor ethnic children."

Don't be afraid to paint vivid, emotional pictures, as long as you get your point across.

11) Send clear, clean copy. The sheer volume of opinion pieces that cross an editor's desk can be dizzying. Some of the larger newspapers receive more than 300, even in a slow week. If your copy isn't completely legible, it will be tossed. Make sure the type is clean and that there are no smudges or written-in manuscript changes. Number your pages and put an identifying word of your title or your name in the top corner of each page. Carefully proofread your manuscript before you send it off.

12) Address your envelope to the right person—by name. Newspaper staffs change often, so call to find out to whom you should address your piece. Unless your opinion piece will die on the vine by the next day, don't submit it by fax. Use the mail; it's cheaper and surer to reach the right person.

13) Don't be coy. Always include your name, address, daytime telephone number, Social Security number (though not all papers pay for opinion pieces), and a brief biography, which ideally will say why you are just the right person to write on this subject (include published credits). The more qualified you are to address the subject, the more chance you have of getting published.

14) Know when to stop. Experts are particularly guilty of overselling their point. They often know so much about a subject that they try to include everything they know. Of course, op-ed editors can cut your article, but that's extra work for them, and they may not want to bother.

>> 69

WRITING THE FAMILIAR ESSAY

BY SHARON HUNT

AS A STUDENT IN PUBLIC SCHOOL IN THE 1960S, I STRUGGLED through essays as dry and unappealing as the secret notes my best friend and I ate before the teacher could read them.

As a writing tutor in college in the 1980s, I struggled through equally dry and unappealing essays written by electronics students who never attended an English class.

Later, as a literary journal editor, I cringed when essays arrived in the mail, and buried them at the bottom of my reading pile. When I could no longer procrastinate, I was often happily surprised by the essays I read. Gone were the dry offerings of seventh graders and future electronics wizards. In their place were essays of such passion I began putting new arrivals at the top of the pile and soon began writing my own.

I hadn't realized earlier what a pleasure familiar essays could be, and how popular they were—and continue to be. They are regularly found in such magazines as *Harper's, The Atlantic Monthly,* and *The New Yorker,* as well as many other publications; in *The New York Times* and a host of other daily and weekly newspapers; and in literary journals and anthologies.

One of the advantages of being an essayist is the range of available—and salable—subject matter. You can write about anything: the seasons, holidays, favorite places; children, parents, companions, and friends; all aspects of life. I pick subjects I feel passionately about. Without that passion, you can't expect to evoke it, or other emotions, in a reader.

Whatever the subject, before I begin to write, I set aside time to think about it. During this germination period, I draw on the journal I keep, a simple, battered notebook that goes everywhere with me.

When lines of conversation or description come to me, I write them down immediately, under a suitable heading. If I don't, I may not recall them later. My working journal also holds essay ideas and research leads (if the topic requires it). In my journal, I also carry on a conversation with myself about the tone or style I want to use in the essay.

In writing essays, I'm very conscious of style, which is a vital part of a familiar essay. Not only does style reflect the writer's distinctive view of a subject, it can also help get specific emotional responses from a reader. If your style is inappropriate for your subject, you won't get the reader response you hoped for. An essay about a debilitating illness, for example, will not evoke reader sympathy if your style is flippant or irreverent. Humor in many instances may backfire, yet in others may work beautifully. If you're uncertain about the right style for an essay, try writing the first page in a couple of different styles, then compare them.

Also, compare the possible voices for writing your essay. Should it be written in the third person, with that omnipotent narrator? Or is the first person, presenting the writer's point of view, a better choice? If you're not sure about which to use, experiment until you find the right one.

I enjoy writing in the first-person voice and find it helpful to imagine I'm carrying on a conversation with someone special as I write. In an essay about my father, entitled "Tell Me," I begin:

Tell me about being a boy in Newfoundland, about going out into the middle of the Atlantic with those fishermen with paws for hands and you not even able to swim.
Tell me about the Lady in White and Mummers at Christmas, ghosts and the women who jumped off the cliff, their purple-blue bodies cradling the rocks that broke them.

Two additional "tell me" paragraphs complete an opening sequence meant to do two things: First, it sets the tone of an inquisitive child wanting to know all about her father before he became her father. Second, this sequence catches readers' attention quickly by offering them a variety of possible story lines. This variety, although narrowed to the limits of essay length, makes readers curious, makes them want to go on reading.

A question or series of questions or a tantalizing or startling fact at the beginning of an essay can also attract readers, as can stating your subject immediately. For example, in an essay for a local newspaper, I wrote:

> I've been saving to buy a piece of land. Just an acre or two; I'm not a greedy person.

Here, there is no doubt about the subject of the essay.

Use short story techniques throughout an essay to keep your readers reading. One of my favorites is selective use of description. In "Tell Me," my father recounted a tragic ferry accident that killed many neighbors and friends. Instead of describing the entire tragedy and focusing on how many were killed and how long it took the ferry to sink, I described incidents following the tragedy:

> . . . barrels of apples floated up on the beach later; someone found a little girl's dress with the price tag still on it.

These selective details give the tragedy a more human dimension. Images of apples meant for a winter's baking, and a child's new dress, never to be worn, emphasize the uncertainty that greets us each day and connects us as human beings. Such connections strengthen an essay and a reader's response to it.

Dialogue can also hold a reader's attention if it sounds real but doesn't have all the real pauses and repetitions that often characterize everyday speech. How can you create such dialogue? Ask yourself if all the "huhs" and "ahs" in the dialogue you've written are necessary to make the person "real," or if they only slow the reader down and add no insight into the person's character. If you feel you can delete such interruptions, do, then read the dialogue aloud. Does it sound real? If it does, you have stayed true to the person's character while removing digressions.

Using anecdotes in an essay gives you an opportunity to "show" rather than "tell," and varying sentence lengths will help create different moods. A reflective essay will benefit from longer sentences, which give a thoughtful quality to the work. On the other hand, short sentences give the work a sense of immediacy. "Tell Me" has a mixture of both. When writing of my father as a teenager, I used sentences like these:

My father could fight. Two stronger, wilder brothers ensured that.

Later, when he and many of the community's men lost their jobs and way of life, longer sentences helped emphasize that more reflective time in his life.

Then the Company closed the mine and put most of the island's men, including my father, out of work for the first time in their lives. The Company closed the mine and changed the island from a thriving community where people painted their houses in the spring and went visiting in the summer to a place mired in government dependence.

Don't overlook the different effects unconventional capitalization and punctuation (or the lack of it) can have. In the above example, I capitalized "Company" to stress the importance of this mining operation to my father's community. Whenever "Company" is mentioned in the essay, it's preceded by "the," further emphasizing its importance. Also, in the second sentence in that example, I didn't use any commas, wanting to give readers a sense of what the people affected felt. *They* had no time to pause, to take a breath and consider their next step. Without the pauses commas allow, readers have to move through that sentence without a pause to stop and reflect, until the sentence is finished.

Finishing a thought or paragraph in an essay requires a transition to the next. A smooth transition greatly improves the flow of an essay, so readers relate ideas to each other without losing the continuity.

Transitional words such as "first," "second," "earlier," "later," "now," and "before" can provide this smooth flow, as can sentence arrangement and word order. "Tell me" repeated at the beginning of the first four paragraphs of my essay is an example of the use of word order to move easily from thought to thought. Another way to accomplish this is to arrange information so that the item mentioned last in one paragraph is mentioned again at the beginning of the next. An essay I wrote about female mentors gave me an opportunity to do this.

There are absolutes in her life. Honesty. Love. Belief. A helping hand. That hand has often been extended to me . . .

A short paragraph ends with the image of a helping hand, while the next continues and expands on that image.

339

One of the pluses of a familiar essay is the denouement, the point at which the essay's various thoughts are tied together to make it stand for something beyond selective description and realistic dialogue; interesting anecdotes and varying sentence lengths; omitted commas and unnecessary capital letters. In my land-hungry essay, the denouement comes near the end. After talking about the kind of land I'd like to buy and where that land might be, I explain my real urge to be a land owner:

I'll wallow in the delight of this being mine to take care of for a while.

Tips for Writing and Marketing Familiar Essays

• Every essay benefits from rewriting until the purpose and flow you want have been achieved.

• Read each essay aloud. Can you follow its logic easily? If not, clarify so that a reader will not be left behind.

• Be sensitive to any possible embarrassment and resentment when writing about relatives or friends.

• Local weeklies or small dailies are good places to start submitting your essays.

• Suggest a regular column to the editor of a local paper. Submit a selection of four to six essays of the same length (this varies depending on editorial requirements) to show you can deliver.

• Read essays in local and national magazines and newspapers to which you'd like to submit your essays. Study the style and subject matter. What is it about these essays that keeps you reading?

>> 70

LETTER TO A YOUNG
ARTICLE WRITER

BY DONALD M. MURRAY

YOUR PIECES ARE FILLED WITH INTERESTING, SPECIFIC INFORMATION; they have a clear focus; they are well written; but they are not likely to be published without revision.

What they lack is what professionals call an edge. The idea does not contain the tension that attracts and holds a reader. Note the first paragraph of my letter. It contains a surprise, an apparent contradiction, a conflict, something unexpected that engages the reader in a conversation. "What does he mean? The articles are written well, with focused information, and they are *not* publishable?" the reader asks, and the writer responds.

Your articles are pleasant and predictable. They do not have an urgency, a significance, an unexpectedness, a tension that will draw in a reader who is not already fascinated by your subject.

Editors find it difficult to describe what is missing in such good writing—and so do I. The problem is not with what is on the paper but what is not. Editors are looking for what they have not seen and cannot command. If editors know what they want, they can order it from professionals on their staff or from familiar free lancers like me. Doris Lessing said, "You have to remember that nobody ever wants a new writer. You have to create your own demand."

The demand is created when a writer expresses an individual, authoritative point of view toward our familiar world in a voice that is appropriate to the topic and the writer's attitude toward it. The voice communicates authority and concern.

Your ideas do not have an essential tension. Some of my daybook lines that have led to writing include:

"I cheered when we dropped the atomic bomb." [I was in the paratroops and scheduled to jump into Tokyo.]

"I'm lucky I had a sickly childhood." [It forced me to exercise my imagination.]

"I'm glad I have an old wife." [We have a shared history.]

"It was good there was no Little League when I was a kid." [We played sandlot ball and were not over-organized by competitive parents.]

My habit is to seek the tensions within my life and the lives of those around me. I inventory what sparks a strong emotional reaction: irony, anger, despair, humor, pain, pleasure, contentment, fear.

I read the mental and daybook or journal notes I make as I lead my life, asking such questions as:

- What surprises me?
- Where's the tension?
- What should be and what is?
- Where's the conflict?
- Where will these ideas, issues, people collide?
- What's the problem?
- What's different from what I expected?
- What are the implications—for me, for my readers?
- What are the connections?
- What contradicts?

Margaret Atwood says, "Good writing takes place at intersections, at what you might call knots, at places where the society is snarled or knotted up." Mary Lee Settle says, "I start my work by asking a question and then try . . . to answer it."

As I question myself, I hear fragments of language. These are rarely sentences, although they may be. Usually they are just phrases, words in collision, or words that connect in unexpected ways. Recently I wrote a column about my grandson learning to walk. The line came from his father, who said Joshua had "to learn to fall to learn to walk." That was an idea; it contained a truth expressed in a line that had a surprising tension.

I record such lines and scratch when they itch. A lead—the opening sentences or paragraphs—can hold an article in place so I can explore it in a draft written days or weeks later. For example, the other day I was doing errands with my wife when I had the following experience, and I immediately wrote (in my head), "have to get glasses tightened." When I got home, I turned the line into a lead:

342

We are driving to Dover, New Hampshire, to shop when Minnie Mae says, "I have to get my sunglasses tightened."

I pull up to Whitehouse Opticians and Minnie Mae asks, "Why are we stopping here?"

"To get your sunglasses tightened."

"They are home on my desk."

[She's just talking. I hear a problem to be solved.]

I have an idea, but that's not enough. In John Jerome's wonderful book on nonfiction writing, *The Writing Trade: A Year in the Life* (Viking, 1992), which should be on your desk, he quotes a colleague as saying that a 600-word essay needs about an idea and a half. That articulated an important truth about all articles for me.

My grandson's learning to fall so he could learn to walk was a good idea, but it was not enough. In writing the article I connected his need to learn to fall with writers, artists, scientists, and entrepreneurs, who need to experience instructive failure to succeed. Then I had an essay.

The anecdote demonstrating the difficulty I (who always want to solve a problem) have communicating with my female companion who is just commenting on life, is an interesting and amusing idea. It articulates a tension most male and female readers have experienced. But it is not yet publishable. I will write it when I come up with the essential extra half of an idea or, more likely, when I start drafting the piece and discover the extra half during the writing.

Your articles stop short of that significant half of an idea, that moment of discovery of a significant extra meaning that you and your reader share in the writing and reading of the essay.

To find that extra meaning I have to write with velocity so that I am thinking on paper, saying what I do not expect to say. Of course you will consider and reconsider, write and rewrite this discovery draft, but for me, it is essential to discover what I have to say by saying it. If I know just what I am going to say when I first start to write an article, the draft is flat, uninteresting. When I discover meaning during the writing, as I have in writing this letter to you, I may have something to share with readers that editors will want to publish.

Good luck. Draw strength from the fact that you can gather specific, revealing information; that you can focus it; that you can write a clear running sentence and a paragraph that develops and communicates a thought or feeling, and then go on to find the edge, the tension, that will make editors accept your articles and invite you to write more.

➤➤ 71

BREAKING INTO
MAGAZINE ARTICLE WRITING

BY CHARLOTTE ANNE SMITH

WHEN MEETING A WRITER, MANY PEOPLE COMMENT THAT THEY'VE always wanted to write. The question is, do they really want to write or do they want to have written? There is a vast difference, and the response to this question, in my opinion, is one of the primary ways to weed out the people who truly want to be writers from those who think being a writer would be glamorous.

There are some other questions that can help clarify these two desires, and you need to ask them of yourself before you embark on this often frustrating, extremely rewarding profession. And, yes, it is a profession, but resign yourself to being asked what you *really* do for a living.

Do you have a passion for the written word? Are you the despair of your family because wherever you are, there is always a pile of books, magazines, and paper? Do you think being a writer would be just the best life ever? Are you one of those people that just *have* to write? If you are, don't give up. That is a pretty good test to determine if you should be a writer.

Now that you have passed that test, let's talk about magazine writing. Nonfiction is easier to break into than fiction—not easy, just *easier*—because there are so many more markets for articles than for short stories. But there is still a lot of competition. In order to sell, you have to be aware of certain basic facts of magazine publishing.

First, be professional. How can you be professional if you've never sold anything? If you've written the right article for a particular magazine and present it in a professional manner, the editor doesn't usually need to know and may not even care if it is your first effort.

Whether you approach an editor by query or in a cover letter accompanying your article, state what is unique about it, compared to others on the same subject. It can be firsthand knowledge, access to documentation or interviews others have not had, specialized training in that field, or just a different viewpoint—i.e., a woman writing about football, a farmer about Wall Street.

For example, I have farmed, raised cattle, operated a bird-dog training kennel, performed in rodeos, trained horses, raised four children, taught Sunday school, played a musical instrument, sung in public, done standup comedy, refinished and reupholstered furniture, built two houses, fished, camped and hiked, and been a professional writer for 24 years. There are publications related to all of these things, and I have sold articles dealing with all of them. My experiences made my articles believable.

You can also use the experiences and expertise of others. My brother was a police officer for years; I have a friend who is a world-renowned livestock auctioneer specializing in thoroughbred horses; others are famous musicians, writers, artists, or just interesting people doing interesting or unusual things. I live in an area whose industries include oil and gas production, coal mining, and agriculture, and I have sold articles on all of these subjects. Some were technical, and I relied on my sources to fill in what I didn't know. The editor didn't care who the expert was, just as long as my article was accurate and the whole thing was readable.

How you present your manuscript is important. Don't submit one full of misspellings and typos. In this day and age, you are going to need equipment that will enable you to turn out a professional-looking manuscript. If you use a typewriter and your finished manuscript is covered with correction fluid, make a clean copy before you submit it.

Just because a market listing says, "replies in two weeks," don't get all upset if you don't hear from the editor by then. (If, on the other hand, the response time goes on much longer than originally indicated, you should contact the editor; things do get lost or forgotten.) If the listing says "don't call," then don't call, and if it says, "query; don't submit the complete manuscript," then follow those instructions. And *don't* send your manuscript by fax unless you know the editor wants to receive submissions that way.

One of the most common complaints editors have about free lancers—and it is a justifiable one—is that they're unfamiliar with the market. Don't send a poem to a publication that never publishes poetry, or an article on cooking wild game to a vegetarian magazine. Write for a sample copy of your target market, buy one on the newsstand, if available, or read several back issues in the library. Carefully reading the magazine you're aiming for will give you a feel for its subject matter, tone, and style. You can get specific information on word length, photo requirements, and method of submission by assiduously studying the market lists in this book.

Don't think that your words are so precious they can't be deleted or changed. Often a rewrite to change length or focus or to include additional information will make the difference between a rejection and a sale. The editor is the buyer; work with him or her. However, it is permissible to object to a suggested change that will destroy the meaning of the article, or will affect your credibility, since credibility is the one commodity a nonfiction writer must maintain to survive.

Ideas for articles are everywhere. If you can't recognize a potential article idea, you're in the wrong business. Everything you see, hear, feel, smell, taste, and touch is a possible article with a potential market. It is your job to make the match. Whatever your interest—a sport, craft, food, profession, hobby, lifestyle, religion—there is a publication (sometimes several) out there devoted to it. Find those magazines, study them, and then develop your article ideas. Markets are everywhere; look for them. Never pass a newsstand without checking it for publications with which you aren't familiar. While waiting for a train in Victoria Station in London, I picked up several magazines on horses and agriculture in England. Soon after I got home I sold an article to a British publication, *Sporting Horse*.

Almost every field has a publication that wants profiles. Consider your family and friends. What professions are they involved in? What are their recreational interests? Have they had a traumatic experience? Won an award or contest? Lived to be 100? The answers to these questions should generate many article ideas.

Train yourself to remember. You never know when what you see, hear, or read will be just right for an article. A fact learned long ago may give you the authenticity needed to make a sale today; an anecdote stored in your memory may be just the thing to put your personal stamp on an article.

Be realistic about what you expect to accomplish. Realize there will

346

be months when you may not make any sales, and many publications still send checks with only two figures on the left of the decimal point. There is also a limit to how much work you can turn out in a given time, and this has to be taken into consideration when you are estimating your potential income. Don't quit your day job the day you decide to become a writer, or even on the day you make your first sale.

Often you won't be paid until weeks or months after you submit your work. Even publications that pay on acceptance may not actually accept the article until several weeks after it is received.

Aim as high as you can. If there are two publications into which your article would fit, always query or submit first to the one that pays more. If one pays on acceptance and the other on publication, but the amount is about the same, go with the pay-on-acceptance publication.

Don't work free. A publication doesn't expect its printer, advertising staff, typesetters or anyone else to work free, so why should the writer? Without the writer they don't have a publication.

I will make two exceptions to that rule. If you find a new publication that may be a steady market and can work out an agreement for payment in the future, go ahead, but have a firm understanding. This will give you credits to show editors, and they don't have to know you weren't paid.

The other exception is a publication dealing with something you are trying to promote—a religion, political viewpoint, or social issue, for instance.

Decide if you want to specialize. If you have expertise in a given field, you may want to write exclusively for that area. However, you may qualify in more than one area and that can make your work more interesting for you and your readers.

Don't expect to get rich, but keep in mind that there are good things in life besides money. I don't know of any other profession as enjoyable, that gives you the freedom to do what you want to do when you want to, that opens up the opportunity to meet so many interesting people— or that would have allowed me to be hugged by Roy Rogers.

➢➢ 72

SCIENCE WRITING TODAY AND TOMORROW

BY PATRICIA BARNES-SVARNEY

I AM TRULY SURROUNDED BY MY WORK: MY COMPUTER RUNS ON megabytes and RAMs; my car moves because of sparks and subsequent combustion, and sports more digital equipment than I care to imagine; and even my gym has the latest techno-gizmo to tell me just how many calories I've used up on a five-mile (albeit stationary) "bike ride." I cannot seem to get away from science and technology—but as a science writer, I do not mind, because it is more fuel for my science articles.

Science and technology encompass all our lives. If you find your hands sweating during the latest Space Shuttle launch, or you enthusiastically tell your friends the reasons why tsunamis crash along a coastline, you may be a potential science writer. And you do not have to be another Albert Einstein, Richard Feynman, or Isaac Asimov to succeed at it.

I became a science writer through the back door. I was a professional scientist who analyzed water samples and plotted flooding along sinuous river systems. A side trip back to college changed my life: The day my professor handed back the first draft of my thesis and said, "This reads like . . . well . . . an article for the general audience," sealed my fate. I have thanked her insight for ten years now.

You do not have to be a scientist or have a science background to write articles and books about science and technology. In fact, it may be helpful for you not to have a science background, because then you won't be caught up in the science jargon. If you are interviewing an astronomer on interstellar objects who says that MACHOs are found at the periphery of our galaxy, you would not just nod your head. You would ask him or her to explain—not only the acronym (Massive

Compact Halo Objects)—but why MACHOs are important to your article.

The best part about science and technology writing is the range of topics from which you can choose—and each of those subjects can be further broken down into narrower topics for other articles. Topics include the physical sciences, (geology, chemistry, etc.); biology (plant, human, viral, bacterial); space science; or medical science. Many science writers also delve into technology: computers, robotics, and electronics. Under technology, a science writer may describe remote sensing techniques used to detect and track volcanic eruption plumes across the planet; or under medical science, show how using supercomputer modeling can help us understand how drugs react within the body.

Science writing does not have to be about current scientific developments; it can also be about science in the past or future. Science past had its wonderful moments of serendipity; science future has its promise of a better life. And do not overlook science fiction for article ideas. After all, most people know about "warp drive," an idea often referred to on "Star Trek." A science writer might ask, "Can we go faster than the speed of light? If we could, what type of propulsion would be needed to catapult a spaceship to such speeds?"

Although there is a myriad of topics to choose from, all science and technology writing must apply to and excite the readers. Will they be able to use the discovery in the present or future? Will it help their children to live happier lives? Does the topic stimulate their imagination, and is it enjoyable to read? Or will the story tell them about a person, place, or thing that they never knew about before?

Now that you have decided to try your hand at writing science, you will need the following:

• *Intense curiosity.* When you are curious about a subject in science, you are more apt to dig deeper, ask for more explanation—and your enthusiasm will show in your writing. An editor once told me, "The attention span of the reader is directly proportional to the writer's interest in the story."

• *An interest in the research.* You may have all the curiosity about a subject, but you also need the tenacity to do the research. Science writers today have it easier than they did in the past: We have access to tremendous amounts of information, not only in libraries, but through

349

computer communication services, where you can find articles on your subject and leads to help you find other sources.

• *Ability to recognize a good idea for a science article.* A good idea for a science article is not "DNA"; a good science article idea is how DNA is being used as genetic "fingerprints" in crime investigations—and how it is also under fire because the technique is so new. Article ideas are everywhere, but the science writer has to know how to focus on that one kernel of interest.

• *Contacts and sources to interview.* A science writer's most valued possession is his or her contact/source list: past interviewees (experts in the fields you are writing about), reference librarians, earlier contacts from science conferences, public information offices of science-oriented institutions, organizations, and universities—and, of course, other science writers.

• *Insistence on accuracy.* The science writer's creed, to borrow from Thoreau, should read, "Simplicity, simplicity—not to mention accuracy, accuracy."

• *Good interpretative skills.* Science writers have a serious responsibility to their readers: They must interpret and present what they uncover in their research and interviews in a clear and interesting way. This interpretation is not always straightforward. I have heard it compared to translating Japanese into English: There are nuances of the Japanese culture integrated into their language that cannot be translated into English. It is often the same with explaining science to the general audience, and as Nobel physicist Richard Feynman once said, not all science can be explained in a basic way. But do not use this as an excuse; a science writer must do the best he or she can to get the subject across to the reader.

Coming up with a good science article idea is not as difficult as it seems. There are many sources that spark ideas: newspapers, science journals, news releases, computer communication services (the ubiquitous "information highway"), and numerous publications from universities and science-oriented organizations—also other people's conversations: I began to research my article on microrobots (for *Sky Magazine*) when I overheard two people joking about "minimachines" taking over the planet Mars. The real microrobots may never take over the red planet, but the suggestion triggered the idea. It also started me on the trail of just how far we have come in space-oriented microrobotic research.

After you come up with a specialized science topic, your first stop should be the library to check on magazines. Read through current magazines and explore magazine topics in the *Readers' Guide to Periodical Literature* (and similar indexes) from the past year or so. This will help you avoid writing about an idea whose time has come and gone; also you will not send a query to a magazine that has just published an article on the same subject with the same angle. If your idea seems to be on track, then gather basic information on the subject from science magazines, brochures, encyclopedias, or books.

Next comes the query, usually a less-than-one-page "outline" (in text form) of your proposed article. The query presents your idea, sources, and credentials to the editor. A word of caution: Know your magazine. Do not send a query on industrial robotics to *Woman's World,* or an idea on the future of the American/Russian cooperation on the Space Station to *Sailing*; but also remember that certain non-science magazines will take science or technology topics, including some inflight and general-interest magazines. Know your science magazines, too: Articles for *Omni* have a different slant from those for *Popular Science.*

The day the editor says, "Go for it," is the day you take all your basic information and outline-query letter, and get to work. Now is also the time to call on your sources for interviews. Some science writers write a sketchy first draft to their article before the interviews—a way to organize their thoughts and frame the questions to ask the interviewee in some semblance of order; other writers do a first draft after the interview. In either case, you will need a list of questions to ask your experts. Always remember that the only dumb question is the one you did not ask.

Writing a publishable science article takes the ability to explain complex concepts without baffling or confusing the readers. One of the best approaches is to discuss the subject or idea in terms the reader can relate to. For example, in my article on agriculture in space (for *Ad Astra*) I wove familiar gardening terms (and references to many gardening problems) into the piece so the readers could relate to growing plants in the Space Station and beyond.

Another strategy to give your science article life is to use anecdotes.

Usually, your interviewees have interesting stories to tell, such as how their discovery was made, or about the first patient to use their new drug. Since the general public often thinks of science as another world, descriptions of the scientists and their surroundings will "humanize" your article, showing that the expert has the same idiosyncrasies that we all have—right down to worries about money or celebrations of victories.

Of course, there are two more qualities that keep all science writers going: patience and perseverance. It takes patience to get an interview with a busy scientist (and sometimes you will not get the interview at all); and patience to see your words in print. Plus, it takes perseverance to understand the intricacies of your science article—and to keep up with the new science discoveries that pop up every week.

There is more than enough science to provide you with subjects for science articles. As a science writer just remember that the universe is now your beat.

➤➤ 73

How to Write a How-To That Sells

By Gail Luttman

Any activity that interests you—from canoeing to cooking to collecting Civil War relics to cutting your own hair—is a potential how-to article. And whether you are an expert or a novice, you are qualified to write about it.

Where to start

The most successful introductions to how-to pieces state a problem and then propose one or more possible solutions, perferably those relating to the seven basic human motivators.

Ego—Does your solution to the problem improve the way you look, the way you feel about yourself, your ability to relate to others?

Economy—Does it save money, protect the environment, improve quality without increasing cost?

Health—Does it give you more energy, promote safety practices, increase your psychological well-being?

Romance—Does it enhance sex appeal, create a cozy atmosphere, improve personal relationships?

Family—Does it entertain children, foster loyalty, help research family history?

Leisure—Does it enliven holiday activities, provide an engrossing hobby, help plan exciting vacations?

Individuality—Does the activity appeal to the universal desire for uniqueness by offering something new, different or better?

These motivators often overlap. A hobby may bring in income. Dieting may improve both health and self-image. An inexpensive bungalow of unusual construction may serve as a romantic retreat. The more motivators you appeal to, the greater interest you will generate in your how-to.

Moving on

After piquing the reader's interest, offer a brief explanation of what the activity involves, couched in enthusiastic words that inspire confidence. Can the skill be learned in five easy steps? Fifteen minutes a day? Does it require a special setting, or will a corner of the garage do? What special tools or materials are needed?

Rather than barrage readers at the beginning with a large number of tools or materials required, you may want to list them in a sidebar, a separate boxed-off article that accompanies the main story. Sidebars are a great way to include data or lengthy explanations without interrupting the narrative flow. Some editors favor articles with one, two, or even three sidebars if the article is very long or complex.

Definitions of unfamiliar terms might go into a vocabulary sidebar, especially when they are numerous; on the other hand, if special words are few or are easy to define, it is better to explain their meanings as you go along.

Whenever possible, describe new concepts by drawing a comparison with something familiar. In a piece about building stone walls, for example, a description of the proper consistency of mortar as "buttery" sparks instant recognition.

Complicated procedures don't seem quite as confusing when written up in short, uncomplicated sentences of the sort found in cookbooks. Explicitness also ensures clarity. Vague directions such as "measure out six to eight cups of water" or "cut two to three yards of string" leave the reader wondering which of the two stated amounts to use.

Clarity is also improved by separating general principles from specific procedures. If you are writing about how to build a chicken coop, for example, after the introductory remarks, explain how the layout and dimensions are established, then include some specific plans. In a how-to about cooking a Christmas goose, first describe how to roast the goose, then offer some favorite recipes. In that way you'll satisfy both the creative reader who likes to improvise and the less adventuresome reader who feels more comfortable with step-by-step instructions.

The final and best way to ensure clarity is with illustrations. The less commonplace the subject, the more important photographs and sketches become, and they are essential when dimensions are involved. In addition, the market is more receptive to illustrated how-tos. But don't despair if you are not an accomplished photographer or artist; many how-to magazines have illustrators who will enhance your article with clear, easy-to-follow illustrations.

Organization

The subject of a how-to usually dictates whether to organize the steps chronologically or to start with simple procedures and work toward difficult ones. If two steps are to be taken at the same time, it is important to make that clear. In bread baking, for instance, point out that yeast should be softening in warm water while the other ingredients are being measured.

Repetition can help or hinder reader understanding. Too much repetition causes readers to lose interest. In a short article, a brief reference to the original explanation is usually all that's needed. But if the article is very long or complex and the explanation is relatively short, repetition is better than asking readers to flip pages back to find the required information.

Include a timetable for each step to help readers gauge their progress. How long does concrete take to set? Eggs to hatch? Wine to ferment? Do varying conditions influence timing? Can or should any deliberate measures be taken to speed things up or slow them down? What specific signs might the reader watch for as the project nears completion?

Finally, what can go wrong? Think twice before including a separate how-not-to section or a trouble-shooting sidebar. Faced with a long list of things that can go wrong, a reader might understandably wonder whether the whole thing is worth the bother. But, in general, as long as a how-to is clearly written and well organized, it doesn't hurt to point out danger spots along the way.

Research, including interviews with appropriate experts, supplies background that adds depth and authority to how-tos, thereby increasing reader interest and credibility. It also helps a writer discover whether his experiences are typical or not. If not, avoid making sweeping or questionable generalizations.

When consulting authoritative sources, watch out for regional varia-

355

tions in the terms and methods you plan to describe, especially when you're writing for a national magazine. Mention chicken wire and a southerner is likely to picture what the westerner calls livestock fencing. Talk about reupholstering a divan or davenport, and there are readers who won't realize you are discussing a couch or a sofa. Before you write your article, look up alternative terminology from other areas.

Voice

Of course, the target audience determines how to approach your subject. If you are describing a new weaving technique to experienced weavers, you may use standard terms freely without defining them. But you should define any words that are specific to the new technique and you should definitely explain why the new technique is worth learning.

It is your job as a how-to writer to make certain that all readers achieve the same level of information by the time they reach the heart of your piece, and to do it without talking down. You can manage this by pretending you are writing a detailed letter to an interested friend.

You will find your most effective how-to voice by writing your article as if you were addressing a particular person who engages you in especially lively conversation. If you can't think of anyone suitable, invent someone. By writing expressly for that single reader, real or fictitious, you will delight all your readers with the personal tone of your how-to.

>> 74

WRITING A LIFE

BY LINDA SIMON

"BIOGRAPHY WORKS IN MYSTERIES," WROTE LEON EDEL, THE MAS-
terful biographer of Henry James. "That is its fascination." Many biographers have likened themselves to detectives trying to find a missing
person—their subject—by searching for clues in letters, diaries, photographs, and whatever other artifacts survive as evidence of their subject's life. Working in public archives and private collections,
biographers read intimate revelations, discover secrets, and ultimately
come to know their subjects better, perhaps, than they know their own
friends and family. The work of a biographer can be difficult, frustrating, and time-consuming; but, as Edel tells us, biography has many
rewards. Biographers learn not only about the particular details of
their subject's life, but also the historical, cultural, and social context
in which they lived; not only about the particular problems and decisions that their subject faced, but something about human nature,
about the dreams and desires that we all share. As a result of their
search into someone else's life, biographers often learn something
about themselves.

Choosing a subject

Who makes a good biographical subject? If we look at library
shelves, we find that in the past biographies were written about famous
men—and a few women. The biographical subject usually was a hero:
someone who had accomplished some great feat, held an important
political position, or made a lasting contribution to the arts. The biographer paid homage to this person's greatness by portraying his life as
exemplary. Catherine Drinker Bowen, who wrote biographies of such
great men as Justice Oliver Wendell Holmes and John Adams, tells us
that writing about heroic figures was, for her, an uplifting experience:

357

> To spend three years or five with a truly great man, reading what he said and wrote, observing him as he errs, stumbles, falls, and rises again; to watch his talent grow . . . this cannot but seize upon a writer, one might almost say transform him. . . . The ferment of genius, Holmes said, is quickly imparted, and when a man is great he makes others believe in greatness. By that token one's life is altered. One has climbed a hill, looked out and over, and the valley of one's own condition will be forever greener.

Biographers today, however, are not likely to share Bowen's belief in heroes. Experience, observation, and a dollop of Freudian psychology has disillusioned many of us. We tend to believe that all people have their weaknesses, flaws, and dark sides. We look for complexities and contradictions—and we find them, even in men and women who have enacted great deeds.

Although many biographies are written about famous men and women, increasingly we find biographies about those who lived relatively ordinary lives. Jean Strouse, for example, decided to write about Alice James, a minor historical figure compared with her brothers, the novelist Henry James and the philosopher William. Alice James, Strouse wrote, "made no claim to have carried on an exemplary struggle or to have achieved anything beyond the private measure of her own experience. To make her into a heroine (or victim-as-heroine) now would be seriously to misconstrue her sufferings and her aims." Still, Strouse believed that Alice James's experiences could illuminate for readers the context of women's lives in the nineteenth century. She believed that writing about "semi-private lives" helps us to enter the world of ordinary men and women—the world, after all, in which most of us live.

If biographers today have a wide range of subjects to choose from, how does one decide? Who is a good subject? Simply put, a good subject, like an interesting friend, is someone whose stories we like to hear, someone we would like to introduce to other people. A good subject is not always likable, but never dull. It is someone whose story has not yet been told, perhaps, or in any case, has not yet been told the way we understand it. We may feel a connection with this subject because we share similar experiences or sensibilities; or we may feel admiration, even envy, for the subject's life. We may be attracted to someone who lived in an exciting time and place, even if that person did not contribute greatly to the excitement. Always, we feel that there is a mystery to be solved: Something about this person is not yet known, and we want to discover it.

I had been reading books by and about American expatriates in Paris, simply for the pleasure of it, when I noticed that Gertrude Stein emerged again and again in memoirs of the period. Surely Stein is an interesting historical figure: an experimenter in poetry and prose whose unconventional appearance and personality made her the center of attention wherever she went. I liked Stein's raunchiness, self-confidence, and literary daring. As I read biographies of Stein—again, simply for the pleasure of immersing myself in the period—I noticed that her companion, Alice B. Toklas, seemed to be a mysterious figure. Was she a kind, protective supporter of Stein? Was she a cold-hearted manipulator? Most biographers portrayed Stein as a dominant force in the household, but was Toklas really in charge? These questions motivated me to see Toklas as a potential biographical subject: She presented a problem for me; she was a mystery.

Although Alice Toklas lived a "semi-private" life in comparison with Gertrude Stein's, still she lived an extraordinary life in comparison with, say, my grandmother or uncle, who did not cavort with the likes of Ernest Hemingway, Pablo Picasso, and F. Scott Fitzgerald. But anyone's grandmother or uncle might be a suitable biographical subject. If your grandmother was an immigrant who kept diaries and sent letters to relatives in her native land, if your uncle was a health food guru who traveled the world teaching new ideas about nutrition, they may be interesting subjects for a full-length biography or a shorter study: an article in a historical journal, for example, or a chapter in a collection of biographical sketches. As a potential biographer, however, you need to ask the same questions about these subjects that you would ask about anyone else: Would my grandmother or uncle interest other people? Is there sufficient source material to give me enough biographical information for my study? Is there a mystery about this person that I want to solve?

Finding clues

Once biographers find a subject, they need to assess whether sufficient biographical material will be available to them. Biographers can write only about someone who has left a paper trail, including letters, journals, creative writing, works of art such as films or paintings, interviews. The biographer must have access to material that can document the subject's life.

If you have chosen a subject who has been written about before, existing biographies can help you to locate archives where there is material about your subject. I knew from biographies of Gertrude Stein that the Stein archives were housed in the American Literature collection at Yale University's Beinecke Library. Many of Toklas's letters were housed there as well. But to find other material, I began a search in the reference room of my local library. There, I examined such sources as the *National Union Catalogue of Manuscript Collections* and the *Directory of Special Libraries and Information Centers* to locate other archives where I guessed that I might find Toklas correspondence or other material. I wrote to these libraries, visited some, ordered photocopies, and began to assemble my own files of source material.

The reference room of a good library contains many directories that lead researchers to archival material. Some of these directories are specialized—focusing on women's history, science, or art, for example. Reference librarians are helpful and knowledgeable about these sources. I have discovered these professionals to be a biographer's best friend.

If you find few sources in library archives, the search becomes a bit more complicated. If your subject has survivors, you need to find out whether material that you need may be in private collections: the attic of your subject's grand-niece or the basement of your subject's ex-wife. Sometimes, survivors are cooperative; sometimes, however, they feel threatened by an interloper who may discover information about the family's life that they wish to be kept private. Although many biographies have been written in the face of survivors' hostility, some biographers find such a situation uncomfortable and stressful. If you are among them, you may want to choose another subject.

Doing it

Researching and writing a biography is not a quick project. It takes time to locate material, time to assemble sources, time to track down clues. You may find yourself spending years formulating a chronology of your subject's life. Anyone beginning a biography needs to have developed strong research skills. Historical writing is good practice, and so is newspaper reporting. Gradually, biographers develop a sense of intuition about their subject, discovering that they can anticipate their subject's reaction to a new acquaintance or a new experience.

Suddenly, they feel it is time to write. When I was working on a biography of Thornton Wilder, I went to visit a charming man who had been a close friend of Wilder's. He began to tell me some stories about Wilder's life—his experiences in the theater, his days as a soldier, his literary friendships—and I found that I could finish sentences: These were stories that I knew in even more detail than Wilder's friend. When I returned home, I began to write the book.

Some biographers write as they research, sketching in the parameters of a life, filling in details as they find them. Some biographers spend twenty years involved in their subject's life, although not all of those years are spent researching and writing. Few writers are able to work on a biography full time, so other tasks—teaching, translating, even doing the laundry—intervene in the research and writing process. Yet biographers admit that even when they are not actually conducting research or writing, their subject becomes a companion, someone they think about often. They begin to see events in their own lives through their subject's eyes; they reflect on their own experiences in light of what they learn about their subject. Biography invites introspection. Personal introspection—thinking about why people behave as they do, about the forces that shape us and the way we affect other people—is good training for the biographer's work.

Biographical problems

In the past few years, biographers have come under attack as being nothing more than burglars, rifling through lingerie drawers and laundry bins, looking for the worst about their subject. Joyce Carol Oates coined the term "pathography" to apply to biographies that present subjects as neurotic, psychotic, depressed, incestuous, alcoholic, or suffering from other antisocial maladies. But these biographies reflect our current intellectual climate more than they reflect the craft of biography.

Certainly the kinds of questions that biographers ask about their subjects have changed over time. Biographers have been influenced by the work of psychologists and social scientists; they examine their subjects from different perspectives, depending on their own ideas

361

about personality development and the cause and effect of behavior. A biography of John Kennedy, written in the 1960s, would have ignored questions about family rivalry and sexual infidelity that biographers feel free to ask twenty years later. A burgeoning interest in biographies of women, beginning in the 1970s, changed both the kinds of questions that biographers asked and the subjects that they chose to write about. In creating a sense of the reality of someone's life, biographers have come to see that the superficial interactions and daily routine may not define an individual. This delving deeply into another personality may seem to some an invasion of privacy. But responsible biographers take their task seriously: They want to find a missing person. Without their efforts, their subject would simply disappear, fade from memory, be lost to history. Biographers keep spirits alive.

➤➤ 75

For Tightwad Travel Writers

By Betty Bezzerides

There's a myth about travel writers: Our friends envision us perpetually snorkeling in Barbados or skiing at St. Moritz, but chances are I'll be driving only twenty miles to the local hot springs instead of hopping a plane to Antigua. While the common constraints of time and money may keep your articles out of the major magazines, they won't keep you from writing and selling travel articles. Here are ten survival tips for travel writers on a tight budget.

1) *Travel close to home.* Using state and regional maps and your home base as a compass point, draw mileage circles. Everything inside the first circle represents day trips; the second circle, weekends; the third circle, long weekends. Then choose an economical mode of transportation. Planes and trains may have to be off limits. There's always your car.

2) *Find a niche.* It might be a general topic, such as close-to-home travel. Or it may be more specific—hiking, biking, parks, food, shopping, museums, local history, or celebrations at those close-to-home destinations.

3) *Look for the offbeat.* Keep your eyes and ears open for the exotic and unusual. To catch my readers' attention, I can count on a bed-and-breakfast visit to a working llama farm, or some "bug time" at a tropical bug museum.

4) *Query local publications.* The high-profile travel magazines probably won't snap up your piece on the village slug races, but there's a good chance the local newspaper will. There are dozens of newspapers

and magazines published in your home state. Many are short-staffed and glad to consider quality free-lance work.

5) *Snoop around.* This goes without saying for all travel writers, of course, but it bears repeating. Your readers trust you to provide accurate, reliable information. Don't lead them into anything you haven't investigated firsthand.

6) *Protect the budget.* Don't hesitate to share your secrets about how to have a good time without spending a lot of money. It may not occur to your readers to shop the local farms for picnic fare, or to calm down travel-weary children at the city park, or to order dinner from the appetizer menu. Show readers how to do it.

7) *Collect free information.* Chambers of commerce, libraries, newspapers, radio, television, travel agents, and friends who travel are all excellent sources. The neighbor who's had a condo in the mountains for ten years will probably be glad to steer you to his favorite restaurant there; a cousin who lives near the hot springs knows the least crowded times to soak. Take advantage of the network.

8) *Use the armchair.* You can put together many travel-related pieces without actually taking a trip. Review travel books. Report on local travel lectures. Share your hard-earned tips on how to travel with children, or how to plan a trip. After years of wandering, I've lost track of how many times people have asked me in disbelief, "How did you ever find that?" Many travelers need a little coaching in off-the-beaten-path adventures.

9) *Pick your friends' brains.* When your close-to-home resources are at a low ebb, be alert for likely candidates to interview when they return from a trip. A geologist friend of mine went to Scotland to retrace the travels of James Hutton, the father of modern geology. A co-worker went kayaking in Belize. A college friend spent a month on the Amazon River. A former boss fished for trout in Patagonia. Friends will usually be glad to share their exploits, enthusiasms, and experiences with you.

10) *Diversify.* Your travels can lead to spin-offs that don't necessarily fit on the travel pages, but can suggest other articles: The insect museum results in a health feature on bugs that bite. The overnight stay at the llama farm leads to a feature on raising llamas. You turn the skeet factory you passed on a back road into an essay on unusual ways of making a living.

You have a nose for the open road. Keep your duffle packed and your antennae tuned for adventure. Observe everything—then write about it!

>> 76

WRITING AND SELLING IN THE NEWSPAPER MARKET

BY JOHANNA S. BILLINGS

ALTHOUGH IT'S NOT EASY TO BREAK INTO THE NEWSPAPER MARKET AS a staff writer, nevertheless, local newspapers are literally begging for free-lance writers, or "stringers," to cover events that the staff writers can't get to.

Both daily and weekly newspapers use stringers. Weeklies generally accept beginning writers because often their staffs are less experienced. Smaller suburban dailies are likely to be receptive to new writers, but the larger dailies usually demand journalism experience.

Breaking in

The best way to sell your work to newspapers is to sell yourself first. Once you have chosen a newspaper, find out who the editor is, and then send a cover letter, including a resumé highlighting your writing credits and "clips" if you have any. A follow-up call should get you an interview, which may be rather informal, especially if you already have some writing experience.

Because most editors are not looking to buy just one article, they seldom want query letters. Instead, they want to cultivate a working relationship with stringers to whom they can give assignments regularly.

As a stringer, you will be doing both "hard news," which refers to government- and other issue-oriented articles, and "features," which include interviews/profiles and community events.

There are no standard rules for article length. Some newspapers have no length guidelines at all; others will tell you before you begin to write exactly how long an article should be.

Article length in newspapers is expressed in inches. The number of words to an inch depends on the size of print and column width of the paper. At the newspaper at which I am currently a stringer, a nine- or ten-inch story is about 800 words, but the same number of words might be eleven or twelve inches at another newspaper.

If you've written for other markets such as magazines, be prepared for a much faster pace. Since newspapers publish roughly thirty times as often as magazines and therefore need thirty times the input, if you want to succeed, you have to write good articles—fast.

Often, particularly at daily newspapers, a stringer will get an assignment without much advance notice. You may get a call Monday afternoon asking if you can cover something that begins at 7:30 that night. And if you're writing for a morning paper, you will be expected to have the story written and in final form by 11 p.m. or midnight.

The "musts"

Both hard news and features are written in much the same way. They must incorporate these elements:

The five W's. *What* is the story about? *Who* is affected by it? *Where* is it happening, and *when*? And most important, *why*? Doing this well means paying attention to details. How much something costs, an address, a person's age, the number of people attending an event are all small details that will make your story complete.

Accuracy. This may seem so basic that it doesn't warrant a mention, but it is crucial. No reader will continue to buy a newspaper if the facts are not reported accurately. And editors will not keep stringers who cannot produce accurate copy.

So, when you conduct an interview or cover a meeting or event, make sure you understand exactly what happened and how, what effects it will have and why it is important. If you have any questions, read previous articles on the subject, or ask sources, editors, and other writers. Then, write your story. When writing about a complicated issue, I try to get phone numbers of key people to call if questions come up while I'm writing.

Balance. Newspapers strive to represent both sides of every story, not the opinion of the writer. If, for example, a zoning board votes to allow an oversized parking lot, explain why the board made that decision. If it wasn't a unanimous vote, be sure to quote people who voted *for* and *against* it. And just as important, be sure to talk to the business people and anyone living nearby who will be affected by the decision.

Let the words of the people you quote speak for themselves, even if you disagree. But remember, the opinions expressed should advance your story, or provide new information, not just repeat information.

The hook. Entice readers at the beginning of your piece with the most interesting item. Newspapers generally present articles in the "inverted pyramid" style, that is, using the most important item first, with the least important at the end. But using the inverted pyramid style is not a hard-and-fast rule. Many of the newspapers I've worked for encourage more flexibility, allowing writers to begin a story with an anecdote or something to catch the reader's attention.

Relevance. Most readers will ask, "What does it mean to me?" before deciding to read on. Put yourself in readers' shoes and ask yourself that question—before you begin writing. For example, what will the zoning hearing mean to the average person reading a story about it— or to the person who is not directly affected but lives or works in the community? Will the new parking lot affect traffic flow? Will a traffic light be necessary? Why did the petitioners need or want a bigger parking lot? Have any residents voiced objections to the new lot? If so, who? Talk to them. Include their opinions in your story.

Generally, the more you include people in a story, the better it will be. If you find that "John Doe" is upset about the new lot, you might lead your story with, "John Doe moved to his present home thirty years ago because he wanted to live in a rural setting. But soon, he will be living next door to So-And-So's new parking lot." Then describe the zoning hearing and decision, moving quickly to represent the views of the zoning board and business owner to make sure your story stays balanced. Personalizing even a hard-news article will make it more interesting to read (and more fun to write).

Do the same with features and stories about community events. Interview people and find out why they came to an event and what they liked or disliked. You might hear about inefficient or rude ticket sales people, something the sponsors would never tell you. Having this information will give your story pizazz.

The fresh approach. This is particularly important when writing about community events. Without new ideas, the preview and after-the-event story can be essentially the same, year after year. It's your job as a stringer to make sure you don't write the same story that appeared in the paper last year. A fresh approach is especially crucial at a weekly because the story might not appear until six days after the area daily already covered it.

While working for a paper in suburban Philadelphia, I did a preview story on the upcoming annual Philadelphia Folk Festival. I had interviewed some volunteers who camped out on the site months before the festival to get the grounds ready, and began my story by focusing on a couple of them. I then gradually worked my way into the nuts and bolts of the festival—how many people were expected to attend, the dates, and the special attractions. The volunteers' experiences served as the thread that tied all the elements of the story together.

Features about individuals who "overcame great obstacles" or "remain positive despite the obstacles" have been done over and over, so taking a fresh perspective is very important. Don't editorialize; just let the person's words speak for themselves, and readers can form their own conclusions.

One last rule: Stringers are often assigned the stories that staff writers can't get to or don't want. But don't look at this as an obstacle. As a stringer, you'll have the luxury of having the time to develop really interesting features.

At first, all your work will be on assignment by the editor. But once you feel comfortable with the business and the writing, you will feel free to suggest ideas for future articles. If it's a viable idea, you'll get the assignment.

➤➤ 77

WRITING THE FEATURE ARTICLE

BY RITA BERMAN

THERE IS A GOOD STEADY MARKET FOR FEATURE ARTICLES. READERS are always looking for ways to improve themselves. Pick up any magazine at the newsstands. What do you see? Articles on how to cope with a teenager or a baby, make tasty meals in 30 minutes, take off ten pounds. How to live longer, happier, wealthier, understand and buy art, learn word processing, or—how to write. All of these feature articles are aimed directly at the reader.

The content of a feature article is more important than the author's name, so the unknown writer has as good an opportunity as the well-known one to have an article accepted, provided that the manuscript is well done and meets the editor's needs.

"Find facts that are new and known by few," an editor told me when I began my writing career. Sounds gimmicky, but it's good advice. Remember that a feature article focuses on the human-interest angle of facts, but this is not a hard and fast rule. Many feature articles are instructive or informational: how-to, how-I, or how-you. The principles of these how-tos (also known as service articles) are that you state the problem, offer a solution, and end with a result. Your advice must guide the readers through the steps taken so that they, too, can recreate your success. Other features are based on interviewing an expert or recognized authority in the field you wish to write about, then in your article, sharing their experiences and knowledge with the reader.

You must do a lot of thinking and planning, as well as gathering and organizing facts. You need to consider the subject of the article; how much readers will be interested in that subject; possible markets; sources that could provide ideas and facts; who might be interviewed for the article; and whether illustrations or photographs may be needed.

By the time you have collected notes, material, photographs, or illustrations, the article may be taking shape in your mind. Before writing your feature, organize your thoughts and material. Know what you want to put into your article, but don't try to keep it all in your head. *Use an outline to get started and stay on track.*

1. On your worksheet, write the working title, which could change after you've written the piece, or as you go along.

Titles are the bait you use to attract editors and readers. Most magazine titles rarely exceed six to eight words. A good title should suggest the contents and tone of the story. Titles cannot be copyrighted, but avoid using one that might be confused with a previously published piece.

2. Jot down a list of words, phrases, or sentences to remind you of all the items and points you wish to cover in your feature.

3. Decide what kind of lead to use to attract the reader:

The question lead: What can you do to get a million dollars?
The controversial statement: It's easy to get a million dollars.
The case history or anecdotal lead: I made my first million—the easy way.
A statement of fact: There are more millionaires than ever.
A descriptive lead: A million dollars in gold lay gleaming in the vault.

A strong lead is crucial in feature writing because this is what draws the reader into the article, and immediately after the lead, you proceed in a way that will sustain that reader's interest and provide the reason or justification for your lead.

This transition from the lead to the text is sometimes referred to as the bridge, hook, angle, or peg of the story.

Example: For one feature, "How We Sold Our Home" (published in *Army, Navy, Air Force Times*), I used a grabber lead about military families being familiar with change-of-station orders, and how we had led a nomadic existence for 12 years.

4. After your lead, what kind of bridge will you use to hold readers' interest?

In my feature, a paragraph stating that about 7 million homes change hands each year provided the bridge; the rest of the piece was my personal story. I involved the readers by informing them that selling our house without using a real estate broker saved us thousands of dollars. That was my response to the reader's natural "what's in it for me?" question. No matter what the subject—going on a cruise, or trying to avoid paying more taxes—readers always ask, "What's in it for me?"

5. The body of your piece. What anecdotes, examples, or facts will you use to prove the point you want to make? For a how-to piece this is where you will describe the pitfalls, things that didn't work, as well as tips that will lead to a satisfactory conclusion.

I continued my home sale feature by describing a few simple steps that should be followed when selling without an agent. Then I was off into the body of the story, repeating and expanding the reasons for selling the house ourselves, and describing how we did it: preparing the house and grounds; pricing the house realistically; and how we saved time and money when we conducted the sale.

6. The conclusion. A final strong paragraph should wrap it all up effectively for the reader.

My last paragraph for "How We Sold Our Home" echoed my lead by referring to military families and their nomadic way of life. This helped reinforce the message to the military readers of *Army, Navy, Air Force Times* that they too might be moving and selling a house sometime in the future.

Do not try to write any of the sections in final form at this stage. The outline should be used as a guide to prompt the flow of thoughts and to keep you moving in the right direction. It will be particularly helpful if for any reason you have to put the article aside.

Writing the rough draft

With the outline to guide you, you will be ready to begin writing your feature. Write directly and simply, as if talking to your readers. Short paragraphs. Write to be understood, not to impress. As your piece begins to take shape, you will have to consider what transitions are needed to take the reader from example to example, and how you will tie the whole thing together. Keep the feature story flowing toward a strong closing paragraph to balance the hard-hitting lead.

Use subheads and a blurb so that readers can grasp the main idea quickly. A blurb is a summary of what the article is about. You need to know this yourself in order to write the feature. If you are unable to compress the scope of the feature into a sentence or two, perhaps you need to think about it some more.

For informational articles, sidebars and boxes keep the article tight and give it impact. In "How We Sold Our Home" I included a box headed "What do real estate terms mean?" listing key words and definitions such as *appraisal, closing costs, earnest money.*

Tell the reader how and where to get more information on the topic, including addresses and phone numbers, if available. If the how-to was based on interviews, give your sources credit for their remarks.

Accuracy is essential in how-to articles, so recheck your facts before you send out the manuscript.

Revision

You should spend almost as much time on revising and rewriting as you spent on thinking, planning, and writing your rough draft. Are the points in good logical order? The best possible words? It's fun to cross out words you have written and substitute new ones that are clearer and give sharper meaning to your story.

If a sentence sounds awkward on rereading, rephrase it. Chop a long sentence into two. Write in simple sentences rather than long, compound or complex ones.

Allow some time to elapse between the first and second draft. If I wait for a day or two, sentences or sections that need reworking seem to leap off the page. Try to read the article aloud, or better still, tape it. Listening to your words will uncover writing weaknesses.

Write to space

The only way you can cut a feature, if it ends up being too long, is to prune throughout. An alternative is to write to space from the outset. Do this by assigning a specific number of words to each section of your outline. As a guide, for a 1,500-word piece you might allot 50 words for the introduction, 150 words for the bridge, 1,200 words for the body of the piece, and 100 words for the conclusion. An average page of typing contains 250 words (25 lines of 10 words), so 1,500 words should run approximately six pages.

Getting the feature published

The usual publication outlet for features is in the monthly or quarterly magazines, thousands of which are published in all regions of the country. New magazines hit the newsstands every month, and the old ones change their formats. In addition, magazines sold by subscription only also have a constant need for steady, reliable writers who can write interesting features. Names and addresses of consumer, special interest, trade, and a host of other magazines can be found in the back of this book; select the best possible markets for your feature.

Many listings request that writers query instead of submitting a completed manuscript. By querying, you find out if—and where—there is interest in your piece. Make a list of markets to query, and send for writers guidelines before you write your query letter. Guidelines provide information on topics that are wanted, word length, preferred submission format, whether photographs are needed, the rights bought, pay scale, and other useful information about editorial needs.

Select one publication and submit a query letter. If you draw a negative response, revise the letter and work your way through the market list. After you get a go-ahead from an editor, you can prepare the article to meet the magazine's editorial needs, and thus increase your chances of being published.

➤➤ 78

BIOGRAPHER AT WORK

BY GALE E. CHRISTIANSON

THE BIOGRAPHER BONDS HIMSELF TO HIS SUBJECT IN A UNION MORE symbiotic than matrimony. Almost never are the two separated during the long months and years of their association, for dreams and nightmares are as much the stuff of writing lives as the countless hours passed in airless archives or mornings wrestling with the blank page.

Thus your subject must be a companion whose character faults, which magnify in the glare of intense scrutiny, are offset by accomplishments sufficiently redeeming to override skepticism and assuage doubt. Such was the case for me with the great Isaac Newton, the subject of my first biography. Though mean-spirited and given to withering tirades against those who challenged his scientific ideas, the inventor of calculus, the mortal who flung gravity across the void, is forever woven into my tapestry of the blessed.

My feelings for Loren Eiseley, the anthropologist, literary naturalist, and author of some of this century's most elegant and evocative essays, are rather more ambivalent. While writing Eiseley's life, I was gradually overwhelmed by his tendency to cast events in conspiratorial hues and to blame everyone but himself for his sufferings. To put it simply: Had I known what I was getting into with Eiseley, I think I would have passed.

Yet the biographer should also be cautious when his prospective subject seems too companionable. Identifying too closely with the subject violates the constraints essential to writing biography. Psychoanalysts term this process "co-creation" or the "commingling of consciousness." Setting out to write the life of another, the biographer is actually carrying on an interior dialogue with himself, while plying his own emotional terrain.

After choosing a subject, the real work begins. Almost every serious

375

biographer (we are not here concerned with so-called celebrity biographies or what I call tabloidism) must face the daunting prospect of burrowing deep into one or more archives. But it is well to complete as much background reading as possible before immersing yourself in the primary sources. Since it is not only unwise but impossible to attempt to include everything about a life, however important, the researcher must be selective. The late Barbara Tuchman characterized biography as a prism of history, while others have likened it to fine portraiture. Leon Edel, best known for his multivolume life of Henry James, speaks of "the figure under the carpet," whose true identity can be resolved only by carefully scrutinizing the tea leaves of research. Whatever the method or the metaphor, the biographer must create a unique angle of vision by fitting keys to locks that yield only to the right questions.

Some biographers enter archives armed with little more than a pencil and a generous supply of 3″ by 5″ cards; others carry laptop computers whose clicking keyboards serve as a constant distraction to those with a sensitive ear. My preference is the portable archives made available via photocopying. With photocopies at one's fingertips, dates, quotations, and myriad other details can be rechecked as often as need be, thus minimizing the number of inadvertent errors that steal into a manuscript.

Moreover, the biographer's perspective is subject to change. This is especially true when dealing with letters, diaries, and notebooks, which may require several readings. Notes are inevitably incomplete and have a way of growing cold during the months or possibly years that may pass before the author returns to them.

But most important to me is that an exact copy recharges the atmosphere as the original did when I first viewed it in the archives. Photocopies are the catalysts of inspiration and of musing, and serve as a constant reminder of the responsibility one bears to one's subject.

Finally, the more quickly material is gathered the sooner one can return home. The costs of photocopying are but a fraction of what it takes to hole up in major cities, where archives tend to be found.

To my continual surprise, I am often asked if I research the *whole* life before I begin to write it. The answer is an emphatic "yes," for, to paraphrase Kierkegaard, a life must be lived forward but it can only be understood backward.

No writer can tell another when enough research is enough, when science must yield to art. This is a personal matter based on a hidden clock whose ticking is as individual as the human thumbprint. But one thing is certain: There will never be a book without writing, and without self-imposed deadlines, the writing will never begin.

To biographers of people who have only recently died, primary sources constitute more than words and images captured on paper. These include the house in which one's subject came into the world, and perhaps left it; the church in which he attended Sunday school; the neighborhood streets along which he bashfully walked hand in hand with his first love; and, if one is very lucky, the living memories of those who grew up with him and took his measure "way back when."

Interviewing friends, relatives, and colleagues of your subject is a tricky albeit rewarding business, best left until you are conversant with the archives. It is only at this point that the right questions can be asked. The web of memory is often very delicate, and responds most sympathetically when probed by a gentle and informed petitioner. And the more you address the same questions to various individuals, the sounder the process. Above all, listen. It is often the seemingly little things these people say that turn out to be the most important.

And what about writing the life of a living person? Having never done so, I can only say, *caveat emptor!* Since the life is not a finished thing, its telling will be superceded by future works based on a sounder perspective. Access to information may also be a problem, even if the subject is cooperative in the beginning. What is gladly given with one hand can be angrily snatched away by the other, especially if the subject's views and those of the biographer clash. With so many other wonderful subjects to choose from, why run the risk?

In her often cited account of Shakespeare's imagined sister, Virginia Woolf asserted that the writer must have "a room of one's own." What is true of the novelist and the poet is no less true of the biographer. "You must have a room, or a certain hour or so a day," wrote the mythographer Joseph Campbell, "where you don't know what was in the newspapers that morning, you don't know who your friends are, you don't know what you owe anybody, you don't know what anybody owes you." This is the place of creation where the writer brings forth what he or she is—and is to be.

Saturated with facts and documents, the writer confronts a ream of blank pages. Do not be surprised or dispirited if nothing happens right away, for obviously a book never writes itself. Someone, presumably the author, must shape the narrative while deciding which details to retain or to cut, which gestures to play up or to play down, which lines to quote or to omit.

A biography can begin at any point in a subject's life, from birth to the deathbed, from the moment when lightning struck, to the transforming pain caused by the loss of a loved one. The tale begins by fitting one of those precious keys into a lock, turning it, and bidding the reader to enter. During my research on Loren Eiseley, for example, it became clear that he had idealized his father, an itinerant hardware salesman who reminded me of no one so much as Willy Loman. Thus the book begins with three-year-old Loren in the arms of Clyde Edwin Eiseley, gazing into the midnight sky of a chill and leafless Nebraska spring in 1910, an incident Loren recounted in an essay penned many years later. The two are transfixed by Halley's comet.

"If you live to be an old man," his father whispered, "you will see it again. It will come back in seventy-five years."

"Yes, Papa," the boy replied dutifully. Tightening his hold on his father's neck, he promised that when he grew old, he would gaze on the comet a second time and remember the person he would always care for more than any other.

Once you begin, set yourself a challenging yet reachable goal. Mine is some 1,000 words a day, the equivalent of about three typed pages. When the gods are kind, as happens on occasion, the total may double, but more often than not I fall a few paragraphs short. I also try to finish a day's writing at a point which will stimulate the creative flow the next morning, the psychological equivalent of priming the pump.

There is much to be gained by reading fine literature while trying to approximate it oneself. The genre does not matter: Novels and essays, short stories and narrative histories, poetry and plays all serve to deepen one's sensibilities.

Your actual voice can also help to locate your literary voice. At day's end, or night's if you are an owl, read your edited work back to yourself aloud. You will not find it easy to ignore dissonant sound waves. Take pleasure in selecting chapter titles as well as epigraphs, if you plan to use them. A copy of *Bartlett's Familiar Quotations* interleaved with scores of ragged markers is a positive sign that you are well on your way. As for the biography itself, keep in mind the fact that Hemingway had thirty titles in reserve, should his editor veto *For Whom the Bell Tolls.*

In time—if you have the determination and the talent—something will happen. You will experience one of those very special days when the narrative voice and the mind become one. It will not last; the days of the storm petrel must inevitably follow. Yet you will also find, when rereading your manuscript for the twentieth time, that you were not appreciably better on your best days than on your worst. Your mind has been operating at two levels, the one conscious but illusory, the other subconscious but real. You have subtly programmed yourself to remain within certain boundaries, both scholarly and aesthetic. You have found your own way of identifying with your subject, and mutual suspicion has yielded to trust. The pages, so pitifully few in the beginning, are piling up with satisfying regularity. You are a biographer.

≫ POETRY

>> 79

TO MAKE A PRAIRIE

BY RITA DOVE

WHEN I WAS INDUCTED INTO PHI BETA KAPPA AT MIAMI UNIVERSITY (Ohio) two decades ago, many of the presiding faculty were aghast when I answered their query concerning my career plans with "I want to be a poet." The implied sentiment was "How can you throw away your education?"—as if declaring one's intention to be a poet was analogous to putting on a dunce cap.

Phi Beta Kappa's motto, "philosophy or the love of knowledge is the guide of life," puts it well. Wisdom is the *guide* of life—not the goal. Intelligence is a desirable commodity, but, as one character in Madeleine L'Engle's book *A Wind in the Door* says, "The naked intellect is an extraordinarily inaccurate instrument." Intellectual achievement requires imagination.

I want to discuss here an activity which, although often smiled at or benevolently dismissed in children, is barely tolerated in adolescents, rarely commended in the boardroom, and, to the best of my knowledge, never encouraged in school—but without which no bridges would soar, no light bulbs burn, and no Greek warships set out upon Homer's "wine-dark sea." That activity is daydreaming—an activity so prevalent that we had to jerryrig a word, an oxymoron of sorts, because, so to speak, the default for dreaming is night. *Daydreaming*. There's a loftier expression for it, of course—reverie. But daydreaming is the word that truly sets us adrift. It melts on the tongue. The French phenomenologist Gaston Bachelard speaks of a "dreaming consciousness" and calls poetic reverie a "phenomenology of the soul," a condition in which "the mind is able to relax, but . . . the soul keeps watch, with no tension, calmed and active."

Many of you have heard the story of Thomas Edison's method for courting inspiration: Whenever he became stymied, he would take a nap, and often the solution to his problem would come to him in his sleep. Herbert Marcuse calls this kind of daydreaming the drive toward *Eros,* as opposed to—what else?—*Thanatos,* or death. And what is the ultimate expression of this drive toward Eros? Child's play, which Marcuse defines by saying that playing as a child plays is its own goal, its own contentment, whereas work serves a purpose that lies outside the self.

When I was a child, I loved math—the neatness of fractions, all those pies sliced into ever-diminishing wedges. I adored unraveling the messy narratives of story problems, reducing them to symbols. I did this with the singlemindedness of a census taker. However, there were two stumbling blocks in my mathematical education. The first occurred when I was forced to drill with flash cards; although there are absolute answers with flash cards, there is no end of the series: One correct solution merely prompts the next problem. Something about this procedure frightened me; I believe I recognized in it some metaphor for the numbing repetitions of daily existence—taking out the garbage, doing the dishes, washing laundry, driving to the office, working from 9 to 5. . . . Here's a poem I wrote on the subject:

Flash Cards

In math I was the whiz kid, keeper of oranges and apples.
What you don't understand, master, my father said; the faster
I answered, the faster they came.

I could see one bud on the teacher's geranium,
one clear bee sputtering at the wet pane.
The tulip trees always dragged after heavy rain
so I tucked my head as my boots slapped home.

My father put up his feet after work
and relaxed with a highball and *The Life of Lincoln.*
After supper we drilled and I climbed the dark

before sleep, before a thin voice hissed
numbers as I spun on a wheel. I had to guess.
Ten, I kept saying, *I'm only ten.*

I hit the second snag in 10th grade, a few weeks into geometry. My homework assignment was to prove a theorem. But how could I even begin if I had to use points and lines and planes in order to prove it—

points with no dimension, lines without thickness, and planes that had no length or width or area or perimeters, but stretched into infinity?

I asked my brother, who was two years older and had weathered geometry without a whimper, but his only advice was "You have to sit down and think about it until you get it." He let me use his desk to do this thinking. And so I sat for twenty minutes, for half an hour, trying to imagine what didn't exist. I began to daydream, and my eyes drifted to the ceiling . . . a plane. No, a representation of a plane; and, though I couldn't see it, the ceiling continued beyond the walls of my brother's room, into the hall and above my bedroom and my parents' bedroom— and if I could imagine the ceiling beyond that closed door, why not a ceiling that went on past the house and the neighborhood, all the way to Forever? Walls met ceiling, forming lines that did the same trick. Where ceiling and two walls met, a point . . .

Geometry

I prove a theorem and the house expands:
the windows jerk free to hover near the ceiling,
the ceiling floats away with a sigh.

As the walls clear themselves of everything
but transparency, the scent of carnations
leaves with them. I am out in the open

and above the windows have hinged into butterflies,
sunlight glinting where they've intersected.
They are going to some point true and unproven.

Some stereotypes

There are a thousand and one myths about artists in general, writers in particular, and specifically poets: Poets, the legend goes, are eccentric, not quite of this world; poets are blessed with imagination that the rest of us can never hope to approach. Poets lead wild—or at the very least, wildly disorganized—lives and say outrageous things in polite company. And lo, poets may even be the prophets of our time. The prevailing notions our society harbors about the creative arts make it difficult for artists, and especially that lofty breed of poets, to be taken seriously.

Oddly enough, there is the converse myth that poetry is difficult—

385

hermetic, cerebral stuff, impossible for the mere mortal to comprehend. I cannot tell you on how many occasions I have read poetry in a church basement or high school classroom, only to have someone come up afterwards and exclaim: "I never knew poetry could be like that—why, that was *fun!*"

What this tells us about our society is that we regard the creative arts with a degree of apprehension, perhaps even suspicion. We do not expect the arts to be accessible, nor do we see any reason to incorporate the arts into our everyday or professional lives. And so, unfortunately, for many students, the years at the university and the few years beyond, in graduate study, may be the last opportunity to live in an environment where intellectual discourse and artistic expression are acknowledged and considered essential.

Of course, stereotypes cut both ways. The flip side of the coin is the assumption that intellect and imagination do not mix. This might be, partly at least, a result of one of our century's most dangerous signs of progress—the concept of specialization.

Let me illustrate this point. In the winter of 1984, when I was giving a series of lectures on the East Coast, a severe storm closed many airports along the seaboard, forcing plane passengers to scramble for the trains. I was on my way to New York City from Providence, Rhode Island, with my husband and infant daughter. The train was so crowded that people were standing—even sitting—in the aisles and in the passageways between cars. In that situation there was no question of chivalry: No one stood up to give me a seat. After about an hour, a seat became free and the young man standing nearest to it—and therefore, according to the laws of survival of the fittest, entitled to it—sat down, then turned and motioned for me to take his place. After another half-hour of travel, the seat next to me became vacant, so I was able to scoot over and give my cavalier a chance to rest his feet.

We began a careful conversation: first about the weather, then my daughter's vital statistics (she was blissfully asleep), and finally, we turned to occupation. "What do you do?" I asked, and was puzzled by his obvious hesitation before the reply came: "I'm . . . I'm a microbiologist." Pause. Then he added, "I usually don't tell people that. It tends to stop conversation."

"So what do you usually tell people?" I asked.

"Oh, that I work in a lab. Or that I study diseases. And what about you?" He turned the tables: "What do you do?" Now it was my turn to hesitate before I answered: "I'm a poet."

"Oh!" he exclaimed. "That's wonderful!"

"And isn't microbiology wonderful, too?" I asked. "Sure," he conceded, "but when I tell people I'm a microbiologist, they're so afraid they won't understand anything I say, they never ask any further. It gets to be a bummer."

"Yeah," I said, "I know what you mean." And I did; many a time I had experienced that awkward silence toward me as a poet. I never knew, however, that there were scientists who suffered the same blues.

"So tell me," I went on, "what exactly *do* you do as a microbiologist?"

What followed was a fascinating account of this man's work with the molecular structure of DNA. He described how, aided by an electron microscope, he "walked" the length of a healthy DNA strand, taking notes along the way on the distinguishing traits of every cell. He then compared these observations with the reports from similar "walks" along DNA strands from people who had multiple sclerosis. By comparing these scientific diaries, he hoped to pinpoint the determining traits for one of the world's most devastating and mysterious diseases.

What impressed me especially about his account was the language he used to describe his work. In order to make this complicated process accessible to a layperson, he resorted to a vivid pictorial—even poetic—vocabulary. When I asked him whether he and his colleagues used the same metaphors in the lab, he seemed surprised. "Well," he replied, "we have specific technical terms of course, but we use some of these words, too. What else can you call it but taking a walk?"

Yes, what else could you call it? Here I was talking with a top-level scientist whose work was so specialized that it had to invent its own language in order to be able to imagine its own investigations. And at this point, when imagination enters, we also enter the domain of poetry.

Making a Prairie

To make a prairie,

Emily Dickinson wrote,

387

> it takes a clover and one bee,
> One clover, and a bee,
> And revery.
> The revery alone will do,
> If bees are few.

To make a prairie—or a light bulb, or the quantum theory of mechanics—you need revery. Daydreaming. The watchful soul in the relaxed mind.

A liberal education is intended to make people flexible, able to cope with the boundless changes that accelerating civilization will confront them with. So much of modern university education has become a closed society with privileged access to certain mysteries, a microcosm where palpable interaction with the physical world has been suspended in the interests of specialized knowledge. The Industrial Revolution, whose most poignant symbol is the assembly line, made specialization practical; now the Technological Revolution, whose symbol might be the silicon chip, makes specialization imperative.

But technological advances also de-emphasize the individual, reducing the grand gestures of the soul to so many impressions on a grain of sand. The humanities, with their insistence on communication and their willingness to admit paradox into the contemplation of truth, are too often silenced by the bully's club of empirical data. There's a Mother Goose rhyme that goes:

> If all the world were paper,
> And all the sea were ink;
> If all the trees were bread and cheese,
> What should we have to drink?

Yes, indeed—for if we assign a category to every wish and leave the fulfillment of these wishes to one discipline, we may be fed but not nourished; someone is sure to forget the lemonade. The groundwork laid in college stresses the connectedness of all learning. The task upon leaving college and entering into the intricacies of a chosen discipline is to avoid being narrowed into a mere functionary of a professional specialization.

How restless and curious the human mind is, how quickly the imagination latches onto a picture, a scene, something volatile and querulous and filled with living, mutable tissue! The mind is informed by the spirit of play. The most fantastical doodles emerge from wandering ballpoint pens in both the classroom and the board meeting. Every discipline is studded with vivid terminology: In geometry various shapes are defined as "random slices of Swiss cheese," chains, or self-squared dragons. There are lady's slippers in botany and wingbacks in football games. There are onomatopoetic bushwhackers in the jungles of Nicaragua; there are doglegs on golf courses and butterfly valves in automobiles. The theory of quark confinement could be a quantum physicist's definition of the human soul. Astronomy has black holes with "event horizons"—the orbital path around a black hole where time stands still, the point beyond which one is drawn inextricably into the core of the imploding star. Every discipline craves imagination, and you owe it to yourself to keep yours alive.

In ancient Rome, every citizen possessed a genius. The genius was a personal spirit that came to every person at birth; it represented the fullness of one's potential powers. This genius was considered a birthright, but it needed to be nourished in order to survive. Now, in our narcissistic age children celebrating a birthday expect gifts to shower upon them from the outside, but the ancient Roman was expected to make a birthday sacrifice to his or her genius. If one served one's genius well during life, the genius became a *lars,* or household god, after one's death. If one neglected one's potential, the genius became a spook, a troublesome spirit who plagued the living.

Poets do not have a monopoly on imagination: the world will be ever unfolding, as long as one can imagine its possibilities, as long as one honors one's spirit—or, as the Romans would have said, one's "genius"—and lets the fresh air blow in, fragrant, from the flowering prairie.

>> 80

POEMS AND MEANING

BY PETER MEINKE

POEMS DON'T HAVE TO MEAN ANYTHING. YOUNG POETS OFTEN MAKE the mistake of thinking they must have Something to Say. It's not that Saying Something is wrong, but it tends to distract from the main objective: saying something memorably, beautifully, permanently. Poetry is news that *stays* news. And what makes it stay news is how it's said, not what it says.

Think of your favorite poems. "Stopping By Woods On A Snowy Evening," by Robert Frost? Lovely description of an all-too-familiar scene, clear as a bell. Or is it? Is it really about death, or even suicide? Well, maybe. It's often what's *not* said that makes poems memorable. T. S. Eliot's "The Love Song of J. Alfred Prufrock"? We have lots of studies of indecisive men: What makes this one unforgettable? Is it about an entire repressed society? Is it about T. S. Eliot? It doesn't matter, does it? Lines like "I have heard the mermaids singing, each to each" will haunt you your entire life.

"O, my Luve's like a red red rose," wrote Robert Burns. This may or may not have been true, but who cares? Or more to the point, "As silent as a mirror is believed / Realities plunge in silence by . . ." is the beginning of Hart Crane's poem, "Legend." I'm not sure what it means (it *seems* to mean something), but I've always loved it. You will have your own examples.

There's a continuum of meaning on which poets position themselves: On one side are poets like Edward Field, who (typically) writes straightforward lines like, "My mother's family was made up of loving women," and on the other, John Ashbery writing "the unplanted cabbages stand tearful out of the mist." The Ashbery school takes the position that meaning is boring and bourgeois: Straight information is too easy. "Tell us something we don't know!" is their cry. The Field side takes the common-sense point of view that poetry belongs to the people, and if it doesn't make sense, who wants it? Surreal gibberish is also easy. (Both sides reflect a Puritan ethic they both deny: *What we do is hard work,* each says, and they're both right.)

Of course I'm exaggerating, but the point I want to make is that *you can station yourself anywhere along the meaning continuum and you will be "right"*: But for the sake of your poetry, let the words, the sounds, the rhythms, the images come first; and let the meaning follow.

And yet. And yet we want poems to mean something to us—and many of them do, but with this startling complication: *They mean different things to different people, and even different things to the same person at different times.* These are the best poems. But anyone who has done a lot of editing for magazines, or judging for contests, will testify to the mind-numbing experience of reading through piles of basically indecipherable poetry. Howard Nemerov, after wading through manuscripts for the lively periodical *Furioso,* most of which apparently followed Archibald MacLeish's dictum, "A poem should not mean / But be," once said: "Well, there they all were, and they didn't mean anything."

I think the best poems *tend* toward meaning, leaving space for us to move around, but at the same time giving us hints, pushing us in a general direction. This doesn't mean that a poem can mean *anything* ("Stopping By Woods," for example, is not about communism. There are no directional hints leading us that way).

To try to trace the development of meaning in a poem, I've chosen semi-randomly one of mine, called "Apples":

> The apple I see and the apple
> I think I see and the apple
> I say I see
> are at least three
> different apples . . .
>   One sympathizes with Dr. Johnson here
> when he kicked a stone
> to dispute the Bishop: such
> airy-fairy distinctions so much
> applesauce!
> And yet when you say
> what I think you say
> in a way that may
> or may not be final I can only hope

> that cold stone that white boulder that . . .
>   iceberg between us
> is not really there but is sliding
> like some titanic idea
> through the North Pole
> in the apple of my eye

What does this poem mean? I wrote it, and I'm not entirely sure! It seems to be a love poem that takes its time getting about its business. Perhaps—translated—it would go like this: Two lovers have had an argument (or something), and one of them is hoping that this coldness on his (or her) lover's part is not permanent but is just passing through. This isn't very interesting, unless you identify with the lovers (which readers of course sometimes do).

What's interesting are the apples.

The poem began, as most of mine do, with a phrase or sentence. I had been talking with a friend about memory, and more or less the first sentence "came out." So I wrote it down in the little notebook I carry around. This, I suppose, is the "inspiration" part of composition. (I visualize the composition of a poem as a series of little explosions, like Chinese firecrackers, each one setting the next one off.)

What I liked about the sentence was the repetition of "apple" four times and "see" three times. When (later, at home) I moved the lines around to emphasize the repetition, I also saw the rhyme of "see" and "three," so I wrote "I say I see" as a separate line, liking the sound and look of it by itself in a five-line stanza (the end words being "apple / apple / see / three / apples"—which is a nice little poem by itself).

While doing this (everything is happening simultaneously in poetry, which is one of the exciting things about writing it) I remembered the famous rebuttal on this general subject that Samuel Johnson made to the Idealist philosopher, Bishop Berkeley. Berkeley had theorized that matter was non-existent (it's all in our heads), and Johnson and Boswell were having a tough time refuting him, until Johnson "struck his foot against a large stone," saying "I refute it *thus*." And thus that old rascal Samuel Johnson entered this poem about apples.

This was a change in direction, so I indented it, and as I tinkered with the poem (the *possible* poem; I didn't know if it would work yet), I could see that "stone" went well with "Johnson" (and then "distinctions"). Dr. Johnson was being playful, so I became playful too—"such airy-fairy distinctions"—and that led me, accidentally, to our slang word for too much fancy talk or overly sophisticated reasoning: "apple-sauce." *Voilà*! We're brought back to the original image of apples, but this time also thinking about language and the strange way that it works. Robert Frost, among many wonderful pronouncements, said the art of poetry involved "the taking advantage of happy accidents."

One question that this section brings up is how much knowledge to expect from a reader. The answer today seems to be—as our canon of required reading shifts, changes, and dwindles—not much. But our task as writers is not to avoid using learned or private references, only to use them clearly and to good effect. The reference to Dr. Johnson and Bishop Berkeley will be familiar to many readers, but those who have never heard of these eighteenth-century gentlemen won't have trouble following the poem. They'll only miss the little pleasure one gets from recognizing an apt illustration—and after all, if they're interested enough, they can look it up!

The poem, despite some rhyme, seemed destined to be in free verse: No set form was emerging. But I saw I could make a kind of loose pattern by making the Dr. Johnson section also five lines, to match the opening sentence; and then reinforce it by end-rhyming "such" and "much" to match "see" and "three" in the first section. Nobody much cares about this sort of thing, or even notices—but it's important that the writer care, trying his or her best to line up "the best words in the best order."

So now I had ten lines, a beginning of sorts, but where was I going? *What did it mean*? Frost said a poem, like a piece of ice, has to glide on its own melting; and as I sat thinking of the lines I had written— mostly about apples—I suddenly understood it was going to be a love poem. Why? I'm not sure, but I think "apple" suggested "Eve," the apple of knowledge, the apple of temptation. And, even closer to this poem, there's the golden apple, the Apple of Discord inscribed "to the fairest" and thrown out by Eris to make trouble among the beautiful goddesses. There are also love-apples (tomatoes) and apple-blossom time—there are so many different apples! I didn't reason all this out, but I'm trying to explain how poems, even little poems like this one, move toward meaning in associative ways.

And because I was also thinking about language, I began to write about how we talk to one another, how easy it is to misunderstand. I

393

had to match those apples verbally (words, like apples, are also different, depending on whether you're saying, hearing, or remembering them). I tried to reproduce the loose rhyme of the first stanza with the "say/say," "may/may" repetitions. I wanted to bring Dr. Johnson's stone back as a kind of metaphor for a lover's spat. That led to the final "idea" of the poem.

I like the "o" sound of "stone" because it went with "hope," and to emphasize it—and it fit emotionally—I made it "cold stone," then "white boulder" (maybe because we've had a driveway with white stones in it). The natural next step from cold stone and white boulder was to think of a glacier or an iceberg.

So the ingredients were all gathered. I hadn't known it when I began, but now I knew I was writing a love poem using apples and icebergs as metaphors for the difficulties of communication. A metaphor doesn't explain anything; rather, it creates a new situation that is in some ways the emotional and intellectual equivalent of an original feeling or thought. I think the appeal of poetry is that this feeling is orchestrated by the power of language to organize what is essentially disorganized experience, a temporary balancing act. *Let the language guide you, and the meaning will follow.* If you reverse that emphasis, you begin heading toward propaganda and advertisement: You're selling something.

What I had left to do in this poem was to tie the two images—apples and icebergs—together in some satisfying way. Is this always necessary? I doubt it, but I like to work that way, the way a musical composition fuses themes at the end. And language came to my rescue, as it tends to do if you're patient. The phrase "apple of my eye" can mean "my true love" or the actual pupil in the middle of my eye; so the most obvious reading of the poem (I think) is that the speaker hopes this misunderstanding is not there permanently but is passing through some cold part (the North Pole) of his lover's mind, and will soon be gone.

It can also mean, however—to hark back to the good Bishop Berkeley—that this idea is really in his own mind; it's something that he's seeing that may or may not be there, it depends where you're standing.

In addition, the word "titanic" darkens the poem considerably. It simply means (the denotation) "enormous," like the ancient Gods, the Titans. But in this context (the Titanic went down in the North Atlan-

394

tic), we can't help but think (the connotation) of the doomed ship. So what began as a fairly lighthearted poem ends ambiguously on a darkening image.

This is a story that has been written about thousands and thousands of times: the progression of love from delight to disaster. I like the idea that this poem mirrors that lifelike situation, really recreates it. I don't think the meaning of the poem is very difficult; it's just that it's like life, a little slippery to get hold of. (What's the meaning of *your* life, or mine?) And yet linguistically it comes together—I hope—to give the reader a sense of closure usually missing from real-life experiences.

I'm not sure this poem is worth all this ink and heavy thinking. I thought I chose it randomly to illustrate the relation of meaning to poetry—and, thinking about it, I now see it's actually *about* meaning, so it may not have been as random as I thought. (I sometimes think *nothing* is random.) Mainly, I wanted to say, trust the language: If it wants to mean something to you, it will.

This is easy to say, and hard to do. We all have ideas that we want to inflict on other people, often very praiseworthy ideas: Love one other, take care of the trees, don't be a pig, etc. But my experience leads me to believe that your ideas are going to come through in spite of yourself, no matter what you do. You don't have to worry about this.

Instead, worry about whether you've used too many adverbs, or what word should end your line. Of course you should be passionate about your poems—there needs to be blood on the page (and tears and gravy, etc.)—but if you need to be told this (BE PASSIONATE!), you're in the wrong line of work, Charlie; get a real job.

Worry about the connotations of your words, and their sounds. Especially their sounds. People—friends, classmates, teachers, reviewers—will disagree on which words go best where. This makes things difficult, but it's the name of the game; it's what poets do.

On the "meaning continuum" I mentioned earlier, I know I'm on the side that favors a high degree of clarity. But I can't help that, and it's not important. Handling the language, with all its wonderful tricks and surprises, to the best of our ability: That's what's important. In a world where everything seems unrelated, chaotic, and fragmented, the language of poetry has this great innate ability to embody the interconnectedness of things: "O, my Luve's like a red red rose." Absolutely.

➤➤81

POETRY AND MEMORY

BY JAMES APPLEWHITE

MEMORY IN THE WIDEST SENSE GOVERNS ALL I DO AS A WRITER, SINCE words, along with the skills acquired for relating them, are stored there. Yet, we aren't aware of the wonder of memory until it falters. Aging makes certain words, especially proper nouns, more difficult to access, in that organic computer-storage we call memory. We're surprised by any difficulty, because the vocabulary, syntax and formal skills we begin learning in childhood have always been spontaneously on hand for our use, as naturally as breathing or walking. Language with its rooting in memory, when we realize its scope and complexity, seems almost miraculous: this vast store to which we're continually adding and, if losing some, not much, in proportion to the total, which seems endlessly elastic.

The operation of memory was central to the argument of E.D. Hirsch's *Cultural Literacy*—a discussion highly relevant to the writer, who always was at first a reader. The words we're reading, apparently, remain only temporarily in a short-term memory, unless they're connected to some pre-existing network of things known. We remember by association, or linkage, and so reading with comprehension requires, in a sense, reading with recognition. We have to recognize the relatedness of what we're newly taking in, to what we already have stored, if there is to be significant understanding and retention. Hirsch argues, therefore, that the new knowledge acquired by the eyes and nerves from words must be connected into the networking of memory, things newly observed attaching themselves to things previously learned.

This means that our understanding of the present, this immediate, passing moment, is conditioned by, and contingent upon, memories from the past. Our eyes interpret not only the letters of words and sentences on the basis of previously acquired knowledge, but also the whole range of experience. We can't conceptualize things, or speak, or write, or take a walk, without using memory.

Writing a poem is therefore an act of memory. The process of arranging old and familiar words into a new order, to embody those conceptions and emotions that always seem different and individual, draws on the long-term storehouse of memory. Writing a poem dramatizes this almost imponderable relation of the present to the past: this moment of consciousness dependent on the deep reservoir of experience. This record of earlier time would lie mute and passive without the moment's articulation. And any current cognitive act would be thin and anonymous without the years' accumulated layers of memory—this basis of who we are. To see a tree as a tree is an act of pattern recognition requiring the past.

Certain poems feature memory explicitly, while all poems implicitly depend on its power. Perhaps such poems are especially moving (I had almost said *memorable*) because they remind us of the relation of the thoughts we think, this minute, to all those preceding thoughts that we cannot now particularly recall, but feel in their cumulative legacy. When the present mind feels the form and texture of a vast, earlier time-scale, one it cannot in detail recall or read, the result may be a profound aesthetic emotion. It is like looking at the ruined masonry of a Gothic abbey: You cannot know the exact history behind these walls and arches, yet you feel the resonance of the past beneath the fissured surface.

I don't think it profitable for a writer to try to *use* memory, directly. Memory is always allowing itself to be used, but won't be coerced; there are better strategies than head-on pressure. Memory has its own processes and its own selectivity. Scenes, faces, bits of story that rise up spontaneously are thus more likely to have an emotive significance than those memories we might deliberately call up.

Really to remember is often to reencounter a part of experience, perhaps distant from present life but still related to it. Profound memory can continue the assimilation of a part of our lives we'd thought we'd finished with, but hadn't. The poetic use of memory is therefore not really separate from that larger meditative attempt to make sense of our lives, of which poetry is part.

As poets, we can intensify this process by focused thinking, not so much on the past itself, as on those issues that *involve* the past: issues

397

of personal identity, confrontations with disappointment or loss, plans for the future that we see as completing long-cherished hopes and ambitions. Just as in keeping a dream-journal one learns to remember dreams better, so consistent meditation and writing can make the past and one's own buried emotions available for poetry. We don't always know how or what we really feel about certain matters—especially those areas of experience involving our childhood. My own experience has shown me that the driving force behind memory is not merely the desire to call up earlier days, but the deeply felt need to reencounter unresolved issues and emotions—the need to understand, to come to terms with, past time.

During the last several years, I've been working on an interrelated set of autobiographical and literary essays. My book of poems, *A History of the River* (Louisiana State University Press), presented a kind of cultural history of my region of the South, ranging from the curing rituals for bright leaf tobacco, through farm artifacts, such as Mason jars, sausage grinders, and mule-drawn plows, through patterns of farmhouse births and deaths and home burials. I was moved to portray the change of the world, as the time-order associated with these earlier objects and practices gave way to the more recent time, surrounding tractors, electrical appliances, mercury vapor farmyard lights, and television sets.

Last spring, I began to write a sequence of more formal poems focused directly on the experience of time. All of them seemed to involve streams, rivers, lakes or the ocean. I thought of them tentatively as *Meditations on Water*. Though my explicit subject was time and its river-like shapes as it flowed by, I was also trying to show how experiences accumulate in the mind, just as a lake holds water which is mostly out of sight. Here is a poem that began as I thought of boat rides on a lake as a child, and the home movies taken there, that extended and represented memory:

Remembering Home Movies on Water

My father cranks the outboard motor. His face
  looks tender
in the camera's fixed light. Beside me sits my
  mother
in her one-piece suit, peering ahead through time,

her face a sphinx-prediction of puzzlements to come:
my amazement at the world, uncertain identity,
courage against death and illness but inability
to assert my own need and course. That route
seemed plowed by the boat's expanding wake,
    the pout
of my mother's lips a judgment on his unwisdom:
this fated, accelerated design, the masculine
    momentum
she deplored and embraced. I also apparently wish
    not
to go on, though summers continued with another
    boat
and larger motor and myself at the helm, driver
so harshly one evening across the wave-cut river
that my girl in front carried bruises across her back
for a week. Her father cursed but she raised her neck
to my lips. I piled weight and muscle into this role
my mother derided, working in the concrete hole
beneath the cars, greasing as automatically as my
    parents
had inserted me into life: these disguises it permits,
these inherited expressions raised dumbly toward
    storm,
as we rush into the imitations from which we've
    come.
Now in this present so seemingly distanced, world-
    different,
I paddle across these circling mirrors to contemplate
their curious accumulation and reflection. Afternoon
sky changes blue into green. Clouds puff dryly
    in the sheen
that's liquid yet develops, a film to be viewed.
Gazing into depths I feel the years' dumb plunges
    flood
back and as Freud knew, that drowned world never
    will change.
I sit on its surface and suffer, accept, mourn,
    rearrange
myself in relation to this deadly dynamic I always
    take
to bed and don't escape: this lost ponderous hidden
    lake.

The lake's depth holds a reservoir of past time that is like the contents of the unconscious. The narrator, in sad recognition that this underwater world "never will change," is somewhat consoled by his sense that the present offers the possibility of new attitudes and relationships to this fixed past.

Other poems I'm working on grew out of recent experiences canoeing or sailing or running beside the Eno River near my house. It seemed that both through my writing and my involvement with water, I was trying to put the first part of my life and the second part together. In one of the poems that resulted, I used memory very centrally, though that had not been my original intention. The kind of writing and thought I'd recently been involved with apparently prepared the way for a spontaneous memory-event, which provided the narrative of the poem.

I had gotten back home almost too late for my customary run by the river, but went out anyway, along the dimming trails of the Eno State Park off Cole Mill Road. I ran deep into the forest and next to the river for a while, its slick quickness maintaining light on the surface, while the trees beside lost detail, becoming humps of shadow. On my way back to the parking area, I passed down into a vale where night had almost fallen. Lightning bugs winked, yellow-green and moving, and a sense of my childhood home came back, at first as a presence and tone without action or shape. A voice from the distant parking lot became a voice from a neighbor's porch. I felt the community gathered around me again and remembered the preacher's term, "communion of saints." When I'd made my slow way back out to the road, I had the shape of a poem in my head. I wrote it out the next day, in the slant-rhymed couplets I've been using lately for meditations. These rhymes, partial and less fully heard, let me say things more explicitly and deliberately, keeping the arguments and questions I want to voice now within the realm of the poetic. Here is the poem.

A Run with the Double River

I returned from the looping trail to Bobbitt's Hole,
finishing in darkness, walking a last half mile.
The footpath dimming among hardwoods angled
   down,
where air felt heavy as breath and a water shone.
Suddenly it was old summer, as lightning-sparks
of insects glowed near and large. A steepening
   of rocks

lay seamed with times like coal, under layers of
  noises.
An owl called, a vole rustled, a sighing like voices
came from trees toward the road. Deeply, I
  remembered:
a time without events, the shadow over a town that
  slumbered
into twilight as the lightning bugs like momentary
  sight
rose sparkling, the scene as if seeing itself in a
  night
wherein minds added up to an awareness and were
  calm.
It felt like our Sunday congregation singing a hymn.
Nothing had gone. Faces of friends, parents, old
  men
I hardly knew looked renewed, individual yet not,
  grown
together in this hum, this single continuing
  evening tone
that collected the drone of the electric fan and dove
  alone
on telephone wires into one thing—all made simple
  again,
as when a garden's leaves rise together after a rain.
But in what medium is this cloud of presences
  stored?
My church had told me of saints gathered unto the
  Lord.
It praised occasions when our single, ephemeral
moments melt together and we feel what is like the
  eternal:
the form within the flowing, shape where past years
  are.
I had entered this under-knowledge, like the river
  aware
of itself. We'd sat as static muttered in our porch's
  radio;
the stories of voices from the chairs around sounded
  low
and ceaselessly, like cicadas crowded into a single
  tree.
The stars pierced near and real. There was no TV.
Such memories seem transmitted by genes instead
  of by wires,
though the footage catalogued in archives aspires
to be this library of the blood. Two currents run
  together,

as clouds and stars paint these streams with passing
  glitter.
The TV in the house with its insistent, loud alarm
distracts from profounder dreaming, yet shows the
  charm
of the race. Its goddesses arouse us to love, and
  heroes kill.
This presentness seems a surface. The river's motion
  is still
though its depth holds a pressure of all early instants,
which roil and swerve and pulse. We run as water
  glints,
as it flashes into a consciousness, that the sky
  imprints
like a source. Each red leaf splashes upon it, come
into a mighty sequence, unique, subsumed in time.

Part of my life I've felt the past as a burden upon me, even as an
oppression. I am a southerner, and share in the South's problem of
history: the feeling I grew up with of having been anticipated by those
fathers and grandfathers and greatgrandfathers who'd bequeathed me
the world in which attitude and actions seemed already determined,
or overdetermined. More recently however, I've felt my separation and
freedom from a regional history which, not in the national consciousness (and sometimes in my own estimation), seems only a stereotypical
relic—a formulaic reiteration—of exhausted prejudice, pride, and
grievances.

What felt so fresh about this descent into a small ravine in the edge
of night was the immediacy of a past that had neither gone stale nor
dwindled into cliché—a past as the presences that inform one's identity, without obtruding their individual outlines. I experienced past
time as a reunion of one part of the self with another. My current
personality felt itself for a moment within a gathering of presences
who had reappeared from deep in my earlier life. They were (and are)
a part of who I am, though I'm not usually aware of that fact.

So as the poet sits writing, figures and images out of the past may
sometimes crowd about. My schoolteacher uncle used to tell me of
Odysseus in the land of the dead, and of how the spirits of the heroes
and heroines of his land collected around him. Since he was still alive,
they wanted him to hear their story, and perhaps to tell it again among
the living. The prophet Tiresias also came forward, and told Odysseus
how he was to get home again successfully. Odysseus may stand for

the poet in relation to deep memory. He or she gathers stories out of cultural and personal history: old stories that will be seen in the new form of their retelling. Like Odysseus, the poet learns from the past how to get back home to the present, how to live in it more vitally, how to proceed into the future. When we've come to the past as free persons, able to accept and internalize its mighty echo, it can send us along our way, abler and more confident, surer of our mission, and of who we are.

A poem is given shape by the poems remembered, collectively, from all the poet's earlier reading: sonnets, blank verse meditations, various kinds of free verse—by the sounds of emphasis and closure, the chiming of stanzas and of rhyme. Poetry is an old story that comes alive again with the new idea. The names and the events and the rhymes are similar but never quite the same. So I say again, the way to use time and memory as a writer is to let it use you. This involves respect toward the past, but not worship. *We* the living are the custodians of all record; we are the only minds of all history now able to reanimate its stories. Ours are the only voices through which the past can speak, in becoming the present and future. Ours is the equal of any time, because it has all times within it. But the empowerment of the past lies buried, unless we can find ways to experience it as alive. The poet occasionally needs to surrender some of his or her conscious intention, even some of the present sense of self, in order to be visited by the times and presences held in the deeper layers of memory. What we remember without usually being aware of it may help us become more truly ourselves as poets.

>> 82

WRITING THE NARRATIVE POEM

BY DEBRA ALLBERY

SOMETIMES AN ORDINARY WORD TAKES ON A MILD HALO—*PATIENCE, provenance, correspondence*—so that the mind in its restless scanning lingers a second to repeat it. Sometimes it's an image that insists—the heavy silhouette of a woman walking toward a row of mailboxes, the last snags of white in a cotton field. The dream-image of a dog, sleek and abject, spotlit, crawling across a gravel road; he glances up at you and the picture fades. Each of these triggers the same recognition of *story*—and each, in time, with careful attention and patience, might become a poem.

I could attempt these "stories" in prose, but I know from experience what would happen. The margins would begin to creep in from either side with each revision; sentences would tighten and straighten themselves into lines. And I'd gradually grow frustrated, ready to cut to the chase, to the reason I was writing in the first place—aiming not so much toward the construction of plots and fleshing-out of characters, but toward the discovery inside a particular moment. For me, a poem is the most natural means toward that discovery.

The narrative poem relates an event in time—a memory, perhaps, a dream: *once, this happened.* Its synopsis might be ordinary, unassuming *(once when I was a child I crossed against the light),* or more startling *(I once lived across the street from a man who killed by dismemberment).* Something in your present has called forth and fixed upon this triggering moment; you write the poem to find out what it has to say about then, about now. In *Memory and Enthusiasm* W.S. DiPiero says that narrative poetry tells "states of becoming," that it "enacts the process of things." In the finished poem the "process of things" is revealed; the significance of that moment, and its relation to the present, becomes clear. The poem may grow out of a fragment, a small story, but the understanding it imparts has a wholeness. The larger story suggests itself around it.

The "narrative" label in contemporary poetry is a loose one. We're not talking here of ballads or epics, but of a general storytelling approach. I wouldn't say that all my poems are narrative, but it's a method I'm drawn to; I like the slight distance it provides, as well as the intimacy of tone it allows. Like a prose story, a narrative poem may concern itself with descriptive passages, characterizations, even dialogue, but it must of course meet any poem's requirements of compression, economy, rhythmic intensity, emotional risk-taking. I try to use as few brushstrokes as possible. Or, to switch the metaphor, the narrative poem should aim to have, as Robert Lowell said of Robert Frost's poetry, "the virtue of a photograph and all the finish of art." It might have a plain and conversational style or a highly rhetorical one, but in no case are its lines merely chopped-up prose. A flexible blank verse has served many narrative poets well, but you might find that shorter or variable line lengths produce musics more suited to your subject.

And your subject? Whatever insists. Whatever, with patience, is revealed. A word repeats itself to you to tell you that there's something important in it you haven't yet heard. An image appears, reappears, and you slowly begin to trace its provenance, detect correspondences. The color of the dog is the color of dust in a cotton field. The woman looks up at you as she lifts her hand to the mailbox. The poem sets its story into motion.

Here are two of my narrative poems* that illustrate the form:

Instinct

Winter was running out before I was ready—
gray clouds scudding flat-bottomed above
the cornfields and small huddles of houses,
the cold low-roofed light breaking open.
There wasn't any work. I took longer walks.
One day I boarded a bus and stepped off here
with two suitcases and my last twenty.

---

*"Next-Door Neighbors" and "Instinct," both of which originally appeared in *The Iowa Review,* are reprinted from Debra Allbery's collection, *Walking Distance* (University of Pittsburgh Press, 1991).

I found a room in this house, three floors
of women keeping out of each other's way.
Lucille, the rickety shadow above me,
has rented her attic room for life.
She scrubs our kitchen sink every morning,
a ritual with rubber gloves and cleanser,
and water boiled in white enamel bowls.

A cellist has moved into the room below me.
She practices at odd hours, scraping
bow against strings, irregular, urgent—
rasping pitches of some mental schism.
It's a quiet house except for her, except
for the undertones of pipes, doors closing,
phones ringing in rooms with no one home.

I hung a bird feeder from the fire escape
outside my window, but they haven't discovered it.
It's not a place birds would think to land.
I watch that little house swinging in gusts
of north wind against a backdrop of brick.
I'm considering South Dakota, Alberta.
Everywhere you move people ask you why.

As far as I know this is part of the story,
these slight intersections of contiguous lives.
The cellist's song rises like the undersides
of memory, the migratory calls of something winged
and flightless. Lucille hangs a sign on the
    basement doorknob
whenever she descends with trash or laundry,
Dont lock this door I am down there.

Next-Door Neighbors

Grant Street was one long Sunday afternoon
in February or March, a few yards of brown grass
thinning and matted, or rubbed away hard.
Our house stayed dark with my mother's pleurisy,
and it made me angry, the way she kept trying
to raise herself up to clean rooms or fix supper.
Then she'd lie down again on the couch, covering
herself tight with two blankets, chilling.
It was Sunday afternoon, foggy, and my father
was playing his Hank Williams record.
He's dozing at the end of the couch, his hand
on my mother's feet, and I go outside to sit
on the porch. Mr. Carter from across the street

pulls up grinning on his Harley and asks me
if I want to take a ride, and I do, but I don't
like his eyes, and besides, I'm not allowed to,
and shake my head no. I'm ten or eleven
with a younger brother and sister somewhere,
but my seeing is short-ranged and telescoped—
cardboard taped to the Carters' front window,
the busted taillight on our old white Comet,
yesterday's *Register,* "The World at Your
　　Doorstep."

Mrs. Carter appears in the broken-paned window,
another black eye, and pulls down the blind.
My mother had called Mrs. Carter to ask if
she'd come over and blow cigarette smoke into
　　her earache,
she had read somewhere that it helped.
But Mrs. Carter said sorry, she couldn't leave the
　　house.
I'd yelled at my mother then why didn't she go
to a doctor, I slammed the door and was sorry.
Now I'm sitting on the step, biting the polish
off my nails. I don't like my coat, it's reversible
and has imitation fur. The snow edging the empty
　　street
looks like coal. Next year Mr. Carter will go
to the electric chair for killing an old man
and his wife and hiding their pieces in his car trunk.
One night I'll forget to kiss my father goodnight
before he drives off to the factory with just one
taillight working, and I'll worry to sleep seeing that,
certain he'll die. I pray for goodness
and mercy every night, I want too many things.

➤➤ 83

POETS, LEARN YOUR TRADE

BY ROBERT MEZEY

I HAVE BEEN ASKED TO OFFER SOME USEFUL ADVICE TO BEGINNING writers and I shall address myself to young poets, since poetry is the art I know best. I confess that I feel a little uncomfortable in this role of wise old counselor, being neither particularly old nor particularly wise and, in fact, in want of advice myself. (What wouldn't I give for a conversation with Robert Frost or John Crowe Ransom or W. H. Auden. There are many things I should like to ask them about this beautiful and difficult art.) Also, I am all too aware that the precepts that immediately spring to mind are the ones that veteran writers always hand out to the young. Nevertheless I will mention a few of them; they are easily summarized, they are no less true for being clichés, and they bear repetition.

First of all, live. Experience, observe, reflect, remember—try to be one of those on whom nothing is lost (in Henry James' great phrase). It is not necessary that your experience be wide, only that it be deep. Think what Emily Dickinson managed to live without—sex, travel, drugs, a career, a lifestyle—and yet few Americans have ever lived as fully, as intensely as she. Live your life. One cannot write out of books.

Read, for after all, one does write out of books also, and poetry is made of poetry. Reading and writing are inseparable; if you are not a reader, you are not a writer. Read history, novels, science, whatever you like, and above all, poetry. As in life, so in reading: Deep is better than wide. And read the best—not your mostly dismal contemporaries, but what has lasted hundreds and thousands of years: Homer, Virgil, Dante, Shakespeare, the King James Bible. Read continually.

Revise what you have written, and then revise it again. You don't want to work all the life out of it, but precision and liveliness and an air of spontaneity are the fruit of long hours of writing and rewriting, of trial and error. First thought is *not* best thought, and poetry, unlike jazz, is not improvisation. In fact, first thoughts tend to be banal, unfocused, conventional, not quite coherent. Most poems require a number of drafts—maybe twenty; maybe fifty. Don't be too easily satisfied.

Those are perhaps the three essential commandments. (If they are not easily obeyed, it may be that you are not destined to be a poet.) But I want to tell you something that nowadays not many others would tell you or even assent to. You must learn to write verse. Not "free" verse, but verse—numbers, measures—call it what you will. It is what poetry has always been written in until the last century or so, and indeed it is only over the last few decades that nonmetrical verse has become the norm (if something which, by definition, violates the norm can *be* a norm). Before you break the rules, you need to know the rules; before you seek novelty, you ought to demonstrate that you know the ancient craft. That is no more than simple honesty and humility. You cannot properly call yourself a poet otherwise. A poet who cannot compose in verse is like a painter who cannot draw or a scientist who does not grasp the scientific method. Besides, as you acquire facility, you will find that verse-making supports your sentences, generates ideas, leads you where you might not otherwise have gone; and you will find what many poets have long known, that free verse is not easier than metrical verse, but much more difficult, and very few can write it well. As André Gide said, art is born of constraint and dies of too much freedom.

How can you go about learning to write in meter? As poets have always learned, by reading good verse and trying to imitate its sounds. You may need to count on your fingers at first, to be sure that you have the permitted number of syllables and the accents in the right positions, but soon you will be able to play by ear. It is useful to have some theoretical understanding, but in the end, an iambic pentameter is a line that sounds like an iambic pentameter, and you must know it the way you know the tune of an old familiar song. Be careful where you look for instruction: Many teachers don't know much about the meters, and these days most poets don't either, and the books can be misleading or flat out wrong. George Stewart's book *The Technique of English Verse* (Holt, Rinehart & Winston) is good; so is James McAuley's *Versification* (Michigan State University Press), the shortest and maybe the best; so is Derek Attridge's *The Rhythms of English Poetry* (Longman). (Remember that good prosodists, though they hear the verse much the same way, may use different terminology or different symbols of scansion.) Be sure you read good models; many contemporary poets who write in meter, or what they call meter, do it atrociously: It is obvious that they don't know how the game is played. You can't go wrong with Marlowe, Herbert, Jonson, Milton, Pope, Tennyson, or Frost, or a hundred others. If you want to read the best of your own times, look for Philip Larkin, Edgar Bowers, Donald Justice, Richard Wilbur, Anthony Hecht, the late distinguished American poet, Henri Coulette, and there are a few others.

All the good poets make up a great free university, which you can attend at any hour of the day or night, choosing whatever teacher you like. Whatever you do, read aloud, both the verse of your models and your own, and listen to it carefully. (It might help to listen to it on tape. It might help to listen to records or tapes of good poets who also read well: Frost, Justice, Larkin, Wilbur, Ransom.)

Once you get the tune fixed in your head, you will have it forever, and you will recognize it in all its many varied patterns. You should, at the very least, be able to write pentameters, tetrameters, and trimeters (the longer and shorter lines are more difficult), and in both strict iambic and loose; common measure and ballad meter; rhymed couplets, tercets, and quatrains; blank verse and passable sonnets. The better you can write in meter, the better you can hear the old verse, and, to some extent, vice versa. And it is essential that you hear the great English poems as they were meant to be heard and that you have some idea of what those poets were trying to do. Otherwise you will have a very imperfect understanding of the poetry of your own language, and that is a serious deficiency in a poet. (Not to say in any cultivated man or woman—after all, accentual-syllabic verse, its invention and development, is one of the glories of our civilization.)

Once you have achieved some mastery of your craft, you can have a go at free verse if you like. Having learnt something about making verse lines that are really lines, you are likelier to do better than if you had never written anything but free. And you may well discover that for all its charms, free verse cannot do nearly as much as metrical verse can, in expressing feeling, in clarifying thought, in varying tempo, in delineating nuances of tone or subtleties of meaning, in em-

410

phasizing, modulating, elevating, clinching both ideas and emotions, and above all, in bringing about that perhaps magical phenomenon that poetry alone is capable of: making us feel that the sounds of the words *are* what is being said, that the sounds somehow deepen, enlarge, enact, embody—in a sense, create—the reality behind them. As Henri Coulette once wrote, "Meter is thinking; it is the basis of intimacy between reader and writer."

These are some of the powers of meter and rhyme, and only the profoundest, sincerest, and most original poet can put them aside, and then only if he knows what he is putting aside. I am no Yeats, God knows, but I urge you, young poets, to do what he urged *his* young fellow poets to do: Learn your trade. Sing whatever is well made.

>> 84

THE POETRY SCENE TODAY

BY DAVID KIRBY

WE ALL KNOW THAT TECHNOLOGY GROWS IN LEAPS AND BOUNDS. Today's computers, for example, make yesterday's models look like Victorian steam engines in comparison. And poetry changes, too. A hundred years ago, formal poetry dominated the scene. Then free verse came along. And now new free-verse forms appear every day. That doesn't mean that formal poetry has disappeared; to the contrary, formal poets are inventing new poem-types of their own. Exactly what kinds of poems are being written today, and how can you write them?

As I see it, there are not just two choices, free verse and formal poetry, but actually six distinct kinds, each with its own particular characteristics.

(1) **Improvisational free verse.** There are really two very different kinds of free-verse poems being written these days, improvisational free verse and formal free verse. Improvisational free verse is like jazz; you make it up as you go. It represents the most obvious extension of what might be called the Walt Whitman tradition in poetry. A poet is most free when he or she is improvising, and thus improvisational free verse has the widest range of the six kinds we're considering here; it extends all the way from the one-stanza poem based on a single insight or observation to the poem that runs for several pages and encompasses a much wider variety of experience.

As written by writers as different as Gwendolyn Brooks, Frank O'Hara, Imamu Amiri Baraka, and William Stafford, the shorter and relatively simple kind of improvisational poem is the most common; it is the kind of poem that most poets are writing these days, and it is what comes to most readers' minds when they think of poetry.

But if you are a free-verse poet who is looking for a challenge, you might consider the long improvisational poem, which may be com-

412

posed of several parts and, for variety's sake, use several contrasting styles. Allen Ginsberg's 1956 Beat masterpiece "Howl" is an excellent example of the long improvisational poem, as are the works of such poets as Norman Dubie, Laura Jensen, Caroline Knox, and Gary Snyder.

(2) **Formal free verse.** This may sound like a contradiction to you, but think of it as a kind of writing that combines the best of the formal and free-verse traditions. Formal free verse is a kind of poetry that has the elegant appearance of formal poetry yet takes advantage of the comparatively greater range of expression we associate with free verse. In its simplest terms, a poem of this kind is a free-verse poem with stanzas and lines of equal length.

Try this: Take one of your free-verse poems, count the number of lines in it, and divide them into stanzas of equal length. Say you have a thirty-line poem; you could make two fifteen-line stanzas, fifteen two-liners, five stanzas of six lines each, six stanzas of five lines, and so on. You don't want to break arbitrarily, of course, but you'll find that the different possibilities will change the way in which you read the poem. After a while, one of them will make more sense than the others. If there is a climactic development near the middle of the poem, for example, then the two fifteen-line stanzas would result in two distinct parts, and the poem as a whole would gain a certain dramatic flair.

But if your original is twenty-nine or thirty-two lines long instead of thirty, you'll have to add a line or cut two. Don't be discouraged: That extra line may just make the point you've been trying to make all along. Or the two you remove may be weak lines that you didn't recognize as such until you had to cut. It never hurts to take another look at a poem, and the formal free-verse method will have you doing just that.

Your final version will be just as expressive as your original, even if you have to add or cut a line or two, yet it will have about it the aura of dignity and composure that the great formal poems have. Every reader wants to have confidence in the poets he reads, and that formal look is an excellent way to establish the poet's authority; it says, "Behold my great shape, dear reader; you haven't read a word yet, but already you can see that a lot of work went into the making of me." Your poem looks good, yet it says what you want—what more could you ask? That's why more and more poets are writing formal free

413

verse these days. Look at the work of Robert Bly, Robert Creeley, James Dickey, and Adrienne Rich. My poem, "Sub Rosa," is an example:

Sub Rosa

Maps would be literal if the normal order
were other than it is: letters would appear across
the faces of cities, and roads would become red lines.
Pages would fly out of books as well and then out
  of windows
to form trees in the yards of the literary.

The trees would shrink to seedlings and then seeds,
which would disappear up the anuses of birds
who would drop them where trees have never grown.
Gasoline would run out of cars and down hoses
into the earth, where it would turn into dinosaurs

who would escape through giant rents in the crust
to lurch down streets crowded with witches,
Manicheans, Confederate soldiers, Hunkpapa Sioux.
Everywhere things would extrude, exfoliate;
poems would be replaced by their meanings.

As for us, nothing would change.
For already when we lie down together or go for
  drives
or simply sit across the table from one another,
each look, each word, each touch bears out
the secret history of the world.

(3) **The New Formalism.** In a sense, there's nothing new about the New Formalism. It's really the Old Formalism being practiced by poets today, so that makes it new. As always, formal poetry requires some very specific skills. If free verse achieves its highest level of success through the appearance of risk and daring (invariably the result of hours of detached, objective revision, of course), formal verse accomplishes what it does through skillful use of rhyme and meter. Occasionally you'll hear someone complain that "poems don't rhyme any more," but that may be because the poems rhyme so subtly that the rhyming isn't apparent. Very few poets use tick-tock AABB rhymes these days. And galloping meters have been replaced by softer rhythms.

Consider these lines that begin Marilyn Hacker's poem "Fourteen" (from her collection *Assumptions*):

> We shopped for dresses which were always wrong:
> sweatshop approximations of the lean-
> lined girls' wear I studied in *Seventeen.*
> The arms pinched, the belt didn't belong. . . .

Here, the poet uses a loose iambic pentameter line, but her ABBA rhyme scheme and her enjambment (or run-on lines) keep the poem from having a singsong sound. The result is a highly formal poem whose emotions are nonetheless expressed in a very natural and unaffected-sounding way. Other poets writing formal verse these days include Van K. Brock, John Hollander, X. J. Kennedy, Barbara F. Lefcowitz, Maura Stanton, and Stephen Yenser.

(4) **Prose poetry.** So far, I've discussed the three main kinds of poetry you're most likely to encounter in books and magazines these days. But another kind is often found there also, and, like free verse, it's an old form that simply gives the appearance of being new. You can find prose poems in the Bible, and they also began appearing in the West in the nineteenth and early-twentieth centuries.

A prose poem is actually a free-verse poem written in paragraphs rather than stanzas, which means that it relies on the allusive, surreal effects of poetry while it disdains the conventions of stanzas and line breaks. There's no hard and fast rule about what goes into a prose poem, but many of them tend to read like fables or dreams or fairy tales. For example, an untitled Charles Simic poem, in his book *The World Doesn't End,* begins: "I was stolen by the gypsies. My parents stole me right back. Then the gypsies stole me again. This went on for some time." A poem like this is intended to induce a dream-like state, and its prose form contributes to that effect, since the action is continuous and without break. As opposed to the impressive grandeur of the formal or the formal free-verse poem, there's a casualness to the prose poem that seduces the reader. A prose poem is like a letter that is found on the sidewalk; who can resist picking it up? William Carlos Williams, Gertrude Stein, and John Ashbery have all written very different kinds of prose poetry, and more poets seem to be trying this appealing form every day.

(5) **Language poetry.** Rather than describe language poetry, let me begin with a stanza from a poem in Michael Palmer's book *Sun:*

> Ideas aren't worth anything
> Today space is splendid
> The mountains have come loose
> Let's unmake something

If the meaning of these lines isn't terribly clear, that's the point: Language poets are trying to break free from the restrictions of conventional middle-class attitudes toward art and life. As a result, their poems often seem bizarre and disorienting. But what poet hasn't strung words together randomly just to hear how they sound? More than any other kind of poetry, language poetry probably embodies the quality that drew most poets to their craft in the first place: the sheer music of it. Consider the poems of Charles Bernstein, Lyn Hejinian, Susan Howe, David Melnick, and Ron Silliman.

(6) **Performance poetry.** If you've ever read a poem and thought, "This would really sound good read aloud," it may be because that poem was written exactly for that purpose. Poets have often sent me their books, but today more and more are sending me tapes of their work as well. When most people hear the phrase "performance artist," they think of some self-dramatizing, avant-garde type, but the oral tradition is as old as the ancient Greeks, and Caribbean and African poets still chant their poems aloud today. If you live in a big city like New York or Chicago, you may be aware already of the "Poetry Slam" contests that take place in bars and coffee houses. Otherwise, contact your local university's English department to find out whether poetry readings are held on campus, and if so, when and where they take place. Also, look for *Stand-Up Poetry,* a collection of performance pieces edited by Charles H. Webb and Suzanne Lummis.

As a poet, surely you've found in this survey a kind of poetry similar to what you are writing at present. Therefore, you might now consider writing a kind of poem you've never tried before. You could end up taking your poetry in an entirely new direction. At the very least, you'll find you've written a "starter" you can use when you go back to the kind of poem you usually write.

>> 85

YESTERDAY'S NOISE: THE POETRY OF CHILDHOOD MEMORY

BY LINDA PASTAN

How sweet the past is, no matter how wrong, or how sad.
How sweet is yesterday's noise.
　　　　—Charles Wright, "The Southern Cross"

I WROTE AN ESSAY TEN YEARS AGO CALLED "MEMORY AS MUSE," AND looking back at it today I am struck by the fact that in the poems I write about childhood now the mood has changed from one of a rather happy nostalgia ("Memory as Muse") to a more realistic, or at least a gloomier, assessment of my own childhood and how it affects me as a writer ("Yesterday's Noise"). Let me illustrate with a poem called "An Old Song," from my most recent book.

An Old Song*

How loyal our childhood demons are,
growing old with us in the same house
like servants who season the meat
with bitterness, like jailers
who rattle the keys
that lock us in or lock us out.

Though we go on with our lives,
though the years pile up
like snow against the door,
still our demons stare at us
from the depths of mirrors
or from the new faces across a table.

And no matter what voice they choose,
what language they speak,
the message is always the same.
They ask "Why can't you do
anything right?" They say
"We just don't love you anymore."

417

As A. S. Byatt said about herself in an interview: "I was no good at being a child." My mother told me that even as a baby I would lie screaming in the crib, clearly terrified of the dust motes that could be seen circling in the sun, as if they were a cloud of insects that were about to swarm and bite me. By the time I was five or six, I had a series of facial tics so virulent that I still can't do the mouth exercises my dentist recommends for fear I won't be able to stop doing them. I'm afraid they'll take hold like the compulsive habits of childhood that led my second-grade teacher to send me from the room until I could, as she put it, control my own face. There was the isolating year (sixth grade) of being the one child nobody would play with, the appointed victim, and there was the even more isolating year (fourth grade) of being, alas, one of the victimizers. There was my shadowy room at bedtime, at the end of a dark hallway, and, until some worried psychologist intervened, no night light allowed.

I thought about calling my last book *Only Child* because something about that condition seemed to define not only me, but possibly writers in general who sit at their desks, necessarily alone, for much of the time. In some ways, of course, it defines all of us, born alone, dying alone, alone in our skins no matter how close we seem to be to others. I tried to capture my particular loneliness as a child, my difficulty in making friends, my search for approval, in what I thought would be the title poem of that book:

Only Child*

Sister to no one,
I watched
the children next door
quarrel and make up
in a code
I never learned
to break.

Go Play!
my mother told me.
Play! said the aunts,
their heads all nodding
on their stems,
a family of rampant
flowers

418

and I a single shoot.
At night I dreamed
I was a twin
the way my two hands,
my eyes,
my feet were twinned.
I married young.

In the fractured light
of memory—that place
of blinding sun or shade,
I stand waiting
on the concrete stoop
for my own children
to find me.

At a reading I gave before a group of Maryland PEN women, some-one who had clearly not read beyond the tables of contents of my books introduced me as a writer of light verse. I remember thinking in a panic that I hardly had a single light poem to read to those expect-ant faces, waiting to be amused. Did I have such an unhappy life, then—wife, mother, grandmother, with woods to walk in, books to read, good friends, even a supportive editor?

I am, in fact, a more or less happy adult, suffering, thank God, from no more than the usual griefs age brings. But I think my poems are colored not only by a possibly somber genetic temperament, but also by my failure at childhood, even when I am not writing about childhood per se. And more and more, as I grow older, those memories them-selves insist upon inserting themselves into my work. Perhaps it is the very way our childhoods change in what I called "the fractured light of memory" that make them such an inexhaustible source of poetry. For me, it is like the inexhaustible subject of the seasons that can be seen in the changeable light of the sun, or the versatile light of the imagination, as benign or malevolent or indifferent, depending upon a particular poet's vision at a particular moment.

I want to reflect a little then on those poems we fish up from the depths of our childhoods. And for any teachers reading this, I want to suggest that assigning poems to student writers that grow out of their childhoods can produce unusually good results, opening up those fro-zen ponds with what Kafka called the axe of poetry.

Baudelaire says that "genius is childhood recalled at will." I had a 19-year-old student once who was not a genius but who complained that he couldn't write about anything except his childhood. Unfortunately, his memory was short, and as a result, all of his poems were set in junior high school. He had taken my course, he told me, in order to find new subjects. I admit that at first glance junior high doesn't seem the most fertile territory for poems to grow in. On the other hand, insecurity, awakening sexuality, fear of failure—many of the great subjects do exist there. It occurred to me that when I was 19, what I usually wrote about were old age and death. Only in my middle years did I start looking back into my own past for the subjects of poems. This started me wondering about the poetry of memory in general. Did other poets, unlike my young students, come to this subject relatively late, as I had? As I looked rather casually and unscientifically through the books on my shelves, it did seem to me that when poets in their twenties and thirties wrote about children, it was usually their own children that concerned them, but when they were in their late forties or fifties or sixties, the children they wrote about tended to be themselves.

Donald Justice, in an interview with *The Missouri Review,* gave as good an explanation of this as anyone. He said, "In the poems I have been thinking of and writing the last few years, I have grown aware that childhood is a subject somehow available to me all over again. The perspective of time and distance alter substance somewhat, and so it is possible to think freshly of things that were once familiar and ordinary, as if they had become strange again. I don't know whether this is true of everybody's experience, but at a certain point childhood seems mythical once more. It did to start with, and it does suddenly again."

There are, first of all, what I call "Poems of the Happy Childhood," Donald Justice's own poem "The Poet At Seven" among them. But for poets less skilled than Justice, there is a danger to such poems, for they can stray across the unmarked but mined border into sentimentality and become dishonest, wishful sort of recollections. When they are working well, however, these "Poems of the Happy Childhood" reflect the Wordsworthian idea that we are born "trailing clouds of glory" and that as we grow older we are progressively despiritualized. Even earlier than Wordsworth, in the mid-17th century, Henry Vaughan anticipated these ideas in his poem, "The Retreat."

I mention Wordsworth and Vaughan because in looking back over the centuries at the work of earlier poets, I find more rarely than I expected poems that deal with childhood at all. Their poems are the exceptions, as are Shakespeare's 30th Sonnet and Tennyson's "Tears, Idle Tears." Perhaps it wasn't until Freud that people started to delve routinely into their own pasts. But nostalgia per se was not so rare, and in a book called *The Uses of Nostalgia: Studies in Pastoral Poetry,* the English critic Laurence Lerner comes up with an interesting theory. After examining pastoral poetry from classical antiquity on, he concludes that pastoral poems express the longing of the poets to return to a childhood arcadia, and that in fact what they longed to return to was childhood itself. He then takes his theory a step further and postulates that the reason poets longed for childhood is simply that they had lost it. He writes, "The list is varied of those who learned to sing of what they loved by losing it. . . . Is that what singing is? Is nostalgia the basis not only of pastoral but of other art too?" Or as Bob Hass puts it in his poem "Meditation at Lagunitas," "All the new thinking is about loss./ In this it resembles all the old thinking."

But though there are some left who think of childhood as a lost arcadia, for the most part Freud changed all of that.

We have in more recent times the idea of poetry as a revelation of the self to the self, or as Marge Perloff put it when describing the poems of Seamus Heaney, "Poetry as a dig."

The sort of poems this kind of digging often provides are almost the opposite of "Poems of the Happy Childhood," and they reflect a viewpoint that is closer to the childhood poems I seem to be writing lately. In fact, a poem like "Autobiographia Literaria" by Frank O'Hara actually consoles the adult by making him remember, albeit with irony in O'Hara's case, how much more unpleasant it was to be a child. If the poetry of memory can console, it can also expiate. In his well-known poem, "Those Winter Sundays," Robert Hayden not only recreates the past but reexamines his behavior there and finds it wanting. The poem itself becomes an apology for his behavior as a boy, and the act of writing becomes an act of repentance.

If you can't expiate the past, however, you can always revise it— and in various and occasionally unorthodox, ways. Donald Justice in the poem "Childhood" runs a list of footnotes opposite his poem, explaining and clarifying. Mark Strand in "The Untelling" reenters the childhood scene as an adult and warns the participants of what is to occur in the future.

Probably the most ambitious thing a poem of childhood memory can accomplish is the Proustian task of somehow freeing us from time itself. Proust is perfectly happy to use random, seemingly unimportant memory sensations as long as they have the power to transport him backwards. When he tastes his madeleine, moments of the past come rushing back, and he is transported to a plane of being on which a kind of immortality is granted. We can grasp for a moment what we can never normally get hold of—a bit of time in its pure state. It is not just that this somehow lasts forever, the way we hope the printed word will last, but that it can free us from the fear of death. To quote Proust: "A minute emancipated from the temporal order had recreated in us for its apprehension the man emancipated from the temporal order." Proust accomplished his journey to the past via the sense or taste, but any sense or combination of senses will do. In my poem "PM/AM," I used the sense of hearing in the first stanza and a combination of sight and touch in the second. Here is the second:

AM**

The child gets up
on the wrong side of the bed.
There are splinters
of cold light on the floor,
and when she frowns
the frown freezes on her face
as her mother has warned her it would.
When she puts her elbows roughly
on the table her father says:
you got up on the wrong side of the bed;
and there is suddenly
a cold river
of spilled milk.
These gestures are merely formal,
small stitches in the tapestry
of a childhood she will remember
as nearly happy. Outside
the snow begins again,
ordinary weather
blurring the landscape
between that time and this,
as she swings her cold legs
over the side of the bed.

But did I really say: "A childhood she will remember as nearly happy"? Whom are you to believe, the poet who wrote that poem years ago or the poet who wrote "An Old Song"? As you see, the past can be reinterpreted, the past can be revised, and the past can also be invented. Sometimes, in fact, one invents memories without even meaning to. In a poem of mine called "The One-Way Mirror Back," I acknowledge this by admitting: "What I remember hardly happened; what they say happened I hardly remember." Or as Bill Matthews put it in his poem "Our Strange and Lovable Weather"—

> . . . any place lies about its weather,
> just as we lie about our childhoods,
> and for the same reason: we can't
> say surely what we've undergone
> and need to know, and need to know.

This "need to know" runs very deep and is one of the things that fuels the poems we write about our childhoods.

But the simplest, the most basic thing such poems provide are the memories themselves, the memories for their own sakes. Here is the third stanza of Charles Simic's poem "Ballad": "Screendoor screeching in the wind/ Mother hobble-gobble baking apples/ Wooden spoons dancing, ah the idyllic life of wooden spoons/ I need a table to spread these memories on." The poem itself, then, can become such a table, a table to simply spread our memories on.

Looking back at some of my own memories, I sometimes think I was never a child at all, but a lonely woman camouflaged in a child's body. I am probably more childlike now. At least I hope so.

---

*"An Old Song" and "Only Child" appear in *Heroes In Disguise,* Norton, 1991.
**"AM" is from *PM/AM:New and Selected Poems,* Norton, 1982.

➤➤ 86

REACHING TOWARD FORM IN YOUR POETRY

BY GREG GLAZNER

ANY ASPIRING POET LOVES TO READ POEMS. IT'S SAFE TO GUESS THAT if you are writing poetry, you have been keeping a mental list of other people's poems—your favorites—for a while now. My list began when I was ten years old. I was fascinated by several of Robert Frost's poems, thanks to a first-rate teacher. (Mrs. Grimes wasn't perfect; she also taught us a terribly sentimental poem, written by a WWII fighter pilot, which began "Oh, I have slipped the surly bonds of earth / And danced the skies on laughter-silvered wings." I still remember the whole poem verbatim.)

Having ignored poetry during my junior high and high school years, I encountered Frost again during my first year in college. "The woods are lovely, dark, and deep," Dr. Brunner half-chanted over the lectern, and my list of favorite poems began growing again—and changing. Over the next fifteen years, poems by Rilke, Stevens, Whitman, Yeats, Dickinson, Kinnell, Milton, Roethke, and many others surpassed Frost's on my list of favorites, but poetry remains as alive for me now (in different ways, of course) as it was when I was a fourth grader, discovering "Stopping by Woods on a Snowy Evening" for the first time.

The love of reading poems is the first drive you need to become a serious poet. Chances are, if you have read this far, you already possess it. The second drive, the desire to develop craft, is especially important in the beginning years. And the third, a fascination with the way form and style turn into content, implying a world, is especially important after some technical problems have been handled.

Even some of the greats have struggled with technique—and the struggle isn't limited to poets. Early on, Charlie Parker, arguably the

greatest musician in the history of jazz, was known as the worst saxophone player in Kansas City. Apparently, he was bad enough that after
the word got out, he couldn't even get an audition. So for a period of
two or three years, he practiced relentlessly with his friend Dizzy
Gillespie, racing through scales, working up various classical pieces.
He claims to have practiced eleven to fifteen hours a day. No wonder
his mature solos would later sound so effortless, so full of vigor and
surprise. His reservoir of technique freed him to focus almost all of
his immense talent into creating an unprecedented kind of music. He
didn't have to think about getting the notes right.

Maybe it's true that poets, like jazz musicians, want nothing more
than to break into a spontaneous, intelligent music. If so, the most
important lesson to learn at the outset, so that later on it can become
as natural and as unconscious as breathing, is this: Almost all of a
poem's power comes from what is suggested, not from what is stated
outright. And of the many ways that poetry can suggest things, three
seem to give beginning poets the most difficulty: voice, tone, and
image.

When I use the word "voice," I mean the personality implied by the
poems' diction and syntax. Maybe such a distinction already sounds
arcane, but it isn't; we instinctively delight in voice in our everyday
lives. Consider this fictitious personal example: Over the Christmas
holidays, when the whole extended family convenes at my parents'
house, somebody gives my mother a new puppy, a three-month-old
Great Dane which promptly eats part of the couch. My grandfather
happens onto the scene of the crime first, smiles, and says, "I reckon
we're just about ready to get shed of a dog." My brother David comes
in and says, "So, looks like Rover here jumped the gun on lunch." And
my mother addresses the dog directly: "Oh, come on. You know better
than that!"

The point is that the way people talk tells us much about their personalities. And the speaker of a poem, while not identical to the poet,
must sound authentic in his or her speech patterns. So when a beginning poet brings into one of my workshops a poem which opens, "The
moss-infested river flowing forth from the verdant mountains. . . . ,"
the voice problem jumps out immediately. For starters, the diction is
generally pitched too high to be believable. But the overly formal
speaker who calls the mountains "verdant" wouldn't use the adjective

425

"moss-infested" in the same breath. So there is a problem with consistency as well. By dropping the diction level and getting the focus away from adjectives, the student writes, "Out of the green mountains, the river choked with moss . . ." and gains much credibility. The voice sounds intelligent, but not stilted.

Beginning poets aren't alone when they encounter substantial difficulties in early drafts of a poem. During the year it took me to write "From the Iron Chair," the nine-page title poem of my book, I filled over three hundred notebook pages with drafts, struggling much of the way. As I worked on the fourth section in particular, the problems in the early drafts all seemed to have to do with tone. By "tone," I mean, of course, the overall mood of a piece of writing.

The first few lines went well enough; only relatively minor changes were necessary. Here are those lines as they appear in the book:

> Down the well of old need,
> down the concrete steps,
> splintered rails, and leaf-rot
>
> of the half-demolished hotel,
> my cousin—one of the last illegal tenants—
> opened the door to his basement.
>
> Inside, there was vodka on his breath
> and a blue-gray static on the air.
> He adjusted a TV wired
>
> to the battery of a car
> and offered me a beer. All I did
> was lean back and take it to my bones,
>
> at twenty that first firing and eviction,
> this last inhabited room
> smelling of booze & glimmering
> like the interior of an age. . . .

Up to this point, the tone was nostalgic, tough, and visceral all at once. It seemed honest. But in what was to follow, the poem took a wrong turn. Here are the next few lines as they appeared in the first draft:

> The weight of twisted beams and bricks
> rose in the mind, at once
> imaginary and real, as if the future

426

had a demolished superstructure—
a brute, invisible weight
and the glut it took to forget it.

What happened to the power of the remembered experience? The tone of "rose in the mind, at once / imaginary and real, as if the future / had a demolished superstructure" is detached, cerebral, so that in context, the lines seem forced and powerless. Here is the same passage rewritten for tone—for the *feel* I had unwittingly abandoned:

We stared into the tube
as if it were enough to change us,

even as the invisible brute weight
of bricks and twisted beams
crushed itself closer like the future.

Twice the ceiling groaned, and I leaned
closer to the sentimental violins.
For an hour my cousin stiffened with me. . . .

While tone and voice work to create the sense that a poem has come from a believable, human origin, images bring the subject matter alive through the senses. Imagery is absolutely central to the work of most poets. Certainly, some great writers have been able to use abstract statement powerfully in poetry; Wallace Stevens comes to mind as a modernist who did so. But in most poems written by beginners, a direct statement of feelings or ideas not embodied in imagery will ring so false and flat that it will ruin the poem. William Carlos Williams' directive, "No ideas but in things," seems tailor-made for aspiring poets learning their craft. Keeping Williams in mind, a young poet whose love poem contains the line "In your absence, I am sleepless with longing," revises it to read, "You are gone, and the streetlight sets off / its blue-white fires across the sheets." The revision gains its power by appealing to the senses of sight and touch. The poem is an aesthetic experience, not amateur philosophy and not diary entry. For most poets, imagery is a crucial way of making a poem live. As the poet Miller Williams once said, "Film it."

Imagery, tone, voice, and many other aspects of craft are addressed in poetry workshops available in almost every corner of the country. A writing workshop can be an excellent way for a poet to improve rapidly, assuming that the teacher is both a good poet and a good

427

teacher—and that the student is motivated. But when, after years of hard work, a poet reaches the level of technical competency, writing as well as thousands of poets whose work fills hundreds of literary magazines in America, what next? What follows the long apprenticeship?

In short, transcending one's own self-imposed strictures. Doesn't the serious poet, having learned to write a modest kind of poem, try to live his way beyond it, reaching toward an understanding of the forms that experiences themselves assume? Think of Galway Kinnell's early poems, heavily influenced by the formalism of the 1950s (some of these are very fine, by the way), and his *The Book of Nightmares*, which moves through the most fundamental, archetypal experiences in jagged, free-verse lines, full of a dark, celebratory, American music. Think of Dickinson cloistered in her father's house, fusing the common measure of the church hymn with her intelligence and solitude, forging her small, powerful hymns to doubt. Think of Charlie Parker breathing out rush after rush of chromatic flourishes, sailing beyond the melody like someone discovering a new kind of grace for an age when all the moorings have come loose.

Young, anyone can set out "like something thrown from the furnace of a star," as Denis Johnson puts it. Poetry touches us easily then, as long as we have the good fortune—as I did in the fourth grade—of being exposed to it in an intelligent way. But for some of us, the experience has such power that we go on to become writers ourselves, governing our lives by the rich, unpredictable cadences of the human voice. In the end, we never know for sure whether we succeed in writing important poetry. But the process—reading, crafting, reaching toward form—is a way of aspiring toward meaning with one's whole being. Anything less is just fooling around with verse.

➤➤87

WRITING POETRY FOR CHILDREN AND YOUNG ADULTS

BY PAT LOWERY COLLINS

FOR YOUNG CHILDREN, A POEM IS A DEEPLY SATISFYING WAY OF LOOK-ing at the world. Fascinated at first by rhyme for its own sake, they soon begin to appreciate poetry that deals with simple concepts. They love slapstick, the wildly impossible, the ridiculous, word play, fanciful questions, clever and unexpected conclusions, twists and turns. They dote on repetition, used to great effect in *A Fine Fat Pig,* by Mary Anne Hoberman, in which the word abracadabra, used as an exclamation, precedes each line describing a zebra.

They revel in the action rhymes, finger play, and later, jump rope games, that depend on onomatopoeia, hyperbole and alliteration, as well as in such farcical verse as *Merry Merry FIBruary,* by Doris Orgel. Using these last two devices and the fun of a deliberate fib, the claim is made that "On the first of FIBruary/Setting out from Hackensack/ My Aunt Selma, in a seashell/ Sailed to Samarkand and back."

Poetry books for this age group are heavily illustrated, not only to complement the words, but also sometimes to explain them. And since poets are usually very visual writers, they will often provide the artist with exciting possibilities for illustrations without really trying.

The combined *Hector Protector* and *As I Went Over the Water* by Maurice Sendak is an unusual case in which poems and illustrations are all of one piece. Words emphasizing the text pepper the illustrations, and much of the action is in the pictures instead of the words. But in most cases, poems, even for the very young, rhymed or unrhymed, should be able to stand on their own.

Sometimes a single poem is used as the entire text for a picture book, illustrated so as to enhance or help to develop a concept or story. The text of my nonfiction book, *I Am an Artist,* is actually one

429

long poem conveying the concept, through the finely detailed paintings of Robin Brickman, that art is a process which begins with our experiences in the natural world.

It's been my observation that children in the middle grades (ages 9–12) are no longer as fascinated by rhyme. To some degree they want a poem to be as profound as what they are experiencing in life, something that takes them seriously. Yet, they still look for poetry that is simple and unlabored. *Haiku,* three unrhymed lines (in Japanese they must consist of 17 syllables) offering an unusual perspective on a spark of reality, is a perfect vehicle. Writing in this form is not as easy as it sounds. To provide an example, I struggled to produce: "Evening/is quietly stitching/the seam of night."

Children of this age are intrigued by the subtlety of haiku, and its shortness is irresistible to those just learning to put their own thoughts on paper.

But humorous, silly verse, either in such traditional forms as the limerick or in new and inventive ways, still holds great appeal. Thus the information that "Oysters/are creatures/without/any features," provided by John Ciardi in *Zoo Doings,* may be better remembered than the multiplication tables.

It is also a good time for books such as *Alice Yazzie's Year,* by Ramona Maher, in which unrhymed poems, each one complete in itself, taken together tell a story of a year in the life of a Navajo girl, a year that holds such mysteries as the birth of a lamb. We are told that "The new lamb sucks/The pinyon burns low/The lamb goes to sleep/His nose is a black star."

Poems about parents quarrelling or grandparents dying are often interspersed with poetry in a lighter vein in collections for this age group. One that does this effectively is *Knock at A Star,* collected by X. J. Kennedy and Dorothy M. Kennedy.

Language for its own sake becomes the focus again for readers about eleven to twelve, when communication with peers, intrigue, and secrets are important. Poetry is then a vehicle to express feelings without exposing them. Tools for this are found in nonsense sounds, obscure meanings, double meanings, rhyme, and, of course, humor. The mystery of nonsense—even an entire made-up language—seems to hold the same allure as it had for the four-year-old. Young readers are all too willing to accept the special logic of Lewis Carroll's "Jabberwocky" and will have no trouble figuring out that when the Jabberwock "came whiffling through the tulgey wood/And burbled as it came," the "beamish boy" slays him as his "vorpal blade went snicker-snack!"

But these same children are also looking for poets able to look at life in the ways that they do. The poetry of Walter de la Mare has a timeless appeal because he affirms feelings that are universal. His book *Peacock Pie* was first published in 1913 and has been in print ever since. I'm currently illustrating a collection for Atheneum called *Sports, Power and Dreams of Glory, Poems Starring Girls,* edited by Isabel Joshlin Glaser, that affirms the dreams and aspirations of young women in such poems as "Abigail," by Kaye Starbird*, which ends by saying, "And while her mother said, 'Fix your looks,'/ Her father added, 'Or else write books.'/ And Abigail asked, 'Is that a dare?' And wrote a book that would curl your hair."

Teenagers may establish a passionate identification with one particular poet as they look for role models, a sense of history, a way to understand the world as it changes in and around them. By this time, they have probably been made aware of the mechanics and craft of poetry and are intrigued by experimentation. They can appreciate any poet whose vision is not too obscure. Because of the need of adolescents to deal with strong feelings and disturbing issues such as death and suicide, they are often attracted to poets with dysfunctional lives, for example, Sylvia Plath and Anne Sexton.

Most poetry for this age group appears in anthologies related to a single theme, to a city or to some historical period.

My own feeling is that even though the poetry you are compelled to write may turn out to have a special appeal for this age group, you will be competing with Shakespeare, T. S. Eliot, Walt Whitman, Emily Dickinson, and a cast of thousands. Of course, there is a lot of wonderful poetry out there for young children too, but not enough of it. And here I think the masters of today are a good match for those of yesterday and have an edge because they speak to the familiar.

But knowing your audience is only a beginning. There are a number of other things you should bear in mind in writing poetry for young people.

---

*Excerpted from "Abigail," in *The Pheasant on Route Seven,* by Kaye Starbird. Copyright ©1968 by Kaye Starbird. Reprinted by permission of Marian Reiner for the author.

Don't fall victim to the mistaken notion that writing poetry for children of any age is easier than writing for adults. Your perspectives and topics may be different, but the skills you must bring to task are the same, skills honed through years of reading good poetry and working to develop your craft. Your most important assets will be a good memory and a strong awareness of the child within you.

It is a common misconception that almost anyone can write poetry for children. It's true we can get away with serving them peanut butter sandwiches for dinner, but it better be creamy peanut butter or the kind with just the right amount of nuts. Just so, the quality of poetry we give our children should be the best available, from the very beginning of their awareness of language.

Another misconception is that almost any idea for a children's book should be written in rhymed verse. Quite the opposite is true. Although there are exceptions, even reasonably good verse will not necessarily make for a more compelling text, and bad verse can, in fact, be deadly. So many "first" manuscripts in verse are submitted to editors that there is almost a universal resistance to them. Here I must admit to being an offender myself with my first book for children, *My Friend Andrew.* Looking back, I realize that any advantage I may have had was somehow knowing enough to keep it simple.

Things I personally object to, not under the control of the poet, are anthologies that include bad poems simply because they're by "good" poets, and minor poems by major poets because they're short; uneven collections by one poet or many; and anthologists who completely overlook contemporary poems and poets. The inability of some editors to recognize good poetry or to appreciate a child's ability to understand abstract concepts is a real problem.

Besides being as meticulous when writing poetry for children as you would be in writing for adults, you should, under penalty of a one-way trip down the rabbit hole, avoid all of the following:

• Poetry that talks down to the reader or is used as a vehicle to deliver a moral or message, unless it is written with good humor, as when Shel Silverstein, in his *Where the Sidewalk Ends,* admonishes readers to "Listen to the Mustn'ts."

• Near rhymes. They stop children in their tracks and detract from the flow of the poem. An example would be "lion's" rhymed with "defiance" and "cat" with "hate" in the poem "My Old Cat," by Hal Summers. *(Knock at A Star)*

• Rhymes that are too cute, convenient, or overused. "Rain" rhymed with "Spain" comes to mind.

• Lazy images. Even well-known poets sometimes do this, settling for the most obvious image, metaphor, or simile as in "wide as the sky."

• Rhyme for rhyme's sake, not because it will assist in saying what you want to say in the most interesting way. If, as with the book, *Madeline,* by Ludwig Bemelmans, it would be hard to imagine your own story being told in any other way, then, by all means, go for it. (I felt this way about *Andrew.*)

• Subject matter inappropriate for the intended age group, sometimes directed more to the parent than the child, or dealing with subjects outside the child's experience.

• Distorted rhyme that's hard to read aloud. Always read your own work aloud to avoid this.

• Poetry that is florid and old-fashioned, written in the accepted style of an earlier period.

• Poetry that is too complex or obscure. Young readers won't want to struggle to understand what may be very personal imagery.

• Writing presented in the form of a poem that isn't poetry by any stretch of the imagination and isn't even good prose.

• Writers who believe they must write like another poet in order to be published.

There was only one Dr. Seuss. If he had insisted on being another Edward Lear, we would have missed his unique vision and voice. If you aren't sure enough of your own voice, keep studying the work of poets you admire—their pace, rhyme schemes and structure—and keep writing until you find how to say what you want to in ways uniquely yours.

Like Valerie Worth, in her *All the Small Poems,* you may have wonderful, quiet perceptions to express about everyday objects and happenings. Borrow her microscope if you must, but wear your prescription lenses and present the world through your observations and special talents, having in mind that building a poem is much like building a block tower: You will be balancing one word or line against another; arranging and rearranging; dropping one word, adding another, until the poem begins to say what you had in mind all along or what may never before have occurred to you. When a poem really comes together, really "happens," it is a moment like no other. You will feel like the child whose tower at long last has reached the sky.

Today, the market for children's poetry is quite different from what it was in the inhospitable 1980s. Then, there were a few poets who had cracked the barrier somewhat earlier and continued to be published, but a limited number of new names came on the scene. Thanks to the firmer financial footing of most book departments for young readers, to some editors who realize that poetry rounds out a list, and to the demand by teachers and librarians, there is currently greater opportunity for new poets. A number of publishing houses are actively seeking poetry for children, but they are highly selective and still apt to overlook a talented newcomer in favor of a poet more likely to turn a profit.

But the field of poetry has never been considered a lucrative one. There are exceptions, as with any art form, and for some poets, who continue to put their words down on paper napkins and laundry lists, there is really no escape.

WRITING THE POETIC SEQUENCE

BY JEFFREY SKINNER

I'D LIKE TO URGE YOU TO A LITTLE GRAND AMBITION. I REALIZE THE oxymoronic character of that phrase, but the poetic sequence as practiced today often contains elements of both transcendence and homeliness, like much of our "postmodern" art, and life. So, please, bear with me.

If we grant that the Adam and Eve of American poetry, Walt Whitman and Emily Dickinson, invented the modern poetic sequence— long, lyrical poems in more or less free-standing sections, connected by tone, texture and theme (rather than by the narrative event and heroic characters of epic)—then it seems natural that every American poet since has at least attempted a long poem to contend with and extend the work of their progenitors.

T. S. Eliot's *The Wasteland,* Ezra Pound's *Cantos,* William Carlos Williams' *Paterson,* Hart Crane's *The Bridge* are some examples of modern poets that come most readily to mind. In the next generation, we might think of John Berryman's *Dream Songs,* Robert Lowell's sonnet sequences, Sylvia Plath's "final" poems. And, to name only a few contemporary examples: Louise Gluck's *Ararat,* Charles Wright's *China Trace,* and Sharon Olds' *The Father.*

This is a cursory list, though even within it one can find an astonishing range of concerns, diction, style, and strategy. I know it's intimidating to begin by mentioning such monuments as *The Wasteland,* but I give them as historical precedent only, not as competitive model. Remember—I said a *little* grand ambition. It is ambitious enough to attempt a sequence on one's own, without bringing Eliot, et al, along for the ride.

We are a diverse and fragmented society, and our poetry reflects this fact. Flexibility of mind and spirit are demanded of us. The juggling act our lives can so easily become is sometimes cause for anxiety, but the other side of this coin is great freedom. At no other moment in history have poets had the opportunity to mix so freely high and low culture, formal and free verse, and language that simultaneously encompasses the diction of the street, the home, the office, the academy and—well, any speech at all—even the jargon of meteorologists.

So—we are free to write a book of sestinas based on the characters in the old Perry Mason television show (*The Whole Truth,* by James Cummins), or a sonnet sequence on rock and roll icons (*Mystery Train,* by David Wojahn). Or we can use free verse and lean more on obsessive character or theme for structuring—as in Sharon Olds' searing vignettes of a father's death *(The Father),* or Charles Wright's booklength sequence of meditative lyrics on the meeting of Eastern and Western views of spiritual regeneration *(China Trace).* The possibilities are infinite. We need not begin with a grand, elevated idea.

How *do* we begin a poetic sequence? Often, the beginnings of a sequence have come for me when I have written a poem I felt did not say all I wanted to say on the subject. But at the same time, I knew that the poem as written was finished: It had a completeness that could not be expanded without distortion. The poem suggested an overarching idea or zone of concern that I wanted to explore from different angles. I sensed that if I continued to build on what the initial poem had established, the resulting group or sequence might acquire an added dimensionality, a depth of field, that the first poem alone did not possess. I felt the pull toward sculpture, if you will, as opposed to the flat canvas.

Here is a poem I wrote some years ago:

Prayer to Owl Hiding in Daylight

Zealot in the trees, hot tiny speck
glowing in the dark of God's endless palm,
forgive me my absences! The clinically depressed
tenements of Bridgeport
ejected me into this calm, and now
there is too much rain, the leaves are pleading,
the green runs. All day, invisibly, you take notes,
like a businessman writing a novel
on his time off, a pale blue spark
snapping between your ears.

When will you visit? We desire visitations
but lack discipline to call them
on, and only our best shoes are shining.
I want claw, want your gold
headlights, your roomy coat of feathers.
I want to sleep days and work nights,
praising silence in high branches.
I want the microtonics of steel
drained from my blood. Oh the eclipse
has come and gone: show yourself.
You'll find my true love and me dreaming
on each other's shoulders, as the baby
breathes out tiny flowers in her crib
and the war continues, silently, elsewhere.

I don't know where this poem came from. Or, to be more precise, I don't know where the first line came from—"Zealot in the trees, hot tiny speck." The words drifted into my mind like a song on the radio; I tuned in. I did not discover until later in the writing that the "Zealot" was an owl. When I did, the poem began to move much faster, and I completed the last third rapidly. Only after it was finished did I notice that the poem was a kind of address, or supplication to the owl. That realization gave me the title.

Now I had a poem that was recognizably mine in language and allusion (new baby, Bridgeport tenements, businessman writing a novel), but that also harked back to earlier periods and cultures, when poetry was taken seriously as ritualistic invocation, a concrete way of knitting together the human and natural worlds, often through the mediation of animals. The poem also seemed conscious of the distance between these two worlds; there was a kind of implied acknowledgment of poetry's functional loss, a sad irony that struck me as essentially contemporary in tone.

These contradictions seemed resonant, and I wanted to explore them further. I began writing other "prayers to animals," setting for myself certain "rules": Each poem must address an undomesticated animal (or insect); I must take the animals as they are, without wrenching them from their natural environment or giving them supernatural attributes; each poem must include my world *as it is,* without idealization; and I must ask something of each animal, something I truly desire. I allowed myself to vary the form of the poems: "Prayer to Sparrow in Two Seasons" was written in tercets, with an iambic pentameter base;

"Prayer to Cottonmouth Blocking the Road to the Pond" seemed to require couplets; "Prayer to Wasp on the Eve of Its Execution," an extended block of varied two- and three-beat lines; and so forth.

I ended up with about fifteen poems in the sequence. It was exciting to follow the implications of an idea, and writing the poems was, as Frost says, "serious play." I did not think about the "great American poetic sequence." I just looked about me for animal subjects, and wrote the next poem.

And this is the attitude I'd suggest you take when writing a sequence: Let yourself be swept up in the idea, yes, but remember that the section or piece you are currently working on deserves your complete attention, and that, day by day, the whole will take care of itself. *Agi quod agis;* Do what you are doing . . .

I have also written a number of sonnet sequences, a formal challenge that comes down to us trailing a long history and its own set of rules. I don't know exactly why the sonnet remains of perennial interest to poets in succeeding generations, but since its invention and right into the present time, the form has drawn poets to test both its resources and its limits. It may be that the sonnet is, in its compactness, and in the buried logic of its movement, a more accurate analogue of human consciousness than anyone has guessed. The poet David St. John calls poems "maps of consciousness"; perhaps the sonnet is, simply, an ideal grid for the linguistic cartographer. . . .

Theory aside, it's clear to me after years of writing and teaching that the formal strictures of a sonnet or sonnet sequence release a paradoxical freedom in the poet. By concentrating on the "boundaries" of fourteen lines, rough iambic pentameter, and end-rhyme, my students find themselves saying surprising, insightful things they just would not have arrived at by writing "free verse." Such discoveries are compounded in the sonnet sequence, where at a certain point the form itself becomes second nature—no longer an impediment of any kind, but rather a powerful tool for unearthing the new.

I have two daughters, now eight and ten years old, but both toddlers when I wrote this poem:

> I wanted a boy, of course, wanted to create
> in my own image, ambitious little god that I am.
> But the long years spent chasing women immoderate-
> ly stacked karma: now I'm surrounded by them.

Human flowers, your natural smell intoxicates
and the fine blond hair I smooth, reading books,
consoling a fall. My own boyhood aches
in me still, burnished wind of summer dusks
comes back: bike-riding through dinner, stickball,
mumbletypeg in the marvelous junkyard; running,
running the long dark length of Grandma's hall
to leap her scented quilt. . . . Oh I've lost nothing,
and need no small version of myself to keep
boy pleasures. A daughter takes a farther reach.

After reading this over, it occurred to me that it might be the beginning of something larger. It engaged many of the themes important to me at that point in my life: the relation of parenting to one's own childhood; the dangerous tendency to view children as extensions of the self; the eternally fascinating and difficult subject of gender difference; and the anxieties raised by simply bringing children into a complex world.

In addition, the poem gave a hint ("your natural smell intoxicates") of the stance succeeding poems might take: they could be written *to* my daughters. The address to a loved one is a time-honored strategy in sonnet sequences and, as is probably obvious by now, I am in favor of the use of traditional poetic form, as long as that form is refreshed and remade by living, contemporary language.

But at that point in their lives neither of my daughters could read; the younger one was not yet talking. How could I suspend my own disbelief in writing poems to people who could not possibly understand?

The solution came in the form of a title for the sequence: "Sonnets to My Daughters Twenty Years in the Future." The poems, or poem, as I now saw it, would be addressed to the women my daughters would become. I would write a "time capsule" poem. This freed me to speak of adult matters in adult terms, though I would still be writing to my flesh and blood. The prospect was, again, exciting, and I plunged in, writing sonnet after sonnet.

I varied the pattern, using both Shakespearean and Petrarchan models. I relied on an iambic pentameter "back beat," though there is much metrical variation in the finished sequence. I also took considerable liberties with end-rhyme exactness, using off, slant, and approximate rhymes whenever I thought it appropriate. My primary goal, while retaining the strong echo of the sonnet form in the reader's mind, was to stay as close to current American speech (as I hear and use it in conversation) as possible. Whatever interest the resulting sequence has, apart from subject matter, is due in large measure to the tension between traditional form and colloquial usage. Purists may object, but to me there is nothing more boring than the tick-tock of a sonnet written to metronomic perfection. *Make it new!* Pound says, and to do that, whether writing in form or free verse, poets must use the language of the time and place they have been given.

One of the advantages of attempting a sequence is that, whatever the eventual success or shortfall of the piece as a whole, one generally ends up with at least a few sections that are salvageable as poems in their own right. When I was writing the sonnets to my daughters, I made it my goal to write fifty of them. But when I reached somewhere around number forty, I felt the impulse fading; the sonnets were becoming mechanical, repetitive. I wrote to my old mentor and friend Philip Levine for advice. "Stop writing," he replied, "when you get tired of reading them." This seemed like excellent counsel; I closed up shop on the sequence and chose and arranged the twenty best sonnets to include in my second collection of poems.

Writing the poetic sequence allows us a kind of relaxed concentration. We escape the pressure of having to say all we know in a single section or poem. Each section opens the way, associatively, to others. The "grid" of a larger structure frees us from the invention of new form every time we set pen to paper. We have the spur of ambition, tempered by the necessity to attend to whatever specific piece of the whole is before us at the moment.

However you begin your sequence—whether with a line, or a poem in which you sense hidden seams of rich material, or the excitement of a formal pattern, or a subject—at some point you will have to decide whether the *idea* of the sequence is important enough to engage you, deeply, on many levels. The writing of a poetic sequence is the construction of a small world, and the heady intensity of that work can be its own reward. Go ahead—try a little grand ambition. You have nothing to lose, and much of delight and discovery to gain.

➤➤ PLAYWRITING

➤➤ 89

STARTING THAT PLAY

BY DAVID COPELIN

YOU WANT TO WRITE A PLAY. DOESN'T EVERYONE? YET NOT EVERY-one who wants to write a play actually writes it. Many would-be play-wrights don't know where to begin. They ask themselves, "Should I start with a theme? Some sort of message? Maybe it's better to start with a plot. People like stories. But haven't all the good stories been deconstructed? Well, then, what about a character in conflict with another character? In conflict with herself? In conflict with the *universe*? Maybe I'd better start with some other essential element. But what might that element be? Is it obvious? Is it esoteric? What *is* it? Oh, maybe I'll take a nap instead."

Ambition sacked by anxiety. Do I exaggerate? Not by much. There's no way to know how many writers with a gift for drama stick to less intimidating literary forms—novels, poems, short stories or cereal-box copy—just because they are unclear about where to start creating a text for the theater.

Shall I tell you where a playwright "should" begin? I could, except that I don't know the One True Answer that the question implies. I'm more comfortable deriving dramatic theory from dramatic practice.

So, I talk with some colleagues. These authors all belong to ThroughLine, a playwrights' group in the San Francisco Bay Area, of which I'm a member. We meet weekly to present, hear, and respond to work in progress. What we have in common is the drive to craft forceful, effective dramas, and to learn what we can from each other. We differ in our writing methods, our visions, our obsessions, our styles, and (you guessed it) where we begin our plays.

Playwright A: "The two most common places to start writing are *character* and *situation*. Questions about situation quickly become questions about character: Who would be in a particular situation?

443

What would they do? How would the situation itself define the characters you'd find there? Or, you can start with specific characters, or character types. If you start with types, you must sculpt them into unique characters by adding traits, or by chipping away at the type until you arrive at an individual. I generally start with a character in mind. Sometimes I see a total personality, sometimes just a single trait. You can also start with a relationship, such as a father and a daughter who don't communicate. Sometimes the key idea is of a relationship that doesn't work, and the play's journey is toward a relationship that *does* function, though on a different level. When you start from a relationship, your task is to show how the people in it are affected by events, whether they change or not."

Playwright B: "Whether they change or not? What do you mean? Somebody's *got* to change, or it's not dramatic. I'm prompted to start with something that I *have* to write about. I don't always know what it is when I start, but I have to find out. And I don't start with character. I start with situation. I ask, 'What would happen if . . . ?' Then I try to find the action that makes what I'm writing a *play* rather than a short story or a novel. It's a plot question; the operative word is *happen*."

Playwright C: "I don't start with either plot or character. I go through a dreamlike process of seeing images. There always seems to be a mask of some kind, an artifice, which I find inherently theatrical. When the picture is strong in my mind, dense and layered, I start to write." C goes on to note that this is purely the way she *begins* a play, that for her, the imagery has to earn its place in the scheme of things. "I'm interested in what this picture means in the continuum. Each event in the world of the play has to connect to something larger than itself."

Playwright D: "I've tried to start with character, but it just doesn't work for me. I also begin by asking, 'What would happen if . . . ?' The question allows me to come up with different scenarios to explore, and it gives me focus and a starting point. I'd love to have strong images and strong characters right from the beginning, but they come naturally as the first question is answered. The story builds the characters."

"Well," says Playwright E, "I start with people and situations from my life, from things that I know. Then I build 'What would happen if . . . ?' and more universal concerns into the action. I try to tell a story. How does the ball roll from what I know into what I don't know?

That's the journey I set out on. And what starts out as real life gradually becomes fiction."

Playwright F also starts from real life, and from memories. "Even when I imagine situations that I haven't been in, they need to feel real to me. They need an emotional similarity to situations that I *have* been in. Then the characters that I find there start to change. Play structure demands that characters change. The images and feelings I start with don't always have action attached, but they lead to images and feelings that do."

Curious (because no one has mentioned it), I ask, "What about theme? Don't any of you start from a theme, or at least a premise?"

Playwright B: "A play speaks as a play speaks. The notion that you can reduce a play to its theme—and that if you can't articulate the theme in a sentence, there's something wrong with the play—is outmoded."

You get the gist. There is not much consensus about the best place to start a play. But after all, during the playwriting process, each element of a play—plot, character, atmosphere, imagery, even the dreaded theme—will get some attention from the author. That being so, it may not really matter which of these elements you tackle first, because you will consider all the others before you're finished.

You might start with the world as you experience it, right on the surface. Some writers begin their plays from newspaper articles. Why not? Seemingly commonplace news often has a hidden poetic dimension. It's a playwright's joy to ferret that out and make it live on stage. Or maybe it's the writer's gift to lend his or her insight, his or her sense of mystery, to something mundane, transforming it into a resonant dramatic event. It's not easy. But this is exactly the challenge that faces any playwright who is comfortable starting with what most people might find ordinary.

Conversely, you might start with something bizarre. The most unlikely tale can make a play, if it has magnetism, forward motion, and something at stake; *we want to see how it comes out*. I have a memory of four erstwhile painters, all sitting mesmerized on my floor, reading the *National Enquirer, not painting*. Did I find a story in the tabloid that later became a play? Did the image of my friends, focused on something other than what they were supposed to be focusing on, induce a drama? Will this anecdote incite *you* to write a play? You see

445

how it works. What's bad for interior decoration can be very good for the theater.

Dreams, daydreams, hallucinations, all are fertile ground for beginning a play. Some writers I know keep "image bank" journals, writing down arresting, detailed visions they see or imagine. If a particular image or series of images retains its potency for you over time, explore it dramatically. Populate it. Set it in motion.

But wait a minute, you say. Aren't *words* the playwright's primary tool? Of course. That's a truth. But is it the *whole* truth? Consider other possibilities. Words are certainly the primary *result* of a playwright's labors, at least on paper, but some dramatists use *actors* as their primary tool, by writing a role for a particular actor, or introducing an object or theme around which actors improvise, and then distilling *their* lines into a drama. This process can be disorganized and unpredictable, but it can also produce exciting results. There's often another side effect: When actors get excited about a play they're working on, they tend to spread the word. Being talked about as an interesting writer is not that unusual; being talked about as someone whose labors may provide employment for performers *is*.

And then there's music. Music is such an effective shortcut to emotions that playwrights have been known to start new scripts by listening to music, using the feelings it evokes to inform their creation of character, setting, atmosphere, even the rhythm of the dialogue. Music can also begin and punctuate a play in performance and bring out the audience's emotions and associated memories, setting them up for guided response to the tale you are presenting—with you doing the guiding. By starting your play with music, especially with the music you listened to as you wrote the first lines, you can, in effect, write the emotional subtext of your play anew every time it is performed.

Some playwrights adapt novels, short stories, even other authors' dramas, into brand-new plays. Where they start writing the new work will obviously depend a lot on what already exists, but even here you can choose where to begin. There is already a literary work with a beginning, a middle, and an end. Should you start at the top, or with the scene that excites you most? Or somewhere else?

The answer to all three questions is "Yes."

By now it should be clear that there are *no* rules about where one "should" begin a play. Beginnings are personal, idiosyncratic. I might start a play in a completely different place from where you would start it. Is there a way to predict from this whose play will be more theatrically persuasive, more successful? I don't think so. No doubt you can start in a place that proves not to be as useful as starting somewhere else might have been, but maybe you need to make the false start in order to recognize the true one later on.

Just *start*. That's the real rule. Procrastination has done more than a gross of drama critics to sabotage playwrights' careers. Wherever you start your play, you'll take a fabulous journey, full of wrong but fascinating turnings, spiced by moments of inspiration that may actually help you solve problems in your script that had seemed insoluble. Or not. You'll write, you'll rewrite, you'll cut. Cutting bad writing is easy. Learning to cut *good* writing that is flawed dramatically, or is misplaced or repetitive, is much harder. Characters will alter when you least expect them to. They may combine, assuming new attributes, changing gender, race or class, or they may disappear entirely. It all depends on where your inspiration, your instincts, and your hard work lead you. Whether your particular talent is for acute observation of the world, or for a strong imaginative interpretation of it, you are creating a new dramatic universe. And no one else could possibly do it quite the way you can.

That's why the best place to start writing your play is . . . *now*.

➤➤ 90

BEFORE YOU TRY BROADWAY . . .

BY ANNA COATES

AS A LOS ANGELES-BASED WRITER, SCRIPT ANALYST, AND DEVOTEE of community theater, I see a lot of plays that could have been a lot better, and I read a lot of scripts that probably should have been shredded at birth.

Which is not necessarily a bad thing.

One of the functions of little theater is to give the playwright a chance to see what works and what doesn't—not on the page, but on the stage, with living, fumbling, stumbling actors. The playwright's duty—alas, oft-neglected—is to figure out what doesn't work, and why, and if necessary to cut and chop or even to begin again.

And in a world that seems unjustly biased toward screenwriters—from Joe Eszterhas and his three-million-dollar *Basic Instinct* to Joe Schmoe and his twenty-thousand-dollar B-flick advance—the playwright has one wonderful advantage over the screenwriter. In addition to basic moral superiority, of course.

The playwright can learn as he goes.

The playwright may aspire to Broadway, but he has a crack at many lesser triumphs along the way. He can tinker with his work, tightening here and lengthening there. Even after he surrenders a script to a director's interpretation, he may continue to edit and rewrite, with or without the director's blessing.

Markets for a stage script can be divided into four categories: *community theater, experimental theater, "legitimate theater"* (aka, the Big Time), and *publication/TV.*

Of course, the categories aren't mutually exclusive. Community theater can mean a show performed on a makeshift stage in a church basement, or an elaborate and well-funded production staged as part of the regular "season" of a repertory house. (You understand, of course, that the term "well-funded" is relative!) Student productions are another type of community theater, and in some college towns they are eagerly awaited as the only theater available.

Community theaters like to produce well-known plays by established playwrights. That gets a little tired when you're seeing *Our Town* or *Streetcar* for the fifth time in six years, but if you think about it, it makes sense. Working with tiny budgets, directors tend to pick shows that are proven winners with broad appeal. They keep in mind that audiences—not to mention casts—may be unseasoned, and will react most favorably to mainstream fare.

This doesn't mean your original light comedy or social drama can't find a home with a little theater—of course it can. But you may need extra patience to find the right house to handle its premiere.

And yes, local companies will occasionally get crazy and go for *experimental theater*. But you're more likely to come across it in a city like Los Angeles or New York with a heavy concentration of actors and writers, an abundance of venues, and a weird (whoops, I mean *varied*) range of tastes.

If you're slathering to do your play on the Great White Way, or at least on cable TV, back up and slow down.

The road to Broadway (and Off-, and off-Off) wends its way through many a community theater and college campus. Sure, your play might be one of the fifteen selected by the O'Neill Theatre Center's National Playwrights Conference. On the other hand, it might be one of the fifteen hundred they reject. And it's within the realm of possibility— just faintly, there at the border—that you'll zap out your first rough script to a cable television company and get a fat check and a contract by FedEx a week later. Certainly, if you're confident about the quality of your work you should try.

But for most mere mortals the way to earn a few credits and learn the ropes is to have their work produced by a small local theater or an undergraduate director.

And that should be pretty easy. After all, an undergraduate director is really just a college kid. And local theaters pay nothing—or maybe carfare—and ought to be happy to get what they can get. Right?

Well, no.

The great majority of scripts submitted to student directors, to little

449

theaters, and to contests will never be produced or optioned because they are badly written.

It's not because the writers are without talent. There is almost always—no, *always*—something positive I can say about a piece of writing, and I'll go out of my way to figure out what it is. Still, it's frustrating and annoying to read script after script in which plots are direct rip-offs from current movies or standard stage productions, down to characters' names and dialogue. Sure, we all know there are only three basic storylines. The trick is to make yours seem fresh.

What directors and readers and editors look for in a script is a storyline that flows and that is logical *within context*. Think about the eternal *Ten Little Indians*. Now, the idea of a disgruntled murderer gathering nine victims and bumping them off slowly and cleverly, one by one, is a bit preposterous, especially in this day of Uzi machine guns and other high tech timesavers. But so cleverly is this story crafted that contemporary audiences are able to lose themselves in the drama and the terror, and suspend disbelief—for ninety minutes, at least.

Realistic dialogue

Beyond plot, what you should be most concerned with is that your script be peopled by believable characters who use realistic, interesting dialogue. Trust me, if you write a terrific story and a potential producer thinks it needs a modified end, or an older main character, or a different setting, she will let you know. Those are very fixable flaws and an excellent piece of work won't remain homeless because of them.

What will get "no thanks" is a hackneyed plot, flat, stereotyped characters, and trite, wooden dialogue.

Stilted dialogue is a common problem. If you want to know how real people speak, listen to them.

Don't be afraid of contractions! You'll seldom hear a person say, "I do not know what I am going to do about it." Most people will say "I don't know what I'm going to do about it." (The exceptions might be a person speaking stiffly, for emphasis, or a non-native speaker. For instance, on the television series *Star Trek: the Next Generation,* Mr. Data's "un-contracted" speech helps define his android character. This device is effective because the other cast members speak naturally.)

When in doubt, read your dialogue aloud.

People sometimes—uh, pause, when they speak. And sometimes they begin sentences with *and* or *but*. But I find writers, are, well . . . reluctant to use hesitation in dialogue.

If you want your hero to say, "Gloria, I—I'm confused. This feeling is so strong. And I don't know what's happening between us," then don't write "Gloria, I am confused. This feeling is so strong. I do not know what is happening between us."

Remember that theoretically the actor should utter only the lines you write. Yes, he may get fed up and throw in an ad-lib and the director may decide to use it. In that case you, the playwright, have not done your job. Dialogue that *works* doesn't tempt actors to rewrite.

(As I'm chasing you with the hickory switch, remember that an early production of your play is your chance to cut and polish for later audiences. Maybe the church-basement director won't allow you to rewrite dialogue mid-production, but you certainly may do so before you resubmit your play to larger regional companies.)

The professional look

Budding playwrights I have found avoid commas although I'm not sure why. Without commas the actors may forget to breathe if you follow me or at least they'll be confused.

An occasional *tpyo* is no big deal, but when every other line of a script contains misspellings like "ocaissional," "privledge," "thier," and "perference," can you blame me for concluding that the writer was just too lazy to consult his dictionary?

Grammar mistakes are irksome, too. No, you don't need perfect diction to write a good script. On the other hand, a writer who aspires to be a professional should certainly know the difference between "lie" and "lay." Your heroine may choose to lay on the bed, but that's a pretty good trick if she's alone in the room. And anyway, isn't this a G-rated production?

The writer should know whether his characters are doing well or doing good (or both). He should know whether that cool rebel flaunts rules or flouts them, and why that kid's new puppy can't be a gift from Daddy and I.

He should know if it's proper to contract *it is* as *its* or if it's not.

Of course, people don't speak perfectly, and judiciously placed solecisms make dialogue ring true. But when *every* character confuses

451

literal and figurative, and says fortuitous when he means fortunate, or infer when he means imply, I begin to suspect the blunders aren't the characters' but the writer's own.

Get the simple stuff straight: Split infinitives will continue to easily slip by me. Likewise sentence fragments.

Dialect trips up a lot of playwrights. No, you don't have to be African-American to create a character who speaks "Black English," and you don't have to be Chinese to write about a fellow from Beijing. But spare me your "G'wan, man, I be jivin' yo' funky sef'" and your "Solly, no speaky Engrish" and most of all, your Southern Belles who say "y'all" when they're speaking to only one person.

If you must indicate a dialect, do it like this:

BELLE

Why, I declare!
(Belle's thick Southern accent makes this sound like, "wha, ah declayuh.")

You need indicate this only once. The director will get the idea, and so will the actress. And both of them will thank you.

Try to keep your set directions to a minimum. Just tell us we're on a pretty beach at sunset, and let the set designer worry about the golden sun and the cry of the gulls and the sails like white wings against the horizon. And keep in mind that the more sets and props your play calls for, the more it will cost to produce.

Keep blocking—the stage directions that show the actors when and how to move—to a minimum. Entrances and exits must be indicated, of course, and long slow clinches are fun to write. But if Tom enters angry, the director will guess that he might slam the door. If Suzy is doing an audience aside, the director will definitely place her downstage. If the phone rings, he can figure out that Jan will need to cross to answer it. O.K.? So indicate movement when necessary to advance the story, and don't leave your actors rooted in place like young saplings. But do have mercy and let the poor director have something to do.

It's scary for a writer to pack up her work and send it out for strangers to peruse. Presumably the fledgling playwright reminds herself that stage companies—local to pro—*want* to like her work. They, like you, are in this biz for the love of the written and spoken word. And besides, who wouldn't like to discover the next Sam Shepard?

What amazes me is that with this in mind, so many scripts are sent out flawed not only in the ways we've discussed above, but badly typed and poorly photocopied.

Neatness counts. Your third-grade teacher told you that and you probably relearned it in college when your psych professor showed you a study indicating that of two term papers *identical* in content the one typed neatly earned higher grades than one full of typos and cross-outs.

So what's the trouble?

I know. It takes a long time to type a hundred pages, doesn't it? It hardly seems worthwhile to retype the whole thing every time you add a couple of paragraphs or take one away.

Stop! You're breaking my heart!

The fact is, if you want to be taken seriously, your script must look professional. That means $8\frac{1}{2}'' \times 11''$ white paper, black ink, margins at the top, bottom, and sides, numbered pages, and invisible corrections or none at all. Absolutely no strike-outs.

Submit a photocopy, never the original. If your script is returned to you clean, there's no reason not to send it out again, but spare us the dog-eared, coffee-ringed, penciled fourth-timers! No one likes to feel like last choice.

The standard format for a play script, adjusted according to number of acts and intended medium and audience, is available from many sources, including books from your local library. But you won't be penalized for indenting dialogue seventeen spaces instead of fifteen, or for numbering your pages at the top center instead of at the top right.

Cover letters

Whether you are submitting your work to a little theater, a contest committee, a cable television director, or a magazine editor, address your cover letter to a specific person *with whom you have spoken,* and who has agreed to look at your work. And I don't want to hear any whining about the cost of toll calls. First of all, most of these people aren't going to want to sit and chat (until they've read your script and realize you're brilliant and incredibly talented). And secondly, are you interested in getting produced or in sitting around complaining about an unavoidable business expense?

If you're submitting your script to a contest or television company, write ahead to request specific instructions about format, formal copyright registration, and whether a signed release is required. But when you want a local theater director to look at your work, it's still necessary to call ahead. By calling in advance, you can make sure that you have the correct contact name and address and that the director is willing to consider your work. Why waste time if she's not? Many directors will look at new plays only between seasons, and if you mail your script to a college theater department in June, it's likely to gather dust at least until September. And remember that your work should *always* go out with the copyright symbol (©) that indicates "copyright protected" at the right-hand top of the cover page.

Like your call, your cover letter should be brief. "Here's the script we talked about, and thanks for your time" will do. If you want to, add a few lines to mention your credits, if you have any, or your credentials, if they're germane. If your script is a comedy about a dairy farmer, and you happen to live on a dairy farm, say so.

Don't send a script replete with four-letter words to a children's playhouse, no matter how the kids in your neighborhood talk. And keep in mind that an all-nude sex comedy isn't likely to play in Peoria.

If you've done your homework and kept set and prop requirements to a minimum, you can say so in your cover letter. But don't use your cover letter to sell the script; it must sell itself. Don't write, "This is a wonderful, rip-roaring comedy full of hilarious moments in the wacky life of a dairy farmer."

With all the pitfalls I've described, what's the worst mistake aspiring playwrights make?

It's not confused plotting or flat characterization or trite dialogue. It's not sloppy typing or garbled cover letters. It's not even forgetting to put your name and phone number somewhere it can be found.

The worst mistake budding playwrights make is *not trying*. Not writing that script, or not polishing it, or not sending it out. Or sending it out only once, then giving up.

You may place your first script its first time out. Or you may place your tenth, its tenth time out, then watch it move along through little theaters and repertory ensembles. And as you look back on all the rejections, you'll realize that you learned something from every one.

I'm rooting for you, so get busy. And, hey—see you on Broadway!

➤➤91

ACT ONE, SCENE ONE:
BEGINNING A PLAY

BY JEFFREY SWEET

NOT SO VERY LONG AGO, IT WAS COMMON PRACTICE TO START A PLAY with a pair of secondary characters in a scene that ran along these lines:

MARY: Young Gregory was out late last night. He finally came back at three in the morning.
JOHN: Did he say anything about where he was or why there's such a big dent in his car?
MARY: No, but he'd had too much to drink, I can tell you that.
JOHN: I wonder if this has anything to do with the letter he received yesterday. The one that made him turn so pale.
MARY: I couldn't say. But this morning at breakfast you could have cut the tension between him and his parents with a knife.

All right, I'm exaggerating, but not by very much. The introductory conversation between two servants, or two gossips in the neighborhood, or a character newly returned from travels asking about events during his absence often kicked off the action. If you can call this action.

The idea behind such scenes was to pump the audience full of the information necessary to understand the subsequent events. Playgoers used to sit patiently for the first ten minutes or so knowing that enduring this sort of exposition was the price they had to pay in order to get to the good stuff. And I'm not talking only about plays by forgotten hacks. The only reason for the lame passage between Camillo and Archidamus in Act One, Scene One of Shakespeare's *The Winter's Tale* is to help the audience get its bearings. (Just because Shakespeare is the best doesn't mean he didn't make his share of mistakes.)

Generally speaking, plays start faster than they used to.

I think this is partially the result of television. Tune into a prime-time drama series, and you'll see something like this in the pre-credits action:

Stand-up comic onstage, telling jokes. Audience laughing. A woman in black carrying a purse slips in through the stage entrance. She moves to a door marked "Dressing Room," enters the room and closes the door behind her. Inside, she switches on the light, looks around, sees a framed photo of an attractive lady sitting on the make-up table. Suddenly, she smashes the photo onto the floor so that the glass from the frame breaks. Onstage, the comic says goodnight and takes his bows. In a cheerful mood, he goes to his dressing room. He switches on the light, takes a step and hears a crunch. He looks down on the floor and sees he has stepped on the glass from the smashed frame. Then he hears a voice: "You were really cooking tonight, Charley. You were killing them." He turns and sees the woman standing behind the door, pointing a small pistol at him. Sweat builds up on his lip. "And I always thought 'die laughing' was an expression," she says. Now she smiles. The camera pulls in on her finger on the trigger. Fade out. Bouncy music kicks in and the credits begin.

Do you want to know who the woman is, why she smashed the picture and whether she's going to ventilate Charley? You've got to stay tuned past the credits and the opening batch of commercials. If you do, you'll probably be willing to sit through some less immediately compelling stuff setting up other characters till the story returns to Charley and his mysterious visitor. And then, odds are, having invested this much time, you'll stick around for the rest of the show. By beginning with a provocative but unexplained incident, the story has been launched, caught your attention and given you enough reason to take the ride to the last stop.

The craft of writing for television has necessarily been affected by the nature of the audience's relation to the medium. Aware that the audience, holding channel changers in their hands, can switch to a competing program at any time, the writers know they have to serve up immediate and pressing reasons for viewers to stick around. Obviously, few are likely to stick around if the show starts with the equivalent of two servants relating offstage events. So a TV script tends to start with a scene that builds to a pressing dramatic question.

Of course, audiences don't come to the theater with channel changers in hand. But, after years of watching the box in their living rooms and getting used to the pacing of tales told there, they come to the theater in the habit of being plunged into the heart of the story quickly. To grab the playgoer fast, many contemporary playwrights have borrowed a leaf from television's book by beginning their plays with characters in the middle of high-energy sequences equivalent to the one introducing Charley's dilemma.

John Guare's remarkable play, *Six Degrees of Separation,* starts with two of the leading characters, Ouisa and Flan Kittredge, excitedly telling the audience about their narrow escape moments before from some unnamed threat, checking to see that none of their valuables has been stolen, savoring how close they may have come to death. Having established their hysteria, Guare then has them take us back several hours to a lower-key scene anticipating the arrival of a friend who is to join them for dinner. With the benefit of hindsight, we know that they will shortly be hyperventilating, and so we watch carefully to see what part this dinner will play in the chain of events that leads to their alarums.

Guare could very well have *started* with the Kittredges discussing their dinner plans and then proceeding with the rest of the play as written. Doing this would not have meant omitting any of his story. But, by kicking the play off with the two in such an agitated state and then flashing back, Guare makes the audience sit up and take notice from the first moment. No coy wooing of the playgoer here; he snares our interest instantly. Knowing that the flashback holds the answer to the question, "What's making the Kittredges so upset?," the audience pays closer attention to the lower-key scene that follows than they would have if the play had started with that scene.

I'm not suggesting that all plays should begin in the middle of action, but quite a few would be improved if they did. I asked the members of a playwriting workshop I run to bring in scripts they were working on, and, as an experiment, we read excerpts from them, each time starting on page ten. In all but two cases, the writers decided their plays actually began better on their tenth pages than on their firsts.

What information was contained in the missing pages? My students discovered that most of it was implicit in the scenes from page 10 on. By beginning in the *middle* of dramatic action—instead of setting up the circumstances in the first ten pages—the playwrights gave the audience the fun of figuring out the circumstances for themselves. Gone were the dull stretches of characters entering the stage, pouring drinks, and slipping in nuggets of self-introduction. Gone, too, were the one-way phone calls designed to sneak in exposition. Rather than switching on and warming up the scripts' motors and then coaxing them up to speed, the plays now had a sense of urgency from the word go, and that urgency made them compelling.

The opening of a play not only gets the story started, it also makes a contract with the audience. The first few minutes virtually announce, "This is the kind of play we're doing," and the audience sets its expectations accordingly. We watch different genres with different expectations. It is very important, then, for the opening of your script to set the audience's expectations correctly. If you break a promise to a friend in real life, you're likely to lose the trust and confidence of that friend. Break a promise to the people who have paid to see your play, and they will respond with confusion and irritation. If, for instance, you begin your play with a pair of bewigged fops trading quips in blank verse, you'd better not suddenly switch in the middle of the second act to a modern psychological thriller. Raising the curtain on a solo figure in black tights on a bare stage miming the life cycle would be a misleading introduction to a Neil Simon-style domestic comedy.

This may sound like very obvious advice, but some very savvy theatrical talents nearly lost a great musical because of such a miscalculation. *A Funny Thing Happened on the Way to the Forum* was trying out in a pre-Broadway engagement in Washington in 1962. According to all accounts, the show was substantially the one we've come to know, but the audiences weren't taking to it. The laughs were few and far between, and each night a dismaying chunk of the audience disappeared at intermission. The perplexed creative team—which included such celebrated figures as George Abbott, Larry Gelbart, Bert Shevelove and Stephen Sondheim—asked director-choreographer Jerome Robbins to take a look and tell them where they were going wrong.

After the performance, Robbins informed them that the problem was with the opening number, a light-hearted little tune called "Love is in the Air," which promised a romantic frolic. What followed instead, however, was an evening of broad jokes, slapstick, and farcical intrigue. Robbins said what was needed was an opening that *promised* broad jokes, slapstick, and farcical intrigue. An opening, he insisted, should promise the audience what in fact a show is going to deliver.

Composer-lyricist Stephen Sondheim went to his piano and wrote a song entitled, "Comedy Tonight," which did just that. According to legend, as soon as it was put in, the reaction to the show turned around completely. What had previously played to indifference now brought cheers. *A Funny Thing Happened* went on to New York, where it received glowing reviews and was proclaimed a hit, all because the opening was changed. It is now counted a classic musical comedy.

Not only do you establish the genre of a show in the first few minutes, you also establish stylistic rights. At the beginning of *Six Degrees of Separation,* Guare swiftly signals the audience that he reserves the right to 1) have any of his characters, at the drop of a hat and without self-consciousness, address the audience directly, and 2) with the briefest of transitions, leap to any other time or place in the story. And, indeed, throughout the script, both major and minor characters feel no compunction about making eye contact with a theater full of playgoers and speaking their minds. What's more, scenes move abruptly back and forth in time and jump, without second thought, from the Kittredges' fancy apartment to Central Park to Greenwich Village and wherever else it is necessary to go to witness the essential events of the story. And, oh yes, the number of laughs at the show's beginning clearly indicates the audience is in for a comedy.

It is a truism among musical theater writers that the opening number is usually the one you write last, because it is only after you've finished the rest of the show that you know what the opening should prepare the audience for. Straight plays are structurally less complicated than musicals, but upon completing a draft, a smart dramatist looks closely at the opening few pages to see if they correctly establish the world and style of the two hours to follow. The audience isn't likely to go through your door if you don't offer them the key to unlock it.

➤➤ 92

BLUEPRINT FOR WRITING A PLAY

BY PETER SAGAL

IF I WEREN'T A PLAYWRIGHT, I'D BE AN ARCHITECT, WHICH ON CERtain days I think is the finest kind of artist there is, because architects create art that is indisputably useful, necessary: Architecture is the art that stitches together the seams of the physical environment. But since I can't draw, I can't do math, and I'm too lazy to undergo all that study, I have to settle for being a playwright. I comfort myself, though, by imagining plays as architecture: art defined by its function, articulated by structure, inspired by the truths about the people who are to use it. Plays, like architecture, are, or should be, useful; they should express their beauty through purpose sheathed with ornament.

So one should go about the business of writing a play with all the dedication, discipline, knowledge, etc. that any fine art requires, but something else, too—something shared again with architecture, and that is a sense of *responsibility*. The architect knows that his or her building may or may not be admired by passers-by, but most definitely it will be used; a mistake on the drawing board may result in discomfort and displeasure for unknown thousands whom the architect failed by making a building that may have been fashionable or pretty but did not *work*, though architects ask people to live and perform their professional and personal functions within such a building. We playwrights ask less but still something substantial: We ask for time. Give us two or three hours of your life, two or three hours that can never be replaced, and we will enclose you in a soundproof room, turn off the lights so you can't read, and forbid you to talk, and we promise that it will be worthwhile.

Your first responsibility as a playwright is to waste no one's time. Consider your audience's attention as a precious gift, a gem, and if you fumble, it's lost forever. Time is a sacred thing, because everyone has only a finite supply of it.

461

Your job as a playwright, then, is to create a series of events, conversations, and images so important that it's worth asking the audience to give up their lives for a while and listen. I think this is the most difficult task in all writing, with the possible exception of book-length epic poetry. You do not have the expansive freedom of the novelist, or the factual safety net of the journalist. There's no tolerance for sloppiness; writing a play is done with a gun to the head. Here's how to do it:

Love your art

The theater won't pay you, won't comfort you, will provide you with little reward, and for that reward will drain your blood. In the best case your writing will be subject to the whims and caprices of actors, technicians, directors, producers; in the worst case, it will be ignored. If very, very successful, it will reach a tiny fraction of the people who watch "Married With Children" on TV, and your financial remuneration will be an even tinier fraction of the amount received by the writers who produce that work and others like it. Don't write for the theater if you want to write for television or the movies, or even for Broadway, which is a fictional place, like the Big Rock Candy Mountain. Write for yourself; write because if you don't you'll go crazy. Write because nothing else in your life compares to the power of creating your own worlds. Write plays because you believe that the experience of people gathering in a theater to see a play is nothing less than sacred. If you don't have the strength of this quasi-religious conviction, then the trials ahead could well overwhelm you.

Study your art

I am continually amazed by how many aspiring playwrights are ignorant of dramatic writing outside of a narrow canon of recognized giants: Shakespeare, Tennessee Williams, Arthur Miller, David Mamet, Sam Shepard, etc. In many cases, the writer sets out to imitate one or more of them. One problem, of course, is that these writers are geniuses, and you can't just imitate their work.

The other problem is that they *aren't* geniuses at all; they were and are working writers who slogged away for years and years, and most of them did their slogging in the theater. There isn't a single great writer for the theater who did not spend a long apprenticeship: Shake-

462

speare, for example, started with the Lord Chamberlain's Men as an actor, writing plays himself only after he had performed uncounted dozens of other, now unknown works.

Such a lengthy servitude isn't necessary, but it is foolish not to recognize such problems as how to make the stage relevant to your life and the lives around you. If you live in a city with an active theater scene, go all the time, particularly to the new plays; the failures will be as educational as the few successes. If you don't have that luxury, then read as much as you can: Read your peers in American playwriting (Tony Kushner, Marlane Meyer, Neal Bell, Jose Rivera, Migdalia Cruz, Wendy Hammond, etc., etc.) and their counterparts in Great Britain; read plays from non-English speaking and non-Western traditions. You will come across hundreds of good ideas and save yourself from making thousands of mistakes. It is idiotic to try to invent the theater from scratch every time you sit down. Depart and rebel, by all means, but know what you are rebelling against.

I am very skeptical of books and articles that offer "rules" for writing, which is why I refuse to offer any specific suggestions to aspiring playwrights, such as, "start in the middle," "make the exposition active," etc. I have arrived at my own set of principles of dramatic writing, but they describe not so much how to write a play, as the kind of play I like. For every one of those rules, there's an exception, and in many cases, the exceptions are brilliant plays. For example, I don't like to have my characters address the audience, offering information about the other characters. That means I'll never write *The Glass Menagerie* or *The Marriage of Bette and Boo,* or even *Henry V,* among the many other plays I admire. The theater, more than any other form of writing, is a living thing: It grows and changes, departing from what just happened and pointing toward what's next. Rules hinder evolution. Further, when you sit down to write, you should be writing from an interior vision of what *your* play *is,* not some acquired idea of what *a* play is *like.* Television writers follow rules, because people who watch television know what they want and watch TV, expecting to get just that. This is the opposite of theater.

Practice your art

Writers in any form have to confront and control the hunger for acclaim. In the theater, this becomes even more difficult because, first, you are collaborating with actors and other artists who are eager to make their mark, and more important, your work is read out loud to large groups of people who might very well make loud noises that indicate approval (or disapproval). It becomes very tempting to get those words out of the word processor, into the hands of actors, and up in front of the audience, and to let the magic of the moment make up for any shortcomings. However, if you remember what I said about responsibility, you will see that this is a pernicious urge to be avoided. The rules of discipline, writing, and constant revision hold as much in playwriting as in poetry—don't buy into the old adage that a playscript is a "blueprint" and can slide by on heart alone. It *is* a blueprint, and it had better be a perfect blueprint or this house won't stand.

So write, write, write; experiment with sound and language and vision and structure. Do not be indulgent. Do not be lazy. Do not put less than perfect words on a stage and hope that the audience will buy them. Don't try to dazzle. Don't coast. Whatever you put on a page, make it your own. Remember, when you sit down to write a play, you are taking the future of an ancient and fragile art form in your hands: A bad play strikes another blow at it, in these wounded and wounding times; a good play breathes new life into the theater, and sends it striding on into a few more hearts, which may, in turn, nourish it after us.

➤➤ 93

ADVICE TO PLAYWRIGHTS

By Janet Neipris

WHEN I BEGIN A PLAYWRITING CLASS, THE FIRST LECTURE IS Fifty Rules to Follow When Writing a Play. Of the fifty rules, forty-nine are structural; only the fiftieth is practical. That rule is, "Make certain you love this project, that you have passion for this play, because you will be working on it for five to ten years, and it is passion that will sustain you." Talent is only one part of playwriting, craft is another, and the third, and perhaps most important, is perseverance.

Recently, I began to write a play at the suggestion of an artistic director of a theatre. The subject—the life and loves of an eminent American playwright—was fascinating, filled with opportunities for research, and eminently commercial. It would be hard to believe this project would not excite any living playwright.

So, I began. But, the more research I did, and the more I learned, the less I was in love with the subject. It remained a good idea, but not for me. The director, who had suggested the play and had promised a staged reading of it, called to ask, "Do you hear the play singing yet?" "No," I replied, "but that will come."

Well, it never did. So, after six months of work, many scenes outlined and written, but no fire from inside, I abandoned the project. It was the most courageous thing I've ever done as a playwright, and with it came the conviction that I was never going to write about something I didn't love. From that moment on, I was certain my actions matched the practical advice I always give young playwrights: WRITE FROM THE HEART.

WRITING YOUR PLAY

1. First, always write out of *passion*. Passion is what sustains perseverance. You have to believe that the play you are writing *must* be

written, and that you are the only one who could tell the story you want to tell in exactly this way.

2. Second, you should be convinced your play is worth developing *artistically,* that its subject matter is of significance and is identifiable to an audience. Always remember you are crafting a piece of dramatic literature. Significant doesn't necessarily mean recreating the Civil War on stage, but rather, that you are writing about a subject that is common to the human heart.

3. Then, you must be convinced your play is worth developing *commercially,* and that an audience will want to pay to come to see it. Your play should either entertain, question, or challenge, and at best, do all three.

4. Always write with the *practical* elements in mind—the set design, costumes, and props. For example, an action that involves fifty elephants or twenty minor characters or a waterfall is certainly impractical, both technically and financially. The writer can, however, be practical without compromising his or her art. For example, if a waterfall is integral to the plot, maybe slides could be suggested, or a backdrop, or sound.

5. Make sure your play is not exactly like this season's hit. The theatre traditionally honors quality, craft, and originality. To create, after all, means to make something where there once was nothing. To create suggests imagining.

6. Write a play that does more than simply mirror reality. Reality is never enough for a complete artistic piece. It is only a beginning. If the audience wanted simple reality, they could just open their windows and look out. Also, be certain never to use a real name for any of your characters. It is the playwright's job to *start* with reality, then *transform* it into a dramatic story.

7. Don't expect to get your script right the first time. You are trying to portray *unique* characters in *conflict,* which leads to *confrontation, resolution,* and *change.* The first draft serves to help you find out what you are writing about. The subsequent drafts, the *rewrites,* are about craft.

8. Before you send the manuscript out, make certain it is the best you can make it. Competition is high, but so is expectation when any publisher or theatre receives a new play. The first chance is the best

chance, so you want to give editors, artistic directors, literary managers, possible producers, and readers the best script possible.

HOW TO BREAK IN

Getting an agent

Do you need an agent in order to get a play produced? Not necessarily, as many theatres and contests do accept scripts that are not represented by an agent. However, having an agent will make it easier to ensure that your script gets a reading. In cases where a regional theatre does require representation, an agent is a necessity. In addition, an agent can be helpful in negotiating a contract with a theatre, a contract that represents you, the playwright, professionally and financially.

1. Get a list of drama agents from one of the following sources:

a. *Dramatists Sourcebook,* published by Theatre Communications Group (TCG), 355 Lexington Ave., New York, NY 10017.
b. *The Dramatists Guild Quarterly,* Summer Directory, published annually by the Dramatists Guild, 234 W. 44th St., Sardi Building, New York, NY 10036.

2. Research *which* agents represent *the kind of plays you write* by reading volumes of *The Best Plays* and *Short Plays* published annually and available in most public libraries. Additional sources include the general drama sections of large bookstores and libraries.

3. Write query letters to agents of interest to you, describing your play briefly and any possible readings or productions of the play. Also, if you have a recommendation from another writer, you can mention the name, but get permission from the writer first.

Then, ask the agent if you may send a script. If you've had no answer a month after sending your script, send a short polite letter asking about its status.

Getting a reading or production

1. Go to local productions in order to familiarize yourself with local directors and actors. Start a notebook listing actors and directors you are interested in working with in the future.

2. Subscribe to *The Dramatists Guild Quarterly,* which lists production possibilities and contests, many of which include production opportunities.

3. Purchase a copy of the *Theatre Directory* from Theatre Communications Group, 355 Lexington Ave., New York, NY 10017. This lists regional theatres and rules for submission of scripts.

4. Join a local theatre group that does play readings and productions. There are such groups in many communities, either attached to a regional theatre or working independently.

5. Try to set up a reading locally or even in your own home. First, discuss your script with a local professional director. Make a list of questions you want to ask about themes, tone, focus, possible cuts, and casting. If you can't make a connection with a local director, you might try to direct this first read-through yourself.

Then, cast the play with local actors or friends. The main purpose of this first reading is for the playwright to "hear" the play. This reading will serve both as an opportunity to plan your second draft of the play, and also for you to align yourself, if possible, with actors and directors in your community. It never hurts to have an actor or director interested in your script. A passionate actor or director who has a script he or she wants to perform or direct is a gift to any playwright.

Getting the play up and alive in any way you can means the project is *in process,* and the *process* of readings and workshop productions (limited rehearsal, staging, and performances) is what ultimately leads to productions.

Don't expect perfection from a reading or production. You are trying to master your craft and improve your playwriting skills. The purpose of early readings or productions is to do your best work, take notes, then rewrite.

Be patient. Playwriting is about talent, craft, and most of all, perseverance and patience. Remember that Beckett sent out the completed draft of *Waiting For Godot* thirty-two times before it was accepted for production.

Getting published

Publishers of plays are listed in the *Dramatists Sourcebook.* A play can only be published if it has been produced, has received good notices, and is deemed commercial, meaning that it will have a future life in regional, community, high school and college theatres. Plays also get published as part of contests.

So, in order to be published, you need either to have a production or win a contest. There are exceptions to these rules, but they are rare. The major publishers of plays are the Dramatists Play Service and the Samuel French Company, as well as Baker's Plays, which publishes children's plays. There are, however, a growing number of smaller and reputable dramatic publishing companies.

Also, there are many young playwrights' competitions throughout the country. If you are a student, consult your English or drama teacher for details. Many of these contests include publication.

Remember, the play belongs to you. Ultimately, if the work is good and you have the endurance of the long distance runner, you will write the play, rewrite, be produced and be published.

>> JUVENILE AND YOUNG ADULT

>> 94

WHY WRITE FOR CHILDREN?

BY ELOISE MCGRAW

WHY DO YOU CHOOSE TO WRITE FOR CHILDREN?" IS A QUESTION I'M often asked. I never have a good simple answer because my reasons are not simple at all. A better question might be not *why* but *how* do I—does anybody—write for the children of today, who are growing up in a world of grim realities that they must take as given and learn to cope with?

One answer to that question is that we must write fiction dealing directly and honestly with these realities, in order to help young readers cope.

Plainly, an aging writer like me, product of a sheltered and lucky life, is not ideal for this job. Nor was the younger—and equally sheltered—writer I was when I first grappled with the problem.

For this is not a new question. A quarter century ago, about the time drugs arrived on junior high school grounds, it suddenly became *the* question among children's writers and editors and other literary people. There was a great deal of talk about the "New Realism" and the "nitty-gritty," and I, for one, worried about it a lot. I was not writing the kind of books that would come to grips with the nitty-gritty, about which I knew very little. I knew I couldn't—what's more, I didn't want to. Even if I tried, they'd be second-rate books. My choice was plain: to go on writing the books I wanted to write (unfashionable, irrelevant or not) or quit writing.

I stuck to my particular cobbler's last, and it turned out to be the sensible choice; the only one, for me. I think it's the sensible choice for children's writers today. Those writers who know what they're talking about and have something real to say about it, will and should write of the violent and gun-ridden world today's children have had foisted upon them. But we others need not leave the field. There is plenty for us to say, too.

What does any child reader, regardless of the traumas of modern-day living, most want and need (consciously or not) from what he reads? It is not necessarily a mirror-image of his own daily life. Back in the early 1970s when the question surfaced before, I read a review by B. J. Chute of a nonfiction book that dealt in part with this issue. The book was excellent and the review favorable, but in Chute's opinion the author "rather underestimates the ability of the so-called under-privileged child to relate to almost any theme, when she asks: 'How do you begin a book that will seem novel and important to children who have known only slums and the worst life has to offer?' Well—" says Chute, "you might begin it, *'Now, my dears,' said old Mrs. Rabbit one morning,* or, *Where's Papa going with that ax?* or *Once upon a time.*" The review goes on to take note of a 10-year-old boy in a Harlem slum who read the myth of Icarus "and said, with touching self-confidence, 'The Greeks thought up this good fable to help me.'"

It is too easy for reading experts (all of them adults) to discuss "the Child." It is no generic "Child" who reads our books, only individual children, and while one child may seize eagerly on a story that mirrors his own life and problems and perhaps makes him feel he is not alone, the next child will turn decisively to something entirely different. To find what? Perspective, maybe. A bigger world.

C. S. Lewis draws a wonderful picture of the effect some fiction can have upon a reader. Suppose, he says, we were all on a ship, and there was trouble among the stewards, one of whom finally slips away from the fierce disputing in the pantries below to take a breather on deck. "Up there, he would taste the salt, he would see the vastness of the water . . . He would remember things like fog, storms, and ice. . . ." Lewis adds that some stories are like that visit to the deck. "They cool us."

In my childhood, I liked to read about characters as different from me as possible, living in foreign or fantastic places, in other times and circumstances. *Not* about children like me—I already knew about them. I can't possibly have been unique. Surely, many children of today who live lives of grim survival must already know all they care to know about such lives, and long for tales of something different, something better. Judging from letters I get from readers, my books speak with meaning and relevance to a good number of today's children, even when I am talking about a boy living three thousand years ago in ancient Egypt, or one roaming the thinly populated Oregon country in the 1840s, or a girl cut adrift in the aftermath of a war nearly ten centuries past. In fact, my modern 4th-to-7th-grade readers respond *especially* to those distant-in-time-and-space boys and girls—characters who apparently speak as directly to them as those in my contemporary novels. But my modern novels have also brought some letters that surprised me, and taught me all over again that children bring questions to fiction that the writer never thought of, and get answers the writer never knew were there.

Not only historical time and distance, but remote planets or imaginary worlds can create a magic far beyond a mere change of scene, and children aren't the only readers who love fairy stories. Indeed, not all children do love them, but as Tolkien's *The Lord of the Rings* so amply proved, a great many grownups do. Tolkien's own theory regarding the appeal of fairy stories is that they allow the reader to become a "sub-creator," a partner in creating a world of his own. Whatever the reason, the popularity of fantasy and science fiction, dragons and rocket ships and wizards has surely never been greater, and it cuts across all age groups, from toddler to senior citizen.

I don't think one can label this sort of thing "escape," unless it is escape from narrow vision, a means of coming up on deck to view a vast starry night. Human beings need boosting out of the groove—pleasant or unpleasant—of daily life, need glimpses of the huge plain of possible experience the groove runs through. Child or adult, we need the shock of sudden perspective, the sight of an unknown, wildly unfamiliar world. An unblinking stare at the all-too-familiar violent streets will seldom give us that. Good imagining often will.

I still have not answered that recurring question—why do I, why do we children's writers, write for youngsters, not for adults?

The slightly supercilious tone in which the question is often asked tends to make writers bristle. Lewis takes it as implying arrested development, and retorts that to treat *adult* as a word of approval, to blush at the suspicion of being childish, is itself a mark of childishness. He thinks all writers—those who write for children and those who don't—simply choose the form best suited to the particular stories they want to tell. Isaac Bashevis Singer, on the occasion of accepting a National Book Award for children's literature, listed ten reasons he wrote for children—out of the five hundred he claimed he had in mind. Some of the least acerbic are: "Children read books, not reviews. They have no use for psychology and detest sociology. They don't try to understand *Finnegans Wake.* They still believe in God, the family, angels, devils, witches, goblins, logic, clarity, punctuation, and other such obsolete stuff. . . ."

My view—and observation—is that any writer soon finds a natural form, a personal gesture, because ideas keep arriving in that form. For example, the characters shaping themselves in my own mind usually turn out to be between ten and fourteen years old. This is no accident; I find children of that age more interesting, as characters to write about, than adults. Adults tend to be already jelled. Deceiving as appearances sometimes are, most grownups have pretty well become whatever they're going to be. A child of eleven or twelve is just in the process of *becoming,* just growing aware of that process, often puzzled by it, and busy coming to grips with how to cope with it. It is at this point in a character's life that I find fertile soil.

So—why do I write for children? Because I like telling stories, specifically the ones *I* want to tell, about the characters that come into *my* head, and I like my freedom to do it the way I choose. And because for me, too, as I write about those other worlds my characters live in, it is a way to leave the hot, crowded rooms below and come up on deck.

➤➤ 95

WRITING MYSTERIES FOR YOUNG READERS

BY WILLO DAVIS ROBERTS

WHAT DOES IT TAKE TO WRITE MYSTERIES FOR YOUNG PEOPLE?

Basically, the requirements are the same as when you write for adults: good characterization, fast-moving plot, entertaining and credible dialogue, and a satisfying resolution. Additionally, however, juvenile book editors expect authors to *be* childlike in their writing, to identify with the targeted age group.

This doesn't mean writing down to young readers; on the contrary, they tend to be discerning and have high standards. I write for them the same way I write for adults—as intelligent, caring, responsible individuals. In many ways I've stayed 11 years old. Certainly, I retain vivid memories of what it was like to be that age, and my books generate numerous letters from readers who identify with my characters in a personal way.

Beginnings with a punchy narrative hook are a must. Start the story on page one. If you can grab a potential reader in the first paragraph, you're off to a good start.

Consider this one, from my book *Nightmare:*

Seconds before the windshield shattered into a crazed, opaque spider web pattern, Nick saw the terrified face that would remain forever imprinted on his mind: eyes wide and unseeing, mouth stretched in a grimace of horror. Nick didn't hear the scream, but he knew there had to be one.

By the bottom of the first page, the reader learns that Nick is having a nightmare about a recent event, and there's a flashback that then leads up to the death of the stranger who fell onto Nick's car. Readers have also learned about Nick's background, his family relationships, and so on. Once it's been established that this is an *action* book, and full of suspense, the reader will be willing to settle for a slower pace until the horror builds again.

The Pet Sitting Peril begins this way:

The hall light was out again. . . . It was the third time in a week. . . . It wasn't that he was afraid of the dark, like a little kid. After all, he was nearly twelve. It was only that it seemed peculiar for a light bulb not to last more than a few days at a time.

A line on page two establishes the boy's uneasy conviction that someone is unscrewing bulbs in a spooky old house. The atmosphere is set. Something fishy is going on. The reader will accept a few pages of background before the suspense once more emerges.

Scared Stiff simply opens with a hint that bad things are coming:

Trouble comes in threes, Pa always said. I knew it was true. When my little brother Kenny broke his arm falling out of a tree, Pa said there'd be two more catastrophes before long, and sure enough, there were.

Because I often base characters on my own children (or, now, my grandchildren), they come alive. They seem real. Readers identify with them strongly, sympathize with them. If you don't know any children the ages of those you write about, find some: in your neighborhood or in a local school.

Your best source for characters may well be yourself. I remember being poor, shy, having an inferiority complex. Children today face far more danger that we did in the thirties and forties. Drugs, crime, broken families, and a breakdown of traditional values make life riskier than it used to be.

But young people have the same basic needs and desires they've always had: families, security, friends, approval, love, recognition. They enjoy adventure; they love a story that scares them. They want to read about kids like themselves who have overcome great odds, who have solved problems, who have triumphed over adversity. Remember what was important to you at 10 or 12, then figure out what the contemporary equivalent would be.

My personal opinions and points of view often appear as those of my primary characters. But don't preach, no matter how strongly you feel about an issue; a *character* may be preachy, but should then be balanced by the views of another character. In my book, *Twisted Sum-*

mer, the children are appalled at being expected to attend a funeral; adult characters provide the necessary counterpoint by holding a memorial service.

Recollections of feelings and impressions from childhood filter into every one of my manuscripts. The aroma of ripe strawberries under a summer sun; my mortification at being cross-examined—and obviously found wanting—by a prominent lady from the church I attended; wearing hand-me-down clothes; the joy of having a whole dollar to spend at the country fair; walking barefoot on the beach; being rescued by a friend when I overestimated my swimming stamina; entering a new class of strangers and knowing I was plain and skinny and unimpressive. All these experiences contribute to my perceptions of the child in my story.

For the most part I write about ordinary people caught up in extraordinary events; everyday children who get involved with criminals (*No Monsters in the Closet, What Could Go Wrong?,* and *Caught!*) and seek their own, kid-level solutions. My recent book, *The Absolutely True Story of My Trip to Yellowstone with the Terrible Rubes,* was based on a trip we took by motorhome with six grandchildren. Did I steal the funny things they said and did? You bet! (I made up the mystery part.)

Adversity is a great place to begin any story. After my father and several of my friends told me about being mistreated as children, I wrote about child abuse, in *Don't Hurt Laurie!* In *Megan's Island* the protagonist struggled, as I did, through many moves and changes in schools that prevented her from either making any friends or learning much of anything. I called on my own teen experience in writing *Baby-Sitting Is A Dangerous Job.*

Every word should be relevant, even in a book-length story. If you've written a scene that doesn't move the story forward, cut it out. And remember that in order to be a story, rather than a slice of life, the primary characters have to be moving toward solving a problem or reaching a goal. Make that problem or goal evident from the beginning. If the middle of the book bogs down, my favorite remedy is to throw another obstacle in the way of the protagonist's progress.

It is perfectly acceptable to use natural disasters—fire, floods, storms, accidents—as obstacles. Do *not* use these events to resolve the puzzle or effect a rescue. Character action should do that.

The beginning writer often tries to write dialogue that "sounds real." There's a risk here. Actual conversation is often full of meaningless and repetitious words and phrases. You might have a character who says, "you know," frequently, but to a reader this quickly becomes tedious. If your characters are eating, you can put in an occasional request for the mustard, but nobody wants to read every "please pass the salt." Read dialogue by the best writers, then follow their examples and practice writing crisp, concise exchanges.

A novice often falls into error by making every character sound alike. Each should have his own vocabulary, emphasis, attitude. As an exercise to vary dialogue, try this: Imagine a woman who has just severely damaged the family car. Write what each of the following people says when she tells them: the mailman (unaffected emotionally or financially); her children (appalled and apprehensive); her mother (concerned about her safety and the husband's reaction); her husband (furious, dismayed, panicked about the cost or loss of insurance, after initial concern for her possible injury); her best friend (sympathy and support). Each of them will have a distinct, separate voice. So should each character.

If you're trying for realism, remember that most parents are caring and conscientious, and probably more sensible than their children. If you portray parents who are selfish and neglectful, to the point where the child suffers considerable anguish over his situation, be sure to indicate that this is *not* common among parents. I once made the mistake of giving my grandchildren what I thought was an amusing book in which the father was a fool in everything he did. My son informed me that he resented having to read a story in which the father came off as a moron. I got the message.

Humor, if not at the expense of parents, teachers, or some unfortunate child, is welcome. Teachers love rereading *The Girl With the Silver Eyes* and *The Magic Book,* because along with laughing students, they have fun. The same is true of *The Minden Curse* and *More Minden Curses,* in which Danny's Irish wolfhound is the biggest and homeliest dog imaginable, and the confusion and trouble he creates is a laughing matter to everyone but Danny and his teacher. But the humor pokes fun at no one, only at life.

It's important to maintain suspense throughout the book. Get as close to the last page as you can before letting the reader off the hook.

Make necessary explanations before the protagonist is out of danger or the last crucial piece of the puzzle falls into place. And keep those explanations brief, or tension will lag. Don't rescue the main character—or let him rescue himself—until the last moment. Remember that the ending is what the reader has been anticipating, the reasons he's kept on reading till that point. He's hoping for a real zinger, for a satisfactory solution, right at the last.

Several other points deserve mention. Avoid writing in a way that would make your book quickly dated. Simply have your characters drop coins into a pay phone, buy movie tickets, get a candy bar, without mentioning specific costs or price.

Slang is trickier. Contemporary slang changes very quickly; what sounds "with it" today may be silly and/or incomprehensible by the time the book appears in print a year or more down the road. Some editors advise avoiding slang altogether, but this is hard to do and still have young characters appear normal.

Profanity may be easier to handle than slang. It is simple to say "he swore" or "he cursed" or some other phrase to convey a character's fury or frustration, without using specific words that may be offensive to some readers.

A final point: Many authors of children's books use crimes that are not major felonies in their mysteries. I almost always write about real crimes—kidnapping, murder, extortion, money laundering, etc.—in which young characters become trapped. I have been criticized for this realism, but almost never by the young readers, who often repeat in letters to me the most graphic or terrifying segments. This is something each writer will have to decide for herself, but don't rule out major crime, thinking it's totally inappropriate for 9- to 12-year-olds. It's all in how you handle it.

Do I write almost exclusively for young people because it's easier? No. In some ways it's more difficult. So if you decide to take an idea you had for an adult mystery and turn it into a juvenile or young adult novel, do it because you like children, identify with them, enjoy them, and can put yourself into the skin of a 12-year-old for 120 to 150 pages.

Chances are the results of your efforts won't be any easier to sell than if you'd written for an adult audience. But maybe you'll turn out a little gem that will become a classic for young readers.

>> 96

MAKING YOUR STORY BREATHE

BY NORMA FOX MAZER

WHEN I PICK UP A BOOK IN THE LIBRARY OR THE BOOKSTORE, I ALWAYS want to know what it's about. Yet when I'm asked the same question about a story on which I'm working, I stumble anxiously over my words. I don't want to answer! I dislike taking the fascination of creating a world and characters and reducing it to a few phrases. All the same, answering this question is what I force myself to do for every book I write. Ideally, I know what the book is "about" (and can state it in a single sentence) *before* I start writing. Sometimes this actually happens.

One night years ago, while I was washing dishes, a sentence appeared in my head. I say "appeared" because it was so clear I seemed to see it: "A girl is kidnapped by her father." I knew at once that I'd been given a gift: a story in seven words. The hard work was over. All I had to do now was ask the myriad questions implicit in that sentence—and answer them by telling a good story. Those questions, beginning with *why? how? when?*, became *Taking Terri Mueller.*

More often, though, rather than a gift, what I have is a muddle. I hate to confess this, after so many years of writing. Doing it right seems simple: Decide what you're going to write about, work a story around it, and go to it. Yeeeaaah! I have written and rewritten hundreds of pages and found myself still sweating out what the story is really about. This happened with my novel, *Missing Pieces.* I began by wanting to write about a close-knit, self-sufficient female household: mother, daughter, and elderly aunt. Right away, I knew the odd house they live in (built on a hill, tiny black-and-white tiles in the hall, kitchen in the basement . . .), I knew Aunt Zis, with her pride and bony shoulders, and I knew a little about Jessie—fuzzy eyebrows and a mouth that worked overtime.

482

I developed Jessie, and a couple of friends for her, each with her own story (racism, shyness); threw in a boy; worked up a love life for her overweight mother, Maribeth; and in an escalating series of scenes went after the main story: the terrors of aging (beloved Aunt Zis) as seen through Jessie's eyes and heart. Early on, to explain this manless family, I wrote a few sentences abut Jessie's father, "the disappearing dude," as she jauntily called him, who'd taken off when she was small.

O.K. The usual rounds of writing and rewriting, and off to the editor at last. The manuscript came back with a three-page comment that boiled down to: too many stories, not enough focus. And, oh, by the way, I'm really interested in that father.

My initial reaction was a snappish, "Well, I'm not!" An attitude. It lasted overnight. But by morning the thought was, "Oh . . . actually, I'm kind of interested in the dude, myself."

I began to tell the same story, but in a new light, focusing on Jessie and her father. I threw out the old title, deleted scenes, recast others, created new ones. Still, it took at least one more major revision before I could put the story into this sentence: *A girl whose father left her years ago is tormented by her desire to know why he did it and who he really was.*

Once a premise is clear, it always seems obvious, and I'm amazed that it eluded me for so long. After it's nailed down, the story opens up for me, and I can go to work on making it breathe. That single sentence (sometimes paragraph) is the spine of the story; around it grows the flesh and blood. And this is where the tools of the trade come into play: *narrative, dialogue, characterization.*

I work to make my story live and breathe (or appear to, anyway; we are illusionists only) in a variety of ways, some hard to describe, others quite pragmatic. Let me get the hard-to-describe stuff out of the way. It has to do with getting to a place that I think of as the free place. In that place, there are no constraints. Scenes appear in my head, words appear on the screen. There is some level of truth or sight here that is exhilarating. It's like crossing a border. On this side, the usual side, I'm walking a path through a dim woods, moving along, but not seeing enough. There are shadows everywhere, and I'm anxious about getting where I'm going.

If I'm lucky and cross the border, everything changes, becomes lighter, vaster, more open. An endless meadow in which I romp and fly. How to get into that meadow, where I'd like to abide? It's not exactly sheer chance, but there's no map, either. Often enough, I'm stuck on the woodsy side, slogging along and devising little tricks and ways of doing things to keep me going forward.

Sculptors start with a lump of clay; writers, with nothing: It's all in the head. When I'm drafting, what I want is something malleable, something to work on—words, scenes, characters. My best trick is to sit in front of the computer wearing my drafting hat, a battered gray fedora, pulled down over my eyes, and type without stopping. The hat over the eyes keeps me from seeing anything but what's on the only screen that matters—the one in my mind.

The next day, before the hat goes on, I look at what I produced. A mess! My heart sinks. With a little effort, I can remember that I've done this 24 times before, and 24 times a novel emerged. But, of course, that was the past and it happened through sheer chance and good luck. This time, I can tell, it's the end of my life as a writer. I don't write stories, I make messes! Still, what are messes for, except to be cleaned up, so I might as well get to it. I start by putting in all the capitals and commas and correcting the spelling. This is soothing. I'm not doing real writing, which means I don't have to be anxious.

It never fails that while I'm doing this, ideas sprout on nearly every line, and one thing leads to another, which leads to a cheerful frame of mind and the possibility that I might still make it as a writer. I do another five or six messy pages. After several months of this routine, I come out from under the hat with a rough, but not impossible, draft.

I begin rewriting and revising. I love this part, but I can still use help. I'll do anything to give it to myself.

Here are a few of my tricks:

1. Eavesdrop. A sentence heard on the fly on a busy New York City street—"They destroyed my innocent childhood"—gave me a sudden insight into Diane, one of Jessie's friends in *Missing Pieces,* and was the basis for at least two important scenes I hadn't known I was going to write.

2. Free write, just as the kids do in school. In *After the Rain,* the letters Rachel writes her brother were never intended for the book. They began as a way for me to get to know more about her.

3. Switch from first person to third, or from third to first. If, for instance, you've written the draft in third person, rewrite your entire manuscript in first person. This doesn't mean merely changing all the "she said"s to "I said"s. It means seeing the story in a fresh way. Third person is the storytelling voice. It has greater freedom than the first person: It's a voice that can know more than the character knows; a voice that can give the viewpoint of more than one character. Transforming a third-person narrative into first person forces a sharper concentration on the character's views, thoughts, and feelings.

How about the reverse? First person is necessarily the narrower vision, but the voice is capable of drawing in the reader more swiftly. The first-person voice rarely stops to notice the scenery (those awful long paragraphs of description I used to think I had to master to be a *real* writer). Only as much of the story can be told as the first-person character is capable of understanding, noticing, and reporting. When your characters are adolescents, this is a severe limitation. First person can also be too talky: Somebody's always in your ear saying, I, I, I, I.

When I rewrite a manuscript into the third person, I always feel grateful for the new notes that are rung, the new details observed. In the third person, things leap out that I, as author, can write into the story but the close-in, first-person viewpoint couldn't notice and still remain a true first person.

4. Take another step with the voice and rewrite the manuscript once more, from third person back to first, or from first person back again to third. Yes, this seems like a lot of work, and it is. But for me, it never fails to add something new, fresh, and vital.

The third-person characters who spent their time in the first person would emerge opened up, with a more intimate tone, while the first-person characters, as a result of their brief third-person lives, now have steadier, quieter, more mature voices.

5. Use pictures. When I was writing *Taking Terri Mueller,* I had a problem with Terri's father; I hated him. He was a great dad, relaxed, loving, and attentive, but I hated him for kidnapping his daughter, and the emotion put me into writer's gridlock. I came across a magazine picture of a man holding a baby up toward his face and smiling with ecstatic love. I ripped the picture out and taped it over my typewriter. Every day, before I did anything else, I looked at that picture and thought, "This is the way Terri's father feels about her. This was how

much he loved her as an infant and has gone on loving her." Finally, I could comprehend how devastating it was for him to think he was going to lose Terri. After that I could write again.

6. Read out loud. The last thing I do is read the manuscript to someone else. The last two words in that sentence are crucial for me. I can read something out loud to myself and be quite satisfied, but when I read the same thing to my husband Harry, the blunders leap out at me. As for silent reading, it's amazing how often my eye skips over sentences on the screen that are awkward or unclear. Unheeding, I speed past the extra adjective, the unneeded adverb, but the moment I have to speak them, I stumble. Narrative holes loom bigger, too, when spoken.

7. Talk the talk. Dialogue is tricky. We all have verbal ticks, but putting them into dialogue rarely works. What do people really say when they get mad, when they're baffled, amused, amazed? I say what I would say, or what I'd like to say. (I'm not confrontational, but I love writing noisy, loud, decisive characters.) Then I write it, then I rewrite it, then I read it out loud.

8. Finally, when you think you have nothing left to do, do this: Go through each chapter as if you *must* cut it by ¼, and be merciless with anything that is repetitious, unclear, clichéd. Be on the lookout, too, for those bits that make you chuckle fondly or glow a little inwardly. Those are nearly always the ones that ought to come out, where the writer is working too hard at being a Wonderful Writer.

Did I say somewhere that when you get the premise, the hard work is over? Silly me. The most dazzling, dramatic idea to come down the pike in the last decade isn't worth much if not brought to life, if the characters don't (as one of my readers once so winningly said) walk alongside the reader. This is what I really want when I write and what all the work and revisions are about: creating a space and a place that is unique, a world the reader enters and might never want to leave.

➤➤97

IF YOU WANT TO WRITE A YOUNG ADULT NOVEL . . .

BY EILEEN CHARBONNEAU

SOME YEARS AGO, I HEARD A WONDERFUL TALK BY MADELEINE L'ENgle, and something she explained has stayed with me ever since. Her strategy for exploring a difficult concept—from the nature of altruism to quantum physics—was to write a young adult novel about it. Her voice rang with such conviction that I didn't believe this was idle flattery to her largely teen-aged audience. More illuminating, that audience was full of good questions about what constitutes character, the patterns of time travel, and how they choose to express themselves as readers, writers, and thinkers. I sat among them, proud and happy to be writing for those same young people.

Make no mistake—young adult novels are real books. Real and very fine novelists write them. The best are full of richness and diversity. They come in all genres—mystery, romance, western, science fiction. They are contemporary and historical. I wrote two novels for grownups (I hesitate to use the term adult novel, for in our culture "adult" has sometimes come to suggest X-rated) before I found the courage to try one for young people. That novel, *The Ghosts of Stony Clove*, turned out to be the first one accepted for publication.

When people express an interest in writing for young adults, the first question I ask is: Why? If they say because they think it might be an easy place to start, I firmly attempt to disabuse them of that notion. Shorter is not easier. In a young adult novel of 40,000 to 70,000 words, every scene must be essential to illuminating character, moving plot, or working on a symbolic level. To do two of these at once is good; to do all three is really impressive.

If my questioners remain undaunted, I ask how well they remember their own teen years. Working for or among young people, eavesdropping at the mall, school, basketball court, rock concert, even having teens in your home are all of great help. But they are not enough. Young people, like all readers, want authenticity—to believe the world you create. They can smell a phony who doesn't remember having been there. Nor will they keep reading a book by a preaching adult, or a writer who doesn't respect them. And of course they deserve that respect, and the truth with a capital T that good fiction provides. So, how well do you remember? Do you have what it takes to explore that tumultuous time of life with the honesty and compassion of a survivor, someone who's found what Dorothy of Kansas was looking for—the intelligence, heart, and courage it takes to become a successful adult?

Still reading? O.K., you're serious. Now for the how-to.

What kind of story should you write? The kind you feel passionate about. I write historical novels because I have an enthusiasm for time traveling that many of my readers share. Through Jeffersonian America, the War of 1812, and Western Expansion, I love letting my readers know that they, in their betwixt-and-between lives, are not alone, even in time. I also write contemporary mysteries. I think the best books in this genre fulfill a longing of young people for justice in a world that is often unfair. All my stories are about the power of loving and being loved, a subject young people agree is worth exploring, for their world craves beauty, too.

Who should tell your story? I wrote *The Ghosts of Stony Clove* in the first-person viewpoint of Ginny Rockwell, a Catskill mountain teenager from early in the last century. I counted my decision a success when readers I meet tell me how well preserved I look! My second book is the first-person narrative of Ginny's teen-aged son, Joshua Woods. In *Honor to the Hills,* it will be Josh's daughter Lily's turn to tell the story of her family's involvement in assisting slaves in their flight to freedom on the Underground Railroad.

For my mysteries I decided on using the limited third-person viewpoint of city-bred Tad Gist and country-raised Linda Tassel, the teens who solve the three novels' crimes. This means that although I tell the story in chapters with alternative "he" and "she" points of view, I stay strictly in the head of Tad or Linda, so my readers can solve the crime along with my protagonists.

I'd suggest the same—a first- or limited third-person—to a YA writer, for these are intimate viewpoints. They help establish closeness and, if done well, readers will identify with and feel for the main characters as they explore their worlds.

A rule of thumb I've heard bandied about is that your protagonist should be a little older than your reader, as young people like to "read up" into their projected futures. It's something to consider, although when I mention this to my own readers, they tend to bristle at the limitation.

Now, how to tell your story? Pressures on today's teenagers are many. They have demanding school work, outside work, and social schedules. Then there's the "reading is no longer cool" syndrome. This one hits teenage boys especially hard. Sometimes it stems from required school reading associated with tests and didactic teaching. What's going to make teenagers realize or remember that reading is a great pleasure? What will make our books bridges that will turn reluctant into lifetime readers? What has worked forever: compelling characters in a good, galloping story.

So, write tight. Don't waste your readers' time. Express yourself in your first draft, communicate in the second, and make your manuscript sing in its third incarnation. And don't let a publisher see anything before that third draft, no matter how long it takes you to get there!

Try to sweeten your story with humor and salt it with excitement. Use all your senses in your writing, and remember that the little-used sense of smell is the gateway to the others.

Borrow the "frozen moment" technique from the Japanese Kabuki theater to slow down time in your breathless action sequences. This impresses on your readers the characters' heightened senses and increases the tension of the scene.

Here's Josh Woods, secure on a tree limb, watching his father face a rabid wolf:

Daddy answered the wolf's low growl with a murmur in a language I didn't understand. His arm reached behind his back where his weapon was slung. As his hand reached cold iron, the wolf sprang.

"Stay back!" he commanded the wolf or me or perhaps us both.

But for me to obey him, I knew, meant to let him die.

My father took the force of the attack squarely. I heard the sickening sound of his head hitting the balsam's protruding roots. The strong hands I'd known all my life were now lost in glistening fur as he struggled to keep the wolf from his throat. His pulse pounded in his neck, so exposed, so fragile.

—*In the Time of the Wolves*

C. H. B. Kitchin has written, "An historian of the future will probably turn, not to blue books or statistics, but to detective stories if he wishes to study the manners of our age." With that in mind, I've tried to structure my young adult mysteries so they not only offer an interesting crime puzzle to solve, but also delve into realities of today's teenagers' lives. In *The Mound-Builders' Secret,* the consequences of our mobile way of life confront Tad as his family moves just before his senior year of high school. Tad explores the effects of living in our multicultural society in *Disappearance at Harmony Festival,* as he tries to understand the culture of Linda's Snowbird Cherokee relatives. In my new book *Blood River,* my teenage couple seeks the stolen Connor Emerald, as Linda recovers from being sexually harassed by a trusted teacher.

Does writing for young adults sound difficult? It should. It is. And it's a difficult field to break into, since it requires that same combination of hard work, luck, and persistence on the path to all publication. Writers magazines and organizations like the YA Network and The Society for Children's Book Writers and Illustrators offer marketing suggestions and provide names of agents who accept work from YA writers.

Keep a sharp eye out for new lines or new companies that publish books for young adults. There has been an increase in paperback original titles in recent years. I placed my first novel with Orchard Books when I read of their call for manuscripts in *The Writer.* I think it helped my chances that Orchard was a new house, willing to take a chance on an unknown. A bookseller who loved *The Ghosts of Stony Clove* recommended me to an editor who dropped into his store one day, saying she was looking for a good writer for her new mystery line. That's how Tad and Linda's adventures began. An editor who enjoyed my writing in another genre asked me if I had a YA available. That led to a happy collaboration and three-book contract with Tor Books. Moral: Treasure your advocates from wherever they come!

Writing for young adults is probably not going to make you rich or famous, so why do writers for young adults keep writing? Many of us see ourselves as promoting a literate future in a dangerous time. We work with editors as dedicated to excellence as we are. And more than in other genres, I find a fine courage among young adult editors and publishers willing to take chances on a character or a story that may not quite fit within a convention—like those musings of Madeleine L'Engle's beloved Time Trilogy or the hero of Jerry Spinelli's *Maniac McGee*. Mark Twain knew this when he wrote his "boys' adventure" stories.

I enjoy the company of other young adult writers. If you decide to join our ranks, I think you'll find us a mutually supportive lot, a happy band of brothers and sisters who do what we do for love of the young adult who picks up our books, and the one still vibrantly alive in all of us. They both deserve our best.

>> 98

Is It Good Enough for Children?

By Madeleine L'Engle

A WHILE AGO WHEN I WAS TEACHING A COURSE ON TECHNIQUES OF fiction, a young woman came up to me and said, "I do hope you're going to teach us something about writing for children, because that's why I'm taking this course."

"What have I been teaching you?" I asked her.

"Well—writing."

"Don't you write when you write for children?"

"Yes, but—isn't it different?"

No, I assured her, it isn't different. The techniques of fiction are the techniques of fiction, and they hold as true for Beatrix Potter as they do for Dostoevsky.

But the idea that writing for children isn't the same as writing for adults is prevalent indeed, and usually goes along with the conviction that it isn't quite as good. If you're a good enough writer for adults, the implication is, of course, you don't write for children. You write for children only when you can't make it in the real world, because writing for children is easier.

Wrong, wrong, wrong!

I had written several regular trade novels before a publisher asked me to write about my Swiss boarding school experiences. Nobody had told me that you write differently when you write for children, so I didn't. I just wrote the best book I possibly could; it was called *And Both Were Young*. After that I wrote *Camilla,* which has been reissued as a young adult novel, and then *Meet the Austins*. It's hard today for me to understand that this simple little book had a very hard time finding a publisher because it's about a death and how an ordinary family reacts to that death. Death at that time was taboo. Children weren't supposed to know about it. I had a couple of offers of publication if I'd take the death out. But the reaction of the family—children as well as the parents—to the death was the core of the book.

Nowadays what we offer children makes *Meet the Austins* seem pale, and on the whole, I think that's just as well, because children know a lot more than most grown-ups give them credit for. *Meet the Austins* came out of my own family's experience with several deaths. To have tried to hide those deaths from our children would have been blind stupidity. All hiding does is confuse children and add to their fears. It is not subject matter that should be taboo, but the way it is handled.

A number of years ago—the first year I was actually making reasonable money from my writing—my sister-in-law was visiting us, and when my husband told her how much I had earned that year, she was impressed and commented, "And to think most people would have had to work so hard for that!"

Well, it is work, it's most certainly work; wonderful work, but work. Revision, revision, revision. Long hours spent not only in the actual writing, but in research. I think the best thing I learned in college was how to do research, so that I could go right on studying after I had graduated.

Of course, it is not *only* work; it is work that makes the incomprehensible comprehensible. Leonard Bernstein says that for him music is cosmos in chaos. That is true for writing a story, too. Aristotle says that what is plausible and impossible is better than what is possible and implausible.

That means that story must be *true,* not necessarily *factual,* but true. This is not easy for a lot of people to understand. When I was a school child, one of my teachers accused me of telling a story. She was not complimenting me on my fertile imagination; she was accusing me of telling a lie.

Facts are fine; we need facts. But story takes us to a world that is beyond facts, out on the other side of facts. And there is considerable fear of this world.

The writer Keith Miller told me of a young woman who was determined that her three preschool children were going to grow up in the real world. She was not, she vowed, going to sully their minds with myth, fantasy, fairy tales. They were going to know the truth—and for truth, read fact—and the truth would make them free.

One Saturday, after a week of rain and sniffles, the sun came out, so she piled the children into her little red VW bug and took them to the Animal Farm. The parking lot was crowded, but a VW bug is small, and she managed to find a place for it. She and the children had a wonderful day, petting the animals, going on rides, enjoying the sunshine. Suddenly, she looked at her watch and found it was far later than she realized. She and the children ran to where the VW bug was parked, and to their horror, found the whole front end was bashed in.

Outraged, she took herself off to the ranger's office. As he saw her approach, he laughed and said, "I'll bet you're the lady with the red VW bug."

"It isn't funny," she snapped.

"Now, calm down, lady, and let me tell you what happened. You know the elephant your children had such fun riding? She's a circus-trained elephant, and she was trained to sit on a red bucket. When she saw your car, she just did what she was trained to do and sat on it. Your engine's in the back, so you can drive it home without any trouble. And don't worry. Our insurance will take care of it. Just go on home, and we'll get back to you on Monday."

Slightly mollified, she and the kids got into the car and took off. But she was later than ever, so when she saw what looked like a very minor accident on the road, she didn't stop, but drove on.

Shortly, the flashing light and the siren came along, and she was pulled over. "Lady, don't you know that in this state it's a crime to leave the scene of an accident?" the trooper asked.

"But I wasn't in an accident," she protested.

"I suppose your car came that way," she said, pointing to the bashed-in front.

"No. An elephant sat on it."

"Lady, would you mind blowing into this little balloon?"

That taught her that facts alone are not enough; that facts, indeed, do not make up the whole truth. After that she read fairy tales to her children and encouraged them in their games of Make Believe and Let's Pretend.

I learned very early that if I wanted to find out the truth, to find out why people did terrible things to each other, or sometimes wonderful things—why there was war, why children are abused—I was more likely to find the truth in story than in the encyclopedia. Again and again I read *Emily of the New Moon,* by Lucy Maud Montgomery, because Emily's father was dying of diseased lungs, and so was mine. Emily had a difficult time at school, and so did I. Emily wanted to be a writer, and so did I. Emily knew that there was more to the world that provable fact, and so did I. I read fairy tales, the myths of all nations, science fiction, the fantasies and family stories of E. Nesbit. I read Jules Verne and H. G. Wells. And I read my parents' books, particularly those with lots of conversation in them. What was not in my frame of reference went right over my head.

We tend to find what we look for. If we look for dirt, we'll find dirt, whether it's there or not. A very nice letter I received from a reader said that she found *A Ring of Endless Light* very helpful to her in coming to terms with the death of a friend, but that another friend had asked her how it was that I used dirty words. I wrote back saying that I was not going to reread my book looking for dirty words, but that as far as I could remember, the only word in the book that could possibly be construed as dirty was *zuggy,* which I'd made up to avoid using dirty words. And wasn't looking for dirty words an ugly way to read a book?

One of my favorite books is Frances Hodgson Burnett's *The Secret Garden.* I read it one rainy weekend to a group of little girls, and a generation later to my granddaughters up in an old brass bed in the attic. Mary Lennox is a self-centered, spoiled-rotten little heroine, and I think we all recognize at least a little of ourselves in her. The secret garden is as much the garden of Mary's heart as it is the physical walled garden. By the end of the book, warmth and love and concern for others have come to Mary's heart, when Colin, the sick boy, is able to walk and run again. And Dickon, the gardener's boy, looks at the beauty of the restored garden and says, "It's magic!" But "magic" is one of the key words that has become taboo to today's self-appointed censors, so, with complete disregard of content, they would add *The Secret Garden* to the pyre. I shudder. This attitude is extreme. It is also dangerous.

It comes down to the old question of separate standards, separate for adults and children. The only standard to be used in judging a children's book is: *Is it a good book?* Is it good enough for me? Because if a children's book is not good enough for all of us, it is not good enough for children.

495

➤➤ 99

WRITING NONFICTION FOR CHILDREN: QUESTIONS AND ANSWERS

BY JAMES CROSS GIBLIN

AMONG THE FIRST AND MOST FREQUENT QUESTIONS ASKED OF WRITERS of children's nonfiction is *Why did you choose to write nonfiction?* My answer is that I'm not sure I did "choose." Instead, nonfiction probably chose me—and it happened at a very early age, as I have a hunch it happens for many nonfiction writers.

When my mother read me Inez Hogan's *The Navajo Twins,* I was fascinated by the description of an arroyo near the twins' home. I lived in Northeastern Ohio and had never seen anything like the desert landscape in which the story was set. In fact, I became so fascinated by it that I went around the house chanting the word *arroyo* over and over, indicating that even at age five I was intrigued by the unusual word and the odd bit of information. And I've continued to be intrigued by such things in my adult life. That's probably why I've explored offbeat subjects like chimney sweeps, eating utensils, windows, and chairs in many of my nonfiction books.

Take a look back at your own childhood. You may detect an early interest in animals, history, airplanes, gardening, or some other subject area that you could draw on for your nonfiction writing if you haven't already.

The next question is generally *Where do you get the ideas for your books?* The answer is, from all sorts of places. The trick is to recognize a good idea when one comes along.

For example, some years ago I saw an exhibit of antique and modern chairs at the Cleveland Museum of Art. The range and variety of chairs on display amazed me, and I thought, "There might be a children's book in this." I picked up the brochure that accompanied the exhibit and, after reading it, was even more convinced of the idea's possibilities.

At the New York Public Library, I delved into several histories of furniture and then drafted a proposal for a book of my own. My editor responded enthusiastically to the idea, and soon I had a contract for *Be Seated: A Book About Chairs.*

Often an idea is suggested to a nonfiction author. For example, after I spoke at one conference, I was asked by a librarian if I'd ever thought of writing a book about unicorns. A month later, at another conference, I was asked the same question.

The second query coming so soon after the first made me think seriously about the idea. Like many writers, I keep a file of newspaper and magazine articles concerning topics that interest me, and I seemed to remember clipping several pieces about unicorns. I riffled through the file, and found three scientific articles dealing with the mythical creature. I reread them, and that was the beginning of my research for *The Truth About Unicorns.*

Wherever an idea comes from, it must strike a deep chord in you, the author. Otherwise, you won't be able to sustain the drive needed to research and write a nonfiction book—a process that can take years. For example, I've jotted down many ideas for books and countless others have been suggested to me, but only a few have called to me the way those for *Be Seated* and *The Truth About Unicorns* did.

Another frequent question is *How do you decide what age group to write for?* The answer depends on three factors that are closely intertwined: (a) your inclinations as an author; (b) the age group you feel would have the strongest interest in the material; and (c) the requirements of the marketplace.

Many nonfiction topics can be explored for all age groups. For example, biographies of George Washington could be—and have been— written for preschoolers, children in the elementary grades, and young adults. I chose to write my biography of Washington as a picture book for first- and second-graders, because I liked the challenge of the picture book format, and because the publisher wanted a biography for that age level.

Other topics are clearly suited to one age group more than another. My book about the deciphering of the Rosetta Stone would be beyond the comprehension of preschoolers and most children in first and second grade. However, it could have been directed toward either the upper elementary or the young adult level.

I decided on the former because I knew that most youngsters study ancient Egypt in the sixth grade. Consequently, I assumed *The Riddle of the Rosetta Stone* would find its largest audience if it were aimed at that age level, and the book's sales so far prove I was right. This shows how important it is to have a sense of the market when you're deciding on the age group for a nonfiction book.

The next question is one of the most basic: *How do you do research?* There's no simple, clear-cut answer to that since each book requires its own research plan, and some are much more complex than others. I usually start the process by letting my mind wander and asking myself, "What subtopics branch out naturally from the main topic?"

For example, with *Let There Be Light,* a history of windows in various cultures and periods, I began my bibliography with books about the history of architecture. From there I got more specific, adding titles about life and dwellings in Africa, the Middle East, the Far East, and the Arctic. Before I was through, I also read books and articles about the Crystal Palace exhibition in Victorian London, the infamous *Kristallnacht* in Nazi Germany, and in this country, the urban riots in which so many windows were smashed during the 1960s.

All of this research gave me a solid foundation on which to build *Let There Be Light.* Like most nonfiction authors, I used only part of the material I'd gathered in the actual writing. But I believe readers can sense the rest, lending credibility and authenticity to the finished book.

Still another question might seem insulting at first hearing, but it's probably not meant to be taken that way: *Do nonfiction writers have to be concerned with literary style?* Of course we do, if we're serious about our work. And a definition of style offered by the French poet, playwright, and filmmaker Jean Cocteau would seem to have a special application to children's nonfiction: "Style is a simple way of saying complicated things."

That definition of Cocteau's is a goal you should constantly aim for in your writing, especially when you're explaining a scientific concept or sketching in the historical background of an event. How do you achieve it? Here are some steps you may find helpful. First, go over the facts in your research notes for a particular section or chapter until you've virtually memorized them. That way you won't have to refer to the notes too often and will be free to draft the text in your own words. Then, work and rework each paragraph until it says what you want to say in the way you want to say it. Besides simplicity, strive for rhythm in the writing. Listen to each sentence in your head as you compose it, and if the words don't flow smoothly, fiddle with them until they do.

Some reviewers have said my books have a "conversational style." If that's true, I think it's because I try to make each sentence *speakable*. That's a distinct advantage today, when even nonfiction books for older children are often read aloud in the classroom.

In the last fifteen or so years, there has been much more emphasis on the visual aspect of children's nonfiction books. So it's not surprising that authors are almost always asked *Are you involved in the illustration of your books—and if so, how?*

Not only am I involved, but—like many nonfiction authors—I'm responsible for gathering most of the illustrations that appear in my books. For example, with *The Truth About Unicorns* I assembled photographs of paintings and tapestries depicting the mythical animal from art museums around the world. To supplement these, I also found pictures of the real narwhal and the one-horned Indian rhinoceros at natural history museums.

However, I was unable to locate illustrations of ancient Greek, Roman, and Chinese unicorns, so the publisher commissioned an artist to draw pictures of them. To help pay for the drawings, I agreed to take a reduced royalty. I felt this was a small price to pay in return for a more attractive and salable book.

Some nonfiction authors still think their work is done when they turn in a manuscript to an editor, and refuse to concern themselves with the illustrations. They're making a big mistake, in my opinion. For if a book isn't well designed and illustrated, it has little chance of succeeding in today's nonfiction marketplace.

Finally, writers are sometimes asked a question which frankly annoys me: *Now that you've mastered nonfiction, would you like to try your hand at fiction?*

The question is annoying because—like the similar question often asked of children's writers, "Would you like to write adult books some day?"—it implies that nonfiction writing is somehow inferior to fiction.

I refuse to accept that notion, probably because I've written my share of fiction and in many ways find that writing nonfiction is a greater challenge; you have to absorb and present a huge amount of information in a clear, accurate, and entertaining manner. Like a writer of fiction, you must find a way to write freely and spontaneously. But at the same time—unlike a fiction writer—you always have to be on guard to make sure you're not omitting or distorting any necessary facts.

It's not easy to rise to this challenge and achieve a happy balance between spontaneity and control, but when you do, the result can be uniquely satisfying. That's why I, for one, would never want to give up writing nonfiction in favor of fiction.

➤➤ 100

CALLING IT QUITS

BY LOIS LOWRY

"You put what in it?" my son asked, his fork halfway to his mouth.
"Ginger snaps," I repeated. "Crushed ginger snaps."
"I thought that's what you said." I watched while he put his fork
back down on his plate and then pushed the plate away from him. It
was clear to me that my son, normally a good sport, was not going to
eat my innovative beef stew.

It was clear to me, after I tasted it myself, that he had made the
right decision.

SOMETIMES IN THE PROCESS OF CREATING, IT IS VERY DIFFICULT TO
know when to quit adding things.

Some years back, I received in the mail the first foreign edition of
my first young adult book, *A Summer to Die*. Fortunately it was
French. Later I would receive, with a gulp of astonishment, the Finn-
ish, the Afrikaans, the Catalan; but this first one was French. French
I can read.

And so I leafed through the pages, savoring the odd, startling sense
of recognition that I had, seeing my own words translated into another language.

On the last page, I read the line of dialogue with which I had concluded the book. "'Meg,' he laughed, putting one arm over my shoulders, 'you were beautiful all along.'" There it was, in French.

But there was something else, as well. I blinked in surprise, seeing
it. In French, the book concluded: "They walked on."

They walked on? Of course they *had* walked on, those two characters, Meg and Will. I knew they had, and I trusted the reader to know
that they had. But I hadn't written that line. The translator had.

I don't know why. I can only guess that the translator simply couldn't resist that urge that makes all of us throw a crushed ginger snap into the stew now and then.

Knowing when to stop is one of the toughest tasks a writer faces.

Is there a rule that one can follow? Probably not. But there is, I think, a test against which the writer can measure his ending, his stopping place.

When something more is going to take place, but the characters have been so fully drawn, and the preceding events so carefully shaped that the reader, on reflection, knows what more will happen, and is satisfied by it—then the book ends.

In essence, you, as writer, will have successfully taught the reader to continue writing the book in his mind.

What about the concept of resolution, then? Isn't the writer supposed to tie up the loose ends of the story neatly at the conclusion? And if everything is neatly packaged and tied, then how on earth can something more take place?

Your story—your plot—your theme—is only a portion of the lives of the characters you have created. Their lives, if you have made them real to the reader, are going to continue in the reader's mind.

Your role is only a part of that process. And you need to know when and how to get out when your role is finished. As author, you tie up and resolve the piece of a life you have chosen to examine. Then you leave, gracefully. The life continues, but you are no longer looking at it.

You have engaged and directed the imagination of the reader; and then you have turned the reader loose.

Writing this, I looked at the endings of some of my own books, to see if they followed any kind of pattern.

In one, *Anastasia on Her Own,* a mother and daughter are laughing and tap-dancing together up a flight of stairs.

In *Find a Stranger, Say Goodbye,* a young girl is packing to go away; she is deciding what to take and what to leave behind.

The narrator and her mother in *Rabble Starkey* are together in a car, heading into a somewhat uncertain future. (Not coincidentally, that book is published in Great Britain under the title *The Road Ahead.*)

The forms of these endings are different. Some are descriptive, some consist of dialogue. Some are lighthearted, others more introspective.

But they do seem to have a few elements in common.

They all include the main character—sometimes more than one—in the final scene.

Each of them, in various forms, reflects a sense of motion, of flow, of moving forward.

And each in its own way contains a kind of conclusive statement.

Anastasia fell in behind her mother and tried to follow the complicated hops, turns, and shuffles her mother was doing. Together they tap-danced down the hall and up the stairs. It was silly, she thought; but it was fun. And it sure felt good, having her mother back in charge.

—Anastasia on Her Own

It was the throwing away that was the hardest. But she did it, until the trunk was packed, the trash can was filled, and the room was bare of everything except the memories; those would always be there, Natalie knew.

—Find a Stranger, Say Goodbye

She sped up a little, driving real careful, and when we went around the curve I looked, and it was all a blur. But there was nothing there. There was only Sweet Hosanna and me, and outside the whole world, quiet in the early morning, green and strewn with brand new blossoms, like the ones on my very best dress.

—Rabble Starkey

The common elements that you can see and hear in those ending paragraphs are a little like the basics in a good stew; maybe you could equate them to a garlic clove, a bay leaf, and a dollop of wine.

As for the crushed ginger snaps? The ingredient that qualifies as overkill and makes the whole thing just a little nauseating?

Well, I confess that those three passages have one more thing in common. Each one was tough to end. Like the translator who added another sentence to my book, I wanted to go on, too. I wanted to add crushed ginger snaps: more sentences, more images, embellishments, explanations, embroidery.

And if I had? Take a look:

She sped up a little, driving real careful, and when we went around the curve I looked, and it was all a blur. But there was nothing there. There was only Sweet Hosanna and me, and outside the whole world, quiet in the early morning, green and strewn with brand new blossoms, like the ones on my very best dress.

What would the future hold for us? I had no way of knowing. But I remembered how, in the past years, my mother had worked and saved to bring us this far. I looked at her now, her eyes intent on the road, and I could see the determination . . .

Et cetera. You can't read it—I couldn't *write* it—without a feeling of wanting to push your plate away. It's too much. It's unnecessary. It is, in a word, sickening.

The letters I get so often from kids provide me, unintentionally, with a reminder of the impact of a good ending. Boy, if anyone in the world knows how to *end,* it's a kid writing a letter.

"Well," they say, "I have to quit now."

≫ 101

NEWS THAT'S FIT FOR FICTION

BY EVE BUNTING

RECENTLY, A PROMOTIONAL POSTER FOR SEVERAL OF MY BOOKS, DE-
signed to look like the front page of a newspaper, carried this headline:

EXTRA, EXTRA, READ ALL ABOUT IT!
ALL THE FICTION THAT'S FIT TO PRINT

The format was no accident. The editors had already commented on
how often the stories I write come straight from newspaper headlines. . . . well, not straight exactly, but by a fairly direct route. My
theory, unconsciously known to me but never actually stated, is that
if a story is dramatic enough, heartbreaking, poignant, or funny enough
to be considered by newspaper editors and published for millions of
people to read, it's a good story.

In my case, I read the newspapers that come to our home rather
superficially. But when an article or essay catches my attention, it gets
my full attention. Never have I said at this point, "I will write a book
about this." What I have said is "Wow! What an interesting story."
Sometimes I clip the piece, sometimes I don't. When I don't I'm often
sorry and find myself, days or weeks later, trying to track it down on
microfilm in my library, unsure of the date when I read it, unsure *where*
I read it. I'm tracking down the story because I can't forget it. And
that is the key. If I can't forget it, that story has touched me in some
deep, heartfelt way. At that point I say: "I want to write about it."

Before I begin, though, there are four questions to consider—the
first I've already answered:

(1) Does the story deeply affect me?

(2) Will it also affect young readers, or does it simply touch on my
personal interests and concerns?

(3) Can I write it so I have a young person as the protagonist, or is it altogether too adult?

(4) Can I see in this an underlying truth that will unfold as the story unfolds? If not it has only surface value and I don't want to do it.

If all of these questions can be answered in the affirmative I am ready to go on to the "thinking through" process, which to my mind is the most valuable time I spend on any book. I will not know it all when I start. That "miserable middle" will still be shadowy. But I will have a strong skeleton, and the theme or unstated message will be fixed in my mind along with a forceful and unflinching ending that I can work toward.

I was sitting one morning at my breakfast table reading my paper. There was a brief paragraph about two young boys who had been walking home from a party the night before. They walked single file along a road where there was no sidewalk. A car came behind them, on the wrong side of the highway, driving at high speed. It hit and killed one boy. The other jumped to safety. "That was the all of it," as we say in Ireland.

But not for me.

The story took hold of my mind and my heart. I imagined the scene . . . the dark road, the shriek of brakes, the car driving on, the boy who had jumped walking unsteadily to where his friend lay motionless on the road, calling his name, knowing he was dead.

I asked myself the four salient questions and was able to answer "yes" to all of them. When I'd thought it through, I had the outline of a plot that told of a quest to find the driver of the killing car, a story of guilt, of revenge, and the maturing of a boy who realizes that things and people are not always what they seem and that revenge can never truly erase sorrow.

Here is the opening paragraph of *A Sudden Silence*, the scene that I visualized so clearly when I first read that sad article in my morning paper.

It was Saturday the 20th of June at 11:30 pm when my brother, Bry, was killed. I'll never forget that date, not if I live to be an old, old man. Coast Highway, shadowed between its tall pole lights, the car suddenly behind Bry and me as we walked single file in the thick grass at the highway's edge. The glare of its white beams; the roar as it passed me where I'd dived sideways, belly down; the thud as it hit him. I'll never forget it.

Naturally, I did not use the boys' real names or the real setting. But the story began with a real happening in the way that so many of my stories do.

One Sunday, I opened the "View" section of my *Los Angeles Times* and saw a group of bizarre pictures. Life-sized wooden dolls, wide-eyed, staring, stood in the front yard of a small, wooden house. There was a photograph of an elderly couple and a close-up of one of the dolls. The accompanying story told of how the couple had always wanted children but had not been able to have them. The husband, a wood carver, made these dolls for his wife, and they became her children. She found or made clothes for them, she gave them names and talked to them. They "talked" back. I stared at the doll. He stared at me. I was mesmerized, hooked. One of the dolls was on view in an art gallery on La Cienega Boulevard in Los Angeles. I visited it. Oh my! The hook was definitely in place.

Could I give these elderly people a real child who would tell my story? Of course. He could be a nephew who is orphaned and comes to live with his mysterious relatives and their even more mysterious children. I called him Matt and gave him a little sister, someone to protect from ghostly or insane happenings. Would young readers be as entranced by the spookiness of this kind of story as I? I'd bet on it. And what would Matt learn? I saw that clearly from the beginning. Aunt Gerda, who is at first to be feared because she is "not like anyone else," is found to be kind, loving and compassionate to the two orphaned children. Is love stronger than fear? In my stories, yes. In life, too.

"Are the ghost children really real?" children ask in their letters.

"If you think they are," I answer.

It's impossible to give a definitive yes or no. Because the author isn't too sure herself, and it's that kind of uncertainty that makes writing fun! And writing *The Ghost Children* was definitely fun.

Sharing Susan was probably taken more directly from a newspaper article than any other book I wrote. Who didn't read about the little girl, accidentally changed with another baby at birth, everyone unsuspecting until one of the girls died. Then the wrenching, heartbreaking complications arose. Should a child be taken from the only parents she has known for thirteen years and sent to strangers who will be her mother and father from now on? The dramatic, misery-making possibilities tore at my imagination.

The writing of *Sharing Susan* presented difficulties. When I write, I usually try to "get rid of the parents" early in the story. That way I am not tempted to have a passive character as my protagonist. I can create one who is independent, who makes decisions on her own, and who can solve her problems without adult help. (Other than her early training, of course, which taught her to be courageous, honest, self-reliant and to ask for help only when it involves her own safety or the safety of others.) I try to send the parents off on a vacation or business trip in Chapter 1 or 2. Or I can have my protagonist go stay with a relative, or go to camp, or keep him or her in school most of the time. Often a mother or father may be out of the picture entirely, and I have a one-parent family that reflects today's society.

In *Sharing Susan,* I had two sets of parents, and many of the decisions being made were *about* Susan, not *by* her. I was forced to have a lot of introspection, slow stuff for young readers. One of my challenges was to keep the plot moving. Strong characterization helped enormously. I had two very different sets of parents with different lifestyles: four complex individuals. My inclination here was to portray one set of parents as mean, demanding, unyielding. That way I could have lots of confrontation and add to Susan's anguish in leaving her familiar home. But I wanted to avoid that trap, which is certainly a cliché and is also scary. A child in such a situation must go where she is sent. What if something like this happened to me, a young reader might ask. Horrifying enough without any additional terror. The book and the idea did spike a lot of imaginations, though, and I must say that most of those who wrote letters to me seemed less than horrified!

Dear Eve:
I've always suspected these weren't my real parents. I am *so different.* Please tell me how I can find out if *I* was changed at birth.
Your friend. . . .
P.S. Up until now I thought I was adopted or left on their doorstep, but they say no. This seems more likely.

Because I know about children's imaginations, I did try to show how extremely rare such an occurrence would be, and I was careful to portray the adults as wise and caring, making the best of a tragic situation and acting in Susan's best interests—at least the way I hope they would be.

In the book, as in real life, I think, Susan is at first prepared to hate her new, upstart mom and dad. She is totally disinterested in the fact that she will have a brother. She enlists her relatives to help her stay where she thinks she belongs, and when that doesn't work she makes her own plans. She'll be so hateful, so ill-mannered, so rotten to that new little brother that these impostor parents will want to send her back. Susan's efforts gave me an opportunity to have Susan "do" instead of being "done to."

In the resolution, Susan understands that she will always be part of both sets of parents, that it is O.K. to love the new ones, too, and that in no way is it disloyal to the mother and father who have cared for her since they brought her home from the hospital, their wonderful, brand-new little girl. She understands that the more love you give, the more you have left to give. And so, happily, Susan is shared.

"But this really happened. Can't you be sued?" I'm asked.

No, it didn't really happen.

I took reality as a jumping-off place, a springboard to my story. My book has different people, acting out in different ways. I am careful never to use the same characteristics, physical, or as far as I know, psychological, of the original players. For instance, in the newspaper article that sparked *Sharing Susan,* the child's biological parents had six or seven other children. In *Sharing Susan,* they had only one. I knew no follow-up to the "real" story until much later, when my book was completed. This was the reality for me. This was what happened. It was Susan's ordeal, and mine. No one else's.

So, read voraciously and clip like a fiend.

Get excited.

Pause.

Question.

Think.

Write.

Take all that fiction that's fit to print—and make it your own.

➤➤ 102

Shaping Children's Fiction: A Three-Step Plan

By Cheryl Fusco Johnson

IF YOU'VE RECENTLY BEGUN WRITING FICTION FOR YOUNG PEOPLE, recognize this as the brave new venture it is. Don't be embarrassed if your first few juvenile manuscripts didn't find acceptance. Writing for children is harder than writing for adults.

Above and beyond all the technical skills any fiction writing requires, crafting juvenile stories and novels demands a special sensitivity to young people's needs. Like many aspiring juvenile writers, you may have directed your previous writing efforts toward adult readers. Three simple steps will help you refocus your thinking so you can create manuscripts that appeal to young readers and the editors who serve them.

Step One. Make sure your story is child-centered. This is harder than it sounds. I've read dozens of manuscripts in which adult characters get more lines of dialogue than younger characters do. Unless you're writing a picture book featuring adult rhinoceroses with childlike personalities, keep the adults in your story from talking too much.

Look at your manuscript. If you see a solid block of dialogue between adult characters, cut that speech out or at least way down. Anything over two or three lines of print amounts to a lecture. Young readers may tolerate adult lectures in real life; they won't put up with them in the stories and books they choose for entertainment.

By limiting adult dialogue, you may avoid other problems as well. Muting or even eliminating adult characters helps keep the young people in your story at center stage, where they belong. At every point in your story, your main character, who's usually a few years older than your readers, should be making his or her own decisions. Resist the impulse to add realism to your story by having Mom or Grandpa suggest—or worse yet, implement—a solution to the main character's dilemma.

Allowing fictional young people to solve their own problems gives real young people the courage to carry on in a world where—outside of the computer lab—their skills, knowledge, and judgment are still inferior to adults'. Don't alienate your readers by having an adult character step in to save their fictional teen-age counterparts. Offer your readers a reassuring glimpse of the self-reliance they desperately want to achieve.

Step Two. Use an appropriate time frame. How much fictional time elapses from the beginning to the end of your story? In general, the time span varies, depending upon the age of the reader: Usually, the younger the target audience, the shorter the story's time span. Choosing an appropriate time frame for your fiction can strengthen its appeal for young readers.

Although novels for adults may cover years or even decades, that length of time is inappropriate for most juvenile books. Even young adult books rarely cover a period longer than the nine months of the school year. Novels for eight-to-twelve-year-olds frequently have a time span that begins the first day of summer vacation and ends when school resumes in the fall. The action in a picture book or a magazine story for very young children may take place during the hours between breakfast and lunch.

The passage of time in juvenile literature should be clearly shown. Sometimes, for example, the time span of stories for the very young does exceed more than a few hours. When it does, authors often help their young readers (or listeners) follow the story line by building their tales around familiar cycles, such as days of the week, the seasons, or months of the year. This technique provides clarity and also a satisfying rhythm that young people can relate to.

Works for teenage readers are more subtly constructed, but they also often incorporate familiar holidays or events that flag the passage of time. Suspense can be heightened by showing the main character struggle to overcome obstacles to attain a goal within a definite time period.

Step Three. Select a setting familiar to children. When choosing the physical setting of your story, remember that children experience the world in a way different from adults. A very young child might crawl into the leg space under a desk to look at a picture book. Older children are likely to read while perched on a desk, back against the wall, or while lying on the floor. Outdoors, children delight in exploring weedy ditches, the crawl space under rambling bushes, or the sheltered patch of dirt beneath an overpass or bridge. Note, also, that the world of young children is, in most ways, more circumscribed than the adult world. Setting a picture book in an unfamiliar place, like an office building or a factory, might confuse young readers. Their outings have probably been limited to places like the doctor's office, the grocery store, the post office, the park or zoo, the babysitter's house or a preschool.

At the other end of the spectrum, the world of older children is, in some ways, broader than that of adults. Personal computers, CD players, video games, answering machines, beepers, camcorders, VCRs, and virtual reality are part of their real world. Writers who didn't grow up with these technological wonders may sometimes include anachronisms in their fiction, with references to outdated items like eight-millimeter cameras, phonographs, and typewriters. This gives a historical rather than a contemporary feel to a story.

Whatever setting you choose, don't go overboard describing it. In general, books and stories for children should have plenty of action and comparatively little scenic description, and the action should start with the opening lines. Experienced juvenile writers build suspense and a sense of excitement into their opening paragraphs.

Take another look at your manuscript. Does the first page show the main character involved in action that reveals something important about his or her personality? Or, like many of the manuscripts written by inexperienced juvenile writers, does yours begin with seven or eight beautifully crafted, but dull, paragraphs describing your character's home, school, or town?

At the beginning of your story, establish a landscape in which your characters can move around, interweaving vivid sensory details with snippets of dialogue and short paragraphs describing riveting action. This fast-paced approach helps snag and retain young readers' attention.

512

Keep in mind that people of all ages read fiction for entertainment. A child-centered manuscript with an appropriate time frame and a familiar setting stands a good chance of satisfying juvenile editors and young readers. Don't sabotage your manuscript's prospects by weighting it down with an obvious moral message.

Respect your readers. If you want young people to adopt certain patterns of behavior, model the behavior of your characters on real life.

>> 103

RESEARCHING NONFICTION FOR
YOUNG READERS

BY NORMAN H. FINKELSTEIN

IF YOUR NONFICTION FOR YOUNG PEOPLE READS LIKE GOOD FICTION, you've got a lot going for you. But no matter how well you tell a tale, there is no substitute for factual, accurate and reliable research. Your readers deserve nothing less.

Don't be put off by stories of nonfiction writers who spend years traveling from one research site to the next to rummage through musty archives and records. You do not need to quit your day job to replicate the lifetime work of scholars.

The financial rewards you will reap as a writer of juvenile nonfiction can rarely support intensive academic research.

Remember, you are writing for young adults and not for doctoral candidates. That means you can generally rely on the basic research of others found in secondary sources for much of the information and data you will need. Still, your writing can succeed only if you make the complex scientific or historical research of others readable and understandable to young readers. Condescension is never permissible.

Where to start? You'll often find succinct overviews and up-to-date information in newspapers and general circulation magazines. I usually consult *The New York Times Index* first. Although it may seem cumbersome, it is also the quickest and most reliable way to locate specific information.

Once I make a list of relevant articles, their dates of publication and page numbers, I then turn to the library's *New York Times* microfilm collection (usually going back to the mid-nineteenth century) for the original full-text articles. Most libraries have reader-printers, so, at a small per-page cost, I can make copies of the relevant articles and take them home for more careful reading.

For magazine articles, there are indexes available in most public libraries; some even provide full text for selected articles. The tried-and-true *Readers' Guide to Periodical Literature* is still the classic key to articles in popular magazines. It is also available as *Wilsondisc* on CD-ROM, which provides abstracts for many articles. These summaries are useful tools in themselves to help narrow your search to the most appropriate articles. The newer *Magazine Index,* also on CD-ROM, provides full-text articles.

I also recommend skimming major books and scholarly journal articles on your topic. Become familiar with the scope of existing research. Soon, you will begin thinking of yourself as one of that field's leading experts. (Don't let that go to your head, however. After all, you are only a beginning expert!) Once you have achieved a general familiarity with the personalities, language, and nuances relevant to your topic, you can then get down to the gritty work of tracking down more specific information.

Writing eight nonfiction books for young readers has taught me a simple, common-sense approach to locating information. I follow a research trail that moves from the general to the specific, using one source to lead to another. My most important tool is a well-organized notetaking system. Use whatever method you wish. The important thing is to build a database of information sources. (Although I am a firmly committed computer user for my writing, I use 4×6 index cards for this stage, a separate card for each information source, print, nonprint or human.)

Where appropriate, I jot down the bibliographic data on books or articles I will need later for footnotes and/or bibliography. (Don't forget the call number and name of the library in which you found a specific book, in case you wish to return to it later.) For human resources, I write down addresses, phone numbers, and where I found the names mentioned. Tracking down information and sources is much like a detective game. One clue leads to another.

Here is my unpatented, common-sense, two-step research plan for tracking down sources:

First, visit the public library.

The preceding quick review of selected published material has already given you a general acquaintance with your topic. Now it's time to build on your basic knowledge by consulting other sources. Jot down a list of possible subjects and key words that describe your topic. A useful initial source I frequently use is a good encyclopedia index. To make sure your words coincide with those used by your library's catalogue, you might also consult the *Library of Congress Subject Headings* volumes (available in all public and university libraries). These headings are almost universally used by libraries. You can also get hints on headings you had not previously considered by checking the subject headings in the Cataloging in Publication (CIP) sections of the books you find. Most books published within the past decade display that information on the copyright page.

Today's newer computerized catalogues enable you to do versatile in-depth searches. Once you have compiled a list of possible books, go to the shelves and pull those that interest you. As you leaf through the books, pay particular attention to two important, yet usually overlooked sections where a good researcher can find lots of useful leads: the acknowledgment page and the notes/bibliography section.

Writers are usually a polite and friendly lot, and they like to thank everyone who helped them on their way to publication. On many acknowledgment pages you will find the names of scholars, librarians, or archivists who helped that writer. Also, footnotes may refer to sources you might not otherwise discover on your own. Bibliographies will guide you to yet other books and journal articles.

Pay particular attention to the mention of specific archives or libraries and the people who work there. That's how I found out about archives I previously didn't know existed, such as the MacArthur Archives in Norfolk, Virginia, and the American Library of Radio and Television at the Thousand Oaks, California Public Library. The result: rewarding research trips to invaluable depositories of memorabilia, documents, and photographs I would have otherwise overlooked.

Although, as I have mentioned earlier, my major research utilizes published secondary sources, I try to include some original research to highlight events or scenarios that my young readers may enjoy or find particularly relevant and to make my book unique.

Before you pawn the family silver and phone the airlines to book expensive reservations to exotic research sites, sit down, pour yourself a fresh cup of coffee, and write letters. I have always found the archivists and librarians I contact by mail to be more than willing to help

516

locate data. Many times, basic research questions can be answered by telephone or letter.

If you have a computer and a modem, try to get an inexpensive Internet connection. (Local universities are the best source for an account, but you will probably need an affiliation. Commercial sources, such as Compuserve, are also available.) Then, from home you can search library catalogues and other databases throughout the world for relevant titles and even full text articles. You could use E-Mail to correspond with experts in your field who may also be on-line.

Don't forget your public library's reference room. There, you will find all sorts of directories and indexes to special museums, archives, libraries, and associations. Browse for additional specialized directories, such as the *Encyclopedia of Associations, The Research Center Directory,* or the *Directory of Special Libraries* to locate specific places with information on your topic. *The Official Museum Directory* may also be useful. For writers looking for historical sources, I recommend the *American History Sourcebook,* edited by Joel Makower. You may be surprised at the number of historical societies and special interest membership groups. There seems to be a society or library for nearly any topic you could possibly imagine.

By now you are thinking, "So many sources, so little time!" There is a wonderful one-volume reference book I often use to consolidate my searches. *The New York Public Library Book of How and Where to Look It Up* (Prentice-Hall, 1991) should be on every nonfiction writer's bookshelf. It includes a list of major reference books on many subjects as well as specific government and special collection sources. Addresses and telephone numbers make it easy for you to get in touch with credible sources.

Second, write letters—to everyone!

In spite of the rising cost of postage, the post office is a writer's most useful research tool. Use the names you've put on the index cards, and write letters to the experts who helped other writers, and to directors of the specific special interest libraries you've tracked down in the directories. Directories of addresses are available in the library or on-line through several data retrieval services. Most people you write to will be gracious and helpful. If they themselves cannot help you with your particular needs, they will often direct you to others who can.

Be professional and businesslike in your correspondence. Type or word process your letter. Use imprinted stationery. Identify your research topic, and introduce yourself. Don't ramble. Have you been previously published? What is your particular interest in the topic? When you write libraries or archives, ask about specific research policies. Would you be welcome to visit? Are there any restrictions on the use of materials? What about copying services? Does the library maintain a photo file that you could use? Are there charges for specific services? What permissions will you need to reproduce material in your book, and, if there are rights and permissions charges for quoting excerpts or reprinting photographs, what are they?

Whenever possible, address your query to a specific person. Provide enough information about your research topics and your credentials to establish your credibility. The more information you provide (as briefly as possible) the easier it is for the archivist or librarian to help you.

Creativity is a full-time job. I firmly believe that every writer worth a publishing contract needs to develop a lifelong affinity for the ancient art of browsing. I've never met a bookstore or library that I didn't like. I learn a lot from roaming through bookstacks and skimming a wide variety of newspapers and magazines, and even the Yellow Pages. I often stumble across unexpected facts and research sources.

Finally, when your book is published, don't forget to cite the sources *you* used, and remember to thank all those wonderful individuals who helped you research your subject. Then, someone else down the road will be able to rely on your experiences just as you were helped by writers who preceded you.

104

Writing Biographies for Young People

By Lou Ann Walker

THE MOMENT I SIGNED THE CONTRACT TO WRITE A BOOK FOR YOUNG people on artist Roy Lichtenstein, I realized I was truly crazy. First of all, I would be writing about a major contemporary figure. He was alive and could kick if he hated what I did. Second, I was going to have to simplify the complex theories behind his art and present those to young readers, keeping in mind that many *adult* museum-goers don't "get" Lichtenstein. Lichtenstein's cartoon-like image of the drowning girl calling to "Brad" to save her floated into my mind: I hoped that Brad was coming for me, too, with a helicopter, a Ph.D. in art history, and a deft touch with the *bon mot*.

My first task was to squelch the panic that comes to virtually every writer. More than anything, I love to tackle what is considered impossible by other writers. I reminded myself that my job as a biographer is to use my ingenuity to circumvent complications. After all, biography is a word from the Greek meaning "record of a life." I began to steep myself in biographies for both adult and younger audiences. The principles I applied were those I have used dozens of times in writing profiles for magazines, as well as my autobiography.

Choosing your subject can be a fascinating process. No one needs to be reminded to write about what he or she knows. But don't be afraid to spread your wings. Look for a subject about whom you'd like to know more. To oversimplify: If you loved physics in college, choose Einstein. Maybe you don't know beans about physics, but you live in Princeton, New Jersey. Einstein again. Say your passion is Ireland. How about William Butler Yeats? If you don't care about Ireland but love poetry, try Yeats again. The point is to broaden your thinking.

The art of persuasion

Along the way, every biographer has to be able to convince someone to cooperate. If your subject is alive, then you have to get that person to talk to you; if dead, then there are descendants or friends of your subject whom you have to convince. Or perhaps it is the research librarian who guards your subject's papers. To paraphrase Janet Malcolm, you've got to seduce. People need to trust you, so you need to be trustworthy. You have to get people to reveal secrets about your subject so you can understand character and motive. But if the people you interview say that certain quotes are off the record, you must honor that restriction. They need to believe that you care about the subject and will be fair during the long, arduous process of writing about that person's life.

There are distinct disadvantages when your subject is alive. He or she may turn down your requests for interviews, and you'll have to be more creative in your approach. Don't give up. You may be intimidated by your subject and thus avoid certain delicate matters, or you may write puffery. Watch out for these pitfalls. Young readers are savvy enough to know when you're purposely hiding the "warts." One of the advantages of a face-to-face interview is that you get to describe the person's environment, clothing, friends, families, pet peeves, enthusiasms—all rich background material.

Read any previously published biographies of your subject to learn what point of view the biographer has taken. Also, you may glean information about the period in which your subject lived. Whether a subject is living or dead, much of a biographer's time is spent in research. Before you meet your subject for the first time, and before you put a word on paper, you must acquire a storehouse of information and read as much as possible of what is already in print. You need to delve into other books not only about your subject, but about and by related people and the relevant historical period. Search *The Readers' Guide to Periodical Literature*. If you're planning to write about a historical figure, don't ignore contemporary magazines, thinking that no one could possibly have written about, say, Alexander Graham Bell or Alexander the Great in the last few years. Somewhere, someone probably has.

In reading *The Lives of the Noble Grecians and Romans,* you'll find that Plutarch understood the interconnection between history and personality and included details that made his characters come alive to readers. Be creative when you look for sources. Digging up little-known, fascinating tidbits can be a great deal of fun. Try obscure museums. Look for videotapes that relate to your subject or the place he lived to help you add flavor to your biography and really understand the person you're writing about. You must constantly ask yourself what motivated your subject to take a specific action or make certain decisions. "Aha!" should become one of your favorite terms, each time you discover a fact or you piece together reasons for behavior.

As you research, make copious notes; I use sticky notes to mark places in books of my own and I make photocopies of important sections. Any notes you take should be in your own words, so that you can distinguish them from the original. Some biographers keep separate file folders for each chapter or topic. I wish I were that well-organized, but I do type up references in separate computer files.

The interview

There is nothing like being able to talk to your subject face to face, querying the whys and wherefores of his or her creativity. At this point you'll be grateful you're prepared. Before that first meeting with your subject, spend several days composing a long, thoughtful list of questions. Conduct preliminary interviews with other sources. If possible, you should have read as much as possible of what the person has written—or seen a substantial amount of his or her artistic creations. There is nothing more embarrassing than asking a question and having the subject say: "Why, that's in the introduction of my first book!" You must always be in control of your interviews and your subject. Don't spend your precious interviewing time apologizing.

I'm a belt-and-suspenders type. With the subject's permission, I run the tape recorder, at the same time writing down the subject's words and noting gestures and facial expressions. I keep my list of questions on a piece of bright-colored paper tucked inside the back of my notepad, so I can flip to it quickly.

And now for a bit of unorthodox advice: If you are writing about a living subject, begin writing *before* your last interview. You need to know where the holes are. What needs qualification and further explanation? Make sure to find out when your subject can be reached for follow-up questions by telephone. But don't abuse that time! Even if your subject is dead, you should begin writing before you've finished your research. I write the first and last chapters so I'll know what my

521

overall focus is and where I'm headed, as well as establishing my tone for the biography. Of course, chapters can be rewritten as you come up with new information, but you never want to be in the terrible situation of having lavished so much time on research (putting off the actual writing!) that you end up without enough time before your deadline to devote yourself to crafting your sentences carefully and analyzing the big picture. One biographer I know has spent years in research and has yet to put a pen to paper. He's the king of extensions. That's not good for your psyche or your bank account.

As you write, scrutinize every sentence. I read my work aloud. Writing for young people has to be even clearer than writing for adults. I study sentences and quotes to make sure they are understandable, but I don't avoid longer words. It's a mistake to "write down" to young readers. If there are a number of technical terms, consider including a glossary at the end of the book. Don't shy away from complicated ideas, either. The mark of a good writer is the ability to communicate virtually anything in terms the reader can understand. If you avoid explaining something, perhaps you don't understand it either. Make your book lively. Remember . . . you're telling a story, so you don't want to bore yourself or anyone else. Try your best to avoid starting with: "So-and-so was born on this date and died on this date." Scramble things up, and begin with a dramatic scene, such as a crisis in your subject's career.

I always like to give my readers a surprise. In *Amy,* my book about a deaf child, I included a photo series of Amy giving a sign language lesson. (The Japanese edition included delightful drawings with these photos.) In writing my Lichtenstein biography, I asked the artist for an art lesson. These components give readers a reason to pick up a book again and again after they've finished the text.

As with anything I write, I try to finish a biography before the deadline so that there is a cooling-off period. When I reread the chapters a few days or weeks later, I see them with a more critical eye.

Test your manuscript on young people, and perhaps a few teachers or parents. Tell them to be brutally honest. Listen carefully to any and all criticism; don't be put off by vague suggestions or strong reactions. Just changing an adjective can improve an entire paragraph or chapter. Not only will these people help you catch errors, but when the book comes out, they will be your greatest promoters. Word of mouth is a vital tool in keeping your published work alive.

If you have ideas for photo resources, mention them to your editor—in most cases, your enthusiasm will spark more care and attention on the part of your editor and the design team. But tread carefully! Many editors prefer writers to stay out of the design process.

Read the galleys for your book as carefully as you'd read a contract with a used-car salesman. Young readers leap on mistakes in any published book.

Now what?

Perhaps more than many adult books, biographies for young people have lives of their own. I'm often asked to give talks at schools, even about books published several years ago—something that doesn't happen very often with adult books—and it's very gratifying. The Authors Guild (330 W. 42nd St., 29th Fl., New York, NY 10036-6902) publishes an excellent guide to negotiating and preparing for in-school talks ($5 for non-members; free for members).

There is something very special about the clear, heartfelt response that you get from young readers. Their agendas aren't hidden. Once at a school book fair, a mother told me that her daughter had read my memoir, written for adults, several years before, and even now as a high school senior, her daughter turned to the book when she needed comforting. At another school, all three fifth-grade classes displayed their beautiful versions of Lichtenstein paintings. The art teacher herself was astonished at how the children expressed their reactions after reading my biography of the artist. As biographers for young readers, you're presenting role models for the next generation. Like adults, they want to learn about how other people overcome adversity. As biographers, we are releasing the creative force in our readers. I can't think of many things more important.

523

105

DISCOVERING STORIES
FOR PICTURE BOOKS

BY BARBARA ABERCROMBIE

YOU ASK YOURSELF WHAT COULD BE SO HARD ABOUT WRITING A PIC-
ture book? It ought to be easy: a short simple story for little kids . . .
kind of an apprenticeship for writing adult fiction. So you write a short
simple story you think children will like, but when you send it out to
publishers it only generates rejection slips. You wonder if there's some
sort of trick to discovering stories that will sell. A right way to do it,
maybe a formula.

There isn't a trick, of course, or a formula, and if there's a right way
to write picture books for children, it's simply being honest about your
own feelings. *Your* feelings, not what you think children should or
should not feel.

What were *your* secret fantasies when you were little? Did you want
to fly? Did you wish you could talk to your cat, or vice versa? Did you
want a larger family, or to be an only child? Were you ever confused
about who you were and what was expected of you? Did you sometimes have the best intentions in the world but find your actions misinterpreted? Did you want to be bigger? Better? Braver? Did your
parents ever embarrass you? Did you feel guilty about being embarrassed? Did you feel too tall, too short, too thin, too fat?

You may notice that things don't change all that much when we grow
up. What we dreamed of, found joy in, hid from, or hoped to change
as children often still concerns us as adults, and out of these concerns
can come the best stories for picture books. It took me a long time to
realize this. When I first attempted writing for children, I believed I
could think and plan my way into a story. But instead, the idea for my
first picture book, *Amanda & Heather & Company,* came to me as an
image, a flash of memory: I remembered how it felt to be a little kid
on an elevator and able to see only adult knees.

I can't tell you how or why this image popped into my head. But I can tell you that by paying attention to the feeling it gave me, of being very small and not understanding adults and their strange rituals, a story evolved about two little girls puzzled by the strange ways grown-ups enjoy themselves at a party. There's nothing about elevators in the story, but there is an illustration (by Mimi Boswell) showing Heather, very small, looking up at a sea of adult knees.

From writing my first picture book, I learned this lesson: Pay attention to your feelings, respect them, and recognize the paradox of thinking that your emotions are unique, yet at the same time *universal*.

One way to get direction into how you felt in the past is through sense memories—concentrating on whatever you absorbed through your five senses during a specific experience. Try it with the following list (you might want to make up your own list later). After each image, shut your eyes for a few moments, relax, and imagine seeing, smelling, tasting, touching, or hearing whatever the image suggests. Choose a specific period in your childhood and pay attention to the feelings that surface with the memory.

Imagine:

* the smell of your classroom the first day of school
* trying on a brand-new pair of shoes
* listening to the sounds of a summer night after you've gone to bed
* eating hot cereal in your kitchen on a cold winter morning
* holding a kitten and running your fingers through its fur
* walking barefoot through grass
* the sound of your parents' voices when they're angry
* opening a present you've longed for (or not getting a present you've longed for)
* your bedroom: what your bed looks like, the things you collect, your favorite toys, the view from the window
* playing a game with your best friend: the sounds, surroundings, feel of the ball or cards or whatever the game is played with

Notice also from this exercise how few words it takes to evoke feelings and memories.

In a picture book as in a poem, each word counts and echoes. In fact, I think a picture book is closer to a poem than to any other form of writing. The story needs to be compressed, yet at the same time each line requires weight and concentration. Dr. Seuss (Theodor Geisel) spoke of "boiling the thing down to the essentials." Simplicity and specific images (including metaphors) are essential. And your story must entertain as well. The sounds and rhythm of the language are vital. Children like to hear a good picture book read over and over again (something rarely true of novels or other forms of written material), but won't want to listen if the story isn't fun.

To understand the power of a picture book, the range and depth and sheer fun it can offer a child, read Maurice Sendak's *Where the Wild Things Are*. Read it over and over, and you'll understand how and why a picture book can endure and resonate, as a poem can. Read *The Story of Ferdinand* by Munro Leaf, too. Written over fifty years ago, this children's classic about a gentle bull who just wants to sit quietly and smell the flowers is an example of what can be done with plot, character, language, humor, and meaning in less than three pages of text. Read and study picture books that were your favorites when you were a child, then read at least fifty examples of picture books that are being published today—not for formulas or rules, but for information and to see what is possible. The best way to learn how to write is to read what you want to write. (This sounds obvious, but I'm always amazed at how many people try to write for children without ever reading what's being published today.)

How do ideas for picture book stories come to you? All I really know for sure is that out of the writing itself comes the story. You take a flash of memory, a true-life incident, a dream, or an observation, and you start writing. You take a cat from your own life and give it to two children in your imagination. You remember what it feels like when a pet is missing. You try what-ifs. What if the father lives in the city with a new wife? What if the girls visit them every weekend? And then suddenly you realize how that situation would connect to the fact that the cat has two homes.

Sometimes inspiration for picture books can come from experiences we have as adults, and then the story itself grows from a blend of reality and imagination. Charlie, the cat in my picture book *Charlie Anderson,* was actually a cat my parents adopted and that, they later discovered, had a second family. I wrote his story through the eyes of two little girls, but only as I wrote did I discover that Sarah and Elizabeth also have two families—a mother in the country and a father and stepmother in the city. I didn't start out to write about children who have two homes because of a divorce; I followed Charlie's life and discovered a more meaningful story as I wrote.

Another source of inspiration for picture books can be an urge to rewrite history, a need to change a sad, factual ending to a happy or more satisfying one. Newspapers can be gold mines for stories you'd like to rewrite. A few years ago I read a letter to Dear Abby about a pet pig named Hamlet who thought he was a dog. His life came to a sad yet predictable end (his name a self-fulfilling prophecy) when his owner had to give him up because of complaints from her suburban neighbors. The grieving owner wrote to Abby to let the world know how good-hearted pigs are and what wonderful pets they make. I was moved by the letter and couldn't get it out of my mind. Finally, I began a story about a pig that would have a happy ending. I worked on it for a long time before I discovered what the story was really about. My pig, renamed Henry, wants to fit into the family that adopted him. He first tries to be a baby, then one of the cats, and then one of the dogs, but he never really belongs or feels appreciated. He can't find happiness because he's always trying to be something he isn't; he feels he's the wrong color, his fur or tail isn't right, or he's too fat. My happy ending has Henry living out the rest of his natural life in a petting zoo, where he's loved and admired for what he is—a magnificent friendly pink pig.

I wrote this story for myself, to make me feel better about the real-life pig who wanted to be a dog. Picture books aren't written for children *out there* in desperate need of being shown the right way to feel and think and live. The child we're really writing for is right inside us. We're writing for the children we were, and the adults we are now. We still want to hear stories that make us laugh at ourselves and the weirdness of the world; stories that tell us we're not the only ones who get into trouble or danger or feel crazy sometimes; stories that will comfort us in the dark.

>> 106

WRITING CHILDREN'S FICTION FOR THE RELIGIOUS MARKET

BY KATHLEEN M. HAYS

RELIGIOUS MAGAZINES OFFER ONE OF THE BEST MARKETS FOR BEGIN-ning writers for children. Because there are dozens of these magazines, some of which are published weekly, there is a continuous need for stories. Also, there is less competition in this market because the payment rate is relatively low. Even so, many writers are reluctant to tackle "religious" stories, but if you are a beginner trying to get your first story published, you may want to reconsider.

Not all religious magazines for children insist on stories with an explicitly religious focus. The non-denominational *Pockets* is a good example. "Kate and the Making-a-Difference-Day Project," which won the annual *Pockets* fiction contest, *embodies* Christian principles rather than *teaches* them. As you become familiar with the children's magazine market, you will discover that many religious magazines want the same kind of story as general interest magazines: lively characters involved in believable situations with resolutions that exemplify wholesome values.

There are many ways to give an otherwise general interest story a religious slant. Consider working a reference to church-going into a bit of dialogue: "Mom was too busy planning some church dinner to listen to me." Or, set your summer sports story at a church camp instead of the local park, or have a quarrel between two friends take place at Sunday school rather than during school recess. Use an indirect biblical reference: "Now I know how the older brother felt when the prodigal son showed up." The advantage of this technique is that the same story may be submitted to both religious and general interest markets without extensive rewriting.

There are some magazines, however—usually those published by conservative religious groups—that want explicitly religious stories. Their editors look for characters who solve problems according to Bible principles, stories that impart basic church doctrine. If you are interested in writing for that part of the market, you need more than a main character who says a prayer or recalls a Bible verse at a critical moment. Your character's religious beliefs must have a direct impact on the outcome of the story. The best way to judge what kind of stories a magazine publishes is to study sample copies.

Writing to theme

Several religious magazines, including *Pockets, R-A-D-A-R,* and *Guideposts for Kids* (formerly *Faith 'n Stuff*), use a "theme list." A theme list for these publications is generally sent with the writer's guidelines and may include suggested Bible verses or ideas for stories and activities. Some writers object to the restrictiveness of writing to theme, but if you can do it, you will increase your chance of selling.

First, read the magazine's theme list in its entirety. Perhaps you have a finished story sitting on your desk at this moment. Does it fit one of the themes? Could it be made to fit?

Don't reject a theme out of hand because it seems difficult. Stories about issues like family and friendship are easy to write, but they also attract other writers. If you can handle a less common theme, you might have a better chance of having your story accepted.

If a theme touches on a problem in your own life, use it as the basis of a story. Don't focus on what happened, but on how you felt about it. Use your feelings of conflict and emotional tension to make your story's main character believable.

I often find it helpful to explore the biblical roots of a theme I am considering. For the *Pockets* topic, "Seeing Others as God Sees Them," I was reminded of the parable of the prodigal son, the young man who wasted his inheritance and came home to find his father waiting with open arms. I have always sympathized with the stay-at-home brother in that story. I'm sure you know him, too—the scowling fellow who went around muttering about people who get the fatted calf. The story I eventually sold to *Pockets* was about a girl who feels slighted when an older stepsister moves in. I doubt if anyone else noticed a connection with the prodigal son's brother, but it made the story work for me.

529

Brainstorm on your theme. Post it where you will see it frequently and can think about it while you're doing other things; give yourself a half hour with a cup of coffee and a blank piece of paper. Jot down anything that comes to mind, no matter how foolish it may look. The trick to brainstorming is to restrain your inner critic long enough to free up the creative part of your mind.

Once you have a list of story ideas to work with, start by defining the main character—boy or girl, age, family situation, personality, perhaps name—and then move on to the plot. What is the main character's goal? What obstacles must he or she overcome to reach it? How is the conflict resolved? Once you have a rough outline, you can start to write, but keep the theme constantly in mind. Make every bit of dialogue and action point toward it.

If at first . . .

You've written your story, polished it, sent it off, and it's been returned. What next? Because you targeted your story for the religious market, you have many other options. Get out your market guide and select another magazine.

After you have tried your preferred markets, give careful consideration to the others. Don't be afraid to send your story to a magazine because the specific beliefs and practices of the parent denomination are unfamiliar to you. An editor who likes your story may be willing to edit a few details to meet the magazine's specific needs.

Think about possible markets before you begin to write. If your story could be suitable for the general interest market, don't make the conclusion hinge on the main character deciding to join a Bible study group. On the other hand, plan in advance how you could strengthen the religious slant.

Pay attention to word limits. *Pockets* and *Guideposts for Kids* have upper limits of about 1500 words, but many general interest magazines are in the 900-word range. For them, shorter is better. A 900-word story probably has twice as many possible markets as one of 1500 words.

Becoming a successful writer for children requires good writing and market savvy. Writing for religious magazines is an excellent way for a beginner to learn the craft and to build a list of credits.

➣➣ EDITING AND MARKETING

➤➤ 107

Confessions of a First Reader

By Roy Sorrels

Your novel, the precious manuscript you've slaved over for months—years, maybe—the one you've revised and edited till it shines like gold, lovingly typed, checked and double-checked for typos, packaged for safety, and mailed off to an editor in a spirit of hopeful optimism, gets passed on by the editor to a free-lance "first reader."

It's every writer's nightmare, but it's also reality. Most manuscripts, even those sent to an editor by a well-known agent, are first read by the editor's in-office assistant, but more often by a first reader.

I was that first reader, for one of the biggest companies in the business. For two years, while writing my own first novel, I dropped by an editor's office once a week to pick up several manuscripts, mostly novels, took them home, read them, and prepared a "reader's report" including a brief plot summary and a paragraph giving my recommendation as to whether it was a "hit" or a "miss" and why.

I gave each manuscript a fair and conscientious read, often speeding up considerably after the first 30 or so pages, when it became abundantly and often painfully clear that what I was reading was unpublishable. Over 90 percent of what I read was, in my opinion, unpublishable, but I really wanted to go to my next meeting with my boss and be able to say, "*This* one is great. Read it! Buy it!"

In the process, I picked up a few extremely valuable tips that helped me write and sell my first novel and several more since. I'd like to share what I learned about any talented writer's chances of eventually getting published.

The first thing aspiring writers must remember is that the editor is their friend. Most writers imagine editors as barriers to their success whose main job is to reject their work. *Not so.* Editors get paid to find good, publishable manuscripts—stuffing form rejection slips into

SASEs is only a disappointing byproduct of that search. They want the manuscript they've just received from a writer to be something great! After all, if editors don't find enough excellent manuscripts, they lose their jobs.

Although it's true that agented material has a strong advantage, even the slush pile gets looked at eventually. Whether your unagented manuscript gets attention or not rests on these six crucial points:

1) Never—*never*—send a manuscript to a publisher unless you have an editor's name, and not just any editor but the right one for your type of book. A manuscript addressed to "Editor" or "To Whom It May Concern" may never reach the editor responsible for the type of book you're submitting. It's relatively simple to get the name of the right editor, but it does require some extra work. If you've written a police procedural, for example, go to your local bookstore or public library to find the name of a publisher who has brought out several police procedural novels. Consult the list of publishers in *Literary Market Place* (available in the reference department of most libraries) for the phone number of that publisher and call and ask for the editorial department. Request the name of the person who handles police procedurals (or whatever category your manuscript is).

I've done this with numerous publishers, and I've always been able to get the name of the appropriate person. If you're asked why you want to know, just tell the truth, and most of the time you'll get the name you're looking for. By addressing your manuscript to a specific editor, it will reach the person who is responsible for the type of material you've written, usually guaranteeing much better attention—even though it may not be accepted.

2) Include a cover letter that's informative, *well-written,* and succinct (rarely more than one page), since you want it to be read. Include brief biographical information, noting any credits or relevant information, and two or three lines about your book. As some wise person once said, "You never get a second chance to make a good first impression," and you want your first impression to show that even though you are perhaps unpublished, you've taken the trouble to learn how a pro acts.

3) As a first reader, I was shocked to see how often beginners reveal their ignorance of the basics of presenting a manuscript. *Neatness counts*—and not simply flawless typing and clean paper that doesn't

look as if it's already been shopped around to every publisher in town, but an overall professional presentation.

4) Once you've succeeded in getting an editor to open to page one of your manuscript, you absolutely must be sure you start with a powerfully effective opening line, first paragraph, and opening page. If what the editor reads on page one grabs or moves or amuses him, then he might read your entire manuscript, or at least pass it on to a reader—and at that point you'll have just as much chance as anybody else of having your manuscript accepted for publication.

5) I often saw the editor I worked for wander over to the slush pile table and riffle quickly through half a dozen manuscripts before handing me one to read. I was mystified: What could she possibly see from ten seconds of flipping pages? When I asked her, she answered, "I'm looking for lots of dialogue." Questioned further, she explained that one of the major flaws in novels from beginning writers was too much narration, not enough lively conversation between characters. Dialogue is vital in getting a reading for an unagented script, not just well-written dialogue, but plenty of it.

6) From slogging through countless bad novels and the occasional one that stood out above the others, I learned that there is absolutely no substitute for the combination of powerful storytelling and vibrant characters. A *story* that is strong and *characters* that come alive on the page will make up for all sorts of other flaws.

But the most important lesson I learned—and I unfailingly applied it to my own beginning novel-writing career—is not to be intimidated by the overwhelming number of submissions publishers receive. So what if Publisher X gets a thousand submissions a week, if 99 percent of them are weak and amateurishly presented? If you've written an excellent novel, and you present it in a professional manner, your chances are as good as any other writer's. Remember, the editor is hungry for good writing.

The motto of every aspiring and not-yet-published writer should always be, "If at first you don't succeed, try again." As a first reader I wrote negative reports on a few books that, a year or two later, I saw in bookstores. One was nominated for a prestigious award. I thought they were dreadful and said so in my reader's reports, but that was simply one person's opinion. Some other first reader, and an editor, obviously loved them. And bought them.

➤➤ 108

EVERYTHING YOU NEED TO KNOW
ABOUT LITERARY AGENTS

BY NANCY LOVE

GETTING STARTED IN THE BOOK WRITING BUSINESS ISN'T GETTING any easier. To the great frustration and annoyance of both writers and literary agents, many large publishing houses no longer accept unsolicited manuscripts. Gone are the slush piles of yore and the excitement when an assistant editor found a gem buried in all those masses of paper. I hear from writers that some editors still do respond to query letters—as opposed to proposals or manuscripts—and instead of a stock, "We don't read unsolicited submissions; get an agent," may actually invite a submission.

For better or for worse, though, agents have increasingly become the keepers of the gates to book-publishing heaven. It's not good for agents when many of us feel as if we're drowning in unsuitable submissions, and it's worse for writers who, in most cases, have to get an agent's attention before they can even try to get an editor's attention.

Who *doesn't* need an agent?

But not everyone needs an agent. Who doesn't? Writers of poetry, articles, and short fiction for magazines can do best on their own, and in fact, probably won't find an agent who will represent them. Writers of text, academic, and professional books—in other words, non-trade (bookstore) books—traditionally sell their own books.

As for writers of trade books, the most successful on their own are the well-connected and the persistent. The well-connected know who they are. They have friends or family who will open some doors for them, or have been approached by a publisher to write a book; or they are so well-known that they need only put out the word for offers to come pouring in. Those in this category will often work with a lawyer who can negotiate and vet the contract.

As for the persistent, they are those hardy and fearless souls who believe they can unlock the doors themselves, and often do, though they often have to approach smaller publishing houses. Some self-publish and can do well if they have a well-defined market—like the Chinese cookbook writer in San Francisco who sells her books at conventions and to people who take her Chinatown tours. A couple I now represent sold 40,000 copies of their self-published book on the joys of Eastern sex through catalogues and advertising and their workshops. Eventually, the business of selling books was taking too much of their time, and I sold reprint rights for their book to a large publishing house only too happy to take over the decidedly unglamorous nitty gritty of the business of promoting and selling.

When do you start looking for an agent?

If you write fiction, after you have finished writing a novel (and have polished it; don't send a "first draft"), you could start your search. Most editors won't read unfinished first novels, therefore, I won't either. There are exceptions to this general rule, of course. Someone famous or with other writing credits can go to an agent with a partial manuscript. A writer with a success or two to his credit will usually be able to show his editor a synopsis of the next book. The advice I always give for short story collections is to try to get some of the stories published in magazines or quarterlies before going for a book.

As for nonfiction, you are ready to talk to an agent when you have a proposal (there are lots of books that will tell you how to do it). If you have some credentials as a journalist, however, an agent might be willing to talk over some ideas with you. If you are a doctor or a physicist or a police officer with an idea but no time or writing skills, a query letter and/or a telephone call is probably your best avenue to an agent who may be able to find a writer to help with a proposal.

Why do you need an agent?

What can an agent do for a writer that a writer can't do for himself or herself, besides having access to editors and saving the writer time?

Here are some of the services that I perform for writers. You decide whether you can do the same or better yourself.

Pre-selling or Getting the Book Together

• When I am approached by editors or packagers with book ideas, I go to the writers I represent, or to others I think would be suitable. Or *I* might come up with ideas that I pass on to my writers.

• Collaborations also often originate with agents. Or if a writer comes to me with a collaboration offer already in place, I can help to negotiate it and try to keep it on course if there are problems.

• Those of us with editorial skills like to think we can make your good ideas better. Often the writer's original idea for fiction or nonfiction needs shaping, focusing, or a little fine-tuning. Maybe it only needs a better title. There's no point in going out with either a nonfiction book proposal or a novel that isn't the best it can possibly be.

Selling

This is what everyone knows agents do. But what does it mean?

• Matchmaking: Selling a book is not like selling widgets. Putting the right editor in the right publishing house together with the right project is more like putting together the right partners in a marriage. John's wife just had a baby so he's going to love this parenting book. Publishing house A favors conservative books and their editor B likes controversial books, so he'll go for this book about how the radical left is corrupting Congress.

• Deal-making: So what's the trick? you might ask. Just take the most money and run. I wish it were that simple. Often the best way to get the most money is an auction, but you can't have an auction without at least two bidders. Three or more would be better. At this point, I call on any reserves of knowledge about herd mentality that might work to stampede the reluctant-to-bid to the table; or if the auction falls through, I regroup to try to get the offer raised. This is the time to stand firm.

There are often other considerations as important to a client as money. For example, what resources will the publisher commit to promoting the book? Control of foreign rights or entertainment rights might be an issue. All these are part of the basic deal that sometimes requires both delicacy and strength to put together.

• Negotiating the contract: Then there are all those fine points in every boilerplate contract. It's my job to know which ones are soft and will yield if I tough it out and which ones are probably engraved in stone. I can hear myself saying, "Well, if you can't give me better percentages on discounts, then give me a cap on how many books can be sold at that discount." Naturally, the more clout a writer has, the easier it is to get concessions. The agent for a writer of three successful books is obviously in a better position to make demands than when she was negotiating a contract for the writer's first novel.

Pre-publication

• Collecting the money. Actually, this starts with signing the contract and in the best cases continues for years after the book comes out. The agent is the collector of advances, royalties, subsidiary rights money. I spend a lot of time tracking and chasing clients' money, and checking royalty statements. I assume it is my responsibility to keep publishers honest and payments on time.

• Acting as liaison between writer and editor, between collaborators, and if necessary between writer and company lawyer on libel and privacy issues. In the best of all possible worlds, nothing goes wrong; in the real world here are a few scenarios from hell that might drag me in as mediator or go-between:

The book is late. Can we get an extension?

The editor leaves. The book is now an "orphan."

The collaborators have stopped talking to each other, and no one knows how or if the book will be completed.

• Promotion and marketing. As it gets closer to publication, I like to do a reality check on the plans of publisher and writer for promoting the book. Sometimes everything is humming along nicely without me. Sometimes I am the one who sets up a meeting of the writer and public relations team (and special sales force if appropriate). I might suggest outside publicity help or coach a writer in the ways she can do it herself.

After publication, I might find myself drawn into the promotion drama when systems break down—where are the books? why can't the writer get on "Oprah"? and other crises.

• Handling subsidiary rights either alone or with subagents. Aggressive pursuit of first serial, entertainment, foreign and other rights is an important link in the money chain and can continue well after the publication of the book.

These are the tangible tasks I find myself occupied with in my role as an agent. The intangible ones might include support, encouragement, and hand-holding, but probably the most important role of an agent is being sensitive to the dreams and goals of each individual, and to help writers reach those, whatever they are, whether money, recognition and/or the pride of having made a contribution to society.

How do you find an agent?

A personal recommendation is the best. Take a lesson from businessman/writer Harvey Mackay and hit your Rolodex. He has thousands of cards on his, but you probably have more possibilities in yours than you realize. Is there a newspaper or magazine editor you've worked with who could suggest an agent, or a writer who has an agent to share? How about your old roommate from college who had a book published? You get the idea. Put the word out and get those phone lines buzzing.

I heard an ingenious idea for identifying a likely agent from a writer who had checked out the acknowledgments in a published book that was similar to his—and found me. It's one way of finding an agent who is successful with your kind of book.

Then, of course, there are listings in reference books for writers. Perhaps the best lists are those that have been pre-screened. For instance, members of the Writers Union rate agents and provide this information to other members. If you belong to the American Society of Journalists and Authors, they will supply you with a list of their members' agents.

Another valuable list is the members of the professional society of agents, the Association of Authors' Representatives, which you can obtain for $5.00 plus a legal-size self-addressed, stamped envelope with 52¢ postage from its office (10 Astor Pl., 3rd Floor, New York, NY 10003). To be eligible for membership, agents have to meet certain book sale requirements and be sponsored by other members. The requirements for listings in *Literary Market Place,* while not as stringent, at least are designed to screen out dabblers and the inexperienced.

Once you've put together a target or targets, the next step is a query letter or a telephone call for information about how the agent prefers to receive submissions. For nonfiction, some of us prefer a query letter first, others a proposal and sample chapters. For fiction, some agents want a query letter, others like sample chapters and a synopsis, still others prefer a full novel. (Always include a self-addressed, stamped envelope if you want your proposal or manuscript returned.)

Agents vary not only in how they want to be approached, but also in what the next steps are in consummating a relationship once the agent offers to represent you. If possible, it is a good idea to meet in order to judge whether the chemistry is right. But at the very least, it's important to discuss the agent's client list, method of operation, and terms. I have an Author-Agent Agreement that spells out the terms of my representation. If the agent of your choice doesn't, be sure you ask questions about charges for expenses that will be passed on to you; what the commission is for subagents, who handle foreign and movie or TV rights; and the provisions for dissolving the relationship if either party decides to pull out.

You will probably want to ask other questions about the working arrangement. Will you be informed of submissions and rejections? Will the agent do multiple or single submissions? I just read a letter from an agent who told a writer that she was sending back his novel because she didn't continue to submit after she had four rejections. I send out many books twelve, even twenty-four times, if that's what it takes to sell them, and I don't think I'm that unusual. Agents differ in many ways, large and small.

I know there's a certain euphoria that settles in when an agent wants to sign you up; I've been on that end myself. But you have to remind yourself that this is a serious business arrangement. You are entrusting your career to a person who will have an important role in your life. Do you trust him/her? Is his/her vision for your future the same as yours? In other words, the question you should ask yourself is not just, How do I get an agent? but How do I get an agent who is right for me?

>> 109

Common Questions About Copyrights

By Howard Zaharoff

To be a good writer, you must understand the basics of writing. To be a published writer, you must understand the basics of manuscript submission and the editorial process.

And to be a successful writer, the owner of a portfolio of published manuscripts, you must also understand the basics of copyright law. As a lawyer who practices in the field, I promise that this isn't too hard. Let me prove it by answering a dozen questions that free lancers often ask.

Before doing so, a few comments. First, the answers I give are based on U.S. law. International issues are mostly ignored. Second, my focus is mainly on works first published or created after March 1, 1989, the last major revision of the Copyright Act (which I refer to below as the "Act"). Third, although the Copyright Office cannot provide legal advice, its Circulars and Public Information Office (call 202/479-0700) provide guidance on many of the following issues. (Start with Circular 1, "Copyright Basics.") There are also many excellent books available, such as Ellen Kozak's *Every Writer's Guide to Copyright & Publishing Law* (Owl, 1990).

1. *What can be copyrighted?* Copyright protects nearly every original piece you write (or draw, compose, choreograph, videotape, sculpt, etc.): not just your novel, article, story or poem, but the software program you create, the advertisements and greeting cards you published, and the love letters you wrote in high school. But copyright does not protect your ideas, only the way you *express* them.

2. *What protection does copyright provide?* A "copyright" is really a bundle of rights. The copyright owner (whom we'll call the "proprietor") controls not only the right to copy the work, but also the rights

542

to prepare "derivative works" (i.e., adaptations, translations, and other modifications), to perform or display the work publicly, and to make the "first sale" of each copy of the work.

3. *What is the duration of copyright protection, and is it renewable?* For works created or first published after 1977, copyright generally lasts 50 years after the death of the author. However, for anonymous or pseudonymous works, or works made "for hire" (see below), the term expires 100 years from creation or 75 years from publication. There are no renewals. (For works published before 1978, the term is 28 years, with right to renew for 47 additional years. See Circular 15, "Renewal of Copyright.")

4. *How do you obtain a copyright?* Copyright protection arises *automatically* as soon as you put your ideas into tangible form. Thus, once on paper, canvas, video, or computer disk, your creation is protected by law.

5. *Is a copyright notice required for protection?* No. Until recently a notice was required on all *published* copies of a work. ("Published" simply means distributed to the public; it does not require printing in a periodical or book.) However, on March 1, 1989, the United States joined the international copyright treaty known as the Berne Convention and removed this requirement for works published after that date.

Still, including a copyright notice alerts everyone to your claim and prevents an infringer from pleading "innocence" (that is, that he had no idea your work was copyrighted). Thus, good reasons remain for including notices on all published copies of your work, and for insisting that your publisher do so.

If you are concerned that your *unpublished* work may be used or copied without permission (e.g., you are circulating copies of your most timely and accomplished piece within your newly formed writers group), you can't lose by including a notice.

6. *What should my copyright notice say?* A proper notice has three elements:

- The international copyright symbol © or the word "Copyright." Most publishers use both. (The abbreviation "Copr" is also acceptable.)
- The year in which the work is first published. (For unpublished works, you may omit a date.)

543

- Your name, or a recognizable abbreviation (e.g., International Business Machines Corporation may use "IBM").

In general, notices should be displayed prominently at the beginning of your work, although any reasonable location is acceptable. If your piece will appear in a magazine, anthology, or other collective work, a single notice in the publisher's name will preserve most of your rights. However, including a separate copyright notice in your own name will clarify that only you, *not* the publisher, has the right to authorize further uses of your work.

7. *Must I register my work with the Copyright Office?* Although registration is not required for copyright protection, it is a precondition to suing for infringement of the copyrights in any work first published in the U.S. (and in the unpublished works of U.S. citizens and residents), and enables you to recover both attorneys' fees and "statutory damages" (i.e. damages of up to $100,000, determined by the judge, which the proprietor may elect to recover from the infringer in lieu of proving and recovering actual losses).

You can register your copyrights at any time during the term of copyright. However, registration within three months of publication generally preserves your rights to all infringement remedies, including statutory damages, while registration within five years of publication provides special benefits in legal proceedings.

8. *How do you register a work?* Copyright Office Form TX is the basic form for nondramatic literary works. Form PA is used to register works of the performing arts, including plays and movies. These one-page forms cost $20 to file and are fairly easy to complete (but only if you read the accompanying instructions!). Adjunct Form GR/CP allows writers to reduce costs by making a single registration for all works published in periodicals within a 12-month period. (You can order forms and circulars over the Hotline, 202/707-9100).

When you apply you must submit one copy of the work, if unpublished, and two copies of the "best edition" of the work, if published. (Only one copy of the best edition is required for contributions to collective works.) The "best edition" is the published edition of highest quality, determined by paper quality, binding, and other factors listed by the Copyright Office (see Circular R7b). For example, if the work

544

was published in both hard and soft covers, the hard cover is normally the best edition.

9. *Should I register my work?* In most cases, no. If your work was published, your publisher may have registered it. If not, failure to register costs you mainly the option for *immediate* relief and statutory damages. Moreover, infringement is the exception and, where it occurs, often can be settled without lawsuits or registration. Besides, most writers earn too little to justify the cost of registration (certainly for articles, poems, and other short works).

10. *What is "public domain" and how can you find out what's there?* Works that are not protected by copyright are said to be in the "public domain"—i.e., freely usable by the public, without the need to get permission or pay a fee. This includes works in which copyright has expired or been lost, works for which copyright is not available, and works dedicated to the public. Although there are many exceptions, *in general* the following are in the public domain:

- Works published more than 75 years ago.
- Works published more than 28 years ago, if the copyright was not renewed.
- Works published without a proper copyright notice before 1978.
- Works published without a proper notice between January 1, 1978 and February 28, 1989 (although the Act enables the proprietor to correct this failure).
- Works created by employees of the Federal government as part of their duties.

For a fee the Copyright Office will examine the status of a work. (See Circular 22, "How to Investigate the Copyright Status of a Work.")

11. *What is fair use?* The Act allows the limited use of others' works for research, teaching, news reporting, criticism, and similar purposes. These permitted uses are called "fair use," although the Act never defines that term. Rather, it lists factors to consider, including the purpose and character of the use (e.g., for-profit vs. teaching), the nature of the work (e.g., a science text vs. a poem), the amount and substantiality of the use, and its effect on the market for the work.

Here are some basic rules that should help you stay on the right side of the law (and help you recognize when someone's use of your work doesn't).

545

• **Copying for noncommercial (e.g., educational) purposes is given wider scope than copying for commercial use.** For example, in general you may quote less of the published writings of a politician in a television docudrama than a history professor may quote in journal articles.

• **Copying factual material gets more latitude than copying fiction.** Fiction contains more of the "originality" protected by the Act: characters and events, sometimes even time and place, derive from the writer's imagination. Facts cannot be copyrighted.

• **Parody is a permissible use, as long as it does not appropriate too much of the original.**

• **Copying from unpublished works without permission is usually considered unfair.** This was illustrated in a 1989 case concerning an unauthorized biography of Scientologist/SF writer L. Ron Hubbard. Referring to an earlier case, in which Random House was enjoined from publishing an unauthorized biography of J. D. Salinger because it infringed copyrights in his unpublished letters, the court wrote that "unpublished works normally enjoy complete protection" from unauthorized publication. (However, legislation is being considered that would expand the application of fair use to unpublished works.)

• **The Act permits certain uses of copyrighted works by libraries, archives, educators, charitable organizations, and others.** See sections 108–110 of the Act and Circular 21.

These rules are complex. Therefore, if you intend to copy more than a negligible amount from another person's work without permission, write to the publisher or copyright owner. Don't take a chance.

12. *What is a "work made for hire," and who owns the rights to these works?* The creator of a work generally owns the copyrights. There is an exception, however, for "works made for hire." Here it is the party who commissions and pays for the work, rather than the actual creator, who owns the copyrights. So when is a work "for hire"?

First, unless expressly excluded by contract, all works created by employees within the scope of their employment are "for hire." (This will normally not include works created on your own time that are unrelated to your employment.) So if you are employed by a news-

546

paper, or hired by a software publisher to write documentation, your employer owns the copyrights in the works you've been paid to create. If you use copies of these works at your next job, you are infringing on your former employer's copyrights.

Second, certain specified categories of works (including translations, compilations, and parts of audiovisual works) are considered "for hire" if they have been specially commissioned and a signed document identifies them as "for hire." Therefore, *if you are not an employee and you haven't agreed in writing that your work is "for hire" (or otherwise assigned your rights), you will generally continue to own the copyrights in your work* even if others paid you to create it (although they will have the right to use your work for the express purposes for which they paid you).

You may wonder about the division of rights when your article, story, or poem is published in a magazine (or other collective work) and there is no written agreement. The Act supplies the answer: The publisher acquires only the right to publish your piece as part of that collective work, of any revision of that work, and of any later collective work in the same series. You retain all other rights, so you are free to revise or remarket your piece.

The above is a *general* discussion of the copyright law as it applies to freelancers. Myriad qualifications and exceptions are not included here. Before making any important copyright decisions consult a knowledgeable copyright lawyer, the Copyright Office, or a trusted publisher or agent with an up-to-date understanding of the law.

➤➤ 110

How to Write Queries That Sell

By Nancy Cornell

ARMED WITH AN IDEA FOR A TERRIFIC ARTICLE, YOU ARE READY TO join hordes of other free lancers in the magazine writing field, right? Wrong! Before writing the article, you have to sell the idea. An irresistible query letter will put you ahead of the mass of other free lancers.

You must make your query appropriate, professional and intriguing to an editor to get your name out of the slush pile and onto a check. Here are six tips for writing a good query:

1) Target appropriate markets, and study them carefully. Read several current issues of the magazine you want to write for. I asked for a sample copy of *Key Horizons,* a closed-circulation magazine (sent only to certain people), and enclosed a large, self-addressed stamped envelope (SASE).

The closer your query matches the articles in the magazine, the better your chance of getting an assignment. Are the magazine's articles written in first person or third? Do they use lots of anecdotes and quotes or more straight exposition? Does the magazine favor human-interest pieces, technology, travel? How long are the articles? After perusing a few copies, you'll recognize the magazine's editorial format.

2) Know the reader. Look at the ads, because they reflect the readers' demographics. Is the model nibbling caviar in a five-star restaurant? Then a proposal entitled "Cost-Cutting Hostels" is about as appropriate as a fur coat in Tahiti. Publications know whom they want to reach—so do successful writers.

Pictures in *Key Horizons* showed models with gray hair and a few wrinkles, ads for hearing aids and retirement centers. Readers of this magazine lead active lives on retirement dollars. Since *Key Horizons* ran a food story in each issue, my query on the benefits of cooking healthful, low-cost meals with peppers interested them.

Editors want articles like the ones they publish, but not the same one they just published. "Browse a dozen copies of the magazine so you don't unknowingly repeat ideas that have run recently," advises former editor and publisher of *Playboy* Nat Lehrman. "This may seem elementary, but the most common complaint heard about writers in an editorial office is: 'Don't these writers read the magazine?'"

3) Be brief. Keep queries to one page, and make the first paragraph, at least the first sentence, sing. Though swamped with submissions, editors notice good queries. My query consisted of three informative, short paragraphs. The first paragraph hooked the editor, the second briefly outlined the article and named an expert I would interview, and the third told some of my writing experience. A zippy title headed the letter.

Analyze your target magazine's article titles. Are they in the form of questions or statements or labels or rhymes? Perhaps they are statistical, paradoxical, or a play on words. Determine the average word length of the titles. Attention to such details helps set your work apart from the competition. Of course, editors often change your title; my title, "Hot 'n' Healthy," became "Hot Stuff." I wish I'd thought of it!

4) Present your query professionally. If a professional-looking query with a promising idea and title reaches an editor the same day as a similar idea filled with grammatical errors and scrawled on mauve stationery, guess which writer gets the go-ahead.

Think of your query letter as a job application, your stand-in for a personal interview. Like an applicant, the letter must be neat, grammatical, and respectful of the editor's time. It must sell itself.

Fussy English teachers pale in comparison to fastidious editors. Misspelled words, typos, or grammatical errors have no place in a professional writer's business.

Since writers and editors rarely meet face to face, a query is often their first contact. Using good quality white or off-white paper for your letterheads, envelopes, and business cards is a must. Though the initial expense may seem high, it's worth the cost, because editors are more disposed to read attractively presented queries.

Letterheads should include your name, address, telephone number, and FAX number, if you have one. Do not have the word "writer" printed on your letterhead, but do put a descriptive word like "Writer" or "Travel Writer" on your business cards. Don't use vertically printed or odd-sized business cards that won't fit into a business card file.

5) After you've written an irresistible query on your professional-looking stationery, send it to the appropriate person at the magazine, not just The Editor. Look at the masthead and address it to a person by name. Skip the publisher and editor-in-chief; aim instead for an editor about the middle of the masthead. If you can't tell if it's a man or a woman, then address the editor by the full name: Dear Leslie Black. Or better still, call the magazine to check the editor's name and exact spelling (and gender, if there is a question about it). This is especially important if the sample issue you have is more than a couple of months old, as editors often move from one publication to another.

6) Keep careful records of queries and follow up on them. On a simple tracking chart, note the date you mailed the query, subject of your proposed article, name and address of the publication, and the name of the editor. Allow room on the chart to note the response and other pertinent information. A weekly glance at the chart will keep you up to date on your queries.

The following is an example of a query letter that used all six tips and resulted in an article published in *Key Horizons* magazine:

Brenda Pace, Editor
Key Horizons
950 N. Meridian, Suite 1200
Indianapolis, IN 46204

Dear Ms. Pace:

Hot 'n' Healthy

Now there's proof positive. Peppers not only taste good but they also help those who eat them to stay healthy. One jalapeno contains more of vitamins A and C than three oranges. Peppers contain no fat and few calories. In addition, delicious Mexican food is easy and inexpensive to prepare.

How would you like my feature story on the healthy habit of eating tasty hot peppers? Along with verified health facts, pepper history and tips for use, the story will include interviews with pepper authorities including Pace Foods' Dr. Lou "Pepper" Rasplicka. I can provide recipes and illustration.

I am a contributor to *New Choices, American Way, Modern Maturity,* and other national publications. Clips and an SASE are enclosed for your convenience. Thank you for considering this query.

Best regards,
s/Nancy Cornell

Key Horizons responded to my query in an unprecedented 12 days; more often, replies take four to six weeks. If there's been no response within that time I send a postcard that reads: "Dear [editor's name]: I wonder if you received my query entitled [name of query] mailed to you on [date]. If not, please let me know, and I'll be happy to send you a copy. If you are still considering it, fine. Take your time. But if you can't use it, please let me know so I may submit it elsewhere."

Surprisingly effective, this polite request usually gets a quick response and, on more than a few occasions, an assignment. Maybe the editor is considering the query and simply needs encouragement.

Because an editor's inaction effectively removes your proposed article from circulation while it's in his or her hands, writers often submit simultaneous queries, sending the same idea (not the same letter) to more than one appropriate publication at the same time. The practice makes good business sense. What if more than one editor wants you to go ahead with your idea? You should be so lucky!

Be sure to send an SASE with your query to assure a reply. Most editors will not respond if you fail to do so. Successful writers get more assignments than rejections because they treat writing as a business, not a hobby. When you get a "go-ahead" in response to your query, write that article in an entertaining and informative manner. Try to make the written piece even better than the query that got you the assignment.

Where to Sell

Where to Sell

More markets and listings than ever before distinguish this year's edition of *The Writer's Handbook*, and writers at all levels of experience should be encouraged by the number and variety of opportunities available to them. Editors, publishers, and producers rely on free lancers for a wide range of material—from articles and fiction to play scripts, poetry, opinion essays, and how-to and children's books—and many are also very receptive to the work of talented newcomers.

Still one of the best markets for beginning free lancers is the field of specialized publications, including city and regional and travel magazines, and those covering such areas as consumer issues, sports, and hobbies and crafts. Editors of these magazines are in constant need of authoritative articles (for which the payment can be quite high), and writers with experience in and enthusiasm for a particular field, whether it's gardening, woodworking, bicycling, antiques, bird watching, bridge, or car repair, can turn their knowledge into article sales. Such interests and activities can generate more than one article if a different angle is used for each magazine and the writer keeps the audience and editorial content firmly in mind.

Magazines devoted to the special concerns of families and parents represent another market with great potential for free lancers—there has been a dramatic increase in the number of publications in this area—and the business, computer, health, and personal finance magazine markets are also very strong, with articles on these topics appearing in almost every publication on the newsstands today. For these subjects, editors are looking for writers who can translate technical material into lively, readable prose, often the most important factor in determining a sale.

While some of the more established markets may seem difficult to break into, especially for the beginner, there are thousands of lesser-known publications where editors will consider submissions from first-time free lancers. City and regional publications offer some of the best opportunities, since these editors generally like to work with local writers and often use a wide variety of material, from features to fillers.

555

Many newspapers accept op-ed pieces, and are most receptive to pieces on topics not covered by syndicated columnists (politics, economics, and foreign affairs); pieces with a regional slant are particularly welcome here.

It is important for writers to keep in mind the number of opportunities that exist for nonfiction, because the paying markets for fiction are somewhat limited. Some general-interest and women's magazines do publish short stories; however, beginners will find these markets extremely competitive, with their work being judged against that of experienced professionals. We recommend that new writers look into the small, literary, and college publications, which always welcome the work of talented beginners. Payment is usually made only in copies, but publication in literary journals can lead to recognition by editors of larger circulation magazines, who often look to the smaller publications for new talent. In addition, a number of regional, specialized, and Sunday magazines use short stories and are particularly interested in local writers.

The market for poetry in general-interest magazines continues to be tight, and the advice for poets, as for fiction writers, is to try to get established and build up a list of publishing credits by submitting material to literary journals. Poets should look also to local newspapers, which often use verse, especially if it is related to holidays or other special occasions.

New playwrights will find that community, regional, and civic theaters and college dramatic groups offer the best opportunities for staged production in this competitive market. Indeed, many of today's well-known playwrights received their first recognition in regional theaters, and aspiring writers who can get their work produced there have taken a significant step toward breaking into the field. In addition to producing plays and giving dramatic readings, many theaters also sponsor competitions or new play festivals.

The market for television and feature film scripts is limited, and most writers break into it only after a careful study of the medium and a long apprenticeship. Writers should be aware of the fact that this market is inaccessible without an agent, and for this reason, we list several agents who are willing to read queries for TV scripts and for screenplays.

While the book publishing field remains extremely competitive, beginners should be especially encouraged by the fact that many houses have committed themselves enthusiastically to launching new novelists. An increasing number of publishers are broadening their nonfiction lines as well—good news especially for authors with a knowledge of or training in a particular field. And while the children's book market is not growing as quickly as in the recent past, a significant number of publishers continue to seek quality titles for their juvenile and young adult lists.

Small presses across the country continue to flourish—in fact, they are currently publishing more books by name authors and more books on mainstream subjects than at any other time in recent years—offering writers an attractive alternative to the big-name companies.

Writers seeking the thrill of competition should review the extensive list of literary prize offers, many of them designed to promote the as yet unpublished author. Nearly all of the competitions listed here are for unpublished manuscripts, and offer publication in addition to a cash prize. The prestige that comes with winning some of the more established awards can do much to further a writer's career, as editors, publishers, and agents are likely to consider the future work of the prize winner more closely.

Though we recommend writers try to market their material on their own, some may be interested in retaining the services of an agent, in which case they will want to consult the list of literary agents, which includes the type of material each agent represents, whether the work of unpublished writers will be considered, and the commission and fees each agent charges his or her clients. (Only those agents that do not charge reading fees are included.)

All information in these lists concerning the needs and requirements of magazines, book publishing companies, and theaters comes directly from the editors, publishers, and directors, but personnel and addresses change, as do requirements. No published listing can give as clear a picture of editorial needs and tastes as a careful study of several issues of a magazine or a book catalogue, and writers should never submit material without first thoroughly researching the prospective market. If a magazine is not available in the local library or on the newsstand, write directly to the editor for the price of a sample copy; contact the publicity department of a book publisher for an up-to-date catalogue, or a theater for a current schedule. Many companies also offer a formal set of writers guidelines, available for an SASE upon request.

ARTICLE MARKETS

The magazines in the following list are in the market for free-lance articles of many types. Unless listings state otherwise, a writer should submit a query first, including a brief description of the proposed article and any relevant qualifications or credits. A few editors want to see samples of published work, if available. Manuscripts must be typed double-space on good white paper (8½ × 11), with name, address, and telephone number at the top left-or right-hand corner of the first page. Do not use erasable or onion skin paper, since it is difficult to work with, and always keep a copy of the manuscript, in case it is lost in the mail. Some publishers will accept—and may in fact prefer—work submitted on computer disk, usually noting the procedure and type of disk in their writers guidelines.

Many publications have writers guidelines outlining their editorial requirements and submission procedures; these can be obtained by sending a self-addressed, stamped envelope (SASE) to the editor. Also, be sure to ask for a sample copy: Editors indicate the most consistent mistake free lancers make is failing to study several issues of the magazine to which they are submitting material.

Submit photos or slides *only* if the editor has specifically requested them. A self-addressed envelope with postage sufficient to cover the return of the manuscript or the answer to a query should accompany all submissions. Response time may vary from two to eight weeks, depending on the size of the magazine and the volume of mail it receives. If an editor doesn't respond within what seems to be a reasonable amount of time, it's perfectly acceptable to send a polite inquiry with an SASE.

GENERAL-INTEREST PUBLICATIONS

ACCENT/TRAVELOG—P.O. Box 10010, Ogden, UT 84409. Attn: Ed. Staff. Articles, 1,000 words, about travel, having fun, fitness, sightseeing, the ordinary and the unusual in foreign and domestic destinations. "Avoid budget approaches and emphasize the use of travel professionals." Must include excellent transparencies. Queries with SASE required. Guidelines. Pays 15¢ a word, $35 for photos, $50 for cover photo, on acceptance.

AIR & SPACE—370 L'Enfant Promenade, 10th Fl., Washington, DC 20024–2518. George Larson, Ed. General-interest articles, 1,000 to 3,500 words, on aerospace experience, past, present, and future; travel, space, history, biographies, essays, commentary. Pays varying rates, on acceptance. Query.

AIR FORCE TIMES—See *Times News Service.*

AMERICAN HERITAGE— 60 Fifth Ave., New York, NY 10011. Richard F. Snow, Ed. Articles, 750 to 5,000 words, on U.S. history and background of American life and culture from the beginning to recent times. No fiction. Pays $300 to $1,500, on acceptance. Query.

AMERICAN JOURNALISM REVIEW— 8701 Adelphi Rd., Adelphi, MD

20783. Rem Rieder, Ed. Articles, 500 to 5,000 words, on print and electronic journalism. Pays 20¢ a word, on publication. Query.

THE AMERICAN LEGION—Box 1055, Indianapolis, IN 46206. Steve Salerno, Ed. Articles, 750 to 2,000 words, on current world affairs, public policy, and subjects of contemporary interest. Pays $400 to $2,000, on acceptance. Query.

AMERICAN VISIONS, THE MAGAZINE OF AFRO-AMERICAN CULTURE—2101 S St. N.W., Washington, DC 20008-4011. Joanne Harris, Ed. Articles, 1,500 words, and columns, 750 to 2,000 words, on African-American history and culture with a focus on the arts. Pays from $100 to $1,000, after publication. Query.

AMERICAS—OAS, 19th and Constitution Ave. N.W., Washington, DC 20006. Rebecca Read Medrano, Ed. Features, 2,500 to 5,000 words, on Latin America and the Caribbean. Wide focus: anthropology, the arts, travel, science, and development. "We prefer stories that can be well illustrated." No political material. Pays from $250, on publication. Query.

ARMY TIMES—See *Times News Service.*

THE ATLANTIC MONTHLY—745 Boylston St., Boston, MA 02116. William Whitworth, Ed. Non-polemical, meticulously researched articles on public issues, politics, social sciences, education, business, literature, and the arts. Ideal length: 3,000 to 6,000 words, though short pieces, 1,000 to 2,000 words, are also welcome and longer text pieces will be considered. Pays excellent rates.

BON APPETIT—6300 Wilshire Blvd., Los Angeles, CA 90048. Barbara Fairchild, Exec. Ed. Articles on fine cooking (menu format or single focus), cooking classes, and gastronomically focused travel. Pays varying rates, on acceptance; buys all rights. Query with samples of published work.

BOSTONIA: THE MAGAZINE OF CULTURE AND IDEAS—10 Lenox St., Brookline, MA 02146. Attn: Ed. Articles, to 3,000 words, on politics, literature, music, art, science, and education, especially from a Boston angle. Pays $150 to $2,500. Queries required.

CAPPER'S—1503 S.W. 42nd St., Topeka, KS 66609-1265. Nancy Peavler, Ed. Articles, 300 to 500 words: human-interest, personal experience for family section, historical. Payment varies, on publication.

CAR AUDIO AND ELECTRONICS—21700 Oxnard St., Woodland Hills, CA 91367. Bill Neill, Ed. Features, 1,000 to 2,000 words, on electronic products for the car: audio systems, security systems, radar detectors, etc. Pays $300 to $1,000, on acceptance.

CHANGE—1319 18th St. N.W., Washington, DC 20036. Attn: Ed. Dept. Well-researched features, 2,500 to 3,500 words, on programs, people, and institutions of higher education; and columns, 700 to 2,000 words. "We can't usually pay for unsolicited articles."

THE CHRISTIAN SCIENCE MONITOR—One Norway St., Boston, MA 02115. Lawrence Goodrich, Features Ed. Articles, 800 words, on arts, education, food, sports, science, and lifestyle; interviews, literary essays for "Home Forum" page; guest columns for "Opinion Page." Pay varies, on acceptance. Original material only.

COLUMBIA—1 Columbus Plaza, New Haven, CT 06510-3326. Richard

McMunn, Ed. Journal of the Knights of Columbus. Articles, 500 to 1,500 words, on a wide variety of topics of interest to K. of C. members, their families, and the Catholic layman: current events, religion, education, art, etc., illustrated with color photos. Pays $250 to $500, including art, on acceptance.

THE COMPASS—365 Washington Ave., Brooklyn, NY 11238. J.A. Randall, Ed. True stories, to 2,000 words, on the sea, sea trades, and aviation. Pays to $1,000, on acceptance. Query with SASE.

CONSUMERS DIGEST—5705 N. Lincoln Ave., Chicago, IL 60659. John Manos, Ed. Articles, 500 to 3,000 words, on subjects of interest to consumers: products and services, automobiles, health, fitness, consumer legal affairs, and personal money management. Photos. Pays from 35¢ to 50¢ a word, extra for photos, on publication. Buys all rights. Query with resumé and published clips.

COSMOPOLITAN—224 W. 57th St., New York, NY 10019. Helen Gurley Brown, Ed. Guy Flatley, Man. Ed. Articles, to 3,000 words, and features, 500 to 2,000 words, on issues affecting young career women. Query.

COUNTRY JOURNAL— 4 High Ridge Park, Stamford, CT 06905. Peter V. Fossel, Ed. Articles, 500 to 1,500 words, for country and small-town residents. Helpful, authoritative pieces; how-to projects, small-scale farming, and gardening. Pays $75 to $500, on acceptance. Send SASE for guidelines. Query with SASE.

DIVERSION MAGAZINE—1790 Broadway, New York, NY 10019. Tom Passavant, Ed.-in-Chief. Articles, 1,200 to 2,200 words, on travel, sports, hobbies, entertainment, food, etc., of interest to physicians at leisure. Photos. Pays from $500, on acceptance. Query. Currently not accepting outside material.

EBONY— 820 S. Michigan, Chicago, IL 60605. Lerone Bennett, Jr., Exec. Ed. "We do not solicit free-lance material."

ESQUIRE—250 W. 55th St., New York, NY 10019. Edward Kosner, Ed.-in-Chief. David Hirshey, Deputy Ed. Articles, 2,500 to 6,500 words, for intelligent adult audience. Pay varies, on acceptance. Query with published clips; complete manuscripts from unpublished writers.

ESSENCE—1500 Broadway, New York, NY 10036. Susan L. Taylor, Ed.-in-Chief. Linda Villarosa, Exec. Ed. Provocative articles, 800 to 2,500 words, about black women in America today: self-help, how-to pieces, business and finance, work, parenting, health, celebrity profiles, and political issues. Pays varying rates, on acceptance. Query required.

FAMILY CIRCLE—110 Fifth Ave., New York, NY 10011. Nancy Clark, Deputy Ed. Articles, to 2,000 words, on "women who have made a difference," marriage, family, and child-rearing issues; consumer affairs, health and fitness, humor and psychology. Pays top rates, on acceptance. Query required.

GLAMOUR—350 Madison Ave., New York, NY 10017. Ruth Whitney, Ed.-in-Chief. Pamela Erens, Articles Ed. Editorial approach is "how-to" for women, 18 to 35. Articles on careers, health, psychology, interpersonal relationships, etc. Fashion, health, and beauty material staff-written. Pays from $1,000 for 1,500-to 2,000-word articles, from $1,500 for longer pieces, on acceptance.

GOOD HOUSEKEEPING—959 Eighth Ave., New York, NY 10019. Joan Thursh, Articles Ed. Articles, 2,500 words, on a unique or trend-setting event; family relationships; personal medical pieces dealing with an unusual illness, treatment, and result; personal problems and how they were solved. Short essays, 750 to 1,000 words, on family life or relationships. Pays first-time writers $500 to $750 for short, essay-type articles; $1,500 to $2,000 for full-length articles, on acceptance. "Payment scale rises for writers with whom we work frequently." Buys all rights, though the writer retains the right to use material from the article as part of a book project. Queries preferred. Guidelines.

GRIT—1503 S.W. 42nd St., Topeka, KS 66609. Michael Scheibach, Ed.-in-Chief. Articles, 500 to 1,200 words, on health, people, home, garden, lifestyle, friends and family, Americana, and travel. Short fiction, 1,000 to 2,000 words (must be addressed to Fiction Ed.). SASE required. Pays 15¢ to 25¢ a word, extra for photos. Query. Send SASE for guidelines and theme calendar.

HARPER'S MAGAZINE— 666 Broadway, New York, NY 10012. Attn: Ed. Articles, 2,000 to 5,000 words. Query with SASE required. Very limited market.

HARROWSMITH COUNTRY LIFE—Ferry Rd., Charlotte, VT 05445. Attn: Ed. Dept. Feature articles, 2,000 to 3,000 words, on country living, gardening, community issues, shelter, how-to and do-it-yourself projects. Short profiles of country careers, news briefs, and natural history. Pays $500 to $1,500 for features, from $50 to $600 for department pieces, on acceptance. Query with SASE required. Guidelines.

HOUSE BEAUTIFUL—1700 Broadway, New York, NY 10019. Elaine Greene, Features Ed. Articles related to the home. Pieces on architecture, design, travel, and gardening. One personal memoir each month, "Thoughts of Home," with high literary standards. Pays varying rates, on acceptance. Query with detailed outline and SASE. Guidelines.

IDEALS—P.O. Box 305300, Nashville, TN 37230. Lisa Thompson, Ed. Articles, 800 to 1,000 words; poetry, 12 to 50 lines. Light, nostalgic pieces. Payment varies. SASE for guidelines.

INQUIRER MAGAZINE—*Philadelphia Inquirer,* P.O. Box 8263, 400 N. Broad St., Philadelphia, PA 19101. Ms. Avery Rome, Ed. Local-interest features, 500 to 7,000 words. Profiles of national figures in politics, entertainment, etc. Pays varying rates, on publication. Query.

KEY HORIZONS—Gateway Plaza, 950 N. Meridian, Suite 1200, Indianapolis, IN 46204. Joan Todd, Man. Ed. General-interest articles and department pieces,1,500 words, for readers ages 50 and older. Topics include personal finance, cooking, family trends, domestic travel, and puzzles. No nostalgia, domestic humor, fillers, or poetry. Pays $25 to $500, $25 to $50 for photos, on publication.

KIWANIS—3636 Woodview Trace, Indianapolis, IN 46268. Chuck Jonak, Man. Ed. Articles, 2,500 words, on home; family; international issues; the social, health, and emotional needs of youth (especially under age 6); career and community concerns of business and professional people. No travel pieces, interviews, profiles. Pays $400 to $1,000, on acceptance. Query. Guidelines.

LADIES' HOME JOURNAL—100 Park Ave., New York, NY 10017. Jane Farrell, Articles Ed. Articles on contemporary subjects of interest to women. "See masthead for specific-topic editors and address appropriate editor." Query with SASE required.

LISTEN MAGAZINE—55 W. Oak Ridge Dr., Hagerstown, MD 21740. Lincoln Steed, Ed. Articles, 1,000 to 1,200 words, on problems of alcohol and drug abuse, for teenagers; personality profiles; self-improvement articles, and drug-free activities. Photos. Pays 5¢ to 7¢ a word, extra for photos, on acceptance. Query. Guidelines.

LOS ANGELES TIMES MAGAZINE—Times Mirror Sq., Los Angeles, CA 90053. John Lindsay, Ed. Dir. Articles, to 5,000 words: general-interest news features, photo spreads, profiles, and narratives focusing on current events. Pays to $4,000, on acceptance. Query required.

MCCALL'S—110 Fifth Ave., New York, NY 10011. Attn: Articles Ed. Articles, 1,000 to 1,800 words, on current issues, human interest, family relationships. Payment varies, on acceptance. SASE.

MADEMOISELLE—350 Madison Ave., New York, NY 10017. Faye Haun, Man. Ed. Articles, 750 to 2,500 words, on subjects of interest to single, working women in their twenties. Reporting pieces, essays, first-person accounts, and humor. No how-to or fiction. Pays excellent rates, on acceptance. SASE required. Query with clips.

MERIDIAN LIFESTYLES—Box 10010, Ogden, UT 84409. Attn: Ed. Dept. Personality profiles, 1,200 words, of celebrities in sports, entertainment, fine arts, science, etc. Celebrities must be nationally or internationally known for their participation in their field, have positive values, and be making a contribution to society. "High-quality color transparencies are a must; query for details." Pays 15¢ a word, $35 for photos, $50 for cover photos, on acceptance.

METROPOLITAN HOME—1633 Broadway, New York, NY 10019. Attn: Articles Dept. Service and informational articles for residents of houses, co-ops, lofts, and condominiums, on real estate, equity, wine and spirits, collecting, trends, travel, etc. Interior design and home furnishing articles with emphasis on lifestyle. Pay varies. Query with clips.

THE MOTHER EARTH NEWS—24 E. 23rd St., 5th Fl., New York, NY 10010. Matthew Scanlon, Ed. Articles for rural and urban readers: home improvements, how-tos, indoor and outdoor gardening, family pastimes, health, food, ecology, energy, and consumerism. Pays varying rates, on acceptance.

MOTHER JONES—731 Market St., Suite 600, San Francisco, CA 94103. Jeffrey Klein, Ed. Investigative articles, political essays, cultural analyses, multicultural issues. "OutFront" pieces, 250 to 500 words. Pays on acceptance. Query with SASE.

MS.—230 Park Ave., 7th Fl., New York, NY 10169. Attn: Manuscript Ed. Articles relating to feminism, women's roles, and social change; reporting, essays, theory, and analysis. No poetry or fiction. Pays market rates. Query with resumé, clips, and SASE.

NATIONAL ENQUIRER—Lantana, FL 33464. Attn: Ed. Dept. Articles, of any length, for mass audience: topical news, the occult, how-to, scientific discoveries, human drama, adventure, personalities. Photos. Pays from $325. Query or send complete manuscript. SASE.

NAVY TIMES—See *Times News Service.*

NEW WOMAN—215 Lexington Ave., New York, NY 10016. Attn: Manuscripts and Proposals. Articles on personal and professional relationships, health, fitness, lifestyle, money, and career issues. Editorial focus is on self-discovery, self-development, and self-esteem. "Read the magazine to become familiar with our needs, and request guidelines with SASE. We look for originality, solid research, and a friendly, accessible style." Pays varying rates, on acceptance.

THE NEW YORK TIMES MAGAZINE—229 W. 43rd St., New York, NY 10036. Attn: Articles Ed. Timely articles, approximately 3,000 words, on news items, forthcoming events, trends, culture, entertainment, etc. Pays to $2,500 for major articles, on acceptance. Query with clips.

THE NEW YORKER—20 W. 43rd St., New York, NY 10036. Send submissions to appropriate Editor (Fact, Fiction, or Poetry). Factual and biographical articles for "Profiles," "Reporter at Large," etc. Pays good rates, on acceptance. Query.

NEWSWEEK—251 W. 57th St., New York, NY 10019–1894. Attn: My Turn. Original opinion essays, 1,000 to 1,100 words, for "My Turn" column; must contain verifiable facts. Submit manuscript with SASE. Pays $1,000, on publication.

OMNI—324 W. Wendover Ave., Suite 200, Greensboro, NC 27408. Keith Ferrell, Ed. Articles, 750 to 3,000 words, on scientific aspects of the future: space, machine intelligence, ESP, origin of life, future arts, lifestyles, etc. Fiction, 2,000 to 10,000 words, should be sent to Ellen Datlow, Fiction Ed., *Omni*, 277 Park Ave., 4th Fl., New York, NY 10172–0003. Pays $750 to $2,500, on acceptance. Query.

PARADE—711 Third Ave., New York, NY 10017. Daren Fonda, Articles Correspondent. National Sunday newspaper magazine. Factual and authoritative articles, 1,000 to 1,500 words, on subjects of national interest: health, consumer and environmental issues, the family, sports, etc. Profiles of well-known personalities and service pieces. No fiction, poetry, games, or puzzles. Pays from $1,000. Query.

PENTHOUSE—1965 Broadway, New York, NY 10023–5965. Peter Bloch, Ed. Lavada B. Nahon, Sr. Ed. General-interest or controversial articles, to 5,000 words. Pays to $1 a word, on acceptance.

PEOPLE WEEKLY—Time-Life Bldg., Rockefeller Ctr., New York, NY 10020. John Saar, Asst. Man. Ed. "Vast majority of material is staff-written." Will consider article proposals, 3 to 4 paragraphs, on timely, entertaining, and topical personalities. Pays good rates, on acceptance.

PLAYBOY—680 N. Lake Shore Dr., Chicago, IL 60611. Peter Moore, Articles Ed. Sophisticated articles, 4,000 to 6,000 words, of interest to urban men. Humor, satire. Pays to $3,000, on acceptance. Query.

PLAYGIRL—801 Second Ave., New York, NY 10017. Laurie Sue Brockway, Ed.-in-Chief. Articles, 1,500 to 3,500 words, on sexuality, relationships, and celebrities for women ages 18 and up. Query with clips. Fiction and nonfiction. Pays negotiable rates, after acceptance.

PSYCHOLOGY TODAY—Sussex Publishing, 49 E. 21st St., New York, NY 10010. Hara E. Marano, Ed. Bimonthly. Articles, 4,000 words, on timely subjects relating to human behavior or the national psyche. Pays varying rates, on publication.

QUEEN'S QUARTERLY—Queens Univ., Kingston, Ont., Canada K7L

3N6. Boris Castel, Ed. Articles, to 5,000 words, on a wide range of topics, and fiction, to 5,000 words. Poetry; send no more than 6 poems. B&W art. Pays to $400, on publication.

READER'S DIGEST—Pleasantville, NY 10570. Kenneth Tomlinson, Ed.-in-Chief. Unsolicited manuscripts will not be read or returned. General-interest articles already in print and well-developed story proposals will be considered. Send reprint or query to any editor on the masthead.

REAL PEOPLE—950 Third Ave., New York, NY 10022–2705. Alex Polner, Ed. True stories, to 500 words, on interesting people, strange occupations and hobbies, eye opening stories about people, places and odd happenings. Pays $25 to $50, on publication; send submissions to "Real Shorts," Brad Hamilton, Ed. Interviews, 1,000 to 1,800 words, with movie or TV actors, musicians, and other entertainment celebrities. Pays $150 to $350, on publication. Query for interviews.

REDBOOK—224 W. 57th St., New York, NY 10019. Harriet Lyons, Sr. Ed. Toni Gerber Hope, Sr. Ed. Articles, 1,000 to 2,500 words, on subjects related to relationships, marriage, sex, current social issues, crime, human interest, health, psychology, and parenting. Payment varies, on acceptance. Query with clips.

ROLLING STONE—1290 Ave. of the Americas, 2nd Fl., New York, NY 10104. Attn: Ed. Magazine of American music, culture, and politics. No fiction. "We rarely accept free-lance material." Query.

THE ROTARIAN—1560 Sherman Ave., Evanston, IL 60201–3698. Willmon L. White, Ed. Articles, 1,200 to 2,000 words, on international social and economic issues, business and management, human relationships, travel, sports, environment, science and technology; humor. Pays good rates, on acceptance. Query.

THE SATURDAY EVENING POST—1100 Waterway Blvd., Indianapolis, IN 46202. Ted Kreiter, Exec. Ed. Family-oriented articles, 1,500 to 3,000 words: humor, preventive medicine, destination-oriented travel pieces (not personal experience), celebrity profiles, the arts, and sciences. Pieces on sports and home repair (with photos). Pays varying rates, on publication. Queries preferred.

SMITHSONIAN MAGAZINE—900 Jefferson Dr., Washington, DC 20560. Marlane A. Liddell, Articles Ed. Articles on history, art, natural history, physical science, profiles, etc. Query with clips and SASE.

SOAP OPERA DIGEST—45 W. 25th St., New York, NY 10010. Jason Bonderoff, Roberta Caploe, Man. Eds. Investigative reports and profiles, to 1,500 words, about New York-or Los Angeles-based soaps. Pays from $250, on acceptance. Query with clips.

SPORTS ILLUSTRATED—1271 Ave. of the Americas, New York, NY 10020. Chris Hunt, Articles Ed. Rarely uses free-lance material. Query.

STAR—660 White Plains Rd., Tarrytown, NY 10591. Attn: Ed. Dept. Topical articles, 50 to 800 words, on show business and celebrities. Pays varying rates.

SUCCESS—230 Park Ave., #7, New York, NY 10169–0014. Scott De-Garmo, Pub./Ed.-in-Chief. Profiles of successful executives, entrepreneurs; management science, psychology, behavior, and motivation articles, 500 to 3,500 words. Query.

TIMES NEWS SERVICE—Army Times Publishing Co., Springfield, VA 22159. Attn: R&R Ed. Articles that are informative, helpful, entertaining, and stimulating to a military audience for "R&R" newspaper section. Pays $75 to $100, on acceptance. Also, 1,000-word articles on careers after military service, travel, books and home entertainment, finance, and education for *Army Times, Navy Times,* and *Air Force Times.* Address Supplements Ed. Pays $125 to $200, on acceptance. Guidelines.

THE TOASTMASTER—P.O. Box 9052, Mission Viejo, CA 92690. Suzanne Frey, Ed. Articles, 1,500 to 2,500 words, on decision making, leadership, language, interpersonal and professional communication, humor, logical thinking, rhetorical devices, public speaking in general, profiles of great orators, speaking techniques, etc. Pays $100 to $250, on acceptance.

TOWN & COUNTRY—1700 Broadway, New York, NY 10019. Pamela Fiori, Ed.-in-Chief. Considers one-page proposals for articles. Include clips and resumé. Rarely buys unsolicited manuscripts.

TRAVEL & LEISURE—1120 Ave. of the Americas, New York, NY 10036. Nancy Novogrod, Ed.-in-Chief. Articles, 800 to 3,000 words, on destinations and leisure-time activities. Regional pieces for regional editions. Pays varying rates, on acceptance. Query.

TROPIC—*The Miami Herald,* One Herald Plaza, Miami, FL 33132. Tom Shroder, Exec. Ed. Essays and articles, 1,000 to 4,000 words, on current trends and issues, light or heavy, for sophisticated audience. No fiction or poetry. Limited humor. Pays $200 to $1,000, on publication. SASE. Allow 4 to 6 weeks for response.

TV GUIDE—Radnor, PA 19088. Barry Golson, Exec. Ed. Short, light, brightly written pieces about humorous or offbeat angles of television and industry trends. (Majority of personality pieces are staff-written.) Pays on acceptance. Query.

VANITY FAIR—350 Madison Ave., New York, NY 10017. Attn: Submissions (Secify News, Arts, or Culture). Pays on acceptance. Query.

VILLAGE VOICE—36 Cooper Sq., New York, NY 10003. Doug Simmons, Man. Ed. Articles, 500 to 2,000 words, on current or controversial topics. Pays $100 to $1,500, on acceptance. Query or send manuscript with SASE.

VISTA—999 Ponce, Suite 600, Coral Gables, FL 33134. Carmen Teresa Roiz, Ed. Articles, to 1,500 words, for English-speaking Hispanic Americans, on job advancement, bilingualism, immigration, the media, fashion, education, medicine, sports, and food. Profiles, 100 words, of Hispanic Americans in unusual jobs; photos welcome. Pays 20¢ a word, on acceptance. Query required. "Sample copy and guidelines free on request."

WASHINGTON POST MAGAZINE—*The Washington Post,* 1150 15th St. N.W., Washington, DC 20071. Liza Mundy, Man. Ed. Essays, profiles, and Washington-oriented general-interest pieces, to 5,000 words, on business, arts and culture, politics, science, sports, education, children, relationships, behavior, etc. Pays from $1,000, after acceptance.

WISCONSIN—*The Milwaukee Journal Magazine,* P.O. Box 661, Milwaukee, WI 53201. Carol Guensburg, Ed. Trend stories, essays, humor, personal-experience pieces, profiles, 500 to 2,500 words, with strong Wisconsin emphasis. Pays $75 to $750, on publication.

WOMAN'S DAY—1633 Broadway, New York, NY 10019. Rebecca Greer, Articles Ed. Articles, 500 to 2,000 words, on subjects of interest to women: marriage, education, family health, child rearing, money management, interpersonal relationships, changing lifestyles, etc. Dramatic first-person narratives about women who have experienced medical miracles or other triumphs, or have overcome common problems, such as alcoholism. SASE required. Pays top rates, on acceptance. Query; unsolicited manuscripts not accepted.

WOMAN'S WORLD—270 Sylvan Ave., Englewood Cliffs, NJ 07632. Attn: Ed. Articles, 600 to 1,800 words, of interest to middle-income women between the ages of 18 and 60, on love, romance, careers, medicine, health, psychology, family life, travel; dramatic stories of adventure or crisis, investigative reports. Send SASE for guidelines. Pays $300 to $900, on acceptance. Query.

YANKEE—Yankee Publishing Co., P.O. Box 520, Dublin, NH 03444. Judson D. Hale, Ed. Articles, to 2,500 words, with New England angle. Photos. Pays $150 to $2,000 (average $800), on acceptance.

YOUR HOME/INDOORS & OUT—Box 10010, Ogden, UT 84409. Attn: Ed. Staff. Articles, 1,000 words with good color transparencies, on fresh ideas in home decor, ranging from floor and wall coverings to home furnishings. Latest in home construction (exteriors, interiors, building materials, design, entertaining, and lifestyle), the outdoors at home (landscaping, pools, patios, gardens, etc.), home management, and home buying and selling. Avoid do-it-yourself approaches. Emphasize the use of professionals. Pays 15¢ a word and $35 for photos, $50 for cover photo, on acceptance. Queries required. Guidelines.

CURRENT EVENTS, POLITICS

THE AMERICAN LEGION—Box 1055, Indianapolis, IN 46206. Steve Salerno, Ed. Articles, 750 to 2,000 words, on current world affairs, public policy, and subjects of contemporary interest. Pays $500 to $2,000, on acceptance. Query.

THE AMERICAN SCHOLAR—1811 Q St. N.W., Washington, DC 20009–9974. Joseph Epstein, Ed. Non-technical articles and essays, 3,500 to 4,000 words, on current affairs, the American cultural scene, politics, arts, religion, and science. Pays to $500, on acceptance.

THE AMICUS JOURNAL—Natural Resources Defense Council, 40 W. 20th St., New York, NY 10011. Kathrin Day Lassila, Ed. Investigative articles, book reviews, essays, and poetry related to national and international environmental policy. Pays varying rates, 30 days after publication. Queries required.

THE ATLANTIC MONTHLY—745 Boylston St., Boston, MA 02116. William Whitworth, Ed. In-depth articles on public issues, politics, social sciences, education, business, literature, and the arts, with emphasis on information rather than opinion. Ideal length is 3,000 to 6,000 words, though short pieces, 1,000 to 2,000 words, are also welcome. Pays excellent rates, on acceptance.

CHURCH & STATE—1816 Jefferson Pl. N.W., Washington, DC 20036. Joseph L. Conn, Man. Ed. Articles, 600 to 2,600 words, on issues of religious liberty and church-state relations. Pays varying rates, on acceptance. Query.

COMMENTARY—165 E. 56th St., New York, NY 10022. Neal Kozodoy, Ed. Articles, 5,000 to 7,000 words, on contemporary issues, Jewish affairs, social sciences, community life, religious thought, culture. Serious fiction; book reviews. Pays on publication.

COMMONWEAL—15 Dutch St., New York, NY 10038. Margaret O'Brien Steinfels, Ed. Catholic. Articles, to 3,000 words, on political, social, religious, and literary subjects. Pays 3¢ a word, on acceptance.

COUNTRY CONNECTIONS—P.O. Box 6748, Pine Mountain Club, CA 93222. Catherine R. Leach, Ed. Articles, to 2,500 words, and fiction, to 1,500 words. Poetry. B&W photos. "Study magazine first. We serve as a forum for public discourse about ethics, politics, social justice, community, city rights, animal and environmental issues, and life in the country." Pays $25 for features, $15 for fiction and poetry, on publication.

THE CRITIC—205 W. Monroe St., 6th Fl., Chicago, IL 60606–5097. Julie Bridge, Ed. Quarterly. "A Journal of American Catholic Culture." Fiction and articles, to 5,000 words. Poetry. "Stories and articles need not be Catholic, but keep in mind the religious affiliation when submitting work. No conservative Roman Catholic tracts; the magazine is moderate to liberal." Pays $25 to $400, on acceptance. Query for articles.

CURRENT HISTORY—4225 Main St., Philadelphia, PA 19127. William W. Finan, Jr., Ed. Country-specific political science and current affairs articles, to 20 pages. Hard analysis written in a lively manner. "We devote each issue to a specific region or country. Writers should be experts with up-to-date knowledge of the region." Queries preferred. Pays $300, on publication.

ENVIRONMENT—1319 18th St. N.W., Washington, DC 20036–1802. Barbara T. Richman, Man. Ed. Articles, 2,500 to 5,000 words, on environmental, scientific, and technological policy and decision-making issues, especially on a global scale. Pays $100 to $300, on publication. Query.

FOREIGN SERVICE JOURNAL—2101 E St. N.W., Washington, DC 20037. Articles of interest to the Foreign Service and the US diplomatic community. Pays to 20¢ a word, on publication. Query.

THE FREEMAN—Foundation for Economic Education, Irvington-on-Hudson, NY 10533. Beth Hoffman, Man. Ed. Articles, to 3,500 words, on economic, political, and moral implications of private property, voluntary exchange, and individual choice. Pays 10¢ a word, on publication.

INQUIRER MAGAZINE—*Philadelphia Inquirer*, P.O. Box 8263, 400 N. Broad St., Philadelphia, PA 19101. Ms. Avery Rome, Ed. Local-interest features, 500 to 7,000 words. Profiles of national figures in politics, entertainment, etc. Pays varying rates, on publication. Query.

IRISH AMERICA—432 Park Ave. S., Suite 1000, New York, NY 10016. Patricia Harty, Ed. Articles, 1,500 to 2,000 words, of interest to Irish-American audience; preferred topics include history, sports, the arts, and politics. Pays 10¢ a word, after publication. Query.

LABOR'S HERITAGE—10000 New Hampshire Ave., Silver Spring, MD 20903. Stuart Kaufman, Ed. Quarterly journal of The George Meany Memorial Archives. Publishes 15-to 30-page documented articles of original research for labor scholars, labor union members, and the general public. Pays in copies.

MIDSTREAM—110 E. 59th St., New York, NY 10022. Joel Carmichael,

Ed. Articles of international and Jewish/Zionist concern. Pays 5¢ a word, after publication. Allow 3 months for response.

MOMENT MAGAZINE— 4710 41st St. N.W., Washington, DC 20016. Andrew Silow-Carroll, Sr. Ed. Sophisticated articles, 2,500 to 5,000 words, on Jewish culture, politics, religion, and personalities. Columns, to 1,500 words, with uncommon perspectives on contemporary issues, humor, strong anecdotes. Book reviews, 400 words. Pays $40 to $600.

MOTHER JONES—731 Market St., Suite 600, San Francisco, CA 94103. Jeffrey Klein, Ed. Investigative articles and political essays. Pays $1,000 to $3,000 for feature articles, after acceptance. Query with clips and SASE required.

THE NATION—72 Fifth Ave., New York, NY 10011. Katrina Vanden Heuvel, Ed. Articles, 1,500 to 2,500 words, on politics and culture from a liberal/left perspective. Pays $75 per published page, to $300, on publication. Query.

THE NEW YORK TIMES MAGAZINE—229 W. 43rd St., New York, NY 10036. Attn: Articles Ed. Timely articles, approximately 4,000 words, on news items, trends, culture, etc. Pays $1,000 for short pieces, from $2,500 for major articles, on acceptance. Query with clips.

THE NEW YORKER—20 W. 43rd St., New York, NY 10036. Attn: Ed., "Comment." Political/social essays, 1,000 words. Payment on acceptance. Query.

ON THE ISSUES—Choices Women's Medical Ctr., Inc., 97–77 Queens Blvd., Forest Hills, NY 11374–3317. Ronni Sandroff, Ed. "The Progressive Woman's Quarterly." Articles, up to 2,500 words, on political or social issues. Movie, music, and book reviews, 500 to 750 words. Query. Payment varies, on publication.

PEACE—P.O. Box 902404, Palmdale, CA 93590–2404. Linda S. James, Ed. Quarterly. Articles and fiction, to 3,000 words, that centers on or refers to the 1960s. Possible topics include life on the road; politics; interviews; and stories from those who fought in the Vietnam War and those who chose not to. Pays to $100, 30 days after publication. Guidelines.

THE PROGRESSIVE— 409 E. Main St., Madison, WI 53703. Matthew Rothschild, Ed. Articles, 1,000 to 3,500 words, on political and social problems. Pays $100 to $300, on publication.

PUBLIC CITIZEN MAGAZINE—1600 20th St. N.W., Washington, DC 20009. Peter Nye, Ed. Investigative reports and articles of timely political interest, for members of Public Citizen: consumer rights, health and safety, environmental protection, safe energy, tax reform, trade, and government and corporate accountability. Photos, illustrations. Payment negotiable.

REASON—3415 S. Sepulveda Blvd., Suite 400, Los Angeles, CA 90034. Attn: Eds. "Free Minds and Free Markets." Articles, 850 to 5,000 words, on politics, economics, and culture "from an individualist's perspective." Pays varying rates, on acceptance. Query.

ROLL CALL: THE NEWSPAPER OF CAPITOL HILL—900 2nd St. N.E., Washington, DC 20002. Stacy Mason, Ed. Factual, breezy articles with political or Congressional angle: Congressional history, human-interest subjects, political lore, etc. Political opinion or commentary on Congressional institutional issues. Pays on publication.

SATURDAY NIGHT—184 Front St. E., Suite 400, Toronto, Ont., Canada M5A 4N3. Kenneth Whyte, Ed. Canada's oldest magazine of politics, social issues, culture, and business. Features, 1,000 to 3,000 words, and columns, 800 to 1,000 words; fiction, to 3,000 words. Must have Canadian tie-in. Payment varies, on acceptance.

VFW MAGAZINE— 406 W. 34th St., Kansas City, MO 64111. Richard K. Kolb, Ed. Local-interest features, 500 to 7,000 words. Profiles of national figures in politics, entertainment, etc. Pays varying rates, on publication. Query.

VILLAGE VOICE—36 Cooper Sq., New York, NY 10003. Doug Simmons, Man. Ed. Articles, 500 to 2,000 words, on current or controversial topics. Pays $100 to $1,500, on publication. Query or send manuscript with SASE.

THE WASHINGTON MONTHLY—1611 Connecticut Ave. N.W., Washington, DC 20009. Charles Peters, Ed. Helpful, informative articles, 1,000 to 4,000 words, on DC-related topics, including politics, and government and the popular culture. Pays 50¢ a word, on publication.

WASHINGTON POST MAGAZINE—*The Washington Post,* 1150 15th St. N.W., Washington, DC 20071. Liza Mundy, Man. Ed. Essays, profiles, and general-interest pieces, to 5,000 words, on Washington-oriented politics and related issues. Pays from $1,000, after acceptance. SASE required.

WHO CARES: A JOURNAL OF SERVICE AND ACTION—1511 K St. N.W., Washington, DC 20005. Leslie Crutchfield, Heather McLeod, News and Features Eds. Chloe Breyer, Photo/Creative Ed. Articles, 1,000 words, on service programs throughout the country for "Partners in Change." Features, 1,500 to 2,500 words, on specific issues related to service and action. "Entrepreneur" pieces, 1,500 to 2,500 words, focus on the business of starting a successful nonprofit. "On Campus," 800 words, on unique service programs that involve college students. "Faith in Service," 1,000 to 1,500 words, on connections between service and spirituality. "Who's Who and What's What," 100-to 400-word news blurbs on service and action. Also, humorous essays, 800 words, and first-person narratives, related fiction, and other creative essays, 800 to 2,000 words. No payment for unsolicited articles. Payment for assigned pieces varies, on publication.

REGIONAL AND CITY PUBLICATIONS

ADIRONDACK LIFE—P.O. Box 97, Jay, NY 12941. Tom Hughes, Ed. Features, to 5,000 words, on outdoor and environmental activities and issues, arts, wilderness, wildlife, profiles, history, and fiction; focus is on the Adirondack Park region of New York State. Pays to 25¢ a word, 30 days after acceptance. Query.

ALABAMA HERITAGE—The Univ. of Alabama, Box 870342, Tuscaloosa, AL 35487–0342. Suzanne Wolfe, Ed. Quarterly. Articles, to 5,000 words, on local, state, and regional history: art, literature, language, archaeology, music, religion, architecture, and natural history. Query, mentioning availability of photos and illustrations. Pays an honorarium, on publication, plus 10 copies. Guidelines.

ALASKA— 808 E St., Suite 200, Anchorage, AK 99501. Tobin Morrison,

Ed. Articles, 2,000 words, on life in Alaska. Pays varying rates, on acceptance. Guidelines.

ALBERTA SWEETGRASS—Aboriginal Multi-Media Society of Alberta, 15001 112th Ave., Edmonton, Alberta, Canada T5M 2V6. R. John Hayes, Asst. Ed. Tabloid. Articles, 200 to 1,000 words (most often 500 to 800 words): features, profiles, and community-based articles all with an Alberta angle.

ALOHA, THE MAGAZINE OF HAWAII AND THE PACIFIC—P.O. Box 3260, Honolulu, HI 96801. Cheryl Chee Tsutsumi, Ed. Articles, 1,500 to 2,500 words, on the life, customs, and people of Hawaii and the Pacific. Poetry. Fiction. Pays $150 to $500 for full-length features, on publication. Query.

AMERICAN DESERT MAGAZINE—12289 Mint Ct., Rancho Cucamonga, CA 91730. Raymond Shadwick, Pub./Ed. Quarterly. Articles, 1,000 to 2,500 words, related to the southwest deserts: desert history, natural features, survival, Native American culture, profiles. Pays 3¢ a word, on publication. Guidelines.

APPRISE—P.O. Box 2954, 1982 Locust Ln., Harrisburg, PA 17105. Jim Connor, Ed. Articles, 1,500 to 3,500 words, of regional (central Pennsylvania) interest, including profiles of notable Pennsylvanians, and broadly based articles of social interest that "enlighten and inform." Pays 10¢ a word, on publication.

ARIZONA HIGHWAYS—2039 W. Lewis Ave., Phoenix, AZ 85009. Robert J. Early, Ed. Articles, 1,600 to 2,000 words, on travel in Arizona; pieces on adventure, humor, lifestyles, nostalgia, history, archaeology, nature, etc. Departments using personal experience pieces include "Mileposts," "Focus on Nature," "Along the Way," "Back Road Adventures," "Hiking," and "Arizona Humor." Pays 35¢ to 55¢ a word, on acceptance. Query required. Guidelines.

ATLANTA—1360 Peachtree St., Suite 1800, Atlanta, GA 30309. Lee Walburn, Ed. Articles, 1,500 to 5,000 words, on Atlanta subjects or personalities. Pays $300 to $2,000, on publication. Query.

ATLANTIC CITY MAGAZINE—P.O. Box 2100, Pleasantville, NJ 08232. Paula Rackow, Ed. Lively articles, 200 to 2,000 words, on Atlantic City and the southern New Jersey shore, for locals and tourists: entertainment, casinos, business, recreation, personalities, lifestyle, local color. Pays $50 to $600, on publication. Query.

BACK HOME IN KENTUCKY—P.O. Box 681629, Franklin, TN 37068–1629. Nanci P. Gregg, Man. Ed. Articles on Kentucky history, travel, craftsmen and artisans, Kentucky cooks, and "colorful" characters; limited personal nostalgia specifically related to Kentucky. Pays $25 to $100 for articles with B&W or color photos. Queries preferred.

BALTIMORE MAGAZINE—16 S. Calvert St., Suite 1000, Baltimore, MD 21202. Ramsey Flynn, Ed. Articles, 500 to 3,000 words, on people, places, and things in the Baltimore metropolitan area. Consumer advice, investigative pieces, profiles, humor, and personal experience pieces. Payment varies, on publication. Query required.

THE BIG APPLE PARENTS' PAPER—36 E. 12th St., New York, NY 10003. Susan Hodara, Ed. Articles, 600 to 750 words, for New York City parents. Pays $50, on publication. Buys first NY-area rights.

BIRMINGHAM—2027 First Ave. N., Birmingham, AL 35203. Joe O'Donnell, Ed. Profiles, business articles, and nostalgia pieces, to 2,500 words, with Birmingham tie-in. Pays $50 to $175, on publication.

BLUE RIDGE COUNTRY—P.O. Box 21535, Roanoke, VA 24018. Kurt Rheinheimer, Ed. Bimonthly. Regional articles, 1,200 to 2,000 words, that "explore and extol the beauty, history, and travel opportunities in the mountain regions of VA, NC, WV, TN, KY, MD, SC, and GA." Color slides or B&W prints considered. Pays $200 for photo-features, on publication. Queries preferred.

BOCA RATON—JES Publishing, Amtec Ctr., Suite 100, 6413 Congress Ave., Boca Raton, FL 33487. Marie Speed, Ed. Articles, 800 to 3,000 words, on Florida topics, personalities, and travel. Pays $50 to $500, on acceptance. Query with clips required.

THE BOSTON GLOBE MAGAZINE—*The Boston Globe*, Boston, MA 02107. Evelynne Kramer, Ed. General-interest articles on regional topics and profiles, 2,500 to 5,000 words. Query and SASE required.

BOSTON MAGAZINE—300 Massachusetts Ave., Boston, MA 02115. Attn: Man. Ed. Informative, entertaining features, 1,000 to 3,000 words, on Boston-area personalities, institutions, and phenomena. Query. Pays to $2,000, on publication.

BOUNDARY WATERS JOURNAL—9396 Rocky Ledge Rd., Ely, MN 55731. Stuart Osthoff, Ed. Articles, 2,000 to 3,000 words, on wilderness, recreation, nature, and conservation in Minnesota's Boundary Waters Canoe Area Wilderness and Ontario's Quetico Provincial Park. Regular features include canoe-route journals, fishing, camping, hiking, cross-country skiing, wildlife and nature, regional lifestyles, history, and events. Pays $200 to $400, on publication; $50 to $150 for photos.

BUFFALO SPREE MAGAZINE—Box 38, Buffalo, NY 14226. Johanna Van De Mark, Ed./Pub. Articles, to 1,800 words, for readers in the western New York region. Pays $75 to $125, $25 for poetry, on publication.

BUSINESS IN BROWARD—P.O. Box 7375, Ft. Lauderdale, FL 33338–7375. Sherry Friedlander, Ed. Published 8 times a year. Articles, 1,000 words, on small business in eastern Florida county. Pay varies, on acceptance.

BUZZ: THE TALK OF LOS ANGELES—11835 W. Olympic Blvd., Suite 450, Los Angeles, CA 90064. Allan Mayer, Ed.-in-Chief. Articles, varying lengths, of particular relevance to readers in southern California. Query. Pays $1 a word, within 30 days of acceptance.

CAPE COD LIFE—P.O. Box 767, Cataumet, MA 02534–0767. Brian F. Shortsleeve, Pub. Articles, to 2,000 words, on current events, business, art, history, gardening, and nautical lifestyle on Cape Cod, Martha's Vineyard, and Nantucket. Pays 10¢ a word, 30 days after publication. Queries preferred.

CARIBBEAN TRAVEL AND LIFE—8403 Colesville Rd., Silver Spring, MD 20910. Veronica Gould Stoddart, Ed. Articles, 500 to 3,000 words, on all aspects of travel, recreation, leisure, and culture in the Caribbean, the Bahamas, and Bermuda. Pays $75 to $550, on publication. Query with published clips.

CAROLOGUE—South Carolina Historical Society, 100 Meeting St., Charleston, SC 29401–2299. Stephen Hoffius, Ed. General-interest articles, to 10 pages, on South Carolina history. Queries preferred. Pays in copies.

CHESAPEAKE BAY MAGAZINE—1819 Bay Ridge Ave., Annapolis, MD 21403. Jean Waller, Ed. Articles, 8 to 10 typed pages, related to the Chesapeake Bay area. Profiles. Photos. Pays on publication. Query.

CHICAGO— 414 N. Orleans, Chicago, IL 60610. Shane Tritsch, Man. Ed. Articles, 1,000 to 5,000 words, related to Chicago. Pays varying rates, on acceptance. Query.

CHICAGO HISTORY— Clark St. at North Ave., Chicago, IL 60614. Rosemary Adams, Ed. Articles, to 4,500 words, on Chicago's urban, political, social, and cultural history. Pays to $250, on publication. Query.

CHICAGO TRIBUNE MAGAZINE—*Chicago Tribune*, 435 N. Michigan Ave., Rm. 532, Chicago, IL 60611. Attn: Ed. Profiles and articles, to 6,000 words, on public and social issues on the personal, local, or national level. Prefer regional slant. Pays $250 to $1,500, on publication. Query.

CITYLIMITS—325 N. Clippert St., Suite B, Lansing, MI 48912. Kelly Rossman-McKinney, Roger Martin, Eds. Upbeat fiction, 1,500 to 2,500 words, of interest to Lansing, MI, area readers. Pays $250, on publication. Query preferred.

COLORADO BUSINESS—7009 S. Potomac, Englewood, CO 80112. Garrison Wells, Ed. Articles, varying lengths, on business, business personalities, and economic trends in Colorado. Pays on publication. Query.

COLORADO HOMES & LIFESTYLES—7009 S. Potomac, Englewood, CO 80112. Karen Coe, Ed. Articles, 1,200 to 1,500 words, on topics related to Colorado: travel, home design and decorating, architecture, gardening, art, antiques, collecting, and entertaining. Pays $125 to $200, on acceptance.

COMMON GROUND MAGAZINE—P.O. Box 99, McVeytown, PA 17051–0099. Ruth Dunmire and Pam Brumbaugh, Eds. Quarterly. General-interest articles, 500 to 5,000 words, related to central Pennsylvania's Juniata River Valley and its rural lifestyle. Related fiction, 1,000 to 2,000 words. Poetry, to 12 lines. Fillers, photos, and cartoons. Pays $25 to $200 for articles, $5 to $15 for fillers, and $5 to $25 for photos, on publication. Guidelines.

CONCORD NORTH—See *New Hampshire Editions*.

CONNECTICUT—789 Reservoir Ave., Bridgeport, CT 06606. Charles Monagan, Ed. Articles, 1,500 to 3,500 words, on Connecticut topics, issues, people, and lifestyles. Pays $500 to $1,200, within 30 days of acceptance.

CONNECTICUT FAMILY—See *New York Family*.

CRAIN'S DETROIT BUSINESS—1400 Woodbridge, Detroit, MI 48207. Cindy Goodaker, Exec. Ed. Business articles, 500 to 1,000 words, about Detroit, for Detroit business readers. Pays $100 to $200, on publication. Query required.

DELAWARE TODAY—P.O. Box 2087, Wilmington, DE 19899. Ted Spiker, Ed. Service articles, profiles, news, etc., on topics of local interest. Pays $75 to $125 for department pieces, $50 to $500 for features, on publication. Queries with clips required.

DETROIT MONTHLY—1400 Woodbridge, Detroit, MI 48207. Megan Swoyer, Man. Ed. Articles on Detroit-area people, issues, lifestyles, and business. Payment varies. Query required.

DOWN EAST—Camden, ME 04843. Davis Thomas, Ed. Articles, 1,500 to 2,500 words, on all aspects of life in Maine. Photos. Pays to 20¢ a word, extra for photos, on acceptance. Query.

EASTSIDE PARENT—Northwest Parent Publishing, 2107 Elliott Ave., #303, Seattle, WA 98121. Ann Bergman, Ed. Articles, 300 to 2,500 words, for parents of children ages 12 and under. Pays $25 to $200, on publication. Queries preferred. Also publishes *Seattle's Child, Portland Parent* and *Pierce County Parent.*

ERIE & CHAUTAUQUA MAGAZINE—317 W. Sixth St., Erie, PA 16507. K. L. Kalvelage, Man. Ed. Feature articles, to 2,500 words, on issues of interest to upscale readers in the Erie, Warren, and Crawford counties (PA), and Chautauqua (NY) county. Pieces with regional relevance. Pays after publication. Query preferred, with writing samples. Guidelines.

FAMILY TIMES—P.O. Box 932, Eau Claire, WI 54702. Ann Gorton, Ed. Articles, from 800 words, for parents in the Chippewa Valley, WI. Pays $35 to $50, on publication. Queries preferred. Guidelines.

FLORIDA KEYS MAGAZINE—P.O. Box 8081, Key West, FL 33041. Gibbons Cline, Ed. Articles, 1,000 to 2,000 words, on the Florida Keys: history, environment, personality profiles, etc. Fillers, humor. Photos. Pays $2 per column inch, on publication.

FLORIDA TREND—Box 611, St. Petersburg, FL 33731–0611. John F. Berry, Ed. Articles on Florida business and businesspeople. Query with SASE required.

FLORIDA WILDLIFE— 620 S. Meridian St., Tallahassee, FL 32399–1600. Attn: Ed. Bimonthly of the Florida Game and Fresh Water Fish Commission. Articles, 800 to 1,500 words, that promote native flora and fauna, hunting, fishing in Florida's fresh waters, outdoor ethics, and conservation of Florida's natural resources. Pays $50 to $300, on publication.

THE GAZETTE—The Sunday Magazine of the *Pittsburgh Post-Gazette*, 34 Blvd. of the Allies, Pittsburgh, PA 15230. Mark S. Murphy, Ed. Well-written, well-organized, in-depth articles of local, regional, or national interest, 3,000 to 4,500 words, on issues, personalities, human interest, historical moments. No fiction, hobbies, how-tos or "timely events" pieces. Pays from $500, on publication. Query.

GEORGIA JOURNAL—The Indispensable Atlanta Co., Inc., P.O. Box 1604, Decatur, GA 30031–1604. David Osier, Ed./Pub. Conoly Hester, Man. Ed. Articles, 200 to 5,000 words, on Georgia's natural and human history and environment; also outdoor adventures, true crime mysteries, people, historical figures, places, events, travel in Georgia. Poetry, to 20 lines, and fiction, to 5,000 words, with Georgia settings; Georgia writers preferred. Pays $50 to $500, on publication.

GRAND RAPIDS—549 Ottawa N.W., Grand Rapids, MI 49503. Carole Valade Smith, Ed. Service articles (dining guide, travel, personal finance, humor) and issue-oriented pieces related to Grand Rapids, Michigan. Pays $35 to $200, on publication. Query.

GULF COAST GOLFER—See *North Texas Golfer.*

HAMPSHIRE WEST—See *New Hampshire Editions.*

HAWAII—1400 Kapiolani Blvd., A25, Honolulu, HI 96814. Jim Borg, Ed.

Bimonthly. Articles, 1,000 to 2,500 words, related to Hawaii. Pays 10¢ a word, on publication. Query.

HIGH COUNTRY NEWS—Box 1090, Paonia, CO 81428. Betsy Marston, Ed. Biweekly. Articles, 2,000 words, and roundups, 750 words, on western environmental issues, public lands management, energy, and natural resource issues; profiles of western innovators; pieces on western politics. "Writers must take regional approach." Poetry. B&W photos. Pays $2 to $4 per column inch, on publication. Query.

HONOLULU—36 Merchant St., Honolulu, HI 96813. John Heckathorn, Ed. Features highlighting contemporary life in the Hawaiian islands: politics, sports, history, people, arts, events. Pays $300 to $700, on acceptance. Queries required.

ILLINOIS ENTERTAINER—124 W. Polk, Suite 103, Chicago, IL 60605. Michael C. Harris, Ed. Articles, 500 to 1,500 words, on local and national entertainment (emphasis on alternative music) in the greater Chicago area. Personality profiles; interviews; reviews. Photos. Pays varying rates, on publication. Query preferred.

INDIANAPOLIS MONTHLY—950 N. Meridian St., Suite 1200, Indianapolis, IN 46204. Sam Stall, Ed. Articles, 200 to 6,000 words, on health, sports, politics, business, interior design, personalities, controversy, and other topics. All material must have an Indianapolis/Indiana focus. Pays $50 to $500, on publication.

INQUIRER MAGAZINE—*Philadelphia Inquirer*, P.O. 8263, 400 N. Broad St., Philadelphia, PA 19101. Ms. Avery Rome, Ed. Articles, 1,500 to 2,000 words, and 3,000 to 7,000 words, on politics, science, arts and culture, business, lifestyles and entertainment, sports, health, psychology, education, religion, and humor. Short pieces, 850 words, for "Up Front." Pays varying rates. Query.

THE IOWAN MAGAZINE—108 Third St., Suite 350, Des Moines, IA 50309. Mark Ingebretsen, Ed. Articles, 1,000 to 3,000 words, on business, arts, people, and history of Iowa. Photos a plus. Payment varies, on acceptance. Query required.

ISLAND LIFE—P.O. Box 929, Sanibel Island, FL 33957. Joan Hooper, Ed. Articles, 500 to 1,200 words, with photos, on wildlife, flora and fauna, design and decor, the arts, shelling, local sports, historical sites, etc., directly related to the islands of Sanibel, Captiva, Marco, Estero, or Gasparilla. No first-person articles. Pays on publication.

JACKSONVILLE—White Publishing Co., 1650 Prudential Dr., Suite 300, Jacksonville, FL 32207. Larry Marscheck, Ed. Service pieces and articles, 1,500 to 2,500 words, on issues and personalities of interest to readers in the greater Jacksonville area. Department pieces, 1,200 to 1,500 words, on business, health, travel, personal finance, real estate, arts and entertainment, sports, food. Home and garden articles on local homeowners, interior designers, etc., 1,000 to 2,000 words. Pays $200 to $500, on publication. Guidelines. Query required.

JOURNAL OF THE WEST—1531 Yuma, Manhattan, KS 66502–4228. Robin Higham, Ed. Articles, to 20 pages, on the history and culture of the West, then and now. Pays in copies.

KANSAS!—Kansas Dept. of Commerce, 700 S.W. Harrison, Suite 1300,

Topeka, KS 66603–3957. Andrea Glenn, Ed. Quarterly. Articles, 1,000 to 1,250 words, on the people, places, history, and events of Kansas. Color slides. Pays to $250, on acceptance. Query.

KANSAS CITY MAGAZINE—7007 College Blvd., Suite 430, Overland Park, KS 66211. Doug Worgul, Ed. Articles, 250 to 3,500 words, of interest to readers in Kansas City. Pays to 30¢ a word, on acceptance. Query.

KENTUCKY LIVING—P.O. Box 32170, Louisville, KY 40232. Donna Bunch Miller, Ed. Articles, 800 to 2,000 words, with strong Kentucky angle: profiles (of people, places, events), history, biography, recreation, travel, leisure or lifestyle, and book excerpts. Pays $125 to $350, on acceptance. Guidelines.

LAKE SUPERIOR MAGAZINE—P.O. Box 16417, Duluth, MN 55816–0417. Paul Hayden, Ed. Articles with emphasis on Lake Superior regional subjects: historical and topical pieces that highlight the people, places, and events that affect the Lake Superior region. Pictorial essays; humor and occasional fiction. Quality photos enhance submission. "Writers must have a thorough knowledge of the subject and how it relates to our region." Pays to $400, extra for photos, on publication. Query.

THE LOOK—P.O. Box 272, Cranford, NJ 07016–0272. John R. Hawks, Pub. Articles, 1,500 to 3,000 words, on fashion, student life, employment, relationships, and profiles of interest to local (NJ) readers ages 16 to 26. Also, beach stories and articles about the New Jersey shore. Pays $30 to $200, on publication.

LOS ANGELES MAGAZINE—1888 Century Park E., Suite 920, Los Angeles, CA 90067. Lew Harris, Ed. Articles, to 3,000 words, of interest to sophisticated, affluent southern Californians, preferably with local focus on a lifestyle topic. Payment varies. Query.

LOS ANGELES READER—5550 Wilshire Blvd., Suite 301, Los Angeles, CA 90036. James Vowell, Ed. Articles, 750 to 5,000 words, on subjects related to the Los Angeles area; special emphasis on feature journalism, entertainment, and the arts. Pays $25 to $500, on publication. Query preferred.

LOUISVILLE—137 W. Muhammad Ali Blvd., Suite 101, Louisville, KY 40202. John Filiatreau, Ed. Articles, 1,000 to 2,000 words, on community issues, personalities, and entertainment in the Louisville area. Photos. Pays from $50, on acceptance. Query; articles on assignment only. Limited freelance market.

MANCHESTER—See *New Hampshire Editions.*

MEMPHIS—MM Corp., Box 256, Memphis, TN 38101. Tim Sampson, Ed. Articles, 1,500 to 4,000 words, on a wide variety of topics related to Memphis and the Mid-South region: politics, education, sports, business, history, etc. Profiles; investigative pieces. Pays $50 to $500, on publication. Query. SASE for guidelines.

METROKIDS—Riverview Plaza, 1400 S. Columbus Blvd., Philadelphia, PA 19147–5526. Nancy Lisagor, Ed. Tabloid. Features and department pieces, 500 to 1,000 words, on regional family travel, dining, and entertainment in the Delaware Valley. Pays $25 to $50, on publication.

MICHIGAN LIVING—1 Auto Club Dr., Dearborn, MI 48126–9982. Len Barnes, Ed. Travel articles, 300 to 2,000 words, on tourist attractions and recreational opportunities in the U.S. and Canada, with emphasis on Michigan: places to go, things to do, costs, etc. Color photos. Pays $55 to $500, (rates vary for photos), on acceptance.

MID-WEST OUTDOORS—111 Shore Dr., Hinsdale, IL 60521-5885. Gene Laulunen, Ed. Articles, to 1,500 words, with photos (no slides), on where, when, and how to fish and hunt, within 500 miles of Chicago. Pays $25, on publication.

MILWAUKEE MAGAZINE—312 E. Buffalo, Milwaukee, WI 53202. John Fennell, Ed. Profiles, investigative articles, and service pieces, 2,000 to 6,000 words; local tie-in a must. No fiction. Pays $400 to $900, on publication. Query preferred.

MINNESOTA MONTHLY—Lumber Exchange Bldg., 10 S. Fifth St., Suite 1000, Minneapolis, MN 55402. Kevin Frazzini, Assoc. Ed. Articles, to 4,000 words, on people, places, events, and issues in Minnesota. Pays $50 to $800, on acceptance. Query.

MONTANA MAGAZINE—P.O. Box 5630, Helena, MT 59604. Beverly R. Magley, Ed. Recreation, travel, general interest, regional profiles, photo-essays. Montana-oriented only. B&W prints, color slides. Pays 15¢ a word, on publication.

MPLS. ST. PAUL—220 S. 6th St., Suite 500, Minneapolis, MN 55402-4507. Brian E. Anderson, Ed. In-depth articles, features, profiles, and service pieces about the Minneapolis-St. Paul area, 300 to 4,000 words. Pays to $2,000.

NAPA VALLEY APPELLATION—P.O. Box 516, Napa, CA 94559. Antonia Allegra, Ed.-in-Chief. Quarterly. Articles, 900 to 1,500 words, on the lifestyles, wines, and gardens of the Napa Valley. Pays $200 to $500, on acceptance.

NASHUA—See *New Hampshire Editions.*

NEBRASKA HISTORY—P.O. Box 82554, Lincoln, NE 68501. James E. Potter, Ed. Articles, 3,000 to 7,000 words, on the history of Nebraska and the Great Plains. B&W line drawings. Pays in copies. Cash prize awarded to one article each year.

NETWORK PUBLICATIONS—See *New Hampshire Editions.*

NEVADA—1800 Hwy. 50 East, Suite 200, Carson City, NV 89710. David Moore, Ed. Articles, 500 to 700 or 1,500 to 1,800 words, on topics related to Nevada: travel, history, profiles, humor, and place. Special section on Nevada events. Photos. Pay varies, on publication.

NEW ALASKAN—P.O. Box 7416, Ketchikan, AK 99901. Jeff Fitzwater, Ed. Articles, 1,000 to 5,000 words, and fiction, must be related to southern Alaska. Pays 2¢ a word, on publication.

NEW FRONTIERS OF NEW MEXICO—P.O. Box 1299, Tijeras, NM 87059. Wally Gordon, Ed./Pub. Fiction and in-depth nonfiction, to 3,000 words, related to New Mexico and the Southwest. Humor, to 1,000 words. Poetry, to 100 lines. Pays $25 to $200, on publication.

NEW HAMPSHIRE EDITIONS—(formerly *Network Publications*) 100 Main St., Nashua, NH 03060. Rick Broussard, Ed. Leeann Boyer, Man. Ed. Lifestyle, business, and history articles with a New Hampshire angle, with sources from all regions of the state, for the company's regional monthlies:

Nashua, Manchester, Concord North, Seacoast, and *Hampshire West.* Query. Payment varies, on publication.

NEW JERSEY MONTHLY—P.O. Box 920, Morristown, NJ 07963–0920. Jenny DeMonte, Ed. Articles, profiles, and service pieces, 1,500 to 3,000 words; department pieces on health, business, education, travel, sports, local politics, and arts with New Jersey tie-in, 750 to 1,500 words. Pays $25 to $100 for shorts, $400 to $700 for departments, $600 to $1,750 for features, on acceptance. Guidelines. Query with clips.

NEW JERSEY REPORTER—The Ctr. for Analysis of Public Issues, 16 Vandeventer Ave., Princeton, NJ 08542. Neil Upmeyer, Ed. Bob Narus, Man. Ed. In-depth articles, 1,000 to 4,000 words, on New Jersey politics and public affairs. Pays $100 to $400, on publication. Query required.

NEW MEXICO MAGAZINE—Lew Wallace Bldg., 495 Old Santa Fe Trail, Santa Fe, NM 87503. Attn: Ed. Articles, 250 to 2,000 words, on New Mexico subjects. No poetry or fiction. Pays about 30¢ a word, on acceptance.

NEW YORK FAMILY—141 Halstead Ave., Suite 3D, Mamaroneck, NY 10543. Felice Shapiro, Pub. Susan Ross, Ed. Betsy Woolf, Sr. Ed. Articles related to family life in New York City. Pays $50 to $100, on publication. Same requirements for *Westchester Family* and *Connecticut Family.*

NEWPORT LIFE—174 Bellevue Ave., Suite 207, Newport, RI 02840. Susan Ryan, Sr. Ed. Quarterly. Articles, 500 to 2,500 words, on the people and places of Newport County: general-interest and historical articles, interviews, profiles, investigative pieces, and photo-features. Departments, 500 to 750 words, include "At the Helm" (on some aspect of boating), "Arts Marquee," "Food for Thought," and "Down to Business." Photos must be available for all articles. Pays 10¢ a word, on publication. Query.

NORTH DAKOTA HORIZONS—P.O. Box 2639, Bismarck, ND 58502. Lyle Halvorson, Ed. Quarterly. Articles, about 3,000 words, on people, places, and events in North Dakota. Photos. Pays $75 to $300, on publication.

NORTH GEORGIA JOURNAL—P.O. Box 127, Roswell, GA 30077. Olin Jackson, Pub./Ed. History, travel, and lifestyle features, 2,000 to 3,000 words, on north Georgia. History features need human-interest approach and must be written in first person; include interviews. Photos a plus. Pays $75 to $250, on acceptance. Query.

NORTH TEXAS GOLFER—9182 Old Katy Rd., Suite 212, Houston, TX 77055. Steve Hunter, Ed. Articles, 800 to 1,500 words, involving local golfers or related directly to north Texas. Pays from $50 to $425, on publication. Query. Same requirements for *Gulf Coast Golfer* (related to south Texas).

NORTHEAST MAGAZINE—*The Hartford Courant,* 285 Broad St., Hartford, CT 06115. Lary Bloom, Ed. Articles and short essays, 750 to 3,000 words, that reflect the concerns of Connecticut residents. Pays $250 to $1,000, on acceptance.

NORTHERN LIGHTS—Box 8084, Missoula, MT 59807–8084. Attn: Ed. Articles, 500 to 3,000 words, about the contemporary West. "We look for beautifully crafted personal essays that illuminate what it means to live in the Rocky Mountain West. We're looking to bust the Hollywood stereotypes." Pays 10¢ a word, on publication.

NORTHWEST PARKS & WILDLIFE—See *Northwest Regional Magazines.*

577

NORTHWEST PRIME TIME JOURNAL—(formerly *Northwest Prime Times*) 10827 N.E. 68th St., Kirkland, WA 98033. Neil Strother, Pub./Ed. News and features on the Northwest for readers 50 and older. Pays $25 to $50, on publication. Limited market.

NORTHWEST REGIONAL MAGAZINES—P.O. Box 18000, Florence, OR 97439–0130. Attn: Dave Peden or Judy Fleagle. All submissions considered for use in *Oregon Coast, Oregon Parks, Northwest Travel*, and *Northwest Parks & Wildlife*. Articles, 800 to 2,000 words, pertaining to the Pacific Northwest, on travel, history, town/city profiles, parks, and nature. News releases, 200 to 500 words. Articles with photos (slides) preferred. Pays $50 to $350, after publication. Guidelines.

NORTHWEST TRAVEL—See *Northwest Regional Magazines.*

OHIO MAGAZINE— 62 E. Broad St., Columbus, OH 43215. John Baskin, Ed. Dir. Profiles of people, cities, and towns of Ohio; pieces on historic sites, tourist attractions, little-known spots. Lengths and payment vary. Query with clips.

OKLAHOMA TODAY—Box 53384, Oklahoma City, OK 73152–9971. Jeanne M. Devlin, Ed. Articles, 1,000 to 4,000 words: travel; profiles; history; nature and outdoor recreation; and arts. All material must have regional tie-in. Pays $75 to $750, on acceptance. Queries preferred. Guidelines.

ORANGE COAST—245-D Fischer Ave., Suite 8, Costa Mesa, CA 92626. Martin J. Smith, Ed. Articles, 2,000 to 3,000 words, of interest to educated Orange County residents. Pieces, 1,000 to 1,500 words, for regular departments including "Coastwatch" (services and products), "Short Cuts" (local phenomena). Query with clips. Pays $400 to $800 for features; $100 to $200 for departments; $25 to $50 for "Short Cuts" and "Coastwatch," after acceptance. Guidelines.

OREGON COAST—See *Northwest Regional Magazines.*

OREGON PARKS—See *Northwest Regional Magazines.*

ORLANDO MAGAZINE—P.O. Box 2207, Orlando, FL 32802. Frederick Abel, Ed. General-interest articles and department pieces, lengths vary, for residents of central Florida. Query with clips.

OTTAWA MAGAZINE—192 Bank St., Ottawa, Ont., Canada K2P 1W8. Mark Sutcliffe, Ed. Articles, investigative journalism, and profiles, 1,500 to 2,000 words, relating to the social issues and cultural and consumer interests of Ottawa City. Pays 30¢ to 50¢ a word, on acceptance. Query with resumé and clips.

OUT WEST: THE NEWSPAPER THAT ROAMS— 408 Broad St., Suite 11, Nevada City, CA 95959. Chuck Woodbury, Ed./Pub. Entertaining and informative articles, 150 to 750 words, and short pieces, 30 to 75 words, on the rural West (not the old West): interesting people, unusual places to stay, offbeat attractions. "Send for a sample of the paper before you submit." Pays about 5¢ a word, on publication.

OUTDOOR TRAVELER, MID-ATLANTIC—WMS Publications, Inc., P.O. Box 2748, Charlottesville, VA 22902. Marianne Marks, Ed. Scott Clark, Assoc. Ed. Articles, 1,500 to 2,000 words, about outdoor recreation, travel, adventure, and nature in the Mid-Atlantic region (NY, PA, NJ, MD, DE, DC, WV, VA, and NC). Departments include "Destinations," 450 to 600 words, on practical and descriptive guides to sports destinations; "Getaways," inns and lodges, including seasonal and outdoor activities; book reviews, 200 words. Pays $375 to $500 for features; payment varies for departments, on publication. Guidelines.

PALM SPRINGS LIFE—Desert Publications, 303 N. Indian Canyon Dr., P.O. Box 2724, Palm Springs, CA 92263. Stewart Weiner, Ed. Articles, 1,000 to 2,000 words, of interest to "wealthy, upscale people who live and/or play in the desert": food, interior design, luxury cars, shopping, sports, homes, personalities, desert issues, arts, and culture. Pays $150 to $400 for features, $30 to $60 for short profiles, on publication. Query required.

PENNSYLVANIA HERITAGE—P.O. Box 1026, Harrisburg, PA 17108–1026. Michael J. O'Malley III, Ed. Quarterly of the Pennsylvania Historical Museum Commission. Articles, 3,000 to 4,000 words, on fine and decorative arts, architecture, archaeology, oral history, exhibits, industry and technology, travel, and folklore, written with an eye toward illustration. Photographic essays. Pieces should "introduce readers to the state's rich culture and historic legacy." Pays $300 to $500 for articles; up to $100 for photos and drawings, on acceptance.

PENNSYLVANIA MAGAZINE—Box 576, Camp Hill, PA 17001–0576. Matthew K. Holliday, Ed. General-interest features with a Pennsylvania focus. All articles must be accompanied by photocopies of possible illustrations. Guidelines.

PERSIMMON HILL—1700 N.E. 63rd St., Oklahoma City, OK 73111. M.J. Van Deventer, Ed. Published by the National Cowboy Hall of Fame. Articles, 1,500 to 2,000 words, on Western history and art, cowboys, ranching, and nature. Top-quality illustrations a must. Pays from $100 to $250, on publication.

PHILADELPHIA—1818 Market St., Philadelphia, PA 19103. Eliot Kaplan, Ed. Articles, 1,000 to 5,000 words, for sophisticated audience, relating to Philadelphia area. No fiction or poetry. Pays on acceptance. Query.

PHOENIX MAGAZINE—5555 N. 7th Ave., Suite B200, Phoenix, AZ 85013. Richard Vonier, Ed. Articles, 1,000 to 3,000 words, on topics of interest to Phoenix-area residents. Pays $300 to $1,000, on publication. Queries preferred.

PIERCE COUNTY PARENT—See *Eastside Parent.*

PITTSBURGH— 4802 Fifth Ave., Pittsburgh, PA 15213. Christopher Fletcher, Ed. Articles, 850 to 3,000 words, with western Pennsylvania slant. Pays on publication.

PORTLAND MONTHLY MAGAZINE—578 Congress St., Portland, ME 04101. Colin Sargent, Ed. Articles on local people, legends, culture, and trends. Fiction, to 750 words. Pays on publication. Query preferred.

PORTLAND PARENT—See *Eastside Parent.*

RECKON—Southern Culture Publications, Hill Hall, Room 301, The Univ. of Mississippi, University, MS 38677. Lynn McKnight, Man. Ed. Quarterly. Fiction, 3,000 to 7,000 words, and non-academic essays, 1,000 to 5,000 words, on the contemporary American South. "Preference is given to prose with a distinct literary tone. Content must be informed, intelligent, and interpretive." No poetry or fillers. Pays 25¢ a word, on publication. Guidelines.

579

RECREATION NEWS—P.O. Box 32335, Washington, DC 20007–0635. M. M. Ghannam, Ed. Articles, 1,500 to 2,000 words, on recreation and travel for government workers in the Washington, DC area. Light, first-person accounts, 800 words, for "Sporting Life" column. "Articles should have a conversational tone that's lean and brisk." Pays $50 for reprints, to $300 for cover articles, on publication. Guidelines. Queries preferred.

RHODE ISLAND MONTHLY—18 Imperial Pl., Providence, RI 02903. Paula M. Bodah, Man. Ed. Features, 1,000 to 4,000 words, ranging from investigative reporting and in-depth profiles to service pieces and visual stories, on Rhode Island and southeastern Massachusetts. Seasonal material, 1,000 to 2,000 words. Fillers, 150 to 500 words, on Rhode Island places, customs, people, events, products and services, restaurants and food. Pays $250 to $1,000 for features; $25 to $50 for shorts, on publication. Query.

ROCKFORD MAGAZINE—99 E. State St., Rockford, IL 61104. Craig Schmidt, Ed. General-interest magazine covering Rockford and northern Illinois. Feature articles, 2,500 to 3,500 words, and departments, 1,500 to 2,000 words, on city and area personalities, politics, events, business, family, travel destinations, home improvement and decor, dining, etc. "Nothing predictable or routine." Payment varies, on acceptance. Query with samples and clips required; no unsolicited manuscripts.

RUNNER TRIATHLETE NEWS—P.O. Box 19909, Houston, TX 77224. Lance Phegley, Ed. Articles on running for road racing and multi-sport enthusiasts in TX, LA, OK, NM, and AR. Payment varies, on publication.

RURALITE—P.O. Box 558, Forest Grove, OR 97116. Attn: Ed. or Feature Ed. Articles, 800 to 2,000 words, of interest to a primarily rural and small-town audience in OR, WA, ID, NV, northern CA, and AK. "Think pieces" affecting rural/urban interests, regional history and celebrations, self-help, profiles, etc. No fiction or poetry. No sentimental nostalgia. Pays $30 to $400, on acceptance. Guidelines. Queries required.

SACRAMENTO MAGAZINE—4471 D St., Sacramento, CA 95819. Krista Hendricks Minard, Ed. Features, 2,500 words, on a broad range of topics related to the region. Department pieces, 1,200 to 1,500 words, and short pieces, 400 words, for "City Lights" column. Pays $75 to $300, on publication. Query.

SAN DIEGO MAGAZINE—4206 W. Point Loma Blvd., P.O. Box 85409, San Diego, CA 92138. Virginia Butterfield, Assoc. Ed. Articles, 1,500 to 3,000 words, on local personalities, politics, lifestyles, business, history, etc., relating to San Diego area. Photos. Pays $250 to $600, on publication. Query with clips.

SAN DIEGO READER—P.O. Box 85803, San Diego, CA 92186. Jim Holman, Ed. Literate articles, 2,500 to 10,000 words, on the San Diego region. Pays $500 to $2,000, on publication.

SAN FRANCISCO EXAMINER MAGAZINE—*San Francisco Examiner,* 110 Fifth St., San Francisco, CA 94103. Attn: Ed. Articles, 1,200 to 3,000 words, on lifestyles, issues, business, history, events, and people in northern California. Pays varying rates. Query.

SAN FRANCISCO FOCUS—2601 Mariposa St., San Francisco, CA 94110–1400. Amy Rennert, Ed. Service features, profiles of local newsmakers, and investigative pieces of local issues, 2,500 to 3,000 words. News items, 250 to 800 words, on subjects ranging from business to arts to politics. Payment varies, on acceptance. Query required.

SAVANNAH MAGAZINE—P.O. Box 1088, Savannah, GA 31402. Georgia R. Byrd, Ed. Articles, 2,500 to 3,500 words, on people and events in and around Savannah and Chatham County. Historical articles, 1,500 to 2,500 words, of local interest. Reviews, 500 to 750 words, of Savannah-based books and authors. Short pieces, 500 to 750 words, on weekend getaways near Savannah. Pays $75 to $350, after acceptance. Submit complete manuscript. Guidelines.

SEACOAST—See *New Hampshire Editions.*

SEATTLE WEEKLY—1008 Western, Suite 300, Seattle, WA 98104. Skip Berger, Ed. Articles, 250 to 4,000 words, from a Northwest perspective. Pays $25 to $800, on publication. Query. Guidelines.

SEATTLE'S CHILD—Northwest Parent Publishing, 2107 Elliott Ave., #303, Seattle, WA 98121. Ann Bergman, Ed. Articles, 400 to 2,500 words, of interest to parents, educators, and childcare providers of children under 12, and investigative reports and consumer tips on issues affecting families in the Puget Sound region. Pays $75 to $400, on publication. Query required.

SENIOR MAGAZINE—3565 S. Higuera St., San Luis Obispo, CA 93401. Attn: Ed. Articles, 600 to 900 words: profiles, travel pieces, articles about new things, places, business, sports, movies, television, and health; book reviews (of new or outstanding older books) of interest to senior citizens in California. Pays $1.50 per inch; $10 to $25 for B&W photos, on publication.

SILENT SPORTS—717 10th St., P.O. Box 152, Waupaca, WI 54981. Attn: Ed. Articles, 1,000 to 2,000 words, on canoeing, bicycling, cross-country skiing, running, hiking, backpacking, and other "silent" sports, in the upper Midwest region. Pays $40 to $100 for features; $20 to $50 for fillers, on publication. Query.

SOUTH CAROLINA HISTORICAL MAGAZINE—South Carolina Historical Society, 100 Meeting St., Charleston, SC 29401–2299. Stephen Hoffius, Ed. Scholarly articles, to 25 pages with footnotes, on all areas of South Carolina history. Pays in copies.

SOUTH CAROLINA WILDLIFE—P.O. Box 167, Columbia, SC 29202–0167. Attn: Man. Ed. Articles, 1,000 to 2,000 words, with regional outdoors focus: conservation, natural history and wildlife, recreation. Profiles. Pays from 10¢ a word. Query.

SOUTH FLORIDA MAGAZINE— 800 Douglas Rd., Suite 500, Coral Gables, FL 33134. Nancy Moore, Ed. Features, 1,100 to 3,500 words, and department pieces, 900 to 1,300 words, on news, profiles, and hot topics related to south Florida. Short, bright items, 200 to 400 words. Pays $75 to $700, within 30 days of acceptance. Query.

SOUTHERN CULTURES—Ctr. for the Study of the American South, Manning Hall, UNC-CH, Chapel Hill, NC 27599–3355. Alecia Holland, Man. Ed. Articles, 15 to 25 typed pages, on folk, popular, and high culture of the South. "We're interested in submissions from a wide variety of intellectual traditions that deal with ways of life, thought, belief, and expression in the United States South." Pays in copies.

SOUTHERN OUTDOORS—5845 Carmichael Rd., Montgomery, AL

36117. Larry Teague, Ed. How-to pieces, 800 to 1,200 words, and 2,000-word how-to and where-to articles on hunting and fishing, for fishermen and hunters in the Southern states. Pays 20¢ a word, on acceptance. Query.

SOUTHWEST ART—5444 Westheimer, Suite 1440, Houston, TX 77056. Susan McGarry, Ed. Articles, 1,200 to 1,800 words, on the artists, art collectors, museum exhibitions, gallery events and dealers, art history, and art trends west of the Mississippi River. Particularly interested in representational or figurative arts. Pays from $400, on acceptance. Query with at least 20 slides of artwork to be featured.

THE STATE: DOWN HOME IN NORTH CAROLINA—128 S. Tryon St., Suite 2200, Charlotte, NC 28202. Scott Smith, Man. Ed. Articles, 750 to 2,000 words, on people, history, and places in North Carolina. Photos. Pays on publication.

SUNSET MAGAZINE— 80 Willow Rd., Menlo Park, CA 94025. William Marken, Ed. Western regional. Limited free-lance market.

SUNSHINE: THE MAGAZINE OF SOUTH FLORIDA—*The Sun-Sentinel,* 200 E. Las Olas Blvd., Ft. Lauderdale, FL 33301–2293. John Parkyn, Ed. Articles, 1,000 to 3,000 words, on topics of interest to south Floridians. Pays $300 to $1,000, on acceptance. Query. Guidelines.

SWEAT—736 E. Loyola Dr., Tempe, AZ 85282. Joan Westlake, Ed. "South West Exercise And Training." Articles, 500 to 1,200 words, on sports or fitness with an Arizona angle. "No personal articles or tales. We want investigative pieces. Articles must relate specifically to Arizona or Arizonans." Pays $25 to $60 for articles; $12 to $70 for photos, on publication. Queries required; no unsolicited manuscripts.

TALLAHASSEE MAGAZINE—P.O. Box 1837, Tallahassee, FL 32302–1837. Dave Fiore, Ed. Articles, 800 to 2,500 words, with a positive outlook on the life, people, and history of the north Florida area. Pays on acceptance. Query.

TEXAS HIGHWAYS MAGAZINE—P.O. Box 141009, Austin, TX 78714–1009. Jack Lowry, Ed. Texas travel, history, and scenic features, 200 to 1,800 words. Pays about 40¢ to 50¢ a word, $80 to $550 per photo. Query. Guidelines.

TEXAS MONTHLY—P.O. Box 1569, Austin, TX 78767–1569. Gregory Curtis, Ed. Features, 2,500 to 5,000 words, and departments, to 2,500 words, on art, architecture, food, education, business, politics, etc. "We like solidly researched pieces that uncover issues of public concern, reveal offbeat and previously unreported topics, or use a novel approach to familiar topics." Pays varying rates, on acceptance. Queries required.

TEXAS PARKS & WILDLIFE—Fountain Park Plaza, 3000 S. Interstate Hwy. 35, Suite 120, Austin, TX 78704. Jim Cox, Sr. Ed. Articles, 800 to 1,500 words, promoting the conservation and enjoyment of Texas wildlife, parks, waters, and all outdoors. Features on hunting, fishing, birding, camping, and the environment. Department pieces, to 1,000 words, for "Parks & Places to Go," "State of Nature," and "Woods and Waters." Photos a plus. Pays to $600, on acceptance; extra for photos.

TIMELINE—1982 Velma Ave., Columbus, OH 43211–2497. Christopher S. Duckworth, Ed. Articles, 1,000 to 6,000 words, on history of Ohio (politics, economics, social, and natural history) for lay readers in the Midwest. Pays $100 to $900, on acceptance. Queries preferred.

TORONTO LIFE—59 Front St. E., Toronto, Ont., Canada M5E 1B3. John Macfarlane, Ed. Articles, 1,500 to 4,500 words, on Toronto. Pays $1,500 to $3,500, on acceptance. Query.

TROPIC—*The Miami Herald,* One Herald Plaza, Miami, FL 33132. Tom Shroder, Exec. Ed. General-interest articles, 750 to 3,000 words, for south Florida readers. Pays $200 to $1,000, on acceptance.

TUCSON LIFESTYLE—Old Pueblo Press, 7000 E. Tanque Verde, Tucson, AZ 85715. Sue Giles, Ed.-in-Chief. Local slant to all articles on businesses, lifestyles, the arts, homes, fashion, and travel in the Southwest. Payment varies, on acceptance. Query preferred.

TWIN CITIES READER—10 S. Fifth St., Minneapolis, MN 55402. David Carr, Ed. Articles, 2 to 4 printed pages, on local public affairs, arts, and general-interest subjects, for readers ages 25 to 44. Pays $5 to $6 per inch, on publication.

VENTURA COUNTY & COAST REPORTER—1567 Spinnaker Dr., Suite 202, Ventura, CA 93001. Nancy Cloutier, Ed. Articles, 3 to 5 pages, on any locally slanted topic. Pays $10, on publication.

VERMONT—14 School St., P.O. Box 288, Bristol, VT 05443. John S. Rosenberg, Ed. Articles on all aspects of contemporary Vermont: its people, culture, politics, and special places. Pays $100 to $800, on publication. Query.

VERMONT LIFE—6 Baldwin St., Montpelier, VT 05602. Tom Slayton, Ed.-in-Chief. Articles, 500 to 3,000 words, on Vermont subjects only. Pays 20¢ a word, extra for photos. Query preferred.

VIRGINIA—The Country Publishers, Inc., P.O. Box 798, Berryville, VA 22611. Garrison Ellis, Ed. Quarterly. "Written for and about people, places, events, and activities in, around, and affecting Virginia." Features, 2,000 to 2,500 words; articles, 1,200 to 1,800 words; humor, folklore, and legend, to 2,000 words; fiction, 1,000 to 1,500 words, with regional setting or reference; related poetry, to 32 lines. Department pieces, 500 to 700 words. Photos. Pays $200 to $300, 30 days after publication.

VIRGINIA BUSINESS—411 E. Franklin St., Suite 105, Richmond, VA 23219. James Bacon, Ed. Articles, 1,000 to 2,500 words, related to the business scene in Virginia. Pays varying rates, on acceptance. Query required.

VIRGINIA WILDLIFE—P.O. Box 11104, Richmond, VA 23230–1104. Attn: Ed. Articles, 1,500 to 2,000 words, on conservation and related topics, including fishing, hunting, wildlife management, outdoor safety, ethics, etc. All material must have Virginia tie-in and be accompanied by color photos. Pays from 15¢ a word, extra for photos, on acceptance. Query with SASE.

WASHINGTON POST MAGAZINE—*The Washington Post,* 1150 15th St. N.W., Washington, DC 20071. Liza Mundy, Man. Ed. Personal-experience essays, profiles, and general-interest pieces, to 6,000 words, on business, arts and culture, politics, science, sports, education, children, relationships, behavior, etc. Articles should be of interest to people living in Washington, DC, area. Pays from $750, on acceptance. Limited market.

THE WASHINGTONIAN—1828 L St. N.W., Suite 200, Washington, DC 20036. John Limpert, Ed. Helpful, informative articles, 1,000 to 4,000 words, on DC-related topics. Pays 50¢ a word, on publication.

WESTCHESTER FAMILY—See *New York Family.*

WESTERN SPORTSMAN—140 Ave. F N., Saskatoon, Sask., Canada S7L 1V8. George Gruenefeld, Ed. Informative articles, to 2,500 words, on hunting, fishing, and outdoor experiences in British Columbia, Alberta, Saskatchewan, and Manitoba. How-tos, humor, cartoons. Photos. Pays $75 to $300, on acceptance.

WESTWAYS—2601 S. Figueroa St., Los Angeles, CA 90007. Attn: Ed. Articles, 1,000 to 3,000 words, and photo-essays, on California, western U.S., greater U.S., and overseas: history, contemporary living, travel, personalities, etc. Photos. Pays from 50¢ a word, extra for photos, on acceptance. Query.

WINDSPEAKER—Aboriginal Multi-Media Society of Alberta, 15001 112th Ave., Edmonton, Alberta, Canada T5M 2V6. Linda Caldwell, Ed. Tabloid. Features, news items, sports, op-ed pieces, columns, etc., 200 to 1,000 words. Pays from $3 per published inch, after publication. Guidelines. Query.

WINDY CITY SPORTS—1450 W. Randolph, Chicago, IL 60607. Jeff Banowetz, Ed. Articles, to 1,000 words, on amateur sports in the Chicago area. Pays $100, on publication. Queries required.

WISCONSIN—*The Milwaukee Journal Magazine,* Journal/Sentinel, Inc., Box 661, Milwaukee, WI 53201. Carol Guensburg, Ed. Articles, 500 to 2,500 words, on business, politics, arts, environment, and social issues with strong Wisconsin emphasis. Personal-experience essays, profiles and investigative articles. Pays $75 to $700, on publication. Query.

WISCONSIN TRAILS—P.O. Box 5650, Madison, WI 53705. Lucy J. Rhodes, Assoc. Ed. Articles, 1,500 to 3,000 words, on regional topics: outdoors, lifestyle, events, history, arts, adventure, travel; profiles of artists, craftspeople, and regional personalities. Pays $150 to $500, on publication. Query.

WISCONSIN WEST MAGAZINE—2645 Harlem St., Eau Claire, WI 54703. Attn: Ed. Articles on current issues for residents of western Wisconsin: profiles of restaurants, weekend leisure activities and getaways, and famous people of western Wisconsin; historical pieces; short humor. Payment varies, on publication.

WYOMING RURAL ELECTRIC NEWS—P.O. Box 380, Casper, WY 82606-0380. Kris Wendtland, Ed. Articles, 500 to 900 words, on issues relevant to rural Wyoming. Articles should support Wyoming's personal and economic growth, social development, and education. Wyoming writers given preference. Pays $20 to $50, on publication.

YANKEE—Yankee Publishing Co., P.O. Box 520, Dublin, NH 03444. Judson D. Hale, Ed. Articles and fiction, 500 to 2,500 words, on New England and New England people. Pays $500 to $2,500 for features, on acceptance.

YANKEE MAGAZINE'S TRAVEL GUIDE TO NEW ENGLAND—33 Union St., Boston, MA 02108. Janice Brand, Ed. Articles, 500 to 2,000 words, on activities, attractions, places to visit in New England. Photos. Pays on acceptance. Query with outline and writing samples required.

TRAVEL ARTICLES

AAA WORLD—See *Car & Travel.*

ACCENT/TRAVELOG—Box 10010, Ogden, UT 84409. Attn: Eds. Articles, 1,000 words, on travel destinations, ways to travel, and travel tips. No budget trips. Pays 15¢ a word, $35 for color photos, on acceptance. Query with SASE.

ADVENTURE ROAD—The Aegis Group, Publishers, 30400 Van Dyke Ave., Warren, MI 48093. Mike Brudenell, Ed. Official publication of the Amoco Motor Club. Articles, 1,500 words, on destinations in North America, Mexico, and the Caribbean. Photos. Pays $500 to $1,000, on acceptance. Query.

AIR FORCE TIMES—See *Times News Service.*

ARIZONA HIGHWAYS—2039 W. Lewis Ave., Phoenix, AZ 85009. Richard G. Stahl, Man. Ed. Informal, well-researched personal-experience and travel articles, 1,600 to 1,800 words, focusing on a specific city or region in Arizona. Also articles dealing with nature, environment, flora and fauna, history, anthropology, archaeology, hiking, boating. Departments for personal-experience pieces include "Focus on Nature," "Along the Way," "Back Road Adventures," "Hiking," and "Arizona Humor." Pays 35¢ to 55¢ a word, on acceptance. Pays $100, on publication. Query with published clips only. Guidelines.

ARMY TIMES—See *Times News Service.*

BIG WORLD—P.O. Box 21, Coraopolis, PA 15108. Jim Fortney, Ed. Bimonthly. Articles, 500 to 4,000 words, that offer advice on working and studying abroad, humorous anecdotes, first-person experiences, or other travel information. "For people who prefer to spend their traveling time responsibly discovering, exploring, and learning, in touch with locals and their traditions, and in harmony with their environment." Pays $10 to $20 for articles, $5 to $20 for photos, on publication.

BLUE RIDGE COUNTRY—P.O. Box 21535, Roanoke, VA 24018. Kurt Rheinheimer, Ed. Regional travel articles, 750 to 1,200 words, on destinations in the mountain regions of VA, NC, WV, TN, KY, MD, SC, and GA. Color slides and B&W prints considered. Pays to $200 for photo-features, on publication. Queries preferred.

CALIFORNIA HIGHWAY PATROLMAN—2030 V St., Sacramento, CA 95818–1730. Carol Perri, Ed. Travel articles, to 2,000 words, focusing on places in California and the West Coast. "We prefer out-of-the-way stops with possibly a California Highway Patrol tie-in instead of regular tourist destinations." Query or send complete manuscript with photos. SASE required. Pays 2½¢ a word, $5 for B&W photos, on publication.

CANADIAN—199 Avenue Rd., Third Fl., Toronto, Ontario, Canada M5R 2J3. Grant N. R. Geall, Pres./Pub. Inflight magazine of Canadian Airlines International. Travel pieces, 800 to 1,000 words. Payment varies, on acceptance. Query.

CANADIAN DIVER & WATERSPORT—See *Diver Magazine.*

CAR & TRAVEL—(formerly *AAA World*) 1000 AAA Dr., Heathrow, FL 32746–5063. Douglas Damerst, Ed. Articles, 600 to 1,500 words, on consumer automotive and travel concerns. Pays $200 to $800, on acceptance. Query with writing samples required. Articles by assignment only.

CARIBBEAN TRAVEL AND LIFE— 8403 Colesville Rd., Suite 830, Silver Spring, MD 20910. Veronica Gould Stoddart, Ed. Lively, informative articles, 500 to 2,500 words, on all aspects of travel, leisure, recreation, and culture in the Caribbean, Bahamas, and Bermuda, for upscale, sophisticated readers. Photos. Pays $75 to $550, on publication. Query.

CHILE PEPPER—P.O. Box 4278, Albuquerque, NM 87196. Melissa Jackson, Man. Ed. First-person food and travel articles, 1,000 to 1,500 words, about spicy world cuisine. Payment varies, on publication. Queries required.

COLORADO HOMES & LIFESTYLES—7009 S. Potomac, Englewood, CO 80112. Karen Coe, Ed. Travel articles, 1,200 to 1,500 words, on cities, regions, establishments in Colorado and contiguous states. Roundups and travel pieces with unusual angles, sidebar, and photos. Pays $150, on acceptance. Query.

CONDE NAST TRAVELER—360 Madison Ave., New York, NY 10017. Alison Humes, Features Ed. Uses very little free-lance material.

THE COOL TRAVELER—P.O. Box 273, Selinsgrove, PA 17870. Bob Moore, Pub./Ed. Bimonthly. Articles, 800 words, including excerpts from diaries and letters written while traveling. "We emphasize 'what happened' rather than 'what to see.'" Pays to $20, on publication.

CRUISE TRAVEL—990 Grove St., Evanston, IL 60201. Robert Meyers, Ed. Charles Doherty, Man. Ed. Ship-, port-, and cruise-of-the-month features, 800 to 2,000 words; cruise guides; cruise roundups; cruise company profiles; travel suggestions for one-day port stops. "Photo-features strongly recommended." Payment varies, on acceptance. Query with sample color photos.

DIVER MAGAZINE—295–10991 Shellbridge Way, Richmond, B.C., Canada V6X 3C6. Stephanie Bold, Ed. Illustrated articles, 500 to 1,000 words, on dive destinations. Shorter pieces are also welcome. "Travel features should be brief and accompanied by excellent slides and/or prints and a map. Unsolicited articles will be reviewed only from August to October and will be considered for *Diver Magazine* and *Canadian Diver & Watersport*." Pays $2.50 per column inch, on publication. Guidelines. Limited market.

ENDLESS VACATION—Box 80260, Indianapolis, IN 46280. Laurie D. Borman, Ed. Travel features, to 1,500 words; primarily on North American destinations, some international destinations. Pays on acceptance. Send SASE for guidelines. Query preferred. Limited market.

FAMILY CIRCLE—110 Fifth Ave., New York, NY 10011. Sylvia Barsotti, Sr. Ed. Travel articles, to 1,500 words. Concept travel pieces should appeal to a national audience and focus on affordable activities for families; prefer service-filled, theme-oriented travel pieces or first-person family vacation stories. Payment varies, on acceptance. Query.

FRIENDLY EXCHANGE—P.O. Box 2120, Warren, MI 48090–2120. Adele Malott, Ed. Articles, 700 to 1,500 words, of interest to active midwestern and western families, on travel and leisure. "Must have 'people' orientation." Photos. Pays $400 to $1,000, extra for photos. Query required. Send SASE for guidelines.

HISTORIC TRAVELER—6405 Flank Dr., Harrisburg, PA 17112. John Stanchak, Ed. "The Guide to Great Historic Destinations." Bimonthly. Articles, 1,500 to 2,000 words, for upscale readers with a strong interest in history. "Accurate information on historic destinations. Possible topics: battlefields, museums, antique shows, events, hotels, inns, transporation, reenactments, preserved communities, and architectural wonders. No South Pacific Islands, Alpine skiing, or Mediterranean cruises." Guidelines. Pays $300 to $500, on acceptance. Query with SASE and clips.

INDIA CURRENTS—P.O. Box 21285, San Jose, CA 95151. Arvind Kumar, Submissions Ed. First-person accounts, 1,200 words, of trips to India or the subcontinent. Helpful tips for first-time travelers. Prefer descriptions of people-to-people interactions. Pays in subscriptions.

INTERNATIONAL LIVING—105 W. Monument St., Baltimore, MD 21201. Kathleen Peddicord, Ed. Dir. Newsletter. Short pieces and features, 200 to 2,000 words, with useful information on investing, shopping, travel, employment, education, real estate, retirement, and lifestyles overseas. Pays $100 to $400, after publication.

ISLANDS—3886 State St., Santa Barbara, CA 93105. Joan Tapper, Ed-in-Chief. Destination features, 2,500 to 4,000 words, on islands around the world as well as department pieces and front-of-the-book items on island-related topics. Pays from 25¢ to 50¢ a word, on acceptance. Query with clips required. Guidelines.

KEY HORIZONS—Gateway Plaza, 950 N. Meridian, Suite 1200, Indianapolis, IN 46204. Joan Todd, Man. Ed. Quarterly. Articles, 1,500 words, on domestic travel for readers 50 and older. Pays $25 to $500, $25 to $50 for photos, on publication.

MICHIGAN LIVING—Automobile Club of Michigan, 1 Auto Club Dr., Dearborn, MI 48126. Len Barnes, Ed. Informative travel articles, 300 to 2,000 words, on U.S. and Canadian tourist attractions and recreational opportunities; special interest in Michigan. Pays $55 to $500 (rates vary for photos), on acceptance.

THE MIDWEST MOTORIST—12901 N. Forty Dr., St. Louis, MO 63141. Michael Right, Ed. Articles, 1,000 to 1,500 words, with color slides, on domestic and foreign travel. Pays from $150, on acceptance.

NATIONAL GEOGRAPHIC—17th and M Sts. N.W., Washington, DC 20036. William Allen, Ed. First-person articles on geography, exploration, natural history, archaeology, and science. Half staff-written; half written by recognized authorities and published authors. Does not consider unsolicited manuscripts.

NATIONAL MOTORIST—Bayside Plaza, 188 The Embarcadero, San Francisco, CA 94105. Jane Offers, Ed. Quarterly. Illustrated articles, 500 to 1,100 words, for California motorists, on motoring in the West, domestic and international travel, car care, roads, personalities, places, etc. Color slides. Pays from 10¢ a word, on acceptance. Pays for photos on publication. SASE required.

NAVY TIMES—See *Times News Service.*

NEW WOMAN—215 Lexington Ave., New York, NY 10016. Attn: Manuscripts and Proposals. Armchair travel pieces; women's personal-experience and "what I learned from this experience" pieces, 800 to 2,500 words. Pays $500 to $2,500, on acceptance. Query required.

NEW YORK DAILY NEWS—220 E. 42nd St., New York, NY 10017. Gunna Bitee Dickson, Travel Ed. Articles, 700 to 900 words, on all manner of travel. Price information must be included. B&W or color photos or slides. Pays $100 to $200 (extra for photos), on publication.

THE NEW YORK TIMES—229 W. 43rd St., New York, NY 10036. Nancy Newhouse, Travel Ed. Query with SASE required; include writer's background, description of proposed article. No unsolicited manuscripts or photos. Pays on acceptance.

NORTHWEST PARKS & WILDLIFE—See *Northwest Regional Magazines.*

NORTHWEST REGIONAL MAGAZINES—P.O. Box 18000, Florence, OR 97439. Attn: Dave Peden or Judy Fleagle. All submissions considered for use in *Oregon Coast, Oregon Parks, Northwest Travel,* and *Northwest Parks & Wildlife.* Articles, 1,200 to 2,000 words, on travel, history, town/city profiles, parks, and nature. News releases, 200 to 500 words. Articles with photos or slides preferred. Pays $50 to $300, after publication. Guidelines.

NORTHWEST TRAVEL—See *Northwest Regional Magazines.*

OREGON COAST—See *Northwest Regional Magazines.*

OREGON PARKS—See *Northwest Regional Magazines.*

OUT WEST: THE NEWSPAPER THAT ROAMS— 408 Broad St., Suite 11, Nevada City, CA 95959. Chuck Woodbury, Ed./Pub. Entertaining and informative articles, 150 to 750 words, and short pieces, 30 to 75 words, on the rural West (not the old West): interesting people, unusual places to stay, offbeat attractions. "Send for a sample of the paper before you submit." Pays about 5¢ a word, on publication.

OUTDOOR TRAVELER, MID-ATLANTIC—WMS Publications, Inc., P.O. Box 2748, Charlottesville, VA 22902. Marianne Marks, Ed. Scott Clark, Assoc. Ed. Articles, 1,500 to 2,000 words, about outdoor recreation, travel, adventure, and nature in the mid-Atlantic region (NY, PA, NJ, MD, DE, DC, WV, VA, and NC). Departments include "Destinations," 450 to 600 words, on practical and descriptive guides to sports destinations; "Lodging," inns and lodges, including seasonal and outdoor activities; book reviews, 200 words. Pays $375 to $500 for features; payment varies for departments, on publication. Guidelines.

RV TIMES MAGAZINE—1100 Welborne Dr., Richmond, VA 23229. Alice P. Supple, Ed. Articles and fiction, 500 to 2,000 words, related to outdoor or leisure activities, travel attractions in the MD, VA, NJ, NY, DE, and PA areas. Pays 7¢ a word (to $90), on publication.

RV WEST MAGAZINE—Vernon Publications, 3000 Northup Way, Suite 200, Bellevue, WA 98009–9643. Michele Andrus Dill, Ed. Dir. Travel and destination articles, 750 to 1,750 words, on where to go and what to do in the 13 western states with your recreational vehicle. Color slides or B&W prints must accompany articles. Pays $1.50 per column inch, on publication. Guidelines.

SACRAMENTO MAGAZINE— 4471 D St., Sacramento, CA 95819. Krista Hendricks Minard, Ed. Articles, 1,000 to 1,500 words, on destinations within a 6-hour drive of Sacramento. Pay varies, on publication. Query.

SPECIALTY TRAVEL INDEX—305 San Anselmo Ave., #313, San Anselmo, CA 94960. C. Steen Hansen, Co-Pub./Ed. Semiannual directory of adventure vacation tour companies, destinations, and vacation packages. Articles, 1,000 to 1,200 words, with how-to travel information, humor, and opinion. Pays 20¢ per word, on publication. Slides and photos considered. Queries preferred.

TEXAS HIGHWAYS MAGAZINE—P.O. Box 141009, Austin, TX 78714–1009. Jack Lowry, Ed. Travel, historical, cultural, scenic features on Texas, 200 to 1,800 words. Pays about 40¢ to 50¢ a word; photos $80 to $500. Guidelines.

TIMES NEWS SERVICE—Army Times Publishing Co., Springfield, VA

22159. Attn: R&R Ed. Travel articles, 700 words, on places of special interest to military people for use in "R&R" newspaper section. "We like travel articles to focus on a single destination but with short sidebar covering other things to see in the area." Pays $100, on acceptance. Pays $35 for color slides or prints. Also, travel pieces, 1,000 words, for supplements to *Army Times*, *Navy Times*, and *Air Force Times*. Address Supplements Ed. Pays $125 to $200, on acceptance. Guidelines.

TRANSITIONS ABROAD—18 Hulst Rd., Box 1300, Amherst, MA 01004–1300. Clay Hubbs, Ed. Articles for overseas travelers of all ages who seek an enriching, in-depth experience of the culture: work, study, travel, budget tips. Progressive emphasis (socially and ecologically responsible travel). Include practical, firsthand information. Emphasis on travel for personal enrichment and education and on establishing meaningful contact with people of host country. "Eager to work with inexperienced writers who travel to learn and want to share information." B&W photos a plus. Pays $1.50 per column inch, after publication. SASE required. Guidelines and editorial calendar.

TRAVEL AMERICA—World Publishing Co., 990 Grove St., Evanston, IL 60201–4370. Randy Mink, Man. Ed. Robert Meyers, Ed. Features, 800 to 1,200 words, on U.S. vacation destinations; also essays, nostalgia, humor, travel tips, and service articles, 800 to 1,000 words. Pays up to $300, on acceptance. Top-quality color slides a must. Query.

TRAVEL & LEISURE—1120 Ave. of the Americas, New York, NY 10036. Nancy Novogrod, Ed.-in-Chief. Articles, 800 to 3,000 words, on destinations and travel-related activities. Regional pieces for regional editions. Short pieces for "Athletic Traveler" and" T&L Reports." Pays on acceptance: $2,500 to $5,000 for features; $750 to $1,500 for regionals; $50 to $300 for short pieces. Query; articles on assignment.

TRAVEL SMART—Dobbs Ferry, NY 10522. Attn: Ed. Short pieces, 250 to 1,000 words, about interesting, unusual and/or economical places. Give specific details on hotels, restaurants, transportation, and costs. Pays on publication. "Send manila envelope with 2 first-class stamps for copy and guidelines."

WESTWAYS—2601 S. Figueroa St., Los Angeles, CA 90007. Attn: Ed. Travel articles, 1,300 to 3,000 words, on where to go, what to see, and how to get there, with an emphasis on southern California and the West. Domestic and foreign travel articles are also of interest. Pays 75¢ a word, on acceptance.

YANKEE MAGAZINE'S TRAVEL GUIDE TO NEW ENGLAND—33 Union St., Boston, MA 02108. Janice Brand, Ed. Articles, 500 to 2,000 words, on destinations in New England. Photos. Pays on acceptance. Query with outline and writing samples.

INFLIGHT MAGAZINES

ABOARD—100 Almeria Ave., Suite 220, Coral Gables, FL 33134. Roberto Casin, Ed. Inflight magazine of 11 Latin American international airlines in Chile, Dominican Republic, Ecuador, Guatemala, El Salvador, Bolivia, Nicaragua, Honduras, Peru, Uruguay, and Paraguay. Articles, 1,200 to 1,500 words, with photos, on these countries and on science, sports, home, fashion, business, ecology, and gastronomy. No political stories. Pays $150, on acceptance and on publication. Query required.

ALASKA AIRLINES MAGAZINE—2701 First Ave., Suite 250, Seattle, WA 98121. Paul Frichtl, Ed. Articles, 250 to 2,500 words, on lifestyle topics, business, travel, and profiles of regional personalities for West Coast business travelers. Payment varies, on publication. Query.

AMERICA WEST AIRLINES MAGAZINE—Skyword Marketing Inc., 4636 E. Elwood St., Suite 5, Phoenix, AZ 85040–1963. Michael Derr, Ed. Mostly business articles; some arts, travel, 500 to 2,000 words. Pays from $250, on publication. Clips and SASE required. Guidelines. Very limited market.

AMERICAN WAY—P.O. Box 619640, DFW Airport, TX 75261–9640. John Ostdick, Ed. American Airlines' inflight magazine. No unsolicited material.

CANADIAN—199 Avenue Rd., Third Fl., Toronto, Ontario, Canada M5R 2J3. Grant N. R. Geall, Pres./Pub. Articles, 1,000 words, on travel for Canadian Airlines International travelers. Payment varies, on acceptance. Query.

HEMISPHERES—1301 Carolina St., Greensboro, NC 27401. Kate Greer, Ed.-in-Chief. United Airlines inflight magazine. Articles, 1,200 to 1,500 words, on business, investing, travel, sports, family, food and wine, etc., that inform and entertain sophisticated, well-traveled readers. "The magazine strives for a unique global perspective presented in a fresh, strong, and artful graphic environment." Pays good rates, on acceptance. Query. Guidelines.

IN-FLIGHT—SCG, Inc. 5110 N. 44th St., Suite 210-L, Phoenix, AZ 85018. Lisa Polacheck, Ed. Bimonthly for KIWI International Airlines. Destination-related features, 600 to 1,600 words, with photos. Columns cover trivia, self-improvement, poignant success stories, and whimsical compositions. Write for current destinations. Payment varies, on publication.

SKY—600 Corporate Dr., Ft. Lauderdale, FL 33334. Lidia de Leon, Ed. Delta Air Lines' inflight magazine. Articles on business, lifestyle, high tech, sports, the arts, etc. Color slides. Pays varying rates, on acceptance. Query with SASE. Guidelines.

SKYVIEW—SCG, Inc., 5110 N. 44th St., Suite 210-L, Phoenix, AZ 85018. Lisa Polacheck, Ed. Magazine of Western Pacific Airlines, serving Denver/Colorado Springs, and various West Coast and Midwest destinations. Destination-related articles, 600 to 1,600 words, with photos. Columns cover money, sports, fashion, and whimsy. Send SASE for current destinations. Payment varies, on publication.

USAIR MAGAZINE—New York Times Custom Publishing, 122 E. 42 St., 14th Fl., New York, NY 10168. Catherine Sabino, Ed. Kathy Passero, Man. Ed. Articles on travel, lifestyle trends, sports, personality profiles, food and wine, shopping, the arts and culture. "Our goal is to provide readers with lively and colorful, yet practical articles that will make their lives and their leisure time more rewarding." Pays good rates, within 60 days of acceptance. Query with clips and SASE; no unsolicited manuscripts or faxes.

WOMEN'S PUBLICATIONS

BBW: BIG BEAUTIFUL WOMAN—9171 Wilshire Blvd., Suite 300, Beverly Hills, CA 90210. Linda Arroz, Ed.-in-Chief. Janey Milstead, Exec. Ed. Articles, 1,500 words, of interest to women ages 25 to 50, especially large-size women, including interviews with successful large-size women and personal accounts of how to cope with difficult situations. Tips on restaurants, airlines, stores, etc., that treat large women with respect. Payment varies, on publication. Query.

BRIDAL GUIDE—Globe Communications Corp., 441 Lexington Ave., New York, NY 10017. Stephanie Wood, Ed.-in-Chief. Cherylann Coutts, Travel Ed. Bimonthly. Articles, 1,500 to 3,000 words, on relationships, sexuality, health and nutrition, psychology, travel, and finance. No wedding planning, beauty, fashion articles; no fiction, essays, poetry. Pays on acceptance. Query with SASE.

BRIDE'S—(formerly *Bride's & Your New Home*) 140 E. 45th St., New York, NY 10017. Sally Kilbridge, Man. Ed. Articles, 800 to 3,000 words, for engaged couples or newlyweds, on wedding planning, relationships, communication, sex, housing, redecorating, finances, careers, remarriage, step-parenting, health, birth control, religion, in-laws. Major editorial subjects: home, wedding, and honeymoon. Pays $200 to $1,000, on acceptance.

COMPLETE WOMAN—875 N. Michigan Ave., Suite 3434, Chicago, IL 60611. Bonnie L. Krueger, Ed. Martha Carlson, Assoc. Ed. Articles, 1,000 to 2,000 words, with how-to sidebars, giving practical advice to women on love, sex, careers, health, personal relationships, etc. Also interested in reprints. Pays varying rates, on publication. Query with clips.

COSMOPOLITAN—224 W. 57th St., New York, NY 10019. Helen Gurley Brown, Ed. Betty Nichols Kelly, Fiction and Books Ed. Articles, to 3,000 words, and features, 500 to 2,000 words, on issues affecting young career women, with emphasis on jobs and personal life. Fiction on male-female relationships: short shorts, 1,500 to 3,000 words; short stories, 3,000 to 4,000 words; condensed published novels, 25,000 words. SASE required. Payment varies.

COUNTRY WOMAN—P.O. Box 989, Greendale, WI 53129. Kathy Pohl, Man. Ed. Profiles of country women (photo-feature packages), inspirational, reflective pieces. Personal-experience, nostalgia, humor, service-oriented articles, original crafts, and how-to features, to 1,000 words, of interest to country women. Pays $25 to $75 for crafts, humor, nostalgia; pays $150 for photo-features, on acceptance.

THE CREATIVE WOMAN—TAPP Group, 126 E. Wing, Suite 288, Arlington Hts., IL 60004. Margaret Choudhury, Ed. Quarterly. Essays, fiction, poetry, criticism, graphic arts, and photography, from a feminist perspective. Send SASE for upcoming themes. Payment varies, on publication.

ELLE—1633 Broadway, New York, NY 10019. Amy Gross, Ed. Dir. Articles, varying lengths, for fashion-conscious women, ages 20 to 50. Subjects include beauty, health, fitness, travel, entertainment, and lifestyles. Pays top rates, on publication. Query required.

ESSENCE—1500 Broadway, New York, NY 10036. Susan L. Taylor, Ed.-in-Chief. Linda Villarosa, Exec. Ed. Provocative articles, 800 to 2,500 words, about black women in America today: self-help, how-to pieces, business and finance, work, parenting, health, celebrity profiles, art, travel, and political issues. Fiction, 800 to 2,500 words. Pays varying rates, on acceptance. Query for articles.

EXECUTIVE FEMALE—30 Irving Pl., New York, NY 10003. Basia Hellwig, Ed.-in-Chief. Articles, 750 to 2,500 words, on managing people, time, money, companies, and careers, for women in business. Pays varying rates, on acceptance. Query.

FAMILY CIRCLE—110 Fifth Ave., New York, NY 10011. Nancy Clark, Deputy Ed. Articles, to 2,000 words, on "women who have made a difference," marriage, family, and child-care and elder-care issues; consumer affairs, psychology, humor, health, nutrition, and fitness. Pays top rates, on acceptance. Query required.

FIRST FOR WOMEN—270 Sylvan Ave., Englewood Cliffs, NJ 07632. Jane Traulsen, Ed. Articles,1,500 to 2,500 words, reflecting the concerns of contemporary women. Not using any fiction at this time. Pay varies, on acceptance. Allow 2 months for response. Query.

GLAMOUR—350 Madison Ave., New York, NY 10017. Pamela Erens, Articles Ed. Ruth Whitney, Ed.-in-Chief. Priscilla Grant, Man. Ed. How-to articles, from 1,500 words, on careers, health, psychology, interpersonal relationships, etc., for women ages 18 to 35. Fashion, entertainment, travel, food, and beauty pieces staff-written. Pays from $500, on acceptance. Query Articles Ed.

GOOD HOUSEKEEPING—959 Eighth Ave., New York, NY 10019. Joan Thursh, Articles Ed. Lee Quarfoot, Fiction Ed. Articles, about 2,500 words, for married working women with children, 18 and under. Social issues, dramatic personal narratives, medical news, marriage, friendship, psychology, crime, finances, work, parenting, and consumer issues. Best places to break in: "Better Way" (short, advice-driven takes on health, money, safety, and consumer issues) and profiles (short takes on interesting or heroic women or families). No submissions on food, beauty, needlework, or crafts. Short stories, 2,000 to 5,000 words, with strong identification for women. Unsolicited fiction not returned; if no response in 6 weeks, assume work was unsuitable. Pays top rates, on acceptance. Query with SASE for nonfiction. Guidelines.

HARPER'S BAZAAR—1700 Broadway, New York, NY 10019. Elizabeth Tilberis, Ed.-in-Chief. Articles, 1,500 to 2,500 words, for active, sophisticated women: the arts, world affairs, food, wine, travel, families, education, careers, health, and sexuality. Payment varies, on acceptance. No unsolicited manuscripts; query with SASE.

IOWA WOMAN—P.O. Box 680, Iowa City, IA 52244. Marianne Abel, Ed. Fiction, poetry, creative nonfiction, book reviews, and personal essays; articles, to 6,500 words, on midwestern history; interviews with prominent women; current social, economic, artistic, and environmental issues. Poems, any length (submit up to 5); photos and drawings. Pays $5 a page, $15 for illustrations, on publication. Queries preferred for articles. Guidelines.

THE JOYFUL WOMAN—P.O. Box 90028, Chattanooga, TN 37412. Joy Rice Martin, Ed. Holly Martin, Ed. Asst. Articles and fiction, 500 to 1,200 words, for "women with a Christian commitment." First-person inspirational true stories, profiles of Christian women, practical and biblically oriented how-to articles. Pays 3¢ to 4¢ a word, on publication. Queries required.

LADIES' HOME JOURNAL—100 Park Ave., New York, NY 10017. Myrna Blyth, Publishing Dir./Ed.-in-Chief. Articles of interest to women. Send queries to: Jane Farrell, Articles Ed. (news/general interest); Mary Hickey, Sr. Ed. (health/medical); Melanie Berger, Assoc. Ed. (celebrity/entertainment); Pamela Guthrie O'Brien, Features Ed. (sex/psychology); Lois Johnson, Beauty

Dir. (beauty/fashion/fitness); Jan Hazard, Food Ed.; Shana Aborn, Features Ed. (personal experience); Mary Mohler, Man. Ed. (children and families). Fiction accepted through literary agents only. True, first-person accounts, 1,000 words, "about the most intimate aspects of our lives" for anonymous "Woman to Woman": Submit typed, double-spaced manuscript with SASE to Box WW, c/o address above; pays $750. Guidelines.

MCCALL'S—110 Fifth Ave., New York, NY 10011. Attn: Articles Ed. Articles, 1,000 to 1,800 words, on current issues, human interest, family relationships. Payment varies, on acceptance.

MADEMOISELLE—350 Madison Ave., New York, NY 10017. Faye Haun, Man. Ed. Articles, 1,500 to 2,500 words, on work, relationships, health, and trends of interest to single, working women in their early to mid-20s. Reporting pieces, essays, first-person accounts, and humor. No how-to or fiction. Pays excellent rates, on acceptance. Submit query with clips and SASE.

MODERN BRIDE—249 W. 17th St., New York, NY 10011. Mary Ann Cavlin, Exec. Ed. Articles, 1,500 to 2,000 words, for bride and groom, on wedding planning, financial planning, juggling career and home, etc. Pays $600 to $1,200, on acceptance.

MS.—230 Park Ave., 7th Fl., New York, NY 10169. Attn: Manuscript Ed. Articles relating to feminism, women's roles, and social change; national and international news reporting, profiles, essays, theory, and analysis. No fiction or poetry accepted, acknowledged, or returned. Query with resumé and published clips.

NA'AMAT WOMAN—200 Madison Ave., Suite 2120, New York, NY 10016. Judith A. Sokoloff, Ed. Articles on Jewish culture, women's issues, social and political topics, and Israel, 1,500 to 3,000 words. Short stories with a Jewish theme. Pays 10¢ a word, on publication.

NEW WOMAN—215 Lexington Ave., New York, NY 10016. Attn: Manuscripts and Proposals. Articles for women ages 25 to 49, on self-discovery, self-development, and self-esteem. Features: relationships, careers, health and fitness, money, fashion, beauty, food and nutrition, travel features with self-growth angle, and essays by and about women pacesetters. Pays about $1 a word, on acceptance. Query with SASE.

ON THE ISSUES—Choices Women's Medical Ctr., Inc., 97–77 Queens Blvd., Forest Hills, NY 11374–3317. Ronni Sandroff, Ed. "The Progressive Woman's Quarterly." Articles, to 2,500 words, on political or social issues. Movie, music, and book reviews, 500 to 750 words. Payment varies, on publication. Query.

PLAYGIRL— 801 Second Ave., New York, NY 10017. Laurie Sue Brockway, Ed.-in-Chief. Erotic entertainment for women. Insightful articles on sexuality and romance; sizzling fiction, humor, and in depth celebrity interviews of interest to contemporary women. Pays varying rates, after acceptance. Query with clips. Guidelines.

RADIANCE: THE MAGAZINE FOR LARGE WOMEN—P.O. Box 30246, Oakland, CA 94604. Alice Ansfield, Ed./Pub. Quarterly. Articles, 1,500 to 2,500 words, that provide information, inspiration, and resources for women all sizes of large. Features include information on health, media, fashion, and politics that relate to issues of body size. Fiction and poetry also welcome. Pays to $100, on publication.

REDBOOK—224 W. 57th St., New York, NY 10019. Harriet Lyons, Sr. Ed. Dawn Raffel, Fiction Ed. Toni Hope, Sr. Ed. For mothers, ages 25 to 45. Short stories, 10 to 15 typed pages; dramatic inspirational narratives, 1,000 to 2,000 words. SASE required. Pays excellent rates, on acceptance. Query with writing samples for articles. Guidelines.

SELF—350 Madison Ave., New York, NY 10017. Attn: Ed. "We no longer accept unsolicited manuscripts or queries."

TODAY'S CHRISTIAN WOMAN— 465 Gundersen Dr., Carol Stream, IL 60188. Ramona Cramer Tucker, Ed. Articles, 1,500 words, that are "warm and personal in tone, full of real-life anecdotes that deal with the following relationships: marriage, parenting, friendship, spiritual life, and self." Humorous anecdotes, 150 words, that have a Christian slant. Payment varies, on acceptance. Queries required. Guidelines.

VIRTUE: THE CHRISTIAN MAGAZINE FOR WOMEN— 4050 Lee Vance View, Colorado Springs, CO 80918. Jeanette Thomason, Ed. Articles and fiction, 1,200 to 1,400 words, on family, marriage, self-esteem, working women, humor, women's spiritual journeys, issues, relationship with family, friends and God. "Provocative, meaningful stories, especially those with bold messages shown in gracious ways." Poetry. Pays 15¢ to 25¢ a word, $25 to $50 for poetry, on publication. Query required.

VOGUE—350 Madison Ave., New York, NY 10017. Attn: Features Ed. Articles, to 1,500 words, on women, entertainment and the arts, travel, medicine, and health. General features. Pays good rates, on acceptance. Query; no unsolicited manuscripts.

WOMAN OF POWER—P.O. Box 2785, Orleans, MA 02653. Charlene McKee, Ed. A magazine of feminism, spirituality, and politics. Articles, to 3,500 words. Each issue explores a special theme. Send SASE for themes and guidelines. Pays in copies and subscription.

WOMAN'S DAY—1633 Broadway, New York, NY 10019. Rebecca Greer, Sr. Articles Ed. Human-interest or helpful articles, to 2,000 words, on marriage, child-rearing, health, careers, relationships, money management. Dramatic first-person narratives of medical miracles, rescues, women's experiences, etc. "We respond to queries promptly; unsolicited manuscripts are returned unread." Pays top rates, on acceptance.

WOMAN'S TOUCH—1445 Boonville, Springfield, MO 65802–1894. Peggy Musgrove, Ed. Aleda Swartzendruber, Assoc. Ed. Inspirational articles, 500 to 1,000 words, for Christian women. Uses some poetry, 50 to 150 words. Pays on acceptance. Submit complete manuscript; allow 3 months for response. Guidelines and editorial calendar.

WOMAN'S WORLD—270 Sylvan Ave., Englewood Cliffs, NJ 07632. Andrea Bien, Feature Ed. Articles, 600 to 1,800 words, of interest to middle-income women between the ages of 18 and 60, on love, romance, careers, medicine, health, psychology, family life, travel; dramatic stories of adventure or crisis, investigative reports. Fast-moving short stories, about 1,900 words, with light romantic theme. (Specify "short story" on outside of envelope.) Mini-mysteries, 1,200 words, with "whodunit" or "howdunit" theme. No science fiction, fantasy, horror, ghost stories, or gratuitous violence. Pays $300 to $900 for articles; $1,000 for short stories; $500 for mini-mysteries, on acceptance. Query for articles. Guidelines.

WOMEN & RECOVERY—Need to Know Press, P.O. Box 1947-2, Cupertino, CA 95015. Sara V. Cole, Ed. Quarterly. Essays, exposés, humor, self-help articles, product or treatment profiles and reviews, opinion pieces, and personal-experience pieces, 1,000 to 2,000 words, related to women's recovery issues (physical, emotional, and spiritual). Poems, cartoons, B&W photos and drawings. Pays $35 to $100 for articles; $15 to $50 for poetry and art, on publication.

WOMEN IN BUSINESS—American Business Women's Assn., 9100 Ward Pkwy., Box 8728, Kansas City, MO 64114-0728. Dawn J. Grubb, Assoc. Ed. How-to business features, 1,000 to 1,500 words, for working women ages 35 to 55, business trends, small-business ownership, self-improvement, and retirement issues. Profiles of ABWA members only. Pays on acceptance. Query required.

WOMEN'S CIRCLE—P.O. Box 299, Lynnfield, MA 01940. Marjorie Pearl, Ed. Success stories on home-based female entrepreneurs. How-to articles on contemporary craft and needlework projects. Unique money-saving ideas and recipes. Pays varying rates, on acceptance.

WOMEN'S SPORTS & FITNESS—2025 Pearl St., Boulder, CO 80302. Mary Duffy, Ed. Articles on fitness, nutrition, outdoor sports; how-tos; profiles; adventure travel pieces; and controversial issues in women's sports, 500 to 2,000 words. Pays on publication.

WORKING MOTHER—Lang Communications, 230 Park Ave., New York, NY 10169. Attn: Ed. Dept. Articles, to 2,000 words, that help women in their task of juggling job, home, and family. "We like pieces that solve or illuminate a problem unique to our readers." Payment varies, on acceptance.

WORKING WOMAN—230 Park Ave., New York, NY 10169. Lynn Povich, Ed.-in-Chief. Articles, 350 to 2,500 words, on business and personal aspects of the lives of executive and managerial women and entrepreneurs. Pays from $300, on acceptance.

MEN'S PUBLICATIONS

ESQUIRE—250 W. 55th St., New York, NY 10019. Edward Kosner, Ed.-in-Chief. David Hirshey, Deputy Ed. Articles, 2,500 to 4,000 words, for intelligent audience. Pays varying rates, on acceptance. Query with clips and SASE.

GALLERY— 401 Park Ave. S., New York, NY 10016-8802. Barry Janoff, Ed.-in-Chief. Rich Friedman, Man. Ed. Articles, investigative pieces, interviews, profiles, to 2,500 words, for sophisticated men. Short humor, satire, service pieces, and fiction. Photos. Pays $500, on publication. Query. Guidelines.

GQ—350 Madison Ave., New York, NY 10017. No free-lance queries or manuscripts.

INSIDE EDGE—258 Harvard St., Suite 329, Brookline, MA 02146. Josie Roth, Ed. Fiction, nonfiction, and humor, 1,000 words, for young men ages 18 to 24. Queries preferred. Pays $250, on publication of second article; first published article receives no payment.

MEN'S FITNESS—21100 Erwin St., Woodland Hills, CA 91367. Attn: Ed. Authoritative and practical articles, 1,500 to 1,800 words, and department pieces, 1,200 to 1,500 words, on sports, fitness, health, nutrition, and men's issues. Pays $500 to $1,000, on acceptance.

MEN'S HEALTH—Rodale Press, 33 E. Minor St., Emmaus, PA 18098. Jeff Csatari, Sr. Ed. Articles, 1,000 to 2,500 words, on fitness, diet, health, relationships, sports, and travel for men ages 25 to 55. Pays from 50¢ a word, on acceptance. Query.

PENTHOUSE—1965 Broadway, New York, NY 10023–5965. Peter Bloch, Ed. Lavada B. Nahon, Sr. Ed. General-interest profiles, interviews, or investigative articles, to 5,000 words. No unsolicited fiction. Pays on acceptance.

PLAYBOY—680 N. Lake Shore Dr., Chicago, IL 60611. Peter Moore, Stephen Randall, Eds. Articles, 3,500 to 6,000 words, and sophisticated fiction, 1,000 to 10,000 words (5,000 preferred), for urban men. (Address fiction to Attn: Fiction Ed.) Humor; satire. Science fiction. Pays to $5,000 for articles and fiction, $2,000 for short-shorts, on acceptance. SASE required.

PLAYERS—8060 Melrose Ave., Los Angeles, CA 90046. L. D. Wills, Ed. Articles, 1,000 to 3,000 words, for black men: politics, economics, travel, fashion, grooming, entertainment, sports, interviews, fiction, humor, satire, health, and sex. Photos a plus. Pays on publication.

ROBB REPORT—1 Acton Pl., Acton, MA 01720. Robert R. Feeman, Ed. Upscale lifestyle magazine for men. Feature articles and regular columns on investment opportunities, exotic cars, classic and collectible autos, investibles and collectibles, technology, lifestyles (fashion, home, trends, food, books, personalities, pets, etc.), boats, travel, business profiles, etc. Pays on publication. Query with SASE and clips.

SENIORS MAGAZINES

AARP BULLETIN—601 E St. N.W., Washington, DC 20049. Elliot Carlson, Ed. Publication of the American Association of Retired Persons. Payment varies, on acceptance. Query required.

ANSWERS: THE MAGAZINE FOR ADULT CHILDREN OF AGING PARENTS—75 Seabreeze Dr., Richmond, CA 94804. Susan R. Keller, Ed./Pub. Features, 1,000 to 1,200 words, written from an emotional viewpoint on caring for an elderly parent. Columns, 800 words, on medication concerns, insurance, legal affairs, emotions, housing issues, products, and health and nutrition. News and book reviews, 50 to 100 words. Payment varies, on publication. Query with outline. Guidelines.

50 AND FORWARD—160 Mayo Rd., Suite 100, Edgewater, MD 21037. Debra Asberry, Ed./Pub. Fiction, 3,000 words, that can be serialized over 3 issues; articles, 800 to 1,200 words; fillers; and B&W art. "Readers are very active, 50 years old and over." Pays $25 to $50, on acceptance.

FLORIDA RETIREMENT LIFESTYLES—Gidder House Publishing, Inc., P.O. Box 161848, Altamonte Springs, FL 32716–1848. Mr. Kerry Smith, Ed. Concise and direct articles, 800 to 1,500 words, that address the issues and concerns of people contemplating a move to Florida for their retirement: financial strategies, retirement communities, recreation, sports, volunteer and educational opportunities, etc. Pays 10¢ a word (to $100), on publication.

GOOD TIMES—Senior Publications, Inc., 5148 Saint-Laurent Blvd.,

Montreal, Quebec, Canada H2T 1R8. Denise B. Crawford, Ed.-in-Chief. Judy Wayland, Asst. Ed. "The Canadian Magazine for Successful Retirement." Celebrity profiles as well as practical articles on health, beauty, cuisine, hobbies, fashion, leisure activities, travel, taxes, legal rights, consumer protection, etc. Payment varies. Query.

GOOD TIMES—1500 Market St., 12th Fl., Centre Sq. E., Philadelphia, PA 19102. Karen Detwiler, Ed.-in-Chief. Lifestyle magazine for mature Pennsylvanians 50 years and older. Articles, 800 to 1,500 words, on medical issues, health, travel, finance, fashion, gardening, fitness, legal issues, celebrities, lifestyles, and relationships. Payment varies, on publication. Query. Guidelines.

GRAND TIMES—P.O. Box 9493, Berkeley, CA 94709–0493. Kira Albin, Man. Ed. Articles and fiction, 600 to 1,800 words, for active retirees in the San Francisco Bay area. "We strive to inform, inspire, and entertain. No articles that play on ageist stereotypes." Pays $15 to $35, on acceptance. Guidelines.

KEY HORIZONS—Gateway Plaza, 950 N. Meridian, Suite 1200, Indianapolis, IN 46204. Joan Todd, Man. Ed. General-interest articles and department pieces, 1,500 words, for readers ages 50 and over in the Midwest, East, and Southwest. Departments include money, health, finance, domestic travel (no first-person pieces), and better living (gardening, cooking, etc.). No nostalgia or first-person retrospectives. Pays $50 to $500, on publication.

LIFE LINES—129 N. 10th St., Rm. 241, Lincoln, NE 68508–3648. Dena Rust Zimmer, Ed. Short stories, "Sports and Hobbies," "Remember When . . . ," and "Travel With . . . ," to 450 words. Poetry, to 50 lines. Fillers and short humor, "the shorter the better." No payment.

MATURE LIFESTYLES—P.O. Box 44327, Madison, WI 53744. Julia Jergensen, Ed. "South Central Wisconsin's Newspaper for the Active 50-Plus Population." Fillers, humor, jokes, and puzzles. No payment.

MATURE LIVING—127 Ninth Ave. N., Nashville, TN 37234. Al Shackleford, Ed. Fiction and human-interest articles, to 1,200 words, for senior adults. Must be consistent with Christian principles. Payment varies, on acceptance.

MATURE OUTLOOK—Meredith Corp., 1912 Grand Ave., Des Moines, IA 50309–3379. Peggy Person, Assoc. Ed. Bimonthly. Upbeat, contemporary articles, varying lengths, for readers 50 and older, travel and leisure topics. Regular columns cover health, money, food, gardening, and people. Third-person stories of real people, 300 to 1,000 words. Pays $125 to $1,000, on acceptance. Query required. Guidelines.

MATURE YEARS—201 Eighth Ave. S., P.O. Box 801, Nashville, TN 37202. Marvin W. Cropsey, Ed. Articles of interest to older adults: health and fitness, personal finance, hobbies and inspiration. Anecdotes, to 300 words, poems, cartoons, jokes, and puzzles for older adults. "A Christian magazine that seeks to build faith. We always show older adults in a favorable light." Include name, address, and social security number with all submissions. Allow 2 months for response.

MILESTONES—246 S. 22nd St., Philadelphia, PA 19103. Cathy Green, Ed. Robert Epp, Dir. Tabloid published 10 times a year. News articles and features, 750 to 1,000 words, on humor, personalities, political issues, etc., for readers 50 and older. Pays $25 for articles, $10 for photos, on publication.

MODERN MATURITY—3200 E. Carson St., Lakewood, CA 90712. J. Henry Fenwick, Ed. Articles, to 2,000 words, on careers, workplace, human interest, living, finance, relationships, and consumerism for readers over 50. Pays $500 to $2,500, on acceptance. Query.

NEW CHOICES FOR RETIREMENT LIVING—28 W. 23rd St., New York, NY 10010. David A. Sendler, Ed.-in-Chief. News and service magazine for people ages 50 to 65. Articles on planning for retirement, health and fitness, financial strategies, housing options, travel, profiles/interviews (celebrities and newsmakers), relationships, leisure pursuits, etc. Payment varies, on acceptance. Query or send complete manuscript.

NEW JERSEY 50+ PLUS—1830 US Rt. 9, Toms River, NJ 08755–1210. Pat Jasin, Ed. Articles on finance, health, travel, and social issues for older readers. Pays in copies. Query required.

RETIRED MILITARY FAMILY—169 Lexington Ave., New York, NY 10016. Liz DeFranco, Ed. Articles, 1,000 to 1,500 words, on travel, finance, food, hobbies, second careers, grandparenting, and other topics of interest to military retirees and their families. Pays to $200, on publication.

THE RETIRED OFFICER MAGAZINE—201 N. Washington St., Alexandria, VA 22314. Attn: Manuscripts Ed. Articles, 800 to 2,000 words, of interest to military retirees and their families. Current military/political affairs, recent military history (especially Vietnam and Korea), military family lifestyles, health, money, second careers. Photos a plus. Pays to $1,000, on acceptance. Queries required. Guidelines.

RX REMEDY—120 Post Rd. W., Westport, CT 06880. Val Weaver, Ed. Bimonthly. Articles, 600 to 2,500 words, on health and medication issues for readers 55 and older. Regular columns include "Housecall" and "The Nutrition Prescription." Query. Pays $1 to $1.25 a word, on acceptance.

SENIOR BEACON—P.O. Box 40126, Georgetown, TX 78628. Carolyn Keeling, Ed. Poetry, to 100 words, and short (one-or 2-line) fillers for seniors in Texas. No payment.

SENIOR HIGHLIGHTS—26081 Merit Cir., Suite 101, Laguna Hills, CA 92653. Julie Puckett, Asst. Ed. Articles, 800 words, on health, money, lifestyles, and travel. No payment. Queries preferred. Responds within 3 months. Guidelines.

SENIOR MAGAZINE—3565 S. Higuera St., San Luis Obispo, CA 93401. Attn: Ed. Articles, 600 to 900 words, of interest to men and women over 40, in the western US: personality profiles, travel pieces, articles about new things, places, business, sports, movies, television, and health. Reviews of new or outstanding older books. Pays $1.50 per inch; $10 to $25 for B&W photos, on publication.

SENIOR TIMES—Suite 814, 1102 Pleasant St., Worcester, MA 01602–1232. Edwin H. Gledhill, Ed. Short stories, 500 to 700 words, of interest to senior citizens. Articles, 500 to 700 words, on arts, entertainment, and positive role models for aging. Poetry, 10 to 200 words. No payment.

SENIOR WORLD NEWSMAGAZINE—1000 Pioneer Way, El Cajon, CA 92020–1923. Laura Impastato, Ed. Articles, 800 to 1,000 words, for active, older adults (over 55). Articles on local, state and national news. Features about celebrities, remarkable seniors, consumer interest, finance and investment, housing, sports, hobbies, collectibles, trends, travel, etc. Health and medicine articles emphasizing wellness, preventive care, and the latest on medical treatments. Pays $75 to $100, on publication.

SENIORS CAPE COD FORUM—72 Winter St., Hyannis, MA 02601. Lisa Shilo Chase, Ed. Local profile pieces, medical news/trends, local trends, and news pieces of interest to seniors. Articles should be 2 double-spaced pages. No payment.

TODAY'S TIMES—100 Annex, 856 Homer St., Vancouver, BC, Canada V6B 2W5. Tony Whitney, Ed. Tabloid. Articles, to 800 words, on travel, transportation, health, entertainment, computers, and other subjects of interest to readers over 50 who live in British Columbia. Payment varies, on publication. Queries required.

WESTCOAST REFLECTIONS—2604 Quadra St., Victoria, BC, Canada V8T 4E4. Jane Kezar, Assoc. Ed. Published 10 times a year "for those 39 and holding." Upbeat, humorous, positive articles, 700 to 1,200 words, on travel, recreation, health and fitness, hobbies, home and garden, cooking, finance, and continuing education. Occasionally uses more serious pieces on housing, finances, and health. Nothing political or religious. "The articles we publish are not necessarily about people over 50, but are for them. Writing style should reflect this; use terminology understood by the mature reader." Pays 10¢ a word, on publication. Queries preferred. Guidelines.

YESTERDAY'S MAGAZETTE—P.O. Box 15126, Sarasota, FL 34277. Ned Burke, Ed. Articles and stories, 500 to 1,000 words, set in the 1920s to '70s. Photos a plus. Traditional poetry, to 24 lines. Pays $5 to $25 for articles, on publication. Pays in copies for short pieces and poetry.

HOME & GARDEN/FOOD & WINE

AMERICAN HOMESTYLE & GARDENING—110 Fifth Ave., New York, NY 10011. Karen Saks, Ed.-in-Chief. Articles on interior design, remodeling, architecture, gardening, and the decorative arts. Payment varies, on acceptance. Query.

AMERICAN ROSE—P.O. Box 30,000, Shreveport, LA 71130. Beth Horstman, Man. Ed. Articles on home rose gardens: varieties, products, helpful advice, rose care, etc.

BETTER HOMES AND GARDENS—1716 Locust St., Des Moines, IA 50309–3023. Jean LemMon, Ed. Articles, to 2,000 words, on money management, health, travel, pets, and cars. Pays top rates, on acceptance. Query.

BON APPETIT—6300 Wilshire Blvd., Los Angeles, CA 90048. Barbara Fairchild, Exec. Ed. Articles on fine cooking (menu format or single focus), cooking classes, and gastronomically focused travel. Pays varying rates, on acceptance. Query with clips.

BRIDE'S—(formerly *Bride's & Your New Home*) 140 E. 45th St., New York, NY 10017. Sally Kilbridge, Man. Ed. Articles, 800 to 3,000 words, for engaged couples or newlyweds on home and redecorating, wedding, and honeymoon. Pays $200 to $1,000, on acceptance.

CANADIAN SELECT HOMES MAGAZINE—(formerly *Select Homes & Foods*) 25 Sheppard Ave. W., Suite 100, North York, Ont., Canada M2N 6S7. Barbara Dixon, Ed. How-to articles, profiles of Canadian homes, renovation, decor, and gardening features, 800 to 1,500 words. Canadian content and locations only. Pays from $400 to $900 (Canadian), on acceptance. Query with international reply coupons. Send SAE with international reply coupons for guidelines.

CHILE PEPPER—P.O. Box 4278, Albuquerque, NM 87196. Melissa Jackson, Man. Ed. Food and travel articles, 1,000 to 1,500 words. "No general and obvious articles, such as 'My Favorite Chile Con Carne.' We want first-person articles about spicy world cuisine." No fillers. Payment varies, on publication. Queries required.

COOKING LIGHT—P.O. Box 1748, Birmingham, AL 35201. Doug Crichton, Ed. Articles on fitness, exercise, health and healthful cooking, nutrition, and healthful recipes. Query.

COOK'S ILLUSTRATED—17 Station St., P.O. Box 569, Brookline, MA 02147. Anne Tuomey, Articles Ed. Bimonthly. Articles with an emphasis on cooking technique, including basic recipes, tips on how to improvise, and sidebars that are "unexpected and complementary." Payment varies, within 60 days of acceptance. Queries preferred. Guidelines.

COUNTRY LIVING—224 W. 57th St., New York, NY 10019. Marjorie E. Gage, Features Ed. Articles, 800 to 1,200 words, on decorating, antiques, cooking, travel, home building, crafts, and gardens. "Most material is written in-house; limited free-lance needs." Payment varies, on acceptance. Query preferred.

EATING WELL—Ferry Rd., P.O. Box 1001, Charlotte, VT 05445–1001. Marcelle DiFalco, Ed. Bimonthly. Feature articles, 2,000 to 5,000 words. Department pieces, 100 to 200 words, for "Nutrition News" and "Marketplace." "We look for strong journalistic voice; authoritative, timely coverage of nutrition issues; healthful recipes that emphasize good ingredients, simple preparation, and full flavor; and a sense of humor." Payment varies, 45 days after acceptance. Query.

ELLE DECOR—1633 Broadway, New York, NY 10019. Charles Bricker, Exec. Ed. Articles, 300 to 1,000 words, on designers and craftspeople (query with photos of the designers and their work) and on houses and apartments "notable for their quirkiness or their beauty, preferably an eclectic combination of the two." Pays $1.25 a word, on publication. Query.

FLOWER & GARDEN MAGAZINE—700 W. 47th St., Suite 310, Kansas City, MO 64112. Attn: Ed. Practical how-to articles, 1,000 words, on lawn and garden advice. Photos a plus. Pays varying rates, on acceptance (on publication for photos). Query.

FOOD & WINE—1120 Ave. of the Americas, New York, NY 10036. Dana Cowin, Ed.-in-Chief. Mary Ellen Ward, Man. Ed. No unsolicited material.

GARDEN DESIGN—100 Ave. of the Americas, 7th Fl., New York, NY 10013. Dorothy Kalins, Ed.-in-Chief. Garden-related features, 500 to 1,000 words, on private, public, and community gardens; articles on art and history as they relate to gardens.

GOURMET: THE MAGAZINE OF GOOD LIVING—Conde Nast, 360 Madison Ave., New York, NY 10017. Attn: Ed. No unsolicited manuscripts; query.

HARROWSMITH COUNTRY LIFE—Ferry Rd., Charlotte, VT 05445.

Attn: Ed. Dept. Features, 3,000 to 4,000 words, on community/small town issues, the environment, rural life, gardening, house design and restoration, building projects, and healthful food. Short pieces for "Gazette" (news briefs) and "Sourcebank" (product and book reviews). Pays $500 to $2,000 for features, $50 to $600 for department pieces, on acceptance. Query required. Guidelines.

THE HERB COMPANION—Interweave Press, 201 E. Fourth St., Loveland, CO 80537. Kathleen Halloran, Ed. Trish Faubion, Man. Ed. Bimonthly. Articles, 1,500 to 3,000 words; fillers, 75 to 150 words. Practical horticultural information, original recipes illustrating the use of herbs, thoroughly researched historical insights, step-by-step instructions for herbal craft projects, profiles of notable individuals in the field, book reviews. Pays $100 per published page, on publication.

HOME GARDEN—1716 Locust St., Des Moines, IA 50309. Douglas A. Jimerson, Ed.-in-Chief. Gardening/lifestyle magazine. No unsolicited manuscripts. Query with resumé.

HOME MAGAZINE—1633 Broadway, 44th Fl., New York, NY 10019. Gale Steves, Ed-in-Chief. Linda Lentz, Articles Ed. Articles of interest to homeowners: architecture, remodeling, decorating, products, project ideas, landscaping and gardening, financial aspects of home ownership, home offices, home-related environmental and ecological topics. Pays varying rates, on acceptance. Query, with 50-to 200-word summary.

HOME MECHANIX—2 Park Ave., New York, NY 10016. Michael Chotiner, Ed. Home improvement articles. Time-or money-saving tips for the home, garage, or yard; seasonal reminders for homeowners. Pays $50, on acceptance.

HOME POOL & BAR-B-QUE—P.O. Box 272, Cranford, NJ 07016–0272. John R. Hawks, Pub. Articles about pool maintenance, design, safety, products, bar-b-que recipes. Pays $30 to $100, on publication.

HORTICULTURE—98 N. Washington St., Boston, MA 02114. Deborah Starr, Exec. Ed. Published 10 times a year. Authoritative, well-written articles, 500 to 2,500 words, on all aspects of gardening. Pays competitive rates, on publication. Query.

HOUSE BEAUTIFUL—1700 Broadway, New York, NY 10019. Elaine Greene, Features Ed. Service articles related to the home. Pieces on design, travel, and gardening. Query with detailed outline and photos if relevant. Guidelines.

HOUSEPLANT MAGAZINE—P.O. Box 1638, Elkins, WV 26241. Larry Hodgson, Ed.-in-Chief. Articles, 700 to 1,500 words, on indoor gardening, travel, humor, hydroponics, plant portraits. Payment varies, on publication. Query.

LOG HOME GUIDE FOR BUILDERS & BUYERS—164 Middle Creek Rd., Cosby, TN 37722. Articles, 500 to 1,500 words, on building new, or restoring old log homes, especially with solar or alternative heating systems, as well as pieces on decorating or profiles of interesting builders of log homes. Pays 20¢ a word, extra for photos, on publication. Limited market. Query.

LOG HOME LIVING—P.O. Box 220039, Chantilly, VA 22022. Roland Sweet, Ed. Articles, 1,000 to 1,500 words, on modern manufactured and hand-crafted kit log homes: homeowner profiles, design and decor features. Pays $200 to $500, on acceptance.

METROPOLITAN HOME—1633 Broadway, New York, NY 10019. Michael Lassell, Articles Dir. Service and informational articles for residents of houses, co-ops, lofts, and condominiums, on real estate, equity, wine and spirits, collecting, trends, travel, etc. Interior design and home furnishing articles with emphasis on lifestyle. Payment varies. Query.

THE MOTHER EARTH NEWS—24 E. 23rd St., 5th Fl., New York, NY 10010. Matthew Scanlon, Ed. Articles on country living: home improvement and construction, how-tos, indoor and outdoor gardening, crafts and projects, etc. Also health, ecology, energy, and consumerism pieces; profiles. Payment varies.

NAPA VALLEY APPELLATION—P.O. Box 516, Napa, CA 94559. Antonia Allegra, Ed.-in-Chief. Quarterly. Articles, 900 to 1,500 words, on the lifestyles, wines, and gardens of the Napa Valley. Pays $200 to $500, on acceptance.

QUICK 'N EASY COUNTRY COOKIN'—Parkside Publications, Inc., P.O. Box 66, Davis, SD 57021–0066. Pam Schrag, Ed. Family-oriented cooking articles, 400 to 500 words and articles with a human-interest/Christian perspective. Pays $10 for articles, on publication. "We also accept short verse, puzzles, and humorous fillers, up to 50 words."

SELECT HOMES & FOODS—See *Canadian Select Homes Magazine.*

VEGGIE LIFE—1041 Shary Cir., Concord, CA 94518. Margo Lemas, Ed. Bimonthly. Features and profiles, 2,000 words, for "people interested in American and ethnic meatless cuisine, organic gardening, environmental issues, and healthy living." Food features (include 8 to 10 recipes); department pieces, 250 to 1,000 words. Payment varies, on acceptance. Queries preferred.

WINE SPECTATOR—387 Park Ave. S., New York, NY 10016. Jim Gordon, Man. Ed. Features, 600 to 2,000 words, preferably with photos, on news and people in the wine world, travel, food, and other lifestyle topics. Pays from $400, extra for photos, on publication. Query required.

WINES & VINES—1800 Lincoln Ave., San Rafael, CA 94901. Philip E. Hiaring, Ed. Articles, 2,000 words, on grape and wine industry, emphasizing marketing, management, and production. Pays 10¢ a word, on acceptance.

WORKBENCH—700 W. 47th St., Suite 310, Kansas City, MO 64112. A. Robert Gould, Exec. Ed. Illustrated how-to articles on home improvement and woodworking, with detailed instructions. Pays from $150 per printed page, on acceptance. Guidelines.

YOUR HOME/INDOORS & OUT—P.O. Box 10010, Ogden, UT 84409. Attn: Ed. Dept. Articles, 1,000 words, with good color transparencies and fresh ideas in all areas of home decor: the latest in home construction (exteriors, interiors, building materials, design); the outdoors at home (landscaping, pools, patios, gardening); home management, buying, and selling. No do-it-yourself pieces. Pays 15¢ a word, $35 for color photos, on acceptance. Query required.

FAMILY & PARENTING MAGAZINES

ADOPTIVE FAMILIES MAGAZINE—(formerly *Ours: The Magazine of Adoptive Families*) 3333 Hwy. 100 N., Minneapolis, MN 55422. Linda Lynch,

Ed. Bimonthly. Articles, 800 to 1,700 words, on living in an adoptive family and other adoption issues. Photos of families, adults, or children. No payment. Query.

AMERICAN BABY—Cahners Childcare Group, 249 W. 17th St., New York, NY 10011. Judith Nolte, Ed. Articles, 1,000 to 2,000 words, for new or expectant parents on prenatal and infant care. Personal experience, 900 to 1,200 words, (do not submit in diary format). Department pieces, 50 to 350 words, for "Crib Notes" (news and feature topics) and "Medical Update" (health and medicine). No fiction, fantasy pieces, dreamy musings, or poetry. Pays $350 to $1,000 for articles, $100 for departments, on acceptance. Guidelines.

ANSWERS: THE MAGAZINE FOR ADULT CHILDREN OF AGING PARENTS—75 Seabreeze Dr., Richmond, CA 94804. Susan R. Keller, Ed./Pub. Features, 1,000 to 1,200 words, written from an emotional viewpoint on caring for an elderly parent. Columns, 800 words, on medication concerns, insurance, legal affairs, emotions, housing issues, products, and health and nutrition. News and book reviews, 50 to 100 words. Payment varies, on publication. Query with outline. Guidelines.

BABY TALK—25 W. 43rd St., New York, NY 10036. Susan Strecker, Ed. Articles, 1,000 to 1,500 words, by parents or professionals, on babies, baby care, etc. No poetry. Pays varying rates, on acceptance. SASE required.

BAY AREA PARENT— 401 Alberto Way, Suite A, Los Gatos, CA 95032–5404. Mary Brence Martin, Ed. Articles, 1,200 to 1,400 words, on local parenting issues for readers in California's Santa Clara County and the South Bay area. Query. Mention availability of B&W photos. Pays 6¢ a word, $10 to $15 for photos, on publication. Also publishes *Valley Parent* for central Contra Costa County and the tri–valley area of Alameda County.

THE BIG APPLE PARENTS' PAPER—36 E. 12th St., New York, NY 10003. Susan Hodara, Ed. Articles, 600 to 750 words, for NYC parents. Pays $35 to $50, on publication. Buys first NY-area rights.

CENTRAL CALIFORNIA PARENT—2037 W. Bullard, #131, Fresno, CA 93711. Sally Cook, Pub. Articles, 500 to 1,500 words, of interest to parents. Payment varies, on publication.

CHRISTIAN HOME & SCHOOL—3350 E. Paris Ave. S.E., Grand Rapids, MI 49512. Gordon L. Bordewyk, Ed. Articles for parents in Canada and the U.S. who send their children to Christian schools and are concerned about the challenges facing Christian families today. Pays $75 to $150, on publication. Send SASE for guidelines or 9"x12" SASE with 4 first-class stamps for guidelines and sample issue.

CHRISTIAN PARENTING TODAY—P.O. Box 36630, Colorado Springs, CO 80936–3663. Brad Lewis, Ed. Articles, 900 to 2,000 words, dealing with raising children with Christian principles. Departments: "Parent Exchange," 25 to 100 words, on problem-solving ideas that have worked for parents; "Life in our House," insightful anecdotes, 25 to 100 words, about humorous things said at home. Queries preferred for articles. Pays 15¢ to 25¢ a word, on publication. Pays $40 for "Parent Exchange," $25 for "Life in our House." Guidelines.

CONNECTICUT FAMILY—See *New York Family*.

EASTSIDE PARENT—Northwest Parent Publishing, 2107 Elliott Ave., #303, Seattle, WA 98121. Ann Bergman, Ed. Articles, 300 to 2,500 words, for parents of children under 12. Readers tend to be professional, two-career families. Pays $25 to $200, on publication. Queries preferred. Also publishes *Seattle's Child, Portland Parent,* and *Pierce County Parent.*

EXCEPTIONAL PARENT—209 Harvard St., Suite 303, Brookline, MA 02146–5005. Stanley D. Klein, Ed. Articles, 1,000 to 1,500 words, for parents raising children with disabilities. Practical ideas and techniques on parenting, as well as the latest in technology, research, and rehabilitation. Pays $25, on publication. Query.

EXPECTING— 685 Third Ave., New York, NY 10017. Evelyn A. Podsiadlo, Ed. Not buying any new material in the foreseeable future.

FAMILY—169 Lexington Ave., New York, NY 10016. Liz DeFranco, Ed. Articles, 1,000 to 2,000 words, of interest to women with children. Topics include: military lifestyle, home decorating, travel, moving, food, personal finances, career, relationships, family, parenting, health and fitness. Pays to $200, on publication.

THE FAMILY: A CATHOLIC PERSPECTIVE—50 St. Pauls Ave., Boston, MA 02130. Sister Mary Lea Hill, Ed. Articles, 800 to 2,000 words, on a broad range of family topics, including marital relationships, parenting, profiles of role-models for Catholic families. Upbeat, thought-provoking, family-oriented fiction, 1,000 to 1,200 words. Views, columns, personal reflections, 800 words; fillers, 50 to 500 words. "Our readers are primarily Roman Catholic parents with children at home." Pays 6¢ to 8¢ a word, on publication. (Pays for fillers on acceptance.) Submit complete manuscripts; no queries and no simultaneous submissions. Does not read submissions in July or August.

FAMILY FUN—Walt Disney Publishing Group, 244 Main St., Northampton, MA 01060. Alexandra Kennedy, Ed. Read-aloud stories, to 750 words, and articles, to 1,500 words, on family activities and "creative parenting." Payment varies, on acceptance. Queries preferred.

FAMILY LIFE—Wenner Media, 1290 Ave. of the Americas, New York, NY 10104–0298. Attn: Ed. Dept. Articles, 1,000 to 4,000 words, on education, travel, money, health, community service, and other subjects of interest to active parents of children ages 3 to 12. Service pieces, 700 to 1,500 words, on sports, lessons, field trips, toys, parties, and pets. Short pieces, 250 to 800 words, on news and activities. Payment varies. Query with clips.

FAMILY TIMES—P.O. Box 932, Eau Claire, WI 54702. Ann Gorton, Ed. Articles, from 800 words, on children and parenting issues: health, education, raising children, how-tos, new studies and programs for educating parents. "Information should be as specific to the Chippewa Valley, WI, as possible. We don't buy humor." Pays $35 to $50, on publication. Guidelines. Query preferred.

FULL-TIME DADS—P.O. Box 577, Cumberland, ME 04021. Stephen Harris, Ed. Fiction, articles, essays, and humor, 600 to 1,200 words, and short poems for fathers who are very involved with their children. "All material must relate to supportive fatherhood." Payment is one copy.

GROWING CHILD/GROWING PARENT—22 N. Second St., P.O. Box 620, Lafayette, IN 47902–0620. Nancy Kleckner, Ed. Articles, to 1,500 words, on subjects of interest to parents of children under 6. No personal experience pieces or poetry. Guidelines.

HOME LIFE—127 Ninth Ave. N., Nashville, TN 37234. Charlie Warren,

Ed.-in-Chief. Southern Baptist. Articles, to 1,500 words, on Christian marriage, parenting, and family relationships. Query with SASE required. Pays from $75 for articles, on acceptance.

JOYFUL CHILD JOURNAL—34 Russell Ave., Buffalo, NY 14214. Karen Spring Stevens, Exec. Ed. Quarterly. Fiction and nonfiction, 500 to 1,000 words, that "explore how society and education can more effectively nurture children (and adults) to express their fullest potential, thus releasing their inner joy. Articles on educating and parenting the whole child (body, mind, and spirit)." Some short poetry. Pays in copies. Queries preferred. Guidelines.

L.A. BABY—See *Wingate Enterprises, Ltd.*

L.A. PARENT—See *Wingate Enterprises, Ltd.*

LIVING WITH TEENAGERS—127 Ninth Ave. N., Nashville, TN 37234. Attn: Ed. Articles from a Christian perspective for parents of teenagers. Send resumé only.

METROKIDS—Riverview Plaza, 1400 S. Columbus Blvd., Philadelphia, PA 19147–5526. Nancy Lisagor, Ed. Tabloid for Delaware Valley families. Features and department pieces, 500 to 1,000 words, on regional family travel, dining, and entertainment. Pays $25 to $50, on publication.

MODERN DAD—7628 N. Rogers Ave., Chicago, IL 60626–1214. Elisa Kronish, Ed. Bimonthly. Fiction and articles, 200 to 3,000 words, that aid, educate, and inform fathers. "We value fathering *and* the family and explore all the possibilities of fatherhood in today's information age." Guidelines. Payment varies, on publication. Query preferred.

MOSAICA DIGEST—242 Fourth St., Lakewood, NJ 08701. Attn: Submission Dept. Joseph Ginberg, Pres. Fiction, 1,500 to 4,000 words; articles, 1,500 to 3,000 words; fillers, 100 to 300 words, of interest to Jewish families. First-person pieces, humor, travel, and history. Articles of Jewish interest are preferred (not articles about religion or religious issues). "We are a family-oriented magazine, and everything must be squeaky clean! No profanity, etc." Reprints are preferred. Pays to $50, on publication.

NEW YORK FAMILY—141 Halstead Ave., Suite 3D, Mamaroneck, NY 10543. Felice Shapiro, Susan Ross, Eds. Articles related to family life in New York City and general parenting topics. Pays $50 to $200. Same requirements for *Westchester Family* and *Connecticut Family.*

OURS: THE MAGAZINE OF ADOPTIVE FAMILIES—See *Adoptive Families Magazine.*

PARENTGUIDE NEWS—419 Park Ave. S., 13th Fl., New York, NY 10016. Jenine M. DeLuca, Ed.-in-Chief. Articles, 1,000 to 1,500 words, related to families and parenting issues: trends, profiles, health, education, special programs, products, etc. Humor and photos also considered.

PARENTING—See *Wingate Enterprises, Ltd.*

PARENTING—301 Howard St., 17th Fl., San Francisco, CA 94105. Attn: Articles Ed. Articles, 500 to 3,500 words, on education, health, fitness, nutrition, child development, psychology, and social issues for parents of young children. Query.

PARENTLIFE—MSN 140, 127 Ninth Ave. N., Nashville, TN 37234. Attn: Ed. Articles on Christian family issues. Resumés only.

PARENTS—685 Third Ave., New York, NY 10017. Ann Pleshette Murphy, Ed. Articles, 1,500 to 2,500 words, on parenting, family, women's and community issues, etc. Informal style with quotes from experts. Pays from $1,000, on acceptance. Query.

PARENT'S DIGEST—100 Park Ave., New York, NY 10017. Mary E. Mohler, Ed.-in-Chief. Published 3 times a year by *Ladies' Home Journal*. Articles, 250 to 2,500 words, for parents; frequently uses reprints. Payment varies, on acceptance. Query.

PIERCE COUNTY PARENT—See *Eastside Parent.*

PORTLAND PARENT—See *Eastside Parent.*

SAN DIEGO PARENT—See *Wingate Enterprises, Ltd.*

SEATTLE'S CHILD—Northwest Parent Publishing, 2107 Elliott Ave., #303, Seattle, WA 98121. Ann Bergman, Ed. Articles, 400 to 2,500 words, of interest to parents, educators, and childcare providers of children under 12, plus investigative reports and consumer tips on issues affecting families in the Puget Sound region. Pays $75 to $400, on publication. Query required.

SESAME STREET PARENTS' GUIDE—One Lincoln Plaza, New York, NY 10023. Anne Heller, Exec. Ed. Articles on children and violence; Susan Schneider, Articles Ed. Articles on educational issues; Nadia Zonis, Medical/Health Ed. Articles, 800 to 2,500 words, on medical, psychological, and educational issues for families with young children (up to 8 years old). Pays 50¢ to $1 per word, up to 6 weeks after acceptance.

THE SINGLE PARENT—Parents Without Partners, Inc., 401 N. Michigan Ave., Chicago, IL 60611. Debbie Olefsky, Ed. Quarterly. Articles, 500 to 1,000 words, addressing the concerns of single parents, including physical and emotional wellness, careers (for adults and youths), and intergenerational issues. Fillers, 300 to 500 words. Prefers pieces that "enlighten and entertain busy people"; no "cutesy or sob stories." No payment.

STEPFAMILIES—Stepfamily Assn. of America, 215 Centennial Mall S., Suite 212, Lincoln, NE 68508–1834. Attn: Ed. Quarterly. Articles, 2 to 4 pages, relevant to stepfamily living. Fillers and poetry. No payment.

TODAY'S FAMILY—P.O. Box 46112, Eden Prairie, MN 55344. Attn: Ed. Quarterly. Articles, 750 to 2,000 words, on "hot topics and fun for every family" and information that helps strengthen families. Departments include "Healthy and Fit Families," "On the School Front," "On the Home Front," "Family Savings," "Random Acts of Caring," "Family Fun and Laughter," and "Family Travel." Pays $10 to $50, on publication. Query preferred.

TWINS—6740 Antioch, Suite 155, Merriam, KS 66204. Jean Cerne, Man. Ed. Bimonthly. Features, 6 to 8 double-spaced pages; columns, 4 to 6 pages. "Twin-specific parenting information, from both the professional (research-based) and personal (hands-on experience) perspectives." Pays varying rates, on publication. Query.

VALLEY PARENT—See *Bay Area Parent.*

WESTCHESTER FAMILY—See *New York Family.*

WINGATE ENTERPRISES, LTD.—P.O. Box 3204, 443 E. Irving Dr., Burbank, CA 91504. Attn: Eds. Publishes city-based parenting magazines with strong "service-to-parent" slant. Articles, 1,200 words, on child development, health, nutrition, and education. *San Diego Parent* covers San Diego area.

Parenting covers the Orange County, CA, area. *L.A. Parent* is geared toward parents of children to age 10; *L.A. Baby* to expectant parents and parents of newborns. Pays $100 to $350, on acceptance. Query.

WORKING MOTHER—Lang Communications, 230 Park Ave., New York, NY 10169. Attn: Ed. Dept. Articles, to 2,000 words, that help women juggle job, home, and family. Payment varies, on acceptance.

LIFESTYLE MAGAZINES

AMERICAN HEALTH—28 W. 23rd St., New York, NY 10010. Attn: Ed. Dept. Lively, authoritative articles, 1,000 to 3,000 words, on scientific and lifestyle aspects of health and fitness; 100-to 500-word news reports. Pays $150 to $250 for news stories; payment varies for features, on acceptance. Query with clips.

AQUARIUS: A SIGN OF THE TIMES—984 Canton St., Roswell, GA 30075. Dan Liss, Ed. Articles, 800 words (with photos or illustrations), on New Age lifestyles and positive thought, holistic health, metaphysics, spirituality, environment. No payment.

BACKHOME—P.O. Box 70, Hendersonville, NC 28793. Lorna K. Loveless, Ed. Articles, 800 to 2,500 words, on home schooling, recycling, home business, healthful cooking. "We hope to provide readers with ways to gain more control over their lives by becoming more self-sufficient: raising their own food, making their own repairs, using alternative energy, etc. We do not promote 'dropping out' of society, but ways to become better citizens and caretakers of the planet." Pays $25 per page; $20 for photos, on publication. Queries preferred.

CAPPER'S—Editorial Dept., 1503 S.W. 42nd St., Topeka, KS 66609–1265. Nancy Peavler, Ed. Human-interest, personal-experience, historical articles, 300 to 700 words. Poetry, to 15 lines, on nature, home, family. Novel-length fiction for serialization. Letters on women's interests, recipes, and hints for "Heart of the Home." Jokes. Children's writing and art section. Pays varying rates, on publication.

CHANGES—U.S. Journal, Inc., 3201 S.W. 15th St., Deerfield Beach, FL 33442–8190. Jeffrey Laign, Ed. "The Recovery Lifestyle Magazine." Bimonthly. Recovery-oriented fiction, 1,500 words, and poetry. Query for non-fiction, 2,000 words. Pays 15¢ a word, on publication.

COUNTRY AMERICA—1716 Locust St., Des Moines, IA 50309–3023. Dick Sowienski, General Interest Ed. Mike Hood, Outdoors Ed. Neil Pond, Entertainment Ed. Peg Brinkhoff, Fashion/Home Ed. Diane Yanney, Food Ed. Bob Ehlert, General Interest Ed. Features on travel, cooking, country heritage, recreation, crafts, homes, gardening, and personalities. "Articles should be light on copy with potential for several color photos." Queries preferred.

COUNTRY CONNECTIONS—P.O. Box 6748, Pine Mountain Club, CA 93222. Catherine R. Leach, Ed. Articles, to 2,500 words, and fiction, to 1,500 words. Poetry. B&W photos. "Study magazine first. We serve as a forum for public discourse about ethics, politics, social justice, community, city rights, animal and environmental issues, and life in the country." Pays $25 for features, $15 for fiction and poetry, on publication.

FATE—P.O. Box 64383, St. Paul, MN 55164–0383. Attn: Ed. Factual fillers and true stories, to 3,000 words, on strange or psychic happenings and mystic personal experiences. Pays 10¢ a word.

FELLOWSHIP—Box 271, Nyack, NY 10960–0271. Richard Deats, Ed. Bimonthly published by the Fellowship of Reconciliation, an interfaith, pacifist organization. Features, 1,500 to 2,000 words, and articles, 750 words, "dealing with nonviolence, opposition to war, and a just and peaceful world community." Photo-essays (B&W photos, include caption information). SASE required. Pays in copies and subscription. Queries preferred.

GERMAN LIFE—Zeitgeist Publishing, 1 Corporate Dr., Grantsville, MD 21536. Michael Koch, Ed. Bimonthly. Articles, 500 to 2,500 words, on German culture, its past and present, and how America has been influenced by its German element: history, travel, people, the arts, and social and political issues. Fillers, 50 to 200 words. Pays $300 to $500 for full-length articles, to $80 for short pieces and for fillers, on publication. Queries preferred.

GOOD TIMES—1500 Market St., 12th Fl., Centre Sq.E., Philadelphia, PA 19102. Karen Detwiler, Ed.-in-Chief. Lifestyle magazine for mature Pennsylvanians 50 years and older. Articles, 1,500 to 2,000 words, on medical issues, health, travel, finance, fashion, gardening, fitness, legal issues, celebrities, lifestyles, and relationships. Guidelines. Payment varies, on publication. Query.

HEART & SOUL—Rodale Press, Inc., 201 E. 42nd St., New York, NY 10017. Stephanie Stokes Oliver, Ed.-in-Chief. Articles, 800 to 1,500 words, on health, beauty, fitness, nutrition, and relationships for African-American readers. "We aim to be the African-American's ultimate guide to a healthy lifestyle." Payment varies, on acceptance. Queries preferred.

ILLYRIA: THE ALBANIAN-AMERICAN NEWSPAPER—2321 Hughes Ave., Bronx, NY 10458. Joseph Finora, Man. Dir. Articles on news, politics, people, sports, history, travel, food, and culture. All articles must relate to Albania or Albanians. Photos. Pays $50 to $70, on publication.

INSIDE MAGAZINE—226 S. 16th St., Philadelphia, PA 19102–3392. Jane Biberman, Ed. Jewish lifestyle magazine. Articles, 1,500 to 3,000 words, on Jewish issues, health, finance, and the arts. Pays $75 to $600, after publication. Queries required; send clips if available.

JEWISH CURRENTS—22 E. 17th St., #601, New York, NY 10003. Morris U. Schappes, Ed. Articles, 2,400 to 3,000 words, on Jewish culture or history: Holocaust resistance commemoration, Black-Jewish relations, Yiddish literature and culture, Jewish labor struggles. "We are a secular Jewish magazine." No fiction. No payment.

THE JEWISH HOMEMAKER—705 Foster Ave., Brooklyn, NY 11230. Mayer Bendet, Ed. Bimonthly. Articles, 1,200 to 2,000 words, for a traditional/Orthodox Jewish audience. Humor. Payment varies, on publication. Query.

LEFTHANDER MAGAZINE—P.O. Box 8249, Topeka, KS 66608–0249. Kim Kipers, Ed. Bimonthly. Articles, 1,500 to 1,800 words, related to left-handedness: profiles of left-handed personalities; performing specific tasks or sports as a lefty; teaching left-handed children. Personal experience pieces for "Perspective." SASE for guidelines. Pays $80 to $100, on publication. Buys all rights. Query.

LIFEPRINTS—P.O. Box 5181, Salem, OR 97304. Carol McCarl, Ed. Quarterly. Articles, 800 to 1,500 words, and poetry, 20 lines, for visually impaired youth and adults. Career opportunities, educational skills, and recreational activities. "We want to give readers an opportunity to learn about interesting and successful people who are blind." Payment varies, on publication. Queries are preferred.

LINK: THE COLLEGE MAGAZINE—The Soho Bldg., 110 Greene St., Suite 407, New York, NY 10012. Ty Wenger, Man. Ed. Lifestyle magazine for college students. News, lifestyle, and issues for college students. Informational how-to and short features, 500 to 800 words, on education news, finances, academics, employment, lifestyles, and trends. Well-researched, insightful, authoritative articles. Queries preferred. Pays $100 to $500, on publication. Guidelines.

MOMENT MAGAZINE— 4710 41st St. N.W., Washington, DC 20016. Andrew Silow-Carroll, Sr. Ed. Sophisticated articles, 2,500 to 5,000 words, on Jewish culture, politics, religion, and personalities. Columns, to 1,500 words, with uncommon perspectives on contemporary issues, humor, strong anecdotes. Book reviews, 400 words. Pays $40 to $600.

NATIVE PEOPLES MAGAZINE—5333 N. 7th St., Suite C-224, Phoenix, AZ 85014–2804. Gary Avey, Ed. Quarterly. Articles, 1,800 to 2,800 words, on the "arts and lifeways" of the native peoples of the Americas; authenticity and positive portrayals of present traditional and cultural practices necessary. Pays 25¢ a word, on publication. Query, including availability of photos.

NATURAL HEALTH: THE GUIDE TO WELL-BEING—17 Station St., Box 1200, Brookline Village, MA 02147. Attn: Ed. Bimonthly. Features, 1,500 to 3,000 words: practical information, new discoveries, and current trends on natural health and living. Topics include natural goods and medicine, alternative health care, nutrition, wellness, personal fitness, and modern holistic teachings. Departments and columns, 250 to 1,000 words. Payment varies, on acceptance.

NEW AGE JOURNAL— 42 Pleasant St., Watertown, MA 02172–2312. Peggy Taylor, Ed. Articles for readers who take an active interest in social change, personal growth, health, and contemporary issues. Features, 2,000 to 4,000 words; columns, 750 to 1,500 words; short news items, 50 words; and first-person narratives, 750 to 1,500 words. Pays varying rates, after acceptance.

NEW CHOICES FOR RETIREMENT LIVING—28 W. 23rd St., New York, NY 10010. Allen J. Sheinman, Articles Ed. David A. Sendler, Ed.-in-Chief. News and service magazine for people ages 50 to 65. Articles on planning for retirement, health and fitness, financial strategies, housing options, travel, profiles/interviews (celebrities and newsmakers), relationships, leisure pursuits, etc. SASE required. Payment varies, on acceptance. Query or send complete manuscript.

NEWPORT LIFE—174 Bellevue Ave., Suite 207, Newport, RI 02840. Susan Ryan, Sr. Ed. Quarterly. Articles, 500 to 2,500 words, on the people and places of Newport County: general-interest and historical articles, interviews, profiles, investigative pieces, and photo-features. Departments, 500 to 750 words, include "At the Helm" (on some aspect of boating), "Arts Marquee," "Food for Thought," and "Down to Business." Photos must be available for all articles. Pays 10¢ a word, on publication. Query.

OUT—The Soho Bldg., 110 Greene St., Suite 600, New York, NY 10012.

Michael Goff, Ed.-in-Chief. Articles, 50 to 8,000 words, on various subjects (current affairs, culture, fitness, finance, etc.) of interest to gay and lesbian readers. "The best guide to what we publish is to read previous issues." Payment varies, on publication. Query. Guidelines.

OUT YOUR BACKDOOR— 4686 Meridian Rd., Williamston, MI 48895. Jeff Potter, Ed. Articles and fiction, 2,500 words, for thrifty, down-to-earth culture enthusiasts. "Budget travel, second-hand treasure, and homespun but high-quality culture all combine to yield an energetic, practical, folksy postmodern magazine." Study sample issue before submitting. Pays in copies.

PALM SPRINGS LIFE—Desert Publications, 303 N. Indian Canyon Dr., P.O. Box 2724, Palm Springs, CA 92263. Stewart Weiner, Ed. Articles, 1,000 to 3,000 words, of interest to "wealthy, upscale people who live and/or play in the desert." Pays $150 to $1,000 for features, $25 to $75 for short profiles, on publication. Query required.

THE PHOENIX—7152 Unity Ave. N., Brooklyn Ctr., MN 55429. Pat Samples, Ed. Tabloid. Articles, 800 to 1,500 words, on recovery, renewal, and growth. Department pieces for "12 Step," "Bodywise," "Family Skills," or "Personal Story." "Our readers are committed to physical, emotional, mental, and spiritual health and well-being. Read a sample copy to see what we publish." Pays 3¢ to 5¢ a word, on publication. Guidelines and calendar.

QUICK 'N EASY COUNTRY COOKIN'—Parkside Publications, Inc., P.O. Box 66, Davis, SD 57021–0066. Pam Schrag, Ed. Family-oriented articles, 400 to 500 words, on cooking, and articles with a human-interest/Christian perspective. Short verse, puzzles, and humorous fillers, up to 50 words. Pays $10 for articles, on publication.

ROBB REPORT—1 Acton Pl., Acton, MA 01720. Robert R. Feeman, Ed. Consumer magazine for the high-end/luxury market. Features on lifestyles, home interiors, boats, travel, investment opportunities, exotic automobiles, business, technology, etc. Payment varies, on publication. Query with SASE and published clips.

USAIR MAGAZINE—NYT Custom Publishing, 122 E. 42nd St., 14th Fl., New York, NY 10168. Catherine Sabino, Ed. Kathy Passero, Man. Ed. USAir inflight magazine. Articles on travel, lifestyle trends, sports, personality profiles, food and wine, shopping, the arts and culture. "Our goal is to provide readers with lively and colorful, yet practical articles that will make their lives and their leisure time more rewarding." Payment made within 60 days of acceptance. Query with clips; no unsolicited manuscripts.

VEGETARIAN VOICE—P.O. Box 72, Dolgeville, NY 13329. Jennie Collura, Sr. Ed. Quarterly. Informative, well-researched and/or inspiring articles, 600 to 1,800 words, on lifestyles and consumer concerns, health, nutrition, animal rights, the environment, world hunger, etc. "Our underlying philosophy is total vegetarian; all our recipes are vegan and we do not support the use of leather, wool, silk, etc." Guidelines. Pays in copies.

VIRTUE: THE CHRISTIAN MAGAZINE FOR WOMEN— 4050 Lee Vance View, Colorado Springs, CO 80918. Jeanette Thomason, Ed. Articles, 1,200 to 1,400 words, on family, marriage, self-esteem, working women; women's relationships with family, friends, and God. Fiction and poetry. Pays 15¢ to 25¢ a word, $25 to $50 for poetry, on publication. Query with SASE required.

WEIGHT WATCHERS MAGAZINE—360 Lexington Ave., New York, NY 10017. Randi Rose, Health Ed. Articles on health, nutrition, fitness, and weight-loss motivation and success. Pays from $500, on acceptance. Query with clips required. Guidelines.

WIRED—544 Second St., San Francisco, CA 94107–1427. Jessie Scanlon, Ed. Assoc. Lifestyle magazine for the "digital generation." Articles, essays, profiles, fiction, and other material that discusses the "meaning and context" of digital technology in today's world. Guidelines. Payment varies, on publication.

YOGA JOURNAL—2054 University Ave., Berkeley, CA 94704. Rick Fields, Ed. Articles, 1,200 to 4,000 words, on holistic health, spirituality, yoga, and transpersonal psychology; New Age profiles; interviews. Pays $100 to $1,200, on acceptance.

SPORTS AND RECREATION

ADVENTURE CYCLIST—Adventure Cycling Assn., P.O. Box 8308, Missoula, MT 59807. Daniel D'Ambrosio, Ed. Articles, 1,200 to 2,500 words: accounts of bicycle tours in the U.S. and overseas, interviews, personal-experience pieces, humor, and news shorts. Pays $25 to $65 per published page.

AKC GAZETTE—(formerly *Pure-Bred Dogs/American Kennel Gazette*) 51 Madison Ave., New York, NY 10010. Mark Roland, Features Ed. "The official journal of the sport of purebred dogs." Articles, 1,000 to 2,500 words, relating to purebred dogs, for serious fanciers. Pays $100 to $300, on acceptance. Queries preferred.

AMERICAN HUNTER—NRA Publications, 11250 Waples Mill Rd., Fairfax, VA 22030. Tom Fulgham, Ed. Articles, 1,400 to 2,000 words, on hunting. Photos. Pays on acceptance. Guidelines.

AMERICAN MOTORCYCLIST—American Motorcyclist Assn., 33 Collegeview Rd., Westerville, OH 43081–1484. Greg Harrison, Ed. Articles and fiction, to 3,000 words, on motorcycling: news coverage, personalities, tours. Photos. Pays varying rates, on publication. Query with SASE.

THE AMERICAN RIFLEMAN—11250 Waples Mill Rd., Fairfax, VA 22030. Mark Keefe, Man. Ed. Factual articles on use and enjoyment of sporting firearms. Pays on acceptance.

AMERICAN SQUAREDANCE MAGAZINE—661 Middlefield Rd., Salinas, CA 93906–1004. Jon Sanborn, Ed. Articles and fiction, 1,000 to 1,500 words, related to square dancing. Poetry. Fillers, to 100 words. Pays $1.50 per column inch.

ATLANTIC SALMON JOURNAL—P.O. Box 429, St. Andrews, N.B., Canada E0G 2X0. Harry Bruce, Ed. Articles, 1,500 to 3,000 words, related to Atlantic salmon: fishing, conservation, ecology, travel, politics, biology, how-tos, anecdotes. Pays $100 to $400, on publication.

BACKPACKER MAGAZINE—Rodale Press, 33 E. Minor St., Emmaus, PA 18098. John Viehman, Exec. Ed. Articles, 250 to 3,000 words, on self-propelled backcountry travel: backpacking, kayaking/canoeing, mountaineering; technique, nordic skiing, health, natural science. Photos. Pays varying rates. Query.

611

THE BACKSTRETCH—P.O. Box 7065, Louisville, KY 40257–0065. Barrett Shaw, Ed. United Thoroughbred Trainers of America. Feature articles, with photos, on subjects related to thoroughbred horse racing. Pays after publication. Sample issue and guidelines on request.

BACKWOODSMAN—P.O. Box 627, Westcliffe, CO 81252. Charlie Richie, Ed. Articles for the twentieth-century frontiersman: muzzleloading, primitive weapons, black powder cartridge guns, woodslore, survival, homesteading, trapping, etc. Historical and how-to articles. No payment.

BASEBALL FORECAST, BASEBALL ILLUSTRATED—See *Hockey Illustrated.*

BASKETBALL FORECAST—See *Hockey Illustrated.*

BASSIN'—NatCom, Inc., 5300 CityPlex Tower, 2448 E. 81st St., Tulsa, OK 74137–4207. Mark Chesnut, Exec. Ed. Articles, 1,200 to 1,400 words, on how and where to bass fish, for the amateur fisherman. Pays $300 to $500, on acceptance. Query.

BASSMASTER MAGAZINE—B.A.S.S. Publications, P.O. Box 17900, Montgomery, AL 36141. Dave Precht, Ed. Articles, 1,500 to 2,000 words, with photos, on freshwater black bass and striped bass. "Short Casts" pieces, 400 to 800 words, on news, views, and items of interest. Pays $200 to $400, on acceptance. Query.

BAY & DELTA YACHTSMAN—2019 Clement Ave., Alameda, CA 94501. Hal Schell, Ed. Cruising stories and features, how-tos. Must have northern California tie-in. Photos and illustrations. Pays varying rates.

BC OUTDOORS—1132 Hamilton St., #202, Vancouver, B.C., Canada V6B 2S2. Karl Bruhn, Ed. Articles, to 1,500 words, on fishing, hunting, conservation, and all forms of non-competitive outdoor recreation in British Columbia and Yukon. Photos. Pays from 20¢ to 27¢ a word, on acceptance.

BICYCLE GUIDE— 6420 Wilshire Blvd., Los Angeles, CA 90048–5515. Garrett Lai, Ed. Articles on cycling history, personality profiles, and photos for all-road cycling enthusiasts. Pays varying rates, on publication. Buys all rights. Query with clips.

BIRD WATCHER'S DIGEST—P.O. Box 110, Marietta, OH 45750. William H. Thompson, III, Ed. Articles, 600 to 2,500 words, for bird watchers: first-person accounts; how-tos; pieces on endangered species; profiles. Pays from $50, on publication. Submit complete manuscript.

BLACK BELT—P.O. Box 918, Santa Clarita, CA 91380–9018. Attn: Ed. Articles related to self-defense: how-tos on fitness and technique; historical, travel, philosophical subjects. Pays $100 to $300, on publication. Guidelines.

BOAT PENNSYLVANIA—Pennsylvania Fish and Boat Commission, P.O. Box 67000, Harrisburg, PA 17106–7000. Art Michaels, Ed. Articles, 200 to 2,500 words, with photos, on boating in Pennsylvania: motorboating, sailing, waterskiing, canoeing, kayaking, and personal watercraft. No pieces on fishing. Pays $50 to $250, on acceptance. Query. Guidelines.

BOUNDARY WATERS JOURNAL—9396 Rocky Ledge Rd., Ely, MN 55731. Stuart Osthoff, Ed. Articles, 2,000 to 3,000 words, on wilderness, recreation, nature, and conservation in Minnesota's Boundary Waters Canoe Area Wilderness and Ontario's Quetico Provincial Park. Regular features include canoe-route journals, fishing, camping, hiking, cross-country skiing, wildlife and nature, regional lifestyles, history, and events. Pays $200 to $400, on publication; $50 to $150 for photos.

BOW & ARROW HUNTING—Box 2429, 34249 Camino Capistrano, Capistrano Beach, CA 92624–0429. Roger Combs, Ed. Dir. Articles, 1,200 to 2,500 words, with B&W photos, on bowhunting; profiles and technical pieces. Pays $100 to $300, on acceptance. Same address and mechanical requirements for *Gun World.*

BOWHUNTER MAGAZINE—Box 8200, Harrisburg, PA 17105–8200. M.R. James, Ed. Informative, entertaining features, 500 to 2,000 words, on bow-and-arrow hunting. Fillers. Photos. "Study magazine first." Pays $50 to $300, on acceptance.

BOWLING—5301 S. 76th St., Greendale, WI 53129. Bill Vint, Ed. Articles, to 1,500 words, on all aspects of bowling, especially human interest. Profiles. "We're looking for unique, unusual stories about bowling people and places and occasionally publish business articles." Pays varying rates, on publication. Query required.

BUCKMASTERS WHITETAIL MAGAZINE—1801 W. Euless Blvd., Suite 150, Euless, TX 76040. Russell Thornberry, Exec. Ed. Semiannual. Articles and fiction, 2,500 words, for serious sportsmen. "Big Buck Adventures" articles capture the details and the adventure of the hunt of a newly discovered trophy. Fresh, new whitetail hunting how-tos; new biological information about whitetail deer that might help hunters; entertaining deer stories; and other department pieces. Photos a plus. Pays $250 to $400 for articles, on acceptance. Guidelines.

CALIFORNIA HORSE REVIEW—See *West Coast Horse Review.*

CANADIAN DIVER & WATERSPORT—See *Diver Magazine.*

CANOE AND KAYAK MAGAZINE—(formerly *Canoe*) P.O. Box 3146, Kirkland, WA 98083. Dennis Stuhaug, Man. Ed. Features, 1,100 to 2,000 words; department pieces, 500 to 1,000 words. Topics include canoeing or kayaking adventures, destinations, boat and equipment reviews, techniques and how-tos, short essays, camping, environment, humor, health, history, etc. Pays $5 per column inch, on publication. Query preferred. Guidelines.

CAR AND DRIVER—2002 Hogback Rd., Ann Arbor, MI 48105. Csaba Csere, Ed.-in-Chief. Articles, to 2,500 words, for enthusiasts, on new cars, classic cars, industry topics. "Ninety percent staff-written. Query with clips. No unsolicited manuscripts." Pays to $2,500, on acceptance.

CAR CRAFT—6420 Wilshire Blvd., Los Angeles, CA 90048. Chuck Schifsky, Ed. Articles and photo-features on high performance street machines, drag cars, racing events; technical pieces; action photos. Pays from $150 per page, on publication.

CASCADES EAST—716 N.E. Fourth St., P.O. Box 5784, Bend, OR 97708. Geoff Hill, Ed./Pub. Articles, 1,000 to 2,000 words, on outdoor activities (fishing, hunting, golfing, backpacking, rafting, skiing, snowmobiling, etc.), history, special events, and scenic tours in central Oregon Cascades. Photos. Pays 5¢ to 10¢ a word, extra for photos, on publication.

CASINO PLAYER—Bayport One, Suite 470, 8025 Black Horse Pike, W. Atlantic City, NJ 08232. Adam Fine, Ed. Articles, 1,000 to 2,000 words, with photos, for beginning to intermediate gamblers, on slots, video poker, and table games. No first-person or real-life gambling stories. Pays from $250, on publication.

CROSS COUNTRY SKIER—1823 Fremont Ave. S., Minneapolis, MN 55403. Jim Chase, Ed. Published October through February. Articles, to 2,000 words, on all aspects of cross-country skiing. Departments, 1,000 to 1,500 words, on ski maintenance, skiing techniques, health and fitness. Pays $300 to $700 for features, $100 to $350 for departments, on publication. Query.

CURRENTS—212 W. Cheyenne Mountain Blvd., Colorado Springs, CO 80906. Greg Moore, Ed. Quarterly. "Voice of the National Organization for River Sports." Articles, 500 to 2,000 words, for kayakers, rafters, and river canoeists, pertaining to whitewater rivers and/or river running. Fillers. B&W action photos. Pays from $40 for articles, $30 to $50 for photos, on publication. Queries preferred.

CYCLE WORLD—1499 Monrovia Ave., Newport Beach, CA 92663. David Edwards, Ed.-in-Chief. Technical and feature articles, 1,500 to 2,500 words, for motorcycle enthusiasts. Photos. Pays on publication. Query.

CYCLING U.S.A.—U.S. Cycling Federation, One Olympic Plaza, Colorado Springs, CO 80909. Frank Stanley, Ed. Articles, 500 to 1,000 words, on bicycle racing. Pays 10¢ to 15¢ a word, on publication. Query.

THE DIVER—P.O. Box 54788, St. Petersburg, FL 33739. Bob Taylor, Ed. Articles on divers, coaches, officials, springboard and platform techniques, training tips, etc. Pays $15 to $35, extra for photos ($5 to $10 for cartoons), on publication.

DIVER MAGAZINE—295–10991 Shellbridge Way, Richmond, B.C., Canada V6X 3C6. Stephanie Bold, Ed. Illustrated articles, 500 to 1,000 words, on dive destinations. Shorter pieces are also welcome. "Travel features should be brief and accompanied by excellent slides and/or prints and a map. Unsolicited articles will be reviewed only from August to October and will be considered for *Diver Magazine* and *Canadian Diver & Watersport*." Pays $2.50 per column inch, on publication. Guidelines. Limited market.

EQUUS—Fleet Street Corp., 656 Quince Orchard Rd., Gaithersburg, MD 20878. Laurie Prinz, Man. Ed. Articles, 1,000 to 3,000 words, on all breeds of horses, covering their health, care, the latest advances in equine medicine and research. "Attempt to speak as one horseperson to another." Pays $100 to $400, on publication.

FAMILY MOTOR COACHING—8291 Clough Pike, Cincinnati, OH 45244-2796. Pamela Wisby Kay, Ed. Articles, 1,500 to 2,000 words, on technical topics and travel routes and destinations accessible by motorhome. Payment varies, on acceptance. Query preferred.

FIELD & STREAM—2 Park Ave., New York, NY 10016. Duncan Barnes, Ed. Articles, 1,500 to 2,000 words, with photos, on hunting, fishing. Short articles, to 1,000 words. Fillers, 75 to 500 words. Cartoons. Pays from $800 for feature articles with photos, $75 to $500 for fillers, $100 for cartoons, on acceptance. Query for articles.

THE FLORIDA HORSE—P.O. Box 2106, Ocala, FL 34478. F. J. Audette, Ed. Articles, 1,500 words, on Florida thoroughbred breeding and racing. Also veterinary articles, financial articles, and articles of general interest. Pays $100 to $200, on publication. Query.

614

FLY FISHERMAN— 6405 Flank Dr., Box 8200, Harrisburg, PA 17105. Philip Hanyok, Man. Ed. Query.

FLY ROD & REEL—P.O. Box 370, Camden, ME 04843. James E. Butler, Ed. Fly-fishing pieces, 2,000 to 2,500 words, and occasional fiction; articles on the culture and history of the areas being fished. Pays on acceptance. Query.

FOOTBALL DIGEST—Century Publishing Co., 990 Grove St., Evanston, IL 60201. Kenneth Leiker, Ed. William Wagner, Assoc. Ed. Articles, 1,500 to 2,500 words, for the hard-core football fan: profiles of pro and college stars, nostalgia, trends in the sport. Pays on publication. Query.

FOOTBALL FORECAST—See *Hockey Illustrated.*

FUR-FISH-GAME—2878 E. Main St., Columbus, OH 43209. Mitch Cox, Ed. Illustrated articles, 800 to 2,500 words, preferably with how-to angle, on hunting, fishing, trapping, dogs, camping, or other outdoor topics. Some humorous or where-to articles. Pays $40 to $150, on acceptance.

GAME AND FISH PUBLICATIONS—P.O. Box 741, Marietta, GA 30061. Attn: Ed. Dept. Publishes 30 monthly outdoor magazines for 48 states. Articles, 1,500 to 2,500 words, on hunting and fishing. How-tos, where-tos, and adventure pieces. Profiles of successful hunters and fishermen. No hiking, canoeing, camping, or backpacking pieces. Pays $125 to $175 for state-specific articles, $200 to $250 for multi-state articles, before publication. Pays $25 to $75 for photos.

GOLF FOR WOMEN—P.O. Box 951989, Lake Mary, FL 32795–1989. Pat Baldwin, Ed.-in-Chief. Golf-related articles of interest to women; fillers and humor. Instructional pieces are staff-written. Pays from 40¢ a word, on publication. Query.

GOLF JOURNAL—Golf House, P.O. Box 708, Far Hills, NJ 07931–0708. Brett Avery, Ed. Articles on golf personalities, history, travel. Humor. Photos. Pays varying rates, on publication.

GOLF MAGAZINE—2 Park Ave., New York, NY 10016. Jim Frank, Ed. Articles, 1,000 words with photos, on golf history and travel (places to play around the world); profiles of professional tour players. Shorts, to 500 words. Pays 75¢ a word, on acceptance. Queries preferred.

GOLF TIPS—Werner Publishing Corp., 12121 Wilshire Blvd., #1220, Los Angeles, CA 90025–1175. Nick Mastroni, Ed. Articles, 500 to 1,500 words, for serious golfers: unique golf instruction, golf products, interviews with pro players. Fillers: short "shotmaking" instruction tips. Queries preferred. Pays $200 to $600, on publication.

THE GREYHOUND REVIEW—National Greyhound Assn., Box 543, Abilene, KS 67410. Tim Horan, Man. Ed. Articles, 1,000 to 10,000 words, pertaining to the greyhound racing industry: how-to, historical nostalgia, interviews. Pays $85 to $150, on publication.

GULF COAST GOLFER—See *North Texas Golfer.*

GUN DIGEST— 4092 Commercial Ave., Northbrook, IL 60062. Ken Warner, Ed. Well-researched articles, to 5,000 words, on guns and shooting, equipment, etc. Photos. Pays from 10¢ a word, on acceptance. Query.

GUN DOG—P.O. Box 35098, Des Moines, IA 50315. Bob Wilbanks, Man. Ed. Features, 1,000 to 2,500 words, with photos, on bird hunting: how-tos, where-tos, dog training, canine medicine, breeding strategy. Fiction. Humor.

Pays $150 to $300 for fillers and short articles, $150 to $400 for features, on acceptance.

GUN WORLD—See *Bow & Arrow Hunting.*

GUNS & AMMO—6420 Wilshire Blvd., Los Angeles, CA 90048. Kevin E. Steele, Ed. Technical and general articles, 800 to 2,500 words, on guns, ammunition, and target shooting. Photos, fillers. Pays from $150, on acceptance.

HANG GLIDING—U.S. Hang Gliding Assn., P.O. Box 1330, Colorado Springs, CO 80901–1330. Gilbert Dodgen, Ed. Articles, 2 to 3 pages, on hang gliding. Pays to $50, on publication. Query.

HOCKEY ILLUSTRATED—Lexington Library, Inc., 233 Park Ave. S., New York, NY 10003. Stephen Ciacciarelli, Ed. Articles, 2,500 words, on hockey players and teams. Pays $125, on publication. Query. Same address and requirements for *Baseball Illustrated, Wrestling World, Pro Basketball Illustrated, Pro Football Illustrated, Baseball Forecast, Pro Football Preview, Football Forecast,* and *Basketball Forecast.*

HORSE & RIDER—12265 W. Bayaud Ave., Suite 300, Lakewood, CO 80228. Sue M. Copeland, Ed. Articles, 500 to 3,000 words, with photos, on western riding and general horse care geared to the performance horse: training, feeding, grooming, health, etc. Pays varying rates, on publication. Buys one-time rights. Guidelines.

HORSEMEN'S YANKEE PEDLAR—83 Leicester St., N. Oxford, MA 01537. Nancy L. Khoury, Pub. News and feature-length articles, about horses and horsemen in the Northeast. Photos. Pays $2 per published inch, on publication. Query.

HORSEPLAY—P.O. Box 130, Gaithersburg, MD 20884. Lisa Kiser, Ed. Articles, 700 to 3,000 words, on eventing, show jumping, horse shows, and dressage for riders, horse owners, and sport horse enthusiasts. Profiles, instructional articles, occasional humor, and competition reports. Pays 10¢ a word for all rights, 9¢ a word for first North American rights, after publication. Query. SASE required. Guidelines.

HOT BOAT—Sport Publications, 8484 Wilshire Blvd., #900, Beverly Hills, CA 90211. Brett Bayne, Ed. Family-oriented articles, 600 to 1,000 words, on motorized water sport events and personalities: general-interest, how-to, and technical features. Pays $85 to $300, on publication. Query.

THE IN-FISHERMAN—Two In-Fish Dr., Brainerd, MN 56401–0999. Doug Stange, Ed. Published 7 times yearly. How-to articles, 1,500 to 4,500 words, on all aspects of freshwater fishing. Humorous or nostalgic looks at fishing, 1,000 to 1,500 words, for "Reflections" column. Pays $250 to $1,000, on acceptance.

INSIDE SPORTS—990 Grove St., Evanston, IL 60201. Kenneth Leiker, Ed. In-depth, insightful sports articles, player profiles. Payment varies, on publication. Query.

INSIDE TEXAS RUNNING—9514 Bristlebrook Dr., Houston, TX 77083–6193. Joanne Schmidt, Ed. Articles and fillers on running in Texas. Pays $35 to $100 for articles, $10 for photos and short fillers, on acceptance.

LAKELAND BOATING—1560 Sherman Ave., Suite 1220, Evanston, IL 60201–5047. Randall W. Hess, Ed. Articles for powerboat owners on the Great

Lakes and other area waterways, on long-distance cruising, short trips, maintenance, equipment, history, regional personalities and events, and environment. Photos. Pays on publication. Query. Guidelines.

MEN'S FITNESS—21100 Erwin St., Woodland Hills, CA 91367. Attn: Ed. Features, 1,500 to 1,800 words, and department pieces, 1,200 to 1,500 words: authoritative and practical articles dealing with fitness, health, and men's issues. Payment varies, on acceptance. Query with relevant clips.

MEN'S HEALTH—Rodale Press, 33 E. Minor St., Emmaus, PA 18098. Jeff Csatari, Sr. Ed. Articles, 1,000 to 2,500 words, on sports, fitness, diet, health, nutrition, relationships, and travel, for men ages 25 to 55. Pays from 50¢ a word, on acceptance. Query.

MICHIGAN OUT-OF-DOORS—P.O. Box 30235, Lansing, MI 48909. Kenneth S. Lowe, Ed. Features, 1,500 to 2,500 words, on hunting, fishing, camping, and conservation in Michigan. Pays $75 to $150, on acceptance.

MID-WEST OUTDOORS—111 Shore Dr., Hinsdale, IL 60521–5885. Gene Laulunen, Ed. Articles, 1,000 to 1,500 words, with photos, on where, when, and how to fish and hunt in the Midwest. No Canadian material. Pays $15 to $35, on publication.

MOTOR TREND—6420 Wilshire Blvd., Los Angeles, CA 90048–5515. C. Van Tune, Ed. Articles, 250 to 2,000 words, on autos, racing, events, and profiles. Photos. Pay varies, on acceptance. Query.

MOTORHOME MAGAZINE—3601 Calle Tecate, Camarillo, CA 93012. Barbara Leonard, Ed. Dir. Articles, to 2,000 words, with color slides, on motorhomes. Also travel and how-to pieces. Pays to $600, on acceptance.

MOUNTAIN BIKE—Rodale Press, 33 E. Minor St., Emmaus, PA 18098. Nelson Pena, Exec. Ed. Articles, 500 to 2,000 words, on mountain-bike touring; major off-road cycling events; political, sport, or land-access issues; riding techniques; fitness and training tips. Pays $100 to $650, on publication. Query.

NATIONAL PARKS MAGAZINE—1776 Massachusetts Ave. N.W., Washington, DC 20036. Sue E. Dodge, Ed. Articles, 1,500 to 2,500 words, on areas in the National Park system, proposed new areas, threats to parks or park wildlife, new trends in park use, legislative issues, and endangered species of plants or animals relevant to national parks. No fiction, poetry, personal narratives, "My trip to . . ." stories, or straight travel pieces. Pays $100 to $800, on acceptance. Query. Guidelines.

NEW YORK OUTDOORS—51 Atlantic Ave., Floral Park, NY 11001. John Tsaousis, Ed. Features, 1,500 to 1,800 words, with color transparencies, on any aspect of outdoor recreation. No hunting or fishing. Pays to $250 for major features. Query preferred.

NORTH TEXAS GOLFER—9182 Old Katy Rd., Suite 212, Houston, TX 77055. Steve Hunter, Ed./Pub. Articles, 800 to 1,500 words, of interest to golfers in north Texas. Pays $50 to $250, on publication. Queries required. Same requirements for *Gulf Coast Golfer* (for golfers in south Texas).

NORTHEAST OUTDOORS—P.O. Box 2180, Waterbury, CT 06722–2180. Michael Griffin, Man. Ed. Articles, 500 to 1,000 words, preferably with B&W photos, on camping and recreational vehicle (RV) touring in northeast U.S.: recommended private campgrounds, camp cookery, recreational vehicle hints. Stress how-to, where-to. Cartoons. Pays $20 to $80, on publication. Guidelines.

OFFSHORE—220 Reservoir St., Needham Heights, MA 02194. Pat Erickson, Ed. Articles, 1,200 to 2,500 words, on boats, people, places, maritime history, and events along the New England, New York, and New Jersey coasts. Writers should be knowledgeable boaters. Photos a plus. Pays $250 to $500.

OPEN WHEEL—P.O. Box 715, Ipswich, MA 01938. Dick Berggren, Ed. Articles, to 6,000 words, on open wheel drivers, races, and vehicles. Photos. Pays to $400 on publication.

OUTDOOR AMERICA—707 Conservation Ln., Gaithersburg, MD 20878–2983. Attn: Articles Ed. Quarterly publication of the Izaak Walton League of America. Articles, 1,250 to 2,000 words, on natural resource conservation issues and outdoor recreation; especially fishing, hunting, and camping. Also, short items, 500 to 750 words. Pays 20¢ a word. Query with published clips.

OUTDOOR CANADA—703 Evans Ave., Suite 202, Toronto, Ont., Canada M9C 5E9. Ms. Teddi Brown, Ed. Published 8 times yearly. Articles, 1,500 to 2,000 words, on fishing, camping, hiking, canoeing, hunting, and wildlife. Pays $200 to $600, on publication.

OUTSIDE—Outside Plaza, 400 Market St., Santa Fe, NM 87501. No unsolicited material.

PADDLER MAGAZINE—P.O. Box 775450, Steamboat Springs, CO 80477. Eugene Buchanan, Ed. Dir. Articles on canoeing, kayaking, rafting, sea kayaking. "Best way to break in is to target a specific department, i.e. 'Hotlines,' 'Paddle People,' etc." Pays $5 an inch, on publication. Query preferred. Guidelines.

PENNSYLVANIA ANGLER—Pennsylvania Fish and Boat Commission, P.O. Box 67000, Harrisburg, PA 17106–7000. Attn: Art Michaels, Ed. Articles, 500 to 3,000 words, with photos, on freshwater fishing in Pennsylvania. Pays $50 to $250, on acceptance. Must send SASE with all material. Query. Guidelines.

PENNSYLVANIA GAME NEWS—Game Commission, 2001 Elmerton Ave., Harrisburg, PA 17110–9797. Bob Mitchell, Ed. Articles, to 2,500 words, on outdoor subjects, except fishing and boating. Photos. Pays from 6¢ a word, extra for photos, on acceptance.

PETERSEN'S BOWHUNTING—6420 Wilshire Blvd., Los Angeles, CA 90048–5515. Greg Tinsley, Ed. How-to articles, 2,000 to 2,500 words, on bowhunting. Also pieces on where to bowhunt, unusual techniques and equipment, and profiles of successful bowhunters will also be considered. Photos must accompany all manuscripts. Pays $300 to $400, on acceptance. Query.

PETERSEN'S HUNTING—6420 Wilshire Blvd., 14th Fl., Los Angeles, CA 90048–5515. Todd Smith, Ed. How-to articles, 2,250 words, on all aspects of sport hunting. B&W photos; color slides. Pays $300 to $500, on acceptance. Query.

PLANE & PILOT—12121 Wilshire Blvd., #1220, Los Angeles, CA 90025–1175. Steve Higginson, Features Ed. Aviation related articles, 1,500 to 3,000 words, targeted to the single engine, piston powered recreational pilot. Training, maintenance, travel, equipment, pilot reports. Occasional features on antique, classic, and kit-or home-built aircraft. Payment varies, on publication. Query preferred.

POWER AND MOTORYACHT—245 W. 17th St., New York, NY 10011. Diane M. Byrne, Assoc. Ed. Articles, 1,000 to 2,000 words, for owners of powerboats, 24 feet and larger. Seamanship, ship's systems, maintenance, sportfishing news, travel destinations, profiles of individuals working to improve the marine environment. "For our readers, powerboating is truly a lifestyle, not just a hobby." Pays $500 to $1,000, on acceptance. Query required.

POWERBOAT—1691 Spinnaker Dr., Suite 206, Ventura, CA 93001. Eric Colby, Ed. Articles, to 1,500 words, with photos, for high performance powerboat owners, on outstanding achievements, water-skiing, competitions; technical articles on hull and engine developments; how-to pieces. Pays $300 to $1,000, on acceptance. Query.

PRACTICAL HORSEMAN—Box 589, Unionville, PA 19375. Mandy Lorraine, Ed. How-to articles conveying experts' advice on English riding, training, and horse care. Pays on acceptance. Query with clips.

PRIVATE PILOT—P.O. Box 6050, Mission Viejo, CA 92690–6050. Joseph P. O'Leary, Ed. Hands-on how-to aviation articles, 1,000 to 3,000 words, for general aviation pilots, aircraft owners, and aviation enthusiasts. Photos. Pays $75 to $450, on publication. Query.

PRO BASKETBALL ILLUSTRATED—See *Hockey Illustrated.*

PRO FOOTBALL ILLUSTRATED, PRO FOOTBALL PREVIEW—See *Hockey Illustrated.*

PURE-BRED DOGS/AMERICAN KENNEL GAZETTE—See *AKC Gazette.*

RESTORATION—P.O. Box 50046, Tucson, AZ 85703–1046. W.R. Haessner, Ed. Articles, 1,200 to 1,800 words, on restoration of autos, trucks, planes, trains, etc., and related building (bridges and structures). Photos. Pays from $25 per page, on publication. Queries required.

RIDER—3601 Calle Tecate, Camarillo, CA 93012. Mark Tuttle Jr., Ed. Articles, to 3,000 words, with slides, on travel, touring, commuting, and camping motorcyclists. Pays $100 to $750, on publication. Query.

ROCK + ICE MAGAZINE—603A S. Broadway, Boulder, CO 80303. Marjorie McCloy, Ed. Bimonthly. Articles, 500 to 6,000 words, and fiction, 1,500 to 4,000 words, for technical rock and ice climbers: sport climbers, mountaineers, alpinists, and other adventurers. Slides and B&W photos considered. Query. Pays $200 per published page.

RUNNER TRIATHLETE NEWS—P.O. Box 19909, Houston, TX 77224. Lance Phegley, Ed. Articles on running for road racing and multi-sport enthusiasts in TX, OK, NM, LA, and AR. Payment varies, on publication.

SAFARI—4800 W. Gates Pass Rd., Tucson, AZ 85745. William Quimby, Publications Dir. Articles, 2,000 words, on worldwide big game hunting. Pays $200, extra for photos, on publication.

SAIL—275 Washington St., Newton, MA 02158–1630. Patience Wales, Ed. Articles, 1,500 to 3,500 words, features, 1,000 to 2,500 words, with photos, on sailboats, equipment, racing, and cruising. How-tos on navigation, sail trim, etc. Pays $75 to $1,000 on publication. Guidelines.

SAILING—125 E. Main St., Port Washington, WI 53074. M. L. Hutchins, Ed. Features, 700 to 1,500 words, with photos, on cruising and racing; first-person accounts; profiles of boats and regattas. Query for technical or how-to pieces. Pays varying rates, 30 days after publication. Guidelines.

SALT WATER SPORTSMAN—77 Franklin St., Boston, MA 02110. Barry Gibson, Ed. Articles, 1,200 to 1,500 words, on how anglers can improve their skills, and on new places to fish off the coast of the U.S. and Canada, Central America, the Caribbean, and Bermuda. Photos a plus. Pays $350 to $700, on acceptance. Query.

SEA, BEST OF BOATING IN THE WEST—17782 Cowan, Suite C, Irvine, CA 92714. Ester Ellis, Sr. Ed. Features, 800 to 1,500 words, and news articles, 200 to 250 words, of interest to West Coast power boaters: profiles of boating personalities, cruise destinations, analyses of marine environmental issues, technical pieces on navigation and seamanship, news from western harbors. No fiction, poetry, or cartoons. Pays varying rates, on publication.

SEA KAYAKER—P.O. Box 17170, Seattle, WA 98107–0870. Christopher Cunningham, Ed. Articles, 400 to 4,500 words, on ocean kayaking. Related fiction. Pays about 12¢ a word, on publication. Query with clips and international reply coupons.

SHOTGUN SPORTS—P.O. Box 6810, Auburn, CA 95604. Frank Kodl, Ed. Articles with photos, on trap and skeet shooting, sporting clays, hunting with shotguns, reloading, gun tests, and instructional shooting. Pays $25 to $200, on publication.

SILENT SPORTS—717 10th St., P.O. Box 152, Waupaca, WI 54981–9990. Attn: Ed. Articles, 1,000 to 2,000 words, on bicycling, cross country skiing, running, canoeing, hiking, backpacking, and other "silent" sports. Must have regional (upper Midwest) focus. Pays $50 to $100 for features; $20 to $50 for fillers, on publication. Query.

SKI MAGAZINE—2 Park Ave., New York, NY 10016. Lisa Gosselin, Exec. Ed. Articles, 1,300 to 2,000 words, for experienced skiers: profiles, and destination articles. Short, 100-to 300-word, news items for "Ski Life" column. Equipment and racing articles are staff-written. Query (with clips) for articles. Pays from $50, on acceptance.

SKIN DIVER MAGAZINE— 6420 Wilshire Blvd., Los Angeles, CA 90048–5515. Bill Gleason, Pub./Ed. Illustrated articles, 500 to 2,000 words, on scuba diving activities, equipment, and dive sites. Pays $50 per published page, on publication.

SKYDIVING MAGAZINE—1725 N. Lexington Ave., DeLand, FL 32724. Michael Truffer, Ed. Timely news articles, 300 to 800 words, relating to sport and military parachuting. Fillers. Photos. Pays $25 to $200, extra for photos, on publication.

SOCCER JR.—27 Unquowa Rd., Fairfield, CT 06430. Joe Provey, Ed. Articles, fiction, and fillers related to soccer for readers in 5th and 6th grade. Pays $450 for features; $250 for department pieces, on acceptance. Query.

SOUTH CAROLINA WILDLIFE—P. O. Box 167, Columbia, SC 29202–0167. John E. Davis, Ed. Articles, 1,000 to 2,000 words, with state and regional outdoor focus: conservation, natural history, wildlife, and recreation. Profiles, how-tos. Pays on acceptance.

SOUTHERN OUTDOORS—5845 Carmichael Rd., Montgomery, AL 36117. Larry Teague, Ed. Essays, 1,200 to 1,500 words, related to the outdoors. Pays 15¢ to 20¢ a word, on acceptance.

SPORT MAGAZINE— 6420 Wilshire Blvd., Los Angeles, CA 90048. Cam Benty, Ed. Dir. No fiction, poetry, or first person. Query with clips.

SPORTS ILLUSTRATED—1271 Ave. of the Americas, New York, NY 10020. Chris Hunt, Articles Ed. Query.

SPUR MAGAZINE—P. O. Box 2123, Augusta, GA 30903–2123. Attn: Ed. Dept. Articles, 300 to 5,000 words, on thoroughbred racing, breeding, polo, show jumping, eventing, and steeplechasing. Profiles of people and farms. Historical and nostalgia pieces. Pays $50 to $400, on publication. Query.

STARTING LINE—P.O. Box 19909, Houston, TX 77224. Lance Phegley, Ed. Quarterly. Articles, 800 to 1,200 words, for coaches, parents, and children, 8 to 18, on training for track and field, cross country, and racewalking, including techniques, health and fitness, nutrition, sports medicine, and related issues. Payment varies, on publication.

STOCK CAR RACING—P.O. Box 715, Ipswich, MA 01938. Dick Berggren, Feature Ed. Articles, to 6,000 words, on stock car drivers, races, and vehicles. Photos. Pays to $400, on publication.

SURFING—P. O. Box 3010, San Clemente, CA 92674. Nick Carroll, Ed. Skip Snead, Asst. Ed. Short newsy and humorous articles, 200 to 500 words. No first-person travel articles. "Knowledge of the sport is essential." Pays varying rates, on publication.

SWEAT—736 E. Loyola Dr., Tempe, AZ 85282. Joan Westlake, Ed. Articles, 500 to 1,200 words, on sports or fitness with an Arizona angle. "No personal articles or tales. We want investigative pieces. Articles must relate specifically to Arizona or Arizonans." Pays $25 to $60 for articles; $12 to $70 for photos, on publication. Queries required; no unsolicited manuscripts.

TENNIS—5520 Park Ave., P. O. Box 0395, Trumbull, CT 06611–0395. Donna Doherty, Ed. Instructional articles, features, profiles of tennis stars, grassroots articles, humor, 800 to 2,000 words. Photos. Pays from $300, on publication. Query.

TENNIS WEEK—341 Madison Ave., #600, New York, NY 10017–3705. Eugene L. Scott, Pub. Kim Kodl, Cherry V. Masih, Merrill Chapman, Man. Eds. In-depth, researched articles, from 1,000 words, on current issues and personalities in the game. Pays $125, on publication.

TRAILER BOATS—20700 Belshaw Ave., Carson, CA 90746–3510. Randy Scott, Ed. Lifestyle, technical and how-to articles, 500 to 2,000 words, on boat, trailer, or tow vehicle maintenance and operation; skiing, fishing, and cruising. Fillers, humor. Pays $100 to $700, on acceptance.

TRAILER LIFE—3601 Calle Tecate, Camarillo, CA 93012. Barbara Leonard, Ed. Articles, to 2,000 words, with photos, on trailering, truck campers, motorhomes, hobbies, and RV lifestyles. How-to pieces. Pays to $600, on acceptance. Guidelines.

TRAILS-A-WAY—Woodall Publishing Co., P.O. Box 5000, Lake Forest, IL 60045–5000. Debbie Harmsen, Ed. RV-related travel articles, 1,000 to 1,200 words, for Midwest camping families. Pay varies, on publication.

VELONEWS—1830 N. 55th St., Boulder, CO 80301. John Wilcockson, Ed. Articles, 500 to 1,500 words, on competitive cycling, training, nutrition; profiles, interviews. No how-to or touring articles. "We focus on the elite of the sport." Pay varies, on publication.

THE WALKING MAGAZINE—9–11 Harcourt, Boston, MA 02116. Seth Bauer, Ed. Articles, 1,500 to 2,000 words, on fitness, health, equipment, nutrition, travel, and adventure, famous walkers, and other walking-related topics. Shorter pieces, 500 to 1,500 words, and essays for "Ramblings" page. Photos welcome. Pays $750 to $2,500 for features, $100 to $600 for department pieces, on acceptance. Guidelines.

WEST COAST HORSE REVIEW—(formerly *California Horse Review*) 9560 S.W. Nimbus, Beaverton, OR 97008. Attn: Ed. Articles, 750 to 2,500 words, on horse training, for professional horsemen; profiles of prominent West Coast horses and riders. Pays $35 to $125, on publication.

THE WESTERN HORSEMAN—P.O. Box 7980, Colorado Springs, CO 80933–7980. Pat Close, Ed. Articles, about 1,500 words, with photos, on care and training of horses; farm, ranch, and stable management; health care and veterinary medicine. Pays to $400, on acceptance.

WESTERN OUTDOORS—3197-E Airport Loop, Costa Mesa, CA 92626. Attn: Ed. Timely, factual articles on fishing, 1,200 to 1,500 words, of interest to western sportsmen. Pays $400 to $500, on acceptance. Query. Guidelines.

WESTERN SPORTSMAN—140 Ave. F N., Saskatoon, Sask., Canada S7L 1V8. George Gruenefeld, Ed. Articles, to 2,500 words, on hunting and fishing in British Columbia, Alberta, Saskatchewan, and Manitoba; how-to pieces. Photos. Pays $75 to $300, on acceptance.

WINDSURFING—P.O. Box 2456, Winter Park, FL 32790. Tom James, Ed. Features, instructional pieces, and tips, by experienced boardsailors. Fast action photos. Pays $50 to $75 for tips, $250 to $300 for features, extra for photos. SASE for guidelines.

WINDY CITY SPORTS—1450 W. Randolph, Chicago, IL 60607. Jeff Banowetz, Ed. Articles, 1,000 words, on amateur sports in Chicago. Pays $100, on publication. Query required.

WOMAN BOWLER—1912 Grand Ave., Des Moines, IA 50309. Paula Marshall, Ed. Profiles, interviews, and news articles, to 1,000 words, for and about women bowlers and the sport of bowling. Pays varying rates, on acceptance. Query with outline.

WOMEN'S SPORTS & FITNESS—2025 Pearl St., Boulder, CO 80302. Mary Duffy, Ed. Articles on fitness, nutrition, outdoor sports; how-tos; profiles; adventure travel pieces; and controversial issues in women's sports, 500 to 2,000 words. Pays on publication.

WRESTLING WORLD—See *Hockey Illustrated*.

YACHTING—2 Park Ave., New York, NY 10016. Charles Barthold, Ed. Articles, 1,500 words, on upscale recreational power and sail boating. How-to and personal-experience pieces. Photos. Pays $350 to $1,000, on acceptance. Queries preferred.

AUTOMOTIVE MAGAZINES

AAA WORLD—See *Car & Travel*.

AMERICAN MOTORCYCLIST—American Motorcyclist Assn., 33 Collegeview Rd., Westerville, OH 43081–1484. Greg Harrison, Ed. Articles and fiction, to 3,000 words, on motorcycling: news coverage, personalities, tours. Photos. Pays varying rates, on publication. Query with SASE.

CAR AND DRIVER—2002 Hogback Rd., Ann Arbor, MI 48105. Csaba Csere, Ed. Articles, to 2,500 words, for enthusiasts, on new cars, classic cars, industry topics. "Ninety percent staff-written. Query with clips. No unsolicited manuscripts." Pays to $2,500, on acceptance.

CAR & TRAVEL—(formerly *AAA World*) 1000 AAA Dr., Heathrow, FL 32746–5063. Douglas Damerst, Ed. Automobile and travel concerns, including automotive travel, purchasing, and upkeep, 750 to 1,500 words. Pays $300 to $600, on acceptance. Query with clips; articles are by assignment only.

CAR AUDIO AND ELECTRONICS—21700 Oxnard St., Woodland Hills, CA 91367. Bill Neill, Ed. Features, 1,000 to 2,000 words, on electronic products for the car: audio systems, security systems, radar detectors, etc.; how to buy them; how they work; how to use them. "To write for us, you must know this subject thoroughly." Pays $200 to $1,000, on acceptance.

CAR CRAFT—6420 Wilshire Blvd., Los Angeles, CA 90048. Chuck Schifsky, Ed. Articles and photo-features on high performance street machines, drag cars, racing events; technical pieces; action photos. Pays from $150 per page, on publication.

CYCLE WORLD—1499 Monrovia Ave., Newport Beach, CA 92663. David Edwards, Ed.-in-Chief. Technical and feature articles, 1,500 to 2,500 words, for motorcycle enthusiasts. Photos. Pays $100 to $200 per page, on publication. Query.

MOTOR TREND—6420 Wilshire Blvd., Los Angeles, CA 90048–5515. C. Van Tune, Ed. Articles, 250 to 2,000 words, on autos, racing, events, and profiles. Photos. Pay varies, on acceptance. Query.

MOTORCYCLIST—6420 Wilshire Blvd., Los Angeles, CA 90048–5515. Mitch Boehm, Ed. Articles, 1,000 to 3,000 words. Photos. Pays $150 to $300 per published page, on publication.

OPEN WHEEL—See *Stock Car Racing*.

RESTORATION—P.O. Box 50046, Tucson, AZ 85703–1046. W.R. Haessner, Ed. Articles, 1,200 to 1,800 words, on restoration of autos, trucks, planes, trains, etc., and related building (bridges, structures, etc.). Photos. Pays from $25 per page, on publication. Queries required.

RIDER—3601 Calle Tecate, Camarillo, CA 93012. Mark Tuttle Jr., Ed. Articles, to 3,000 words, with color slides, on travel, touring, commuting, and camping motorcyclists. Pays $100 to $750, on publication. Query.

ROAD KING—Hammock Publishing, 3322 W. End Ave., Suite 700, Nashville, TN 37203. Tom Berg, Ed. Bill Hudgins, Ed. Dir. Bimonthly. Articles, 300 to 1,500 words, on business of trucking from a driver's point of view; profiles of drivers and their rigs; technical aspects of trucking equipment; trucking history; travel destinations near major interstates; humor; fillers. No fiction. Include clips with submission. Pays negotiable rates, on publication.

STOCK CAR RACING—P.O. Box 715, Ipswich, MA 01938. Dick Berggren, Ed. Features, technical automotive pieces, and profiles of interesting racing personalities, to 6,000 words, for oval track racing enthusiasts. Fillers. Pays $75 to $350, on publication. Same requirements for *Open Wheel.*

TRUCKERS/USA—P.O. Box 323, Windber, PA 15963. David Adams, Ed.

Articles, 500 to 1,000 words, on the trucking business and marketing. Poetry and trucking-related fiction. Pays $50 for articles, $10 for poems, on publication.

FITNESS MAGAZINES

AMERICAN FITNESS—15250 Ventura Blvd., Suite 200, Sherman Oaks, CA 91403. Peg Jordan, Ed. Rhonda Wilson, Man. Ed. Articles, 500 to 1,500 words, on exercise, health, trends, sports, nutrition, alternative paths, etc. Illustrations, photos.

FIT MAGAZINE—(formerly *New Body*) 1700 Broadway, New York, NY 10019. Nicole Dorsey, Ed. Lively, readable service-oriented articles, 800 to 1,200 words, on exercise, nutrition, lifestyle, diet, and health for women ages 18 to 35. Writers should have some background in or knowledge of the health field. Also considers 500-word essays for "How I Lost It" column by writers who have lost weight and kept it off. Pays $100 to $300, on publication. Query.

FITNESS—Gruner & Jahr USA Publishing, 110 Fifth Ave., New York, NY 10011. Rona Cherry, Ed. Articles, 500 to 2,000 words, on health, exercise, sports, nutrition, diet, psychological well-being, alternative therapies, sex, and beauty for readers around 30 years old. Pays $1 per word, on acceptance. Queries required.

IDEA PERSONAL TRAINER— 6190 Cornerstone Ct. E., Suite 204, San Diego, CA 92121–3773. Terese Hannon, Asst. Ed. Association publication for personal fitness trainers. Articles on exercise science; program design; profiles of successful trainers; business, legal, and marketing topics; tips for networking with other trainers and with allied medical professionals; client counseling; and training tips. "What's New" column includes industry news, products, and research. Payment varies, on acceptance. Query.

IDEA TODAY— 6190 Cornerstone Ct. E., Suite 204, San Diego, CA 92121–3773. Terese Hannon, Asst. Ed. Practical articles, 1,000 to 3,000 words, on new exercise programs, business management, nutrition, sports medicine, dance-exercise, and one-to-one training techniques. Articles must be geared toward the aerobics instructor, exercise studio owner or manager, or personal trainer. No consumer or general health articles. Payment is negotiable, on acceptance. Query preferred.

INSIDE TEXAS RUNNING— 9514 Bristlebrook Dr., Houston, TX 77083–6193. Joanne Schmidt, Ed. Articles and fillers on running in Texas. Pays $35 to $100, $10 to $25 for photos, on acceptance.

MEN'S FITNESS—21100 Erwin St., Woodland Hills, CA 91367. Peter Sikowitz, Ed.-in-Chief. Features, 1,500 to 1,800 words, and department pieces, 1,200 to 1,500 words: "authoritative and practical articles dealing with fitness, health, and men's issues." Pays $500 to $1,000, on acceptance. Limited market.

MEN'S HEALTH—Rodale Press, 33 E. Minor St., Emmaus, PA 18098. Jeff Csatari, Sr. Ed. Articles, 1,000 to 2,500 words, on fitness, diet, health, relationships, sports, and travel, for men ages 25 to 55. Pays from 50¢ a word, on acceptance. Query.

NATURAL HEALTH: THE GUIDE TO WELL-BEING—17 Station St., Box 1200, Brookline Village, MA 02147. Bimonthly. Features, 1,500 to 3,000 words: practical information, new discoveries, and current trends about natural health and living. Topics include: natural goods and medicines, alternative health care, nutrition, wellness, personal fitness, and modern holistic teachings. Departments and columns, 250 to 1,000 words. Pays varying rates, on acceptance.

NEW BODY—See *Fit Magazine.*

THE PHYSICIAN AND SPORTSMEDICINE— 4530 W. 77th St., Minneapolis, MN 55435. Terry Monahan, Exec. Ed. News and feature articles. Clinical articles must be co-authored by physicians. Sports medicine angle necessary. Pays $150 to $1,000, on acceptance. Query. Guidelines.

SHAPE—21100 Erwin St., Woodland Hills, CA 91367–3772. Elizabeth Turner, Asst. Ed. Articles, 1,200 to 1,500 words, with new and interesting ideas on the physical and mental side of getting and staying in shape; reports, 300 to 400 words, on journal research. Payment varies, on publication. Guidelines. Limited market; most bylines by experts.

SWEAT—736 E. Loyola Dr., Tempe, AZ 85282. Joan Westlake, Ed. Articles, 500 to 1,200 words, on sports or fitness with an Arizona angle. "No personal articles or tales. We want investigative pieces. Articles must relate specifically to Arizona or Arizonans." Pays $25 to $60 for articles; $12 to $70 for photos, on publication. Queries required; no unsolicited manuscripts.

TOTAL HEALTH—165 N. 100 E. #2, St. George, UT 84770. Robert L. Smith, Ed. Articles, 1,200 to 1,400 words, on fitness, diet, preventive health care, and mental health. Pays $50 to $75, on publication. Queries preferred.

VEGETARIAN TIMES—P.O. Box 570, Oak Park, IL 60303. Toni Apgar, Ed. Dir. Articles, 1,200 to 2,500 words, on vegetarian cooking, nutrition, health and fitness, and profiles of prominent vegetarians. "News Items" and "In Print" (book reviews), to 500 words. "Herbalist" pieces, to 1,800 words, on medicinal uses of herbs. Queries required. Pays $75 to $1,000, on acceptance. Guidelines.

VIM & VIGOR— 8805 N. 23rd Ave., Suite 400, Phoenix, AZ 85021. Fred Petrovsky, Ed. Positive articles, with accurate medical facts, on health and fitness, 1,200 to 2,000 words, by assignment only. Writers may submit qualifications for assignment. Pays $500, on acceptance. Guidelines.

THE WALKING MAGAZINE— 9–11 Harcourt, Boston, MA 02116. Seth Bauer, Ed. Articles, 1,500 to 2,500 words, on fitness, health, equipment, nutrition, travel and adventure, famous walkers, and other walking-related topics. Shorter pieces, 150 to 800 words, and essays for "Ramblings" page. Photos welcome. Pays $750 to $1,800 for features, $100 to $500 for department pieces, within a week of acceptance. Guidelines.

WEIGHT WATCHERS MAGAZINE—360 Lexington Ave., New York, NY 10017. Randi Rose, Health Ed. Articles on health, nutrition, fitness, and weight-loss motivation and success. Pays from $500, on acceptance. Query with clips required. Guidelines.

WOMEN'S SPORTS & FITNESS—2025 Pearl St., Boulder, CO 80302. Mary Duffy, Ed. Articles on fitness, nutrition, outdoor sports; how-tos; profiles; adventure travel pieces; and controversial issues in women's sports, 500 to 2,000 words. Pays on publication.

YOGA JOURNAL—2054 University Ave., Berkeley, CA 94704. Rick Fields, Ed. Articles, 1,200 to 4,000 words, on holistic health, meditation, consciousness, spirituality, and yoga. Pays $50 to $800, on publication.

YOUR HEALTH—1720 Washington Blvd., Box 10010, Ogden, UT 84409. Attn: Ed. Staff. Articles, 1,000 words, on individual health care needs: fitness, low-impact aerobics, nutrition, prevention and treatment, etc. Color photos required. Pays 15¢ a word, on acceptance.

CONSUMER/PERSONAL FINANCE

BLACK ENTERPRISE—130 Fifth Ave., New York, NY 10011. Earl G. Graves, Ed. Articles on money management, careers, political issues, entrepreneurship, high technology, and lifestyles for black professionals. Profiles. Pays on acceptance. Query.

COMPLETE WOMAN—875 N. Michigan Ave., Suite 3434, Chicago, IL 60611. Bonnie Krueger, Ed. Martha Carlson, Assoc. Ed. Articles, 1,000 to 2,000 words, with how-to sidebars, giving advice to women. Also interested in reprints. Pays varying rates, on publication. Query with clips.

CONSUMERS DIGEST—5705 N. Lincoln Ave., Chicago, IL 60659. John Manos, Ed. Articles, 500 to 3,000 words, on subjects of interest to consumers: products and services, automobiles, travel, health, fitness, consumer legal affairs, and personal money management. Photos. Pays from 35¢ to 50¢ a word, extra for photos, on acceptance. Query with resumé and clips.

ESSENCE—1500 Broadway, New York, NY 10036. Susan L. Taylor, Ed.-in-Chief. Linda Villarosa, Ed. Articles, 800 to 2,500 words, for black women in America today, on business and finance, as well as health, art, travel, politics, and celebrity profiles, self-help pieces, how-tos. Payment varies, on acceptance. Query.

FAMILY CIRCLE—110 Fifth Ave., New York, NY 10011. Nancy Clark, Deputy Ed. Susan Sherry, Sr. Ed. Enterprising, creative, and practical articles, 1,000 to 1,500 words, on investing, smart ways to save money, secrets of successful entrepreneurs, and consumer news on smart shopping. Pays $1 a word, on acceptance. Query with clips.

FAMILY LIFE—Wenner Media, 1290 Ave. of the Americas, New York, NY 10104–0298. Attn: Ed. Dept. Articles, 1,000 to 4,000 words, on money and finances of interest to active parents of children ages 3 to 12. Other subjects of interest include education, travel, health, community service. Payment varies. Query with clips.

GOOD HOUSEKEEPING—959 Eighth Ave., New York, NY 10019. Joan Thursh, Articles Ed. Short advice-driven articles on money, finances, consumer issues, health, and safety for "Better Way" section. Pays good rates, on acceptance. Guidelines.

HOME MECHANIX—2 Park Ave., New York, NY 10016. Michael Chotiner, Ed. Home improvement articles, remodeling, maintenance, home finances. Time-or money-saving tips for the home, garage, or yard; seasonal reminders for homeowners. Pays $50, on acceptance.

KEY HORIZONS—Gateway Plaza, 950 N. Meridian, Suite 1200, Indianapolis, IN 46204. Joan Todd, Man. Ed. General-interest articles and department pieces, 1,500 words, for readers ages 50 and over in the Midwest, East, and Southwest. Departments include money, finance, domestic travel (no first-person pieces), and better living (gardening, cooking, etc.), health. No nostalgia or first-person retrospectives. Pays $50 to $500, on publication.

KIPLINGER'S PERSONAL FINANCE MAGAZINE—1729 H St. N.W., Washington, DC 20006. Attn: Ed. Dept. Articles on personal finance (i.e., buying insurance, mutual funds). Pays varying rates, on acceptance. Query required.

KIWANIS—3636 Woodview Trace, Indianapolis, IN 46468. Chuck Jonak, Man. Ed. Articles, 2,500 words, on financial planning for younger families and retirement planning for older people. Pays $400 to $1,000, on acceptance. Query required.

MODERN BRIDE—249 W. 17th St., New York, NY 10011. Mary Ann Cavlin, Exec. Ed. Articles, 1,500 to 2,000 words, for bride and groom, on wedding planning, financial planning, juggling career and home, etc. Pays $600 to $1,200, on acceptance.

MODERN MATURITY—3200 E. Carson St., Lakewood, CA 90712. Annette Winter, Sr. Ed. Articles, 300 to 2,000 words, on a wide range of financial topics of interest to people over 50. Pays to $1 a word, on acceptance. Queries required.

THE MONEYPAPER—1010 Mamaroneck Ave., Mamaroneck, NY 10543. Vita Nelson, Ed. Financial news and money-saving ideas; particularly interested in information about companies with dividend reinvestment plans. Brief, well-researched articles on personal finance, money management: saving, earning, investing, taxes, insurance, and related subjects. Pays $75 for articles, on publication. Query with resumé and writing sample.

NEW CHOICES FOR RETIREMENT LIVING—28 W. 23rd St., New York, NY 10010. Allen J. Sheinman, Articles Ed. David A. Sendler, Ed.-in-Chief. News and service magazine for people ages 50 to 65. Articles on retirement planning, financial strategies, housing options, as well as health and fitness, travel, leisure pursuits, etc. Payment varies, on acceptance.

NEW WOMAN—215 Lexington Ave., New York, NY 10016. Attn: Manuscripts and Proposals. Articles for women ages 25 to 49, on careers, money, relationships, health and fitness, fashion, beauty, food and nutrition, travel with a self-growth angle. Pays about $1 a word, on acceptance. Query with SASE.

OUT—The Soho Bldg., 110 Greene St., Suite 600, New York, NY 10012. Michael Goff, Ed.-in-Chief. Articles, 50 to 8,000 words, on finance and other subjects for gay and lesbian readers. Guidelines. Query.

RETIRED MILITARY FAMILY—169 Lexington Ave., New York, NY 10016. Liz DeFranco, Ed. Articles, 1,000 to 1,500 words, on finance, second careers and other topics of interest to military retirees and their families. Pays to $200, on publication.

ROBB REPORT—1 Acton Pl., Acton, MA 01720. Robert R. Feeman, Ed. Features on investment opportunities for high-end/luxury market. Lifestyle articles, home interiors, boats, travel, exotic automobiles, business, technology, etc. Payment varies, on publication. Query with SASE and clips.

SENIOR HIGHLIGHTS—26081 Merit Cir., Suite 101, Laguna Hills, CA 92653. Julie Puckett, Asst. Ed. Articles, 800 words, on money, lifestyles, health, and travel. No payment. Guidelines. Query with SASE.

WOMAN'S DAY—1633 Broadway, New York, NY 10019. Rebecca Greer, Sr. Articles Ed. Articles, to 2,000 words, on financial matters of interest to a broad range of women. Pays top rates, on acceptance. Query; no unsolicited manuscripts.

WOMEN IN BUSINESS—American Business Women's Assn., 9100 Ward Pkwy., Box 8728, Kansas City, MO 64114–0728. Dawn J. Grubb, Assoc. Ed. How-to business features, 1,000 to 1,500 words, for working women ages 35 to 55, business trends, small-business ownership, self-improvement, and retirement issues. Pays on acceptance. Query.

YOUR MONEY—5705 N. Lincoln Ave., Chicago, IL 60659. Dennis Fertig, Ed. Informative, jargon-free personal finance articles, to 2,500 words, for the general reader, on investment opportunities and personal finance. Pays 40¢ a word, on acceptance. Query with clips for assignment. (Do not send manuscripts on disks.)

BUSINESS AND TRADE PUBLICATIONS

ABA JOURNAL—American Bar Assn., 750 N. Lake Shore Dr., Chicago, IL 60611. Gary A. Hengstler, Ed./Pub. Articles, to 3,000 words, on law-related topics: current events in the law and ideas that will help lawyers practice better and more efficiently. Writing should be in an informal, journalistic style. Pays from $1,000, on acceptance; buys all rights.

ACCESSORIES MAGAZINE—50 Day St., Norwalk, CT 06854. Karen Alberg, Ed. Dir. Articles, with photos, for women's fashion accessories buyers and manufacturers. Profiles of retailers, designers, manufacturers; articles on merchandising and marketing. Pays $75 to $100 for short articles, from $100 to $300 for features, on publication. Query.

ACROSS THE BOARD—845 Third Ave., New York, NY 10022. Karen Bodner, Asst. to the Ed. Articles, 1,000 to 4,000 words, on a variety of topics of interest to business executives; straight business angle not required. Payment varies, on publication.

ALTERNATIVE ENERGY RETAILER—P.O. Box 2180, Waterbury, CT 06722. John Florian, Ed. Dir. Feature articles, 1,000 words, for retailers of hearth products, including appliances that burn wood, coal, pellets, and gas, and hearth accessories and services. Interviews with successful retailers, stressing the how-to. B&W photos. Pays $200, extra for photos, on publication. Query.

AMERICAN DEMOGRAPHICS—P.O. Box 68, Ithaca, NY 14851–9989. Brad Edmondson, Ed.-in-Chief. Articles, 500 to 2,000 words, on the 4 key elements of a consumer market (its size, its needs and wants, its ability to pay, and how it can be reached), with specific examples of how companies market to consumers. Readers include marketers, advertisers, and strategic planners. Pays $100 to $500, on acceptance. Query.

AMERICAN MEDICAL NEWS—515 N. State St., Chicago, IL 60610. Ronni Scheier, Topic Ed. Public health articles, 900 to 1,500 words, on socio-economic developments of interest to physicians across the country. No pieces on health, clinical treatments, or research. Pays $500 to $1,500, on acceptance. Query required. Guidelines.

THE AMERICAN SALESMAN—P.O. Box 1, Burlington, IA 52601–0001. Barbara Boeding, Ed. Articles, 900 to 1,200 words, on techniques for increasing sales. Author photos requested on article acceptance. Pays 3¢ a word, on publication. Buys all rights. Guidelines.

AMERICAN SCHOOL & UNIVERSITY—P.O. Box 12901, 9800 Metcalf, Overland Park, KS 66212–2215. Joe Agron, Ed. Articles and case studies, 1,200 to 1,500 words, on design, construction, operation, and management of school and university facilities. Queries preferred.

ARCHITECTURE—1130 Connecticut Ave. N.W., Suite 625, Washington, DC 20036. Address Man. Ed. Articles, to 3,000 words, on architecture, building technology, professional practice. Pays 50¢ a word.

AREA DEVELOPMENT MAGAZINE—400 Post Ave., Westbury, NY 11590. Geraldine Gambale, Ed. Articles for top executives of industrial companies on sites and facility planning. Pays 25¢ per word. Query.

ART BUSINESS NEWS—19 Old King's Hwy. S., Darien, CT 06820. Sarah Seamark, Ed. Articles, 1,000 words, for art dealers and framers, on trends and events of national importance to the art industry, and relevant business subjects. Pays on publication. Query preferred.

AUTOMATED BUILDER—P.O. Box 120, Carpinteria, CA 93014. Don Carlson, Ed. Articles, 500 to 750 words, on various types of home manufacturers and dealers with slides or color prints. Pays $300, on acceptance, for articles with photos. Query required.

BARRON'S—200 Liberty St., New York, NY 10281. Edwin A. Finn, Ed. Investment-interest articles. Query.

BEAUTY EDUCATION—3 Columbia Cir., Albany, NY 12212. Catherine Frangie, Pub. Articles, 750 to 1,000 words, that provide beauty educators, trainers, and professionals in the cosmetology industry with information, skills, and techniques on such topics as hairstyling, makeup, aromatherapy, retailing, massage, and beauty careers. Send SASE for editorial calendar and themes. Pays in copies. Query.

BICYCLE RETAILER AND INDUSTRY NEWS—502 W. Cordova Rd., Santa Fe, NM 87501. Marc Sani, Ed. Articles, 50 to 1,200 words, on employee management, employment strategies, and general business subjects for bicycle manufacturers, distributors, and retailers. Pays 20¢ a word (higher rates for more complex articles), plus expenses, within 30 days of publication. Query.

BOATING INDUSTRY—Argus Business, 5 Penn Plaza, 13th Fl., New York, NY 10001–1810. Richard W. Porter, Ed. Articles, 1,000 to 2,500 words, on recreational marine products, management, merchandising and selling, for boat dealers. Photos. Pays varying rates, on publication. Query.

BOOKPAGE—ProMotion, Inc., 2501 21st Ave. S., Suite 5, Nashville, TN 37212. Ann Meador Shayne, Ed. Book reviews, 500 words, for a tabloid used by booksellers to promote new titles, authors, and bookstores. Query with writing samples and areas of interest; Editor will make assignments for reviews. Pays in copies. Guidelines.

BUILDER—Hanley-Wood, Inc., One Thomas Cir. N.W., Suite 600, Washington, DC 20005. Noreen S. Welle, Ed. Articles, to 1,500 words, on trends and news in home building: design, marketing, new products, etc. Pays negotiable rates, on acceptance. Query.

BUSINESS—P.O. Box 10010, 1720 Washington Blvd., Ogden, UT 84409. Attn: Editorial Staff. Informative articles, 1,000 words, on business concerns of the businessperson/entrepreneur in U.S. and Canada. Color photos. Pays 15¢ a word, $35 for photos, $50 for cover photos, on acceptance. Query. Guidelines.

CAMPGROUND MANAGEMENT—P.O. Box 5000, Lake Forest, IL 60045–5000. Mike Byrnes, Ed. Detailed articles, 500 to 2,000 words, on managing recreational vehicle campgrounds. Photos. Pays $50 to $200, after publication.

CHIEF EXECUTIVE—733 Third Ave., 21st Fl., New York, NY 10017. J.P. Donlon, Ed. CEO bylines. Articles, 2,500 to 3,000 words, on management, financial, or business strategies. Departments, 1,200 to 1,500 words, on investments, amenities, and travel. Features on CEOs at leisure, Q&A's with CEOs, other topics. Pays varying rates, on acceptance. Query required.

CHINA, GLASS & TABLEWARE—368 Essex Ave., Bloomfield, NJ 07003. Amy Stavis, Ed. Case histories and interviews, 1,500 to 2,500 words, with photos, on merchandising of china and glassware. Pays $65 per page, on publication. Query.

CHRISTIAN RETAILING—600 Rinehart Rd., Lake Mary, FL 32746. Carol Chapman Stertzer, Man. Ed. Articles, 1,500 to 2,300 words, on new products, industry news, or topics related to running a profitable Christian retail store. Pays $50 to $300, on publication.

CLEANING AND MAINTENANCE MANAGEMENT MAGAZINE—13 Century Hill Dr., Latham, NY 12110–2197. Anne Dantz, Ed. Articles, 500 to 1,200 words, on managing efficient cleaning and custodial/maintenance operations, profiles, photo-features, or general-interest articles directly related to the industry; also technical/mechanical how-tos. Photos encouraged. Pays to $200 for features, on publication. Query. Guidelines.

COMMERCIAL CARRIER JOURNAL—Chilton Way, Radnor, PA 19089. Paul Richards, Man. Ed. Thoroughly researched articles on private fleets and for-hire trucking operations. Pays from $50, on acceptance. Queries required.

COMPUTER GRAPHICS WORLD—10 Tara Blvd., Suite 500, Nashua, NH 03062–2801. Stephen Porter, Ed. Articles, 1,000 to 3,000 words, on computer graphics and multimedia technology and their use in science, engineering, architecture, film and broadcast, and interactive entertainment areas. Photos. Pays $600 to $1,000 per article, on acceptance. Query.

CONCORD NORTH—See *New Hampshire Editions.*

CONCRETE INTERNATIONAL—Box 19150, 22400 W. Seven Mile Rd., Detroit, MI 48219–1849. William J. Semioli, Assoc. Pub./Ed. Articles, 6 to 12 double-spaced pages, on concrete construction, design, and technology with drawings and/or photos. Pays $100 per printed page, on publication. Query.

THE CONSTRUCTION SPECIFIER—Construction Specifications Institute, 601 Madison St., Alexandria, VA 22314. Jack Reeder, Ed. Technical articles, 1,000 to 3,000 words, on the "nuts and bolts" of commercial construction, for architects, engineers, specifiers, contractors, and manufacturers. Pays 15¢ per word, on publication.

CONVENIENCE STORE NEWS—7 Penn Plaza, New York, NY 10001. Maureen Azzato, Exec. Ed. Features and news items, 500 to 750 words, for convenience store owners and operators. Photos, with captions. Pays $3 per column inch or negotiated price for features; extra for photos, on publication. Query.

CONVERTING MAGAZINE—1350 E. Touhy Ave., P.O. Box 5080, Des Plaines, IL 60017–5080. Mark Spaulding, Ed.-in-Chief. Business articles, 750 to 1,500 words, serving the technical, trends, and productivity information needs of flexible-packaging converting companies, as well as manufacturers of labels, paperboard cartons, and other converted products. Payment varies, on publication. Query required.

COOKING FOR PROFIT—P.O. Box 267, Fond du Lac, WI 54936–0267. Colleen Phalen, Pub./Ed.-in-Chief. Articles, of varying lengths, for foodservice professionals: profiles of successful restaurants, chains, and franchises, schools, hospitals, nursing homes, or other "institutional feeders"; also case studies on successful energy management. Payment varies, on publication.

CRAIN'S CHICAGO BUSINESS—740 Rush St., Chicago, IL 60611. Jay McCormick, Man. Ed. Business articles about the Chicago metropolitan area exclusively.

DAIRY FOODS MAGAZINE—Cahners Publishing Co., 1350 E. Touhy Ave., Des Plaines, IL 60018. Ellen Mather, Ed. Articles, to 2,500 words, on innovative dairies, dairy processing operations, marketing successes, new products for milk handlers and makers of dairy products. Fillers, 25 to 150 words. Payment varies.

DENTAL ECONOMICS—P.O. Box 3408, Tulsa, OK 74101. Dick Hale, Ed. Articles, 1,200 to 3,500 words, on business side of dental practice, patient and staff communication, personal investments, etc. Pays $100 to $400, on acceptance.

DRAPERIES & WINDOW COVERINGS—450 Skokie Blvd., Suite 507, Northbrook, IL 60062. Katie Sosnowchik, Ed. Articles, 1,000 to 2,000 words, for retailers, wholesalers, designers, and manufacturers of draperies and window, wall, and floor coverings. Profiles, with photos, of successful businesses in the industry; management-and marketing-related articles. Pays $150 to $250, after acceptance. Query.

DRUG TOPICS—5 Paragon Dr., Montvale, NJ 07645–1742. Valentine A. Cardinale, Ed. News items, 500 words, with photos, on pharmacists and associations. Merchandising features, 1,000 to 1,500 words. Pays $100 to $150 for news, $200 to $400 for features, on acceptance. Query for features.

EMERGENCY—6300 Yarrow Dr., Carlsbad, CA 92009–1597. Doug Fiske, Ed. Articles, to 3,000 words, of interest to paramedics, emergency medical technicians, flight nurses, and other pre-hospital personnel; disaster management, advanced and basic life support, assessment, treatment. Pays $100 to $400 for features, $50 to $300 for departments. Photos are a plus. Guidelines and editorial calendar available.

EMPLOYEE SERVICES MANAGEMENT—NESRA, 2211 York Rd., Suite 207, Oak Brook, IL 60521–2371. Cynthia M. Helson, Ed. Articles, 1,200 to 2,500 words, for human resource and employee service professionals.

THE ENGRAVERS JOURNAL—26 Summit St., P.O. Box 318, Brighton, MI 48116. Rosemary Farrell, Man. Ed. Articles, of varying lengths, on topics related to the engraving industry or small business. Pays $60 to $175, on acceptance. Query.

ENTREPRENEUR—2392 Morse Ave., Irvine, CA 92714. Rieva Lesonsky, Ed.-in-Chief. Articles for established and aspiring independent business owners, on all aspects of running a business. Pay varies, on acceptance. Query required.

EQUIPMENT WORLD—P.O. Box 2029, Tuscaloosa, AL 35403. Marcia Gruver, Ed. Features, 500 to 1,500 words, for contractors who buy, sell, and use heavy equipment; articles on equipment selection, application, maintenance, management, and replacement. Pay varies, on acceptance.

EXECUTIVE FEMALE—30 Irving Pl., New York, NY 10003. Basia Hellwig, Ed.-in-Chief. Articles, 750 to 2,500 words, on managing people, time, money, companies, and careers, for women in business. Pays varying rates, on acceptance. Query.

FARM JOURNAL—1500 Market St., Philadelphia, PA 19102-2181. Earl Ainsworth, Ed. Practical business articles, 500 to 1,500 words, with photos, on growing crops and raising livestock. Pays 20¢ to 50¢ a word, on acceptance. Query required.

FINANCIAL WORLD—1328 Broadway, New York, NY 10001. Douglas A. McIntyre, Pub. Features and profiles of large companies and financial institutions and the people who run them. Pays varying rates, on publication. Query required.

FISHING TACKLE RETAILER MAGAZINE—P.O. Box 17151, Montgomery, AL 36141–0151. Dave Ellison, Ed. Articles, 300 to 1,250 words, for merchants who carry angling equipment. Business focus is required, and writers should provide practical information for improving management and merchandising. Pays varying rates, on acceptance.

FITNESS MANAGEMENT—P.O. Box 1198, Solana Beach, CA 92075. Edward H. Pitts, Ed. Authoritative features, 750 to 2,500 words, and news shorts, 100 to 750 words, for owners, managers, and program directors of fitness centers. Content must be in keeping with current medical practice; no fads. Pays 8¢ a word, on publication. Query.

FLORIST—29200 Northwestern Hwy., P.O. Box 2227, Southfield, MI 48037–2227. Barbara Koch, Man. Ed. Articles, to 2,000 words, with photos, on retail florist shop management.

FLOWERS &—Teleflora Plaza, Suite 118, 12233 W. Olympic Blvd., Los Angeles, CA 90064. Joanne Jaffe, Ed.-in-Chief. Articles, 500 to 1,500 words, with how-to information for retail florists. Pays 30¢ a word, on acceptance. Query with clips.

FOOD MANAGEMENT—122 E. 42nd St., Suite 900, New York, NY 10168. Donna Boss, Ed. Articles on food service in hospitals, nursing homes, schools, colleges, prisons, businesses, and industrial sites. Trends, legislative issues, and how-to pieces, with management tie-in. Query.

THE FUTURE, NOW: INNOVATIVE VIDEO—Blue Feather Co., N8494 Poplar Grove Rd., P.O. Box 669, New Glarus, WI 53574–0669. Jennifer M. Jarik, Ed. Bimonthly. Articles, to 2 pages, on new ideas in the video industry. Pays from $75 to $100, on publication.

GARDEN DESIGN—100 Ave. of the Americas, 7th Fl., New York, NY 10013. Dorothy Kalins, Ed.-in-Chief. Garden-related features, 500 to 1,000 words, on private, public, and community gardens; articles on art and history as they relate to gardens. Pays from 50¢ a word, on acceptance. Guidelines.

GENERAL AVIATION NEWS & FLYER—P.O. Box 39099, Tacoma, WA 98439–0099. Dave Sclair, Pub. Articles, 500 to 2,500 words, of interest to "general aviation" pilots. Pays to $3 per column inch (approximately 40 words); $10 for B&W photos; to $50 for color photos; within a month of publication.

GOLF COURSE NEWS—38 Lafayette St., Yarmouth, ME 04096. Hal Phillips, Ed. Features, 500 to 1,000 words, on all aspects of golf course maintenance, design, building, and management. Pays $200, on acceptance.

GOVERNMENT EXECUTIVE—1501 M St. N.W., Washington, DC 20005. Timothy Clark, Ed. Articles, 1,500 to 3,000 words, for civilian and military government workers at the management level.

GREENHOUSE MANAGEMENT & PRODUCTION—(formerly *Greenhouse Manager*) P.O. Box 1868, Fort Worth, TX 76101–1868. David Kuack, Ed. How-to articles, innovative production and/or marketing techniques, 500 to 1,800 words, accompanied by color slides, of interest to professional greenhouse growers. Pays $50 to $300, on acceptance. Query required.

HAMPSHIRE WEST—See *New Hampshire Editions.*

HEALTH FOODS BUSINESS—2 University Plaza, Suite 204, Hackensack, NJ 07601. Gina Geslewitz, Ed. Articles, 1,200 words, with photos, profiling health food stores. Pays on publication. Query. Guidelines.

HEALTH PROGRESS— 4455 Woodson Rd., St. Louis, MO 63134–3797. Judy Cassidy, Ed. Journal of the Catholic Health Association. Features, 2,000 to 4,000 words, on hospital and nursing home management and administration, medical-moral questions, health care, public policy, technological developments in health care and their effects, nursing, financial and human resource management for health-care administrators, and innovative programs in hospitals and long-term care facilities. Payment negotiable. Query.

HEATING/PIPING/AIR CONDITIONING—2 Prudential Plaza, 180 N. Stetson Ave., Suite 2555, Chicago, IL 60601. Robert T. Korte, Ed. Articles, to 5,000 words, on heating, piping, and air conditioning systems in industrial plants and large buildings; engineering information. Pays $60 per printed page, on publication. Query.

HOSPITALS & HEALTH NETWORKS—737 N. Michigan Ave., Chicago, IL 60611. Mary Grayson, Ed. Articles, 800 to 900 words, for hospital administrators. Query.

HUMAN RESOURCE EXECUTIVE—747 Dresher Rd., Horsham, PA 19044–0980. David Shadovitz, Ed. Profiles and case stories, 1,800 to 2,200 words, of interest to people in the personnel profession. Pays varying rates, on acceptance. Queries required.

INC.—38 Commercial Wharf, Boston, MA 02110. George Gendron, Ed. No free-lance material.

INCOME OPPORTUNITIES—1500 Broadway, Suite 600, New York, NY 10036–4015. Linda Molner, Ed.-in-Chief. Helpful articles, 1,000 to 2,500 words, on how to make money full-or part-time; how to start a successful small business, improve sales, work at home, mail order, franchising, etc. Pays varying rates, on acceptance.

INDEPENDENT BUSINESS—125 Auburn Ct., Suite 100, Thousand Oaks, CA 91362. Maryann Hammers, Sr. Ed. Articles, 500 to 2,000 words, of practical interest and value to small business owners. Guidelines. Pays $200 to $1,500, on acceptance. Query.

INDEPENDENT LIVING PROVIDER—150 Motor Pkwy., Suite 420, Hauppauge, NY 11788–5145. Anne Kelly, Ed. Articles, 1,500 to 3,000 words, on the sales and services of home medical equipment dealers. Pays 15¢ a word, on publication. Query.

INSTANT & SMALL COMMERCIAL PRINTER—P.O. Box 1387, Northbrook, IL 60065. Anne Marie Mohan, Ed. Articles, 3 to 6 typed pages, for operators and employees of printing businesses specializing in retail printing and/or small commercial printing: case histories, how-tos, technical pieces, small-business management. Pays $150 to $250, extra for photos, on publication. Query.

INTERNATIONAL BUSINESS—9 E. 40th St., 10th Fl., New York, NY 10016. Lori Ioannou, Ed.-in-Chief. Articles, 1,000 to 1,500 words, on global marketing strategies. Short pieces, 500 words, with tips on operating abroad. Profiles, 750 to 3,000 words, on individuals or companies. Pays 80¢ to $1 a word, on acceptance and on publication. Query with clips.

JEMS, JOURNAL OF EMERGENCY MEDICAL SERVICES—P.O. Box 2789, Carlsbad, CA 92018. Marion Garza, Ed. Coord. Articles, 1,500 to 3,000 words, of interest to emergency medical providers (EMTs, paramedics, nurses, and physicians) who work in the EMS industry worldwide.

LLAMAS—P.O. Box 100, Herald, CA 95638. Cheryl Dal Porto, Ed. "The International Camelid Journal," published 7 times yearly. Articles, 300 to 3,000 words, of interest to llama and alpaca owners. Pays $25 to $300, extra for photos, on publication. Query.

LP-GAS MAGAZINE—131 W. First St., Duluth, MN 55802. Zane Chastain, Ed. Articles, 1,500 to 2,500 words, with photos, on LP-gas dealer operations: marketing, management, etc. Photos. Pays to 15¢ a word, extra for photos, on acceptance. Query.

MACHINE DESIGN—Penton Publications, 1100 Superior Ave., Cleveland, OH 44114. Ronald Khol, Ed. Articles, to 10 typed pages, on mechanical and electromechanical design topics for engineers. Pays varying rates, on publication. Submit outline or brief description.

MAINTENANCE TECHNOLOGY—1300 S. Grove Ave., Barrington, IL 60010. Robert C. Baldwin, Ed. Technical articles with how-to information on increasing the reliability and maintainability of electrical and mechanical systems and equipment. Readers are managers, supervisors, and engineers in all industries and facilities. Payment varies, on acceptance. Query.

MANAGE—2210 Arbor Blvd., Dayton, OH 45439. Doug Shaw, Ed. Articles, 800 to 1,000 words, on management and supervision for first-line and middle managers. "Please indicate word count on manuscript and enclose SASE." Pays 5¢ a word.

MANAGING OFFICE TECHNOLOGY—1100 Superior Ave., Cleveland, OH 44114. Lura Romei, Ed. Articles, 3 to 4 double-spaced, typed pages, on new concepts, management techniques, technologies, and applications for management executives. Payment varies, on acceptance. Query preferred.

MANCHESTER—See *New Hampshire Editions.*

MEMPHIS BUSINESS JOURNAL— 88 Union, Suite 102, Memphis, TN 38103. Barney DuBois, Ed. Articles, to 2,000 words, on business, industry trade, agri-business and finance in the mid-South trade area. Pays $80 to $200, on acceptance. "Not considering free-lance material at this time."

MIX MAGAZINE— 6400 Hollis St., Suite 12, Emeryville, CA 94608. Blair Jackson, Exec. Ed. Articles, varying lengths, for professionals, on audio, audio post-production, sound production, live sound, and music entertainment technology. Pay varies, on publication. Query.

MODERN HEALTHCARE—740 N. Rush St., Chicago, IL 60611. Clark Bell, Ed. News weekly covers management, finance, building design and construction, and new technology for hospitals, health maintenance organizations, nursing homes, and other health care institutions. Pays $200 to $400, on publication. Query; very limited free-lance market.

MODERN TIRE DEALER—P.O. Box 3599, Akron, OH 44309-3599. Lloyd Stoyer, Ed. Tire retailing and automotive service articles, 1,000 to 1,500 words, with photos, on independent tire dealers and retreaders. Pays $300 to $450, on publication. Query; articles by assignment only.

NASHUA—See *New Hampshire Editions.*

NATIONAL FISHERMAN—121 Free St., P.O. Box 7438, Portland, ME 04112. James W. Fullilove, Ed. Articles, 200 to 2,000 words, aimed at commercial fishermen and boat builders. Pays $4 to $6 per inch, extra for photos, on publication. Query preferred.

NATION'S BUSINESS—1615 H St. N.W., Washington, DC 20062–2000. Articles on small-business topics, including management advice and success stories. Pays negotiable rates, on acceptance. Guidelines.

NEEDLEWORK RETAILER—P.O. Box 2438, Ames, IA 50010. Heidi A. Bomgarden, Ed. Bimonthly. Articles, 500 to 1,000 words, for owners and managers of independent needlework retail stores. Profiles of needlework shop owners; articles about a successful store event or promotion. "Articles should be written with the needlework retailer specifically in mind and stress the uniqueness of the store, promotion, etc., and how it can be profitable to the readers." Pays varying rates, on acceptance.

NEPHROLOGY NEWS & ISSUES/NORTH AMERICA—15150 N. Hayden Rd., Suite 101, Scottsdale, AZ 85260. Mark Neumann, Ed. News articles, human-interest features, and opinion essays on dialysis, kidney transplants, and kidney disease. Also publishes *Nephrology News & Issues/Europe* for the European renal care community.

NEW CAREER WAYS NEWSLETTER— 67 Melrose Ave., Haverhill, MA 01830. William J. Bond, Ed. How-to articles, 1,500 to 2,000 words, on new ways to succeed at work in the 1990s. Pays varying rates, on publication. Query with outline and SASE. Same address and requirements for *Workskills Newsletter.*

NEW HAMPSHIRE EDITIONS—100 Main St., Nashua, NH 03060. Rick Broussard, Ed. Leeann Boyer, Man. Ed. Lifestyle, business, and history articles with a New Hampshire angle, with sources from all regions of the state, for the company's regional monthlies: *Nashua, Manchester, Concord North, Seacoast* (formerly *Hampshire East*), and *Hampshire West*. Payment varies, on publication.

THE NORTHERN LOGGER AND TIMBER PROCESSOR—Northeastern Logger's Assn., Inc., P.O. Box 69, Old Forge, NY 13420. Eric A. Johnson, Ed. Features, 1,000 to 2,000 words, of interest to the forest product industry. Photos. Pays varying rates, on publication. Query preferred.

NSGA RETAIL FOCUS—National Sporting Goods Assoc., 1699 Wall St., Suite 700, Mt. Prospect, IL 60056. Bob Nieman, Ed. Members magazine. Articles, 1,000 to 1,500 words, on sporting goods industry news and trends, the latest in new product information, and management and store operations. Payment varies, on publication. Query.

OPPORTUNITY MAGAZINE—18 E. 41st St., New York, NY 10017. I. J. Eisenstadter, Ed. Articles, 900 to 1,500 words, on sales psychology, sales techniques, successful small business careers, self-improvement. Pays $25 to $50, on publication.

OPTOMETRIC ECONOMICS—American Optometric Assn., 243 N. Lindbergh Blvd., St. Louis, MO 63141–7881. Gene Mitchell, Man. Ed. Articles, 1,000 to 3,000 words, on private practice management for optometrists; direct, conversational style with how-to advice on how optometrists can build, improve, better manage, and enjoy their practices. Short humor and photos. Payment varies, on acceptance. Query.

PARTY & PAPER RETAILER—70 New Canaan Ave., Norwalk, CT 06850. Trisha McMahon Drain, Ed. Articles, 800 to 1,000 words, that offer employee, management, and retail marketing advice to the party or stationery store owner: display ideas, success stories, financial advice, legal advice. "Articles grounded in facts and anecdotes are appreciated." Pay varies, on publication. Query with published clips.

PET BUSINESS—7-L Dundas Cir., Greensboro, NC 27407. Rita Davis, Ed. Brief, documented articles on animals and products found in pet stores; research findings; legislative/regulatory actions; business and marketing tips and trends. Pays $4 per column inch, on publication; pays $20 for photos.

PET PRODUCT NEWS & PSM—P.O. Box 6050, Mission Viejo, CA 92690. Scott McElhaney, Ed. Articles, 1,000 to 1,200 words, with photos, on pet shops, and pet and product merchandising. No fiction or news clippings. Pays $175 to $350, extra for photos. Query.

PHOTO MARKETING—3000 Picture Pl., Jackson, MI 49201. Gary Pageau, Exec. Ed. Business articles, 1,000 to 3,500 words, for owners and managers of camera/video stores or photo processing labs. Pays $150 to $500, extra for photos, on acceptance. Query; no unsolicited manuscripts.

PHYSICIAN'S MANAGEMENT—7500 Old Oak Blvd., Cleveland, OH 44130. Bob Feigenbaum, Ed. Articles, 1,500 words, on finance, investments, malpractice, and office management for primary care physicians. No clinical pieces. Pays $125 per printed page, on acceptance. Query.

PIZZA TODAY—P.O. Box 1347, New Albany, IN 47151. Bruce Allar, Ed. Articles, to 2,500 words, on pizza business management for pizza entrepreneurs. Pizza business profiles. Pays $75 to $150 per published page, on publication. Query.

P.O.B.—Business News Publishing, 755 W. Big Beaver Rd., Suite 100, Troy, MI 48084. Victoria L. Dickinson, Ed. Technical and business articles, 1,000 to 4,000 words, for professionals and technicians in the surveying and mapping fields. Technical tips on field and office procedures and equipment maintenance. Pays $150 to $400, on acceptance.

POLICE MAGAZINE— 6300 Yarrow Dr., Carlsbad, CA 92009–1597. Randall Resch, Ed. Articles and profiles, 1,000 to 3,000 words, on specialized groups, equipment, issues, and trends of interest to people in the law enforcement profession. Pays $100 to $300, on acceptance. Query.

POOL & SPA NEWS—3923 W. Sixth St., Los Angeles, CA 90020. News articles for the swimming pool, spa, and hot tub industry. Pays from 10¢ to 15¢ a word, extra for photos, on publication. Query.

PRO—1233 Janesville Ave., Fort Atkinson, WI 53538. Karla Raye Cuculi, Ed. Articles, 1,000 to 1,500 words, on business management for owners of lawn maintenance firms. Pays $150 to $250, on publication. Query.

PUBLISH—Integrated Media, Inc., 501 Second St., San Francisco, CA 94107. Jake Widman, Ed. Features, 1,500 to 2,000 words, and reviews, 400 to 800 words, on all aspects of computerized publishing. Pays $400 to $600 for reviews, $850 to $1,200 for full-length features, on acceptance.

QUICK PRINTING— 445 Broad Hollow Rd., Melville, NY 11747. Jean Scott, Asst. Ed. Articles, 1,500 to 2,500 words, of interest to owners and operators of quick print shops, copy shops, and small commercial printers, on how to make their businesses more profitable; include figures. Pays from $75, on acceptance.

REGARDIE'S—1010 Wisconsin Ave. N.W., Suite 600, Washington, DC 20007. Richard Blow, Ed. Profiles and investigations of the "high and mighty" in the DC area. "We require aggressive reporting and imaginative, entertaining writing." Pays 75¢ a word, on publication. Queries required.

REMODELING—Hanley-Wood, Inc., One Thomas Cir. N.W., Suite 600, Washington, DC 20005. Wendy A. Jordan, Ed. Articles, 250 to 1,700 words, on remodeling and industry news for residential and light commercial remodelers. Pays on acceptance. Query.

RESTAURANTS USA—1200 17th St. N.W., Washington, DC 20036–3097. Jennifer Batty, Ed. Publication of the National Restaurant Assn. Articles, 1,000 to 1,500 words, on the food service and restaurant business. Restaurant experience preferred. Pays $350 to $800, on acceptance. Query.

ROOFER MAGAZINE—12734 Kenwood Ln., Bldg. 73, Ft. Myers, FL 33907. Angela Hutto, Ed. Technical and non-technical articles, human-interest pieces, 500 to 1,000 words, on roofing-related topics: new roofing concepts, energy savings, pertinent issues, roofing contractor profiles, industry concern. Humorous items welcome. No general business or computer articles. Include photos. Pays negotiable rates, on publication. Guidelines.

THE ROTARIAN—1560 Sherman Ave., Evanston, IL 60201–3698. Willmon L. White, Ed. Articles, 1,200 to 2,000 words, on international social and economic issues, business and management, environment, science and technology. "No political or religious subjects." Pays good rates, on acceptance. Query.

RV BUSINESS—2575 Vista Del Mar Dr., Ventura, CA 93001. Sherman

Goldenberg, Ed.-in-Chief. Articles, to 1,500 words, on RV industry news and product-related features. Articles on legislative matters affecting the industry. General business features rarely used. Pays varying rates.

SAFETY COMPLIANCE LETTER—24 Rope Ferry Rd., Waterford, CT 06386. Michele Rubin, Ed. Interview-based articles, 800 to 1,250 words, for corporate safety managers, on successful safety and health programs and issues in the workplace. Pays to 15¢ a word, on acceptance. Query.

SAFETY MANAGEMENT—24 Rope Ferry Rd., Waterford, CT 06386. Heather Vaughn, Ed. Interview-based articles, 1,100 to 1,500 words, for safety professionals, on improving workplace safety and health. Pays to 15¢ a word, on acceptance. Query.

SALES & MARKETING MANAGEMENT—Bill Communications, Inc., 355 Park Ave. S., New York, NY 10010. Charles Butler, Ed. Features and short articles of interest to sales and marketing executives. Looking for practical "news you can use." Pays varying rates, on acceptance. Queries preferred.

SEACOAST—See *New Hampshire Editions*.

SIGN BUSINESS—P.O. Box 1416, Broomfield, CO 80038. Regan Dickinson, Man. Ed. Articles specifically targeted to the sign business. Prefer step-by-step how-to features. Pays $50 to $200, on publication.

SMALL PRESS REVIEW—Dustbooks, P.O. Box 100, Paradise, CA 95967. Len Fulton, Ed./Pub. Reviews, 200 words, of small literary books and magazines; tracks the publishing of small publishers and small-circulation magazines. Pays 10¢ a word, on acceptance. Query.

SOFTWARE MAGAZINE—One Research Dr., Suite 400B, Westborough, MA 01581. Mike Bucken, Ed. Technical features, to 3,500 words, for computer-literate MIS audience, on how various software products are used. Pays about $750 to $1,000, on publication. Query required. Calendar of scheduled editorial features available.

SOUTHERN LUMBERMAN—P.O. Box 681629, Franklin, TN 37068-1629. Nanci P. Gregg, Man. Ed. Articles on sawmill operations, interviews with industry leaders, how-to technical pieces with an emphasis on increasing sawmill production and efficiency and new installation. "Always looking for 'sweetheart' mill stories; we publish one per month." Pays $100 to $250 for articles with B&W photos. Queries preferred.

SOUVENIRS AND NOVELTIES—7000 Terminal Sq., Suite 210, Upper Darby, PA 19082. Articles, 1,500 words, quoting souvenir shop managers on items that sell, display ideas, problems in selling, industry trends. Photos. Pays from $1 per column inch, extra for photos, on publication.

STONE WORLD—(formerly *Tile World/Stone World*) 1 Kalisa Way, Suite 205, Paramus, NJ 07652. Michael Reis, Ed. Articles, 750 to 1,500 words, on new trends in installing and designing with stone. For architects, interior designers, design professionals, and stone fabricators and dealers. Pays $4 per column inch, on publication. Query.

TANNING TRENDS—3101 Page Ave., Jackson, MI 49203–2254. Kristen Miller-Gledhill, Ed. Articles on small businesses and skin care for tanning salon owners. Scientific pro-tanning articles and "smart tanning" pieces. Query for profiles. "Our aim is to boost salon owners to the 'next level' of small business ownership. Focus is on business principles with special emphasis on public relations and marketing." Payment varies, on publication.

TEA & COFFEE TRADE JOURNAL—130 W. 42nd St., New York, NY 10036. Jane P. McCabe, Ed. Articles, 3 to 5 pages, on trade issues of importance to the tea and coffee industry. Pays $5 per published inch, on publication. Query.

TEXTILE WORLD—4170 Ashford-Dunwoody Rd. N.E., Suite 420, Atlanta, GA 30319. Mac Isaacs, Ed. Articles, 500 to 2,000 words, with photos, on manufacturing and finishing textiles. Pays varying rates, on acceptance.

TILE WORLD/STONE WORLD—See *Stone World.*

TODAY'S OR NURSE—Slack, Inc., 6900 Grove Rd., Thorofare, NJ 08086. Frances R. DeStefano, Man. Ed. Clinical or general articles, from 2,000 words, of direct interest to operating room nurses.

TOURIST ATTRACTIONS AND PARKS—7000 Terminal Sq., Suite 210, Upper Darby, PA 19082. Articles, 1,500 words, on successful management of parks and leisure attractions. News items, 250 and 500 words. Pays 7¢ a word, on publication. Query.

TRAILER/BODY BUILDERS—P.O. Box 66010, Houston, TX 77266. Paul Schenck, Ed. Articles on engineering, sales, and management ideas for truck body and truck trailer manufacturers. Pays from $100 per printed page, on acceptance.

TRAINING MAGAZINE—50 S. Ninth St., Minneapolis, MN 55402. Jack Gordon, Ed. Articles, 1,000 to 2,500 words, for managers of training and development activities in corporations, government, etc. Pays to 25¢ a word, on acceptance. Query.

TREASURY & RISK MANAGEMENT—111 W. 57th St., New York, NY, 10019. Anthony Baldo, Ed. Ann Gram, Art Dir. Bimonthly. Articles, 200 to 3,000 words, on treasury management for corporate treasurers, CFOs, and vice presidents of finance. Pays 50¢ to $1 a word, on acceptance. Query.

TRUCKERS/USA—P.O. Box 323, Windber, PA 15963. David Adams, Ed. Articles, 500 to 1,000 words, on the trucking business and marketing. Trucking-related poetry and fiction. Payment varies, on publication.

UNIQUE OPPORTUNITIES—455 S. 4th Ave., #1236, Louisville, KY 40202. Bett Coffman, Asst. Ed. Articles, 2,000 to 3,000 words, that cover the economic, business, and career-related issues of interest to physicians who are interested in relocating. Doctor profiles, 500 words. "Our goal is to educate physicians about how to evaluate career opportunities, negotiate the benefits offered, plan career moves, and provide information on the legal and economic aspects of accepting a position." Pays 50¢ a word for features; $100 to $200 for profiles, on acceptance. Query.

VENDING TIMES—1375 Broadway, New York, NY 10018. Arthur E. Yohalem, Ed. Features and news articles, with photos, on vending machines. Pays varying rates, on acceptance. Query.

WINES & VINES—1800 Lincoln Ave., San Rafael, CA 94901. Philip E. Hiaring, Ed. Articles, 2,000 words, on grape and wine industry, emphasizing marketing, management, and production. Pays 10¢ a word, on acceptance.

WOODSHOP NEWS—Pratt St., Essex, CT 06426-1185. Ian C. Bowen, Ed. Features, one to 3 typed pages, for and about people who work with wood: business stories, profiles, news. Pays from $3 per column inch, on publication. Queries preferred.

WORKBOAT—P.O. Box 1348, Mandeville, LA 70470. Don Nelson, Ed. Features, to 2,000 words, and shorts, 500 to 1,000 words, providing current, lively information for workboat owners, operators, crew, suppliers, and regulators. Topics include construction and conversion; diesel engines and electronics; politics and industry; unusual vessels; new products; and profiles. Payment varies, on acceptance and on publication. Queries preferred.

WORKING WOMAN—230 Park Ave., New York, NY 10169. Lynn Povich, Ed. Articles, 350 to 2,500 words, on business and personal aspects of working women's lives. Pays from $300, on acceptance.

WORKSKILLS NEWSLETTER—See *New Career Ways Newsletter.*

WORLD OIL—Gulf Publishing Co., P.O. Box 2608, Houston, TX 77252–2608. Robert E. Snyder, Ed. Engineering and operations articles, 3,000 to 4,000 words, on petroleum industry exploration, drilling, or production. Photos. Pays from $50 per printed page, on acceptance. Query.

WORLD SCREEN NEWS—1123 Broadway, Suite 901, New York, NY 10010. George P. Winslow, Ed. Features and short pieces on trends in the business of international television programming (network, syndication, cable, and pay). Pays to $750, after publication.

WORLD WASTES—6151 Powers Ferry Rd. N.W., Atlanta, GA 30339. Bill Wolpin, Ed./Pub. Case studies, market analysis, and how-to articles, 1,000 to 2,000 words, with photos of refuse haulers, recyclers, landfill operators, resource recovery operations, and transfer stations, with solutions to problems in the field. Pays from $125 per printed page, on publication. Query preferred.

IN-HOUSE/ASSOCIATION MAGAZINES

Publications circulated to company employees (sometimes called house magazines or house organs) and to members of associations and organizations are excellent, well-paying markets for writers at all levels of experience. Large corporations publish these magazines to promote good will, familiarize readers with the company's services and products, and interest customers in these products. And many organizations publish house magazines designed to keep their members abreast of the issues and events concerning a particular cause or industry. Always read an in-house magazine before submitting an article; write to the editor for a sample copy (offering to pay for it) and the editorial guidelines. Stamped, self-addressed envelopes (SASEs) should be enclosed with any query or manuscript. The following list includes a sampling of publications in this large market.

AARP BULLETIN—601 E St. N.W., Washington, DC 20049. Elliot Carlson, Ed. Publication of the American Association of Retired Persons. Payment varies, on acceptance. Query required.

AMERICAN HOW-TO—12301 Whitewater Dr., Suite 260, Minnetonka, MN 55343. Tom Sweeney, Ed. Bimonthly magazine for members of The Handyman Club of America. Articles, 1,000 to 1,500 words, for homeowners interested in do-it-yourself projects. Carpentry, plumbing, electrical work, landscaping, masonry, tools, woodworking, and new products. Payment is 50¢ a word, on acceptance. Queries preferred. Send SASE for editorial calendar with upcoming themes.

CALIFORNIA HIGHWAY PATROLMAN—2030 V St., Sacramento, CA 95818–1730. Carol Perri, Ed. Articles on transportation safety, California history, travel, consumerism, past and present vehicles, humor, special holidays, general items, etc. Photos a plus. Buys one-time rights; pays 2½¢ a word, $5 for B&W photos, on publication. Guidelines and/or sample copy with 9x11 SASE.

CATHOLIC FORESTER—355 Shuman Blvd., P.O. Box 3012, Naperville, IL 60566–7012. Dorothy Deer, Ed. Official publication of the Catholic Order of Foresters, a fraternal life insurance company for Catholics. General-interest articles and fiction, to 1,500 words, that deal with contemporary issues; no moralizing, explicit sex or violence. Pays from 10¢ a word, on acceptance.

COLUMBIA—1 Columbus Plaza, New Haven, CT 06510–0901. Richard McMunn, Ed. Journal of the Knights of Columbus. Articles, 1,500 words, for Catholic families. Must be accompanied by color photos or transparencies. No fiction. Pays to $500 for articles and photos, on acceptance.

THE COMPASS—365 Washington Ave., Brooklyn, NY 11238. J.A. Randall, Ed. Articles, to 2,000 words, on the sea and deep sea trade; also articles on aviation. No fiction, poetry, or first-person accounts. Pays to $1,000, on acceptance. Query with SASE.

FOCUS—Turnkey Publishing, P.O. Box 200549, Austin, TX 78720. Doug Johnson, Ed. Magazine of the North American Data General Users Group. Articles, 700 to 4,000 words, on Data General computers. Photos a plus. Pays to $50, on publication. Query required.

FORD NEW HOLLAND NEWS—See *New Holland News*.

THE FURROW—Deere & Co., John Deere Rd., Moline, IL 61265. George R. Sollenberger, Exec. Ed. Specialized, illustrated articles on farming. Pays to $1,000, on acceptance.

HARVARD MAGAZINE—7 Ware St., Cambridge, MA 02138–4001. John Rosenberg, Ed. Liam Rector, Poetry Ed. Articles, 500 to 5,000 words, with a connection to Harvard University. Short, serious, literary poetry. Pays from $100, on publication. Query required.

IDEA PERSONAL TRAINER—6190 Cornerstone Ct. E., Suite 204, San Diego, CA 92121–3773. Therese Hannon, Asst. Ed. Association publication for personal fitness trainers. Articles on exercise science; program design; profiles of successful trainers; business, legal, and marketing topics; tips for networking with other trainers and with allied medical professionals; client counseling; and training tips. "What's New" column includes industry news, products, and research. Payment varies, on acceptance. Query.

KIWANIS—3636 Woodview Trace, Indianapolis, IN 46268. Chuck Jonak, Man. Ed. Articles, 2,500 words (sidebars, 250 to 350 words), on lifestyle, relationships, world view, education, trends, small business, religion, health, etc. No travel pieces, interviews, profiles. Pays $400 to $1,000, on acceptance. Query.

THE LION—300 22nd St., Oak Brook, IL 60521. Robert Kleinfelder, Sr. Ed. Official publication of Lions Clubs International. Articles, 800 to 2,000 words, and photo-essays, on club activities. Pays from $100 to $700, including photos, on acceptance. Query.

MAQUETTE—International Sculpture Ctr., 1050 17th St. N.W., Suite 250, Washington, DC 20036. Penelope Kiser, Ed. Membership magazine of the

International Sculpture Center, devoted to the advancement of contemporary sculpture. Articles, 1,500 to 2,500 words. Payment varies, on publication. Query required.

NETWORK NEWS—9710 S. 700 E., Bldg. A, Suite 206, Sandy, UT 84070. Linda Boyer, Ed. Official publication of the Network Professional Association. Humorous editorial articles, 600 to 800 words, on computing, especially networking. Submit with SASE for reply only; manuscripts will not be returned. Pays 30¢ a word, after acceptance.

NEW HOLLAND NEWS—(formerly *Ford New Holland News*) New Holland, Inc., P.O. Box 1895, New Holland, PA 17557. Attn: Ed. Articles, to 1,500 words, with strong color photo support, on agriculture and rural living. Pays on acceptance. Query.

OPTIMIST MAGAZINE— 4494 Lindell Blvd., St. Louis, MO 63108. Dennis R. Osterwisch, Ed. Articles, to 1,000 words, on activities of local Optimist Club, and techniques for personal and club success. Pays from $100, on acceptance. Query.

PUBLIC CITIZEN MAGAZINE—1600 20th St. N.W., Washington, DC 20009. Peter Nye, Ed. Investigative reports and articles of timely political interest, for members of Public Citizen: consumer rights, health and safety, environmental protection, safe energy, tax reform, trade, and government and corporate accountability. Photos, illustrations. Payment negotiable.

RESTAURANTS USA—1200 17th St. N.W., Washington, DC 20036-3097. Jennifer Batty, Ed. Publication of the National Restaurant Assn. Articles, 1,000 to 1,500 words, on the food service and restaurant business. Restaurant experience preferred. Pays $350 to $800, on acceptance. Query.

THE RETIRED OFFICER MAGAZINE—201 N. Washington St., Alexandria, VA 22314. Address the Manuscripts Ed. Articles, 1,800 to 2,000 words, of interest to military retirees and their families. Current military/national affairs: recent military history, health/medicine, and second-career opportunities. No fillers. Photos a plus. Pays to $1,000, on acceptance. Query. Guidelines.

THE ROTARIAN—1560 Sherman Ave., Evanston, IL 60201-3698. Willmon L. White, Ed. Publication of Rotary International, world service organization of business and professional men and women. Articles, 1,200 to 2,000 words, on international social and economic issues, business and management, human relationships, travel, sports, environment, science and technology; humor. Pays good rates, on acceptance. Query.

SCULPTURE—International Sculpture Ctr., 1050 17th St. N.W., Suite 250, Washington, DC 20036. Suzanne Ramljak, Ed. Bimonthly magazine of the International Sculpture Center. (Also available on newsstands.) Articles on sculpture, sculptors, collections of sculpture, books on sculpture, criticism, etc. Payment varies, on publication. Query.

SILVER CIRCLE— 4900 Rivergrade Rd., Irwindale, CA 91706. Jay Binkly, Ed. National consumer-interest quarterly. Consumer service articles, 800 to 2,500 words, on careers, money, health, home, auto, gardening, food, travel, hobbies, etc. Pays $250 to $1,500, on acceptance. Query.

VFW MAGAZINE— 406 W. 34th St., Kansas City, MO 64111. Richard K. Kolb, Ed. Magazine for Veterans of Foreign Wars and their families. Articles, to 1,500 words, on current issues and military history, with veteran angle.

Photos. Pays to $500 for unsolicited articles, extra for photos, on acceptance. Guidelines.

WOMEN IN BUSINESS—9100 Ward Pkwy., Box 8728, Kansas City, MO 64114–0728. Dawn J. Grubb, Assoc. Ed. Bimonthly publication of the American Business Women's Association. How-to features, 1,000 to 1,500 words, for career women from 25 to 55 years old, on business trends, small-business ownership, self-improvement, and retirement issues. Profiles of ABWA members only. Guidelines. Pays 15¢ a published word, on acceptance. Query.

RELIGIOUS MAGAZINES

ADVANCE—See *Enrichment: A Journal for Pentecostal Ministry.*

AMERICA—106 W. 56th St., New York, NY 10019–3893. George W. Hunt, S.J., Ed. Articles, 1,000 to 2,500 words, on current affairs, family life, literary trends. Pays $75 to $150, on acceptance.

AMERICAN BIBLE SOCIETY RECORD—1865 Broadway, New York, NY 10023. Clifford P. Macdonald, Man. Ed. Material related to work of American Bible Society: translating, publishing, distributing. Pays on acceptance. Query.

AMERICAN JEWISH HISTORY—American Jewish Historical Society, 2 Thornton Rd., Waltham, MA 02154. Dr. Marc Lee Raphael, Ed. Academic articles, 15 to 30 typed pages, on the settlement, history, and life of Jews in North and South America. Queries preferred. No payment.

AMIT WOMAN—817 Broadway, New York, NY 10003–4761. Micheline Ratzersdorfer, Ed. Articles, 1,000 to 2,000 words, of interest to Jewish women: Middle East, Israel, history, holidays, travel. Pays to $75, on publication.

ANGLICAN JOURNAL—600 Jarvis St., Toronto, Ont., Canada M4Y 2J6. Attn: Ed. National newspaper of the Anglican Church of Canada. Articles, to 1,200 words, on current events and human-interest subjects in a religious context. Pays $200 to $500, on acceptance. Query.

ANNALS OF ST. ANNE DE BEAUPRÉ—P.O. Box 1000, St. Anne de Beaupré, Quebec, Canada G0A 3C0. Roch Achard, C.Ss.R., Ed. Articles, 500 to 1,500 words, that promote devotion to St. Anne and Christian family values. "Write something inspirational, educational, objective, and uplifting." No poetry. Pays 3¢ to 4¢ a word, on acceptance.

BAPTIST LEADER—American Baptist Churches-USA, P.O. Box 851, Valley Forge, PA 19482–0851. D. Ng, Ed. Practical how-to or thought-provoking articles, 1,200 to 2,000 words, for local church lay leaders, pastors, and Christian education staff.

BIBLE ADVOCATE—P.O. Box 33677, Denver, CO 80233. Roy Marrs, Ed. Articles, 1,000 to 2,500 words, and fillers, 100 to 500 words, on Bible passages and Christian living. Poetry, 5 to 25 lines, on religious themes. Opinion pieces, to 700 words. "Be familiar with the doctrinal beliefs of the Church of God (Seventh Day). For example, they don't celebrate a traditional Easter or Christmas." Pays $10 per page (to $25) for articles, $5 for poetry, on publication. Guidelines.

BRIGADE LEADER—Box 150, Wheaton, IL 60189. Deborah Christensen, Man. Ed. Inspirational articles, 1,000 words, for Christian men who

643

lead boys. "Most articles are written on assignment by experts; very few free lancers used. Query with clips and we'll contact you if we need you for an assignment." Pays $60 to $150.

CATHOLIC DIGEST—P.O. Box 64090, St. Paul, MN 55164–0090. Attn: Articles Ed. Articles, 1,000 to 3,500 words, on Catholic and general subjects. Fillers, to 300 words, on instances of kindness rewarded, for "Hearts Are Trumps"; accounts of good deeds, for "People Are Like That." Pays from $200 for original articles, $100 for reprints, on acceptance; $4 to $50 for fillers, on publication. Guidelines.

CATHOLIC NEAR EAST MAGAZINE—1011 First Ave., New York, NY 10022–4195. Michael La Civita, Ed. Bimonthly publication of Catholic Near East Welfare Assoc., a papal agency for humanitarian and pastoral support. Articles, 1,500 to 2,000 words, on people of the Middle East, northeast Africa, India, and eastern Europe: their faith, heritage, culture, and present state of affairs. Special interest in Eastern Christian churches. Color photos for all articles. Pays 20¢ a word. Query.

CATHOLIC TWIN CIRCLE—15760 Ventura Blvd., Suite 1201, Encino, CA 91436. Loretta G. Seyer, Ed. Features, how-tos, and interviews, 1,000 to 2,000 words, of interest to Catholic families; include photos. Opinion or inspirational columns, 600 to 800 words. Strict attention to Catholic doctrine required. Enclose SASE. Pays from 10¢ a word for articles, $50 for columns, on publication.

CHARISMA & CHRISTIAN LIFE—600 Rinehart Rd., Lake Mary, FL 32746. Lee Grady, Ed. Dir. Charismatic/evangelical Christian articles, 1,500 to 2,500 words, for developing the spiritual life. News stories, 300 to 1,500 words. Photos. Pays varying rates, on publication.

THE CHRISTIAN CENTURY—407 S. Dearborn St., Chicago, IL 60605. James M. Wall, Ed. Ecumenical. Articles, 1,500 to 3,000 words, with a religious angle, on political and social issues, international affairs, culture, the arts. Poetry, to 20 lines. Photos. Pays about $50 per printed page, extra for photos, on publication.

CHRISTIAN EDUCATION COUNSELOR—1445 Boonville Ave., Springfield, MO 65802–1894. Sylvia Lee, Ed. Articles, 1,000 to 1,500 words, on teaching and administrating Christian education in the local church, for local Sunday school and Christian school personnel. Pays 5¢ to 10¢ a word, on acceptance.

CHRISTIAN EDUCATION JOURNAL—Scripture Press Ministries, P.O. Box 650, Glen Ellyn, IL 60138. Leslie H. Stobbe, Exec. Ed. Articles, 5 to 15 typed pages, on Christian education topics. Pays $100, on publication. Guidelines.

CHRISTIAN HOME & SCHOOL—3350 E. Paris Ave. S.E., Grand Rapids, MI 49512. Gordon L. Bordewyk, Ed. Articles for parents in Canada and the U.S. who send their children to Christian schools and are concerned about the challenges facing Christian families today. Pays $75 to $150, on publication. Guidelines.

CHRISTIAN MEDICAL & DENTAL SOCIETY JOURNAL—P.O. Box 5, Bristol, TN 37621–0005. David B. Biebel, D. Min., Ed. Articles, 8 to 10 double-spaced pages, for Christian medical and dental professionals. Queries preferred. Pays to $50, on publication. Guidelines.

CHRISTIAN PARENTING TODAY—4050 Lee Vance View, Colorado

Springs, CO 80918. Brad Lewis, Ed. Articles, 900 to 2,000 words, dealing with raising children with Christian principles. Departments: "Parent Exchange," 25 to 100 words on problem-solving ideas that have worked for parents; "Life in Our House," insightful anecdotes, 25 to 100 words, about humorous things said at home. Pays 15¢ to 25¢ a word, on publication. Pays $40 for "Parent Exchange," $25 for "Life in our House." Guidelines; send SASE.

CHRISTIAN SINGLE—127 Ninth Ave. N., Nashville, TN 37234–0140. Stephen Felts, Ed. Articles, 600 or 1,200 words, for single adults about leisure activities, issues related to single parents, inspiring personal experiences, humor, life from a Christian perspective. Payment varies, on acceptance. Query. Guidelines.

CHRISTIAN SOCIAL ACTION—100 Maryland Ave. N.E., Washington, DC 20002. Lee Ranck, Ed. Articles, 1,500 to 2,000 words, on social issues for concerned persons of faith. Pays $75 to $125, on publication.

CHRISTIANITY TODAY—465 Gundersen Dr., Carol Stream, IL 60188. Michael G. Maudlin, Man. Ed. Doctrinal social issues and interpretive essays, 1,500 to 3,000 words, from evangelical Protestant perspective. No fiction or poetry. Pays $200 to $500, on acceptance. Query.

CHURCH & STATE—1816 Jefferson Pl. N.W., Washington, DC 20036. Joseph L. Conn, Man. Ed. Articles, 600 to 2,600 words, on issues of religious liberty and church-state relations. Pays varying rates, on acceptance. Query.

CHURCH EDUCATOR—Educational Ministries, Inc., 165 Plaza Dr., Prescott, AZ 86303. Robert G. Davidson, Ed. How-to articles, to 1,750 words, on Christian education: activity projects, crafts, learning centers, games, bulletin boards, etc., for all church school, junior and high school programs, and adult study group ideas. Allow 3 months for response. Pays 3¢ a word, on publication.

THE CHURCH HERALD— 4500 60th St. S.E., Grand Rapids, MI 49512–9642. Jeffrey Japinga, Ed. Reformed Church in America. Articles, 500 to 1,500 words, on Christianity and culture, politics, marriage, and home. Pays $50 to $125. Query.

THE CHURCH MUSICIAN—127 Ninth Ave. N., Nashville, TN 37234. Jere Adams, Ed. Articles on choral techniques, instrumental groups, worship planning, music administration, directing choirs (all ages), rehearsal planning, music equipment, new technology, drama/pageants and related subjects, hymn studies, book reviews, and music-related fillers. Pays 5½¢ a word, on acceptance.

COLUMBIA—1 Columbus Plaza, New Haven, CT 06510–0901. Richard McMunn, Ed. Knights of Columbus. Articles, 1,500 words, for Catholic families. Must be accompanied by color photos or transparencies. No fiction. Pays to $500 for articles with photos, on acceptance.

COMMENTARY—165 E. 56th St., New York, NY 10022. Neal Kozodoy, Ed. Articles, 5,000 to 7,000 words, on contemporary issues, Jewish affairs, social sciences, religious thought, culture. Serious fiction; book reviews. Pays on publication.

COMMONWEAL—15 Dutch St., New York, NY 10038. Margaret O'Brien Steinfels, Ed. Catholic. Articles, to 3,000 words, on political, religious, social, and literary subjects. Pays 3¢ a word, on acceptance.

COMPASS: A JESUIT JOURNAL—Box 400, Sta. F, 50 Charles St. E., Toronto, Ont., Canada M4Y 2L8. Robert Chodos, Ed. Essays, 1,500 to 2,500 words, on current religious, political, and cultural topics. "We are ecumenical in spirit and like to provide a forum for lively debate and an ethical perspective on social and religious questions." Query preferred. Pays $100 to $500, on publication.

THE COVENANT COMPANION—5101 N. Francisco Ave., Chicago, IL 60625. John E. Phelan, Ed. Articles, 1,000 words, with Christian implications published for members and attenders of Evangelical Covenant Church, "aimed at gathering, enlightening, and stimulating devotion to Jesus Christ and the living of the Christian life." Poetry. Pays $15 to $35, on publication.

CRUSADER—P.O. Box 7259, Grand Rapids, MI 49510. G. Richard Broene, Ed. Fiction, 900 to 1,500 words, and articles, 400 to 1,000 words, for boys ages 9 to 14 that show how God is at work in their lives and in the world around them. Also, short fillers. Pays 4¢ to 5¢ a word, on acceptance.

DAILY WORD—Unity Village, MO 64065. Colleen Zuck, Ed. Daily lessons, 25 lines (double-spaced), that may be based on an affirmation, a Bible text, or an idea that has been helpful in meeting some situation in your life. Pays $30, on acceptance, plus copies. Guidelines.

DAUGHTERS OF SARAH—2121 Sheridan Rd., Evanston, IL 60201. Elizabeth Anderson, Ed. Quarterly. Articles, 750 to 2,500 words, on theology, social issues, and personal experiences of Christian feminism. Poetry, to 500 words, and occasional fiction, to 2,000 words, from a Christian feminist perspective. Guidelines and themes. No simultaneous submissions. Query preferred.

DECISION—Billy Graham Evangelistic Assn., 1300 Harmon Pl., P.O. Box 779, Minneapolis, MN 55440–0779. Roger C. Palms, Ed. Christian testimonies and teaching articles on evangelism and Christian nurturing, 1,500 to 1,800 words. Vignettes, 400 to 1,000 words. Pays varying rates, on publication.

DISCOVERIES—WordAction Publishing Co., 6401 The Paseo, Kansas City, MO 64131. Attn: Asst. Ed. Weekly take-home paper designed to correlate with Evangelical Sunday school curriculum. Fiction, 500 to 700 words, for 8- to 10-year-olds. Stories should feature contemporary, true-to-life characters and should illustrate character building and scriptural application. No poetry. SASE required. Pays 5¢ a word, on publication. Guidelines.

DREAMS & VISIONS—Skysong Press, 35 Peter St. S., Orillia, Ont., Canada L3V 5A8. Steve Stanton, Ed. New frontiers in Christian fiction. Eclectic fiction, 2,000 to 6,000 words, that "has literary value and is unique and relevant to Christian readers today." Pays ½¢ per word.

ENRICHMENT: A JOURNAL FOR PENTECOSTAL MINISTRY—(formerly *Advance*) 1445 Boonville Ave., Springfield, MO 65802. Wayde Goodell, Ed. Articles, 1,200 to 1,500 words, slanted to ministers, on preaching, doctrine, practice; how-to features. Pays to 10¢ a word, on acceptance.

EVANGEL—Light and Life Press, Box 535002, Indianapolis, IN 46253– 5002. Carolyn Smith, Ed. Free Methodist. Personal experience articles, 1,000 words; short devotional items, 300 to 500 words; fiction, 1,200 words, showing personal faith in Christ to be instrumental in solving problems. Pays 4¢ a word for articles, $10 for poetry, on publication.

EVANGELIZING TODAY'S CHILD—Box 348, Warrenton, MO 63383–

0348. Attn: Ed. Articles, 1,200 to 1,500 words, for Sunday school teachers, Christian education leaders, and children's workers. Feature articles should include teaching principles, instruction for the reader, and classroom illustrations. "Impact" articles, 700 to 900 words, show the power of the Gospel in or through the life of a child; "Resource Center," 200-to 300-word teaching tips. Also short stories, 800 to 1,000 words, of contemporary children dealing with problems; must have a scriptural solution. Pays 10¢ to 12¢ a word for articles; $15 to $25 for "Resource Center" pieces; 8¢ a word for short stories, on publication. Guidelines.

FAITH TODAY—Box 8800, Sta. B, Willowdale, Ontario, Canada M2K 2R6. Brian C. Stiller, Ed. Articles, 1,500 words, on current issues relating to the church in Canada. Pays negotiable rates, on publication. Queries required.

THE FAMILY: A CATHOLIC PERSPECTIVE—50 St. Pauls Ave., Boston, MA 02130. Sister Mary Lea Hill, Ed. Articles, 800 to 2,000 words, on a broad range of family topics, including marital relationships, parenting, profiles of role-models for Catholic families. Upbeat, thought-provoking, family-oriented fiction, 1,000 to 1,200 words. Views, columns, personal reflections, 800 words; fillers, 50 to 500 words. "Our readers are primarily Roman Catholic parents with children at home." Submit complete manuscripts; no queries and no simultaneous submissions. Pays 8¢ to 10¢ a word, on publication. (Pays for fillers on acceptance.) Does not read submissions in July or August.

THE FAMILY DIGEST—P.O. Box 40137, Fort Wayne, IN 46804. Corine B. Erlandson, Ed. Articles, 750 to 1,100 words, on family life, Catholic subjects, seasonal, parish life, prayer, inspiration, how-to, spiritual life, for the Catholic reader. Also publishes short humorous anecdotes drawn from personal experience and light-hearted cartoons. Pays 5¢ a word; $10 for personal anecdotes; $20 for cartoons, on acceptance.

FELLOWSHIP—Box 271, Nyack, NY 10960–0271. Richard Deats, Ed. Bimonthly published by the Fellowship of Reconciliation, an interfaith, pacifist organization. Articles, 750 and 1,500 to 2,000 words; B&W photo-essays, on active nonviolence, opposition to war. "Articles for a just and peaceful world community." Pays in copies and subscription. Queries preferred.

FELLOWSHIP IN PRAYER—291 Witherspoon St., Princeton, NJ 08542. Articles, to 1,500 words, relating to prayer, meditation, and the spiritual life as practiced by men and women of all faith traditions. Pays in copies. Guidelines.

FOURSQUARE WORLD ADVANCE—1910 W. Sunset Blvd., Suite 200, P.O. Box 26902, Los Angeles, CA 90026. Ronald D. Williams, Ed. Official publication of the International Church of the Foursquare Gospel. Religious fiction and nonfiction, 1,000 to 1,200 words, and religious poetry. Pays $75, on publication. Guidelines.

FRIENDS JOURNAL—1501 Cherry St., Philadelphia, PA 19102–1497. Vinton Deming, Ed. Articles, to 2,000 words, reflecting Quaker life today: commentary on social issues, experiential articles, Quaker history, world affairs. Poetry, to 25 lines, and Quaker-related humor and crossword puzzles also considered. Pays in copies. Guidelines.

GLORY SONGS—127 Ninth Ave. N., Nashville, TN 37234. Jere V. Adams, Ed. For volunteer and part-time music directors and members of church choirs. Very easy music and accompaniments designed specifically for the small church (4 to 6 songs per issue). Includes 8-page pull-out with articles for choir members on leisure reading, music training, and choir projects. Pays 5½¢ per word, on acceptance.

GROUP, THE YOUTH MINISTRY MAGAZINE—Box 481, Loveland, CO 80539. Rick Lawrence, Ed. Interdenominational magazine for leaders of junior and senior high school Christian youth groups. Articles, 500 to 1,700 words, about practical youth ministry principles, techniques, or activities. Short how-to pieces, to 300 words. Pays to $200 for articles, $25 for department pieces, on acceptance. Guidelines.

GUIDE—Review and Herald Publishing Assn., 55 W. Oak Ridge Dr., Hagerstown, MD 21740. Stories, to 1,200 words, for Christian youth, ages 10 to 14. Pays 3¢ to 4¢ a word, on acceptance.

HERALD OF HOLINESS— 6401 The Paseo, Kansas City, MO 64131. Attn: Man. Ed. Church of the Nazarene. Articles, 800 to 2,000 words, about distinctive Nazarenes, Christian family life and marriage, a Christian approach to social issues, seasonal material, and short devotional articles. Pays 4¢ to 5¢ a word, within 30 days of acceptance. Submit complete manuscript. Guidelines.

HOME LIFE—127 Ninth Ave. N., Nashville, TN 37234. Charlie Warren, Ed.-in-Chief. Leigh Neely, Man. Ed. Southern Baptist. Fiction, personal experience, and articles on Christian marriage, parenthood, and family relationships. Human-interest pieces, 200 to 1,500 words; cartoons and short verse related to family. Query with SASE required. Pays on acceptance.

INDIAN LIFE—Box 3765, Sta. B, Winnipeg, MB, Canada R2W 3R6. Attn: Acquisitions Ed. Christian teaching articles and testimonials of Native Americans, 1,000 to 1,200 words. "Our magazine is designed to help the North American Indian Church speak to the social, cultural, and spiritual needs of Native people." Writing should be at a seventh-grade reading level. "We prefer Native writers who write from within their culture. Read the magazine before submitting." Queries preferred.

INSIDE MAGAZINE—226 S. 16th St., Philadelphia, PA 19102–3392. Jane Biberman, Ed. Jewish lifestyle magazine. Articles, 1,500 to 3,000 words, on Jewish issues, health, finance, and the arts. Pays $75 to $600, after publication. Queries required; send clips if available.

JEWISH CURRENTS—22 E. 17th St., #601, New York, NY 10003. Morris U. Schappes, Ed. Articles, 2,400 to 3,000 words, on Jewish history, Jewish secularism, progressivism, labor struggle, Holocaust resistance, Black-Jewish relations, Israel, Yiddish culture. "We are pro-Israel though non-Zionist and a secular magazine; no religious articles." Overstocked with fiction and poetry. No payment.

THE JEWISH HOMEMAKER—705 Foster Ave., Brooklyn, NY 11230. Mayer Bendet, Ed. Bimonthly. Articles, 1,200 to 2,000 words, for a traditional/Orthodox Jewish audience. Humor. Payment varies, on publication. Query.

THE JEWISH MONTHLY—B'nai B'rith International, 1640 Rhode Island Ave. N.W., Washington, DC 20036. Jeff Rubin, Ed. Articles, 500 to 3,000 words, on politics, religion, history, culture, and social issues of Jewish concern with an emphasis on people. Pays 10¢ to 25¢ a word, on publication. Query with clips.

JOURNAL OF CHRISTIAN NURSING—P.O. Box 1650, Downers Grove, IL 60515. Judy Shelly, Sr. Ed. Articles, 8 to 12 double-spaced pages, that help

648

Christian nurses view nursing practice through the eyes of faith: spiritual care, ethics, values, healing and wholeness, psychology and religion, personal and professional ethics, etc. Priority given to nurse authors, though work by non-nurses will be considered. Opinion pieces, to 4 pages, for "The Last Word" section. Pays $25 to $80. Guidelines and editorial calendar.

THE JOYFUL WOMAN—P.O. Box 90028, Chattanooga, TN 37412. Joy Rice Martin, Ed. Articles and fiction, 500 to 1,200 words, for Christian women: first-person inspirational true stories, profiles of Christian women, practical and Bible-oriented how-to articles. Pays 3¢ to 4¢ a word, on publication. Queries required; no unsolicited manuscripts.

LEADERSHIP— 465 Gundersen Dr., Carol Stream, IL 60188. Kevin A. Miller, Ed. Articles, 500 to 3,000 words, on administration, finance, and/or programming of interest to ministers and church leaders. Personal stories of crisis in ministry. "We deal mainly with the how-to of running a church. We're not a theological journal but a practical one." Pays $50 to $350, on acceptance.

LIBERTY MAGAZINE—12501 Old Columbia Pike, Silver Spring, MD 20904–1608. Clifford R. Goldstein, Ed. Timely articles, to 2,500 words, and photo-essays, on religious freedom and church-state relations. Pays 6¢ to 8¢ a word, on acceptance. Query.

LIGHT AND LIFE—P.O. Box 535002, Indianapolis, IN 46253–5002. Robert Haslam, Ed. Fresh, lively articles about practical Christian living, and sound treatments of vital issues facing the Evangelical in contemporary society. Pays 4¢ a word, on publication.

LIGUORIAN—Liguori, MO 63057–9999. Rev. Allan Weinert, Ed. Catholic. Articles and short stories, 1,500 to 2,000 words, on Christian values in modern life. Pays 10¢ to 12¢ a word, on acceptance.

THE LIVING LIGHT—U.S. Catholic Conference, Dept. of Education, Box 45, The Catholic Univ. of America, Washington, DC 20064. Berard L. Marthaler, Exec. Ed. Theoretical and practical articles, 1,500 to 4,000 words, on religious education, catechesis, and pastoral ministry.

LIVING WITH TEENAGERS—127 Ninth Ave. N., Nashville, TN 37234. Articles, 600 to 1,200 words, told from a Christian perspective for parents of teenagers; first-person approach preferred. Queries welcome; SASE required. Pay is negotiable and made on acceptance.

THE LOOKOUT— 8121 Hamilton Ave., Cincinnati, OH 45231. Simon J. Dahlman, Ed. Articles, 500 to 2,000 words, on spiritual growth, family issues, applying Christian faith to current issues, and people overcoming problems with Christian principles. Inspirational or humorous shorts, 500 to 800 words; fiction, to 2,000 words. Pays 6¢ to 12¢ a word, on acceptance.

THE LUTHERAN— 8765 W. Higgins Rd., Chicago, IL 60631. Edgar R. Trexler, Ed. Articles, to 1,600 words, on Christian ideology, personal religious experiences, social and ethical issues, family life, church, and community. Pays $100 to $600, on acceptance. Query required.

MARRIAGE PARTNERSHIP—Christianity Today, Inc., 465 Gundersen Dr., Carol Stream, IL 60188. Ron Lee, Ed. Articles, 500 to 2,000 words, related to marriage, for men and women who wish to fortify their relationship. Cartoons, humor, fillers. Pays $50 to $300, on acceptance. Query required.

MARYKNOLL—Maryknoll, NY 10545. Joseph Veneroso, M. M., Ed.

Frank Maurovich, Man. Ed. Magazine of the Catholic Foreign Mission Society of America. Articles, 800 to 1,000 words, and photos relating to missions or missioners overseas. Pays $150, on acceptance. Payment for photos made on publication.

MATURE LIVING—127 Ninth Ave. N., Nashville, TN 37234. Al Shackleford, Ed. Fiction and human-interest articles, to 1,200 words, for senior adults. Must be consistent with Christian principles. Payment varies, on acceptance.

MATURE YEARS—201 Eighth Ave. S., P.O. Box 801, Nashville, TN 37202. Marvin W. Cropsey, Ed. Nondenominational quarterly. Articles, 1,500 to 2,000 words, on retirement or related subjects, inspiration. Humorous and serious fiction, 1,500 to 1,800 words. Travel pieces with religious slant. Poetry, to 14 lines. Include social security number with manuscript. Guidelines.

THE MENNONITE—P.O. Box 347, Newton, KS 67114. Gordon Houser, Ed. Larry Penner, Asst. Ed. Articles, 1,000 words, that emphasize Christian themes. Pays 5¢ a word, on publication. Guidelines.

MESSENGER OF THE SACRED HEART— 661 Greenwood Ave., Toronto, Ont., Canada M4J 4B3. Articles and short stories, about 1,500 words, for American and Canadian Catholics. Pays from 4¢ a word, on acceptance.

MIDSTREAM—110 E. 59th St., New York, NY 10022. Joel Carmichael, Ed. Jewish/Zionist-interest articles and book reviews. Fiction, to 3,000 words, and poetry. Pays 5¢ a word, after publication. Allow 3 months for response.

THE MIRACULOUS MEDAL— 475 E. Chelten Ave., Philadelphia, PA 19144–5785. John W. Gouldrick, C.M., Ed. Dir. Catholic. Fiction, to 2,400 words. Religious verse, to 20 lines. Pays from 2¢ a word for fiction, from 50¢ a line for poetry, on acceptance.

MODERN LITURGY—160 E. Virginia St., #290, San Jose, CA 95112. Nick Wagner, Ed. Practical, imaginative how-to help for Roman Catholic liturgy planners. Pays in copies and subscription. Query required.

MOMENT MAGAZINE— 4710 41st St. N.W., Washington, DC 20016. Suzanne Singer, Man. Ed. Sophisticated, issue-oriented articles, 2,000 to 4,000 words, on Jewish topics. Nonfiction only. Pays $150 to $400, on publication.

MOMENTUM—National Catholic Educational Assn., 1077 30th St. N.W., Suite 100, Washington, DC 20007–3852. Patricia Feistritzer, Ed. Articles, 500 to 1,500 words, on outstanding programs, issues, and research in education. Book reviews. Pays $25 to $75, on publication. Query.

MOODY MAGAZINE— 820 N. La Salle Blvd., Chicago, IL 60610. Andrew Scheer, Man. Ed. Anecdotal articles, 1,200 to 2,000 words, on the evangelical Christian experience in the home, the community, and the workplace. Pays 15¢ to 20¢ a word, on acceptance. Query.

THE NATIONAL CHRISTIAN REPORTER—See *The United Methodist Reporter.*

NEW COVENANT—200 Noll Plaza, Huntington, IN 46750. Jim Manney, Ed. Articles and testimonials, 1,000 to 4,000 words, that foster renewal in the Catholic Church, especially the charismatic, ecumenical, and evangelical dimensions of that renewal. Pays from 15¢ a word, on acceptance. Queries preferred.

NEW ERA—50 E. North Temple, Salt Lake City, UT 84150. Richard M.

Romney, Man. Ed. Articles, 150 to 1,500 words, and fiction, to 2,000 words, for young Mormons. Poetry; photos. Pays 5¢ to 10¢ a word, 25¢ a line for poetry, on acceptance. Query.

NEW WORLD OUTLOOK— 475 Riverside Dr., Rm. 1333, New York, NY 10115. Alma Graham, Ed. Articles, 500 to 2,000 words, illustrated with color photos, on United Methodist missions and Methodist-related programs and ministries. Focus on national, global, and women's and children's issues, and on men and youth in missions. Pays on publication. Query.

OBLATES—15 S. 59th St., Belleville, IL 62223–4694. Mary Mohrman, Manuscripts Ed. Christine Portell, Man. Ed. Articles, 500 to 600 words, that inspire, uplift, and motivate through positive Christian values in everyday life. Inspirational poetry, to 16 lines. Pays $80 for articles, $30 for poems, on acceptance. Send 2 first-class stamps and SASE for guidelines and sample copy. Send complete manuscript only.

OUR FAMILY—Box 249, Battleford, Sask., Canada S0M 0E0. Nestor Gregoire, Ed. Articles, 1,000 to 3,000 words, for Catholic families, on modern society, family, marriage, current affairs, and spiritual topics. Humor; verse. Pays 7¢ to 10¢ a word for articles, 75¢ to $1 a line for poetry, on acceptance. SAE with international reply coupons required with all submissions. Guidelines.

PARENTLIFE—MSN 140, 127 Ninth Ave. N., Nashville, TN 37234. Attn: Ed. Informative articles and personal experience pieces, 800 to 1,200 words, relating to family and the preschool child, written with a Christian perspective. Payment varies, on acceptance.

PASTORAL LIFE—Box 595, Canfield, OH 44406–0595. Anthony L. Chenevey, Ed. Articles, 2,000 to 2,500 words, addressing the problems of pastoral ministry. Pays 4¢ a word, on publication. Guidelines.

PATHWAYS—Christian Board of Publication, Box 179, St. Louis, MO 63166. Christine Hershberger Miner, Ed. Fiction, 100 to 800 words; articles, 600 to 1,000 words; and poetry, to 20 lines, for 12- to 16-year-olds. Pays 3¢ a word for prose, from $3 for poetry, on acceptance. Guidelines.

PENTECOSTAL EVANGEL—1445 Boonville Ave., Springfield, MO 65802. Hal Donaldson, Ed. Assemblies of God. Religious, personal experience, and devotional articles, 400 to 1,000 words. Pays 7¢ a word, on acceptance.

THE PENTECOSTAL MESSENGER—P.O. Box 850, Joplin, MO 64802. Peggy Allen, Man. Ed. Articles, 500 to 2,000 words, that deal with Christian commitment: human interest, inspiration, social and religious issues, Bible topics, and seasonal material. Pays 1½¢ per word, on publication. Guidelines.

PERSPECTIVE—Pioneer Clubs, Box 788, Wheaton, IL 60189. Rebecca Powell Parat, Ed. Articles, 750 to 1,500 words, that provide growth for adult club leaders in leadership and relationship skills and offer encouragement and practical support. Readers are lay leaders of Pioneer Clubs for boys and girls (age 2 to 12th grade). "Most articles written on assignment; writers familiar with Pioneer Clubs who would be interested in working on assignment should contact us." Queries preferred. Pays $40 to $90, on acceptance. Guidelines.

PIME WORLD—17330 Quincy St., Detroit, MI 48221. Paul W. Witte, Man. Ed. Articles, 600 to 1,200 words, on Catholic missionary work in Asia, West Africa, and Latin America. Color photos. No fiction or poetry. Pays 6¢ a word, extra for photos, on publication.

POWER AND LIGHT— 6401 The Paseo, Kansas City, MO 64131. Beula J. Postlewait, Preteen Ed. Fiction, 400 to 800 words, for grades 5 and 6, defining Christian experiences and demonstrating Christian values and beliefs. Pays 5¢ a word for multi-use rights, on publication.

THE PREACHER'S MAGAZINE—10814 E. Broadway, Spokane, WA 99206. Randal E. Denny, Ed. Scholarly and practical articles, 700 to 2,500 words, on areas of interest to Christian ministers: church administration, pastoral care, professional and personal growth, church music, finance, evangelism. Pays 3½¢ a word, on publication. Guidelines.

PRESBYTERIAN RECORD—50 Wynford Dr., North York, Ont., Canada M3C 1J7. John Congram, Ed. Fiction and nonfiction, 1,500 words, and poetry, any length. Short items, to 800 words, of a contemporary and often controversial nature for "Full Count." The purpose of the magazine is "to provide news, not only from our church but the church-at-large, and to fulfill both a pastoral and prophetic role among our people." Queries preferred. SAE with international reply coupons required. Pays about $50 (Canadian), on publication. Guidelines.

PRESBYTERIAN SURVEY—See *Presbyterians Today.*

PRESBYTERIANS TODAY—(formerly *Presbyterian Survey*) 100 Witherspoon, Louisville, KY 40202–1396. Catherine Cottingham, Man. Ed. Articles, 1,200 words, of special interest to members of the Presbyterian Church (USA). Pays to $200, before publication.

PURPOSE— 616 Walnut Ave., Scottdale, PA 15683–1999. James E. Horsch, Ed. Fiction, nonfiction, and fillers, to 750 words, on Christian discipleship and church-year related themes, with good photos; pieces of history, biography, science, hobbies, from a Christian perspective; Christian problem solving. First-person pieces preferred. Poetry, to 12 lines. "Send complete manuscript; no queries." Pays to 5¢ a word, to $2 a line for poetry, on acceptance.

QUAKER LIFE—Friends United Meeting, 101 Quaker Hill Dr., Richmond, IN 47374–1980. Johan Maurer, Ed. Ben Richmond, Man. Ed. News and analysis, devotional and study articles for members of Friends United Meeting, other Friends (Quakers), evangelical Christians, religious pacifists. Personal testimonies. Poetry. Guidelines. Pays in copies.

QUEEN OF ALL HEARTS—26 S. Saxon Ave., Bay Shore, NY 11706– 8993. J. Patrick Gaffney, S.M.M., Ed. Publication of Montfort Missionaries. Articles and fiction, 1,000 to 2,000 words, related to the Virgin Mary. Poetry. Pay varies, on acceptance.

RECONSTRUCTIONISM TODAY—30 Old Whitfield Rd., Accord, NY 12404. Lawrence Bush, Ed. Articles on contemporary Judaism and Jewish culture. No fiction or poetry. Pays in copies and subscription.

RESPONSE: A CONTEMPORARY JEWISH REVIEW—27 W. 20th St., 9th Fl., New York, NY 10011–3707. Yigal Schleifer, David R. Adler, Eds. Michael Steinberg, Asst. Ed. Fiction, to 25 double-spaced pages, in which Jewish experience serves as controlling influence. Articles, to 25 pages, with a focus on Jewish issues. Poetry, to 80 lines, and book reviews. Pays in copies. Guidelines.

REVIEW FOR RELIGIOUS—3601 Lindell Blvd., St. Louis, MO 63108. David L. Fleming, S.J., Ed. Informative, practical, or inspirational articles,

1,500 to 5,000 words, from a Catholic theological or spiritual point of view. Pays $6 per page, on publication. Guidelines.

ST. ANTHONY MESSENGER—1615 Republic St., Cincinnati, OH 45210–1298. Norman Perry, O.F.M., Ed. Articles, 2,000 to 3,000 words, on personalities, major movements, education, family, religious and church issues, spiritual life, and social issues. Human-interest pieces. Humor; fiction, 2,000 to 3,000 words. Articles and stories should have religious implications. Query for nonfiction. Pays 14¢ a word, on acceptance.

ST. JOSEPH'S MESSENGER—P.O. Box 288, Jersey City, NJ 07303–0288. Sister Ursula Maphet, Ed. Inspirational articles, 500 to 1,000 words, and fiction, 1,000 to 1,500 words. Verse, 4 to 40 lines. Payment varies, on publication.

SEEK—8121 Hamilton Ave., Cincinnati, OH 45231. Eileen H. Wilmoth, Ed. Articles and fiction, to 1,200 words, on inspirational and controversial topics and timely religious issues. Christian testimonials. Pays 5¢ to 7¢ a word, on acceptance. SASE for guidelines.

THE SENIOR MUSICIAN—127 Ninth Ave. N., Nashville, TN 37234. Jere V. Adams, Ed. Quarterly. For music directors, pastors, organists, pianists, choir coordinators. Easy choir music for senior adult choirs to use in worship, ministry, and recreation. Also includes leisure reading, music training, fellowship suggestions, and choir projects for personal growth. Pays 5½¢ a word, on acceptance.

SHARING THE VICTORY—Fellowship of Christian Athletes, 8701 Leeds Rd., Kansas City, MO 64129. John Dodderidge, Ed. Articles, interviews, and profiles, to 1,000 words, for co-ed Christian athletes and coaches in junior high, high school, college, and pros. Pays from $50, on publication. Query required.

SIGNS OF THE TIMES—P. O. Box 5353, Nampa, ID 83653–5353. Marvin Moore, Ed. Seventh-Day Adventists. Articles, 500 to 2,000 words: features on Christians who have performed community services; first-person experiences, to 1,000 words; health, home, marriage, human-interest pieces; inspirational articles. Pays to 20¢ a word, on acceptance. Send 9x12 SASE for sample and guidelines.

SISTERS TODAY—The Liturgical Press, St. John's Abbey, Collegeville, MN 56321–7500. Articles, 500 to 3,500 words, on theology, social justice issues, and religious issues for women and the Church. Poetry, to 34 lines. Pays $5 per printed page, $10 per poem, on publication; $50 for color cover photos and $25 for B&W inside photos. Send articles to: Sister Mary Anthony Wagner, O.S.B., Ed., St. Benedict's Convent, St. Joseph, MN 56374–2099. Send poetry to: Sister Virginia Micka, C.S.J.,1884 Randolph Ave., St. Paul, MN 55105.

SOCIAL JUSTICE REVIEW—3835 Westminster Pl., St. Louis, MO 63108–3409. Rev. John H. Miller, C.S.C., Ed. Articles, 2,000 to 3,000 words, on social problems in light of Catholic teaching and current scientific studies. Pays 2¢ a word, on publication.

SPIRITUAL LIFE—2131 Lincoln Rd. N.E., Washington, DC 20002–1199. Edward O'Donnell, O.C.D., Ed. Professional religious journal. Religious essays, 3,000 to 5,000 words, on spirituality in contemporary life. Pays from $50, on acceptance. Guidelines.

STANDARD—6401 The Paseo, Kansas City, MO 64131. Articles and fiction, 300 to 1,700 words; true experiences; poetry, to 20 lines; fiction with Christian emphasis but not overtly preachy; cartoons in good taste. Pays 3½¢ a word, on acceptance.

SUNDAY DIGEST— 4050 Lee Vance View, Colorado Springs, CO 80918–7100. John Schinkel, Ed. Articles, 500 to 1,600 words, on Christian faith in contemporary life; inspirational and how-to articles. Pays on acceptance.

TEACHERS INTERACTION—3558 S. Jefferson Ave., St. Louis, MO 63118. Jane Haas, Ed. Helpful articles, 800 to 1,200 words, for Christian teachers and how-to pieces, to 100 words, specifically for Lutheran Church-Missouri Synod volunteer church school teachers. Pays $20 to $100, on publication. Limited free-lance market.

THEOLOGY TODAY—Box 29, Princeton, NJ 08542. Thomas G. Long, Ed. Patrick D. Miller, Ed. Articles, 1,500 to 3,500 words, on theology, religion, and related social and philosophical issues. Literary criticism. Pays $75 to $200, on publication.

TODAY'S CHRISTIAN WOMAN— 465 Gundersen Dr., Carol Stream, IL 60188. Ramona Cramer Tucker, Ed. Articles, 1,500 words, that are "warm and personal in tone, full of real-life anecdotes that deal with the following relationships: marriage, parenting, friendship, spiritual life, and self." Humorous anecdotes, 150 words, that have a Christian slant. Payment varies, on acceptance. Queries required. Guidelines.

THE UNITED CHURCH OBSERVER— 478 Huron St., Toronto, Ont., Canada M5R 2R3. Factual articles, 1,500 to 2,500 words, on religious trends, human problems, social issues. No poetry. Pays after publication. Query.

THE UNITED METHODIST REPORTER—P.O. Box 660275, Dallas, TX 75266–0275. John Lovelace, Ed. United Methodist newspaper. Religious features, to 500 words. Religious verse, 4 to 12 lines. Photos. "Tight-deadline, time-sensitive, nationally circulated weekly newspaper." Pays 4¢ a word, on publication. Send for guidelines. Same address and requirements for *The National Christian Reporter* (interdenominational).

UNITED SYNAGOGUE REVIEW—155 Fifth Ave., New York, NY 10010. Lois Goldrich, Ed. Articles, 1,000 to 1,200 words, on issues of interest to Conservative Jewish community. Query.

UNITY MAGAZINE—1901 N.W. Blue Pkwy., Unity School of Christianity, Unity Village, MO 64065. Philip White, Ed. Religious and inspirational articles, 1,000 to 1,800 words, on health and healing, Bible interpretation, and the metaphysical. Poems. Pays 20¢ a word, on acceptance.

VIRTUE: THE CHRISTIAN MAGAZINE FOR WOMEN— 4050 Lee Vance View, Colorado Springs, CO 80918. Jeanette Thomason, Ed. Articles and fiction for Christian women. Journalistic reports on women's issues and women's lives and their spiritual journeys. Query for articles; SASE required. Guidelines.

THE WAR CRY—The Salvation Army, P.O. Box 269, Alexandria, VA 22313. Attn: Ed.-in-Chief. Inspirational articles, to 800 words, addressing modern life and issues. Color photos. Pays 20¢ a word for articles, $75 to $150 for photos, on acceptance.

WITH: THE MAGAZINE FOR RADICAL CHRISTIAN YOUTH—722 Main St., Box 347, Newton, KS 67114. Eddy Hall and Carol Duerksen, Eds.

Fiction, 500 to 2,000 words; nonfiction, 500 to 1,600 words; and poetry, to 50 lines for Mennonite and Brethren teenagers. "Wholesome humor always gets a close read." B&W 8x10 photos accepted. Payment is 5¢ a word, on acceptance (3¢ a word for reprints).

WOMAN'S TOUCH—1445 Boonville, Springfield, MO 65802–1894. Peggy Musgrove, Ed. Aleda Swartzendruber, Assoc. Ed. Articles, 500 to 1,000 words, that provide help and inspiration to Christian women, strengthening family life, and reaching out in witness to others. Uses some poetry and fillers, 50 to 150 words. Submit complete manuscript. Allow 3 months for response. Payment varies, on acceptance. Guidelines and editorial calendar.

WORLD VISION MAGAZINE—P.O. Box 9716, Federal Way, WA 98063–9716. Bruce Brander, Man. Ed. Thoroughly researched articles, 1,200 to 2,000 words, on worldwide poverty, evangelism, the environment, and justice. Include reputable sources and strong anecdotes. "Turning Points," first-person articles, 450 to 700 words, about a life-changing, spiritual experience related to serving the poor. "We like articles to offer positive ways Christians can make a difference." Query required. Payment negotiable, made on acceptance.

YOUNG SALVATIONIST—The Salvation Army, 615 Slaters Ln., P.O. Box 269, Alexandria, VA 22313. Attn: Lesa Davis, Prod. Mgr. Articles, 600 to 1,200 words, that teach the Christian view of everyday living, for teenagers. Short shorts, first-person testimonies, 600 to 800 words. Pays 15¢ a word (10¢ a word for reprints), on acceptance. SASE required. Send 8½x11 SASE (3 stamps) for theme list, guidelines, and sample copy.

YOUR CHURCH— 465 Gundersen Dr., Carol Stream, IL 60188. Richard Doebler, Man. Ed. Articles, to 1,000 words, about church business administration. Pays about 10¢ a word, on acceptance. Query required. Guidelines.

HEALTH

ACCENT ON LIVING—P. O. Box 700, Bloomington, IL 61702. Raymond C. Cheever, Pub. Betty Garee, Ed. Articles, 250 to 1,000 words, about physically disabled people, including their careers, recreation, sports, self-help devices, and ideas that can make daily routines easier. Good photos a plus. Pays 10¢ a word, on publication. Query.

AMERICAN BABY—Cahners Childcare Group, 249 W. 17th St., New York, NY 10011. Judith Nolte, Ed. Articles, 1,000 to 2,000 words, for new or expectant parents on prenatal and infant care. Personal experience, 900 to 1,200 words, (do not submit in diary format). Department pieces, 50 to 350 words, for "Crib Notes" (news and feature topics) and "Medical Update" (health and medicine). No fiction, fantasy pieces, dreamy musings, or poetry. Pays $350 to $1,000 for articles, $100 for departments, on acceptance. Guidelines.

AMERICAN FITNESS—15250 Ventura Blvd., Suite 200, Sherman Oaks, CA 91403. Peg Jordan, Ed. Rhonda Wilson, Man. Ed. Articles, 500 to 1,500 words, on exercise, health, trends, sports, nutrition, alternative paths, etc. Illustrations, photos.

AMERICAN HEALTH—28 W. 23rd St., New York, NY 10010. Attn: Ed. Dept. Lively, authoritative articles, 1,000 to 3,000 words, on scientific and lifestyle aspects of health and fitness; 100-to 500-word news reports. Query with clips. Pays $250 ($50 kill fee) for news stories; 75¢ to $1 per word for features (kill fee is 25% of assigned fee), on acceptance.

AMERICAN JOURNAL OF NURSING—555 W. 57th St., New York, NY 10019. Santa J. Crisall, Clinical Dir. Articles, 1,500 to 2,000 words, with photos or illustrations, on nursing or disease processes. Query.

AQUARIUS: A SIGN OF THE TIMES—984 Canton St., Roswell, GA 30075. Dan Liss, Ed. Tabloid. Articles, 800 words (plus photo or illustration) on holistic health, metaphysics, spirituality, and the environment. "We are a great way for new writers to get clips." No payment.

ARTHRITIS TODAY—The Arthritis Foundation, 1314 Spring St. N.W., Atlanta, GA 30309. Cindy McDaniel, Ed. Research, self-help, how-to, general interest, general health, and lifestyle topics, and inspirational articles, 750 to 3,000 words, and short fillers, 100 to 250 words. "The magazine is written to help people with arthritis live more productive, independent, and pain-free lives." Pays $500 to $1,000 and up for articles, $100 to $250 for short fillers, on acceptance.

BABY TALK—35 W. 43rd St., New York, NY 10036. Susan Strecker, Ed. Articles, 1,000 to 1,500 words, by parents or professionals, on babies and baby care, etc. No poetry. Pay varies, on acceptance. SASE required.

BETTER HEALTH—1450 Chapel St., New Haven, CT 06511. Magaly Oliver, Pub. Dir. Wellness and prevention magazine affiliated with The Hospital of Saint Raphael in New Haven. Upbeat articles, 2,000 to 2,500 words, that encourage a healthier lifestyle. Articles must contain quotes and narrative from healthcare professionals at Saint Raphael's and other local services. No first-person or personal experience articles. Pays $500, on acceptance. Query with SASE.

COPING: LIVING WITH CANCER—P.O. Box 682268, Franklin, TN 37068. Tricia Brown, Ed. Uplifting and practical articles for people living with cancer: medical news, lifestyle issues, and inspiring personal essays. No payment.

DIABETES SELF-MANAGEMENT—150 W. 22nd St., New York, NY 10011. James Hazlett, Ed. Articles, 2,000 to 4,000 words, for people with diabetes who want to know more about controlling and managing it. Up-to-date and authoritative information on nutrition, pharmacology, exercise physiology, technological advances, self-help, and other how-to subjects. "Articles must be useful, instructive, and must have immediate application to the day-to-day life of our readers. We do not publish personal experience, profiles, exposés, or research breakthroughs." Query with one-page rationale, outline, writing samples, and SASE. Pays from $500, on acceptance. Buys all rights.

EATING WELL—Ferry Rd., P.O. Box 1001, Charlotte, VT 05445–1001. Marcelle DiFalco, Ed. Bimonthly. "A food book with a health perspective." Feature articles, 2,000 to 5,000 words, for readers who "know that what they eat directly affects their well-being, and believe that with the right approach, one can enjoy both good food and good health." Department pieces, 100 to 200 words, for "Nutrition News" and "Marketplace." "We look for strong journalistic voice; authoritative, timely coverage of nutrition issues; healthful recipes that emphasize good ingredients, simple preparation, and full flavor; and a sense of humor." Pays varying rates, 45 days after acceptance. Query.

FIT MAGAZINE—(formerly *New Body*) 1700 Broadway, New York, NY

10019. Nicole Dorsey, Ed. Well-researched, service-oriented articles, 800 to 1,200 words, on exercise, nutrition, lifestyle, diet, and health for women ages 18 to 35. Also considers submissions, 500 words, for "How I Lost It" column, in which writers tell how they lost weight and have kept it off. Writers should have some background in or knowledge of the health field. Pays $100 to $300, on publication. Send detailed query.

FITNESS—Grune & Jahr USA Publishing, 110 Fifth Ave., New York, NY 10011. Rona Cherry, Ed. Articles, 500 to 2,000 words, on health, exercise, sports, nutrition, diet, psychological well-being, alternative therapies, sex, and beauty. Average reader is 30 years old. Pays $1 a word, on acceptance. Query required.

HEALTH—301 Howard St., 18th Fl., San Francisco, CA 94105. Amanda Uhry, Ed. Asst. Articles, 1,200 words, for "Food," "Fitness," "Vanities," "Money," "Mind," and "Relationships" departments. Pays $1,800, on acceptance. Query with clips and SASE required.

HEART & SOUL—Rodale Press, Inc., 201 E. 42nd St., New York, NY 10017. Stephanie Stokes Oliver, Ed.-in-Chief. Articles, 800 to 2,000 words, on health, beauty, fitness, nutrition, and relationships for African-American readers. Pays varying rates, on acceptance. Queries preferred.

HOSPITALS & HEALTH NETWORKS—737 N. Michigan Ave., Chicago, IL 60611. Mary Grayson, Ed. Articles, 800 to 900 words, for hospital administrators, on financing, staffing, coordinating, and providing facilities for health care services. Query.

IDEA PERSONAL TRAINER—6190 Cornerstone Ct. E., Suite 204, San Diego, CA 92121–3773. Terese Hannon, Asst. Ed. Association publication for personal fitness trainers. Articles on exercise science; program design; profiles of successful trainers; business, legal, and marketing topics; tips for networking with other trainers and with allied medical professionals; client counseling; and training tips. "What's New" column includes industry news, products, and research. Payment varies, on acceptance. Query.

IDEA TODAY—6190 Cornerstone Ct. E., Suite 204, San Diego, CA 92121–3773. Terese Hannon, Asst. Ed. Practical articles, 1,000 to 3,000 words, on new exercise programs, business management, nutrition, sports medicine, dance-exercise, and one-to-one training techniques. Articles must be geared toward the aerobics instructor, exercise studio owner or manager, or personal trainer. No consumer or general health pieces. Payment negotiable, on acceptance. Query preferred.

INDEPENDENT LIVING PROVIDER—150 Motor Parkway, Suite 420, Hauppauge, NY 11788–5145. Anne Kelly, Ed. Articles, 1,500 to 3,000 words, on sales and service by home medical equipment dealers. Possible topics: home health care, careers, travel, sports, family life, and sexuality. Pays 10¢ a word, $15 per photo, on publication. Query.

LET'S LIVE—P.O. Box 74908, Los Angeles, CA 90004. Beth Salmon, Ed.-in-Chief. Articles, 1,000 to 1,500 words, on preventive medicine and nutrition, alternative medicine, diet, vitamins, herbs, exercise, recipes, and natural beauty. Pays $150, on publication. Query.

MEDIPHORS—P.O. Box 327, Bloomsburg, PA 17815. Dr. Eugene D. Radice, Ed. "A Literary Journal of the Health Professions." Short stories, essays, and commentary, 3,000 words, related to medicine and health. Poetry, to 30 lines. "We are not a technical journal of science. We do not publish research or review articles, except of a historical nature." Pays in copies. Guidelines.

NATURAL FOOD & FARMING—Natural Food Associates, P.O. Box 210, Atlanta, TX 75551. Bill Francis, Ed. Articles, to 2,000 words, on health and nutrition. "We want articles that emphasize the relationship between agriculture, environmental issues, and preventive medicine with human health as a common denominator; teach the value of natural, poison-free food produced on living, fertile soil; expose the dangers of chemicals in our food, land, and water; and strive to convince others that good food and better health are necessary to save our civilization." Pays $25, on acceptance, plus 5¢ a word immediately after publication.

NATURAL HEALTH: THE GUIDE TO WELL-BEING—17 Station St., Box 1200, Brookline Village, MA 02147. Attn: Ed. Bimonthly. Features, 1,500 to 3,000 words, on holistic health, natural foods, herbal remedies, etc., and interviews. Departments and columns, 250 to 1,000 words. Photos. Pays varying rates, on acceptance.

NEW BODY—See *Fit Magazine.*

NURSING 96—1111 Bethlehem Pike, P.O. Box 908, Springhouse, PA 19477–0908. Patricia Nornhold, Clinical Dir. Most articles are clinically oriented, and are written by nurses for nurses. Also covers legal, ethical, management, and career aspects of nursing; narratives about personal nursing experiences. No poetry. Pays $25 to $300, on publication. Query.

NUTRITION HEALTH REVIEW—P.O. Box 406, Haverford, PA 19041. Frank Ray Rifkin, Ed. Quarterly tabloid. Articles on medical progress, information relating to nutritional therapy, genetics, psychiatry, behavior therapy, surgery, pharmacology, animal health; vignettes relating to health and nutrition. "Vegetarian-oriented; we do not deal with subjects that favor animal testing, animal foods, cruelty to animals or recipes that contain animal products." Humor, cartoons. Pays on publication. Query.

PATIENT CARE—5 Paragon Dr., Montvale, NJ 07645. Jeffrey H. Forster, Ed. Articles on medical care, for primary-care physicians; mostly staff-written. Pays varying rates, on publication. Query; all articles assigned.

THE PHOENIX—7152 Unity Ave. N., Brooklyn Ctr., MN 55429. Pat Samples, Ed. Tabloid. Articles, 800 to 1,500 words, on recovery, renewal, and growth. Department pieces for "12 Step," "Bodywise," "Family Skills," or "Personal Story." "Our readers are committed to physical, emotional, mental, and spiritual health and well-being. Read a sample copy to see what we publish." Pays 3¢ to 5¢ a word, on publication. Guidelines and calendar.

THE PHYSICIAN AND SPORTSMEDICINE—4530 W. 77th St., Minneapolis, MN 55435. Terry Monahan, Exec. Ed. News and feature articles; clinical articles coauthored with physician. Sports medicine angle necessary. Pays $150 to $1,000, on acceptance. Query. Guidelines.

A POSITIVE APPROACH—P.O. Box 910, Millville, NJ 08332. Patricia Johnson, Ed. Articles, 500 words, on all aspects of the positive-thinking disabled/handicapped person's private and business life. Well-researched articles of interest to the visually and hearing impaired, veterans, the arthritic, and all categories of the disabled and handicapped, on interior design, barrier-free architecture, gardening, wardrobe, computers, and careers. No fiction or poetry. Pays in copies.

PREVENTION—33 E. Minor St., Emmaus, PA 18098. Lewis Vaughn, Man. Ed. Query required. No guidelines available. Limited market.

PSYCHOLOGY TODAY—Sussex Publishing, 49 E. 21st St., New York, NY 10010. Hara E. Marano, Ed. Bimonthly. Articles, 4,000 words, on timely subjects and news. Pays varying rates, on publication.

RX REMEDY—120 Post Rd. W., Westport, CT 06880. Val Weaver, Ed. Bimonthly. Articles, 600 to 2,500 words, on health and medication issues for readers 55 and older. Regular columns include "Housecall" and "The Nutrition Prescription." Query. Pays $1 to $1.25 a word, on acceptance.

TANNING TRENDS—3101 Page Ave., Jackson, MI 49203-2254. Kristen Miller-Gledhill, Ed. Articles on skin care and "smart tanning" for tanning salon owners. "We promote tanning clients responsibly and professionally." Payment varies, on publication.

TODAY'S OR NURSE—Slack Inc., 6900 Grove Rd., Thorofare, NJ 08086. Frances R. DeStefano, Man. Ed. Clinical or general articles, from 2,000 words, of direct interest to operating room nurses.

TOTAL HEALTH—165 N. 100 E. #2, St. George, UT 84770. Robert L. Smith, Ed. Articles, 1,200 to 1,400 words, on preventive health care, fitness, diet, and mental health. Color or B&W photos. Pays $50 to $75, on publication.

VEGETARIAN TIMES—P.O. Box 570, Oak Park, IL 60303. Toni Apgar, Ed. Dir. Articles, 1,200 to 2,500 words, on vegetarian cooking, nutrition, health and fitness, and profiles of prominent vegetarians. "News Items" and "In Print" (book reviews), to 500 words. "Herbalist" pieces, to 1,800 words, on medicinal uses of herbs. Queries required. Pays $75 to $1,000, on acceptance. Guidelines.

VEGETARIAN VOICE—P.O. Box 72, Dolgeville, NY 13329. Jennie Collura, Sr. Ed. Quarterly. Informative, well-researched and/or inspiring articles, 600 to 1,800 words, on health, nutrition, animal rights, the environment, world hunger, etc. Pays in copies. Guidelines.

VIBRANT LIFE—55 W. Oak Ridge Dr., Hagerstown, MD 21740. Attn: Ed. Features, 750 to 1,500 words, on total health: physical, mental, and spiritual. Upbeat articles on the family and how to live happier and healthier lives; Christian slant. Pays $80 to $250, on acceptance.

VIM & VIGOR— 8805 N. 23rd Ave., Suite 400, Phoenix, AZ 85021. Fred Petrovsky, Ed. Positive health and fitness articles, 1,200 to 2,000 words, with accurate medical facts. By assignment only; writers with feature- or news-writing ability may submit qualifications for assignment. Pays $500, on acceptance. Guidelines.

THE WALKING MAGAZINE— 9-11 Harcourt, Boston, MA 02116. Seth Bauer, Ed. Articles, 1,500 to 2,500 words, on fitness, health, equipment, nutrition, travel and adventure, famous walkers, and other walking-related topics. Shorter pieces, 150 to 800 words, and essays for "Ramblings" page. Photos welcome. Pays $750 to $1,800 for features, $100 to $500 for department pieces, on acceptance. Guidelines.

WOMEN & RECOVERY—Need to Know Press, P.O. Box 1947-2, Cupertino, CA 95015. Sara V. Cole, Ed. Quarterly. Essays, exposés, humor, self-help articles, product or treatment profiles and reviews, opinion pieces, 1,000 to 2,000 words, related to women's recovery issues (physical, emotional, and spiritual). Poems, cartoons, B&W photos and drawings. Pays $35 to $100 for articles; $15 to $50 for poetry and art, on publication.

YOGA JOURNAL—2054 University Ave., Berkeley, CA 94704. Rick Fields, Ed. Articles, 1,200 to 4,000 words, on holistic health, meditation, consciousness, spirituality, and yoga. Pays $100 to $1,200, on acceptance.

YOUR HEALTH—5401 N.W. Broken Sound Blvd., Boca Raton, FL 33487. Susan Gregg, Ed.-in-Chief. Health and medical articles, 1,000 to 2,000 words, for a lay audience. Queries preferred. Pays $75 to $200, on publication.

YOUR HEALTH—1720 Washington Blvd., Box 10010, Ogden, UT 84409. Attn: Ed. Staff Articles, 1,000 words, on individual health care needs: prevention, treatment, low-impact aerobics, fitness, nutrition, etc. Color photos required. Pays 15¢ a word, on acceptance. Guidelines.

EDUCATION

ACTIVITY RESOURCES—P.O. Box 4875, Hayward, CA 94540. Mary Laycock, Ed. Math educational material only for books geared to grades K through 8. Submit complete book manuscript. Royalty.

AMERICAN SCHOOL & UNIVERSITY—P.O. Box 12901, 9800 Metcalf, Overland Park, KS 66212-2215. Joe Agron, Ed. Articles and case studies, 1,200 to 1,500 words, on design, construction, operation, and management of school and university facilities. Queries preferred.

BEAUTY EDUCATION—3 Columbia Cir., Albany, NY 12212. Catherine Frangie, Pub. Articles, 750 to 1,000 words, that provide beauty educators, trainers, and professionals in the cosmetology industry with information, skills, and techniques on such topics as hairstyling, makeup, aromatherapy, retailing, massage, and beauty careers. Send SASE for editorial calendar and themes. Pays in copies. Query.

THE BOOK REPORT—Linworth Publishing, 480 E. Wilson Bridge Rd., Suite L, Worthington, OH 43085-2372. Carolyn Hamilton, Ed./Pub. "The Journal for Secondary School Librarians." Articles by school librarians or other educators about practical aspects of running a school library. Write for themes and guidelines. Also publishes *Library Talk,* "The Magazine for Elementary School Librarians" and *Technology Connection,* "The Magazine for Library and Media Specialists."

CAREERS & THE DISABLED—See *Minority Engineer.*

CHANGE—1319 18th St. N.W., Washington, DC 20036. Attn: Ed. Columns, 700 to 2,000 words, and in-depth features, 2,500 to 3,500 words, on programs, people, and institutions of higher education. "We can't usually pay for unsolicited articles."

CHRISTIAN EDUCATION JOURNAL—Scripture Press Ministries, P.O. Box 650, Glen Ellyn, IL 60138. Leslie H. Stobbe, Exec. Ed. Articles, 5 to 15 typed pages, on Christian education topics. Pays $100, on publication. Guidelines.

THE CLEARING HOUSE—Heldref Publications, 1319 18th St. N.W., Washington, DC 20036. Judy Cusick, Man. Ed. Bimonthly for middle level and high school teachers and administrators. Articles, 2,500 words, related to education: useful teaching practices, research findings, and experiments. Some opinion pieces and satirical articles related to education. Pays in copies.

EQUAL OPPORTUNITY—See *Minority Engineer.*

FOUNDATION NEWS—1828 L St. N.W., Washington, DC 20036. Jody Curtis, Ed. Articles, to 2,000 words, on national or regional activities supported by, or of interest to, grantmakers fiand the nonprofit sector. Query.

GIFTED EDUCATION PRESS QUARTERLY—P.O. Box 1586, 10201 Yuma Ct., Manassas, VA 22110. Maurice Fisher, Pub. Articles, to 4,000 words, written by educators, laypersons, and parents of gifted children, on the problems of identifying and teaching gifted children and adolescents. "Interested in incisive analyses of current programs for the gifted and recommendations for improving the education of gifted students. Particularly interested in advocacy for gifted children, biographical sketches of highly gifted individuals, and the problems of teaching humanities, science, ethics, literature, and history to the gifted. Looking for highly imaginative and knowledgeable writers." Pays in subscription. Query required.

THE HISPANIC OUTLOOK IN HIGHER EDUCATION—17 Arcadian Ave., Paramus, NJ 07652. Attn: Ed. Articles, 1,500 to 2,000 words, on the issues, concerns, and potential models for furthering the academic results of Hispanics in higher education. Queries are preferred. Payment varies, on publication.

HOME EDUCATION MAGAZINE—P.O. Box 1083, Tonasket, WA 98855–1083. Helen E. Hegener, Man. Ed. Informative articles, 750 to 2,000 words, on all aspects of the growing homeschool movement. Send complete manuscript or detailed query with SASE. Pays 45¢ per column inch, on publication.

THE HORN BOOK MAGAZINE—11 Beacon St., Suite 1000, Boston, MA 02108. Attn: Ed. Articles, 600 to 2,800 words, on books for young readers and related subjects for librarians, teachers, parents, etc. Payment varies, on publication. Query.

INDEPENDENT LIVING PROVIDER—See *Minority Engineer.*

INSTRUCTOR MAGAZINE—Scholastic, Inc., 555 Broadway, New York, NY 10012. Mickey Revenaugh, Ed. Articles, 300 to 1,500 words, for teachers in grades K through 8. Payment varies, on acceptance.

ITC COMMUNICATOR—International Training in Communication, P.O. Box 1809, Sutter Creek, CA 95685. JoAnn Levy, Ed. Educational articles, 200 to 800 words, on leadership, language, speech presentation, procedures for meetings, personal and professional development, written and spoken communication techniques. SASE required. Pays in copies.

JOYFUL CHILD JOURNAL—34 Russell Ave., Buffalo, NY 14214. Karen Spring Stevens, Exec. Ed. Quarterly. Fiction and nonfiction, 500 to 1,000 words, that "explore how society and education can more effectively nurture children (and adults) to express their fullest potential, thus releasing their inner joy. Articles on educating and parenting the whole child (body, mind, and spirit)." Some short poetry. Queries preferred. Guidelines. Pays in copies.

LEADERSHIP PUBLISHERS, INC.—P.O. Box 8358, Des Moines, IA 50301–8358. Attn: Dr. Lois F. Roets. Educational materials for talented and gifted students, grades K to 12. Send SASE for catalogue and guidelines before submitting. Pays in royalty for books, and flat fee for booklets.

LEARNING—1607 Battleground Ave., Greensboro, NC 27408. Attn: Manuscript Ed. Articles that help teachers deal with issues such as stress, motivation, burnout, and other self-improvement topics; successful teaching strategies to reach today's kids; and ideas to get parents involved. SASE required. Pays $15 to $300. Allow 6 months for response.

LIBRARY TALK—See *The Book Report.*

MEDIA & METHODS—1429 Walnut St., Philadelphia, PA 19102. Michele Sokoloff, Ed. Dir. Articles, 800 to 1,000 words, on media, technologies, and methods used to enhance instruction and learning in K through 12th-grade classrooms. Pays $50 to $200, on publication. Query required.

MINORITY ENGINEER—150 Motor Pkwy., Suite 420, Hauppauge, NY 11788–5145. James Schneider, Ed. Articles, 1,000 to 1,500 words, for college students, on career opportunities; techniques of job hunting, and role-model profiles of professional minority engineers. Interviews. Pays 10¢ a word, on publication. Query. Also publishes: *Equal Opportunity*; *Careers & the Dis-ABLED*, query James Schneider; *Woman Engineer* and *Independent Living Provider*, query Editor Anne Kelly.

MOMENTUM—National Catholic Educational Assn., 1077 30th St. N.W., Suite 100, Washington, DC 20007–3852. Patricia Feistritzer, Ed. Articles, 500 to 1,500 words, on outstanding programs, issues, and research in education. Book reviews. Query or send complete manuscript. No simultaneous submissions. Pays $25 to $75, on publication.

SCHOOL ARTS MAGAZINE—50 Portland St., Worcester, MA 01608. Eldon Katter, Ed. Articles, 800 to 1,000 words, on art education with special application to the classroom: successful and meaningful approaches to teaching art, innovative art projects, uncommon applications of art techniques or equipment, etc. Photos. Pays varying rates, on publication. Guidelines.

SCHOOL SAFETY—National School Safety Ctr., 4165 Thousand Oaks Blvd., Suite 290, Westlake Village, CA 91362. Ronald D. Stephens, Exec. Ed. Published 8 times during the school year. Articles, 2,000 to 3,000 words, of use to educators, law enforcers, judges, and legislators on the prevention of drugs, gangs, weapons, bullying, discipline problems, and vandalism; also on-site security and character development as they relate to students and schools. No payment.

SESAME STREET PARENTS' GUIDE—One Lincoln Plaza, New York, NY 10023. Susan Schneider, Articles Ed. Articles, 800 to 2,500 words, on educational issues for families with young children (up to 8 years old). Pays 50¢ to $1 per word, within 6 weeks of acceptance.

TEACHING K-8— 40 Richards Ave., Norwalk, CT 06854. Patricia Broderick, Ed. Dir. Articles, 1,200 words, on the profession of teaching children. Pays to $35, on publication. Queries are not necessary.

TECH DIRECTIONS—Box 8623, Ann Arbor, MI 48107. Paul J. Bamford, Man. Ed. Articles, one to 10 double-spaced typed pages, for teachers and administrators in industrial, technology, and vocational educational fields, with particular interest in classroom projects, computer uses, and legislative issues. Pays $10 to $150, on publication. Guidelines.

TECHNOLOGY CONNECTION—See *The Book Report.*

TODAY'S CATHOLIC TEACHER—330 Progress Rd., Dayton, OH 45449.

Mary Noschang, Ed. Articles, 600 to 800 words, 1,000 to 1,200 words, and 1,200 to 1,500 words, on education, parent-teacher relationships, innovative teaching, teaching techniques, etc., of use to educators in Catholic schools. Pays $65 to $250, on publication. SASE required. Query. Guidelines.

WOMAN ENGINEER—See *Minority Engineer.*

FARMING AND AGRICULTURE

ACRES USA—P.O. Box 8800, Metairie, LA 70011. Fred C. Walters, Ed. Articles on sustainable agriculture: technology, case reports, "hands-on" advice. "Our emphasis is on production of quality food without the use of toxic chemicals." Pays 5¢ a word, on publication.

AMERICAN BEE JOURNAL—51 N. Second St., Hamilton, IL 62341. Joe M. Graham, Ed. Articles on beekeeping, for professionals. Photos. Pays 75¢ a column inch, extra for photos, on publication.

BEE CULTURE—623 W. Liberty St., Medina, OH 44256. Mr. Kim Flottum, Ed. Basic how-to articles, 500 to 2,000 words, on keeping bees and selling bee products. Slides or B&W prints. Payment varies, on acceptance and on publication. Queries preferred.

BEEF—7900 International Dr., Suite 300, Minneapolis, MN 55425. Joe Roybal, Ed. Articles on beef cattle feeding, cowherds, stocker operations, and related phases of the cattle industry. Pays to $300, on acceptance.

THE BRAHMAN JOURNAL—P.O. Box 220, Eddy, TX 76524–0220. Joe Brockett, Ed. Articles on Brahman cattle only. Photos. Pays $150 to $300, on publication. Queries preferred.

BUCKEYE FARM NEWS—Ohio Farm Bureau Federation, 2 Nationwide Plaza, Box 479, Columbus, OH 43216–0479. Lynn Echelberger, Copy Ed. Articles, to 600 words, related to agriculture. Pays on publication. Query. Limited market.

DAIRY GOAT JOURNAL—W. 2997 Markert Rd., Helenville, WI 53137. Dave Thompson, Ed. Articles, to 1,500 words, on successful dairy goat owners, youths and interesting people associated with dairy goats. "Especially interested in practical husbandry ideas." Photos. Pays $50 to $150, on publication. Query.

FARM AND RANCH LIVING—5400 S. 60th St., Greendale, WI 53129. Nick Pabst, Ed. Articles, 2,000 words, on rural people and situations; nostalgia pieces; profiles of interesting farms and farmers, ranches and ranchers. Pays $15 to $400, on acceptance and on publication.

FARM INDUSTRY NEWS—7900 International Dr., Minneapolis, MN 55425. Joe Degnan, Ed. Articles for farmers, on new products, machinery, equipment, chemicals, and seeds. Pays $350 to $500, on acceptance. Query required.

FARM JOURNAL—1500 Market St. Philadelphia, PA 19102-2181. Earl Ainsworth, Ed. Articles, 500 to 1,500 words, with photos, on the business of farming. Pays 20¢ to 50¢ a word, on acceptance. Query.

FARM SUPPLY RETAILING—P.O. Box 23536, Minneapolis, MN 55423–0536. Joseph Rydholm, Ed. Profiles, 1,400 words, of successful farm supply retailers and articles on running/managing a small business, preferably slanted to the farm supply retailer. Photos. Pays $150 to $200 for articles; $25 to $75 for photos, on publication.

FORD NEW HOLLAND NEWS—See *New Holland News.*

THE FURROW—Deere & Co., John Deere Rd., Moline, IL 61265. George Sollenberger, Exec. Ed. Specialized, illustrated articles on farming. Pays to $1,000, on acceptance.

HARROWSMITH COUNTRY LIFE—Ferry Rd., Charlotte, VT 05445. Attn: Ed. Dept. Articles, 2,000 to 4,000 words, on country living, gardening, home building and restoration, cooking, and do-it-yourself building projects. News briefs for "Gazette." Product and book reviews for "Sourcebank." Pays $500 to $2,000 for features, $50 to $600 for department pieces, on acceptance. Query required. Send SASE for guidelines.

THE LAND—P.O. Box 3169, Mankato, MN 56002–3169. Randy Frahm, Ed. Articles on Minnesota agriculture and rural issues. Pays $25 to $45, on acceptance. Query required.

NATIONAL CATTLEMEN—5420 S. Quebec St., Englewood, CO 80111–1904. Kendal Frazier, Ed. Colleen Church, Dir. of Publications. Articles, 1,200 words, related to the cattle industry. Payment varies, on publication.

NATURAL FOOD & FARMING—Natural Foods Associates, P.O. Box 210, Atlanta, TX 75551. Bill Francis, Ed. Articles, to 2,000 words, on health and nutrition. "We want articles that emphasize the relationship between agriculture, environmental issues, and preventive medicine with human health as a common denominator; teach the value of natural, poison-free food produced on living, fertile soil; expose the dangers of chemicals in our food, land, and water; and strive to convince others that good food and better health are necessary to save our civilization." Pays $25, on acceptance, plus 5¢ a word immediately after publication.

NEW HOLLAND NEWS—(formerly *Ford New Holland News*) New Holland, Inc., P.O. Box 1895, New Holland, PA 17557–0903. Attn: Ed. Articles, to 1,500 words, with strong color photo support, on agriculture and rural living. Pays on acceptance. Query.

OHIO FARMER—1350 W. Fifth Ave., Columbus, OH 43212. Tim White, Ed. Technical articles on farming, rural living, etc., in Ohio. Pays $50 per column, on publication.

ONION WORLD—P.O. Box 1467, Yakima, WA 98907–1467. D. Brent Clement, Ed. Production and marketing articles, to 1,500 words (preferred length 1,200 words), for commercial onion growers and shippers. "Research oriented articles are of definite interest. No gardening articles." Pays about $125, on publication. Query preferred.

PEANUT FARMER—3000 Highwoods Blvd., Suite 300, Raleigh, NC 27604–1029. Mary Evans, Man. Ed. Articles, 500 to 2,000 words, on production and management practices in peanut farming. Pays $50 to $350, on publication.

PENNSYLVANIA FARMER—P.O. Box 4475, Gettysburg, PA 17325. John R. Vogel, Ed. Articles on farmers in PA, NJ, DE, MD, and WV; timely business-of-farming concepts and successful farm management operations. Short pieces on humorous experiences in farming. Payment varies, on publication.

PROGRESSIVE FARMER—2100 Lakeshore Dr., Birmingham, AL 35209. Toni Holifield, Ed. Asst. Articles, to 5 double-spaced pages (3 pages preferred), on farmers or new developments in agriculture; rural communities; and personal business issues concerning the farmstead, home office, relationships, worker safety, finances, taxes, and regulations. Pays $50 to $400, on publication. Query.

RURAL HERITAGE—281 Dean Ridge Ln., Gainesboro, TN 38562. Gail Damerow, Ed. How-to and feature articles, 1,200 to 1,600 words, related to rural living and draft horses, mules, and oxen. Short pieces, to 800 words, also considered. Pays 5¢ a word, $10 for photos, on publication. SASE for guidelines.

SHEEP! MAGAZINE—W. 2997 Markert Rd., Helenville, WI 53137. Dave Thompson, Ed. Articles, to 1,500 words, on successful shepherds, woolcrafts, sheep raising, and sheep dogs. "Especially interested in people who raise sheep successfully as a sideline enterprise." Photos. Pays $80 to $150, extra for photos, on publication. Query.

SMALL FARM TODAY—3903 W. Ridge Trail Rd., Clark, MO 65243–9525. Paul Berg, Man. Ed. Agriculture articles, 800 to 1,800 words, on preserving and promoting small farming, rural living, and "agripreneurship." How-to articles on alternative crops, livestock, and direct marketing. Pays 3½¢ a word, on publication. Query.

SMALL FARMER'S JOURNAL—P.O. Box 1627, Dept. 106, Sisters, OR 97759. Address the Eds. How-tos, humor, practical work horse information, livestock and produce marketing, gardening information, and articles appropriate to the independent family farm. "Also actively seeking manuscripts with regional (Northwest) interest." Pays negotiable rates, on publication. Query.

SUCCESSFUL FARMING—1716 Locust St., Des Moines, IA 50309–3023. Gene Johnston, Man. Ed. Articles on farm production, business, and families; also farm personalities, health, leisure, and outdoor topics. Pays varying rates, on acceptance.

TOPICS IN VETERINARY MEDICINE—1600 Paoli Pike, W. Chester, PA 19380. Kathleen Etchison, Ed. Technical articles, 1,200 to 1,500 words, and clinical features, 500 words, on veterinary medicine. Photos. Pays $300, $150 for shorter pieces, extra for photos, on publication.

WALLACES FARMER—6200 Aurora Ave., Suite 609E, Urbandale, IA 50322–2838. Monte Sesker, Ed. Features, 600 to 700 words, on farming in Iowa; methods and equipment; interviews with farmers. Query. Payment varies, on acceptance.

THE WESTERN PRODUCER—Box 2500, Saskatoon, Saskatchewan, Canada S7K 2C4. Address Man. Ed. Articles, to 800 words (prefer under 600 words), on agricultural and rural subjects, preferably with a Canadian slant. Photos. Pays from 15¢ a word; $20 to $40 for B&W photos; to $100 for color photos, on acceptance.

WYOMING RURAL ELECTRIC NEWS—P.O. Box 380, Casper, WY 82606–0380. Kris Wendtland, Ed. Articles, 500 to 900 words, on issues relevant to rural Wyoming. Articles should support Wyoming's personal and economic growth, social development, and education. Wyoming writers given preference. Pays $20 to $50, on publication.

ENVIRONMENT AND CONSERVATION

AMERICAN FORESTS—1516 P St. N.W., Washington, DC 20005. Bill Rooney, Ed. Well-documented articles, to 2,000 words, with photos, on the use, enjoyment, and management of forests. Photos. Pays on acceptance.

THE AMICUS JOURNAL—Natural Resources Defense Council, 40 W. 20th St., New York, NY 10011. Kathrin Day Lassila, Ed. Quarterly. Articles and book reviews on national and international environmental topics. (No fiction, speeches, or product reports accepted.) Pays varying rates, 30 days after publication. Query required.

ANIMALS—350 S. Huntington Ave., Boston, MA 02130. Joni Praded, Dir./Ed. Informative, well-researched articles, to 2,500 words, on animal protection, national and international wildlife, pet care, conservation, and environmental issues that affect animals. No personal accounts or favorite pet stories. Pays from $350, on acceptance. Query.

ATLANTIC SALMON JOURNAL—P.O. Box 429, St. Andrews, N.B., Canada E0G 2X0. Harry Bruce, Ed. Articles, 1,500 to 3,000 words, related to Atlantic salmon: fishing, conservation, ecology, travel, politics, biology, how-tos, anecdotes. Pays $100 to $400, on publication.

AUDUBON—700 Broadway, New York, NY 10003. Michael W. Robbins, Ed. Bimonthly. Articles, 300 to 4,000 words, on conservation and environmental issues, natural history, ecology, and related subjects. Payment varies, on acceptance. Query.

BIRD WATCHER'S DIGEST—P.O. Box 110, Marietta, OH 45750. William H. Thompson, III, Ed. Articles, 600 to 2,500 words, for bird watchers: first-person accounts; how-tos; pieces on endangered species; profiles. Pays from $50, on publication. Submit complete manuscript.

E: THE ENVIRONMENTAL MAGAZINE—Earth Action Network, Inc., P.O. Box 5098, Westport, CT 06881. Jim Motavalli, Man. Ed. Environmental features, 4,000 words, and news for departments: 400 words for "In Brief"; and 1,000 words for "Currents." Pays 20¢ a word, on publication. Query.

EQUINOX—25 Sheppard Ave. W., Suite 100, North York, Ont., Canada M2N 6S7. Jim Cormier, Ed. Alan Morantz, "Nexus" Ed. Articles, 3,000 to 6,000 words, on popular geography, wildlife, astronomy, science, the arts, travel, and adventure. Department pieces, 300 to 800 words, for "Nexus" (science and medicine). Pays $1,500 to $3,500 for features, $100 to $500 for short pieces, on acceptance.

FLORIDA WILDLIFE— 620 S. Meridian St., Tallahassee, FL 32399–1600. Attn: Ed. Bimonthly of the Florida Game and Fresh Water Fish Commission. Articles, 800 to 1,200 words, that promote native flora and fauna, hunting, fishing in Florida's fresh waters, outdoor ethics, and conservation of Florida's natural resources. Pays $50 to $400, on publication.

HARROWSMITH COUNTRY LIFE—Ferry Rd., Charlotte, VT 05445. Attn: Ed. Dept. Feature articles, 1,000 to 3,000 words, on practical country living, gardening, rural and community issues, the environment, house profiles (design, construction, and restoration). How-to and do-it-yourself building, country skills, gardening projects, healthful cooking, news briefs, and product and book reviews. Pays $500 to $1,500 for features; $50 to $600 for department pieces. Query required. Guidelines.

NATIONAL GEOGRAPHIC—1145 17th St. N.W., Washington, DC 20036. William Allen, Ed. First-person, general-interest, heavily illustrated articles on science, natural history, exploration, and geographical regions. Written query required.

NATIONAL PARKS MAGAZINE—1776 Massachusetts Ave. N.W., Washington, DC 20036. Sue E. Dodge, Ed. Articles, 1,500 to 2,500 words, on areas in the National Park system, proposed new areas, threats to parks or park wildlife, new trends in park use, legislative issues, and endangered species of plants or animals relevant to national parks. No fiction, poetry, personal narratives, "My trip to . . . ," or straight travel pieces. Pays $100 to $800, on acceptance. Query. Guidelines.

NATIONAL WILDLIFE— 8925 Leesburg Pike, Vienna, VA 22184. Mark Wexler, Ed. Articles, 1,000 to 2,500 words, on wildlife, conservation, environment; outdoor how-to pieces. Photos. Pays on acceptance. Query.

NATURE CONSERVANCY—1815 N. Lynn St., Arlington, VA 22209. Mark Cheater, Ed. Membership publication. Very limited market. Not looking for new writers.

OUTDOOR AMERICA—707 Conservation Ln., Gaithersburg, MD 20878–2983. Attn: Articles Ed. Quarterly publication of the Izaak Walton League of America. Articles, 1,250 to 2,000 words, on natural resource conservation issues and outdoor recreation; especially fishing, hunting, and camping. Short items, 500 to 750 words. Pays 20¢ a word. Query with clips.

OUTDOOR TRAVELER, MID-ATLANTIC—WMS Publications, Inc., P.O. Box 2748, Charlottesville, VA 22902. Marianne Marks, Ed. Scott Clark, Assoc. Ed. Articles, 1,500 to 2,000 words, about outdoor recreation, travel, adventure, and nature in the mid-Atlantic region (NY, PA, NJ, MD, DE, DC, WV, VA, and NC). Departments include "Destinations," 450 to 600 words, on practical and descriptive guides to sports destinations; "Lodging," inns and lodges, including seasonal and outdoor activities; book reviews, 200 words. Pays $375 to $500 for features; payment varies for departments, on publication. Guidelines.

PACIFIC DISCOVERY—California Academy of Sciences, Golden Gate Park, San Francisco, CA 94118–4599. Gordy Slack, Assoc. Ed. Quarterly. Well-researched articles, 1,500 to 3,000 words, on natural history and preservation of the environment. Pays 25¢ a word, before publication. Query.

SEA FRONTIERS— 400 S.E. Second Ave., 4th Fl., Miami, FL 33131. Bonnie Bilyeu Gordon, Ed. Illustrated articles, 500 to 3,000 words, on scientific advances related to the sea; biological, physical, chemical, or geological phenomena; ecology; conservation, etc., written in a popular style for lay readers. Send SASE for guidelines. Pays 25¢ a word, on acceptance. Query.

SMITHSONIAN MAGAZINE— 900 Jefferson Dr., Washington, DC 20560. Marlane A. Liddell, Articles Ed. Articles on history, art, natural history, physical science, profiles, etc. Query with clips.

SPORTS AFIELD—250 W. 55th St., New York, NY 10019. Terry McDonell, Ed. Articles, 500 to 2,000 words, with quality photos, on hunting, fishing, nature, survival, conservation, ecology, personal experiences. How-to pieces; humor, fiction. Payment varies, on acceptance.

TEXAS PARKS & WILDLIFE—Fountain Park Plaza, 3000 S. Interstate Hwy. 35, Suite 120, Austin, TX 78704. Jim Cox, Sr. Ed. Articles, 800 to 1,500 words, promoting the conservation and enjoyment of Texas wildlife, parks, waters, and all outdoors. Features on hunting, fishing, birding, camping, and the environment. Department pieces, to 1,000 words, for "Parks & Places to Go," "State of Nature," and "Woods and Waters." Photos a plus. Pays to $600, on acceptance; extra for photos.

VIRGINIA WILDLIFE—P.O. Box 11104, Richmond, VA 23230–1104. Attn: Ed. Articles, 1,500 to 2,000 words, on conservation and related topics, including fishing, hunting, wildlife management, outdoor safety, ethics, etc. All material must have Virginia tie-in and be accompanied by color photos. Pays from 15¢ a word, extra for photos, on acceptance. Query.

WILDLIFE CONSERVATION—The Wildlife Conservation Society, Bronx, NY 10460. Nancy Simmons, Sr. Ed. First-person articles, 1,500 to 2,000 words, on "popular" natural history, "based on author's research and experience as opposed to textbook approach." Payment varies, on acceptance. Guidelines.

MEDIA AND THE ARTS

AHA! HISPANIC ARTS NEWS—Assoc. of Hispanic Arts, 173 E. 116th St., New York, NY 10029–1302. Dolores Prida, Ed. Editorials, profiles, opportunities for artists, monthly calendars. Query.

THE AMERICAN ART JOURNAL—730 Fifth Ave., Suite 205, New York, NY 10019–4105. Jayne A. Kuchna, Ed. Scholarly articles, 2,000 to 10,000 words, on American art of the 17th through the early 20th centuries. Photos. Pays $200 to $500, on acceptance.

AMERICAN INDIAN ART MAGAZINE—7314 E. Osborn Dr., Scottsdale, AZ 85251. Roanne P. Goldfein, Ed. Detailed articles, 10 double-spaced pages, on American Indian arts: painting, carving, beadwork, basketry, textiles, ceramics, jewelry, etc. Pays varying rates, on publication. Query.

AMERICAN JOURNALISM REVIEW— 8701 Adelphi Rd., Adelphi, MD 20783. Rem Rieder, Ed. Articles, 500 to 5,000 words, on print or electronic journalism, ethics, and related issues. Pays 20¢ a word, on publication. Query.

AMERICAN THEATRE—355 Lexington Ave., New York, NY 10017. Jim O'Quinn, Ed. Features, 500 to 2,500 words, on the theater and theater-related subjects. Departments include "People," "In Print," "Trends," and "Media." Payment varies, on publication. Query.

AMERICAN VISIONS, THE MAGAZINE OF AFRO-AMERICAN CULTURE—2101 S St. N.W., Washington, DC 20008–4011. Joanne Harris, Ed. Articles, 1,500 words, and columns, 750 to 2,000 words, on African-American culture with a focus on the arts. Pays from $100 to $1,000, on publication. Query.

ART & ANTIQUES—3 E. 54th St., 11th Fl., New York, NY 10022. Mark Mayfield, Ed. Investigative pieces or personal narratives, 1,500 words, and news items, 300 to 500 words, on art or antiques. Pays 50¢ to $1 a word, on publication. Query.

ARTS ATLANTIC—145 Richmond St., Charlottetown, P.E.I., Canada C1A 1J1. Joseph Sherman, Ed. Articles and reviews, 600 to 3,000 words, on visual, performing, and literary arts primarily in Atlantic Canada. Also, "idea and concept" articles of universal appeal. Query.

AT THE CROSSROADS—P.O. Box 317, Sta. P, Toronto, Ontario, Canada M5S 2S8. Karen Augustine, Ed.-in-Chief. Published 3 times a year. "A journal for women artists of African descent." Fiction, to 6 typed pages, and nonfiction, to 16 pages: interviews and profiles; news; reviews of black cultural events, concerts, books, dance, theatre, and music. "We are looking for fresh, challenging articles, columns, and opinion pieces. Get as creative and controversial as you want. No anti-black or homophobic material." Pays in honorarium or subscription.

BLUEGRASS UNLIMITED—Box 111, Broad Run, VA 22014–0111. Peter V. Kuykendall, Ed. Articles, to 3,500 words, on bluegrass and traditional country music. Photos. Pays 8¢ to 10¢ a word, extra for photos.

BRIGHT LIGHTS FILM JOURNAL—P.O. Box 420987, San Francisco, CA 94142–0987. Gary Morris, Ed.-in-Chief. Quarterly. Publishes film analysis, commentary, and history, 1,000 to 10,000 words, with an emphasis on social and cultural forces that shape films, past and present. "We deal with all forms of to independent and world cinema, from 'high art' films to mainstream Hollywood." Payment is in copies.

CAMERA & DARKROOM—9171 Wilshire Blvd., Suite 300, Beverly Hills, CA 90210. Ana Jones, Ed. Articles on photographic techniques and photographic portfolios, 1,000 to 2,500 words, with photos, for all levels of photographers. Pays $100 to $750. Query.

THE CHURCH MUSICIAN—127 Ninth Ave. N., Nashville, TN 37234. Jere V. Adams, Ed. Articles on choral techniques, instrumental groups, worship planning, music administration, directing choirs (all ages), rehearsal planning, music equipment, new technology, drama/pageants and related subjects, hymn studies, book reviews, and music-related fillers. Pays 5½¢ a word, on acceptance.

CLASSICAL MUSIC MAGAZINE—106 Lakeshore Rd. E., Suite 212, Mississauga, Ont., Canada L5G 1E3. Derek Deroy, Ed. Feature articles, 1,500 to 3,500 words, and short pieces, to 500 words. Interviews, personality profiles, book reviews, historical articles. "All articles should pertain to the world of classical music. No academic analysis. A solidly researched historical article with source references, or an interview with a famous classical personality are your best bets." Guidelines. Pays $100 to $500 (Canadian) for articles, $35 to $75 for short pieces, on publication.

DANCE MAGAZINE—33 W. 60th St., New York, NY 10023. Richard Philp, Ed.-in-Chief. Features on dance, personalities, techniques, health issues, and trends. Photos. Query; limited free-lance market.

DANCE TEACHER NOW—3101 Poplarwood Ct., Suite 310, Raleigh, NC 27604. K.C. Patrick, Ed. Articles, 1,000 to 3,000 words, for professional dance educators, senior students, and other dance professionals on practical information for the teacher and/or business owner; economic and historical issues related to the profession. Profiles of schools, methods, and people who are leaving their mark on dance. Must be thoroughly researched. Photos a plus. Pays $200 to $350, on acceptance. Query preferred.

DECORATIVE ARTIST'S WORKBOOK—1507 Dana Ave., Cincinnati, OH 45207. Sandra Carpenter, Ed. How-to articles, 1,000 to 1,500 words, on decorative painting. "Painting projects only, not crafts." Profiles, 500 words, of up-and-coming painters for "The Artist of the Issue" column. Pays $150 to $250 for features; $85 for profiles, on acceptance. Query required.

DOUBLETAKE—Ctr. for Documentary Studies at Duke Univ., 1317 W. Pettigrew St., Durham, NC 27705. Attn: Manuscript Ed. Quarterly. Realistic fiction, to 5,000 words, narrative poetry (submit up to 6 poems), book excerpts, personal experience, essays, humor, and cultural criticism. Color or B&W photo-essays, works in progress, and proposals "in the broadest definition of documentary work." (Submit up to 60 slides.) "We want to be a magazine where image and word have equal weight." Pays $1,000 for fiction and nonfiction, $2 a line for poetry, on acceptance. Guidelines. Query for nonfiction.

DRAMATICS—Educational Theatre Assoc., 3368 Central Pkwy., Cincinnati, OH 45225–2392. Don Corathers, Ed. Articles, interviews, how-tos, 750 to 4,000 words, for high school students of the performing arts with an emphasis on theater practice: acting, directing, playwriting, technical subjects. Prefer articles that "could be used by a better-than-average high school teacher to teach students something about the performing arts." Pays $25 to $300 honorarium. Complete manuscripts preferred; graphics and photos accepted.

THE ENGRAVERS JOURNAL—26 Summit St., P. O. Box 318, Brighton, MI 48116. Rosemary Farrell, Man. Ed. Articles, varying lengths, on topics related to the engraving industry and small business operations. Pays $60 to $175, on acceptance. Query.

ENTERTAINMENT WEEKLY—1675 Broadway, New York, NY 10019. Attn: Ed. Letters to the editor are published on the "Mail" page. Include name, address, and telephone number. No payment.

FILM QUARTERLY—Univ. of California Press Journals, 2120 Berkeley Way, Berkeley, CA 94720. Ann Martin, Ed. Historical, analytical, and critical articles, to 6,000 words; film reviews, book reviews. Guidelines.

FLUTE TALK—Instrumentalist Publishing Co., 200 Northfield Rd., Northfield, IL 60093. Kathleen Goll-Wilson, Ed. Articles, 6 to 12 typed pages, on flute performance, music, and pedagogy; fillers; photos and line drawings. Thorough knowledge of music or the instrument a must. Pays honorarium, on publication. Queries preferred.

GLORY SONGS—127 Ninth Ave. N., Nashville, TN 37234. Jere V. Adams, Ed. For volunteer and part-time music directors and members of church choirs. Very easy music and accompaniments designed specifically for the small church (4 to 6 songs per issue). Includes 8-page pull-out with articles for choir members on leisure reading, music training, and choir projects. Pays 5½¢ per word, on acceptance.

GUITAR PLAYER MAGAZINE—411 Borel Ave., Suite 100, San Mateo, CA 94402. Attn: Ed. Articles, 1,500 to 5,000 words, on guitarists, guitars, and related subjects. Pays $100 to $400, on acceptance. Buys one-time and reprint rights.

INDIA CURRENTS—P.O. Box 21285, San Jose, CA 95151. Arvind Kumar, Submissions Ed. Fiction, to 1,800 words, and articles, to 800 words, on Indian culture in the United States and Canada. Articles on Indian arts, entertainment, and dining. Also music reviews, 300 words; book reviews, 300 to 400 words; commentary on national or international events affecting the lives of Indians, 800 words. Pays in subscriptions. Guidelines.

JAZZIZ—3620 N.W. 43rd St. #D, Gainesville, FL 32606. Roy Parkhurst, Sr. Ed. Feature articles on all aspects of adult contemporary music: interviews, profiles, concept pieces. Departments include reviews of a variety of music genres, radio, and video. Emphasis on new releases. Send resumé with manuscript. Pays varying rates, on acceptance. Query.

LIVING BLUES—Hill Hall, Room 301, Univ. of Mississippi, University, MS 38677. David Nelson, Ed. Articles, 1,500 to 10,000 words, about living African-American blues artists. Interviews. Occasional retrospective/historical articles or investigative pieces. Pays $75 to $200, on publication; $25 per B&W photo. Query.

MAQUETTE—International Sculpture Ctr., 1050 17th St. N.W., Suite 250, Washington, DC 20036. Penelope Kiser, Ed. Articles, 1,500 to 2,500 words, on contemporary sculpture. Payment varies, on publication. Query required.

MODERN DRUMMER—12 Old Bridge Rd., Cedar Grove, NJ 07009. Ronald L. Spagnardi, Ed. Articles, 500 to 2,000 words, on drumming: how-tos, interviews. Pays $50 to $500, on publication.

NEW ENGLAND ENTERTAINMENT DIGEST—P.O. Box 88, Burlington, MA 01803. Julie Ann Charest, Ed. News and features on the arts and entertainment industry in New England. Pays $10 to $35, on publication.

PERFORMANCE—1101 University Dr., Suite 108, Fort Worth, TX 76107. Don Waitt, Pub./Ed.-in-Chief. Reports on the touring industry: concert promoters, booking agents, concert venues and clubs, as well as support services, such as lighting, sound, and staging companies.

PETERSEN'S PHOTOGRAPHIC— 6420 Wilshire Blvd., Los Angeles, CA 90048-5515. Geoffrey B. Engel, Ed. Articles and how-to pieces, with photos, on travel, video, and darkroom photography, for beginners, advanced amateurs, and professionals. Pays $125 per printed page, on publication.

PLAY—3620 N.W. 43rd St. #D, Gainesville, FL 32606. William Stephenson, Sr. Ed. Features, articles, and departments covering educational entertainment products for children: music, spoken word, video, electronics, books, computers, games, and other interactive toys. Targeted to parents; also includes clinical discussions of child development. Pays varying rates, on acceptance. Query.

PLAYBILL—52 Vanderbilt Ave., New York, NY 10017. Judy Samelson, Ed. Sophisticated articles, 700 to 1,800 words, with photos, on theater and subjects of interest to theatergoers. Pays $100 to $750, on acceptance.

POPULAR PHOTOGRAPHY—1633 Broadway, New York, NY 10019. Jason Schneider, Ed.-in-Chief. How-to articles, 500 to 2,000 words, for amateur photographers. Query with outline and photos.

PREVUE—P.O. Box 974, Reading, PA 19603. J. Steranko, Ed. Lively articles, interviews, and illustrated features on women and the arts (film and TV actresses, singers, comics, dancers, strippers, artists, celebrities, models, etc.). Pays varying rates, on acceptance. Query with clips.

ROLLING STONE—1290 Ave. of the Americas, 2nd Fl., New York, NY 10104. Attn: Ed. Magazine of American music, culture, and politics. No fiction. Query; no unsolicited manuscripts. Rarely accepts free-lance material.

SCULPTURE—International Sculpture Ctr., 1050 17th St. N.W., Suite 250, Washington, DC 20036. Suzanne Ramljak, Ed. Bimonthly. Articles on sculpture, sculptors, collections of sculpture, books on sculpture, criticism, etc. Payment varies, on publication. Query.

THE SENIOR MUSICIAN—127 Ninth Ave. N., Nashville, TN 37234. Jere V. Adams, Ed. Quarterly music periodical. Easy choir music for senior adult choirs to use in worship, ministry, and recreation. Also includes leisure reading, music training, fellowship suggestions, and choir projects for personal growth. For music directors, pastors, organists, pianists, choir coordinators. Pays 5½¢ a word, on acceptance.

SHEET MUSIC MAGAZINE—223 Katonah Ave., Katonah, NY 10536. Josephine Sblendorio, Man. Ed. Pieces, 1,000 to 2,000 words, for pianists and organists, on musicians and composers, how-tos, and book reviews, to 500 words; no hard rock or heavy metal subjects. Pays $75 to $200, on publication.

SOUTHWEST ART—5444 Westheimer, Suite 1440, Houston, TX 77056. Susan McGarry, Ed. Articles, 1,200 to 1,800 words, on the artists, art collectors, museum exhibitions, gallery events and dealers, art history, and art trends west of the Mississippi River. Particularly interested in representational or figurative arts. Pays from $400, on acceptance. Query with at least 20 slides of artwork to be featured.

STAGE DIRECTIONS—SMW Communications, Inc., 3101 Poplarwood Ct., Suite 310, Raleigh, NC 27604. Stephen Peithman, Ed. How-to articles, to 2,000 words, on acting, directing, costuming, makeup, lighting, set design and decoration, props, special effects, fundraising, and audience development for readers who are active in all aspects of community, regional, academic, or youth theater. Short pieces, 400 to 500 words, "are a good way to approach us first." Pays 10¢ a word, on publication. Guidelines.

STORYTELLING MAGAZINE—P.O. Box 309, Jonesborough, TN 37659. Attn: Eds. Features, 1,000 to 3,000 words, related to the oral tradition and stories, to 1,200 words, written in the oral tradition. News items, 200 to 400 words, and photos reflecting unusual storytelling events/applications. Themes for each issue; query first or send SASE to request topics. "We're looking for meaty free-lance work that reflects the ongoing dynamics of a reviving oral tradition." Pays 10¢ a word.

TCI—32 W. 18th St., New York, NY 10011. Patricia MacKay, Pub. David Barbour, Ed. Articles, 500 to 2,500 words, on design, technical, and management aspects of theater, opera, dance, television, and film for those in performing arts and the entertainment trade. Pays on acceptance. Query.

U.S. ART—220 S. Sixth St., Suite 500, Minneapolis, MN 55402. Frank J. Sisser, Ed./Pub. Features and artist profiles, 2,000 words, for collectors of limited-edition art prints. Pays $400 to $450, within 30 days of acceptance. Query.

VIDEOMAKER—P.O. Box 4591, Chico, CA 95927. Stephen Muratore, Ed. Authoritative, how-to articles geared to hobbyist and professional video camera/camcorder users: instructionals, editing, desktop video, audio and video production, innovative applications, tools and tips, industry developments, new products, etc. Pays varying rates, on publication. Queries preferred.

WEST ART—P.O. Box 6868, Auburn, CA 95604–6868. Martha Garcia, Ed. Features, 350 to 700 words, on fine arts and crafts. No hobbies. Photos. Pays 50¢ per column inch, on publication. SASE required.

WILDLIFE ART— 4725 Highway 7, P.O. Box 16246, St. Louis Park, MN 55416–0246. Rebecca Hakala Rowland, Ed. Informative, thought-provoking articles, 500 to 2,500 words, on wildlife and art topics. Many features spotlight individual artists; query with photos or slides of artist's work. Guidelines. Payment varies, on acceptance. Query required.

HOBBIES, CRAFTS, COLLECTING

ALL ABOUT BEER—See *Suds 'n Stuff.*

AMERICAN HOW-TO—12301 Whitewater Dr., Suite 260, Minnetonka, MN 55343. Tom Sweeney, Ed. Bimonthly. Articles, 1,000 to 1,500 words, for homeowners interested in do-it-yourself projects. Carpentry, plumbing, electrical work, landscaping, masonry, tools, woodworking, and new products. Payment is 50¢ a word, on acceptance. Send SASE for editorial calendar with upcoming themes. Queries preferred.

AMERICAN WOODWORKER—Rodale Press, 33 E. Minor St., Emmaus, PA 18098. David Sloan, Ed. "A how-to bimonthly for the woodworking enthusiast." Technical or anecdotal articles, to 2,000 words, relating to woodworking or furniture design. Fillers, drawings, slides and photos considered. Pays from $150 per published page, on publication; regular contributors paid on acceptance. Queries preferred. Guidelines.

ANCESTRY—P.O. Box 476, Salt Lake City, UT 84110. Loretto Szucs, Acquisitions Ed. Bimonthly for genealogists and hobbyists who are interested in getting the most out of their research. Articles, 1,500 to 4,000 words, that instruct (how-tos, research techniques, etc.) and inform (new research sources, new collections, etc.). No family histories, genealogies, or pedigree charts. Pays $25 to $75, on publication. Guidelines.

THE ANTIQUE TRADER WEEKLY—Box 1050, Dubuque, IA 52004. Carolyn Clark, Ed. Articles, 1,000 to 2,000 words, on all types of antiques and collectors' items. Photos. Pays from $25 to $200, on publication. Buys all rights. Query preferred.

ANTIQUES & AUCTION NEWS—P.O. Box 500, Mount Joy, PA 17552. Attn: Ed. Weekly newspaper. Factual articles, 600 to 1,500 words, on antiques, collectors, collections, and places of historic interest. Photos. Pays $5 to $20, after publication. Query required.

ANTIQUEWEEK—P.O. Box 90, Knightstown, IN 46148. Tom Hoepf, Ed., Central Edition; Connie Swaim, Ed., Eastern Edition. Weekly antique, auction, and collectors' newspaper. Articles, 500 to 1,500 words, on antiques, collectibles, restorations, genealogy, auction and antique show reports. Photos. Pays from $40 to $150 for in-depth articles, on publication. Query. Guidelines.

AQUARIUM FISH—P.O. Box 6050, Mission Viejo, CA 92690. Edward Bauman, Ed. Articles, 2,000 to 4,000 words, on freshwater, saltwater, and pond fish, with or without color transparencies. (No "pet fish" stories.) Payment varies, on publication.

AUTOGRAPH COLLECTOR MAGAZINE—510-A S. Corona Mall, Corona, CA 91720. Kevin Sherman, Ed. Articles, 1,000 to 3,500 words, on all areas of autograph collecting: preservation, framing, and storage, specialty collections, documents and letters, collectors and dealers. Payment varies. Queries preferred.

673

BECKETT BASEBALL CARD MONTHLY—15850 Dallas Pkwy., Dallas, TX 75248. Mike Payne, Ed. Articles, 500 to 2,000 words, geared to baseball-card collecting, with an emphasis on the pleasures of the hobby. "We accept no stories with investment tips." Pays $100 to $250, on acceptance. Query. Guidelines.

BECKETT BASKETBALL MONTHLY—15850 Dallas Pkwy., Dallas, TX 75248. Randy Cummings, Assoc. Ed. Articles, 400 to 1,000 words, on the sports-card hobby, especially basketball card collecting for readers 10 to 25. Query. Pays $100 to $250, on acceptance. Also publishes *Beckett Football Card Monthly, Beckett Focus on Future Stars, Beckett Hockey Monthly,* and *Beckett Racing Monthly.* SASE for guidelines.

BIRD TALK—Box 6050, Mission Viejo, CA 92690. Julie Rach, Ed. Articles for pet bird owners: care and feeding, training, safety, outstanding personal adventures, exotic birds in their native countries, profiles of celebrities' pet birds, travel to bird parks or shows. Good transparencies a plus. Pays 10¢ a word, after publication. Query required.

BIRD WATCHER'S DIGEST—P.O. Box 110, Marietta, OH 45750. William H. Thompson III, Ed. Articles, 600 to 3,000 words, on bird-watching experiences and expeditions: information about rare sightings; updates on endangered species. Pays from $50, on publication. Allow 8 weeks for response.

CARD COLLECTOR'S PRICE GUIDE—See *Combo.*

CARD PLAYER—3140 S. Polaris #8, Las Vegas, NV 89102. Linda Johnson, Pub. "The Magazine for Those Who Play to Win." Articles on poker events, personalities, legal issues, new casinos, tournaments, and prizes. Also articles on strategies, theory and game psychology to improve poker play. Occasionally uses humor, cartoons, puzzles, or anecdotal material. Pays $35 to $100, on publication; $15 to $35 for fillers. Guidelines.

THE CAROUSEL NEWS & TRADER— 87 Park Ave. W., Suite 206, Mansfield, OH 44902. Attn: Ed. Features on carousel history and profiles of amusement park operators and carousel carvers of interest to band organ enthusiasts, carousel art collectors, preservationists, amusement park owners, artists, and restorationists. Pays $50 per published page, after publication. Guidelines.

CHESS LIFE—186 Rt. 9W, New Windsor, NY 12553–7698. Glenn Petersen, Ed. Articles, 500 to 3,000 words, for members of the U.S. Chess Federation, on news, profiles, technical aspects of chess. Features on all aspects of chess: history, humor, puzzles, etc. Fiction, 500 to 2,000 words, related to chess. Photos. Pays varying rates, on acceptance. Query; limited free-lance market.

CLASSIC TOY TRAINS—21027 Crossroads Cir., Waukesha, WI 53187. Attn: Ed. Articles, with photos, on toy train layouts and collections. Also toy train manufacturing history and repair/maintenance. Pays $75 per printed page, on acceptance. Query.

COLLECTING TOYS—21027 Crossroads Cir., Waukesha, WI 53187. Tom Hammel, Ed. Bimonthly. Articles of varying lengths for a "nostalgia/collecting magazine that recalls the great toys of the 1940s and '70s." Profiles of toy collectors, designers, and manufacturers; articles for toy collectors. Color photos. Pays $75 to $100 per page.

COLLECTOR EDITIONS—170 Fifth Ave., New York, NY 10010. Joan

Muyskens Pursley, Ed. Articles, 750 to 1,500 words, on collectibles, mainly contemporary limited-edition figurines, plates, and prints. Pays $150 to $350, within 30 days of acceptance. Query with photos.

COLLECTORS JOURNAL—P.O. Box 601, Vinton, IA 52349. Cristina McCormick Hurley, Ed. Weekly tabloid. Features, to 2,000 words, on antiques and collectibles. Pays $10 for articles, $15 for articles with photos, on publication.

COLLECTORS NEWS—P.O. Box 156, Grundy Ctr., IA 50638. Linda Kruger, Ed. Articles, to 1,000 words, on private collections, antiques, and collectibles, especially 20th-century nostalgia, Americana, glass and china, music, furniture, transportation, timepieces, jewelry, farm-related collectibles, and lamps; include quality color or B&W photos. Pays $1 per column inch; $25 for front-page color photos, on publication.

COMBO—(formerly *Card Collector's Price Guide* and *Comic Book Collector*) 155 E. Ames Ct., Plainview, NY 11803. Ian M. Feller, Ed. Articles, from 800 words, related to non-sports cards (comic cards, TV/movie cards, science fiction cards, etc.) and comic books; collecting and investing; fillers. Queries preferred. Pays to 10¢ a word, on publication.

COMIC BOOK COLLECTOR—See *Combo*.

COUNTRY FOLK ART MAGAZINE—8393 E. Holly Rd., Holly, MI 48442–8819. Judith Karns, Man. Ed. Articles on decorating, gardening, collectibles; how-to pieces, 750 to 1,000 words, with a creative slant on American folk art; profiles of artisans. Pays $150 to $300, on acceptance. Submit pieces on seasonal topics one year in advance.

CRAFTS 'N THINGS—2400 Devon, Suite 375, Des Plaines, IL 60018–4618. Julie Stephani, Ed. How-to articles on all kinds of crafts projects, with instructions. Send manuscript with instructions and photograph of the finished item. Pays $50 to $250, on acceptance.

CROSS-STITCH SAMPLER—P.O. Box 718, Ingomar, PA 15127. Deborah A. Novak, Ed. Articles, 500 to 1,500 words, about counted cross-stitch, drawn thread, or themes revolving around stitching (samplers, needlework tools, etc.). Pays varying rates, on acceptance. Queries required.

DOG FANCY—P.O. Box 6050, Mission Viejo, CA 92690. Kim Thornton, Ed. Articles, 1,500 to 3,000 words, on dog care, health, grooming, breeds, activities, events, etc. Photos. Payment varies, on publication.

DOLLMAKER'S JOURNAL—Firefly Group, 2900 W. Anderson Ln., #20–244, Austin, TX 78757–1124. Barbara Johnson, Ed. Quarterly. Articles and how-to pieces for dollmakers. Pays in copies or ad space. Query required.

FIBERARTS—50 College St., Asheville, NC 28801. Ann Batchelder, Ed. Published 5 times yearly. Articles, 400 to 2,000 words, on contemporary trends in fiber sculpture, weaving, surface design, quilting, stitchery, papermaking, felting, basketry, and wearable art. Pays varying rates, on publication. Query with photos of subject, outline, and synopsis.

FINESCALE MODELER—P.O. Box 1612, Waukesha, WI 53187. Bob Hayden, Ed. How-to articles for people who make nonoperating scale models of aircraft, automobiles, boats, figures. Photos and drawings should accompany articles. One-page model-building hints and tips. Pays from $40 per published page, on acceptance. Query preferred.

GAMES—19 W. 21st St., Suite 1002-W, New York, NY 10010. R. Wayne Schmittberger, Ed.-in-Chief. "The magazine for creative minds at play." Features and short articles on games and playful, offbeat subjects. Visual and verbal puzzles, pop culture quizzes, brainteasers, contests, game reviews. Pays top rates, on publication. Send SASE for guidelines; specify writer's, crosswords, variety puzzles, or brainteasers.

HERITAGE QUEST—American Genealogical Lending Library, P.O. Box 329, Bountiful, UT 84011. Leland Meitzler, Ed. Bimonthly. Genealogy how-to articles, 2 to 4 pages; national, international, or regional in scope. Pays $30 per published page, on publication.

THE HOME SHOP MACHINIST—2779 Aero Park Dr., Box 1810, Traverse City, MI 49685. Joe D. Rice, Ed. How-to articles on precision metalworking and foundry work. Accuracy and attention to detail a must. Pays $40 per published page, extra for photos and illustrations, on publication. Guidelines.

KITPLANES—P.O. Box 6050, Mission Viejo, CA 92690. Dave Martin, Ed. Articles geared to the growing market of aircraft built from kits and plans by home craftsmen, on all aspects of design, construction, and performance, 1,000 to 4,000 words. Pays $60 per page, on publication.

LOST TREASURE—P.O. Box 1589, Grove, OK 74344. Grace Michael, Man. Ed. How-to articles, legends, folklore, and stories of lost treasures. Also publishes *Treasure Facts*: how-to information for treasure hunters (hunt strategies, techniques, pitfalls, how to increase finds, use equipment, locate treasure, etc), club news, who's who in treasure hunting, tips, etc. *Treasure Cache* (annual): articles on documented treasure caches with sidebar telling how to search for cache highlighted in article. Pays 4¢ a word, $5 for photos, $100 for cover photos.

LOTTOWORLD MAGAZINE—2150 Goodlette Rd., Suite 200, Naples, FL 33940. Barry Miller, Man. Ed. Articles of interest to readers, over 18 years old, who play the lottery. Human-interest pieces on lottery winners and losers, winning systems, advice on predicting numbers and increasing your odds of winning, competition between state lotteries, etc. Payment varies, 30 days after publication.

THE MIDATLANTIC ANTIQUES MAGAZINE—P.O. Box 908, Henderson, NC 27536. Lydia Stainback, Ed. Articles, 500 to 2,000 words, on antiques, collectibles, and related subjects. "We need show and auction reporters." Payment varies, on publication. Queries are preferred.

MILITARY HISTORY—741 Miller Dr. S.E., #D2, Leesburg, VA 22075. Jon Guttman, Ed. Bimonthly. Features, 4,000 words with 500-word sidebars, on the strategy, tactics, and personalities of military history. Department pieces, 2,000 words, on espionage, weaponry, perspectives, and travel. No fiction. Pays $200 to $400, on publication. Guidelines. Query.

MINIATURE QUILTS—See *Traditional Quiltworks*.

MODEL RAILROADER—21027 Crossroads Cir., P.O. Box 1612, Waukesha, WI 53187. Andy Sperandeo, Ed. Articles on model railroads, with photos of layout and equipment. Pays $90 per printed page, on acceptance. Query.

MOTOR BOATING & SAILING—250 W. 55th St., 4th Fl., New York, NY 10019–5905. Peter A. Janssen Ed./Pub. Articles, 1,500 words, on buying, maintaining, and enjoying boats. "Appeal to the dreams, adventures, and the lifestyles of committed boat owners." Hard-core, authoritative how-to. Payment varies, on acceptance. Query.

NEEDLEWORK RETAILER—P.O. Box 2438, Ames, IA 50010. Heidi A. Bomgarden, Ed. Articles, 500 to 1,000 words, on how to run a small needlework business. "Articles must specifically address the needlework business; general articles about small business will not be accepted." Pays varying rates, on acceptance.

NEW ENGLAND ANTIQUES JOURNAL— 4 Church St., Ware, MA 01082. Jody Young, Gen. Mgr. Julie Murkette, Man. Ed. Well-researched articles, to 2,500 words, on antiques of interest to collectors and/or dealers; auction and antiques show reviews, to 1,000 words; antiques market news, to 500 words; photos desired. Pays to $150, on publication. Query or send manuscript. Reports in 2 to 4 weeks.

NOSTALGIA WORLD—Box 231, North Haven, CT 06473. Richard Mason, Jr., Ed. Features, 3,000 words, and other articles, 1,500 words, on all kinds of collectibles: records, TV memorabilia (Munsters, Star Trek, Dark Shadows, Elvira, etc.), comics, gum cards, toys, sheet music, monsters, magazines, dolls, movie posters, etc. Pays $10 to $25, on publication.

NUTSHELL NEWS—21027 Crossroads Cir., P.O. Box 1612, Waukesha, WI 53187. Sybil Harp, Ed. Articles, 1,200 to 1,500 words, for dollhouse-scale miniatures enthusiasts, collectors, craftspeople, and hobbyists. Interested in artisan profiles, tours of collections, and how-to projects. "Writers must be knowledgeable miniaturists." Color slides or B&W prints required. Pays $50 per page, part on acceptance, balance on publication. Query.

PETERSEN'S PHOTOGRAPHIC— 6420 Wilshire Blvd., Los Angeles, CA 90048. Geoffrey B. Engel, Ed. How-to articles on all phases of still photography of interest to the amateur and advanced photographer. Pays about $125 per printed page for article accompanied by photos, on publication.

POPULAR MECHANICS—224 W. 57th St., New York, NY 10019. Deborah Frank, Man. Ed. Articles, 300 to 1,500 words, on latest developments in mechanics, industry, science, telecommunications; features on hobbies with a mechanical slant; how-tos on home and shop projects; features on outdoor adventures, boating, and electronics. Photos and sketches a plus. Pays to $1,500; to $500 for short pieces, on acceptance. Buys all rights.

QUILTING INTERNATIONAL—All American Crafts, Inc., 243 Newton-Sparta Rd., Newton, NJ 07860. Marion Buccieri, Ed. Bimonthly. Articles, 800 to 1,000 words, on contemporary quilts and related topics, as well as traditional and contemporary quilt patterns. Pays $75 to $200, on publication. Query.

QUILTING TODAY—See *Traditional Quiltworks.*

RAILROAD MODEL CRAFTSMAN—P.O. Box 700, Newton, NJ 07860–0700. William C. Schaumburg, Ed. How-to articles on scale model railroading; cars, operation, scenery, etc. Pays on publication.

RESTORATION—P.O. Box 50046, Tucson, AZ 85703–1046. W.R. Haessner, Ed. Articles, 1,200 to 1,800 words, on restoring and building chairs, machines, boats, autos, trucks, planes, trains, toys, tools, etc. Photos and art required. Pays $50 per page, on publication. Query.

SCHOOL MATES—U.S. Chess Federation, 186 Rte. 9W, New Windsor, NY 12553–7698. Brian Bugbee, Ed. Articles and fiction, 250 to 800 words, and short fillers, related to chess for beginning chess players (primarily children, 8 to 16). "Primarily instructive material, but there's room for fun puzzles, cartoons, anecdotes, etc. All chess related. Articles on chessplaying celebrities are always of interest to us." Pays from $20, on publication. Query; limited free-lance market.

73 AMATEUR RADIO—WGI, 70 Rte. 202N, Peterborough, NH 03458. David Cassidy, Assoc. Pub./Ed. Articles, 1,500 to 3,000 words, for electronics hobbyists and amateur radio operators. Pays $50 to $250.

SEW NEWS—P.O. Box 1790, News Plaza, Peoria, IL 61656. Linda Turner Griepentrog, Ed. Articles, to 3,000 words, "that teach a specific technique, inspire a reader to try new sewing projects, or inform a reader about an interesting person, company, or project related to sewing, textiles, or fashion." Emphasis is on fashion (not craft) sewing. Pays $25 to $400, on acceptance. Queries required; no unsolicited manuscripts accepted.

THE SEWING ROOM— 816 W. Bannock St., Suite 502, Boise, ID 83702–5850. Andrea Simmonsen, Asst. Ed. Articles and columns, 500 to 2,500 words, on basic sewing techniques, projects for and by children, updating old clothing, and one-day projects. Fillers and sewing tips. Color photos. Pays $450 to $600 for articles; $20 to $100 for fillers; $50 to $150 for photos, on acceptance.

SPORTS CARD TRADER—155 E. Ames Ct., Plainview, NY 11803. Attn: Ed. Office. Articles, from 1,000 words, related to all sports cards, especially baseball, football, basketball, and hockey cards; collecting and investing. Fillers. Pays 10¢ a word, on publication. Queries preferred.

SUDS 'N STUFF—(formerly *All About Beer*) Bosak Publishing, 4764 Galicia Way, Oceanside, CA 92056. Bunny Bosak, Assoc. Ed. Bimonthly. Articles on breweries and beer. Pays varying rates, after publication. Queries preferred.

TEDDY BEAR REVIEW—Collector Communications Corp., 170 Fifth Ave., New York, NY 10010. Stephen L. Cronk, Ed. Articles on antique and contemporary teddy bears for makers, collectors, and enthusiasts. Pays $50 to $200, within 30 days of acceptance. Query with photos.

THREADS MAGAZINE—Taunton Press, 63 S. Main St., Box 5506, Newtown, CT 06470. Attn: Ed. Bimonthly. Technical pieces on garment construction by writers who are expert sewers, knitters, quilters, and other craftspeople. Pays $150 per published page, on publication.

TRADITIONAL QUILTWORKS—Chitra Publications, 2 Public Ave., Montrose, PA 18801. Attn: Ed. Team. Specific, quilt-related how-to articles, 700 to 1,500 words. Patterns, features, and department pieces. Queries preferred. Pays $75 per published page, on publication. Also publishes *Quilting Today* and *Miniature Quilts*.

TREASURE CACHE and TREASURE FACTS—See *Lost Treasure.*

TROPICAL FISH HOBBYIST—1 T.F.H. Plaza, Neptune City, NJ 07753. Ray Hunziker, Ed. Articles, 1,000 to 3,000 words, for beginning and experienced tropical and marine fish enthusiasts. Photos. Pays $35 to $250, on acceptance. Query.

WEST ART—Box 6868, Auburn, CA 95604–6868. Martha Garcia, Ed. Features, 350 to 700 words, on fine arts and crafts. No hobbies. Photos. Pays 50¢ per column inch, on publication. SASE required.

WESTERN & EASTERN TREASURES—P.O. Box 1598, Mercer Island,

WA 98040–1598. Rosemary Anderson, Man. Ed. Illustrated articles, to 1,500 words, on treasure hunting and how-to metal-detecting tips. Pays 2¢ a word, extra for photos, on publication.

WILDFOWL CARVING AND COLLECTING—Stackpole Magazines, 500 Vaughn St., Harrisburg, PA 17110. Cathy Hart, Ed.-in-Chief. How-to and reference articles, of varying lengths, on bird carving; collecting antique and contemporary carvings. Pays varying rates, on acceptance. Query.

WIN MAGAZINE—120 S. San Fernando Blvd., Suite 439, Burbank, CA 91502. Joey Sinatra, Ed. Gambling-related articles, 1,600 to 2,500 words, and fiction. Pays on publication.

WOODENBOAT MAGAZINE—P.O. Box 78, Brooklin, ME 04616. Matthew Murphy, Ed. How-to and technical articles, 4,000 words, on construction, repair, and maintenance of wooden boats; design, history, and use of wooden boats; and profiles of outstanding wooden boat builders and designers. Pays $150 to $200 per 1,000 words. Query preferred.

WOODWORK— 42 Digital Dr., Suite 5, Novato, CA 94949. John McDonald, Ed. Bimonthly. Articles for woodworkers on all aspects of woodworking (simple, complex, technical, or aesthetic). Pays $150 per published page; $35 for "Techniques," on publication. Queries or outlines (with slides) preferred.

WORKBASKET MAGAZINE—700 W. 47th St., Suite 310, Kansas City, MO 64112. Kay M. Olson, Ed. Instructions and models for original knit, crochet, and tat items. (Designs must fit theme of issue.) How-tos on crafts and gardening, 400 to 1,200 words, with photos. Pays on acceptance; negotiable rates for instructional items.

WORKBENCH—700 W. 47th St., Suite 310, Kansas City, MO 64112. A. Robert Gould, Exec. Ed. Articles on do-it-yourself home improvement and maintenance projects and general woodworking articles for beginning and expert craftsmen. Complete working drawings with accurate dimensions, step-by-step instructions, lists of materials, in-progress photos, and photos of the finished product must accompany submission. Pays from $150 per published page, on acceptance. Query.

YELLOWBACK LIBRARY—P.O. Box 36172, Des Moines, IA 50315. Gil O'Gara, Ed. Articles, 300 to 2,000 words, on boys'/girls' series literature (Hardy Boys, Nancy Drew, Tom Swift, etc.) for collectors, researchers, and dealers. "Especially welcome are interviews with, or articles by past and present writers of juvenile series fiction." Pays in copies.

YESTERYEAR—P.O. Box 2, Princeton, WI 54968. Michael Jacobi, Ed. Articles on antiques and collectibles for readers in WI, IL, IA, MN, and surrounding states. Photos. Will consider regular columns on collecting or antiques. Pays from $10, on publication. Limited market.

ZYMURGY—Box 1510, Boulder, CO 80306–1510. Dena Nishek, Ed. Articles appealing to beer lovers and homebrewers. Pays in merchandise and books. Query.

POPULAR & TECHNICAL SCIENCE, COMPUTERS

AD ASTRA—National Space Society, 922 Pennsylvania Ave. S.E., Washington, DC 20003–2140. Pat Dasch, Ed.-in-Chief. Lively, non-technical features, to 3,000 words, on all aspects of international space program. Particularly interested in "Living in Space" articles; space settlements; lunar and Mars bases. Pays $150 to $200, on publication. Query. Guidelines.

AMERICAN HERITAGE OF INVENTION & TECHNOLOGY— 60 Fifth Ave., New York, NY 10011. Frederick Allen, Ed. Quarterly. Articles, 2,000 to 5,000 words, on history of technology in America, for the sophisticated general reader. Pays on acceptance. Query.

THE ANNALS OF IMPROBABLE RESEARCH—AIR, P.O. Box 380853, Cambridge, MA 02238. Marc Abrahams, Ed. Science humor, science reports and analysis, one to 4 pages. Brief science-related poetry. B&W photos. "This journal is the place to find the mischievous, funny, iconoclastic side of science." No payment. Guidelines.

ARCHAEOLOGY—135 William St., New York, NY 10038. Peter A. Young, Ed.-in-Chief. Articles on archaeology by professionals or lay people with a solid knowledge of the field. Pays $250 to $500, on publication. Query required.

ASTRONOMY—P.O. Box 1612, Waukesha, WI 53187. Robert Burnham, Ed. Articles on astronomy, astrophysics, space programs, research. Hobby pieces on equipment; short news items. Pays varying rates, on acceptance.

BIOSCIENCE—American Institute of Biological Science, 730 11th St. N.W., Washington, DC 20001. Anna Maria Gillis, Features Ed. Articles, 2 to 4 journal pages, on new developments in biology or on science policy, for professional biologists. Style should be journalistic. Pays $300 per journal page, on publication. Query required.

C/C++ USERS JOURNAL—1601 W. 23rd St., Suite 200, Lawrence, KS 66046–4153. Marc Briand, Man. Ed. Practical, how-to articles, 2,500 words (including up to 250 lines of code) on C/C++ programming. Algorithms, class designs, book reviews, tutorials. No programming "religion." Pays $110 per published page of text, $90 per published page of code, on publication. Query required. Guidelines.

COMPUTERSCENE MAGAZINE—3507 Wyoming Blvd. N.E., Albuquerque, NM 87111. Greg Hanson, Man. Ed. Laine Douglas Shomaker, Asst. Ed. Computer-related articles and fiction, 800 to 1,500 words. "We provide New Mexico computer users with entertaining and informative articles on all aspects of computers: hardware, software, technology, productivity, advice, personal experience, even computer-related fiction." Fillers, 400 to 800 words. Pays $40 to $57, on publication. Guidelines and editorial calendar.

DATA COMMUNICATIONS—1221 Ave. of the Americas, New York, NY 10020. Don Marks, Sr. Technology Ed. Technical articles, 2,000 to 5,000 words, on communications networks. Readers are managers of multinational computer networks. Payment varies; made on acceptance and on publication. Also publishes *Data Communications International* and *Data Communications Asia-Pacific*.

DIEHARD MAGAZINE—LynnCarthy Industry, Inc., P.O. Box 392, Boise, ID 83701. Attn: Ed. "The Flyer for Commodore 8 Bitters." Programs, reviews, tutorials, and humor, 500 to 3,000 words. Articles on all technical aspects of Commodore usage, especially on C/PM and machine language. Pays $20 to $200, on acceptance. Submit disk or hard copy.

ELECTRONICS NOW—500-B Bi-County Blvd., Farmingdale, NY 11735.

Brian C. Fenton, Ed. Technical articles, 1,500 to 3,000 words, on all areas related to electronics. Pays $50 to $500 or more, on acceptance.

ENVIRONMENT—1319 18th St. N.W., Washington, DC 20036–1802. Barbara T. Richman, Man. Ed. Factual and analytical articles, 2,500 to 5,000 words, on scientific, technological, and environmental policy and decision-making issues, especially on a global scale. Pays $100 to $300. Query.

THE FUTURIST—World Future Society, 7910 Woodmont Ave., Suite 450, Bethesda, MD 20814. Cynthia G. Wagner, Man. Ed. Features, 1,000 to 5,000 words, on subjects pertaining to the future: environment, education, business, science, technology, etc. Submit complete manuscript with brief bio (or CV) and SASE. Pays in copies.

HOBSON'S CHOICE: SCIENCE FICTION AND TECHNOLOGY—The Starwind Press, P.O. Box 98, Ripley, OH 45167. Attn: Submissions Ed. Articles and literary criticism, 1,000 to 5,000 words, for readers interested in science and technology. Also science fiction and fantasy, 2,000 to 10,000 words. Pays 1¢ to 4¢ a word, on acceptance. Query for nonfiction.

HOME OFFICE COMPUTING—Scholastic, Inc., 411 Lafayette St., New York, NY 10003. Bernadette Grey, Ed.-in-Chief. Articles, 3,000 words, that provide readers with practical information on how to run their businesses and use technology more effectively. Profiles of small-business owners. Education and entertainment pieces, 800 to 1,500 words, for "Family Computing" section. Writers must be familiar with microcomputers and software, home office products, and issues affecting small and home businesses. Payment varies, on acceptance.

HOMEPC—CMP Publications, 600 Community Dr., Manhasset, NY 11030–5772. Andrea Linne, Features Ed. Articles that help home computer users get the most out of their PCs. Payment varies, on acceptance. Query with clips and resumé required.

INFOMART MAGAZINE—Infomart Corporate Communications, 1950 Stemmons Fwy., Suite 6038, Dallas, TX 75207. Elizabeth Gustwick, Ed. Articles, 800 to 2,500 words, on business applications of information technology systems. Payment is negotiable. Query.

LINK-UP—2222 River Rd., King George, VA 22485. Loraine Page, Ed. Dir. Articles about online services, the Internet, and CD-ROM for the computer owner who uses this technology for business, home, and educational use. Pays $90 to $220 for articles, on publication. Photos a plus.

MICROCOMPUTER JOURNAL—76 N. Broadway, Hicksville, NY 11801. Art Salsberg, Ed.-in-Chief. How-to features, technical tutorials, servicing and construction projects related to personal computer and microcontroller equipment and software. Emphasizes enhancements, modifications, and applications. Lengths vary. Pays $90 to $150 per published page, after acceptance. Query with outline required.

NATURAL HISTORY—American Museum of Natural History, Central Park W. at 79th St., New York, NY 10024. Bruce Stutz, Ed.-in-Chief. Informative articles, to 3,000 words, on anthropology and natural sciences. "Strongly recommend that writers send SASE for guidelines and read our magazine." Pays from $1,000 for features, on acceptance. Query.

NETWORK NEWS—9710 S. 700 E., Bldg. A, Suite 206, Sandy, UT 84070. Linda Boyer, Ed. Humorous editorial articles, 600 to 800 words, on computing, especially networking. "Readers are computer professionals who are concerned with the multivendor network computing world." Pays 30¢ a word, after acceptance. Submit with SASE for reply only; manuscripts will not be returned.

OMNI—324 W. Wendover Ave., Suite 200, Greensboro, NC 27408. Keith Ferrell, Ed. Quarterly print version; monthly online (electrical) version. Articles, 750 to 3,500 words, on scientific aspects of the future: space colonies, cloning, machine intelligence, ESP, origin of life, future arts, lifestyles, etc. Fiction, 2,000 to 10,000 words, should be sent to Ellen Datlow, Fiction Ed., *Omni*, 277 Park Ave., 4th Fl., New York, NY 10172–0003. Pays $800 to $3,500, $175 for short items, on acceptance. Query.

PC GRAPHICS & VIDEO—201 E. Sandpointe Ave., Suite 600, Santa Ana, CA 92707. Gene Smarte, Ed. Applications of graphics and video on pc-compatible computers for professionals and enthusiasts. Pays flat rate. Query.

POPULAR ELECTRONICS—500-B Bi-County Blvd., Farmingdale, NY 11735. Carl Laron, Ed. Features, 1,500 to 2,500 words, for electronics hobbyists and experimenters. "Our readers are science and electronics oriented, understand computer theory and operation, and like to build electronics projects." Fillers and cartoons. Pays $25 to $500, on acceptance.

POPULAR SCIENCE—2 Park Ave., New York, NY 10016. Fred Abatemarco, Ed. Articles, with photos, on developments in applied science and technology. Short illustrated articles on new inventions and products; photo-essays, book excerpts. Payment varies, on acceptance.

PUBLISH—Integrated Media, Inc., 501 Second St., San Francisco, CA 94107. Jake Widman, Ed. Features, 1,500 to 2,000 words, and reviews, 400 to 800 words, on all aspects of computerized publishing. Pays $400 to $600 for reviews, $850 to $1,200 for full-length features, on acceptance.

RESELLER MAGAZINE—(formerly *Vertical Application Reseller*) 275 Washington St., Newton, MA 02158. John Russell, Ed. Articles, 500 to 1,200 words, that emphasize profitable strategies for value-added resellers, systems, integrators, software developers, and VAR-consultants. "Magazine sections include how-tos for selling, marketing, customer, technology, business, and verticals." Payment varies. Query.

SEA FRONTIERS—400 S.E. Second Ave., 4th Fl., Miami, FL 33131. Bonnie Bilyeu Gordon, Ed. Illustrated articles, 500 to 3,000 words, on scientific advances related to the sea; biological, physical, chemical, or geological phenomena; ecology; conservation, etc., written in a popular style for lay readers. Pays 25¢ a word, on acceptance. Query. Guidelines.

SKY & TELESCOPE—Sky Publishing Corp., P.O. Box 9111, Belmont, MA 02178–9111. Timothy Lyster, Man. Ed. Articles for amateur and professional astronomers worldwide. Department pieces for "Amateur Astronomers," "Astronomical Computing," "Telescope Making," "Observer's Page," and "Gallery." Also, 1,000-word opinion pieces, for "Focal Point." Mention availability of diagrams and other illustrations. Pays 10¢ to 25¢ a word, on publication. Query required.

TECHNOLOGY REVIEW—MIT, W59–200, Cambridge, MA 02139. Steven J. Marcus, Ed. General-interest articles on technology and its implications. Payment varies, on acceptance. Query.

VERTICAL APPLICATION RESELLER—See *Reseller Magazine.*

WORDPERFECT MAGAZINES—MS 7300, 270 W. Center St., Orem, UT 84057. Attn: Ed. Features, 1,400 to 1,800 words, and columns, 1,200 to 1,400 words, on how-to subjects with easy-to-follow instructions that familiarize readers with WordPerfect software. Avoid jargon. Pays $400 to $700, on acceptance. Query. Guidelines.

ANIMALS

AKC GAZETTE—(formerly *Pure-Bred Dogs/American Kennel Gazette*) 51 Madison Ave., New York, NY 10010. Mark Roland, Features Ed. "The official journal for the sport of purebred dogs." Articles, 1,000 to 2,000 words, relating to serious breeders of purebred dogs. Pays from $250 to $350, on acceptance. Query preferred.

ANIMAL PRESS—1815 Hancock St., San Diego, CA 92110. Renee Vititoe, Ed. Articles and fiction, 1,000 words. Well-written human interest, educational, or newsworthy articles about pets. No animal activist material. Pays $25 to $50, after publication.

ANIMALS—350 S. Huntington Ave., Boston, MA 02130. Joni Praded, Dir./Ed. Informative, well-researched articles, to 2,500 words, on animal protection, national and international wildlife, pet care, conservation, and environmental issues that affect animals. No personal accounts or favorite pet stories. Pays from $350, on acceptance. Query.

AQUARIUM FISH—P.O. Box 6050, Mission Viejo, CA 92690. Edward Bauman, Ed. Articles, 2,000 to 4,000 words, on freshwater, saltwater, and pond fish, with or without color transparencies. (No "pet fish" stories.) Payment varies, on publication.

BIRD TALK—Box 6050, Mission Viejo, CA 92690. Julie Rach, Ed. Articles for pet bird owners: care and feeding, training, safety, outstanding personal adventures, exotic birds in their native countries, profiles of celebrities' birds, travel to bird parks or bird shows. Pays 7¢ to 10¢ a word, after publication. Query required; good transparencies a plus.

CAT FANCY—P.O. Box 6050, Mission Viejo, CA 92690. Debbie Phillips-Donaldson, Ed. Nonfiction, to 3,000 words, on cat care, health, grooming, etc. Pays 5¢ to 10¢ a word, on publication. Query with SASE required.

DAIRY GOAT JOURNAL—W. 2997 Markert Rd., Helenville, WI 53137. Dave Thompson, Ed. Articles, to 1,500 words, on successful dairy goat owners, youths and interesting people associated with dairy goats. "Especially interested in practical husbandry ideas." Photos. Pays $50 to $150, on publication. Query.

DOG FANCY—P.O. Box 6050, Mission Viejo, CA 92690. Kim Thornton, Ed. Articles, 1,500 to 3,000 words, on dog care, health, grooming, breeds, activities, events, etc. Photos. Payment varies, on publication.

DOG WORLD—PJS Publishing Inc., 29 N. Wacker Dr., Chicago, IL 60606–3298. Donna L. Marcel, Ed. Articles, to 3,000 words, for breeders, pet owners, exhibitors, kennel operators, veterinarians, handlers, and other pet professionals on all aspects of pet care and responsible ownership: health care, training, legal rights, animal welfare, etc. Allow 4 months for response. Pays $50 to $500, on publication. Queries required. Guidelines.

EQUUS—Fleet Street Corp., 656 Quince Orchard Rd., Gaithersburg, MD 20878. Laurie Prinz, Man. Ed. Articles, 1,000 to 3,000 words, on all breeds of horses, covering their health and care as well as the latest advances in equine medicine and research. "Attempt to speak as one horseperson to another." Pays $100 to $400, on publication.

THE FLORIDA HORSE—P.O. Box 2106, Ocala, FL 34478. F.J. Audette, Ed. Articles, 1,500 words, on Florida thoroughbred breeding and racing. Also veterinary articles, financial articles, and articles of general interest. Pays $100 to $200, on publication.

HORSE & RIDER—12265 W. Bayaud Ave., Suite 300, Lakewood, CO 80228. Sue M. Copeland, Ed. Articles, 500 to 3,000 words, with photos, on western training and general horse care: feeding, health, grooming, etc. Pays varying rates, on publication. Guidelines.

HORSE ILLUSTRATED—P.O. Box 6050, Mission Viejo, CA 92690. Audrey Pavia, Ed. Articles, 1,500 to 2,500 words, on all aspects of owning and caring for horses. Photos. Pays $200 to $300, on publication. Query.

HORSEMEN'S YANKEE PEDLAR—83 Leicester St., N. Oxford, MA 01537. Nancy L. Khoury, Pub. News and feature-length articles, about horses and horsemen in the Northeast. Photos. Pays $2 per published inch, on publication. Query.

HORSEPLAY—P.O. Box 130, Gaithersburg, MD 20884. Lisa M. Kiser, Ed. Articles, 700 to 3,000 words, on eventing, show jumping, horse shows, dressage, driving, and fox hunting for horse owners and English riders. Profiles, instructional articles, occasional humor, and competition reports. Pays 10¢ a word or flat fee, after publication; buys all rights. Query with SASE. Guidelines.

LLAMAS—P.O. Box 100, Herald, CA 95638. Cheryl Dal Porto, Ed. "The International Camelid Journal," published 7 times yearly. Articles, 300 to 3,000 words, of interest to llama and alpaca owners. Pays $25 to $300, extra for photos, on publication. Query.

MUSHING—P.O. Box 149, Ester, AK 99725-0149. Todd Hoener, Pub. How-tos, innovations, history, profiles, interviews, and features related to sled dogs, 1,500 to 2,000 words, and department pieces, 500 to 1,000 words, for competitive and recreational dog drivers and skijorers. International audience. Photos. Pays $20 to $250, on publication. Queries preferred. Guidelines.

PRACTICAL HORSEMAN—Box 589, Unionville, PA 19375. Mandy Lorraine, Ed. How-to articles on English riding, training, and horse care. Payment varies, on acceptance. Query with clips.

PURE-BRED DOGS/AMERICAN KENNEL GAZETTE—See *AKC Gazette.*

SHEEP! MAGAZINE—W. 2997 Markert Rd., Helenville, WI 53137. Dave Thompson, Ed. Articles, to 1,500 words, on successful shepherds, woolcrafts, sheep raising, and sheep dogs. "Especially interested in people who raise sheep successfully as a sideline enterprise." Photos. Pays $15 to $150, extra for photos, on acceptance. Query.

TROPICAL FISH HOBBYIST—1 T.F.H. Plaza, Neptune City, NJ 07753. Ray Hunziker, Ed. Articles, 1,000 to 3,000 words, for beginning and experienced tropical and marine fish enthusiasts. Photos. Pays $35 to $250, on acceptance. Query.

THE WESTERN HORSEMAN—P.O. Box 7980, Colorado Springs, CO 80933–7980. Pat Close, Ed. Articles, 1,500 words, with photos, on care and training of horses; farm, ranch, and stable management; health care and veterinary medicine. Pays to $400, on acceptance.

WILDLIFE CONSERVATION—The Wildlife Conservation Society, Bronx, NY 10460. Nancy Simmons, Sr. Ed. Articles, 1,500 to 2,000 words, that "probe conservation controversies to search for answers and help save threatened species." Payment varies, on acceptance. Guidelines.

TRUE CRIME

DETECTIVE CASES—See *Globe Communications Corp.*

DETECTIVE DRAGNET—See *Globe Communications Corp.*

DETECTIVE FILES—See *Globe Communications Corp.*

FRONT PAGE DETECTIVE—Reese Communications, Inc., 460 W. 34th St., New York, NY 10001. Rose Mandelsberg, Ed.-in-Chief. True detective stories, 5,000 to 6,000 words, with detective work, mystery, and some kind of twist. No fiction. Good color photos of victim, perpetrator, crime scene, or detective may accompany article. Pays $250 to $500 for articles, to $200 for photos. Query.

FUGITIVE!—848 Dodge Ave., Suite 240, Evanston, IL 60202. Lawrence Shulruff, Ed. Articles, 600 to 800 words, on unsolved crimes and criminals at large. "Provide details about case. We encourage readers to contact police with tips about cases in each issue. Articles shouldn't be gory. Photos or composites of suspect are required." Query required. Pays $50 to $150, on acceptance.

GLOBE COMMUNICATIONS CORP.—1350 Sherbrooke St. W., Suite 600, Montreal, Quebec, Canada H3G 2T4. Dominick A. Merle, Ed. Factual accounts, 3,500 to 6,000 words, of "sensational crimes, preferably sex crimes, either pre-trial or after conviction." All articles will be considered for *Startling Detective, True Police Cases, Detective Files, Headquarters Detective, Detective Dragnet,* and *Detective Cases.* Query with pertinent information, including dates, site, names, etc. Pays $250 to $350, on acceptance; buys all rights.

HEADQUARTERS DETECTIVE—See *Globe Communications Corp.*

INSIDE DETECTIVE—Reese Communications, Inc., 460 W. 34th St., New York, NY 10001. Rose Mandelsberg, Ed.-in-Chief. Timely, true detective stories, 5,000 to 6,000 words, or 10,000 words. No fiction. Color photos of victim, killer, crime scene, or officer who headed investigation. Pays $250 to $500 for articles, to $200 for photos, on acceptance. Query.

MASTER DETECTIVE—Reese Communications, Inc., 460 W. 34th St., New York, NY 10001. Rose Mandelsberg, Ed.-in-Chief. Detailed articles, 5,000 to 6,000 words, with photos, on current cases, emphasizing human motivation and detective work. Also publish longer articles, 10,000 words. No fiction. Clear, color photos of victim, crime scene, perpetrator, and officer who led case. Pays $250 to $500, to $200 for photos, on acceptance. Query.

OFFICIAL DETECTIVE—Reese Communications, Inc., 460 W. 34th St., New York, NY 10001. Rose Mandelsberg, Ed.-in-Chief. True detective stories, 5,000 to 6,000 words, on current investigations, strictly from the investigator's point of view. No fiction. Clear color photos of victim, killer, crime scene, or lead officer on case. Pays $250 ($500 for double-length pieces), to $200 for photos, on acceptance. Query.

P.I. MAGAZINE: AMERICA'S PRIVATE INVESTIGATION JOURNAL— 755 Bronx Ave., Toledo, OH 43609. Bob Mackowiak, Ed. Profiles of professional investigators containing true accounts of their most difficult cases. Pays $50 to $75, plus copies, on publication.

STARTLING DETECTIVE—See *Globe Communications Corp.*

TRUE DETECTIVE—Reese Communications, Inc., 460 W. 34th St., New York, NY 10001. Rose Mandelsberg, Ed.-in-Chief. Articles, from 5,000 to 10,000 words, with photos, on current police cases, emphasizing detective work and human motivation. No fiction. Photos of perpetrator, victim, crime scene, or officer who spearheaded case. Pays $250 to $500, to $200 for photos, on acceptance. Query.

TRUE POLICE CASES—See *Globe Communications Corp.*

MILITARY

AIR FORCE TIMES—See *Times News Service.*

ARMY MAGAZINE—2425 Wilson Blvd., Arlington, VA 22201–3385. Mary B. French, Ed.-in-Chief. Features, 1,000 to 2,000 words, on military subjects. Essays, humor, history (especially World War II), news reports, first-person anecdotes. Pays 12¢ to 18¢ a word, $25 to $50 for anecdotes, on publication. Guidelines.

ARMY RESERVE MAGAZINE—1815 N. Ft. Myer Dr., #305, Arlington, VA 22209–1805. Lt. Col. Jim Nielsen, Ed. Articles, 1,000 words, on military training and the history of the Army Reserve; profiles, 250 words, of interesting people in Army Reserve; military family life, humor, and anecdotes. Submit manuscripts with high-quality color slides or photos. No payment. Query. Guidelines.

ARMY TIMES—See *Times News Service.*

FAMILY—169 Lexington Ave., New York, NY 10016. Liz DeFranco, Ed. Articles, 1,000 to 2,000 words, of interest to military women with children. Pays to $200, on publication. Guidelines.

LEATHERNECK—Box 1775, Quantico, VA 22134–0776. William V. H. White, Ed. Articles, to 3,000 words, with photos, on U.S. Marines. Pays $50 per printed page, on acceptance. Query.

MARINE CORPS GAZETTE—Box 1775, Quantico, VA 22134. Col. John E. Greenwood, Ed. Military articles, 500 to 2,000 words and 2,500 to 5,000 words. "Our magazine serves primarily as a forum for active duty officers to exchange views on professional, Marine Corps-related topics. Opportunity for 'outside' writers is limited." Queries preferred.

MILITARY—2122 28th St., Sacramento, CA 95818. Lt. Col. Michael Mark, Ed. Articles, 600 to 2,500 words, on firsthand experience in military service: World War II, Korea, Vietnam, and all current services. "Our magazine is about military history by the people who served. They are the best historians." No payment.

MILITARY HISTORY—741 Miller Dr. S.E., #D2, Leesburg, VA 22075.

Jon Guttman, Ed. Bimonthly. Features, 4,000 words with 500-word sidebars, on the strategy, tactics, and personalities of military history. Department pieces, 2,000 words, on espionage, weaponry, perspectives, and travel. Pays $200 to $400, on publication. Query. Guidelines.

NAVY TIMES—See *Times News Service.*

RETIRED MILITARY FAMILY—169 Lexington Ave., New York, NY 10016. Liz DeFranco, Ed. Articles, 1,000 to 1,500 words, of interest to military retirees and their families: travel, finance, food, hobbies, second careers, grandparenting, etc. Pays to $200, on publication.

THE RETIRED OFFICER MAGAZINE—201 N. Washington St., Alexandria, VA 22314. Attn: Manuscripts Ed. Articles, 800 to 2,000 words, of interest to military retirees and their families. Current military/political affairs: recent military history (especially Vietnam and Korea), health, money, military family lifestyles, and second-career job opportunities. Photos a plus. Pays to $1,000, on acceptance. Queries required; no unsolicited manuscripts. Guidelines.

TIMES NEWS SERVICE—Army Times Publishing Co., Springfield, VA 22159. Attn: R&R Ed. Free-lance material for "R&R" newspaper section. Articles about military life and its problems, as well as interesting things people are doing. Travel articles, 700 words, on places of interest to military people. Profiles, 600 to 700 words, on interesting members of the military community. Personal-experience essays, 750 words. No fiction or poetry. Pays $75 to $100, on acceptance. Also articles, 1,000 words, for supplements to *Army Times*, *Navy Times*, and *Air Force Times*. Address Supplements Ed. Pays $125 to $200, on acceptance. Guidelines.

VFW MAGAZINE— 406 W. 34th St., Kansas City, MO 64111. Richard K. Kolb, Ed. Magazine for Veterans of Foreign Wars and their families. Articles, 1,500 words, on current events, veteran affairs, and military history with veteran angle. Photos. Pays to $500, extra for photos, on acceptance. Query. Guidelines.

HISTORY

ALABAMA HERITAGE—The Univ. of Alabama, Box 870342, Tuscaloosa, AL 35487–0342. Suzanne Wolfe, Ed. Quarterly. Articles, to 5,000 words, on local, state, and regional history: art, literature, language, archaeology, music, religion, architecture, and natural history. Pays an honorarium, on publication, plus 10 copies. Query, mentioning availability of photos and illustrations. Guidelines.

AMERICAN HERITAGE— 60 Fifth Ave., New York, NY 10011. Richard F. Snow, Ed. Articles, 750 to 5,000 words, on U.S. history and background of American life and culture from the beginning to recent times. No fiction. Pays from $300 to $1,500, on acceptance. Query.

AMERICAN HERITAGE OF INVENTION & TECHNOLOGY— 60 Fifth Ave., New York, NY 10011. Frederick Allen, Ed. Quarterly. Articles, 2,000 to 5,000 words, on history of technology in America, for the sophisticated general reader. Pays on acceptance. Query.

AMERICAN HISTORY—(formerly *American History Illustrated*) 6405 Flank Dr., P.O. Box 8200, Harrisburg, PA 17105. Attn: Ed. Articles, 3,000 to 5,000 words, soundly researched. Style should be popular, not scholarly. No travelogues, fiction, or puzzles. Pays $300 to $650, on acceptance. Query required.

AMERICAN JEWISH HISTORY—American Jewish Historical Society, 2 Thornton Rd., Waltham, MA 02154. Dr. Marc Lee Raphael, Ed. Articles, 15 to 30 typed pages, on American Jewish history. No payment. Queries preferred.

CAROLOGUE—South Carolina Historical Society, 100 Meeting St., Charleston, SC 29401–2299. Stephen Hoffius, Ed. General-interest articles, to 10 pages, on South Carolina history. Pays in copies. Queries preferred.

CHICAGO HISTORY—Clark St. at North Ave., Chicago, IL 60614. Rosemary Adams, Ed. Articles, to 4,500 words, on political, social, and cultural history of Chicago. Pays to $250, on publication. Query.

EARLY AMERICAN LIFE—Box 8200, Harrisburg, PA 17105–8200. Mimi Handler, Ed. Illustrated articles, 1,000 to 3,000 words, on early American life: arts, crafts, furnishings, gardens, and architecture before 1850. Pays $50 to $500, on acceptance. Query.

EIGHTEENTH-CENTURY STUDIES—Dept. of English, CB 3520, Greenlaw Hall, Univ. of North Carolina, Chapel Hill, NC 27599. Attn: Eds. Quarterly. Articles, to 6,500 words, on all aspects of the eighteenth century, especially those that are interdisciplinary or that are of general interest to scholars working in other disciplines. Blind submission policy: Submit 2 copies of manuscript; author's name and address should appear only on separate title page. No payment.

GOLDENSEAL—The Cultural Ctr., 1900 Kanawha Blvd. E., Charleston, WV 25305–0300. Ken Sullivan, Ed. Features, 3,000 words, and shorter articles, 1,000 words, on traditional West Virginia culture and history. Oral histories, old and new B&W photos, research articles. Pays to $200, on publication. Guidelines.

THE HIGHLANDER—P.O. Box 397, Barrington, IL 60011. Angus Ray, Ed. Bimonthly. Articles, 1,300 to 1,900 words, related to Scottish history. "We do not use any articles on modern Scotland or current problems in Scotland." Pays $100 to $150, on acceptance.

HISTORIC TRAVELER—6405 Flank Dr., Harrisburg, PA 17112. John Stanchak, Ed. Bimonthly. Articles, 1,500 to 2,000 words, for upscale readers with a strong interest in history and historic sites. "Accurate information on historic destinations. Possible topics: battlefields, museums, antique shows, events, hotels, inns, transporation, reenactments, preserved communities, and architectural wonders. No South Pacific Islands, Alpine skiing, or Mediterranean cruises." Pays $300 to $500, on acceptance. Query with SASE and clips. Guidelines.

HISTORY NEWS—AASLH, 530 Church St., Suite 600, Nashville, TN 37219–2325. LuAnne Sneddon, Ed. History-related articles, 2,500 to 3,500 words, about museums, historical societies and sites, libraries, etc.; "In My Opinion" pieces, 1,000 words; "Technical Leaflets," 5,000 words. B&W photos. No payment made. Submit 2 copies of manuscript. Guidelines.

JOURNAL OF THE WEST—1531 Yuma, Manhattan, KS 66502–4228. Robin Higham, Ed. Articles, to 20 pages, devoted to the history and the culture of the West, then and now. B&W photos. Pays in copies.

LABOR'S HERITAGE—10000 New Hampshire Ave., Silver Spring, MD

20903. Stuart Kaufman, Ed. Quarterly journal of The George Meany Memorial Archives. Articles, 15 to 30 pages, for labor scholars, labor union members, and the general public. Pays in copies.

MILITARY—2122 28th St., Sacramento, CA 95818. Lt. Col. Michael Mark, Ed. Military history by people who served in the military. First-hand experiences, 600 to 2,500 words, of service in World War II, Korea, Vietnam, and more recent times. No payment.

MILITARY HISTORY—741 Miller Dr. S.E., #D2, Leesburg, VA 22075. Jon Guttman, Ed. Bimonthly. Features, 4,000 words with 500-word sidebars, on the strategy, tactics, and personalities of military history. Department pieces, 2,000 words, on espionage, weaponry, personalities, perspectives, and travel. Pays $200 to $400, on publication. Query. Guidelines.

MONTANA, THE MAGAZINE OF WESTERN HISTORY—225 N. Roberts St., Box 201201, Helena, MT 59620–1201. Charles E. Rankin, Ed. Authentic articles, 3,500 to 5,500 words, on the history of the American and Canadian West; new interpretive approaches to major developments in western history. Footnotes or bibliography must accompany article. "Strict historical accuracy is essential." No fiction. No payment made. Queries preferred.

NEBRASKA HISTORY—P.O. Box 82554, Lincoln, NE 68501. James E. Potter, Ed. Articles, 3,000 to 7,000 words, relating to the history of Nebraska and the Great Plains. B&W line drawings. Allow 60 days for response. Pays in copies. Cash prize awarded to one article each year.

OLD WEST—P.O. Box 2107, Stillwater, OK 74076. John Joerschke, Ed. Thoroughly researched and documented articles, 1,500 to 4,500 words, on the history of the American West. B&W 5x7 photos to illustrate articles. Pays 3¢ to 6¢ a word, on acceptance. Queries are preferred.

PENNSYLVANIA HERITAGE—P.O. Box 1026, Harrisburg, PA 17108–1026. Michael J. O'Malley III, Ed. Quarterly of the Pennsylvania Historical and Museum Commission. Articles, 3,000 to 4,000 words, that "introduce readers to the state's rich culture and historic legacy." Pays $300 to $500, up to $100 for photos or drawings, on acceptance.

PERSIMMON HILL—1700 N.E. 63rd St., Oklahoma City, OK 73111. M.J. Van Deventer, Ed. Published by the National Cowboy Hall of Fame. Articles, 1,500 to 2,000 words, on Western history and art, cowboys, ranching, and nature. Top-quality illustrations with captions a must. Pays from $100 to $250, on publication.

PROLOGUE—National Archives, NECP, Washington, DC 20408. Dr. Henry J. Gwiazda, Ed. Quarterly. Articles, varying lengths, based on the holdings and programs of the National Archives, its regional archives, and the presidential libraries. Pays in copies. Query.

SOUTH CAROLINA HISTORICAL MAGAZINE—South Carolina Historical Society, 100 Meeting St., Charleston, SC 29401–2299. Stephen Hoffius, Ed. Scholarly articles, to 25 pages including footnotes, on South Carolina history. "Authors are encouraged to look at previous issues to be aware of previous scholarship." Pays in copies.

TRUE WEST—P.O. Box 2107, Stillwater, OK 74076–2107. John Joerschke, Ed. True stories, 500 to 4,500 words, with photos, about the Old West to 1930. Some contemporary stories with historical slant. Source list required. Pays 3¢ to 6¢ a word, extra for B&W photos, on acceptance.

THE WESTERN HISTORICAL QUARTERLY—Utah State Univ., Logan, UT 84322–0740. Clyde A. Milner II, Ed. Original articles about the American West, the Westward movement from the Atlantic to the Pacific, twentieth-century regional studies, Spanish borderlands, Canada, northern Mexico, Alaska, and Hawaii. No payment made.

YESTERDAY'S MAGAZETTE—P.O. Box 15126, Sarasota, FL 34277. Ned Burke, Ed. Articles and fiction, to 1,000 words, on the 1920s through '70s, nostalgia and memories of people, places, and things. Traditional poetry, to 24 lines. Pays $5 to $25, on publication. Pays in copies for poetry and short pieces. Guidelines.

COLLEGE, CAREERS

THE BLACK COLLEGIAN—140 Carondelet St., New Orleans, LA 70130. Sonya Stinson, Ed. Articles, to 2,000 words, on experiences of African-American students, careers, and how-to subjects. Pays on publication. Query.

BYLINE—Box 130596, Edmond, OK 73013. Marcia Preston, Ed.-in-Chief. General fiction, 2,000 to 4,000 words. Nonfiction: 1,500-to 1,800-word features and 300-to 750-word special departments. Poetry, 10 to 30 lines preferred. Nonfiction and poetry must be about writing. Humor, 400 to 750 words, about writing. "We seek practical and motivational material that tells writers how they can succeed, not why they can't. Overdone topics: writers' block, the muse, rejection slips." Pays $5 to $10 for poetry; $15 to $35 for departments; $50 for features and $100 short fiction, on acceptance.

CAMPUS LIFE— 465 Gundersen Dr., Carol Stream, IL 60188. Harold Smith, Exec. Ed. Fiction and humor, reflecting Christian values, 1,000 to 3,000 words, for high school and college students. Pays from $150 to $400, on acceptance. Limited free-lance market. Published writers only. Queries required.

CAREER DIRECTIONS—21 N. Henry St., Edgerton, WI 53534. Diane Everson, Pres. and Pub. Tabloid. "Current News & Career Opportunities for Students." Career-related articles, 500 to 1,500 words, "mostly how-to." Pays $50 to $150, on acceptance. Also publishes the newsletter *Career Waves*, "leading ideas for career development professionals."

CAREER WAVES—See *Career Directions*.

CAREER WORLD—General Learning Corp., 60 Revere Dr., Northbrook, IL 60062–1563. Carole Rubenstein, Sr. Ed. Published monthly, September through May. Gender-neutral articles about specific occupations and career development for junior and senior high school audience. Query with clips and resumé. Payment varies, on publication.

CAREERS AND THE COLLEGE GRAD—260 Center St., Holbrook, MA 02343. Jennifer Most, Ed. Annual. Career-related articles, 1,500 to 2,000 words, for junior and senior liberal arts students. Career-related fillers, 500 words and line art or color prints. Queries preferred. No payment. Same address and requirements for *Careers and the MBA* (semiannual) for first-and second-year MBA students, and *Careers and the Engineer* (semiannual) for junior and senior engineering students.

CAREERS & THE DISABLED—See *Minority Engineer*.

CAREERS AND THE ENGINEER—See *Careers and the College Grad*.

CAREERS AND THE MBA—See *Careers and the College Grad.*

CIRCLE K—3636 Woodview Trace, Indianapolis, IN 46268–3196. Nicholas K. Drake, Exec. Ed. Serious and light articles, 1,500 to 2,000 words, on careers, college issues, trends, leadership development, self-help, community service and involvement. Pays $150 to $400, on acceptance. Queries preferred.

COLLEGE BROADCASTER—National Assn. of College Broadcasters, 71 George St., Box 1824, Providence, RI 02912–1824. Attn: Ed. Quarterly. Articles, 500 to 2,000 words, on college radio and TV station operations and media careers. Pays in copies. Query.

EQUAL OPPORTUNITY—See *Minority Engineer.*

FLORIDA LEADER—c/o Oxendine Publishing, P.O. Box 14081, Gainesville, FL 32604–2081. Kay Quinn, Man. Ed. Published 3 times a year. Articles, 800 to 1,000 words, for Florida college students. "Focus on leadership, career success, profiles of growth careers in Florida and the Southeast." Pays $35 to $50, on publication.

LINK: THE COLLEGE MAGAZINE—The Soho Building, 110 Greene St., Suite 407, New York, NY 10012. Ty Wenger, Ed.-in-Chief. News, lifestyle, and issues for college students. Informational how-to and short features, 500 to 800 words, on education news, finances, academics, employment, lifestyles, and trends. Well-researched, insightful, authoritative articles. Pays $100 to $500, on publication. Queries preferred. Guidelines.

MINORITY ENGINEER—150 Motor Parkway, Suite 420, Hauppauge, NY 11788–5145. James Schneider, Exec. Ed. Articles, 1,000 to 1,500 words, for college students, on career opportunities; techniques of job hunting; developments in and applications of new technologies. Interviews. Profiles. Pays 10¢ a word, on publication. Query. Same address and requirements for *Woman Engineer* (address Anne Kelly), and *Equal Opportunity* and *Careers & the DisABLED* (address James Schneider).

ONCE UPON A TIME—553 Winston Ct., St. Paul, MN 55118. Audrey B. Baird, Ed. "A Publication for Children's Writers and Illustrators." Quarterly. Articles, to 900 words: questions, insights, tips and experiences (no fiction) on the writing and illustrating life by published and unpublished writers. B&W artwork. No payment.

STUDENT LEADER—c/o Oxendine Publishing Inc., P.O. Box 14081, Gainesville, FL 32604–2081. Kay Quinn, Man. Ed. Semiannual. "The Magazine for America's Most Outstanding Students." Articles, 800 to 1,000 words, on leadership issues and career and college success. "Include quotes from faculty, corporate recruiters, current students, recent alumni." Pays $50 to $150, on publication.

STUDENT LEADERSHIP—P.O. Box 7895, Madison, WI 53707–7895. Jeff Yourison, Ed. Articles, to 2,000 words, and poetry for Christian college students. All material should reflect a Christian world view. Queries required.

UCLA MAGAZINE—405 Hilgard Ave., Los Angeles, CA 90024–1391. Jeffrey Hirsch, Ed. Quarterly. Articles, 2,000 words, must be related to UCLA through research, alumni, students, etc. Pays to $2,000, on acceptance. Queries required.

UNIQUE OPPORTUNITIES—455 S. 4th Ave., #817, Louisville, KY 40202. Bett Coffman, Asst. Ed. Articles, 2,000 to 3,000 words, that cover economic, business, and career-related issues of interest to physicians who are looking for their first practice or looking to make a career move. Doctor profiles, 500 words. "Our goal is to educate physicians about how to evaluate career opportunities, negotiate the benefits offered, plan career moves, and provide information on the legal and economic aspects of accepting a position." Pays 50¢ a word for features; $100 to $200 for profiles, on acceptance. Query.

WOMAN ENGINEER—See *Minority Engineer.*

OP-ED MARKETS

THE ARGUS LEADER—P.O. Box 5034, Sioux Falls, SD 57117–5034. Rob Swenson, Editorial Page Ed. Articles, to 850 words, on a wide variety of subjects for "Different Voices" column. Prefer local writers with an expertise in their subject. No payment. Guidelines.

THE ATLANTA CONSTITUTION—P.O. Box 4689, Atlanta, GA 30302. Teresa Weaver, Op-Ed Ed. Articles related to the Southeast, Georgia, or the Atlanta metropolitan area, 200 to 800 words, on a variety of topics: law, economics, politics, science, environment, performing and manipulative arts, humor, education; religious and seasonal topics. Pays $75 to $125, on publication. Submit complete manuscript.

THE BALTIMORE SUN—P.O. Box 1377, Baltimore, MD 21278–0001. Hal Piper, Opinion-Commentary Page Ed. Articles, 600 to 1,500 words, on a wide range of topics: politics, education, foreign affairs, lifestyles, etc. Humor. Payment varies, on publication. Exclusive rights: MD and DC.

THE BOSTON GLOBE—P.O. Box 2378, Boston, MA 02107–2378. Marjorie Pritchard, Ed. Articles, to 700 words, on economics, education, environment, foreign affairs, and regional interest. Pays $100, on publication. Send complete manuscript. Exclusive rights: New England.

BOSTON HERALD—One Herald Sq., Boston, MA 02106. Attn: Editorial Page Ed. Pieces, 600 to 800 words, on economics, foreign affairs, politics, regional interest, and seasonal topics. Prefer submissions from regional writers. Payment varies, on publication. Exclusive rights: MA, RI, and NH.

THE CHARLOTTE OBSERVER—P.O. Box 30308, Charlotte, NC 28230–0308. Jane McAlister Pope, Ed. Well-written, thought-provoking articles, to 700 words. "We are only interested in articles on local (Carolinas) issues or that use local examples to illustrate other issues." Pays $50, on publication. No simultaneous submissions in NC or SC.

THE CHICAGO TRIBUNE— 435 N. Michigan Ave., Chicago, IL 60611. Marcia Lythcott, Op-Ed Page Ed. Pieces, 800 to 1,000 words, on domestic and international affairs, environment, regional interest, and personal essays. SASE required.

THE CHRISTIAN SCIENCE MONITOR—One Norway St., Boston, MA 02115. Stacy Teicher, Opinion Page Coordinator. Pieces, 750 to 900 words, on domestic and foreign affairs, economics, education, environment, law, media, and politics. Pays $100, on acceptance. Retains all rights for 90 days after publication.

THE CLEVELAND PLAIN DEALER—1801 Superior Ave., Cleveland, OH 44114. Robert Stock, Assoc. Ed. Pieces, 700 to 900 words, on a wide variety of subjects. Pays $50, on publication.

DENVER POST—P.O. Box 1709, Denver, CO 80201. Bob Ewegen, Ed. Articles, 400 to 700 words, with local or regional angle. No payment for freelance submissions. Query.

DES MOINES REGISTER—P.O. Box 957, Des Moines, IA 50304. Attn: "Opinion" Page Ed. Articles, 500 to 750 words, on all topics. Prefer Iowa subjects. Pays $35 to $75, on publication. Exclusive rights: IA.

DETROIT FREE PRESS—321 W. Lafayette Blvd., Detroit, MI 48226. Attn: Op-Ed Ed. Opinion pieces, to 800 words, on domestic and foreign affairs, economics, education, environment, law, politics, and regional interest. Priority given to local writers or topics of local interest. Pays $50 to $100, on publication. Query. Exclusive rights: MI and northern OH.

THE DETROIT NEWS—615 W. Lafayette Blvd., Detroit, MI 48226. Attn: Richard Burr. Pieces, 500 to 750 words, on a wide variety of subjects. Pays $75, on publication.

FRESNO BEE—1626 E St., Fresno, CA 93786–0001. Karen Baker, Ed. Articles, 750 words, by central California writers only.

INDIANAPOLIS STAR—P.O. Box 145, Indianapolis, IN 46206–0145. John H. Lyst, Ed. Articles, 700 to 800 words. Pays $40, on publication. Exclusive rights: IN.

JOURNAL AMERICAN—P.O. Box 90130, Bellevue, WA 98009–9230. Craig Groshart, Editorial Page Ed. Articles, to 600 words, by local authors on local and regional issues. "Very limited market." No payment.

LONG BEACH PRESS-TELEGRAM—604 Pine Ave., Long Beach, CA 90844. Larry Allison, Ed. Articles, 750 to 900 words, on regional topics. Pays $75, on publication. Exclusive rights: Los Angeles area.

LOS ANGELES TIMES—Times Mirror Sq., Los Angeles, CA 90053. Bob Berger, Op-Ed Ed. Commentary pieces, 650 to 700 words, on many subjects. "Not interested in nostalgia or first-person reaction to faraway events. Pieces must be exclusive." Payment varies, on publication. Limited market. SASE required.

LOUISVILLE COURIER-JOURNAL—525 W. Broadway, Louisville, KY 40202. Attn: Op-Ed Ed. Pieces, 750 words, on regional topics. Local writers preferred. Pays $25 to $50, on publication. Very limited market.

THE NEW YORK TIMES—229 W. 43rd St., New York, NY 10036. Attn: Op-Ed Ed. Opinion pieces, 650 to 800 words, on any topic, including public policy, science, lifestyles, and ideas, etc. Include your address, daytime phone number, and social security number with submission. "If you haven't heard from us within 2 weeks, you can assume we are not using your piece. Include SASE if you want work returned." Pays on publication. Buys first North American rights.

NEWSDAY—"Viewpoints," 235 Pinelawn Rd., Melville, NY 11747. Noel Rubinton, "Viewpoints" Ed. Pieces, 700 to 800 words, on a variety of topics. Pays $150, on publication.

THE ORANGE COUNTY REGISTER—P.O. Box 11626, Santa Ana, CA 92711. K.E. Grubbs, Jr., Ed. Articles on a wide range of local and national issues and topics. Pays $50 to $100, on publication.

THE OREGONIAN—1320 S.W. Broadway, Portland, OR 97201. Attn: Op-Ed Ed. Articles, 900 to 1,000 words, of news analysis from Pacific Northwest writers or on regional topics. Pays $100 to $150, on publication. Send complete manuscript.

PITTSBURGH POST GAZETTE—34 Blvd. of the Allies, Pittsburgh, PA 15222. John Allison, Contributions Ed. Articles, to 1,000 words, on a variety of subjects. No whimsy. Pays $60 to $150, on publication. SASE required.

PORTLAND PRESS HERALD—P.O. Box 1460, Portland, ME 04104–5009. Attn: Op-Ed Page Ed. Articles, 750 words, on any topic with state tie-in. No payment without prior agreement. Exclusive rights: ME.

THE REGISTER GUARD—P.O. Box 10188, Eugene, OR 97440. Don Robinson, Editorial Page Ed. All subjects; regional angle preferred. Pays $25 to $50, on publication. Very limited use of non-local writers.

THE SACRAMENTO BEE—2100 Q St., Sacramento, CA 95852. William Kahrl, Opinion Ed. Op-ed pieces, to 750 words; state and regional topics preferred. Pays $150, on publication.

ST. LOUIS POST-DISPATCH—900 N. Tucker Blvd., St. Louis, MO 63101. Donna Korando, Commentary Ed. Articles, 700 words, on economics, education, science, politics, foreign and domestic affairs, and the environment. Pays $70, on publication. "Goal is to have half of the articles by local writers."

ST. PAUL PIONEER PRESS—345 Cedar St., St. Paul, MN 55101. Ronald D. Clark, Ed. Articles, to 750 words, on a variety of topics. Strongly prefer authors or topics with a connection to the area. Pays $75, on publication.

ST. PETERSBURG TIMES—Box 1121, 490 First Ave. S., St. Petersburg, FL 33731. Jon East, "Perspective" Section Ed. Authoritative articles, to 2,000 words, on current political, economic, and social issues. Payment varies, on publication. Query.

THE SAN FRANCISCO CHRONICLE—901 Mission St., San Francisco, CA 94103. Dean Wakefield, Open Forum Ed. Articles, 400 and 650 words, "that represent lively writing, are pertinent to public policy debates, and move the debate forward." Pays to $150 (usually $75 to $100 for unsolicited pieces), on publication.

SAN FRANCISCO EXAMINER—110 5th St., San Francisco, CA 94103. Attn: Op-Ed Ed. Well-written articles, 500 to 650 words, double-spaced; preference given to local and state issues and to subjects bypassed by most news media. No sports. No first-run movies. Payment varies, on publication.

USA TODAY—1000 Wilson Blvd., Arlington, VA 22229. Juan J. Walte, Ed./Columns. Articles, 600 words, on current public policy issues. Very limited market. Pays $200, on publication. Query.

THE WALL STREET JOURNAL—Editorial Page, 200 Liberty St., New York, NY 10281. David B. Brooks, Op-Ed Ed. Articles, to 1,500 words, on politics, economics, law, education, environment, humor (occasionally), and foreign and domestic affairs. Articles must be timely, heavily reported, and of national interest by writers with expertise in their field. Pays $150 to $300, on publication.

WASHINGTON TIMES—3600 New York Ave. N.E., Washington, DC 20002. Frank Perley, Articles and Opinion Page Ed. Articles, 800 to 1,000 words, on a variety of subjects. No pieces written in the first-person. "Syndicated columnists cover the 'big' issues; find an area that is off the beaten path." Pays $150, on publication. Exclusive rights: Washington, DC, and Baltimore area.

ADULT MAGAZINES

CHIC—9171 Wilshire Blvd., Suite 300, Beverly Hills, CA 90210. Scott Schalin, Exec. Ed. Sex-related articles, interviews, erotic fiction, 2,500 words. Query for articles. Pays $500 for articles, $350 for fiction, on acceptance.

D-CUP—Swank Publications, Inc., 210 Rte. 4 E., Suite 401, Paramus, NJ 07652. Bob Rosen, Ed. Erotic fiction and articles, 2,000 to 2,500 words. Pays $100 to $250, on publication.

FORUM, THE INTERNATIONAL JOURNAL OF HUMAN RELATIONS—277 Park Ave., New York, NY 10172. V. K. McCarty, Assoc. Pub./ Ed. Dir. Erotic fiction and couple-oriented articles focusing on sex information. Pays from $1,000, on acceptance.

GALLERY—401 Park Ave. S., New York, NY 10016–8802. Barry Janoff, Ed.-in-Chief. Rich Friedman, Man. Ed. Articles, investigative pieces, interviews, profiles, to 2,500 words, for sophisticated men. Short humor, satire, service pieces, and fiction. Photos. Pays varying rates, on publication. Query. Guidelines.

GENESIS—110 E. 59th St., Suite 3100, New York, NY 10022. Michael Banka, Pub. Steve Glassman, Man. Ed. Articles, 2,000 words. Sexually explicit nonfiction features, 2,000 words. Photo-essays. Pays 60 days after acceptance. Query with clips.

PENTHOUSE—1965 Broadway, New York, NY 10023. Peter Bloch, Ed. Lavada B. Nahon, Sr. Ed. Articles, to 5,000 words: general-interest profiles, interviews (with introduction), and investigative pieces. Pays on acceptance.

PLAYBOY—680 N. Lake Shore Dr., Chicago, IL 60611. Peter Moore, Stephen Randall, Articles Eds. Articles, 3,500 to 6,000 words, and sophisticated fiction, 1,000 to 10,000 words (5,000 preferred), for urban men. Humor; satire. Science fiction. Pays to $5,000 for articles, to $5,000 for fiction, $2,000 for short-shorts, on acceptance.

PLAYERS—8060 Melrose Ave., Los Angeles, CA 90046. L. D. Wills, Ed. Articles, 1,000 to 3,000 words, for black men: politics, economics, travel, fashion, grooming, entertainment, sports, interviews, fiction, humor, satire, health, and sex. Photos a plus. Pays on publication.

PLAYGIRL—801 Second Ave., New York, NY 10017. Laurie Sue Brockway, Ed.-in-Chief. Articles, 1,500 to 4,000 words, for women 18 and older. Erotic fiction, 1,000 to 3,500 words. Pays varying rates, on acceptance.

VARIATIONS, FOR LIBERATED LOVERS—277 Park Ave., New York, NY 10172. V. K. McCarty, Ed. Dir./Assoc. Pub. First-person true narrative descriptions of "a couple's enthusiasm, secrets, and exquisitely articulated sex scenes squarely focused within one of the magazine's pleasure categories." Pays $400, on acceptance.

WILDE—530 Howard St., Suite 400, San Francisco, CA 94105. John Fall, Ed. Investigative news features, commentary, interviews, and profiles for gay and bisexual men. Also, erotic and nonerotic fiction, 4,000 words. Erotic photos. Payment varies, on publication. Queries preferred.

FICTION MARKETS

This list gives the fiction requirements of general- and special-interest magazines, including those that publish detective and mystery, science fiction and fantasy, romance and confession stories. Other good markets for short fiction are the *College, Literary, and Little Magazines* where, though payment is modest (usually in copies only), publication can bring the work of a beginning writer to the attention of editors at the larger magazines. Juvenile fiction markets are listed under *Juvenile, Teenage, and Young Adult Magazines.* Publishers of book-length fiction manuscripts are listed under *Book Publishers.*

All manuscripts must be typed double-space and submitted with self-addressed envelopes bearing postage sufficient for the return of the material. If a manuscript need not be returned, note this with the submission, and enclose an SASE or a self-addressed, stamped postcard for editorial reply. Use good white paper; onion skin and erasable bond are not acceptable. *Always* keep a copy of the manuscript, since occasionally material is lost in the mail. Magazines may take several weeks—often longer—to read and report on submissions. If an editor has not reported on a manuscript after a reasonable length of time, write a brief, courteous letter of inquiry.

GENERAL FICTION

ABORIGINAL SF—P.O. Box 2449, Woburn, MA 01888–0849. Charles C. Ryan, Ed. Stories, 2,500 to 7,500 words, with a unique scientific idea, human or alien character, plot, and theme of lasting value; "must be science fiction; no fantasy, horror, or sword and sorcery." Pays $250. Guidelines.

AFRICAN VOICES—270 W. 96th St., New York, NY 10025. Carolyn A. Butts, Exec. Ed. Bimonthly. Humorous, erotic, and dramatic fiction, 500 to 2,500 words, by ethnic writers. Nonfiction, 500 to 1,500 words: investigative articles, artist profiles, essays, and first-person narratives. Poetry, to 50 lines. Pays $25 for fiction, on publication, plus 10 copies of magazine. (Payment varies for nonfiction.)

AIM MAGAZINE—P.O. Box 20554, Chicago, IL 60620. Ruth Apilado, Ed. Short stories, 800 to 3,000 words, geared to proving that people from different backgrounds are more alike than they are different. Story should not moralize. Pays from $15 to $25, on publication. Annual contest.

ALFRED HITCHCOCK MYSTERY MAGAZINE—1540 Broadway, New York, NY 10036. Cathleen Jordan, Ed. Well-plotted, plausible mystery, suspense, detection and crime stories, to 14,000 words; "ghost stories, humor, futuristic or atmospheric tales are all possible, as long as they include a crime or the suggestion of one." Pays 8¢ a word, on acceptance. Guidelines.

ALOHA, THE MAGAZINE OF HAWAII AND THE PACIFIC—P.O. Box 3260, Honolulu, HI 96801. Cheryl Tsutsumi, Ed. Fiction to 2,000 words, with a Hawaii focus. Pays $150 to $300, on publication. Query.

AMAZING STORIES—201 Sheridan Springs Rd., Lake Geneva, WI 53147. Mr. Kim Mohan, Ed. Original, previously unpublished science fiction, fantasy, and horror, 1,000 to 20,000 words. Pays 6¢ to 10¢ a word, on acceptance.

THE AMERICAN VOICE—332 W. Broadway, Suite 1215, Louisville, KY 40202. Frederick Smock, Ed. Avant-garde, literary fiction, nonfiction, and well-crafted poetry, any length (shorter works are preferred). "Please read our journal before attempting to submit." Payment varies, on publication.

ANALOG SCIENCE FICTION AND FACT—1540 Broadway, New York, NY 10036. Stanley Schmidt, Ed. Science fiction, with strong characters in believable future or alien setting: short stories, 2,000 to 7,500 words; novelettes, 10,000 to 20,000 words; serials, to 70,000 words. Pays 5¢ to 8¢ a word, on acceptance. Query for novels.

ASIMOV'S SCIENCE FICTION MAGAZINE—1540 Broadway, 15th Fl., New York, NY 10036. Gardner Dozois, Ed. Short science fiction and fantasies, to 15,000 words. Pays 6¢ to 8¢ a word, on acceptance. Guidelines.

THE ATLANTIC MONTHLY—745 Boylston St., Boston, MA 02116. William Whitworth, Ed. Short stories, 2,000 to 6,000 words, of highest literary quality, with "fully developed narratives, distinctive characterization, freshness in language, and a resolution of some kind." Pays $2,500, on acceptance.

THE BELLETRIST REVIEW—Marmarc Publications, 17 Farmington Ave., Suite 290, Plainville, CT 06062. Marlene Dube, Ed. Semiannual. Fiction, 1,500 to 5,000 words: adventure, contemporary, erotica, psychological horror, humor, literary, mainstream, suspense, and mystery. No fantasy, juvenile, westerns, overblown horror, or confessional pieces. Pays in copies.

BOYS' LIFE—1325 W. Walnut Hill Ln., P.O. Box 152079, Irving, TX 75015–2079. Attn: Fiction Ed. Publication of the Boy Scouts of America. Humor, mystery, science fiction, adventure, 1,200 words, for 8- to 18-year-old boys; study back issues. Pays from $750, on acceptance. Guidelines.

BUFFALO SPREE MAGAZINE—Box 38, Buffalo, NY 14226. Johanna Van De Mark, Ed./Pub. Fiction and humor, to 2,000 words, for readers in the western New York region. Pays $100 to $125, on publication.

BYLINE—Box 130596, Edmond, OK 73013. Marcia Preston, Ed.-in-Chief. Kathryn Fanning, Man. Ed. General fiction, 2,000 to 4,000 words. Nonfiction: 1,500- to 1,800-word features and 300- to 750-word special departments. Poetry, 10 to 30 lines preferred. Nonfiction and poetry must be about writing. Humor, 400 to 750 words, about writing. "We seek practical and motivational material that tells writers how they can succeed, not why they can't. Overdone topics: writers' block, the muse, rejection slips." Pays $5 to $10 for poetry; $15 to $35 for departments; $50 for features; and $100 for short fiction, on acceptance. Guidelines.

CAPPER'S—1503 S.W. 42nd St., Topeka, KS 66609–1265. Nancy Peavler, Ed. Fiction, 7,500 to 40,000 words (12,000 to 20,000 words preferred), for serialization. No profanity, violence, or explicit sex. Pays $75 to $400, on publication.

CATHOLIC FORESTER—355 Shuman Blvd., P.O. Box 3012, Naperville, IL 60566–7012. Dorothy Deer, Ed. Official publication of the Catholic Order of Foresters. Fiction, to 2,000 words (prefer shorter); "looking for more contemporary, meaningful stories dealing with life today." No sex or violence or "preachy" stories; religious angle not required. Pays 10¢ a word, on acceptance.

CHANGES—U.S. Journal, Inc., 3201 S.W. 15th St., Deerfield Beach, FL 33442–8190. Jeffrey Laign, Ed. "The Recovery Lifestyle Magazine." Recovery-oriented fiction, 1,500 words, and poetry. Articles, 2,000 words, and poetry.

CHESS LIFE—186 Rt. 9W, New Windsor, NY 12553–7698. Glenn Petersen, Ed. Fiction, 500 to 2,000 words, related to chess for members of the U.S. Chess Federation. Also, articles, 500 to 3,000 words, on chess news, profiles, technical aspects of chess. Pays varying rates, on acceptance. Query; limited market.

CITYLIMITS—325 N. Clippert St., Suite B, Lansing, MI 48912. Kelly Rossman-McKinney, Roger Martin, Eds. Upbeat fiction, 1,500 to 2,500 words, of interest to Lansing, MI, area readers. Pay $250, on publication. Query preferred.

COBBLESTONE: THE HISTORY MAGAZINE FOR CHILDREN—7 School St., Peterborough, NH 03458–1454. Meg Chorlian, Ed. Fiction, 500 to 800 words, for children aged 8 to 14 years; must relate to theme. Pays 20¢ to 25¢ a word, on publication. Guidelines.

COMMENTARY—165 E. 56th St., New York, NY 10022. Neal Kozodoy, Man. Ed. Fiction, of high literary quality, on contemporary social or Jewish issues. Pays on publication.

COMMON GROUND MAGAZINE—P.O. Box 99, McVeytown, PA 17051–0099. Ruth Dunmire and Pam Brumbaugh, Eds. Quarterly. Fiction, 1,000 to 2,000 words, related to Central Pennsylvania's Juniata River Valley. Pays $25 to $200, on publication. Guidelines.

COUNTRY WOMAN—P.O. Box 989, Greendale, WI 53129. Kathy Pohl, Man. Ed. Fiction, 750 to 1,000 words, of interest to rural women; protagonist must be a country woman. "Stories should focus on life in the country, its problems and joys, as experienced by country women; must be upbeat and positive." Pays $90 to $125, on acceptance.

CRICKET—Box 300, Peru, IL 61354–0300. Marianne Carus, Ed.-in-Chief. Fiction, 200 to 2,000 words, for 9- to 14-year-olds. Pays to 25¢ a word, on publication.

DISCOVERIES—WordAction Publishing Co., 6401 The Paseo, Kansas City, MO 64131. Attn: Asst. Ed. Weekly take-home paper designed to correlate with Evangelical Sunday school curriculum. Fiction, 500 to 700 words, for 8- to 10-year-olds. Stories should feature contemporary, true-to-life characters and should illustrate character building and scriptural application. No poetry. Pays 5¢ a word, on publication. Guidelines.

DOGWOOD TALES MAGAZINE—P.O. Box 172068, Memphis, TN 38187. Attn: Ed. Bimonthly "for the fiction lover in all of us." Short stories, 250 to 6,000 words (prefer no more than 3,000 words), in any genre except religion or pornography. "Stories should be fresh, well-paced, and have strong endings." Contests. Guidelines.

ELLERY QUEEN'S MYSTERY MAGAZINE—1540 Broadway, New York, NY 10036. Janet Hutchings, Ed. High-quality detective, crime, and mystery stories, 1,500 to 6,000 words. Also "Minute Mysteries," 250 words, short verses, limericks, and novellas, to 17,000 words. "We like a mix of classic detection and suspenseful crime." "First Stories" by unpublished writers. Pays 3¢ to 8¢ a word, on acceptance.

ESQUIRE—250 W. 55th St., New York, NY 10019. Edward Kosner, Ed.-in-Chief. Send finished manuscript of short story; submit one at a time. No full-length novels. No pornography, science fiction, or "true romance" stories.

EVANGEL—Light and Life Press, Box 535002, Indianapolis, IN 46253–5002. Carolyn Smith, Ed. Free Methodist. Fiction, to 1,200 words, with personal faith in Christ shown as instrumental in solving problems. Pays 4¢ a word, on publication.

FAMILY FUN—Walt Disney Publishing Group, 244 Main St., Northampton, MA 01060. Alexandra Kennedy, Ed. Stories, 750 words, for parents to read aloud to children. Articles, to 1,500 words, on family activities and "creative parenting." Payment varies, on acceptance.

FICTION INTERNATIONAL—English Dept., San Diego State Univ., San Diego, CA 92182–8140. Harold Jaffe, Ed. Post-modernist and politically committed fiction and theory. Write for current theme. Submit between September 1st and December 15th.

FLY ROD & REEL—P.O. Box 370, Camden, ME 04843. James E. Butler, Ed. Occasional fiction, 2,000 to 2,500 words, related to fly fishing. Special annual fiction issue published in summer. Payment varies, on acceptance.

GALLERY—401 Park Ave. S., New York, NY 10016–8802. Barry Janoff, Ed. Dir. Rich Friedman, Man. Ed. Fiction, to 3,000 words, for sophisticated men. "We are not looking for science fiction, mystery, 40s-style detective, or stories involving aliens from other planets. We do look for interesting stories that enable readers to view life in an off-beat, unusual, or insightful manner: fiction with believable characters and actions. We encourage quality work from unpublished writers." Pays $500, on publication.

GLIMMER TRAIN PRESS—812 S.W. Washington St., Suite 1205, Portland, OR 97205. Susan Burmeister-Brown, Ed. Fiction, 1,200 to 7,500 words. "Eight stories in each quarterly magazine." Pays $500, on acceptance. Submit material in January, April, July, and October; allow 3 months for response. "Send SASE for guidelines before submitting."

GOOD HOUSEKEEPING—959 Eighth Ave., New York, NY 10019. Lee Quarfoot, Fiction Ed. Short stories, 1,000 to 3,000 words, with strong identification figures for women, by published writers and "beginners with demonstrable talent." Novel condensations or excerpts from about-to-be-published books only. "Writers whose work interests us will hear from us within 4 to 6 weeks of receipt of manuscript. Please send inexpensive copies of your work; and do not enclose SASEs or postage. We can no longer return or critique manuscripts. We do accept multiple submissions." Pays top rates, on acceptance.

GRIT—1503 S.W. 42nd St., Topeka, KS 66609. Michael Scheibach, Ed.-in-Chief. Short stories, 2,200 to 2,500 words; occasionally shorter stories, 800 to 2,000 words. Articles, 500 to 1,200 words, on interesting people and topics. Should be upbeat, inspirational, wholesome; of interest to all ages. No reference to drinking, smoking, drugs, sex, or violence. Also publishes some short poetry and true-story nostalgia. Pays 12¢ to 25¢ a word, extra for photos, on publication. All fiction submissions should be marked "Fiction Dept." Guidelines.

GUIDEPOSTS FOR KIDS—P.O. Box 538A, Chesterton, IN 46304. Mary Lou Carney, Ed. Bible-based bimonthly for 7- to 12-year-olds. Problem fiction, mysteries, historicals, 1,000 words, with "realistic dialogue and sharp imagery. No preachy stories about Bible-toting children." Pays $200 to $400 for all rights, on acceptance. No reprints.

HARDBOILED—Gryphon Publications, P.O. Box 209, Brooklyn, NY 11228–0209. Gary Lovisi, Ed. Hard, cutting-edge crime fiction, to 3,000 words, "with impact. It's a good idea to read an issue before submitting a story." Payment varies, on publication. Query for articles, book and film reviews.

HARPER'S MAGAZINE— 666 Broadway, New York, NY 10012. Attn: Eds. Will consider unsolicited fiction manuscripts. No poetry. Query for non-fiction (very limited market).

HIGHLIGHTS FOR CHILDREN— 803 Church St., Honesdale, PA 18431–1824. Kent L. Brown Jr., Ed. Fiction on sports, humor, adventure, mystery, etc., 900 words, for 8- to 12-year-olds. Easy rebus form, 100 to 120 words, and easy-to-read stories, to 500 words, for beginning readers. "We are partial to stories in which the protagonist solves a dilemma through his or her own resources." Pays from 14¢ a word, on acceptance. Buys all rights.

HOMETOWN PRESS—2007 Gallatin St., Huntsville, AL 35801. Jeffrey C. Hindman, M.D., Ed.-in-Chief. Fiction, 800 to 2,500 words, well-crafted and tightly written, suitable for family reading. New and unpublished writers welcome. Guidelines.

INSIDE EDGE—258 Harvard St., Suite 329, Brookline, MA 02146. Josie Roth, Ed. Fiction and humor, 1,000 words, for young men ages 18 to 24. Pays $250, on publication of second story; first published piece receives no payment.

THE JOYFUL WOMAN—P.O. Box 90028, Chattanooga, TN 37412. Joy Rice Martin, Ed. Fiction, 500 to 1,200 words, for women with a "Christian commitment." Also first-person inspirational true stories. Pays 3¢ to 4¢ a word, on publication.

LADIES' HOME JOURNAL—100 Park Ave., New York, NY 10017. Fiction generally accepted through agents only.

THE LOOKOUT— 8121 Hamilton Ave., Cincinnati, OH 45231. Simon J. Dahlman, Ed. Short-shorts, 500 to 2,000 words, with moral or Christian themes. No historical fiction, science fiction, or fantasy. Pays to 9¢ a word, on acceptance.

LOUIS L'AMOUR WESTERN MAGAZINE—1540 Broadway, New York, NY 10036. Elana Lore, Ed. Well-written western short stories, to 12,000 words. "Our focus is on traditional western short stories, but we will also consider Native American, modern, and mystery-oriented westerns." Pays 8¢ a word, on acceptance.

THE MAGAZINE OF FANTASY AND SCIENCE FICTION—Box 11526, Eugene, OR 97440. Kristine Kathryn Rusch, Ed. Fantasy and science fiction stories, to 15,000 words. Pays 5¢ to 7¢ a word, on acceptance.

MATURE LIVING— 127 Ninth Ave. N., Nashville, TN 37234. Al Shackleford, Ed. Fiction, 900 to 1,200 words, for senior adults. Must be consistent with Christian principles. Pays $75, on acceptance.

MIDSTREAM—110 E. 59th St., New York, NY 10022. M. S. Solow, Man. Ed. Fiction on Jewish themes, to 3,000 words. Pays 5¢ a word, after publication. Allow 3 months for response.

NA'AMAT WOMAN—200 Madison Ave., 21st Fl., New York, NY 10016. Judith A. Sokoloff, Ed. Short stories, approximately 2,500 words, with Jewish theme. Pays 8¢ a word, on publication.

NEW MYSTERY MAGAZINE—The Flatiron Bldg., 175 Fifth Ave., Suite 2001, New York, NY 10010–7703. Charles Raisch, Ed. Quarterly. Mystery, crime, detection, and suspense short stories, 2,000 to 6,000 words, with "sympathetic characters and visual scenes." Book reviews, 250 to 2,000 words, of upcoming or recently published novels. Pays 3¢ to 10¢ a word, on publication. No guidelines; study back issues.

THE NEW YORKER—20 W. 43rd St., New York, NY 10036. Attn: Fiction Dept. Short stories, humor, and satire. Payment varies, on acceptance.

OMNI—277 Park Ave., 4th Fl., New York, NY 10172–0003. Ellen Datlow, Fiction Ed. Strong, realistic science fiction. "We want to intrigue our readers with mind-broadening, thought-provoking stories that will excite their sense of wonder." Some contemporary hard-edged fantasy. No sword-and-sorcery, space opera, or supernatural stories. (Note: Nonfiction should be sent to Keith Ferrell, Ed., *Omni*, 324 W. Wendover Ave., Suite 200, Greensboro, NC 27408.) Pays from $1,300 to $2,250, on acceptance.

PENTHOUSE—277 Park Ave., 4th Fl., New York, NY 10172–0003. Peter Bloch, Ed. Lavada B. Nahon, Sr. Ed. for women's erotic fiction.

PLAYBOY— 680 N. Lake Shore Dr., Chicago, IL 60611. Alice K. Turner, Fiction Ed. Limited market.

PLAYGIRL— 801 Second Ave., New York, NY 10017. Laurie Sue Brochway, Ed.-in-Chief. Contemporary, erotic fiction, from a female perspective, 3,000 to 4,000 words. "Fantasy Forum," 1,000 to 2,000 words. Pays from $500; $25 to $100 for "Fantasy Forum," after acceptance.

POWER AND LIGHT— 6401 The Paseo, Kansas City, MO 64131. Beula J. Postlewait, Preteen Ed. Fiction, 500 to 800 words, for grades 5 to 6, defining Christian experiences and values. Pays 5¢ a word for multiple-use rights, on publication.

PURPOSE— 616 Walnut Ave., Scottdale, PA 15683–1999. James E. Horsch, Ed. Fiction, 750 words, on problem solving from a Christian point of view. Poetry, 3 to 12 lines. Pays to 5¢ a word for fiction; to $1 per line for poetry, on acceptance.

QUEEN'S QUARTERLY—Queens Univ., Kingston, Ont., Canada K7L 3N6. Attn: Fiction Ed. Fiction, to 5,000 words, in English and French. Pays to $300, on publication.

RANGER RICK— 8925 Leesburg Pike, Vienna, VA 22184–0001. Deborah Churchman, Fiction Ed. Action-packed nature- and conservation-related fiction, to 900 words, for 6- to 12-year-olds. No anthropomorphism. "Multicultural stories welcome." Pays to $550, on acceptance. Usually buys all rights. Guidelines.

REDBOOK—224 W. 57th St., New York, NY 10019. Dawn Raffel, Fiction Ed. Fresh, distinctive short stories, of interest to women. No unsolicited poetry, novellas, or novels accepted. Pays from $1,500 for short stories (to 25 pages), on acceptance. Allow 12 weeks for reply.

ST. ANTHONY MESSENGER—1615 Republic St., Cincinnati, OH 45210–1298. Norman Perry, O.F.M., Ed. Barbara Beckwith, Man. Ed. Fiction that makes readers think about issues, lifestyles, and values. Pays 14¢ a word, on acceptance. Queries or manuscripts accepted.

SASSY— 6420 Wilshire Blvd., Los Angeles, CA 90048–5515. Attn: Tommi Lewis. Short stories for girls age 16 to 21. Payment varies, on acceptance.

SCHOOL MATES—U.S. Chess Federation, 186 Rte. 9W, New Windsor, NY 12553–7698. Brian Bugbee, Ed. Fiction and articles, 250 to 800 words, and short fillers, related to chess for beginning chess players (primarily children, ages 6 to 16). "Instructive, but there's room for fun puzzles, anecdotes, etc. All chess related." Pays from $20, on publication. Query; limited free-lance market.

SEA KAYAKER—P.O. Box 17170, Seattle, WA 98107–0870. Christopher Cunningham, Ed. Short stories exclusively related to ocean kayaking, 1,000 to 3,000 words. Pays on publication.

SEVENTEEN— 850 Third Ave., New York, NY 10022. Joe Bargmann, Fiction Ed. High-quality, literary short fiction, to 4,000 words. Pays on acceptance.

SPORTS AFIELD—250 W. 55th St., New York, NY 10019. Terry McDonell, Ed. Occasional fiction, 1,500 words, on hunting, fishing, outdoor and nature-related topics. Humor. Payment varies, on acceptance.

STRAIGHT— 8121 Hamilton Ave., Cincinnati, OH 45231. Carla Crane, Ed. Well-constructed fiction, 1,000 to 1,500 words, showing Christian teens using Bible principles in everyday life. Contemporary, realistic teen characters a must. Most interested in school, church, dating, and family life stories. Pays 3¢ to 7¢ a word, on acceptance. Guidelines.

'TEEN— 6420 Wilshire Blvd., Los Angeles, CA 90048–5515. Attn: Fiction Dept. Short stories, 2,500 to 4,000 words: mystery, teen situations, adventure, romance, humor for teens. Pays from $200, on acceptance.

TEEN LIFE—1445 Boonville Ave., Springfield, MO 65802–1894. Tammy Bicket, Ed. Fiction, to 1,200 words, for 13- to 19-year-olds. Articles, 500 to 1,000 words. Strong evangelical emphasis a must: believable characters working out their problems according to biblical principles. Buys first rights; pays on acceptance. Reprints considered.

TQ/TEEN QUEST—2221 W. Walnut Hill Ln., Irving, TX 75038. Christopher Lyon, Ed. Fiction, 1,000 to 2,000 words, for Christian teens. Pays 10¢ to 15¢ a word, on publication.

TRUCKERS/USA—P.O. Box 323, Windber, PA 15963. David Adams, Ed. Trucking-related articles, poetry, and fiction, to 1,000 words. Payment varies, on publication.

TRUE CONFESSIONS—233 Park Ave. S., New York, NY 10003. Pat Byrdsong, Ed. Romantic stories, 5,000 to 8,000 words: true-to-life drama, passion, intrigue, etc. Also short stories, 1,000 to 2,000 words. Pays after publication. Buys all rights.

VIRGINIA—The Country Publishers, Inc., P.O. Box 798, Berryville, VA 22611. Garrison Ellis, Ed. Quarterly. Fiction, 1,500 to 2,000 words, with Virginia setting or reference. Pays $200 to $300, 30 days after publication.

VIRTUE: THE CHRISTIAN MAGAZINE FOR WOMEN— 4050 Lee Vance View, Colorado Springs, CO 80918. Jeanette Thomason, Ed. Fiction, 1,200 to 1,400 words, with a Christian slant; inspirational, women's spiritual journeys, women's perspectives. Pays 15¢ to 22¢ a word, on publication. Query for articles.

WESTERN PEOPLE—Box 2500, Saskatoon, Sask., Canada S7K 2C4. Attn: Ed. Short stories, 1,000 to 2,500 words, on subjects or themes of interest to rural readers in western Canada. Pays $100 to $175, on acceptance. Enclose international reply coupons and SAE.

WILDFOWL—1901 Bell Ave., Suite #4, Des Moines, IA 50315. R. Sparks, Man. Ed. Occasional fiction, humor, related to duck hunters and wild-fowl. Pays $400, on acceptance.

WIN MAGAZINE—120 S. San Fernando Blvd., Suite 439, Burbank, CA 91502. Joey Sinatra, Ed. Gambling-related fiction, 1,600 to 2,500 words. Pays on publication.

WOMAN'S WORLD—270 Sylvan Ave., Englewood Cliffs, NJ 07632. Attn: Fiction Dept. Fast-moving short stories, about 1,900 words, with light romantic theme. (Specify "short story" on outside of envelope.) Mini-mysteries, 1,200 words, with "whodunit" or "howdunit" theme. No science fiction, fantasy, or historical romance and no horror, ghost stories, or gratuitous violence; no holiday themes. "Dialogue-driven romances help propel the story." Pays $1,000 for short stories, $500 for mini-mysteries, on acceptance.

YANKEE—Yankee Publishing Co., P.O. Box 520, Dublin, NH 03444. Judson Hale, Ed. Edie Clark, Fiction Ed. High-quality, literary short fiction, to 3,000 words, with New England setting; no sap buckets or lobster pot stereotypes. Pays $1,000, on acceptance.

DETECTIVE AND MYSTERY

ALFRED HITCHCOCK MYSTERY MAGAZINE—1540 Broadway, New York, NY 10036. Cathleen Jordan, Ed. Well-plotted, previously unpublished mystery, detective, suspense, and crime short stories, to 14,000 words. Submissions by new writers strongly encouraged. Pays 8¢ a word, on acceptance. No multiple submissions, please. (Submissions sent to *AHMM* are not considered for, or read by, *Ellery Queen's Mystery Magazine*.) Guidelines with SASE.

ARMCHAIR DETECTIVE—129 W. 56th St., New York, NY 10019. Kate Stine, Ed.-in-Chief. Judi Vause, Man. Ed. Articles on mystery and detective fiction; biographical sketches, reviews, etc. No fiction. Pays $10 a printed page; reviews are unpaid.

ELLERY QUEEN'S MYSTERY MAGAZINE—1540 Broadway, New York, NY 10036. Janet Hutchings, Ed. Detective, crime, and mystery fiction, approximately 1,500 to 6,000 words. Occasionally publishes novelettes, to 20,000 words, by established authors and humorous mystery verse. No sex, sadism, or sensationalism. Particularly interested in new writers and "first stories." Pays 3¢ to 8¢ a word, on acceptance.

HARDBOILED—Gryphon Publications, P.O. Box 209, Brooklyn, NY 11228–0209. Gary Lovisi, Ed. Hard, cutting-edge crime fiction, to 3,000 words. B&W drawings (send photocopies only). Payment varies, on publication. Query for articles, book and film reviews.

MURDEROUS INTENT—P.O. Box 5947, Vancouver, WA 98668–5947. Margo Power, Ed./Pub. Quarterly. Mystery and suspense stories and mystery-related articles, 2,000 to 4,000 words; fillers, to 750 words; poems, to 60 lines. "We see way too many stories of husband and wife bumping each other off. We love humor in mysteries. Surprise us!" Pays $10, on acceptance. Query for nonfiction.

NEW MYSTERY MAGAZINE—The Flatiron Bldg., 175 Fifth Ave., Suite 2001, New York, NY 10010–7703. Charles Raisch, Ed. Quarterly. Mystery, crime, detection, and suspense short stories, 2,000 to 6,000 words. No true crime. Book reviews, 250 to 2,000 words, of upcoming or recently published novels. Pays $15 to $300, on publication. Guidelines.

OVER MY DEAD BODY!—P.O. Box 1778, Auburn, WA 98071–1778. Cherie Jung, Features Ed. Mystery, suspense, and crime fiction, to 4,000 words. Author profiles, interviews, and mystery-related travel, 750 to 1,500 words. Fillers, to 100 words. Include B&W photos. "We are entertainment for mystery fans, from cozy to hardboiled and everything in between." Pays 1¢ a word for fiction; $10 to $25 for nonfiction; $5 for fillers; $10 to $25 for illustrations, on publication.

SCIENCE FICTION AND FANTASY

ABERRATIONS—P.O. Box 460430, San Francisco, CA 94146. Richard Blair, Man. Ed. Michael Andre-Driussi, Sr. Fiction Ed. Science fiction, horror, and fantasy, to 8,000 words. "Experimental, graphic, multi-genre is O.K. with science fiction/fantasy/horror tie-in." Pays ¼¢ a word, on publication. Guidelines.

ABORIGINAL SF—P.O. Box 2449, Woburn, MA 01888–0849. Charles C. Ryan, Ed. Short stories, 2,500 to 7,500 words, and poetry, one to 2 typed pages, with strong science content, lively, unique characters, and well-designed plots. No sword and sorcery or fantasy. Pays $250 for fiction, $20 for poetry, $4 for science fiction jokes, and $20 for cartoons, on publication.

ABSOLUTE MAGNITUDE—P.O. Box 13, Greenfield, MA 01302. Warren Lapine, Ed. Quarterly. Technical science fiction, 1,000 to 25,000 words. No fantasy, horror, satire, or funny science fiction. Pays 3¢ a word (1¢ a word for reprints), on publication. Guidelines.

AMAZING STORIES—201 Sheridan Springs Rd., Lake Geneva, WI 53147. Mr. Kim Mohan, Ed. Original, previously unpublished science fiction, fantasy, and horror, 1,000 to 25,000 words. Pays 6¢ to 10¢ a word, on acceptance.

ANALOG SCIENCE FICTION AND FACT—1540 Broadway, New York, NY 10036. Stanley Schmidt, Ed. Science fiction with strong characters in believable future or alien setting: short stories, 2,000 to 7,500 words; novelettes, 10,000 to 20,000 words; serials, to 80,000 words. Also uses future-related articles. Pays to 7¢ a word, on acceptance. Query for serials and articles.

ARGONAUT—P.O. Box 4201, Austin, TX 78765. Michael E. Ambrose, Ed. Often overstocked. Query first to find out if we're open to submissions. "Hard" science fiction, to 7,500 words, and science fiction dealing with the sciences, intergalactic or interplanetary adventure. Poetry, to 30 lines, with a science fiction focus. No fantasy, horror, interviews, reviews, or seasonal material. Reports in 6 weeks. Pays in 3 copies.

ASIMOV'S SCIENCE FICTION MAGAZINE—1540 Broadway, 15th Fl.,

New York, NY 10036. Gardner Dozois, Ed. Short, character-oriented science fiction and fantasy, to 15,000 words. Pays 5¢ to 8¢ a word, on acceptance. Guidelines.

CENTURY—Century Publishing, Inc., P.O. Box 150510, Brooklyn, NY 11215–0510. Robert K.J. Killheffer, Ed. Literary science fiction, fantasy, and magic realism, 1,000 and 20,000 words. Pays 4¢ to 6¢ a word, on acceptance.

DRAGON MAGAZINE—201 Sheridan Springs Rd., Lake Geneva, WI 53147. Mr. Kim Mohan, Ed. Barbara G. Young, Fiction Ed. Articles, 1,500 to 7,500 words, on fantasy and science fiction role-playing games. Fantasy, 1,500 to 8,000 words. Pays 6¢ to 8¢ a word for fiction, on acceptance. Pays 4¢ a word for articles, on publication. Guidelines.

FANGORIA—475 Park Ave. S., 8th Fl., New York, NY 10016. Anthony Timpone, Ed. Published 10 times yearly. Movie, TV, and book previews, reviews, and interviews, 1,800 to 2,500 words, in connection with upcoming horror films. "A strong love of the genre and an appreciation and understanding of the magazine are essential." Pays $175 to $225, on publication.

FANTASY & TERROR—See *Fantasy Macabre.*

FANTASY MACABRE—P.O. Box 20610, Seattle, WA 98102. Jessica Salmonson, Ed. Fiction, to 3,000 words, including translations. "We look for a tale that is strong in atmosphere, with menace that is suggested and threatening rather than the result of dripping blood and gore." Pays 1¢ a word, to $30 per story, on publication. Also publishes *Fantasy & Terror* for poetry-in-prose pieces.

HAUNTS—Nightshade Publications, Box 8068, Cranston, RI 02920–0068. Joseph K. Cherkes, Ed. Horror, science/fantasy, and supernatural short stories with strong characters, 1,500 to 8,000 words. No explicit sexual scenes or gratuitous violence. Pays ½¢ to 1¢ a word, on publication. Manuscripts read January through June.

HOBSON'S CHOICE: SCIENCE FICTION AND TECHNOLOGY—The Starwind Press, P.O. Box 98, Ripley, OH 45167. Attn: Submissions Ed. Science fiction and fantasy, 2,000 to 10,000 words. Articles and literary criticism, 1,000 to 5,000 words, for readers interested in science and technology. Pays 1¢ to 4¢ a word, on acceptance. Query for nonfiction.

THE LEADING EDGE—3163 JKHB, Provo, UT 84602. Alex Grover, Ed. Semiannual. Short stories, 3,000 to 12,000 words, and some experimental fiction; poems, to 600 lines; and articles, to 8,000 words, on science, scientific speculation, and literary criticism. "Do not send originals; manuscripts are marked and critiqued by staff." Pays $10 to $100, on publication. Guidelines.

LORDS OF THE ABYSS: TALES OF SUPERNATURAL HORROR—Stygian Vortex Publications, 6634 Atlanta St., Hollywood, FL 33024–2965. Glenda Woodrum, Ed.-in-Chief. John R. Osborne, Asst. Ed. Annual. Stories by and for supernatural horror enthusiasts. No length limits on fiction; query for stories over 10,000 words. Some book, movie, and role-playing game reviews, to 500 words. "No serial killers, rapists, insane people, child molesters, demonically possessed vehicles, or psycho killers." Pays 50¢ per published page; $1 per poem, on publication, and one copy. Guidelines.

THE MAGAZINE OF FANTASY AND SCIENCE FICTION—P.O. Box 11526, Eugene, OR 97440. Kristine Kathryn Rusch, Ed. Fantasy and science fiction stories, to 10,000 words. Pays 5¢ to 7¢ a word, on acceptance.

MAGIC REALISM—P.O. Box 922648, Sylmar, CA 91392–2648. C. Darren Butler, Ed. Julie Thomas, Man. Ed. Quarterly. Stories, to 7,500 words (4,000 words preferred), of magic realism, exaggerated realism, some genre fantasy/ dark fantasy. Occasionally publish glib fantasy like that found in folktales, fairy tales, and myths. No occult, sleight-of-hand magicians, or wizards/witches. Pays $2 per published page for prose; $3 per page for poetry. Guidelines.

MARION ZIMMER BRADLEY'S FANTASY MAGAZINE—P.O. Box 249, Berkeley, CA 94701. Marion Zimmer Bradley, Ed. Quarterly. Well-plotted stories, 3,500 to 4,000 words. Action and adventure fantasy "with no particular objection to modern settings." Send SASE for guidelines before submitting. Pays 3¢ to 10¢ a word, on acceptance.

NEURONET: STORIES FROM THE CYBERLAND—Stygian Vortex Publications, 6634 Atlanta St., Hollywood, FL 33024–2965. Glenda Woodrum, Ed.-in-Chief. John R. Osborne, Asst. Ed. Annual. Cyberpunk fiction. "All stories should be hard-hitting, gritty, and filled with the grim nature of the cyberpunk future." No length limits. Pays 50¢ per published page, $1 per poem, on publication, plus one copy. Query for stories over 10,000 words. Guidelines.

NEXT PHASE—Phantom Press Publications, 5A Green Meadow Dr., Nantucket Island, MA 02554. Kim Guarnaccia, Ed. Science fiction, fantasy, experimental fiction, and commentary, to 3,000 words, and interviews with authors, poets, or artists. Poetry, any length. "We prefer environmentally or socially conscious fiction." Pays in copies.

OMNI—277 Park Ave., 4th Fl., New York, NY 10172–0003. Ellen Datlow, Fiction Ed. Strong, realistic science fiction, 2,000 to 10,000 words, with good characterizations. "We want to intrigue our readers with mindbroadening, thought-provoking stories that will excite their sense of wonder." Some fantasy. No horror, ghost, or sword and sorcery tales. (Nonfiction, 750 to 3,000 words, should be sent to Keith Ferrell, Ed., *Omni,* 324 W. Wendover Ave., Suite 200, Greensboro, NC 27408.) Pays $1,300 to $2,250, on acceptance.

ONYX MAGAZINE—850 S. Lake Park Ave. #6, Hobart, IN 46342. Tim Snodgrass, Ed. Quarterly. Humorous science fiction, fantasy, and horror, to 12 pages, single-spaced. Personal-experience essays, to 8 pages, on science fiction/fantasy conventions. Poems, limericks, fillers, drawings, humorous cartoons. Pays in copies.

PIRATE WRITINGS—53 Whitman Ave., Islip, NY 11751. Edward J. McFadden, Pub./Ed. Tom Piccirilli, Assoc. Ed. Mystery, science fiction, fantasy, 250 to 6,000 words. Poetry, to 20 lines. Pays 1¢ to 5¢ a word, on publication.

PLOT MAGAZINE—Calypso Publishing, P.O. Box 1351, Sugar Land, TX 77487–1351. Christina C. Russell, Man. Ed. Fantasy, science fiction, horror, suspense, and speculative fiction, to 7,500 words. "The magazine is designed to encourage new and emerging writers. If your story can give us gooseflesh, we want to see it." Pays $10 for stories, $5 for line drawings, on acceptance.

PULPHOUSE: A FICTION MAGAZINE—P.O. Box 1227, Eugene, OR 97440. Dean Wesley Smith, Ed. Fantasy, science fiction, horror, mysteries, mainstream, and westerns, 5,000 words. Pays 4¢ to 7¢ a word, before publication.

SCAVENGER'S—519 Ellinwood, Osage City, KS 66523. Janet Fox, Ed. Flash fiction, 1,200 words, in the genres of science fiction, fantasy, horror, and mystery. Articles, 1,000 words, pertaining to writing and art in those genres. Poems, to 10 lines, and humor, 500 to 700 words, for writers and artists. "Most of the content is market information." Pays $4 for fiction, articles, and cover art; $2 for humor, poems, and inside art, on acceptance.

SCIENCE FICTION CHRONICLE—P.O. Box 022730, Brooklyn, NY 11202–0056. Andrew Porter, Ed. News items, 200 to 500 words, for science fiction and fantasy readers, professionals, and booksellers. No fiction. Pays 3½¢ to 5¢ a word, on publication. Query.

THE SCREAM FACTORY—Deadline Press, 16473 Redwood Lodge Rd., Los Gatos, CA 95030. Bob Morrish, Ed. Quarterly. Articles, 1,000 to 7,000 words, on all facets of horror fiction and film. Interviews, 750 to 4,000 words, with authors and directors; brief, analytical reviews, 100 to 400 words, of old and new books. No fiction. Pays ½¢ a word, on publication. Query.

SHADOW SWORD—Stygian Vortex Publications, 6634 Atlanta St., Hollywood, FL 33024–2965. Glenda J. Woodrum, Ed. Quarterly. Stories, articles, and artwork by and for fantasy enthusiasts: heroic fantasy, sword and sorcery, high fantasy, and dark fantasy. "No 'cute' stories or fantasies set in a version of the real technological world." Pays 50¢ per published page, $1 for poetry, and one copy, on publication. Query for stories over 10,000 words. Guidelines.

SHAPESHIFTER!—Stygian Vortex Publications, 6634 Atlanta St., Hollywood, FL 33024–2965. John R. Osborne, Ed. Annual. Stories, articles, and artwork on lycanthropes, shape-changers, and partly human creatures. Some role-playing game-related material and book or movie reviews. Query for stories over 10,000 words. "We prefer stories in which the shapeshifters are the heroes/protagonists, not stories in which they ravage a small town, etc." Pays one copy plus 50¢ a page, on publication. Guidelines.

SIRIUS VISIONS—Claddagh Press, 1075 N.W. Murray Rd., Suite 161, Portland, OR 97229. Marybeth H. O'Halloran, Ed. Published 8 times a year. Fiction, 1,000 to 7,500 words, including science fiction, fantasy, magical realism, humor, and "space opera." "Some reason to feel hopeful at the end is essential. No horror, gore, or dark fantasy." Pays 1¢ to 3¢ a word, on or before publication.

STARQUEST S.F. MAGAZINE—5727 Rosemead Blvd., #136, Temple City, CA 91780. Joe Fekete, Ed.-in-Chief. Science fiction, fantasy, and speculative fiction, to 5,000 words; critiques and articles, to 2,500 words; short rhyming poetry, preferably limericks. B&W drawings. Pays in copies.

TWISTED—P.O. Box 1249, Palmetto, GA 30268–1249. Christine Hoard, Ed. Fiction and articles, to 5,000 words; poetry, to one page. "No sword and sorcery or hard science fiction. We prefer adult-oriented horror and dark fantasy." Pays in copies. Query. Guidelines.

2AM MAGAZINE—P.O. Box 6754, Rockford, IL 61125–1754. Gretta M. Anderson, Ed. Fiction, of varying lengths. "We prefer dark fantasy/horror; great science fiction and sword and sorcery stories are welcome." Profiles and intelligent commentaries. Poetry, to 50 lines. Pays from ½¢ a word, on acceptance. Guidelines.

WEIRD TALES—See *Worlds of Fantasy & Horror*.

WORLDS OF FANTASY & HORROR—(formerly *Weird Tales*) 123 Crooked Ln., King of Prussia, PA 19406–2570. George Scithers, Pub. Darrell

Schweitzer, Ed. Quarterly. Fantasy and horror (no science fiction), to 7,000 words. Pays 3¢ to 6¢ a word, on acceptance. Guidelines.

ZERO GRAVITY FREEFALL—30210 S.E. Lake Retreat S. Dr., Ravensdale, WA 98051. Margaret Danielson, Ed. Fiction (no fantasy or horror), to 5,000 words, and nonfiction (reviews, analysis, interviews, columns), to 2,000 words, that "speculate on the future state of humankind or reflect upon its past achievements." Poetry. Artists should send queries with their portfolios. Pays to 3¢ a word, on publication. Query for nonfiction.

CONFESSION AND ROMANCE

BLACK CONFESSIONS—See *Black Romance.*

BLACK ROMANCE—233 Park Ave. S., New York, NY 10003. Marcia Y. Mahan, Ed. Romance fiction, 5,800 to 6,000 words, and service articles on beauty, health, and relationship tips, 800 to 1,000 words, for black female readers. Queries preferred. Pays $75 to $125, on publication. Also publishes *Black Secrets, Bronze Thrills, Black Confessions,* and *Jive.* Guidelines.

BLACK SECRETS—See *Black Romance.*

BRONZE THRILLS—See *Black Romance.*

INTIMACY—233 Park Ave. S., 5th Fl., New York, NY 10003. Marcia Y. Mahan, Ed. Fiction, 5,000 to 5,800 words, for black women ages 18 to 45; must have contemporary plot and contain 2 romantic and intimate love scenes. Pays $75 to $100, on publication. Guidelines.

JIVE—See *Black Romance.*

MODERN ROMANCES—233 Park Ave. S., New York, NY 10003. Eileen Fitzmaurice, Ed. Romantic and topical confession stories, 2,000 to 10,000 words, with reader-identification and strong emotional tone. Pays 5¢ a word, after publication. Buys all rights.

ROMANTIC INTERLUDES—P.O. Box 760, Germantown, MD 20875. Attn: Ed. Bimonthly. Romantic fiction, 1,200 to 6,000 words. No graphic sex or violence. Romantic poetry, 100 words. Pays half on acceptance, half on publication. Guidelines.

TRUE CONFESSIONS—233 Park Ave. S., New York, NY 10003. Pat Byrdsong, Ed. Timely, emotional, first-person stories, 2,000 to 10,000 words, on romance, family life, and problems of today's young blue-collar women. Pays 5¢ a word, after publication.

TRUE EXPERIENCE—233 Park Ave. S., New York, NY 10003. Claire Cloutier LeBlanc, Ed. Alison M. Way, Assoc. Ed. Realistic first-person stories, 1,000 to 10,000 words, on family life, single life, love, romance, overcoming hardships, mysteries. Pays 3¢ a word, after publication.

TRUE LOVE—233 Park Ave. S., New York, NY 10003. Kristina M. Kracht, Ed. Fresh, young, true-to-life romance stories, on love and topics of current interest. Must be written in the past tense and first person. Pays 3¢ a word, after publication. Guidelines.

TRUE ROMANCE—233 Park Ave. S., New York, NY 10003. Pat Vitucci, Ed. True or true-to-life, dramatic and/or romantic first-person stories, 2,000 to 9,000 words. Love poems. "We enjoy working with new writers." Reports in 3 to 5 months. Pays 3¢ a word, a month after publication.

POETRY MARKETS

The following list includes markets for both serious and light verse. Although major magazines pay good rates for poetry, the competition to break into print is very stiff, since editors use only a limited number of poems in each issue. On the other hand, college, little, and literary magazines use a great deal of poetry, and though payment is modest—usually in copies—publication in these journals can establish a beginning poet's reputation, and can lead to publication in the major magazines. Poets will also find a number of competitions offering cash awards for unpublished poems in the *Literary Prize Offers* list, as well as opportunities to have their book-length poetry manuscripts published.

ALOHA, THE MAGAZINE OF HAWAII AND THE PACIFIC—P.O. Box 3260, Honolulu, HI 96801. Cheryl Chee Tsutsumi, Ed. Poetry relating to Hawaii. Pays $30 per poem, on publication.

AMERICA—106 W. 56th St., New York, NY 10019. Patrick Samway, S.J., Literary Ed. Serious poetry, preferably in contemporary prose idiom, 10 to 25 lines. Occasional light verse. Submit 2 or 3 poems at a time. Pays $1.40 per line, on publication. Guidelines.

THE AMERICAN SCHOLAR—1811 Q St. N.W., Washington, DC 20009–9974. Joseph Epstein, Ed. Highly original poetry for college-educated, intellectual readers. Pays $50, on acceptance.

THE ATLANTIC MONTHLY—745 Boylston St., Boston, MA 02116. Peter Davison, Poetry Ed. Previously unpublished poetry of highest quality. Limited market; only 2 to 3 poems an issue. Interested in new poets. Occasionally uses light verse. "No simultaneous submissions; we make prompt decisions." Pays excellent rates, on acceptance.

CAPPER'S—1503 S.W. 42nd St., Topeka, KS 66609–1265. Nancy Peavler, Ed. Free verse, light verse, traditional, nature, and inspirational poems, 4 to 16 lines, with simple everyday themes. Submit up to 6 poems at a time. Pays $10 to $15, on acceptance.

CHILDREN'S PLAYMATE—P.O. Box 567, Indianapolis, IN 46206. Sandy Grieshop, Ed. Poetry for children, 6 to 8 years old, on good health, nutrition, exercise, safety, seasonal and humorous subjects. Pays from $15, on publication. Buys all rights.

THE CHRISTIAN SCIENCE MONITOR—One Norway St., Boston, MA 02115. Elizabeth Lund, The Home Forum. Finely crafted poems that celebrate the extraordinary in the ordinary. Seasonal material always needed. No violence, sensuality, or racism. Short poems preferred; submit no more than 5 poems at a time. Pays varying rates, on publication.

COMMONWEAL—15 Dutch St., New York, NY 10038. Rosemary Deen, Poetry Ed. Catholic. Serious, witty poetry. Pays 50¢ a line, on publication. No submissions accepted June to September.

COMPLETE WOMAN—Dept. P, 875 N. Michigan Ave., Suite 3434, Chicago, IL 60611. Attn: Poetry Ed. Send poetry with SASE. Pays in one copy.

COSMOPOLITAN—224 W. 57th St., New York, NY 10019. Rachel Zalis, Poetry Ed. Poetry about relationships and other topics of interest to young, active women. Pays $25, on acceptance.

COUNTRY WOMAN—P.O. Box 989, Greendale, WI 53129. Kathy Pohl, Man. Ed. Traditional rural poetry and light verse, 4 to 30 lines, on rural experiences and country living; also seasonal poetry. Poems must rhyme. Pays $10 to $25, on acceptance.

EVANGEL—Box 535002, Indianapolis, IN 46253-5002. Carolyn Smith, Ed. Free Methodist. Devotional or nature poetry, 8 to 16 lines. Pays $10, on publication.

THE ILLINOIS ARCHITECTURAL AND HISTORICAL REVIEW—202 S. Plum, Havana, IL 62644. David Alan Badger, Ed. Quarterly. Poems, to 40 lines, related to Illinois, especially its history, architecture, or historical figures. Submit to Gene Fehler, Poetry Ed., 106 Laurel Ln., Seneca, SC 29678. No other free-lance material used. Pays in copies.

MATURE YEARS—201 Eighth Ave. S., P.O. Box 801, Nashville, TN 37202. Marvin W. Cropsey, Ed. United Methodist. Poetry, to 14 lines, on preretirement, retirement, Christianity, inspiration, seasonal subjects, aging. No "saccharine" poetry. Submit up to 6 poems at a time. Pays 50¢ to $1 per line.

MIDSTREAM—110 E. 59th St., New York, NY 10022. M.S. Solow, Poetry Ed. Poetry of Jewish interest. "Brevity highly recommended." Pays $25, on publication. Allow 3 months for response.

THE MIRACULOUS MEDAL— 475 E. Chelten Ave., Philadelphia, PA 19144-5785. John W. Gouldrick, C.M., Ed. Catholic. Religious verse, to 20 lines. Pays 50¢ a line, on acceptance.

MODERN BRIDE—249 W. 17th St., New York, NY 10011. Mary Ann Cavlin, Exec. Ed. Short verse of interest to bride and groom. Pays $25 to $35, on acceptance.

THE NATION—72 Fifth Ave., New York, NY 10011. Grace Schulman, Poetry Ed. Poetry of high quality. Pays after publication.

NATIONAL ENQUIRER—Lantana, FL 33464. Darryl C. Wrobel, Asst. Ed. Short poems, with traditional rhyming verse, of an amusing, philosophical, or inspirational nature. No experimental poetry. Original epigrams, humorous anecdotes, and "daffynitions." Submit seasonal/holiday material at least 2 months in advance. Pays $25, after publication.

THE NEW REPUBLIC—1220 19th St. N.W., Washington, DC 20036. Attn: Poetry Ed. Pays $75, after publication.

THE NEW YORKER—20 W. 43rd St., New York, NY 10036. Attn: Poetry Ed. First-rate poetry. Pays top rates, on acceptance.

PATHWAYS—Christian Board of Publication, Box 179, St. Louis, MO 63166. Christine Hershberger Miner, Ed. Short poems for 12- to 15-year-olds. Pays 30¢ a line, on publication.

PURPOSE—616 Walnut Ave., Scottdale, PA 15683–1999. James E. Horsch, Poetry Ed. Poetry, to 8 lines, with challenging Christian discipleship angle. Pays 50¢ to $1 a line, on acceptance.

RADIANCE: THE MAGAZINE FOR LARGE WOMEN—P.O. Box 30246, Oakland, CA 94604. Alice Ansfield, Ed./Pub. Quarterly. Poetry for women. Payment varies, on publication.

ST. JOSEPH'S MESSENGER—P.O. Box 288, Jersey City, NJ 07303–0288. Sister Ursula Maphet, Ed. Light verse and traditional poetry, 4 to 40 lines. Pays $5 to $20, on publication.

THE SATURDAY EVENING POST—P.O. Box 567, Indianapolis, IN 46206. Steven Pettinga, Post Scripts Ed. Light verse and humor. No conventional poetry. Pays $15, on publication.

THE UNITED METHODIST REPORTER—P.O. Box 660275, Dallas, TX 75266–0275. John Lovelace, Ed. Religious verse, 4 to 16 lines. Pays $2, on acceptance.

WESTERN PEOPLE—P.O. Box 2500, Saskatoon, Sask., Canada S7K 2C4. Michael Gillgannon, Man. Ed. Short poetry with Western Canadian themes. Pays on acceptance. Send international reply coupons.

YANKEE—Yankee Publishing Co., P.O. Box 520, Dublin, NH 03444. Jean Burden, Poetry Ed. Serious poetry of high quality, to 30 lines. Pays $50 per poem for all rights, $35 for first rights, on publication.

YESTERDAY'S MAGAZETTE—P.O. Box 15126, Sarasota, FL 34277. Ned Burke, Ed. Traditional poetry, to 24 lines. Pays in copies for poetry and short pieces.

GREETING CARDS & NOVELTY ITEMS

Companies selling greeting cards and novelty items (T-shirts, coffee mugs, buttons, etc.) often have their own specific requirements for submitting ideas, verse, and artwork. In general, however, each verse or message should be typed double-space on a 3x5 or 4x6 card. Use only one side of the card, and be sure to put your name and address in the upper left-hand corner. Keep a copy of every verse or idea you send. (It's also advisable to keep a record of what you've submitted to each publisher.) Always enclose an SASE, and do not send out more than ten verses or ideas in a group to any one publisher. Never send original artwork unless a publisher indicates a definite interest in using your work.

AMBERLEY GREETING CARD COMPANY—11510 Goldcoast Dr., Cincinnati, OH 45249–1695. Ned Stern, Ed. Humorous ideas for cards: birthday, illness, friendship, anniversary, congratulations, "miss you," etc. Pays $150. Buys all rights. Send SASE for market letter before submitting ideas.

AMERICAN GREETINGS—One American Rd., Cleveland, OH 44144. Kathleen McKay, Ed. Recruitment. Study current offerings and query before submitting.

BLUE MOUNTAIN ARTS, INC.—P.O. Box 1007, Boulder, CO 80306. Attn: Ed. Staff, Dept. TW. Poetry and prose about love, friendship, family, philosophies, etc. Also material for special occasions and holidays: birthdays, get well, Christmas, Valentine's Day, Easter, etc. Submit seasonal material 4 months in advance of holiday. No artwork or rhymed verse. Include SASE. Pays $200 per poem.

BRILLIANT ENTERPRISES—117 W. Valerio St., Santa Barbara, CA 93101–2927. Ashleigh Brilliant, Ed. Illustrated epigrams. Send SASE for the price of a catalogue and samples. Pays $40, on acceptance.

CONTEMPORARY DESIGNS—P.O. Box 60, Gilbert, IA 50105–0060. Sallie Abelson, Ed. Short, positive, humorous sayings for coffee mugs, T-shirts, memo pads, etc. "We are in need of sayings that fit into the following categories: college students, Jewish, camp, teacher, working world. We are not interested in puns, gross ideas, poetry, or prose. No need to enclose artwork; however, if you have a picture idea, you may draw it out or describe it." Submit each idea separately on 3x5 cards. Include writer's name and address on each card. Responds in 6 weeks. Pays from $35, on acceptance. Guidelines.

CONTENOVA GIFTS—735 Park North Blvd., Suite 114, Clarkston, GA 30021–1971. Vicki Boynton, Dir. of Marketing. Catchy, humorous, and sentimental one-liners for ceramic gift mugs. Submit on 3x5 cards; up to 15 ideas at a time. Payment varies, on acceptance. Guidelines.

DAYSPRING GREETING CARDS—P.O. Box 1010, Siloam Springs, AR 72761. Ann Woodruff, Ed. Religious/Christian cards. Uses unrhymed (preferred) and rhymed messages, traditional and light verse (various lengths) for humorous, inspirational, juvenile, and religious cards: anniversary, birthday, holidays, congratulations, friendship, get well, graduation, keep in touch, love, miss you, new baby, please write, sympathy, thank you, wedding, etc. Submit holiday/seasonal material one year ahead. Pays $35 to $50, on acceptance. Guidelines.

DESIGN DESIGN, INC.—P.O. Box 2266, Grand Rapids, MI 49501–2266. Don Kallil, Ed. Tom Vituj, Creative Dir. Humorous and sentimental ideas for greeting cards, mugs, T-shirts, and note pads. Everyday (birthday, get well, just for fun, etc.) and seasonal (Christmas, Valentine's Day, Easter, Mother's Day, Father's Day, Graduation, Halloween, Thanksgiving) material. Payment varies, on publication.

EPHEMERA, INC.—P.O. Box 490, Phoenix, OR 97535. Attn: Ed. Provocative, irreverent, and outrageously funny slogans for novelty buttons and magnets. Submit typed list of slogans with an SASE. Pays $25 per slogan, on publication. Guidelines.

HALLMARK CARDS, INC.—Box 419580, Mail Drop 216, Kansas City, MO 64141–6580. Write Carol King for submission agreement. Work is on assignment basis only. Free lancers must show exceptional originality and style not available from in-house employees and must have previous writing experience.

OATMEAL STUDIOS—Box 138 TW, Rochester, VT 05767. Attn: Ed. Humorous, clever, and new ideas needed for all occasions. Send legal-size SASE for guidelines.

PARAMOUNT CARDS—P.O. Box 6546, Providence, RI 02940-6546. Attn: Editorial Freelance. Humorous card ideas for birthday, relative's birthday, friendship, romance, get well, Christmas, Valentine's Day, Easter, Mother's Day, Father's Day, and Graduation. Submit each idea (5 to 10 per submission) on 3x5 card with name and address on each. Payment varies, on acceptance.

PLUM GRAPHICS—P.O. Box 136, Prince Station, New York, NY 10012. Yvette Cohen, Ed. Editorial needs change frequently; write for guidelines. Queries required. Pays $40 per card, on publication.

RED FARM STUDIO—1135 Roosevelt Ave., P.O. Box 347, Pawtucket, RI 02862. Attn: Production Coord. Traditional cards for graduation, wedding, birthday, get well, anniversary, friendship, new baby, sympathy, and Christmas. No studio humor. Pays $3 a line.

REGENCY THERMOGRAPHERS—(formerly *Williamhouse-Regency, Inc.*) 64 N. Conahan Dr., P.O. Box 2009, Hazelton, PA 18201. Burt Dolgin, Ed. Captions for wedding invitations only. Pays $25 per caption, on acceptance. Write for specifications sheet.

ROCKSHOTS, INC.—632 Broadway, New York, NY 10012. Bob Vesce, Ed. Adult, provocative, humorous gag lines for greeting cards. Submit on 4x5 cards with SASE. Pays $50 per line, on acceptance. Guidelines.

SANGAMON COMPANY—Route 48 W., P.O. Box 410, Taylorville, IL 62568. Attn: Ed. Dept. "We will send writer's guidelines to experienced free lancers before reviewing any submissions. We work on assignment." Pays competitive rates, on acceptance.

SUNRISE PUBLICATIONS, INC.—P.O. Box 4699, Bloomington, IN 47402-4699. Attn: Text Ed. Original copy for holiday and everyday cards. "Submit up to 15 verses, one to 4 lines, on 3x5 cards; simple, to-the-point ideas that could be serious, humorous, or light-hearted, but sincere, without being overly sentimental. Rhymed verse not generally used." Allow 3 months for response. Pays standard rates. Guidelines.

VAGABOND CREATIONS, INC.—2560 Lance Dr., Dayton, OH 45409. George F. Stanley, Jr., Ed. Greeting cards with graphics only on cover (no copy) and short punch line inside: birthday, everyday, Valentine's Day, Christmas, and graduation. Mildly risqué humor with double entendre acceptable. Ideas for illustrated theme stationery. Pays $15, on acceptance.

WARNER PRESS PUBLISHERS—P.O. Box 2499, Anderson, IN 46018. Robin Fogle, Product Ed. Writers must send SASE for guidelines before submitting." Religious themes, sensitive prose, and inspirational verse for boxed cards, posters, and calendars. Pays $20 to $35, on acceptance. Also accepts ideas for coloring and activity books.

WEST GRAPHICS PUBLISHING—385 Oyster Point Blvd., #7, S. San Francisco, CA 94080. Attn: Production Dept. Outrageous humor concepts, all occasions (especially birthday) and holidays, for photo and illustrated card lines. Submit on 3x5 cards: concept on one side; name, address, and phone number on other. Pays $100, 30 days after publication.

WILLIAMHOUSE-REGENCY, INC.—See *Regency Thermographers.*

COLLEGE, LITERARY, AND LITTLE MAGAZINES

The thousands of literary journals, little magazines, and college quarterlies published today welcome work from novices and pros alike; editors are always interested in seeing traditional and experimental fiction, poetry, essays, reviews, short articles, criticism, and satire, and as long as the material is well-written, the fact that a writer is a beginner doesn't adversely affect his or her chances for acceptance.

Most of these smaller publications have small budgets and staffs, so they may be slow in their reporting time—several months is not unusual. In addition, they usually pay only in copies of the issue in which published work appears and some—particularly college magazines—do not read manuscripts during the summer.

Publication in the literary journals can, however, lead to recognition by editors of large-circulation magazines, who read the little magazines in their search for new talent. There is also the possibility of having one's work chosen for reprinting in one of the prestigious annual collections of work from the little magazines.

Because the requirements of these journals differ widely, it is always important to study recent issues before submitting work to one of them. Large libraries may carry a variety of journals, or a writer may send a postcard to the editor and ask the price of a sample copy. When submitting a manuscript, always enclose a self-addressed envelope, with sufficient postage for its return, or an SASE for editorial reply only, if the manuscript need not be returned.

For a complete list of literary and college publications and little magazines, writers may consult such reference works as *The International Directory of Little Magazines and Small Presses*, published annually by Dustbooks (P.O. Box 100, Paradise, CA 95967).

AFRICAN AMERICAN REVIEW—Dept. of English, Indiana State Univ., Terre Haute, IN 47809. Joe Weixlmann, Ed. Essays on African American literature, theater, film, art, and culture; interviews; poems; fiction; and book reviews. Submit up to 6 poems. Pays an honorarium and copies. Query for book review assignments; send 3 copies of all other submissions. Responds in 3 months.

AFRICAN VOICES—270 W. 96th St., New York, NY 10025. Carolyn A.

Butts, Exec. Ed. Bimonthly. Humorous, erotic, and dramatic fiction, 500 to 2,500 words, by ethnic writers. Nonfiction, 500 to 1,500 words, including investigative articles, artist profiles, essays, and first-person narratives. Pays $25 for fiction (payment varies for nonfiction), plus 10 copies of issue, on publication.

AGNI—(formerly *The Agni Review*) Dept. TW, Boston Univ., Creative Writing Program, 236 Bay State Rd., Boston, MA 02215. Askold Melnyczuk, Ed. Erin Belieu, Man. Ed. Short stories, poetry, and essays. Manuscripts read October 1 to April 30.

ALABAMA LITERARY REVIEW—Troy State Univ., Smith 253, Troy, AL 36082. Theron Montgomery, Chief Ed. Semiannual. Contemporary, literary fiction and nonfiction, 3,500 words, and poetry, to 2 pages. Thought-provoking B&W photos. Pays in copies (honorarium when available). Responds within 3 months.

ALASKA QUARTERLY REVIEW—Univ. of Alaska Anchorage, 3211 Providence Dr., Anchorage, AK 99508. Attn: Eds. Short stories, novel excerpts, short plays, and poetry (traditional and unconventional forms). Submit manuscripts between August 15 and May 15. Pays in copies (and honorarium when funding is available).

ALBATROSS—P.O. Box 7787, North Port, FL 34287–0787. Richard Smyth, Richard Brobst, Eds. High-quality poetry; especially interested in ecological and nature poetry written in narrative form. Interviews with well-known poets. Submit 3 to 5 poems at a time with brief bio. Pays in copies.

AMELIA—329 E St., Bakersfield, CA 93304. Frederick A. Raborg, Jr., Ed. Poetry, to 100 lines; critical essays, to 2,000 words; reviews, to 500 words; belles lettres, to 1,000 words; fiction, to 4,500 words; fine pen-and-ink sketches; photos. Pays $35 for fiction and criticism, $10 to $25 for other nonfiction and artwork, $2 to $25 for poetry. Annual contest.

THE AMERICAN BOOK REVIEW—Publications Ctr., Univ. of Colorado, English Dept., Box 494, Boulder, CO 80309. Don Laing, Man. Ed. Literary book reviews, 700 to 1,200 words. Pays $50 honorarium and copies. Query with clips of published reviews.

AMERICAN LITERARY REVIEW—Univ. of North Texas, P.O. Box 13827, Denton, TX 76203–6827. Barbara Rodman, Ed. Short fiction, to 30 double-spaced pages, and poetry (submit 3 to 5 poems). Pays in copies.

THE AMERICAN POETRY REVIEW—1721 Walnut St., Philadelphia, PA 19103. Attn: Eds. Highest quality contemporary poetry. Responds in 10 weeks.

AMERICAN QUARTERLY—Dept. of English, Georgetown Univ., Washington, DC 20057. Lucy Maddox, Ed. Scholarly essays, 5,000 to 10,000 words, on any aspect of U.S. culture. Pays in copies.

THE AMERICAN SCHOLAR—1811 Q St. N.W., Washington, DC 20009–9974. Joseph Epstein, Ed. Articles, 3,500 to 4,000 words, on science, politics, literature, the arts, etc. Book reviews. Pays to $500 for articles, $100 for reviews, on publication.

THE AMERICAN VOICE—332 W. Broadway, Suite 1215, Louisville, KY 40202. Frederick Smock, Ed. Published 3 times per year. Avant-garde, literary fiction, nonfiction, and well-crafted poetry, any length (shorter works are preferred). "Please read our journal before attempting to submit." Payment varies, on publication.

AMERICAN WRITING— 4343 Manayunk Ave., Philadelphia, PA 19128. Alexandra Grilikhes, Ed. Semiannual. "We encourage experimentation, new writing that takes risks with form, point of view, language, perceptions. We're interested in the voice of the loner, states of being, and initiation." Fiction and nonfiction, to 3,500 words, and poetry. Pays in copies.

AMHERST REVIEW—Box 1811, Amherst College, P.O. Box 5000, Amherst, MA 01002–5000. Molly Lyons, Ed. Fiction, to 6,000 words. Submit material September through February only. Pays in copies.

ANOTHER CHICAGO MAGAZINE—3709 N. Kenmore, Chicago, IL 60613. Attn: Ed. Semiannual. Fiction, essays on literature, and poetry. "We want writing that's urgent, new, and lives in the world." Pays $5 to $50, on acceptance.

ANTIETAM REVIEW—7 W. Franklin St., Hagerstown, MD 21740. Susanne Kass and Ann Knox, Eds.-in-Chief. Fiction, to 5,000 words; poetry and photography. Submissions from natives or residents of MD, PA, WV, VA, DE, or DC only. Pays from $20 to $100. Guidelines. Manuscripts read September through January.

THE ANTIGONISH REVIEW—St. Francis Xavier Univ., P.O. Box 5000, Antigonish, N.S., Canada B2G 2W5. George Sanderson, Ed. Poetry; short stories, essays, book reviews, 1,800 to 2,500 words. Pays in copies.

ANTIOCH REVIEW—P.O. Box 148, Yellow Springs, OH 45387–0148. Robert S. Fogarty, Ed. Timely articles, 2,000 to 8,000 words, on social sciences, literature, and humanities. Quality fiction. Poetry. No inspirational poetry. Pays $10 per printed page, on publication. Poetry considered from September to May; other material considered year-round.

APALACHEE QUARTERLY—Apalachee Press, P.O. Box 10469, Tallahassee, FL 32302. Barbara Hamby, Rikki Clark, Monifa Love, Kim MacQueen, Lara Moody, Eds. Experimental fiction, to 30 manuscript pages; poems (submit 3 to 5). Pays in copies. Manuscripts read September to May.

APPALACHIA—5 Joy St., Boston, MA 02108. Parkman D. Howe III, Poetry Ed. Semiannual publication of the Appalachian Mountain Club. Oldest mountaineering journal in the country covers nature, conservation, climbing, hiking, canoeing, and ecology. Poems, to 30 lines. Pays in copies.

ARACHNE—162 Sturges St., Jamestown, NY 14701–3233. Susan L. Leach, Ed. Semiannual. Fiction, to 1,500 words. Poems (submit up to 7). "We are looking for rural material and would like first publication rights." No simultaneous submissions. Pays in copies. Manuscripts read in January and July.

ARIZONA COWBOY CONNECTION MAGAZINE—(formerly *Arizona Cowboy Poets Magazine*) P.O. Box 498, Prescott, AZ 86302. Sally Harper Bates, Geri Davis, Eds. Cowboy and western poetry, any length. Articles, 250 to 500 words, on cowboy views, themes, lifestyles, and attitudes; articles about families involved in the Arizona livestock community. Pays in copies.

ARIZONA QUARTERLY—Univ. of Arizona, Main Library B-541, Tucson, AZ 85721. Edgar A. Dryden, Ed. Criticism of American literature and culture from a theoretical perspective. No poetry or fiction. Pays in copies.

ART TIMES—P.O. Box 730, Mt. Marion, NY 12456. Raymond J. Steiner, Ed. Cheryl A. Rice, Poetry Ed. Fiction, to 1,500 words, and poetry, to 20 lines, for literate, art conscious readers (generally over 40 years old). Feature essays on the arts are staff-written. Pays $25 for fiction, in copies for poetry, on publication.

ARTFUL DODGE—College of Wooster, Wooster, OH 44691. Daniel Bourne, Ed. Annual. Fiction, to 20 pages. Literary essays, especially those involving personal narrative, to 15 pages. Poetry, including translations of contemporary poets; submit 3 to 6 poems at a time; long poems encouraged. Pays $5 per page, on publication, plus 2 copies. Manuscripts read year-round.

THE ASIAN PACIFIC AMERICAN JOURNAL—The Asian American Writers' Workshop, 37 St. Marks Pl., New York, NY 10003–7801. Curtis Chin, Man. Dir. Short stories, excerpts from longer fiction works, and essays, 2,000 to 3,000 words, by emerging or established Asian American writers. Poetry (submit 4 to 6 poems). Pays in copies. Query required for reviews and interviews; queries preferred for other articles.

THE ATLANTEAN PRESS REVIEW—P.O. Box 7336, Crescent Branch, Golden, CO 80403. Patricia LeChevalier, Ed. Romantic-realism: adventure, suspense, detective and romance stories, and serious fiction. Essays on various aspects of romantic art and art history. Structured rhyming poems. No horror, supernatural, erotica, or religious material. Pays $15 to $125, half on acceptance, half on publication.

AURA LITERARY/ARTS REVIEW—P.O. Box 76, Univ. Ctr., UAB, Birmingham, AL 35294. Steve Mullen, Ed. Fiction and essays on literature, to 5,000 words; book reviews, to 4,000 words; poetry; photos. Pays in copies. Guidelines.

BANEKE—P.O. Box 2417, Gainesville, FL 32602. Jorge Ibanez, Ed. Articles, book reviews, and interviews on Latino writers and artists. Pays in copies. Query preferred.

BELLES LETTRES—11151 Captain's Walk Ct., N. Potomac, MD 20878–0441. Janet Mullaney, Ed. Published 3 times a year; devoted to literature by or about women. Articles, 250 to 2,000 words: reviews, interviews, rediscoveries, and retrospectives; columns on publishing news, reprints, and nonfiction titles. Query required. Pays in copies (plus honorarium if funds available).

THE BELLINGHAM REVIEW—The Signpost Press Inc., 1007 Queen St., Bellingham, WA 98226. Knute Skinner, Ed. Semiannual. Fiction, to 5,000 words, and poetry, any length. Pays in copies and subscription. Manuscripts read from September 1 to March 1.

BELLOWING ARK—P.O. Box 45637, Seattle, WA 98145. Robert R. Ward, Ed. Bimonthly. Short fiction, poetry, and essays of varying lengths, that portray life as a positive, meaningful process. B&W photos; line drawings. Pays in copies. Manuscripts read year-round.

THE BELOIT FICTION JOURNAL—Box 11, Beloit College, Beloit, WI 53511. Fred Burwell, Ed. Short fiction, one to 35 pages, on all themes. No pornography, political propaganda, religious dogma. Pays in copies. Manuscripts read September to May.

BELOIT POETRY JOURNAL—RFD 2, Box 154, Ellsworth, ME 04605. Attn: Ed. Strong contemporary poetry, of any length or in any mode. Pays in copies. Guidelines.

BLACK BEAR REVIEW—Black Bear Publications, 1916 Lincoln St., Croydon, PA 19021–8026. Ave Jeanne, Ed. Semiannual. Book reviews and contemporary poetry. "We publish poems with social awareness, but any well-written piece is considered." Pays in one copy.

BLACK RIVER REVIEW—855 Mildred Ave., Lorain, OH 44052–1213. Deborah Gilbert and Kaye Coller, Eds. Contemporary poetry, fiction (to 4,000 words), essays, short book reviews, B&W artwork. No greeting card verse or slick magazine prose. Submit between January 1 and May 1. Pays in copies. Guidelines.

THE BLACK WARRIOR REVIEW—The Univ. of Alabama, P.O. Box 2936, Tuscaloosa, AL 35486–2936. Mark S. Drew, Ed. Fiction; poetry; translations; reviews and essays. Pays $5 to $10 per page, $25 to $35 per poem, on publication. Annual awards. Manuscripts read year-round.

THE BLOOMSBURY REVIEW—1028 Bannock St., Denver, CO 80204–4037. Tom Auer, Ed. Marilyn Auer, Assoc. Ed. Book reviews, publishing features, interviews, essays, poetry. Pays $5 to $25, on publication.

BLUE UNICORN—22 Avon Rd., Kensington, CA 94707. Attn: Ed. Published in October, February, and June. "We are looking for originality of image, thought, and music; we rarely use poems over a page long." Submit up to 5 poems. Artwork used occasionally. Pays in one copy.

BLUELINE—English Dept., SUNY, Potsdam, NY 13676. Anthony Tyler, Ed. Essays and fiction, to 3,500 words, on Adirondack region or similar areas. Poems, to 75 lines; submit no more than 5. Pays in copies. Manuscripts read September to November 30.

BORDERLANDS: TEXAS POETRY REVIEW—P.O. Box 49818, Austin, TX 78765. Attn: Ed. Semiannual. "Outward-looking" poetry of a political, spiritual, ecological, or social nature. Bilingual writers and writers from Texas and the Southwest given special attention. Send up to 5 pages of unpublished poetry. Essays, to 3,000 words, on contemporary poets, especially those from the Southwest. Pays one copy. Query for essays.

BOSTON REVIEW—E53, Room 407, 30 Wadsworth, MIT, Cambridge, MA 02139. John Thompson, Man. Ed. Reviews and essays, 800 to 3,000 words, on literature, art, music, film, photography. Original fiction, to 5,000 words. Poetry. Pays $40 to $100. Manuscripts read year-round.

BOTTOMFISH—21250 Stevens Creek Blvd., Cupertino, CA 95014. Robert Scott, Ed. Annual. Stories, vignettes, and experimental fiction, to 5,000 words. Free verse or traditional poetry, any subject, any length. "Our purpose is to give national exposure to new writers and new styles of creative writing. We publish at the end of March each year." Pays in copies. Manuscripts read July 1 to February 1.

BOULEVARD—P.O. Box 30386, Philadelphia, PA 19103. Richard Burgin, Ed. Published 3 times a year. High-quality fiction and articles, to 30 pages; poetry. Pays to $250, on publication.

THE BRIDGE—14050 Vernon St., Oak Park, MI 48237. Jack Zucker, Ed. Helen Zucker, Fiction Ed. Mitzi Alvin, Poetry Ed. Manon Meilgaard, Assoc. Fiction Ed. Semiannual. Fiction, 7,500 words, and poetry, to 200 lines. Pays in copies.

BUCKNELL REVIEW—Bucknell Univ., Lewisburg, PA 17837. Attn: Ed. Interdisciplinary journal in book form. Scholarly articles on arts, science, and letters. Pays in copies.

718

CALLALOO—Dept. of English, Univ. of Virginia, Charlottesville, VA 22903. Charles H. Rowell, Ed. Fiction, poetry, drama, and popular essays by, and critical studies and bibliographies on Afro-American, Caribbean, and African artists and writers. Payment varies, on publication.

CALLIOPE—Creative Writing Program, Roger Williams Univ., Bristol, RI 02809–2921. Martha Christina, Ed. Short stories, to 2,500 words; poetry. Pays in copies and subscription. No submissions April through July.

CALYX, A JOURNAL OF ART & LITERATURE BY WOMEN—P.O. Box B, Corvallis, OR 97339. M. Donnelly, Man. Ed. Fiction, 5,000 words; book reviews, 1,000 words (please query about reviews); poetry, to 6 poems. Include short bio. Pays in copies. Guidelines. Submissions accepted October 1 to November 15 and March 1 to April 15.

CANADIAN FICTION MAGAZINE—Box 1061, Kingston, Ontario, Canada K7L 4Y5. Attn: Ed. High-quality short stories, novel excerpts, and experimental fiction, to 5,000 words, by Canadians. Interviews with Canadian authors; translations. Pays $10 per page, on publication. Annual prize, $500. Manuscripts read year-round.

THE CAPE ROCK—Dept. of English, Southeast Missouri State Univ., Cape Girardeau, MO 63701. Harvey E. Hecht, Ed. Semiannual. Poetry, to 70 lines, and B&W photography. (One photographer per issue; pays $100.) Pays in copies and $200 for best poem in each issue. Manuscripts read August to April.

THE CARIBBEAN WRITER—Univ. of the Virgin Islands, RR 02, Box 10,000, Kingshill, St. Croix, USVI 00850. Erika J. Waters, Ed. Annual. Fiction (to 15 pages, submit up to 2 stories) and poems (no more than 5); the Caribbean should be central to the work. Blind submissions policy: place title only on manuscript; name, address, and title of manuscripts on separate sheet. Pays in copies. Annual deadline is September 30.

THE CAROLINA QUARTERLY—Greenlaw Hall CB#3520, Univ. of North Carolina, Chapel Hill, NC 27599–3520. Amber Vogel, Ed. Fiction, to 7,000 words, by new or established writers. Poetry, to 300 lines. Manuscripts read year-round.

CATALYST—236 Forsyth St., Suite 400, Atlanta, GA 30303. Pearl Cleage, Ed. Semiannual. Fiction, to 3,000 words, and poetry. Pays $10 to $200, on publication. Guidelines and themes. Responds in 6 months.

THE CENTENNIAL REVIEW—312 Linton Hall, Michigan State Univ., E. Lansing, MI 48824–1044. R.K. Meiners, Ed. Articles, 3,000 to 5,000 words, on sciences, humanities, and interdisciplinary topics. Pays in copies.

CENTURY—Century Publishing, Inc., P.O. Box 150510, Brooklyn, NY 11215–0510. Robert K.J. Killheffer, Ed. Literary science fiction, fantasy, and magic realism, 1,000 and 20,000 words. Pays 4¢ to 6¢ a word, on acceptance.

THE CHARITON REVIEW—Truman State Univ., Kirksville, MO 63501. Jim Barnes, Ed. Highest quality poetry and fiction, to 6,000 words. Modern and contemporary translations. "The only guideline is excellence in all matters."

CHICAGO REVIEW—5801 S. Kenwood Ave., Chicago, IL 60637. David Nicholls, Ed. Laura Reed-Morrisson, Fiction Ed. Angela Sorby, Poetry Ed. Jennifer Sampson, Nonfiction Ed. Essays, interviews, reviews, fiction, translations, poetry. Pays in copies plus one year's subscription. Manuscripts read year-round; replies in 2 to 3 months.

CHIRON REVIEW—522 E. South Ave., St. John, KS 67576–2212. Michael Hathaway, Ed. Contemporary fiction, to 4,000 words; articles, 500 to 1,000 words; and poetry, to 30 lines. Photos. Pays in copies. Poetry and chapbook contests; SASE for details.

CICADA—329 E St., Bakersfield, CA 93304. Frederick A. Raborg, Jr., Ed. Quarterly. Single haiku, sequences, or garlands; essays about the forms; haibun and fiction (one story per issue) related to haiku or Japan. Pays in copies.

CIMARRON REVIEW—205 Morrill Hall, Oklahoma State Univ., Stillwater, OK 74078–0135. Gordon Weaver, Ed. Poetry, fiction, essays. Seeks an individual, innovative style that focuses on contemporary themes. Pays $50 for stories and essays; $15 for poems, plus one-year subscription. Manuscripts read year-round.

CINCINNATI POETRY REVIEW—Humanities Dept., College of Mt. St. Joseph, Cincinnati, OH 45233. Jeffrey Hillard, Ed. Semiannual. Poetry of all types. Pays in copies.

CLOCKWATCH REVIEW—Dept. of English, Illinois Wesleyan Univ., Bloomington, IL 61702–2900. James Plath, Ed. Semiannual. Fiction, to 4,000 words, and poetry, to 36 lines. "Our preference is for fresh language, a believable voice, a mature style, and a sense of the unusual in the subject matter." Pays $25 for fiction, $5 for poetry, on acceptance, plus copies. Manuscripts read year-round.

COLLAGES & BRICOLAGES—P.O. Box 86, Clarion, PA 16214. Marie-José Fortis, Ed. Annual. Fiction and nonfiction, plays, interviews, book reviews, and poetry. Surrealistic, feminist, and expressionistic drawings in ink. "I seek innovation and honesty. The magazine often focuses on one subject; query for themes." Pays in copies. Manuscripts read August through October.

COLUMBIA: A MAGAZINE OF POETRY & PROSE— 404 Dodge, Columbia Univ., New York, NY 10027. Attn: Ed. Semiannual. Fiction and nonfiction; poetry; essays; interviews; visual art. Pays in copies. Guidelines. Manuscripts read September to May.

THE COMICS JOURNAL—Fantagraphics, Inc., 7563 Lake City Way, Seattle, WA 98115. Attn: Man. Ed. "Looking for free-lancers with working knowledge of the diversity and history of the comics medium." Reviews, 2,500 to 5,000 words; domestic and international news, 500 to 7,000 words; "Opening Shots" editorials, 500 to 1,500 words; interviews; and features, 2,500 to 5,000 words. Query for news and interviews. Pays 2¢ a word, on publication. Guidelines.

COMMON JOURNEYS— 4136 43rd Ave. S, Minneapolis, MN 55406. Leslie Keyes, Ed. Semiannual literary journal "on the illness experience." Creative, compelling nonfiction, 1,200 words, related to chronic pain or illness. Poetry, to 30 lines. "General tone should be realistic but hopeful." Pays one copy.

CONFRONTATION—Dept. of English, C.W. Post of L. I. U., Brookville, NY 11548. Martin Tucker, Ed. Serious fiction, 750 to 6,000 words. Crafted poetry, 10 to 200 lines. Pays $10 to $100, on publication.

THE CONNECTICUT POETRY REVIEW—P.O. Box 818, Stonington, CT 06378. J. Claire White and Harley More, Eds. Poetry, 5 to 20 lines, and reviews, 700 words. Pays $5 per poem, $10 per review, on acceptance. Manuscripts read September to January and April to June.

CONNECTICUT RIVER REVIEW—327 Seabury Dr., Bloomfield, CT 06002. Ben Brodinsky, Ed. Semiannual. Poetry. Submit 3 to 5 poems, to 40 lines. Pays in one copy. Guidelines.

THE COOL TRAVELER—P.O. Box 273, Selinsgrove, PA 17870. Bob Moore, Pub./Ed. Bimonthly. Articles, 800 words, including excerpts from diaries and letters written while traveling. "We are a literary newsletter about place and experience; we emphasize 'what happened' rather than 'what to see.'" Pays to $20, on publication.

CQ/CALIFORNIA STATE POETRY QUARTERLY—California State Poetry Society, Box 7126, Orange, CA 92613. Attn: Ed. Board. Poetry, to 60 lines. All poets welcome. Payment is one copy. Responds within 3 months.

CRAZY QUILT—P.O. Box 632729, San Diego, CA 92163–2729. Attn: Eds. Fiction, to 4,000 words, poetry, one-act plays, and literary criticism. Also B&W art, photographs. Pays in copies. Manuscripts read year-round.

THE CREAM CITY REVIEW—Box 413, Univ. of Wisconsin, Milwaukee, WI 53201. Mark Drechsler and Andrew Rivera, Eds.-in-Chief. Semiannual. "We serve a national audience interested in a diversity of writing (in terms of style, subject, genre) and writers (gender, race, class, publishing history, etc.). Both well-known and newly published writers of fiction, poetry, and essays are featured, along with B&W artwork." Pays in copies. Manuscripts read year-round; responds in 8 weeks (not as quickly during the summer).

THE CREATIVE WOMAN—TAPP Group, 126 East Wing, Suite 288, Arlington Hgts., IL 60004. Margaret Choudhury, Ed. Quarterly. Essays, fiction, poetry, criticism, graphic arts, and photography, from a feminist perspective. SASE for upcoming themes. Payment varies, on publication.

THE CRESCENT REVIEW—P.O. Box 15069, Chevy Chase, MD 20825. J.T. Holland, Ed. Semiannual. Short stories only. Pays in copies. Manuscripts read July through October and January through April.

THE CRITIC—205 W. Monroe St., 6th Fl., Chicago, IL 60606–5097. Julie Bridge, Ed. Quarterly. "A Journal of American Catholic Culture." Fiction and articles, to 5,000 words. Poetry. "Stories and articles need not be Catholic, but keep in mind the religious affiliation when submitting work. No conservative Roman Catholic tracts; the magazine is moderate to liberal." Pays $25 to $400, on acceptance. Query for articles.

CUMBERLAND POETRY REVIEW—P.O. Box 120128, Acklen Sta., Nashville, TN 37212. Attn: Eds. High-quality poetry and criticism; translations. Send up to 6 poems with brief bio. No restrictions on form, style, or subject matter. Pays in copies.

CUTBANK—Eng. Dept., Univ. of Montana, Missoula, MT 59812. Attn: Eds. Semiannual. Fiction, to 40 pages, (submit one story at a time) and poems (submit up to 5 poems). All manuscripts are considered for the Richard Hugo Memorial Poetry Award and the A.B. Guthrie, Jr. Short Fiction Award. Pays in copies. Guidelines. Manuscripts read August 15 to March 15.

DENVER QUARTERLY—Univ. of Denver, Denver, CO 80208. Bin

Ramke, Ed. Literary, cultural essays and articles; poetry; book reviews; fiction. Pays $5 per printed page, after publication.

DESCANT—Texas Christian Univ., T.C.U. Box 32872, Fort Worth, TX 76129. Betsy Colquitt, Stanley Trachtenberg, Harry Opperman, and Steve Sherwood, Eds. Fiction, to 6,000 words. Poetry, to 40 lines. No restriction on form or subject. Pays in copies. Frank O'Connor Award ($500) is given each year for best short story published in the volume. Submit material September through May only.

THE DEVIL'S MILLHOPPER—The Devil's Millhopper Press, USC/Aiken, 171 University Pkwy., Aiken, SC 29801–6309. Stephen Gardner, Ed. Poetry. Send SASE for guidelines and contest information. Pays in copies.

DEXTER REVIEW—P.O. Box 8418, Ann Arbor, MI 48107. Ronald Farrington Sharp, Ed. Annual. Non-genre fiction, to 3,000 words; poetry, to 3 pages; art-related essays and short interviews, to 3,000 words. No formula romances, detectives, space aliens. Pays in copies. Guidelines. Manuscripts read January through May. Contests; SASE for details.

THE DISTILLERY—Motlow State Community College, P.O. Box 88100, Tullahoma, TN 37388. Stuart Bloodworth and Linda Rollins, Eds. Semiannual. Fiction, 4,000 words; poetry, 100 lines; critical essays, photos and drawings. Regional authors preferred. Pays in copies.

DOG RIVER REVIEW—5976 Billings Rd., Parkdale, OR 97041–9610. Laurence F. Hawkins, Ed. Poetry, fiction, plays, book reviews, and related articles, to 2,500 words. B&W art. No religious or greeting card verse. Pays in copies.

DREAMS & VISIONS—Skysong Press, R. R. 1, Washago, Ontario, Canada L0K 2B0. Steve Stanton, Ed. Eclectic fiction, 2,000 to 6,000 words, that is "in some way unique and relevant to Christian readers today." Pays in copies, with $100 honorarium to best of the year.

EARTH'S DAUGHTERS—P.O. Box 41, Central Park Sta., Buffalo, NY 14215. Attn: Ed. Published 3 times a year. Fiction, to 1,000 words, poetry, to 40 lines, and B&W photos or drawings. "Finely crafted work with a feminist theme." Pays in copies. SASE for guidelines and themes.

ECLECTIC RAINBOWS—1538 Tennessee Walker Dr., Roswell, GA 30075. Linda T. Dennison, Ed./Pub. Semiannual. Features and profiles, 1,000 to 3,000 words, and personal experience and humor, to 1,500 words. Creative nonfiction, interviews, fiction, and poetry having to do with "the people, places, and things that make a positive difference in our lives." Pays $25, on publication.

ELF: ECLECTIC LITERARY FORUM—P.O. Box 392, Tonawanda, NY 14150. C. K. Erbes, Ed. Fiction, 3,500 words. Essays on literary themes, 3,500 words. Poetry, to 30 lines. Allow 4 to 6 weeks for response. Pays in 2 copies.

EUREKA LITERARY MAGAZINE—Eureka College, P.O. Box 280, Eureka, IL 61530. Loren Logsdon, Ed. Semiannual. Fiction, 25 to 30 pages, and poetry, submit up to 4 poems at a time. "We seek to promote no specific political agenda or literary theory. We strive to publish the best of the fiction and poetry submitted to us." Pays in copies.

EVENT—Douglas College, Box 2503, New Westminster, BC, Canada V3L 5B2. David Zieroth, Ed. Short fiction, reviews, poetry. Pays $22 per printed page, on publication.

722

EXPRESSIONS—P.O. Box 16294, St. Paul, MN 55116. Sefra Kobrin Pitzele, Ed. Semiannual. Literature and art by people with disabilities and ongoing illnesses. Fiction and articles, to 2,500 words. Poetry, to 64 lines. B&W artwork. "We hope to be a place where talented people who may have limited energy, finances, or physical ability can be published." Pays in copies. Guidelines.

FARMER'S MARKET—Elgin Community College, 1700 Spartan Dr., Elgin, IL 60123-7193. Attn: Ed. Short stories, to 30 pages, and poetry. Pays in copies and subscription.

FATHOMS—2020 W. Pensacola, Unit 46, #549, Tallahassee, FL 32304. Rex West, Poetry Ed. Todd Pierce, Fiction Ed. Semiannual. Short stories and "flash" fiction, to 2,000 words. Poetry, to 100 lines. Pays in one copy.

FEELINGS—Anderie Poetry Press, P.O. Box 85, Easton, PA 18044-0085. Carl and Carole Heffley, Eds. "America's Beautiful Poetry Magazine." Quarterly. Submit up to 3 poems, 30 lines each, "that convey an immediate sense of recognition, intensity of thought, and heart-to-heart communication." Awards 3 editor's choice prizes of $10, plus readers' choice award of $10, each issue.

FICTION INTERNATIONAL—English Dept., San Diego State Univ., San Diego, CA 92182-0295. Harold Jaffe, Ed. Post-modernist and politically committed fiction and theory. Pays in copies. Manuscripts read from September 1 to December 15.

THE FIDDLEHEAD—Campus House, Univ. of New Brunswick, Fredericton, N.B., Canada E3B 5A3. Attn: Ed. Serious fiction, 2,500 words, preferably by Canadians. Pays about $10 per printed page, on publication. SAE with international reply coupons required. Manuscripts read year-round.

FIELD—Rice Hall, Oberlin College, Oberlin, OH 44074. Stuart Friebert, David Young, Eds. Serious poetry, any length, by established and unknown poets; essays on poetics by poets. Translations by qualified translators. Payment varies, on publication. Manuscripts read year-round.

FINE MADNESS—P.O. Box 31138, Seattle, WA 98103-1138. Attn: Ed. Poetry, to 10 pages. Fiction by invitation only. Pays in copies. No simultaneous submissions. Guidelines.

FIVE FINGERS REVIEW—P.O. Box 15426, San Francisco, CA 94115. Published once or twice a year. "Writing with a sense of experimentation, an awareness of tradition, and a willingness to explore artistic boundaries." Pays in copies.

FLYWAY—(formerly *Poet & Critic*) 203 Ross Hall, Iowa State Univ., Ames, IA 50011-1201. Stephen Pett, Ed. Poetry, fiction, creative nonfiction, and reviews. Pays in copies. Manuscripts read September through May.

FOLIO—Dept. of Literature, American Univ., Washington, DC 20016. Attn: Ed. Semiannual. Fiction, poetry, translations, and essays. Photos and drawings. Pays in 2 copies. Submissions read September through March. Contest.

FOOTWORK, THE PATERSON LITERARY REVIEW—Poetry Ctr., Passaic County Comm. College, College Blvd., Paterson, NJ 07505-1179. Maria Mazziotti Gillan, Ed. High-quality fiction and poetry, to 10 pages. Pays in copies. Manuscripts read January through May.

723

THE FORMALIST—320 Hunter Dr., Evansville, IN 47711. William Baer, Ed. Metrical poetry, to 2 pages, including blank verse, couplets, and traditional forms such as sonnets, ballads, villanelles, etc. "Sound and rhythm make poetry what it is."

THE FRACTAL—George Mason Univ., 4400 University Dr., Fairfax, VA 22030–4444. David Gardner, Sr. Ed. Literary fiction and poetry and academic nonfiction. Science fiction, fantasy, and horror stories of varying lengths. Guidelines. Pays $25 for fiction; $50 for nonfiction; $5 for poetry, on publication.

FREE INQUIRY—P.O. Box 664, Buffalo, NY 14226. Paul Kurtz, Ed. Tim Madigan, Exec. Ed. Articles, 500 to 5,000 words, for "literate and lively readership. Focus is on criticisms of religious belief systems, and how to lead an ethical life without a supernatural basis." Pays in copies.

FUGUE—Univ. of Idaho, English Dept., Brink Hall, Room 200, Moscow, ID 83843. Address Exec. Ed. Literary digest of the Univ. of Idaho. Fiction, to 7,000 words. Nonfiction, to 2,000 words, on writing. Poetry, any style, 100 lines. "We try to give new writers in all classifications of fiction and poetry a chance at publication." Manuscripts not returned; include SASE for editorial reply. Guidelines. Pays honorarium and one copy.

FULL-TIME DADS—P.O. Box 577, Cumberland, ME 04021. Stephen Harris, Ed. Fiction, articles, essays, and humor, 600 to 1,200 words, and short poems for fathers who are very involved with their children. "All material must relate to supportive fatherhood." Payment is one copy.

THE GEORGIA REVIEW—Univ. of Georgia, Athens, GA 30602–9009. Stanley W. Lindberg, Ed. Stephen Corey, Assoc. Ed. Short fiction; literary, interdisciplinary, and personal essays; book reviews; poetry; artwork. Translations and novel excerpts strongly discouraged. No simultaneous submissions. Manuscripts read September through May.

THE GETTYSBURG REVIEW—Gettysburg College, Gettysburg, PA 17325. Peter Stitt, Ed. Quarterly. Poetry, fiction, essays, and essay reviews, 1,000 to 20,000 words. "Review sample copy before submitting." Pays $2 a line for poetry; $25 per printed page for fiction and nonfiction. Allow 3 to 6 months for response. No simultaneous submissions.

GLIMMER TRAIN PRESS—812 S.W. Washington St., Suite 1205, Portland, OR 97205. Susan Burmeister-Brown, Ed. Quarterly. Fiction, 1,200 to 7,500 words. Eight stories in each issue. Pays $500, on acceptance. Submit material in January, April, July, and October. Allow 3 months for response. Short story award for new writers; SASE for details.

GOTHIC JOURNAL—19210 Forest Rd. N., Forest Lake, MN 55025–9766. Kristi Lyn Glass, Pub. Bimonthly. News and reviews for readers, writers, and publishers of romantic suspense, romantic mystery, and gothic, supernatural, and woman-in-jeopardy romance novels. Articles, 1,000 to 2,000 words, on gothic and romantic suspense topics; author profiles, 3,000 to 4,000 words; book reviews, 250 to 500 words. Pays $20 for articles, $30 for author profiles, on publication.

GRAHAM HOUSE REVIEW—Box 5000, Colgate Univ., Hamilton, NY 13346. Peter Balakian, Ed. Bruce Smith, Ed. Poetry, translations, and essays on modern poets. Payment depends on grants. Manuscripts read year-round; responds within 8 weeks.

GRAIN—Box 1154, Regina, Sask., Canada S4P 3B4. Geoffrey Ursell, Ed. Short stories, to 30 typed pages; poems, send up to 8; visual art. Pays $30 to $100 for stories and poems, $100 for cover art, $30 for other art. SAE with international reply coupons required. Manuscripts read year-round.

GRAND STREET—131 Varick St., #906, New York, NY 10013. Jean Stein, Ed. Quarterly. Poetry, any length. Pays $3 a line, on publication. Will not read unsolicited fiction or essays.

GREEN'S MAGAZINE—P.O. Box 3236, Regina, Sask., Canada S4P 3H1. David Green, Ed. Fiction for family reading, 1,500 to 4,000 words. Poetry, to 40 lines. No simultaneous submissions. Pays in copies. International reply coupons must accompany U.S. manuscripts. Manuscripts read year-round.

THE GREENSBORO REVIEW—Dept. of English, Univ. of North Carolina, Greensboro, NC 27412-5001. Jim Clark, Ed. Semiannual. Poetry and fiction. Submission deadlines: September 15 and February 15. Pays in copies. Writer's guidelines and guidelines for literary awards issue available.

HALF TONES TO JUBILEE—Pensacola Junior College, English Dept., 1000 College Blvd., Pensacola, FL 32504. Walter F. Spara, Ed. Fiction, to 1,500 words, and poetry, to 60 lines. Pays in copies. Manuscripts read August 15 to May 15. Contest.

HARP-STRINGS—P.O. Box 640387, Beverly Hills, FL 34464. Madelyn Eastlund, Ed. Poems, 14 to 80 lines, on a variety of topics and in many forms. No light verse, "prose masquerading as poetry," confessions, or raw guts poems. Pays in copies.

HAUNTS—Nightshade Publications, Box 8068, Cranston, RI 02920–0068. Joseph K. Cherkes, Ed. Short stories, 1,500 to 8,000 words: horror, science-fantasy, and supernatural tales with strong characters. Pays ½¢ to 1¢ a word, on publication. Manuscripts read January 1 to June 1.

HAWAII REVIEW—Dept. of English, Univ. of Hawaii, 1733 Donagho Rd., Honolulu, HI 96822. Michelle Y. Viray, Ed.-in-Chief. Quality fiction, poetry, interviews, essays, and literary criticism reflecting both regional and global concerns. Manuscripts read year-round.

HAYDEN'S FERRY REVIEW—Box 871502, Arizona State Univ., Tempe, AZ 85287–1502. Attn: Ed. Semiannual. Fiction, essays, and poetry (submit up to 6 poems). Include brief bio and SASE. Deadline for Spring/Summer issue is September 30; Fall/Winter issue, February 28. Pays in copies.

THE HEARTLANDS TODAY—Firelands Writing Ctr. of Firelands College, Huron, OH 44839. Larry Smith and Nancy Dunham, Eds. Fiction, 1,000 to 4,500 words, and nonfiction, 1,000 to 3,000 words, about the contemporary Midwest. Poetry (submit 3 to 5 poems). "Writing must be set in the Midwest, but can include a variety of themes." B&W photos. Pays $10 to $20 honorarium, plus copies. Query for current themes.

THE HIGHLANDER—P.O. Box 397, Barrington, IL 60011. Angus Ray, Ed. Bimonthly. Articles, 1,300 to 1,900 words, related to Scottish history. "We do not want articles on modern Scotland or current problems in Scotland." Pays $100 to $150, on acceptance.

THE HOLLINS CRITIC—P.O. Box 9538, Hollins College, Roanoke, VA 24020. John Rees Moore, Ed. Published 5 times a year. Features an essay on a contemporary fiction writer or poet, cover sketch, brief biography, and book list. Also, book reviews and poetry. Pays $25 for poetry, on publication.

HOME LIFE—127 Ninth Ave. N., Nashville, TN 37234. Charlie Warren, Ed.-in-Chief. Southern Baptist. Short lyrical verse: humorous, marriage and family, seasonal, and inspirational. Query for family-oriented articles, 600 to 1,800 words. Also uses one piece of fiction each month. Pays to $24 for poetry, from $75 for articles, on acceptance.

HOME PLANET NEWS—P.O. Box 415, Stuyvesant Sta., New York, NY 10009. Enid Dame and Donald Lev, Eds. Quarterly art tabloid. Fiction, to 8 typed pages; reviews, 3 to 5 pages; and poetry, any length. "We are looking for quality poetry, fiction, and discerning literary and art reviews." Query for nonfiction. Pays in copies and subscription. Manuscripts read February 1 to May 31.

HOWLING DOG— 8419 Rhode, Utica, MI 48317. Dorothy Donovan, Ed. Semiannual. "Strange" fiction, to 1,000 words. Free verse, avant-garde, wild poetry, to 5 pages. "We are looking for pieces with a humorous perspective toward society's problems." Pays in copies.

HURRICANE ALICE: A FEMINIST QUARTERLY—207 Lind Hall, 207 Church St. S.E., Minneapolis, MN 55455. Attn: Ed. Articles, fiction, essays, interviews, and reviews, 500 to 3,000 words, with feminist perspective. Pays in copies.

HYPHEN MAGAZINE—P.O. Box 516, Somonauk, IL 60552. Attn: Ed. Original fiction, poetry, interviews, articles, reviews, and columns, as well as artwork. Pays in copies.

THE ILLINOIS REVIEW— 42401 English Dept., Illinois State Univ., Normal, IL 61790–4240. Jim Elledge, Ed. Semiannual. Poems, prose poems, short-short fiction, stories, novel excerpts, one-act plays, translations, essays, and book reviews. "Open to mainstream and alternative material by established or unknown writers." B&W cover art and photos. Pays in copies. Manuscripts read August 1 to May 1; responds in one to 2 months.

IN MY SHOES— 410 E. Park St., Archer, FL 32618. April Burk, Ed. "Personal stories from the journey of life." True stories, memoirs, and "as told to" articles, 1,500 words. No fiction or confession. Departments (also 1,500 words) include "Heart & Soul," inspirational, heartwarming pieces; "Tongue Flap," humor; and "Tread Marks," personal experience travel pieces. Pays in copies.

IN THE COMPANY OF POETS—P.O. Box 10786, Oakland, CA 94610. Jacalyn Robinson, Ed./Pub. Quarterly. Fiction and creative essays, to 2,500 words, for a wide multicultural range of readers. Poems of any length. Drawings and photos. Pays in 3 copies. Guidelines. Manuscripts read year-round.

INDIANA REVIEW—316 N. Jordan Ave., Indiana Univ., Bloomington, IN 47405. Shirley Stephenson, Ed. Geoffrey Pollock, Assoc. Ed. Fiction with an emphasis on storytelling and sophistication of language. Poems that are well-executed and ambitious. Pays $5 per page. Manuscripts read year-round.

INTERGALACTIC POETRY MESSENGER—Flutter By Press, 252 Nassau St., Princeton, NJ 08540. Bruce Wilpon, Ed. Fiction and nonfiction, to 10 pages; poetry, submit up to 10. Essays, cartoons, photos, illustrations, short humor. "Readership includes poets, writers, the young at heart. Our aim is to expand the readership of poetry journals with our graphics parade. We publish serious work in a mirthful, accessible format." Queries preferred. Payment varies, on publication.

726

INTERIM—Dept. of English, Univ. of Nevada, Las Vegas, NV 89154–5034. A. Wilber Stevens, Ed. Semiannual. Poetry, any form or length, and fiction, to 7,500 words (uses no more than 2 stories per issue). Pays in copies and 2-year subscription. Responds in 2 months.

THE IOWA REVIEW—EPB 308, Univ. of Iowa, Iowa City, IA 52242. David Hamilton, Ed. Essays, poems, stories, reviews. Pays $10 a page for fiction and nonfiction, $1 a line for poetry, on publication. Manuscripts read September 1 through April 15.

IOWA WOMAN—P.O. Box 680, Iowa City, IA 52244. Marianne Abel, Ed. Fiction, poetry, creative nonfiction, book reviews, and personal essays; articles, to 6,500 words, on midwestern history; interviews with prominent women; current social, economic, artistic, and environmental issues. Poems, any length (submit up to 5); photos and drawings. Queries preferred for articles. Pays $5 a page, $15 for illustrations, on publication. Guidelines.

JACARANDA REVIEW—Dept. of English, Univ. of California, Los Angeles, CA 90024. Bruce Kijewski, Ed. Laurence Roth, Poetry Ed. Semiannual. Fiction, to 50 pages, and poetry (submit up to 3 poems). No payment.

THE JAMES WHITE REVIEW—P.O. Box 3356, Butler Quarter Sta., Minneapolis, MN 55403. Phil Willkie, Pub. "A Gay Men's Literary Quarterly." Short stories, to 9,000 words, and poetry, to 250 lines. Book reviews. Responds in 3 months.

JAPANOPHILE—Box 223, Okemos, MI 48864. Earl R. Snodgrass, Ed. Fiction, to 4,000 words, with a Japanese setting. Each story should have at least one Japanese character and at least one non-Japanese. Articles, 2,000 words, that celebrate Japanese culture. "We seek to promote Japanese-American understanding. We are not about Japan-bashing or fatuous praise." Pays to $20, on publication. Annual short story contest; deadline December 31.

JOYFUL NOISE—31 St. Anthony Ln., Glenville, NY 12302. Fred Dandino, Pub. Carole Dandino, Ed. Semiannual. Fiction, 500 words; nonfiction, 250 to 500 words; poetry, anecdotes, recipes, limericks, puzzles, and letters, any length. "We accept only material from people who are physically challenged. When submitting, please tell us what your disability is. We're always on the lookout for humorous stories." Send complete manuscript; no queries. Responds in 2 months. Pays in copies. Guidelines.

KALEIDOSCOPE—United Disability Services, 326 Locust St., Akron, OH 44302–1876. Darshan Perusek, Ph.D., Ed.-in-Chief. Semiannual. Fiction, essays, interviews, articles, and poetry relating to disability and the arts, to 5,000 words. Photos a plus. "We present balanced, realistic images of people with disabilities and publish pieces that challenge stereotypes." Submissions accepted from writers with or without disabilities. Pays $10 to $125. Guidelines recommended. Manuscripts read year-round; response may take up to 6 months.

KALLIOPE: A JOURNAL OF WOMEN'S ART—Florida Community College at Jacksonville, 3939 Roosevelt Blvd., Jacksonville, FL 32205. Attn: Ed. Fiction, to 2,500 words; poetry; interviews of women writers, to 2,000 words; and B&W photos of fine art. Query for interviews only. Pays in copies.

KANSAS QUARTERLY—English Dept., Kansas State Univ., Manhattan,

KS 66506. Attn: Ed. Literary criticism, art, and history. Fiction and poetry. Pays in copies. Two series of annual awards.

KARAMU—Dept. of English, Eastern Illinois Univ., Charleston, IL 61920. Peggy Brayfield, Ed. Contemporary or experimental fiction. Creative nonfiction prose, personal essays, and memoir pieces. Poetry. Pays in copies. Manuscripts read year-round; best time to submit is January to May.

THE KENYON REVIEW—Kenyon College, Gambier, OH 43022. David H. Lynn, Ed. Quarterly. Fiction, poetry, essays, literary criticism, and reviews. "We appreciate manuscripts from writers who read the magazine." Pays $10 a printed page for prose, $15 a printed page for poetry, on publication. Manuscripts read September through March.

KINESIS—P.O. Box 4007, Whitefish, MT 59937. Leif Peterson, Ed./Pub. Fiction, essays, and reviews, 2,000 to 6,000 words; poetry, to 60 lines. "Make sure it moves!" Pays in copies and subscription.

KIOSK—c/o English Dept., 306 Clemens Hall, SUNY Buffalo, Buffalo, NY 14226. Mary Obropta, Ed. Robert Rebein, Fiction Ed. A.M. Allcott, Poetry Ed. Fiction, to 20 pages, with a "strong sense of voice, narrative direction, and craftsmanship." Poetry "that builds possibilities for dramatic dialogue." Address appropriate editor. Pays in copies. Manuscripts read September 1 to April 15.

LAMBDA BOOK REPORT—1625 Connecticut Ave. N.W., Washington, DC 20009. Jim Marks, Ed. Reviews and features, 500 to 1,100 words, of gay and lesbian books. Pays $15 to $60, 30 days after publication. Queries preferred.

LATINO STUFF REVIEW—P.O. Box 440195, Miami, FL 33144. Nilda Cepero-Llevada, Ed./Pub. Short stories, 3,000 words; poetry, to one page; criticism and essays on literature, the arts, social issues. Bilingual publication focusing on Latino topics. Pays in copies.

THE LEADING EDGE—3163 JKHB, Provo, UT 84602. Michael Carr, Ed. Semiannual. Science fiction and fantasy, 3,000 to 12,000 words; poetry, to 600 lines; and articles, to 8,000 words, on science, scientific speculation, and literary criticism. "Do not send originals; manuscripts are marked and critiqued by staff." Pays $10 to $100, on publication. Guidelines.

LIGHT—Box 7500, Chicago, IL 60680. John Mella, Ed. Quarterly. Light verse. Also fiction, reviews, and essays, to 2,000 words. Fillers, humor, jokes, quips. "If it has wit, point, edge, or barb, it will find a home here." Cartoons and line drawings. Pays in copies. Query for nonfiction.

LILITH, THE INDEPENDENT JEWISH WOMEN'S MAGAZINE—250 W. 57th St., New York, NY 10107. Susan Weidman Schneider, Ed. Fiction, 1,500 to 2,000 words, on issues of interest to Jewish women.

LITERAL LATTE— 61 E. 8th St., Suite 240, New York, NY 10003. Jenine Gordon, Ed./Pub. Bimonthly distributed to cafés and bookstores in New York City. Fiction and personal essays, to 6,000 words; poetry, to 2,000 words; B&W art. Pays in subscription and copies.

LITERARY MAGAZINE REVIEW—English Dept., Kansas State Univ., Manhattan, KS 66506. Attn: Ed. Reviews and articles concerning literary magazines, 1,000 to 1,500 words, for writers and readers of contemporary literature. Pays modest fees and in copies. Query.

THE LITERARY REVIEW—Fairleigh Dickinson Univ., 285 Madison

Ave., Madison, NJ 07940. Walter Cummins, Ed.-in-Chief. Jill Kushner, Man. Ed. Martin Green, Harry Keyishian, William Zander, Eds. Serious fiction; poetry; translations; essays and reviews on contemporary literature. Pays in copies.

LONG SHOT—P.O. Box 6238, Hoboken, NJ 07030. Danny Shot and Nancy Mercado, Eds. Fiction, poetry, and nonfiction, to 10 pages. B&W photos and drawings. Pays in copies.

THE LONG STORY—18 Eaton St., Lawrence, MA 01843. Attn: Ed. Stories, 8,000 to 20,000 words; prefer stories with a moral/thematic core, particularly about poor and working class people. Pays in copies. Manuscripts read year-round.

THE LONGNECK—208 S. Crawford Rd., Vermillion, SD 57069. J.D. Erickson, Ed. Essays and fiction, 2,000 words. Vignettes, nostalgia. Poetry; submit no more than 5 poems. No religious material. Deadline: March 1 annually. Payment is in copies.

LYNX EYE—c/o Scribblefest Literary Group, 1880 Hill Dr., Los Angeles, CA 90041. Pam McCully, Kathryn Morrison, Eds. Quarterly. Short stories, vignettes, novel excerpts, one-act plays, essays, belle lettres, satires, and reviews, 500 to 5,000 words; poetry, to 30 lines; and fillers, to 250 words. Pays $10, on publication.

MAGIC REALISM—Pyx Press, P.O. Box 922648, Sylmar, CA 91392-2648. C. Darren Butler, Ed. Quarterly. Stories, to 7,500 words (4,000 words preferred), and poetry, any length, of magic realism, exaggerated realism, some genre fantasy/dark fantasy. Occasionally publish glib fantasy like that found in folktales, fairy tales, and myths. No occult, sleight-of-hand magicians, or wizards/witches. Pays $2 per published page, plus copy. Contest; SASE for details.

THE MALAHAT REVIEW—Univ. of Victoria, P.O. Box 1700, MS 8524, Victoria, BC, Canada V8W 2Y2. Derk Wynand, Ed. Fiction and poetry, including translations. Pays from $25 per page, on acceptance.

MANY MOUNTAINS MOVING—420 22nd St., Boulder, CO 80302. Naomi Horii, Ed. Published 3 times yearly. Fiction, nonfiction, and poetry by writers of all cultures. Pays in copies.

MASSACHUSETTS REVIEW—Memorial Hall, Univ. of Massachusetts, Amherst, MA 01003. Attn: Ed. Literary criticism; articles on public affairs, scholarly disciplines. Essays. Short fiction, 15 to 25 pages. Poetry. Pays $50, on publication. Manuscripts read November through May.

MEDIPHORS—P.O. Box 327, Bloomsburg, PA 17815. Eugene D. Radice, MD, Ed. "A literary journal of the health professions." Short stories, essays, and commentary, 3,000 words. "Topics should have some relation to medicine and health, but may be quite broad." Poems, to 30 lines. Humor. Pays in copies. Guidelines.

MICHIGAN HISTORICAL REVIEW—Clarke Historical Library, Central Michigan Univ., Mt. Pleasant, MI 48859. Attn: Ed. Semiannual. Scholarly articles related to Michigan's political, social, economic, and cultural history; articles on American, Canadian, and Midwestern history that directly or indirectly explore themes related to Michigan's past. Manuscripts read year-round.

MICHIGAN QUARTERLY REVIEW—3032 Rackham Bldg., Univ. of Michigan, Ann Arbor, MI 48109. Laurence Goldstein, Ed. Scholarly essays on all subjects; fiction; poetry. Pays $8 a page, on publication. Annual contest for authors published in the journal.

MID-AMERICAN REVIEW—Dept. of English, Bowling Green State Univ., Bowling Green, OH 43403. George Looney, Ed. Wayne Barham, Assoc. Ed. High-quality fiction, poetry, articles, translations, and reviews of contemporary writing. Fiction to 5,000 words, (query for longer work). Reviews, articles, 500 to 2,500 words. Pays to $50, on publication (pending funding). Manuscripts read September through May.

MIDWEST QUARTERLY—Pittsburg State Univ., Pittsburg, KS 66762. James B. M. Schick, Ed. Scholarly articles, 2,500 to 5,000 words, on contemporary academic and public issues; poetry. Pays in copies. Manuscripts read year-round.

THE MINNESOTA REVIEW—Dept. of English, E. Carolina Univ., Greenville, NC 27858. Attn: Ed. Politically committed fiction, 1,000 to 6,000 words; nonfiction, 5,000 to 7,500 words; and poetry, 3 pages maximum, for readers committed to social issues, including feminism, neomarxism, etc. Pays in copies. Responds in 2 to 4 months.

MISSISSIPPI REVIEW—Ctr. for Writers, Univ. of Southern Mississippi, Southern Sta., Box 5144, Hattiesburg, MS 39406–5144. Frederick Barthelme, Ed. Serious fiction, poetry, criticism, interviews. Pays in copies.

THE MISSOURI REVIEW—1507 Hillcrest Hall, Univ. of Missouri-Columbia, Columbia, MO 65211. Greg Michalson, Man. Ed. Speer Morgan, Ed. Poems, of any length. Fiction and essays. Pays $20 per printed page, on contract. Manuscripts read year-round.

MODERN HAIKU—P.O. Box 1752, Madison, WI 53701–1752. Robert Spiess, Ed. Haiku and articles about haiku. Pays $1 per haiku, $5 a page for articles. Manuscripts read year-round.

MONTHLY REVIEW—122 W. 27th St., New York, NY 10001. Paul M. Sweezy, Harry Magdoff, Eds. Analytical articles, 5,000 words, on politics and economics, from independent socialist viewpoint. Pays $25 for reviews, $50 for articles, on publication.

MOVING OUT: A FEMINIST LITERARY AND ARTS JOURNAL—P.O. Box 21249, Detroit, MI 48221. Poetry, fiction, articles, and art by women. Submit 4 to 6 poems at a time. Pays in copies.

MUDDY RIVER POETRY REVIEW—89 Longwood Ave., Brookline, MA 02146. Zvi A. Sesling, Ed. Semiannual. Poems. "While free verse is preferred, nothing will be rejected if it is quality." No previously published poems. Payment is one copy.

NEBO: A LITERARY JOURNAL—Dept. of English and Foreign Languages, Arkansas Tech. Univ., Russellville, AR 72801–2222. Attn: Ed. Poems (submit up to 5); mainstream fiction, to 3,000 words; critical essays, to 10 pages. Pays in one copy. Guidelines. Offices closed May through August. "Best time to submit is November through February."

NEGATIVE CAPABILITY—62 Ridgelawn Dr. E., Mobile, AL 36608. Sue Walker, Ed. Poetry, any length; fiction, essays, art. Contests.

NEW AUTHOR'S JOURNAL—1542 Tibbits Ave., Troy, NY 12180. Mario V. Farina, Ed. Fiction, to 3,000 words, and poetry. Topical nonfiction, to 1,000 words. Pays in copies and subscription. Manuscripts read year-round.

NEW DELTA REVIEW—c/o Dept. of English, Louisiana State Univ., Baton Rouge, LA 70803–5001. Nicola Mason, Catherine Williamson, Eds. Semiannual. Fiction and nonfiction, to 5,000 words. Submit up to 4 poems, any length. Also essays, interviews, reviews, and B&W photos or drawings. "We want to see your best work, even if it's been rejected elsewhere." Pays in copies. Manuscripts read year-round.

NEW ENGLAND REVIEW—Middlebury College, Middlebury, VT 05753. Stephen Donadio, Ed. Fiction, nonfiction, and poetry of varying lengths. Also, speculative and interpretive essays, critical reassessments, statements by artists working in various media, interviews, testimonials, letters from abroad. "We are committed to exploration of all forms of contemporary cultural expresssion." Pays $10 per page ($20 minimum), on publication. Manuscripts read September to May.

NEW ENGLAND WRITERS' NETWORK—P.O. Box 483, Hudson, MA 01749–0483. Glenda Baker, Ed.-in-Chief. Short stories and novel excerpts, to 2,000 words. All genres except pornography. Personal and humorous essays, to 1,000 words. Upbeat, positive poetry, to 32 lines. Pays $10 for stories; pays in copies for other material. Query for all how-tos and creative technique articles. Guidelines. Submit fiction and essays June 1 to August 31 only. Poetry may be submitted year-round.

NEW LETTERS—Univ. House, Univ. of Missouri-Kansas City, 5101 Rockhill Rd., Kansas City, MO 64110–2499. James McKinley, Ed.-in-Chief. Fiction, 3,500 to 5,000 words. Poetry, submit 3 to 6 poems at a time. SASE for literary awards guidelines. Manuscripts read October 15 to May 15.

NEW ORLEANS REVIEW—Loyola Univ., New Orleans, LA 70118. Attn: Ed. Literary or film criticism, to 3,000 words. Serious fiction and poetry.

THE NEW PRESS LITERARY QUARTERLY—53–35 Hollis Court Blvd., Flushing, NY 11365. Bob Abramson, Pub. Quarterly. Fiction and nonfiction, to 2,500 words. Poetry to 200 lines. Pays $15 for prose. Contests.

THE NEW YORK QUARTERLY—P.O. Box 693, Old Chelsea Sta., New York, NY 10113. William Packard, Ed. Published 3 times a year by The National Quarterly Foundation. Poems of any style and persuasion, well written and well intentioned. Pays in copies. Manuscripts read year-round. SASE required.

NEXUS—Wright State Univ., W016A Student Union, Dayton, OH 45435. Ted Cains, Ed. Tara Miller, Man. Ed. Poetry, hard-hitting fiction, photography. One-act plays. Essays on obscure poets, artists, and musicians. Pays in copies.

NIGHTSUN—School of Arts & Humanities, Frostburg State Univ., Frostburg, MD 21532–1099. Douglas DeMars, Ed. Annual. Short stories, about 3 pages, and poems, to 40 lines. Payment is 2 copies. Manuscripts read September 1 to May 1.

NIMROD—2210 S. Main St., Tulsa, OK 74114–1190. Attn: Ed. Publishes 2 issues annually, one awards and one thematic. Quality poetry and fiction, experimental and traditional. Pays $5 a page (to $25) and copies. Annual awards for poetry and fiction. Guidelines.

96 INC.—P.O. Box 15559, Boston, MA 02215. Attn: Ed. Semiannual. Fiction, 1,000 to 7,500 words, interviews, and poetry of varying length. Pays $10 to $25, on publication.

THE NORTH AMERICAN REVIEW—Univ. of Northern Iowa, Cedar Falls, IA 50614–0516. Peter Cooley, Poetry Ed. Poetry of high quality. Pays from $20 per poem, on publication. Manuscripts read year-round.

NORTH ATLANTIC REVIEW—15 Arbutus Ln., Stony Brook, NY 11790–1408. John Gill, Ed. Annual. Fiction and nonfiction, to 5,000 words; fillers, humor, photographs and illustrations. A special section on social or literary issues is a part of each issue. Pays in copies. Responds in 5 or 6 months.

THE NORTH DAKOTA QUARTERLY—Univ. of North Dakota, Grand Forks, ND 58202–7209. Attn: Ed. Essays in the humanities and social sciences; fiction, reviews, and poetry. Limited market. Pays in copies and subscription.

NORTHEASTARTS—Boston Arts Organization, Inc., JFK Sta., P.O. Box 6061, Boston, MA 02114. Mr. Leigh Donaldson, Ed. Fiction and nonfiction, to 750 words; poetry, to 30 lines; and short essays and reviews. "Both published and new writers are considered. No obscene or offensive material." Payment is 2 copies.

THE NORTHERN READER—Savage Press, Box 115, Superior, WI 54880. Mike Savage, Ed. Bimonthly. Reminiscence pieces, to 1,500 words. Fiction, to 2,000 words. Free verse and metrical poetry, essays, and fillers. Pays in copies. Guidelines.

NORTHWEST REVIEW—369 PLC, Univ. of Oregon, Eugene, OR 97403. Elizabeth Claman, Fiction Ed. Fiction, commentary, essays, and poetry. Reviews. Pays in copies. Guidelines.

OASIS—P.O. Box 626, Largo, FL 34649–0626. Neal Storrs, Ed. Short fiction and literary essays, to 7,000 words, poetry, and translations from French, German, Italian, or Spanish. Nonfiction on any subject. "Style is paramount." Pays $15 to $50 for prose, $5 per poem, on publication. Guidelines. Responds quickly.

OFFERINGS—P.O. Box 1667, Lebanon, MO 65536. Velvet Fackeldey, Ed. Quarterly. Poetry, to 30 lines, traditional and free verse. No payment.

THE OHIO REVIEW—Ellis Hall, Ohio Univ., Athens, OH 45701–2979. Wayne Dodd, Ed. Short stories, poetry, essays, reviews. Pays $5 per page for prose, $1 a line for poetry, plus copies, on publication. SASE required. Submissions read September through May.

ONIONHEAD—Arts on the Park, Inc., 115 N. Kentucky Ave., Lakeland, FL 33801–5044. Attn: Ed. Council. Short stories, to 4,000 words; essays, to 2,500 words; and poetry, to 60 lines; on provocative social, political, and cultural observations and hypotheses. Pays in copies. Send SASE for Wordart poetry contest information. Manuscripts read year-round; responds in 8 weeks.

ORANGE COAST REVIEW—Dept. of English, Orange Coast College, 2701 Fairview Rd., Costa Mesa, CA 92628–5005. Short stories, poetry, essays, and interviews, any length. Submit material from December 1 to April 1. Allow 6 to 8 weeks for response. Pays $5 for poetry, 1¢ per word for prose.

OREGON EAST—Hoke College Ctr., EOSC, La Grande, OR 97850. Attn: Ed. Short fiction, nonfiction, to 3,000 words, one-act plays, poetry, and high-contrast graphics. Pays in copies. Manuscripts read September through March.

OTHER VOICES—Univ. of Illinois at Chicago, Dept. of English (M/C 162), 601 S. Morgan St., Chicago, IL 60607-7120. Lois Hauselman, Ruth Canji, Tina Peano, Eds. Semiannual. Fresh, accessible short stories, one-act plays, and novel excerpts, to 5,000 words. Pays in copies and modest honorarium. Manuscripts read October to April.

OUTERBRIDGE—College of Staten Island, English Dept. 2S-218, 2800 Victory Blvd., Staten Island, NY 10314. Charlotte Alexander, Ed. Annual. Well-crafted stories, about 20 pages, and poetry, to 4 pages, "directed to a wide audience of literate adult readers." Pays in 2 copies. Manuscripts read September to June.

PAINTBRUSH: A JOURNAL OF CONTEMPORARY MULTICULTURAL LITERATURE—Language & Literature, Northeast Missouri State Univ., Kirksville, MO 63501. Ben Bennani, Ed. Annual. Book reviews, to 1,500 words, and serious, sophisticated poems (submit 3 to 5). Query preferred for book reviews. Pays in copies.

PAINTED BRIDE QUARTERLY—230 Vine St., Philadelphia, PA 19106. Marion Wrenn, Kathleen Volk-Miller, Eds. Fiction and poetry of varying lengths. Pays $5, plus subscription.

PANDORA—2063 Belford, Holly, MI 48442. Meg Mac Donald, Ed. Character-oriented science fiction and fantasy. Poetry. "Read magazine before submitting." Closed to unsolicited material at this time; query.

THE PARIS REVIEW—541 E. 72nd St., New York, NY 10021. Attn: Fiction and Poetry Eds. Fiction and poetry of high literary quality. Pays on publication.

PARNASSUS—41 Union Sq. W., Rm. 804, New York, NY 10003. Herbert Leibowitz, Ed. Critical essays and reviews on contemporary poetry. International in scope. Pays in cash and copies. Manuscripts read year-round.

PARTISAN REVIEW—Boston Univ., 236 Bay State Rd., Boston, MA 02215. William Phillips, Ed.-in-Chief. Edith Kunzweil, Ed. Serious fiction, poetry, and essays. Payment varies. No simultaneous submissions. Manuscripts read year-round.

PASSAGER: A JOURNAL OF REMEMBRANCE AND DISCOVERY—c/o Univ. of Baltimore, 1420 N. Charles St., Baltimore, MD 21201-5779. Kendra Kopelke, Ed. Fiction and essays, 4,000 words, of "remembrance and discovery." Poetry, to 40 lines. "We publish writers of all ages, but with an emphasis on new older writers." Pays in copies.

PASSAGES NORTH—Kalamazoo College, 1200 Academy St., Kalamazoo, MI 49006. Michael Barrett, Ed. Semiannual; published in December and June. Poetry, fiction, essays, interviews, visual art. Pays in copies. Manuscripts read September to June.

THE PENNSYLVANIA REVIEW—Univ. of Pittsburgh, Dept. of English, 526 Cathedral of Learning, Pittsburgh, PA 15260. Attn: Ed. Fiction, to 5,000 words, book reviews, interviews with authors, and poems (send up to 6). Pays in copies. Manuscripts read September through March only.

PEQUOD—New York Univ., English Dept., 19 University Pl., 2nd Fl., New York, NY 10003. Mark Rudman, Ed. Semiannual. Short stories, essays, and literary criticism, to 10 pages; poetry and translations, to 3 pages. Pays honorarium, on publication.

733

PIEDMONT LITERARY REVIEW—Bluebird Ln., Rt. #1, Box 1014, Forest, VA 24551. Evelyn Miles, Man. Ed. Quarterly. Poems, any length and style (prefer rhyme and meter); submit up to 5 poems to William R. Smith, Poetry Ed., 3750 Woodside Ave., Lynchburg, VA 24503. Submit Asian verse to Dorothy McLaughlin, 10 Atlantic Rd., Somerset, NJ 08873. Submit prose, to 2,500 words, to Dr. Olga Kronmeyer, 25 W. Dale Dr., Lynchburg, VA 24501. No pornography. Pays one copy.

PIG IRON PRESS—P.O. Box 237, Youngstown, OH 44501–0237. Jim Villani, Ed. Fiction and nonfiction, to 8,000 words. Poetry, to 100 lines. Write for upcoming themes. Pays $5 per published page or poem, on publication. Manuscripts read year-round. Responds in 3 months.

PIVOT—250 Riverside Dr., #23, New York, NY 10025. Martin Mitchell, Ed. Annual. Poetry, to 75 lines. Pays 2 copies. Manuscripts read January 1 to June 1.

PLOT MAGAZINE—Calypso Publishing, P.O. Box 1351, Sugar Land, TX 77487–1351. Christina C. Russell, Man. Ed. Fantasy, science fiction, horror, suspense, and speculative fiction, to 7,500 words. "The magazine is designed to encourage new and emerging writers. If your story can give us gooseflesh, we want to see it." Pays $10 for stories, $5 for line drawings, on acceptance.

PLOUGHSHARES—Emerson College, 100 Beacon St., Boston, MA 02116–1596. Attn: Ed. Serious fiction, to 6,000 words. Poetry (submit up to 5 poems at a time). Pays $10 per page ($40 to $200), on publication, plus 2 copies and subscription. Manuscripts read August through March. Guidelines.

POEM—c/o English Dept., U.A.H., Huntsville, AL 35899. Nancy Frey Dillard, Ed. Serious lyric poetry. Pays in copies. Manuscripts read year-round (best times to submit are December to March and June to September).

POET & CRITIC—See *Flyway*.

POET LORE—The Writer's Ctr., 4508 Walsh St., Bethesda, MD 20815. Sunil Freeman, Man. Ed. Philip K. Jason and Geraldine Connolly, Exec. Eds. Original poetry, all kinds. Translations, reviews, and critical essays. Pays in copies. Annual narrative poetry contest.

POET MAGAZINE—P.O. Box 54947, Oklahoma City, OK 73154. Attn: Ed. Quarterly. "Dedicated to publishing poets at all levels. New and experienced poets encouraged to submit." Submit copies (not originals) of up to 5 poems, any form, and articles of any length on subjects related to poetry. Include one loose first-class stamp (not SASE) for editorial reply; manuscripts will not be returned. Payment is one copy. Guidelines.

POETRY—60 W. Walton St., Chicago, IL 60610. Joseph Parisi, Ed. Poetry of highest quality. Submit 3 to 4 poems. Allow 10 to 12 weeks for response. Pays $2 a line, on publication.

POETRY EAST—DePaul Univ., English Dept., 802 W. Belden Ave., Chicago, IL 60614–3214. Marilyn Woitel, Man. Ed. Semiannual. Poetry, essays, and translations. "Please send a sampling of your best work. Do not send book-length manuscripts without querying first." Pays in copies.

THE POET'S PAGE—821 S. First St., Princeton, IL 61356. Ione K. Pence, Ed./Pub. Quarterly. Poetry, any length, any style, any topic. Articles and essays on poetry and poetic forms, poets, styles, etc. Pays in copies.

POTOMAC REVIEW—P.O. Box 134, McLean, VA 22101–0134. Jack Harrison, Ed. Quarterly. Fiction and literary essays, to 2,500 words. Poetry, to 2 pages. Pays in copies.

PRAIRIE SCHOONER—201 Andrews Hall, Univ. of Nebraska, Lincoln, NE 68588–0334. Hilda Raz, Ed. Short stories, poetry, essays, book reviews, and translations. Pays in copies. SASE required. Manuscripts read September through May; responds in 3 months. Annual contests.

PRIMAVERA—Box 37–7547, Chicago, IL 60637. Attn: Editorial Board. Annual. Fiction and poetry that focuses on the experiences of women; author need not be female. B&W photos and drawings. No simultaneous submissions. Pays in 2 copies. Responds within 3 months.

PRISM INTERNATIONAL—E462–1866 Main Mall, Dept. of Creative Writing, Univ. of British Columbia, Vancouver, B.C., Canada V6T 1Z1. Attn: Ed. High-quality fiction, poetry, drama, creative nonfiction, and literature in translation, varying lengths. Include international reply coupons. Pays $20 per published page. Annual short fiction contest.

PROLIFIC WRITER'S MAGAZINE—P.O. Box 554, Oradell, NJ 07649. Brian Konradt, Ed. Fiction (no science fiction or fantasy) and nonfiction, to 3,000 words. Poetry, any length; fillers; B&W art. Pays in copies.

PROOF ROCK—P.O. Box 607, Halifax, VA 24558. Don Conner, Fiction Ed. Serena Fusek, Poetry Ed. Fiction, to 2,500 words. Poetry, to 32 lines. Reviews. Pays in copies.

PUCKERBRUSH REVIEW—76 Main St., Orono, ME 04473–1430. Constance Hunting, Ed. Semiannual. Literary fiction, criticism, and poetry of various lengths, "to bring literary Maine news to readers." Pays in 2 copies. Manuscripts read year-round.

PUDDING MAGAZINE: THE INTERNATIONAL JOURNAL OF APPLIED POETRY—c/o Pudding House Writers Resource Ctr., Bed & Breakfast for Writers, Johnstown, OH 43031. Jennifer Bosveld, Ed. Poems on popular culture, social concerns, personal struggle; poetry therapy that has been revised for art's sake; articles/essays on poetry in the human services. Manuscripts read year-round.

PUERTO DEL SOL—New Mexico State Univ., Box 3E, Las Cruces, NM 88003–0001. Kevin McIlvoy, Antonya Nelson, Eds. Short stories and personal essays, to 30 pages; novel excerpts, to 65 pages; articles, to 45 pages, and reviews, to 15 pages. Poetry, photos. Pays in copies. Manuscripts read September 1 to April 1.

PULPHOUSE: A FICTION MAGAZINE—P.O. Box 1227, Eugene, OR 97440. Dean Wesley Smith, Ed. Fiction, 5,000 words: science fiction, fantasy, horror, mystery, romance, western, and mainstream. Occasionally uses poetry. Pays 4¢ to 7¢ a word, before publication.

QUARTERLY WEST—317 Olpin Union, Univ. of Utah, Salt Lake City, UT 84112. M.L. Williams and Lawrence Coates, Eds. Fiction, short-shorts, poetry, translations, and reviews. Pays $25 to $50 for stories, $15 to $50 for poems. Manuscripts read year-round. Biennial novella competition in even-numbered years.

RAG MAG—P.O. Box 12, Goodhue, MN 55027–0158. Beverly Voldseth, Ed. Semiannual. Eclectic fiction and nonfiction, art, photos. Poetry, any length. No religious writing. Pays in copies. Manuscripts read year-round.

RAMBUNCTIOUS REVIEW—1221 W. Pratt Blvd., Chicago, IL 60626. Mary Alberts, Richard Goldman, Nancy Lennon, Beth Hausler, Eds. Fiction, to 12 pages; poems, submit up to 5 at a time. Pays in copies. Manuscripts read September through May. Contests.

RECONSTRUCTION—1563 Massachusetts Ave., Cambridge, MA 02138. Randall Kennedy, Pub. Quarterly. Articles, 2,000 to 40,000 words, on "important political, social, and cultural issues involving race relations. We are particularly concerned with providing a forum for uninhibited commentary on African-American politics, society, and culture." Payment is negotiable. Queries preferred.

RED CEDAR REVIEW—Dept. of English, 17-C Morrill Hall, Michigan State Univ., E. Lansing, MI 48824–1036. Laura Klynstra, Poetry Ed. Tom Bissell, Fiction Ed. Fiction, to 5,000 words, and poetry (submit up to 5 poems). Pays in copies. Manuscripts read year-round.

THE REDNECK REVIEW OF LITERATURE—1556 S. Second Ave., Pocatello, ID 83204. Penelope Reedy, Ed. Semiannual. Fiction, to 2,500 words, on the contemporary American West; essays and book reviews, 300 to 1,500 words; poetry and drama. Pays in copies. Manuscripts read year-round.

REVIEW: LATIN AMERICAN LITERATURE AND ARTS—Americas Society, 680 Park Ave., New York, NY 10021. Alfred J. MacAdam, Ed. Semiannual. Work in English translation by and about young and established Latin American writers; essays and book reviews considered. Send queries for 1,000- to 1,500-word manuscripts, and short poem translations. Payment varies, on acceptance.

RIVER CITY—Dept. of English, Univ. of Memphis, Memphis, TN 38152. Paul Naylor, Ed. Poems, short stories, essays, and interviews. No novel excerpts. Pay varies according to grants. Manuscripts read September through April. Contests.

RIVER STYX—3207 Washington Ave., St. Louis, MO 63103. Attn: Ed. Published 3 times a year. Poetry, fiction, personal essays, literary interviews, and B&W photos. Payment is $8 per printed page and 2 copies. Manuscripts read September 1 to October 31; reports in 12 weeks.

RIVERSIDE QUARTERLY—Box 958, Big Sandy, TX 75755. Leland Sapiro, Ed. Science fiction and fantasy, to 3,500 words; reviews, criticism, any length; poetry and letters. "Read magazine before submitting." Send poetry to Sheryl Smith, 515 Saratoga #2, Santa Clara, CA 95050. Pays in copies.

ROANOKE REVIEW—Roanoke College, Salem, VA 24153. Robert R. Walter, Ed. Quality short fiction, to 5,000 words, and poetry, to 100 lines. Pays in copies.

ROCKFORD REVIEW—P.O. Box 858, Rockford, IL 61105. David Ross, Ed.-in-Chief. Quarterly. Fiction, essays, and satire, 250 to 1,300 words. Experimental and traditional poetry, to 50 lines (shorter works preferred). One-act plays and other dramatic forms, to 10 pages. "We prefer genuine or satirical human dilemmas with coping or non-coping outcomes that ring the reader's bell." Submit up to 3 works at a time. Pays in copies; 2 $25 Editor's Choice Prizes awarded each issue.

ROSEBUD—P.O. Box 459, Cambridge, WI 53523. Rod Clark, Ed. Quarterly. Fiction, articles, profiles, 1,200 to 1,800 words, and poems; love, alienation, travel, humor, nostalgia, and unexpected revelation. Pays $45 plus copies, on publication. Guidelines.

SAN FERNANDO POETRY JOURNAL—18301 Halstead St., Northridge, CA 91325. Richard Cloke, Ed. Quality poetry, 20 to 100 lines, with social content; scientific, philosophical, and historical themes. Pays in copies.

SANSKRIT LITERARY/ART PUBLICATION—Cone Ctr., Univ. of North Carolina/Charlotte, Charlotte, NC 28223–0001. Attn: Ed. Annual. Poetry, short fiction, photos, and fine art.

SANTA BARBARA REVIEW—104 La Verada Ln., Santa Barbara, CA 93108. P.S. Leddy, Ed. Short stories, novellas, and occasionally plays. Biographies and essays, to 6,500 words. Poems. Translations. B&W photos. Pays in copies. Query for novellas and nonfiction.

SATYAGRAHA MAGAZINE—P.O. Box 11275, Berkeley, CA 94712. Ken Boyte, Ed. Semiannual. Articles, to 1,200 words, on progressive issues, and poetry, to 50 lines. Fillers; B&W photos and art. Pays in copies.

SCANDINAVIAN REVIEW—725 Park Ave., New York, NY 10021. Attn: Ed. Published 3 times a year. Essays on contemporary Scandinavia: arts, sciences, business, politics, and culture of Scandinavia. Fiction and poetry, translated from Nordic languages. Pays from $100, on publication.

SCRIVENER—McGill Univ., 853 Sherbrooke St. W., Montreal, Quebec, Canada H3A 2T6. Ursula Hines, Ed. Poems, submit 5 to 15; prose, to 20 pages; reviews, to 5 pages. Photography and graphics. Pays in copies.

THE SEATTLE REVIEW—Padelford Hall, GN-30, Univ. of Washington, Seattle, WA 98195. Donna Gerstenberger, Ed. Short stories, to 20 pages, poetry, essays on the craft of writing, and interviews with northwest writers. Payment varies. Manuscripts read September 1 through May 31.

SENECA REVIEW—Hobart & William Smith Colleges, Geneva, NY 14456. Deborah Tall, Ed. Poetry, translations, and essays on contemporary poetry. Pays in copies. Manuscripts read September 1 to May 1.

SHORT FICTION BY WOMEN—Box 1254, Old Chelsea Sta., New York, NY 10011. Rachel Whalen, Ed. Semiannual. Short stories, novellas, and novel excerpts, to 20,000 words, by women writers. No horror, romance, or mystery fiction. Payment varies, on publication. Manuscripts read year-round. Guidelines.

SING HEAVENLY MUSE! WOMEN'S POETRY & PROSE—P.O. Box 13320, Minneapolis, MN 55414. Attn: Ed. Short stories and essays, to 5,000 words. Poetry. Query for themes and reading periods. Pays in copies.

SIRIUS VISIONS—Claddagh Press, 1075 N.W. Murray Rd., Suite 161, Portland, OR 97229. Marybeth H. O'Halloran, Ed. Published 8 times a year. Fiction, 1,000 to 7,500 words, including science fiction, fantasy, magical realism, humor, and "space opera." "Some reason to feel hopeful at the end is essential. No horror, gore, or dark fantasy." Pays 1¢ to 3¢ a word, on or before publication.

SKYLARK—2200 169th St., Hammond, IN 46323–2094. Pamela Hunter, Ed. "The Fine Arts Annual of Purdue Calumet." Fiction and articles, to 4,000 words. Poetry, to 21 lines. B&W prints and drawings. Pays in one copy. Manuscripts read November 1 through April 30 for fall publication.

THE SLATE—P.O. Box 581189, Minneapolis, MN 55458–1189. Rachel

Fulkerson, Ed. Published 3 times a year. Short fiction, poetry, nonfiction, and essays. "We are dedicated to reviving a cultural interest in the written word and to nourishing the relationship between writer and reader." Pays in copies. Manuscripts read year-round.

SLIPSTREAM—Box 2071, Niagara Falls, NY 14301. Attn: Ed. Contemporary poetry, any length. Pays in copies. Query for themes. Guidelines. Annual poetry chapbook contest has a December 1 deadline; send SASE for details. Fiction overstocked; query.

THE SMALL POND MAGAZINE—P.O. Box 664, Stratford, CT 06497–0664. Napoleon St. Cyr, Ed. Published 3 times a year. Fiction, to 2,500 words; poetry, to 100 lines. Pays in copies. Query for nonfiction. Include short bio. Manuscripts read year-round.

SMALL PRESS REVIEW—Box 100, Paradise, CA 95967. Len Fulton, Ed. Reviews, 200 words, of small, literary books and magazines. Query. Pays 10¢ a word, on acceptance.

SNAKE NATION REVIEW—Snake Nation Press, 110 #2 W. Force, Valdosta, GA 31601. Roberta George, Ed. Quarterly. Short stories, novel chapters, and informal essays, 5,000 words, and poetry, to 60 lines. Pays in copies and prizes.

SNOWY EGRET—P.O. Box 9, Bowling Green, IN 47833. Karl Barnebey and Philip Repp, Eds. Poetry, fiction, and nonfiction, to 10,000 words. Natural history from artistic, literary, philosophical, and historical perspectives. Pays $2 per page for prose; $2 to $4 for poetry, on publication. Manuscripts read year-round.

SONORA REVIEW—Dept. of English, Univ. of Arizona, Tucson, AZ 85721. Attn: Fiction, Poetry, or Nonfiction Ed. (Address appropriate genre editor.) Annual contests. Simultaneous submissions accepted (except for contest entries). Manuscripts read year-round.

THE SOUTH CAROLINA REVIEW—Dept. of English, Clemson Univ., Clemson, SC 29634–1503. Elizabeth Boleman-Herring, Man. Ed. Semiannual. Fiction, essays, reviews, and interviews, to 4,000 words. Poems. Send complete manuscript plus diskette. Send SASE or E-mail address for guidelines. Pays in copies. Response time is 6 to 9 months. Manuscripts read September through May (but not in December).

SOUTH DAKOTA REVIEW—Box 111, Univ. Exchange, Vermillion, SD 57069–2390. Brian Bedard, Ed. Exceptional fiction, 3,000 to 5,000 words, and poetry, 10 to 25 lines. Critical articles, especially on American literature, Western American literature, theory and esthetics, 3,000 to 5,000 words. Pays in copies. Manuscripts read year-round; slower response time in the summer.

THE SOUTHERN CALIFORNIA ANTHOLOGY—c/o Master of Professional Writing Program, WPH 404, Univ. of Southern California, Los Angeles, CA 90089–4034. James Ragan, Ed.-in-Chief. Fiction, to 20 pages, and poetry, to 5 pages. Pays in copies. Manuscripts read September to May.

SOUTHERN EXPOSURE—P.O. Box 531, Durham, NC 27702. Pat Arnow, Ed. Quarterly forum on "Southern movements for social change." Short stories, to 4,500 words, essays, investigative journalism, and oral histories, 500 to 4,500 words. Pays $25 to $200, on publication. Query.

SOUTHERN HUMANITIES REVIEW—9088 Haley Ctr., Auburn Univ.,

AL 36849. Dan R. Latimer, Virginia M. Kouidis, Eds. Short stories, essays, and criticism, 3,500 to 15,000 words; poetry, to 2 pages. Responds within 3 months. SASE required.

SOUTHERN POETRY REVIEW—Dept. of English, Univ. of North Carolina, Charlotte, NC 28223. Ken McLaurin, Ed. Poems. No restrictions on style, length, or content. Manuscripts read September through May.

THE SOUTHERN REVIEW— 43 Allen Hall, Louisiana State Univ., Baton Rouge, LA 70803–5005. James Olney and Dave Smith, Eds. Emphasis on contemporary literature in United States and abroad with special interest in southern culture and history. Fiction and essays, 4,000 to 8,000 words. Serious poetry of highest quality. Pays $12 a page for prose, $20 a page for poetry, on publication. No manuscripts read in the summer.

SOUTHWEST REVIEW—307 Fondren Library W., Box 374, Southern Methodist Univ., Dallas, TX 75275. Elizabeth Mills, Sr. Fiction Ed. "A quarterly that serves the interests of the region but is not bound by them." Fiction, essays, poetry, and interviews with well-known writers, 3,000 to 7,500 words. Pays varying rates. Manuscripts read September 1 through May 31.

SOU'WESTER—Southern Illinois Univ. at Edwardsville, Edwardsville, IL 62026–1438. Fred W. Robbins, Ed. Nancy Avdoian, Poetry Ed. Roger Ridenour, Fiction Ed. Fiction, to 8,000 words. Poetry, any length. Pays in copies. Manuscripts not read in August.

THE SOW'S EAR POETRY REVIEW—19535 Pleasant View Dr., Abingdon, VA 24211–6827. Attn: Ed. Quarterly. Eclectic poetry and art. Submit one to 5 poems, any length, plus a brief biographical note. Interviews, essays, and articles, any length, about poets and poetry are also considered. B&W photos and drawings. Payment is one copy. Poetry and chapbook contests; send SASE for guidelines.

SPARROW MAGAZINE—Sparrow Press, 103 Waldron St., W. Lafayette, IN 47906. Felix Stefanile, Ed./Pub. Contemporary (14-line) sonnets, and occasionally formal poems in other structures. Submit up to 5 poems. Pays $3 per poem, on publication. A $25 sonnet prize is awarded to a contributor in each issue.

SPECTRUM—Anna Maria College, Box 72-A, Paxton, MA 01612–1198. Robert H. Goepfert, Ed. Scholarly articles, 3,000 to 15,000 words; short stories, to 10 pages; and poetry, to 2 pages; book reviews, photos, and artwork. Pays $20 plus 2 copies. Manuscripts read September 1 to May 10.

THE SPOON RIVER POETRY REVIEW—Dept. of English, Stevenson Hall, Illinois State Univ., Normal, IL 61790–4240. Lucia Cordell Getsi, Ed. Poetry, any length. Pays in copies. Editors' Prize Contest; SASE for details.

SPSM&H—329 E St., Bakersfield, CA 93304. Frederick A. Raborg, Jr., Ed. Single sonnets, sequences, essays about the sonnet form, short fiction in which the sonnet plays a part, books, and anthologies. Pays $10, plus copies, for fiction and essays.

THE STABLE COMPANION—P.O. Box 6485, Lafayette, IN 47903. Susanna Brandon, Pub. Quarterly. "The Literary Magazine for Horse Lovers." Fiction and nonfiction, to 5,000 words, on horse-related topics, recent or historical, humorous or serious. No how-to pieces on riding or horse care. Poetry, to 40 lines. "We're looking for dramatic tension, high interest, character development, and dialogue in both fiction and nonfiction." Pays in copies. Guidelines.

STAND MAGAZINE—122 Morris Rd., Lacey's Spring, AL 35754. Daniel Schenker and Amanda Kay, U.S. Eds. (179 Wingrove Rd., Newcastle upon Tyne NE4 9DA UK) British quarterly. Fiction, 2,000 to 5,000 words, and poetry to 100 lines (submit up to 6 poems). No formulaic verse.

STARQUEST S.F. MAGAZINE—5727 Rosemead Blvd., #136, Temple City, CA 91780. Joe Fekete, Ed.-in-Chief. Science fiction, fantasy, and speculative fiction, to 5,000 words; critiques and articles, to 2,500 words; short rhyming poetry, preferably limericks. B&W drawings. Pays in copies.

STORY QUARTERLY—P.O. Box 1416, Northbrook, IL 60065. Anne Brashler, Diane Williams, Eds. Short stories and interviews. Pays in copies. Manuscripts read year-round.

THE STYLUS—9412 Huron Ave., Richmond, VA 23294. Roger Reus, Ed. Annual. "An open forum for intelligent, well-researched articles on a variety of authors and literary topics." Limited fiction market. Pays in copies. Query preferred.

THE SUN—The Sun Publishing Co., 107 N. Roberson St., Chapel Hill, NC 27516. Sy Safransky, Ed. Essays, interviews, and fiction, to 7,000 words; poetry; photos, illustrations, and cartoons. "We're interested in all writing that makes sense and enriches our common space." Pays $100 for fiction, to $300 for nonfiction, $25 for poetry, on publication.

SYCAMORE REVIEW—Purdue Univ., Dept. of English, West Lafayette, IN 47907. Michael S. Manley, Ed.-in-Chief. Semiannual. Poetry, short fiction (no genre fiction), personal essays, drama, and translations. Pays in copies. Manuscripts read September to April.

TAR RIVER POETRY—Dept. of English, East Carolina Univ., Greenville, NC 27834. Peter Makuck, Ed. Poetry and reviews. "Interested in skillful use of language, vivid imagery. Less academic, more powerful poetry preferred." Pays in copies. Submit from September to November or January to April.

THE TEXAS REVIEW—English Dept., Sam Houston State Univ., Huntsville, TX 77341. Paul Ruffin, Ed. Fiction, poetry, articles, to 20 typed pages. Reviews. Pays in copies and subscription.

THEMA—Box 74109, Metairie, LA 70033–4109. Virginia Howard, Ed. Fiction, to 20 pages, and poetry, to 2 pages, related to theme. Pays $25 per story; $10 per short-short; $10 per poem; $10 for B&W art/photo, on acceptance. Send SASE for themes and guidelines.

THEMA 360 DEGREES: ART & LITERARY REVIEW—980 Bush St., Suite 200, San Francisco, CA 94109. Karen Kinnison, Ed. Quarterly art and literary review, featuring fiction and poetry (any length), artwork, graphic imagery, and "art-text," words mixed with images. Send photocopies and photographs only. Pays in copies.

THE THREEPENNY REVIEW—P.O. Box 9131, Berkeley, CA 94709. Wendy Lesser, Ed. Fiction, to 5,000 words. Poetry, to 100 lines. Essays, 1,500 to 3,000 words, on books, theater, film, dance, music, art, television, and politics. Pays to $200, on acceptance. Limited market. Guidelines. Manuscripts read September through May.

TIGHTROPE—323 Pelham Rd., Amherst, MA 01002. Ed Rayher, Ed. Limited-edition, letterpress semiannual. Poetry, any length. Pays in copies. Manuscripts read year-round.

TOMORROW MAGAZINE—P.O. Box 148486, Chicago, IL 60614–8486. Tim W. Brown, Ed. Poetry. Fiction and novel excerpts, 2,000 words. Pays in copies.

TOUCHSTONE—P.O. Box 8308, Spring, TX 77387. Bill Laufer, Pub. Annual. Fiction, 750 to 2,000 words: mainstream, experimental. Interviews, essays, reviews. Poetry, to 40 lines. Pays in copies. Manuscripts read year-round.

TREASURE HOUSE—Treasure House Publishing, 1106 Oak Hill Ave., #3A, Hagerstown, MD 21742. Attn: Ed.-in-Chief. Fiction, 1,500 to 3,000 words, and poetry. Submit poems (up to 10) to: Ed., *Treasure House*, c/o 1420 N St. N.W., #912-E, Washington, DC 20005. (Submit fiction to Hagerstown address.) Pays in copies. Guidelines.

TRIQUARTERLY—Northwestern Univ., 2020 Ridge Ave., Evanston, IL 60208–4302. Attn: Ed. Serious, aesthetically informed and inventive poetry and prose, for an international and literate audience. Pays $20 per page for prose, $1.50 per line for poetry. Manuscripts read October through March. Allow 10 to 12 weeks for reply.

TRIVIA—P.O. Box 9606, N. Amherst, MA 01059–9606. Kay Parkhurst, Ed. Semiannual journal of radical feminist writing. Literary essays, experimental prose, translations, interviews, and reviews. "After-readings": personal accounts of the writer's reaction to books or other writings by women. Pays in copies. Guidelines. Manuscripts read year-round.

2AM MAGAZINE—P.O. Box 6754, Rockford, IL 61125–1754. Gretta Anderson, Ed. Poetry, articles, reviews, and personality profiles, 500 to 2,000 words, as well as fantasy, horror, and some science fiction/sword-and-sorcery short stories, 500 to 5,000 words. Pays ½¢ a word, on acceptance. Manuscripts read year-round.

UNSOMA—349 Davis Rd., Pelzer, SC 29669. Penegashega Nick, Ed. Articles, poetry, essays, prose, B&W art, exposés, erotica. "Radical, political, A to Z, anything and everything that twists the mind, soothes the soul, enlightens the lost." Pays in copies.

URBANUS MAGAZINE—(formerly *Urbanus/Raisirr*) P.O. Box 192561, San Francisco, CA 94119. G. Manson, Sr. Ed. Published 3 times a year. Fiction and nonfiction, 1,000 to 5,000 words, and poetry, to 40 lines, that reflect postmodernist influences for a "readership generally impatient with the mainstream approach." B&W photos and drawings. Pays 1¢ a word; $5 a page for poetry, on acceptance. Query for reading periods.

VERVE—P.O. Box 3205, Simi Valley, CA 93093. Ron Reichick, Ed. Contemporary fiction and nonfiction, to 1,000 words, that fit the theme of the issue. Poetry, to 2 pages; submit up to 5 poems. Pays in one copy. Query for themes.

THE VILLAGER—135 Midland Ave., Bronxville, NY 10708. Amy Murphy, Ed. Mary Hazzah, Fiction/Articles Ed. Mrs. Joseph Aiello, Poetry Ed. Fiction, 900 to 1,500 words, "in good taste": mystery, adventure, humor, romance. Short, preferably seasonal poetry. Pays in copies.

VINCENT BROTHERS REVIEW— 4566 Northern Cir., Riverside, OH

45424–5733. Kimberly Willardson, Ed. Published 3 times a year. Fiction, non-fiction, poetry, fillers, and B&W art. "Read back issues before submitting." Pays from $10 for fiction and nonfiction, plus 2 copies; payment for all other work is 2 copies. Guidelines.

VIRGINIA QUARTERLY REVIEW—One W. Range, Charlottesville, VA 22903. Attn: Ed. Quality fiction and poetry. Serious essays and articles, 3,000 to 6,000 words, on literature, science, politics, economics, etc. Pays $10 per page for prose, $1 per line for poetry, on publication.

VISIONS INTERNATIONAL—1110 Seaton Ln., Falls Church, VA 22046. Bradley R. Strahan, Ed. Published 3 times a year. Poetry, to 30 lines, and B&W drawings. (Query first for art.) "Nothing amateur or previously published. Read magazine before submitting." Pays in copies (or honorarium when funds available). Manuscripts read year-round.

WASCANA REVIEW—c/o Dept. of English, Univ. of Regina, Regina, Sask., Canada S4S 0A2. Kathleen Wall, Ed. Short stories, 2,000 to 6,000 words; critical articles on short fiction and poetry; poetry. Pays $3 per page for prose, $10 for poetry, after publication.

WASHINGTON REVIEW—P.O. Box 50132, Washington, DC 20091–0132. Clarissa Wittenberg, Ed. Poetry; articles on literary, performing and fine arts in the Washington, D.C., area. Fiction, 1,000 to 2,500 words. Area writers preferred. Pays in copies. Responds in 3 months.

WEBSTER REVIEW—English Dept., SLCC—Meramec, 11333 Big Bend Rd., St. Louis, MO 63122. Robert Boyd, Greg Marshall, Eds. Fiction; poetry; interviews; essays; translations. Pays in copies. Manuscripts read September through May.

WEST BRANCH—Bucknell Hall, Bucknell Univ., Lewisburg, PA 17837. Karl Patten, Robert Taylor, Eds. Poetry and fiction. Pays in copies and subscriptions.

WESTERN HUMANITIES REVIEW—Univ. of Utah, Salt Lake City, UT 84112. Amanda Pecor, Man. Ed. Quarterly. Fiction and essays, to 30 pages, and poetry. Pays $50 for poetry, $150 for short stories and essays, on publication. Manuscripts read October through June; responds in 3 to 6 months.

THE WILLIAM AND MARY REVIEW—P.O. Box 8795, College of William and Mary, Williamsburg, VA 23187–8795. Laura Sims, Ed. Annual. Fiction, critical essays, and interviews, 2,500 to 7,500 words; poetry, all genres (submit 5 to 8 poems). Pays in copies. Manuscripts read September through April. Responds in 3 months.

WILLOW SPRINGS—MS-1, Eastern Washington Univ., Cheney, WA 99004–2496. Attn: Ed. Fiction, poetry, translation, and art. Length and subject matter are open. Pays $10 for poetry; $35 for prose, on publication. Manuscripts read September 15 to May 15.

WIND MAGAZINE—P.O. Box 24548, Lexington, KY 40524. Steven R. Cope and Charlie G. Hughes, Eds. Semiannual. Short stories and poems. Reviews of books from small presses, to 250 words, and news of interest to the literary community. Pays in copies. Manuscripts read year-round.

THE WINDLESS ORCHARD—Dept. of English, Indiana-Purdue Univ., Ft. Wayne, IN 46805. Robert Novak, Ed. Contemporary poetry. Pays in copies. SASE required. Manuscripts read year-round.

WINDSOR REVIEW—Dept. of English, Univ. of Windsor, Windsor, Ont., Canada N9B 3P4. Wanda Campbell, General Ed. Short stories, poetry, and original art. Pays $15 to $50, on publication. Responds in one to 3 months.

WITHOUT HALOS—Ocean County Poets Collective, P.O. Box 1342, Point Pleasant Beach, NJ 08742. Frank Finale, Ed. Submit 3 to 5 poems (to 2 pages) between January 1 and June 30. Pays in copies.

WITNESS—Oakland Community College, 27055 Orchard Lake Rd., Farmington Hills, MI 48334. Peter Stine, Ed. Thematic journal. Fiction and essays, 5 to 20 pages, and poems (submit up to 3). Pays $6 per page for prose, $10 per page for poetry, on publication.

WOMAN OF POWER—P.O. Box 2785, Orleans, MA 02653. Charlene McKee, Ed. A magazine of feminism, spirituality, and politics. Nonfiction, to 5,000 words. Send SASE for issue themes and guidelines. Pays in copies and subscription. Manuscripts read year-round.

WONDER MAGAZINE—2770 Fairlane Dr., Doraville, GA 30340–3230. Rod Bennett, Ed. Semiannual. Articles, to 4,000 words, on "the fanciful," on science fiction personalities, "or on any subject that touches the sense of wonder in all of us." Fiction. Pays to $50, on publication. Query.

THE WORCESTER REVIEW—6 Chatham St., Worcester, MA 01609. Rodger Martin, Ed. Poetry (submit up to 5 poems at a time), fiction, critical articles about poetry, and articles and reviews with a New England connection. Pays in copies. Responds within 6 months.

WORDWRIGHTS—The Argonne Hotel Press, 1620 Argonne Pl. N.W., Washington, DC 20009. R.D. Baker, Pub. Quarterly. Fiction and nonfiction, 1,000 to 5,000 words. Poetry, to 50 lines. Pays in copies.

THE WORMWOOD REVIEW—P.O. Box 4698, Stockton, CA 95204–0698. Marvin Malone, Ed. Quarterly. Poetry and prose-poetry, 4 to 400 lines. "We encourage wit and conciseness." Pays 3 to 20 copies or cash equivalent.

WRITERS FORUM—Univ. of Colorado, 1420 Austin Bluffs Pkwy., Colorado Springs, CO 80933–7150. C. Kenneth Pellow, Ed. Annual. Mainstream and experimental fiction, 1,000 to 8,000 words. Poetry (one to 5 poems per submission). Emphasis on western themes and writers. Pays in copies. Manuscripts read September through February.

WRITERS' INTERNATIONAL OPEN FORUM—P.O. Box 516, Tracyton, WA 98393–0516. Sandra Haven, Ed. Dir. Fiction, 500 to 1,500 words, all genres except horror. "We help writers improve skills and marketability through the exchange of ideas and responses to our published stories by our subscribers." *Special Juniors Edition*: Stories, to 2,000 words, and essays, 1,200 words, written by and for children 9 to 16 years old. *Special Seniors Edition*: Fiction, to 2,000 words, and essays to 1,200 words, written for and by seniors. Pays from $5, on acceptance.

XANADU—Box 773, Huntington, NY 11743–0773. Mildred Jeffrey, Weslea Sidon, Lois V. Walker, Sue Kain, Eds. Poetry on a variety of topics; no length restrictions. Articles on poetry. Pays in copies. Manuscripts read September through June.

YALE REVIEW—Yale Univ., P.O. Box 208243, New Haven, CT 06520–8243. J.D. McClatchy, Ed. Serious poetry, to 200 lines, and fiction, 3,000 to 5,000 words. Pays average of $300.

YARROW—English Dept., Lytle Hall, Kutztown State Univ., Kutztown, PA 19530. Harry Humes, Ed. Semiannual. Poetry. "Just good, solid, clear writing. We don't have room for long poems." Pays in copies. Manuscripts read year-round.

ZYZZYVA—41 Sutter, Suite 1400, San Francisco, CA 94104. Howard Junker, Ed. Publishes work of West Coast writers only: fiction, essays, and poetry. Pays $50 to $250, on acceptance. Manuscripts read year-round.

HUMOR, FILLERS, AND SHORT ITEMS

Magazines noted for their excellent filler departments, plus a cross-section of publications using humor, short items, jokes, quizzes, and cartoons, follow. However, almost all magazines use some type of filler material from time to time, and writers can find dozens of markets by studying copies of magazines at a library or newsstand.

ADVENTURE CYCLIST—Adventure Cycling Assn., P.O. Box 8308, Missoula, MT 59807. Daniel D'Ambrosio, Ed. News shorts from the bicycling world for "In Bicycle Circles." Pays $5 to $10, on publication.

AMERICAN SPEAKER—Attn: Current Comedy, 1101 30th St. N.W., Washington, DC 20007. Aram Bakshian, Ed.-in-Chief. Original, funny, performable jokes on news, fads, topical subjects, business, etc., for "Current Comedy" section of *American Speaker* Magazine. Jokes for roasts, retirement dinners, and for speaking engagements. Humorous material specifically geared for public speaking situations such as microphone feedback, introductions, long events, etc. Also interested in longer original jokes and anecdotes that can be used by public speakers. No poems, puns, ethnic jokes, or sexist material. Pays $12, on publication. Guidelines.

AMERICAN WOODWORKER—Rodale Press, 33 E. Minor St., Emmaus, PA 18098. David Sloan, Ed. Fillers relating to woodworking or furniture design. Guidelines.

THE ANNALS OF IMPROBABLE RESEARCH—AIR, P.O. Box 380853, Cambridge, MA 02238. Marc Abrahams, Ed. Science humor, science reports and analysis, one to 4 pages. B&W photos. "This journal is the place to find the mischievous, funny, iconoclastic side of science. An insider's journal that lets anyone sneak into the company of wonderfully mad scientists." No payment. Guidelines.

ARMY MAGAZINE—2425 Wilson Blvd., Arlington, VA 22201-3385. Mary B. French, Ed.-in-Chief. True anecdotes on military subjects. Pays $25 to $50, on publication.

THE ATLANTIC MONTHLY—745 Boylston St., Boston, MA 02116.

Attn: Ed. Sophisticated humorous or satirical pieces, 1,000 to 3,000 words. Some light poetry. Pays from $500 for prose, on acceptance.

ATLANTIC SALMON JOURNAL—P.O. Box 429, St. Andrews, N.B., Canada E0G 2X0. Harry Bruce, Ed. Fillers, 50 to 100 words, on salmon politics, conservation, and nature. Pays $25 for fillers, on publication.

BICYCLING—33 E. Minor St., Emmaus, PA 18098. Attn: Eds. Anecdotes, helpful cycling tips, and other items for "Bike Shorts" and "Tip Talk" sections, 150 to 250 words. Pays $25 to $50, on acceptance.

BYLINE—Box 130596, Edmond, OK 73013. Marcia Preston, Ed.-in-Chief. Humor, 200 to 400 words, about writing. Pays $15 to $20 for humor, on acceptance.

CAPPER'S—1503 S.W. 42nd St., Topeka, KS 66609–1265. Nancy Peavler, Ed. Letters, to 300 words, sharing heartwarming experiences, nostalgic accounts, household hints, poems, and recipes, for "Heart of the Home." Pieces, to 600 words, on people or groups who are making a difference, for "Community Heartbeat." Jokes, submit up to 6 at a time. Pays varying rates (and in gift certificates), on publication.

CASCADES EAST—716 N. E. 4th St., P. O. fiBox 5784, Bend, OR 97708. Kim Hogue, Ed. Fillers related to travel, history, and recreation in central Oregon. Pays 5¢ to 10¢ a word, extra for photos, on publication.

CATHOLIC DIGEST—P.O. Box 64090, St. Paul, MN 55164–0090. Attn: Filler Ed. Articles, 200 to 500 words, on instances of kindness, for "Hearts Are Trumps." Stories about conversions, for "Open Door." Reports of tactful remarks or actions, for "The Perfect Assist." Accounts of good deeds, for "People Are Like That." Humorous pieces, 50 to 300 words, on parish life, for "In Our Parish." Amusing signs, for "Signs of the Times." Jokes; fillers. No fiction. Pays $4 to $50, on publication.

CHICKADEE—179 John St., Suite 500, Toronto, Ont., Canada M5T 3G5. Lizann Flatt, Ed. Juvenile poetry, 10 to 15 lines. Fiction, 800 words. Pays on acceptance. Enclose international reply coupons.

CHILDREN'S PLAYMATE—1100 Waterway Blvd., P.O. Box 567, Indianapolis, IN 46206. Sandy Grieshop, Ed. Articles and fiction, puzzles, games, mazes for 6- to 8-year-olds, emphasizing health, fitness, sports, safety, and nutrition. Pays to 17¢ a word (varies on puzzles), on publication.

THE CHURCH MUSICIAN—127 Ninth Ave. N., Nashville, TN 37234. Jere V. Adams, Ed. Humorous fillers with a music slant for church music leaders, pastors, organists, pianists, and members of the music council or other planning groups. (No clippings.) Pays 5½¢ a word, on publication.

COLUMBIA JOURNALISM REVIEW—Columbia Univ., 700 Journalism Bldg., New York, NY 10027. Gloria Cooper, Man. Ed. Amusing mistakes in news stories, headlines, photos, etc. (original clippings required), for "Lower Case." Pays $25, on publication.

COMBO—155 E. Ames Ct., Plainview, NY 11803. Ian M. Feller, Ed. Fillers related to non-sports cards (comic cards, TV/movie cards, science fiction cards, etc.) and comic books. Pays 10¢ a word, on publication.

COUNTRY WOMAN—P. O. Box 989, Greendale, WI 53129. Kathy Pohl, Man. Ed. Short rhymed verse, 4 to 20 lines, seasonal and country-related. All material must be positive and upbeat. Pays $10 to $15, on acceptance.

CRACKED—Globe Communications, Inc., 441 Lexington Ave., 2nd Fl., New York, NY 10017. Lou Silverstone, Andy Simmons, Eds. Humor, one to 5 pages, for 12- to 15-year-old readers. "Queries are not necessary, but read the magazine before submitting material!" Pays from $100 per page, on acceptance.

CYCLE WORLD—1499 Monrovia Ave., Newport Beach, CA 92663. David Edwards, Ed.-in-Chief. News items on motorcycle industry, legislation, trends. Pays on publication.

ESSENCE—1500 Broadway, New York, NY 10036. Linda Villarosa, Ed. Short items, 500 to 750 words, for black women on work, parenting, and health. Payment varies, on acceptance.

FACES—Cobblestone Publishing, 7 School St., Peterborough, NH 03458–1454. Carolyn P. Yoder, Ed. Puzzles, mazes, crosswords, and picture puzzles for children. Send SASE for list of monthly themes before submitting.

THE FAMILY: A CATHOLIC PERSPECTIVE—50 St. Pauls Ave., Boston, MA 02130. Sr. Theresa Frances Myers, Ed. Fillers, 50 to 500 words; and views, columns, personal reflections, 800 words, for Roman Catholic parents with children at home. Pays for fillers on acceptance.

FAMILY CIRCLE—110 Fifth Ave., New York, NY 10011. Uses some short humor, 750 words. No fiction. Payment varies, on acceptance.

THE FAMILY DIGEST—P.O. Box 40137, Fort Wayne, IN 46804. Corine B. Erlandson, Ed. Family- or Catholic parish-oriented humor. Anecdotes, to 250 words, of funny or unusual real-life parish and family experiences. Pays $10, on acceptance.

FARM AND RANCH LIVING—5400 S. 60th St., Greendale, WI 53129. Nick Pabst, Ed. Fillers on rural people and living, 200 words. Pays from $15, on acceptance and publication.

FATE—P.O. Box 64383, St. Paul, MN 55164–0383. Attn: Ed. Factual fillers, to 300 words, on strange or psychic happenings. True stories, to 500 words, on proof of survival or mystic personal experiences. Pays 10¢ a word for fillers, $25 for strange/psychic happenings. Guidelines.

FIELD & STREAM—2 Park Ave., New York, NY 10016. Duncan Barnes, Ed. Fillers on hunting, fishing, camping, etc., to 500 words. Cartoons. Pays $75 to $250 for fillers, $100 for cartoons, on acceptance.

FINESCALE MODELER—P.O. Box 1612, Waukesha, WI 53187. Bob Hayden, Ed. One-page hints and tips on building nonoperating, scale models. Payment varies, on acceptance.

GAMES—19 W. 21st St., Suite 1002, New York, NY 10010. R. Wayne Schmittberger, Ed.-in-Chief. Pencil puzzles, visual brainteasers, and pop culture tests. Humor and playfulness a plus; quality a must. Pays top rates, on publication.

GERMAN LIFE—Zeitgeist Publishing, 1 Corporate Dr., Grantsville, MD 21536. Michael Koch, Ed. Fillers, 50 to 200 words, on German culture, its past and present, and how America has been influenced by its German element: history, travel, people, the arts, and social and political issues. Articles, 500 to 2,000 words. Pays to $80 for fillers; $300 to $500 for articles, on publication. Queries preferred for articles.

GLAMOUR—350 Madison Ave., New York, NY 10017. Attn: Viewpoint

Ed. Articles, 1,000 words, for "Viewpoint" section: opinion pieces for women. Pays $500, on acceptance.

THE HERB COMPANION—Interweave Press, 201 E. Fourth St., Loveland, CO 80537. Kathleen Halloran, Ed. Trish Faubion, Man. Ed. Bimonthly. Fillers, 75 to 150 words, for herb enthusiasts: practical horticultural tips, original recipes using herbs, etc. Payment varies, on publication.

THE JEWISH HOMEMAKER—705 Foster Ave., Brooklyn, NY 11230. Mayer Bendet, Ed. Humor and fillers for traditional/Orthodox Jewish audience. Payment varies, on publication.

MAD MAGAZINE—1700 Broadway, 5th Fl., New York, NY 10019. Attn: Eds. Humorous pieces on a wide variety of topics. Two- to 8-panel cartoons (not necessary to include sketches with submission). Pays top rates, on acceptance. Guidelines strongly recommended.

MATURE LIVING—127 Ninth Ave. N., MSN 140, Nashville, TN 37234. Attn: Ed. Brief, humorous, original items; 25-line profiles with action color photos; "Grandparents Brag Board" items; Christian inspirational pieces for senior adults, 125 words. Pays $10 to $20.

MATURE YEARS—201 Eighth Ave. S., P.O. Box 801, Nashville, TN 37202. Marvin W. Cropsey, Ed. Poems, cartoons, puzzles, jokes, anecdotes, to 300 words, for older adults. Allow 2 months for manuscript evaluation. "A Christian magazine that seeks to build faith. We always show older adults in a favorable light." Include name, address, social security number with all submissions.

MID-WEST OUTDOORS—111 Shore Dr., Hinsdale, IL 60521–5885. Gene Laulunen, Man. Ed. Where to and how to fish and hunt in the Midwest, 700 to 1,500 words, with 2 photos (no slides). Pays $15 to $35, on publication.

MODERN BRIDE—249 W. 17th St., New York, NY 10011. Mary Ann Cavlin, Exec. Ed. Humorous pieces, 500 to 1,000 words, for brides. Pays on acceptance.

NATIONAL ENQUIRER—Lantana, FL 33464. Darryl C. Wrobel, Asst. Ed. Short, humorous or philosophical fillers, witticisms, anecdotes, jokes, tart comments. Original items only. Short poetry with traditional rhyming verse, amusing, philosophical, or inspirational in nature. No obscure or artsy poetry. Submit seasonal/holiday material at least 3 months in advance. Pays $25, after publication.

THE NEW HUMOR MAGAZINE—Box 216, Lafayette Hills, PA 19444. Edward Savaria, Jr., Ed. Quarterly. Fiction, interviews, and profiles, up to 1,000 words; short poetry, jokes, and fillers. "We would edit out all truly gross humor and anything that elicits loud groans. Please, no X-rated jokes or stories." Pays $50 to $300 for stories and articles, $5 to $25 for jokes and fillers, on acceptance.

THE NEW YORKER—20 W. 43rd St., New York, NY 10036. Attn: Newsbreaks Dept. Amusing mistakes in newspapers, books, magazines, etc. Pays from $10, extra for headings and tags, on acceptance.

OPTOMETRIC ECONOMICS—American Optometric Assn., 243 N. Lindbergh Blvd., St. Louis, MO 63141. Gene Mitchell, Man. Ed. Short humor for optometrists. Payment varies, on acceptance.

OUTDOOR LIFE—2 Park Ave., New York, NY 10016. Vin T. Sparano,

Ed. Short instructive items, 900 to 1,100 words, on hunting, fishing, boating, and outdoor equipment; regional pieces on lakes, rivers, specific geographic areas of special interest to hunters and fishermen. Photos. No fiction or poetry. Pays $300 to $350, on acceptance.

PLAYBOY— 680 N. Lake Shore Dr., Chicago, IL 60611. Attn: Party Jokes Ed. or After Hours Ed. Jokes; short original material on new trends, lifestyles, personalities; humorous news items. Pays $100 for jokes, on publication; $50 to $350 for "After Hours" items, on publication.

PLAYGIRL— 801 Second Ave., New York, NY 10017. Attn: Man. Ed. Humorous pieces, 800 to 1,500 words, looking on romance and relationships with a sexual twist, from male or female perspective, 800 to 1,000 words, for "Playgirl Punchline." Pays varying rates, after acceptance. Query.

READER'S DIGEST—Pleasantville, NY 10570. Consult "Contributor's Corner" page for guidelines. No submissions acknowledged or returned.

REAL PEOPLE— 950 Third Ave., 16th Fl., New York, NY 10022. Brad Hamilton, Ed. True stories, to 500 words, about interesting people for "Real Shorts" section: strange occurrences, everyday weirdness, etc.; may be funny, sad, or hair-raising. Also humorous items, to 75 words, taken from small-circulation magazines, newspapers, etc. Pays $25 to $50, on publication.

RHODE ISLAND MONTHLY—18 Imperial Pl., Providence, RI 02903. Paula M. Bodah, Man. Ed. Short pieces, to 500 words, on Rhode Island and southeastern Massachusetts: places, customs, people and events. Pays $150 to $350. Query.

ROAD KING—Hammock Publishing, 3322 W. End Ave., Suite 700, Nashville, TN 37203. Attn: Fillers Ed. Trucking-related cartoons and fillers. Payment is negotiable, on publication.

THE ROTARIAN—1560 Sherman Ave., Evanston, IL 60201–3698. Willmon L. White, Ed. Occasional humor articles. Payment varies, on acceptance. No payment for fillers, anecdotes, or jokes.

SACRAMENTO MAGAZINE— 4471 D St., Sacramento, CA 95819. Krista Minard, Ed. "City Lights," interesting and unusual people, places, and behind-the-scenes news items, to 400 words. All material must have Sacramento tie-in. Payment varies, on publication.

THE SEWING ROOM— 816 W. Bannock St., Suite 502, Boise, ID 83702–5850. Andrea Simonsen, Asst. Ed. Fillers and sewing tips on basic sewing techniques, projects for and by children, updating old clothes, and one-day projects. Pays $20 to $100 for fillers, on acceptance.

THE SINGLE PARENT—Parents Without Partners, Inc., 401 N. Michigan Ave., Chicago, IL 60611. Debbie Olefsky, Ed. Quarterly. Fillers, 300 to 500 words, addressing the concerns of the single parent. No payment.

SKI MAGAZINE—2 Park Ave., New York, NY 10016. Lisa Gosselin, Exec. Ed. Short, 100- to 300-word items on events and people in skiing for "Ski Life" department. Humor, 300 to 2,000 words, related to skiing. Pays on acceptance.

SPORTS AFIELD—250 W. 55th St., New York, NY 10019. Attn: Almanac Ed. Unusual, useful tips, anecdotes, 100 to 300 words, for "Almanac" section: hunting, fishing, camping, boating, etc. Photos. Pays on publication.

SPORTS CARD TRADER—155 E. Ames Ct., Plainview, NY 11803. Douglas Kale, Ed. Fillers related to collecting and investing in sports cards, especially baseball, football, basketball, and hockey cards. (Also articles on investing in sports cards or memorabilia.) Pays 10¢ a word, on publication.

STAR—660 White Plains Rd., Tarrytown, NY 10591. Attn: Ed. Topical articles, 50 to 800 words, on show business and celebrities. Pays varying rates.

STITCHES, THE JOURNAL OF MEDICAL HUMOUR—16787 Warden Ave., R.R. #3, Newmarket, Ont., Canada L3Y 4W1. Simon Hally, Ed. Humorous pieces, 250 to 2,000 words, for physicians. "Most articles have something to do with medicine." Short humorous verse and original jokes. Pays 30¢ to 40¢ (Canadian) a word; $50 (Canadian) for cartoons, on publication.

TECH DIRECTIONS—Box 8623, Ann Arbor, MI 48107. Paul J. Bamford, Man. Ed. Cartoons, puzzles, brainteasers, and humorous anecdotes of interest to technology and industrial education teachers and administrators. Pays $20 for cartoons; $25 for puzzles, brainteasers, and other short classroom activities; $5 for humorous anecdotes, on publication.

THOUGHTS FOR ALL SEASONS: THE MAGAZINE OF EPIGRAMS—478 N.E. 56th St., Miami, FL 33137. Michel P. Richard, Ed. Epigrams and puns, one to 4 lines, and poetry, to one page. "Writers are advised not to submit material until they have examined a copy of the magazine." Payment is one copy.

TOUCH—Box 7259, Grand Rapids, MI 49510. Carol Smith, Man. Ed. Puzzles based on the NIV Bible, for Christian girls ages 8 to 14. Pays $10 to $15 per puzzle, on acceptance. Send SASE for theme update.

TRAVEL SMART—Dobbs Ferry, NY 10522. Attn: Ed. Interesting, unusual travel-related tips. Practical information for vacation or business travel. Fresh, original material. Pays $5 to $150. Query for over 250 words.

TRUE CONFESSIONS—233 Park Ave. S., New York, NY 10003. Pat Byrdsong, Ed. Warm, inspirational first-person fillers, to 300 words, about love, marriage, family life, prayer for "Woman to Woman," "My Moment with God," "My Man," and "Incredible But True." Also, short stories, 1,000 to 2,000 words. Pays after publication. Buys all rights.

WISCONSIN TRAILS—P.O. Box 5650, Madison, WI 53705. Attn: Ed. Short fillers, 300 words, about Wisconsin: places to go, things to do, etc. Pays $50, on publication.

WOMEN'S GLIB—P.O. Box 259, Bala Cynwyd, PA 19004. Rosalind Warren, Ed. Annual. Feminist humor, 2 to 10 pages, funny one-liners, and brief, rhymed poems. Submissions accepted from women only. No pieces on diet, weight loss, body image, or romance. Cartoons. Pays from $5 per page, on publication, plus copies.

JUVENILE AND YOUNG ADULT MAGAZINES

JUVENILE MAGAZINES

AMERICAN GIRL—8400 Fairway Pl., P.O. Box 998, Middleton, WI 53562-0998. Attn: Magazine Dept. Asst. Bimonthly. Articles, to 800 words, and contemporary or historical fiction, to 3,000 words, for girls ages 8 to 12. "We do not want 'teenage' material, i.e. articles on romance, make-up, dating, etc." Payment varies, on acceptance. Query for articles; include photo leads with historical queries.

BABYBUG—P.O. Box 300, Peru, IL 61354. Marianne Carus, Ed.-in-Chief. Very simple stories, rhymes, poems, activities for infants and toddlers, 6 months to 2 years. Pays from $25, on publication.

BOYS' QUEST—P.O. Box 227, Bluffton, OH 45817–4610. Attn: Ed. Bi-monthly. Fiction and nonfiction, 500 words, for boys ages 6 to 10. "We are looking for articles, stories, and poetry that deal with timeless topics such as pets, nature, hobbies, science, games, sports, careers, simple cooking, etc." B&W photos a plus. Pays 5¢ a word, on publication. Guidelines.

CALLIOPE: WORLD HISTORY FOR YOUNG PEOPLE—Cobblestone Publishing, Inc., 7 School St., Peterborough, NH 03458. Rosalie Baker and Charles Baker, Eds. Theme-based magazine, published 5 times yearly. Articles, 750 words, with lively, original approach to world history (East/West) through the Renaissance. Shorts, 200 to 750 words, on little-known information related to issue's theme. Fiction, to 1,200 words: historical, biographical, adventure, or retold legends. Activities for children, to 800 words. Poetry, to 100 lines. Puzzles and games. Pays 10¢ to 17¢ a word, on publication. Guidelines and themes.

CHICKADEE—The Young Naturalist Foundation, 179 John St., Suite 500, Toronto, Ont., Canada M5T 3G5. Lizann Flatt, Ed. Adventure, historical, folktale, mystery, and humorous stories for 3- to 9-year-olds. Also puzzles, activities, and observation games. No religious material. Pays varying rates, on acceptance. Submit complete manuscript with $1.50 check or money order for return postage.

CHILD LIFE—1100 Waterway Blvd., P.O. Box 567, Indianapolis, IN 46206. Lise Hoffman, Ed. Articles, 600 to 800 words, for 9- to 11-year-olds. Fiction and humor, to 1,200 words, with emphasis on health, fitness, nutrition, and sports. General interest. Poetry. Puzzles. Photos. Pays 10¢ a word, extra for photos, on publication. Buys all rights.

CHILDREN'S DIGEST—1100 Waterway Blvd., P.O. Box 567, Indianapolis, IN 46206. Sandy Grieshop, Ed. Health and general-interest publication for preteens. Informative articles, 500 to 1,200 words, and fiction (especially realistic, adventure, mystery, and humorous), 500 to 1,500 words. Historical and biographical articles. Poetry and activities. Pays from 10¢ a word, from $15 for poems, on publication.

CHILDREN'S PLAYMATE—1100 Waterway Blvd., P.O. Box 567, Indianapolis, IN 46206. Lise Hoffman, Ed. General-interest and health-related short stories, 500 to 600 words, for 6- to 8-year-olds. Simple science articles and how-to crafts pieces with brief instructions. "All About" features, about 500 words, on health, fitness, nutrition, safety, and exercise. Poems, puzzles, dot-to-dots, mazes, hidden pictures. Pays to 17¢ a word, from $15 for poetry, on publication. Buys all rights.

CLUBHOUSE—Box 15, Berrien Springs, MI 49103. Krista Phillips, Ed. Action-oriented Christian stories, 800 to 1,200 words. Children in stories should be wise, brave, funny, kind, etc. Pays $25 to $35 for stories.

COBBLESTONE: THE HISTORY MAGAZINE FOR CHILDREN—

7 School St., Peterborough, NH 03458–1454. Meg Chorlian, Ed. Theme-related articles, biographies, plays, and short accounts of historical events, 700 to 800 words, for 8- to 15-year-olds; also supplemental nonfiction, 300 to 600 words. Fiction, to 800 words. Activities, to 700 words: crafts, recipes, etc., that can be done either by children alone or with adult supervision. Poetry, to 100 lines. Crossword and other word puzzles using the vocabulary of the issue's theme. Pays 20¢ to 25¢ a word, on publication. (Payment varies for activities and poetry.) Guidelines and themes.

CRAYOLA KIDS—Meredith Publishing, 1912 Grand Ave., Des Moines, IA 50309–3379. Deborah Gore Ohrn, Ed. Bimonthly for readers 3 to 8 years old. Stories, 150 to 250 words; hands-on crafts and activities, one to 4 pages. Interviews. Pays $100 to $250, on publication. Query with resumé and work samples.

CRICKET—Box 300, Peru, IL 61354–0300. Marianne Carus, Ed.-in-Chief. Articles and fiction, 200 to 1,500 words, for 9- to 14-year-olds. Poetry, to 30 lines. Pays to 25¢ a word, to $3 a line for poetry, on publication. Guidelines.

DISCOVERIES—WordAction Publishing Co., 6401 The Paseo, Kansas City, MO 64131. Attn: Asst. Ed. Weekly designed to correlate with Evangelical Sunday school curriculum. Fiction, 500 to 700 words, for 8- to 10-year-olds should feature contemporary, true-to-life character and illustrate character building and scriptural application. No poetry. Pays 5¢ a word, on publication. Guidelines.

THE DOLPHIN LOG—The Cousteau Society, 870 Greenbrier Cir., Suite 402, Chesapeake, VA 23320. Elizabeth Foley, Ed. Articles, 400 to 600 words, on a variety of topics related to our global water system: marine biology, ecology, natural history, and water-related subjects, for 7- to 13-year-olds. No fiction. Pays $25 to $150, on publication. Query.

FACES—Cobblestone Publishing, 7 School St., Peterborough, NH 03458–1454. Carolyn P. Yoder, Asst. Pub. In-depth feature articles, 800 words, with an anthropology theme. Shorts, 300 to 600 words, related to themes. Fiction, to 800 words, on legends, folktales, stories from around the world, etc., related to theme. Activities, to 700 words, including recipes, crafts, games, etc., for children. Pays 20¢ to 25¢ a word. Guidelines and themes.

FIELD & STREAM—2 Park Ave., New York, NY 10016. Duncan Barnes, Ed. Articles, to 600 words, on hunting and fishing, real-life adventure, how-to projects, natural phenomena and history, conservation, and sporting ethics for *Field and Stream Jr.*, a special section aimed at 8- to 12-year-olds. Puzzles and fillers, 25 to 100 words. Pays from $75 to $650, on acceptance. Queries preferred.

THE FRIEND—50 E. North Temple, 23rd Floor, Salt Lake City, UT 84150. Vivian Paulsen, Man. Ed. Stories and articles, 1,000 to 1,200 words. Stories, to 250 words, for younger readers and preschool children. Pays from 9¢ a word, from $25 per poem, on acceptance. Prefers completed manuscripts.

GIRLS' LIFE—Monarch Avalon, Inc., 4517 Harford Rd., Baltimore, MD 21214. Kelly White, Sr. Ed. Features of various lengths and one-page fillers that will entertain and educate girls ages 7 to 14. Payment varies, on publication. Query with resumé and clips. Guidelines.

GUIDEPOSTS FOR KIDS—P.O. Box 538A, Chesterton, IN 46304. Mary Lou Carney, Ed. Issue-oriented, thought-provoking articles, 1,000 to 1,500 words. "Things kids not only need to know, but want to know." Fiction: historicals and mysteries, 700 to 1,300 words, and contemporary stories, 1,000 words. "Not preachy. Dialogue-filled and value-driven." Pays competitive rates, on acceptance. Query for articles.

HIGHLIGHTS FOR CHILDREN— 803 Church St., Honesdale, PA 18431–1824. Beth Troop, Manuscript Coord. Christine Clark, Assoc. Ed. Stories and articles, to 900 words, for 8- to 12-year-olds: humorous pieces, sports stories, stories that treat holidays in unusual ways (overstocked with Halloween material), retellings of legends and myths, and articles about children who are engaged in the arts. Fiction should have strong plot, believable characters, story line that holds reader's interest from beginning to end. No crime or violence. For articles, cite references used and qualifications. Easy rebus-form stories. Easy-to-read stories, 300 to 600 words, with strong plots. Pays from 14¢ a word, on acceptance.

HOPSCOTCH, THE MAGAZINE FOR GIRLS—P.O. Box 164, Bluffton, OH 45817–0164. Marilyn Edwards, Ed. Bimonthly. Articles and fiction, 600 to 1,000 words, and short poetry for girls ages 6 to 12. Special interest in articles, with photos, about girls involved in worthwhile activities. "We believe young girls deserve the right to enjoy a season of childhood before they become young adults; we are not interested in such topics as sex, romance, cosmetics, hairstyles, etc." Pays 5¢ to 7¢ a word, on publication.

HUMPTY DUMPTY'S MAGAZINE—1100 Waterway Blvd., P.O. Box 567, Indianapolis, IN 46206. Janet Flynn Hoover, Ed. General-interest publication with an emphasis on health and fitness for 4- to 6-year-olds. Easy-to-read fiction, to 500 words, some with health and nutrition, safety, exercise, or hygiene as theme; humor and light approach preferred. Creative nonfiction, including photo stories. Crafts with clear, brief instructions. No-cook recipes using healthful ingredients. Short verse, narrative poems. Pays to 22¢ a word, from $15 for poems, on publication. Buys all rights.

JACK AND JILL—1100 Waterway Blvd., P.O. Box 567, Indianapolis, IN 46206. Daniel Lee, Ed. Articles, 500 to 800 words, for 7- to 10-year-olds, on sports, fitness, health, nutrition, safety, exercise. Features, 500 to 700 words, on history, biography, life in other countries, etc. Fiction, to 700 words. Short poems, games, puzzles, projects, recipes. Photos. Pays 10¢ to 20¢ a word, extra for photos, on publication.

JUNIOR TRAILS—1445 Boonville Ave., Springfield, MO 65802–1894. Sinda Zinn, Ed. Fiction, 1,000 to 1,500 words, with a Christian focus, believable characters, and moral emphasis. Articles, 300 to 500 words, on science, nature, biography. Pays 2¢ or 3¢ a word, on acceptance.

KID CITY—Children's Television Workshop, 1 Lincoln Plaza, New York, NY 10023. Attn: Fiction Ed. Short stories, to 500 words; factual articles; interviews and features on kids in sports, TV, or movies; animal stories; crafts, activities, games and comics that teach. Send complete manuscript for fiction; query for nonfiction. Pays $250 to $400, on acceptance. Guidelines.

LADYBUG—P.O. Box 300, Peru, IL 61354–0300. Marianne Carus, Ed.-in-Chief. Paula Morrow, Ed. Picture stories, read-aloud stories, fantasy, folk and fairy tales, 300 to 750 words, for 2- to 6-year-olds; poetry, to 20 lines; songs and rhymes; crafts, activities, and games, to 4 pages. Pays to 25¢ a word for stories and articles; to $3 a line for poetry, on publication. Guidelines.

MY FRIEND—Daughters of St. Paul, 50 St. Pauls Ave., Boston, MA 02130. Sister Anne Joan, Ed. "The Catholic Magazine for Kids." Readers are 6 to 12 years old. General-information articles, media literacy, lives of saints, etc., 150 to 600 words. Some humorous poetry, 6 to 8 lines. Buys first rights. Fiction overstocked. Pays $20 to $150 for articles, $5 to $20 for fillers. Query for artwork. Guidelines.

NATIONAL GEOGRAPHIC WORLD—1145 17th St. N.W., Washington, DC 20036–4688. Susan Tejada, Ed. Picture magazine for young readers, ages 8 and older. Natural history, adventure, archaeology, geography, science, the environment, and human interest. Proposals for picture stories only. No unsolicited manuscripts.

NEW MOON, THE MAGAZINE FOR GIRLS AND THEIR DREAMS— P.O. Box 3620, Duluth, MN 55803–3620. Joe Kelly, Man. Ed. "Our goal is to celebrate girls and support their efforts to hang on to their voices, strengths, and dreams as they move from being girls to becoming women." Profiles of girls and women, 300 to 1,000 words. Science and math experiments, 300 to 600 words. Submissions from both girls and adults. Queries preferred. Pays 5¢ to 8¢ a word, on publication. Also publishes companion letter, *New Moon Parenting: For Adults Who Care About Girls.*

ODYSSEY: SCIENCE THAT'S OUT OF THIS WORLD—Cobblestone Publishing, 7 School St., Peterborough, NH 03458–1454. Elizabeth Lindstrom, Ed. Features, 750 words, on astronomy, space science, and other related physical sciences for 8- to 14-year-olds. Science-related fiction, myths, legends, and science fiction stories. Experiments and games. Pays 20¢ to 25¢ a word, on publication. Guidelines and themes.

ON THE LINE—616 Walnut, Scottdale, PA 15683–1999. Mary Clemens Meyer, Ed. Weekly paper for 10- to 14-year-olds. Nature, general nonfiction, and how-to articles, 350 to 500 words; fiction, 900 to 1,200 words; poetry, puzzles, cartoons. Pays to 4¢ a word, on acceptance.

OWL—Owl Communications, 179 John St., Suite 500, Toronto, Ont., Canada M5T 3G5. Nyla Ahmad, Ed. Articles, 500 to 1,000 words, for 8- to 12-year-olds, about animals, science, people, technology, new discoveries, activities. Pays varying rates, on acceptance. Guidelines.

PLAYS, THE DRAMA MAGAZINE FOR YOUNG PEOPLE—120 Boylston St., Boston, MA 02116–4615. Elizabeth Preston, Man. Ed. Wholesome one-act comedies, dramas, skits, satires, farces, and creative dramatic material suitable for school productions at junior high, middle, and lower grade levels. Plays with modern settings preferred. Also uses dramatized classics, folktales and fairy tales, puppet plays. No religious plays or musicals. Pays good rates, on acceptance. Buys all rights. Query for classics, folk and fairy tales. Guidelines.

POCKETS—1908 Grand Ave., Box 189, Nashville, TN 37202–0189. Janet Knight, Ed. Ecumenical magazine for 6- to 12-year-olds. Fiction and scripture stories, 600 to 1,500 words; short poems; games and family communication activities; role model stories; and stories about children involved in justice and environmental projects. Pays from 12¢ a word, $25 to $50 for poetry, on acceptance. Guidelines and themes. Annual fiction contest; send SASE for details.

POWER AND LIGHT—6401 The Paseo, Kansas City, MO 64131. Beula

J. Postlewait, Preteen Ed. Fiction, 500 to 800 words, for grades 5 and 6, with Christian emphasis. Cartoons and puzzles. Pays 5¢ a word for multi-use rights, 1¾¢ a word for reprints. Pays $15 for cartoons and puzzles.

R-A-D-A-R—Standard Publishing, 8121 Hamilton Ave., Cincinnati, OH 45231. Elaina Meyers, Ed. Weekly Sunday school take-home paper. Articles, 400 to 650 words, on nature, hobbies, crafts. Short stories, 900 to 1,000 words: mystery, sports, school, family, with 12-year-old as main character; serials, 2,000 words. Christian emphasis. Poems to 12 lines. Pays to 7¢ a word, to 50¢ a line for poetry, on acceptance.

RANGER RICK—National Wildlife Federation, 8925 Leesburg Pike, Vienna, VA 22184–0001. Gerald Bishop, Ed. Articles, to 900 words, on wildlife, conservation, natural sciences, and kids in the outdoors, for 6- to 9-year-olds. Nature-related fiction, mysteries, fantasies, and science fiction welcome. Games (no crosswords or word-finds), crafts, humorous poems, outdoor activities, and puzzles. For nonfiction, query with sample lead, list of references, and names of experts you plan to contact. Guidelines. Pays to $550, on acceptance.

SESAME STREET MAGAZINE—One Lincoln Plaza, New York, NY 10023. Anne Heller, Exec. Ed. Articles on children and violence: Susan Schneider, Articles Ed. Articles on educational issues: Nadia Zonis, Medical/Health Ed. Articles, 800 to 2,500 words, on medical, psychological, and educational issues for families with young children (up to 8 years old). Pays 50¢ to $1 per word, up to 6 weeks after acceptance.

SHOFAR—43 Northcote Dr., Melville, NY 11747. Gerald H. Grayson, Ed. Short stories, 500 to 750 words; articles, 250 to 750 words; poetry, to 50 lines; short fillers, games, puzzles, and cartoons for Jewish children, 8 to 13. All material must have a Jewish theme. Pays 10¢ a word, on publication. Submit holiday pieces at least 6 months in advance.

SKIPPING STONES—P.O. Box 3939, Eugene, OR 97403. Arun N. Toké, Exec. Ed. "A Multicultural Children's Magazine." Articles, approximately 500 words, relating to community and family, religions, culture, nature, traditions, and cultural celebrations in other countries, for 7- to 15-year-olds. "Especially invited to submit are children from cultural backgrounds other than European-American and/or those with physical challenges. We print art, poetry, songs, games, stories, and photographs from around the world and include many different languages (with English translation)." Payment is one copy, on publication. Guidelines.

SOCCER JR.—27 Unquowa Rd., Fairfield, CT 06430. Joe Provey, Ed. Fiction and fillers about soccer for readers ages 8 and up. Pays $450 for a feature or story; $250 for department pieces, on acceptance. Query.

SPIDER—P.O. Box 300, Peru, IL 61354. Attn: Submissions Ed. Fiction, 300 to 1,000 words, for 6- to 9-year-olds: realistic, easy-to-read stories, fantasy, folk and fairy tales, science fiction, fables, myths. Articles, 300 to 800 words, on nature, animals, science, technology, environment, foreign culture, history (include short bibliography with articles). Serious, humorous, or nonsense poetry, to 20 lines. Puzzles, activities, and games, to 4 pages, also considered. Pays 25¢ a word, $3 per line for poetry, on publication.

SPORTS ILLUSTRATED FOR KIDS—Time & Life Bldg., Rockefeller Ctr., New York, NY 10020. Stephen Malley, Sr. Ed. Articles, 1,000 to 1,500 words, and short features, 500 to 600 words, for 8- to 13-year-olds. "Most articles are staff-written. Department pieces are the best bet for free lancers." Departments: "My Worst Day," 600 words, an athlete's account as told to a writer; "Curveballs," 150 words, wacky sports trivia; "Tips from the Pros" and "Legends," 400 words, about sports figures of the past. Pays $500 for departments, $1,000 to $1,250 for articles, on acceptance. Query required.

STONE SOUP, THE MAGAZINE BY CHILDREN—Box 83, Santa Cruz, CA 95063–0083. Gerry Mandel, Ed. Stories, free-verse poems, plays, book reviews by children under 14. "Preference given to writing based on real-life experiences." Pays $10.

STORY FRIENDS—Mennonite Publishing House, Scottdale, PA 15683. Marjorie Waybill, Ed. Stories, 350 to 800 words, for 4- to 9-year-olds, on Christian faith and values in everyday experiences. Poetry. Pays to 5¢ a word, to $10 per poem, on acceptance.

SUPERSCIENCE BLUE—Scholastic, Inc., 555 Broadway, New York, NY 10012. Attn: Ed. Science news and hands-on experiments for grades 4 through 6. Article topics are staff-generated and assigned to writers. For consideration, send children's and science writing clips to Editor. Include large SASE for editorial calendar and sample issue. Pays $50 to $500, on acceptance.

3–2–1 CONTACT—Children's Television Workshop, 1 Lincoln Plaza, New York, NY 10023. Curtis Slepian, Ed. Entertaining and informative articles, 600 to 1,000 words, for 8- to 14-year-olds, on all aspects of science, computers, scientists, and children who are learning about or practicing science. Pays $75 to $500, on acceptance. No fiction. Query.

TOUCH—Box 7259, Grand Rapids, MI 49510. Carol Smith, Man. Ed. Upbeat fiction and features, 500 to 1,000 words, for Christian girls ages 8 to 14; personal life, nature, crafts. Poetry, puzzles. Pays 2½¢ a word, extra for photos, on acceptance. Query with SASE for theme update.

TURTLE MAGAZINE FOR PRESCHOOL KIDS—1100 Waterway Blvd., Box 567, Indianapolis, IN 46206. Janet Hoover, Ed. Heavily illustrated articles with an emphasis on health and nutrition for 2- to 5-year-olds. Humorous, entertaining fiction. Also crafts and activities pieces and simple science experiments. Simple poems. Stories-in-rhyme and read-aloud stories, to 500 words. Pays to 20¢ a word for stories; from $15 for poems; payment varies for activities, on publication. Buys all rights. Guidelines.

U.S. KIDS—1100 Waterway Blvd., P.O. Box 567, Indianapolis, IN 46206. Steve Charles, Health/Fitness Ed. Articles, to 1,000 words, on issues related to kids ages 5 to 10, fiction, true-life adventures, science and nature topics. Special emphasis on health and fitness. Fiction with real-world focus; no fantasy.

VENTURE—Christian Service Brigade, P.O. Box 150, Wheaton, IL 60189. Deborah Christensen, Ed. Fiction and nonfiction, 1,000 words, for 8- to 11-year-old boys involved in Stockade. "Think like a boy this age. They want action, adventure, and humor. They also need to see how faith in God affects every area of life and is more than just a prayer to get out of trouble." Humor and fillers; color photos also accepted. Pays 5¢ to 10¢ a word, on publication.

WONDER TIME—6401 The Paseo, Kansas City, MO 64131. Lois Perrigo, Ed. Stories, 250 to 350 words, for 6- to 8-year-olds, with Christian emphasis to correlate with Sunday school curriculum. Pays $25 for stories, on production.

YOUNG JUDEAN—50 W. 58th St., New York, NY 10019. Jonathan Mayo,

Ed. Quarterly. Articles, 500 to 1,000 words, with photos, for 9- to 12-year-olds, on Israel, Jewish holidays, Jewish-American life, Jewish history. Fiction, 800 to 1,000 words, on Jewish themes. Fillers, humor, reviews. No payment.

YOUTH UPDATE—*St. Anthony Messenger Press,* 1615 Republic St., Cincinnati, OH 45210. Attn: Ed. "Articles for Catholic teens that address timely topics. Avoid cuteness; glib phrases and clichés; academic or erudite approaches; preachiness." Pays on acceptance, 14¢ a word. Query with outline.

ZILLIONS—Consumers Union of the United States, 101 Truman Ave., Yonkers, NY 10703–9925. Moye Thompson, Man. Ed. Bimonthly. Articles, 1,000 to 1,500 words, on consumer education (money, product testing, health, etc.), for children, preteens, and young teens. "We are the *Consumer Reports* for kids." Pays $500 to $1,500, on publication. Guidelines.

YOUNG ADULT MAGAZINES

ALIVE NOW!—P.O. Box 189, Nashville, TN 37202. Attn: Ed. Short essays, 250 to 400 words, with Christian emphasis for adults and young adults. Poetry, one page. B&W photos. Pays $20 to $30, on publication. Query with SASE for themes.

BOYS' LIFE—1325 W. Walnut Hill Ln., P.O. Box 152079, Irving, TX 75015–2079. Attn: Ed. Publication of Boy Scouts of America. Articles and fiction, 500 to 1,500 words, for 8- to 18-year-old boys. Pays from $350 for major articles, $750 for fiction, on acceptance. Query for articles; send complete manuscript for fiction.

BREAKAWAY— 8605 Explorer Dr., Colorado Springs, CO 80920. Michael Ross, Ed. Fiction, to 1,800 words, and real-life adventure articles, to 1,500 words. Humor and interesting facts, 500 to 800 words. Readers are 12- to 16-year-old Christian boys. "Must have a male slant." Pays 12¢ to 15¢ a word, on acceptance. Guidelines.

CAMPUS LIFE— 465 Gundersen Dr., Carol Stream, IL 60188. Harold Smith, V.P./Ed. Articles reflecting Christian values and world view, for high school and college students. Humor, general fiction, and true, first-person experiences. "If we have a choice of fiction, how-to, and a strong first-person story, we'll go with the true story every time." Photo-essays, cartoons. Pays 10¢ to 20¢ a word, on acceptance. Query.

CHALLENGE—1548 Poplar Ave., Memphis, TN 38104–2493. Jeno Smith, Ed. Southern Baptist. Articles, to 800 words, for 12- to 18-year-old boys, on teen issues, current events. Photo-essays on Christian sports personalities. Pays 4½¢ a word, extra for photos, on acceptance.

CRACKED—Globe Communications, Inc., 441 Lexington Ave., 2nd Fl., New York, NY 10017. Lou Silverstone, Andy Simmons, Eds. Humor, one to 5 pages, for 12- to 15-year-old readers. "Read magazine before submitting." Pays $100 per page, on acceptance.

EXPLORING—P.O. Box 152079, 1325 W. Walnut Hill Ln., Irving, TX 75015–2079. Scott Daniels, Exec. Ed. Publication of Boy Scouts of America. Articles, 500 to 1,500 words, for 14- to 21-year-old boys and girls, on teenage trends, college, computer games, music, education, careers, "Explorer" activities (hiking, canoeing, camping), and program ideas for meetings. No controversial subjects. Pays $150 to $500, on acceptance. Query. Guidelines.

FREEWAY—See *Zelos.*

KEYNOTER—3636 Woodview Trace, Indianapolis, IN 46268. Julie A. Carson, Exec. Ed. Articles, 1,500 to 1,800 words, for high school leaders: general-interest features; self-help; contemporary teenage problems. No fillers, poetry, first-person accounts, or fiction. Pays $150 to $300, on acceptance. Query preferred.

LISTEN MAGAZINE—55 W. Oak Ridge Dr., Hagerstown, MD 21740. Lincoln Steed, Ed. Articles, 1,200 to 1,500 words, providing teens with "a vigorous, positive, educational approach to the problems arising from the use of tobacco, alcohol, and other drugs." Pays 5¢ to 7¢ a word, on acceptance.

THE LOOK—P.O. Box 272, Cranford, NJ 07016–0272. John R. Hawks, Pub. Articles, 1,500 to 3,000 words, on fashion, student life, employment, relationships, and profiles of interest to local (NJ) readers ages 16 to 26. Also, beach stories and articles about the New Jersey shore. Pays $30 to $200, on publication.

MERLYN'S PEN: THE NATIONAL MAGAZINES OF STUDENT WRITING—P.O. Box 1058, Dept. WR, East Greenwich, RI 02818. R. James Stahl, Ed. *Intermediate Edition*: writing by students in grades 6 through 9. Short stories, to 3,500 words; reviews; travel pieces; and poetry, to 100 lines. *Senior Edition*: for writers in grades 9 through 12. Fiction, 3,500 words. Poetry, to 200 lines. Responds with a brief critique in 10 weeks. Pays in copies. Guidelines.

NEW ERA—50 E. North Temple, Salt Lake City, UT 84150. Richard M. Romney, Ed. Articles, 150 to 1,500 words, and fiction, to 2,000 words, for young Mormons. Poetry. Photos. Pays 5¢ to 20¢ a word, 25¢ a line for poetry, on acceptance. Query.

REACT—c/o *Parade Magazine*, 711 Third Ave., New York, NY 10017. Attn: Articles Ed. Weekly. Articles, to 1,000 words, on national and international news, entertainment, sports, social issues, and profiles of notable young people for readers 11 to 15. Fillers, to 250 words, on news, sports, and entertainment. Payment varies, on acceptance. Query.

SASSY—6420 Wilshire Blvd., Los Angeles, CA 90048–5515. Attn: Tommi Lewis. Short stories for girls ages 16 to 21. Payment varies, on acceptance.

SEVENTEEN—850 Third Ave., New York, NY 10022. Joe Bargmann, Sr. Ed. Articles, to 2,500 words, on subjects of interest to teenagers. Sophisticated, well-written fiction, 1,000 to 4,000 words, for young adults. Personal essays, to 1,200 words, by writers 21 and younger for "Voice." Pays varying rates, on acceptance.

STRAIGHT—8121 Hamilton Ave., Cincinnati, OH 45231. Carla J. Crane, Ed. Articles on current situations and issues for Christian teens. Humor. Well-constructed fiction, 1,000 to 1,200 words, showing teens using Christian principles. Poetry by teenagers. Photos. Pays about 3¢ to 7¢ a word, on acceptance. Send SASE for guidelines.

'TEEN—6420 Wilshire Blvd., Los Angeles, CA 90048–5515. Attn: Ed. Short stories, 2,500 to 4,000 words: mystery, teen situations, adventure, romance, humor for teens. Pays from $200, on acceptance. Buys all rights.

TEEN LIFE—1445 Boonville Ave., Springfield, MO 65802–1894. Tammy Bicket, Ed. Articles, 500 to 1,000 words, and fiction, to 1,200 words, for 13- to 19-year-olds; strong evangelical emphasis. Interviews with Christian ath-

757

letes and other well-known Christians; true stories; up-to-date factual articles. Send SASE for current topics. Pays on acceptance.

TEEN POWER—Box 632, Glen Ellyn, IL 60138. Amy J. Cox, Ed. Take-home Sunday school paper. True-to-life fiction or first-person (as told to), true teen experience stories with Christian insights and conclusion, 700 to 1,000 words. Include photos. Pays 7¢ to 10¢ a word, extra for photos, on acceptance.

TIGER BEAT—Sterling/MacFadden Partnership, 233 Park Ave. S., New York, NY 10003. Louise Barile, Ed. Articles, to 4 pages, on young people in show business and the music industry. Pays varying rates, on acceptance. Query.

TQ/TEEN QUEST—2845 W. Airport Freeway, Suite 137, Irving, TX 75062. Christopher Lyon, Ed. Articles and well-crafted fiction, 2,000 words, for Christian teens. Cartoons and color slides. Pays 10¢ to 15¢ a word, on publication.

YM—685 Third Ave., New York, NY 10017. Maria Baugh, Man. Ed. Articles, to 2,500 words, on entertainment, lifestyle, fashion, beauty, relationships, health, for women ages 14 to 19. Payment varies, on acceptance. Query with clips.

YOUNG AND ALIVE—4444 S. 52nd St., Lincoln, NE 68506. Richard J. Kaiser, Man. Ed. M. Marilyn Brown, Ed. Quarterly. Feature articles, 800 to 1,400 words, for blind and visually impaired young adults on adventure, biography, camping, careers, health, history, hobbies, holidays, marriage, nature, practical Christianity, sports, and travel. Photos. Pays 3¢ to 5¢ a word, $5 to $20 for photos, on acceptance. Guidelines.

YOUNG SALVATIONIST—The Salvation Army, 615 Slaters Ln., P.O. Box 269, Alexandria, VA 22313. Attn: Youth Ed. Articles for teens, 800 to 1,200 words, with Christian perspective; fiction, 800 to 1,200 words; short fillers. Pays 10¢ a word, on acceptance.

YOUNG SCHOLAR—Suite 1, 4905 Pine Cone Dr., Durham, NC 27707. Greg Sanders, Man. Ed. Articles, 1,200 to 1,500 words, for bright high school students. Departments include "News to Use," 325 words; "Performance," 750 words; "Mindstuff," 350 word-reviews of older books; "What's Hot Now," 100 to 250 words, on interesting, worthwhile products. "The magazine is not about school; it's about learning and living the learning lifestyle. Our readers are very sophisticated. Don't write anything elementary, preachy, or thoughtless." Pays $100 to $400 for articles, $25 to $250 for department pieces, on acceptance. Queries preferred. Guidelines.

ZELOS—(formerly *Freeway*) Box 632, Glen Ellyn, IL 60138. Amy J. Cox, Ed. First-person true stories, personal experience, how-tos, humor, fiction, to 1,000 words, for 15- to 20-year-olds. Send photos, if available. Occasionally publishes poetry. Must have Christian emphasis. Pays 7¢ to 10¢ a word.

THE DRAMA MARKET

Community, regional, and civic theaters and college dramatic groups offer the best opportunities today for playwrights to see their work produced, whether on the stage or in dramatic readings. Indeed, aspiring playwrights will be encouraged to hear that many well-known playwrights received their first recognition in the regional theaters. Payment is generally nominal, but regional and university theaters usually buy only the right to produce a play, and all further rights revert to the author. Since most directors like to work closely with authors on any revisions necessary, theaters will often pay the playwright's expenses while in residence during rehearsals. The thrill of seeing your play come to life on the stage is one of the pleasures of being on hand for rehearsals and performances.

Aspiring playwrights should query college and community theaters in their region to find out which ones are interested in seeing original scripts. Dramatic associations of interest to playwrights include the Dramatists Guild (234 W. 44th St., New York, NY 10036), and Theatre Communications Group, Inc. (355 Lexington Ave., New York, NY 10017), which publishes the annual *Dramatists Sourcebook*. *The Playwright's Companion*, published by Feedback Theatrebooks (305 Madison Ave., Suite 1146, New York, NY 10165), is an annual directory of theaters and prize contests seeking scripts. See the *Organizations for Writers* list for details on dramatists' associations.

Some of the theaters on the following list require that playwrights submit all or some of the following with scripts—cast list, synopsis, resumé, recommendations, return postcard—and with scripts and queries, SASEs must always be enclosed. Playwrights may also wish to register their material with the U.S. Copyright Office. For additional information about this, write Register of Copyrights, Library of Congress, Washington, DC 20559.

REGIONAL AND UNIVERSITY THEATERS

ACTORS THEATRE OF LOUISVILLE—316 W. Main St., Louisville, KY 40202. Michael Bigelow Dixon, Lit. Mgr. Ten-minute comedies and dramas, to 10 pages; include SASE. Annual contest. Guidelines.

A. D. PLAYERS—2710 W. Alabama, Houston, TX 77098. Attn: Lit. Mgr. Jeannette Clift George, Artistic Dir. Full-length or one-act comedies, dramas, musicals, children's plays, and adaptations with Christian world view. Submit resumé, cast list, and synopsis with SASE. Readings. Pays negotiable rates.

ALABAMA SHAKESPEARE FESTIVAL—The State Theatre, #1 Festival Dr., Montgomery, AL 36117–4605. Bob Vardaman, Lit. Assoc. Full-length scripts with southern and/or African-American themes, issues, or history and scripts with southern and/or African-American authors. Send resumé and synopsis in June.

ALLIANCE THEATRE COMPANY—1280 Peachtree St. N.E., Atlanta, GA 30309. Attn: Lit. Dept. Full-length comedies and dramas especially those that "deal with moral/spiritual questions of life in multicultural America." Query with synopsis and up to ten pages of sample dialogue; no unsolicited scripts. Pay varies.

AMERICAN LITERATURE THEATRE LAB—Fountain Theatre, 5060 Fountain Ave., Los Angeles, CA 90029. Simon Levy, Prod. Dir. One-act and full-length stage adaptations of classic and contemporary American literature.

759

Sets and cast size are unrestricted. Send synopsis and SAS postcard. Rate of payment is standard, as set by the Dramatists Guild.

AMERICAN LIVING HISTORY THEATER—P.O. Box 2677, Hollywood, CA 90078. Dorene Ludwig, Artistic Dir. One-act, historically accurate (primary source materials only) dramas dealing with marketable or known American historical and literary characters and events. Submit treatment and letter with SASE. Responds within 6 months. Pays varying rates.

AMERICAN PLACE THEATRE—111 W. 46th St., New York, NY 10036. Elise Thoron, Artistic Assoc. "No unsolicited manuscripts accepted. Writers may send a synopsis and the first 20 pages with SASE. We seek challenging, innovative works and do not favor obviously commercial material."

AMERICAN REPERTORY THEATRE— 64 Brattle St., Cambridge, MA 02138. Steven Maler, Artistic Assoc. for New Plays. No unsolicited manuscripts or samples.

AMERICAN STAGE COMPANY—FDU, Box 336, Teaneck, NJ 07666. James Vagias, Exec. Prod. Full-length comedies, dramas, and musicals for cast of 5 or 6 and single set. No unsolicited scripts.

AMERICAN THEATRE OF ACTORS—314 W. 54th St., New York, NY 10019. James Jennings, Artistic Dir. Full-length dramas for a cast of 2 to 6. Submit complete play and SASE. Reports in one to 2 months.

MAXWELL ANDERSON PLAYWRIGHTS SERIES, INC.—11 Esquire Rd., Norwalk, CT 06851. Muriel Nussbaum, Ken Parker, Artistic Dirs. Produces 6 professional staged readings of new plays each year in Greenwich, CT. Send complete script with SASE.

ARENA STAGE—Sixth and Maine Ave. S.W., Washington, DC 20024. Cathy Madison, Lit. Mgr. No unsolicited manuscripts; send synopsis and first 10 pages of dialogue.

ARKANSAS REPERTORY THEATRE COMPANY— 601 S. Main, P.O. Box 110, Little Rock, AR 72203–0110. Brad Mooy, Lit. Mgr. Full-length comedies, dramas, and musicals; prefer up to 8 characters. Send synopsis, cast list, resumé, and return postage; do not send complete manuscript. Reports in 3 months.

ARTREACH TOURING THEATRE—3074 Madison Rd., Cincinnati, OH 45209. Kathryn Schultz Miller, Artistic Dir. One-act dramas and adaptations for touring family theater; up to 3 cast members, simple sets. Submit script with synopsis, cast list, resumé, recommendations, and SASE. Payment varies.

BARTER THEATER—P.O. Box 867, Abingdon, VA 24210. Richard Rose, Artistic Dir. Full-length dramas, comedies, adaptations, musicals, and children's plays. Submit synopsis, dialogue sample, and SASE. Allow 6 to 8 months for report. Payment rates negotiable.

BERKELEY REPERTORY THEATRE—2025 Addison St., Berkeley, CA 94704. Sharon Ott, Artistic Dir. No unsolicited manuscripts; agent submissions or professional recommendations only. Responds in 3 to 4 months.

BERKSHIRE THEATRE FESTIVAL—Box 797, Stockbridge, MA 01262. Arthur Storch, Artistic Dir. Full-length comedies, musicals, and dramas; cast to 8. Submit through agent only.

BOARSHEAD THEATER— 425 Cesar Chavez Ave., Lansing, MI 48933.

760

John Peakes, Artistic Dir. Full-length comedies and dramas with simple sets and cast of up to 10. Send precis, 5 to 10 pages of dialogue, cast list with descriptions. SAS postcard for reply.

BRISTOL RIVERSIDE THEATRE—Box 1250, Bristol, PA 19007. Susan D. Atkinson, Producing/Artistic Dir. Full-length plays with up to 10 actors and a simple set.

CALIFORNIA UNIVERSITY THEATRE—California, PA 15419. Dr. Richard J. Helldobler, Chairman. Unusual, avant-garde, and experimental one-act and full-length comedies and dramas, children's plays, and adaptations. Cast size varies. Submit synopsis with short, sample scene(s). Payment available.

CENTER STAGE—700 N. Calvert St., Baltimore, MD 21202. James Magruder, Resident Dramaturg. Full-length comedies, dramas, translations, adaptations. No unsolicited manuscripts. Send synopsis, a few sample pages, resumé, cast list, and production history. Allow 8 to 10 weeks for reply.

CHILDSPLAY, INC.—Box 517, Tempe, AZ 85280. David Saar, Artistic Dir. Multigenerational plays running 45 to 120 minutes: dramas, musicals, and adaptations for family audiences. Productions may need to travel. Submissions accepted July through December. Reports in 2 to 6 months.

CIRCLE REPERTORY COMPANY—632 Broadway, 6th Fl., New York, NY 10012. Austin Pendleton, Artistic Dir. "We accept scripts submitted by agents." Offers criticism "as often as possible." Reports in 6 months. Readings.

CITY THEATRE COMPANY—57 S. 13th St., Pittsburgh, PA 15203. Gwen Orel, Lit. Dir. Full-length cutting-edge comedies and dramas; especially interested in women and minorities. Cast to 10; simple sets. Query September to May. Royalty.

CLASSIC STAGE COMPANY—136 E. 13th St., New York, NY 10003. Patricia Taylor, Man. Dir. David Esbjornson, Artistic Dir. Full-length adaptations and translations of existing classic literature. Submit synopsis with cast list and SASE, September to May. Offers readings. Pays on royalty basis.

THE CONSERVATORY THEATRE ENSEMBLE—c/o Tamalpais High School, 700 Miller Ave., Mill Valley, CA 94941. Daniel Caldwell, Artistic Dir. Comedies, dramas, children's plays, adaptations, and scripts addressing high school issues for largely female cast (about 3 women per man). "One-act plays of approximately 30 minutes are especially needed, as we produce 40 short plays each season using teenage actors." Send synopsis and resumé.

CREATIVE THEATRE—102 Witherspoon St., Princeton, NJ 08540. Pamela Hoffman, Artistic Dir. Participatory plays for children, grades K through 6; cast of 4 to 6; arena or thrust stage. Submit manuscript with synopsis and cast list. Pay varies.

CROSSROADS THEATRE CO.—7 Livingston Ave., New Brunswick, NJ 08901. Ricardo Khan, Artistic Dir. Sydné Mahone, Dir. of Play Development. Full-length and one-act dramas, comedies, musicals, and adaptations; issue-oriented experimental plays that offer honest, imaginative, and insightful examinations of the African-American experience. Also interested in African and Caribbean plays and plays exploring cross-cultural issues. Queries only, with synopsis, cast list, resumé, and SASE.

DELAWARE THEATRE COMPANY—200 Water St., Wilmington, DE

19801–5030. Cleveland Morris, Artistic Dir. Full-length comedies, dramas, and musicals dealing with interracial dynamics in America. Contemporary or historical settings. Prefer cast of no more than 10. Send synopsis or complete script; SASE required. Reports in 6 months. Write for details of Connections competition.

DENVER CENTER THEATRE COMPANY—1050 13th St., Denver, CO 80204. Attn: Lit. Dir. Readings and productions of new works presented throughout the year. Send letter of inquiry, synopsis, 10 pages of dialogue, and resumé of writing experience. Stipend and housing provided for workshops.

DETROIT REPERTORY THEATRE—13103 Woodrow Wilson Ave., Detroit, MI 48238. Barbara Busby, Lit. Mgr. Full-length comedies and dramas. Enclose SASE. Pays royalty.

STEVE DOBBINS PRODUCTIONS—650 Geary Blvd., San Francisco, CA 94102. Alan Ramos, Lit. Dir. Full-length comedies, dramas, and musicals. Cast of up to 12. Query with synopsis and resumé. No unsolicited manuscripts. Reports in 6 months. Offers workshops and readings. Pays 6% of gross.

DORSET THEATRE FESTIVAL—Box 519, Dorset, VT 05251. Jill Charles, Artistic Dir. Full-length comedies, musicals, dramas, and adaptations for up to 8 cast members; simple set preferred. Agent submissions and professional recommendations only. Pays varying rates. Residencies at Dorset Colony House for Writers available October to June; inquire.

EAST WEST PLAYERS—4424 Santa Monica Blvd., Los Angeles, CA 90029. Tim Dang, Artistic Dir. Ken Narasaki, Dramaturg. Produces 4 to 5 new plays annually. Original plays, translations, adaptations, musicals, and youth theater, "all of which must illuminate the Asian or Asian-American experience, or resonate in a significant fashion if cast with Asian-American actors." Readings. Prefer to see query letter with synopsis and 10 pages of dialogue; complete scripts also considered. Reports in 5 to 6 weeks for query; 6 months for complete script.

EMPIRE THEATER—Box 132048, Houston, TX 77219–2048. Michael J. Ferrand, Man. Dir. Full-length comedies. Payment varies. Also sponsors Houston Theater Festival: one-act plays, to 45 minutes, and more risqué plays, to 60 minutes. Deadline: January 15.

ENSEMBLE STUDIO THEATRE—549 W. 52nd St., New York, NY 10019. Attn: Lit. Mgr. Send full-length or one-act comedies and dramas with resumé and SASE, September to April. Rarely pays for scripts. Fifteen readings of new plays per year.

FLORIDA STUDIO THEATRE—1241 N. Palm Ave., Sarasota, FL 33577. Chris Angermann, New Play Development. Innovative plays with universal themes. Query with synopsis and SASE. Also accepting musicals.

WILL GEER THEATRICUM BOTANICUM—Box 1222, Topanga, CA 90290. Attn: Lit. Dir. All types of scripts for outdoor theater, with large playing area. Submit synopsis with SASE. Pays varing rates.

EMMY GIFFORD CHILDREN'S THEATER—3504 Center St., Omaha, NE 68105. James Larson, Artistic Dir. Theatre for young audiences. Referrals only.

THE GOODMAN THEATRE—200 S. Columbus Dr., Chicago, IL 60603. Susan V. Booth, Lit. Mgr. Queries from recognized literary agents or producing organizations required for full-length comedies or dramas. No unsolicited scripts.

THE GUTHRIE THEATER—725 Vineland Pl., Minneapolis, MN 55403. Attn: Lit. Dept. Full-length comedies, dramas, and adaptations of world's classics. Manuscripts accepted only from recognized theatrical agents. Query with detailed synopsis and cast size. Reports in 2 to 4 months.

HIPPODROME STATE THEATRE—25 S.E. Second Pl., Gainesville, FL 32601. David Boyce, Dramaturg. Full-length plays with unit sets and casts of up to 10. Agent submissions and professional recommendations only.

HOLLYWOOD THESPIAN COMPANY—12838 Kling St., Studio City, CA 91604–1127. Rai Tasco, Artistic Dir. Full-length comedies and dramas for integrated cast. Include cast list and SAS postcard with submission.

HONOLULU THEATRE FOR YOUTH—2846 Ualena St., Honolulu, HI 96819. Peter C. Brosius, Artistic Dir. Plays, 60 to 90 minutes, for young people and family audiences. Adult casts. Contemporary issues, Pacific themes, etc. Unit sets, small cast. Query or send cover letter with synopsis, cast list, and SASE. Royalties negotiable.

HORIZON THEATRE COMPANY—P. O. Box 5376, Station E, Atlanta, GA 30307. Jeffrey and Lisa Adler, Artistic Dirs. Full-length comedies, dramas, and satires. Encourages submissions by women writers. Cast of no more than 10. Submit synopsis with cast list, resumé, and recommendations. Pays percentage. Readings. Reports in 6 months.

HUNTINGTON THEATRE COMPANY—252 Huntington Ave., Boston, MA 02115. Jayme Koszyn, Dramaturg. Full-length comedies and dramas. Query with synopsis, cast list, resumé, recommendations, and SAS postcard.

ILLINOIS THEATRE CENTER— 400 Lakewood Blvd., Park Forest, IL 60466. Steve S. Billig, Artistic Dir. Full-length comedies, dramas, musicals, and adaptations, for unit/fragmentary sets, and up to 8 cast members. Send summary and SAS postcard. No unsolicited manuscripts. Pays negotiable rates. Workshops and readings offered.

ILLUSTRATED STAGE COMPANY—Box 640063, San Francisco, CA 94164–0063. Steve Dobbins, Artistic Dir. Full-length comedies, dramas, and musicals for a cast of up to 18. Query with synopsis and SASE. No unsolicited manuscripts. Offers workshops and readings.

INVISIBLE THEATRE—1400 N. First Ave, Tucson, AZ 85719. Deborah Dickey, Lit. Mgr. Letter of introduction from theatre professional must accompany submissions for full-length comedies, dramas, musicals, and adaptations. Submit after September '96. Cast of up to 10; simple set. Also one-act plays. Pays royalty.

JEWISH REPERTORY THEATRE—1395 Lexington Ave., New York, NY 10128. Ran Avni, Artistic Dir. Full-length comedies, dramas, musicals, and adaptations, with up to 10 cast members, relating to the Jewish experience. Pays varying rates. Enclose SASE.

KUMU KAHUA THEATRE, INC.— 46 Merchant St., Honolulu, HI 96813. Dennis Carroll, Artistic Dir. Full-length plays especially relevant to life in Hawaii. Prefer simple sets for arena and in-the-round productions. Submit resumé and synopsis January through April. Pays $35 per performance. Readings. Contests.

763

LIVE OAK THEATRE—200 Colorado, Austin, TX 78701. Tom Byrne, Lit. Mgr. Full-length plays and adaptations. "Special interest in producing works of Texan and southern topics and new American plays." No musicals. Send letter of inquiry with SASE. Contest; send SASE for details. Guidelines.

LOS ANGELES DESIGNERS' THEATRE—P. O. Box 1883, Studio City, CA 91614–0883. Richard Niederberg, Artistic Dir. Full-length comedies, dramas, musicals, fantasies, or adaptations. Religious, political, social, and controversial themes encouraged. Nudity, "adult" language, etc., O.K. "Please detail in the cover letter what the writer's proposed involvement with the production would be beyond the usual. Do not submit material that needs to be returned." Payment varies.

THE MAGIC THEATRE—Fort Mason Ctr., Bldg. D, San Francisco, CA 94123. Cathy Clark, Lit. Mgr. Comedies and dramas. "Special interest in poetic, non-linear, and multicultural work for mainstage productions, workshops, and readings." Query with synopsis, resumé, first 10 to 20 pages of script, and SASE; no unsolicited manuscripts. Pays varying rates.

MANHATTAN THEATRE CLUB—453 W. 16th, New York, NY 10011. Attn: Kate Loewald. Full-length and one-act comedies, dramas, and musicals. No unsolicited manuscripts or queries; agent submissions only.

MILL MOUNTAIN THEATRE—One Market Sq., Second Fl., Roanoke, VA 24011–1437. Jo Weinstein, Lit. Mgr. One-act comedies and dramas, 25 to 40 minutes. For full-length plays, send letter, resumé, and synopsis. Payment varies.

MISSOURI REPERTORY THEATRE—4949 Cherry St., Kansas City, MO 64110. Felicia Londré, Dramaturg. Full-length comedies and dramas. Query with synopsis, cast list, resumé, and SAS postcard. Royalty. Allow 6 months for response.

MUSICAL THEATRE WORKS—440 Lafayette St., New York, NY 10003. Andrew Barrett, Lit. Mgr. Full-length musicals, for a cast of up to 15. Submit manuscript and cassette score with SASE. Responds in 4 to 6 months.

NATIONAL BLACK THEATRE—2033 Fifth Ave., Harlem, NY 10035. Attn: Tunde Samuel. Drama, musicals, and children's plays. "Scripts should reflect African and African-American lifestyle. Historical, inspirational, and ritualistic forms appreciated." Workshops and readings.

NATIONAL PLAYWRIGHTS CONFERENCE, EUGENE O'NEILL THEATRE CENTER—234 W. 44th St., Suite 901, New York, NY 10036. Mary F. McCabe, Conference Administrator. Annual competition to select new stage plays and teleplays/screenplays for development during the summer at organization's Waterford, CT location. Submission deadline: December 1. Send #10-size SASE in the fall for guidelines. Pays stipend, plus travel/living expenses during conference.

NEW THEATRE, INC.—169 Massachusetts Ave., Boston, MA 02115. Attn: NEWorks Submissions Program. New full-length scripts for readings, workshop, and main stage productions. Include SASE.

NEW TUNERS/PERFORMANCE COMMUNITY—1225 W. Belmont Ave., Chicago, IL 60657. Allan Chambers, Artistic Dir. of Development. Full-length musicals only, for cast to 15; no wing/fly space. Send query with brief synopsis, cassette tape of score, cast list, resumé, SASE, and SAS postcard. Pays on royalty basis.

NEW YORK SHAKESPEARE FESTIVAL/JOSEPH PAPP PUBLIC THE-ATER— 425 Lafayette St., New York, NY 10003. Shelby Jiggetts, Lit. Mgr. Plays and musical works for the theater, translations, and adaptations. Submit sample dialogue with synopsis, cassette (for musicals), and SASE. Allow 4 to 6 months for response.

NEW YORK STATE THEATRE INSTITUTE—155 River St., Troy, NY 12180. Attn: Patricia Di Benedetto Snyder, Producing Artistic Dir. Emphasis on new, full-length plays and musicals for family audiences. Submit complete script (with tape for musicals) or query with synopsis and cast list. Payment varies.

ODYSSEY THEATRE ENSEMBLE—2055 S. Sepulveda Blvd., Los Angeles, CA 90025. Ron Sossi, Artistic Dir. Full-length comedies, dramas, musicals, and adaptations: provocative subject matter, or plays that stretch and explore the possibilities of theater. Query Jan Lewis, Lit. Mgr., with synopsis, 8 to 10 pages of sample dialogue, and resumé. Pays variable rates. Allow 2 to 6 months for reply to script; 2 to 4 weeks for queries. Workshops and readings.

OLDCASTLE THEATRE COMPANY—Bennington Center for the Arts, P.O. Box 1555, Bennington, VT 05201. Eric Peterson, Dir. Full-length comedies, dramas, and musicals for a small cast (up to 10). Submit synopsis and cast list in the winter. Reports in 6 months. Offers workshops and readings. Pays expenses for playwright to attend rehearsals. Royalty.

PENGUIN REPERTORY COMPANY—Box 91, Stony Point, Rockland County, NY 10980. Joe Brancato, Artistic Dir. Full-length comedies and dramas with cast size to 5. Submit script, resumé, and SASE. Payment varies.

PENNSYLVANIA STAGE— 837 Linden St., Allentown, PA 18101. Attn: Lit. Dir. Full-length plays with cast of 4 to 10; no more than 2 sets. Send synopsis, cast list, and SASE to Outreach/Literary Dept. Allow 6 months for reply. Staged readings possible.

PEOPLE'S LIGHT AND THEATRE COMPANY—39 Conestoga Rd., Malvern, PA 19355. Alda Cortese, Lit. Mgr. One-act or full-length comedies, dramas, adaptations. No unsolicited manuscripts; query with synopsis, 10 pages of script required. Reports in 6 months. Payment negotiable.

PIER ONE THEATRE—Box 894, Homer, AK 99603. Lance Petersen, Lit. Dir. Full-length and one-act comedies, dramas, musicals, children's plays, and adaptations. Submit complete script; include piano score with musicals. "We are now concentrating on plays by Alaskan playwrights or of special significance to the Alaskan experience." Pays 8% of ticket sales for mainstage musicals; other payment varies.

PLAYHOUSE ON THE SQUARE—51 S. Cooper in Overton Sq., Memphis, TN 38104. Jackie Nichols, Artistic Dir. Full-length comedies, dramas; cast of up to 15. Contest deadline is April for fall production. Pays $500.

PLAYWRIGHTS HORIZONS— 416 W. 42nd St., New York, NY 10036. Address Literary Dept. Full-length, original comedies, dramas, and musicals by American authors. No one-acts or screenplays. Synopses discouraged; send resumé and SASE, include tape for musicals. Off Broadway contract.

PLAYWRIGHTS' PLATFORM—164 Brayton Rd., Boston, MA 02135. Attn: Lit. Dir. Script development workshops and public readings for New England playwrights only. Full-length and one-act plays of all kinds. No sexist or racist material. Residents of New England send scripts with short synopsis, resumé, SAS postcard, and SASE. Readings conducted at Massachusetts College of Art (Boston).

POPLAR PIKE PLAYHOUSE—7653 Old Poplar Pike, Germantown, TN 38138. Frank Bluestein, Artistic Dir. Full-length and one-act comedies, dramas, musicals, and children's plays. Submit synopsis with SAS postcard and resumé. Pays $300.

PRINCETON REPERTORY COMPANY—17 Hulfish St., Suite 260, Palmer Sq. N., Princeton, NJ 08542. Victoria Liberatori, Artistic Dir. Full-length comedies and dramas for a cast of up to 5. One set. Submit synopsis with resumé, cast list, and 3-page dialogue sample. Do not submit complete script. "Scripts with socially relevant themes that move beyond domestic drama preferred." Readings offered. Responds within one year.

THE PUERTO RICAN TRAVELING THEATRE—141 W. 94th St., New York, NY 10025. Miriam Colon Valle, Artistic Dir. Full-length and one-act comedies, dramas, and musicals; cast of up to 8; simple sets. "We prefer plays based on the contemporary Hispanic experience, material with social, cultural, or psychological content." Payment negotiable.

THE REPERTORY THEATRE OF ST. LOUIS—Box 191730, St. Louis, MO 63119. Attn: Lit. Dir. Query with brief synopsis, technical requirements, and cast size. Unsolicited manuscripts will be returned unread.

THE ROAD COMPANY—P.O. Box 5278 EKS, Johnson City, TN 37603. Robert H. Leonard, Artistic Dir. Christine Murdock, Lit. Mgr. Full-length and one-act comedies, dramas with social/political relevance; experimental forms welcome. Send synopsis, cast list, and production history, if any. Pays negotiable rates. Reports in 6 to 12 months.

ROUND HOUSE THEATRE—12210 Bushey Dr., Silver Spring, MD 20902. Attn: Production Office Mgr. Full-length comedies, dramas, and adaptations; cast of up to 10; prefer simple set. Send one-page synopsis. No unsolicited manuscripts.

SALT AND PEPPER MIME COMPANY/NEW ENSEMBLE ACTORS THEATRE—320 E. 90th St., #1B, New York, NY 10128. Ms. Scottie Davis, Man. Prod. One-acts, all types, especially those conducive to "nontraditional" casting. "Very interested in pieces suitable to surrealistic or mimetic concept in philosophy or visual style." One- or 2-person cast. Send resumé, SAS postcard, cast list, and synopsis to 250 W. 65th St., New York, NY 10023. Scripts reviewed from May to September. Works also considered for readings, storyplayers, experimental development, and readers theater. Royalty.

SEATTLE REPERTORY THEATRE—155 Mercer St., Seattle, WA 98109. Daniel Sullivan, Artistic Dir. Full-length comedies, dramas, and adaptations. Submit synopsis, 10-page sample, SAS postcard, and resumé to Kurt Beattie, Artistic Assoc. New plays series with workshops each spring.

SOCIETY HILL PLAYHOUSE—507 S. 8th St., Philadelphia, PA 19147. Walter Vail, Dramaturg. Full-length dramas, comedies, and musicals with up to 6 cast members and simple set. Submit synopsis and SASE. Reports in 6 months. Nominal payment.

SOUTH COAST REPERTORY—P. O. Box 2197, Costa Mesa, CA 92628. John Glore, Lit. Mgr. Full-length comedies, dramas, musicals, juveniles. Query with synopsis and resumé. Payment varies.

766

SOUTHERN APPALACHIAN REPERTORY THEATRE—P.O. Box 620, Mars Hill, NC 28754. James W. Thomas, Artistic Dir. Full-length comedies, dramas, musicals, and plays including (but not limited to) scripts with Appalachian theme. Submit resumé, recommendations, full script, and SASE. Send SASE for information on Southern Appalachian Playwright's Conference (held in January each year). Pays $500 royalty if play is selected for production during the summer season. Deadline for submissions is October 1 each year.

STAGE ONE: THE LOUISVILLE CHILDREN'S THEATRE—425 W. Market St., Louisville, KY 40202. Attn: Lit. Dir. Adaptations of classics and original plays for children ages 4 to 18. Submit script with resumé and SASE. Reports in 4 months.

STAGES REPERTORY THEATRE—3201 Allen Pkwy., #101, Houston, TX 77019. Beth Sanford, Assoc. Artistic Dir. Unproduced new works: full-length dramas, comedies, translations, and adaptations, with small casts and simple sets. Submit synopsis; no unsolicited scripts. Send for guidelines for Texas playwrights' festival held in the spring.

MARK TAPER FORUM—135 N. Grand Ave., Los Angeles, CA 90012. Oliver Mayer, Lit. Assoc. Full-length comedies, dramas, musicals, juveniles, adaptations. Query.

THE TEN MINUTE MUSICALS PROJECT—Box 461194, W. Hollywood, CA 90046. Michael Koppy, Prod. One-act musicals. Include audio cassette, libretto, and lead sheets with submission. "We are looking for complete short musicals." Pays $250.

THEATER ARTISTS OF MARIN—Box 150473, San Rafael, CA 94915. Charles Brousse, Artistic Dir. Full-length comedies, dramas, and musicals for a cast of 2 to 8. Submit complete script with SASE. Reports in 4 to 6 months. Three showcase productions each year.

THEATER MU—1201 Yale Pl., #911, Minneapolis, MN 55403. Rick Shiomi, Artistic Dir. Luu Pham, Lit. Dir. Full-length and one-act comedies and dramas for primarily Asian-American cast. Submit synopsis with cast list, return post card, resumé, recommendations, and SASE. Allow 6 months for response. Also sponsors New Eyes Festival with staged readings for selected scripts. No payment.

THEATRE AMERICANA—Box 245, Altadena, CA 91001. Attn: Lit. Dir. Full-length comedies and dramas, preferably with American theme. No children's plays. Language and subject matter should be suitable for a community audience. Send bound manuscript with cast list, resumé, and SASE, by January 31. No payment. Allow 3 to 6 months for reply. Submit no more than 2 entries per season.

THEATRE ON THE SQUARE—450 Post St., San Francisco, CA 94102. Jonathan Reinis, Artistic Dir. Full-length comedies, dramas, and musicals for 15-person cast. Submit cast list and script with SASE. Reports in 30 days.

THEATRE/TEATRO—Bilingual Foundation of the Arts, 421 N. Ave., #19, Los Angeles, CA 90031. Guillermo Reyes, Lit. Mgr. Margarita Galban, Artistic Dir. Full-length plays about the Hispanic experience; small casts. Submit manuscript with SASE. Pays negotiable rates.

THEATREWORKS—470 San Antonio Rd., Palo Alto, CA 94306. Attn: Lit. Dept. Full-length comedies, dramas, and musicals. Submit complete script or synopsis with SAS postcard and SASE, cast list, theatre resumé, and production history. For musicals, include cassette of up to 6 songs and lyrics for all songs. Responds in 2 months for submissions made March to August; 4 months for submissions September to February. Payment is negotiable.

THEATREWORKS/USA— 890 Broadway, 7th Fl., New York, NY 10003. Barbara Pasternack, Lit. Mgr. One-hour children's musicals and plays with music for 5-person cast. Playwrights must be within commutable distance to New York City. Submit outline or treatment, sample scenes, and music in spring, summer. Pays royalty and commission.

WALNUT STREET THEATRE COMPANY—9th and Walnut Sts., Philadelphia, PA 19107. Beverly Elliott, Lit. Mgr., Main Stage. Full-length comedies, dramas, musicals, and popular, upbeat adaptations; also, one- to 4-character plays for studio stage. Submit 20 sample pages with SAS postcard, cast list, and synopsis. Musical submissions must include an audio tape. Reports in 5 months. Payment varies.

THE WESTERN STAGE—156 Homestead Ave., Salinas, CA 93901. Tom Humphrey, Artistic Dir. Joyce Lower, Dramaturg. The Salinas River Playwriting Festival, September through October in even-numbered years. Presentations in theater, dance, music, the visual arts, film, poetry. Also workshops, classes, displays, etc. Write for guidelines and required application.

WOOLLY MAMMOTH THEATRE COMPANY—1401 Church St. N.W., Washington, DC 20005. Jim Byrnes, Lit. Mgr. Looking for offbeat material, unusual writing. Unsolicited scripts accepted. Payment varies.

GARY YOUNG MIME THEATRE—23724 Park Madrid, Calabasas, CA 91302. Gary Young, Artistic Dir. Comedy monologues and vignettes, for children and adults, one to 90 minutes; casts of one man or one man and one woman, and portable set. Pays varying rates. Enclose SAS postcard, resumé, recommendations, cast list, and synopsis.

PLAY PUBLISHERS

ALABAMA LITERARY REVIEW—Troy State Univ., 253 Smith Hall, Troy, AL 36082. Theron Montgomery, Ed. Full-length and one-act comedies and dramas, to 50 pages. Query preferred. Responds to queries in 2 weeks; 2 to 3 months for complete manuscripts. Do not submit material in August. Payment is in copies; honorarium when available.

AMELIA—329 E St., Bakersfield, CA 93304. Frederick A. Raborg, Jr., Ed. One-act comedies and dramas; no longer than 45 minutes running time. Responds in 2 to 3 months. Payment is $35, on acceptance.

ANCHORAGE PRESS—Box 8067, New Orleans, LA 70182. Attn: Ed. Plays and musicals that have been proven in multiple production, for children ages 6 to 18. "We publish 8 to 10 new playbooks and one to 3 new hardcover books each year." Royalty.

ART CRAFT PUBLISHING COMPANY—P.O. Box 1058, Cedar Rapids, IA 52406. Attn: Ed. Two- and 3-act comedies, mysteries, farces, and musicals and one-act comedies or dramas, with one interior setting and a large cast for production by middle, junior, and senior high school students. Pays royalty or flat fee.

BAKER'S PLAYS—100 Chauncy St., Boston, MA 02111. Attn: Ed.

Scripts for amateur production: one-act plays, children's plays, musicals, religious drama, full-length plays for high school production. Allow 4 months for response.

BLIZZARD PUBLISHING—73 Furby St., Winnipeg, Manitoba, Canada R3C 2A2. Anna Synenko, Acquisitions Ed. One-act and full-length dramas, children's plays, and adaptations. Responds in 3 to 4 months. Royalty. Queries preferred.

CALLALOO—Dept. of English, Univ. of Virginia, Charlottesville, VA 22903. Charles H. Rowell, Ed. One-act dramas by and about African-American, Caribbean, and African writers. Scripts read September through May. Responds in 3 to 6 months. Payment varies, on publication.

CHICAGO PLAYS, INC.—2632 N. Lincoln Ave., Chicago, IL 60614. Jill Murray, Pres. Full-length and one-act comedies, dramas, musicals, children's plays, and adaptations. "Submissions must have received a professional production in the Chicago area." Responds in 4 to 6 months. Royalty.

CHILDREN'S PLAYMATE—1100 Waterway Blvd., P.O. Box 567, Indianapolis, IN 46206. Sandy Grieshop, Ed. Plays for children ages 6 to 8. Special emphasis on health, nutrition, exercise, and safety. Pays up to 17¢ a word, on publication.

I. E. CLARK, PUBLISHERS—St. John's Rd., P.O. Box 246, Schulenburg, TX 78956. Debra Drabek, Ed. One-act and full-length plays and musicals, for children, young adults, and adults. Serious drama, comedies, classics, fairytales, melodramas, and holiday plays. "We seldom publish a play that has not been produced." Responds in 2 to 6 months. Royalty.

COLLAGES & BRICOLAGES—P.O. Box 86, Clarion, PA 16214. Marie-José Fortis, Ed. One-act comedies and dramas. Manuscripts read August through November; responds in one to 3 months. Payment is in copies.

CONFRONTATION—Dept. of English, C.W. Post of L.I.U., Greenvale, NY 11548. Martin Tucker, Ed. One-act comedies, dramas, and adaptations. Manuscripts read September through May. Responds in 6 to 8 weeks. Pays, $25 to $100, on publication.

CONTEMPORARY DRAMA SERVICE—Meriwether Publishing Co., Box 7710, 885 Elkton Dr., Colorado Springs, CO 80903. Arthur Zapel, Ed. Easy-to-stage comedies, skits, one-acts, musicals, puppet scripts, and full-length plays for schools and churches. (Junior high through college level; no elementary level material.) Adaptations of classics and improvised material for classroom use. Comedy monologues and duets. Chancel drama for Christmas and Easter church use. Enclose synopsis. Books on theater arts subjects, scene books, and anthologies. Textbooks for speech and drama. Pays by fee arrangement or royalty.

DRAMATIC PUBLISHING—311 Washington St., Woodstock, IL 60098. Sarah Clark, Ed. Full-length and one-act plays and musicals for the stock, amateur, and children's theater market. Royalty. Responds within 16 weeks.

DRAMATICS—Educational Theatre Assoc., 3368 Central Pkwy., Cincinnati, OH 45225–2392. Don Corathers, Ed. One-act and full-length plays for high school production. Pays $100 to $400 for one-time, non-exclusive publications rights, on acceptance.

ELDRIDGE PUBLISHING COMPANY—P. O. Box 1595, Venice, FL

34284. Nancy Vorhis, Ed. Dept. One-act and full-length plays and musicals suitable for performance by schools, churches, and community theatre groups. Comedies, tragedies, dramas, skits, spoofs, and religious plays (Christmas and Easter); easy costuming and scenery. Submit complete manuscript with cover letter, biography, and SASE. Responds in 2 months. Flat fee for one-act and religious plays, paid on publication; royalties for full-length plays.

SAMUEL FRENCH, INC.— 45 W. 25th St., New York, NY 10010. Lawrence R. Harbison, Ed. Full-length plays for dinner, community, stock, college, and high school theaters. One-act plays, 30 to 45 minutes. Children's plays, 45 to 60 minutes. Royalty.

HEUER PUBLISHING COMPANY—Drawer 248, Cedar Rapids, IA 52406. C. Emmett McMullen, Ed. One-act comedies and dramas for contest work; two- and three-act comedies, mysteries, or farces, and musicals, with one interior setting, for middle school and high school production. Pays royalty or flat fee.

LYNX EYE—c/o Scribblefest Literary Group, 1880 Hill Dr., Los Angeles, CA 90041. Pam McCully, Kathryn Morrison, Co-Eds. One-act plays, 500 to 5,000 words, for thoughtful adults who enjoy interesting reading and writing. Also, short stories, vignettes, novel excerpts, essays, belle lettres, satires, and reviews; poetry, to 30 lines; fillers, to 250 words. Pays $10, on publication.

MODERN INTERNATIONAL DRAMA—Theatre Dept., SUNY, P.O. Box 6000, Binghamton, NY 13902–6000. George E. Wellwarth, Man. Ed. Semiannual. Full-length and one-act translations of previously untranslated modern (20th century) plays. No adaptations. Queries preferred. Responds in one month. Pays in copies, on publication.

NATIONAL DRAMA SERVICE—MSN 170, 127 Ninth Ave. N., Nashville, TN 37234. Attn: Ed. Scripts, 2 to 7 minutes long: drama in worship, puppets, clowns, Christian comedy, mime, movement, readers theater, creative worship services, and monologues. "We publish dramatic material that communicates the message of Christ. We want scripts that will give even the smallest church the opportunity to enhance their ministry with drama." Payment varies, on acceptance. Guidelines.

PIONEER DRAMA SERVICE—P. O. Box 4267, Englewood, CO 80155. Attn: Ed. Full-length and one-act plays; plays for young audiences; musicals, melodramas, and Christmas plays. No unproduced plays or plays with largely male casts or multiple sets. Query. Outright purchase or royalty.

PLAYERS PRESS, INC.—P.O. Box 1132, Studio City, CA 91614–0132. Robert W. Gordon, Ed. One-act and full-length comedies, dramas, and musicals. "No manuscript will be considered unless it has been produced." Query with manuscript-size SASE and 2 #10 SASEs for correspondence. Include resumé and/or biography. Responds in 3 to 12 months. Royalty.

PLAYS, THE DRAMA MAGAZINE FOR YOUNG PEOPLE—120 Boylston St., Boston, MA 02116–4615. Elizabeth Preston, Man. Ed. One-act plays, with simple contemporary sets, for production by young people, 7 to 17: comedies, dramas, farces, skits, holiday plays. Also adaptations of classics, biography plays, puppet plays, and creative dramatics. No musicals or plays with religious themes. Maximum lengths: lower grades, 10 double-spaced pages; middle grades, 15 pages; junior and senior high, 20 pages. Pays good rates, on acceptance. Buys all rights. Query for adaptations. Guidelines.

PRISM INTERNATIONAL—Dept. of Creative Writing, Univ. of British Columbia, E462–1866 Main Mall, Vancouver, BC, Canada V6T 1Z1. Attn: Ed. One-act plays. Responds in 2 to 3 months. Pays $20 per page, on publication.

THE RADIO PLAY—The Public Media Foundation, 100 Boylston St., Suite 230, Boston, MA 02116. Valerie Henderson, Exec. Prod. Original radio plays and radio dramatizations of American classics in the public domain, 28 to 29 pages, to fit a 30-minute program format. Query for dramatizations only. Send SASE for style sheet.

RAG MAG—P.O. Box 12, Goodhue, MN 55027. Beverly Voldseth, Ed. Semiannual. Full-length and one-act comedies and dramas. Query with 3 to 7 pages of play and SASE. Pays in copies.

ROCKFORD REVIEW—P.O. Box 858, Rockford, IL 61105. David Ross, Ed. One-act comedies, dramas, and satires, to 1,300 words. "We prefer genuine or satirical human dilemmas with coping or non-coping outcomes that ring true." Pays in copies (plus invitation to attend reading-reception in the fall). Two $25 Editor's Choice Prizes awarded each issue.

SINISTER WISDOM—P.O. Box 3252, Berkeley, CA 94703. Akiba Onada-Sikwoia, Ed. Quarterly. One-act (no longer than 15 pages) lesbian drama. "We are particularly interested in work that reflects the diversity of our experiences: as lesbians of color, ethnic lesbians, Jewish, old, young, working class, poor, disabled, fat. Only material by born-woman lesbians is considered." Responds in 3 to 9 months; write for upcoming themes. Payment is in 2 copies, on publication. SASE.

SMITH AND KRAUS, INC.—P.O. Box 127, Main St., Lyme, NH 03768. Marisa Smith, Pres. Full-length and one-act dramas for adults and young actors; monologue anthologies. Send query and synopsis. Response time is 3 months. Pays on acceptance and on publication.

THE TV AND FILM SCRIPT MARKET

The almost round-the-clock television offerings on commercial, educational, and cable TV stations, in addition to the hundreds of films released yearly, may lead free-lance writers to believe that opportunities to sell scripts or program ideas are infinite. Unfortunately, this is not true. With few exceptions, producers and programmers do not consider scripts submitted directly to them, no matter how good they are. In general, free lancers can achieve success in this nearly closed field by concentrating on getting their fiction (short stories and novels) and nonfiction published in magazines or books, combed diligently by producers for possible adaptations. A large percentage of the material offered over all types of networks (in addition to the motion pictures made in Hollywood) is in the form of adaptations of published material.

Writers who want to try their hand at writing directly for this very limited market should be prepared to learn the special techniques and acceptable format of scriptwriting, either by taking a workshop through a university or at a writers conference, or by reading one or more of the many books that have been written on this subject. Also, experience in playwriting and a knowledge of dramatic structure gained through working in amateur, community, or professional theaters can be helpful.

Knowledge of the TV and film industry is vital to the scriptwriter, and trade magazines will keep the writer abreast of current events. *The Hollywood Reporter* (5055 Wilshire Blvd., Los Angeles, CA 90036–4396) publishes daily industry news, including information on rewrites underway, book adaptations, deal-making, etc. Writers may also want to check *Variety* (5700 Wilshire Blvd., Suite 120, Los Angeles, CA 90036) for trade news.

Writers may wish to register their story, treatment, series format, or script with the Writers Guild of America; to protect themselves from legal battles, many producers will not look at a script unless it has been registered with the Guild. This registration does not confer statutory rights, but it does supply evidence and date of authorship. Registration is effective for ten years, and is renewable after that. The WGA's registration service is available for a fee of $10 to $23 for members and $17 to $57 for non-members. For more information, write to: Registration Service, Writers Guild of America East, Inc., 555 W. 57th St., New York, NY 10019. Dramatic material can also be registered with the U.S. Copyright Office (Register of Copyrights, Library of Congress, Washington, DC 20559).

Since virtually all TV and film producers will read scripts and queries submitted only through recognized agents, we've included in this section a list of agents willing to read queries for TV scripts or screenplays. These agents have indicated that they do not charge a reading fee, and most charge the standard 10% commission for dramatic material; however, writers are advised to write directly for details on each agent's policy. Most of the major film studios will deal only with those agents who are Writers Guild of America signatories; such agents are required, under contract with the guild, to charge their clients no more than a 10% commission. Writers seeking representation for their screenplays should note, therefore, that an agent charging over 10% commission on a screenplay will be unable to show that script to the major studios.

The Association of Authors' Representatives (10 Astor Pl., 3rd Floor, New York, NY 10003) will send a list of member agents upon receipt of a self-addressed, legal-sized envelope with 55¢ postage, and a $5 check or money order. *Literary Market Place* (Bowker), available in most libraries, includes a list of agents; and *Literary Agents of North America* (Author Aid/Research Associates International, 340 E. 52nd St., New York, NY 10022; (212) 758–4213) provides detailed information on agents and their needs and is available through the publisher. Most of the agents listed below prefer queries and/or synopses, and will not reply unless the standard SASE has been enclosed; never send a complete manuscript unless it has been requested. Agents indicating they will consider multiple queries (i.e., queries the author has sent simultaneously to other agents) do so with the understanding that the author has made note of it in the query. A list of network (ABC, NBC, CBS, FOX) shows, agents, and production companies may be found in *Ross Reports Television*, published monthly by Television Index, Inc., (40–29 27th St., Long Island City, NY 11101; (718) 937–3990).

TV AND FILM SCRIPT AGENTS

AARDVARK LITERARY AGENTS—3908 Harlem Rd., Suite 104, Amherst, NY 14226. Attn: Kate Berman or Jim Fair. Screenplays. Query with bio/resumé; no multiple queries. Commission: 10%. Fees: photocopying, shipping.

BERMAN, BOALS, & FLYNN, INC.—225 Lafayette St., # 1207, New York, NY 10012. Attn: Lois Berman, Judy Boals, or Jim Flynn. Screenplays, teleplays, and stage plays. Unpublished, unproduced writers considered. Query with SASE, bio, and resumé. Commission: 10%. Fees: photocopying.

BRET ADAMS LTD.— 448 W. 44th St., New York, NY 10036. Attn: Mary Harden. Screenplays, teleplays, and stage plays. Unproduced writers considered. Query with synopsis, bio, resumé, and SASE. Commission: 10%. Fees: none.

LEE ALLAN AGENCY—P.O. Box 18617, Milwaukee, WI 53218. Attn: Mr. Lee A. Matthias. Screenplays. Query only, with SASE; multiple queries O.K. Commission: 10%. Fees: photocopying, shipping.

MARCIA AMSTERDAM AGENCY— 41 W. 82nd St., #9A, New York, NY 10024. Attn: Marcia Amsterdam. Screenplays and teleplays: comedy, romance, psychological suspense. Query with resumé; multiple queries O.K.; three-week exclusive for requested submissions. Commission: 10% screenplays. Fees: photocopying and shipping.

THE AUTHOR'S AGENCY—3355 N. Five Mile Rd., Suite 332, Boise, ID 83713–3925. Attn: R.J. Winchell. Screenplays and teleplays. Unproduced writers considered. Send complete typewritten manuscript with SASE. Commissions: 10%. Fees: none. "Our interests are broad. We support writers as they persevere toward excellence."

ROBERT A. FREEDMAN DRAMATIC AGENCY, INC.—1501 Broadway, Suite 2310, New York, NY 10036. Attn: Robert A. Freedman or Selma Luttinger. Screenplays, teleplays, and stage plays. Send query only; multiple queries O.K. Commission: standard. Fees: photocopying.

THE CHARLOTTE GUSAY LITERARY AGENCY—10532 Blythe Ave., Los Angeles, CA 90064. Screenplays. Query with outline, sample pages, bio/resumé, and SASE; no multiple queries. Commission: 10%.

BARBARA HOGENSON AGENCY—19 W. 44th St., Suite 1000, New York, NY 10036. Attn: Barbara Hogenson. Screenplays, teleplays, and stage plays. Query with bio and synopsis; multiple queries O.K. Commission: 10% (screenplays, teleplays); 15% (books). Fees: none.

OTTO R. KOZAK LITERARY AGENCY—P.O. Box 152, Long Beach, NY 11561. Screenplays and teleplays only. Unpublished and unproduced writers considered. Query with outline or treatment; no multiple queries. Commission: 10%. Fees: none.

THE SHUKAT COMPANY, LTD.—340 W. 55th St., Suite 1A, New York, NY 10019. Attn: Scott Shukat, Pat McLaughlin. Screenplays and stage plays. Unpublished, unproduced writers occasionally considered. Query with outline, sample pages, and bio; no multiple queries. Commission: 15%. Fees: none. "Since this is a small office, we will reply only if we are interested in the material. SASE not necessary."

RENAISSANCE/H.N. SWANSON, INC.—8523 Sunset Blvd., Los Angeles, CA 90069. Attn: Joel Gotler, Pres. Screenplays and teleplays. Unpublished, unproduced writers sometimes considered. Query first; no multiple queries. Commission: 10%. Fees: none.

THE TANTLEFF OFFICE—375 Greenwich St., Suite 700, New York, NY 10013. Attn: Jill Bock. Screenplays and teleplays. Query with synopsis, up to 10 sample pages, bio/resumé; multiple queries O.K. Commission: 10%. Fees: none.

ANN WRIGHT REPRESENTATIVES—165 W. 46th St., Suite 1105, New York, NY 10036–2501. Attn: Dan Wright. Screenplays and teleplays. Query with bio/resumé; no multiple queries. Commission: 10%. Fees: photocopying, shipping.

BOOK PUBLISHERS

The following list includes the major book publishers for adult and juvenile fiction and nonfiction and a representative number of small publishers from across the country.

Before submitting a complete manuscript to an editor, it is advisable to send a brief query letter describing the proposed book, and an SASE. The letter should also include information about the author's special qualifications for dealing with a particular topic and any previous publication credits. An outline of the book (or a synopsis for fiction) and a sample chapter may also be included.

While it is common practice to submit a book manuscript to only one publisher at a time, it is becoming more and more acceptable to submit the same query or proposal to more than one editor simultaneously. When sending multiple queries, *always* make note of it in each submission.

Book manuscripts may be sent in typing paper boxes (available from a stationery store) and sent by first-class mail, or, more common and less expensive, by "Special Fourth Class Rate—Manuscript." For rates, details of insurance, and so forth, inquire at your local post office. With any submission to a publisher, be sure to enclose sufficient postage for the manuscript's return.

Royalty rates for hardcover books usually start at 10% of the retail price of the book and increase after a certain number of copies have been sold. Paperbacks generally have a somewhat lower rate, about 5% to 8%. It is customary for the publishing company to pay the author a cash advance against royalties when the book contract is signed or when the finished manuscript is received. Some publishers pay on a flat-fee basis.

While most of the publishers on this list consider either unsolicited manuscripts or queries, an increasing number now read only agented submissions. Since finding an agent is not an easy task, especially for newcomers, writers are advised to try to sell their manuscripts directly to the publisher first. Should this fail, the *Literary Agents* list notes, among many other details, whether the work of unpublished writers is considered.

ABINGDON PRESS—P.O. Box 801, Nashville, TN 37202. Mary Catherine Dean, Sr. Ed. General-interest books: mainline, social issues, marriage/family, self-help, exceptional people. Query with outline and one or 2 sample chapters. Guidelines.

ACADEMY CHICAGO PUBLISHERS—363 W. Erie St., Chicago, IL 60610. Anita Miller, Ed. General adult fiction; classic mysteries with emphasis on character and/or puzzle. History; biographies; travel; books by and about women. Also interested in reprinting books dropped by other houses, including academic titles and anthologies. Query with 4 sample chapters. SASE required. Royalty.

ACCENT PUBLICATIONS—Box 36640, 7125 Disc Dr., Colorado Springs, CO 80936. Mary Nelson, Man. Ed. Nonfiction church resources covering every facet of Christian education for the local church; evangelical Christian perspective; no trade books. "Request guidelines before querying." Query with sample chapters and SASE. Royalty. Paperback only.

ACE BOOKS—200 Madison Ave., New York, NY 10016. Susan Allison, V.P., Ed.-in-Chief. Science fiction and fantasy. Query with first 3 chapters and outline to Laura Anne Gilman, Ed. Royalty.

ACTIVITY RESOURCES—P.O. Box 4875, Hayward, CA 94540. Mary Laycock, Ed. Math educational material only. "Our main focus is on grades K through 8." Submit complete manuscript. Royalty.

ADAMA BOOKS—See *Modan Publishing*.

ADDISON-WESLEY PUBLISHING CO.—One Jacob Way, Reading, MA 01867–3999. Attn: Ed. Dept. Adult nonfiction on current topics including science, health, psychology, business, biography, child care, etc. Specializing in literary nonfiction. Royalty.

ALASKA NORTHWEST BOOKS—2208 N.W. Market St., Suite 300, Seattle, WA 98107. Marlene Blessing, Ed.-in-Chief. Nonfiction, 50,000 to 100,000 words, with an emphasis on natural world and history of Alaska and the Pacific Northwest: travel books; cookbooks; field guides; children's books; outdoor recreation; natural history; native culture; lifestyle. Send query or sample chapters with outline. Guidelines.

ALGONQUIN BOOKS OF CHAPEL HILL—Box 2225, Chapel Hill, NC 27515. Shannon Ravenel, Ed. Dir. Trade books, fiction and nonfiction, for adults.

ALYSON PUBLICATIONS—P.O. Box 4371, Los Angeles, CA 90078.

Attn: Ed. Gay and lesbian adult fiction and nonfiction books, from 65,000 words. *Alyson Wonderland* imprint: Children's picture books with gay and lesbian themes; young adult titles, from 65,000 words. Query with outline and sample chapters. Royalty.

ALYSON WONDERLAND—See *Alyson Publications.*

AMERICAN EDUCATION PUBLISHING—150 E. Wilson Bridge Rd., Suite 145, Columbus, OH 43085. Attn: Ed. Dir. Children's books, 32 to 64 pages. Submit complete manuscript. Royalty.

AMERICAN PARADISE PUBLISHING—P.O. Box 37, St. John, USVI 00831. Gary M. Goodlander, Ed. "We are interested in 'hopelessly local' books, between 80 and 300 pages. We need useful, practical books that help our Virgin Island readers lead better and more enjoyable lives." Guidebooks, cookbooks, how-to books, books on sailing, yacht cruising, hiking, snorkeling, sportfishing, local history, and West Indian culture, specifically aimed at Caribbean readers/tourists. Query with outline and sample chapters. Royalty.

THE AMERICAN PSYCHIATRIC PRESS—1400 K St. N.W., Washington, DC 20005. Carol C. Nadelson, M.D., Ed.-in-Chief. Books that interpret scientific and medical aspects of psychiatry for a lay audience and that address specific psychiatric problems. Authors must have appropriate credentials to write on medical topics. Query required. Royalty.

AMPERSAND PRESS—Creative Writing Program, Roger Williams Univ., Bristol, RI 02809. Martha Christina, Dir. Fiction and poetry, chapbooks and full-length. Query only. Royalty.

ANCHORAGE PRESS—Box 8067, New Orleans, LA 70182. Attn: Acquisitions Ed. Dramatic publishers. Plays for children ages 4 to 18. "We publish 8 to 10 new playbooks and one to 3 new hardcover books each year." Royalty.

AND BOOKS—702 S. Michigan, South Bend, IN 46601. Janos Szebedinsky, Ed. Adult nonfiction. Topics include computers, fine arts, health, philosophy, regional subjects, and social justice.

ANHINGA PRESS—P.O. Box 10595, Tallahassee, FL 32302–0595. Rick Campbell, Ed. Poetry books. (Publishes two books a year.) Query or send complete manuscripts. Flat fee. Annual poetry prize of $1,000 plus publication; send SASE for details.

APPALACHIAN MOUNTAIN CLUB BOOKS—5 Joy St., Boston, MA 02108. Attn: Ed. Dept. Regional (New England) and national nonfiction titles, 250 to 400 pages, for adult audience; juvenile and young adult nonfiction. Topics include guidebooks on non-motorized backcountry recreation, nature, mountain history/biography, search and rescue, conservation, and environmental management. Query with outline and sample chapters. Multiple queries considered. Royalty.

APPLE SOUP BOOKS—See *Alfred A. Knopf Books for Young Readers.*

ARCADE PUBLISHING—141 Fifth Ave., New York, NY 10010. Richard Seaver, Pub./Ed. Fiction and nonfiction. No longer accepting children's books. No unsolicited manuscripts. Query.

ARCHWAY PAPERBACKS—Pocket Books, 1230 Ave. of the Americas, New York, NY 10020. Patricia MacDonald, Ed. Dir. Young adult contemporary fiction (suspense thrillers, romances) and nonfiction (popular current topics),

776

for ages 12 to 16. Send query, outline, sample chapters to Attn: Manuscript Proposals.

ARCSOFT PUBLISHERS—P.O. Box 179, Hebron, MD 21830. Anthony Curtis, Pres. Nonfiction hobby books for beginners: personal computing, space science, desktop publishing, journalism. Hobby electronics for laymen and consumers, beginners and novices. Outright purchase and royalty basis. Query. Paperback only.

ARMSTRONG PUBLISHING CORP.—55 Old Post Rd., #2, P.O. Box 1678, Greenwich, CT 06836. Herbert M. Johnson, Ed. George F. Johnson, Ed. Fiction and nonfiction picture books, 24 to 48 pages, for readers ages 3 to 11. Distributed through Taylor Publishing Company. Royalty.

ASTARTE SHELL PRESS—P.O. Box 3648, Portland, ME 04104. Sapphire, Ed. Books on theology, politics, and social issues from a feminist/woman's perspective. No poetry. Send sample chapters or complete manuscripts. Royalty.

AUGUST HOUSE—P.O. Box 3223, Little Rock, AR 72203. Books pertaining to folklore, folktales, and storytelling. Storytelling resources: picture books (featuring traditional folktales), folktale collections, instructional/how-to books, and personal story collections. Submit query letter or proposal with sample chapters.

AVALON BOOKS—401 Lafayette St., New York, NY 10003. Hank Kennedy, Pres. Marcia Markland, VP/Pub. Eleanor Wickland, Assoc. Ed. Hardcover books, 40,000 to 50,000 words: romances, mysteries, and westerns. No explicit sex. Query with first 3 chapters and outline; nonreturnable. SASE for guidelines.

AVERY PUBLISHING GROUP—120 Old Broadway, Garden City Park, NY 11040. Attn: Man. Ed. Nonfiction, from 40,000 words, on health, childbirth, child care, healthful cooking. Query with SASE. Royalty.

AVON BOOKS—1350 Ave. of the Americas, New York, NY 10019. Robert Mecoy, Ed.-in-Chief. Genre fiction, general nonfiction, historical romance, 60,000 to 200,000 words. *Avon Hardcover*: Adult commercial fiction and nonfiction. Send one- or 2-page query describing book (including its length). *Avo-Nova*: science fiction, 75,000 to 100,000 words. Query with synopsis and sample chapters. Ellen Edwards, Historical Romance; John Douglas, Science Fiction; Chris Miller, Fantasy. *Camelot Books*: Ellen Krieger, Ed. Fiction and nonfiction for 7-to 10-year-olds. Query. *Flare Books*: Ellen Krieger, Ed. Fiction and nonfiction for 12-year-olds and up. Query. Royalty. Paperback only.

AVONOVA—See *Avon Books*.

BACKCOUNTRY PUBLICATIONS—See *The Countryman Press, Inc.*

BAEN BOOKS—Baen Enterprises, P.O. Box 1403, Riverdale, NY 10471–1403. Jim Baen, Pres./Ed.-in-Chief. Strongly plotted science fiction; innovative fantasy. Query with synopsis and manuscript. Advance and royalty. Guidelines available for letter-sized SASE.

BAKER BOOK HOUSE—P. O. Box 6287, Grand Rapids, MI 49516–6287. Jane Schrier, Asst. to the Dir. of Pub. Religious nonfiction: books for trade, clergy, seminarians, collegians. Religious fiction. Royalty.

BALBOA—See *Tiare Publications*.

BALLANTINE BOOKS—201 E. 50th St., New York, NY 10022. Attn: Ed.-in-Chief. General fiction and nonfiction. Query.

BALSAM PRESS—36 E. 22nd St., 9th Fl., New York, NY 10010. Barbara Krohn, Exec. Ed. General and illustrated adult nonfiction. Query. Royalty.

BANTAM BOOKS—1540 Broadway, New York, NY 10036. Irwyn Applebaum, Pres./Pub. Adult fiction and nonfiction. Mass-market titles, submit queries to the following imprints: *Crime Line*, crime and mystery fiction; *Domain*, frontier fiction, historical sagas, traditional westerns; *Spectra*, science fiction and fantasy; *Bantam Nonfiction*, wide variety of commercial nonfiction, including true crime, health and nutrition, sports, reference. Agented queries and manuscripts only.

BANTAM, DOUBLEDAY, DELL—See *Bantam Books, Doubleday and Co.*, and *Dell Books.*

BARRICADE BOOKS—150 Fifth Ave., New York, NY 10011. Lyle Stuart, Pub. General nonfiction, celebrity biographies, controversial subjects. No fiction. Send synopsis only with SASE. Modest advances against royalties.

BARRON'S—250 Wireless Blvd., Hauppauge, NY 11788. Grace Freedson, Acquisitions Ed. Juvenile nonfiction (science, nature, history, hobbies, and how-to) and picture books for ages 3 to 6. Adult nonfiction (business, pet care, childcare, sports). Query with SASE. Guidelines.

BAUHAN, PUBLISHER, WILLIAM L.—Box 443, Dublin, NH 03444. William L. Bauhan, Ed. Biographies, fine arts, gardening, architecture, and history books with an emphasis on New England. Submit query with outline and sample chapter.

BEACH BOOKS—See *National Press Books, Inc.*

BEACON PRESS—25 Beacon St., Boston, MA 02108. Attn: Dir. Deb Chasman, Sr. Ed. General nonfiction: world affairs, women's studies, anthropology, history, philosophy, religion, gay and lesbian studies, environment, nature writing, African-American studies, Asian-American studies, Native-American studies. Series: "Concord Library" (nature writing); "Barnard New Women Poets"; "Black Women Writers" (fiction); "Men and Masculinity" (nonfiction). Query. SASE required.

BEAR & COMPANY, INC.—P.O. Drawer 2860, Santa Fe, NM 87504. Barbara Clow, Ed. Nonfiction "that will help transform our culture philosophically, environmentally, and spiritually." Query with outline, sample chapters, and SASE. Royalty.

BEECH TREE BOOKS—See *William Morrow and Co., Inc.*

BEHRMAN HOUSE—235 Watchung Ave., W. Orange, NJ 07052. Adam Siegel, Projects Ed. Adult and juvenile nonfiction, varying lengths, in English and in Hebrew, on Jewish subject matter. Query with outline and sample chapters. Flat fee.

BERKLEY PUBLISHING GROUP—200 Madison Ave., New York, NY 10016. Lou Aronica, Pub. General-interest fiction and nonfiction; science fiction, suspense, and mystery novels; romance. Submit through agent only. Publishes both reprints and originals. Paperback books, except for some hardcover mysteries and science fiction. Young adult books: Laura Anne Gilman, Ed. Horror, suspense, adventure, and romance. Query required.

THE BESS PRESS—P.O. Box 22388, Honolulu, HI 96823. Revé Shapard,

Ed. Nonfiction books about Hawaii, Asia, and the Pacific for adults, children, and young adults. Submit outline with sample chapters or complete manuscript. Royalty.

BETHANY HOUSE PUBLISHERS—11300 Hampshire Ave. S., Minneapolis, MN 55438. Attn: Ed. Dept. Religious fiction and nonfiction. Query with sample chapters. Royalty.

BETTER HOMES AND GARDENS BOOKS—See *Meredith Corp. Book Group.*

BINFORD & MORT PUBLISHING—1202 N.W. 17th Ave., Portland, OR 97209. J.F. Roberts, Ed. Books on subjects related to the Pacific Coast and the Northwest. Lengths vary. Query. Royalty.

BIRCH LANE PRESS—See *Carol Publishing Group.*

BLACK BUTTERFLY CHILDREN'S BOOKS—Writers and Readers Publishing, 625 Broadway, New York, NY 10012. Patricia Allen, Man. Ed. Titles featuring black children and other children of color. Picture books for children up to 11; board books for toddlers; juvenile fiction for all ages. Query. Royalty.

BLACK BUZZARD PRESS—1110 Seaton Ln., Falls Church, VA 22046. Bradley R. Strahan, Ed. Poetry manuscripts, to 60 pages. Query. Royalty.

BLAIR, PUBLISHER, JOHN F.—1406 Plaza Dr., Winston-Salem, NC 27103. Carolyn Sakowski, Pres. Books from 50,000 words: biography, history, folklore, and guidebooks, with southeastern tie-in. Query. Royalty.

BLUE DOLPHIN PUBLISHING, INC.—P.O. Box 1920, Nevada City, CA 95959. Paul M. Clemens, Ed. Books, 200 to 300 pages, on comparative spiritual traditions, lay and transpersonal psychology, self-help, health, healing, and social ecology. Query with outline and sample chapters. Royalty.

BONUS BOOKS—160 E. Illinois St., Chicago, IL 60611. Anne Barthel, Ed. Nonfiction; topics vary widely. Query with sample chapters and SASE. Royalty.

BOTTOM DOG PRESS—c/o Firelands College, Huron, OH 44839. Larry Smith, Dir. Collections of personal essays, 50 to 200 pages, and poetry for chapbook publication and anthologies. "Interested writers should query with SASE for information on current anthology projects." Royalty.

BOYDS MILLS PRESS—815 Church St., Honesdale, PA 18431. Beth Troop, Manuscript Coord. Hardcover trade books for children. Fiction: picture books; middle-grade fiction with fresh ideas and involving story; young adult novels of literary merit. Nonfiction should be "fun, entertaining, and informative." Send outline and sample chapters for young adult novels and nonfiction, complete manuscripts for all other categories. Royalty.

BRANDEN PUBLISHING COMPANY—17 Station St., Box 843, Brookline Village, MA 02147. Attn: Ed. Dept. Novels, biographies, and autobiographies. Especially books by or about women, 250 to 350 pages. Also considers queries on history, computers, business, performance arts, and translations. Query only with SASE. Royalty.

BRAZILLER PUBLISHERS, GEORGE—60 Madison Ave., New York, NY 10010. Attn: Ed. Dept. Fiction and nonfiction. Mostly art, art history; some profiles of writers, collections of essays and short stories, anthologies. Send art history manuscripts to Adrienne Baxter, Ed.; others to Fiction Editor. Send outline with sample chapters. Payment varies.

BREAKAWAY BOOKS—336 W. 84th St., #4, New York, NY 10024. Garth Battista, Pub. Literary sports novels and single stories and poems, any length, for anthology series. "Our goal is to bring to light literary writing on the athletic experience." Royalty.

BRETT BOOKS, INC.—P.O. Box 290–637, Brooklyn, NY 11229–0011. Barbara J. Brett, Pres./Pub. Nonfiction for adult trade market. "Submit a query letter of no more than 2 pages, stating your professional background and summarizing your book proposal in 2 to 4 paragraphs." SASE. Royalty.

BRISTOL PUBLISHING ENTERPRISES—P.O. Box 1737, San Leandro, CA 94577. Patricia J. Hall, Ed. *Nitty Gritty Cookbooks*: 120-recipe manuscripts. Query with outline, sample chapters, SASE. Royalty.

BROADMAN AND HOLMAN PUBLISHERS—127 Ninth Ave. N., Nashville, TN 37234. Richard P. Rosenbaum, Jr., Ed. Dir. Religious and inspirational nonfiction. Query with SASE. Royalty.

BROADWAY BOOKS—1540 Broadway, New York, NY 10036. William Shinker, Ed. Adult fiction and nonfiction. Query. Royalty.

BUCKNELL UNIVERSITY PRESS—Bucknell Univ., Lewisburg, PA 17837. Mills F. Edgerton, Jr., Dir. Scholarly nonfiction. Query. Royalty.

BULFINCH PRESS—34 Beacon St., Boston, MA 02108. Attn: Ed. Dept. Books on fine arts and photography. Query with outline or proposal and vita.

C&T PUBLISHING—5021 Blum Rd., #1, Martinez, CA 94553. Todd Hensley, Pres. Quilting books, 64 to 200 finished pages. "Our focus is how-to, although we will consider picture, inspirational, or history books on quilting." Send query, outline, or sample chapters. Multiple queries considered. Royalty.

CALYX BOOKS—P.O. Box B, Corvallis, OR 97339. Margarita Donnelly, Ed. Beverly McFarland, Ed. Feminist publisher. Novels, short stories, poetry, nonfiction, translations, and anthologies by women. Send SASE for guidelines before submitting. Limited market.

CAMELOT BOOKS—See *Avon Books*.

CANDLEWICK PRESS—2067 Massachusetts Ave., Cambridge, MA 02140. Attn: Ed. Dept. "Unfortunately, we are no longer able to consider any unsolicited material; it will be returned unread."

CAROL PUBLISHING GROUP—600 Madison Ave., New York, NY 10022. Allan J. Wilson, Ed. General nonfiction. *Citadel Press*: biography (celebrity preferred), autobiography, film, history, and self-help, 70,000 words. *Birch Lane Press*: adult nonfiction, 75,000 words. *Lyle Stuart*: adult nonfiction, 75,000 words, of a controversial nature, gaming, etc.; address Hillel Black, Ed. Also *University Books*. Query with SASE required. Royalty.

CAROLRHODA BOOKS—241 First Ave. N., Minneapolis, MN 55401. Rebecca Poole, Ed. Complete manuscripts for ages 4 to 12: biography, science, nature, history, photo-essays; historical fiction, 10 to 15 pages, for ages 6 to 10. Guidelines. Hardcover.

CAROUSEL PRESS—P.O. Box 6061, Albany, CA 94706–0061. Stephanie Dillon, Ed. Travel guides, especially family-oriented. Send letter, table of contents, and sample chapter. "We publish one or 2 new books each year and will consider out-of-print books that the author wants to update." Modest advance and royalty.

CARROLL AND GRAF PUBLISHERS, INC.—260 Fifth Ave., New York, NY 10001. Kent E. Carroll, Exec. Ed. General fiction and nonfiction. No unagented submissions.

CARTWHEEL BOOKS—555 Broadway, New York, NY 10012. Tina Lynch, Asst. to Ed. Dir. Picture books, fiction, and nonfiction, to about 1,000 words, for children, preschool to third grade. Royalty or flat fee. Query; no unsolicited manuscripts.

CASSANDRA PRESS—P.O. Box 150868, San Rafael, CA 94915. Attn: Ed. Dept. New age, holistic health, metaphysical, and psychological books. Query with outline and sample chapters, or complete manuscript. Include SASE. Royalty (no advance).

THE CATHOLIC UNIVERSITY OF AMERICA PRESS— 620 Michigan Ave. N.E., Washington, DC 20064. David J. McGonagle, Dir. Scholarly nonfiction: American and European history (both ecclesiastical and secular); Irish studies; American and European literature; philosophy; political theory; theology. Query with prospectus, annotated table of contents, or introduction and resumé. Royalty.

CHATHAM PRESS—P. O. Box A, Old Greenwich, CT 06870. Roger H. Lourie, Man. Dir. Books on the Northeast coast, gardening, New England maritime subjects, and the ocean. Large photography volumes. Query with outline, sample chapters, illustrations, and SASE. Royalty.

CHELSEA GREEN PUBLISHING CO.—P.O. Box 428, White River Junction, VT 05001. Jim Schley, Ed. Nonfiction: natural history, environmental issues, energy and shelter, and lifestyle books with strong backlist potential. Query with outline and SASE. Not considering any unsolicited manuscripts at this time. Royalty.

CHICAGO REVIEW PRESS— 814 N. Franklin St., Chicago, IL 60610. Amy Teschner, Ed. Nonfiction: activity books for young children, project books for ages 10 to 18, general nonfiction, architecture, pregnancy, how-to, popular science, and regional gardening and other regional topics. Query with outline and sample chapters.

CHILDREN'S LIBRARY PRESS—P.O. Box 1919, Joshua Tree, CA 92252. Attn: Acquisitions Ed. Texts for picture books. Submit complete manuscript. Royalty.

CHILTON BOOK CO.— One Chilton Way, Radnor, PA 19089. Christopher J. Kuppig, Gen. Mgr. *Wallace-Homestead Books.* Antiques and collectibles, sewing and crafts, professional/technical, and automotive topics. Query with outline, sample chapter, and SASE.

CHINA BOOKS—2929 24th St., San Francisco, CA 94110. James J. Wang, Sr. Ed. Books relating to China or Chinese culture. Adult nonfiction, varying lengths. Juvenile picture books, fiction, nonfiction, and young adult books. Query. Royalty.

CHRONICLE BOOKS—275 Fifth St., San Francisco, CA 94103. Attn: Ed. Dept. Topical nonfiction, history, biography, art, photography, architecture, design, nature, food, regional topics. Fiction. Children's books. Send proposal with SASE.

CITADEL PRESS—See *Carol Publishing Group.*

CLARION BOOKS—215 Park Ave. S., New York, NY 10003. Dorothy

Briley, Ed.-in-Chief/Pub. Fiction, nonfiction, and picture books: short novels and lively stories for ages 6 to 10 and 8 to 12, historical fiction, humor; picture books for infants and children to age 7; biography, natural history, social studies, American and world history for readers 5 to 8, and 9 up. Royalty. Hardcover.

CLEIS PRESS—P.O. Box 14684, San Francisco, CA 94114. Frédérique Delacoste, Ed. Fiction and nonfiction, 200 pages, by women. No poetry. Send SASE with 2 first-class stamps for catalogue before querying. Royalty.

COBBLEHILL BOOKS—375 Hudson St., New York, NY 10014. Joe Ann Daly, Ed. Dir. Rosanne Lauer, Exec. Ed. Fiction and nonfiction for preschoolers through junior high school. Query for manuscripts longer than picture books; send complete manuscript with SASE for picture books. Royalty.

COFFEE HOUSE PRESS—27 N. 4th St., Suite 400, Minneapolis, MN 55401. Attn: C. Hickman. Literary fiction (no genres). Query with SASE.

COMING OF AGE PRESS—14045 Robins Run, Austin, TX 78737. Connie Burton, Pub. Juvenile fiction and nonfiction, young adult books, women's fiction and nonfiction, and picture books. "We are dedicated to humane and hopeful ideals portrayed in beautiful books, carefully constructed and illustrated." Submit outline with sample chapters (complete manuscript for picture books). Royalty or flat fee.

CONCORDIA PUBLISHING HOUSE—3558 S. Jefferson Ave., St. Louis, MO 63118. Attn: Ed. Dept. Practical nonfiction with explicit religious content, conservative Lutheran doctrine. Children's fiction with explicit Christian content. No poetry. Query. Royalty.

CONFLUENCE PRESS—Lewis Clark State College, 500 8th Ave., Lewiston, ID 83502–2698. James Hepworth, Dir. Fiction, nonfiction, and poetry, of varying lengths, "to promote and nourish young writers, in particular, to achieve literary and artistic excellence." Send query, outline, and sample chapters. Flat fee or royalty.

CONSUMER REPORTS BOOKS—101 Truman Ave., Yonkers, NY 10703. Mark Hoffman, Ed. Medicine/health, food/nutrition, personal finance, retirement planning, automotive, home maintenance. Submit complete manuscript, or send contents, outline, 3 chapters, and resumé.

CONTEMPORARY BOOKS, INC.—2 Prudential Plaza, Suite 1200, Chicago, IL 60601–6790. Nancy Crossman, Ed. Dir. Trade nonfiction, 100 to 400 pages, on health, fitness, sports, cooking, humor, business, popular culture, biography, real estate, finance, women's issues. Query with outline, sample chapters, and SASE. Royalty.

COPPER BEECH BOOKS—The Millbrook Press, 2 Old New Milford Rd., Brookfield, CT 06804. Sheilah Holmes, Ed. Nonfiction books for children, preschool to age 12. Series include books based on words, on "what if" scenarios, and world mysteries and "fact or fiction" issues. Query with outline and sample chapter. Royalty.

COTLER BOOKS, JOANNA—See *HarperCollins Children's Books.*

THE COUNTRYMAN PRESS, INC.—P.O. Box 175, Woodstock, VT 05091–0175. Laura Jorstad, Man. Ed. Imprints: *Backcountry Publications, Foul Play Press.* Nonfiction: Country living; gardening; nature/environment; how-to; travel guidebooks; regional guidebooks on hiking, walking, canoeing, bicycling, mountain biking, cross-country skiing, and flyfishing for all parts of the country. Fiction: mystery. Submit query or outline and 3 sample chapters, along with SASE. Royalty.

CRAFTSMAN BOOK COMPANY— 6058 Corte del Cedro, P.O. Box 6500, Carlsbad, CA 92018. Laurence D. Jacobs, Ed. How-to construction and estimating manuals and software for professional builders, 450 pages. Query. Royalty. Paperback.

CREATIVE ARTS BOOK CO.— 833 Bancroft Way, Berkeley, CA 94710. Donald S. Ellis, Pub. Adult nonfiction: women's issues, music, African-American and Asian, and California topics. Query with outline, sample chapters, SASE. Royalty.

CRIME LINE—See *Bantam Books.*

THE CROSSING PRESS—P.O. Box 1048, Freedom, CA 95019. Elaine Goldman Gill, John Gill, Pubs. Health, holistic health, men's studies, feminist studies, spiritual works, gay topics, cookbooks. Royalty.

CROWN BOOKS FOR YOUNG READERS—201 E. 50th St., New York, NY 10022. Simon Boughton, Pub. Dir. Arthur Levine, Ed.-in-Chief. Children's nonfiction (science, sports, nature, music, and history) and picture books for ages 3 and up. Query. Guidelines.

CROWN PUBLISHERS—201 E. 50th St. New York, NY 10022. Attn: Ed. Adult fiction and nonfiction.

DANIEL AND COMPANY, JOHN—P.O. Box 21922, Santa Barbara, CA 93121. John Daniel, Pub. Books, to 200 pages, in the field of belles lettres and literary memoirs; stylish and elegant writing; essays and short fiction dealing with social issues; one poetry title per year. Send synopsis or outline with no more than 50 sample pages and SASE. Allow 6 to 8 weeks for response. Royalty.

DAVIS PUBLICATIONS, INC.—50 Portland St., Worcester, MA 01608. Wyatt Wade, Ed. Books for the art education market; mainly for teachers of art, grades K through 12, 100 to 300 manuscript pages. Must have an educational component. Grades K through 8, address Claire M. Golding; grades 9 through 12, address Helen Ronan. Query with outline and sample chapters. Royalty.

DAW BOOKS, INC.—375 Hudson St., 3rd Fl., New York, NY 10014–3658. Elizabeth R. Wollheim, Ed.-in-Chief. Sheila E. Gilbert, Sr. Ed. Peter Stampfel, Submissions Ed. Science fiction and fantasy, 60,000 to 120,000 words. Royalty.

DAWN PUBLICATIONS—14618 Tyler Foote Rd., Nevada City, CA 95959. Glenn J. Hovemann, Ed. Dept. Nature awareness books highlighting nature's power to enliven the human soul. Health and healing books that aim to help people rise to their highest potential, physically, mentally, and spiritually. Children's picture books with a positive, uplifting message to awaken a sense of appreciation and kinship with nature. Submit table of contents, synopsis, sample chapters. For children's works, submit complete manuscript and specify intended age. Guidelines. Royalty.

DEARBORN FINANCIAL PUBLISHING, INC.—155 N. Wacker Dr., Chicago, IL 60606–1719. Anita A. Constant, Sr. V.P. Books on financial services, real estate, banking, small business, etc. Query with outline and sample chapters. Royalty and flat fee.

DEL REY BOOKS—201 E. 50th St., New York, NY 10022. Shelly Shapiro, Exec. Ed. Veronica Chapman, Sr. Ed. Science fiction and fantasy, 60,000 to 120,000 words; first novelists welcome. Material must be well paced with logical resolutions. Fantasy with magic basic to plotline. Send manuscript or outline with 3 sample chapters. Include manuscript-size SASE. Royalty.

DELACORTE PRESS—1540 Broadway, New York, NY 10036. Leslie Schnur, Jackie Farber, Trish Todd, Jackie Cantor, Eds. Adult fiction and nonfiction. Accepts fiction (mystery, young adult, romance, fantasy, etc.) from agents only.

DELANCEY PRESS—P.O. Box 40285, Philadelphia, PA 19106. Wesley Morrison, Ed. Dir. All types of nonfiction, 60,000 words. No fiction. Query. Royalty.

DELL BOOKS—1540 Broadway, New York, NY 10036. Attn: Editorial Dept., Book Proposal. Commercial fiction and nonfiction, family sagas, historical romances, war action, general fiction, occult/horror/psychological suspense, true crime, men's adventure. Send narrative synopsis for fiction (to 4 pages) or outline (also to 4 pages) for nonfiction. Enclose SASE. No poetry. Allow 2 to 3 months for response.

DEVIN-ADAIR PUBLISHERS, INC.—6 N. Water St., Greenwich, CT 06830. J. Andrassi, Ed. Books on conservative affairs, Irish topics, photography, Americana, self-help, health, gardening, cooking, and ecology. Send outline, sample chapters, and SASE. Royalty.

DI CAPUA BOOKS, MICHAEL—See *HarperCollins Children's Books.*

DIAL PRESS—1540 Broadway, New York, NY 10036. Susan Kamil, Ed. Dir. Quality fiction and nonfiction. No unsolicited material.

DOMAIN—See *Bantam Books.*

DOUBLEDAY AND CO.—1540 Broadway, New York, NY 10036. Arlene Friedman, Pub./Pres. Proposals from literary agents only. No unsolicited material.

DOWN HOME PRESS—P.O. Box 4126, Asheboro, NC 27204. Jerry Bledsoe, Ed. Nonfiction books related to the Carolinas and the South. Query or send complete manuscript. Royalty.

DUNNE BOOKS, THOMAS—175 Fifth Ave., New York, NY 10010. Thomas L. Dunne, Ed. Adult fiction (mysteries, trade, etc.) and nonfiction (history, biographies, science, politics, etc.). Query with outline, sample chapters, and SASE. Royalty.

DUQUESNE UNIVERSITY PRESS—600 Forbes Ave., Pittsburgh, PA 15282–0101. Attn: Ed. Dept. Scholarly publications in the humanities and social sciences; creative nonfiction (book-length only) by emerging writers. Guidelines.

DUTTON ADULT—375 Hudson St., New York, NY 10014. Arnold Dolin, Ed. Dir. Fiction and nonfiction books. Manuscripts accepted only from agents or on personal recommendation.

DUTTON CHILDREN'S BOOKS—375 Hudson St., New York, NY 10014. Lucia Monfried, Ed.-in-Chief. Picture books, easy-to-read books; fiction and nonfiction for preschoolers to young adults. Submit outline and first 3 chapters with query for fiction and nonfiction, complete manuscripts for picture books and easy-to-read books. Manuscripts should be well written with fresh ideas and child appeal. Include SASE.

EAKIN PRESS—P.O. Drawer 90159, Austin, TX 78709–0159. Melissa Roberts, Sr. Ed. Adult nonfiction, 60,000 to 80,000 words: Texana, regional cookbooks, Mexico and the Southwest, WWII, military. Children's books: history, culture, geography, etc., of Texas and the Southwest. Juvenile picture books, 5,000 to 10,000 words; fiction, 20,000 to 30,000 words; young adult fiction, 25,000 to 40,000 words. Query. Royalty.

EASTERN WASHINGTON UNIVERSITY PRESS—Mail Stop 14, Eastern Washington Univ., 526 5th St., Cheney, WA 99004–2431. Attn: Eds. Literary essays, history, social commentary, and other academic subjects. Limited fiction (one title every 2 years or so). One or 2 books of poetry, 60 to 150 pages, each year. "We are a small regional university press, publishing titles that reflect regional service, our international contacts, our strong creative writing program, and research and interests of our exceptional faculty." Query with outline. Royalty.

THE ECCO PRESS—100 W. Broad St., Hopewell, NJ 08525. Daniel Halpern, Ed. Fiction, poetry, literary criticism, and translations. Send query and sample chapter.

EERDMANS PUBLISHING COMPANY, INC., WM. B.—255 Jefferson Ave. S.E., Grand Rapids, MI 49503. Jon Pott, Ed.-in-Chief. Protestant, Roman Catholic, and Orthodox theological nonfiction; American religious history; ethics; philosophy; history; spiritual growth. For children's religious books, query Amy Eerdmans, Children's Book Ed. Royalty.

ELDER BOOKS—P.O. Box 490, Forest Knolls, CA 94933. Attn: Ed. Books related to aging, health, and Alzheimer's. Human-interest, how-to, and inspirational books. Send complete manuscript; no multiple submissions. Allow 3 months for response. Royalty.

ELEMENT BOOKS— 42 Broadway, Rockport, MA 01966. Paul Cash, Acquisitions Ed. Books on world religions, ancient wisdom, astrology, meditation, and women's studies. Study recent catalogue. Query with outline and sample chapters. Royalty.

EMC CORP.—300 York Ave., St. Paul, MN 55101. Eileen Slater, Ed. Vocational, career, and consumer education textbooks. Royalty. No unsolicited manuscripts.

ENSLOW PUBLISHERS, INC.—P.O. Box 605, 44 Fadem Rd., Springfield, NJ 07081. Brian D. Enslow, Ed./Pub. Nonfiction books for young people. Areas of emphasis are children's and young adult books for ages 10 to 18 in the fields of social studies, science, and biography. Also reference books for all ages and easy reading books for teenagers.

EPICENTER PRESS—P.O. Box 60529, Fairbanks, AK 99706. Lael Morgan, Ed. Quality nonfiction trade books, contemporary western art and photography titles, and destination travel guides emphasizing the Pacific Northwest. "We are a regional press whose interests include but are not limited to the arts, history, environment, and diverse cultures and lifestyles of the North Pacific and high latitudes." Flat fee.

ERIKSSON, PUBLISHER, PAUL S.—P.O. Box 62, Forest Dale, VT 05745. Attn: Ed. Dept. General nonfiction (send outline and cover letter); some fiction (send 3 chapters with query). Royalty.

EVANS & CO., INC., M.—216 E. 49th St., New York, NY 10017. Attn: Ed. Dept. Books on humor, health, self-help, popular psychology, and cookbooks. Western fiction for adults; fiction and nonfiction for young adults. Query with outline, sample chapter, and SASE. Royalty.

EVENT HORIZON PRESS—P.O. Box 867, Desert Hot Springs, CA 92240. Joseph Cowles, Pub. Adult fiction and nonfiction. Poetry books, from 50 pages. Query.

EXCALIBUR PUBLICATIONS—Box 36, Latham, NY 12110–0036. Alan M. Petrillo, Ed. Books on military history, firearms history, antique arms and accessories, military personalities, tactics and strategy, history of battles. Query with outline and sample chapters. SASE. Royalty or flat fee.

FABER AND FABER—53 Shore Dr., Winchester, MA 01890. Attn: Ed. Dept. Novels, anthologies, and nonfiction books on topics of popular culture and general interest. Query with SASE. Royalty.

FACTS ON FILE PUBLICATIONS— 460 Park Ave. S., New York, NY 10016. Susan Schwartz, Ed. Dir. Reference and trade books on science, health, literature, language, history, the performing arts, ethnic studies, popular culture, sports, etc. (No fiction, poetry, computer books, technical books or cookbooks.) Query with outline, sample chapter, and SASE. Royalty. Hardcover.

FANFARE—1540 Broadway, New York, NY 10036. Beth de Guzman, Wendy McCurdy, Sr. Eds. Shawna Summers, Assoc. Ed. Historical and contemporary adult women's fiction, about 90,000 to 150,000 words. Study field before submitting. Query. Paperback and hardcover.

FARRAR, STRAUS & GIROUX—19 Union Sq. W., New York, NY 10003. Adult and juvenile literary fiction and nonfiction. No guidelines or catalogue available.

FAWCETT/IVY BOOKS—201 E. 50th St., New York, NY 10022. Barbara Dicks, Exec. Ed. Adult mysteries, regencies, and historical romances, 75,000 to 120,000 words. Mysteries and problem novels, 60,000 to 70,000 words, for young adults. "In the last year, all our acquisitions have been through agents." Query with outline and sample chapters. Average response time is 3 to 6 months. Royalty.

THE FEMINIST PRESS AT THE CITY UNIVERSITY OF NEW YORK— 311 E. 94th St., New York, NY 10128. Florence Howe, Pub. Reprints of significant "lost" fiction, original memoirs, autobiographies, biographies; multicultural anthologies; handbooks; bibliographies. "We are especially interested in international literature, women and peace, women and music, and women of color." Royalty.

FINE, DONALD I.—375 Hudson St., New York, NY 10014. Attn: Ed. Dept. Literary and commercial fiction. General nonfiction. No queries or unsolicited manuscripts. Submit through agent only.

FIREBRAND BOOKS—141 The Commons, Ithaca, NY 14850. Nancy K. Bereano, Ed. Feminist and lesbian fiction and nonfiction. Royalty. Paperback and library edition cloth.

FIRESIDE BOOKS—1230 Ave. of the Americas, New York, NY 10020. No unsolicited manuscripts.

FLARE BOOKS—See *Avon Books*.

FLORES PUBLICATIONS, J.—P.O. Box 830131, Miami, FL 33283–0131.

Eli Flores, Ed. Books, 30,000 to 80,000 words, on business, personal finance. Query with outline and sample chapters. Royalty.

FONT & CENTER PRESS—P.O. Box 95, Weston, MA 02193. Ilene Horowitz, Ed./Pub. Cookbooks. How-to books. Alternative history for adults and young adults. Send proposal, outline, and sample chapter(s). Responds in 3 months. SASE. Royalty.

FORTRESS PRESS— 426 S. Fifth St., Box 1209, Minneapolis, MN 55440. Dr. Marshall D. Johnson, Dir. Books in the areas of biblical studies, theology, ethics, and church history for academic and professional markets, including libraries. Query.

FOUL PLAY PRESS—See *The Countryman Press, Inc.*

THE FREE PRESS— 866 Third Ave., New York, NY 10022. Michael Jacobs, Ed. Trade books.

FREE SPIRIT PUBLISHING— 400 First Ave. N., Suite 616, Minneapolis, MN 55401–1730. M. Elizabeth Salzmann, Ed. Asst. Adult books, varying lengths, related to raising, counseling, and/or educating children. Very limited market for juvenile fiction and picture books (pre-K through 12th grade) on self-esteem, emotional or mental health, social skills, school success, self-help for kids, etc. Query with outline and sample chapter for nonfiction; complete manuscript for juvenile fiction. "Request free catalogue and submission guidelines before submitting." Royalty.

FULCRUM PUBLISHING—350 Indiana St., Suite 350, Golden, CO 80401. Attn: Submissions Dept. Adult trade nonfiction: travel, nature, American history, biography, self-help, and gardening. No fiction. Send cover letter, sample chapters, table of contents, author credentials, and market analysis. Royalty.

FULL COURT PRESS BOOKS—See *National Press Books, Inc.*

GARLIC PRESS—See *National Press Books, Inc.*

GARRETT PARK PRESS—P.O. Box 190, Garrett Park, MD 20896. Robert Calvert, Jr., Pub. Reference books on career education, occupational guidance, and financial aid only. Query required. Multiple queries discouraged. Royalty.

GEORGIA STATE UNIVERSITY BUSINESS PRESS—University Plaza, Atlanta, GA 30303–3093. Attn: Ed. Dept. Books, software, research monographs, and directories in the business sciences and related disciplines.

GERINGER BOOKS, LAURA—See *HarperCollins Children's Books.*

GIBBS SMITH PUBLISHER—P.O. Box 667, Layton, UT 84401. Madge Baird, Ed. Dir. Adult nonfiction. Query. Royalty.

GINIGER CO. INC., THE K.S.—250 W. 57th St., Suite 519, New York, NY 10107. Attn: Ed. Dept. General nonfiction. Query with SASE; no unsolicited manuscripts. Royalty.

GLENBRIDGE PUBLISHING LTD.— 6010 W. Jewell Ave., Lakewood, CO 80232. James A. Keene, Ed. Nonfiction books on a variety of topics, including business, history, and psychology. Query with sample chapter. Royalty.

GLOBE PEQUOT PRESS, THE— 6 Business Park Rd., Box 833, Old Saybrook, CT 06475. Laura Strom, Acquisitions Ed. Nonfiction with national and regional focus; travel; outdoor recreation; personal finance; home-based business; cooking. Query with sample chapter, contents, and one-page synopsis. SASE required. Royalty or flat fee.

GOLD EAGLE—See *Worldwide Library.*

GOLDEN PRESS—See *Western Publishing Co., Inc.*

GOLDEN WEST PUBLISHERS— 4113 N. Longview, Phoenix, AZ 85014. Hal Mitchell, Ed. Cookbooks and nonfiction Western history and travel books. Query. Royalty or flat fee.

GOODFELLOW PRESS—7710 196th Ave. N.E., Redmond, WA 98053. Pamela R. Goodfellow, Pub. Novels, 85,000 to 120,000 words, about men and women dealing with their worlds, overcoming obstacles, and fulfilling dreams. Send for guidelines. Royalty.

GRAYWOLF PRESS—2402 University Ave., Suite 203, St. Paul, MN 55114. Attn: Ed. Dept. Literary fiction (short story collections and novels), poetry, and essays.

GREAT QUOTATIONS—1967 Quincy Ct., Glendale Heights, IL 60139. Ringo Suek, Ed. General adult titles, 80 to 200 pages, with strong, clever, descriptive titles and brief, upbeat text. "We publish small, quick-read gift books." Query with outline and sample chapters or send complete manuscript. Royalty.

GREENWILLOW BOOKS—1350 Ave. of the Americas, New York, NY 10019. Susan Hirschman, Ed.-in-Chief. Children's books for all ages. Picture books.

GROSSET AND DUNLAP, INC.—200 Madison Ave., New York, NY 10016. Jane O'Connor, Pub. Mass-market children's books. Query required. Royalty.

GROVE/ATLANTIC MONTHLY PRESS— 841 Broadway, New York, NY 10003–4793. Morgan Entrekin, Pub. Distinguished fiction and nonfiction. Query; no unsolicited manuscripts. Royalty.

GULLIVER BOOKS—See *Harcourt Brace & Co. Children's Book Div.*

HACHAI PUBLISHING—156 Chester Ave., Brooklyn, NY 11218. Dina Rosenfeld, Ed. Full-color children's picture books, 32 pages, for readers ages 2 to 8; Judaica, Bible tales. Query or send complete manuscript. Flat fee.

HAMMOND, INC.—515 Valley St., Maplewood, NJ 07040. Charles Lees, Ed. Nonfiction: cartographic reference, travel. Query with outline and sample chapters. SASE required. Payment varies.

HANCOCK HOUSE PUBLISHERS, LTD.—1431 Harrison Ave., Blaine, WA 98230. Attn: Ed. Dept. Adult nonfiction: guidebooks, biographies, natural history, popular science, conservation, animal husbandry, falconry, and sports. Some juvenile nonfiction. Query with outline and sample chapters or send complete manuscript. Multiple queries considered. Royalty.

HARCOURT BRACE & CO.—525 B St., Suite 1900, San Diego, CA 92101. Attn: Ed. Dept. Adult trade nonfiction and fiction. No unsolicited manuscripts or queries.

HARCOURT BRACE & CO. CHILDREN'S BOOK DIV.—525 B St., Suite 1900, San Diego, CA 92101–4495. Attn: Manuscript Submissions. Juvenile fiction and nonfiction for beginning readers through young adults under the following imprints: *HB Children's Books, Gulliver Books, Jane Yolen Books, Odyssey Paperbacks,* and *Voyager Paperbacks.* Submissions accepted from agents only.

HARCOURT BRACE PROFESSIONAL PUBLISHING—525 B St., Suite 1900, San Diego, CA 92101. Attn: Ed. Dept. Professional books for practitioners in accounting, auditing, tax. Query required. Royalty.

HARDSCRABBLE BOOKS—See *Univ. Press of New England.*

HARLEQUIN BOOKS/CANADA—225 Duncan Mill Rd., Don Mills, Ont., Canada M3B 3K9. *Mira Books*: Dianne Moggy, Sr. Ed. Contemporary women's fiction, 100,000 words. Query. *Harlequin Superromance*: Paula Eykelhof, Sr. Ed. Contemporary romance, 85,000 words, with a mainstream edge. Query. *Harlequin Temptation*: Birgit Davis-Todd, Sr. Ed. Sensuous, humorous contemporary romances, 60,000 words. Query.

HARLEQUIN BOOKS/U.S.—300 E. 42nd St., 6th Fl., New York, NY 10017. Debra Matteucci, Sr. Ed. Contemporary romances, 70,000 to 75,000 words. Send for tip sheets. *Harlequin American Romances*: bold, exciting romantic adventures, "where anything is possible and dreams come true." *Harlequin Intrigue*: set against a backdrop of mystery and suspense, worldwide locales. Query. Paperback.

HARPERCOLLINS CHILDREN'S BOOKS—10 E. 53rd St., New York, NY 10022–5299. Katrin Magnusson, Admin. Coord. Picture books, chapter books, and fiction and nonfiction for middle-grade and young adult readers. "Our imprints (*HarperTrophy* paperbacks, *Joanna Cotler Books, Michael di Capua Books, Harper Junior Books*, and *Laura Geringer Books*) are committed to producing imaginative and responsible children's books. All publish from preschool to young adult titles." Guidelines. Royalty.

HARPERCOLLINS PUBLISHERS—10 E. 53rd St., New York, NY 10022–5299. Adult Trade Department: Address Man. Ed. Fiction, nonfiction (biography, history, etc.), reference. Submissions from agents only. College texts: Address College Dept. No unsolicited manuscripts; query only.

HARPERCOLLINS SAN FRANCISCO—1160 Battery St., San Francisco, CA 94111–1213. Attn: Acquisitions Ed. Books on spirituality and religion. No unsolicited manuscripts; query required.

HARPERCOLLINS WEST—1160 Battery St., San Francisco, CA 94111–1213. Attn: Acquisitions Ed. General interest books and information products about the Pacific Northwest, northern California, the Rocky Mountain region, southern California, the Southwest, and the Pacific Rim. "We want to combine unique titles of local and regional interest with those of importance to the national book markets." Query. Royalty.

HARPERPRISM—10 E. 53rd St., New York, NY 10022–5299. John Silbersack, Ed.-in-Chief. Christopher Schelling, Exec. Ed. Caitlin Blasdell, Asst. Ed. Science fiction/fantasy. No unsolicited manuscripts; query.

HARPERTROPHY—See *HarperCollins Children's Books.*

HARVARD COMMON PRESS—535 Albany St., Boston, MA 02118. Bruce Shaw, Ed. Adult nonfiction: cookbooks, travel guides, books on family matters, health, small business, etc. Send outline and sample chapters or complete manuscript. SASE. Royalty.

HARVARD UNIVERSITY PRESS—79 Garden St., Cambridge, MA 02138–1499. No free-lance submissions.

HARVEST HOUSE PUBLISHERS—1075 Arrowsmith, Eugene, OR 97402. LaRae Weiker, Ed. Mgr. Nonfiction with evangelical theme: how-tos, marriage, women, contemporary issues. Fiction. No biographies, autobiographies, history, music books, or poetry. Query with SASE.

HAWORTH PRESS, INC.—10 Alice St., Binghamton, NY 13904–1580. Bill Palmer, Ed. Scholarly press interested in research-based adult nonfiction: psychology, social work, women's studies, family and marriage; some recreation and entertainment. Send outline with sample chapters or complete manuscript. Royalty.

HAY HOUSE—P.O. Box 6204, Carson, CA 90749–6204. Attn: Ed. Dir. Metaphysical books on health, self-awareness, spiritual growth, and the environment. Query with outline and sample chapters. Royalties.

HAZELDEN EDUCATIONAL MATERIALS—Box 176, Center City, MN 55012. Betty Christiansen, Assoc. Ed. Self-help books, 100 to 400 pages, relating to addiction, recovery, spirituality, and wholeness. Query with outline and sample chapters. Multiple queries considered. Royalty.

HEALTH COMMUNICATIONS, INC.—3201 S.W. 15th St., Deerfield Beach, FL 33442. Christine Belleris, Ed. Dir. Books, 250 pages, on self-help, recovery, and personal growth for adults. Query with outline and sample chapter, or send manuscript with SASE. Royalty.

HEALTH PRESS—P.O. Box 1388, Santa Fe, NM 87504. Diane Fraser, Ed. Health-related adult and children's books, 100 to 300 pages. "We're seeking cutting-edge, original manuscripts that will excite, educate, and help readers." Author must have credentials, or preface/intro must be written by M.D., Ph.D., etc. Controversial topics are desired; must be well researched and documented. Submit outline, table of contents, and first chapter with SASE. Royalty.

HEARST BOOKS and HEARST MARINE BOOKS—See *William Morrow and Co., Inc.*

HEINEMANN—361 Hanover St., Portsmouth, NH 03801. Attn: Ed. Dept. Practical theatre, world literature, and literacy education. Query.

HEMINGWAY WESTERN STUDIES SERIES—Boise State Univ., 1910 University Dr., Boise, ID 83725. Tom Trusky, Ed. Artists' and eccentric books (multiple editions) relating to Rocky Mountain environmental, racial, religious, gender and other public issues. Guidelines.

HERALD PRESS—616 Walnut Ave., Scottdale, PA 15683. Attn: Ed. Dept. Christian books for adults and children: inspiration, Bible study, self-help, devotionals, current issues, peace studies, church history, missions, evangelism, family life, fiction, and personal experience. Send one-page summary and 2 sample chapters. Royalty.

HIGGINSON BOOK COMPANY—148 Washington St., Salem, MA 01970. E. Wheeldon, Ed. Dept. Nonfiction genealogy and local history, 20 to 1,000 pages. Specializes in reprints. Query. Royalty.

HIGHSMITH PRESS—P.O. Box 800, Fort Atkinson, WI 53538–0800. Donald Sager, Pub. Adult books, 80 to 360 pages, on professional library science, education, and reference. Teacher activity and curriculum resource books, 48 to 240 pages, for pre-K through 12. Query with outline and sample chapters. Royalty.

HOLIDAY HOUSE, INC.— 425 Madison Ave., New York, NY 10017. Margery S. Cuyler, V. P. Ashley Mason, Assoc. Ed. General juvenile fiction and nonfiction. Submit complete manuscript or 3 sample chapters and summary; enclose SASE. Royalty. Hardcover only.

HOLT AND CO., HENRY—115 W. 18th St., New York, NY 10011. Bruno Quinson, Pub. Distinguished works of biography, history, fiction, and natural history; humor; child activity books; parenting books; books for the entrepreneurial business person; and health books. "Virtually all submissions come from literary agents or from writers whom we publish. We do not accept unsolicited submissions."

HOME BUILDER PRESS—Nat'l Assoc. of Home Builders, 1201 15th St. N.W., Washington, DC 20005–2800. Doris M. Tennyson, Sr. Ed. How-to and business management books, 150 to 200 manuscript pages, for builders, remodelers, and developers. Writers should be experts in homebuilding, remodeling, land development and related aspects of the building industry. Query with outline and sample chapter. Royalty. For author's packet, call John Tuttle (800) 368–5242, ext. 222.

HOUGHTON MIFFLIN COMPANY—222 Berkeley St., Boston, MA 02116–3764. Attn: Ed. Dept. Fiction: literary, historical. Nonfiction: history, biography, psychology. No unsolicited submissions. Children's book division, address Children's Trade Books: picture books, fiction, and nonfiction for all ages. Query. Royalty.

HP BOOKS—200 Madison Ave., New York, NY 10016. Attn: Ed. Dept. Illustrated how-tos on cooking, gardening, automotive topics. Query with SASE. Royalty.

HUMANICS PUBLISHING GROUP—P.O. Box 7400, Atlanta, GA 30309. W. Arthur Bligh, Acquisitions Ed. Inspiring trade books, 100 to 300 pages: self help, spiritual, instructional, and health for body, mind, and soul. "We are interested in books that people go to for help, guidance, and inspiration." Query with outline required. Royalty.

HUNGRY MIND PRESS—57 Macalester St., St. Paul, MN 55105. David Unowsky, Ed. Gail See, Ed. Biographies and memoirs; contemporary affairs; cookbooks; cultural criticism; nature writing; spiritual reflection; and travel essays. "Books that examine the human experience, encourage reflection, and enrich everyday life. We want to involve writers in the planning and marketing of their books and build a strong relationship with booksellers." Query with outline. Royalty.

HUNTER PUBLISHING, INC.—300 Raritan Center Pkwy., Edison, NJ 08818. Kim André, Acquisitions Dept. Adventure travel guides to the U.S., South America, and the Caribbean.

HYPERION—114 Fifth Ave., New York, NY 10011. Material accepted from agents only. No unsolicited manuscripts or queries considered.

INDIANA UNIVERSITY PRESS— 601 N. Morton St., Bloomington, IN 47404–3797. Attn: Ed. Dept. Scholarly nonfiction, especially cultural studies, literary criticism, music, history, women's studies, African-American studies, science, philosophy, African studies, Middle East studies, Russian studies, anthropology, regional, etc. Query with outline and sample chapters. Royalty.

INTERNATIONAL MARINE—Box 220, Camden, ME 04843. Jonathan Eaton, Ed. Dir., John Kettlewell, Acquisitions Ed. Books on boating (sailing and power).

INTIMATE MOMENTS—See *Silhouette Books.*

IRON CROWN ENTERPRISES—P.O. Box 1605, Charlottesville, VA 22902. Jessica Ney-Grimm, Ed. Supplemental texts, 80,000 to 230,000 words, to accompany fantasy role-playing games. Extremely specific market. "Study one of our existing products before querying." Royalty or flat fee.

ISLAND PRESS—1718 Connecticut Ave. N.W., Suite 300, Washington, DC 20009. Charles C. Savitt, Pub. Nonfiction focusing on natural history, literary science, the environment, and natural resource management. "We want solution-oriented material to solve environmental problems. For our imprint, *Shearwater Books*, we want books that express new insights about nature and the environment." Query or send manuscript. SASE required.

JAI PRESS, INC.—55 Old Post Rd., #2, P.O. Box 1678, Greenwich, CT 06836. Herbert Johnson, Ed. Research and technical reference books on such subjects as business, economics, management, sociology, political science, and computer science. Query or send complete manuscript. Royalty.

JALMAR PRESS—2625 Skypark Dr., Suite 204, Torrance, CA 90505. Catherine Montgomery, Dir. Acquisitions & Development. Nonfiction books for parents and teachers to help students increase self-awareness. Multiple queries considered. Submit outline. Royalty.

JAMES BOOKS, ALICE—Univ. of Maine at Farmington, 98 Main St., Farmington, ME 04938. Jean Amaral, Program Dir. "Shared-work cooperative" publishes books of poetry (72 to 80 pages) by writers living in New England. Manuscripts read in September and January. "We emphasize the publication of poetry by women and poets of color, but also welcome and publish manuscripts by men." Authors paid with 100 copies of their books. Write for guidelines. Holds national competition for Beatrice Hawley Award; see Literary Prize Offers.

THE JOHNS HOPKINS UNIVERSITY PRESS—2715 N. Charles St., Baltimore, MD 21218. No unsolicited poetry or fiction considered.

JOHNSON BOOKS, INC.—1880 S. 57th Ct., Boulder, CO 80301. Barbara Mussil, Pub. Nonfiction: environmental subjects, archaeology, geology, natural history, astronomy, travel guides, outdoor guidebooks, fly fishing, regional. Query. Royalty.

JONATHAN DAVID PUBLISHERS, INC.—68–22 Eliot Ave., Middle Village, NY 11379. Alfred J. Kolatch, Ed.-in-Chief. General nonfiction (how-to, sports, cooking and food, self-help, etc.) and books on Judaica. Query with outline, sample chapter, resumé, and SASE. Royalty or outright purchase.

JOVE BOOKS—200 Madison Ave., New York, NY 10016. Fiction and nonfiction. No unsolicited manuscripts.

JUST US BOOKS—356 Glenwood Ave., East Orange, NJ 07017. Cheryl Hudson, Ed. Children's books celebrating African-American heritage. Picture books, 24 to 32 pages. Chapter books and biographies, from 2,500 words. Queries with SASE required; no unsolicited manuscripts. Royalty or flat fee.

KALMBACH BOOKS—21027 Crossroads Cir., Waukesha, WI 53187.

Terry Spohn, Sr. Acquisitions Ed. Adult nonfiction, 18,000 to 50,000 words, on scale modeling, model railroading, miniatures, and amateur astronomy. Send outline with sample chapters. Accepts multiple queries. Royalty.

KAR-BEN COPIES— 6800 Tildenwood Ln., Rockville, MD 20852. Judye Groner, Ed. Books on Jewish themes for preschool and elementary children (to age 9): picture books, fiction, and nonfiction. Complete manuscript preferred; SASE. Flat fee and royalty.

KEATS PUBLISHING, INC.—27 Pine St., Box 876, New Canaan, CT 06840. Norman Goldfind, Pub. Nonfiction: health, how-to. Query. Royalty.

KENSINGTON BOOKS— 850 Third Ave., New York, NY 10022. Sarah Gallick, Exec. Ed. Mainstream fiction and nonfiction. Mysteries. Send synopsis and sample chapters. Royalty.

KENT STATE UNIVERSITY PRESS—Kent State Univ., Kent, OH 44242. John T. Hubbell, Dir. Julia Morton, Sr. Ed. Interested in scholarly works in history, biography, archaeology, the arts; literary studies of high quality; titles of regional Ohio interest; and general nonfiction.

KIVAKI PRESS—585 E. 31st St., Durango, CO 81301. Greg Cumberford, Pub. Nonfiction books for the academic, holistic health, and environmental markets covering such topics as person/place narratives, ecological restoration, deep ecology, and indigenous epistemologies. Complete manuscript may be submitted on disk with hard copy of synopsis. If not submitting on disk, send synopsis only for manuscripts over 200 pages. Royalty. Reports in 6 to 8 weeks.

KNOPF BOOKS FOR YOUNG READERS, ALFRED A.—201 E. 50th St., New York, NY 10022. Arthur Levine, Ed.-in-Chief. *Apple Soup Books.* Distinguished juvenile fiction and nonfiction. Query; no unsolicited manuscripts. Royalty. Guidelines.

KNOPF, INC., ALFRED A.—201 E. 50th St., New York, NY 10022. Attn: Sr. Ed. Distinguished adult fiction and general nonfiction. Query. Royalty.

KODANSHA AMERICA, INC.—114 Fifth Ave., New York, NY 10011. Attn: Ed. Dept. Books, 50,000 to 200,000 words, on cross-cultural, Asian and other international subjects. Query with outline, sample chapters, and SASE. Royalty.

LAREDO PUBLISHING—22930 Lockness Ave., Torrance, CA 90501. Sam Laredo, Ed. Bilingual and ESL (English as a second language) titles in Spanish and English. Children's fiction and young adult titles. Query with outline. Royalty.

LARK BOOKS—50 College St., Asheville, NC 28801. Rob Pulleyn, Pub. Distinctive books for creative people in crafts, how-to, leisure activities, and "coffee table" categories. Query with outline. Royalty.

LAUREL-LEAF—1540 Broadway, New York, NY 10036. Attn: Ed. Dept. Unsolicited young adult manuscripts are accepted only for the Delacorte Press Prize for a first young adult novel; see Literary Prize Offers.

LEADERSHIP PUBLISHERS, INC.—P.O. Box 8358, Des Moines, IA 50301–8358. Dr. Lois F. Roets, Ed. Educational materials for talented and gifted students, grades K to 12, and teacher reference books. No fiction or poetry. Send SASE for catalogue and writer's guidelines before submitting. Query or send complete manuscript. Royalty for books; flat fee for booklets.

793

LEE & LOW BOOKS—95 Madison Ave., New York, NY 10016. Philip Lee, Pub. Elizabeth Szabla, Ed.-in-Chief. Focus is on fiction and nonfiction picture books for children ages 4 to 10. "Our goal is to meet the growing need for books that address children of color and to provide books on subjects and stories they can identify with. Of special interest are stories set in contemporary America. Folklore and animal stories discouraged." Include SASE with any submission. Royalty or flat fee.

LEISURE BOOKS—276 Fifth Ave., New York, NY 10001. Sharon Morey, Ed. Historical romances, from 110,000 words; *Love Spell,* futuristic, time-travel, and historical romances from 100,000 words. Query with synopsis, sample chapters, and SASE. Royalty.

LIFETIME BOOKS, INC.—2131 Hollywood Blvd., Hollywood, FL 33020. Brian Feinblum, Sr. Ed. Nonfiction (200 to 300 pages): general interest, how-to, business, health, and inspiration. Query with letter or outline and sample chapter, SASE. Royalty. Send 9x12 SASE with 5 first-class stamps for catalogue.

LINCOLN-HERNDON PRESS, INC.— 818 S. Dirksen Pkwy., Springfield, IL 62703. Shirley A. Buscher, Asst. Pub. American humor that reveals American history. Humor collections. Query.

LITTLE, BROWN & CO.—1271 Ave. of the Americas, New York, NY 10020. Attn: Ed. Dept. Fiction, general nonfiction, sports books; divisions for law and medical texts. Query only.

LITTLE, BROWN & CO. CHILDREN'S BOOK DEPT.—34 Beacon St., Boston, MA 02108. Attn: Ed. Dept. Juvenile fiction and nonfiction and picture books. No unsolicited manuscripts. Agented material only.

LLEWELLYN PUBLICATIONS—P.O. Box 64383, St. Paul, MN 55164–0383. Nancy J. Mostad, Acquisitions Mgr. Books, from 75,000 words, on subjects of self-help, how-to, alternative health, astrology, metaphysics, new age, and the occult. Metaphysical/occult fiction. "We're interested in any kind of story (romance, mystery, historical, gothic, science, adventure), just as long as the theme is some aspect of authentic occultism." Query with sample chapters. Multiple queries considered. Royalty.

LODESTAR—375 Hudson St., New York, NY 10014. Virginia Buckley, Ed. Dir. Fiction (picture books to young adult, mystery, fantasy, science fiction, western) and nonfiction (science, contemporary issues, nature, history) considered for ages 9 to 11, 10 to 14, and 12 up. Also fiction and nonfiction picture books for ages 4 to 8. "We are not accepting submissions at this time, but writers may query."

LOTHROP, LEE & SHEPARD BOOKS—1350 Ave. of the Americas, New York, NY 10019. Susan Pearson, Ed.-in-Chief. Juvenile fiction and nonfiction, picture books. No unsolicited material. Royalty.

LOUISIANA STATE UNIVERSITY PRESS—P.O. Box 25053, Baton Rouge, LA 70894–5053. Attn: Acquisitions Ed. Scholarly adult nonfiction, dealing with the U.S. South, its history and its culture. Query with outline and sample chapters. Royalty.

LOVE SPELL—See *Leisure Books.*

LOVEGRAM ROMANCES—See *Zebra Books.*

LOVESWEPT—1540 Broadway, New York, NY 10036. Beth de Guzman,

Sr. Ed. Shawna Summers, Assoc. Ed. Adult contemporary romances, approximately 55,000 to 60,000 words. Study field before submitting. Query required. Paperback only.

LOYOLA UNIVERSITY PRESS—3441 N. Ashland Ave., Chicago, IL 60657-1397. Joseph Downey, S.J., Ed. Religious and ethics-related material for college-educated Christian readers. *Campion Book Series*: art, literature, and religion; contemporary Christian concerns; Jesuit studies; Chicago books. *Values and Ethics Series*: scholarly books centered on the theme of values and ethics, but stressing readability and topical relevance. Nonfiction, 200 to 400 pages. Query with outline. Royalty.

LUCENT BOOKS—P.O. Box 289011, San Diego, CA 92198-9011. Bonnie Szumski, Man. Ed. Lori Shein, Ed. Books, 18,000 to 25,000 words, for junior high/middle school students. "Overview" series: current issues (political, social, historical, environmental topics). Other series include "World History," "Great Battles," "The Way People Live" (exploring daily life and culture of communities worldwide, past and present). No unsolicited material; work is by assignment only. Flat fee. Query for guidelines and catalogue.

LYLE STUART—See *Carol Publishing Group*.

LYONS & BURFORD, PUBLISHERS—31 W. 21st St., New York, NY 10010. Peter Burford, Ed. Books, 100 to 300 pages, related to the outdoors (camping, gardening, natural history, etc.) or sports. Query with outline. Royalty.

MCCLANAHAN BOOK CO.—23 W. 26th St., New York, NY 10010. Elise Donner, Ed. Dir. Mass-market books for children, preschool to third grade. "Most books published as part of a series." Submit complete manuscript. Flat fee.

MCELDERRY BOOKS, MARGARET K.—866 Third Ave., New York, NY 10022. Margaret K. McElderry, V.P./Pub. Emma Dryden, Ed. Picture books; quality fiction; fantasy; beginning chapter books; humor; realism; and nonfiction.

MCFARLAND & COMPANY, INC., PUBLISHERS—Box 611, Jefferson, NC 28640. Robert Franklin, Ed.-in-Chief. Scholarly and reference books, from 225 manuscript pages, in many fields, except mathematical sciences. No new age, inspirational, children's, poetry, fiction, or exposés. Submit complete manuscripts or query with outline and sample chapters. Royalty.

MCGUINN & MCGUIRE PUBLISHING, INC.—P.O. Box 20603, Bradenton, FL 34203. Christopher Carroll, Man. Ed. Books, 55,000 to 100,000 words: business, history, and biography titles. "We especially like to see authors who have researched the market as completely as they researched their topic." Send complete manuscript or query with outline and sample chapters, SASE. Royalty.

MCKAY COMPANY, DAVID—201 E. 50th St., New York, NY 10022. No unsolicited manuscripts.

MACMILLAN GENERAL REFERENCE—(formerly *Prentice Hall Press*) 15 Columbus Cir., New York, NY 10023. Attn: Ed. Dept. General reference and travel books. Query required. Royalty.

MACMURRAY & BECK, INC.—P.O. Box 150717, Lakewood, CO 80215. Frederick Ramey, Exec. Dir. Quality fiction and nonfiction. Royalty.

795

MAGINATION PRESS—19 Union Sq. W., New York, NY 10003. Susan Kent Cakars, Ed. Children's picture books dealing with the psychotherapeutic treatment or resolution of serious childhood problems. Picture books for children 4 to 8; nonfiction for children 8 to 13. Most books are written by mental health professionals. Submit complete manuscript. Royalty.

MARKOWSKI INTERNATIONAL PUBLISHERS—One Oakglade Cir., Hummelstown, PA 17036. Michael A. Markowski, Ed. Nonfiction, from 30,000 words: popular health and fitness, marriage and human relations, personal and career development, self-help, sales and marketing, leadership training, network marketing, motivation, success, and Christian topics. Also various aviation and model aviation topics. "We are interested in how-to, motivational, and instructional books of short to medium length that will serve recognized and emerging needs of society." Query with outline and 3 sample chapters. Royalty.

MEADOWBROOK PRESS—18318 Minnetonka Blvd., Deephaven, MN 55391. Attn: Submissions Ed. Upbeat, useful books, 60,000 words, on pregnancy, childbirth, and parenting; shorter works of humor, party planning, children's activities. Query with outline, sample chapters, and qualifications. Royalty or flat fee.

MEGA-BOOKS, INC.—(formerly *Mega-Books of New York*) 116 E. 19th St., New York, NY 10003. Carol Gilbert, Man. Ed. Book packager. Young adult books, 150 pages, children's books. Query for guidelines. SASE with resumé. Flat fee.

MENTOR BOOKS—375 Hudson St., New York, NY 10014. Attn: Eds. Nonfiction originals for the college and high school market. Query required. Royalty.

MERCURY HOUSE—201 Filbert St., Suite 400, San Francisco, CA 94133. Thomas Christensen, Exec. Ed. Quality fiction and nonfiction, including biography, literary travel, environment, philosophy/personal growth, translation, and memoir. Query with outline, sample chapters, and SASE. Limited fiction market.

MEREDITH CORP. BOOK GROUP—*Better Homes and Gardens Books*, 1716 Locust St., Des Moines, IA 50309–3023. Kay Sanders, Exec. Ed. Books on gardening, crafts, decorating, cooking and food; mostly staff-written. "Interested in free-lance writers with expertise in these areas." Limited market. Query with SASE.

MESSNER, JULIAN—Simon & Schuster Educational Group, Silver Burdett Press, 299 Jefferson Rd., P.O. Box 480, Parsippany, NJ 07054–0480. John Dooling, Pub. Curriculum-oriented nonfiction. General nonfiction for ages 8 to 14: science, nature, biography, history, social issues, and hobbies. Lengths vary. Royalty.

THE MICHIGAN STATE UNIVERSITY PRESS—1405 S. Harrison Rd., Suite 25, E. Lansing, MI 48823–5202. Attn: Ed. Dept. Scholarly nonfiction, with concentrations in history, regional history, African sources, business, and Civil War. Submit prospectus, table of contents, and sample chapters to Editor-in-Chief. Authors should refer to *The Chicago Manual of Style, 14th Edition*, for formats and styles.

MILKWEED EDITIONS— 430 First Ave. N., Suite 400, Minneapolis, MN 55401–1743. Emilie Buchwald, Ed. "We publish excellent award-winning fiction, poetry, essays, and nonfiction, the kind of writing that makes for good reading." Publishes about 15 books a year. Submit complete manuscript. Royalty. Also publishes *Milkweeds for Young Readers*: high quality novels and biographies for middle grades.

THE MILLBROOK PRESS—2 Old New Milford Rd., Brookfield, CT 06804. Sarah DeCapua, Manuscript Coord. Nonfiction for early elementary grades through grades 7 and up, appropriate for the school and public library market, encompassing curriculum-related topics and extracurricular interests. Some picture books. Query with outline and sample chapter. Royalty.

MILLS & SANDERSON, PUBLISHERS—P.O. Box 833, Bedford, MA 01730–0833. Jan H. Anthony, Pub. Books, 200 pages, for series on family problem solving/psychotherapy or contemporary American biographies. Query. Royalty.

MINSTREL BOOKS—1230 Ave. of the Americas, New York, NY 10020. Patricia MacDonald, VP/Ed. Dir. Middle-grade fiction and nonfiction for ages 7 to 11. Scary stories, fantasies, school stories, adventures, animal stories; no picture books. Send query, outline, sample chapters to Attn: Manuscript Proposals.

MIRA BOOKS—See *Harlequin Books/Canada*.

THE MIT PRESS—55 Hayward St., Cambridge, MA 02142. Larry Cohen, Asst. Dir. Books on computer science/artificial intelligence; cognitive sciences; economics; architecture; aesthetic and social theory; linguistics; technology studies; environmental studies; and neuroscience.

MODAN PUBLISHING—P.O. Box 1202, Bellmore, NY 11710. Bennett Shelkowitz, Man. Dir. Adult nonfiction. Young adult fiction and nonfiction. Children's picture books. Books with international focus or related to political or social issues. *Adama Books*: Judaica and Hebrew books from Israel.

MONDO PUBLISHING—One Plaza Rd., Greenvale, NY 11548. Attn: Submissions Ed. Picture books, nonfiction, and early chapter books for readers ages 4 to 8. "We want to create beautiful books that children can read on their own and find so enjoyable that they'll want to come back to them time and time again." Query or send complete manuscript. Royalty.

MOON HANDBOOKS—Moon Publications, Inc., P.O. Box 3040, Chico, CA 95927–3040. Taran March, Exec. Ed. Travel guides, 400 to 600 pages. Will consider multiple submissions. Query. Royalty.

MOREHOUSE PUBLISHING— 871 Ethan Allen Hwy., Suite 204, Ridgefield, CT 06877. Deborah Grahame-Smith, Ed. E. Allen Kelley, Pub. Theology, pastoral care, church administration, spirituality, Anglican studies, history of religion, books for children, youth, elders, etc. Query with outline, contents, and sample chapter. SASE required. Royalty.

MORRIS, JOSHUA—See *Reader's Digest Young Families, Inc.*

MORROW AND CO., INC., WILLIAM—1350 Ave. of the Americas, New York, NY 10019. Attn: Eds. Adult fiction and nonfiction: no unsolicited manuscripts. *Beech Tree Books* and *Mulberry Books* (children's paperbacks), Amy Cohn, Ed. Dir.; *Hearst Books* (general nonfiction) and *Hearst Marine Books*, Ann Bramsom, Ed. Dir.; *Morrow Junior Books* (children's books for all ages), David Reuther, Ed.-in-Chief.

MOUNTAIN PRESS PUBLISHING—1301 S. 3rd W., P.O. Box 2399, Missoula, MT 59806. Attn: John Rimel. Nonfiction, 300 pages: natural history, field guides, geology, horses, Western history, Americana, outdoor guides, and fur trade lore. Query with outline and sample chapters; multiple queries considered. Royalty.

THE MOUNTAINEERS BOOKS—1011 S.W. Klickitat Way, Suite 107, Seattle, WA 98134. Margaret Foster, Ed.-in-Chief. Nonfiction books on non-competitive aspects of outdoor sports such as mountaineering, backpacking, walking, trekking, canoeing, kayaking, bicycling, skiing; independent adventure travel. Field guides, how-to and where-to guidebooks, biographies of outdoor people; accounts of expeditions. Natural history and conservation. Submit sample chapters and outline. Royalty.

MOYER BELL—Kymbolde Way, Wakefield, RI 02879. Jennifer Moyer, Pub. Adult fiction, nonfiction, and poetry. Query with sample chapter or send complete manuscript. Royalty.

MUIR PUBLICATIONS, JOHN—P.O. Box 613, Santa Fe, NM 87504–0613. Steven Cary, Pres. Travel guidebooks for adults. Nonfiction for children, 8 to 12, primarily in the areas of science and intercultural issues. Send manuscript or query with sample chapters. No fiction. Royalty or work for hire.

MULBERRY BOOKS—See *William Morrow and Co., Inc.*

MUSTANG PUBLISHING CO., INC.—Box 3004, Memphis, TN 38173. Rollin A. Riggs, Ed. Nonfiction for 18- to 40-year-olds, specializing in travel, humor, and how-to. Send queries for 100- to 300-page books, with outlines and sample chapters. Royalty. SASE required.

THE MYSTERIOUS PRESS—Time and Life Bldg., 1271 Ave. of the Americas, New York, NY 10020. William Malloy, Ed.-in-Chief. Mystery/suspense novels. Agented manuscripts only.

NAIAD PRESS, INC.—Box 10543, Tallahassee, FL 32302. Barbara Grier, Ed. Adult fiction, 52,000 to 55,000 words, with lesbian themes and characters: mysteries, romances, gothics, ghost stories, westerns, regencies, spy novels, etc. Query with letter and one-page précis only. Royalty.

NATIONAL PRESS BOOKS, INC.—7200 Wisconsin Ave., Suite 212, Bethesda, MD 20814. Talia Greenberg, Ed. Nonfiction: history, criminology, reference and health; parenting; business, management, and automotive titles. Imprints include *Beach Books, Full Court Press Books, Garlic Press, Pandemonium Books, Plain English Press,* and *Zenith Editions.* Query with outline and sample chapters. Royalty.

NATUREGRAPH PUBLISHERS—P.O. Box 1075, Happy Camp, CA 96039. Barbara Brown, Ed. Nonfiction: Native-American culture, natural history, outdoor living, land, gardening, Indian lore, and how-to. Query. Royalty.

THE NAVAL INSTITUTE PRESS—Annapolis, MD 21402. Attn: Acquisitions Dept. Nonfiction, 60,000 to 100,000 words: military histories; biographies; ship guides; how-tos on boating and navigation. Occasional fiction, 75,000 to 110,000 words. Query with outline and sample chapters. Royalty.

NELSON, INC., THOMAS—Nelson Pl. at Elm Hill Pike, P.O. Box 141000, Nashville, TN 37214–1000. Attn: Submissions Ed. Religious and general fiction and inspirational nonfiction for adults and teens. Query with outline, resumé, sample chapter, and SASE. Allow 18 weeks for response.

NEW LEAF PRESS, INC.—P.O. Box 311, Green Forest, AR 72638. Jim

Fletcher, Acquisitions Ed. Nonfiction, 100 to 400 pages, for Christian readers: self-help, how to live the Christian life, devotionals, gift books. Query with outline and sample chapters, or submit complete manuscript. Royalty.

THE NEW PRESS— 450 W. 41st St., New York, NY 10036. Andre Schiffrin, Dir. Serious nonfiction: history, economics, education, politics. Fiction in translation. Query required.

NEW RIVERS PRESS— 420 N. 5th St., Suite 910, Minneapolis, MN 55401. C.W. Truesdale, Ed./Pub. Collections of short stories, essays, and poems from emerging writers in upper Midwest. Query.

NEW SOCIETY PUBLISHERS— 4527 Springfield Ave., Philadelphia, PA 19143. Attn: Ed. Dept. Nonfiction books on fundamental social change through nonviolent social action. Request guidelines before submitting proposal. SASE required.

NEW WORLD LIBRARY—58 Paul Dr., San Rafael, CA 94903. Attn: Submissions Ed. Nonfiction, especially leading-edge inspirational/self-help books, enlightened business, Native American studies, classic wisdom, African-American studies, women's studies. "Aim for intelligent, aware audience, interested in personal and planetary transformation." Query with outline and SASE. Multiple queries accepted. Royalty.

NEWCASTLE PUBLISHING—13419 Saticoy St., N. Hollywood, CA 91605. Al Saunders, Pub. Nonfiction manuscripts, 200 to 250 pages, for older adults on personal health, health care issues, and relationships. "We are not looking for fads or trends. We want books with a long shelf life." Multiple queries considered. Royalty.

NEWMARKET PRESS—18 E. 48th St., New York, NY 10017. Esther Margolis, Pub. Nonfiction on health, psychology, self-help, child care, parenting, music, and film. Query required. Royalty.

NITTY GRITTY BOOKS—See *Bristol Publishing Enterprises.*

NORTHLAND PUBLISHING—P.O. Box 1389, Flagstaff, AZ 86002. Erin Murphy, Ed. Nonfiction books on natural history; fine arts; Native American culture, myth, art, and crafts; and cookbooks. Unique children's books, to 1,500 words. Prefer Southwest/West regional themes. Query with outline, sample chapter, potential market for proposed adult books. For children's books, send complete manuscript. "Include SASE with all submissions and queries. No queries by phone or fax." Royalty.

NORTHWORD PRESS, INC.—Box 1360, 7520 Highway 51, Minocqua, WI 54548. Barbara K. Harold, Man. Ed. Nonfiction nature and wildlife books, from 25,000 words. Send for catalogue. Royalty or flat fee.

NORTON AND CO., INC., W.W.—500 Fifth Ave., New York, NY 10110. Liz Malcolm, Ed. High-quality fiction and nonfiction. No occult, paranormal, religious, genre fiction (formula romance, science fiction, westerns), cookbooks, arts and crafts, young adult, or children's books. Query with synopsis, 2 to 3 chapters (including first chapter), and resumé. Return postage and packaging required. Royalty.

ODYSSEY PAPERBACKS—See *Harcourt Brace & Co. Children's Book Div.*

THE OLIVER PRESS—Josiah King House, 2709 Lyndale Ave. S., Minneapolis, MN 55408. James Satter, Ed. Collective biographies for young adults.

Submit proposals for books, 20,000 words, on people who have made an impact in such areas as history, politics, crime, science, and business. Flat fee (approximately $1,000).

OPEN HAND PUBLISHING—P.O. Box 22048, Seattle, WA 98122. Pat Andrus, Acquisitions Ed. Books that reflect the diverse cultures within the United States, with emphasis on the African American. "Our mission is to publish books which will promote positive social change as well as better understanding between all people." Query. Royalty.

ORCHARD BOOKS—95 Madison Ave., New York, NY 10016. Neal Porter, Pres./Pub. Hardcover picture books. Fiction for middle grades and young adults. Nonfiction and photo-essays for young children. Submit complete manuscript. Royalty.

OREGON STATE UNIVERSITY PRESS—101 Waldo Hall, Corvallis, OR 97331. Attn: Ed. Dept. Scholarly books in a limited range of disciplines and books of particular importance to the Pacific Northwest. Query with summary of manuscript.

OSBORNE/MCGRAW HILL—2600 Tenth St., Berkeley, CA 94710. Scott Rogers, Sr. Acquisitions Ed. Microcomputer books for general audience. Query. Royalty.

OUR SUNDAY VISITOR PUBLISHING—200 Noll Plaza, Huntington, IN 46750. Jacquelyn M. Lindsey, Acquisitions Ed. Catholic-oriented books of various lengths. No fiction. Query with outline and sample chapters. Royalty.

THE OVERLOOK PRESS—149 Wooster St., New York, NY 10012. Tracy Carns, Ed. Dir. Literary fiction, some fantasy/science fiction, foreign literature in translation, general nonfiction, including art, architecture, design, film, history, biography, crafts/lifestyle, martial arts, Hudson Valley regional interest, and children's books. Query with outline, sample chapters and SASE. Royalty.

OWEN PUBLISHERS, INC., RICHARD C.—P.O. Box 585, Katonah, NY 10536. Janice Boland, Ed., Dept. TW. Fiction and nonfiction. Brief storybooks, approximately 45 to 100 words, suitable for 5-, 6-, and 7-year-old beginning readers for the "Ready to Read" program. Royalties for writers. Flat fee for illustrators. Writers must send SASE for guidelines before submitting.

OXFORD UNIVERSITY PRESS—198 Madison Ave., New York, NY 10016. Attn: Ed. Dept. Authoritative books on literature, history, philosophy, etc.; college textbooks, medical, scientific, technical and reference books. Query. Royalty.

PANDEMONIUM BOOKS—See *National Press Books, Inc.*

PANTHEON BOOKS—201 E. 50th St., New York, NY 10022. Attn: Ed. Dept. Quality fiction and nonfiction. Query required. Royalty.

PAPIER-MACHE PRESS—135 Aviation Way, #14, Watsonville, CA 95076. Sandra Martz, Ed. Fiction, poetry, and nonfiction books; 4 to 6 books annually. "We emphasize, but are not limited to, the publication of books and related items for midlife and older women." Write for guidelines. Query. Royalty.

PARA PUBLISHING—P.O. Box 2206–238, Santa Barbara, CA 93118–2206. Dan Poynter, Ed. Adult nonfiction books on parachutes and skydiving only. Author must present evidence of having made at least 1,000 jumps. Query. Royalty.

PARAGON HOUSE—370 Lexington Ave., New York, NY 10017. Michael Giampaoli, Pub. Serious nonfiction, including history, reference, literature, philosophy, religion, and current affairs. Query. Royalty.

PARENTING PRESS—#F, P.O. Box 75267, Seattle, WA 98125. John Shoemaker, Assoc. Ed. Choice-oriented parenting books, 112 pages. Skill-building and problem-solving children's books, 30 to 60 pages. "Send SASE for guidelines and booklist, then query with outline and sample chapters." Royalty.

PAULIST PRESS—997 Macarthur Blvd., Mahwah, NJ 07430. Donald Brophy, Man. Ed. Adult nonfiction, 100 to 400 pages; and picture books, 8 to 10 pages, for readers 5 to 7 or 8 to 10. For adult books, query with outline and sample chapters. For juvenile books, submit complete manuscript to Karen Scialabba, Ed. Royalty.

PEACHTREE PUBLISHERS, LTD.— 494 Armour Cir. N.E., Atlanta, GA 30324. Attn: Ed. Dept. Wide variety of children's books, fiction and nonfiction. No religious material, science fiction/fantasy, romance, mystery/detective, historical fiction; no business, scientific, or technical books. Send outline and sample chapters. SASE required. Royalty. No unsolicited submissions from unpublished authors at this time.

PELICAN PUBLISHING CO., INC.—1101 Monroe St., Gretna, LA 70053. Nina Kooij, Ed. General nonfiction: Americana, regional, architecture, travel, cookbooks. Royalty.

PENGUIN BOOKS—375 Hudson St., New York, NY 10014. Attn: Ed. Dept. Adult fiction and nonfiction paperbacks. Royalty.

PEREGRINE SMITH BOOKS—P.O. Box 667, Layton, UT 84041. Theresa Desmond, Ed. Juvenile books: western/cowboy; activity; how-to; nature/environment; and biography/ethnic. Fiction picture books, to 2,000 words; nonfiction picture books, to 4,000 words; chapter books, to 10,000 words, for readers 5 to 11. Royalty.

THE PERMANENT PRESS—Noyac Rd., Sag Harbor, NY 11963. Judith Shepard, Ed. Original and arresting novels. Query. Royalty.

PERSPECTIVES PRESS—P.O. Box 90318, Indianapolis, IN 46290–0318. Pat Johnston, Pub. Books on infertility, adoption, closely related reproductive health and child welfare issues (foster care, etc.). Also picture books, 32 pages, for children to 10 years old. "Writers must read our guidelines before submitting." Query. Royalty.

PETERSON'S/PACESETTER BOOKS—202 Carnegie Ctr., P.O. Box 2123, Princeton, NJ 08543–2123. Andrea Pedolsky, Exec. Ed. Books that bring a new point of view to perennial business topics or identify new issues and developments in the business world. "We want books that can bring something new to businesspeople's lives, that show the human side of the business world, that have a sense of humor." Submit proposal with one sample chapter. Royalty.

PHILOMEL BOOKS—200 Madison Ave., New York, NY 10016. Patricia Lee Gauch, Ed. Dir. Juvenile picture books, young adult fiction, and some biographies. Fresh, original work with compelling characters and "a truly childlike spirit." Query required.

PINEAPPLE PRESS—P.O. Drawer 16008, Southside Sta., Sarasota, FL 34239. June Cussen, Ed. Serious fiction and nonfiction, Florida-oriented,

60,000 to 125,000 words. Query with outline, sample chapters, and SASE. Royalty.

PINNACLE BOOKS— 850 Third Ave., New York, NY 10022. Paul Dinas, Exec. Ed. Nonfiction books: true crime, celebrity biographies, and humor. Unsolicited material not accepted.

PIPPIN PRESS—229 E. 85th St., Gracie Sta., Box 1347, New York, NY 10028. Barbara Francis, Pub. High-quality picture books for preschoolers; small chapter books for ages 6 to 10, emphasizing humor and fantasy, humorous mysteries; imaginative nonfiction for children of all ages. Query with SASE only; no unsolicited manuscripts. Royalty.

PLAIN ENGLISH PRESS—See *National Press Books, Inc.*

PLANET DEXTER—Addison-Wesley Publishing Co., One Jacob Way, Reading, MA 01867–3999. Elizabeth Doyle, Ed. Nonfiction educational books for children ages 5 to 12. "Our goal is to create book-based products with an accompanying toy, electronic gadget, craft item, or learning tool." No fiction or poetry. No textbook-style academic writing. SASE required.

PLAYERS PRESS, INC.—P.O. Box 1132, Studio City, CA 91614. Robert Gordon, Ed. Plays and musicals for children and adults; juvenile and adult nonfiction related to theatre, film, television, and the performing arts. Lengths vary. Query. Royalty.

PLENUM PUBLISHING CORP.—233 Spring St., New York, NY 10013. Linda Greenspan Regan, Sr. Ed. Trade nonfiction, approximately 300 pages, on popular science, criminology, psychology, sociology, anthropology, and health. Query required. Royalty. Hardcover.

PLUME BOOKS—375 Hudson St., New York, NY 10014. Attn: Ed. Dept. Nonfiction: hobbies, business, health, cooking, child care, psychology, history, popular culture, biography, and politics. Fiction: serious literary and gay. Query.

POCKET BOOKS—1230 Ave. of the Americas, New York, NY 10020. William R. Grose, Exec. VP/ Ed. Dir. Gina Centrello, Pub./Pres. Original fiction and nonfiction. Mystery line: police procedurals, private eye, and amateur sleuth novels, 60,000 to 70,000 words. Royalty.

POPULAR PRESS—Bowling Green State Univ., Bowling Green, OH 43403. Ms. Pat Browne, Ed. Nonfiction, 250 to 400 pages, examining some aspect of popular culture. Query with outline. Flat fee or royalty.

POTTER, CLARKSON—201 E. 50th St., New York, NY 10022. Lauren Shakely, Ed.-in-Chief. General trade books. Submissions accepted through agents only.

PRAEGER PUBLISHERS— 88 Post Rd. W., Westport, CT 06880–4232. James Dunton, Pub. General nonfiction; scholarly and textbooks. Query with outline. Royalty.

PRENTICE HALL PRESS—See *Macmillan General Reference.*

PRIMA PUBLISHING—P.O. Box 1260, Rocklin, CA 95677. Ben Dominitz, Pub. Jennifer Basye, Ed. Nonfiction on variety of subjects, including business, health, and cookbooks. "We want books with originality, written by highly qualified individuals." Royalty.

PROMPT PUBLICATIONS—2647 Waterfront Pkwy. E. Dr., Suite 300,

Indianapolis, IN 46214–2041. Attn: Acquisitions Ed. Nonfiction softcover technical books on electronics, how-to, troubleshooting and repair, electrical engineering, video and sound equipment, cellular technology, etc., for all levels of technical experience. Query with outline, sample chapters, author bio, and SASE. Royalty.

PRUETT PUBLISHING COMPANY—2928 Pearl, Boulder, CO 80301. Jim Pruett, Pres. Nonfiction: outdoors and recreation, western U.S. history, travel, natural history and the environment, fly fishing. Query. Royalty.

PUTNAM'S SONS, G.P.—200 Madison Ave., New York, NY 10016. Attn: Ed. Dept. General trade nonfiction, fiction. Query Nancy Paulson, Pres. and Pub., for children's books. No unsolicited manuscripts. Royalty.

QUARRY PRESS—P.O. Box 1061, Kingston, Ontario, Canada K7L 4Y5. Adult fiction and nonfiction. "We are known for publishing new and innovative Canadian writing." Query with outline, synopsis, and sample chapters. Royalty.

QUEST BOOKS—306 W. Geneva Rd., P. O. Box 270, Wheaton, IL 60189–0270. Brenda Rosen, Exec. Ed. Nonfiction books on Eastern and Western religion and philosophy, holism, healing, transpersonal psychology, men's and women's spirituality, Native-American spirituality, meditation, yoga, ancient wisdom. Query. Royalty.

RAGGED MOUNTAIN PRESS—Box 220, Camden, ME 04843. Jonathan Eaton, Ed. Dir. John Kettlewell, Acquisitions Ed. Books on outdoor recreation.

RAINTREE STECK-VAUGHN PUBLISHERS—National Education Corp., 466 Southern Blvd., Chatham, NJ 07928. Walter Kossmann, Ed. Nonfiction books, 5,000 to 30,000 words, for school and library market: biographies for grades 3 and up; and science, social studies, and history books for primary grades through high school. Query with outline and sample chapters; SASE required. Flat fee and royalty.

RANDOM HOUSE, INC.—201 E. 50th St., New York, NY 10022. Attn: Ed. Dept. General fiction and nonfiction. Agented material only.

RANDOM HOUSE JUVENILE DIV.—201 E. 50th St., New York, NY 10022. Kate Klimo, Pub. Dir. Fiction and nonfiction for beginning readers; paperback fiction line for 7-to 9-year-olds. No unsolicited manuscripts. Agented material only.

READER'S DIGEST KIDS—See *Reader's Digest Young Families, Inc.*

READER'S DIGEST YOUNG FAMILIES, INC.—221 Danbury Rd., Wilton, CT 06897. Willy Derraugh, Pub. Children's books for readers ages 2 to 11. Imprints include: *Reader's Digest Kids,* high-quality, fully illustrated information and reference books; *Joshua Morris,* imaginative and uniquely formatted novelty books and book kits, with an emphasis on information and learning; *Wishing Well,* novelty formats. Address submissions to an imprint's Acquisitions Ed.

THE RED SEA PRESS—11-D Princess Rd., Suites D, E, F, Lawrenceville, NJ 08648. Kassahun Checole, Pub. Adult nonfiction, 360 double-spaced manuscript pages. "We focus on nonfiction material with a specialty on the Horn of Africa." Query. Royalty.

RED WAGON BOOKS—Harcourt, Brace & Co. Children's Books, 525

B St., Suite 1900, San Diego, CA 92101–4495. Attn: Acquisitions Ed. No unsolicited material.

REGNERY PUBLISHING, INC.— 422 First St. S.E., Suite 300, Washington, DC 20003. Attn: Ed. Dept. Nonfiction books. Query. Royalty.

RENAISSANCE HOUSE—541 Oak St., P. O. Box 177, Frederick, CO 80530. Eleanor H. Ayer, Ed. Regional guidebooks. Guidebooks on CO, AZ, CA, and the Southwest. "We use only manuscripts written to our specifications for new or ongoing series." Submit outline and short bio. Royalty.

REPUBLIC OF TEXAS PRESS—See *Wordware Publishing.*

RISING TIDE PRESS—5 Kivy St., Huntington Sta., New York, NY 11746. Lee Boojamra, Ed. Books for, by, and about lesbians. Fiction, 60,000 to 80,000 words: romance, mystery, and science fiction/fantasy. Nonfiction, 40,000 to 60,000 words. Royalty. Reports in 3 months. SASE for guidelines.

RIZZOLI INTERNATIONAL PUBLICATIONS, INC.—300 Park Ave. S., New York, NY 10010. Manuela Soares, Children's Book Ed. Original manuscripts that introduce children to fine art, folk art, and architecture of all cultures for a small list. Nonfiction and fiction for all ages. Query with SASE or response card. Royalty.

ROC—375 Hudson St., New York, NY 10014. Amy Stout, Exec. Ed. Jennifer Smith, Asst. Ed. Science fiction, fantasy. Query.

ROCKBRIDGE PUBLISHING—P.O. Box 351, Berryville, VA 22611. Katherine Tennery, Ed. Book-length nonfiction on the Civil War, Virginia history, and travel guides to Virginia. Query. Royalty.

RODALE PRESS—33 E. Minor St., Emmaus, PA 18098. Pat Corpora, Pub. Books on health, gardening, homeowner projects, cookbooks, inspirational topics, pop psychology, woodworking, natural history. Query with outline and sample chapter. Royalty and outright purchase. In addition: "We're always looking for truly competent free lancers to write chapters for books conceived and developed in-house"; payment on a work-for-hire basis; address Bill Gottlieb, Ed.-in-Chief.

ROYAL FIREWORKS PRESS—1 First Ave., Unionville, NY 10988. Charles Morgan, Ed. Adult science fiction and mysteries. Juvenile and young adult fiction, biography, and educational nonfiction. Submit complete manuscripts. No multiple queries. Royalty.

RUNNING PRESS—125 S. 22nd St., Philadelphia, PA 19103. Attn: Exec. Ed. Trade nonfiction: art, craft, how-to, self-help, science, lifestyles. Young adult books and interactive packages. Query. Royalty.

RUTLEDGE HILL PRESS—211 Seventh Ave. N., Nashville, TN 37219. Tracey Menges, Ed. Southern-interest fiction and market-specific nonfiction. Query with outline and sample chapters. Royalty.

ST. ANTHONY MESSENGER PRESS—1615 Republic St., Cincinnati, OH 45210–1298. Lisa Biedenbach, Man. Ed. Inspirational nonfiction for Catholics, supporting a Christian lifestyle in our culture; prayer aids, scripture, church history, education, practical spirituality, parish ministry, liturgy resources. Query with 500-word summary. Royalty.

ST. MARTIN'S PRESS—175 Fifth Ave., New York, NY 10010. Attn: Ed. Dept. General adult fiction and nonfiction. Query. Royalty.

SANDLAPPER PUBLISHING, INC.—P.O. Drawer 730, Orangeburg, SC 29116–0730. Amanda Gallman, Book Ed. Nonfiction books on South Carolina history, culture, cuisine. Query with outline, sample chapters, and SASE.

SASQUATCH BOOKS—1008 Western Ave., #300, Seattle, WA 98104. Attn: Ed. Dept. Regional books by West Coast authors on a wide range of nonfiction topics: travel, natural history, gardening, cooking, history, children's and public affairs. Books must have a West Coast angle. Query with SASE. Royalty.

SCARECROW PRESS—P.O. Box 4167, Metuchen, NJ 08840. Norman Horrocks, V.P./Editorial. Reference works and bibliographies, from 150 pages, especially in the areas of cinema, TV, radio, and theater, mainly for use by libraries. Query or send complete manuscript; multiple queries considered. Royalty.

SCHOCKEN BOOKS—201 E. 50th St., New York, NY 10022. Attn: Ed. Dept. General nonfiction: Judaica, women's studies, education, history, religion, psychology. Query with outline and sample chapter. Royalty.

SCHOLASTIC, INC.—555 Broadway, New York, NY 10012. No unsolicited manuscripts.

SCHOLASTIC PROFESSIONAL BOOKS— 411 Lafayette St., New York, NY 10003. Attn: Shawn Richardson. Books by and for teachers of kindergarten through eighth grade. *Instructor Books*: practical, activity/resource books on teaching reading and writing, science, math, etc. *Teaching Strategies Books*: 64 to 96 pages on new ideas, practices, and approaches to teaching. Query with outline, sample chapters or activities, contents page, and resume. Flat fee or royalty. Multiple queries considered. SASE for guidelines.

SCHWARTZ BOOKS, ANNE—1230 Ave. of the Americas, New York, NY 10020. Anne Schwartz, Ed. Picture books through juvenile fiction and nonfiction as well as illustrated collections. Query; no unsolicited manuscripts.

SCOTT, FORESMAN AND CO.— 1900 E. Lake Ave., Glenview, IL 60025. Neil Topham, Pres. Elementary and secondary textbooks. Royalty or flat fee.

SCRIBNER—1230 Ave. of the Americas, New York, NY 10020. Attn: Ed. Dept. No unsolicited manuscripts.

SEASIDE PRESS—See *Wordware Publishing*.

SHAW PUBLISHERS, HAROLD—388 Gunderson Dr., Box 567, Wheaton, IL 60189. Joan L. Guest, Man. Ed. Nonfiction, 120 to 220 pages, with an evangelical Christian perspective. Some teen and adult fiction and literary books. Query. Flat fee or royalty.

SHEARWATER BOOKS—See *Island Press*.

SIERRA CLUB BOOKS—100 Bush St., San Francisco, CA 94104. Attn: Ed. Dept. Nonfiction: environment, natural history, the sciences, outdoors and regional guidebooks, nature photography; juvenile fiction and nonfiction. Query with SASE. Royalty.

SIGNAL HILL PUBLICATIONS—1320 Jamesville Ave., Box 131, Syracuse, NY 13210. Jennifer Lashley, Ed. Fiction and nonfiction, 5,000 to 9,000 words, and poetry for adults who read at low levels, for use in adult basic education programs, volunteer literacy organizations, and job training programs. Query with outline, synopsis, and one to 3 sample chapters. "Read guidelines first. Do not submit material for juvenile or teenage readers." Royalty or flat fee.

SIGNATURE BOOKS, INC.—564 W. 400 North, Salt Lake City, UT 84116–3411. Attn: Board of Dirs. Adult fiction and nonfiction, from 100 pages. Adult poetry from 80 pages. Royalty.

SILHOUETTE BOOKS—300 E. 42nd St., New York, NY 10017. Isabel Swift, Ed. Dir. *Silhouette Romances*: Anne Canadeo, Sr. Ed. Contemporary romances, 53,000 to 58,000 words. *Special Edition*: Tara Gavin, Sr. Ed. Sophisticated contemporary romances, 75,000 to 80,000 words. *Silhouette Desire*: Lucia Macro, Sr. Ed. Sensuous contemporary romances, 53,000 to 60,000 words. *Intimate Moments*: Leslie Wainger, Sr. Ed./Ed. Coord. Sensuous, exciting contemporary romances, 80,000 to 85,000 words. *Silhouette Yours Truly*: Melissa Senate, Ed. Contemporary, fun romances with written word (literary) hook. Historical romance: 95,000 to 105,000 words, and more; query with synopsis and 3 sample chapters to Tracy Farrell, Sr. Ed. Query with synopsis and SASE to appropriate editor. Tipsheets available.

SILVER MOON PRESS—126 Fifth Ave., Suite 803, New York, NY 10011. Eliza Booth, Ed. Juvenile titles for a multicultural audience, ages 6 to 9 and 8 to 12. Historical fiction, 64 to 80 pages, and books on science also considered. Query with outline; multiple queries accepted. Payment varies.

SIMON & SCHUSTER—1230 Ave. of the Americas, New York, NY 10020. Adult books: No unsolicited material.

SIMON & SCHUSTER BOOKS FOR YOUNG READERS—1230 Ave. of the Americas, New York, NY 10020. Stephanie Owens Lurie, V.P./Ed. Dir. Books for ages preschool through high school: picture books to young adult; nonfiction for all age levels. Hardcover only. Send complete manuscript for picture books; synopsis and 3 chapters for novels; query for nonfiction. SASE required for reply.

SINGER MEDIA CORP.—Seaview Business Park, 1030 Calle Cordillera, #106, San Clemente, CA 92673. Kurt Singer, Pres. Packages books for US and foreign book publishers. Foreign reprint rights to books in fields of business, management, self-help, romance and mysteries, psychology, and documentary videos. Advance against royalties.

SKYLARK BOOKS—See *Yearling Books*.

THE SMITH—69 Joralemon St., Brooklyn, NY 11201. Harry Smith, Ed. Fiction and nonfiction, from 64 pages, and poetry, 48 to 112 pages. "While publishing at a high level of craftsmanship, we have pursued the increasingly difficult, expensive and now relatively rare policy of keeping our titles in print over the decades." Query with outline and sample chapters. Royalty.

SMITH AND KRAUS, INC.—P.O. Box 127, Main St., Lyme, NH 03768. Marisa Smith, Pres. Books related to theater, including anthologies of monologues, works by modern playwrights, and career development for actors. Full-length or one-act dramas that have been produced in the past year. Also, books for young actors. Send query and synopsis. Response time is 3 months. Pays on acceptance and on publication.

SMITH RESEARCH ASSOCIATES—564 W. 400 North, Salt Lake City, UT 84116–3411. George D. Smith, Ed. Utah history and Mormon studies, from 250 pages.

SOHO PRESS—853 Broadway, New York, NY 10003. Juris Jurjevics, Ed. Mysteries, thrillers, and contemporary fiction and nonfiction, from 60,000 words. Send SASE and complete manuscript. Royalty.

SOUTHERN ILLINOIS UNIVERSITY PRESS—P.O. Box 3697, Carbondale, IL 62902–3697. James Simmons, Ed. Dir. Nonfiction in the humanities, 200 to 400 pages. Query with outline and sample chapters. Royalty.

SOUTHERN METHODIST UNIVERSITY PRESS—Box 415, Dallas, TX 75275. Kathryn Lang, Sr. Ed. Literary fiction. Nonfiction: scholarly studies in religion, medical ethics (death and dying); film, theater; scholarly works on Texas or Southwest. No juvenile material, science fiction, or poetry. Query. Royalty.

SPECIAL EDITION—See *Silhouette Books.*

SPECTACLE LANE PRESS—Box 34, Georgetown, CT 06829. Attn: Ed. Dept. Humor books, 500 to 5,000 words, on subjects of strong, current interest, illustrated with cartoons. Buys text or text/cartoon packages. Occasional nonfiction, non-humor books on provocative subjects of wide concern. Royalty.

SPECTRA BOOKS—1540 Broadway, New York, NY 10036. Jennifer Hershey, Exec. Ed. Tom Dupree, Sr. Ed. Science fiction and fantasy, with emphasis on storytelling and characterization. Query with SASE; no unsolicited manuscripts. Royalty.

STACKPOLE BOOKS—5067 Ritter Rd., Mechanicsburg, PA 17055. Judith Schnell, Ed. Dir. Adult books on the outdoors. Nature, fishing, crafts/hobbies, woodworking, military history, sporting literature, cooking/gardening, and hunting. Query. Royalty.

STANDARD PUBLISHING—8121 Hamilton Ave., Cincinnati, OH 45231. Attn: Acquisitions Coord. Fiction for children based on Bible or with moral tone. Christian education. Conservative evangelical. Guidelines.

STANFORD UNIVERSITY PRESS—Stanford Univ., Stanford, CA 94305–2235. Norris Pope, Ed. "For the most part, we publish academic scholarship." No original fiction or poetry. Query with outline and sample chapters. Royalty.

STEERFORTH PRESS—105–106 Chelsea St., Box 70, S. Royalton, VT 05068. Michael Moore, Ed. Adult nonfiction and some literary fiction. Twelve books a year: serious works of history, biography, politics, current affairs. Query with SASE. Royalty.

STEMMER HOUSE PUBLISHERS, INC.—2627 Caves Rd., Owings Mills, MD 21117. Barbara Holdridge, Ed. Juvenile picture books and adult nonfiction. Specializes in art, design, cookbooks, children's, and horticultural titles. Query with SASE. Royalty.

STERLING PUBLISHING CO., INC.—387 Park Ave. S., New York, NY 10016. Sheila Anne Barry, Acquisitions Mgr. How-to, hobby, woodworking, health, fiber arts, crafts, dolls and puppets, ghosts, wine, nature, oddities, new consciousness, puzzles, juvenile humor and activities, juvenile nature and science, medieval history, Celtic topics, gardening, alternative lifestyle, business, pets, recreation, sports and games books, reference, and home decorating. Query with outline, sample chapter, and sample illustrations. Royalty.

STONEYDALE PRESS—205 Main St., Drawer B, Stevensville, MT 59870. Dale A. Burk, Ed. Adult nonfiction, primarily how-to, on outdoor recreation with emphasis on big game hunting. "We're a very specialized market. Query with outline and sample chapters essential." Royalty.

STOREY COMMUNICATIONS—Schoolhouse Rd., Pownal, VT 05261. Gwen Steege, Sr. Ed. How-to books for country living. Adult books, 100 to 350 pages, on gardening, animals, crafts, building, cooking, beer, and how-to. Juvenile nonfiction, 64 to 160 pages, on gardening, crafts, and cooking. Royalty or flat fee.

STORY LINE PRESS—Three Oaks Farm, Brownsville, OR 97327–9718. Robert McDowell, Ed. Fiction, nonfiction, and poetry of varying lengths. Query. Royalty.

STRAWBERRY HILL PRESS—3848 S.E. Division St., Portland, OR 97202–1641. Carolyn Soto, Ed. Nonfiction: biography, autobiography, history, cooking, health, how-to, philosophy, performance arts, and Third World. Query with sample chapters, outline, and SASE. Royalty.

SUNDANCE PUBLISHING—P.O. Box 1326, Taylor Rd., Littleton, MA 01460. Gare Thompson, Publisher. Curriculum materials to accompany quality children's, young adult, and adult literature. *Sundance Big Books* feature multi-cultural characters and themes. Royalty or flat fee.

TAB BOOKS—Professional Book Group, McGraw-Hill, Inc., Blue Ridge Summit, PA 17294. Ron Powers, Ed. Dir. Nonfiction: electronics, computers, vocational how-to, aviation, science fair projects, business start up, science and technology, juvenile science, technician-level automotive, marine and outdoor life, military history, and engineering. Royalty or flat fee.

TAMBOURINE BOOKS—1350 Ave. of the Americas, New York, NY 10019. Paulette C. Kaufmann, V.P./Ed.-in-Chief. Picture books, fiction, and nonfiction for all ages in general trade market.

TAYLOR PUBLISHING CO.—1550 W. Mockingbird Ln., Dallas, TX 75235. Macy Jaggers, Asst. Ed. Adult nonfiction: gardening, sports, health, popular culture, celebrity biographies, parenting, home improvement, nature/outdoors. Juvenile nonfiction: first-person accounts of the lives of athletes and other celebrities. Query with outline, sample chapters, author bio, and SASE. Royalty.

TEMPLE UNIVERSITY PRESS—Broad and Oxford Sts., Philadelphia, PA 19122. Michael Ames, Ed. Adult nonfiction. Query with outline and sample chapters. Royalty.

TEN SPEED PRESS—P.O. Box 7123, Berkeley, CA 94707. Attn: Ed. Dept. Self-help and how-to on careers, recreation, etc.; natural science, history, cookbooks. Query with outline, sample chapters, and SASE. Paperback. Royalty.

THUNDER'S MOUTH PRESS—632 Broadway, 7th Fl., New York, NY 10012. Neil Ortenberg, Ed. Mainly nonfiction: current affairs, popular culture, memoirs, and biography, to 300 pages. Royalty.

TIARE PUBLICATIONS—P.O. Box 493, Lake Geneva, WI 53147. Gerry L. Dexter, Ed. Books of interest to radio hobbyists, 60,000 to 100,000 words: jazz discographies and commentaries, *Balboa* imprint. Query with outline and sample chapters. Royalties.

TIME-LIFE FOR CHILDREN—777 Duke St., Alexandria, VA 22314. Mary Saxton, Ed. Juvenile books. Publishes series of 12 to 24 volumes (no single titles), so author must have a series concept. Send SASE for required release form before submitting material. Payment is flat fee.

TIMES BOOKS—201 E. 50th St., New York, NY 10022. Steve Wasserman, Ed. Dir. No unsolicited manuscripts or queries accepted.

TOPAZ—375 Hudson St., New York, NY 10014. Constance Martin, Ed. Historical romance. Query.

TOR BOOKS—175 Fifth Ave., 14th Fl., New York, NY 10010. Patrick Nielsen Hayden, Sr. Ed. , science fiction and fantasy. Melissa Ann Singer, Sr. Ed., general fiction. Books from 60,000 words. Query with outline and sample chapters. Royalty.

TOUCHSTONE—1230 Ave. of the Americas, New York, NY 10020. Attn: Ed. No unsolicited manuscripts.

TRICYCLE PRESS—Ten Speed Press, P.O. Box 7123, Berkeley, CA 94707. Nicole Geiger, Ed. Children's books: Picture books, submit complete manuscripts. Activity books, submit about 20 pages and complete outline. "Real life" books that help children cope with issues. SASE required. Do not send original artwork. Responds in 10 weeks. Royalty.

TROLL ASSOCIATES—100 Corporate Dr., Mahwah, NJ 07430. M. Francis, Ed. Juvenile fiction and nonfiction. Query preferred. Royalty or flat fee.

TSR, INC.—201 Sheridan Springs Rd., Lake Geneva, WI 53147. Attn: Manuscript Ed. Epic high fantasy, gritty, action-oriented fantasy, Gothic horror, some humorous young adult fantasy, some science fiction, about 100,000 words. Query. Advance royalty.

TUDOR PUBLISHERS, INC.—P.O. Box 38366, Greensboro, NC 27438. Pam Cox, Ed. Helpful nonfiction books for senior citizens, teenagers, and minorities. Young adult biographies and occasional young adult novels. Reference library titles. Occasional high-quality adult fiction. Send proposal or query with sample chapters. Royalty.

TWENTY-FIRST CENTURY BOOKS—115 W. 18th St., New York, NY 10011. Attn: Submissions Ed. Juvenile nonfiction, 20,000 to 30,000 words, for use in schools and libraries. Science, history, health, biography, and social studies books for grades 5 and up. "Books are published primarily in series of 4 or more; not all titles are necessarily by the same author." Submit outline and sample chapters. Royalty.

TYNDALE HOUSE—351 Executive Dr., Box 80, Wheaton, IL 60189. Ron Beers, V.P. Juvenile and adult fiction and nonfiction on subjects of concern to Christians. Picture books with religious focus for preschool and early readers. Query.

UAHC PRESS—838 Fifth Ave., New York, NY 10021. Aron Hirt-Manheimer and David Kasakove, Eds. Religious educational titles on or related to Judaism. Adult nonfiction; juvenile picture books, fiction, nonfiction, and young adult titles. Query with outline. Royalty.

UNIVERSITY BOOKS—See *Carol Publishing Group.*

UNIVERSITY OF ALABAMA PRESS—P.O. Box 870380, Tuscaloosa, AL 35487–0380. Attn: Ed. Dept. Scholarly and general regional nonfiction. Submit to appropriate editor: Malcolm MacDonald, Ed. (history, public administration, political science); Nicole Mitchell, Ed. (English, rhetoric and communication, Judaic studies, women's studies); Judith Knight, Ed. (archaeology, anthropology). Send complete manuscript. Royalty.

UNIVERSITY OF ARIZONA PRESS—1230 N. Park Ave., Suite 102, Tucson, AZ 85719. Stephen Cox, Dir. Joanne O'Hare, Sr. Ed. Christine R. Szuter, Acquiring Ed. Amy Chapman Smith, Acquiring Ed. Scholarly and popular nonfiction: Arizona, American West, anthropology, archaeology, environmental science, Latin America, Native Americans, natural history, space sciences, women's studies. Query with outline and sample chapters or send complete manuscript. Royalty.

UNIVERSITY OF CALIFORNIA PRESS—2120 Berkeley Way, Berkeley, CA 94720. Attn: Acquisitions Dept. Scholarly nonfiction. Query with cover letter, outline, sample chapters, curriculum vitae, and SASE.

UNIVERSITY OF GEORGIA PRESS—330 Research Dr., Athens, GA 30602–4901. Karen Orchard, Ed. Short story collections and poetry, scholarly nonfiction and literary criticism, Southern and American history, regional studies, biography and autobiography. For nonfiction, query with outline and sample chapters. Poetry collections considered in Sept. and Jan. only; short fiction in June and July only. A $10 fee is required for all poetry and fiction submissions. Royalty. SASE for competition guidelines.

UNIVERSITY OF ILLINOIS PRESS—1325 S. Oak St., Champaign, IL 61820. Richard L. Wentworth, Ed.-in-Chief. Short story collections, 140 to 180 pages; nonfiction; and poetry, 70 to 100 pages. Rarely considers multiple submissions. Query. Royalty. "Not accepting unsolicited manuscripts."

UNIVERSITY OF MASSACHUSETTS PRESS—Box 429, Amherst, MA 01004–0429. Clark Dougan, Sr. Ed. Query with SASE.

UNIVERSITY OF MINNESOTA PRESS—2037 University Ave. S.E., Minneapolis, MN 55455. Biodun Iginla, Ed. Janaki Bakhle, Ed. Nonfiction: media studies, literary theory, critical aesthetics, philosophy, cultural criticism, regional titles, 50,000 to 225,000 words. Query with detailed prospectus or introduction, table of contents, sample chapter, and resumé. Royalty.

UNIVERSITY OF MISSOURI PRESS—2910 LeMone Blvd., Columbia, MO 65201–8227. Beverly Jarrett, Dir./Ed.in-Chief. Mr. Clair Wilcox, Acquisitions Ed. Scholarly books on American and European history; American, British, and Latin American literary criticism; political philosophy; intellectual history; regional studies; and short fiction.

UNIVERSITY OF NEBRASKA PRESS—312 N. 14th St., Lincoln, NE 68588–0484. Attn: Eds. Specializes in the history of the American West, Native-American studies, and literary criticism. Send proposals with summary, 2 sample chapters, and resumé. See Literary Prize Offers for annual North American Indian Prose Award.

UNIVERSITY OF NEW MEXICO PRESS—Univ. of New Mexico, Albuquerque, NM 87131. Elizabeth C. Hadas, Ed. Dir. David V. Holtby, Larry Ball, Dana Asbury, and Barbara Guth, Eds. Scholarly nonfiction on social and cultural anthropology, archaeology, Western history, art, and photography. Query. Royalty.

UNIVERSITY OF NORTH CAROLINA PRESS—P.O. Box 2288, Chapel Hill, NC 27515–2288. David Perry, Ed. General-interest books (75,000 to 125,000 words) on the lore, crafts, cooking, gardening, travel, and natural history of the Southeast. No fiction or poetry. Query preferred. Royalty.

UNIVERSITY OF NORTH TEXAS PRESS—P.O. Box 13856, Denton, TX 76203–6586. Frances B. Vick, Dir. Charlotte M. Wright, Ed. Books on Western Americana, Texan culture, women's studies, multicultural studies, and folklore. Series include: "War and the Southwest" (perspectives, histories, and memories of war from authors living in the Southwest); "Western Life Series"; "Philosophy and the Environment Series"; and "Texas Writers" (critical biographies of Texas writers). Send manuscript or query with sample chapters; no multiple queries. Royalty.

UNIVERSITY OF OKLAHOMA PRESS—1005 Asp Ave., Norman, OK 73019–0445. John Drayton, Asst. Dir. Books, to 300 pages, on the history of the American West, Indians of the Americas, congressional studies, classical studies, literary criticism, and natural history. Query. Royalty.

UNIVERSITY OF PITTSBURGH PRESS—127 N. Bellefield Ave., Pittsburgh, PA 15260. Attn: Eds. Scholarly nonfiction; poetry. Query.

UNIVERSITY OF TENNESSEE PRESS—293 Communications Bldg., Knoxville, TN 37996–0325. Attn: Acquisitions. Nonfiction, regional trade, and regional fiction, 200 to 300 manuscript pages. No poetry. Query with outline and sample chapters. Royalty.

UNIVERSITY OF WISCONSIN PRESS—114 N. Murray St., Madison, WI 53715–1199. Attn: Acquisitions Ed. Scholarly nonfiction and regional books. Offers Brittingham Prize in Poetry and Pollak Prize in Poetry; query for details.

UNIVERSITY PRESS OF COLORADO—P.O. Box 849, Niwot, CO 80544. Attn: Ed. Dept. Scholarly books in the humanities, social sciences, and applied sciences. Fiction for new series.

UNIVERSITY PRESS OF FLORIDA—15 N.W. 15th St., Gainesville, FL 32611–2079. Walda Metcalf, Ed.-in-Chief/Assoc. Dir. Nonfiction, 150 to 350 manuscript pages, on regional studies, Native Americans, folklore, women's studies, Latin-American studies, contemporary literary criticism, sociology, anthropology, archaeology, international affairs, labor studies, and history. Poetry. Royalty.

THE UNIVERSITY PRESS OF KENTUCKY— 663 S. Limestone St., Lexington, KY 40508–4008. Nancy Grayson Holmes, Ed.-in-Chief. Scholarly books in the major fields. Serious nonfiction of general interest. Books related to Kentucky and the Ohio Valley, the Appalachians, and the South. No fiction, drama, or poetry. Query.

UNIVERSITY PRESS OF MISSISSIPPI—3825 Ridgewood Rd., Jackson, MS 39211–6492. Seetha Srinivasan, Ed.-in-Chief. Scholarly and trade titles in American literature, history, and culture; southern studies; African-American, women's and American studies; social sciences; popular culture; folklife; art and architecture; natural sciences; and other liberal arts.

UNIVERSITY PRESS OF NEW ENGLAND—23 S. Main St., Hanover,

NH 03755–2048. Attn: Ed. Dept. General and scholarly nonfiction. American, British, and European history, literature, literary criticism, creative fiction and nonfiction, and cultural studies. Jewish studies, women's studies, studies of the New England region, environmental studies, and other policy issues. *Hardscrabble Books* imprint: New England fiction.

VAN NOSTRAND REINHOLD—115 Fifth Ave., New York, NY 10003. Brian D. Heer, Pres./CEO, Marianne Russell, VP-Editorial. Business, professional, scientific, and technical publishers of applied reference works. Hospitality, culinary, architecture, graphic and interior design, industrial and environmental health and safety, computer science, engineering, and technical management.

VIKING—375 Hudson St., New York, NY 10014. Barbara Grossman, Pub. Fiction and nonfiction. Nonfiction: psychology, sociology, child-rearing and development, cookbooks, sports, and popular culture. Query. Royalty.

VIKING CHILDREN'S BOOKS—375 Hudson St., New York, NY 10014. Attn: Ed. Dept. Fiction and nonfiction, including biography, history, and sports, for ages 7 to 14. Humor and picture books for ages 2 to 6. Query Children's Book Dept. with outline and sample chapter. SASE required. Royalty.

VILLARD BOOKS—201 E. 50th St., New York, NY 10022. Craig Nelson, V.P./Exec. Ed. Fiction, sports, inspiration, how-to, biography, humor, etc. "We look for authors who are promotable and books we feel we can market well." Royalty.

VINTAGE BOOKS—201 E. 50th St., New York, NY 10022. Attn: Ed. Dept. Quality fiction and serious nonfiction. Query with sample chapters for fiction; query for nonfiction.

VOYAGER PAPERBACKS—See *Harcourt Brace & Co. Children's Book Div.*

WALKER AND COMPANY—435 Hudson St., New York, NY 10014. Attn: Ed. Dept. Adult fiction: mysteries, westerns. Adult nonfiction: Americana, biography, history, science, natural history, medicine, psychology, parenting, sports, outdoors, reference, popular science, self-help, business, and music. Juvenile nonfiction, including biography, science, history, music, and nature. Juvenile fiction: Middle grade and young adult novels. Query with synopsis and SASE. Guidelines. Royalty.

WALLACE-HOMESTEAD BOOKS—See *Chilton Book Co.*

WARNER BOOKS—1271 Ave. of the Americas, New York, NY 10020. Mel Parker, Pub., Warner Paperbacks. No unsolicited manuscripts or proposals.

WASHINGTON SQUARE PRESS—1230 Ave. of the Americas, New York, NY 10020. Amy Einhorn, Ed. Dir. Adult fiction. "We're not looking for 'hip' fiction. We're more about discovering future classics and bringing timeless novels to a broader audience." Query. Royalty. Paperback.

WASHINGTON STATE UNIVERSITY PRESS—Cooper Publications Bldg., Pullman, WA 99164–5910. Glen Lindeman and Keith Petersen, Eds. Books on northwest history, prehistory, and culture, 200 to 350 pages. Send complete manuscript. Royalty.

WASHINGTON WRITERS PUBLISHING HOUSE—P.O. Box 15271,

Washington, DC 20003. Attn: Ed. Dept. Poetry books, 50 to 60 pages, by writers in the greater Washington, DC, area only. Send SASE for guidelines.

WATTS, FRANKLIN—95 Madison Ave., New York, NY 10016. Attn: Submissions. Curriculum-oriented nonfiction for grades 4 to 12, including science, history, social studies, and biography. Query with SASE required.

WEISS ASSOCIATES, DANIEL—33 W. 17th St., New York, NY 10011. Sigrid Berg, Ed. Asst. Book packager. A few parenting and self-help books. Young adult books, 45,000 words; middle grade books, 33,000 words; elementary books, 10,000 to 12,000 words. Query with outline and 2 sample chapters. Royalty and flat fee.

WESLEYAN UNIVERSITY PRESS—110 Mt. Vernon St., Middletown, CT 06459–0433. Eileen McWilliam, Dir. Wesleyan Poetry series: 64 to 80 pages. Query. Royalty.

WESTERN PUBLISHING CO., INC.—850 Third Ave., New York, NY 10022. Robin Warner, V.P./Pub. Alice Bregman, Marilyn Salomon, Ed. Dirs. Children's fiction and nonfiction: picture books, storybooks, concept books, novelty books. Adult nonfiction: field guides. No unsolicited manuscripts. Same address and requirements for *Golden Press,* Kenn Goin, Ed. Royalty or flat fee.

WHISPERING COYOTE PRESS—300 Crescent Ct., Suite 1150, Dallas, TX 75201. Ms. Lou Alpert, Ed. Picture books, 32 pages, for readers ages 4 to 12. Submit complete manuscript with SASE. Royalty.

WHITE PINE PRESS—10 Village Sq., Fredonia, NY 14063. Elaine La-Mattina, Ed. Novels, books of short stories, and essay collections, 250 to 350 pages. Query with outline and sample chapters. Royalty.

WHITECAP BOOKS—351 Lynn Ave., N. Vancouver, BC, Canada V7J 2C4. Colleen MacMillan, Pub. Juvenile books, 72 to 84 pages, and adult books, varying lengths, on such topics as natural history, gardening, parenting, history and regional subjects. Query with table of contents, synopsis, and one sample chapter. Flat fee or royalty.

WHITMAN, ALBERT—6340 Oakton, Morton Grove, IL 60053. Kathleen Tucker, Ed. Picture books for preschool children; novels, biographies, mysteries, and general nonfiction for middle-grade readers. Submit complete manuscript for picture books, 3 chapters and outline for longer fiction; query for nonfiction. Royalty.

WILDERNESS PRESS—2440 Bancroft Way, Berkeley, CA 94704. Thomas Winnett, Ed. Nonfiction: outdoor sports, recreation, and travel in the western U.S. Royalty.

WILEY & SONS, JOHN—605 Third Ave., New York, NY 10158–0012. Attn: Ed. Dept. Nonfiction: science/technology; business/management; real estate; travel; cooking; biography; psychology; computers; language; history; current affairs; health; finance. Send proposals with outline, author vita, market information, and sample chapter. Royalty.

WILLIAMSON PUBLISHING CO.—Church Hill Rd., Charlotte, VT 05445. Attn: Nonfiction Ed. Activity books for children. Adult hands-on books for country living. Writers must send for guidelines before submitting material.

WILLOW CREEK PRESS—Number 1, Fifty One Centre, P.O. Box 881, Minocqua, WI 54548. Tom Petrie, Ed. Books, 25,000 to 50,000 words, on nature, wildlife, and outdoor sports. Query with sample chapters. No fiction. Royalty.

WILLOWISP PRESS— 801 94th Ave. N., St. Petersburg, FL 33702. Attn: Acquisitions Ed. Juvenile books for pre-K through grade 8. Picture books, 300 to 800 words. Fiction, 14,000 to 18,000 words, for grades 3 through 5; 20,000 to 24,000 words for grades 5 through 8. Requirements for nonfiction vary. Query with outline, sample chapter, and SASE. Guidelines. Royalty or flat fee.

WILSHIRE BOOK COMPANY—12015 Sherman Rd., N. Hollywood, CA 91605. Melvin Powers, Pub. Nonfiction: self-help, motivation, inspiration, psychology, spirituality, how-to, entrepreneurship, mail order, and horsemanship; how to make money doing business on computer bulletin boards, especially step-by-step instructions for home-based businesses. Fiction: adult fables, 35,000 to 45,000 words, that teach principles of psychological growth or offer guidance in living. Send synopsis/detailed chapter outline, 3 chapters, and SASE. Royalty.

WINDSWEPT HOUSE PUBLISHERS—Mt. Desert, ME 04660. Jane Weinberger, Pub. Children's picture books; young adult novels; adult fiction and nonfiction. Query.

WISHING WELL—See *Reader's Digest Young Families, Inc.*

WOODBINE HOUSE— 6510 Bells Mill Rd., Bethesda, MD 20817. Susan Stokes, Ed. Books for or about people with disabilities only. No personal accounts, poetry, or books that can be marketed only through bookstores. Query or submit complete manuscript with SASE. Guidelines. Royalty.

WORDWARE PUBLISHING—1506 Capital Ave., Plano, TX 75074. Russell A. Stultz, Ed., *Wordware Computer Books.* Mary Goldman, Ed., *Republic of Texas Press.* Texana, Western, and Southwest regional books. *Seaside Press,* city and regional guides and religion. Query with sample chapters, length estimate, and manuscript completion date. Royalty.

WORKMAN PUBLISHING CO., INC.—708 Broadway, New York, NY 10003. Attn: Ed. Dept. General nonfiction. Normal contractual terms based on agreement.

WORLDWIDE LIBRARY—225 Duncan Mill Rd., Don Mills, Ont., Canada M3B 3K9. Randall Toye, Ed. Dir. Feroze Mohammed, Sr. Ed. Action adventure series for *Gold Eagle* imprint; mystery fiction reprints only. No unsolicited manuscripts or queries.

YEARLING BOOKS—1540 Broadway, New York, NY 10036. Attn: Ed. Dept. Books for K through 6. Manuscripts accepted from agents only. Same address and requirements for *Skylark Books.*

YOLEN BOOKS, JANE—See *Harcourt Brace & Co. Children's Book Div.*

ZEBRA BOOKS— 850 Third Ave., New York, NY 10022. Ann LaFarge, Exec. Ed. Popular fiction: horror; historical romance; *Lovegram Romances* (120,000 words); regencies (80,000 to 120,000 words); sagas; westerns; some nonfiction. Submissions must be addressed to a particular editor.

ZENITH EDITIONS—See *National Press Books, Inc.*

Z-FAVE— 850 Third Ave., 16th Fl., New York, NY 10022. Elise Donner, Exec. Ed. Series and single titles for 8-to 16-year-olds. Send complete synopsis and sample chapters or complete synopsis and complete manuscript. Royalty.

ZINO PRESS CHILDREN'S BOOKS—2348 Pinehurst Dr., Middleton, WI 53562. Judith Laitman, Pres. Picture books and nonfiction books for children. Flat fee.

ZONDERVAN PUBLISHING HOUSE—5300 Patterson S.E., Grand Rapids, MI 49530. Attn: Manuscript Review. Christian titles. General fiction and nonfiction; academic and professional books. Query with outline, sample chapter, and SASE. Royalty. Guidelines.

UNIVERSITY PRESSES

University presses generally publish books of a scholarly nature or of specialized interest by authorities in a given field. A few publish fiction and poetry. Many publish only a handful of titles a year. Always query first. Do not send a manuscript until you have been invited to do so by the editor. Several of the following presses and their detailed editorial submission requirements are included in the *Book Publishers* list.

BOISE STATE UNIVERSITY—See *Hemingway Western Studies Series.*

BOWLING GREEN STATE UNIVERSITY—See *Popular Press.*

BUCKNELL UNIVERSITY PRESS—Bucknell University, Lewisburg, PA 17837.

CAMBRIDGE UNIVERSITY PRESS—40 W. 20th St., New York, NY 10011–4211.

THE CATHOLIC UNIVERSITY OF AMERICA PRESS—620 Michigan Ave. N.E., Washington, DC 20064.

COLUMBIA UNIVERSITY PRESS—562 W. 113th St., New York, NY 10025.

DUKE UNIVERSITY PRESS—Box 90660, Durham, NC 27708–0660.

DUQUESNE UNIVERSITY PRESS—600 Forbes Ave., Pittsburgh, PA 15282–0101.

FORDHAM UNIVERSITY PRESS—University Box L, Bronx, NY 10458–5172.

GEORGIA STATE UNIVERSITY BUSINESS PRESS—University Plaza, Atlanta, GA 30303–3093.

HEMINGWAY WESTERN STUDIES SERIES—Boise State Univ., 1910 University Dr., Boise, ID 83725.

INDIANA UNIVERSITY PRESS—601 N. Morton St., Bloomington, IN 47404–3797.

THE JOHNS HOPKINS UNIVERSITY PRESS—2715 N. Charles St., Baltimore, MD 21218.

KENT STATE UNIVERSITY PRESS—Kent State Univ., Kent, OH 44242.

LOUISIANA STATE UNIVERSITY PRESS—P.O. Box 25053, Baton Rouge, LA 70894–5053.

LOYOLA UNIVERSITY PRESS—3441 N. Ashland Ave., Chicago, IL 60657–1397.

THE MICHIGAN STATE UNIVERSITY PRESS—1405 S. Harrison Rd., Suite 25, E. Lansing, MI 48823–5202.

THE MIT PRESS—Acquisitions Dept., 55 Hayward St., Cambridge, MA 02142.

NEW YORK UNIVERSITY PRESS—70 Washington Sq. S., New York, NY 10012.

OHIO STATE UNIVERSITY PRESS—180 Pressey Hall, 1070 Carmack Rd., Columbus, OH 43210.

OREGON STATE UNIVERSITY PRESS—101 Waldo Hall, Corvallis, OR 97331.

THE PENNSYLVANIA STATE UNIVERSITY PRESS—University Support Bldg. 1, Suite C, University Park, PA 16802.

POPULAR PRESS—Bowling Green State Univ., Bowling Green, OH 43403.

PRINCETON UNIVERSITY PRESS—41 William St., Princeton, NJ 08540.

SOUTHERN ILLINOIS UNIVERSITY PRESS—Box 3697, Carbondale, IL 62902–3697.

SOUTHERN METHODIST UNIVERSITY PRESS—Box 415, Dallas, TX 75275.

STANFORD UNIVERSITY PRESS—Stanford University, Stanford, CA 94305–2235.

STATE UNIVERSITY OF NEW YORK PRESS—State Univ. Plaza, Albany, NY 12246–0001.

SYRACUSE UNIVERSITY PRESS—1600 Jamesville Ave., Syracuse, NY 13244–5160.

TEMPLE UNIVERSITY PRESS—Broad and Oxford Sts., Philadelphia, PA 19122.

UNIVERSITY OF ALABAMA PRESS—P.O. Box 870380, Tuscaloosa, AL 35487–0380.

UNIVERSITY OF ARIZONA PRESS—1230 N. Park Ave., Suite 102, Tucson, AZ 85719.

UNIVERSITY OF CALIFORNIA PRESS—2120 Berkeley Way, Berkeley, CA 94720.

UNIVERSITY OF CHICAGO PRESS—5801 Ellis Ave., Chicago, IL 60637–1496.

UNIVERSITY OF GEORGIA PRESS—330 Research Dr., Athens, GA 30602–4901.

UNIVERSITY OF ILLINOIS PRESS—1325 S. Oak St., Champaign, IL 61820.

UNIVERSITY OF MASSACHUSETTS PRESS—Box 429, Amherst, MA 01004–0429.

UNIVERSITY OF MICHIGAN PRESS—P.O. Box 1104, 839 Greene St., Ann Arbor, MI 48106–1104.

UNIVERSITY OF MINNESOTA PRESS—2037 University Ave. S.E., Minneapolis, MN 55455.

UNIVERSITY OF MISSOURI PRESS—2910 LeMone Blvd., Columbia, MO 65201–8227.

UNIVERSITY OF NEBRASKA PRESS—312 N. 14th St., Lincoln, NE 68588–0484.

UNIVERSITY OF NEW MEXICO PRESS—Univ. of New Mexico, Albuquerque, NM 87131.

UNIVERSITY OF NORTH CAROLINA PRESS—P.O. Box 2288, Chapel Hill, NC 27515–2288.

UNIVERSITY OF NORTH TEXAS PRESS—P.O. Box 13856, Denton, TX 76203–6586.

UNIVERSITY OF NOTRE DAME PRESS—University of Notre Dame, Notre Dame, IN 46556.

UNIVERSITY OF OKLAHOMA PRESS—1005 Asp Ave., Norman, OK 73019–0445.

UNIVERSITY OF PITTSBURGH PRESS—127 N. Bellefield Ave., Pittsburgh, PA 15260.

UNIVERSITY OF SOUTH CAROLINA PRESS—University of South Carolina, Carolina Plaza, 8th Fl., Columbia, SC 29208.

UNIVERSITY OF TENNESSEE PRESS—293 Communications Bldg., Knoxville, TN 37996–0325.

UNIVERSITY OF UTAH PRESS—101 U.S.B., Salt Lake City, UT 84112.

UNIVERSITY OF WASHINGTON PRESS—P.O. Box 50096, Seattle, WA 98145–5096.

UNIVERSITY OF WISCONSIN PRESS—114 N. Murray St., Madison, WI 53715–1199.

UNIVERSITY PRESS OF COLORADO—P.O. Box 849, Niwot, CO 80544.

UNIVERSITY PRESS OF FLORIDA—15 N.W. 15th St., Gainesville, FL 32611–2079.

THE UNIVERSITY PRESS OF KENTUCKY—663 S. Limestone St., Lexington, KY 40508–4008.

UNIVERSITY PRESS OF MISSISSIPPI—3825 Ridgewood Rd., Jackson, MS 39211–6492.

UNIVERSITY PRESS OF NEW ENGLAND—23 S. Main St., Hanover, NH 03755–2048.

THE UNIVERSITY PRESS OF VIRGINIA—Box 3608, Univ. Sta., Charlottesville, VA 22903.

WASHINGTON STATE UNIVERSITY PRESS—Cooper Publications Bldg., Pullman, WA 99164–5910.

WAYNE STATE UNIVERSITY PRESS— 4809 Woodward Ave., Detroit, MI 48201.

WESLEYAN UNIVERSITY PRESS—110 Mt.Vernon St., Middletown, CT 06459–0433.

YALE UNIVERSITY PRESS—Box 209040, 92A Yale Sta., New Haven, CT 06520–9040.

SYNDICATES

Syndicates buy material from writers and artists to sell to newspapers all over the country and the world. Authors are paid either a percentage of the gross proceeds or an outright fee.

Of course, features by people well known in their fields have the best chance of being syndicated. In general, syndicates want columns that have been popular in a local newspaper, perhaps, or magazine. Since most syndicated fiction has been published previously in magazines or books, beginning fiction writers should try to sell their stories to magazines before submitting them to syndicates.

Always query syndicates before sending manuscripts, since their needs change frequently, and be sure to enclose SASEs with queries and manuscripts.

ARKIN MAGAZINE SYNDICATE—500 Bayview Dr., N. Miami Beach, FL 33160. Joseph Arkin, Ed. Dir. Articles, 750 to 2,200 words, for trade and professional magazines. Must have small-business slant, be written in layman's language, and offer solutions to business problems. Articles should apply to many businesses, not just a specific industry. No columns. Pays 3¢ to 10¢ a word, on acceptance. SASE required; query not necessary.

CONTEMPORARY FEATURES SYNDICATE—P. O. Box 1258, Jackson, TN 38302–1258. Lloyd Russell, Ed. Articles, 1,000 to 10,000 words: how-to, money savers, business, etc. Self-help pieces for small business. Pays from $25, on acceptance. Query.

HARRIS & ASSOCIATES FEATURES—350 Sharon Park Dr., Q-1, Menlo Park, CA 94025. Dick Harris, Ed. Sports-and family-oriented features, to 1,200 words; fillers and short humor, 500 to 800 words. Queries preferred. Pays varying rates.

HISPANIC LINK NEWS SERVICE—1420 N St. N.W., Washington, DC 20005. Charles A. Ericksen, Ed. Trend articles, opinion and personal experience pieces, and general features with Hispanic focus, 650 to 700 words; editorial cartoons. Pays $25 for op-ed columns and cartoons, on acceptance. Guidelines.

THE HOLLYWOOD INSIDE SYNDICATE—Box 49957, Los Angeles, CA

90049–0957. John Austin, Dir. Feature articles, 750 to 2,500 words, on TV and film personalities with B&W photo(s). Article suggestions for 3-part series. Pieces on unusual medical and scientific breakthroughs. Pays on percentage basis for features, negotiated rates for ideas, on publication.

NATIONAL NEWS BUREAU—P.O. Box 43039, Philadelphia, PA 19129. Harry Jay Katz, Ed. Articles, 500 to 1,500 words, interviews, consumer news, how-tos, travel pieces, reviews, entertainment pieces, features, etc. Pays on publication.

NEW YORK TIMES SYNDICATION SALES—122 E. 42nd St., New York, NY 10168. Gloria Brown Anderson, Exec. Ed. Previously published health, lifestyle, and entertainment articles only, to 1,500 words. Query with published article or tear sheet and SASE. Pays 50% royalty on collected sales.

OCEANIC PRESS SERVICE—Seaview Business Park, 1030 Calle Cordillera, Unit #106, San Clemente, CA 92673. Peter Carbone, General Mgr. Buys reprint rights for foreign markets, on previously published novels, self-help, and how-to books; interviews with celebrities; illustrated features on celebrities, family, health, beauty, personal relationships, etc.; cartoons, comic strips. Pays on acceptance or half on acceptance, half on syndication. Query.

SINGER MEDIA CORP.—1030 Calle Cordillera, #106, San Clemente, CA 92673. Helen J. Lee, Ed. U.S. and/or foreign reprint rights to published romance books, historical novels, gothics, and mysteries (published during last 25 years); business management titles, self-help, and computer. Biography, women's interest, all lengths. Home repair, psychological quizzes. Interviews with celebrities. Humor. Illustrated columns, cartoons, comic strips. Pays on percentage basis or by outright purchase.

TRIBUNE MEDIA SERVICES—435 N. Michigan Ave., #1500, Chicago, IL 60611. Mark Mathes, Man. Ed. Continuing columns, comic strips, features, electronic databases.

UNITED FEATURE SYNDICATE—200 Park Ave., New York, NY 10166. Diana Loevy, V.P./ Exec. Ed. Syndicated columns; no one-shots or series. Payment by contractual arrangement. Send samples with SASE.

UNITED PRESS INTERNATIONAL—1400 Eye St. N.W., Washington, DC 20005. Robert A. Martin, Man. Ed., International. Tobin Beck, Man. Ed., North America. No free-lance material.

LITERARY PRIZE OFFERS

Each year many important literary contests are open to free-lance writers from all genres. Writers seeking publication of their book-length poetry manuscripts are encouraged to enter the several contests in this list that offer publication as the prize; many presses that once considered unsolicited poetry manuscripts by emerging or unpublished writers now limit their reading of such manuscripts to those entered in their contests for new writers. The summaries given below are intended merely as guides; since submission requirements are more detailed than space allows, writers should send SASE for complete guidelines before entering any contest. Writers are also advised to check the monthly "Prize Offers" column of *The Writer* Magazine (120 Boylston St., Boston, MA 02116–4615) for additional contest listings and up-to-date contest requirements. Deadlines are annual unless otherwise noted.

ACADEMY OF AMERICAN POETS—Walt Whitman Award, 584 Broadway, Suite 1208, New York, NY 10012–3250. An award of $5,000 plus publication is offered for a book-length poetry manuscript by a poet who has not yet published a volume of poetry. Deadline: November 15.

ACADEMY OF MOTION PICTURE ARTS AND SCIENCES—The Nicholl Fellowships, Dept. WR, 8949 Wilshire Blvd., Beverly Hills, CA 90211–1972. Up to 5 fellowships of $25,000 each are awarded for original screenplays that display exceptional craft and engaging storytelling. Deadline: May 1.

ACTORS' PLAYHOUSE—National Children's Theatre Festival, Miracle Theatre, 280 Miracle Mile, Coral Gables, FL 33134. Attn: Judy Buckland, Education Dir. A prize of $1,200 plus production is awarded for the best musical, 45 to 60 minutes long, for ages 5 to 12; $800 plus production is awarded for the best play, 40 to 50 minutes long, for ages 12 to 17. Deadline: December 1.

ACTORS THEATRE OF LOUISVILLE—Ten-Minute Play Contest, 316 W. Main St., Louisville, KY 40202–4218. A prize of $1,000 is offered for a previously unproduced 10-page script. Deadline: December 1.

AMERICAN ACADEMY OF ARTS AND LETTERS—Richard Rogers Awards, 633 W. 155th St., New York, NY 10032. Offers subsidized productions or staged readings in New York City by a nonprofit theater for a musical, play with music, thematic review, or any comparable work other than opera. Deadline: November 1.

AMERICAN ANTIQUARIAN SOCIETY—Fellowships for Historical Research, 185 Salisbury St., Worcester, MA 01609–1634. Attn: John B. Hench. At least 3 fellowships are awarded to creative and performing artists, writers, filmmakers, and journalists for research on pre-20th century American history. Residencies are 4 to 8 weeks; travel expenses and stipends of $1,200 per month are offered. Deadline: October 1.

AMERICAN FICTION/NEW RIVERS PRESS—Fiction Awards, P.O. Box 229, Moorhead State Univ., Moorhead, MN 56563. Attn: Alan Davis, Ed. Prizes of $1,000, $500, and $250 are awarded for short stories, to 10,000 words. The stories of up to 20 finalists are published in the *American Fiction* anthology. Deadline: May 1.

THE AMERICAN-SCANDINAVIAN FOUNDATION—Translation Prize, 725 Park Ave., New York, NY 10021. A prize of $2,000 is awarded for an outstanding English translation of poetry, fiction, drama, or literary prose originally written in Danish, Finnish, Icelandic, Norwegian, or Swedish. Deadline: June 1.

ANHINGA PRESS—Anhinga Prize for Poetry, P.O. Box 10595, Tallahassee, FL 32302–0595. A $2,000 prize will be awarded for an unpublished full-length collection of poetry, 48 to 72 pages, by a poet who has published no more than one full-length collection. Deadline: March 15.

ARMY MAGAZINE—Essay Contest, 2425 Wilson Blvd., Arlington, VA 22201. Prizes of $1,000, $500, and $250 plus publication are awarded for essays on a given theme. Deadline: May 31.

THE ASSOCIATED WRITING PROGRAMS—Awards Series, Tallwood House, Mail Stop 1E3, George Mason Univ., Fairfax, VA 22030. In the categories of poetry, short fiction, the novel, and nonfiction, the prize is book publication and a $2,000 honorarium. Deadline: February 29.

ASSOCIATION OF JEWISH LIBRARIES—Sydney Taylor Manuscript Competition, 1327 Wyntercreek Ln., Dunwoody, GA 30338. Attn: Paula T. Sandfelder, Coordinator. Offers $1,000 for the best fiction manuscript, 64 to 200 pages, by an unpublished book author, writing for readers 8 to 11. Stories must have a positive Jewish focus. Deadline: January 15.

ASTRAEA NATIONAL LESBIAN ACTION FOUNDATION—Emerging Writers Awards, Lesbian Writers Fund, 666 Broadway, Suite 520, New York, NY 10012. Five awards of $11,000 each are given to lesbian writers of fiction or poetry whose work includes some lesbian content. Writers must have published at least one piece in a newspaper, periodical, or anthology, and must not have published more than one book. Deadline: March 1.

AUSTIN PEAY STATE UNIVERSITY—Rainmaker Awards in Poetry, P.O. Box 4565, Clarksville, TN 37044. A prize of $500 plus publication in *Zone 3* is awarded for the best poem. Deadline: January 1.

BAKER'S PLAYS—High School Playwriting Contest, 100 Chauncy St., Boston, MA 02111. Plays about the high school experience, written by high school students, are eligible for awards of $500, $250, and $100. Deadline: January 31.

BANTAM DOUBLEDAY DELL BOOKS FOR YOUNG READERS—Marguerite de Angeli Prize, Dept. BFYR, 1540 Broadway, New York, NY 10036. A prize of $1,500 and a $3,500 advance against royalties is awarded for a middle-grade fiction manuscript that explores the diversity of the American experience. Open to U.S. and Canadian writers who have not previously published a novel for middle-grade readers. Deadline: June 30.

BELLES LETTRES—Personal Essay Contest, 11151 Captain's Walk Ct., N. Potomac, MD 20878. A prize of publication plus $500 is awarded for the best personal essay of up to 2,000 words, on any topic. Deadline: August 31.

THE BELLINGHAM REVIEW—Tobias Wolff Award in Fiction/49th Parallel Poetry Award, MS-9053, Western Washington Univ., Bellingham, WA 98225. Tobias Wolff Award in Fiction: Offers prizes of $250 plus publication, $150, and $100 for a short story or novel excerpt. Deadline: February 29. Annie Dillard Award in Nonfiction: Offers prizes of $250 plus publication, $150, and $100 for previously unpublished essays. Deadline: April 30. 49th Parallel Poetry Award: Offers publication and prizes of $150, $100, and $50 for individual poems. Deadline: December 1.

BEVERLY HILLS THEATRE GUILD/JULIE HARRIS PLAYWRIGHT AWARD—2815 N. Beachwood Dr., Los Angeles, CA 90068. Attn: Marcella Meharg. Offers prize of $5,000, plus possible $2,000 for productions in Los Angeles area, for previously unproduced and unpublished full-length play. A $2,000 second prize and $1,000 third prize are also offered. Deadline: November 1.

BIRMINGHAM-SOUTHERN COLLEGE—Hackney Literary Awards,

BSC A-3, Birmingham, AL 35254. A prize of $2,000 is awarded for an unpublished novel, any length. Deadline: September 30. Also, a $2,000 prize is shared for the winning short story, to 5,000 words, and poem of up to 50 lines. Deadline: December 31.

BLUE MOUNTAIN CENTER—Richard J. Margolis Award, 101 Arch St., 9th Fl., Boston, MA 02110. A prize of $1,000 is awarded annually to a promising journalist, poet, or essayist whose work combines warmth, humor, wisdom, and a concern with social issues. Applications should include up to 30 pages of published or unpublished work. Deadline: July 1.

BOISE STATE UNIVERSITY—Eccentric Format Book Competition, Hemingway Western Studies Ctr., Boise, ID 83725. Tom Trusky, Ed. A prize of $500 and publication is awarded for up to 3 books; manuscripts (text and/or visual content) and proposals are considered for the short-run printing of books on public issues, especially the Inter-Mountain West. Deadline: December 1.

BOSTON MAGAZINE—Fiction Contest, 300 Massachusetts Ave., Boston, MA 02115. Publication and $500 are awarded for the best short story on a given theme, up to 3,000 words, set in or around Boston. Deadline: September 1.

BOSTON REVIEW—Short Story Contest, E53–407, MIT, Cambridge, MA 02139. A prize of $300 plus publication is awarded for the best previously unpublished story of up to 4,000 words. Deadline: October 1.

BUCKNELL UNIVERSITY—The Philip Roth Residence in Creative Writing, Stadler Ctr. for Poetry, Bucknell Univ., Lewisburg, PA 17837. Attn: John Wheatcroft, Dir. The fall residency may be used by a writer, over 21, not currently enrolled in a university, to work on a first or second book. The residency is awarded in odd-numbered years to a fiction writer, and in even-numbered years to a poet. Deadline: March 1.

CASE WESTERN RESERVE UNIVERSITY—Marc A. Klein Playwriting Award, Dept. of Theater Arts, 10900 Euclid Ave., Cleveland, OH 44106–7077. A prize of $1,000 plus production is offered for an original, previously unproduced full-length play by a student currently enrolled at an American college or university. Deadline: May 15.

CHELSEA AWARD COMPETITION—P.O. Box 1040, York Beach, ME 03910. Attn: Ed. Prizes of $500 plus publication are awarded for the best unpublished short fiction and poetry. Deadlines: June 15 (fiction); December 15 (poetry).

CHICAGO TRIBUNE—Nelson Algren Awards, 435 N. Michigan Ave., Chicago, IL 60611. A first prize of $5,000 and 3 runner-up prizes of $1,000 are awarded for outstanding unpublished short stories, 2,500 to 10,000 words, by American writers. Deadline: February 1.

CLAREMONT GRADUATE SCHOOL—Kingsley Tufts Poetry Awards, 160 E. 10th St., Claremont, CA 91711. An award of $50,000 is given to an American poet whose work is judged most worthy. An award of $5,000 is given to an emerging poet whose work displays extraordinary promise. Books of poetry published or manuscripts completed in the calendar year are considered. Deadline: December 15.

CLAUDER COMPETITION—P.O. Box 383259, Cambridge, MA 02238–3259. Awards $3,000 plus professional production for a full-length play by a

New England writer. Runner-up prizes of $500 and a staged reading also awarded. Deadline: June 30 (of odd-numbered years).

CLEVELAND STATE UNIVERSITY POETRY CENTER—Poetry Ctr. Prize, Dept. of English, Rhodes Tower, Rm. 1815, 1983 E. 24th St., Cleveland, OH 44115–2440. Publication and $1,000 are awarded for a previously unpublished book-length volume of poetry. Deadline: March 1.

COALITION FOR THE ADVANCEMENT OF JEWISH EDUCATION—David Dornstein Memorial Creative Writing Contest, 261 W. 35th St., Fl. 12A, New York, NY 10001. A prize of publication and $1,000 is awarded for the best original, previously unpublished short story, to 5,000 words, on a Jewish theme or topic, by a writer age 18 to 35. Deadline: December 31.

COLONIAL PLAYERS, INC.—Promising Playwright Award, 99 Great Lake Dr., Annapolis, MD 21403. Attn: Frank Moorman. A prize of $750 plus possible production will be awarded for the best full-length play by a resident of MD, DC, VA, WV, DE, or PA. Deadline: December 31 (of even-numbered years).

COMMUNITY CHILDREN'S THEATRE OF KANSAS CITY—8021 E. 129th Terrace, Grandview, MO 64030. Attn: Mrs. Blanche Sellens, Dir. A prize of $500, plus production, is awarded for the best play, up to one hour long, to be performed by adults for elementary school audiences. Deadline: January 31.

THE CRITIC—Short Story Contest, Thomas More Assoc., 205 W. Monroe St., 6th Floor, Chicago, IL 60606–5097. Original, unpublished short stories are eligible for the prize of $500 plus publication. Deadline: September 1 (of even-numbered years).

CUMBERLAND POETRY REVIEW—Robert Penn Warren Poetry Prize Competition, P.O. Box 120128, Nashville, TN 37212. Three poems of up to 100 lines each may be submitted for prizes of $500, $300, and $200. Deadline: March 15.

EUGENE V. DEBS FOUNDATION—Bryant Spann Memorial Prize, Dept. of History, Indiana State Univ., Terre Haute, IN 47809. Offers a prize of $1,000 for a published or unpublished article or essay on themes relating to social protest or human equality. Deadline: April 30.

DEEP SOUTH WRITERS CONFERENCE—Contest Clerk, Drawer 44691, Univ. of Southwestern Louisianna, Lafayette, LA 70504–4691. Prizes ranging from $50 to $300 are offered for unpublished manuscripts in the following categories: short fiction, novel, nonfiction, poetry, drama, and French literature. Deadline: July 15. Miller Award: offers $500 for a play dealing with some aspect of the life of Edward de Vere (1550–1604), the 17th Earl of Oxford. Deadline: July 15 (of odd-numbered years).

DELACORTE PRESS—Prize for First Young Adult Novel, Bantam Doubleday Dell BFYR, 1540 Broadway, New York, NY 10036. A writer who has not previously published a young adult novel may submit a book-length manuscript with a contemporary setting suitable for readers ages 12 to 18. The prize is $1,500, a $6,000 advance, and hardcover and paperback publication. Deadline: December 31.

BARBARA DEMING MEMORIAL FUND, INC.—Money for Women, P.O. Box 40–1043, Brooklyn, NY 11240–1043. Attn: Pam McAllister, Administrator. Grants of up to $1,000 are awarded semiannually to individual feminists in the arts whose work addresses women's concerns and/or speaks for peace and justice from a feminist perspective. Deadlines: June 30; December 31.

DRURY COLLEGE—Playwriting Contest, 900 N. Benton Ave., Springfield, MO 65802. Attn: Sandy Asher, Writer-in-Residence. Prizes of $300 and 2 $150 honorable mentions, plus possible production, are awarded for original, previously unproduced one-act plays. Deadline: December 1 (of even-numbered years).

DUBUQUE FINE ARTS PLAYERS—One-Act Playwriting Contest, 1321 Tomahawk Dr., Dubuque, IA 52003. Attn: Jennie G. Stabenow, Coordinator. Prizes of $600, $300 and $200 plus possible production are awarded for unproduced, original one-act plays of up to 40 minutes. Deadline: January 31.

DUKE UNIVERSITY—Dorothea Lange-Paul Taylor Prize, Prize Committee, Ctr. for Documentary Studies, Box 90802, Duke Univ., Durham, NC 27708–0802. A grant of up to $10,000 is awarded to a writer and photographer working together in the formative stages of a documentary project that will ultimately result in a publishable work. Deadline: January 31.

EIGHTH MOUNTAIN PRESS—Poetry Prize, 624 Southeast 29th Ave., Portland, OR 97214. A prize of a $1,000 advance plus publication is awarded for a poetry manuscript, 50 to 120 pages, by a woman writer. Deadline: February 1 (of even-numbered years).

ELF: ECLECTIC LITERARY FORUM—Ruth Cable Memorial Prize, P.O. Box 392, Tonawanda, NY 14150. Awards of $500 and 3 $50 prizes are given for poems up to 50 lines. Deadline: March 31.

ELMIRA COLLEGE—Playwriting Award, Dept. of Theatre, Elmira College, Elmira, NY 14901. Attn: Prof. Amnon Kabatchnik, Artistic Dir. A prize of $1,000 plus production is awarded for the best original full-length play. Deadline: June 1 (of even-numbered years).

EMPORIA STATE UNIVERSITY—Bluestem Award, English Dept., Emporia State Univ., Emporia, KS 66801–5087. A prize of $1,000 plus publication is awarded for a previously unpublished book of poems by a U.S. author. Deadline: March 1.

ENSEMBLE THEATRE—George Hawkins Play Contest, 3535 Main St., Houston, TX 77002. Offers $500 plus production for an original one-act play or musical, using adult actors, for African-American audiences, ages 6 to 16. Deadline: March 15.

THE FLORIDA REVIEW—Short Fiction Contest, Dept. of English, Univ. of Central Florida, Orlando, FL 32816–0001. Attn: Russell Kesler, Ed. Prizes of $500 and $200 plus publication are offered for short stories of up to 7,500 words. Deadline: June 15.

FLORIDA STATE UNIVERSITY—World's Best Short Short Story Contest, English Dept., Florida State Univ., Tallahassee, FL 32306. Attn: Jerome Stern. A prize of $100, a box of Florida oranges, and publication are offered for the best short short story, 250 words. Deadline: February 15.

FLORIDA STATE UNIVERSITY CREATIVE WRITING PROGRAM—Richard Eberhart Prize in Poetry, English Dept., F.S.U., Tallahassee, FL 32306. A $300 prize and publication in *Sun Dog: The Southeast Review,* is awarded for the best unpublished poem of 30 to 100 lines. Deadline: September 15.

FLORIDA STUDIO THEATRE—Shorts Contest, 1241 N. Palm Ave., Sarasota, FL 34236. Attn: Christian Angermann. Short scripts, songs, and other performance pieces on a given theme are eligible for a prize of $500. Deadline: February 15.

THE FORMALIST—Howard Nemerov Sonnet Award, 320 Hunter Dr., Evansville, IN 47711. A prize of $1,000 plus publication is offered for a previously unpublished, original sonnet. Deadline: June 15.

FOUR WAY BOOKS—Poetry Contests, P.O. Box 607, Marshfield, MA 02050. Intro Series in Poetry: A prize of $1,000 plus publication is awarded for a book-length collection of poems by a poet who has not previously published a book of poetry. Award Series in Poetry: A prize of $1,500 plus publication is awarded for a book-length collection of poems by a poet who has published at least one collection of poetry. Deadline: April 30.

GEORGE MASON UNIVERSITY—Greg Grummer Award in Poetry, *Phoebe: A Journal of Literary Arts*, 4400 Univ. Dr., Fairfax, VA 22030. A prize of $500 plus publication is offered for an outstanding previously unpublished poem. Deadline: December 15.

THE GEORGE WASHINGTON UNIVERSITY—Jenny McKean Moore Writer-in-Washington, Dept. of English, The George Washington Univ., Washington, DC 20052. Attn: Prof. Christopher Sten. A salaried teaching position for 2 semesters is offered to a creative writer (of various mediums in alternate years) having "significant publications and a demonstrated commitment to teaching. The writer need not have conventional academic credentials." The 1996–97 position was awarded to a poet. Deadline: November 15.

GLIMMER TRAIN PRESS—Semiannual Short Story Award for New Writers, 812 S.W. Washington St., #1205, Portland, OR 97205. Writers whose fiction has never appeared in a nationally distributed publication are eligible to enter their stories of 1,200 to 7,500 words. Prizes are $1,200 plus publication, $500, and $300. Deadlines: March 31; September 30.

GREENFIELD REVIEW LITERARY CENTER—North American Native Authors First Book Awards, P.O. Box 308, 2 Middle Grove Rd., Greenfield Ctr., NY 12833. Attn: Joseph Bruchac, Dir. Native Americans of American Indian, Aleut, Inuit, or Metis ancestry who have not yet published a book are eligible to enter poetry, 48 to 100 pages, and prose, 120 to 240 pages (fiction or nonfiction) for publication. Deadline: May 1.

GROLIER POETRY PRIZE—6 Plympton St., Cambridge, MA 02138. Two $150 honorariums are awarded for poetry manuscripts of up to 10 double-spaced pages, including no more than 5 previously unpublished poems, by writers who have not yet published a book of poems. Deadline: May 1.

HEEKIN GROUP FOUNDATION—Fiction Fellowships Competition, 68860 Goodrich Rd., Sisters, OR 97759. Awards the following fellowships to beginning career writers: 2 $1,500 Tara Fellowships in Short Fiction; 2 $3,000 James Fellowships for a Novel in Progress; one $2,000 Mary Moloy Fellowship for a Children's Working Novel; and one $2,000 Siobhan Fellowhip for a Nonfiction Essay. Writers who have never published a novel, a children's novel, more than 5 short stories in national publication, or an essay are eligible to enter. Deadline: December 1.

KEY WEST HEMINGWAY DAYS FESTIVAL—Writing Contests, P.O. Box 4045, Key West, FL 33041. First Novel Contest: $1,000 plus literary representation for an unpublished first novel. Deadline: May 1. Young Writers' Scholarships: 2 $1,000 prizes for 6 pages of fiction, nonfiction, or poetry by college-bound high school juniors or seniors. Deadline: May 1. Short Story Contest: $1,000 plus festival airfare, and 2 $500 prizes for short stories, 3,000 words or fewer. Deadline: June 1.

HIGHLIGHTS FOR CHILDREN—Fiction Contest, 803 Church St., Honesdale, PA 18431. Three $1,000 prizes plus publication are offered for stories on a given subject, up to 900 words. The theme for 1996: "Stories about children in today's world." Deadline: February 29.

HILTON-LONG POETRY FOUNDATION—Naomi Long Madgett Poetry Award, c/o Lotus Press, Inc., P.O. Box 21607, Detroit, MI 48221. A prize of $500 plus publication will be awarded to an African-American writer for a previously unpublished collection of poems, 60 to 80 pages. Deadline: April 1.

RUTH HINDMAN FOUNDATION—H.E. Francis Award, Dept. of English, Univ. of Alabama, Huntsville, AL 35899. A prize of $1,000 plus publication is awarded for a short story of up to 5,000 words. Deadline: December 31.

L. RON HUBBARD'S WRITERS OF THE FUTURE CONTEST—P.O. Box 1630, Los Angeles, CA 90078. Unpublished fiction writers are eligible to enter science fiction or fantasy short stories under 10,000 words, or novellas under 17,000 words. Quarterly prizes: $1,000, $750, and $500. Annual prize: $4,000. Deadlines: March 31; June 30; September 30; December 31.

HUMBOLDT STATE UNIVERSITY—Raymond Carver Short Story Contest, English Dept., Humbolt State Univ. Arcata, CA 95521–4957. Offers a $500 first prize, plus publication in the literary journal *Toyon*, and a $250 second prize for an unpublished short story, to 25 pages, by a writer living in the U.S. Deadline: November 1.

ICS BOOKS, INC.—"No S---! There I Was . . ." Contest, 1370 E. 86th Pl., Merrillville, IN 46410. Prizes of $2,000 and $500 plus publication are offered for humorous, tall tales. Deadline: December 1.

INSTITUTE OF HISPANIC CULTURE—José Martí Award, 3400 Bissonnet, Suite 135, Houston, TX 77005–2153. Prize of $1,000, $600, and $400 are awarded for essays, 15 to 20 pages, on a given theme. Deadline: August 31.

IOWA WOMAN—Writing Contest for Women, P.O. Box 680, Iowa City, IA 52244. Women writers may enter short fiction, essays, or poems for a $500 first prize, $250 second prize, and publication. Deadline: December 31.

IUPUI CHILDREN'S THEATRE—Playwriting Competition, Indiana Univ.-Purdue Univ. at Indianapolis, 525 N. Blackford St., Indianapolis, IN 46202–3120. Offers 4 $1,000 prizes plus staged readings for plays for young people. Deadline: September 1 (of even-numbered years).

ALICE JAMES BOOKS—Beatrice Hawley Award, Univ. of Maine at Farmington, 98 Main St., Farmington, ME 04938. A prize of publication plus 100 free copies is offered for the best poetry manuscript, 60 to 70 pages. Deadline: January 15.

JEWISH COMMUNITY CENTER THEATRE—Dorothy Silver Playwriting Competition, 3505 Mayfield Rd., Cleveland Heights, OH 44118. Attn: Elaine Rembrandt, Dir. Offers $1,000 and a staged reading for an original, previously unproduced full-length play, on some aspect of the Jewish experience. Deadline: December 15.

THE CHESTER H. JONES FOUNDATION—National Poetry Competition, P. O. Box 498, Chardon, OH 44024. Prizes of $1,000, $750, $500, and $250, as well as several $50 and $10 prizes are awarded for original, unpublished poems of up to 32 lines. Deadline: March 31.

JAMES JONES SOCIETY—First Novel Fellowship, c/o Dept. of English, Wilkes Univ., Wilkes-Barre, PA 18766. An award of $2,500 is offered for a first novel-in-progress by an American. Deadline: March 1.

THE JOURNAL: THE LITERARY MAGAZINE OF O.S.U.—The Ohio State Univ. Press, 180 Pressey Hall, 1070 Carmack Rd., Columbus, OH 43210–1002. Attn: David Citino, Poetry Ed. Awards $1,000 plus publication for at least 48 pages of original, unpublished poetry. Deadline: September 30.

KALLIOPE: A JOURNAL OF WOMEN'S ART—Sue Saniel Elkind Poetry Contest, Florida Community College at Jacksonville, 3939 Roosevelt Blvd., Jacksonville, FL 32205. Publication and $1,000 are awarded for the best poem, under 50 lines, written by a woman. Deadline: October 15.

KEATS/KERLAN MEMORIAL FELLOWSHIP—The Ezra Jack Keats/Kerlan Collection Memorial Fellowship Committee, 109 Walter Library, 117 Pleasant St. S.E., Univ. of Minnesota, Minneapolis, MN 55455. A $1,500 fellowship is awarded to a talented writer and/or illustrator of children's books who wishes to use the Kerlan Collection for furtherance of his or her artistic development. Deadline: May 1.

KENT STATE UNIVERSITY PRESS—Stan and Tom Wick Poetry Prize, P.O. Box 5190, Kent, OH 44242–0001. Publication and $1,000 are offered for a book of poems, 48 to 68 pages, by a writer who has not previously published a collection of poetry. Deadline: May 1.

JACK KEROUAC LITERARY PRIZE—Lowell Celebrates Kerouac! Festival, P.O. Box 8788, Lowell, MA 01853. A prize of $500 and festival reading are awarded for an unpublished work of fiction, nonfiction, or poetry relating to themes expressed in Kerouac's work. Deadline: August 1.

LA JOLLA FESTIVAL—International Imitation Raymond Chandler Writing Competition, c/o Friends of the La Jolla Library, 6632 Aveûida Manana, La Jolla, CA 92037. Prizes of $500, $300, and $200 will be awarded for manuscripts, 500 words, that imitate or parody Raymond Chandler's writing style and subject matter. Deadline: August 1.

LINCOLN COLLEGE—Billee Murray Denny Poetry Award, 300 Keokuk St., Lincoln, IL 62656. Attn: Janet Overton. Prizes of $1,000, $500, and $250 are offered for original, unpublished poems by poets who have never published a book of poetry. Deadline: May 31.

LIVE OAK THEATRE—New Play Award, 200 Colorado St., Austin, TX 78701. Attn: Tom Byrne, Lit. Mgr. Offers $1,000 plus possible production for the best full-length, unproduced, unpublished play. Deadline: November 1.

LODI ARTS COMMISSION—Drama Festival, 125 S. Hutchins St., Suite D, Lodi, CA 95240. A prize of $1,000 plus production is awarded for a full-length play; a prize of $500 plus production is awarded for a children's play. Deadline: April 1 (of odd-numbered years).

LOVE CREEK PRODUCTIONS—One-Ace Play Festivals, 47 El Dorado Pl., Weehawken, NJ 07087–7004. One-act plays based on designated themes are awarded production; winners receive prizes of $200 to $300. Deadline: March 31; May 31; July 31; Sept. 30.

827

AMY LOWELL POETRY TRAVELLING SCHOLARSHIP—Choate, Hall & Stewart, Exchange Pl., 53 State St., Boston, MA 02109–2891. Attn: F. Davis Dassori, Jr. A scholarship of approximately $29,000 is awarded for a poet to spend the year abroad to advance the art of poetry. Deadline: October 15.

THE MADISON REVIEW—Dept. of English, 600 N. Park St., Helen C. White Hall, Univ. of Wisconsin-Madison, Madison, WI 53706. Phyllis Smart Young Prize in Poetry: awards $500 plus publication for a group of 3 unpublished poems. Chris O'Malley Prize in Fiction: awards $500 plus publication for an unpublished short story. Deadline: September 30.

MARTIN FOUNDATION FOR THE CREATIVE ARTS—Frank Waters Southwest Writing Award, P.O. Box 1357, Ranchos de Taos, NM 87529. Attn: Mag Dimond. A first prize of $2,000 plus publication, and 2 $2,000 honorable mentions, are offered for novels on a designated theme (in 1996: "The Non-Urban West"). Writers from the following states are eligible: NM, AZ, NV, UT, CO, TX. Deadline: August 31.

MASQUE THEATRE OF TEMPLE TERRACE—Playwriting Competition, P.O. Box 291212, Tampa, FL 33687–1212. Attn: Contest Coordinator. Prizes of $500 plus production, $100, and $50 are awarded for previously unpublished, unproduced, full-length plays; no children's plays or musicals. Deadline: February 28.

MID-LIST PRESS—First Series Awards, 4324 12th Ave. S., Minneapolis, MN 55407–3218. Publication and an advance against royalties are awarded for first books in the following categories: a novel in any genre, from 50,000 words; poetry, from 65 pages; short fiction, from 50,000 words; creative nonfiction, from 50,000 words. Deadline: February 1 (novel and poetry); July 1 (short fiction and creative nonfiction).

MIDWEST RADIO THEATRE WORKSHOP—MRTW Script Contests, 915 E. Broadway, Columbia, MO 65201. Workshop Script Contest: offers $800 in prizes, to be divided among 2 to 4 winners, and free workshop participation for contemporary radio scripts, 25 to 30 minutes long. Deadline: November 15.

MIDWEST THEATRE NETWORK—Rochester Playwright Festival, 5031 Tongen Ave. N.W., Rochester, MN 55901. Five to 8 scripts of various lengths and types are chosen for festival production. Deadline: November 15.

MILKWEED EDITIONS— 430 First Ave. N., Suite 400, Minneapolis, MN 55401–1743. Awards are for manuscripts already accepted for publication by the press. National Fiction Prize: A $2,000 prize, an advance, and royalties are awarded for the best novel, novella, or collection of short fiction; writers who have previously published a book-length collection of fiction or at least 3 short stories or novellas are eligible. Prize for Children's Literature: A cash prize, advance, and royalties are awarded for the best children's novel or biography that embodies humane values; writers who have published books or at least 3 short stories for children or adults are eligible. Deadline: year-round.

MILL MOUNTAIN THEATRE—New Play Competition, 2nd Floor, One Market Square, Roanoke, VA 24011–1437. Attn: Jo Weinstein. Offers a $1,000 prize and staged reading, with possible full production, for an unpublished, unproduced, full-length or one-act play or musical. Cast size to 10. Deadline: January 1.

MISSISSIPPI REVIEW—Prize for Short Fiction, The Ctr. for Writers, Univ. of Southern Mississippi, Box 5144, Hattiesburg, MS 39406–5144. Attn:

R. Fortenberry. Publication and $1,000 are offered for the best short story; runner-up stories will be published. Deadline: March 31.

THE MISSOURI REVIEW—Editors' Prize, 1507 Hillcrest Hall, UMC, Columbia, MO 65211. Publication plus $1,000 is awarded for short fiction and essay manuscripts, 25 pages, and $500 for the winning poetry manuscript, 10 pages. Deadline: October 15.

MOTHER TONGUE PRESS—Poetry Chapbook Contest, 290 Fulford-Ganges Rd., Salt Spring Island, BC V8K 2K6, Canada. Attn: Mona Fertig. Two $300 prizes plus publication are awarded for unpublished 10-to 15-page poetry manuscripts in Canadian and international categories. Deadline: November 30.

THE MOUNTAINEERS BOOKS—The Barbara Savage/"Miles from Nowhere" Memorial Award, 1001 S. W. Klickitat Way, Suite 201, Seattle, WA 98134. Attn: Donna DeShazo, Dir. Offers a $3,000 cash award, plus publication and a $12,000 advance against royalties for an outstanding unpublished, book-length manuscript of a nonfiction, personal-adventure narrative. Deadline: October 1 (of even-numbered years).

NATIONAL ENDOWMENT FOR THE ARTS—Nancy Hanks Center, 1100 Pennsylvania Ave. N.W., Rm. 722, Washington, DC 20506. Attn: Dir., Literature Program. Offers fellowships to writers and translators of poetry, fiction, plays, and creative nonfiction. Deadline: varies.

NATIONAL FEDERATION OF STATE POETRY SOCIETIES—Poetry Manuscript Contest, 3520 State Rte. 56, Mechanicsburg, OH 43044. Attn: Amy Zook, Chairman. A prize of $1,000 is awarded for the best manuscript of poetry, 35 to 60 pages. Deadline: October 15.

NATIONAL POETRY SERIES—P.O. Box G, Hopewell, NJ 08525. Attn: Emily Wylie, Coordinator. Sponsors Annual Open Competition for unpublished book-length poetry manuscripts. Five manuscripts are selected for publication, and each winner receives a $1,000 award. Deadline: February 15.

NEGATIVE CAPABILITY—Fiction/Poetry Contests, 62 Ridgelawn Dr. E., Mobile, AL 36608. Attn: Sue Walker. Eve of St. Agnes Poetry Award: offers $1,000 plus publication for an original, unpublished poem. Deadline: January 15. Short Fiction Award: offers $1,000 for a previously unpublished story, 1,500 to 4,500 words. Deadline: December 1.

NEW ENGLAND POETRY CLUB—Annual Contests, 10 Baker Pl., Newton, MA 02162–1301. Attn: David Ellis. Prizes range from $100 to $500 in various contests for members, nonmembers, and students. Deadline: June 30.

NEW ENGLAND THEATRE CONFERENCE—John Gassner Memorial Playwriting Award, c/o Dept. of Theatre, Northeastern Univ., 360 Huntington Ave., Boston, MA 02115. A $500 first prize and a $250 second prize are offered for unpublished, unproduced full-length plays written by New England residents or members of the NETC. Deadline: April 15.

NEW LETTERS—Univ. of Missouri-Kansas City, 5100 Rockhill Rd., Kansas City, MO 64110–2499. Offers $750 for the best short story, to 5,000 words; $750 for the best group of 3 to 6 poems; $500 for the best essay, to 5,000 words. The work of each winner and first runner-up will be published. Deadline: May 15.

NEWPORT WRITERS CONFERENCE—CWA Writing Contest, P.O. Box

12, Newport, RI 02840–0001. A prize of $250 plus free conference tuition is offered for short stories, to 2,000 words, and poetry, any length. Deadline: June 1.

NIMROD/HARDMAN AWARDS—*Nimrod International Journal,* 2010 Utica Sq., Suite 707, Tulsa, OK 74114-1635. Katherine Anne Porter Prize: offers prizes of $1,000 and $500 for fiction, to 7,500 words. Pablo Neruda Prize: offers prizes of $1,000 and $500 for one long poem or a selection of poems. Deadline: April 15.

NORTH CAROLINA WRITERS' NETWORK—International Literature Prizes, 3501 Hwy. 54 W., Studio C, Chapel Hill, NC 27516. Thomas Wolfe Fiction Prize: offers $500 for a previously unpublished short story or novel excerpt. Deadline: August 31. Paul Green Playwrights Prize: offers $500 for a previously unproduced, unpublished play. Deadline: September 30. Randall Jarrell Poetry Prize: offers $500 for a previously unpublished poem. Deadline: November 1.

NORTHEASTERN UNIVERSITY PRESS—Samuel French Morse Poetry Prize, English Dept., 406 Holmes, Northeastern Univ., Boston, MA 02115. Attn: Prof. Guy Rotella, Chairman. Offers $500 plus publication for a full-length poetry manuscript by a U.S. poet who has published no more than one book of poems. Deadline: August 1 (for inquiries); September 15 (for entries).

NORTHERN KENTUCKY UNIVERSITY—Y.E.S. New Play Festival, Dept. of Theatre, Highland Hts., KY 41099–1007. Attn: Mike King, Project Dir. Awards 3 $400 prizes plus production for previously unproduced full-length plays and musicals. Deadline: October 15 (of even-numbered years).

NORTHERN MICHIGAN UNIVERSITY—Mildred & Albert Panowski Playwriting Competition, Forest Roberts Theatre, Northern Michigan Univ., 1401 Presque Isle Ave., Marquette, MI 49855–5364. Awards $2,000, plus production for an original, full-length, previously unproduced and unpublished play. Deadline: November 15.

O'NEILL THEATER CENTER—National Playwrights Conference, 234 W. 44th St., Suite 901, New York, NY 10036. Attn: Mary F. McCabe. Offers stipend, staged readings, and room and board at the conference, for new stage and television plays. Deadline: December 1.

OFF CENTER THEATER—Women Playwright's Festival, Tampa Bay Performing Arts Ctr., P.O. Box 518, Tampa, FL 33601. A $1,000 prize, production, and travel are offered for the best play about women, written by a woman; runner-up receives staged reading. Deadline: September 15.

OLD DOMINION UNIVERSITY—See Univ. of North Texas Press.

THE PARIS REVIEW—Poetry and Fiction Prizes, 541 E. 72nd St., New York, NY 10021. Bernard F. Connors Prize: offers $1,000 plus publication for a previously unpublished poem. Deadline: May 1. Aga Khan Prize: offers $1,000 plus publication for a previously unpublished short story. Deadline: June 1.

PEN CENTER USA WEST—Grants for Writers with HIV/AIDS, 672 S. Lafayette Park Pl., #41, Los Angeles, CA 90057. Grants of $1,000 are awarded to writers with HIV/AIDS to continue and/or finish a current literary project. Writers living in the western U.S. who have been actively involved in creating literary work during the past 3 years are eligible to apply. Deadline: September 30.

PEN/JERARD FUND AWARD—PEN American Ctr., 568 Broadway, New York, NY 10012. Attn: John Morrone, Programs & Publications. Offers $4,000 to beginning female writers for a work-in-progress of general nonfiction. Applicants must have published at least one article in a national magazine or major literary magazine, but not more than one book of any kind. Deadline: January 1 (of odd-numbered years).

PEN WRITERS FUND—PEN American Ctr., 568 Broadway, New York, NY 10012. Attn: India Amos, Writers Fund Coordinator. Grants and interest-free loans of up to $500 are available to published writers or produced playwrights facing unanticipated financial emergencies. If the emergency is due to HIV-and AIDS-related illness, professional writers and editors qualify for grants of up to $1,000 through the Fund for Writers and Editors with AIDS; all applications and decisions are confidential. Deadline: year-round.

PEN WRITING AWARDS FOR PRISONERS—PEN American Center, 568 Broadway, New York, NY 10012. County, state, and federal prisoners are eligible to enter one unpublished manuscript in each of 4 categories: poetry, to 100 lines, fiction, drama, and nonfiction, to 5,000 words. Prizes of $100, $50, and $25 are awarded in each category. Deadline: September 1.

PEREGRINE SMITH POETRY SERIES—Gibbs Smith, Publisher, P.O. Box 667, Layton, UT 84041. Offers a $500 prize plus publication for a previously unpublished 64-page poetry manuscript. Deadline: April 30.

PETERLOO POETS—Open Competition, 2 Kelly Gardens, Calstock, Cornwall PL18 9SA, U.K. Attn: Harry Chambers. Prizes totalling 5,100 British pounds, including a grand prize of £3,000 plus publication, are awarded for poems of up to 40 lines. Deadline: March 1.

PHILADELPHIA FESTIVAL OF WORLD CINEMA—"Set in Philadelphia" Screenwriting Competition, 3701 Chestnut St., Philadelphia, PA 19104. A $5,000 prize is awarded for the best screenplay, 85 to 130 pages, set primarily in the greater Philadelphia area. Deadline: January 1.

PIG IRON PRESS—Kenneth Patchen Competition, P.O. Box 237, Youngstown, OH 44501. Awards paperback publication, $100, and 50 copies of the winning manuscript of fiction (in even-numbered years) and poetry (in odd-numbered years). Deadline: December 31.

PIONEER DRAMA SERVICE—Shubert Fendrich Memorial Playwriting Contest, P.O. Box 4267, Englewood, CO 80155–4267. A prize of publication plus a $1,000 advance is offered for a previously produced, though unpublished, full-length play suitable for community theater. Deadline: March 1.

PIRATE'S ALLEY FAULKNER SOCIETY—William Faulkner Creative Writing Competition, 632 Pirate's Alley, New Orleans, LA 70116. Prizes are $7,500 for an unpublished novel of over 50,000 words; $2,500 for a novella of under 50,000 words; $1,500 for a short story of under 15,000 words; and $1,500 for a personal essay under 2,500 words. All awards include additional prize money to be used as an advance against royalties to encourage publisher interest. Deadline: April 1.

PLAYBOY—College Fiction Contest, 680 N. Lakeshore Dr., Chicago, IL 60611. Prizes of $3,000 plus publication, and $500, are offered for a short story, up to 25 pages, by a college student. Deadline: January 1.

PLAYHOUSE-ON-THE-SQUARE—New Play Competition, 51 S. Cooper, Memphis, TN 38104. Attn: Mr. Jackie Nichols, Exec. Dir. A stipend plus production is awarded for a full-length, previously unproduced play or musical. Deadline: April 1.

THE PLAYWRIGHTS' CENTER—Jerome Fellowships, 2301 Franklin Ave. E., Minneapolis, MN 55406. Five emerging playwrights are offered a $7,000 stipend and 12-month residency; housing and travel are not provided. Deadline: September 15.

THE PLUM REVIEW—Poetry and Fiction Contests, P.O. Box 1347, Philadelphia, PA 19105–1347. Publication and $500 are awarded for previously unpublished poems in any form or style. Deadline: February 28. Publication and $500 are awarded for fiction of any length, style, and subject matter. Deadline: November 30.

POCKETS—Fiction Contest, c/o Lynn W. Gilliam, Assoc. Ed., P.O. Box 189, Nashville, TN 37202–0189. A $1,000 prize goes to the author of the winning 1,000-to 1,600-word story for children in grades 1 to 6. Deadline: August 15.

POET LORE—John Williams Andrews Narrative Poetry Competition, The Writer's Ctr., 4508 Walsh St., Bethesda, MD 20815. A prize of $350 plus publication is awarded for the best unpublished, original narrative poem of at least 100 lines. Deadline: November 30.

POETRY SOCIETY OF AMERICA—15 Gramercy Park, New York, NY 10003. Prizes are offered in contests for unpublished poems, open to nonmembers: The $2,750 Robert H. Winner Award for up to 10 poems by a writer over 40 who has published no more than one book; the $500 George Bogin Memorial Award for 4 or 5 poems taking a stand against oppression; and a $100 Student Poetry Award. Deadline: December 22.

EMILY POWELL LITERARY AWARDS—8F Hudson Harbour Dr., Poughkeepsie, NY 12601. Attn: Victor L. Gregurick. Prizes of $200, $150, $100, and $50 are awarded for unpublished poems, up to 100 lines; a $50 prize for "Best Line Drawing" is also awarded. Deadline: August 15.

PRISM INTERNATIONAL—Short Fiction Contest, Creative Writing Dept., Univ. of B.C., E466–1866 Main Mall, Vancouver, B.C., V6T 1Z1. Publication, a $2,000 first prize, and five $200 prizes are awarded for stories of up to 25 pages. Deadline: December 1.

PURDUE UNIVERSITY PRESS—Verna Emery Poetry Award, 1532 South Campus Courts-E, W. Lafayette, IN 47907–1532. Unpublished collections of original poetry, 60 to 90 pages, are considered for an award of publication plus royalties. Deadline: January 31.

QUARTERLY REVIEW OF LITERATURE—Poetry Awards, 26 Haslet Ave., Princeton, NJ 08540. Four to 6 prizes of $1,000, publication, and 100 books are awarded for 60-to 100-page manuscripts of poetry, poetic plays, long poems, or poetry in translation. Deadlines: May 31; November 30.

QUICK BROWN FOX PUBLISHERS—Short Story and Poetry Contest, Dept. TW, P.O. Box 7894, Athens, GA 30604–7894. Attn: Dr. Charles Connor. Prizes of $500 and $100 are awarded for stories of up to 3,000 words. A $100 prize is awarded for the best poem of up to 16 lines. Deadline: March 1.

RANDOM HOUSE JUVENILE BOOKS—Dr. Seuss Picturebook Award Contest, 201 E. 50th St., New York, NY 10022. A prize of $25,000 plus publication is awarded for a picturebook manuscript by an author/illustrator who has not published more than one book. Deadline: December 1 (of even-numbered years).

REDNECK REVIEW OF LITERATURE—Fiction Contest, 1556 S. Second Ave., Pocatello, ID 83204. Publication and prizes of $250 and $150 are offered for the best contemporary previously unpublished short stories that challenge "Western American Mythology." Deadline: July 15.

RIVER CITY—Writing Awards in Fiction, Dept. of English, Memphis State Univ., Memphis, TN 38152. Awards of $2,000 plus publication, $500, and $300 are offered for previously unpublished short stories, to 7,500 words. Deadline: December 1.

ROME ART & COMMUNITY CENTER—Milton Dorfman Poetry Prize, 308 W. Bloomfield St., Rome, NY 13440. Offers prizes of $500, $200, and $100 plus publication for the best original, unpublished poems. Deadline: November 1.

IAN ST JAMES AWARDS—c/o The New Writers' Club Ltd., P.O. Box 101, Tunbridge Wells, Kent TN4 8YD, England. Attn: Merric Davidson. Offers 20 prizes of 250 to 5,000 British pounds plus publication for short stories. Deadline: February 29.

ST. MARTIN'S PRESS/MALICE DOMESTIC CONTEST—Thomas Dunne Books, 175 Fifth Ave., New York, NY 10010. Offers publication plus a $10,000 advance against royalties, for a best first traditional mystery novel. Deadline: October 15.

ST. MARTIN'S PRESS/PRIVATE EYE NOVEL CONTEST—PWA Contest, 175 Fifth Ave., New York, NY 10010. The writer of the best first private eye novel, from 60,000 words, receives publication plus $10,000 against royalties. Deadline: August 1.

SARABANDE BOOKS—Poetry and Short Fiction Prizes, 2234 Dundee Rd., Suite 200, Louisville, KY 40205. Prizes are $2,000, publication, and a standard royalty contract in the competition for the Kathryn A. Morton Prize in Poetry (for a collection of poems, from 48 pages) and the Mary McCarthy Prize in Short Fiction (for a collection of short stories or novellas, 150 to 300 pages). Deadline: February 15.

SIENA COLLEGE—International Playwrights' Competition, Siena College, 515 Loudon Rd., Loudonville, NY 12211–1462. Offers $2,000 plus campus residency expenses for the winning full-length script; no musicals. Deadline: June 30 (of even-numbered years).

SIERRA—Nature-Writing Contest, 730 Polk St., San Francisco, CA 94109. As many as 3 previously unpublished essays, to 2,000 words, on any aspect of the natural world, are chosen for publication. Deadline: February 1.

SIERRA REPERTORY THEATRE—Taylor Playwriting Award, P. O. Box 3030, Sonora, CA 95370. Attn: Dennis Jones, Producing Dir. Offers $500, plus possible production, for a full-length play or musical that has received no more than 2 productions or staged readings. Deadline: August 31.

SNAKE NATION PRESS—Fiction and Poetry Contests, 110 #2 W. Force St., Valdosta, GA 31601. Attn: Nancy Phillips. Violet Reed Haas Prize: Offers publication plus $500 for a previously unpublished book of poetry, 50 to 75 pages. Deadline: January 15. *Snake Nation Review* Contest Issues: Prizes are publication plus $300, $200, and $100 for short stories; $100, $75, and $50 for poems. Deadlines: April 1; September 1.

SOCIETY OF AMERICAN TRAVEL WRITERS FOUNDATION—Lowell Thomas Travel Journalism Award, 4101 Lake Boone Trail, Suite 201, Raleigh, NC 27607. Prizes totalling $11,000 are offered for published and broadcast work by U.S. and Canadian travel journalists. Deadline: January 31.

SONORA REVIEW—Contests, Univ. of Arizona, Dept. of English, Tucson, AZ 85721. Poetry Contest: offers $500 plus publication for the best poem. Deadline: July 1. Short Story Contest: offers $500 plus publication for the best short story. Deadline: December 1.

SONS OF THE REPUBLIC OF TEXAS—Summerfield G. Roberts Award, General Office, 5942 Abrams Rd., Suite 222, Dallas, TX 75231. A prize of $2,500 is awarded for published or unpublished creative writing on the Republic of Texas, 1836–1846. Deadline: January 15.

THE SOUTHERN ANTHOLOGY—The Southern Prize, 2851 Johnson St., #321, Lafayette, LA 70503. A prize of $600 and publication are awarded for the best original, previously unpublished short story or novel excerpt, up to 7,500 words, or poem. Deadline: May 30.

SOUTHERN APPALACHIAN REPERTORY THEATRE—Playwrights' Conference, P.O. Box 620, Mars Hill, NC 28754–0620. Attn: Ms. Gaynelle M. Caldwell, Jr. Unproduced, unpublished scripts will be considered; up to 5 playwrights are selected to attend the conference and hear their plays read by professional actors; full production is possible. Deadline: October 1.

SOUTHERN POETRY REVIEW—Guy Owen Poetry Prize, Dept. of English, UNCC, Charlotte, NC 28223. Attn: Ken McLaurin, Ed. A prize of publication plus $500 is awarded for the best original, previously unpublished poem. Deadline: April 30.

THE SOW'S EAR PRESS—19535 Pleasant View Dr., Abingdon, VA 24211–6827. Chapbook Competition: offers a prize of $500 plus 50 published copies for the best poetry manuscript, as well as 2 $100 prizes. Deadline: April 30. Poetry Competition: offers prizes of $500, $100, and $50 for a previously unpublished poem of any length. Deadline: October 31.

SPOON RIVER POETRY REVIEW—Editors' Prize, 4240 Dept. of English, Illinois State Univ., Normal, IL 61790–4240. Publication and a $500 prize, as well as 2 $50 prizes, are awarded for single poems. Deadline: May 1.

STAND MAGAZINE—Short Story Competition, 179 Wingrove Rd., Newcastle upon Tyne, NE4 9DA, England. Prizes totalling 2,500 British pounds, including a £1,500 first prize, are awarded for previously unpublished stories under 8,000 words. Winning stories are published in *Stand Magazine*. Deadline: March 31 (of odd-numbered years).

STATE UNIVERSITY OF NEW YORK AT STONY BROOK—Short Fiction Prize, Dept. of English, Humanities Bldg., State Univ., Stony Brook, NY 11794–5350. Attn: Carolyn McGrath. A prize of $1,000 is offered for the best short story, up to 5,000 words, written by an undergraduate currently enrolled full-time in an American or Canadian college. Deadline: February 28.

STORY LINE PRESS—Nicholas Roerich Prize, Three Oaks Farm, Brownsville, OR 97327–9718. A prize of $1,000 plus publication is awarded for an original book of poetry by a poet who has never before published a book of poetry. Deadline: October 15.

SUNY FARMINGDALE—Paumanok Poetry Award, Visiting Writers Program, Knapp Hall, SUNY Farmingdale, Farmingdale, NY 11735. Prizes of $1,000 and 2 $500 prizes are offered for entries of 5 to 7 poems. Deadline: September 15.

SYRACUSE UNIVERSITY PRESS—John Ben Snow Prize, 1600 Jamesville Ave., Syracuse, NY 13244–5160. Attn: Dir. Awards a $1,500 advance, plus publication, for an unpublished book-length nonfiction manuscript about New York State, especially upstate or central New York. Deadline: December 31.

TEN MINUTE MUSICALS PROJECT—Box 461194, W. Hollywood, CA 90046. Attn: Michael Koppy, Prod. Musicals of 7 to 14 minutes are eligible for a $250 advance against royalties and musical anthology productions at theaters in the U.S. and Canada. Deadline: August 31.

THEATRE MEMPHIS—New Play Competition, P.O. Box 240117, Memphis, TN 38124–0117. The prize is $1,500 plus production for the best full-length play. Deadline: July 1, 1996 (held every 3 years).

DAVID THOMAS CHARITABLE TRUST—Open Competitions, P.O. Box 4, Nairn IV12 4HU, England. The trust sponsors a number of theme-based poetry and short story contests open to beginning writers, with prizes ranging from £25 to £1,200. Deadline: January 15.

THE THURBER HOUSE—Thurber House Residencies, 77 Jefferson Ave., Columbus, OH 43215. Attn: Michael J. Rosen, Lit. Dir. Three-month residencies and stipends of $5,000 each are awarded in the categories of writing, playwriting, and journalism. Winners have limited teaching responsibilities with The Ohio State Univ.. Deadline: December 15.

TOWNGATE THEATRE—Playwriting Contest, Oglebay Institute, Oglebay, Wheeling, WV 26003. Offers $300 plus production for an unproduced, full-length, non-musical play. Deadline: January 1.

TRITON COLLEGE—Salute to the Arts Poetry Contest, 2000 Fifth Ave., River Grove, IL 60171. Winning original, unpublished poems, to 60 lines, on designated themes, are published by Triton College. Deadline: April 1.

UNICO NATIONAL—Ella T. Grasso Literary Award Contest, 72 Burroughs Pl., Bloomfield, NJ 07003. A prize of $1,000 is awarded for the best essay or short story, 1,500 to 2,000 words, on the Italian-American experience. Deadline: April 1.

U.S. NAVAL INSTITUTE—Arleigh Burke Essay Contest, *Proceedings Magazine*, 118 Maryland Ave., Annapolis, MD 21402–5035. Attn: Bert Hubinger. Awards prizes of $3,000, $2,000, and $1,000 plus publication, for essays on the advancement of professional, literary, or scientific knowledge in the naval or maritime services, and the advancement of the knowledge of sea power. Deadline: December 1. Also sponsors several smaller contests; deadlines vary.

UNIVERSITY OF AKRON PRESS—The Akron Poetry Prize, 374B Bierce Library, Akron, OH 44325–1703. Publication and $500 are offered for a previously unpublished collection of poems. Deadline: June 30.

UNIVERSITY OF ARKANSAS PRESS—Arkansas Poetry Award, 201 Ozark Ave., Fayetteville, AR 72701. Awards publication of a 50-to 80-page poetry manuscript to a writer who has never had a book of poetry published. Deadline: May 1.

UNIVERSITY OF CALIFORNIA IRVINE—Chicano/Latino Literary Contest, Dept. of Spanish and Portuguese, UCI Irvine, CA 92717. Attn: Juan Bruce-Novoa, Dir. A first prize of $1,000 plus publication, and prizes of $500 and $250 are awarded in alternating years for poetry, drama, novels, and short stories. Deadline: April 30.

UNIVERSITY OF COLORADO—Nilon Award for Excellence in Minority Fiction, Fiction Collective Two, English Dept. Publications Ctr., Campus Box 494, Boulder, CO 80309–0494. Awards $1,000 plus joint publication for original, unpublished, book-length fiction, in English, by a U.S. citizen. Open to writers of the following ethnic minorities: African American, Hispanic, Asian, Native American or Alaskan Native, and Pacific Islander. Deadline: November 30.

UNIVERSITY OF GEORGIA PRESS—Flannery O'Connor Award for Short Fiction, Athens, GA 30602. Two prizes of $1,000 plus publication are awarded for a book-length collection of short fiction. Deadline: July 31.

UNIVERSITY OF GEORGIA PRESS CONTEMPORARY POETRY SERIES—Athens, GA 30602–4901. Offers publication of manuscripts from poets who have published at least one volume of poetry. Deadline: January 31. Publication of book-length poetry manuscripts is offered to poets who have never had a book of poems published. Deadline: September 30.

UNIVERSITY OF HAWAII AT MANOA—Kumu Kahua Playwriting Contest, Dept. of Drama and Theatre, 1770 East-West Rd., Honolulu, HI 96822. Awards $500 for a full-length play, and $200 for a one-act, set in Hawaii and dealing with some aspect of the Hawaiian experience. Also conducts contest for plays written by Hawaiian residents. Deadline: January 1.

UNIVERSITY OF IOWA—Iowa Publication Awards for Short Fiction, Dept. of English, 308 English Philosophy Bldg., Iowa City, IA 52242–1492. The John Simmons Short Fiction Award and the Iowa Short Fiction Award, both for unpublished full-length collections of short stories, offer publication under a standard contract. Deadline: September 30.

UNIVERSITY OF IOWA PRESS—The Iowa Poetry Prize, 119 W. Park Rd., 100 Kuhl House, Iowa City, IA 52242–1000. Two $1,000 prizes, plus publication, are awarded for poetry manuscripts, 50 to 150 pages, by writers who have published at least one book of poetry. Deadline: March 31.

UNIVERSITY OF LOUISVILLE—*The Louisville Review*, 315 Bingham Humanities, Louisville, KY 40292. Attn: Karen Mann Johns, Ed. Writers of the best poetry, up to 7 pages, and fiction, up to 20 pages, each receive $500 plus publication. Deadline: December 31.

UNIVERSITY OF MASSACHUSETTS PRESS—Juniper Prize, Amherst, MA 01003. Offers a prize of $1,000 plus publication for a book-length manuscript of poetry; awarded in odd-numbered years to writers who have never published a book of poetry, and in even-numbered years to writers who have published a book or chapbook of poetry. Deadline: September 30.

UNIVERSITY OF NEBRASKA PRESS—North American Indian Prose Award, 312 N. 14th St., Lincoln, NE 68588–0484. Previously unpublished book-length manuscripts of biography, autobiography, history, literary criticism, and essays will be judged for originality, literary merit, and familiarity with North American Indian life. A $1,000 advance and publication are offered. Deadline: July 1.

UNIVERSITY OF NORTH TEXAS PRESS—Short Fiction Contest,

American Literary Review, P.O. Box 13827, Denton, TX 76203. Attn: Shawn Behlen. Publication and prizes of $300, $150, and $75 are offered for unpublished short fiction of up to 10,000 words. Deadline: December 15. Vassar Miller Prize in Poetry, c/o English Dept., Old Dominion Univ., Norfolk, VA 23529. Attn: Scott Cairns, Series Ed. Publication and $500 are awarded for an original, unpublished poetry manuscript, 50 to 80 pages. Deadline: November 30.

UNIVERSITY OF PITTSBURGH PRESS—127 N. Bellefield Ave., Pittsburgh, PA 15260. Agnes Lynch Starrett Poetry Prize: offers $2,500 plus publication in the Pitt Poetry Series for a book-length collection of poems by a poet who has not yet published a volume of poetry. Deadline: April 30. Drue Heinz Literature Prize: offers $10,000 plus publication and royalty contract for an unpublished collection of short stories or novellas, 150 to 300 pages, by a writer who has previously published a book-length collection of fiction or at least 3 short stories or novellas in nationally distributed magazines. Deadline: August 31.

UNIVERSITY OF SOUTHERN CALIFORNIA—Ann Stanford Poetry Prize, Master of Professional Writing Program, WPH 404, Univ. of Southern California, Los Angeles, CA 90089–4034. Publication plus prizes of $750, $250, and $100 are awarded; submit up to 5 poems. Deadline: April 15.

UNIVERSITY OF WISCONSIN PRESS POETRY SERIES—114 N. Murray St., Madison, WI 53715. Attn: Ronald Wallace, Ed. Previously unpublished manuscripts, 50 to 80 pages, are considered for the Brittingham Prize in Poetry and the Felix Pollak Prize in Poetry, each offering $1,000 plus publication. Deadline: October 1.

THE UNTERBERG POETRY CENTER OF THE 92ND STREET Y—"Discovery"/*The Nation*, 1395 Lexington Ave., New York, NY 10128. Four prizes of $300, publication, and a reading are awarded for original 10-page manuscripts by writers who have not yet published a book of poetry. Deadline: February 1.

VETERANS OF FOREIGN WARS—Voice of Democracy Audio Essay Competition, VFW National Headquarters, 406 W. 34th St., Kansas City, MO 64111. Several national scholarships totalling $109,000 are awarded to high school students for short, tape-recorded essays. Themes change annually. Deadline: November 15.

VILLA MONTALVO—Biennial Poetry Competition, P.O. Box 158, Saratoga, CA 95071. Residents of CA, NV, OR, and WA are eligible to enter poems in any style for prizes of: $1,000 plus an artist residency at Villa Montalvo, $500, and $300, as well as 8 prizes of $25. Deadline: October 1 (of odd-numbered years).

WAGNER COLLEGE—Stanley Drama Award, Dept. of Humanities, Howard Ave. & Campus Rd., Staten Island, NY 10301. Awards $2,000 for an original, previously unpublished and unproduced full-length play or musical or thematically related one-acts. Deadline: September 1.

WASHINGTON PRIZE FOR FICTION—1301 S. Scott St., #424, Arlington, VA 22204. Attn: Larry Kaltman, Dir. Offers $3,000, $2,000, and $1,000 for unpublished novels or short story collections, at least 65,000 words. Deadline: November 30.

WHITE PINE PRESS—Poetry Prize, 10 Village Sq., Fredonia, NY 14063. A prize of publication plus $500 is awarded for an original book-length manuscript of poetry. Deadline: December 1.

WHITE-WILLIS THEATRE—New Playwrights Contest, 5266 Gate Lake Rd., Ft. Lauderdale, FL 33319. Offered are a $500 prize plus production for the winning unpublished, unproduced full-length play. Deadline: September 1.

TENNESSEE WILLIAMS FESTIVAL—Univ. of New Orleans, Metro College Conference Services, ED 122, New Orleans, LA 70148. A $1,000 prize plus a staged reading and full production are offered for an original, unpublished one-act play on an American subject. Deadline: December 31.

WORD WORKS—Washington Prize for Fiction, P. O. Box 42164, Washington, DC 20015. A prize of $1,000 plus publication is offered for an unpublished volume of poetry by a living American poet. Deadline: March 1.

WRITERS AT WORK—Fellowship Competition, P.O. Box 1146, Centerville, UT 84014–5146. Prizes of $1,500 plus publication, and $500, in fiction and poetry categories, are awarded for excerpts of unpublished short stories, novels, essays, or poetry. Open to any writer who has not yet published a book-length volume of original work. Deadline: March 15

THE WRITER'S VOICE—Annual Writing Awards, 5 W. 63rd St., New York, NY 10023. Capricorn Awards for writers over 40: $1,000 for a 48-to 68-page manuscript of poetry, and for the first 150 pages of a novel. Open Voice Awards: $500 each for published or unpublished writers of up to 10 pages of fiction or poetry. Deadline: December 31.

YALE UNIVERSITY PRESS—Yale Series of Younger Poets Prize, Box 92A, Yale Sta., New Haven, CT 06520. Attn: Ed. Series publication is awarded for a book-length manuscript of poetry written by a poet under 40 who has not previously published a volume of poems. Deadline: February 29.

YOUNG PLAYWRIGHTS, INC.—Young Playwrights Festival, Dept. T, 321 W. 44th St., Suite 906, New York, NY 10036. Festival productions and readings are awarded for the best plays by writers 18 or younger. Deadline: October 15.

WRITERS COLONIES

Writers colonies offer isolation and freedom from everyday distractions and a quiet place for writers to concentrate on their work. Though some colonies are quite small, with space for just three or four writers at a time, others can provide accommodations for as many as thirty or forty. The length of a residency may vary, too, from a couple of weeks to five or six months. These programs have strict admissions policies, and writers must submit a formal application or letter of intent, a resumé, writing samples, and letters of recommendation. As an alternative to the traditional writers colony, a few of the organizations listed offer writing rooms for writers who live nearby. Write for application information first, enclosing a stamped, self-addressed envelope. Residency fees listed are subject to change.

THE EDWARD F. ALBEE FOUNDATION, INC.
14 Harrison St.
New York, NY 10013
(212) 266–2020
David Briggs, *Foundation Secretary*
    Located on Long Island, "The Barn," or the William Flanagan Memorial Creative Persons Center, is maintained by the Albee Foundation. "The standards for admission are, simply, talent and need." Ten to twelve writers are accepted each season for one-month residencies, available from June 1 to October 1; applications, including writing samples, project description, and resumé, are accepted from January 1 to April 1. There is no fee, though residents are responsible for their own food and travel expenses.

ALTOS DE CHAVÒN
c/o Parsons School of Design
2 W. 13th St., Rm. 707
New York, NY 10011
(212) 229–5370
Stephen D. Kaplan, *Arts/Education Director*
    Altos de Chavòn is a nonprofit center for the arts in the Dominican Republic committed to education, design innovation, international creative exchange, and the promotion of Dominican culture. Residencies average 12 weeks and provide the emerging or established artist an opportunity to live and work in a setting of architectural and natural beauty. All artists are welcome to apply, though writers should note there are no typewriters, the library is oriented more toward the design profession, and the apartments housing writers also accommodate university students. Two to three writers are chosen each year for the program. The fee is $300 per month for an apartment with kitchenette; linen and cleaning services are available at an extra cost. Applications include a letter of interest, writing sample, and resumé; artists are chosen in July.

MARY ANDERSON CENTER FOR THE ARTS
101 St. Francis Dr.
Mount St. Francis, IN 47146
(812) 923–8602
Susan Culberson Fey, *Assistant Director*
    Founded in 1989, the artists' residency and retreat is situated on the grounds of a Franciscan friary. Space is available for six residents at a time, including private rooms, working space, and a visual artists' studio; meals are provided. Two-week to three-month residencies are available

and are granted based on project proposal and the artist's body of work; applications are accepted year-round. Fees are $25 per day, plus $15 to apply.

ATLANTIC CENTER FOR THE ARTS
1414 Art Center Ave.
New Smyrna Beach, FL 32168
(904) 427–6975
Nicholas Conroy, *Program Director*
 The center is located on the east coast of central Florida, with 67 acres of pristine hammockland on a tidal estuary. All buildings, connected by raised wooden walkways, are handicapped accessible and air conditioned. The center provides a unique environment for sharing ideas, learning, and collaborating on interdisciplinary projects. Master artists meet with mid-career artists for readings and critiques, with time out for individual work. Residencies are three weeks. Fees are $100 a week for tuition and $25 a day for housing; off-site, tuition-only plans are available; financial aid is limited. Application deadlines vary.

BERLINER KÜNSTLERPROGRAM
Artists-in-Berlin Program
950 Third Ave.
New York, NY 10022
(212) 758–3223
Dr. Rolf Hoffmann, *Director*
 One-year residencies are offered to well-known and emerging writers, painters, sculptors, and composers to promote cultural exchange. Up to 20 residencies are offered for periods beginning between January 1 and June 30. Room, board, travel, and living expenses are awarded. Residents may bring spouse and children. Application, project description, and copies of publications are due by January 1 of the year preceding the residency.

BLUE MOUNTAIN CENTER
Blue Mountain Lake, NY 12812–0109
(518) 352–7391
Harriet Barlow, *Director*
 Hosts month-long residencies for artists and writers from mid-June to late October. Established fiction and nonfiction writers, poets, and playwrights whose work evinces social and ecological concern are eligible; 14 residents are accepted per session. Residents are not charged for their time at Blue Mountain, although all visitors are invited to contribute to the studio construction fund. There is no application form; apply by sending a brief biographical sketch, a plan for work at Blue Mountain, five to 10 slides or a writing sample of any length, an indication of preference for an early summer, late summer, or fall residence, and a $20 application fee, attention: *Admissions Committee.* Applications are due February 1.

BYRDCLIFFE ARTS COLONY
Artists' Residency Program
Woodstock Guild
34 Tinker St.
Woodstock, NY 12498
(914) 679–2079
Attn: *Director*
 The Villetta Inn, located on the 400-acre arts colony, offers private rooms, a communal kitchen, and a peaceful environment for fiction writ-

ers, poets, playwrights, and visual artists. Residencies from one to four months are offered from June to September. Fees are $400 to $500 per month; limited financial assistance available. Submit application, resumé, writing sample, reviews, and references; the deadline is in mid-April.

THE CAMARGO FOUNDATION
W-1050 First National Bank Bldg.
332 Minnesota St.
St. Paul, MN 55106–1312
Ricardo Bloch, *Administrative Assistant*

The Camargo Foundation maintains a center of studies in France for the benefit of nine scholars and graduate students each semester who wish to pursue projects in the humanities relative to France and Francophone culture. In addition, one artist, one composer, and one writer are accepted each semester. The foundation offers furnished apartments and a reference library in the city of Cassis. Research should be at an advanced stage and not require resources unavailable in the Marseilles-Aix-Cassis region. Fellows must be in residence at the foundation; the award is exclusively a residential grant. Application materials include: application form, curriculum vitae, three letters of recommendation, and project description. Writers, artists, and composers are required to send work samples. Applications are due February 1.

CENTRUM
P.O. Box 1158
Port Townsend, WA 98368
(360) 385–3102
Carol Jane Bangs, *Program Manager*

Writers are awarded one-month residencies between September and May. Applicants selected by a peer jury receive free housing and a $300 stipend. Previous residents may return on a space-available basis for a fee of $300 a month. Applications are due October 1.

CHATEAU DE LESVAULT
Writers Retreat Program
Onlay
58370 Villapourion
France
(33) 86–84–32–91; fax: (33) 86–84–35–78
Bibbi Lee, *Director*

This French country residence is located in western Burgundy, in the national park of Le Morvan. Five large rooms, fully equipped for living and working, are available October through April, for one month or longer. Residents in this small artists' community have access to the entire chateau, including the salon, library, and grounds. The fee is 4,500 francs (approximately $900) per month, or 2,500 francs for two weeks, and includes room, board, and utilities. Apply by writing to the selection committee, including project description, two references, writing samples, and publications list, if available. Applications are handled on a first-come basis.

CURRY HILL/GEORGIA
c/o 404 Crestmont Ave.
Hattiesburg, MS 39401–7211
(601) 264–7034
Mrs. Elizabeth Bowne, *Director*

This one-week retreat for eight fiction and nonfiction writers is offered for two sessions each spring (March 31 to April 6, and April 14 to 20, 1996) by writer/teacher Elizabeth Bowne. "I care about writers and am delighted and enthusiastic when I can help develop talent." A $500 fee covers meals and lodging at Curry Hill, a family plantation home near Bainbridge, Georgia. Applicants are accepted on a first-come basis.

DJERASSI RESIDENT ARTISTS PROGRAM
2325 Bear Gulch Rd.
Woodside, CA 94062–4405
(415) 747–1250; fax: (415) 747–0105
Attn: *Program Assistant*

The Djerassi Program offers living and work spaces in a rural, isolated setting to writers, visual artists, choreographers, and composers seeking undisturbed time for creative work. Residencies usually last one month; 60 artists are accepted each year. There are no fees other than the $25 application fee. Applications, with resumé and documentation of recent creative work, are due February 15.

DORLAND MOUNTAIN ARTS COLONY
Box 6
Temecula, CA 92593
(909) 676–5039
Attn: *Admissions Committee*

Dorland is a nature preserve and "primitive retreat for creative people" located in the Palomar Mountains of Southern California. "Without electricity, residents find a new, natural rhythm for their work." Novelists, playwrights, poets, nonfiction writers, composers, and visual artists are encouraged to apply for residencies of one to two months. The fee of $150 a month includes cottage, fuel, and firewood. Send SASE for application; deadlines are March 1 and September 1.

DORSET COLONY HOUSE
Box 519
Dorset, VT 05251
(802) 867–2223
John Nassivera, *Director*

Writers and playwrights are offered low-cost room with kitchen facilities at the historic Colony House in Dorset, Vermont. Residencies are one week to two months, and are available between September 15 and June 1. Applications are accepted year-round, and up to eight writers stay at a time. The fee is $95 per week; financial aid is limited. For more information, send SASE.

FINE ARTS WORK CENTER IN PROVINCETOWN
24 Pearl St.
Provincetown, MA 02657
Fred Leebron, *Acting Executive Director*

Fellowships, including living and studio space and monthly stipends, are available at the Fine Arts Work Center on Cape Cod, for fiction writers, poets, and playwrights to work independently. Residencies are for seven months, October through May; apply before February 1 deadline. Eight first-year fellows and two second-year fellows are accepted. Send SASE for details.

THE GELL WRITERS CENTER
Writers & Books
740 University Ave.
Rochester, NY 14607
(716) 473–2590
Joe Flaherty, *Director*

The Center, on Canandaigua Lake, is found in the Finger Lakes region of New York, and includes 24 acres of woodlands. Two separate living quarters, with private bath and work area, are available for $35 per night. All serious writers are welcome; reservations made on a first-come basis.

GLENESSENCE WRITERS COLONY
1447 W. Ward Ave.
Ridgecrest, CA 93555
(619) 446–5894
Allison Swift, *Director*

Glenessence is a luxury villa located in the Upper Mojave Desert, offering private rooms with bath, pool, spa, courtyard, shared kitchen, fitness center, and library. Children, pets, and smoking are prohibited. Residencies are offered at $565 per month; meals are not provided. Reservations are made on a first-come basis.

THE TYRONE GUTHRIE CENTRE
Annaghmakerrig, Newbliss
County Monaghan
Ireland
(353) 47–54003; fax: (353) 47–54380
Bernard Loughlin, *Director*

Set on a 400-acre country estate, the center offers peace and seclusion to writers and other artists to enable them to get on with their work. All art forms are represented. One-to three-month residencies are offered throughout the year, at the rate of 1,200 to 1,600 pounds (about $1,920 to $2,560) per month, depending on the season; financial assistance is available to Irish citizens only. A number of longer term self-catering houses in the old farmyard are also available at £300 per week. Writers may apply for acceptance year-round.

THE HAMBIDGE CENTER
P.O. Box 339
Rabun Gap, GA 30568
(706) 746–5718
Judy Barber, *Director*

The Hambidge Center for Creative Arts and Sciences is located on 600 acres of quiet woods in the north Georgia mountains. Seven private cottages are available for fellows, who are asked to contribute $125 per week. Two-week to two-month residencies, from May to October, and limited winter residencies are offered to serious artists from all disciplines. Send SASE for application form. Application deadline: January 31.

843

HEADLANDS CENTER FOR THE ARTS
944 Fort Barry
Sausalito, CA 94965
(415) 331–2787
Programs for 1996 at the Headlands Center, located on 13,000 acres of open coastal space, are available to residents of Ohio, North Carolina, and California. Application requirements vary by state. Decisions are announced in October for residencies beginning in February. Send SASE for more information.

HEDGEBROOK
2197 E. Millman Rd.
Langley, WA 98260
(360) 321–4786
Attn: *Director*
Hedgebrook provides women writers, published or not, of all ages and from all cultural backgrounds, with a natural place to work. Established in 1988, the retreat is located on 30 acres of farmland and woods on Whidbey Island in Washington State. Each writer has her own cottage, equipped with electricity and woodstove. A bathhouse serves all six cottages. Writers gather for dinner in the farmhouse every evening and frequently read in the living room/library afterwards. Limited travel scholarships are available. Residencies range from one week to three months. April 1 is the application deadline for residencies from mid-June to mid-December; September 30 for mid-January to late May. Applicants are chosen by a selection committee composed of writers. There is a $15 fee to apply; send SASE for application.

KALANI HONUA RETREAT & CULTURAL CENTER
Artist-in-Residence Program
RR2, Box 4500
Pahoa, HI 96778
(808) 965–7828
Richard Koob, *Program Coordinator*
Located in a rural coastal setting of 20 botanical acres, Kalani Honua hosts and sponsors educational programs "with the aloha experience that is its namesake: harmony of heaven and earth." Residencies range from two weeks to two months and are available throughout the year. Fees range from $26 to $43 per day, excluding meals. Applications accepted year-round.

LEIGHTON STUDIOS
Office of the Registrar
The Banff Centre for the Arts
Box 1020, Station 28
107 Tunnel Mountain Dr.
Banff, Alberta T0L 0C0
Canada
(403) 762–6180; (800) 565–9989; fax: (403) 762–6345
Theresa Boychuck, *Registrar*
The Leighton Studios are open year-round, providing time and space for artists to produce new work. Established writers, composers, musicians, and visual artists of all nationalities are encouraged to apply. Artists

844

working in other mediums at the conceptual state of a project will also be considered. Weekly fees (Canadian dollars): $301 studio; $203 single room; $94.50 meals (optional). Reductions in the studio fee are available to applicants demonstrating financial need. Applications are accepted at any time. Space is limited; apply at least six months prior to preferred starting date. Write for application form.

THE MACDOWELL COLONY
100 High St.
Peterborough, NH 03458
(603) 924–3886
Pat Dodge, *Admissions Coordinator*

Studios, room, and board are available for writers to work without interruption in a woodland setting. Selection is competitive. Apply by January 15 for stays May through August; April 15 for September through December; and September 15 for January through April. Residencies last up to eight weeks, and 80 to 90 writers are accepted each year. Send SASE for application.

THE MILLAY COLONY FOR THE ARTS
P.O. Box 3
Austerlitz, NY 12017–0003
(518) 392–3103
Gail Giles, *Assistant Director*

At Steepletop, the former home of Edna St. Vincent Millay, writers are provided studios, living quarters, and meals at no cost. Residencies last one month. Application deadlines are February 1, May 1, and September 1. Send SASE for more information and application.

MOLASSES POND WRITERS' RETREAT AND WORKSHOP
RR 1, Box 85C
Milbridge, ME 04658
(207) 546–2506
Martha Barron Barrett and Sue Wheeler, *Coordinators*

Led by published authors who teach writing at the University of New Hampshire. The one-week workshop is held in June and includes time set aside for writing, as well as manuscript critique and writing classes. Up to 10 writers participate, staying in five lakeside cottages with private work space and kitchen. Classes and communal dinner held in the main lodge. The $350 fee covers lodging, dinners, and tuition. Applicants must be serious about their work. No children's literature or poetry. Submit statement of purpose and 15 to 20 pages of fiction or nonfiction between March 1 and April 1.

JENNY MCKEAN MOORE WRITER-IN-WASHINGTON
Dept. of English
The George Washington University
Washington, DC 20052
Attn: Prof. Christopher Sten

The fellowship allows for a writer to teach two paid semesters at The George Washington University. Teaching duties include a fiction workshop each semester for students from the metropolitan community who may have had little formal education; and one class each semester for university students. Applications include letter, resumé, mention of teaching experience and other qualifications. The application deadline is November 15.

THE N.A.L.L. ASSOCIATION
232, Boulevard de Lattre
06140 Vence
France
(33) 93–58–13–26; fax: (33) 93–58–09–00
Attn: *Director*

This international center for writers and artists is located on eight acres of the Mediterranean village of Vence. Residents stay in cottages equipped with kitchen, bath, and private garden. One afternoon a week is set aside for residents to discuss their work with local artists over tea. Six-month residencies are encouraged. Cottages are rented at various rates, to members of the N.A.L.L. (Nature, Art, and Life League); membership is 500 francs (about $100) per year. Meals are not included. Submit resumé, writing sample, and project description. Applications are accepted year-round.

THE NORTHWOOD UNIVERSITY
Alden B. Dow Creativity Center
3225 Cook Rd.
Midland, MI 48640–2398
(517) 837–4478
Carol B. Coppage, *Director*

The Fellowship Program allows individuals time away from their on-going daily routines to pursue their project ideas without interruption. A project idea should be innovative, creative, and have potential for impact in its field. Four eight-week residencies, lasting from early-June to early-August, are awarded yearly. There is a $10 application fee. A $750 stipend plus room and board are provided. No spouses or families. Applications are due December 31.

PALENVILLE INTERARTS COLONY
2 Bond St.
New York, NY 10012
(518) 678–3332
Joanna Sherman, *Artistic Director*

The Palenville residency program has been temporarily suspended.

RAGDALE FOUNDATION
1260 N. Green Bay Rd.
Lake Forest, IL 60045
(708) 234–1063
Michael Wilkerson, *Director*

Uninterrupted time and peaceful space allow writers a chance to finish works in progress, to begin new works, to solve thorny creative problems, and to experiment in new genres. The foundation is located 30 miles north of Chicago, on 40 acres of prairie. Residencies of two weeks to two months are available for writers, artists, and composers. The fee is $15 a day; some full and partial fee waivers available, based solely on financial need. Send SASE for deadline information. Late applications considered when space is available. Application fee: $20.

846

SASKATCHEWAN WRITERS GUILD
Writers/Artists Colonies and Individual Retreats
P.O. Box 3986
Regina, Saskatchewan S4P 3R9
Canada
(306) 757–6310
Attn: *Director*

The Saskatchewan Colonies are at three locations: St. Peter's Abbey, near Humboldt, provides a six-week summer colony (July-August) and a two-week winter colony in February, for up to eight writers and artists at a time; applicant stays vary. Individual retreats of up to a month are offered year-round at St. Peter's, for up to three residents at a time. Emma Lake, near Prince Albert, is the site of a two-week residency in August. The newly established Riverhurst Colony, ideal for the writer interested in an isolated setting, is open for two weeks, dates to be determined. A fee of $100 a week includes room and board. Submit application form, resumé, project description, two references, and a 10-page writing sample. Saskatchewan residents are given preference. Apply two to three months in advance.

THE JOHN STEINBECK ROOM
Long Island University
Southampton Campus Library
Southampton, NY 11968
(516) 287–8382
Robert Gerbereux, *Library Director*

The John Steinbeck Room at Long Island University provides a basic research facility to writers who have either a current contract with a book publisher or a confirmed assignment from a magazine editor. The room is available for a period of six months with one six-month renewal permissible. Send SASE for application.

THE THURBER HOUSE RESIDENCIES
c/o Thurber House
77 Jefferson Ave.
Columbus, OH 43215
(614) 464–1032; fax: (614) 228–7445
Michael J. Rosen, *Literary Director*

Residencies in the restored home of James Thurber are awarded to journalists, poets, and playwrights. Residents work on their own writing projects, and in addition to other duties, teach one class at the Ohio State University. A stipend of $5,000 per quarter is provided. A letter of interest and curriculum vitae must be received by December 15, at which time applications are reviewed for the upcoming academic year.

UCROSS FOUNDATION
Residency Program
2836 U.S. Hwy. 14–16 East
Clearmont, WY 82835
(307) 737–2291
Elizabeth Guheen, *Executive Director*

Residencies, two to eight weeks, in the foothills of the Big Horn Mountains in Wyoming, allow writers, artists, and scholars to concentrate on their work without interruption. Two residency sessions are scheduled annually: February to June and August to December. There is no charge for room, board, or studio space. Application deadlines are March 1 for the fall session and October 1 for the spring session. Send SASE for more information.

VERMONT STUDIO CENTER
P.O. Box 613NW
Johnson, VT 05656
(802) 635–2727; fax: (802) 635–2730
Attn: *Registrar*

The Vermont Studio Center offers two-week studio sessions for up to 12 writers from February through April, led by prominent writers and teachers focusing on fiction, creative nonfiction, and poetry. Independent writers' retreats from two to 12 weeks are available year-round for those seeking more solitude. Room, working studio, and meals are included in all programs. Fees are $1,200 for the two-week studio session, and $750 for a two-week independent retreat. Financial assistance is available based on need. Applications are accepted year-round.

VILLA MONTALVO ARTIST RESIDENCY PROGRAM
P.O. Box 158
Saratoga, CA 95071
(408) 741–3421
Lori A. Wood, *Program Director*

Villa Montalvo, in the foothills of the Santa Cruz Mountains, offers one-to three-month, free residencies to writers and artists. Several merit-based fellowships are available. The application deadlines are September 1 and March 1; send SASE for forms.

VIRGINIA CENTER FOR THE CREATIVE ARTS
Sweet Briar, VA 24595
(804) 946–7236
William Smart, *Director*

A working retreat for writers, composers, and visual artists in Virginia's Blue Ridge Mountains. Residencies from one week to two months are available year-round. Application deadlines are the 15th of January, May, and September; about 300 residents are accepted each year. A limited amount of financial assistance is available. Send SASE for more information.

THE WRITERS ROOM
10 Astor Pl., 6th Fl.
New York, NY 10003
(212) 254–6995
Donna Brodie, *Executive Director*

Located in Greenwich Village, the Writers Room provides highly subsidized work space to all types of writers at all stages of their careers. "We offer urban writers a quiet place to escape from noisy neighbors, children, roommates, and other distractions of city life." The room holds 33 desks separated by partitions, a typing room with seven desks, a kitchen, and a library. Open 24 hours a day, 365 days a year. The fee is $165 per quarter.

THE WRITERS STUDIO
The Mercantile Library Association
17 E. 47th St.
New York, NY 10017
(212) 755–6710
Harold Augenbraum, *Director*
The Writers Studio is a quiet place in which writers can rent space conducive to the production of good work. A carrel, locker, small reference collection, electrical outlets, and membership in the Mercantile Library of New York are available at the cost of $200 per three-month residency. Submit application, resumé, and writing samples; applications are considered year-round.

HELENE WURLITZER FOUNDATION OF NEW MEXICO
Box 545
Taos, NM 87571
(505) 758–2413
Henry A. Sauerwein, Jr., *Executive Director*
Rent-free and utility-free studios in Taos are offered to writers and artists in all media. "All artists are given the opportunity to be free of the shackles of a 9-to-5 routine." Length of residency varies from three to six months. The foundation is open from April 1 through September 30. Residencies are assigned one to two years in advance.

YADDO
Box 395
Saratoga Springs, NY 12866–0395
(518) 584–0746; fax: (518) 584–1312
Lesley M. Leduc, *Program Coordinator*
Visual artists, writers, choreographers, dancers, composers, and collaborators are invited for stays from two weeks to two months. Room, board, and studio space are provided. Voluntary payment of $20 a day is suggested. No artist deemed worthy of admission by the judging panels will be denied admission on the basis of an inability to contribute. Deadlines are January 15 and August 1. There is a $20 application fee; send SASE for form.

WRITERS CONFERENCES

Each year, hundreds of writers conferences are held across the country. The following list, arranged by state, represents a sampling of conferences; each listing includes the location of the conference, the month during which it is usually held, and the name and address of the person from whom specific information may be received. Additional conferences are listed annually in the May issue of *The Writer* Magazine (120 Boylston St., Boston, MA 02116–4615).

ALABAMA

AL/GA SCBWI SPRINGMINGLE—Gulf Shores, AL. February. Send SASE to Joan Broerman, Reg. Advisor, SCBWI, 1616 Kestwick Dr., Birmingham, AL 35226.

AL/GA SCBWI "WRITING AND ILLUSTRATING FOR KIDS"—Birmingham, AL. October. Send SASE to Joan Broerman, Reg. Advisor, SCBWI, 1616 Kestwick Dr., Birmingham, AL 35226.

WRITING TODAY—Birmingham, AL. April. Write Martha Andrews, Dir., Birmingham-Southern College, Box 549003, Birmingham, AL 35254.

ALASKA

SITKA SYMPOSIUM ON HUMAN VALUES & THE WRITTEN WORD—Sitka, AK. June. Write Carolyn Servid, Dir., Island Institute, P.O. Box 2420, Sitka, AK 99835.

ARKANSAS

ARKANSAS WRITERS' CONFERENCE—Little Rock, AR. June. Write Clovita Rice, Dir., Arkansas Writers' Conference, 1115 Gillette Dr., Little Rock, AR 72227.

OZARK CREATIVE WRITERS CONFERENCE—Eureka Springs, AR. October. Write Peggy Vining, 6817 Gingerbread Ln., Little Rock, AR 72204.

CALIFORNIA

CHRISTIAN COMMUNICATORS CONFERENCE—Fullerton, CA. July. Write Susan Titus Osborn, Co-Dir., 3133 Puente St., Fullerton, CA 92635.

CHRISTIAN "WRITERS IN THE REDWOODS" RETREAT—Occidental, CA. November. Write Elaine Wright Colvin, Alliance Redwoods, 6250 Bohemian Hwy., Occidental, CA 95465.

MOUNT HERMON CHRISTIAN WRITERS CONFERENCE—Mount Hermon, CA. March, April. Write David R. Talbott, Dir., Mount Hermon Assn., P.O. Box 413, Mount Hermon, CA 95041–0413.

NAPA VALLEY WRITERS' CONFERENCE—St. Helena, CA. August. Write John Leggett, Co-Dir., Napa Valley College, 1088 College Ave., St. Helena, CA 94574.

ROUND TABLE COMEDY WRITERS CONVENTION—Palm Springs, CA. July. Write Linda Perret, Dir., 30941 W. Agoura Rd., Ste. 228, Westlake Village, CA 91361.

SANTA BARBARA WRITERS CONFERENCE—Santa Barbara, CA. June. Write Barnaby Conrad, Dir., Box 304, Carpinteria, CA 93014.

SQUAW VALLEY COMMUNITY OF WRITERS—Squaw Valley, CA. July, August. Write Oakley Hall, Dir., Squaw Valley Community of Writers, P.O. Box 2352, Olympic Valley, CA 96146.

WRITERS AND ILLUSTRATORS CONFERENCE IN CHILDREN'S LITERATURE—Marina Del Rey, CA. August. Write Lin Oliver, Dir., SCBWI, 22736 Vanowen, Ste. 106, West Hills, CA 91307.

WRITERS' FORUM—Pasadena, CA. March. Write Meredith Brucker, Dir., Community Education, Pasadena City College, 1570 E. Colorado Blvd., Pasadena, CA 91106.

COLORADO

COLORADO CHRISTIAN WRITERS CONFERENCE—Boulder, CO. March. Write Debbie Barker, Dir., 67 Seminole Ct., Lyons, CO 80540.

COLORADO GOLD CONFERENCE—Denver, CO. September. Write Lee Karr, Dir., Rocky Mountain Fiction Writers, P.O. Box 260244, Denver, CO 80226–0244.

1996 NATIONAL WRITERS ASSOCIATION SUMMER CONFERENCE—Denver, CO. June. Write Sandy Whelchel, Dir., National Writers Assn., 1450 S. Havana, Ste. 424, Aurora, CO 80012.

STEAMBOAT SPRINGS WRITERS CONFERENCE—Steamboat Springs, CO. July. Write Harriet Freiberger, Dir., P.O. Box 774284, Steamboat Springs, CO 80477.

CONNECTICUT

WESLEYAN WRITERS CONFERENCE—Middletown, CT. June. Write Anne Greene, Dir., Wesleyan Writers Conference, Wesleyan Univ., Middletown, CT 06459.

FLORIDA

CHRISTIAN WRITERS' INSTITUTE FLORIDA CONFERENCE—Orlando, FL. February. Write Dottie McBroom, Dir., Christian Writers' Institute, P.O. Box 952248, Lake Mary, FL 32795–2248.

FLORIDA REGION SCBWI CONFERENCE—Palm Springs, FL. September. Write Barbara Casey, Dir., 2158 Portland Ave., Wellington, FL 33414.

KEY WEST LITERARY SEMINAR: "AMERICAN WRITERS AND THE NATURAL WORLD"—Key West, FL. January. Write Miles Frieden, Dir., Key West Literary Seminar, 419 Petronia St., Dept. TW, Key West, FL 33040.

SLEUTHFEST '96 MYSTERY/SUSPENSE/TRUE CRIME CONFERENCE—Fort Lauderdale, FL. March. Write Dianne Ell, Mystery Writers of America, 1432 S.E. 8th St., Deerfield Beach, FL 33441.

SOUTHWEST FLORIDA WRITERS' CONFERENCE—Fort Myers, FL. February. Write Joanne Hartke, Dir., Edison Community College, P.O. Box 60210, Fort Myers, FL 33906–6210.

SPACE COAST WRITERS GUILD ANNUAL CONFERENCE—Cocoa Beach, FL. November. Write Dr. Edwin J. Kirschner, Pres., Space Coast Writers Guild, Box 804, Melbourne, FL 32902.

"WRITING THE AUTOBIOGRAPHY IN YOUR OWN WORDS"—Sarasota, FL. November. Write Hannelore Hahn, Dir., International Women's Writing Guild, P.O. Box 810, Gracie Station, New York, NY 10028.

GEORGIA

AMERICAN CHRISTIAN WRITERS CONFERENCE—Atlanta, GA. October. Write Reg Forder, Dir., American Christian Writers, P.O. Box 5168, Phoenix, AZ 85010.

CURRY HILL PLANTATION WRITERS' RETREAT—Bainbridge, GA. March, April. Write Elizabeth Bowne, Dir., 404 Crestmont Ave., Hattiesburg, MS 39401–7211.

MOONLIGHT AND MAGNOLIAS CONFERENCE—Atlanta, GA. September. Send SASE to Lillian Richey, Dir., 4605 Settles Point Rd., Suwanee, GA 30174.

SANDHILLS WRITERS' CONFERENCE—Augusta, GA. May. Write Maxine Allen, Augusta College, Cont. Education, 2500 Walton Way, Augusta, GA 30904.

SOUTHEASTERN WRITER'S CONFERENCE—St. Simons Island, GA. June. Write Pat Laye, Co-Dir., Rt. 1, Box 102, Cuthbert, GA 31740.

IDAHO

"WRITE TO BE READ" WORKSHOP—Nampa, ID. October. Write Norman B. Rohrer, Dir., 260 Fern Ln., Hume, CA 93628.

ILLINOIS

1996 AMERICAN MEDICAL WRITERS ASSOCIATION ANNUAL CONFERENCE—Chicago, IL. November. Write Lillian Sablack, Dir., AMWA, 9650 Rockville Pike, Bethesda, MD 20814.

23RD ANNUAL MISSISSIPPI VALLEY WRITERS CONFERENCE—Rock Island, IL. June. Write Bess Pierce, 734 18th Ave. A, Moline, IL 61265.

AUTUMN AUTHORS' AFFAIR—Lisle, IL. October. Write Nancy McCann, Dir., Love Designers Writers' Club, 1507 Burnham Ave., Calumet City, IL 60409.

CHRISTIAN WRITERS' INSTITUTE ANNUAL CONFERENCE—Glen Ellyn, IL. June. Write Dottie McBroom, Dir., Christian Writers' Institute, P.O. Box 952248, Lake Mary, FL 32795–2248.

INDIANA

BUTLER UNIVERSITY MIDWINTER CHILDREN'S LITERATURE CONFERENCE—Indianapolis, IN. February. Send SASE to Shirley Daniell, Butler Univ. Midwinter Children's Literature Conference, 4600 Sunset Ave., Indianapolis, IN 46208.

MIDWEST WRITERS WORKSHOP—Muncie, IN. July. Write Earl L. Conn, Dir., Midwest Writers Workshop, Dept. of Journalism, Ball State Univ., Muncie, IN 47306.

IOWA

IOWA SUMMER WRITING FESTIVAL—Iowa City, IA. June, July. Write Peggy Houston, Dir., Iowa Summer Writing Festival, 116 International Center, Univ. of Iowa, Iowa City, IA 52242.

KANSAS

WRITERS WORKSHOP IN SCIENCE FICTION—Lawrence, KS. July. Write James Gunn, Dir., English Dept., Univ. of Kansas, Lawrence, KS 66045.

KENTUCKY

19TH ANNUAL APPALACHIAN WRITERS WORKSHOP—Hindman, KY. July, August. Write Mike Mullins, Dir., Box 844, Hindman Settlement School, Hindman, KY 41822.

LOUISIANA

WRITERS' GUILD OF ACADIANA ANNUAL CONFERENCE—Lafayette, LA. March. Write Leigh Simmons, Dir., 220 Doucet Rd., 164H, Lafayette, LA 70503.

MAINE

56TH STATE OF MAINE WRITERS' CONFERENCE—Ocean Park, ME. August. Write Richard F. Burns, Dir., P.O. Box 7146, Ocean Park, ME 04063–7146.

STONECOAST WRITERS' CONFERENCE—Freeport, ME. July. Write Barbara Hope, Dir., Summer Session Office, Univ. of Southern Maine, 96 Falmouth St., Portland, ME 04103.

WELLS WRITERS' WORKSHOP—Wells, ME. May, September. Write Victor A. Levine, Dir., 69 Broadway, Concord, NH 03301.

MARYLAND

SANDY COVE CHRISTIAN WRITERS CONFERENCE—North East, MD. October. Write Gayle Roper, Dir., R.D. 6, Box 112, Coatesville, PA 19320.

MASSACHUSETTS

AMHERST BOOK AND PLOW FESTIVAL—Amherst, MA. September. Write Dian Mandle, Dir., 11 Spring St., Amherst, MA 01002.

CAPE COD WRITERS' CONFERENCE—Craigville, MA. August. Write Marion Vuilleumier, Dir., Cape Cod Writers' Center, c/o Conservatory, Rt. 132, W. Barnstable, MA 02668.

NATURE AND SCIENCE WRITING—Bermuda. March. Write Bill Sargent, Dir., 15 Henley St., F, Charlestown, MA 02129.

MICHIGAN

AMERICAN CHRISTIAN WRITERS CONFERENCE—Detroit, MI. June. Write Reg Forder, Dir., American Christian Writers, P.O. Box 5168, Phoenix, AZ 85010.

MINNESOTA

MINNEAPOLIS WRITERS' WORKSHOP—Minneapolis, MN. August. Write Colleen Campbell, Dir., P.O. Box 24356, Minneapolis, MN 55424.

OUTDOOR WRITERS ASSOCIATION OF AMERICA ANNUAL CONFERENCE—Duluth, MN. June. Write Eileen King, 2017 Cato Ave., Ste. 101, State College, PA 16801–2768.

SPLIT ROCK ARTS PROGRAM—Duluth, MN. July, August. Write Andrea Gilats, Dir., 306 Wesbrook Hall, Univ. of Minnesota, 77 Pleasant St. S.E., Minneapolis, MN 55455.

MISSOURI

AMERICAN CHRISTIAN WRITERS CONFERENCE—St. Louis, MO. June. Write Reg Forder, Dir., American Christian Writers, P.O. Box 5168, Phoenix, AZ 85010.

MARK TWAIN WRITERS CONFERENCE—Hannibal, MO. June. Write Dr. James C. Hefley, Dir., Hannibal-LaGrange College, 921 Center St., Hannibal, MO 63401.

SCBWI "WRITING FOR CHILDREN" WORKSHOP—Springfield, MO. October. Write Sandy Asher, Dir., Drury College, 900 N. Benton Ave., Springfield, MO 65802.

MONTANA

ENVIRONMENTAL WRITING INSTITUTE—Corvallis, MT. May. Write Hank Harrington, Dir., Environmental Studies Program, Univ. of Montana, Missoula, MT 59812.

YELLOW BAY WRITERS' WORKSHOP—Flathead Lake, MT. August. Write Lee Hynson, Dir., Yellow Bay Writers' Workshop, Ctr. for Cont. Education, Univ. of Montana, Missoula, MT 59812.

NEVADA

READING AND WRITING THE WEST—Reno, NV. July. Write Stephen Tchudi, Dir., Dept. of English, (098) Univ. of Nevada, Reno, NV 89557–0031.

NEW HAMPSHIRE

18TH ANNUAL FESTIVAL OF POETRY—Franconia, NH. July, August. Write Donald Sheehan, Dir., The Frost Place, Box 74, Franconia, NH 03580.

NEW JERSEY

TRENTON STATE COLLEGE WRITERS CONFERENCE—Trenton, NJ. April. Write Jean Hollander, Dir., Writers Conference, English Dept., Hillwood Lakes CN 4700, Trenton, NJ 08650–4700.

NEW MEXICO

SOUTHWEST WRITERS WORKSHOP 14TH ANNUAL CONFERENCE—Albuquerque, NM. August. Write Dir., Southwest Writers Workshop, 1338 Wyoming N.E., Ste. B, Albuquerque, NM 87112.

NEW YORK

25TH ANNUAL ASJA WRITERS' CONFERENCE—New York, NY. May. Write Alexandra Cantor Owens, Dir., ASJA, 1501 Broadway, Ste. 302, New York, NY 10036.

"THE BIG APPLE WORKSHOPS AND OPEN HOUSE"—New York, NY. April, October. Write Hannelore Hahn, Dir., International Women's Writing Guild, P.O. Box 810, Gracie Station, New York, NY 10028.

"FROM DREAM TO REALITY" CONFERENCE—Melville, NY. March. Send SASE to Charlene Goldsmith-Bjelke, Co-Chair, Romance Writers of America, P.O. Box 3722, Grand Central Station, New York, NY 10163-3722.

HIGHLIGHTS FOUNDATION WRITERS WORKSHOP—Chautauqua, NY. July. Write Jan Keen, Dir., Highlights Foundation, 814 Court St., Honesdale, PA 18431.

HOFSTRA UNIVERSITY SUMMER WRITERS CONFERENCE—Hempstead, NY. July. Write Lewis Shena, Dir., UCCE (Liberal Arts), 110 Hofstra Univ., Hempstead, NY 11550-1090.

MANHATTANVILLE'S WRITERS' WEEK—Purchase, NY. June. Write Dean Ruth Dowd, Dir., Manhattanville College, 2900 Purchase St., Purchase, NY 10577.

ROBERT QUACKENBUSH'S CHILDREN'S BOOK WRITING AND IL-LUSTRATING WORKSHOPS—New York, NY. July. Write Robert Quackenbush, Dir., Quackenbush Studios, 460 E. 79th St., New York, NY 10021.

THE WRITER IN YOU—New York, NY. May. Write John Lehman, Weekend Seminars, 315 E. Water St., Cambridge, WI 53523.

NORTH CAROLINA

DUKE UNIVERSITY WRITERS' WORKSHOP—Durham, NC. June. Write Georgann Eubanks, Dir., Box 90703, Durham, NC 27708-0703.

THE WRITER'S ROUNDTABLE—Wilmington, NC. Late Summer. Write Jack Fryar, Dir., Writer's Roundtable, 2801 Lyndon Ave., Wilmington, NC 28405.

OHIO

28TH ANNUAL MIDWEST WRITERS' CONFERENCE—Canton, OH. October. Write Gregg L. Andrews, Dir., Midwest Writers' Conference, 6000 Frank Ave. N.W., Canton, OH 44720.

13TH ANNUAL WESTERN RESERVE WRITERS CONFERENCE—Kirtland, OH. September. Write Lea Leever Oldham, Dir., 34200 Ridge Rd., #110, Willoughby, OH 44094.

51TH ANNUAL WRITERS MINI-CONFERENCE—Kirtland, OH. March. Write Lea Leever Oldham, Dir., 34200 Ridge Rd., #110, Willoughby, OH 44094.

ANTIOCH WRITERS' WORKSHOP—Yellow Springs, OH. July. Write Judy DaPolito, Dir., Antioch Writers' Workshop, P.O. Box 494, Yellow Springs, OH 45387.

THE COLUMBUS WRITERS CONFERENCE—Columbus, OH. September. Write Angela Palazzolo, Dir., P.O. Box 20548, Columbus, OH 43220.

THE HEIGHTS WRITER'S CONFERENCE—Beachwood, OH. May. Write Lavern Hall, Dir., Writer's World Press, P.O. Box 24684, Cleveland, OH 44124–0684.

SELF-PUBLISHING YOUR OWN BOOK—Kirtland, OH. February, April, August, October. Write Lea Leever Oldham, Dir., 34200 Ridge Rd., #110, Willoughby, OH 44094.

WRITING FOR MONEY WORKSHOP—Mayfield, OH. March, May, November. Write Lea Leever Oldham, Dir., 34200 Ridge Rd., #110, Willoughby, OH 44094.

OKLAHOMA

5TH ANNUAL NORTHWEST OKLAHOMA WRITER'S WORKSHOP—Enid, OK. Spring. Write Dr. Earl Mabry, Dir., P.O. Box 1308, Enid, OK 73702.

OKLAHOMA FALL ARTS INSTITUTE'S WRITING WORKSHOP—Lone Wolf, OK. October. Write Mary Gordon Taft, Dir., Oklahoma Arts Institute, P.O. Box 18154, Oklahoma City, OK 73154.

OPPORTUNITY 1996—Norman, OK. March. Write Lura Nell Tolle, National League of American Pen Women, Box 312, Hydro, OK 73048–0312.

OREGON

HAYSTACK WRITING PROGRAM—Cannon Beach, OR. June, August. Write Maggie Herrington, Dir., P.S.U. Extended & Summer Programs, P.O. Box 1491, Portland, OR 97207.

WINTER AND SUMMER FISHTRAP—Wallowa Lake, OR. February, July. Write Rich Wandschneider, Dir., Fishtrap, P.O. Box 38, Enterprise, OR 97828.

"WRITING THE AUTOBIOGRAPHY IN YOUR OWN WORDS"—Wilsonville, OR. October. Write Hannelore Hahn, International Women's Writing Guild, P.O. Box 810, Gracie Station, New York, NY 10028.

PENNSYLVANIA

ANNUAL PENNWRITERS CONFERENCE—Grantville, PA. May. Write C.J. Houghtaling, Dir., R.R. 2, Box 241, Middlebury Center, PA 16935.

CUMBERLAND VALLEY FICTION WRITERS WORKSHOP—Carlisle, PA. June. Write Judy Gill, Dir., Dept. of English, Dickinson College, P.O. Box 1773, Carlisle, PA 17013–2896.

MID-ATLANTIC MYSTERY BOOK FAIR & CONVENTION—Philadelphia, PA. November. Write Deen Kogan, Dir., 507 S. 8th St., Philadelphia, PA 19147.

MONTROSE CHRISTIAN WRITERS' CONFERENCE—Montrose, PA. July. Write Jill Meyers, Dir., Montrose Bible Conference, P.O. Box 159, Montrose, PA 18801–1059.

WRITING FOR PUBLICATION—Pittsburgh, PA. April. Write Rev. Mary

Lee Talbot, Pittsburgh Theological Seminary, 616 N. Highland Ave., Pittsburgh, PA 15206.

TENNESSEE

RHODES WRITING CAMP—Memphis, TN. June. Write Dr. Beth Kamhi, Dir., Dept. of English, Rhodes College, 2000 North Pkwy., Memphis, TN 38112.

TEXAS

AMERICAN CHRISTIAN WRITERS CONFERENCE—Dallas, TX. May. Write Reg Forder, Dir., American Christian Writers, P.O. Box 5168, Phoenix, AZ 85010.

AUSTIN WRITERS' LEAGUE SPRING WORKSHOPS—Austin, TX. March through September. Write Angela Smith, Dir., Austin Writers' League, 1501 W. 5th St., Ste. E-2, Austin, TX 78703.

CRAFT OF WRITING CONFERENCE—Richardson, TX. September. Write Janet Harris, Dir., Univ. of Texas, P.O. Box 830688, MS CN1.1, Richardson, TX 75083–0688.

ROMANCE WRITERS OF AMERICA 16TH ANNUAL CONFERENCE—Dallas, TX. July. Write Angela Butterworth, Dir., Romance Writers of America, 13700 Veterans Memorial, #315, Houston, TX 77014.

TCU/CHISHOLM TRAIL WRITERS CONFERENCE—Fort Worth, TX. June. Write Diane Lovin, Texas Christian Univ., Box 32927, Fort Worth, TX 76129.

VERMONT

BREAD LOAF WRITERS' CONFERENCE—Ripton, VT. August. Write Michael Collier, Dir., Bread Loaf Writers' Conference, Middlebury College, Middlebury, VT 05753.

NEW ENGLAND WRITERS CONFERENCE—Windsor, VT. July. Write Frank & Susan Anthony, Dirs., Box 483, Windsor, VT 05089.

VIRGINIA

CHRISTOPHER NEWPORT UNIVERSITY WRITERS' CONFERENCE—Newport News, VA. April. Write Terry Cox-Joseph, Dir., Office of Cont. Education, Christopher Newport Univ., 50 Shoe Ln., Newport News, VA 23606.

HIGHLAND SUMMER CONFERENCE—Radford, VA. June. Write Dr. Grace Toney Edwards, Dir., HSC Appalachian Regional Studies Ctr., P.O. Box 7014, Radford Univ., Radford, VA 24142.

SHENANDOAH INTERNATIONAL PLAYWRIGHTS RETREAT—Staunton, VA. August, September. Write Robert Graham Small, Dir., Pennyroyal Farm, Rt. 5, Box 167F, Staunton, VA 24401.

SHENANDOAH VALLEY WRITERS' GUILD—Middletown, VA. June. Write Prof. F.H. Cogan, Dir., Lord Fairfax Community College, P.O. Box 47, Middletown, VA 22645.

VIRGINIA CHRISTIAN WRITERS CONFERENCE—Roanoke, VA. April. Send SASE to Betty Robertson, CCM Publishing, Box 12624, Roanoke, VA 24027.

WASHINGTON

CLARION WEST SCIENCE FICTION & FANTASY WRITERS WORK-SHOP—Seattle, WA. June, July. Write Leslie Howle, Dir., 340 15th Ave. E., Ste. 350, Seattle, WA 98112.

PACIFIC NORTHWEST WRITERS CONFERENCE—Seattle, WA. July. Write Judy Bodmer, Dir., PNWC, 2033 6th Ave., #804, Seattle, WA 98121–2546.

PORT TOWNSEND WRITERS' CONFERENCE—Port Townsend, WA. July. Write Carol Jane Bangs, Dir., Centrum, Box 1158, Port Townsend, WA 98368.

SEATTLE CHRISTIAN WRITERS CONFERENCE—Seattle, WA. February, May, October. Write Elaine Wright Colvin, Dir., Writers Information Network, P.O. Box 11337, Bainbridge Island, WA 98110.

WRITER'S WEEKEND AT THE BEACH—Ocean Park, WA. February. Write Pat Rushford, Co-Dir., P.O. Box 877, Ocean Park, WA 98640.

WISCONSIN

GREEN LAKE WRITERS CONFERENCE—Green Lake, WI. July. Write Jan DeWitt, Dir., Green Lake Conference Ctr., W2511 State Hwy. 23, Green Lake, WI 54941–9300.

SCBWI WISCONSIN FALL RETREAT—Madison, WI. October. Send SASE to Patricia Curtis Pfitsch, Dir., Rt. 1, Box 137, Gays Mills, WI 54631.

STATE ARTS COUNCILS

State arts councils sponsor grants, fellowships, and other programs for writers. To be eligible for funding, a writer *must* be a resident of the state in which he is applying. For more information, write to the addresses below. Telephone numbers are listed; 1–800 numbers are toll free for in-state calls only; numbers preceded by TDD indicate Telecommunications Device for the Deaf; TTY indicates Teletypewriter.

ALABAMA STATE COUNCIL ON THE ARTS
One Dexter Ave.
Montgomery, AL 36130
(334) 242–4076; fax: (334) 240–3269
Albert B. Head, *Executive Director*

ALASKA STATE COUNCIL ON THE ARTS
411 W. 4th Ave., Suite 1E
Anchorage, AK 99501–2343
(907) 269–6610
Shannon Planchon, *Grants Officer*

ARIZONA COMMISSION ON THE ARTS
417 W. Roosevelt
Phoenix, AZ 85003
(602) 255–5882
Tonda Gorton, *Literature Director*

ARKANSAS ARTS COUNCIL
1500 Tower Bldg.
323 Center St.
Little Rock, AR 72201
(501) 324–9766; fax: (501) 324–9154
Mona Hughes, *Assistant Director*

CALIFORNIA ARTS COUNCIL
Public Information Office
1300 I St., Suite 930
Sacramento, CA 95814
(916) 322–6555; fax: (916) 322–6575; TDD: (916) 322–6569

COLORADO COUNCIL ON THE ARTS
750 Pennsylvania St.
Denver, CO 80203–3699
(303) 894–2617; fax: (303) 894–2615
Fran Holden, *Executive Director*

CONNECTICUT COMMISSION ON THE ARTS
227 Lawrence St.
Hartford, CT 06106
(203) 566–4770; fax: (203) 566–6462
John Ostrout, *Executive Director*

DELAWARE DIVISION OF THE ARTS
Carvel State Building
820 N. French St.
Wilmington, DE 19801
(302) 577–3540; fax: (302) 577–6561
Barbara King, *Artist Fellowship Coordinator*

FLORIDA ARTS COUNCIL
Dept. of State
Div. of Cultural Affairs
The Capitol
Tallahassee, FL 32399–0250
(904) 487–2980; fax: (904) 922–5259; TTY: (904) 488–5779
Attn: Ms. Peyton Fearington

859

GEORGIA COUNCIL FOR THE ARTS
530 Means St. N.W., Suite 115
Atlanta, GA 30318
(404) 651–7920; fax: (404) 651–7922
Caroline Ballard Leake, *Executive Director*
Ann R. Davis, *Grants Manager, Literature*

HAWAII STATE FOUNDATION ON CULTURE AND THE ARTS
44 Merchant St.
Honolulu, HI 96813
(808) 586–0300; fax: (808) 586–0308
Wendell P.K. Silva, *Executive Director*

IDAHO COMMISSION ON THE ARTS
Box 83720
Boise, ID 83720–0008
(208) 334–2119
Attn: Diane Josephy Peavey

ILLINOIS ARTS COUNCIL
James R. Thompson Center
100 W. Randolph, Suite 10–500
Chicago, IL 60601
(312) 814–4990; (800) 237–6994; fax: (312) 814–1471
Richard Gage, *Director of Communication Arts*

INDIANA ARTS COMMISSION
402 W. Washington St., Rm. 072
Indianapolis, IN 46204–2741
(317) 232–1268; TDD: (317) 233–3001
Dorothy Ilgen, *Executive Director*

IOWA ARTS COUNCIL
Capitol Complex
600 E. Locust
Des Moines, IA 50319–0290
(515) 281–4006; fax: (515) 242–6495
Attn: Bruce Williams

KANSAS ARTS COMMISSION
Jayhawk Tower
700 S.W. Jackson, Suite 1004
Topeka, KS 66603–3758
(913) 296–3335; fax: (913) 296–4989; TTY: (800) 766–3777
Robert T. Burtch, *Editor*

KENTUCKY ARTS COUNCIL
31 Fountain Pl.
Frankfort, KY 40601
(502) 564–3757; fax: (502) 564–2839; TDD: (502) 564–3757
Louis S. DeLuca, *Executive Director*

LOUISIANA STATE ARTS COUNCIL
Box 44247
Baton Rouge, LA 70804
(504) 342–8200; fax: (504) 342–8173
James Borders, *Executive Director*

MAINE ARTS COMMISSION
25 State House Station
Augusta, ME 04333–0025
(207) 287–2724; fax: (207) 287–2335; TDD: (207) 287–6740
Alden C. Wilson, *Director*

MARYLAND STATE ARTS COUNCIL
Artists-in-Education
601 N. Howard St.
Baltimore, MD 21201
(410) 333–8232; fax: (410) 333–1062
Linda Vlasak, *Program Director*
Pamela Dunne, *AIE Program Assistant*

MASSACHUSETTS CULTURAL COUNCIL
120 Boylston St., 2nd Floor
Boston, MA 02116–4802
(617) 727–3668; (800) 232–0960; TTY: (617) 338–9153
Attn: Ricardo Barreto

MICHIGAN COUNCIL FOR ARTS AND CULTURAL AFFAIRS
1200 Sixth St., Suite 1180
Detroit, MI 48226–2461
(313) 256–3731
Betty Boone, *Executive Director*

MINNESOTA STATE ARTS BOARD
Park Square Court
400 Sibley St., Suite 200
St. Paul, MN 55101–1949
(612) 215–1600; (800) 8MN-ARTS; fax: (612) 215–1602
Karen Mueller, *Artist Assistance Program Associate*

COMPAS: WRITERS & ARTISTS IN THE SCHOOLS
305 Landmark Center
75 W. Fifth St.
St. Paul, MN 55102
(612) 292–3254; fax: (612) 292–3258
Daniel Gabriel, *Director*

MISSISSIPPI ARTS COMMISSION
239 N. Lamar St., Suite 207
Jackson, MS 39201
(601) 359–6030; fax: (601) 359–6008
Betsy Bradley, *Executive Director*

MISSOURI ARTS COUNCIL
Wainwright Office Complex
111 N. 7th St., Suite 105
St. Louis, MO 63101–2188
(314) 340–6845; fax: (314) 340–7215
Michael Hunt, *Program Administrator for Literature*

MONTANA ARTS COUNCIL
316 N. Park Ave., Suite 252
Helena, MT 59620
(406) 444–6430; fax: (406) 444–6548
Fran Morrow, *Director of Artists Services*

NEBRASKA ARTS COUNCIL
3838 Davenport St.
Omaha, NE 68131–2329
(402) 595–2122; fax: (402) 595–2334
Jennifer Severin, *Executive Director*

NEVADA STATE COUNCIL ON THE ARTS
Capitol Complex
602 N. Curry St.
Carson City, NV 89710
(702) 687–6680; fax: (702) 687–6688
Susan Boskoff, *Executive Director*

NEW HAMPSHIRE STATE COUNCIL ON THE ARTS
Phenix Hall
40 N. Main St.
Concord, NH 03301–4974
(603) 271–2789; fax: (603) 271–3584; TDD: (800) 735–2964
Audrey Sylvester, *Artist Services Coordinator*

NEW JERSEY STATE COUNCIL ON THE ARTS
Grants Office, Fellowships
CN 306
Trenton, NJ 08625
(609) 292–6130
S. Rink, *Grants Coordinator*

NEW MEXICO ARTS DIVISION
228 E. Palace Ave.
Santa Fe, NM 87501
(505) 827–6490; fax: (505) 827–6043
Randy Forrester, *Local Arts Coordinator*

NEW YORK STATE COUNCIL ON THE ARTS
915 Broadway
New York, NY 10010
(212) 387–7028; fax: (212) 387–7164
Kathleen Masterson, *Director, Literature Program*

NORTH CAROLINA ARTS COUNCIL
Dept. of Cultural Resources
Raleigh, NC 27601–2807
(919) 733–7897; fax: (919) 715–5406
Deborah McGill, *Literature Director*

NORTH DAKOTA COUNCIL ON THE ARTS
418 E. Broadway, Suite 70
Bismarck, ND 58501
(701) 328–3954; fax: (701) 328–3963
Patsy Thompson, *Executive Director*

OHIO ARTS COUNCIL
727 E. Main St.
Columbus, OH 43205–1796
(614) 466–2613; fax: (614) 466–4494
Bob Fox, *Literature Program Coordinator*

STATE ARTS COUNCIL OF OKLAHOMA
P.O. Box 52001–2001
Oklahoma City, OK 73152–2001
(405) 521–2931; fax: (405) 521–6418
Betty Price, *Executive Director*

OREGON ARTS COMMISSION
775 Summer St. N.E.
Salem, OR 97310
(503) 986–0084; fax: (503) 986–0260
Attn: Peter Sears

PENNSYLVANIA COUNCIL ON THE ARTS
Room 216, Finance Bldg.
Harrisburg, PA 17120
(717) 787–6883
Marcia Salvatore, *Literature and Theatre Programs*
Diane Young, *Artists-in-Education Program*

RHODE ISLAND STATE COUNCIL ON THE ARTS
95 Cedar St., Suite 103
Providence, RI 02903
(401) 277–3880
Randall Rosenbaum, *Executive Director*

SOUTH CAROLINA ARTS COMMISSION
1800 Gervais St.
Columbia, SC 29201
(803) 734–8696
Steven Lewis, *Director, Literary Arts Program*

SOUTH DAKOTA ARTS COUNCIL
230 S. Phillips Ave., Suite 204
Sioux Falls, SD 57102–0788
(605) 367–5678
Attn: Dennis Holub

TENNESSEE ARTS COMMISSION
404 James Robertson Pkwy., Suite 160
Nashville, TN 37243–0780
(615) 741–1701; fax: (615) 741–8559
Attn: Alice Swanson

TEXAS COMMISSION ON THE ARTS
Visual and Communication Arts
P.O. Box 13406
Austin, TX 78711–3406
(512) 463–5535; fax: (512) 475–2699
Rita Starpattern, *Program Administrator*

UTAH ARTS COUNCIL
617 E. South Temple
Salt Lake City, UT 84102–1177
(801) 533–5895; fax: (801) 533–6196
Guy Lebeda, *Literary Coordinator*

VERMONT COUNCIL ON THE ARTS
136 State St.
Montpelier, VT 05602
(802) 828–3291; fax: (802) 828–3363
Cornelia Carey, *Grants Officer*

VIRGINIA COMMISSION FOR THE ARTS
223 Governor St.
Richmond, VA 23219
(804) 225–3132
Peggy J. Baggett, *Executive Director*

WASHINGTON STATE ARTS COMMISSION
234 E. 8th Ave.
P.O. Box 42675
Olympia, WA 98504–2675
(206) 753–3860
Bitsy Bidwell, *Community Arts Development Manager*

WEST VIRGINIA DEPT. OF EDUCATION AND THE ARTS
Culture and History Division
The Cultural Center, Capitol Complex
1900 Kanawha Blvd. E.
Charleston, WV 25305
(304) 558–0220
Lakin Ray Cook, *Executive Director*

WISCONSIN ARTS BOARD
101 E. Wilson St., 1st Floor
Madison, WI 53702
(608) 266–0190; fax: (608) 267–0380
Dean Amhaus, *Executive Director*

ORGANIZATIONS FOR WRITERS

ACADEMY OF AMERICAN POETS
584 Broadway, Suite 1208
New York, NY 10012
(212) 274–0343; fax: (212) 274–9427
Jonathan Galassi, *President*

The academy was founded in 1934 to support American poets at all stages of their careers and to foster the appreciation of contemporary poetry. The largest organization in the country dedicated specifically to the art of poetry, the academy sponsors a number of prizes and programs: an annual fellowship for distinguished poetic achievement; the Tanning prize, the largest annual literary award in the U.S.; the Lenore Marshall Poetry Prize; the James Laughlin Award; the Walt Whitman Award; the Harold Morton Landon Translation Award; poetry prizes and colleges and universities; and the American Poets Fund and the Atlas Fund, which provide financial assistance to poets and publishers of poetry. Readings, lectures, and regional symposia take place at various New York City locations and other locations in the United States. Membership is open to all. Annual dues: $25 and up.

AMERICAN CRIME WRITERS LEAGUE
455 Crescent Ave.
Buffalo, NY 14214
Joan Hess, *President*
Douglas Anderson, *Membership Chair*

A national organization of working professional mystery authors. To be eligible for membership in ACWL you must have published at least one of the following: one full-length work of crime fiction or nonfiction; three short stories; or three nonfiction crime articles. The bimonthly *ACWL BULLETin* features articles by reliable experts and an exchange of information and advice among professional writers. Annual dues: $35.

AMERICAN MEDICAL WRITERS ASSOCIATION
9650 Rockville Pike
Bethesda, MD 20814
(301) 493–0003; fax: (301) 493–6384; e-mail: amwa@amwa.org
Lillian Sablack, *Executive Director*

Members of the association are engaged in biomedical communications. Any person actively interested in or professionally associated with any medium of medical communication is eligible for membership. Annual dues: $75.

AMERICAN SOCIETY OF JOURNALISTS AND AUTHORS, INC.
1501 Broadway, Suite 302
New York, NY 10036
(212) 997–0947
Alexandra Cantor, *Executive Director*
A nationwide organization of independent writers of nonfiction dedicated to promoting high standards of nonfiction writing through monthly meetings, annual writers' conferences, etc. The ASJA offers extensive benefits and services including referral services, numerous discount services, and the opportunity to explore professional issues and concerns with other writers. Members also receive a monthly newsletter with confidential market information. Membership is open to professional freelance writers of nonfiction; qualifications are judged by the membership committee. Call or write for application details.

ASSOCIATED WRITING PROGRAMS
Tallwood House, Mail Stop 1E3
George Mason University
Fairfax, VA 22030
(703) 993–4301; fax: (703) 993–4302
Attn: *Membership*
The AWP seeks to serve writers and teachers in need of community, support, information, inspiration, contacts, and ideas. Provides publishing opportunities, job listings, and an active exchange of ideas on writing and teaching, including an annual conference. Members receive six issues of *AWP Chronicle* and eight issues of *AWP Job List*. Publications include *The AWP Official Guide to Creative Writing Programs*. Annual dues: $50, *individual*; $20, *student*.

THE AUTHORS GUILD, INC.
330 W. 42nd St., 29th Fl.
New York, NY 10036–6902
(212) 563–5904; fax: (212) 564–5363; e-mail: Authors@pipeline.com
Attn: *Membership Committee*
Membership offers writers of all genres legal advice, reviews of publishing and agency contracts, and access to seminars and symposiums around the country on subjects of concern to authors. The Authors Guild also lobbies on behalf of all authors on issues such as copyright, taxation, and freedom of expression. A writer who has published a book in the last seven years with an established publisher, or has published three articles in periodicals of general circulation within the last eighteen months is eligible for active voting membership. An unpublished writer who has just received a contract offer may be eligible for associate membership. All members of the Authors Guild automatically become members of its parent organization, the Authors League of America. Annual dues: $90.

866

THE AUTHORS LEAGUE OF AMERICA, INC.
330 W. 42nd St.
New York, NY 10036–6902
(212) 564–8350; fax: (212) 564–5363; e-mail: Authors@pipeline.com
Attn: *Membership Committee*

A national organization representing over 14,000 authors and dramatists on matters of joint concern, such as copyright, taxes, and freedom of expression. Membership is restricted to authors and dramatists who are members of the Authors Guild and the Dramatists Guild. Matters such as contract terms and subsidiary rights are in the province of the two guilds.

BLACK THEATRE NETWORK
Box 11502
Fisher Bldg. Station
Detroit, MI 48211
(419) 372–2350
Lundeana Thomas, *President*

The Black Theatre Network is a national non-profit organization devoted to exposing all people to the beauty and complexity of black theater, and to preserving the art form for future generations. The BTN sponsors an annual national conference, and the Randolph Edmonds Young Scholars Competition. Publications include the quarterly *BTNews, The Black Theatre Directory,* and *Black Voices,* a guide to plays by black authors. Annual dues: $35, *student & retiree;* $60, *individual;* $95, *organization.*

THE DRAMATISTS GUILD
234 W. 44th St.
New York, NY 10036–3909
(212) 398–9366
Peter Stone, *President;* Todd Neal, *Director of Membership*

A professional association of playwrights, composers, and lyricists, the guild was established to protect dramatists' rights and to improve working conditions. Services include use of the guild's contracts; a toll-free number for members in need of business counseling; a discount ticket service; access to two health insurance programs and a group term life insurance plan; a reference library; and a Committee for Women. Publications include *The Dramatists Guild Quarterly, The Dramatists Guild Resource Directory,* and *The Dramatists Guild Newsletter.* All playwrights, produced or not, are eligible for membership. Annual dues: $125, *active;* $75, *associate;* $50, *subscribing;* $35, *student.*

INTERNATIONAL ASSOCIATION OF THEATRE FOR CHILDREN AND YOUNG PEOPLE
2707 E. Union
Seattle, WA 98122
(206) 392–2147
Jolly Sue Baker, *Executive Director*

The development of professional theater for young audiences and international exchange are the organization's primary mandates. Provides a link between professional theaters, artists, directors, training institutions, and arts agencies; sponsors festivals and forums for interchange among theaters and theater artists. Annual dues: $50, *individual*; $25, *student and retiree*.

THE INTERNATIONAL WOMEN'S WRITING GUILD
Box 810, Gracie Station
New York, NY 10028–0082
(212) 737–7536; fax: (212) 737–9469
Hannelore Hahn, *Executive Director & Founder*
     Founded in 1976, serving as a network for the personal and professional empowerment of women through writing. Services include six issues of a 32-page newsletter, a list of literary agents and publishing services, access to health insurance plans at group rates, access to writing conferences and related events throughout the U.S., including the annual summer conference at Skidmore College in Saratoga Springs, NY, regional writing clusters, and year-round supportive networking. Any woman may join regardless of portfolio. Annual dues: $35; $45 *international*.

MIDWEST RADIO THEATRE WORKSHOP
KOPN
915 E. Broadway
Columbia, MO 65201
(314) 874–5676; fax: (314) 499–1662; e-mail: Kopn@thoughtport.com
Steve Donofrio, *Director*
     Founded in 1979, the MRTW is the only national resource for American radio dramatists, providing referrals, technical assistance, educational materials, and workshops. MRTW coordinates an annual national radio script contest, publishes an annual radio scriptbook, and distributes a script anthology with primer. Send SASE for more information.

MYSTERIES FOR MINORS—(See *Sisters in Crime*)

MYSTERY WRITERS OF AMERICA, INC.
17 E. 47th St., 6th Floor
New York, NY 10017
(212) 888–8171
Priscilla Ridgway, *Executive Director*
     The MWA exists for the purpose of raising the prestige of mystery and detective writing, and of defending the rights and increasing the income of all writers in the field of mystery, detection, and fact crime writing. Each year, the MWA presents the Edgar Allan Poe Awards for the best mystery writing in a variety of fields. The four classifications of membership are: *active*, open to any writer who has made a sale in the field of mystery, suspense, or crime writing; *associate*, for professionals in allied fields/ writers in other fields; *corresponding*, for writers living outside the U.S.; *affiliate*, for unpublished writers. Annual dues: $65; $32.50 *corresponding members*.

NATIONAL ASSOCIATION OF SCIENCE WRITERS, INC.
P.O. Box 294
Greenlawn, NY 11740
(516) 757–5664
Diane McGurgan, *Administrative Secretary*
     The NASW promotes the dissemination of accurate information regarding science through all media, and conducts a varied program to in-

crease the flow of news from scientists, to improve the quality of its presentation, and to communicate its meaning to the reading public. Anyone who has been actively engaged in the dissemination of science information is eligible to apply for membership. Active members must be principally involved in reporting on science through newspapers, magazines, TV, or other media that reach the public directly. Associate members report on science through limited-circulation publications and other media. Annual dues: $60.

THE NATIONAL LEAGUE OF AMERICAN PEN WOMEN, INC.
The Pen Arts Building
1300 17th St. N.W.
Washington, DC 20036–1973
(202) 785–1997
Dr. Fran T. Carter, *National President*
Founded in 1897, the league promotes development of the creative talents of professional women in the arts. Membership is through local branches, available by invitation from current members in the categories of Art, Letters, and Music.

THE NATIONAL WRITERS ASSOCIATION
1450 S. Havana, Suite 424
Aurora, CO 80012
(303) 751–7844
Sandy Whelchel, *Executive Director*
New and established writers, poets, and playwrights throughout the U.S. and Canada may become members of the NWA, a full-time, customer-service-oriented association founded in 1937. Members receive a bimonthly newsletter, *Authorship*, and may attend the annual June conference. Annual dues: $60, *professional*; $50, *regular*; add $25 outside the U.S., Canada, and Mexico.

NATIONAL WRITERS UNION
873 Broadway, #203
New York, NY 10003
(212) 254–0279
Jonathan Tasini, *President*
Dedicated to bringing about equitable payment and fair treatment of free-lance writers through collective action. Membership is over 4,000 and includes book authors, poets, cartoonists, journalists, and technical writers in 13 chapters nationwide. The union offers its members contract and agent information, group health insurance, press credentials, grievance handling, a quarterly magazine, and sample contracts and resource materials. It sponsors workshops and seminars across the country. Membership is open to writers who have published a book, play, three articles, five poems, one short story or an equivalent amount of newsletter, publicity, technical, commercial, government, or institutional copy, or have written an equivalent amount of unpublished material and are actively seeking publication. Annual dues: $75 to $175.

869

NEW DRAMATISTS
424 W. 44th St.
New York, NY 10036
(212) 757-6960
Elana Greenfield, *Director of Artistic Programs*

New Dramatists is dedicated to finding gifted playwrights and giving them the time, space, and tools to develop their craft. Services include readings and workshops; a director-in-residence program; national script distribution for members; artist work spaces; international playwright exchange programs; script copying facilities; and a free ticket program. Membership is open to residents of New York City and the surrounding tri-state area. National memberships are offered to those outside the area who can spend time in NYC in order to take advantage of programs. Apply between July 15 and September 15. No annual dues.

NORTHWEST PLAYWRIGHTS GUILD
Box 9218
Portland, OR 97207-9218
(503) 222-7010
Bill Johnson, *Office Manager*

The guild supports and promotes playwrights living in the Northwest through play development, staged readings, and networking for play competitions and production opportunities. Members receive monthly and quarterly newsletters. Annual dues: $25.

OUTDOOR WRITERS ASSOCIATION OF AMERICA, INC.
2017 Cato Ave., Suite 101
State College, PA 16801-2768
(814) 234-1011
James W. Rainey, *Executive Director*

A non-profit, international organization representing professional communicators who report and reflect upon America's diverse interests in the outdoors. Membership, by nomination only, includes a monthly publication, *Outdoors Unlimited*; annual conference; annual membership directory; contests. The association also provides scholarships to qualified students.

PEN AMERICAN CENTER
568 Broadway
New York, NY 10012
(212) 334-1660
Karen Kennerly, *Executive Director*

PEN American Center is one of more than 120 centers worldwide that compose International PEN. The 2,800 members of the American Center are poets, playwrights, essayists, editors, and novelists, as well as literary translators and those agents who have made a substantial contribution to the literary community. PEN American headquarters is in New York City, and branches are located in Boston, Chicago, New Orleans, Portland, Oregon, and San Francisco. Among the activities, programs, and services sponsored are literary events and awards, outreach projects to encourage reading, assistance to writers in financial need, and international and domestic human rights campaigns on behalf of many writers, editors, and journalists censored or imprisoned because of their writing.

Membership is open to writers who have published two books of literary merit, as well as editors, agents, playwrights, and translators who meet specific standards; apply to membership committee.

THE PLAYWRIGHTS' CENTER
2301 Franklin Ave. E.
Minneapolis, MN 55406
(612) 332–7481
David Moore, Jr., *Executive Director*
The Playwrights' Center fuels the contemporary theater by providing services that support the development and public appreciation of playwrights and playwriting. Members receive applications for all programs, a calendar of events, eligibility to participate in special activities, including classes, outreach programs, and PlayLabs. Annual dues: $35.

POETRY SOCIETY OF AMERICA
15 Gramercy Park
New York, NY 10003
(212) 254–9628
Elise Paschen, *Executive Director*
Founded in 1910, the PSA seeks to raise the awareness of poetry, to deepen the understanding of it, and to encourage more people to read, listen to, and write poetry. To this end, the PSA presents national series of readings including "Tributes in Libraries" and "Poetry in Public Places," mounts poetry posters on mass transit vehicles through "Poetry in Motion," and broadcasts an educational poetry series on cable television. The PSA also offers annual contests for poetry (many open to non-members), seminars, poetry festivals, and publishes a newsletter. Annual dues: $40.

POETS AND WRITERS, INC.
72 Spring St.
New York, NY 10012
(212) 226–3586
Elliot Figman, *Executive Director*
Poets & Writers, Inc., was founded in 1970 to foster the development of poets and fiction writers and to promote communication throughout the literary community. A non-membership organization, it offers a nationwide information center for writers; *Poets & Writers Magazine* and other publications; as well as support for readings and workshops at a wide range of venues.

ROMANCE WRITERS OF AMERICA
13700 Veterans Memorial Dr., Suite 315
Houston, TX 77014
(713) 440–6885; fax: (713) 440–7510
Allison Kelley, *Executive Manager*
An international organization with over 150 local chapters across the U.S. and Canada; membership is open to any writer, published or unpublished, interested in the field of romantic fiction. Annual dues of $60, plus $10 application fee for new members; benefits include annual conference, contest, market information, and bimonthly newsmagazine, *Romance Writers' Report*.

871

SCIENCE-FICTION AND FANTASY WRITERS OF AMERICA, INC.
5 Winding Brook Dr., #1B
Guilderland, NY 12084
Peter Dennis Pautz, *Executive Secretary*

An organization whose purpose it is to foster and further the professional interests of science fiction and fantasy writers. Presents the annual Nebula Award for excellence in the field and publishes the *Bulletin* for its members (also available to non-members).

Any writer who has sold a work of science fiction or fantasy is eligible for membership. Annual dues: $50, *active* ; $35, *affiliate*; plus $10 installation fee; send for application and information.

SISTERS IN CRIME
860 N. Lake Shore Dr., #5K
Chicago, IL 60611–1753
(312) 587–8997; fax: (312) 587–9969
Barbara D'Amato, *President*

Sisters in Crime was founded in 1986 to combat discrimination against women in the mystery field, educate publishers and the general public as to inequalities in the treatment of female authors, and raise the level of awareness of their contribution to the field. Membership is open to all and includes writers, readers, editors, agents, booksellers, and librarians. Publications include a quarterly newsletter and membership directory. Annual dues: $25, U.S.; $30, foreign. Members interested in mysteries for young readers may join Mysteries for Minors (Patricia Elmore, Chair, P.O. Box 442124, Lawrence, KS 66044–8933) with no additional dues.

SMALL PRESS GENRE ASSOCIATION
P.O. Box 6301
Concord, CA 94524
(510) 254–7442
Joe Morey, *President*

The SPGA is a new international service organization for writers of any genre, illustrators, editors, and publishers of material related to the genres of science fiction, fantasy, horror, western, mystery and its subgenres. Members receive six issues of the *Genre Press Digest*, market news, awards, yearly showcase book of members work, membership directory, critique services, grievance arbitration, and research assistance. Annual dues: $25, U.S. and Canada; $30, *international.*

SOCIETY FOR TECHNICAL COMMUNICATION
901 N. Stuart St., #904
Arlington, VA 22203–1854
(703) 522–4114
William C. Stolgitis, *Executive Director*

A professional organization dedicated to the advancement of the theory and practice of technical communication in all media. The 19,000 members in the U.S. and other countries include technical writers and editors, publishers, artists and draftsmen, researchers, educators, and audiovisual specialists. Annual dues: $95.

872

SOCIETY OF AMERICAN TRAVEL WRITERS
4101 Lake Boone Trail, Suite 201
Raleigh, NC 27607
(919) 787–5181
Susan Rexer, *Administrative Coordinator*
The Society of American Travel Writers represents writers and other professionals who strive to provide travelers with accurate reports on destinations, facilities, and services. Membership is by invitation. Active membership is limited to salaried travel writers and free lancers who have a steady volume of published or distributed work about travel. Initiation fees: $200, *active*; $400, *associate*. Annual dues: $120, *active*; $240, *associate*.

SOCIETY OF CHILDREN'S BOOK WRITERS & ILLUSTRATORS
22736 Vanowen St., Suite 106
West Hills, CA 91307
(818) 888–8760
Lin Oliver, *Executive Director*
A national organization of authors, editors, publishers, illustrators, filmmakers, librarians, and educators, the SCBWI offers a variety of services to people who write, illustrate, or share an interest in children's literature. Full memberships are open to those who have had at least one children's book or story published. Associate memberships are open to all those with an interest in children's literature. Annual dues: $50.

SOCIETY OF ENVIRONMENTAL JOURNALISTS
P.O. Box 27280
Philadelphia, PA 19118
(215) 247–9710; fax: (215) 247–9712; e-mail: SEJOffice@aol.com
WWW: http://www.tribnet.com/environ/env—home.htm
Beth Parke, *Executive Director*
Dedicated to improving the quality, accuracy, and visibility of environmental reporting, the society serves 1,000 members with a quarterly newsletter, the *SEJournal*, national and regional conferences, computer online services on AOL, compuserve, and the World Wide Web, and an annual directory. Annual dues: $35; $30, *student*.

SOCIETY OF PROFESSIONAL JOURNALISTS
16 S. Jackson St.
Greencastle, IN 46135–0077
(317) 653–3333
Greg Christopher, *Executive Director*
With 14,000 members and 300 chapters, the society seeks to serve the interests of print, broadcast, and wire journalists. Services include legal counsel on journalism issues, jobs-for-journalists career search program, professional development seminars, and awards that encourage journalism. Members receive *Quill*, a monthly magazine that explores current issues in the field. SPJ promotes ethics and freedom of information programs. Annual dues: $66, *professional*; $33, *student*.

873

THE SONGWRITERS GUILD FOUNDATION
1560 Broadway, Suite 1306
New York, NY 10036
(212) 768–7902; fax: (212) 768–9048
George Wurzbach, *National Projects Director*
Open to published and unpublished songwriters, the Guild provides members with contracts, reviews contracts, collects royalties from publishers, offers group health and life insurance plans, conducts workshops and critique sessions, and provides a songwriting collaboration service. Annual dues: $55, *associate*; $70 and up, *full member.*

THEATRE COMMUNICATIONS GROUP
355 Lexington Ave.
New York, NY 10017
(212) 697–5230
John Sullivan, *Executive Director*
TCG, a national organization for the American theater, provides services to facilitate the work of playwrights, literary managers, and other theater professionals and journalists. Publications include the quarterly bulletin *PlaySource*, which circulates information on new plays, translations, and adaptations to more than 300 TCG constituent theaters and to potential producers. Also publishes the annual *Dramatists Sourcebook* and a line of theater books including plays and translations. Individual members receive *American Theatre* Magazine. Annual dues: $35, *individual.*

WESTERN WRITERS OF AMERICA, INC.
1012 Fair St.
Franklin, TN 37064
(615) 791–1444
James A. Crutchfield, *Secretary/Treasurer*
Membership is open to qualified professional writers of fiction and nonfiction related to the history and literature of the American West. Its chief purpose is to promote a more widespread distribution, readership, and appreciation of the West and its literature. Holds annual convention in the last week of June. Sponsors annual Spur Awards, Owen Wister Award, and Medicine Pipe Bearer's Award for published work and produced screenplays. Annual dues: $60.

WRITERS GUILD OF AMERICA, EAST, INC.
555 W. 57th St.
New York, NY 10019
(212) 767–7800
Mona Mangan, *Executive Director*

WRITERS GUILD OF AMERICA, WEST, INC.
8955 Beverly Blvd.
West Hollywood, CA 90048
Address as of February 1, 1996: 7000 W. 3rd St., Los Angeles, CA 90048
(310) 550–1000
Brian Walton, *Executive Director*
The Writers Guild of America (East and west) represents writers in motion pictures, broadcast, cable and new media industries, including news and entertainment. In order to qualify for membership, a writer must

874

fulfill current requirements for employment or sale of material in one of these fields.

The basic dues are $25 per quarter for WGA West and $12.50 per quarter for WGAE. In addition, there are quarterly dues based on percentage of the member's earnings in any one of the fields over which the guild has jurisdiction. The initiation fee is $1,000 for WGAE, for writers living east of the Mississippi, and $2,500 for WGA west, for those living west of the Mississippi.

WRITERS INFORMATION NETWORK
P.O. Box 11337
Bainbridge Island, WA 98110
(206) 842–9103; fax: (206) 842–0536
Elaine Wright Colvin, *Director*

W.I.N. was founded in 1983 to provide a link between Christian writers and the religious publishing industry. Offered are a bimonthly newsletter, market news, editorial services, advocacy and grievance procedures, referral services, and conferences. Annual dues: $25; $35, *foreign*.

LITERARY AGENTS

As the number of book publishers that will consider only agented submissions grows, more writers are turning to agents to sell their manuscripts. The agents in the following list handle literary material, and in some cases, stage plays. Included in each listing are such important details as type of material represented, submission procedure, and commission. Since agents derive their income from the sales of their clients' work, they must represent writers who are selling fairly regularly to good markets. Nonetheless, many of the agents listed here note they will consider unpublished writers. Always query an agent first, and enclose a self-addressed, stamped envelope; most agents will not respond without it. Do not send any manuscripts until the agent has asked you to do so; and be wary of agents who charge fees for reading manuscripts. All of the following agents have indicated they do *not* charge reading fees, and those who pass on postage, phone, or photocopying fees to their clients have indicated such.

To learn more about agents and their role in publishing, the Association of Authors' Representatives, Inc., publishes a code of ethics as well as an up-to-date list of AAR members, available for $5 (check or money order) and a 55¢ legal-size SASE. Write to: Association of Authors' Representatives, Inc., 10 Astor Pl., 3rd Floor, New York, NY 10003.

Other lists of agents and their policies can be found in *Literary Market Place*, a directory found in most libraries, and in *Literary Agents of North America (Author Aid/Research Associates International, 340 E. 52nd St., New York, NY 10022)*.

AARDVARK LITERARY AGENTS—3908 Harlem Rd., Suite 104, Amherst, NY 14226. Attn: Kate Berman, Jim Fair. Adult fiction, nonfiction, and plays. Young adult novels considered; no poetry, no children's stories. Unpublished writers considered. Submit outline with complete manuscript and SASE. Multiple queries O.K. Commission: 10%. Fees: photocopying, shipping.

LEE ALLAN AGENCY—P.O. Box 18617, Milwaukee, WI 53218. Attn: Mr. Lee A. Matthias. Adult genre fiction, nonfiction, and juvenile books for all ages. Unpublished writers considered. Query with SASE; multiple queries O.K. Commission: 15%. Fees: photocopying, overnight shipping, phone. "Go to a bookstore and locate the exact place in the store where your book would be displayed. If it realistically fits a popular market niche, is not derivative or imitative, meets the size constraints, and you can't make it any better yourself, you are ready to find an agent."

JAMES ALLEN LITERARY AGENT—538 East Hartford St., P.O. Box 278, Milford, PA 18337. Attn: James Allen. Adult fiction. Query with 2-to 3-page synopsis; no multiple queries. Commission: 10% domestic, 20% foreign. Fees: photocopying, shipping. "My list is quite full; though I'm always willing to consider material, I'm mainly interested in taking on only people with previous book-length fiction publishing credits."

MARCIA AMSTERDAM AGENCY—41 W. 82nd St., #9A, New York, NY 10024. Attn: Marcia Amsterdam. Adult and young adult fiction; mainstream nonfiction. Query; multiple queries O.K.; two-to three-week exclusive on requested material. Commission: 15% domestic. Fees: standard costs.

ARCADIA—20A Old Neversink Rd., Danbury, CT 06811. Attn: Victoria Gould Pryor. Adult fiction and nonfiction. Unpublished writers considered. Query with SASE; multiple queries O.K. Commission: 15%. Fees: photocopying.

THE AUTHOR'S AGENCY—3355 N. Five Mile Rd., Suite 332, Boise, ID 83713–3925. Attn: R.J. Winchell. Adult fiction and nonfiction; stage plays. Unpublished writers considered. Submit complete typewritten manuscript with SASE. Commission: 15% books; 10% scripts. Fees: none. "Our interests are broad."

THE AXELROD AGENCY—54 Church St., Lenox, MA 01240. Adult fiction and nonfiction. Unpublished writers considered. Query; multiple queries O.K. Commission: 10% domestic, 20% foreign. Fees: photocopying.

MALAGA BALDI LITERARY AGENCY, INC.—Box 591, Radio City Station, New York, NY 10101. Attn: Malaga Baldi. Adult fiction and nonfiction. Unpublished writers considered. Query first. "If I am interested, I ask for proposal, outline, and sample pages for nonfiction, complete manuscript for fiction." Multiple queries O.K. Commission: 15%. Fees: none. Response time: 10 weeks minimum.

THE BALKIN AGENCY—P.O. Box 222, Amherst, MA 01004. Attn: Rick Balkin. Adult nonfiction. Unpublished writers considered. Query with outline; no multiple queries. Commission: 15% domestic, 20% foreign. Fees: none. "Most interested in serious nonfiction."

VIRGINIA BARBER AGENCY—101 Fifth Ave., New York, NY 10003.

Adult fiction and nonfiction. Query with outline, sample pages, and bio/resumé. No multiple queries. Commission: 15% domestic, 20% foreign. Fees: photocopying.

LORETTA BARRETT BOOKS—101 Fifth Ave., New York, NY 10003. Attn: Loretta Barrett. Adult fiction and nonfiction. Unpublished writers considered. Query with outline and bio/resumé; no multiple queries. Commission: 15%. Fees: phone. Response time: 4 weeks; "please do not call before then."

REID BOATES LITERARY AGENCY—Box 328, 69 Cooks Crossroad, Pittstown, NJ 08867–0328. Attn: Reid Boates. Adult mainstream fiction and nonfiction. Unpublished writers considered. Query; no multiple queries. Commission: 15%. Fees: none.

BOOKSTOP LITERARY AGENCY—67 Meadow View Rd., Orinda, CA 94563. Attn: Kendra Marcus. Juvenile fiction only. Unpublished writers considered. Send complete manuscript with SASE. Commission: 15%. Fees: photocopying, shipping.

GEORGES BORCHARDT, INC.—136 E. 57th St., New York, NY 10022. Adult fiction and nonfiction. Unpublished writers considered by recommendation only. No unsolicited queries or submissions. Commission: 15%. Fees: photocopying, shipping.

BRANDT & BRANDT LITERARY AGENTS—1501 Broadway, New York, NY 10036. Adult fiction and nonfiction. Unpublished writers considered occasionally. Unsolicited query by letter only; no multiple queries. Commission: 15%. Fees: photocopying.

THE HELEN BRANN AGENCY—94 Curtis Rd., Bridgewater, CT 06752. Attn: Genny Ross. Adult fiction and nonfiction. Unpublished writers considered. Query; no multiple queries. Commission: 15%. Fees: none.

CURTIS BROWN LTD.—10 Astor Pl., New York, NY 10003. General trade fiction and nonfiction; also juvenile. Unpublished writers considered. Query; no multiple queries. Commission: unspecified. Fees: photocopying; express mail.

ANDREA BROWN LITERARY AGENCY—P.O. Box 429, El Granada, CA 94018. Attn: Andrea Brown. Juvenile fiction and nonfiction only. Unpublished writers considered. Query with outline, sample pages, bio/resumé, and SASE; no faxes. Commission: 15% domestic; 20% foreign. Fees: none.

JANE JORDAN BROWNE—Multimedia Product Development, 410 S. Michigan Ave., Rm. 724, Chicago, IL 60605. Attn: Jane Jordan Browne. Adult fiction and nonfiction; juvenile books for all ages. Query with SASE; multiple queries O.K. Commission: 15% domestic, 20% foreign. Fees: photocopying; foreign fax, phone, postage.

KNOX BURGER ASSOCIATES, LTD.—39½ Washington Square S., New York, NY 10012. Adult fiction and nonfiction; no science fiction, fantasy, or romance. Unpublished writers considered. Query with SASE; no multiple queries. Commission: 15%. Fees: photocopying.

SHEREE BYKOFSKY ASSOCIATES, INC.—211 E. 51st St., Suite 11D, New York, NY 10022. Adult nonfiction. Unpublished writers considered. Query with outline, up to 3 sample pages or proposal, and SASE. Multiple queries O.K. if indicated as such. Commission: 15%. Fees: none.

MARTHA CASSELMAN—P.O. Box 342, Calistoga, CA 94515–0342.

Nonfiction, especially interested in cookbooks. Also young adult. Unpublished writers considered. Query with outline, sample pages, bio/resumé, and SASE for return. Multiple queries O.K. if noted as such. Commission: 15%. Fees: photocopying, express mail; overseas mail, phone, fax.

JULIE CASTIGLIA AGENCY—1155 Camino del Mar, Suite 510, Del Mar, CA 92014. Attn: Julie Castiglia. Fiction: mainstream and literary. Nonfiction: psychology, health, finance, women's issues, science, biography, business, outdoors. Query with outline, sample pages, and bio/resumé. No multiple queries. Commission: 15%. Fees: photocopying, shipping. "Please do not query on the phone. Attend workshops and writers' conferences before approaching an agent."

HY COHEN LITERARY AGENCY, LTD.—111 W. 57th St., New York, NY 10019. Attn: Hy Cohen. Adult fiction, nonfiction, and juvenile. Unpublished writers considered. Unsolicited queries and manuscripts O.K., "with SASE, please!" Multiple submissions considered. Commission: 10% domestic, 20% foreign. Fees: phone, photocopying, postage. "I rarely respond well to first-person narrative. Good luck!"

RUTH COHEN, INC.—P.O. Box 7626, Menlo Park, CA 94025. Attn: Ruth Cohen. Adult fiction and occasionally, nonfiction; quality juvenile fiction and nonfiction. Unpublished writers considered. Query with first 10 pages, outline, bio/resumé, and SASE. Commission: 15%. Fees: some shipping.

JOANNA LEWIS COLE— 404 Riverside Dr., New York, NY 10025. Juvenile fiction and nonfiction, all ages. Unpublished writers considered. Send query letter with SASE; multiple queries O.K. Commission 10% to15%. Fees: none.

DON CONGDON ASSOCIATES, INC.—156 Fifth Ave., Suite 625, New York, NY 10010. Adult fiction and nonfiction. Unpublished writers considered occasionally. Query with outline; no multiple queries. Commission: 10% domestic. Fees: photocopying.

THE DOE COOVER AGENCY—58 Sagamore Ave., Medford, MA 02155. Attn: Doe Coover, Colleen Mohyde. Adult fiction and general nonfiction. Unpublished writers considered. Query with outline, sample pages, bio/resumé, and SASE; multiple queries O.K. Commission: 15%. Fees: photocopying.

RICHARD CURTIS ASSOCIATES, INC.—171 E. 74th St., New York, NY 10021. Adult nonfiction. Unpublished writers considered. Query with bio/resumé; no multiple queries. Commission: 15% domestic, 20% foreign. Fees: photocopying, shipping.

DARHANSOFF & VERRILL LITERARY AGENCY—179 Franklin St., New York, NY 10013. Adult fiction and nonfiction. Unpublished writers considered. Unsolicited queries "only with recommendations." Commission: 15% domestic, 20% foreign. Fees: none.

ELAINE DAVIE LITERARY AGENCY— 620 Park Ave., Rochester, NY 14607. Attn: Elaine Davie. Adult fiction and nonfiction; "we specialize in popular/commercial novels by and for women, especially romance." Unpublished writers considered. Query with outline and sample pages. Multiple submissions O.K. Commission: 15%. Fees: none.

ANITA DIAMANT AGENCY, INC.—310 Madison Ave., #1105, New York, NY 10017. Attn: Anita Diamant. Adult fiction: literary, mystery, romance. Also nonfiction "anything not technical," and young adult. Query with outline, sample pages, and bio/resumé; no multiple queries. Commission: 15%. Fees: none.

SANDRA DIJKSTRA LITERARY AGENCY—1155 Camino del Mar, Suite 515C, Del Mar, CA 92014. Attn: Debra Ginsberg. Adult and children's fiction and nonfiction. Query with outline and bio/resumé. For fiction, submit first 50 pages and synopsis; for nonfiction, submit proposal. Commission: 15% domestic, 20% foreign. Fees: none.

THE JONATHAN DOLGER AGENCY— 49 E. 96th St., 9B, New York, NY 10128. Attn: Tom Wilson. Adult trade fiction and nonfiction. Considers unpublished writers. Query with outline and SASE. Commission: 15%. Fees: photocopying, shipping. "No category mysteries, romance, or science fiction."

DWYER & O'GRADY, INC.—P.O. Box 239, East Lempster, NH 03605. Attn: Elizabeth O'Grady. Branch office: P.O. Box 790, Cedar Key, FL 32625. Children's picture books for ages 6 to 12, with strong story line, dialogue, and character development. Unpublished writers considered. Query with bio/resumé; no multiple queries. Commission: 15%. Fees: photocopying, shipping. "Our primary focus is the representation of illustrators who also write their own stories; however, we represent several adult authors who write for the children's market."

JANE DYSTEL LITERARY MANAGEMENT—One Union Square W., Suite 904, New York, NY 10003. Attn: Jane Dystel, Miriam Goderich. Adult fiction and nonfiction. Unpublished writers considered. Query with bio/resumé; no multiple queries. Commission: 15%. Fees: shipping.

EDUCATIONAL DESIGN SERVICES—P.O. Box 253, Wantaugh, NY 11793. Attn: Bertram L. Linder. Educational texts only. Unpublished writers considered. Query with outline, sample pages or complete manuscript, bio/resumé, and SASE. No multiple queries. Commission: 15%. Fees: none.

ETHAN ELLENBERG LITERARY AGENCY—548 Broadway, Suite 5E, New York, NY 10012. Attn: John Ciatron. Adult fiction (suspense, romance, science fiction, fantasy) and nonfiction (health, spirituality, business, popular science); juvenile books. Unpublished writers considered. Query with outline, sample pages, and SASE; multiple queries O.K. Commission: 15%. Fees: photocopying, shipping.

ANN ELMO AGENCY— 60 E. 42nd St., New York, NY 10165. Attn: Lettie Lee. Branch office: 756 Neilson St., Berkeley, CA 94707. Adult fiction, nonfiction, and plays. Juvenile books for middle grades and up; no picture books. Unpublished writers considered. Query with outline, sample pages, and bio/resumé. No multiple queries. Commission: 15%. Fees: none.

FELICIA ETH—555 Bryant St., Suite 350, Palo Alto, CA 94301. Attn: Felicia Eth. Adult fiction, "highly selective, mostly contemporary." Also nonfiction. Unpublished writers considered. Query with outline, sample pages, and bio/resumé. Multiple queries O.K. if noted. Commission: 15% domestic, 20% foreign. Fees: photocopying. "I am a small, highly personal agency, not right for everyone but very committed to those I work with. I tend to work with writers based either on the West Coast or at least west of the Mississippi."

FARBER LITERARY AGENCY—14 E. 75th Ave. S.E., New York, NY 10021. Attn: Ann Farber. Adult fiction, nonfiction, and stage plays; juvenile books. Unpublished writers considered. Query with outline, sample pages, and SASE. Commission: 15% "with services of attorney." Fees: photocopying.

FLANNERY LITERARY—34–36 28th St., #5, Long Island City, NY 11106–3516. Attn: Jennifer Flannery. Adult fiction and nonfiction; juvenile books for all ages. Unpublished writers considered. Query; multiple queries O.K. Commission: 15%. Fees: none.

ROBERT A. FREEDMAN DRAMATIC AGENCY, INC.—1501 Broadway, Suite 2310, New York, NY 10036. Attn: Robert A. Freedman or Selma Luttinger. Stage plays. Send query only; multiple queries O.K. Commission: standard. Fees: photocopying.

SAMUEL FRENCH, INC.— 45 W. 25th St., New York, NY 10010. Attn: Lawrence Harbison, Ed. Stage plays. Unpublished writers considered. Submit complete manuscript; multiple submissions O.K. Commission: 10%. Fees: none.

JAY GARON-BROOKE ASSOCIATES—101 W. 55th St., #5K, New York, NY 10019. Adult fiction and nonfiction. Unpublished writers considered. Query with outline, bio/resume, and SASE; no multiple queries. Commission: 15% domestic, 30% foreign. Fees: photocopying.

GOLDFARB & GRAYBILL—918 16th St. N.W., Suite 400, Washington, DC 20006. Attn: Nina Graybill. Adult fiction and nonfiction. No poetry, romance, science fiction, or children's books. Query with bio/resume; for fiction, include a synopsis, sample chapter. Multiple queries O.K. Commission: 15%. Fees: photocopying, shipping. "We appreciate clear, succinct, well-written, grammatical query letters and samples."

GOODMAN ASSOCIATES—500 West End Ave., New York, NY 10024. Attn: Elise Simon Goodman. Adult fiction and nonfiction. Unpublished writers considered. Query with outline, sample pages, and bio/resume. Multiple queries O.K. Commission: 15% domestic, 20% foreign. Fees: photocopying, long-distance phone, overseas postage.

SANFORD J. GREENBURGER—55 Fifth Ave., 15th Fl., New York, NY 10003. Attn: Faith Hornby Hamlin. Adult fiction (no science fiction, fantasy, or romance) and nonfiction, including sports books; juvenile picture books. Unpublished writers considered. Query with outline, sample pages, bio/resume, and SASE; multiple queries O.K. Commission: 15% domestic; 20% foreign. Fees: photocopying.

MAIA GREGORY ASSOCIATES—311 E. 72nd St., New York, NY 10021. Adult nonfiction only. Unpublished writers considered. Query with sample pages and bio/resume. No multiple queries. Commission: 15%. Fees: none.

HEACOCK LITERARY AGENCY, INC.—1523 Sixth St., Suite 14, Santa Monica, CA 90401. Attn: Rosalie Heacock, Pres. Adult fiction and nonfiction. Unpublished writers considered. Query with outline, 20 sample pages, bio/resume, and SASE. Multiple queries O.K., if mentioned. Commission: 15% for first $50,000 per year, then 10% for balance of year. Fees: out-of-pocket expenses. "The agency offers thoughtful representation and provides sounding board for new book ideas for established clientele. Please write your query letter as well as you write your original manuscript, for it is the first sample of your writing that the agent will see and evaluate. Good luck!"

FREDERICK HILL ASSOCIATES—1842 Union St., San Francisco, CA 94123. Attn: Bonnie Nadell. Branch office: 8446½ Melrose Pl., Los Angeles, CA 90069. Adult fiction and nonfiction. Unpublished writers considered.

Query with outline and bio/resumé; multiple queries O.K. Commission: 15%. Fees: photocopying, postage.

JOHN L. HOCHMANN BOOKS—320 E. 58th St., New York, NY 10022. Attn: John L. Hochmann. Nonfiction: biography, social history, college textbook. Unpublished writers considered, "provided they present evidence of substatial expertise in the field they are writing about." Query with outline, sample pages, and bio/resumé. No multiple queries. Commission: 15% U.S./Canadian; plus 15% foreign language and U.K. Fees: photocopying. "Do not submit jacket copy. Submit outlines and proposals that include evaluations of competing books."

BARBARA HOGENSON AGENCY—19 W. 44th St., Suite 1000, New York, NY 10036. Attn: Barbara Hogenson. Adult fiction, nonfiction, and plays. Query; multiple queries O.K. Commission: 15% books, 10% scripts. Fees: none.

HULL HOUSE LITERARY AGENCY—240 E. 82nd St., New York, NY 10028. Attn: David Stewart Hull, Pres. New writers contact Lydia Mortimer, Associate. Nonfiction: true crime, biography, military, general history. Fiction, especially crime fiction. Query with outline and bio/resumé; include sample pages with nonfiction queries only. Multiple queries O.K. Commission: 15% domestic; 10% foreign. Fees: photocopying, overseas fax and postage.

IMG/JULIAN BACH LITERARY AGENCY—22 E. 71st St., New York, NY 10021. Attn: Julian Bach, Carolyn Krupp. Adult fiction and nonfiction. Unpublished writers considered. Query with outline, sample pages, and bio/resumé. No multiple queries. Commission: 15%. Fees: photocopying.

INTERNATIONAL PUBLISHER ASSOCIATES, INC.—304 Guido Ave., Lady Lake, FL 32159. Attn: J. DeRogatis, Exec. Vice Pres. Adult fiction and nonfiction. Unpublished writers considered. Query with outline and sample pages; multiple queries O.K. Commission: 15% domestic, 20% foreign. Fees: photocopying, shipping, "on acceptance."

SHARON JARVIS & CO.—Toad Hall, Inc., Laceyville, PA 18623. Adult fiction and nonfiction. Unpublished writers considered. Query with bio/resumé; no multiple queries. Commission: 15%. Fees: photocopying. "Pay attention to what's selling and what's commercial."

JCA LITERARY AGENCY, INC.—27 W. 20th St., Suite 1103, New York, NY 10011. Adult fiction and nonfiction. Unpublished writers considered. Query with sample pages; multiple queries O.K. Commission: 15% domestic, 20% foreign. Fees: photocopying, shipping. "Be as straightforward and to-the-point as possible. Don't try to hype us or bury us in detail."

LOUISE B. KETZ AGENCY—1485 First Ave., Suite 4B, New York, NY 10021. Attn: Louise B. Ketz. Adult nonfiction on science, business, sports, history, and reference. Considers unpublished writers "with proper credentials." Query with outline and bio/resumé; multiple queries occasionally considered. Commission: 10% to 15%. Fees: photocopying and shipping.

KIDDE, HOYT & PICARD—335 E. 51st St., New York, NY 10022. Attn: Katharine Kidde, Laura Langlie. General interest/trade nonfiction on current affairs, social sciences, and the arts. Adult mainstream fiction; some literary, mysteries, romances, thrillers. No science fiction, horror, or poetry. Unpublished writers not considered, "but we'll consider writers who have published short fiction or nonfiction—a published book is not necessary." Query with 2 or 3 chapters, synopsis, and bio/resumé. Multiple queries O.K. Commission: 15%. Fees: photocopying, postage.

KIRCHOFF/WOHLBERG, INC.—866 United Nations Plaza, Suite 525, New York, NY 10017. Attn: Liza Voges, Julie Alperen. Juvenile fiction and nonfiction only. Unpublished writers considered. Query; multiple submissions O.K. Commission: 15%. Fees: none.

HARVEY KLINGER, INC.—301 W. 53rd St., New York, NY 10019. Attn: Harvey Klinger. Adult fiction and nonfiction. Unpublished writers considered. Query with outline, sample pages, and bio/resumé. No multiple queries. Commission: 15% domestic, 25% foreign. Fees: photocopying, shipping.

BARBARA S. KOUTS—P.O. Box 560, Bellport, NY 11713. Attn: Barbara S. Kouts. Adult fiction, nonfiction; juvenile books for all ages. Unpublished writers considered. Query with bio/resumé. Multiple queries O.K. Commission: 10%. Fees: photocopying. "Send your best work always!"

EDITE KROLL LITERARY AGENCY—12 Grayhurst Pk., Portland, ME 04102. Attn: Edite Kroll. Adult fiction and nonfiction; juvenile fiction. Unpublished writers considered. Query with outline, sample pages, bio, and SASE; multiple queries O.K. Commission: 15% domestic; 20% foreign. Fees: photocopying. "Keep queries brief. No phone or fax queries."

PETER LAMPACK AGENCY, INC.—551 Fifth Ave., Suite 1613, New York, NY 10176. Attn: Sandra Blanton, Agent. Deborah T. Brown, Assoc. Agent. Literary and commercial fiction; "We like both contemporary relationship works and historical fiction in addition to thrillers, psychological suspense, mystery, action-adventure. We do not do romance, science fiction, or horror." Also biography/autobiography, nonfiction on politics, finance, and law written by experts in the fields. Unpublished writers considered. Query with synopsis; outline and bio/resumé for nonfiction. Sample pages will be solicited after queries. Multiple queries O.K. Commission: 15%. Fees: photocopying.

THE ROBERT LANTZ-JOY HARRIS AGENCY—156 Fifth Ave., Suite 617, New York, NY 10010. Adult fiction and nonfiction. Unpublished writers considered. Query with outline, sample pages, and bio/resumé. No multiple queries. Commission: 15%. Fees: photocopying, shipping.

MICHAEL LARSEN/ELIZABETH POMADA—1029 Jones St., San Francisco, CA 94109. Attn: M. Larsen, nonfiction; E. Pomada, fiction. Fiction: literary, commercial, and genre. Nonfiction: general, including pop psychology and science, biography, business, nature, health, history, arts, travel. Unpublished writers welcome. Query for fiction with first 30 pages, synopsis, SASE, and phone number; send #10 SASE for brochure. For nonfiction, query by phone: (415) 673-0939. Multiple queries O.K., "as long as we're told." Commission: 15%. Fees: none.

THE MAUREEN LASHER AGENCY—P.O. Box 888, Pacific Palisades, CA 90272. Attn: Ann Cashman. Adult fiction and nonfiction. Unpublished writers considered. Query with outline, sample pages, and bio/resumé. No multiple queries. Commission: 15%. Fees: none.

LEVANT & WALES, INC.—108 Hayes St., Seattle, WA 98108. Attn: Elizabeth Wales, Valerie Griffith. Adult fiction and nonfiction. Unpublished writers considered. Query with outline, sample pages, and bio/resumé. Mulitple queries O.K. Commission: 15%. Fees: photocopying.

ELLEN LEVINE LITERARY AGENCY, INC.—15 E. 26th St., Suite 1801,

New York, NY 10010. Adult fiction and nonfiction; juvenile material. Unpublished writers considered. Query with SASE. Commission: 15% domestic; 20% foreign. Fees: photocopying, shipping.

LICHTMAN, TRISTER, SINGER & ROSS—1666 Connecticut Ave. N.W., Suite 501, Washington, DC 20009. Attn: Gail Ross, Howard Yoon. Adult nonfiction. Unpublished writers considered. Query with outline, sample pages, resumé, and SASE. Multiple queries O.K. Commission: 15%. Fees: none.

NANCY LOVE LITERARY AGENCY—250 E. 65th St., New York, NY 10021. Mostly nonfiction, including alternative health care, parenting, spiritual and inspirational books, crime, self-help; some fiction, but no genres except mysteries and thrillers. Unpublished writers considered. Query; no multiple submissions on novels. Commission: 15%. Fees: photocopying.

DONALD MAASS LITERARY AGENCY—157 W. 57th St., Suite 1003, New York, NY 10019. Attn: Donald Maass, Pres. Jennifer Jackson, Associate. Adult fiction, specializing in genres: science fiction, fantasy, mystery, suspense, historical. Unpublished writers considered. Query; multiple queries O.K. if noted as such. Commission: 15% domestic; 20% foreign. Fees: none.

GERARD MCCAULEY AGENCY, INC.—P.O. Box 844, Katonah, NY 10536. Attn: Gerard F. McCauley. Adult nonfiction. Unpublished writers considered. Query; no multiple queries. Commission: 15%. Fees: postage.

GINA MACCOBY LITERARY AGENCY—1123 Broadway, Suite 1009, New York, NY 10010. Adult fiction and nonfiction; juvenile for all ages. Unpublished writers considered. Query; multiple queries O.K. Commission: 15%. Fees: photocopying, overseas postage, bank charges for converting foreign currencies.

CAROL MANN LITERARY AGENCY—55 Fifth Ave., New York, NY 10003. Attn: Carol Mann. Gail Geinberg, subsidiary rights. Adult nonfiction and some fiction Query; multiple queries O.K. Commission: 15%. Fees: photocopying, shipping.

MANUS ASSOCIATES, INC.— 417 E. 57th St., Suite 5D, New York, NY 10022. Attn: Janet Manus. Branch office: 430 Cowper St., Palo Alto, CA 94301. Adult fiction and nonfiction. No science fiction, category romance, or military books. Unpublished writers considered. Query with outline, sample pages, and bio/resumé. Multiple queries O.K. "on occasion." Commission: 15%. Fees: photocopying, shipping.

ELISABETH MARTON AGENCY—One Union Square W., Rm. 612, New York, NY 10003-3303. Attn: Tonda Marton. Stage plays only. Unproduced playwrights considered. Query; multiple queries O.K. Commission: 10%. Fees: none.

JED MATTES, INC.—2095 Broadway, #302, New York, NY 10023-2895. Adult fiction and nonfiction. Unpublished writers considered. Query; multiple queries O.K. Commission: 15% domestic; 20% foreign. Fees: none.

HELMUT MEYER LITERARY AGENCY—330 E. 79th St., New York, NY 10021. Attn: Helmut Meyer, Literary Agent. Adult fiction and nonfiction. Phone queries preferred: (212) 288-2421. For letter queries, include outline, sample pages, and bio/resumé. No multiple queries. Commission: 15%. Fees: none.

HENRY MORRISON, INC.—Box 235, Bedford Hills, NY 10507. Adult fiction and nonfiction; book-length only. Unpublished writers considered. Query with outline; multiple queries O.K. Commission: 15% domestic; 20% foreign. Fees: photocopying, shipping. "We are concentrating on a relatively small list of clients, and work toward building them in the U.S. and international marketplaces. We tend to avoid autobiographical novels and extremely literary novels, but always seek good nonfiction on major political and historical subjects."

RUTH NATHAN AGENCY— 80 Fifth Ave., Suite 706, New York, NY 10011. Art books, decorative arts, show business, biography. Selected historical fiction, pre-1500. No unsolicited manuscripts. Commission: 15%. Fees: photocopying, shipping. "To writers seeking an agent: Please note what my specialties are. Do not send science fiction, fantasy, children's books, or business books."

NEW ENGLAND PUBLISHING ASSOCIATES—P.O. Box 5, Chester, CT 06412. Attn: Elizabeth Frost Knappman or Edward W. Knappman. Adult nonfiction. Unpublished writers considered. Query; "send a carefully thought-out, market-driven proposal with concept statement, market analysis, competitive survey, author bio, annotated chapter outline, and 50–70 pages of sample chapters." Commission: 15%. Fees: none.

THE RICHARD PARKS AGENCY—138 E. 16th St., 5B, New York, NY 10003. Adult nonfiction; fiction by referral only. Unpublished writers considered. Query with SASE; multiple queries O.K. if noted as such. Commission: 15% domestic; 20% foreign. Fees: photocopying. "No phone calls or faxed queries, please."

L. PERKINS ASSOCIATES—5800 Arlington Ave., Suite 18J, Riverdale, NY 10471. Attn: Lori Perkins or Peter Rubie. Adult fiction and nonfiction. Unpublished writers considered. Query with outline, sample pages, bio/resumé; multiple queries O.K. Commission: 15% domestic; 20% foreign. Fees: photocopying, shipping. "No unprofessional presentation or behavior; keep queries simple, direct, and to the point."

JAMES PETER ASSOCIATES, INC.—P.O. Box 772, Tenafly, NJ 07670. Attn: Bert Holtje. Adult nonfiction. Unpublished writers considered. Query with outline, sample pages, and bio/resumé. No multiple queries. Commission: 15%. Fees: none.

ALISON PICARD, LITERARY AGENT—P.O. Box 2000, Cotuit, MA 02635. Attn: Alison Picard. Adult fiction, nonfiction, and juvenile. Unpublished writers considered. Query; multiple queries O.K. Commission: 15%. Fees: none.

SUSAN ANN PROTTER—110 W. 40th St., Suite 1408, New York, NY 10018. Adult fiction and nonfiction only, specializing in mysteries, contemporary thrillers and science fiction, health, psychology, self-help, popular science, medicine, and parenting. Query by mail only, with description, bio/resumé, synopsis, and SASE. Commission: unspecified. Fees: $10 handling fee for requested manuscripts to cover cost of return.

ROBERTA PRYOR, INC.—24 W. 55th St., New York, NY 10019. Attn: Roberta Pryor. Adult fiction, nonfiction, current affairs, biographies, ecology. Unpublished writers considered. Query with outline, sample pages, and bio/resumé. Multiple queries O.K. Commission: 15% domestic; 10% foreign and film. Fees: photocopying, express mail. "When submitting book proposals, taboo is the coy refusal to give away any plot resolution. How do we know the author can resolve his plot, take care of loose ends? Some applicants feel a copywriter's approach, i.e. jacket copy come-on will tickle our fancy. Not so."

RAINES & RAINES—71 Park Ave., Suite 4A, New York, NY 10016. Attn: Keith Korman, Joan Raines, Theron Raines. Adult fiction, nonfiction, and juvenile books for all ages. No unpublished writers considered. Query; no multiple queries. Commission: 15% domestic; 20% foreign. Fees: photocopying. "Keep query to one page."

HELEN REES LITERARY AGENCY—308 Commonwealth Ave., Boston, MA 02115. Adult fiction and nonfiction. Unpublished writers considered. Query with outline, bio/resumé, and sample to 50 pages. No multiple queries. Commission: 15%. Fees: none.

JANE ROTROSEN AGENCY—318 E. 51st St., New York, NY 10022. Attn: Ruth Kagle, Andrea Cirillo, Meg Ruley. Branch office: P.O. Box 1331, Taos, NM 87571. Attn: Stephanie Tade. Adult fiction and nonfiction. Unpublished writers considered. Query; multiple queries O.K. Commission: 15% domestic; 20% foreign. Fees: none.

PESHA RUBINSTEIN LITERARY AGENCY—37 Overlook Terr., #1D, New York, NY 10033. Attn: Pesha Rubinstein. Commercial fiction and nonfiction. Contemporary women's fiction. Juvenile books. No young adult fiction, science fiction, or fantasy. Unpublished writers considered. Query with first 10 pages; multiple queries O.K. Commission: 15% domestic, 20% foreign. Fees: photocopying. "Don't tell me you'll make me rich. Do tell me the ending of the story in the synopsis."

RUSSELL-SIMENAUER LITERARY AGENCY, INC.—P.O. Box 43267, Upper Monclair, NJ 07043. Attn: Jacqueline Simenauer, Margaret Russell. Phone: (201) 746-0539; fax: (201) 746-0754. Fiction: literary, commercial, mysteries, historical novels, first novels. Nonfiction: pop psychology, self-help; medical, nutrition, sexuality, New-Age spirituality; women's and men's issues, investigative journalism, true crime, adventure, business, celebrities. Query with outline, sample pages, bio/resumé. Multiple queries O.K. Commission: 15% domestic, 25% foreign. Fees: shipping, phone, photocopying.

RUSSELL & VOLKENING, INC.—50 W. 29th St., New York, NY 10001. Adult and juvenile fiction and nonfiction. Unpublished writers considered. Query with letter and SASE. No multiple queries. Commission: 10%. Fees: none.

SANDUM & ASSOCIATES—144 E. 84th St., New York, NY 10028. Attn: Howard E. Sandum. Adult fiction and nonfiction. Unpublished writers considered. Query with sample pages and bio/resumé. Multiple queries O.K. Commission: 15% domestic; 10% when foreign or TV/film subagents are used. "We do not consider manuscripts in genres such as science fiction, romance, or horror unless surpassing literary qualities are present."

THE SHUKAT COMPANY, LTD.—340 W. 55th St., Suite 1A, New York, NY 10019. Attn: Scott Shukat, Pat McLaughlin. Stage plays. Unpublished writers occasionally considered. Query with outline and sample pages. No multiple queries. Commission: 15%. Fees: none.

BOBBE SIEGEL, RIGHTS LITERARY AGENT—41 W. 83rd St., New York, NY 10024. Attn: Bobbe Siegel. Adult fiction and nonfiction. Unpublished writers considered. Query; multiple queries O.K. Commission: 15%. Fees: photocopying. "Keep query short, to the point, and literate. Don't sing your own praises; manuscript should speak for itself."

F. JOSEPH SPIELER LITERARY AGENCY—154 W. 57th St., Rm. 135, New York, NY 10019. Attn: F. Joseph Spieler, Lisa M. Ross, John F. Thornton, Literary Agents. Branch office: The Spieler Agency West, 1760 Solano Ave., Suite 300, Berkeley, CA 94707. Attn: Victoria Shoemaker, Agent. Adult fiction and nonfiction; also juvenile for all ages. Unpublished writers considered. Query with outline; no multiple queries. Commission: 15%. Fees: none.

GLORIA STERN AGENCY—2929 Buffalo Speedway, #2111, Houston, TX 77098. Attn: Gloria Stern. Adult nonfiction. Query with short outline, bio/resumé, and one chapter. Multiple queries O.K. Commission: 15%. Fees: photocopying.

GUNTHER STUHLMANN, AUTHOR'S REPRESENTATIVE—P.O. Box 276, Becket, MA 01223. Attn: Barbara Ward. Literary fiction and nonfiction, especially biography, letters, and history. No mysteries, romance, science fiction, or adventure. Unpublished writers sometimes considered. Query with letter and SASE; no multiple queries. Commission: 10% North America; 15% Britain and Commonwealth; 20% foreign. "We take on few new clients at this time."

TARC LITERARY AGENCY—4725 E. Sunrise Dr., #219, Tucson, AZ 85718. Attn: Martha Gore. Adult fiction and nonfiction; multicultural juvenile books. Unpublished writers considered. Query with bio and resumé. Commission: 15% domestic; 20% foreign. Fees: photocopying, shipping.

SUSAN P. URSTADT, INC.—P.O. Box 1676, New Canaan, CT 06840. Attn: Susan Urstadt. Adult nonfiction, specializing in art, antiques, architecture, popular reference, crafts, travel, health, careers, regional books, etc. Unpublished writers considered. Query with outline, sample pages, overview of the market and competition, bio/resumé, and SASE. No multiple queries. Commission:15%. Fees: none. "We look for dedicated, cheerful, long-term authors of high quality who want to build writing careers with care."

JOHN A. WARE LITERARY AGENCY—392 Central Park W., New York, NY 10025. Attn: John Ware. Adult fiction: literate, accessible, noncategory fiction, plus thrillers and mysteries. Adult nonfiction: biography, history, current affairs, investigative journalism, social criticism, Americana and folklore, science, medicine, sports, memoir. Unpublished writers considered. Query; multiple queries O.K. Commission: 15% domestic, 20% foreign. Fees: photocopying. "No phone queries, please, without referral."

WATKINS/LOOMIS AGENCY—133 E. 35th St., Suite One, New York, NY 10016. Attn: Lily Oei. Adult fiction and nonfiction. Unpublished writers considered. Query with SASE; no multiple queries. Commission: 15%. Fees: none.

SANDRA WATT & ASSOCIATES—8033 Sunset Blvd., Suite 4053, Los Angeles, CA 90046. Attn: Sandra Watt. Adult fiction and nonfiction. Unpublished writers considered. Query with bio/resumé; multiple submissions O.K. Commission: 15%. Fees: marketing fees for shipping, phone, faxes, for new writers only. "We're old fashioned. We love good writing."

WIESER & WIESER, INC.—118 E. 25th St., 2nd Fl., New York, NY 10010. Attn: Olga Wieser. Adult fiction and nonfiction. Unpublished writers considered. Query with outline and bio/resumé. No multiple queries. Commission: 15%. Fees: photocopying, shipping.

WITHERSPOON ASSOCIATES—157 W. 57th St., Suite 700, New York, NY 10019. Adult fiction and nonfiction. Unpublished writers considered. Query with sample pages; no multiple queries. Commission: 15%. Fees: none.

RUTH WRESCHNER, AUTHORS' REPRESENTATIVE—10 W. 74th St., New York, NY 10023. Attn: Ruth Wreschner. Adult fiction (mainstream novels, genre books, mysteries, romance) and nonfiction (by experts in a particular field); also young adult. No pornography, incest, or sexual abuse. Unpublished writers considered. Query with outline, sample pages, and bio/resumé. Multiple queries O.K. Commission: 15% domestic; 20% foreign. Fees: photocopying and postage.

ANN WRIGHT REPRESENTATIVES—165 W. 46th St., Suite 1105, New York, NY 10036–2501. Attn: Dan Wright, Literary Dept. Adult fiction. Unpublished writers considered. Query with bio/resumé. No multiple queries. Commission: 10% to 20%. Fees: photocopying, shipping.

WRITERS HOUSE—21 W. 26th St., New York, NY 10010. Attn: John Abraham, fiction. John Hodgeman, nonfiction. Beth Feinberg, juvenile and young adult. Liza Landsman, multimedia. Adult fiction, and nonfiction; juvenile for all ages; and young adult. Unpublished writers considered. "Query with one-page letter on why your project is excellent, what it's about, and why you're the wonderful author to write it." No multiple queries. Commission: 15% domestic; 20% foreign. Fees: out-of-pocket expenses only.

WRITERS' PRODUCTIONS—P.O. Box 630, Westport, CT 06881. Attn: David L. Meth. Adult fiction and nonfiction, both of literary quality. Children's books that fit into multimedia fantasies. Unpublished writers considered. Query with outline, 30 to 50 sample pages, and bio/resumé. Multiple queries considered, but not preferred. Commission: 15% domestic; 25% foreign, dramatic, multimedia, software sales, licensing, and merchandising. Fees: photocopying, shipping. "Send your best, most professional written work. Research your market, know your field."

SUSAN ZECKENDORF ASSOCIATES, INC.—171 W. 57th St., New York, NY 10019. Attn: Susan Zeckendorf. Fiction: literary fiction; mysteries; thrillers; women's commercial fiction. Nonfiction: science; music; biography; social history. Unpublished writers considered. Query with outline and bio/resumé. Commission: 15% domestic; 20% foreign. Fees: photocopying. "Keep your description of the work brief."

GEORGE ZIEGLER—160 E. 97th St., Suite 4A, New York, NY 10029. Nonfiction, "preferably by a writer who has the scholarly credentials for the subject." Unpublished writers considered. Query; multiple queries O.K. Commission: 15%. Fees: none. "The query should tell me what the project is about, not how good the author thinks it is."

Glossary

Advance — The amount a publisher pays a writer before a book is published; it is deducted from the royalties earned from sales of the finished book.

Agented material — Submissions from literary or dramatic agents to a publisher. Some publishing companies accept agented material only.

All rights — Some magazines purchase all rights to the material they publish, which means that they can use it as they wish, as many times as they wish. They cannot purchase all rights unless the writer gives them written permission to do so.

Assignment — A contract, written or oral, between an editor and writer, confirming that the writer will complete a specific project by a certain date, and for a certain fee.

B&W — Abbreviation for black-and-white photographs.

Book outline — Chapter-by-chapter summary of a book, frequently in paragraph form, allowing an editor to evaluate the book's content, tone, and pacing, and determine whether he or she wants to see the entire manuscript for possible publication.

Book packager — Company that puts together all the elements of a book, from initial concept to writing, publishing, and marketing it. Also called **book producer** or **book developer.**

Byline — Author's name as it appears on a published piece.

Clips — Copies of a writer's published work, often used by editors to evaluate the writer's talent.

Column inch — One inch of a typeset column; often serves as a basis for payment.

Contributor's copies — Copies of a publication sent to a writer whose work is included in it.

Copy — Manuscript pages before they are set into type.

Copy editing — Line-by-line editing to correct errors in spelling, grammar, and punctuation, and inconsistencies in style. Differs from **content editing**, which evaluates flow, logic, and overall message.

Copyright — Legal protection of creative works from unauthorized use. Under the law, copyright is secured automatically when the work is set down for the first time in written or recorded form.

Cover letter — A brief letter that accompanies a manuscript or book proposal. A cover letter is *not* a **query letter.**

Deadline — The date on which a written work is due at the editor's office, agreed to by author and editor.

Draft — A complete version of an article, story, or book. **First drafts** are often called **rough drafts**.

Fair use — A provision of the copyright law allowing brief passages of copyrighted material to be quoted without infringing on the owner's rights.

Feature — An article that is generally longer than a news story and whose main focus is an issue, trend, or person.

Filler — Brief item used to fill out a newspaper or magazine column; could be a news item, joke, anecdote, or puzzle.

First serial rights — The right of a magazine or newspaper to publish a work for the first time in any periodical. After that, all rights revert to the writer.

Galleys — The first typeset proofs of a manuscript, before they are divided into pages.

Ghostwriter — Author of books, articles, and speeches that are credited to someone else.

Glossy — Black-and-white photo with a shiny, rather than a matte, finish.

Hard copy — The printed copy of material written on a computer.

Honorarium — A modest, token fee paid by a publication to an author in gratitude for a submission.

International reply coupon (IRC) — Included with any correspondence or submission to a foreign publication; allows the editor to reply by mail without incurring cost.

Kill fee — Fee paid for an article that was assigned but subsequently not published; usually a percentage of the amount that would have been paid if the work had been published.

Lead time — Time between the planning of a magazine or book and its publication date.

Libel — A false accusation or published statement that causes a person embarrassment, loss of income, or damage to reputation.

Little magazines — Publications with limited circulation whose content often deals with literature or politics.

Mass market — Books appealing to a very large segment of the reading public and often sold in such outlets as drugstores, supermarkets, etc.

Masthead — A listing of the names and titles of a publication's staff members.

Ms — Abbreviation for manuscript; mss is the plural abbreviation.

Multiple submissions — Also called **simultaneous submissions**. Complete manuscripts sent simultaneously to different publications. Once universally discouraged by editors, the practice is gaining more acceptance, though some still frown on it. **Multiple queries** are generally accepted, however, since reading them requires less of an investment in time on the editor's part.

On speculation — Editor agrees to consider a work for publication "on speculation," without any guarantee that he or she will ultimately buy the work.

One-time rights — Editor buys manuscript from writer and agrees to publish it one time, after which the rights revert to the author for subsequent sales.

Op-ed — A newspaper piece, usually printed opposite the editorial page, that expresses a personal viewpoint on a timely news item.

Over-the-transom — Describes the submission of unsolicited material by a free-lance writer; the term harks back to the time when mail was delivered through the open window above an office door.

Payment on acceptance — Payment to writer when manuscript is submitted.

Payment on publication — Payment to writer when manuscript is published.

Pen name — A name other than his or her legal name that an author uses on written work.

Public domain — Published material that is available for use without permission, either because it was never copyrighted or because its copyright term is expired. Works published at least 75 years ago are considered in the public domain.

Q-and-A format — One type of presentation for an interview article, in which questions are printed, followed by the interviewee's answers.

Query letter — A letter—usually no longer than one page—in which a writer proposes an article idea to an editor.

Rejection slip — A printed note in which a publication indicates that it is not interested in a submission.

Reporting time — The weeks or months it takes for an editor to evaluate a submission.

Reprint rights — The legal right of a magazine or newspaper to print an article, story, or poem after it has already appeared elsewhere.

Royalty — A percentage of the amount received from retail sales of a book, paid to the author by the publisher. For hardcovers, the royalty is generally 10% on the first 5,000 copies sold; 12½% on the next 5,000 sold; 15% thereafter. Paperback royalties range from 4% to 8%, depending on whether it's a trade or mass-market book.

SASE — Self-addressed, stamped envelope, required with all submissions—either for return of material or (if you don't need material returned) for editor's reply.

Slush pile — The stack of unsolicited manuscripts in an editor's office.

Tear sheets — The pages of a magazine or newspaper on which an author's work is published.

Unsolicited submission — A manuscript that an editor did not specifically ask to see.

Work for hire — When a work is written on a "for hire" basis, all rights in it become the property of the publisher. Though the work-for-hire clause applies mostly to work done by regular employees of a company, some editors offer work-for-hire agreements to free lancers. Think carefully before signing such agreements, however, since by doing so you will essentially be signing away your rights and will not be able to try to resell your work on your own.

Writers guidelines — A formal statement of a publication's editorial needs, payment schedule, deadlines, and other essential information.

INDEX TO MARKETS

899

912